UNIVERSITY CASEBOOK SERIES®

PRACTICING ENVIRONMENTAL LAW

TODD AAGAARD
Vice Dean and Professor of Law
Villanova University School of Law

DAVE OWEN
Professor of Law
UC Hastings College of the Law

JUSTIN PIDOT
Associate Professor of Law
University of Denver Sturm College of Law

FOUNDATION
PRESS

University Casebook Series is a trademark registered in the U.S. Patent and Trademark Office.

© 2017 LEG, Inc. d/b/a West Academic
    444 Cedar Street, Suite 700
    St. Paul, MN 55101
    1-877-888-1330

Printed in the United States of America

ISBN: 978-1-63459-307-6

PREFACE

Learning environmental law presents a challenge. On the one hand, students are drawn to the subject by an interest in—indeed, often, a deep passion for—helping to solve pressing problems that threaten human health and the natural environment. On the other hand, environmental law is largely composed of statutes and regulations, and those statutes and regulations are often lengthy, technical, and complex. The fundamental challenge for an environmental law course, therefore, is to help students understand the often difficult materials that comprise environmental law without losing the excitement that brought them to the field.

In our experiences as environmental lawyers, however, the practice of environmental law does not have this problem. Environmental law comes alive in practice. What can seem impenetrable as a student becomes clearer and more compelling when approached through real-world problems.

For that reason, our casebook injects a practice orientation into environmental law pedagogy, hopefully making learning environmental law as interesting as practicing it. In the process, we aim to teach you the skills emphasized in a doctrinal course: learning substantive principles, reading text closely, identifying ambiguity and unresolved issues, and creating arguments that appropriately rely on relevant legal authorities. But by emphasizing the practice of environmental law, we also aim to teach you skills more often associated with experiential learning, including the integration of multiple, diverse sources of legal authority; problem-solving; fact-based advocacy; tactical judgment; and negotiation.

To accomplish these objectives, this book incorporates several distinctive attributes. Approaching the book with these attributes in mind will help you make the most of the learning opportunities they provide.

- *Practice-based exercises.* Each chapter contains a series of practice-based exercises. At the conclusion of most chapters, a longer capstone problem reinforces concepts from the chapter and provides a deeper examination of a cutting-edge environmental problem. The problems are integrative and application-oriented, illustrating how legal problems arise in the real world, how a single problem may implicate multiple legal issues, how science and economics affect environmental decision-making, and how addressing a problem may require drawing on multiple types and sources of information and authority. The problems also ask you to think critically about the interests and values you are seeking to advance.

- *Broad range of materials.* Attorneys who practice environmental law rely on a much broader range of materials than just the leading Supreme Court cases and scholarly articles that fill most casebooks. Environmental lawyers do consult leading cases and some scholarly articles, but they also work with statutes, regulations, lower court opinions, agency orders, permits, technical reports, and guidance documents. Our casebook includes materials of all these types, giving you experience in reading and analyzing different documents. Our casebook also helps you to understand the differences among the different types of documents and the relationships between them—issues that generate many legal disputes in environmental law practice.

- *Balance of standard-setting and standard application.* Environmental law casebooks tend to focus on cases challenging EPA regulations. Most situations that environmental lawyers encounter in practice, by contrast, involve questions about how statutes and regulations apply to a particular factual scenario, and are less likely to involve purely legal questions about the validity of regulations. Our casebook includes a more equal balance between standard-setting cases and standard-application cases. Standard application also provides a useful vehicle for detailed factual analysis and advocacy, another important skill that law school may not have given you enough opportunities to develop.

Our book is organized into eight chapters. The first two chapters provide the conceptual, analytical, and historical foundation for a study of environmental law:

- Chapter 1 (Introduction) introduces the field of environmental law. It examines major themes in the field by posing a series of seven basic questions that underlie environmental policymaking: Is something happening to the environment? Should we respond? Should the response be legal? Who should respond? What legal tools should we use? What should the intensity of the response be? Upon whom should the burdens of responding (or not responding) fall?

- Chapter 2 (Background Principles) provides an overview of areas that, although not specific to environmental law, are of central importance to understanding it. Environmental statutes were enacted against a historical backdrop of common-law torts doctrines and the structural backdrop of the Constitution. Principles and methods of statutory interpretation provide tools for interpreting environmental legislation. Because much of environmental law involves delegations of authority to administrative agencies, practicing environmental law requires an understanding of administrative law, which governs the activities of those agencies.

Each of the remaining six chapters examines a major environmental topic and the principal federal statute that addresses it:

- Chapter 3 addresses air pollution and the Clean Air Act;

- Chapter 4 addresses water pollution and the Clean Water Act;

- Chapter 5 addresses hazardous waste management and the Resource Conservation and Recovery Act (RCRA);

- Chapter 6 addresses hazardous waste site cleanup and the Comprehensive Environmental Response, Compensation, and Liability Act (CERCLA);

- Chapter 7 addresses environmental impact analysis and the National Environmental Policy Act (NEPA); and

- Chapter 8 addresses biodiversity protection and the Endangered Species Act.

These chapters generally follow a common structure. They explain the environmental problem, summarize the historical developments that led to enactment of the key federal statute, examine the key components of the statutory program using practice-based exercises, and finally conclude with a capstone question. If we have succeeded in producing the casebook we set out to write, you will finish your course with an understanding of why environmental law matters and how environmental law looks in practice—and hopefully with your initial excitement and passion for environmental issues not just intact, but deepened.

As we complete the project of writing the first edition of this book, Donald Trump has just been elected President, moving environmental law into a new and uncertain phase. Much is still unknown about what the new Trump Administration will pursue as its environmental agenda, and how Congress, the courts, interest groups, states, and the public will react. Undoubtedly, however, the path that environmental law takes in this next phase will depend on a complex mix of factors, including the legislative, administrative, and judicial processes that are entailed in both pursuing and opposing attempts to change environmental law. We hope the practice-based approach embodied in this casebook will help a new generation of lawyers confront the immense challenges of this next phase of environmental law's history. And we hope to give you a good start on your path toward a meaningful career in a subject area that we love, and that is now as crucially important as ever.

TODD AAGAARD
DAVE OWEN
JUSTIN PIDOT

January 31, 2017

SUMMARY OF CONTENTS

TABLE OF CONTENTS

TABLE OF CASES

The principal cases are in bold type.

UNIVERSITY CASEBOOK SERIES®

PRACTICING ENVIRONMENTAL LAW

CHAPTER 1

INTRODUCTION

I. INTRODUCTION

One day in September, 1970, a schoolgirl in Maine sat down and wrote a letter to one of her senators. In it, she described the condition of the Little Androscoggin River, which flowed through her town:

> in any Season you can smell the most sickening smell on earth! At the mouth of the brook, frogs have been seen gasping for air. . . . My uncle works for the government and just came back from Argentina. He almost died when he saw the river. He used to swim and fish in the river. But now fish have been seen floating down the river dead. . . . I am sick of the river like this. Please do something about it.[1]

She was hardly the only one complaining. Across the nation, people were becoming increasingly frustrated with, and worried about, pollution of their air and water. Rivers across much of the country were choked with industrial and human waste. The previous year, an oil spill off the coast of Santa Barbara had become a national news story. Extreme air pollution events were also recurring phenomena. Among the most infamous, and deadly, were a 1954 episode that turned Donora, Pennsylvania to nighttime darkness at noon and a 1966 air pollution event that killed well over 100 New Yorkers. *See* Jody Freeman, *The Story of Chevron: Environmental Law and Administrative Discretion*, in ENVIRONMENTAL LAW STORIES 171, 175–76 (Richard Lazarus & Oliver Houck, eds. 2005). And while almost no one was thinking about this at the time, the same activity that created New York City's killer fog—burning fossil fuels—was beginning to change concentrations of greenhouse gases in the earth's atmosphere, and thus beginning to create what has become the defining environmental challenge of our present times.

But the schoolgirl's letter (and many other complaints like it) went to a sympathetic reader and arrived at a fortuitous time. Over the next few years, Ed Muskie, the Senator who received the letter, and his colleagues did indeed do something about problems like the pollution in the Little Androscoggin River. They passed a series of statutes that still define the field of environmental law.

In the process, they also created a new practice area for lawyers. This book will introduce you to that practice area. It will help you

---

[1] Letter from Suzanne Clune to Sen. Edmund Muskie, Sept. 7, 1970, https://www.mainememory.net/media/pdf/25726.pdf.

understand the environmental problems that environmental laws confront, the structure of those laws, and the basic challenges that underlie them. But this book is not just a theoretical summary of a legal area or a primer on its doctrines. It also will introduce you to the day-to-day work of practicing environmental law. Every day, across the country, thousands of lawyers spend their days thinking about how to advocate for a cleaner and healthier environment, or about how to help clients succeed and prosper in a world where environmental protection is a legal priority. Many others, even though they do not consider themselves environmental law practitioners, must address environmental laws from time to time. Our most basic goal, in this book, is to prepare you to join their ranks.

A. HOW THIS BOOK IS STRUCTURED

This book begins by introducing some questions that recur whenever the legal system confronts an environmental problem. These basic challenges and questions cut across the field, and you will revisit them repeatedly in the chapters that follow. Chapter 1 also provides a brief history of environmental law in the United States, and it closes with a discussion problem focused on environmental justice.

Chapter 2 introduces you to the overlap between environmental law and three other legal subject areas: torts, constitutional law, and administrative law. In the latter two units of this chapter, you may re-read some cases that you covered in a constitutional or administrative law course, and that is no coincidence. Over the past fifty years, environmental law has become thoroughly intertwined with administrative and constitutional law, and many seminal cases in both of those subject areas have emerged out of environmental conflicts.

The remaining chapters introduce you to specific subject areas within the field of environmental law: air quality, water quality, hazardous waste management, hazardous waste site cleanup, environmental impact assessment, and endangered species protection. In each chapter, you will learn not just about key doctrinal issues, but also about the tactical questions that attorneys in these subfields routinely confront. In other words, you will get a window into what an environmental lawyer actually does.

Environmental law is a large and growing field, and that means any casebook must leave out some important subject matter. This book is no exception, and three omissions are particularly important. First, this casebook focuses primarily on federal, rather than state, environmental law. That is less of an omission than it might initially seem, for much of state environmental law is based on federal law (and some federal environmental laws imitated analogous state laws). If you understand federal environmental laws, you are well on your way to understanding their state counterparts. But not all state environmental law parallels federal law, and you will want to be alert to the differences as you enter practice.

Second, this book focuses primarily on pollution control laws. With the exception of some materials in the chapters on environmental impact assessment, water quality, and biodiversity protection, this book generally does not address the extraction of resources from the environment, or our efforts to preserve those resources in place. Our primary focus instead is the control of pollution. If you are interested in those subjects, a class in natural resources law would be a good follow-up and complement to this class.

Third, this book focuses almost exclusively on the United States' domestic environmental laws, and leaves international environmental law and the laws of other countries for other courses.

B. How to Learn from This Book

The format of this book is different from that of a typical legal casebook. Most of the teaching units revolve around discussion problems. The problems will present you with a fact pattern and a legal question (or questions), and the materials that follow will provide you with the legal authority you need to answer that question. Often the answers will be contestable, and the materials will provide fodder for competing arguments on all sides. The legal questions will not all turn solely on interpreting and applying legal authority. Sometimes you'll need to think about whether bringing or defending a case will make sense, even if the law seems to be on your side. And sometimes resolving the matter will require you to negotiate a deal rather than strategize your way through litigation.

The premise of this format is that people learn best by learning actively. You will learn more, we think, by searching governing law—and your own good judgment—for answers than by simply reading and critiquing a series of appellate decisions. This format also will give you more exposure to the kinds of analytical and strategic thinking that are the bread and butter (and, we think, the most interesting part) of environmental law practice. Similarly, the problems will introduce you to many of the different kinds of documents that practicing environmental lawyers use—and produce.

That format will require you to approach class preparation a little bit differently. Initially, when you are preparing a problem, you should keep in mind that it will take more time than just reading and briefing a case. You will need to refer back and forth between the question and the supporting legal materials, and that will slow you down. It can be particularly time-consuming when you are reading excerpts from statutes and regulations. Statutory and regulatory interpretation are core skills for an environmental lawyer, and this book will confront you with many opportunities to build those skill sets. And one of the most important skills for a lawyer reading statutes is the ability to read slowly, methodically, and carefully.

In addition, you will want to think strategically as you read the problems. Environmental law, like most legal subject areas, sometimes presents lawyers with easy questions, but the problems in this book often present close calls (though, of course, you may argue otherwise). So think carefully, as you read, about which arguments would help your client prevail, and which materials would best support those arguments, and also about which arguments would leave you most vulnerable.

II. THE BASIC QUESTIONS OF ENVIRONMENTAL LAW

In 1999, two researchers published a study calling attention to the presence of pharmaceuticals in surface waterways. Christian G. Daughton & Thomas A. Ternes, *Pharmaceuticals and Personal Care Products in the Environment: Agents of Subtle Change?*, 107 ENVTL. HEALTH PERSP. 907 (1999). The pharmaceuticals were present, the researchers wrote, because when people excrete drugs, or when they flush spare pills down the toilet, the drugs pass through sewage treatment systems and enter aquifers, rivers, and lakes. The implications seemed frightening. If drugs are in the water around us, then fish, frogs, plants, and everything else in those waters are exposed to those drugs. So, too, are people. Engineers did not design water treatment systems to remove pharmaceuticals, and we therefore ingest a cocktail of drugs every time we drink out of the faucet.

Before you swear off drinking water, read on, for there is a catch. The study found the pharmaceuticals only in trace quantities, most measured in parts per trillion. By design, most drugs are effective in very low concentrations, but these concentrations were very, very, very low. Consequently, researchers immediately began to ask whether aquatic species or people would even be affected by the traces of pharmaceuticals they were ingesting. Perhaps these new discoveries, scary as they sounded, just showed that chemical detection tests had become extraordinarily sensitive, not that people, plants, or animals were at risk.

Another set of questions also arose: what, if anything, should law do about this situation? Should Congress, or a state legislature, pass laws designed to get pharmaceuticals out of drinking water? Should an administrative agency act? A court? And how should the answers to those questions be decided: would science, economics, or ethics, or something else offer the answer? If there was to be a legal response, how should those laws work, and would they actually be effective? And upon whom should the burden of complying with those laws fall?

To environmental lawyers, these are familiar questions. At least some of them arise with nearly every problem that environmental law now addresses, and with a great many problems that environmental law does not yet respond to at all. Whether the issue is smog, bacterial contamination of waterways, oil pollution at old gas stations, the disappearance of a rare animal species, or a changing global climate, environmental problems present certain common questions for policymakers and lawyers. We highlight each of those questions in the paragraphs that follow, and as you will see from later chapters, people's disparate answers often inform their positions in environmental law's great clashes. This chapter thus will introduce you to the foundational challenges of environmental law.

A. IS SOMETHING HAPPENING TO THE ENVIRONMENT?

In 1969, in one of the seminal moments in environmental law history, the Cuyahoga River caught on fire. A spark from a passing railroad fell to the surface of the river, where it landed on a floating scum of flammable pollutants, and soon the surface of the river was shooting up flames and black smoke. To anyone watching, it would have been obvious immediately that something was happening to the environment, and that, from the perspective of a fish or a person, what was happening was not good.

But the world is not always so clear. Quite often, the first question in any environmental controversy is whether something actually is happening to the environment—and, if something is happening, what exactly its consequences are. Are trace quantities of pharmaceuticals even present in a waterway? If they are, are they affecting fish, or people? If they are affecting fish or people, are the consequences actually bad, and if they are, how bad are they?

Each of these questions, in turn, poses numerous subsidiary questions. Take the question whether trace quantities of pharmaceuticals in a waterway are affecting fish or people. What conditions might be associated with exposure to pharmaceuticals? Are these conditions being observed in fish or people? Where these conditions are observed, are they being caused by exposure to pharmaceuticals or something else? These subsidiary questions, like the larger questions, are often extremely difficult to answer definitively. Data about environmental conditions are often sparse or nonexistent. Establishing causation is difficult at best, and sometimes impossible, especially where (as is often the case) a particular adverse outcome, such as cancer, has numerous potential causes.

Examples of these questions abound in environmental law. In the early years of the field, classic court cases turned on questions about whether lead emissions were hazardous to public health, or whether drinking water laced with asbestos fibers increased risks of cancer. *See Ethyl Corp. v. EPA*, 541 F.2d 1 (D.C. Cir. 1976) (en banc); *Reserve Mining Co. v. Environmental Protection Agency*, 514 F.2d 492 (8th Cir. 1975). More recently, much of the public debate over climate change has focused on questions about whether humans really are changing the climate. Sometimes the debates are premised on misunderstanding,[2] and sometimes subsequent research resolves the questions. But quite often, scientists are unsure whether some human activity is affecting the environment. Or, alternatively, they understand some effects but not others, and that uncertainty takes years to resolve.

B. SHOULD WE RESPOND?

Even if something might be, or even is, happening to the environment, a second question still arises: should we do anything about it? Sometimes the answer might be obvious; if an environmental problem poses an imminent danger to human health, the key question should be how to respond, not whether to do so. But if the threat is not so certain, or doesn't directly affect people, and the costs of responding appear to be real and substantial, then what should we do? And what ethical or moral theory should we even use to judge whether a change is good or bad?

1. RISK AND PRECAUTION

The first of these questions spawns many of environmental policymaking's most vigorous debates, and the example of pharmaceuticals in drinking water can help explore the competing views. One might say that we should never risk exposing our bodies to an unnatural contaminant with uncertain health risks. Environmental lawyers generally refer to this view as the "precautionary principle." In its strongest form, it asserts that people should not carry out activities that might pose environmental risks until they demonstrate that those activities are in fact safe.

But that is nonsense, say the precautionary principle's harshest critics. In their view, the precautionary principle "leads in no direction at all," for some degree of risk is unavoidable in life. Cass Sunstein, *Beyond the Precautionary Principle*, 151 U. PA. L. REV. 1003, 1004 (2003). A law banning trace pharmaceuticals from surface water might effectively stop drug sales, and how then would we reduce the risk and the misery associated with human illness? Or, alternatively, that law might require

---

[2] Two prominent examples involve climate change and genetically modified foods. Much of the *political* debate about climate change focuses on whether people really are changing the climate, even though that debate was settled in the scientific community decades ago. Similarly, much of the debate about genetically modified foods turns on the perceived public health threats of consuming GMOs, even though most scientists agree there is hardly any evidence of such risks. *See* NATIONAL ACADEMIES OF SCIENCE, ENGINEERING, AND MEDICINE, GENETICALLY ENGINEERED CROPS: EXPERIENCES AND PROSPECTS (2015) (summarizing the scientific literature).

municipal wastewater treatment systems to install treatment systems so expensive that the cities would no longer have money to fund schools or hire police. The risks of an uneducated and unprotected populace would replace the risks of trace quantities of pharmaceuticals. These dilemmas are everywhere, according to the precautionary principle's critics, and the precautionary principle really is just a call for a myopic focus on a particular subset of risks.

If the critics are right, and the precautionary principle leads nowhere, what principles should replace it? One alternative is something of an inverse precautionary principle, in which economic activity is presumptively allowable unless regulators convincingly prove that the activity places humans or the environment at risk. That may not strike you as a persuasive view, but it appears often in environmental debates. Consider, for example, the many politicians who have argued that we should not endanger our economy by responding to an uncertain threat like climate change. Similarly, it is not hard to imagine pharmaceutical companies arguing that until scientists are sure that trace quantities of drugs are harming the environment, no regulatory response should occur. In the eyes of the companies, the burdens imposed by regulation may be concrete and real, but the potential benefits may seem speculative.

A compromise view would suggest that we should weigh risks against risks, accepting that no path is free of danger or uncertainty, and should follow the least risky course. Or, perhaps, we should place a slight thumb on the scales in favor of environmental protection, or in favor of the economic status quo, or, perhaps, in favor of technological innovation. The differences between those positions may seem abstract, but they can make huge differences in our actual responses to environmental problems.

2.   ETHICAL THEORIES OF ENVIRONMENTAL PROTECTION

Another basic philosophical question infuses these debates: what ethical theories should we use to judge which environmental changes are bad—and, if they are bad, how bad they really are? In evaluating whether to regulate pharmaceuticals in drinking water, should we take a purely utilitarian stance, in which all that matters is aggregate social welfare? And if so, should that just be the welfare of people, or should natural systems also count? Or, alternatively, should we use ethical theories that ground our environmental obligations in relationships that transcend utilitarian calculations?

In one of the most influential texts in American environmentalist thought, naturalist Aldo Leopold took the latter view. He argued that a "land ethic" should inform all human interactions with the environment. "All ethics," he wrote, so far evolved rest upon a single premise: that the individual is part of a community of interdependent parts. * * * The land ethic simply enlarges the boundaries of the community to include soils, waters, plants, and animals, or collectively: the land.

This sounds simple: do we not already sing our love for and obligation to the land of the free and the home of the brave? Yes, but just what and whom do we love? Certainly not the soil, which we are sending helter-skelter downriver. Certainly not the waters, which we assume have no function except to turn turbines, float barges, and carry off sewage. Certainly not the plants, of which we exterminate whole communities without batting an eye. Certainly not the animals, of which we have already extirpated many of the largest and most beautiful species. A land ethic of course cannot prevent the alteration, management, and use of these 'resources,' but it does affirm their right to continued existence, and, at least in spots, their continued existence in a natural state.

In short, a land ethic changes the role of Homo sapiens from a conqueror of the land-community to plain member and citizen of it. It implies respect for his fellow members, and also respect for the community as such. * * *

A thing is right when it tends to preserve the integrity, stability, and beauty of the biotic community. It is wrong when it tends otherwise.

ALDO LEOPOLD, A SAND COUNTY ALMANAC, WITH ESSAYS ON CONSERVATION FROM ROUND RIVER 239–40, 262 (1966).

If one adopts that ethic, then perhaps depositing pharmaceuticals in waterways is wrong not because (or at least not just because) it might harm the people who drink that water, but because it harms the waterway itself.

But Leopold's view has critics. One of the most famous responses comes from economist William Baxter:

Recently scientists have informed us that use of DDT in food production is causing damage to the penguin population. For the present purposes let us accept that assertion as an indisputable scientific fact. The scientific fact is often asserted as if the correct implication—that we must stop agricultural use of DDT followed from the mere statement of the fact of penguin damage. But plainly it does not follow * * *.

* * * Damage to penguins, or sugar pines, or geological marvels is, without more, simply irrelevant. One must go further, by my

criteria, and say: Penguins are important because people enjoy seeing them walk about rocks; and furthermore, the well-being of people would be less impaired by halting use of DDT than by giving up penguins. In short, my observations about environmental problems will be people-oriented, as are my criteria. I have no interest in preserving penguins for their own sake.

It may be said by way of objection to this position, that it is very selfish of people to act as if each person represented one unit of importance and nothing else was of any importance. It is undeniably selfish. Nevertheless I think it is the only tenable starting place for analysis for several reasons. First, no other position corresponds to the way most people really think and act—i.e., corresponds to reality.

Second, this attitude does not portend any massive destruction of nonhuman flora and fauna, for people depend on them in many obvious ways, and they will be preserved because and to the degree that humans do depend on them.

Third, what is good for humans is, in many respects, good for penguins and pine trees—clean air for example. So that humans are, in these respects, surrogates for plant and animal life.

Fourth, I do not know how we could administer any other system. Our decisions are either private or collective. Insofar as Mr. Jones is free to act privately, he may give such preferences as he wishes to other forms of life: he may feed birds in winter and do with less himself, and he may even decline to resist an advancing polar bear on the ground that the bear's appetite is more important than those portions of himself that the bear may choose to eat. In short my basic premise does not rule out private altruism to competing life-forms, It does rule out, however, Mr. Jones' inclination to feed Mr. Smith to the bear, however hungry the bear, however despicable Mr. Smith.

Insofar as we act collectively on the other hand, only humans can be afforded an opportunity to participate in the collective decisions. Penguins cannot vote now and are unlikely subjects for the franchise—pine trees more unlikely still. Again each individual is free to cast his vote so as to benefit sugar pines if that is his inclination. But many of the more extreme assertions that one hears from some conservationists amount to tacit assertions that they are specially appointed representatives of sugar pines, and hence that their preferences should be weighted more heavily than the preferences of other humans who do not enjoy equal rapport with "nature." The simplistic assertion that agricultural use of DDT must stop at once because it is harmful to penguins is of that type.

Fifth, if polar bears or pine trees or penguins, like men, are to be regarded as ends rather than means, if they are to count in our calculus of social organization, someone must tell me how much each one counts, and someone must tell me how these life-forms are to be permitted to express their preferences, for I do not know either answer. If the answer is that certain people are to hold their proxies, then I want to know how those proxy-holders are to be selected: self-appointment does not seem workable to me.

Sixth, and by way of summary of all the foregoing, let me point out that the set of environmental issues under discussion—although they raise very complex technical questions of how to achieve any objective—ultimately raise a normative question: what ought we to do? Questions of ought are unique to the human mind and world-they are meaningless as applied to a nonhuman situation.

WILLIAM F. BAXTER, PEOPLE OR PENGUINS: THE CASE FOR OPTIMAL POLLUTION (1974).

The disagreement between Leopold and Baxter is not quite as stark as these passages might initially suggest. In other passages, Leopold makes clear that he views human interests as very important. And, as Baxter repeatedly notes, a person with an entirely anthropocentric and utilitarian worldview could still be an ardent environmentalist; the natural environment can be very helpful and valuable to humans. Nevertheless, there are circumstances when these kinds of ethical choices can lead people to starkly different views about how environmental controversies should be resolved.

C. SHOULD THE RESPONSE BE LEGAL?

Imagine, for purposes of argument, that scientists are convinced that pharmaceuticals in drinking water are harming people and the environment and that there is a widespread consensus that something ought to be done about it. Why should we invoke law as a response? After all, other tools are available. Government agencies could (and in fact do) launch information campaigns encouraging people not to flush unused pills down the toilet. They also could (and in fact do) use other voluntary measures, like offering people opportunities to drop off unused pills for proper disposal. Consumers could decline to use drugs that are particularly likely to contaminate waterways, or could even use boycotts to encourage drug companies to find better ways to control the full life cycles of the chemicals they produce.

There are many reasons why these tools might seem more appealing than a legal response. Law, at its core, is a set of rules backed by the coercive power of government, which means it is always at least somewhat heavy-handed. Particularly in a society committed to liberty and freedom, people often prefer a lighter touch. Laws also are not always effective tools. Enforcing a prohibition against pill-flushing, for example, might be so difficult that there is no sense in trying.

So why use law? One of the classic answers to this question is that voluntary, non-legal measures are unlikely to work. And the most famous articulation of that answer comes from an essay, penned by ecologist Garrett Hardin, called *The Tragedy of the Commons*. The essay excerpt below explains Hardin's analysis and then, at the end, briefly applies it to the greatest environmental challenge of our era.

Barton H. Thompson, Jr., *Tragically Difficult: The Obstacles to Governing the Commons*
30 ENVTL. L. 241 (2000)

In 1968 Garrett Hardin published his famous and oft-cited article "The Tragedy of the Commons," examining the overuse of commonly shared resources. Hardin chose his title well. The problem of the tragedy of the commons has been recognized since at least the days of Aristotle. But Hardin gave the problem a vivid and visceral name that quickly captures our attention and tells us much of what we need to know.

Anyone who has studied the environment for very long understands the tragedy of the commons. When a resource is freely available to everyone in common, everyone has an incentive to take as much of that resource as they want, even though the collective result may be the destruction of the resource itself. Society as a whole would be better off restraining consumption and preserving the resource. But the rational action for each individual is to consume to her heart's content. Because no one can bind anyone else's actions, not consuming simply makes one a patsy. To each individual, moreover, her own actions seem insignificant. Holding back will lead to a marginal improvement, if any, in the condition of the resource. Even those who recognize and bemoan the oncoming tragedy of overuse will often conclude that it makes no sense not to join others in depleting the resource. The high road leads nowhere. The cumulative result of reasonable individual choices is collective disaster.

Most of the recent academic literature on the tragedy of the commons examines why some commons do *not* lead to tragic consequences. Elinor Ostrom and others have shown that local communities throughout the world sometimes have been able to avoid the tragedy through the development of local management institutions. Psychologists also have conducted experiments to determine which conditions maximize the chances that individual resource users will limit their consumption even when trapped in the logic of the commons. These experiments suggest that resource users are more likely to restrict their consumption when they receive prompt feedback on the impact of their extractions, when their behavior is visible to others, when they can communicate with their fellow resource users, and when the users share a group identity. The message of both fieldwork and experimental commons is that tragedy is not inevitable. With the right conditions, resource users can avoid depleting the resource.

* * * Academics not only have explained the structural fabric of the tragedy of the commons, but also have identified a number of workable solutions. One frequently promoted solution is to privatize the commons. Both field investigations and social science experiments have shown that privatization, when possible, is typically a particularly effective solution to the tragedy of the commons. When a resource can be privatized, the resource owners will incur the entire cost of overuse and thus carefully husband the resource. A related solution is to unitize the resource: organize a single operator to manage exploitation of the resource and divide any profits among the community of resource users or owners. When privatization or unitization is not possible—and frequently such solutions are not workable for technological or cultural reasons— government or community regulation can limit overuse of the commons. The government can restrict the total number of cattle being grazed in the common pasture, cap extractions of petroleum, or control discharges of pollutants into a surface stream. Local communities can establish and enforce informal rules.

Despite multiple workable solutions to the tragedy of the commons, however, governments and other institutions have found it extremely difficult to address many of the most important commons dilemmas facing the world today. Resource users, moreover, have typically been the most vociferous critics of proposed solutions. In a number of important commons contexts, resource users have vehemently denied that there is a problem (despite relatively substantial evidence that a serious problem exists), argued that intervention by the government or other outside institutions is unnecessary (despite repeated failures by the community of resource users themselves to voluntarily or collectively limit resource use), and opposed suggested solutions as unfair and unwise. The question that impels this Essay is why it has proven so difficult to implement effective solutions and, more specifically, why resource users have proven not only unreceptive, but affirmatively hostile, to such solutions.

One should not expect that solving the tragedy of the commons will be easy. Just as the tragedy of the commons presents a collective action problem, so do attempts to solve the problem. Solving the tragedy of the commons is an example of a public good because all users of the commons benefit from a solution. No individual resource user may see why it is in her particular advantage to rush out and spend political and other resources trying to solve the tragedy. Let Joe take the lead, Jill thinks. But of course the problem is that Joe, in turn, waits for Jill to take the lead, and both wait for Bob. The result, according to political economists, is that everyone holds back and nothing gets done.

* * * The danger of global climate change presents a slightly different form of commons dilemma. Rather than taking something *out* of the commons, people are putting something *in*—CO_2 and other greenhouse gases. It also is not simply a narrow class of the population that is feeding the potential tragedy; virtually everyone is contributing to the problem. But global climate change is still a classic example of the tragedy of the commons. Because atmospheric use is free to all, businesses, individuals, and governmental entities internationally use it as a great waste repository, resulting in the current tremendous threat to the world's climatic system.

While the tragedy of the commons provides one classic explanation for legal protection of the environment, it is not the only one. Environmental regulation also might be desirable because, in its absence, people will not have sufficient information to make informed decisions about environmental consequences. Or it might be desirable to prevent vulnerable people who lack political power from being harmed by those with greater influence. It might also save us from ourselves; many environmental laws function to limit exploitation or pollution of natural systems, even though it might be profitable in the short-term, so that our quality of life will be sustainable into the future. There are also more cynical explanations. Sometimes government regulation allows businesses that can accommodate the regulatory regime to gain a competitive advantage over those that do not, and sometimes it allows political leaders and advocacy groups to claim the mantle of environmental savior even when the laws they are supporting are unlikely to have any particular positive effect.

In short, there are many reasons, some of them compelling, to bring the coercive force of law to bear on environmental problems. Nevertheless, as you work your way through this book, and as you confront environmental problems in the real world, it is worthwhile to consider whether non-legal responses might complement legal ones, or might even eliminate any need for legal intervention.

D. WHO SHOULD RESPOND?

If people agree that an environmental change is occurring and is problematic, and that it deserves a legal response, that leads to another difficult question: who should respond?

There are many possible answers. Congress, the judiciary, and the executive branch all could take the lead, and within the executive branch, responses could come from the chief executive and his or her close subordinates or from administrative agencies. There also are also multiple levels of government within the United States. Federal, state, and local governments all could—and often do—respond to environmental problems. Moreover, branches of government and levels of government often work together (and sometimes in opposition) to address particular environmental problems.

The responses also can come from outside of government. Many large corporate firms now use internal environmental governance systems, which mimic elements of public environmental law but rely on private corporate management institutions for their implementation. Increasingly, large corporations impose environmental (and labor) standards on their suppliers, and some of those standards often reach across international boundaries and exceed the demands of environmental law. Consequently, for some companies, the most important environmental "regulator" is a purchaser like WalMart, not a government agency. *See generally* Michael P. Vandenbergh, *Private Environmental Governance*, 99 CORNELL L. REV. 129 (2013). Similarly, government agencies often contract out some of their environmental work, and private businesses routinely lean on the expertise of consultants (and, of course, lawyers) to help them comply with the mandates of environmental law. For decades, private advocacy groups like the Natural Resources Defense Council and the Sierra Club have worked constantly to influence the development and implementation of environmental law. Consequently, few environmental controversies are addressed purely within public or private spheres, and environmental policymaking often blurs the boundaries between those realms.

Image courtesy of Michael Vandenbergh

Environmental law also often presents questions about what kinds of qualifications and expertise environmental decision-makers should have. For example, should highly trained experts with specialized, technical knowledge decide what to do about pharmaceuticals in drinking water? That may seem logical, for many environmental issues implicate complex questions of environmental science, engineering, and economics. But even experts have their biases—the worldviews of engineers, economists, and scientists can be very different from each other's, and also from those of lay people—and sometimes technocratic decision can be opaque and exclusive. Alternatively, environmental decision-making could be highly participatory, with decisions made largely in response to popular preferences. But while that may sound democratic, what happens if public preferences are poorly informed? Consider, for example, the plausible possibilities that lay people will react to stories of pharmaceuticals in drinking water with unjustified alarm—or unjustified complacency. These tensions between populist and technocratic decision-making, and between different types of technocrats, also recur throughout environmental law.

All of these questions about who should act (or not act) drive a substantial part of the work of environmental lawyers. They are a central focus of Chapter 2, which addresses the intersections between environmental law and tort, constitutional, and administrative law. And they will continue to arise throughout the rest of the book.

E. WHAT LEGAL TOOLS SHOULD WE USE?

Suppose that people agree that an environmental problem exists, that it merits a legal response, and that, say, the federal government should lead that response. What sort of legal tools should it use?

Responding to a problem like pharmaceuticals in drinking water requires much more than just a legal declaration that the problem ought to go away. Instead, lawmakers must figure out how to actually change the status quo. For most environmental problems, there are many possible ways to do this (and for some, there may be no good way at all). You will spend much of the rest of this course exploring the options, but a short preview may be helpful at this early stage. As you read, consider which, if any, of these tools might respond effectively to the presence of pharmaceuticals in drinking water.

1. TORTS

As the next chapter will discuss in more depth, there was a time not so long ago when environmental law, to the extent it existed, was mostly tort law. People harmed by pollution turned to claims like nuisance or trespass to seek redress. While torts now play a secondary role in environmental law, they still are important in some realms, like dealing with injuries from exposure to toxic chemicals. And the tort system remains available as an option when new environmental problems emerge. So, for example, an environmental lawyer concerned about pharmaceuticals in drinking water might consider whether a public or private nuisance claim or a product liability theory offers a viable response. In addition, tort principles such as joint and several liability and proximate causation have been integrated into many statutory programs.

2. PROPERTY

Torts were not the only common law doctrine that people used to address environmental problems. Another path to environmental protection may be to create (or clarify) property rights in natural resources.

That may seem odd, for political debates have conditioned us to think of property rights and environmental regulation as natural enemies. But if one cause of environmental degradation is that resources are shared by many people but controlled by none, leading to a tragedy of the commons, then giving people defined property rights in the resource may improve long-term stewardship. People are more likely to take care of land, for example, if clear ownership rights ensure that no one else can poach resources that are preserved.

3. INFORMATION

A very different form of environmental regulation relies on information disclosure. That could happen in a variety of ways. First, lawmakers could require decision-makers to gather and disclose information about the environmental consequences of their actions. In theory, that process of gathering and disclosing information would better inform the decision-makers themselves, and also would facilitate better public debate about environmental decisions. The leading example of this regulatory approach is the National Environmental Policy Act, which you will study in Chapter 7.

Second, lawmakers could require businesses (or public entities) to disclose information about their environmental performance. So, for example, regulators could require businesses to disclose how many tons of toxic chemicals they have released into the environment, or how much of a pollutant their wastewater discharges or smokestack emissions contain. Regulators then could use that information to support policymaking or enforcement. Or that information could work without additional government involvement. It could alert consumers that a company's environmental performance is poor, leading those consumers to avoid the company's products. Or it could cause investors to worry that a company engages in poor environmental management and thus presents a risky investment choice.

4.   PRESCRIPTIVE REGULATION

The most important legal tools for an environmental lawyer to understand are prescriptive regulatory systems. Generally speaking, these systems identify specific actions that regulated entities must or must not take. Environmental lawyers often break the world of prescriptive and proscriptive regulations down into two categories, each described in more detail below. Each category pervades the world of environmental law.

a.   Laws That Require Specific Actions

The first category includes laws that demand, or prohibit, certain actions. Such laws are sometimes referred to as "command and control" regulation. A law that requires coal-fired power plants to install scrubbers—which are a specific kind of pollution control technology—is the classic example of this kind of requirement. Another example is a mandate for construction companies to place hay bales at the perimeters of their sites to filter sediment out of stormwater runoff. A third, to return to our pharmaceutical example, might be to ban drugs that seem particularly persistent in water and are particularly harmful to aquatic species.

b.   Performance Standards

A performance standard specifies the outcome that a regulated entity must achieve, not the method by which it must reach that outcome. So, for example, an air quality regulator might establish a limit on the amount of sulfur dioxide that coal-fired power plants can emit, but allow the power plants to decide whether to achieve that standard by installing scrubbers or using low-sulfur coal. Water quality regulators might limit the amount of sediment that can leave a construction site but let construction companies to figure out how to comply with those limits.

5. ECONOMIC INCENTIVES AND TRADING

In environmental law's early years, prescriptive regulatory systems dominated the field. Regulators saw clear advantages in those systems; most importantly, they were often relatively easy to enforce. But many economists, and a growing number of lawyers, argued that prescriptive regulatory approaches were inefficient. They proposed two alternatives, each of which has become increasingly important to the practice of environmental law.

a. Tradable Permit Systems

The first alternative to become popular is something known as environmental trading (you probably have also heard the phrase cap-and-trade). A simple example illustrates the concept and its appeal:

> Suppose that two factories each emit 1000 tons per year of volatile organic compounds (VOCs), which are a common class of air pollutants. Suppose that regulators want to cut those emissions by half. And suppose, also, that because of differences in the technology they use, the two factories will incur different costs to abate pollution. Factory A will have to spend $50 for each ton/year of reduction, while factory B will need to spend $100 for each ton/year.

> If regulators just impose a performance standard, and require each facility to cut its pollution in half, the aggregate cost will be the sum of A's and B's abatement costs, captured by the simple equation below:

> Total cost = (500 × 50) + (500 × 100) = 75,000

> But imagine if the regulator assigns A and B an entitlement to emit half their present level but allows them to trade shares. And imagine that A realizes it can cut seventy-five percent of its pollution without an increase in its per-ton abatement costs. A then could cut its pollution by seventy-five percent and sell a credit to B for the excess twenty-five percent reduction, thus letting B reduce its pollution by only twenty-five percent. And suppose B realizes it would be cheaper to buy that credit than to reduce its pollution by a full fifty percent, so it happily makes the deal with A. Aggregate pollutant emissions would be exactly the same, but aggregate costs would now be lower, as shown by the equation below:

> Total cost = (750 × 50) + (250 × 100) = 62,500

This second option is a simple version of environmental trading. Note that it has produced the same environmental outcome while distributing the burdens of compliance to the entity able to bear those burdens with the lowest cost—a result that, in theory, is optimal for everyone involved.

As you'll see from the chapters that follow, regulators now use trading systems in a wide variety of environmental realms. As you will also see, in practice, trading systems are almost invariably more complicated than this stylized example. Some involve huge numbers of actors, rather than just simple exchanges between two factories, and some involve trading things that are less fungible than tons of sulfur dioxide. Even tons of sulfur dioxide are unlikely to be truly fungible in the real world; trading will shift the location of emissions, and those locations may be important. But even as the systems become more complicated, this basic economic argument provides their underlying rationale.

b.   Fees and Taxes

An alternative way to regulate through economic incentives is to put a direct price on environmental harms—or on activities that lead to them. This can be done through fees or taxation. The most famous example of this approach is something known as a carbon tax, which places a tax on the carbon dioxide emissions that cause the lion's share of climate change. But other examples exist, and many others are possible.

The basic theory supporting these taxes comes from the work of an economist named Arthur Pigou. Pigou, like many economists, was concerned with something called an externality, which is a cost that a firm does not factor into its economic decision-making—usually because it is borne by someone else. Externalities are everywhere in environmental law; the pollution that a factory sends to its neighbors is a classic example. Pigou hypothesized that a tax on pollution would compel the emitting factory to incorporate into its decision-making the costs it imposes on others, and thus would lead to a more socially optimal level of pollution—while also generating revenue.

As of this writing, taxation plays a fairly small role in the United States' environmental regulatory systems. But the idea of environmental taxation has become increasingly prominent in discussions of potential environmental reforms, and a carbon tax is now a widely-discussed option, favored by many economists, for responding to climate change.

6.   PLANNING SCHEMES

In addition to these different regulatory tools, environmental laws often require planning. A typical planning provision will specify some outcome that should be achieved and then require some other entity to come up with and implement a plan to attain that outcome. Air quality regulation provides a classic example. Under Clean Air Act sections 108, 109, and 110, the federal government sets national ambient air quality standards, but it delegates to the states the responsibility and the authority to adopt and implement plans that will attain those standards.

In practice, environmental planning requirements often work in concert with other regulatory systems. State planners will likely use some mix of informational requirements, prescriptive regulatory systems, and incentives to attain the desired environmental outcome. The planning requirement thus really functions as a system for delegating bounded authority, not as a substitute for alternative regulatory approaches.

7. PROCEDURAL AND SUBSTANTIVE REGULATIONS

As you learn about different regulatory tools, one last distinction will be helpful to keep in mind. Environmental lawyers often distinguish between procedural and substantive regulatory requirements. Procedural requirements generally specify the process some decision-maker must complete before it takes actions that affect the environment. So, for example, a procedural provision of an environmental law might require a public agency to consider public comments before making its decision. A substantive requirement, by contrast, governs the content of the ultimate decision. A prohibition on harms to rare animals is a classic example of a substantive prohibition.

Environmental law is filled with both kinds of provisions, and some sections of environmental laws contain both procedural and substantive requirements.

8. SUBSIDIES AND CONSTRUCTION

People often think of environmental regulation as something that stands in tension with the construction of infrastructure. Sometimes that view is accurate. But environmental laws have often encouraged people to build things as a way of protecting the environment.

Perhaps the most famous, and environmentally successful, example of this is the program for wastewater treatment plant construction in the 1972 Federal Water Pollution Control Act (now known as the Clean Water Act). In addition to authorizing strict regulation of water pollutant dischargers, the Act also authorized massive expenditures on water treatment. Those expenditures affected the politics of the act by also making it a jobs bill, and by leading some opponents, including President Nixon, to express concern about massive costs. Other examples are more indirect. Many environmental restrictions create the need for compliance infrastructure, and designing and building that infrastructure puts some people to work, even as it increases costs for other entities.

This list of tools may seem dauntingly long. And the realities of environmental law are even more complicated than the list suggests. Individual environmental statutes—even seemingly simple ones—often draw upon a variety of different regulatory tools. And sometimes regulatory tools that appear, on paper, to fall neatly within one category will function quite differently in practice. If you delve into the vast literature on environmental law, you are likely to find a fair amount of casual pigeonholing of environmental statutes. The Clean Water Act, someone might tell you, is a prescriptive statute, and the National Environmental Policy Act is informational. Beware of those simple characterizations. In the real world, the tools we have described are often employed in combination, and many regulatory systems defy any kind of simple classification.

F. WHAT SHOULD THE INTENSITY OF THE RESPONSE BE?

Of all the questions raised by environmental challenges, one probably recurs more than any other. How stringent should environmental law be? Or, to put the question differently, how should environmental law balance the benefits of solving or preventing environmental problems against the costs of compliance? Our pharmaceutical dilemma would almost certainly raise this question. If pharmaceuticals in water seem to pose only modest ecological and human health risks, and the costs of keeping them out of waterways would be large, how much (if any) protection should the law require?

In part, this question just revisits our earlier questions about precaution and environmental ethics. But another thorny question is often intertwined with those ethical questions: how should we go about measuring the benefits and burdens of regulation? That second question is at the heart of one of the most heated debates of environmental policy-making (and of regulatory theory more generally): what role should formal cost-benefit analysis play in environmental policymaking?

To understand that debate, it may be helpful to know something about what cost-benefit analysis is and how it came to be a part of environmental law. Generally speaking, a cost-benefit analysis tries, to the maximum extent feasible, to place dollar values on the costs of a regulatory measure, to place dollar values on the benefits, and to weigh them against each other. A strict cost-benefit test then might rule out any regulatory option whose quantified benefits do not outweigh its quantified costs, while a less strict test might simply use the cost-benefit analysis as a common-sense check on regulatory decision-making. Similarly, a strict cost-benefit test might set the stringency of a regulation at the point at which the marginal cost of any increase in regulatory stringency exceeds the marginal benefits.

Cost-benefit analysis first evolved as a method for evaluating federal water projects. During President Jimmy Carter's administration, at a time when the costs of implementing environmental and workplace safety laws were coming into sharper focus, it began to emerge as a more general tool for evaluating regulatory policy. President Ronald Reagan then elevated the importance and visibility of cost-benefit analysis by issuing an executive order mandating cost-benefit analysis for any major agency rulemaking. Every president since has affirmed or retained that requirement, though Presidents Clinton and Obama both issued orders that would make formal cost-benefit analyses a few shades less determinative of policy outcomes. The Reagan executive order also delegated oversight over cost-benefit analyses to the Office of Information and Regulatory Affairs (OIRA), a sub-agency within the Office of Management and Budget, which is itself a part of the White House, and that oversight role has stayed with OIRA ever since.

Cost-benefit analysis has been controversial. Its advocates assert that it provides a valuable check on what otherwise might be myopic agency decision-making, preventing EPA, for example, from prioritizing environmental improvements over all other social values. They also argue that it accords with the way people in the real world make decisions, or at least should; finances are undeniably important, and reasonable people routinely weigh the pros and cons of alternative courses of action. Finally, they argue that it brings some transparency to governmental decision-making. Numbers can be manipulated, as even the strongest advocates of cost-benefit analysis would concede, but, they argue, it is easier to spot the flaws in a quantitative analysis than to pick apart a decision that an agency just chalks up to intuition or informed professional judgment. *See, e.g.,* John Graham, *Saving Lives through Administrative Law and Economics*, 157 U. PA. L. REV. 395 (2008); CASS R. SUNSTEIN, THE COST-BENEFIT STATE: THE FUTURE OF REGULATORY PROTECTION (2003).

The critics, meanwhile, have lobbed a series of charges against formal cost-benefit analysis. *See, e.g.,* Frank Ackerman & Lisa Heinzerling, *Pricing the Priceless: Cost-Benefit Analysis of Environmental Protection*, 150 U. PA. L. REV. 1553 (2002). They argue that it is inherently biased against environmental protection, because industry's costs are easy to estimate (and exaggerate), while environmental benefits are inherently difficult to quantify. Consider, for example, a cost-benefit analysis of pharmaceuticals in drinking water; how exactly would one put a price on genetic deformities in fish, particularly if one isn't sure how likely those deformities are to occur? While those non-quantified costs can be noted, people tend to fixate on the numbers, and things that can't be quantified often drop out of the policymaking calculus. The critics also charge that cost-benefit analysis is ethically suspect. It requires placing numeric values on human life, which strikes most people as odd, and in OIRA's traditional practices, it also requires placing a lesser value on deaths or other harms in the future than deaths

The work of Richard Revesz and Michael Livermore provides an interesting third position in this debate. They have argued that when setting national ambient air quality standards—a process in which EPA legally is forbidden to consider regulatory costs—EPA has routinely set standards *less* stringent than those its own cost-benefit analyses would have required. Based on these findings, they argue that cost-benefit analysis could lead to stronger environmental protection and ought to have more of a role in regulatory decision-making. *See* Michael A. Livermore & Richard L. Revesz, *Rethinking Health-Based Environmental Standards*, 89 N.Y.U. L. REV. 1184 (2014).

that occur at present. Finally, the critics of cost-benefit analysis have launched a furious institutional critique against OIRA. According to many accounts, the agency is staffed by economists with a cultural bias against regulation and a weak understanding of the risks to which agencies are responding, and it operates without any of the transparency that is normally required by administrative law (and by OIRA's own governing rules). *See, e.g.,* Daniel A. Farber & Anne Joseph O'Connell, *The Lost World of Administrative Law*, 92 TEX. L. REV. 1136 1165–67, 1175 (2014). The result, some critics allege, is that OIRA's cost-benefit analyses are essentially anti-regulatory hatchet jobs.

For most environmental lawyers, these questions about OIRA and formal cost-benefit analysis are just an academic debate—or a debate limited to high-level policymakers and their advisors. Only if you become heavily involved in federal environmental rulemaking processes are you likely to spend much time reading formal cost-benefit analyses, and only a subset of the lawyers who participate in rulemakings are likely to confront legal questions about when cost-benefit analysis should occur and how it should be used. Similarly, most lawyers who engage in legislative environmental advocacy are unlikely to spend much time debating requirements for formal cost-benefit analysis. Most lawmaking happens at state levels, and few state agencies have enough resources to actually complete formal cost-benefit analyses.

You are likely, however, to confront some of the deeper questions lurking beneath these debates. In courtrooms, agency decision-making processes, and legislative chambers, advocates routinely debate the pros and cons of different policy options. And in those debates, questions about the role of economics, and about who supplies and who weighs the numbers, are likely to recur again and again.

G. UPON WHOM SHOULD THE BURDENS OF RESPONDING (OR NOT RESPONDING) FALL?

In a traditional and formal cost-benefit analysis, the primary focus of the inquiry is on *aggregate* costs and *aggregate* benefits. Who bears those costs and benefits is not of primary concern. And through the early years of environmentalism, most environmentalists did not think much about which people bore the burdens of environmental pollution. If asked, they would likely have said something like, "we all do," or "everyone does, except the big companies that are despoiling the earth."

In the late 1980s and early 1990s, the emergence of the environmental justice movement shattered that complacency. A 1987 study, commissioned by the United Church of Christ, found that hazardous waste landfills were disproportionately likely to be sited in low-income neighborhoods populated primarily by people of color. UNITED CHURCH OF CHRIST, TOXIC WASTES AND RACE IN THE UNITED STATES (1987). Similar studies followed, and with them, two charges. One was directed against society generally: environmental justice advocates argued that the United States had chosen to lay the heaviest burdens of environmental pollution upon people of color, and that this choice was motivated by racism. A second charge was directed at the environmental movement. Environmentalists, according to environmental justice advocates, had spent too much time on causes that mostly benefited people who were white and wealthy—like preserving beautiful wilderness areas for hikers, or keeping industrial development out of wealthy suburban neighborhoods—and not nearly enough time worrying about the places where poor and non-white people lived and worked. *See* Richard J. Lazarus, *Pursuing "Environmental Justice": The Distributional Effects of Environmental Protection*, 87 NW. U. L. REV. 787, 788–89 (1993) (summarizing critiques). The environmentalists were no better than the society around them, according to this charge. Sometimes they were worse. For environmentalists, many of whom saw themselves as heirs to the civil rights movement, that was a harsh message to receive.

The emergence of the environmental justice movement provoked several reactions. Environmental groups and government agencies attempted reforms. Many environmental groups now pursue environmental justice initiatives, focus to a greater extent on urban pollution issues, and have made deliberate efforts to reach out to and include people of color. Some state and federal environmental agencies have also made efforts to integrate environmental justice into their decision-making. At the international level, environmental justice concerns play a prominent role in debates over climate change, which remains a problem to which comparatively wealthy and predominantly white countries in the Global North disproportionately contribute and from which residents of the Global South are likely to suffer the most harm.

Meanwhile, at academic levels, researchers began studying the racial and socioeconomic dynamics of environmental harms more intensively. Some of the resulting studies presented a more complicated story than the original UCC reports. *See, e.g.,* Vicki Been & Francis Gupta, *Coming to the Nuisance or Going to the Barrios: A Longitudinal Analysis of Environmental Justice Claims*, 24 ECOLOGY L.Q. 1 (1997) (finding mixed evidence, some of which suggests that the siting of hazardous waste facilities influences the demographics of communities rather than the other way around). But other recent studies still show that poor and minority communities, at least in some parts of the country, continue to bear the heaviest burdens from environmental pollution. *See, e.g.,* Lara Cushing et al., *Racial/Ethnic Disparities in Cumulative Environmental Health Impacts in California: Evidence from a Statewide Environmental Justice Screening Tool*, 106 AM. J. PUB. HEALTH 2341 (2015) (finding continued disparities).

III. THE HISTORY OF ENVIRONMENTAL LAW

Even before the American Revolution, the colonists were passing laws and litigating cases that we might now label as environmental. In the Nineteenth Century, American courts continued this tradition, considering several blockbuster cases addressing environmental problems. But the idea of environmentalism, and the associated idea of a discrete field of environmental law, did not coalesce and emerge as a force until the 1960s. The field you are entering, therefore, is quite young, and in some ways has only just begun to move past its formative stages. And the debates of the 1960s and 1970s are not that different from—and can sometimes help you make sense of—the debates of today.

The excerpt below chronicles environmental law's first few decades. If you are interested in a more detailed account, we recommend Professor Lazarus's book, *The Making of Environmental Law* (2004), which tells a similar story in greater depth.

Richard J. Lazarus, *The Greening of America and the Graying of United States Environmental Law: Reflections on Environmental Law's First Three Decades in the United States*

20 VA. ENVTL. L.J. 75 (2001)

Those of us who have spent our professional lives as practicing lawyers, teachers, and scholars steeped in environmental law often lose sight of the discipline's relative youth. Yet, prior to 1970, environmental protection law in the United States was essentially nonexistent. Of course, there were a few, isolated states pursuing fledgling efforts, and there were common law property and tort doctrines that some of the more activist judges were willing to invoke on behalf of environmental concerns in private and public lawsuits. But there was nothing even remotely resembling a comprehensive legal regime for regulating pollution of the air, water, or land.

There was no national clean air legislation, no federal clean water act program, no hazardous waste or toxic substance laws. There was not even a federal environmental protection agency prior to the 1970s (and virtually no state agency analogues). The federal pollution control authorities that did exist were greatly fragmented amongst several agencies, and they possessed relatively weak statutory powers, much of which consisted of little more than providing financial and technical assistance to state and local governments.

Ten years later, a relative blink of an eye for the lawmaking process in most moments of history, the legal landscape transformed completely. There were hundreds of pages of federal environmental protection statutes, and thousands of pages of federal regulations and less formal agency regulatory guidance documents. There was also a federal environmental agency, the United States Environmental Protection Agency ('EPA'), which was primarily responsible for the implementation of the host of newly enacted environmental protection laws. Although the EPA was shy of the full-fledged cabinet-level status many environmentalists had sought, the agency possessed a powerful array of statutory authorities. These authorities provided for the EPA's promulgation of pollution control standards and, through a variety of financial incentives and sanctions, for its oversight of state governmental efforts to achieve compliance with such standards within their respective jurisdictions.

A. *The First Generation of U.S. Environmental Protection Law*

What did the first generation of laws look like? There was, at the very outset, the National Environmental Policy Act ('NEPA'), literally signed into law on the first day of the decade, January 1, 1970. NEPA requires federal agency assessment of the environmental impacts of proposed federal agency action and possible alternatives. Although NEPA's essentially procedural requirement had a massive impact on governmental decision-making, the federal legislative enactments during the early 1970s that imposed substantive requirements were even more significant.

Three of these substantive laws were the Clean Air Act of 1970, the Federal Water Pollution Control Act Amendments of 1972 (now, as further amended, referred to as the Clean Water Act), and the Endangered Species Act Amendments of 1973. These laws were dramatic, sweeping, and apparently uncompromising. Each of these laws imposed a series of specific statutory commands on polluting activities. They did not rely primarily on voluntary behavioral changes in response to mere exhortation. Nor did they turn, in the first instance, principally to financial incentives or otherwise seek to enlist market incentives to achieve their environmental protection objectives. They instead sought to identify classes and categories of polluting or environmentally destructive activities that threatened human health and the environment, and then to impose stringent standards on their performance.

The restrictions were generally not based on economic feasibility but rather on far more demanding norms. Some were based on technological standards designed not simply to replicate existing pollution control technology but rather, in effect, to force industry to develop new technology capable of substantially more reductions in existing levels of pollution. Other standards directly required that certain environmental or human health risks be eliminated regardless of either economic or technological feasibility, even if (in theory) compliance with such a standard could occur only upon shutdown of the polluting activity.

These first generation laws were also remarkably aspirational in scope and in their mandates. The standards, and corresponding deadlines for their accomplishment, were exceedingly ambitious, if not unrealistic. Indeed, as discussed below, although such ambitious laws necessarily made a strong symbolic societal statement regarding the importance of environmental protection and the need for fundamental change in humankind's relation to the natural environment, they also unwittingly triggered a pathological cycle of crisis, controversy, and public distrust, which has since hampered needed reform.

The Clean Air Act, for instance, required the Administrator of the EPA to promulgate and, in short order (by 1975) achieve nationally uniform ambient air quality standards that would protect public health, with an adequate margin of safety and public welfare. The Clean Water Act, enacted as the Federal Water Pollution Control Act Amendments in 1972, was equally demanding. The 1972 enactment sought fishable and swimmable waters everywhere by 1983 and zero discharge of pollutants by 1985, and it made unlawful any discharge of pollutants into navigable waters absent a permit issued by the EPA. The Endangered Species Act of 1973 was not nearly as sweeping in its scope as the others, but set requirements that unsettled existing standards of conduct. The ESA mandated that federal agencies ensure that their actions were not likely to jeopardize the continued existence of endangered or threatened species, or result in the destruction or adverse modification of their habitat. The mandate was absolute.

B.   Roots of the First Generation Laws

The natural question that arises is what prompted this dramatic legal transformation. Part of the explanation finds it roots in the way that a series of news media events captured the attention of the American public in the late 1960s, culminating in the first celebration of 'Earth Day' in the spring of 1970. Certainly to be included in those triggering events would be the publication of Rachel Carson's book, Silent Spring, in 1962, which raised public concerns about the adverse health effects of pesticides. Two other important public viewpoint-forming events both occurred in 1969: the Santa Barbara oil spill off the California coast and the 'burning' of the Cuyahoga River in Ohio, each of which was the subject of considerable television news coverage.

The time was also ripe in the United States for consensus. The civil rights movement and the antiwar movement had polarized the nation in the 1960s. Many citizens were ready for an issue about which there could be a national consensus rather than further polarization. To a large extent, the environmental movement satisfied that need.

Indeed, for that reason, many elected officials saw the environmental movement as a basis for political self-promotion. Environmental issues were largely ignored during the 1969 Presidential election, but by 1969 and 1970, both Democrats in Congress and Republicans in the White House sought to demonstrate their environmental credentials to enhance their competing aspirations for national office. The lofty goals and stringent requirements of the Clean Air Act, for instance, resulted in part from a competition between President Richard Nixon and Senator Edward Muskie, with each seeking to 'out-environmental' the other in their respective willingness to propose ever tougher restrictions on air pollution.

The emergence of strong national environmental public interest organizations during this period also fueled the explosion in environmental lawmaking activities. New organizations, such as the Environmental Defense Fund and Natural Resources Defense Council, joined longstanding, but recently invigorated entities, such as the Sierra Club, National Audubon Society, and National Wildlife Federation, to push for tougher environmental laws. These organizations prodded through lobbying, lawsuits, legislative, executive, and judicial decision makers to be more responsive to environmental concerns.

Legislative action was critical because, after all, only the U.S. Congress is empowered to pass laws such as the Clean Air Act, Clean Water Act, and Endangered Species Act. But the courts likewise served a crucial historical function. They acted both independent of, and in some respects, in collaboration with, Congress.

Many judges viewed environmental lawsuits as akin to the civil rights suits of the prior decade: proper occasions for heightened judicial attention on behalf of societal concerns likely to be given short shrift in the democratic process. Those judges, accordingly, sought to relax standing barriers that might otherwise restrict judicial access for those environmental citizen suits. They sought to apply more exacting standards of judicial review to ensure that environmental concerns were not ignored by executive and legislative branch policymakers. In addition, they frequently read more into the meaning of the statutes than many lawmakers likely had specifically contemplated when voting in favor of their passage.

* * * These judicial rulings also had the practical effect of providing the environmental community with enormous political leverage before Congress. Environmentalists, and politicians vying to enhance their environmental credentials, were not the only parties seeking comprehensive federal environmental legislation. Industry, too, sought such legislation; indeed, the regulated community did so quite urgently.

Many judicial rulings and state legislative actions favorable to the environment had left industry unsettled about what was, and what was going to be, required of them. Indeed, in certain areas, industry faced legal prohibitions of conduct in which they had long engaged. The regulated community, accordingly, needed to restore some order through federal legislative action. Environmentalists effectively exploited industry's need by insisting upon exceedingly demanding statutory requirements. The strict requirements of the Clean Air Act, Clean Water Act, and the National Forest Management Act can all be traced to such prior judicial rulings and state legislative initiatives.

Finally, the far reaching nature of the laws is also likely a reflection of American culture. The 1960s were divisive times, but they also offered the nation a shared moment of self-congratulation. President John Kennedy had boldly announced at the outset of the decade that the United States would land a man on the moon by the decade's end, and, in 1969, the nation did so. To many, cleaning up the environment presented a similar challenge—a challenge made all the more compelling by those first solitary pictures of Earth taken from outer space. The nation, it seemed, needed only to pursue its environmental protection goals with the same uncompromising determination and technological ingenuity that had characterized the space program. If it did, the United States could also achieve goals—zero discharge into waters of the United States and compliance with ambient air quality standards within five years—that might at the outset seem wholly out of reach.

C. Challenge and Response: The Emergence of a Second Generation of Environmental Laws

It is, of course, far easier to set an ambitious goal than it is to meet one, and, almost as soon as these first generation laws were passed, it seemed as if they might well have a short half-life. Industry resisted their implementation, as did many state governments who concluded that the federal legislation improperly usurped state sovereignty.

The greatest challenge the laws faced, however, was the energy crisis of the mid-1970s. Industry promoted the notion, readily embraced by many politicians, that the energy needs of the nation were both more pressing than and inconsistent with environmental protection concerns. The country's need, for instance, to rely on abundant domestic supplies of coal, rather than petroleum imports, might require relaxing air pollution control requirements inconsistent with increased coal combustion. Likewise, the need to explore, extract, and transport domestic energy reserves of coal, petroleum, and natural gas would likely require relaxation of environmental restrictions that impeded or otherwise made such activities more costly.

The 'energy/environment' confrontation, however, ultimately fell far short of dismantling the first generation laws of the early 1970s. At the instigation of environmental citizen suits, courts insisted on strict implementation of those laws, resulting in a series of negotiated settlements between government and environmental interests, as well as judicial orders outlining schedules for agency compliance with statutory requirements. Although Congress amended the laws in certain respects, it did so without abandoning the law's basic structure and rigor. Congress extended some deadlines, fine-tuned some requirements to add incremental flexibility, and mostly relaxed standards only in terms of their application to the daily behavior of individual citizens (e.g., driving) rather than the conduct of industry.

Indeed, rather than abandon the first generation of environmental protection laws, Congress expanded upon them in the second half of the first decade. Congress enacted a new series of laws at least as ambitious and sweeping, and in some respects, even more so. These 'second generation laws' are distinguishable from the first generation largely because they tend to focus on a particular type of pollutant, rather than the identity of the particular environmental media in which pollutants are released. Hence, while the Clean Air Act, Clean Water Act, and

Endangered Species Act focused on air, water, and wildlife (and habitat), the Toxic Substances Control Act ('TSCA') and Resource Conservation and Recovery Act ('RCRA'), adopted in 1976, and the Comprehensive Environmental Response, Compensation, and Liability Act ('CERCLA'), each focused on that subset of more dangerous, i.e., toxic or hazardous, pollutants and substances regardless of the environmental media in which they were found.

RCRA and TSCA were both classic, prospective, and comprehensive regulatory laws. They included both health-based provisions and technology-based provisions, with some consideration of costs versus benefits. The theoretical justification for these laws was the need to supplement the media-based laws, which risked simply chasing toxic pollutants from one media to the next, with some laws that looked at the larger, overall picture. RCRA and TSCA were meant to close the 'last remaining loophole' in environmental law.

CERCLA likewise focused on 'hazardous' substances, but was fundamentally different in its orientation than any other previous legislation. It was a retrospective liability law, not a prospective regulatory enactment. CERCLA was designed to provide for cleanup of abandoned and inactive hazardous waste sites, and to assign liability to the responsible parties for those cleanup costs. The other laws, with their prospective focus, generally neglected to deal with the legacies of decades of inadequate controls. Instead, they likely exacerbated the problem. By significantly increasing the costs of doing business, the prospective laws inevitably generated more abandoned and inactive sites as business sought to avoid the new, more stringent requirements (and associated liabilities) by simply closing down.

CERCLA's liability scheme was wholly unprecedented when enacted, at least in terms of U.S. law. It assigns liability for cleanup costs not just to current owners and operators of the site, but to all past and previous owners of the site at the time of waste disposal. Also included within the liability net are any persons who generated the hazardous substances that were disposed on the site, as well as parties who transported substances to the site. Moreover, because liability is strict, and almost always joint and several (because the harm is indivisible), any one of these parties may be held liable for the entire cleanup costs.

D. Concluding Thoughts

The overall transformation of U.S. law from 1970 through 1980 is astounding. The environmental improvements were minimal and some activities escaped the most demanding environmental protection requirements altogether. Nonetheless, in many respects, there were substantial improvements in the resulting quality of the environment in the United States during this time period. Still, perhaps the fairest characterization of the laws is that they permitted the U.S. economy to continue to grow without the kind of massive environmental degradation that might have otherwise occurred and which certainly has been experienced elsewhere.

There was, however, during that first formative decade, the planting of seeds of unrest that have since persisted and tended to undermine environmental law's ability to reform itself in response to changing information and circumstances. The promises not kept, however unrealistic they may have been, were broken at a cost. They helped to create a pathological cycle of distrust that has since plagued U.S. environmental law. When aspirational promises of clean air, clean water, and species preservation were not met, the debates and discussions regarding environmental law and policy became dominated by accusations of incompetence, exchanges of blame, and worse. Ironically, the general pattern was to respond to those discussions by enacting statutes that made even grander promises which, when not met, triggered a further cycle of blame and distrust.

U.S. governmental institutions have frequently exacerbated rather than redressed this dilemma. These institutions are founded upon deep-seated skepticism of those who wield government authority and they seek, through the checks and balances embraced by the U.S. tripartite system of government, to curb potential governmental overreaching and any single branch's abuse of the public trust. During environmental law's first decade in the United States, repeated failures to meet statutory promises suggested agency abuse of its public trust as public aspirations went unmet. At the same time, various interests exploited to their own advantage the institutional forces of distrust embedded within the American system. The result has been the pattern of agency crisis and controversy and a cycle of regulatory failure, which first began during the 1970s.

III. The Transformation of American Law in Response to Environmentalism: The Second Decade

Modern environmental law's second decade in the United States began as tumultuously as the first but with a very different evolutionary spin. Immediately on the heels of congressional passage of CERCLA, the most far-reaching of all the environmental statutes, President Ronald Reagan took office. He favored a substantial cutback of environmental regulation and took concerted action to accomplish that end.

By the end of the decade, however, no such rollback had occurred, notwithstanding a series of Presidential efforts. Instead, Congress passed federal environmental statutes that were even more demanding than they had been at the start of the decade. Even more significantly, the environmental protection laws were themselves only the most formal expression of environmental law in the United States. Environmentalism, and its underlying values, priorities, and information, had triggered a sweeping transformation of legal rules across a broad spectrum of areas of law in the United States.

A. Regulatory Reform, Deregulation, and the Legislative Backlash

When President Ronald Reagan took office in January 1981, significant cutbacks on federal environmental protection law seemed inevitable. Candidate Reagan had campaigned on a platform that seemed to leave little room for comprehensive federal pollution control requirements. He had campaigned on themes antithetical to much federal environmental law: against 'big government;' against the federal government diminishing the power of state governments to decide for themselves how to govern; and against government rules and regulations that restricted industry and substituted governmental determinations of proper industrial conduct for basic economic forces supplied by a free market.

During his campaign, Reagan also specifically singled out federal environmental laws on each of these grounds. He complained that many environmental restrictions were extreme: they improperly usurped state sovereignty, they cost too much, they stifled needed economic growth, and they reflected the views of a radical fringe rather than mainstream America. It is therefore not surprising that President Reagan, immediately upon taking office, reportedly sought to nominate to the position of the EPA Administrator someone willing to 'bring EPA to its knees.'

Surprisingly, the popular President's efforts were not only stymied but actually prompted a legislative backlash that ultimately generated even more stringent environmental protection laws. The Reagan Administration's efforts at deregulation unwittingly fueled the public's pre-existing distrust of government—the legacy of the first decade's series of failed promises—especially the public's readiness to believe that the government might be compromising public health concerns in order to bolster the corporate profits of industry. The environmental community in the United States took effective advantage of public concern—vigorously promoting public outrage—and, as a result, substantially increased both their own financial resources and membership as well as their lobbying clout before Congress.

The Reagan Administration's short-term solution was to replace its initial head of the EPA, who had sought to decrease the agency's budget, with a highly regarded individual with strong environmental credentials. The long-term impact of the Administration's effort to cut back on federal environmental protection laws, however, was precisely the opposite from the Administration's original policy objective. Congress responded to the public's disapproval of deregulatory efforts by amending the federal environmental protection laws in a manner designed both to make them stronger and to reduce executive branch discretion to diminish their effectiveness in the future.

Hence, environmental laws that in the 1970s had conferred considerable discretion on the EPA regarding how best to meet strict environmental goals now commenced to dictate to the agency not only the statutory ends, but the precise means as well. Even those statutory amendments that retained some discretion in the EPA to develop environmental protection requirements in the first instance imposed strict deadlines on their promulgation. Furthermore, in the event those deadlines were not met, the amendments mandated the automatic triggering of stringent requirements, including absolute prohibitions on specified waste disposal activities.

From 1981 through 1990, Congress substantially amended virtually all of the major environmental protection laws. Congress amended the Endangered Species Act in 1982, the Resource Conservation and Recovery Act in 1984, CERCLA in 1986, the Clean Water Act in 1987, and the Clean Air Act in 1990. These detailed, prescriptive amendments converted what had been open-ended statutes, tens of pages in length, into statutes of several hundred pages in length. Congress had, in effect, deprived the executive branch of much of the environmental policymaking authority that the latter had historically enjoyed. Although the Clean Air Act included, for the first time, a major program dependent on market incentives (tradeable emission rights to control acid deposition), the statutes generally adhered to a 'command and control' regime of strict technology and health-based standards.

B.   The 'Greening' of U.S. Law

The significance for environmental law of the 1980s, however, was not confined either to the nation's rebuff of the Reagan Administration's deregulatory efforts or Congress detailed amendments of both first and second generation environmental statutes. Virtually all of U.S. law was 'greened' during the 1980s. The environmental protection laws were simply the most obvious, surface expression of the legal transformation.

The emergence of environmental law in the United States underwent, especially in the second decade, a general process of assimilation as the teachings and values of environmentalism infused one category of legal rules after another, transforming our nation's laws in response to the public's demand for environmental protection. Areas of the law as diverse as administrative, bankruptcy, civil rights, corporate, free speech, insurance, international, remedies, securities, and tax law each underwent (and are still undergoing) a significant process of transformation in response to the public's desire to have a legal system that better reflects the public's environmental protection goals. Legal rules invariably express a balance struck—an equilibrium—between competing values. Modern environmentalism challenged many of those settled equilibria.

It challenged: (1) administrative law principles that limited judicial review of environmental lawsuits; (2) limitations on tort liability that made recovery of environmental harm more difficult; (3) property law rules that promoted environmentally destructive activities; (4) limitations on corporate liability that made it difficult to hold corporations responsible for environmental harm they caused; (5) bankruptcy rules that frequently kept economic actors from paying the full cost of environmental harm they had created; and (6) civil rights laws that considered housing, employment, and education needs, but gave too little attention to the civil rights dimension of clean air and clean water. In response, legal doctrine in each of these areas evolved during the 1980s.

C.   The Expanding Practice of Environmental Law

Another important feature of U.S. environmental law in the 1980s was the way in which the practice of environmental law grew exponentially. At the beginning of the decade, environmental law was a fairly narrow specialty. Many firms had no lawyers that specialized in the area, and those that did generally included environmental law as a subpart of their litigation sections. Few corporations possessed in-house environmental law expertise.

By the end of the 1980s, the number of practitioners of environmental law had dramatically increased. Environmental law became one of the 'hot' specialties. Law firms were eager to find lawyers with expertise in the area, and law students enrolled in record numbers of environmental law courses. Every major law firm boasted of its own environmental law practice; some large firms employed as many as 100 lawyers practicing primarily environmental law. Sizeable law firms specializing almost exclusively in environmental law also developed. Virtually every major corporation hired in-house counsel knowledgeable about environmental law.

A similar explosion in environmental counsel occurred in the public sector. The U.S. Department of Justice had approximately 15 lawyers working full time on environmental enforcement matters at the outset of the 1980s. By the end of the 1980s, there were more than 150 enforcement lawyers. The U.S. Environmental Protection Agency employed approximately fifty-two lawyers when it commenced operations in the early 1970s, but employed more than 800 by the early 1990s. Similar patterns were likely mimicked throughout state and local governments, where the vast majority of environmental enforcement actually occurs.

No doubt the primary reason for this dramatic expansion in environmental law expertise was CERCLA's unprecedented and sweeping liability regime and the threat of possible criminal prosecution for felony violations of environmental statutes, both of which dominated the decade of the 1980s. Expanded civil and criminal liability provided the private sector (and many public sector entities as well) with a huge incentive to hire lawyers to represent them in pending CERCLA actions and, even more importantly, to advise them regarding future compliance to minimize their possible future liability and exposure to felony prosecution. Moreover, because CERCLA liability, in particular, swept so broadly—bringing within its liability net every major Fortune 500 company as well as many small companies, nonprofit medical and educational institutions, and even the government itself—the combined need for environmental counsel was massive in the mid- to late-1980s.

D. Concluding Thoughts

With everyone claiming to be an environmentalist, U.S. environmental law's second decade ended in many significant respects the way the first decade began. The politically disastrous rejection of President Reagan's effort at the beginning of the decade to dismantle much of the federal environmental protection arsenal prompted most policymakers to shy away from any pretense of an effort to challenge the propriety of increasingly stringent federal environmental protection requirements.

During the 1988 Presidential elections, both major party candidates (George Bush and Michael Dukakis) claimed environmental credentials. Each promised significant new initiatives to protect the natural environment. Upon his subsequent election, President George Bush delivered on his promise by providing crucial support to amendments to the Clean Air Act, which had been stalemated in Congress for more than a decade. The resulting Clean Air Act Amendments of 1990 imposed sweeping, comprehensive, and demanding requirements that largely perpetuated, through detailed elaboration and supplementation, the Act's initial 1970 regulatory regime.

Environmental law no longer seemed to be at risk of wholesale abandonment, but to have come of age. After two decades, it was increasingly seen as part of the settled legal landscape, as reflected both in the environmental protection laws themselves and in the host of legal rules that had been effectively 'greened' in other intersecting, yet nonetheless diverse, areas of law. The major perceived challenges concerned how best to achieve the next stages of pollution control and, in particular, how best to channel limited resources to those environmental protection problems that presented the most serious risks. Although the precise terms of the laws seemed constantly in flux, however, no wholesale abandonment of the law's basic goals and regulatory frameworks seemed in the offing.

IV. A Surprise Attack, Persistent Controversies, and the Emergence of International Environmental Law in the Domestic Arena: The Third Decade

Appearances are often as deceiving in law as they are in life; the close of environmental law's second decade was no exception. The early 1990s revealed once again how abruptly the political winds surrounding environmental law can dramatically shift. Environmental programs that seemed a matter of shared consensus became, virtually without warning, the subject of radical, yet broad-based efforts at their legislative unraveling. Unlike in the 1980s, however, Congress now supported reform, and the executive branch was in opposition. Nevertheless, somewhat astonishingly, the legislative reform effort dissipated almost as dramatically as it arose, leaving the entire federal program largely intact. Indeed, it is the phenomenon of relatively little legislative action that may prove to be one of the significant legacies of the 1990s.

A less obvious but still significant catalyst for reform can be found in the changing nature of the federal judiciary in the United States. More than a decade of conservative judicial appointments from 1981 through 1992 created a federal judiciary in the 1990s wholly unlike one that welcomed, indeed affirmatively instigated, the development of tough environmental protection requirements in the 1970s. The full implications of that shift are still not clear, but there has been an increasing number of judicial rulings in environmental law's third decade that are openly skeptical of the expansive application of strict environmental requirements.

Although congressional reform efforts have since diminished, the controversies that precipitated those efforts have not disappeared. Prominently left in the legislative wake are several persistent, growing controversies related to U.S. environmental law that require resolution if yet another massive, unpredictable reform effort is to be avoided. Some of these controversies relate to longstanding disputes pertaining to the structure of governmental decision making in the United States. Federal and state governments have long debated, and frequently differed, on how best to allocate environmental law and policymaking authority between their respective sovereign authorities and, within each sovereign, between their various branches of government.

* * * Environmental law's third decade momentarily began with George Bush, the self-declared 'environmental President,' but quickly shifted in the early 1990s to an emphasis on regulatory retrenchment. His Vice-President made environmental deregulation a major executive branch initiative, culminating in a formal moratorium on regulations, including several significant environmental protection programs.

The most remarkable challenge to federal environmental protection laws, however, came several years later in 1994, with the election of

Republican majorities to both the House and Senate of Congress. The Republicans campaigned on the basis of a program they dubbed as the 'Contract With America,' the full implications of which for environmental law became apparent only in the immediate aftermath of their election. The Contract targeted federal environmental protection programs more than any other area of the law for significant curtailment.

Republican majorities in both chambers moved swiftly on several legislative fronts to convert their agenda into positive law. They proposed legislation that would have replaced environmental standards based on minimum standards of human health and technology-forcing requirements. In their place would be environmental standards based on cost/benefit analyses, comparative risk assessment, and other economic efficiency criteria. Environmentalists have long complained that such standards inevitably decrease environmental protection by discounting environmental values not susceptible to monetary valuation and environmental risks not certain to occur.

Other aspects of the new Republican majority agenda similarly promised a radical overhaul of the existing federal environmental law programs. They included legislation that would limit Congress' ability to enact so-called 'unfunded mandates,' which require action by state governments without providing the states with the funding necessary to do so. Proponents of this legislation repeatedly cited federal environmental laws as examples of laws that, because they necessarily rely on state and local implementation, included such improper mandates.

Other bills promised 'regulatory relief' designed to make it harder for government to promulgate regulations that impose economic costs on industry. Here too, proponents singled out costly environmental requirements as justifying these reforms. The bills proposed, inter alia, imposing on federal agencies multiple layers of procedural requirements and heightened standards of judicial review, each of which would be likely to chill agency implementation of environmental protection rules.

Finally, the Republican 'Contract' sought to cut back on environmental law through budgetary reductions and disincentives. For instance, within the broader context of reducing the national debt, the new Republican legislative majorities proposed budgets that singled out environmental protection for some of the most severe reductions. Their budgets reportedly would have reduced the EPA's enforcement dollars by up to forty percent.

The even more sweeping proposals, however, related to proposed budgetary disincentives. The 'Contract' included bills that called for compensating private property owners for any economic loss they might suffer because of federal restrictions on the use of their property. The legislative proposal singled out for such treatment environmental restrictions, especially those related to water quality control and endangered species protection. The legislative hearings in support of such a compensation requirement, accordingly, sought to highlight the (greatly exaggerated) plights of small land owners that retained no economic use of their land because of environmental restrictions.

The practical effect of the proposed laws would be to confer on those who owned private property rights in natural resources an economic right—compensable if diminished—to engage in the very kind of environmentally destructive conduct that the environmental laws had deemed unlawful. The most likely programmatic effect of such a damage remedy, which was estimated to cost the federal government billions of dollars if enacted and the environmental laws fully implemented, would be for those federal agencies responsible for implementing federal environmental laws to minimize their liability by curbing their implementation and enforcement efforts. No doubt to ensure just that result, the proposed legislation called for the damage remedies to be paid out of the agency's own operating budget, rather than out of general U.S. Treasury funds.

Any one of these legislative proposals, if enacted, could have fundamentally changed the structure of federal environmental law. Their cumulative impact would have been as revolutionary as the lawmaking effort that created modern environmental protection law in the early 1970s. For much of 1994, moreover, congressional passage of at least several of these initiatives seemed a virtual certainty.

Remarkably, however, practically none of these varied proposals became law (although some proposals are still pending). The reform efforts dissipated almost as quickly they formed. In a reversal of roles, while the legislative branch in 1994 sought to reform environmental law, the executive branch sought to preserve it. In the 1980s, the executive branch had sought to obtain many similar changes, only to be rebuffed by Congress, but when Congress was instigating the reforms in 1994, the executive branch maintained the opposition.

The executive branch also used the same tactics against Congress that Congress had used against it a decade beforehand. Just as Congress had effectively exploited the public's distrust of government efforts to protect the environment in the 1980s to defeat that earlier reform effort, so too the executive branch now pursued an identical strategy to block Congress. The President, Vice President, and the EPA Administrator repeatedly characterized Congress as seeking to undermine public health and environmental quality at the behest of industry profits. The American public, always ready to perceive environmental protection in such stark terms, and prone to expect such a political sell-out, responded in a manner that ultimately deprived the legislative reform effort of its political strength. Hence, the third major effort in as many decades to dismantle the demanding framework of U.S. environmental law, like the two before it, fell flat.

———————

Lazarus wrote his article in 2001, so it does not cover a lot of recent history. In the years since, some of the trends he described have continued, while other new ones have emerged.

Federal legislative stalemate. In the 1990s, as Lazarus explains, Congress considered major changes to environmental laws, but legislative stalemates and the threat of presidential vetoes prevented those changes from being enacted. Very little has changed. Since 1990, Congress has rejected proposals for major retrenchments to environmental laws, and it also has not passed any major legislation responding to emerging problems like climate change. At the federal level, only fisheries law (revised in 1996 and again in 2002) and the Toxic Substances Control Act (revised in 2016) have seen significant changes.

State legislatures, by contrast, have been much more active in the environmental realm. Some have passed landmark new environmental legislation. California's AB–32, which creates a sweeping regulatory scheme designed to reduce greenhouse gas emissions, is one of the most ambitious examples. Others have taken major steps to limit the scope of environmental regulations.

Administrative reforms. While Congress has done very little to change environmental *statutory* law, administrative agencies have made major changes through rulemakings, adjudications, and evolving practices. One recent article summarizes the resulting dynamics:

> We might start by acknowledging that the legislators of the 1970s and 1980s, for all their foresight, underestimated the complexities of the tasks they assigned to administrative regulators. In particular, they underestimated the extent to which environmental progress would require picky, detailed attention to thousands of small threats.* * * The Congresses of environmental law's early years gave regulators the authority to respond to those problems, but neither they nor the agencies they empowered had the toolboxes or the experience to undertake the difficult, and sometimes intrusive, tasks involved in administering this brave new regime. What followed, then, was a long period when the gaps between environmental mandates and actual practice were extraordinarily large and agencies weren't quite sure how those gaps could be closed—and in which some efforts at closure were both clumsy and ineffective.

Things are very different now. The United States may no longer pass significant environmental statutes; the glory years of environmental legislating are over. But the other key story of the last thirty years has been the evolution of administrative protections. Across many different subfields of environmental law, agencies have moved, slowly and fitfully, toward expanding and improving the protections offered within existing statutory bounds. Central to that movement has been an increasing intolerance of harms that might once have been written off as *de minimis*. The shift is by no means complete; there are still many gaps between the ambitions of the statutes of the 1970s and 1980s and the regulatory practices of the present day. And figuring out ways to use limited, and often declining, staffing levels and budgets to regulate increasing numbers of pollution sources remains an enormous challenge for environmental agencies. But from hazardous waste management to stormwater regulation to stream fills, environmental law is filled with examples of gradually increasing regulatory protection.

Regulated industries (and regulated governmental entities and individuals) have sometimes been implacable opponents of those changes. But at the same time agencies have learned to protect more, they also have learned to protect in ways more solicitous of the regulated, and the regulated have learned to work with the new regulatory regimes. General permits, compensatory mitigation programs, and more cooperative enforcement regimes, to provide a few examples, have all been designed to make regulation work better for industry. And the growth of the environmental consulting industry, the emergence of private certification systems, and an increasing embrace of environmental management systems and self-auditing programs, to provide a few more examples, have all offered industries ways to take charge of their own compliance, and to integrate environmental requirements into functioning business models.

Dave Owen, *Little Streams and Legal Transformations*, 2017 UTAH L. REV. ___, ___.

The Emergence of Climate Change. In the 1970s, scientists were already thinking about climate change, but legislators were not. Even in 2001, when Richard Lazarus wrote his historical article, climate change law was still primarily an aspiration (or, for some, a fear). Now, climate change dominates environmental policy debates, and figuring out whether and how to respond to climate change has become a central question for many subfields of environmental law.

Because of that importance, a basic primer on climate change may help prepare you for the rest of this course.[3] In short, climate change occurs because some gases—carbon dioxide is the most important one—function like a greenhouse roof, letting light in but slowing the outward flow of heat. Life depends on this greenhouse effect; without it, the earth would be uninhabitably cold. But as greenhouse gas concentrations rise, the amount of heat retained by the earth's atmosphere also increases, raising average global temperatures.

For many decades, greenhouse gas concentrations have indeed been rising. The primary cause is fossil fuel combustion, which releases carbon dioxide into the atmosphere. Other major contributing activities include deforestation and agricultural practices, which release methane, another important greenhouse gas, and which also reduce the earth's capacity to pull carbon dioxide back out of the atmosphere. Climate models predict that this warming will continue for centuries. But the degree of future warming—and, accordingly, the intensity of secondary consequences—will depend primarily on how much more greenhouse gases humans emit into the atmosphere.

This warming is already having, and will continue to have, a variety of secondary consequences. Sea levels are rising, partly because polar ice caps are melting and partly because water expands as it warms. Those rising seas will place low-lying coastal areas around the world at risk, and are likely to eventually inundate some areas that currently host large populations. Extreme weather, including heat waves, droughts, and floods, will become increasingly common. Water supplies in many areas will become more erratic. Habitat zones will shift toward the poles and toward higher elevations. And plant, animal, and human communities all will need to adjust to the resulting shifts. Some other consequences are less certain, as is the degree to which these consequences will occur. But many changes are already underway.

While these changes are threatening, the challenges of responding to climate change are substantial. Climate change is a global problem, and that means any comprehensive solution will necessitate multinational cooperation. Climate change also arises largely from activities carried out by large and powerful industries, and that fuels potent opposition to new regulatory changes. In another sense, climate change arises out of the everyday behaviors of billions of people—with very few exceptions, anyone who drives a car or lives in a house is a contributor—and requiring people to use new technologies or change their daily lives is not easy. Climate change also is difficult for law to address partly because the links between our actions and the resulting

---

[3]   For an authoritative, but accessible and nicely illustrated, summary of climate change science, see NATIONAL ACADEMY OF SCIENCES, CLIMATE CHANGE: EVIDENCE, IMPACTS, AND CHOICES (2012).

environmental changes are hard to perceive. When an oil spill pollutes a river, the cause and the effect tend to be palpably obvious, and it is generally easy for people to understand the need for a response. But we cannot see our tailpipe emissions changing the climate. Indeed, because weather is naturally variable, and because climate change is not affecting all places equally, it is sometimes hard for people who are not climate scientists to perceive that the climate is changing at all. A problem that is hard to perceive and difficult to address does not lend itself to easy responses.

Yet environmental law is responding, and in the chapters that follow, you'll see many examples of people trying to apply old environmental laws to this relatively new problem. Over the course of your careers, the environmental laws associated with climate change are likely to evolve. But the nature of that evolution is far from certain.

The Partial Merger of Energy and Environmental Law. The growing importance of climate change has contributed to another important evolution in environmental law. Increasingly, environmental law and energy law are merged fields. They never were entirely separate; from the outset of environmental law's modern era, people have recognized many environmental issues arise from the extraction, transportation, and combustion of fossil fuels. But the integration between the fields continues to grow, to the point where it is now nearly impossible to separate them. Consequently, many of the fact patterns you read in the pages that follow will overlap with the field of energy law.

The 2016 Election. As this book goes to press, a president who has emphatically denied the existence of climate change is assuming office, and a political party that has been generally hostile—at least in recent years—to environmental regulation holds both branches of Congress and will likely soon have appointed a majority of the Justices of the United States Supreme Court. A push for legislative and administrative changes to environmental laws is all but certain to occur. But the scope of that push, and its resonance with Congress as a whole, remain to be seen. The long-term implications for environmental law also are far from clear, and they will depend upon the actions of many people, including, perhaps, you.

IV. CAPSTONE PROBLEM: LITIGATING ENVIRONMENTAL JUSTICE?

Most of the chapters in this book include a capstone discussion problem, which is designed to integrate the concepts you learned in that chapter and to extend your knowledge in new directions. The capstone problem in this first chapter is a little different, for it focuses on just one issue: environmental justice. But it will also introduce you to one of the most basic skills an environmental lawyer must possess: the ability to read governing law and figure out whether or not a client has a sound basis for a legal claim. It also will introduce you to a second skill that many lawyers do not encounter until they enter practice: understanding what levers, beyond courtroom advocacy, lawyers might use to advance their clients' interests.

You are an attorney in a rapidly-growing western metropolitan area. The region was built up around highways—public transit systems are minimal—but reliance on automobiles seems to be causing problems. Traffic has become increasingly bad, and so has air pollution. On hot summer days and during winter temperature inversions, thick smog envelops much of the region.

Highway planners are under heavy pressure to do something to relieve the traffic, and their proposed solution has been wider roads. More specifically, they propose to add two lanes to a major arterial highway that accesses the city's downtown from its western suburbs. To suburban residents, this sounds like an ideal solution; they anticipate reduced commute times. Developers who hope to continue the suburbs' outward expansion are similarly pleased by the proposal. But residents of the city neighborhoods adjacent to the proposed highway expansion are not pleased at all. And your clients—a coalition of community groups from those urban neighborhoods—are leading the opposition.

The residents are concerned about noise and health. Multiple studies have shown that pollution levels tend to be higher in close proximity to highways, and have also shown lasting health effects upon the people— particularly children and the elderly—who live near heavy traffic. Asthma and other respiratory problems are already common in the neighborhoods near the highway. More lanes will mean more cars, the residents fear, and that will only make the problems worse.

The residents also see the proposed highway expansion as the latest episode in a long and ugly history. When the highway was first built, it, like many highways in the United States, bisected an established neighborhood populated primarily by people of color. The presence of the highway irrevocably altered the character of that neighborhood, even as it provided conveniences for, and facilitated the growth of, nearby suburbs, which then were almost exclusively white. Both the urban neighborhoods and the adjacent suburbs now are more racially mixed than they were in the 1960s, when the highway was first built. But about sixty percent of the urban neighborhood residents are people of color, while the surrounding suburbs still are about seventy-five percent white. One neighborhood activist bluntly captures the prevailing sentiment in her community: "this is just more environmental racism, plain and simple."

The highway expansion will require approvals from both the Federal Highway Administration (which will provide key funding) and the state highway department. Your task is to figure out whether you have any legal basis for challenging those approvals. More specifically, your challenge is to determine whether you can base a successful legal claim on the fact that pollution from the highway expansion will disproportionately affect people of color (another attorney in your office is researching whether you could bring claims under the Clean Air Act or the National Environmental Policy Act). Community activists have repeatedly explained to you that what they would like, most of all, is "to get a court to recognize that we have suffered racial injustice, and to put a stop to it."

Can you find a legal basis to support that claim? Please assume that you have scoured the administrative record and records from public hearings, and that they reveal very little concern for the health impacts on your clients' communities. No one outside the communities seemed to care much about those health impacts, but nowhere in the record can you find a statement like, "well, we don't need to worry about what happens to those people because they're black and Latino." The statements you find instead are all about alleviating traffic jams.

As you consider the legal materials, you also should think about other forms of activism. Sometimes bringing a lawsuit would be unwise even if the law is on your side. Conversely, sometimes even a losing lawsuit can help bring attention to your cause or rally a community into action. And whether or not you bring a lawsuit, you probably should think about what else you and your client should do to advance its cause. In short, thinking about whether your case will win or lose in court is only part of an environmental lawyer's job, and only part of what you should consider as you analyze this problem.

For any claim alleging racial injustice, you might look first to the United States Constitution.

U.S. Constitution, Fourteenth Amendment

* * * No state shall . . . deny to any person within its jurisdiction the equal protection of the laws.

A huge body of case law, some of which you may have reviewed in a constitutional law course, has grown out of those few words. To date, however, the body of cases addressing environmental justice claims is tiny, and it does not include any cases from the United States Supreme Court. The summaries and short excerpts below instead come from two key non-environmental cases.

Washington v. Davis
426 U.S. 229 (1976)

[The District of Columbia required all applicants for police positions to take a written test, and applicants had to obtain a threshold score in order to be hired. African-American applicants failed the test at much higher rates than white applicants, and two applicants challenged the test, arguing that the disparate rates of failure demonstrated that the test was unconstitutionally discriminatory.]

* * * The central purpose of the Equal Protection Clause of the Fourteenth Amendment is the prevention of official conduct discriminating on the basis of race. It is also true that the Due Process Clause of the Fifth Amendment contains an equal protection component prohibiting the United States from invidiously discriminating between individuals or groups. *Bolling v. Sharpe*, 347 U.S. 497 (1954). But our cases have not embraced the proposition that a law or other official act, without regard to whether it reflects a racially discriminatory purpose, is unconstitutional solely because it has a racially disproportionate impact.

* * * The school desegregation cases have also adhered to the basic equal protection principle that the invidious quality of a law claimed to be racially discriminatory must ultimately be traced to a racially discriminatory purpose. That there are both predominantly black and predominantly white schools in a community is not alone violative of the Equal Protection Clause. The essential element of De jure segregation is "a current condition of segregation resulting from intentional state action.

* * * This is not to say that the necessary discriminatory racial purpose must be express or appear on the face of the statute, or that a law's disproportionate impact is irrelevant in cases involving Constitution-based claims of racial discrimination. A statute, otherwise neutral on its face, must not be applied so as invidiously to discriminate on the basis of race. *Yick Wo v. Hopkins*, 118 U.S. 356 (1886). * * *

Necessarily, an invidious discriminatory purpose may often be inferred from the totality of the relevant facts, including the fact, if it is true, that the law bears more heavily on one race than another. It is also not infrequently true that the discriminatory impact in the jury cases for example, the total or seriously disproportionate exclusion of Negroes from jury venires may for all practical purposes demonstrate unconstitutionality because in various circumstances the discrimination is very difficult to explain on nonracial grounds. Nevertheless, we have not held that a law, neutral on its face and serving ends otherwise within the power of government to pursue, is invalid under the Equal Protection Clause simply because it may affect a greater proportion of one race than of another. Disproportionate impact is not irrelevant, but it is not the sole touchstone of an invidious racial discrimination forbidden by the Constitution. Standing alone, it does not trigger the rule, *McLaughlin v. Florida*, 379 U.S. 184 (1964), that racial classifications are to be subjected to the strictest scrutiny and are justifiable only by the weightiest of considerations.

Village of Arlington Heights v. Metropolitan Housing Development Corp.
429 U.S. 252 (1977)

[A developer sought to build a low- and moderate-income housing development in Arlington Heights, a relatively affluent and overwhelmingly white suburb of Chicago. When the city effectively foreclosed the project by denying a rezoning request, the developer and an individual plaintiff sued, alleging an equal protection violation.]

Our decision last Term in *Washington v. Davis*, 426 U.S. 229 (1976), made it clear that official action will not be held unconstitutional solely because it results in a racially disproportionate impact. "Disproportionate impact is not irrelevant, but it is not the sole touchstone of an invidious racial discrimination." Id., at 242. Proof of racially discriminatory intent or purpose is required to show a violation of the Equal Protection Clause. * * *

Davis does not require a plaintiff to prove that the challenged action rested solely on racially discriminatory purposes. Rarely can it be said that a legislature or administrative body operating under a broad mandate made a decision motivated solely by a single concern, or even that a particular purpose was the "dominant" or "primary" one. In fact, it is because legislators and administrators are properly concerned with balancing numerous competing considerations that courts refrain from reviewing the merits of their decisions, absent a showing of arbitrariness or irrationality. But racial discrimination is not just another competing consideration. When there is a proof that a discriminatory purpose has been a motivating factor in the decision, this judicial deference is no longer justified.

Determining whether invidious discriminatory purpose was a motivating factor demands a sensitive inquiry into such circumstantial and direct evidence of intent as may be available. The impact of the official action whether it "bears more heavily on one race than another," *Washington v.*

Davis, supra, 426 U.S. at 242, may provide an important starting point. Sometimes a clear pattern, unexplainable on grounds other than race, emerges from the effect of the state action even when the governing legislation appears neutral on its face. *Yick Wo v. Hopkins*, 118 U.S. 356 (1886); *Guinn v. United States*, 238 U.S. 347 (1915); *Lane v. Wilson*, 307 U.S. 268 (1939); *Gomillion v. Lightfoot*, 364 U.S. 339 (1960). The evidentiary inquiry is then relatively easy. But such cases are rare. Absent a pattern as stark as that in *Gomillion* or *Yick Wo*, impact alone is not determinative, and the Court must look to other evidence.

The historical background of the decision is one evidentiary source, particularly if it reveals a series of official actions taken for invidious purposes. * * * The specific sequence of events leading up the challenged decision also may shed some light on the decisionmaker's purposes. * * * Departures from the normal procedural sequence also might afford evidence that improper purposes are playing a role. Substantive departures too may be relevant, particularly if the factors usually considered important by the decisionmaker strongly favor a decision contrary to the one reached.

The legislative or administrative history may be highly relevant, especially where there are contemporary statements by members of the decisionmaking body, minutes of its meetings, or reports. * * *

The foregoing summary identifies, without purporting to be exhaustive, subjects of proper inquiry in determining whether racially discriminatory intent existed. With these in mind, we now address the case before us.

* * * We also have reviewed the evidence. The impact of the Village's decision does arguably bear more heavily on racial minorities. Minorities constitute 18% of the Chicago area population, and 40% of the income groups said to be eligible for Lincoln Green. But there is little about the sequence of events leading up to the decision that would spark suspicion. The area around the Viatorian property has been zoned R–3 since 1959, the year when Arlington Heights first adopted a zoning map. Single-family homes surround the 80-acre site, and the Village is undeniably committed to single-family homes as its dominant residential land use. The rezoning request progressed according to the usual procedures. The Plan Commission even scheduled two additional hearings, at least in part to accommodate MHDC and permit it to supplement its presentation with answers to questions generated at the first hearing.

The statements by the Plan Commission and Village Board members, as reflected in the official minutes, focused almost exclusively on the zoning aspects of the MHDC petition, and the zoning factors on which they relied are not novel criteria in the Village's rezoning decisions. There is no reason to doubt that there has been reliance by some neighboring property owners on the maintenance of single-family zoning in the vicinity. The Village originally adopted its buffer policy long before MHDC entered the picture and has applied the policy too consistently for us to infer discriminatory purpose from its application in this case. Finally, MHDC called one member of the Village Board to the stand at trial. Nothing in her testimony supports an inference of invidious purpose.

In sum, the evidence does not warrant overturning the concurrent findings of both courts below. Respondents simply failed to carry their burden of proving that discriminatory purpose was a motivating factor in the Village's decision. This conclusion ends the constitutional inquiry. The court of Appeals' further finding that the Village's decision carried a discriminatory "ultimate effect" is without independent constitutional significance.

In addition to constitutional theories, civil rights litigants have sometimes tried to ground their claims in Title VI of the Civil Rights Act of 1964, and on implementing regulations drafted by federal agencies. Your research quickly forecloses that as a promising avenue for claims. In a series of decisions in the 2000s, federal courts determined that no private right of action exists under Title VI or under agency implementing regulations. That means such claims are foreclosed to private clients like yours, even if the statute itself or the agency implementing regulations might appear to forbid the conduct you would like to challenge. *See* Brendan Cody, *Note: South Camden Citizens in Action: Siting Decisions, Disparate Impact Discrimination, and Section 1983*, 29 ECOLOGY L.Q. 231 (2002).

That leaves you with another potential avenue. In 1994, President Bill Clinton issued Executive Order 12898, which addresses environmental justice. Executive orders are binding upon federal agencies until they are revoked by the president or trumped by a statute. This order has been neither revoked nor trumped, so it remains good law. Can it help you?

Executive Order 12,898
59 Fed. Reg. 7629 (1994)

By the authority vested in me as President by the Constitution and the laws of the United States of America, it is hereby ordered as follows:

Section 1–1. Implementation.

1–101. Agency Responsibilities.

To the greatest extent practicable and permitted by law, and consistent with the principles set forth in the report on the National Performance Review, each Federal agency shall make achieving environmental justice part of its mission by identifying and addressing, as appropriate, disproportionately high and adverse human health or environmental effects of its programs, policies, and activities on minority populations and low-income populations in the United States and its territories and possessions, the District of Columbia, the Commonwealth of Puerto Rico, and the Commonwealth of the Mariana Islands.

* * * 1–103. Development of Agency Strategies.

(a) Except as provided in section 6–605 of this order, each Federal agency shall develop an agency-wide environmental justice strategy, as set forth in subsections (b)–(e) of this section that identifies and addresses disproportionately high and adverse human health or environmental effects of its programs, policies, and activities on minority populations and low-income populations. The environmental justice strategy shall list programs, policies, planning and public participation processes, enforcement, and/or rulemakings related to human health or the environment that should be revised to, at a minimum:

(1) promote enforcement of all health and environmental statutes in areas with minority populations and low-income populations;

(2) ensure greater public participation;

(3) improve research and data collection relating to the health of and environment of minority populations and low-income populations; and

(4) identify differential patterns of consumption of natural resources among minority populations and low-income populations. In addition, the environmental justice strategy shall include, where appropriate, a timetable for undertaking identified revisions and consideration of economic and social implications of the revisions.

* * * Sec. 2–2. Federal Agency Responsibilities for Federal Programs.

Each Federal agency shall conduct its programs, policies, and activities that substantially affect human health or the environment, in a manner that ensures that such programs, policies, and activities do not have the effect of excluding persons (including populations) from participation in, denying persons (including populations) the benefits of, or subjecting persons (including populations) to discrimination under, such programs, policies, and activities, because of their race, color, or national origin.

[Eds. note: we have omitted provisions addressing information gathering and research and fish consumption advisories.]

* * * Sec. 5–5. Public Participation and Access to Information.

(a) The public may submit recommendations to Federal agencies relating to the incorporation of environmental justice principles into Federal agency programs or policies. Each Federal agency shall convey such recommendations to the Working Group.

(b) Each Federal agency may, whenever practicable and appropriate, translate crucial public documents, notices, and hearings relating to human health or the environment for limited English speaking populations.

(c) Each Federal agency shall work to ensure that public documents, notices, and hearings relating to human health or the environment are concise, understandable, and readily accessible to the public.

(d) The Working Group shall hold public meetings, as appropriate, for the purpose of fact-finding, receiving public comments, and conducting inquiries concerning environmental justice. The Working Group shall prepare for public review a summary of the comments and recommendations discussed at the public meetings.

Sec. 6–6. General Provisions.

6–601. Responsibility for Agency Implementation.

The head of each Federal agency shall be responsible for ensuring compliance with this order. Each Federal agency shall conduct internal reviews and take such other steps as may be necessary to monitor compliance with this order.

* * * 6–609. Judicial Review.

This order is intended only to improve the internal management of the executive branch and is not intended to, nor does it create any right, benefit, or trust responsibility, substantive or procedural, enforceable at law or equity by a party against the United States, its agencies, its officers, or any person. This order shall not be construed to create any right to judicial review involving the compliance or noncompliance of the United States, its agencies, its officers, or any other person with this order.

WILLIAM J. CLINTON

THE WHITE HOUSE,

February 11, 1994.

———————

Environmental activism (or defending against environmental activism) does not just mean filing or responding to lawsuits. Sometimes it does not involve lawsuits at all. The essay below, written by Luke Cole, a prominent environmental justice attorney, explains and evaluates several different models of environmental justice lawyering. As you read, consider whether and how you might draw upon the different advocacy models and strategies Cole describes in advocating for your clients.

Luke W. Cole, *Macho Law Brains, Public Citizens, and Grassroots Activists: Three Models of Environmental Advocacy*
14 VA. ENVTL. L.J. 687, 689-703 (1995)

This essay will briefly sketch three models of environmental advocacy: the professional model, the participatory model, and the power model. I also use the colloquial descriptions "macho law brain," "public citizen," and "grassroots activist" to describe the stereotypical adherent to each respective model. These models are necessarily caricatures, resembling "real life" only in a broad sense. These models do not necessarily describe particular situations, but serve as teaching tools for examining different styles of environmental advocacy.

Using a generic administrative process for granting land use permits, the article will describe each model and its efficacy for poor people and people of color engaged in environmental struggles. I conclude that the power model of environmental advocacy will achieve the best results for communities, and that community groups and advocates should use a complementary approach including both the power and the participatory models.

* * * Recognizing that U.S. residents have a strong interest in their environment, over the last twenty years, Congress and state legislatures have included public participation provisions in a number of environmental laws. These provisions generally have several features in common: opportunities for public input during the environmental decision making process; a requirement that agencies respond to that public input; and sections allowing lawsuits by the public (known as "citizen suits") to enforce the law. Some laws include provisions for technical assistance grants to local groups in order to help them assume a more active role in the process.

* * * B. *The Professional Model*

The professional model is grounded in the idea that the attorney is an expert and will best represent a group's interests during the permitting process. Because of his or her training and skills, the attorney plays a central role in the permitting process, representing the client group in all fora.

[Cole then describes how the attorney, often working with experts, will help clients participate in multiple phases of the permitting process.]

Finally, if the decisionmakers decide against the client group, the attorney can sue to block the project. Adherents to the professional model enjoy this phase of the process the most, and often look for "test cases" in order to influence the law. A quick glance through any environmental law casebook will reveal the names of the nation's most prominent and leading environmental groups, many of which use the professional model of advocacy.

*** C. The Participatory Model

While the professional model essentially revolves around the attorney, the participatory model aims to maximize community involvement in the administrative permitting process. This model seeks to present client voices at every opportunity afforded by the process.

[Cole then describes how an attorney using the participatory model would work with clients to help them understand the process and to facilitate their participation in that process.]

The participatory model essentially accepts the system and encourages participation in it. An adherent might believe that environmental decision making would be fairer if people had more access to the system. Citizen victories in siting battles reinforce a sense that the system works and a belief that the voices of the people can be heard. This belief in the system contrasts with the skepticism felt by advocates of the power model.

*** D. The Power Model

Adherents of the power model believe that the system is stacked and that no amount of participation by itself will change the relations of power that give rise to environmental degradation. Advocates of the power model are convinced that more access to the system means nothing without power within that system. If it is used at all, the public participation process is viewed as a vehicle for organizing communities and a means to community empowerment. By bringing people together to realize and exercise their collective strength, practitioners of the power model target the root of community problems—powerlessness.

Three central ideas define the power model. First, it eschews the public participation process as co-optive. Second, it focuses on the actual leverage point in the process—the decision by officials. Third, it emphasizes strategies to influence the decisionmakers. These strategies offer a significant opportunity for environmental justice advocates.

*** 1. A Step-by-Step Process

The power model relies on a step-by-step analysis of the power dynamics of the decision. Key questions to be asked and answered include:

1) Who are the actual decisionmakers? An elected city council or board of supervisors usually makes the ultimate decision, even though a local appointed body, such as a planning commission or zoning board, may make an initial decision on a project.

2) Where do the individual decisionmakers stand on the project? Client groups can ascertain the various viewpoints through meetings with the elected official or her staff or through research into press archives at a local newspaper or TV station.

3) How can the group shift or neutralize its opponents in the decision-making body? This may take a variety of forms, depending on the timing as well as the energy, resources, and the creativity of the group. Community groups in California have made neighborhood struggles city-wide issues by appearing at candidate forums during election years and asking pointed questions. Other groups have worked with local decisionmakers to pass ordinances against various forms of pollution. In smaller communities, group members have campaigned for and won seats on the decision making body. Participation in the political process is not necessary, however, in order to pressure an elected official. Groups have distributed "WANTED" posters with the official's name, face, and "crimes" listed; groups have picketed or held sit-ins at an official's office; groups have joined local elected officials at their churches to pray for the official; and some groups have launched boycotts of businesses owned by elected officials. Other groups have organized "toxic tours" of heavily-polluted neighborhoods to educate the media, decisionmakers, and out-of-town supporters. Many groups have formed partnerships with other local institutions such as churches, medical centers, and schools to broaden the group's appeal and reach. The possibilities are limited only by the imagination of the community group and its advocates.

4) How can the group solidify its position with supporters on the decision-making body? Ensuring that the supporters of the client group adhere to their position is just as important as targeting the client group's opponents. Client groups can influence decisionmakers in positive ways by creating positive press through events such as "plant a tree for councilmember X," or presenting "community leadership" awards. Other ideas may include volunteering in a decisionmaker's office, working on their campaigns, or holding fundraising events for them.

5) Who are the group's potential allies, both in the community and regionally? Coalitions and networks are crucial ingredients in the environmental justice movement. The successful merger of diverse constituencies into broad-based local campaigns or regional networks can be instrumental in winning the fight at hand and leaving a viable structure for future battles.

2. The Process in Practice

The power model recognizes that taking part in the permitting process is often futile for residents of low-income communities and communities of color who cannot muster the political power within the system to compete with well-connected and financed companies. Some environmental review processes do not even acknowledge these communities, let alone study them for potential impact. Many groups have taken part in the permitting process for a proposed facility, and earnestly presented damning evidence about a company, project, or technology that all experts agree is bad, only to see the permit approved by their elected representatives. Such communities learn the hard way that the public participation process is not designed to hear and address their concerns, but instead to manage, diffuse, and ultimately co-opt community opposition to projects.

The power model is more concerned with building viable community organizations than with winning any particular permitting battle. The model recognizes that communities must take ownership of the struggle "and ultimately their own communities." Redlining, racism, unemployment, and crime are long-term problems for low-income communities that long outlive fights over particular facilities. Ideally, environmental justice strategies that build local power will have an impact on these long-term problems. Many community organizations created during the heat of local environmental fights have become creative, contributing community forces for social and economic justice.

Because of its focus on building power, rather than using the system, the power model provides a less clear role for the attorney than the participatory model. However, the experience of the Center on Race, Poverty, and the Environment indicates that a lawyer can still provide valuable services to a client group within the parameters of the power model. First, the attorney may know of or have previously represented groups in other communities that have organized successful campaigns against similar projects. The attorney can direct his or her clients to these groups for assistance, or develop tactics based on the strategies used by those other groups. Second, the lawyer may be more familiar with the local power structure, and thus better able to identify how best to leverage decisionmakers. Finally, the attorney can counsel his or her clients about the legality of specific protests, demonstrations, and civil disobedience actions.

The power model has one significant downside. If it fails and the decisionmakers approve the project, the community group may be precluded from pursuing a lawsuit. Most administrative processes require a potential litigant to exhaust his or her administrative remedies before filing suit. If a community group has ignored the administrative process, the group will almost certainly be barred from suing to overturn that process. If a group is allowed to sue, it has not taken part in building a strong administrative record with which to challenge the decision, making success less likely.

NOTES

1.   Early in the excerpt, Cole states that most environmental groups prefer the professional model. Later, he offers a scathing critique of that model:

> The professional model concentrates power, decision making, and activity in the attorney. A community group plays little, if any, role besides lending its name to legal proceedings in order to provide standing for the suit. * * * But, when the hearing room is empty of all but lawyers, the decisionmakers infer that the community concern about the project is not significant.

> How are the clients educated? The clients have no role in the professional model, and thus gain no insight into either the process or substance of their own claim. Since the attorney does all the work, the clients are not educated as to the dangers of a particular proposal, or the alternatives to it. Also, they learn nothing about the permitting process, which may become even more daunting to them because "only the lawyer can do it." Perhaps the most important and most damaging effect of the professional model is the group's realization that it has no role to play in resolving its own problems.

> * * * Unfortunately, the professional model is entirely ineffective at building the environmental justice movement at the local level. By taking all the power out of the community and putting it in the hands of the lawyer, the professional model leaves no responsibility to the local movement. In fact, use of the professional model has made many communities skeptical about working with the legal system at all. Taking events that would have been good organizing tools—like public hearings—and putting them in the hands of the lawyer actively discourages movement building. To the extent that it impedes a strong local group from developing and joining regional networks, the professional model has a detrimental effect on the national environmental justice movement.

> * * * Like applying a Band-Aid to skin cancer, this style of advocacy does not change the status quo—the symptom may be covered up, but the malady lingers on. Communities are typically chosen for noxious land uses because they are politically and economically powerless. Thus, the noxious land use is merely a symptom of the larger problem of powerlessness. If an attorney steps in without involving the community and defeats the noxious land use through inspired legal argument, only the symptom is removed. By teaching communities that they have no role in solving the problems which

affect them, the professional model reinforces powerlessness and is thus antithetical to environmental justice.

Cole, *supra*, at 703-705.

This is a harsh critique, and you might wonder why any activist group would employ such a model. In response, most environmental groups would be quick to note, as Cole himself notes, that this description is a caricature; they would probably say they utilize hybrids of all three models—and that, in response to critiques from Cole and others, they have worked to achieve more community involvement and empowerment. But there are reasons why an environmental group (or any kind of group engaged in activist lawyering) might prefer something close to the professional model. Most importantly, it often requires less time from the attorneys. Organizing and educating a community group can be extremely time-consuming—particularly if its membership shifts or if it is staffed by volunteers with limited time to devote to the cause—and the budgets of activist groups and the lawyers who represent them are often quite limited. Additionally, an attorney's or technical expert's knowledge is often worth something. Attorneys or experts may understand the law or science of an environmental controversy in ways that clients will not, even with an extensive investment in education, and there may be times when a more attorney-directed process best serves the client's long-term interests. That means attorneys representing community groups—or, for that matter, any kind of client—often must make difficult choices about how much to educate and involve the client and how much to rely on the attorneys' own legal expertise.

Test your knowledge with a Chapter 1 online quiz in CasebookPlus™.

CHAPTER 2

BACKGROUND PRINCIPLES

Although the environmental statutes enacted in the 1970s were in many respects revolutionary, they were not written in isolation. Congress and state legislatures wrote environmental statutes against a historical backdrop of centuries-old torts doctrines. They also wrote against the structural backdrop of a constitutional system that maintains important limits on the roles of federal and state governments, and of the branches within those governments. Thus, the practice of environmental law under federal and state statutes necessarily intersects with tort law and constitutional law. Much of environmental law also involves delegations of authority to administrative agencies. Practicing environmental law therefore requires a sophisticated understanding of administrative law, which governs the activities of those agencies. This chapter examines these intersections.

I. TORTS

Over one hundred years ago, the State of Missouri found itself aggrieved by water pollution coming from its neighbors in Illinois. The United States Supreme Court explained the basic facts of the case:

> This is a suit brought by the state of Missouri to restrain the discharge of the sewage of Chicago through an artificial channel into the Desplaines river, in the state of Illinois. That river empties into the Illinois river, and the latter empties into the Mississippi at a point about 43 miles above the city of St. Louis. It was alleged in the bill that the result of the threatened discharge would be to send 1,500 tons of poisonous filth daily into the Mississippi, to deposit great quantities of the same upon the part of the bed of the lastnamed river belonging to the plaintiff, and so to poison the water of that river, upon which various of the plaintiff's cities, towns, and inhabitants depended, as to make it unfit for drinking, agricultural, or manufacturing purposes.

Missouri v. Illinois, 200 U.S. 496, 517 (1906). No statute provided a basis for Missouri's lawsuit—indeed, an Illinois statute allegedly *authorized* Chicago's activities. Missouri instead argued that Chicago's sewage discharges were creating a nuisance.

At the time, nuisance claims were a common legal response to environmental problems. For most of the United States' history, people who were harmed by pollution turned to tort claims. Sometimes they won, and some of the victories were epic in their scope. In *People v. Gold Run Ditch & Mining Co.*, for example, the California Supreme Court put an end to hydraulic gold mining in the state, stopping a practice that had unearthed much of the gold from the Sierra Nevada, but that had also flushed millions of tons of gravel into the state's rivers. 4 P. 1152 (Cal. 1884). Sometimes the plaintiffs lost. Missouri, for example, would have to wait many more years for legal restraints on Chicago sewage. The Supreme Court found that the evidence of impacts upon St. Louis was equivocal, and in any event, discharging waste directly to the river was the general practice at that time. Chicago was hardly the only culprit. 200 U.S. at 521–26.

With the rise of statutory and administrative law, tort law no longer holds primacy in the field of environmental law. But it is still present, and in some parts of the field, it remains important. That is particularly true where pollution harms individuals who hope to recover damages for injuries to their health or to their property; most statutory environmental laws do not provide for that remedy, or allow it only for a limited set of governmental plaintiffs. This subpart will introduce (or reintroduce) you to some of the tort principles that environmental plaintiffs invoke in environmental cases (some of which are called "toxic tort" cases) and then will discuss challenges associated with applying tort law to modern environmental regulation. It will end with recent litigation raising difficult questions about the role of judge-made law in this modern statutory age.

A. TORTS AND ENVIRONMENTAL LAW: THE BASICS

Many of the torts you learned about in your first year have at least some potential relevance to environmental law. A few are particularly important.

1. NUISANCE

Nuisance claims are among the most common types of environmental tort claims. They come in two varieties. "A private nuisance," according to the Restatement, "is a nontrespassory invasion of another's interest in the private use and enjoyment of land." Restatement (Second) of Torts § 821D. A public nuisance, in contrast, "is an unreasonable interference with a right common to the general public." *Id.* § 821B.

Nuisance claims arise in a variety of contexts, but the classic nuisance claim is a factory sending pollution onto its neighbors' property. *See, e.g., Boomer et al. v. Atlantic Cement Co.*, 257 N.E.2d 870 (1970) (addressing a dispute between a cement factory and its neighbors).

2. TRESPASS

Trespass liability, according to the Restatement (Second) of Torts, arises when "[o]ne * * * intentionally

(a)   enters land in the possession of the other, or causes a thing or a third person to do so, or

(b)   remains on the land, or

(c)   fails to remove from the land a thing which he is under a duty to remove.

Restatement (Second) of Torts § 158. The classic trespass case involves a person going onto someone else's land, but some courts have applied trespass principles to the migration of pollution. *See, e.g., Mangini v. Aerojet-General Corp.*, 281 Cal. Rptr. 827 (Cal. Ct. App. 1991) (holding that the plaintiff landowners could bring a trespass claim against a company that had contaminated the landowners' property with rocket fuel).

3. NEGLIGENCE, STRICT LIABILITY, PRODUCT LIABILITY

Toxic tort claims are often based in negligence, strict liability, or product liability, alleging that a toxin manufactured or released by the defendant has harmed the plaintiff's health or property. Although the elements necessary to state a claim differ somewhat among negligence, strict liability, and product liability, the principal challenge across all three of these causes of action in a toxic tort case is proving general and specific causation. Plaintiffs must show both (1) that the toxin is generally "capable of causing injuries like that suffered by the plaintiff in human beings subjected to the same level of exposure as the plaintiff" (general causation), and (2) that the toxin released or manufactured by the defendant caused the plaintiff's injury (specific causation). *Bonner v. ISP Techs., Inc.*, 259 F.3d 924 (8th Cir. 2001) (affirming a verdict in favor of a worker who suffered cognitive impairment and personality disorders after being exposed to an organic solvent manufactured by the defendant); *see also, e.g., Atkins v. Ferro Corp.*, 534 F. Supp. 2d 662 (M.D. La. 2008) (granting summary judgment against residents who sued a chemical plant and manager for injuries allegedly caused by hydrochloric acid emitted from the plant during a fire, on the ground that the residents did not prove they were exposed to harmful levels of the acid or were injured thereby).

These causation standards are often difficult to satisfy because of scientific uncertainties and a lack of data about specific exposure levels. Courts also often grapple with the admissibility of expert scientific evidence regarding causation. *See, e.g., Zellers v. NexTech Ne., LLC*, 533 F. App'x 192 (4th Cir. 2013) (affirming the exclusion of a physician's proffered expert opinion that the plaintiff's exposure to refrigerant gas caused her neurological impairments, when the physician did not identify the intensity, duration, or level of the plaintiff's exposure).

PROBLEMS: APPLYING TORT LAW TO ENVIRONMENTAL LAW

Because you probably have already taken a full course in torts, our review of tort law will be brief. The problems below will introduce you to some of the circumstances in which a plaintiff might bring an environmental tort case—and to some of the challenges of bringing such claims. For each, consider what tort claim(s) the potential plaintiff might be able to bring and whether those claims should prevail.

1. Your client owns a gas station. That gas station, like most gas stations, stores its gasoline in large underground storage tanks (USTs). For years, and unbeknownst to your client, one of his USTs leaked, and when the leaking gasoline hit the water table, it began to flow laterally. A six-inch-thick layer of gasoline now sits on top of the water table beneath your client's neighbor's land—and her house. The fumes have invaded her basement, and she says they give her constant headaches (gasoline does contain many toxic constituents, so her complaint is plausible). She also worries that her basement might explode. Does she have a potential tort claim against your client? If so, how strong is it?

2. Your client owns a sand and gravel mine. She has owned that mine for twenty years. The mine is located in a rural area in Wisconsin. The surrounding area is rural, with a mix of woodlands and farms.

Five years ago, a couple from Chicago bought a nearby farmhouse and converted it to a bed and breakfast. They were charmed by the area's bucolic character, and they loved the idea of a farm-to-table restaurant, but they and their guests have been taken aback by the noise and dust emanating from your client's sand and gravel operation. Now they are suing your client. Their complaint alleges that the dust and noise have made their outdoor spaces unpleasant on many summer and fall days, driving guests away and damaging their business.

Your client's mine doesn't make much money, and she wants to make this lawsuit go away quickly. Can you obtain a motion to dismiss? Remember that a judge, when considering such a motion, must assume the truth of any well-pleaded fact. What if the case goes to the merits? Based on the limited facts provided, do you think your client will prevail?

3. You live in an old, established neighborhood in a suburb of a major Midwestern city. You love your neighborhood, but it has an unfortunate tendency to flood. In major rainstorms, murky, polluted-looking standing water two or three feet deep can fill your street—and your basement. The resulting damage has cost you tens of thousands of dollars. You bought the house ten years ago, and you've been flooded three times in that span. Your neighbors, several of whom have lived in the neighborhood much longer than you, have told you that this kind of thing never used to happen.

By talking to an environmental engineer, you learn a few things about the causes of this flooding. One probable cause, he says, is climate change, which is expected to increase the severity of precipitation events. The other primary culprits are developments uphill from you. Nearby areas used to contain a mix of forests and marshes, with a few pockets of residential development. But in recent years, developers have cut down the forests and filled more and more of the marshes. By replacing forest and marsh with pavement and roofs, your engineer tells you, the developers have taken a landscape that once stored stormwater in swamps, trees, and subsurface aquifers and converted it to one where stormwater flows rapidly over roofs and pavement and into storm drains. The storm drains then clog, because they weren't built to handle the volume of water they are now receiving, and your neighborhood floods.

Through a little bit of additional research, you learn that no one developer is responsible for more than 10% of the overall development. You also learn that your city, which permitted all the development, has near-complete immunity from tort suits. And you learn that while many states have property law doctrines that define landowners' obligations with respect to surface water drainage, your state does not.

Do you have a viable tort claim?

To answer these questions, your starting point would likely be your state's statutory provisions defining torts, and also its body of tort case law. For this problem, however, the materials are more truncated. Please assume that your state has based its tort law on the Restatement (Second) of Torts— as many states indeed have done—and evaluate potential claims based on the Restatement excerpts below.

Restatement (2d) of Torts

§ 821A.   Types of Nuisance

In this Restatement "nuisance" is used to denote either

    (a) a public nuisance as defined in § 821B, or

    (b) a private nuisance as defined in § 821D. * * *

§ 821D.   Private Nuisance

A private nuisance is a nontrespassory invasion of another's interest in the private use and enjoyment of land.

§ 821E.   Who Can Recover For Private Nuisance

For a private nuisance there is liability only to those who have property rights and privileges in respect to the use and enjoyment of the land affected, including

    (a) possessors of the land,

(b) owners of easements and profits in the land, and

(c) owners of nonpossessory estates in the land that are detrimentally affected by interferences with its use and enjoyment.

§ 821F.   Significant Harm

There is liability for a nuisance only to those to whom it causes significant harm, of a kind that would be suffered by a normal person in the community or by property in normal condition and used for a normal purpose.

§ 822. General Rule

One is subject to liability for a private nuisance if, but only if, his conduct is a legal cause of an invasion of another's interest in the private use and enjoyment of land, and the invasion is either

(a) intentional and unreasonable, or

(b) unintentional and otherwise actionable under the rules controlling liability for negligent or reckless conduct, or for abnormally dangerous conditions or activities.

§ 824. Type of Conduct Essential to Liability

The conduct necessary to make the actor liable for either a public or a private nuisance may consist of

(a) an act; or

(b) a failure to act under circumstances in which the actor is under a duty to take positive action to prevent or abate the interference with the public interest or the invasion of the private interest.

§ 825. Intentional Invasion—What Constitutes

An invasion of another's interest in the use and enjoyment of land or an interference with the public right, is intentional if the actor

(a) acts for the purpose of causing it, or

(b) knows that it is resulting or is substantially certain to result from his conduct.

§ 826. Unreasonableness of Intentional Invasion

An intentional invasion of another's interest in the use and enjoyment of land is unreasonable if

(a) the gravity of the harm outweighs the utility of the actor's conduct, or

(b) the harm caused by the conduct is serious and the financial burden of compensating for this and similar harm to others would not make the continuation of the conduct not feasible.

§ 827. Gravity of Harm—Factors Involved

In determining the gravity of the harm from an intentional invasion of another's interest in the use and enjoyment of land, the following factors are important:

(a) The extent of the harm involved;

(b) the character of the harm involved;

(c) the social value that the law attaches to the type of use or enjoyment invaded;

(d) the suitability of the particular use or enjoyment invaded to the character of the locality; and

(e) the burden on the person harmed of avoiding the harm.

§ 828. Utility of Conduct—Factors Involved

In determining the utility of conduct that causes an intentional invasion of another's interest in the use and enjoyment of land, the following factors are important:

(a) the social value that the law attaches to the primary purpose of the conduct;

(b) the suitability of the conduct to the character of the locality; and

(c) the impracticability of preventing or avoiding the invasion.

§ 829. Gravity vs. Utility—Conduct Malicious or Indecent

An intentional invasion of another's interest in the use and enjoyment of land is unreasonable if the harm is significant and the actor's conduct is

(a) for the sole purpose of causing harm to the other; or

(b) contrary to common standards of decency.

§ 829A.   Gravity vs. Utility—Severe Harm

An intentional invasion of another's interest in the use and enjoyment of land is unreasonable if the harm resulting from the invasion is severe and greater than the other should be required to bear without compensation.

§ 830. Gravity vs. Utility—Invasion Avoidable

An intentional invasion of another's interest in the use and enjoyment of land is unreasonable if the harm is significant and it would be practicable for the actor to avoid the harm in whole or in part without undue hardship.

> **§ 831. Gravity vs. Utility—Conduct Unsuited To Locality**
>
> An intentional invasion of another's interest in the use and enjoyment of land is unreasonable if the harm is significant, and
>
> (a) the particular use or enjoyment interfered with is well suited to the character of the locality; and
>
> (b) the actor's conduct is unsuited to the character of that locality.
>
> **§ 840D.   Coming To the Nuisance**
>
> The fact that the plaintiff has acquired or improved his land after a nuisance interfering with it has come into existence is not in itself sufficient to bar his action, but it is a factor to be considered in determining whether the nuisance is actionable.

B. THE CHALLENGES OF TORT-BASED ENVIRONMENTAL LAW

Tort law is no longer central to environmental law. There are some environmental lawyers and scholars who lament that change. *See, e.g.,* Roger E. Meiners & Bruce Yandle, *Common Law Environmentalism*, 94 PUB. CHOICE 49 (1998). They argue that the tort system (and property law) offered many advantages over a legal system governed primarily by detailed statutes and regulations and administered by government agencies. The more mainstream view, however, is that the tort system was never particularly well-suited for responding to the challenges of environmental law. The following excerpt explains many of the primary concerns.

Albert C. Lin, Beyond Tort: *Compensating Victims of Environmental Toxic Injury*
78 S. CAL. L. REV. 1439, 1441–59 (2005)

The difficulties of proving causation in [environmental] cases confound environmental tort plaintiffs. Assuming that victims are even aware that they have been injured, victims must overcome gaps in knowledge regarding causation, risk, and harm to obtain compensation for their injuries. The characteristics of environmental toxic injuries complicate efficient liability determinations. These injuries tend to involve a large number of persons exposed to significant, albeit low, probability risks. A long latency period between exposure and illness and multiple alternate causes of illness exacerbate this causation problem. These difficulties, combined with the costs of litigation, result in the systematic undercompensation of environmental tort victims and the systematic underdeterrence of polluters.

* * * The paradigmatic traditional tort case involves a single identifiable plaintiff, a single identifiable defendant, and a readily determinable cause of the tortious event. For example, a pedestrian struck by a car can identify the driver of the car and the driver's negligence as the cause of the pedestrian's resulting injuries. Although the parties may dispute the driver's negligence or the harm suffered by the plaintiff, the judicial process is well equipped to determine such issues. Our judicial system is similarly able to handle classic strict liability claims, such as a dynamite explosion, a sudden flood from a reservoir, or even a catastrophic Bhopal-type accident.[1] In such cases, cause and effect are readily identifiable. An environmental tort plaintiff, however, often faces far more formidable problems of proof. As an initial matter, courts generally apply a negligence standard rather than a strict liability standard to ordinary economic activities. Only where a polluter is engaged in abnormally dangerous activities do courts apply a strict liability standard. Furthermore, environmental tort plaintiffs must overcome the high hurdles of causation and latency of harm.

1.   Latency of Harm

Latency of harm complicates proving causation with any environmental disease that takes time to develop. For example, consider an individual who is diagnosed with cancer many years after an exposure to carcinogenic pollutants released from an industrial facility. Over the course of a lifetime, this individual has been exposed to numerous carcinogens through various pathways, including air, water, and food supply. In contrast to the paradigmatic tort plaintiff described above, this plaintiff's injury is latent, appearing some time after exposure. The length of the latency period may vary among individuals. Thus, even when a population is exposed simultaneously to a pollutant, incidences of disease occur over a period of time that can span several decades.

This latency and lack of simultaneity make evidence more difficult to gather. For example, victims may not have been aware of their first exposure to a toxic substance. Therefore, years later, they will likely be unable to prove the fact, timing, or extent of exposure. Exposure often occurs at low levels over extended periods of time. The passage of time not only complicates proof, but also increases the risk that a defendant will no longer be financially viable, assuming that the defendant can even be identified. Compounding plaintiffs' difficulties, statutes of limitations may bar suit, although some jurisdictions have rules tolling the statutory period until the time when the injury is discovered.

---

[1]   Eds.: Here, the author is referring to a catastrophic release of methyl isocyanate, a toxic gas, from a Union Carbide plant in Bhopal, India, in 1984. The release killed 2,000 people and injured 200,000. *See* Stuart Diamond, *The Bhopal Disaster: How It Happened*, N.Y. TIMES, Jan. 28, 1985.

2.   Causation

An even greater barrier faced by plaintiffs is causation. Toxic tort plaintiffs typically must establish two types of causation. First, a plaintiff must prove general causation—that a substance is capable of causing the injury at issue. Second, a plaintiff must prove specific causation—that exposure to the substance in fact caused that plaintiff's injury. The scientific uncertainty that surrounds causation can make these burdens insurmountable.

A few diseases, such as asbestosis, are so-called "signature diseases"—diseases that are extremely rare in the general population, but far more prevalent in persons exposed to a particular substance. These illnesses can be traced to exposure to a specific substance. Illnesses involving environmental toxic exposure, however, often can result from multiple causes. For example, an individual instance of lung cancer might be attributed to exposure to tobacco smoke, exposure to pollutants from a nearby factory, or exposure to pollutants from traffic on a local highway. Separating the roles of the potential causal agents, which may interact in complex ways, is often problematic, if not impossible. Unlike our automobile accident example, there is usually no obvious evidence that a particular agent caused the plaintiff's harm in environmental tort cases.

* * * The difficulties of overcoming latency and proving causation undermine the tort system's ability to meet its principal objectives. The tort system is said to have three primary objectives: (1) compensation, (2) deterrence, and (3) corrective justice. Compensation is provided to plaintiffs who can demonstrate that they were harmed by the activities of others. Here, the tort system essentially serves as social insurance by spreading the costs of accidents to risk creators and their consumers. Deterrence is achieved through the threat of financial liability—economically rational actors are forced to take into account the impacts of their activities on others. Proponents of efficient deterrence argue that liability rules should be designed to induce efficient levels of activity and care. Proponents of corrective justice contend that those responsible for violating other persons' autonomy should restore those persons to their preinjury status. In environmental toxic tort cases, the tort system fails to serve any of these objectives well.

1.   Undercompensation

Given the difficulties discussed above, environmental tort plaintiffs often face very limited prospects for obtaining compensation. * * * [M]ost instances of environmental injury involve widely dispersed and commonly released pollutants such as sulfur dioxide or fine particulate matter. Victims tend to suffer cancer, heart disease, respiratory illness, and other maladies not readily traced to potential defendants. Although the exact number of uncompensated deaths and illnesses is uncertain, studies indicate this number is substantial.

* * * Like all tort plaintiffs, those few environmental tort victims who can demonstrate liability receive only partial compensation once attorneys' fees are paid. According to a recent estimate, of each dollar spent in insured tort cases, twenty-two cents compensates for economic loss, twenty-four cents compensates for noneconomic loss, and the remaining fifty-four cents goes to attorneys and administrative costs. These figures are consistent with previous studies that have found that tort plaintiffs recover less than half of the total amount expended by defendants and their insurers. The difficulties of proving causation make it likely that the share of proceeds going toward compensation is even lower in environmental toxic injury cases.

The chance of a plaintiff's successful recovery is further eroded by the legal remoteness of damages, the difficulty of valuing subjective losses, and the difficulty of accounting for the increased risk of latent harms. Damages are often paid years after a victim has been injured; thus, the recovery may be of little use to the victim. Often, only the victim's survivors receive the benefit of any recovery. Furthermore, the tort system's general lack of oversight and coordination adds to the inequities—dissimilar awards are common for similarly situated victims. Finally, if a defendant becomes insolvent, remaining plaintiffs will be unable to secure compensation.

* * * [T]he overall problems of proof suggest that victims of environmental pollution are being dramatically undercompensated as a group. As the American Law Institute remarked: "[T]he large gap between potential and actual [environmental] tort claims . . . is at least as serious a social and legal problem as is the surplus of claims that is popularly supposed to afflict other areas of personal injury."

2.   Underdeterrence

Like compensation, deterrence is a basic objective of the tort system that fails in environmental toxic injury cases. * * * With respect to environmental toxic injuries, underdeterrence is virtually guaranteed. Assessing future liability is clouded by ignorance of the dangers, by the scope of exposure, and by the low probability that defendants will be held responsible for those dangers. Most air and water pollution impose small costs on a large number of people. They are thus unlikely to warrant the costs of litigation for any individual victim. In addition, potential defendants are likely to discount the long-term negative effects of present decisions because plaintiffs' injuries will not arise until far into the future. When injuries do arise, plaintiffs will face numerous problems of proving causation. Corporations generally amortize such future costs by incorporating a discount rate into their calculations of future cash flow.

If an injury does not occur until twenty or thirty years after exposure, the discounted value of the injury is likely to approach zero.

Moreover, organizations may be deterred only to the extent that decisionmakers in the organization bear responsibility for their decisions. This is unlikely to happen where injuries are latent. Internal corporate structures may not provide the proper incentives to corporate decisionmakers, who may not be with the corporation decades later when liability is imposed. Liability insurance, where available, further reduces corporate decisionmakers' incentives to consider the full cost of negative externalities. This is especially so if insurance premiums fail to reflect the risks associated with a particular insured's activities.

Not surprisingly, the limited empirical data available suggests that common law tort litigation has had little deterrent effect on polluter behavior. The exceptions are instances where a harm can be readily linked to a large and isolated pollution source. * * * For most sources of common pollutants, however, victims simply cannot show causation, and polluters, who face almost no risk of liability, are undeterred.

3. Corrective Justice

The third objective of the tort system is to provide corrective justice, which has been defined as "the defendant's obligation to compensate for harm that she has caused wrongfully or in violation of the plaintiff's rights." With environmental toxic injuries, the tort system fails to provide corrective justice to victims for many of the same reasons that it fails to achieve compensation and deterrence. Here again, the causation inquiry is critical. Many commentators consider causation central to corrective justice because it establishes the essential nexus between the parties by identifying the specific victim of the injurer's acts. Yet the obstacles to proving causation in environmental toxic tort cases often prevent any such nexus from being established.

———————

C. TORTS AND ENVIRONMENTAL LAW IN THE AGE OF STATUTES

As the excerpt above explains, many problems and challenges can arise when plaintiffs try to remedy environmental harms through the tort system. Those problems and challenges help explain why environmental advocates turned their attention from the common law to Congress and state legislatures. To a great extent, environmentalists succeeded in their legislative advocacy, and that success created a new question: to what extent did the emergent statutory regimes displace the traditional role of tort law? That question is thoroughly intertwined with related questions about institutional competence: to what extent should judges, rather than legislatures or administrative agencies, still play leading roles in developing the frontiers of environmental law?

Those questions have arisen repeatedly for traditional air and water pollution. *See, e.g. City of Milwaukee v. Illinois and Michigan*, 451 U.S. 304 (1981) (holding that a *federal* common law nuisance claim was preempted by the Clean Water Act); *International Paper Co. v. Ouellette*, 479 U.S. 481 (1987) (holding that the Clean Water Act did not preempt a claim brought under the nuisance law of the state in which a discharge occurred). Then, in the mid-2000s, a new type of environmental tort litigation emerged. Coalitions of environmental groups and states began filing nuisance claims against major emitters of greenhouse gases. One of the resulting decisions appears below.

As you read, please be aware that the decision you are reading was reversed by the United States Court of Appeals for the Second Circuit, which held that the case did *not* present a political question, and also rejected several other arguments for dismissal. *Connecticut v. American Electric Power Co.*, 415 F.3d 50 (2nd Cir. 2009). The United States Supreme Court then reversed the Second Circuit, but on different grounds; it held that the Clean Air Act had displaced federal common law nuisance claims against greenhouse gas emitters. *American Electric Power Co. v. Connecticut*, 564 U.S. 410 (2011). The opinion that follows therefore is no longer good law, and some other judges have found its reasoning unpersuasive. But we have included it because it presents, in nicely distilled form, some of the thorniest questions that arise when a modern court confronts a sweeping common law environmental claim. So consider, as you read, what you would have done if you were Judge Preska, and the nation's most ambitious environmental tort case landed in your courtroom. Would you have come to a similar result? And how, if you were arguing the case on appeal, might you have tried to persuade the Second Circuit that Judge Preska's decision was right or wrong?

Connecticut v. American Electric Power Co., Inc.

406 F. Supp. 2d 265 (S.D.N.Y. 2005)

■ PRESKA, DISTRICT JUDGE.

The Framers based our Constitution on the idea that a separation of powers enables a system of checks and balances, allowing our Nation to thrive under a Legislature and Executive that are accountable to the People, subject to judicial review by an independent Judiciary. *See Federalist Paper* No. 47 (1788); U.S. Const. arts. I, II, III. While, at times, some judges have become involved with the most critical issues affecting America, political questions are not the proper domain of judges. *See, e.g.,*

Baker v. Carr, 369 U.S. 186 (1962); *Nixon v. United States,* 506 U.S. 224 (1993). Were judges to resolve political questions, there would be no check on their resolutions because the Judiciary is not accountable to any other branch or to the People. Thus, when cases present political questions, "judicial review would be inconsistent with the Framers' insistence that our system be one of checks and balances." *Nixon,* 506 U.S. at 234–35. As set out below, cases presenting political questions are consigned to the political branches that are accountable to the People, not to the Judiciary, and the Judiciary is without power to resolve them. This is one of those cases.

BACKGROUND

The States of Connecticut, New York, California, Iowa, New Jersey, Rhode Island, Vermont, and Wisconsin and the City of New York (the "State Plaintiffs") and the Open Space Institute, Inc. ("OSI"), the Open Space Conservancy, Inc., and the Audubon Society of New Hampshire (the "Private Plaintiffs") (collectively, "Plaintiffs") bring the above-captioned actions against American Electric Power Company, Inc., American Electric Power Service Corporation (together, "AEP"), the Southern Company ("Southern"), Tennessee Valley Authority ("TVA"), Xcel Energy Inc. ("Xcel"), and Cinergy Corporation ("Cinergy") (collectively, "Defendants") under federal common law or, in the alternative, state law, to abate what Plaintiffs describe as the "public nuisance" of "global warming." Defendants now move to dismiss the complaints for, *inter alia,* lack of jurisdiction and failure to state a claim upon which relief can be granted. For the reasons set forth below, Defendants' motions are granted.

The State Plaintiffs, claiming to represent the interests of more than 77 million people and their related environments, natural resources, and economies, and the Private Plaintiffs, non-profit land trusts, bring these federal common law public nuisance actions to abate what they allege to be Defendants' contributions to the phenomenon commonly known as global warming. Plaintiffs assert that the Defendants collectively emit approximately 650 million tons of carbon dioxide annually, that carbon dioxide is the primary greenhouse gas, and that greenhouse gases trap atmospheric heat and cause global warming.

As part of their venue allegations, Plaintiffs maintain that global warming will cause irreparable harm to property in New York State and New York City and that it threatens the health, safety, and well-being of New York's citizens, residents, and environment.

According to the complaints, Defendants "are the five largest emitters of carbon dioxide in the United States" and their emissions "constitute approximately one quarter of the U.S. electric power sector's carbon dioxide emissions." According to the complaints, U.S. electric power plants are responsible for "ten percent of worldwide carbon dioxide emissions from human activities."

State Plaintiffs assert that global warming has already occurred in the form of a documented increase in average temperatures in the United States of between .74 and 5 degrees Fahrenheit since 1900, and a decline in snowfall and the duration of snow cover in recent decades. In addition to what State Plaintiffs say are these already-documented climate changes, the United States Environmental Protection Agency (the "EPA") projects an increase in temperature of approximately 4 to 5 degrees by the year 2100. State Compl. Private Plaintiffs assert that the Intergovernmental Panel on Climate Change projects that the global average surface air temperature will increase approximately 2.5 to 10.4 degrees Fahrenheit from the year 1990 to 2100.

Plaintiffs say the natural processes that remove carbon dioxide from the atmosphere now are unable to keep pace with the level of carbon dioxide emissions. As a result, Plaintiffs allege, carbon dioxide levels have increased approximately 34% since the industrial revolution began, causing increased temperatures. Plaintiffs further allege that because the planet's natural systems take hundreds of years to absorb carbon dioxide, Defendants' past, present, and future emissions will remain in the atmosphere and contribute to global warming for many decades and, possibly, centuries. Although Plaintiffs acknowledge that there is some dispute about the rate and intensity of the process of global climate change, Plaintiffs say official reports from American and international scientific bodies demonstrate the clear scientific consensus that global warming has begun, is altering the natural world, and will accelerate over the coming decades unless action is taken to reduce emissions of carbon dioxide.

Congress has recognized that carbon dioxide emissions cause global warming and that global warming will have severe adverse impacts in the United States, but it has declined to impose any formal limits on such emissions. *See, e.g.,* The Global Climate Protection Act of 1987, P.L. 100–204, Title XI, §§ 1102–03, reprinted at 15 U.S.C. § 2901 note. However, Congress and the Executive Branch have taken several steps to better understand and address the complex issue of global warming. As early as 1978, Congress established a "national climate program" to improve understanding of global climate change through research, data collection, assessments, information dissemination, and international cooperation. *See* National Climate Program Act of 1978, 15 U.S.C. §§ 2901, et seq. Two years later, in the Energy Security Act, Pub. L. No. 96–294, tit. VII, § 711, 94 Stat. 611, 774–75 (1980), Congress directed the Office of Science and Technology Policy to engage the National Academy of Sciences in a study of the "projected impact, on the level of carbon dioxide in the atmosphere, of fossil fuel combustion, coal-conversion and related synthetic fuels activities" authorized by the Energy Security Act. In the Global Climate Protection Act of 1987, Congress directed the Secretary of State to coordinate U.S. negotiations concerning global climate change. *See* 15 U.S.C. § 2901 note; *see also id.* § 2952(a) (directing the President and Secretary of State in 1990 to "initiate discussions" with other nations for agreements on climate research).

In 1990, Congress enacted the Global Change Research Act, 15 U.S.C. §§ 2931–2938, which established a ten-year research program for global climate issues, *id.* § 2932, directed the President to establish a research program to "improve understanding of global change," *id.* § 2933, and provided for scientific assessments every four years that "analyze[ ] current trends in global change," *id.* § 2936(3). Congress also established a program to research agricultural issues related to global climate change, Pub. L. No. 101–624, tit. XXIV, § 2402, 104 Stat. 4058, 4058–59 (1990), and, two years later, directed the Secretary of Energy to conduct several assessments related to greenhouse gases and report to Congress, Energy Policy Act of 1992, Pub. L. No. 102–486, § 1604, 106 Stat. 2776, 3002.

In 1992, as a result of the negotiations authorized by the Global Climate Protection Act of 1987, President George H.W. Bush signed, and the Senate ratified, the United Nations Framework Convention on Climate Change ("UNFCCC"), which brought together a coalition of countries to work toward a coordinated approach to address the international issue of global warming. Following ratification of the UNFCCC, member nations negotiated the Kyoto Protocol, which called for mandatory reductions in the greenhouse gas emissions of developed nations. *See* UNFCCC, Kyoto Protocol (Dec. 11, 1997).

Although President William Jefferson Clinton signed the Kyoto Protocol, it was not presented to the Senate, which formally expressed misgivings over the prospect that the potential economic burdens of carbon dioxide reductions would be shouldered exclusively by developed nations, such as the United States. S. Res. 98, 105th Cong. (1997) (resolving by vote of 95–0 to urge the President not to sign any agreement that would result in serious harm to the economy or that did not include provisions regarding the emissions of developing nations). Thereafter, Congress passed a series of bills that affirmatively barred the EPA from implementing the Protocol. *See* Pub. L. No. 105–276, 112 Stat. 2461, 2496 (1998); Pub. L. No. 106–74, 113 Stat. 1047, 1080 (1999); Pub. L. No. 106–377, 114 Stat. 1141, 1441A–41 (2000). The EPA has ruled that the Clean Air Act does not authorize carbon dioxide regulation. Control of

Emissions from New Highway Vehicles and Engines, 68 Fed. Reg. 52,922 (Sept. 8, 2003).[2]

President George W. Bush opposes the Protocol because it exempts developing nations who are major emitters, fails to address two major pollutants, and would have a negative economic impact on the United States. *See* Transcript, President Bush Discusses Global Climate Change (Jun. 11, 2001). Instead, the policy of the current administration "emphasizes international cooperation and promotes working with other nations to develop an efficient and coordinated response to global climate change," which the EPA describes as a "prudent," "realistic and effective long-term approach to the global climate change issue." 68 Fed. Reg. at 52933.

Here, to curtail Defendants' contribution to global warming, Plaintiffs "seek an order (i) holding each of the Defendants jointly and severally liable for contributing to an ongoing public nuisance, global warming, and (ii) enjoining each of the Defendants to abate its contribution to the nuisance by capping its emissions of carbon dioxide and then reducing those emissions by a specified percentage each year for at least a decade." According to Plaintiffs, the unspecified reductions they seek "will contribute to a reduction in the risk and threat of injury to the plaintiffs and their citizens and residents from global warming."

By way of a variety of motions, supported by Unions for Jobs, as amicus, Defendants move to dismiss the complaints against them on several grounds. First, Defendants contend that Plaintiffs have failed to state a claim upon which relief can be granted because: (1) there is no recognized federal common law cause of action to abate greenhouse gas emissions that allegedly contribute to global warming; (2) separation of powers principles preclude this Court from adjudicating these actions; and (3) Congress has displaced any federal common law cause of action to address the issue of global warming. Second, Defendants contend that this Court lacks jurisdiction over Plaintiffs' claims because: (1) Plaintiffs do not have standing to sue on account of global warming and (2) Plaintiffs' failure to state a claim under federal law divests the Court of § 1331 jurisdiction. In addition to advancing these primary arguments, Defendants Southern, TVA, Xcel, and Cinergy move to dismiss for lack of personal jurisdiction, and TVA moves to dismiss because, as an agency and instrumentality of the United States, it claims that it cannot be sued for a tort when the subject of the lawsuit is the actions it performs as part of its discretionary functions.

---

[2]   Eds.: This EPA ruling was later set aside by the Supreme Court in *Massachusetts v. EPA*, 549 U.S. 497 (2007), an excerpt from which appears later in this casebook, and that you may have read in your course in constitutional law. But at the time Judge Preska issued her decision, the Supreme Court had not yet ruled, and a divided panel of the D.C Circuit had just dismissed the plaintiffs' challenge to EPA's ruling. *Massachusetts v. EPA*, 415 F.3d 50 (D.C. Cir. 2005).

DISCUSSION

* * * The threshold jurisdictional question in this case is whether the complaints raise non-justiciable political questions that are beyond the limits of this Court's jurisdiction. * * *

To determine if a case is justiciable in light of the separation of powers ordained by the Constitution, a court must decide "whether the duty asserted can be judicially identified and its breach judicially determined, and whether protection for the right asserted can be judicially molded." *Baker v. Carr,* 369 U.S. 186, 198 (1962). Six situations have been recognized as indicating the existence of a non-justiciable political question:

> [1] a textually demonstrable constitutional commitment of the issue to a coordinate political department; or [2] a lack of judicially discoverable and manageable standards for resolving it; or [3] the impossibility of deciding without an initial policy determination of a kind clearly for nonjudicial discretion; or [4] the impossibility of a court's undertaking independent resolution without expressing lack of the respect due coordinate branches of the government; or [5] an unusual need for unquestioning adherence to a political decision already made; or [6] the potentiality of embarrassment from multifarious pronouncements by various departments on one question.

Vieth v. Jubelirer, 541 U.S. 267, 277–78 (2004) (quoting *Baker v. Carr,* 369 U.S. 186, 217 (1962)). Although several of these indicia have formed the basis for finding that Plaintiffs raise a non-justiciable political question, the third indicator is particularly pertinent to this case.

As noted above, a non-justiciable political question exists when a court confronts "the impossibility of deciding without an initial policy determination of a kind clearly for nonjudicial discretion." *Vieth,* 541 U.S. at 278. As the Supreme Court has recognized, to resolve typical air pollution cases, courts must strike a balance "between interests seeking strict schemes to reduce pollution rapidly to eliminate its social costs and interests advancing the economic concern that strict schemes [will] retard industrial development with attendant social costs." *Chevron U.S.A., Inc. v. Natural Res. Def. Council, Inc.,* 467 U.S. 837, 847 (1984). In this case, balancing those interests, together with the other interests involved, is impossible without an "initial policy determination" first having been made by the elected branches to which our system commits such policy decisions, *viz.,* Congress and the President.

Plaintiffs advance a number of arguments why theirs is a simple nuisance claim of the kind courts have adjudicated in the past, but none of the pollution-as-public-nuisance cases cited by Plaintiffs has touched on so many areas of national and international policy. The scope and magnitude of the relief Plaintiffs seek reveals the transcendently legislative nature of this litigation. Plaintiffs ask this Court to cap carbon dioxide emissions and mandate annual reductions of an as-yet-unspecified percentage. Such relief would, at a minimum, require this Court to: (1) determine the appropriate level at which to cap the carbon dioxide emissions of these Defendants; (2) determine the appropriate percentage reduction to impose upon Defendants; (3) create a schedule to implement those reductions; (4) determine and balance the implications of such relief on the United States' ongoing negotiations with other nations concerning global climate change; (5) assess and measure available alternative energy resources; and (6) determine and balance the implications of such relief on the United States' energy sufficiency and thus its national security—all without an "initial policy determination" having been made by the elected branches.

Defendants have set forth just a few of the difficult "initial policy determination[s]" that would have to be made by the elected branches before any court could address these issues:

> [G]iven the numerous contributors of greenhouse gases, should the societal costs of reducing such emissions be borne by just a segment of the electricity-generating industry and their industrial and other consumers?

> Should those costs be spread across the entire electricity-generating industry (including utilities in the plaintiff States)? Other industries?

> What are the economic implications of these choices?

> What are the implications for the nation's energy independence and, by extension, its national security?

Def. Memo. at 7–8.

If there is any doubt as to the complexity of the "initial policy determination[s]" that must be made by the elected branches before a non-elected court can properly adjudicate a global warming nuisance claim, one need only look to the statements of the EPA, the agency in which "Congress has vested administrative authority" over the "technically complex area of environmental law," *New England Legal Foundation v. Costle*, 666 F.2d 30, 33 (2d Cir. 1981), and which has been grappling with the proper approach to the issue of global climate change for years. For example:

> It is hard to imagine any issue in the environmental area having greater "economic and political significance" than regulation of activities that might lead to global climate change. 68 Fed. Reg. 52922, 52928 (Sept. 8, 2003).

> The issue of global climate change ... has been discussed extensively during the last three Presidential campaigns; it is the subject of debate and negotiation in several international bodies; and numerous bills have been introduced in Congress over the last 15 years to address the issue. 68 Fed. Reg. at 52928.

> Unilateral [regulation of carbon dioxide emissions in the United States] could also weaken U.S. efforts to persuade key developing countries to reduce the [greenhouse gas] intensity of their economies. 68 Fed. Reg. at 52931.

> Unavoidably, climate change raises important foreign policy issues, and it is the President's prerogative to address them. 68 Fed. Reg. at 52931.

> Virtually every sector of the U.S. economy is either directly or indirectly a source of [greenhouse gas] emissions, and the countries of the world are involved in scientific, technical, and political-level discussions about climate change. 68 Fed. Reg. at 52928.

Considering these statements in no way undermines the longstanding principle that the judicial branch, not the political branches, determines, on a case-by-case basis, when a political question is raised. Looking at the past and current actions (and deliberate inactions) of Congress and the Executive within the United States and globally in response to the issue of climate change merely reinforces my opinion that the questions raised by Plaintiffs' complaints are non-judiciable political questions.

The parties dispute what effect, if any, the relief sought by Plaintiffs would have on United States foreign relations. Plaintiffs contend that there would no effect because the "[o]fficial United States policy is to reduce domestic emissions." Pl. Opp. at 20. Plaintiffs cite, *inter alia,* EPA and DOE's promotion of voluntary efforts to reduce greenhouse gas emissions, the President's statement that "[we] can make great progress in reducing emissions, and we will. Yet, even that isn't enough," Congress' commissioning of research on technologies to reduce carbon dioxide emissions, and the UNFCCC's references to limiting emissions. Pl. Opp. at 21. However, official United States policy is expressed by statutes and treaties in force, not press releases. And in interpreting a statute, "[o]ne must . . . listen attentively to what it does not say." Felix Frankfurter, *Some Reflections on the Reading of Statutes,* 47 COLUM. L. REV. 527, 535–36 (1947). The explicit statements of Congress and the Executive on the issue of global climate change in general and their specific refusal to impose the limits on carbon dioxide emissions Plaintiffs now seek to impose by judicial fiat confirm that making the "initial policy determination[s]" addressing global climate change is an undertaking for the political branches.

Because resolution of the issues presented here requires identification and balancing of economic, environmental, foreign policy, and national security interests, "an initial policy determination of a kind clearly for non-judicial discretion" is required. *Vieth,* 541 U.S. at 278 (quoting *Baker,* 369 U.S. at 212). Indeed, the questions presented here "uniquely demand single-voiced statement of the Government's views." *Baker,* 369 U.S. at 211. Thus, these actions present non-justiciable political questions that are consigned to the political branches, not the Judiciary.

NOTES

1. As you evaluate Judge Preska's decision, it may be worthwhile to consider the institutional resources her chambers could have drawn upon to resolve the case if it had continued on to the merits. Federal district court judges work alone; they are not part of panels. They generally have two clerks for research and writing support, and both most likely are recent law school graduates. There is no guarantee that either a judge or her clerks have ever taken a course in environmental law, let alone developed expertise in the science or economics of climate change. And a typical federal district court judge will have dozens—perhaps hundreds—of other cases on her docket. Doctrine aside, one might understand why a federal court judge would be reluctant to take on a case of this magnitude and technical complexity.

   In your authors' experience, it is very important for environmental lawyers to be aware of these concerns. Environmental law is hard for many judges and clerks, as well as many law students, and environmental cases often involve large and complex factual records. An attorney who can make the subject accessible, therefore, will often gain a competitive edge.

2. *Connecticut v. American Electric Power Co.* was one of several nuisance cases involving climate change. Another prominent case involved the Kivalina, a Native American village on the coast of Alaska. The Kivalina plaintiffs argued that climate change was literally destroying their town; a combination of rising seas and retreating sea ice had exposed them to storms that were damaging buildings and would force the residents to move. In contrast to the *Massachusetts v. EPA* plaintiffs, they asked for damages rather than for injunctive relief. But that turned out to be a distinction without a difference. A federal district court dismissed the case on political question and standing grounds. *Native Village of Kivalina v. Exxon-Mobil Corp.*, 663 F. Supp. 2d 863 (N.D. Cal. 2009). The plaintiffs appealed, but the Ninth Circuit upheld the dismissal, though on a different legal theory. Following the Supreme Court's decision in *American Electric Power Co. v.*

Connecticut, it held that the plaintiffs' claims were displaced by the Clean Air Act. 696 F.3d 849 (9th Cir. 2012).

3.   Federal courts have not resolved the question of whether the state common law remains available to plaintiffs seeking to sue greenhouse gas emitters, and generally federal courts have been more willing to conclude that federal statutes displace federal common law than that they preempt state common law.

II. INTRODUCTION TO STATUTORY INTERPRETATION

As the *American Electric Power Company* litigation ultimately demonstrated, environmental law is now primarily the domain of statutes (and administrative lawmaking, a subject for later in this chapter). One consequence of the importance of statutes is that statutory interpretation is now a key part of the day-to-day work of environmental lawyering—as well as lawyering in many other realms. It also will be an essential skill as you work through the remaining pages of this book. But reading statutes can be difficult. To help you navigate the challenges of statutory interpretation, the pages that follow provide an overview of statutory interpretation techniques.

We have built much of the overview around a real case (and a case you might have already read if you have taken a course in statutory interpretation). That case is *Babbitt v. Sweet Home Chapter of Communities for a Great Oregon*, 515 U.S. 687 (1996) and it involved a timber industry challenge to regulations implementing section nine of the Endangered Species Act (ESA). The key details of the case appear in the excerpt below:

Section 9(a)(1) of the Act provides the following protection for endangered species:

Except as provided in sections 1535(g)(2) and 1539 of this title, with respect to any endangered species of fish or wildlife listed pursuant to section 1533 of this title it is unlawful for any person subject to the jurisdiction of the United States to—

* * *

(B) take any such species within the United States or the territorial sea of the United States." 16 U.S.C. § 1538(a)(1).

Section 3(19) of the Act defines the statutory term "take":

"The term 'take' means to harass, harm, pursue, hunt, shoot, wound, kill, trap, capture, or collect, or to attempt to engage in any such conduct." 16 U.S.C. § 1532(19).

The Act does not further define the terms it uses to define "take." The Interior Department regulations that implement the statute, however, define the statutory term "harm":

> "*Harm* in the definition of 'take' in the Act means an act which actually kills or injures wildlife. Such act may include significant habitat modification or degradation where it actually kills or injures wildlife by significantly impairing essential behavioral patterns, including breeding, feeding, or sheltering." 50 C.F.R. § 17.3 (1994).

This regulation has been in place since 1975.

515 U.S. at 690–91.

In the late 1990s, the Fish and Wildlife Service began threatening to enforce this provision against timber companies that cut down trees used as habitat by northern spotted owls and red-cockaded woodpeckers—both of which were protected species. A lawsuit followed, culminating in the Supreme Court decision excerpted above. The decision has become famous among statutory interpretation scholars as well as environmental lawyers.

A. LEGISLATIVE SUPREMACY

The foundational principle of statutory interpretation is that an interpreting court or agency should give effect to the intent of the legislature. A judge's role, as the Supreme Court has repeatedly stressed, is to faithfully implement the law set forth by Congress (unless the law passed by Congress is unconstitutional).

This principle informed the Court's deliberations in *Sweet Home*, for all of the authors of all of the opinions began with the premise that their job was to discern Congressional intent. But a much more explicit, and famous, articulation of this principle comes from another classic ESA case. *Tennessee Valley Authority v. Hill* involved a clash between the ESA, which, in that case, was protecting a two-inch fish called a snail darter, and the Tennessee Valley Authority's plans to dam part of the Little Tennessee River. 437 U.S. 153 (1978). The Supreme Court Justices appear to have agreed, unanimously, that stopping the dam to protect the fish would be just plain silly.[3] But the majority also agreed that the ESA required that construction be stopped. As Justice Burger, writing for the majority, explained, "[o]ur individual appraisal of the wisdom or unwisdom of a particular course consciously selected by the Congress is to be put aside in the process of interpreting a statute. Once the meaning

---

[3] For an extended argument that stopping the dam was not silly at all, as well as a recounting of the rich backstory and epilogue to the Supreme Court's decision, see ZYGMUNT J.B. PLATER, THE SNAIL DARTER AND THE DAM: HOW PORK-BARREL POLITICS ENDANGERED A LITTLE FISH AND KILLED A RIVER (2015). Plater represented the plaintiffs in *TVA v. Hill*.

of an enactment is discerned and its constitutionality determined, the judicial process comes to an end." *Id.* at 194.[4]

B. THE IMPORTANCE OF PLAIN LANGUAGE

In addition to agreeing that Congressional intent should govern, judges generally agree that the actual text of a statute is the most important tool for its interpretation. Some judges—Justice Scalia was the most prominent example—have argued that the statutory text is the *only* tool that matters, while others just consider statutory text to be very important evidence of Congressional intent. But the three primary rules of statutory interpretation, according to a statement widely attributed to Supreme Court Justice Felix Frankfurter, are "(1) read the statute, (2) read the statute, and (3) read the statute." HENRY J. FRIENDLY, BENCHMARKS 202 (1967).

But how does one make sense of statutory text? As you have no doubt learned in your legal education, and in your life outside law school, words are not always clear. The chronic indeterminacy of language makes "read the statute" necessary but insufficient advice. Indeed, that indeterminacy was central to the *Sweet Home* decision. Does "take" refer only to an intentional act by which someone takes possession of a thing? Or might it reach more broadly to encompass acts that result in unintentional but foreseeable harm? Either interpretation seems plausible. To address these kinds of ambiguities, lawyers often turn to a series of interpretive tools.

1. DEFINITIONS

Many statutes contain definition sections, and if a statute defines a term, that definition governs—even if it is at odds with common usage of the word. That means paying attention to statutory definitions is very important. Consider, for example, the Resource Conservation and Recovery Act's (RCRA) definition of the key phrase "solid waste." To most of us, the meaning of that phrase is intuitively obvious, and it would exclude wastes in liquid or gaseous form. But the statute defines "solid waste," as "any garbage, refuse, sludge from a waste treatment plant, water supply treatment plant, or air pollution control facility and other discarded material, including solid, liquid, semisolid, or contained gaseous material." 42 U.S.C. § 6903(27). And that statutory definition trumps the conventional meaning of the word "solid."

For that reason, the majority in *Sweet Home* devoted much of its opinion to interpreting the statutory definition of "take." That, in turn, meant focusing heavily on the term "harm," which, because it appears to

---

[4] In his notes about the case, Justice Marshall put the point more succinctly: "Congress can be a jackass." Holly Doremus, *The Story of TVA v. Hill, in* ENVIRONMENTAL LAW STORIES 109, 130 (Richard J. Lazarus & Oliver A. Houck, eds. 2005).

be the broadest term in the definition of "take," became the crucial word in the case. As Justice Stevens' majority opinion explained, in responding to Justice Scalia's dissent, "[I]mportantly, Congress explicitly defined the operative term 'take' in the ESA, no matter how much the dissent wishes otherwise, thereby obviating the need for us to probe its meaning as we must probe the meaning of the undefined subsidiary term 'harm.'" 515 U.S. at 697 n.10.

2. CONVENTIONAL MEANING AND TERMS OF ART

While most statutes define some terms, they tend to leave most words and phrases undefined. For language without a statutory definition, the common meaning generally governs, and lawyers will often turn to dictionaries and to conventional usage to discern what that common meaning is. In her concurring opinion in *Sweet Home*, Justice O'Connor provided a classic example of this kind of reasoning. She argued that, under any ordinary understanding of the term, activities that impair animals' feeding, sheltering, or breeding would count as "harm." 515 U.S. at 710.

Occasionally, however, a statute will use a term of art—that is, a word or phrase that has a distinct meaning to a particular audience. In his dissent in *Sweet Home*, Justice Scalia argued that ESA section 9 presented such a situation. The term "take," he argued, had a long-established meaning in the common law of wildlife, and it referred to the intentional act of taking possession of an animal or plant. An act that incidentally impacted an endangered animal, he argued, did not fit within the traditional understanding of this legal term of art. 515 U.S. at 717.

3. CONTEXT

When interpreting a statute, you will often zero in on a few sentences, or even a few words. That is important; sometimes entire cases turn on the meaning of a single sentence, or even just one word. But you should not ignore the larger context of those words. Sometimes a phrase that seems ambiguous in isolation will become clear when considered in combination with the sentences that surround it. And sometimes a particular subsection of a statute will make more sense when you consider how that subsection interacts with other provisions of the statute.

In *Sweet Home*, Justice Stevens' majority opinion included a classic example of this form of analysis. Justice Stevens noted that other sections of the statute allowed legal authorizations for "incidental takes"—in other words, takes that occurred as collateral and unintended consequences of otherwise lawful activity—and that these authorizations were conditioned on taking steps to reduce and compensate for the damage done to the species' habitat. If the take prohibition did not encompass habitat modification, he argued, then these other provisions, which appeared to provide exceptions to a prohibition on habitat modification, would be superfluous. *See* 515 U.S. at 700–01.

4. SEMANTIC CANONS OF CONSTRUCTION

When interpreting statutes, lawyers also often turn to semantic canons of construction, which, in less fancy terms, are just rules of thumb for making sense of statutory language. Statutory interpretation scholars have identified a long list of such canons, and while the list is too long for us to reproduce here, the *Sweet Home* case can introduce you to some particularly important ones.

One is known as a canon against redundancy (courts also often use the word surplusage). This canon reflects an assumption that Congress does not include redundant or meaningless words in statutes. In *Sweet Home*, for example, the majority argued that "unless the statutory term 'harm' encompasses indirect as well as direct injuries, the word has no meaning that does not duplicate the meaning of other words that § 3 uses to define 'take.' A reluctance to treat statutory terms as surplusage supports the reasonableness of the Secretary's interpretation." 515 U.S. at 697–98.

In dissent, Justice Scalia responded with two different, and closely-related, canons. One, known as *ejusdem generis* (many canons have Latin names), holds that a catch-all term included in a list takes meaning consistent with the theme emerging from the remaining words in that list. Therefore, if all the other terms in the definition—"harass . . . pursue, hunt, shoot, wound, kill, trap, capture, or collect"—referred to intentional acts directed at the animal in question, then harm, too, should be interpreted only as referring to intentional acts. 515 U.S. at 719–21. Closely related is another canon, *noscitur a sociis*, which basically means that a word is known by the company it keeps.

You might notice that some of these canons seem to point in opposite directions. That, for years, has been the classic critique of canons of construction; for every canon, the famous legal scholar Karl Llewellyn once argued, there is an equal and opposite canon. Karl N. Llewellyn, *Remarks on the Theory of Appellate Decision and the Rules or Canons of about How Statutes are to be Construed*, 3 VAND. L. REV. 395 (1950). So what good are they, you might wonder? One answer is that they are tactically useful. Invoking a canon can add heft to your legal arguments, even if your opponents might deploy another canon in rebuttal; reaching stalemate in a canon battle can be better than unilateral disarmament. Another answer is that considering how canons of construction might apply to a statutory passage can sometimes help you anticipate and evaluate interpretations that differ from the one you reached at first. You will likely find, as you read statutes, that you sometimes arrive rather quickly and confidently at decisions about what they mean—but that other reasonable and intelligent people arrive quickly at different judgments. And if one of those other people is a judge or agency administrator (or just your supervising attorney), and you have not anticipated the alternative interpretation, that can be a problem. So you may be wise to think of canons of construction, and of statutory interpretation techniques more generally, not just as tools for argument, but also as checks against hasty and overly confident conclusions.

C. INTERPRETIVE AIDS BEYOND THE PLAIN LANGUAGE OF THE STATUTE

Statutory language is very, very important to statutory interpretation. But it isn't always everything; judges and practicing lawyers also sometimes draw upon other sources to discern Congressional intent.

1. SUBSTANTIVE CANONS OF CONSTRUCTION

Substantive canons of construction are presumptions designed to achieve or to avoid particular outcomes. A classic example of a substantive canon of construction is the rule of lenity, which creates a presumption that ambiguous criminal statutes will be interpreted in ways that favor a defendant. In *Sweet Home*, for example, the plaintiffs attempted to invoke the rule of lenity, arguing that ambiguities in the ESA—which allows for criminal enforcement—should be interpreted in a manner favorable to potential defendants. 515 U.S. at 704 n.18. The Court rejected that argument, but it nevertheless illustrates how a substantive canon of construction might be used.

The rule of lenity is just one of many substantive canons of construction, and there are again too many for us to list all of them. But two are particularly important for environmental law. One is the canon of constitutional avoidance. A judge invoking this canon will generally select a statutory interpretation that avoids raising a constitutional question. In other words, if that judge is choosing between statutory interpretations A and B, and interpretation A would raise a constitutional issue but interpretation B would not, the canon favors interpretation B. Another important canon, which often blurs with the canon of constitutional avoidance, holds that statutes should be interpreted in ways that respect certain core values like protecting traditional areas of state authority. As you will see from the water quality materials in Chapter 5, both of these canons have played important roles in Supreme Court cases addressing the scope of federal jurisdiction under the Clean Water Act.

2.   PURPOSE

When interpreting statutes, judges (and agencies) will often consider the purpose of the statute. Sometimes that purpose is plainly evident from the actual words of a statute; Congress often declares its aims. But in some cases, judges have interpreted a statute based on a broader sense of congressional goals, even when that sense was not anchored in—or was even at odds with—specific words from the statute. *See generally* John F. Manning, *What Divides Textualists from Purposivists?*, 106 COLUM. L. REV. 70 (2006).

Proponents of "purposivist" interpretation argue that this is the best way to remain truly faithful to Congressional intent. Words, they note, often fail us; sometimes they just come out wrong, and we don't say what we really mean. Or sometimes we can't anticipate the circumstances in which a law would be applied, and following the literal language of the statute in that unexpected circumstance would undermine the goals of its drafters. If our listeners or readers try, in those situations, to look past the literal words we said, and to do what we really want, they are honoring our intent, not subverting it.

But critics of this form of interpretation have powerful arguments. Congress votes only on the actual words of a statute, they argue, not on unrecorded understandings. Giving effect to what lawmakers may have meant, rather than what they said, might subvert the lawmaking process. In addition, critics of purpose-based interpretation often note that different members of Congress have different purposes in mind, and that statutes are often compromises among competing purposes. If, for example, the Supreme Court were to interpret ESA section 9 so as to best protect species, might that not subvert a competing goal of maintaining some limits on federal regulatory authority? *See Bennett v. Spear*, 520 U.S. 154, 176–77 (1997) (opining that the ESA reflects both an "overall goal of species preservation" and a countervailing goal to "avoid needless economic dislocation produced by agency officials zealously but unintelligently pursuing their environmental objectives").

Occasionally, the debate about whether to consider purpose in addition to text will be important to the resolution of a statutory interpretation question. Usually it does not matter much. Few judges (or agency decision-makers) are purists when it comes to textualism or purposivism. With most judges, you will be most effective if you can ground your arguments in the literal text of the statute *and* can explain how your proposed interpretation comports with some sensible statutory purpose.

3. LEGISLATIVE HISTORY

In deciding *Sweet Home*, both the majority and the dissenting opinions discussed the legislative history of the ESA. That means they considered the context in which the statute was passed, the evolution of the statute through multiple drafts, and the committee reports and Congressional debates that surrounded the statute's passage.

Once upon a time, this was a standard and unquestioned practice. Court opinions interpreting environmental statutes often contained many pages summarizing the legislative history of the statute and drawing key conclusions from that history. And attorneys litigating environmental cases spent many hours mining legislative history for key details. But in the 1980s, a group of judges—again led by Justice Scalia—began questioning the courts' reliance on legislative history. Their critique had several key points. First, and most importantly, they noted that Congress votes on statutory text, not legislative history. Second, they argued that legislative history was often crafted strategically, sometimes by legislators (or staff members) who hoped to obtain through judicial interpretations a statutory meaning they could never get passed as explicit text. Third, the critics noted that legislative history is often quite ambiguous, and that this ambiguity invited attorneys and judges to make strategic and selective use of legislative history. As D.C. Circuit judge Harold Leventhal said, citing favorable legislative history can be like "looking over a crowd and picking out your friends." Patricia M. Wald, *Some Observations on the Use of Legislative History in the 1981 Supreme Court Term*, 68 IOWA L. REV. 195, 214 (1983). For this reason, Justice Scalia hardly ever discussed legislative history, and his *Sweet Home* dissent, in which he made what the majority described as a "welcome but selective foray into legislative history," was a true outlier. 515 U.S. at 705.

Legislative history still has its defenders, who generally argue that courts are foolish to disregard contextual clues about statutory meaning. But the Justice Scalia-led critique has resonated enough that legislative history is generally somewhat less important than it used to be. For some judges, it is not important at all. In many states, the general rule is that a court should consult legislative history only if a statute is ambiguous on its face. *E.g. Ennabe v. Manosa*, 319 P.3d 201, 215 (Cal. 2014).

4. JUSTICE, FAIRNESS, EFFICIENCY, COMMON SENSE

Any time you are trying to anticipate how a statute will be interpreted, or to persuade a decision-maker to interpret a statute in a particular way, you will want to consider whether your preferred interpretation will strike a judge as just, sensible, or fair. This may sound like an odd statement; didn't this section begin with the principle that a judge must uphold Congressional intent even if she finds that intent to be unwise? But that advice is important for two key reasons.

The first, and less important, reason is that sometimes judges will disregard the plain language of a statute if they find that language to be absurd. Judges taking this approach will sometimes just presume that Congress never could have intended that literal result, but other judges will argue that they have a responsibility to help shape the law in ways that make it better.

The more important reason is that people tend to read language in ways that comport with their sense of fairness and justice. The *Sweet Home* case also seems to exemplify this, as will many of the other environmental decisions you read. The majority opinion and Justice O'Connor's concurrence both strike a generally sympathetic tone toward the project of providing regulatory protection for wildlife, and both uphold the federal government's ability to provide that protection. Justice Scalia's dissent, by contrast, leaves little doubt about his views of federal regulatory protection of wildlife on private land. In his second sentence, he asserted that "[t]he Court's holding that the hunting and killing prohibition incidentally preserves habitat on private lands imposes unfairness to the point of financial ruin—not just upon the rich, but upon the simplest farmer who finds his land conscripted to national zoological use." 515 U.S. at 714.

Sweet Home is just one case, but broader empirical studies suggest that ideology and policy preferences do influence judicial decision-making, even in statutory interpretation cases. *See, e.g.,* Richard L. Revesz, *Environmental Regulation, Ideology, and the D.C. Circuit*, 83 VA. L. REV. 1717 (1997); Thomas J. Miles & Cass R. Sunstein, *Do Judges Make Regulatory Policy? An Empirical Investigation of Chevron*, 73 U. CHI. L. REV. 823, 847–65 (2006); Jason J. Czarnezki, *An Empirical Investigation of Judicial Decisionmaking, Statutory Interpretation, and the Chevron Doctrine in Environmental Law*, 79 U. COLO. L. REV. 767 (2008). Importantly, none of those studies suggests that ideology is *completely* outcome-determinative; you can still win a case before a decision-maker who disagrees with your client's policy positions, and you can still lose before a sympathetic judge. But the studies do underscore the importance of framing your specific statutory arguments within a policy argument that will appeal to the judge or judges you appear before.

Additionally, what is true of judges is likely to be true of practicing attorneys, including you: you're likely to read statutes in ways that comport with your policy preferences. That can be dangerous, particularly if you represent clients with whom you sympathize, because you may fail to anticipate the different interpretations reached by a judge or other decision-maker who does not share your sympathies.

D. DEFERENCE AND AGENCY INTERPRETATIONS

The final statutory interpretation principle in this discussion overlaps with administrative law. Often, in the environmental law realm, judges must review agency interpretations of statutes. The question then arises: should the judge take a completely fresh look at the statute's meaning, or should the judge interpret the statute with deference given to the agency's interpretation? The usual answer is that the judge will accord some deference to the agency, but we will explain that answer in more detail below.

III. INTRODUCTION TO ADMINISTRATIVE LAW

Environmental law is largely administrative law. Although Congress and state legislatures play an essential role by enacting statutes, and courts by adjudicating cases, the overwhelming majority of environmental law is created, implemented, and adjudicated by federal and state administrative agencies. Thus, to understand and practice environmental law requires a strong understanding of administrative law. Attorneys who do not have a robust appreciation for administrative law can commit serious errors that prejudice their clients—for example, forgoing opportunities to challenge agency actions in court by missing deadlines, waiving arguments, or filing suit in the wrong court.

A. WHY ADMINISTRATION?

The importance of government agencies, and of administrative law, to environmental law is now an established reality. But why do administrative agencies play such an important role in this field? Policymakers would generally cite two primary explanations.

First, environmental law depends on technical expertise. To understand environmental controversies, and to implement environmental law, often requires some understanding of natural sciences, including biology, chemistry, and physics. Solutions to environmental problems often require engineering. And, as you have already seen from chapter 1, assessments of environmental problems and the designs of regulatory solutions to those problems are both highly intertwined with economics. In American governance, we typically look to administrative agencies to supply that kind of technical expertise. The United States Environmental Protection Agency, for example, has many more scientists, economists, and engineers on its staff than does Congress, and that staffing leaves it better equipped to respond to environmental controversies. Assigning environmental governance to agencies with technical expertise also has another potential benefit. In theory, at least, it might limit the influence of short-term political calculations on environmental decision-making.

Second, environmental law requires a lot of work. Effectively implementing environmental law requires developing and updating hundreds of standards, issuing thousands of permits, conducting investigations, bringing enforcement actions, and providing public education and outreach—among other tasks. Congress simply does not have enough people to do all of this, and the President him- or herself is much too busy. The same is true at the state level. State environmental agencies often complain of low funding levels and understaffing, but they still have resource advantages over legislatures—some of which, in smaller states, serve only part-time. Consequently, in environmental law, as in most other fields of regulatory governance, agencies do the day-to-day work of turning statutory environmental laws into actual governance.

But the emphasis on agencies also generates some of environmental law's recurring controversies. The idea that agencies are technically expert and politically insulated is a double-edged sword. It raises the appealing possibility of decisions grounded in impartial science, but it also raises the threat that policy-laden decisions will be made without accountability to the public. The very idea of the impartial expert also is widely contested. In the 1970s, when Congress enacted environmental laws, trust in government experts was far lower than in the 1930s, when the idea of the impartial expert was at its apex. Many of the public participation provisions and deadlines embedded in environmental laws, and in administrative law more generally, respond to that distrust. Despite those public participation provisions, levels of trust in government continue to decline. Today, some worry that expert agencies are even more susceptible to "capture,"—being subject to undue influence by interest groups—than are elected officials, while others worry that agencies will be so focused on their regulatory missions that they will ignore the collateral costs of regulation. Consequently, critics on all sides of environmental controversies often charge that government agencies are overly bureaucratic and insufficiently responsive to public preferences.

For practicing environmental lawyers, disagreements over the justifications for, and problems with, administrative governance are not just abstractions. If you pursue a career in this realm, you will likely find that debates about administrative governance and administrative law creep into your daily work, at least some of the time. Nonetheless, administrative agencies are now thoroughly entrenched in environmental law. For that reason—and whether you favor strong administrative governance or not—developing an understanding of government agencies, and of the body of law that governs them, will be essential to your success as an environmental lawyer (and it may be essential to your success as a lawyer in any field).

B. THE STRUCTURE OF ADMINISTRATIVE LAWMAKING

As noted, most environmental law is set forth in regulations issued by administrative agencies. But administrative agencies are creatures of statute, meaning that they are created by statute and have legal authority only insofar as they have been given that authority by Congress (or, at the state level, by a state legislature). Congress, in turn, can act only within its enumerated powers under the Constitution. Thus, we can understand environmental law as a hierarchical pyramid:

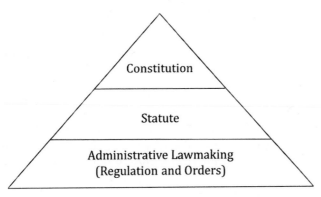

Learning environmental law requires studying the detailed administrative regulations and orders that comprise the bulk of environmental law, but also the more general statutes that authorize those regulations and orders, while always keeping in mind the very broadly stated provisions of the Constitution that authorize those statutes.

For example, as you will study in Chapter 4, new stationary sources of air pollution are subject to extensive requirements, including emissions limitations, set forth in New Source Performance Standards regulations issued by EPA. These regulations are authorized by Clean Air Act § 111, which directs EPA to issue regulations "establishing Federal standards of performance for new sources" of air pollution. 42 U.S.C. § 7411(b)(1)(B). The Clean Air Act is valid because air pollution involves "Commerce * * * among the several States," an area in which the Commerce Clause of Article I, Section 8, authorizes Congress to act.

C. THE PROCESS OF ADMINISTRATIVE LAWMAKING

As for the process by which agencies issue regulations, the Administrative Procedure Act (APA), which Congress enacted in 1946, establishes a generic blueprint for the procedures of administrative agencies. 5 U.S.C. §§ 551–559, 701–706. States have their own administrative procedure acts, which generally follow the model created by the APA. The APA divides the world of administrative outputs into two primary categories: (1) regulations, which arise from rulemaking processes; and (2) orders, which arise from adjudication. In addition to regulations and orders, administrative agencies also produce huge volumes of handbooks, guidance documents, interpretive rules, and other statements that, while not themselves law, are designed to guide internal agency practices and to help regulated entities understand the law and anticipate agency priorities and preferences. Below, we describe each of those categories in more detail.

a.   Rulemaking and Regulations

Agency regulations come from rulemaking, and, with limited exceptions, administrative rulemaking entails four main steps:

- Advance Notice of Proposed Rulemaking (optional): The agency indicates a regulatory objective and solicits public input.

- Proposed Rule: The agency proposes a draft rule for public comment and explains its rationale for the rule, including factual data, methodology, and legal interpretations and policy considerations that formed the basis for the proposed rule.

- Public Comment: The agency provides an opportunity for the public to comment on the proposed rule.

- Final Rule: The agency issues its final rule, along with an explanation of any changes from the proposed rule, a summary of the comments it received, and its responses to those comments.

Each of these steps—the advanced noticed of proposed rulemaking (if there is one), the proposed rule, and the final rule—are published in the *Federal Register*, which is published daily, along with an accompanying discussion known as the *preamble* that explains the rule. In addition, the final rule, once issued, is codified in the *Code of Federal Regulations*, which is published annually. If you want to see a currently effective regulation, the best place to look is the Code of Federal Regulations. If you want to understand the background or historical development of a rule, you will want to use the Federal Register.

Some statutes, such as the Clean Air Act, contain their own rulemaking provisions. *See, e.g.*, 42 U.S.C. § 7607(d). Others, like the National Environmental Policy Act, create additional layers of procedure for rulemakings in a variety of contexts. *See* Chapter 3, *infra*.

b.   Adjudication and Orders

Under the APA, an adjudication is any administrative process that culminates in an order. The APA defines order broadly, and the term encompasses actions like permitting and licensing. Many of the agency decision-making processes that allow people to take specific actions affecting the environment—filling wetlands, for example, or obtaining a permit to emit air pollutants—therefore qualify as adjudications.

Under the APA, adjudications can be either formal or informal. Formal adjudications are somewhat like courtroom proceedings; they involve formal procedures for introducing evidence and providing briefing, and the ultimate decision will be made by an administrative law judge. Informal adjudication is a broader catch-all category, and it can include decisions made through fairly ad-hoc procedures. In nearly all adjudications, agencies will apply existing law to the specific facts of the matter before them, much like a judge applying law to the facts of a case. But agencies also sometimes announce new legal principles in orders, much like a judge developing new principles of common law.

Most agencies allow internal appellate review of orders. EPA, for example, contains an entity known as the "Environmental Appeals Board," to which the decisions of individual administrative law judges can be appealed. Orders also can be challenged in court, but in some circumstances litigants must try appealing decisions within the agency— a process referred to as exhausting administrative remedies—before they can bring a suit in court. Specific provisions of statutes or regulations determine whether exhaustion is required, and attorneys must pay close attention to such requirements or risk losing a client's case by filing a lawsuit without completing the necessary steps.

c.   Guidance Documents, Policy Statements, Interpretive Rules, Handbooks

In addition to regulations and orders, which carry the force of law, agencies also produce large volumes of non-binding materials designed to explain to regulated entities—and to agency staff—how the agency interprets governing law, and how that law should be implemented. These advisory documents come in a wide variety of forms. And sometimes they are not even documents; at some point in your career, you will probably find yourself calling agency staff to get advice on how specific legal provisions are interpreted, or listening to (or delivering) an agency presentation on similar subject matter. They also arise from a variety of processes. Some come from forms of rulemaking and may even be recorded in the Federal Register, while with others, the process of creation is much more informal.

All of this guidance material has, in theory, a salutary purpose: it helps people understand what the law is and what agency priorities are. It therefore helps agencies act with greater consistency and protects regulated entities against unpleasant surprises. For these reasons, finding, reading, and understanding administrative guidance is a large part of the work of lawyers for regulated entities; indeed, much of that guidance is written with the expectation that compliance lawyers will use it to inform their clients' decisions. But there is a potential dark side to reliance on guidance documents. The critical view is perhaps best encapsulated in an excerpt from *Appalachian Power Co. v. EPA*, 208 F.3d 1015 (D.C. Cir. 2000):

> The phenomenon we see in this case is familiar. Congress passes a broadly worded statute. The agency follows with regulations containing broad language, open-ended phrases, ambiguous standards and the like. Then as years pass, the agency issues circulars or guidance or memoranda, explaining, interpreting, defining and often expanding the commands in the regulations. One guidance document may yield another and then another and so on. Several words in a regulation may spawn hundreds of pages of text as the agency offers more and more detail regarding what its regulations demand of regulated entities. Law is made, without notice and comment, without public participation, and without publication in the Federal Register or the Code of Federal Regulations. With the advent of the Internet, the agency does not need these official publications to ensure widespread circulation; it can inform those affected simply by posting its new guidance or memoranda or policy statement on its web site. An agency operating in this way gains a large advantage. "It can issue or amend its real rules, i.e., its interpretative rules and policy statements, quickly and inexpensively without following any statutorily prescribed procedures." Richard J. Pierce, Jr., *Seven Ways to Deossify Agency Rulemaking*, 47 ADMIN. L. REV. 59, 85 (1995). The agency may also think there is another advantage—immunizing its lawmaking from judicial review.

D. JUDICIAL REVIEW OF ADMINISTRATIVE AGENCY ACTION

As that last sentence suggests, judicial review of administrative decisions is an important part of administrative law. Oversight from judges, according to conventional administrative law theory, is one crucial way in which the American legal system balances the need for agency-based governance with the need for accountability and the rule of law. But environmental lawyers often confront questions about judicial review. A few are particularly recurrent and important:

- When is judicial review available?
- Who has standing to bring a challenge?
- In what court may the challenge be brought?
- What evidence will the court consider?
- What standard of review will the court use?

The discussion below addresses four of those five questions. The remaining question—who has standing—we will revisit later in this chapter, when we discuss the intersections between environmental and constitutional law.

a.   Timing

When an individual or organization objects to a "final agency action" taken by an administrative agency, it can sue the agency under the judicial review provisions of the Administrative Procedure Act (APA). 5 U.S.C. §§ 701–706 (excerpted *infra*). Some statutes, such as the Clean Air Act, contain judicial review provisions similar to the APA, *see* 42 U.S.C. § 7607(b), (d)(9) (excerpted *infra*), as well as citizen-suit provisions that allow suits against an agency when it has failed to perform one of its mandatory duties under the statute, *see* 42 U.S.C. § 7604(a)(2).

The requirement for final agency action is similar to the constitutional requirement for a "ripe" decision. Both final agency action doctrine and ripeness doctrine preclude lawsuits until the agency has reached the end of its decision-making process. In some circumstances, ripeness doctrine prevents challenges to even a final agency action until that action has been applied in some real world context and caused tangible consequences. They are designed, in other words, to stop litigants from suing agencies for things those agencies might do, but have not actually done yet, or for actions that might turn out to be inconsequential.

In addition to protecting agencies from suits that are filed too early, administrative law doctrines also protect agencies against lawsuits that are filed too late. Some of that protection comes from statutes of limitations. Judicial review provisions of environmental statutes often have stringent statutes of limitations, *see* 42 U.S.C. § 7607(c) (requiring petitions for review of certain EPA actions under the Clean Air Act to be filed within sixty days), as opposed to the more generous six-year limitations period that applies to APA claims. Protection also can come from constitutional doctrines like mootness, which precludes lawsuits from continuing when a court can no longer provide meaningful relief.

b.   Which Court?

In general, suits challenging the actions of federal agencies must be brought in federal district court. Some statutes, however, provide for petitions for review filed directly in federal courts of appeal. *See* 42 U.S.C. § 7607(b) (excerpted *infra*). In such cases, the parties are called petitioner and respondent instead of plaintiff and defendant. When a statute includes a specialized judicial review provision, a would-be plaintiff cannot choose instead to file suit under the general cause of action created by the APA. In other words, if a statute allows for a petition for review in a court of appeals, a litigant must follow that procedure.

More complicated questions can arise when the challenged agency decision is made by a state agency. State agency decisions generally are reviewable in state court. But challengers sometimes do not want to be in state court—environmental plaintiffs are often pressing politically unpopular positions, which they do not want to litigate before locally-elected judges—and questions therefore arise about the extent to which state agency decisions may be challenged in federal court. For full exploration of those questions, we recommend a course on the federal courts.

c.   What Evidence?

Most administrative decision-making processes will create an *administrative record* composed of the materials the agency considered while reaching its decision. In defending an action challenged in court, the agency may not rely on information outside of the record. This can get an agency in trouble when it finds that it must justify its action by relying on outside information it did not invoke during the administrative process. But the principle limiting courts to the administrative record is a double-edged sword that can limit those challenging agency action as well. A court reviewing the agency's action cannot consider the challengers' information if it comes from outside of the record. And an argument may be deemed waived if it was not raised before the agency during the administrative process. Although this may strike some litigants as an unfair technicality, the requirement allows the agency to consider an argument and respond to it, making any changes or correcting any errors, prior to finalizing its decision.

d.   What Standard of Review?

To prevail in a court challenge to an agency action, a litigant typically must show that the agency has acted in a manner that is "arbitrary, capricious, an abuse of discretion, or otherwise not in accordance with law." 5 U.S.C. § 706. Courts reviewing a claim that an agency action is arbitrary and capricious are deferential to the agency's factual conclusions, although the court will make sure that the agency has adequately explained its decision. A defect in an agency action may be procedural, such as neglecting to allow sufficient opportunity for public comment, or substantive, such as adopting a regulation that is inconsistent with the governing statute. If the court reviewing the agency action finds defects in the action, it remands the action back to the agency for the agency to correct the errors found by the court.

Courts also often give deference to an agency's legal conclusions. In *Chevron, U.S.A., Inc. v. Natural Resources Defense Council, Inc.*, 467 U.S. 837 (1984), the Supreme Court set forth a two-step test for determining when to defer to an agency's interpretation of a statute the agency administers. First, if the intent of Congress is clear from the statute, then that unambiguously expressed congressional intent controls, and the agency's interpretation receives no deference. Second, if the statute's meaning is not clear, a court defers to the agency's interpretation if it is reasonable. *Id.* at 844. This *Chevron* framework typically applies when an agency

> The APA and some other statutes also refer to a substantial evidence standard of review. Most practicing lawyers and judges will tell you that substantial evidence review is just arbitrary and capricious review by another name. *See, e.g., Mem'l Hosp./Adair Cty. Health Ctr. v. Bowen*, 829 F.2d 111 (D.C. Cir. 1987) (noting that the substantial evidence standard and arbitrary and capricious standard "require equivalent levels of scrutiny"). But there are a few outlying court decisions suggesting that the substantial evidence standard is meaningfully different. *See, e.g., Aqua Slide 'N' Dive Corp. v. Consumer Prod. Safety Comm'n*, 569 F.2d 831, 841 (5th Cir. 1978) (suggesting that the substantial evidence standard may in some circumstances be stricter than the arbitrary and capricious standard).

interprets its statute through a formal and binding process, such as notice and comment rulemaking or formal adjudication. *Christensen v. Harris Cty.*, 529 U.S. 576, 587 (2000). Less formal interpretations, such as an interpretation in a nonbinding guidance document, are usually given less deference. *See Skidmore v. Swift & Co.*, 323 U.S. 134, 140 (1944) (holding that such interpretations are "entitled to respect" to the extent that they have the "power to persuade"). Courts also give deference to an agency's interpretation of its own regulation regardless of the form in which that interpretation is articulated, if the regulation is ambiguous and the agency's interpretation is reasonable. *Auer v. Robbins*, 519 U.S. 452 (1997); *Bowles v. Seminole Rock & Sand Co.*, 325 U.S. 410 (1945). Under this framework, the Supreme Court has even considered the position articulated in a litigation brief as a basis for deferring to an agency's interpretation of its regulations. *See Coeur Alaska, Inc. v. Southeastern Alaska Conservation Council*, 557 U.S. 261, 274 (2009). Some Justices have recently been critical of *Auer/Seminole Rock* deference, indicating that the doctrine may be in some jeopardy. *See, e.g., Perez v. Mortgage Bankers Ass'n*, 135 S. Ct. 1199, 1225 (2015) (Thomas, J., concurring in the judgment); *Decker v. Nw. Envtl. Def. Ctr.*, 133 S. Ct. 1326, 1340 (2013) (Scalia, J., dissenting).

PROBLEM: CHALLENGING AN EPA RULE

You are an attorney in the legal department of an Alabama company that manufactures construction equipment. A team of engineers working for your company recently designed a new type of diesel-powered mechanical excavator that works far more efficiently than existing excavators.

Suppose that two years ago EPA issued new emissions standards for excavators. In developing the standards, EPA assumed that all excavators use the technology of the best existing excavator and did not anticipate development of your company's technology. At the time, your company was working to develop the new technology, but did not want to reveal its plans to its competitors and so decided not to submit a comment on the proposed rule.

Your company's engineers believe that, even with all possible pollution control equipment, the new excavator's emissions will exceed—that is, violate—the EPA standards by ten percent. The overall emissions for each job, however, will be lower, because your excavators will get jobs done faster and use less power. But EPA's standards establish a maximum allowable level of emissions per amount of power the equipment uses each hour it is in operation, not for each job it does, and the standards therefore do not account for the efficiency advantages your company's equipment would offer. The company hopes to begin manufacturing and selling the excavator three months from now.

Concerned about the impact of the emissions standards on your company's ability to sell the excavator in the United States, the general counsel of the company wrote a letter to EPA asking whether the emissions standards applies to the new excavator despite its enhanced efficiency. The letter argued that "in light of EPA's ultimate goal of reducing air pollution, it would be nonsensical and irrational for the agency to prohibit the sale of our new equipment, which will ultimately emit less air pollutants due to its greater efficiency, even though it would technically violate of the standards."

EPA responded with a letter stating, in relevant part, "Application of the relevant emissions standards is determined by the language of the standards themselves, which by your own admission encompass your new equipment. Accordingly, it would appear that the emissions standards do apply."

The general counsel of the company has asked you to advise her of potential actions the company can take to challenge the application of the emissions standards to the new excavator. Together with the general counsel, you have identified the following specific questions for analysis:

a.   Can the company sue EPA to challenge the rule setting the emissions standard? If so, in what court should the company bring suit?

b.   Can the company sue EPA to challenge EPA's letter? If so, in what court should the company bring suit?

 c. If the company sues EPA, what would the company have to show in order to prevail? What arguments might the company make to satisfy this burden? How likely is the company to prevail, based on the information you have at hand? What additional information might be relevant?

 d. If the company cannot sue EPA to challenge the rule, how else might the company be able to protect its interests?

 e. If EPA initiates an enforcement action against the company for violations of the emissions standards, can the company argue in defense that the standards are arbitrary and capricious as applied to the new excavator?

Generally judicial review of administrative agency actions is governed by the APA. The Clean Air Act, however, includes its own judicial review provisions that augment the APA, set forth below. Although the overall framework for judicial review under these Clean Air Act provisions closely resembles judicial review under the APA, there are a few important differences.

CAA § 307, 42 U.S.C. § 7607. Administrative proceedings and judicial review

(b) Judicial review

(1) A petition for review of action of the Administrator in promulgating any national primary or secondary ambient air quality standard, any emission standard or requirement under section 7412 of this title, any standard of performance or requirement under section 7411 of this title, any standard under section 7521 of this title (other than a standard required to be prescribed under section 7521(b)(1) of this title), any determination under section 7521(b)(5) of this title, any control or prohibition under section 7545 of this title, any standard under section 7571 of this title, any rule issued under section 7413, 7419, or under section 7420 of this title, or any other nationally applicable regulations promulgated, or final action taken, by the Administrator under this chapter may be filed only in the United States Court of Appeals for the District of Columbia. A petition for review of the Administrator's action in approving or promulgating any implementation plan under section 7410 of this title or section 7411(d) of this title, any order under section 7411(j) of this title, under section 7412 of this title, under section 7419 of this title, or under section 7420 of this title, or his action under section 1857c–10(c)(2)(A), (B), or (C) of this title (as in effect before August 7, 1977) or under regulations thereunder, or revising regulations for enhanced monitoring and compliance certification programs under section 7414(a)(3) of this title, or any other final action of the

Administrator under this chapter (including any denial or disapproval by the Administrator under subchapter I of this chapter) which is locally or regionally applicable may be filed only in the United States Court of Appeals for the appropriate circuit. Notwithstanding the preceding sentence a petition for review of any action referred to in such sentence may be filed only in the United States Court of Appeals for the District of Columbia if such action is based on a determination of nationwide scope or effect and if in taking such action the Administrator finds and publishes that such action is based on such a determination. Any petition for review under this subsection shall be filed within sixty days from the date notice of such promulgation, approval, or action appears in the Federal Register, except that if such petition is based solely on grounds arising after such sixtieth day, then any petition for review under this subsection shall be filed within sixty days after such grounds arise. The filing of a petition for reconsideration by the Administrator of any otherwise final rule or action shall not affect the finality of such rule or action for purposes of judicial review nor extend the time within which a petition for judicial review of such rule or action under this section may be filed, and shall not postpone the effectiveness of such rule or action.

(2)   Action of the Administrator with respect to which review could have been obtained under paragraph (1) shall not be subject to judicial review in civil or criminal proceedings for enforcement. Where a final decision by the Administrator defers performance of any nondiscretionary statutory action to a later time, any person may challenge the deferral pursuant to paragraph (1). * * *

(d) Rulemaking

* * *

(3)   In the case of any rule to which this subsection applies, notice of proposed rulemaking shall be published in the Federal Register, as provided under section 553(b) of Title 5, shall be accompanied by a statement of its basis and purpose and shall specify the period available for public comment (hereinafter referred to as the "comment period"). The notice of proposed rulemaking shall also state the docket number, the location or locations of the docket, and the times it will be open to public inspection. The statement of basis and purpose shall include a summary of—

(A)   the factual data on which the proposed rule is based;

(B)   the methodology used in obtaining the data and in analyzing the data; and

(C)   the major legal interpretations and policy considerations underlying the proposed rule.

The statement shall also set forth or summarize and provide a reference to any pertinent findings, recommendations, and comments by the Scientific Review Committee established under section 7409(d) of this title and the National Academy of Sciences, and, if the proposal differs in any important respect from any of these recommendations, an explanation of the reasons for such differences. All data, information, and documents referred to in this paragraph on which the proposed rule relies shall be included in the docket on the date of publication of the proposed rule. * * *

(5)   In promulgating a rule to which this subsection applies (i) the Administrator shall allow any person to submit written comments, data, or documentary information; (ii) the Administrator shall give interested persons an opportunity for the oral presentation of data, views, or arguments, in addition to an opportunity to make written submissions; (iii) a transcript shall be kept of any oral presentation; and (iv) the Administrator shall keep the record of such proceeding open for thirty days after completion of the proceeding to provide an opportunity for submission of rebuttal and supplementary information.

(6)(A)   The promulgated rule shall be accompanied by (i) a statement of basis and purpose like that referred to in paragraph (3) with respect to a proposed rule and (ii) an explanation of the reasons for any major changes in the promulgated rule from the proposed rule.

(B)   The promulgated rule shall also be accompanied by a response to each of the significant comments, criticisms, and new data submitted in written or oral presentations during the comment period.

(C)   The promulgated rule may not be based (in part or whole) on any information or data which has not been placed in the docket as of the date of such promulgation.

(7)(A)   The record for judicial review shall consist exclusively of the material referred to in paragraph (3), clause (i) of paragraph (4)(B), and subparagraphs (A) and (B) of paragraph (6).

(B)   Only an objection to a rule or procedure which was raised with reasonable specificity during the period for public comment (including any public hearing) may be raised during judicial review. If the person raising an objection can demonstrate to the Administrator that it was impracticable to raise such objection within such time or if the grounds for such objection arose after the period for public comment (but within the time specified for judicial review) and if such objection is of central relevance to the outcome of the rule, the Administrator shall convene a proceeding for reconsideration of the rule and provide the same procedural rights as would have been afforded had the information been available at the time the rule was proposed. If the Administrator refuses to convene such a proceeding, such person may seek review of such refusal in the United States court of appeals for the appropriate circuit (as provided in subsection (b) of this section). Such reconsideration shall not postpone the effectiveness of the rule. The effectiveness of the rule may be stayed during such reconsideration, however, by the Administrator or the court for a period not to exceed three months.

(8) The sole forum for challenging procedural determinations made by the Administrator under this subsection shall be in the United States court of appeals for the appropriate circuit (as provided in subsection (b) of this section) at the time of the substantive review of the rule. No interlocutory appeals shall be permitted with respect to such procedural determinations. In reviewing alleged procedural errors, the court may invalidate the rule only if the errors were so serious and related to matters of such central relevance to the rule that there is a substantial likelihood that the rule would have been significantly changed if such errors had not been made.

(9) In the case of review of any action of the Administrator to which this subsection applies, the court may reverse any such action found to be—

    (A)   arbitrary, capricious, an abuse of discretion, or otherwise not in accordance with law;

    (B)   contrary to constitutional right, power, privilege, or immunity;

    (C)   in excess of statutory jurisdiction, authority, or limitations, or short of statutory right; or

    (D)   without observance of procedure required by law, if (i) such failure to observe such procedure is arbitrary or capricious, (ii) the requirement of paragraph (7)(B) has been met, and (iii) the condition of the last sentence of paragraph (8) is met. * * *

The following case, although not a leading case from the Supreme Court, provides a clear explanation of some of the principles governing when an interested party can challenge an agency position in court.

Independent Equipment Dealers Ass'n v. EPA

372 F.3d 420 (D.C. Cir. 2004)

■ ROBERTS, CIRCUIT JUDGE:

Petitioner Independent Equipment Dealers Association (IEDA) is a trade association of independent dealers of heavy construction and industrial equipment, such as cranes, large forklifts, and generators. IEDA dealers are "independent" in the sense that they are not affiliated with any manufacturer. In December 2002, IEDA wrote to EPA seeking EPA's concurrence in its interpretation of emissions regulations pertaining to "nonroad engines"—engines used in such heavy construction and industrial equipment. *See generally* 40 C.F.R. pt. 89. Four weeks later, EPA replied that it did not concur in IEDA's proffered interpretation. IEDA then filed this petition for review claiming that EPA, by its letter, had substantively amended its regulations concerning nonroad engines, and in so doing had failed to comply with the notice-and-comment requirements of Section 307(d) of the Clean Air Act, 42 U.S.C. § 7607(d)(3). IEDA alternatively contends that EPA's letter violated the Clean Air Act's prohibition on agency action that is arbitrary or capricious. *See id.* § 7607(d)(9)(A). We conclude that we lack jurisdiction and accordingly dismiss the petition for review.

I.

Since 1996, EPA has regulated nonroad engines by requiring their manufacturers to obtain a "certificate of conformity" indicating compliance with EPA emissions standards before selling such engines or importing them into the United States. 40 C.F.R. §§ 89.105, 89.1003(a)(1); *see also* 42 U.S.C. § 7547(a) (authorizing regulation of nonroad engines); *id.* § 7522(a)(1) (prohibiting the sale, distribution, or importation of any uncertified new motor vehicle engine). Manufacturers are not required to obtain certificates of conformity for each individual engine or engine model, but rather for each "engine family." 40 C.F.R. § 89.105. EPA defines an engine family as a group of engines "expected to have similar emission characteristics throughout their useful life periods"—a categorization based on the design and emissions characteristics of the engines. *Id.* § 89.116. The application for the certificate of conformity must include "[a]n unconditional statement certifying that all engines in the engine family comply with all requirements of this part [40 C.F.R. pt. 89] and the Clean Air Act." *Id.* § 89.115(d)(10). * * *

In furtherance of this regulatory regime, EPA also requires manufacturers to affix to each new engine an "emission control information label" that identifies the engine and states that it conforms to all EPA emissions standards and regulations. *Id.* § 89.110, (b)(10). On a practical level, this engine label demonstrates to dealers, purchasers, and enforcement inspectors that the engine is covered by an EPA certificate of conformity. Unlabeled engines are presumed to be uncertified.

Many nonroad engines are manufactured outside the United States. Engines covered by a certificate of conformity may be imported into the United States subject only to ordinary customs regulations. Engines not covered by a manufacturer's certificate of conformity may only be imported if they comply with EPA's Independent Commercial Importers (ICI) program. 40 C.F.R. § 89.601 et seq. The chief burden associated with the ICI program is that after the importer has obtained a certificate of conformity for the engine family, the importer still must test one of every three imported engines for compliance with Part 89 emissions regulations. According to EPA, each test costs between $15,000 and $30,000, depending on the engine. Additionally, since it is the importer, not the manufacturer, who obtains a certificate of conformity for the engines, all other Part 89 requirements—labeling, recall and warranty, etc.—run to the importer rather than the manufacturer. *See* 40 C.F.R. § 89.610. The ICI importer thus steps into the shoes of the manufacturer, assuming all the obligations that would ordinarily fall upon the manufacturer.

The market for nonroad engines in the United States is segmented between original engine manufacturers (OEMs), who sell the equipment they manufacture through networks of authorized dealers, and independent equipment dealers, who are not affiliated with an OEM. Independent dealers make their way in the market by re-selling equipment, frequently at lower prices than the OEMs. The collapse of the Asia-Pacific Rim economy in the late 1990s offered a unique opportunity to enterprising independent equipment dealers. In the deeply distressed Asian construction market, equipment distributors found themselves with bloated inventories and few prospects of selling that equipment locally. Sensing an arbitrage opportunity, some U.S. independent dealers bought equipment at depressed prices in Asia, and then imported the equipment into the United States. Of course, the Asian equipment could be legally imported only if it were covered by a manufacturer's certificate of conformity or had been taken through the costly and time-consuming ICI process. Few independent dealers availed themselves of the ICI program; the lack of significant EPA enforcement of Part 89 regulations made importation of uncertified equipment a much more lucrative path.

The importation of low-priced Asian equipment—EPA-certified and otherwise—by independent dealers into the United States market had the predictable effect of undermining the pricing power of the OEMs in the United States. OEMs have a difficult time selling a machine for $50,000 when an independent dealer is selling the identical machine for $35,000, having purchased it in Korea for $20,000.

The OEMs appealed to EPA for increased enforcement of Part 89 regulatory requirements. In November 1998, EPA and the Associated Equipment Distributors, a trade association of authorized dealers, hosted a workshop to explain the Part 89 requirements as they pertained to imported engines. At the workshop, EPA vowed to enforce the regulations, and the Customs Service explained that it would impound any engine lacking an EPA emissions control information label.

EPA followed up in February 2000 with an Enforcement Alert announcing its intention to increase enforcement of certificate of conformity and emission control information label requirements with regard to imported nonroad engines. In that document, EPA emphasized that all engines imported into the U.S. must be covered by a certificate of conformity and must bear an EPA-compliant emissions control information label. In a "Fact and Fiction" segment, EPA also cautioned that many engines obtained overseas were not eligible for importation:

> Fiction: An uncertified engine having similar or even identical emission characteristics as a certified engine should be able to be imported.

> Fact: Manufacturers may produce engines that are identical to U.S. certified versions but the engines are not intended for the U.S. market. These engines are not certified and may not be imported unless they are produced under an EPA-issued certificate, [and] are properly labeled. . . .

> Note how the court describes a long series of communications between EPA and industry. This is typical of administrative environmental regulation, and you can safely assume that lawyers on all sides were heavily involved in those communications. Your legal education may have conditioned you to identify lawyering primarily with courtroom proceedings, but this case provides just one of many possible examples of how much lawyering occurs before a case is ever filed.

EPA soon reiterated this position in response to an inquiry from authorized dealers. OEMs asked whether manufacturers could adopt a program of destination-specific labeling of engines, thereby indicating which engines are and which are not covered by a certificate of conformity. EPA responded that "[t]he manufacturer is not only allowed to place a destination-specific label on a non-certified engine intended for sale elsewhere than the United States, but also is encouraged to do this." EPA explained that

> the key distinction for imported engines . . . is whether the manufacturer intended the engine to be covered by a certificate or not to be covered by a certificate. . . .

> In your scenario, the manufacturer has chosen, for whatever reason, to not include under certificate coverage the engines intended for sale elsewhere than the U.S., and so it will not place the EPA required emission label on the engines. This step is correct.

EPA was even more explicit in its 2001 response to an inquiry from an engine manufacturer. There EPA wrote, "[m]anufacturers also may choose . . . to produce engines which will not be covered by an EPA certificate, because they will be sold elsewhere than the U.S.," even though "[t]hese non-certified engines may be physically identical to engines which the manufacturer chooses to be covered by an EPA certificate."

The OEMs then—with EPA's blessing—took the position that only those engines they intended to import into the United States were covered by EPA certificates of conformity, and began affixing EPA emissions control labels only to those engines. This had the desired effect; independent dealers seeking access to the United States market were left only with the much less attractive option of importing uncertified machines through the ICI process, even though many of those engines—according to IEDA—were identical in all respects to engines to which OEMs had affixed labels.

IEDA believes this destination-specific labeling program violates EPA's Part 89 regulations. IEDA wrote to EPA to raise the question of whether "engines that are 'identical' to an EPA certified version can be designated 'uncertified' by the engine manufacturer under the regulations at 40 C.F.R. Part 89." IEDA stated its view that because certificates of conformity apply to "engine families and not to individual engines," and because "the engine family is defined by its physical characteristics," "all engines that have the same physical characteristics . . . are covered by the certificate of conformity issued to the engine family." IEDA sought EPA's concurrence in this conclusion and also IEDA's view that all manufacturers' Part 89 obligations, including warranty, recall, and defect reporting requirements, and, crucially, the emissions control information label requirement, apply to all such covered engines.

EPA responded that it did not concur in IEDA's interpretation of the Part 89 regulations. EPA stated that "[n]either the Clean Air Act [n]or our regulations impose [Part 89] requirements on engines that the manufacturer did not introduce or intend for introduction into U.S. commerce." It explained that the "requirement to divide a 'manufacturer's product line' into engine families in 40 C.F.R. § 89.116 refers to that portion of the product line intended for sale in the U.S." Thus, contrary to IEDA's interpretation, a manufacturer was empowered to "identify which of its engines are covered by its certificate of conformity and which are not." This identification was typically accomplished, said

EPA, through the affixing (or not) of the emissions control information label.

Unsatisfied with that response, IEDA filed the instant petition for review.

II.

IEDA contends that the EPA Letter adds a manufacturer "intent" element to the definition of an "engine family," and thus substantively amends the Part 89 regulations—specifically 40 C.F.R. § 89.116—without satisfying the notice-and-comment requirements of the Clean Air Act. *See* 42 U.S.C. § 7607(d)(3). Alternatively, IEDA claims that the EPA Letter violates the Act's prohibition on regulation that is "arbitrary, capricious, an abuse of discretion, or otherwise not in accordance with law." *Id.* § 7607(d)(9)(A). * * *

Both EPA and Intervenor-Respondent Engine Manufacturers Association have raised numerous challenges to our jurisdiction over IEDA's petition for review, among them that the EPA Letter does not constitute "final action" within the meaning of the judicial review provision of the Act, *id.* § 7607(b). As we are a court of limited jurisdiction, we are obliged to consider these jurisdictional objections before addressing the merits of IEDA's substantive claims.

At the outset, we observe that EPA's claim that its letter does not constitute "final action" seems somewhat inartful in view of its concurrent insistence that the interpretation of the certificate of conformity regulations contained therein *is* final and not subject to change.

This line of argument becomes more understandable when one considers the dual requirements for "final agency action": (1) that the action be final—*i.e.,* not tentative or interlocutory; and (2) that the action be one from which "rights or obligations have been determined" or from which "legal consequences will flow." *Bennett v. Spear,* 520 U.S. 154, 177–78 (1997) (internal quotation omitted). The Government's brief makes clear that its underlying objection is not so much to the first element—concerning finality—as it is to the second—concerning the types of agency action suitable for review. EPA's brief does not assert that its interpretation is tentative or interlocutory; it does, however, forcefully argue that the EPA Letter is legally insignificant. So rather than ask—awkwardly—whether an interpretation the parties agree is not subject to change is *final,* we instead frame our inquiry as whether the EPA Letter setting out that interpretation constitutes reviewable agency action.

In answering that question, we start with the acknowledgment that the term "agency action" undoubtedly has a broad sweep. *See, e.g., FTC v. Standard Oil Co. of Cal.,* 449 U.S. 232, 238 n.7 (1980); *Whitman v.*

American Trucking Ass'ns, 531 U.S. 457, 478 (2001). But we also have long recognized that the term is not so all-encompassing as to authorize us to exercise "judicial review [over] everything done by an administrative agency." *Hearst Radio, Inc. v. FCC*, 167 F.2d 225, 227 (D.C. Cir. 1948). Here, common sense, basic precepts of administrative law, and the Administrative Procedure Act itself all point to the conclusion that the EPA Letter to IEDA is not reviewable agency action.

The answer seems obvious once we examine the concrete impact the EPA Letter had on IEDA and its members—in short, none whatsoever. As discussed above, the EPA Letter merely restated in an abstract setting—for the umteenth time—EPA's longstanding interpretation of the Part 89 certificate of conformity regulations. The Letter neither announced a new interpretation of the regulations nor effected a change in the regulations themselves. The Letter was purely informational in nature; it imposed no obligations and denied no relief. Compelling no one to do anything, the letter had no binding effect whatsoever—not on the agency and not on the regulated community. It was, as EPA describes it, "the type of workaday advice letter that agencies prepare countless times per year in dealing with the regulated community." At oral argument, counsel for IEDA appeared to concede that such a letter, unless it wrought a regulatory change, would be an insufficient basis for jurisdiction.

That concession is in accordance with our prior decisions. We have held that we lacked authority to review claims where "an agency merely expresses its view of what the law requires of a party, even if that view is adverse to the party." *AT&T v. EEOC*, 270 F.3d 973, 975 (D.C. Cir. 2001); *see also DRG Funding Corp. v. HUD*, 76 F.3d 1212, 1214 (D.C. Cir. 1996) (holding unreviewable an agency order that "does not itself adversely affect complainant but only affects his rights adversely on the contingency of future administrative action" (internal quotation omitted)). Similarly, we have held often enough that when an "agency has not yet made any determination or issued any order imposing any obligation . . . , denying any right . . . , or fixing any legal relationship," the agency action was not reviewable. *Reliable Automatic Sprinkler Co. v. CPSC*, 324 F.3d 726, 732 (D.C. Cir. 2003) (citing *Role Models Am., Inc. v. White*, 317 F.3d 327, 331–32 (D.C. Cir. 2003)). "[P]ractical consequences," such as the threat of "having to defend itself in an administrative hearing should the agency actually decide to pursue enforcement," are insufficient to bring an agency's conduct under our purview. *Id.*

Moreover, our "reopening doctrine" specifically spells out the circumstances when an agency's discussion of its existing regulations *can* ripen into an "opportunity for renewed comment and objection" to those regulations. *Ohio v. EPA*, 838 F.2d 1325, 1328 (D.C. Cir. 1988). Implicit in the very concept of a reopening doctrine is the notion that regulations and interpretations that have not been reopened by agency action remain at repose and are not newly reviewable. This, of course, makes good sense. Just as it would be folly to allow parties to challenge a regulation anew each year upon the annual re-publication of the Code of Federal Regulations, so too it is silly to permit parties to challenge an established regulatory interpretation each time it is repeated. Such a regime would quickly muzzle any informal communications between agencies and their regulated communities—communications that are vital to the smooth operation of both government and business. * * *

Our conclusion that the EPA Letter is not reviewable agency action means that we lack jurisdiction to consider the merits of IEDA's substantive claims under the Act. *See* 42 U.S.C. § 7607(b). This conclusion obviates the necessity of considering the Government's and the Intervenor's other jurisdictional arguments.

The petition for review is dismissed for lack of jurisdiction.

Why didn't IEDA just challenge EPA's Part 89 regulations? Does the answer to that question help your analysis of your company's ability to sue EPA?

The *Independent Equipment Dealers Association* case makes clear that not all grievances against EPA can form the basis for a justiciable lawsuit. The following case addresses the standards that apply to a court's consideration of the merits of a suit against an agency.

Husqvarna AB v. EPA

254 F.3d 195 (D.C. Cir. 2001)

■ KAREN LeCRAFT HENDERSON, CIRCUIT JUDGE:

The petitioners, Husqvarna AB *et al.* (Husqvarna), seek review of the Phase 2 Emission Standards for New Nonroad Spark-Ignition Handheld Engines promulgated by the respondent, the U.S. Environmental Protection Agency (EPA), under the authority of section 213 of the Clean Air Act (CAA), 42 U.S.C. § 7547. Husqvarna contends that the final rule is arbitrary and capricious because the EPA failed to select the emission standards that represent the best balance of the factors identified in CAA section 213. It also maintains that the regulatory alternative chosen by the EPA is not supported by substantial evidence in the record. Finally, Husqvarna alleges procedural error stemming from inadequate notice and opportunity to comment. Because each of these arguments lacks merit, we deny Husqvarna's petition.

I.   Background

In 1990 the Congress amended the CAA and added section 213, which authorizes the EPA to set emissions standards for "nonroad engines and vehicles." Section 213 required the EPA to adopt emission standards by 1993 and to revise them as appropriate thereafter. The EPA missed the statutory deadline and a lawsuit to enforce the statute was filed, which has resulted in the district court's monitoring of the EPA's compliance.

In establishing emission standards, the EPA created two categories of small spark-ignition (SI) engines: nonhandheld and handheld.[1]

The EPA further divided handheld engines into three classes-Classes III, IV and V-based on engine size, with Class III encompassing the smallest and Class V the largest handheld engines. The domestic handheld engine industry includes 22 manufacturers, including Husqvarna, Stihl, John Deere, Shindaiwa, Kawasaki, Echo, Ryobi and Honda, which manufacture a total of 186 engine families. These manufacturers primarily use two-stroke engines in handheld products because of their high power-to-weight ratios and low cost. A two-stroke engine is an internal combustion engine that accomplishes the operations of intake, compression, expansion and exhaust in two piston strokes rather than four.

The EPA has regulated emissions from handheld engines in two phases. In Phase 1, the EPA proposed short-term new engine standards based in part on standards California had adopted for similar engines. In January 1998 the EPA proposed Phase 2 emission standards for handheld engines that were slightly more stringent than those in Phase 1. The proposed Phase 2 standards were expected to reduce hydrocarbons (HC) and oxides of nitrogen (NO_x) emissions by 30 per cent beyond Phase 1 standards by the year 2025. The proposal called for a reduction in emissions for Class III, IV and V engines to 210, 172 and 116 grams per kilowatt-hour (g/kWhr),[4] respectively. In response to the proposal, the EPA received input from manufacturers indicating that lower emission levels were feasible.[5] And in late 1998 a portion of the handheld engine industry suggested that it would support final $HC+NO_x$ standards of 72 g/kW-hr for Classes III and IV and 87 g/kW-hr for Class V (72–72–87).

On December 2, 1998 John Deere Consumer Products, Inc. (Deere), which appeared as an intervenor before this court, recommended that the EPA consider stricter Phase 2 standards in light of its recent development of "compression wave technology" (CWT), which promised

---

[1]   Nonhandheld engines tend to be large and include engines that power lawnmowers and garden tractors. Handheld engines are smaller and are used in equipment such as chainsaws, leaf blowers and weed trimmers.

[4]   Grams per kilowatt-hour (g/kW-hr) is used to measure the mass of pollutants (grams) emitted per quantum of work (kW-hr) the engine performs.

[5]   "Lower" emission levels equate to stricter standards and presumably cleaner air.

to significantly reduce emissions from handheld engines. CWT uses compressed air to improve fuel injection in the combustion chamber of a two-stroke engine, resulting in almost all of the fuel being combusted. Deere stated that CWT was adaptable to all sizes of two-stroke engines and could meet a 72 g/kW-hr $HC+NO_x$ standard in 2001.

On July 28, 1999 the EPA published a Supplemental Notice of Proposed Rulemaking (Supplemental Proposal), which proposed emission limits of 50 g/kW-hr for Classes III and IV with phase-in between 2002 and 2006 and an emission limit of 72 g/kW-hr for Class V with phase-in between 2004 and 2008. In addition to CWT, the Supplemental Proposal identified three other technologies-stratified scavenging, miniature four-stroke engines and catalysts-that could be utilized by manufacturers to meet the Phase 2 standards. The Supplemental Proposal also contained an averaging, banking and trading (ABT) program to give handheld engine manufacturers flexibility in meeting the more stringent Phase 2 standards. Under the proposed program, manufacturers would declare a family emission limit (FEL) for each engine family. Manufacturers need only ensure that average emissions from all of their engine families meet the emission standards for the given model year. They could also generate bankable emission credits based on the differences between the FEL and the Phase 2 standards for the applicable model year.

Many manufacturers, including Husqvarna, commented on the Supplemental Proposal. The public comment period closed on September 17, 1999, although the EPA agreed to consider additional comments filed within 30 days therefrom. It also continued to meet with interested manufacturers after the close of the comment period. The final Phase 2 emission standards for handheld SI engines were published on April 25, 2000. In the final rule, the EPA adopted the 50–50–72 $HC+NO_x$ emission standards proposed in the Supplemental Proposal, but with an implementation schedule of four years instead of the five as proposed. The decision rested on the EPA's determination that "rapid technological advances" in the handheld engine industry warranted a more expeditious implementation. While noting that "not all of the technologies . . . have yet been demonstrated in mass-produced production engines operated under typical in-use conditions," the EPA identified the following technologies as likely to meet the newly adopted standards: Class III (CWT & low-medium efficiency catalyst; stratified scavenging with lean combustion & medium-high efficiency catalyst; four-stroke), Class IV (CWT; CWT & low efficiency catalyst; stratified scavenging with lean combustion & medium efficiency catalyst; four-stroke) and Class V (CWT; four-stroke; stratified scavenging with lean combustion). The EPA explained that changes in equipment design could allay safety concerns about the use of catalysts. It also determined that the Phase 2 standards were cost-effective. Finally, the EPA revised the ABT program to avoid a delay in the shift to cleaner engines. Husqvarna challenges all of these parts of the final rule.

II. Analysis

"Our analysis is guided by the deference traditionally given to agency expertise, particularly when dealing with a statutory scheme as unwieldy and science-driven as the Clean Air Act." *Appalachian Power Co. v. EPA*, 135 F.3d 791, 801–02 (D.C. Cir. 1998). Under section 307(d)(9) of the CAA, we reverse agency action found to be "arbitrary, capricious, an abuse of discretion, or otherwise not in accordance with law." 42 U.S.C. § 7607(d)(9)(A). Questions of statutory interpretation are governed by the familiar two-step test set forth in *Chevron, U.S.A., Inc. v. NRDC*, 467 U.S. 837, 842–43 (1984). The court first asks "whether Congress has directly spoken to the precise question at issue," in which case it "must give effect to the unambiguously expressed intent of Congress." *Id*. If the "statute is silent or ambiguous with respect to the specific issue," the court moves to the second step and defers to the agency's interpretation as long as it is "based on a permissible construction of the statute." *Id*. at 843. We will strike down the rulemaking for procedural error "only if the errors were so serious and related to matters of such central relevance to the rule that there is a substantial likelihood that the rule would have been significantly changed if such errors had not been made." CAA § 307(d)(8), 42 U.S.C. § 7607(d)(8).

In challenging the EPA's handheld engine Phase 2 emission standards, Husqvarna raises three claims. First, it asserts that the EPA's choice of the 50–50–72 emission standards contravenes the best balance requirement of CAA section 213. Second, it maintains that the final rule is arbitrary and capricious because it is not supported by substantial evidence in the record. Finally, it argues that the EPA failed to comply with the procedural requirements of CAA section 307(d).

A. CAA Section 213

Section 213(a)(3) of the CAA requires the EPA to promulgate standards that "shall achieve the greatest degree of emission reduction achievable through the application of technology which the Administrator determines will be available for the engines or vehicles to which such standards apply, giving appropriate consideration to the cost of applying such technology within the period of time available to manufacturers and to noise, energy, and safety factors associated with the application of such technology." 42 U.S.C. § 7547(a)(3). Husqvarna maintains that the 50–50–72 emission standards do not represent the "best balance" of these factors for the industry. We disagree that a "best balance" of the kind Husqvarna contemplates is required. The EPA did not deviate from its statutory mandate or frustrate congressional will by placing primary significance on the "greatest degree of emission reduction achievable" and by considering cost, noise, energy and safety factors as important but secondary factors. The overriding goal of the section is air quality and the other listed considerations, while significant, are subordinate to that goal. The record indicates that the EPA considered each of the factors listed in section 213 and nothing suggests that "the agency *abandoned* its obligation to balance the statutory factors and select the best balance for a predominant segment of industry from the alternatives before it." Contrary to Husqvarna's claim, the EPA did not single out a single engine technology and use it as a benchmark to set standards. Rather, it set the emission standards with four different engine technologies in mind. * * *

In sum, we defer to the EPA's selection of emission standards under section 213. The record shows that the EPA reasonably arrived at what it determined was the best regulatory standard by ascertaining the greatest degree of emission reduction achievable while giving appropriate consideration to cost, noise, energy and safety factors.

B.   Substantial Evidence

CAA section 213 is a technology-forcing standard. *See* 42 U.S.C. § 7547(a)(3); 42 U.S.C. § 7547(b). * * * "Congress intended the agency to project future advances in pollution control capability. It was 'expected to press for development and application of improved technology rather than be limited by that which exists today.'" *NRDC v. EPA*, 655 F.2d 318, 328 (D.C. Cir. 1981) (quoting S. Rep. No. 91–1196, at 24 (1970)). Husqvarna acknowledges that the statute is technology-forcing but challenges whether EPA projections of future advances in pollution control capability are supported by substantial evidence. It asserts that the EPA * * * selected emission standards that are not technologically feasible * * *. We find these claims without merit.

* * * [S]ubstantial evidence supports the EPA's determination that the Phase 2 standards can be achieved through the application of the identified technologies-CWT, stratified scavenging, miniature four-stroke engines and catalysts. The record indicates that these engine technologies are already capable of meeting an emission limit of 72 g/kW-hr, with the four-stroke engine technology currently meeting the 50 g/kWhr standard. The EPA found that the two-stroke technologies-CWT and stratified scavenging—can also currently meet the 50 g/kW-hr standard with the addition of a catalyst. Husqvarna offers no theoretical objections to the technologies' capacity to meet the emission standards within the phase-in period. " 'In the absence of theoretical objections to the technology, the agency need only identify the major steps necessary for development of the device, and give plausible reasons for its belief that the industry will be able to solve these problems in the time remaining. The EPA is not required to rebut all speculation that unspecified factors may hinder "real world" emission control.' " *NRDC v.*

Thomas, 805 F.2d 410, 434 (D.C. Cir. 1986) (quoting *NRDC*, 655 F.2d at 334). Husqvarna criticizes the performance of the various engine technologies but cannot show that the remaining issues related to design, implementation, mass production, performance, heat and weight cannot be solved through innovation and equipment redesign. It also questions the adequacy of the time period to solve these issues. Substantial evidence, however, supports the EPA's determination that the continued rapid development of engine technologies makes it probable that CWT, stratified scavenging, four-stroke engine and catalyst technologies will enable manufacturers to comply with the emission standards within the phase-in period.

Accordingly, we conclude that the final rule is supported by substantial evidence.

C.   Procedural Errors

Section 307(d)(9) of the CAA provides that a court may reverse agency action if it was promulgated "without observance of procedure required by law, if (i) such failure to observe such procedure is arbitrary or capricious, (ii) the requirement of paragraph (7)(B) has been met, and (iii) the condition of the last sentence of paragraph (8) is met." 42 U.S.C. § 7607(d)(9)(D). Paragraph 7(B) limits judicial review to objections "raised with reasonable specificity during the period for public comment," or on reconsideration if "it was impracticable to raise such objection within such time . . . and if such objection is of central relevance to the outcome of the rule." 42 U.S.C. § 7607(d)(7)(B). Finally, the last sentence of section 307(d)(8) provides that "[i]n reviewing alleged procedural errors, the court may invalidate the rule only if the errors were so serious and related to matters of such central relevance to the rule that there is a substantial likelihood that the rule would have been significantly changed if such errors had not been made." 42 U.S.C. § 7607(d)(8).

Husqvarna contends that the EPA failed to comply with section 307(d)(3)(a) of the CAA, which requires that a notice of proposed rulemaking "be accompanied by a statement of its basis and purpose" and "include a summary of [ ] the factual data on which the proposed rule is based." 42 U.S.C. § 7607(d)(3). It also argues that the agency failed to comply with section 307(d)(4)(B)(i), which dictates that "all written comments and documentary information on the proposed rule received from any person for inclusion in the docket during the comment period shall be placed in the docket." 42 U.S.C. § 7607(4)(B)(i). Husqvarna alleges that these failures denied it sufficient opportunity to comment on the relevant technologies as well as on the ABT program as it appeared in the final rule. We find these claims without merit. First, the Supplemental Proposal specifically referred to the technologies that would serve as the basis of the 50–50–72 emission standards-CWT, miniature four-stroke engines, stratified scavenging and catalysts.

Husqvarna and other manufacturers had ample opportunity to comment on the technologies. In fact, the bulk of Husqvarna's substantive claims revolves around the EPA's treatment of the comments they in fact submitted. The EPA even extended the time to accept public input until 30 days after close of the public comment period to provide manufacturers like Husqvarna with more opportunity to comment. Second, Husqvarna had opportunity to comment on the proposed ABT program. The final ABT provisions were a logical outgrowth of those proposed in the Supplemental Proposal, even though they were in part based on comments received during the 30 day extension period. The Supplemental Proposal gave Husqvarna fair notice of the subjects and issues involved in formulating the ABT program. Likewise, the four-year phase-in period was a logical outgrowth of the proposed five-year implementation schedule. Finally, even if the EPA committed procedural error, Husqvarna failed to show it was "so serious and related to matters of such relevance to the rule that there is a substantial likelihood that the rule would have been significantly changed if such error [ ] had not been made." 42 U.S.C. § 7607(d)(8). Husqvarna was unable to establish a substantial likelihood that the rule would have been significantly changed if it had had an expanded opportunity to comment. Accordingly, we find Husqvarna's claims of procedural error without merit.

III. Conclusion

In sum, we reject Husqvarna's substantive and procedural challenges to the Phase 2 Emission Standards for New Nonroad Spark-Ignition Handheld Engines. Accordingly, and for the reasons set forth in this opinion, the petition for review is

Denied.

IV. CONSTITUTIONAL LAW AND ENVIRONMENTAL LAW

In the American legal system, constitutions are trump cards, and the United States Constitution is the highest trump card of all. Environmental law is no exception to this general principle. Constitutional provisions provide the underlying authority for federal environmental regulation, but they also establish boundaries upon that authority. The United States Constitution also defines limits on state environmental regulatory authority.

This subsection reviews—briefly—those limits, many of which you probably explored in greater depth in a course in Constitutional Law.

A. THE CONSTITUTION AND CONGRESSIONAL AUTHORITY

As the Introduction to Section III noted, Congress can act only within its enumerated powers under the Constitution. As a consequence of this limitation, no statute is valid unless if falls within at least one of Congress's constitutional powers. Three constitutional clauses have particular relevance to environmental statutes: the Interstate Commerce Clause, the Property Clause, and the Treaty Clause.

1. INTERSTATE COMMERCE CLAUSE

The Interstate Commerce Clause empowers Congress to enact statutes pertaining to "commerce * * * among the several states." U.S. CONST. art. I, § 8. The Commerce Clause power encompasses "three broad categories of activity that Congress may regulate": (a) use and misuse of the channels of interstate commerce; (b) instrumentalities of interstate commerce, or persons or things in interstate commerce; and (c) activities that substantially affect interstate commerce. *United States v. Lopez*, 514 U.S. 549, 558–59 (1995). Because most pollution statutes regulate commercial conduct that affects interstate commerce, the Commerce Clause has often been cited as the justification for federal pollution statutes. *See, e.g., Hodel v. Virginia Surface Mining and Reclamation Ass'n*, 452 U.S. 264, 282 (1981) ("[T]he power conferred by the Commerce Clause [is] broad enough to permit congressional regulation of activities causing air or water pollution, or other environmental hazards that may have effects in more than one State"); *United States v. Ho*, 311 F.3d 589 (5th Cir. 2002) (affirming, against a Commerce Clause challenge, the conviction of a contractor who violated asbestos work practice standards promulgated under the Clean Air Act, reasoning that asbestos removal is a commercial activity that, in the aggregate, affects the interstate commercial real estate market); *United States v. Olin Corp.*, 107 F.3d 1506, 1510–11 (11th Cir. 1997) (upholding the Comprehensive Environmental Response, Compensation, and Liability Act (CERCLA) as a valid exercise of the Commerce Clause power even as applied to "intrastate, on-site waste disposal" because "unregulated management of hazardous substances, even strictly within individual states, significantly impacts interstate commerce").

Despite these broad validations of federal authority to regulate pollution, the Supreme Court has twice since 2000 expressed skepticism that the Commerce Clause grants Congress broad regulatory powers over small, intrastate waters. *Solid Waste Agency of N. Cook Cty. v. U.S. Army Corps of Engineers*, 531 U.S. 159, 174 (2001) (stating that such powers "would result in a significant impingement of the States' traditional and primary power over land and water use"); *Rapanos v. United States*, 547 U.S. 715, 738 (2006) (plurality) (opining that extension of federal regulatory authority to intermittently flowing waters would represent an "unprecedented intrusion into traditional state authority" that might exceed the scope of the Commerce Clause). It remains to be seen whether these expressions of concern will result in actual constitutional rulings that limit federal authority over environmental resources.

Within the field of environmental law, the other primary focus of Commerce Clause litigation has been section nine of the ESA. So far, challenges to the constitutionality of ESA section nine have been uniformly unsuccessful once they have reached the appellate court. But while he was a judge on the D.C. Circuit, Chief Justice Roberts penned a dissent from a denial of rehearing en banc expressing skepticism that the Commerce Clause supports protecting endangered species that live entirely within a single state. *See Rancho Viejo, LLC v. Norton*, 334 F.3d 1158, 1161 (D.C. Cir. 2003) (Roberts, J., dissenting from denial of rehearing en banc). In keeping with that view, a federal district court recently held that a regulation prohibiting the take of Utah prairie dogs on non-federal land exceeds the scope of the Commerce Clause. *People for Ethical Treatment of Prop. Owners v. U.S. Fish & Wildlife Serv.*, 57 F. Supp. 3d 1337, 1344 (D. Utah 2014). The decision is being appealed to the Tenth Circuit.

2. PROPERTY CLAUSE

The Property Clause gives Congress "Power to dispose of and make all needful Rules and Regulations respecting the Territory or other Property belonging to the United States." U.S. CONST., art. IV, § 3. To the extent environmental resources are "Property belonging to the United States," the Property Clause gives Congress broad authority to enact legislation to protect such resources. For natural resources statutes that govern the management of federal lands and waters, this is a powerful justification. In *Kleppe v. New Mexico*, 426 U.S. 529 (1976), for example, the Supreme Court upheld the Wild Free-Roaming Horses and Burros Act as a valid exercise of Congress' power under the Property Clause, even though the statute may conflict with some state laws and may have some effect on private lands. The Property Clause has less effect on pollution statutes, where the environmental resources are generally not owned by the federal government.

3. TREATY CLAUSE

The Treaty Clause gives the President the "Power, by and with the Advice and Consent of the Senate, to make Treaties." U.S. CONST. art. II, § 2. The Necessary and Proper Clause of Article I, in turn, gives Congress power to make all laws necessary and proper for carrying into execution the powers conferred in the Constitution, which include the Treaty Power. U.S. CONST. art I, § 8. On its face, this combination might seem to give Congress the power to enact any statute in furtherance of a treaty.

As the United States has entered into many treaties aimed at environmental protection, such an interpretation could justify many potential and existing federal environmental statutes.

Older Supreme Court precedent provides some support for this position. In *Missouri v. Holland*, 252 U.S. 416 (1920), the Supreme Court upheld an international migratory bird treaty as a valid exercise of the Treaty Power, in that the treaty involves a matter of "national interest" that "can be protected only by national action in concert with that of another power." *Id.* at 435. Because the treaty was valid, the Migratory Bird Treaty Act, which Congress enacted to implement the treaty, was valid as well. *Id. Missouri v. Holland* thus seems to give Congress expansive legislative powers to effectuate valid international treaties.

A non-environmental case—*Bond v. United States*, 134 S. Ct. 2077 (2014), recently raised questions about *Holland*'s precedential value. Carol Anne Bond used toxic chemicals to attempt to injure another woman, who was having an affair with Bond's husband. Bond was convicted of violating the Chemical Weapons Convention Implementation Act of 1998, which Congress enacted to implement the international Convention on the Prohibition of the Development, Production, Stockpiling, and Use of Chemical Weapons and on Their Destruction. A treaty aimed at banning chemical weapons was clearly a valid exercise of the Treaty Power, but Bond argued that the chemical weapons statute nevertheless exceeded Congress's authority to legislate. The Supreme Court held that, to avoid constitutional problems that might arise if the chemical weapons statute were interpreted too broadly, the statute should not be read to reach "local criminal conduct" such as Bond's. *Id.* at 2090. The *Bond* case, although it did not articulate a test for the constitutional limits of Congress's authority to legislate in furtherance of an international treaty, seems to indicate—more so than *Missouri v. Holland*—that such limits exist and might present a significant constraint on Congress's legislative authority. Thus, after *Bond*, it is unclear to what extent the Treaty Power gives Congress authority to enact legislation not otherwise supported by one of the enumerated powers in Article I, Section 8.

B. CONSTITUTIONAL LIMITS ON STATE AUTHORITY

1. DORMANT COMMERCE CLAUSE

Although the Commerce Clause is phrased in terms of granting regulatory power to Congress, the Clause also implicitly precludes states from unjustifiably discriminating against or burdening interstate commerce—an application known as the Dormant Commerce Clause. *See, e.g., Oregon Waste Sys., Inc. v. Dep't of Envtl. Quality of State of Or.*, 511 U.S. 93, 98 (1994). State laws that affect interstate commerce in ways that are discriminatory—that is, selectively benefit in-state economic interests and burden out-of-state economic interests—are generally per se invalid. *Hughes v. Oklahoma*, 441 U.S. 322, 336, 344 n.6 (1979). State laws that only incidentally affect interstate commerce are valid unless "the burden imposed on such commerce is clearly excessive in relation to the putative local benefits." *Pike v. Bruce Church, Inc.*, 397 U.S. 137, 142 (1970).

The Dormant Commerce Clause has been used to strike down a variety of state laws perceived by courts as discriminatory, including laws relating to the environment but motivated by economic rather than environmental protection concerns. Many of these pertain to solid waste disposal. *See, e.g.*, *C & A Carbone, Inc. v. Town of Clarkstown*, 511 U.S. 383 (1994) (invalidating a local ordinance that required solid waste processed or handled within the town to be processed at the town's transfer station); *Chemical Waste Management, Inc. v. Hunt*, 504 U.S. 334 (1992) (invalidating a state law that imposed surcharges on the disposal of out-of-state solid waste); *Philadelphia v. New Jersey*, 437 U.S. 617 (1978) (invalidating a state law prohibiting the importation of waste from out of state).

On the other hand, when courts have believed a state or local law was enacted for the legitimate purpose of environmental protection or resource conservation, and the law treats out-of-state concerns equitably, courts have tended to find the law valid. *See, e.g.*, *Minnesota v. Clover Leaf Creamery Co.*, 449 U.S. 456, 471 (1981) (upholding a Minnesota law that prohibited selling milk in plastic, nonreturnable milk containers, even though the law would incidentally benefit Minnesota firms that produced pulpwood containers at the expense of non-Minnesota firms that produced nonreturnable plastic jugs); *Rocky Mountain Farmers Union v. Corey*, 730 F.3d 1070 (9th Cir. 2013) (upholding state Low Carbon Fuel Standard regulations despite their burden on out-of-state corn ethanol producers); *Nat'l Elec. Mfrs. Ass'n v. Sorrell*, 272 F.3d 104 (2d Cir. 2001) (upholding Vermont statute requiring labeling of mercury-containing lamps).

2. SUPREMACY   CLAUSE,   PREEMPTION,   AND   COOPERATIVE FEDERALISM

The Supremacy Clause of Article VI of the United States Constitution provides that federal laws "shall be the supreme Law of the Land." U.S. CONST. art VI, § 2. State law thus cannot legalize conduct that is unlawful under federal law. In addition, if Congress wants to, it can preempt even state regulation that does *not* conflict with federal requirements. With a few exceptions, Congress has not chosen to preempt states' ability to enact environmental laws that are more protective than federal standards. Many federal environmental laws, however, preempt states' ability to weaken the protections in federal law.

Our discussion here focuses primarily on the relationships between the federal government and the states (and, by extension, local governments), largely because those relationships are so important to the field of environmental law. But in some parts of the country, another influential set of actors shares the stage. Those actors are Native American tribes. Tribes assume a variety of roles in environmental law. Because their identity is often closely tied to land, and to other natural resources, they can be important beneficiaries of environmental law, and they sometimes assume special status as legal trustees of environmental resources. Within their reservations, they also can assume authority for implementing environmental law. Because of the United States' history of discrimination against Native Americans, impacts upon tribes can raise important environmental justice issues. And because tribal activities can sometimes pollute the environment, tribes sometimes are regulated entities under environmental law.

As you learn it in law school, constitutional law tends to focus on cases that set boundaries on federal and state authority, not on the zones in which both the federal and state governments may act. But because the Commerce Clause gives Congress broad authority to address environmental concerns, and states retain their police power to regulate within their borders, and the Supremacy Clause readily allows concurrent federal and state regulatory authority, most environmental governance occurs in spheres where the states and the federal government (and, often, local governments as well) share legal authority. Most environmental lawyers therefore spend more time sorting out relationships in shared regulatory space than they spend determining the legal limits on federal or state spheres.

One method for sharing authority is something known as "cooperative federalism." In cooperative federalism regimes, the federal government passes a comprehensive statute that applies across the nation. But it gives states the option of assuming responsibility for implementing the statute, or at least key parts of it. That implementing authority generally comes with discretion, and a state that assumes implementing authority will make many important decisions about regulations, permit terms, and enforcement priorities. In a cooperative federalism scheme, states generally retain the authority to adopt environmental protection standards that are more stringent than the federal baseline.

Cooperative federalism schemes are quite common in environmental law. Because of their prevalence, environmental lawyers routinely work with (or for) state regulatory authorities, even if much of their work involves federal environmental laws. Of course, the federal government does remain involved. Some environmental regulatory programs cannot be delegated to the states, and even where delegation does occur, state environmental regulators generally receive oversight and technical support from their federal counterparts. Federal environmental agencies also have offices across the nation, and much environmental law implementation therefore involves teamwork between state and regional federal environmental staff.

C. TAKINGS DOCTRINE

An additional limitation on governmental regulatory authority (state, local, or federal) comes from the Takings Clause in the Fifth Amendment of the United States Constitution, and from analogous provisions of state constitutional and statutory law. The Fifth Amendment states, in relevant part, "nor shall private property be taken without just compensation." The United States Supreme Court has repeatedly held that regulations may trigger this prohibition if they go "too far" toward limiting property rights. *Pennsylvania Coal Co. v. Mahon,* 260 U.S. 393, 415 (1922). But many environmental laws limit some people's property rights (and also protect the property rights of others), and the Supreme Court has also stated that " 'government regulation—by definition—involves the adjustment of rights for the public good,' * * * [and] '[g]overnment hardly could go on if to some extent values incident to property could not be diminished without paying for every such change in the general law." *Lingle v. Chevron U.S.A. Inc.,* 544 U.S. 528, 538 (2005) (quoting *Andrus v. Allard,* 444 U.S. 51, 65 (1979) and *Pa. Coal Co. v. Mahon,* 260 U.S. at 413). Striking a balance between those dueling principles, and figuring out when environmental regulations go too far and constitute takings, has become a recurrent issue.

This issue has come up most often with regulatory limitations on development; it comes up much more rarely with pure pollution control requirements. In particular, three types of environmental law provisions are responsible for generating a disproportionate share of takings cases. One is section 404 of the Clean Water Act, which prohibits landowners from filling streams or wetlands without a permit, and analogous wetland protections under state law. *See, e.g. Palazzolo v. Rhode Island,* 533 U.S. 606 (2001). Similarly, many state law restrictions on land use are designed at least partly to protect the environment, and those too are often subject to takings challenges. *See, e.g., Tahoe-Sierra Preservation Council v. Tahoe Regional Planning Agency*, 535 U.S. 302 (2002). Finally, regulated entities have sometimes brought takings challenges to land and water use restrictions under the Endangered Species Act. *See* Robert Meltz, *The Endangered Species Act (ESA) and Claims of Property Rights Takings* (Congressional Research Service, 2013).

Takings doctrine is notoriously complicated, but a simple primer should provide you with at least a general understanding of the field. When an alleged taking occurs through government regulation, courts will generally analyze a claim using three factors: the diminution in property value; the nature of the government action; and the extent, if any, of interference with reasonable investment-backed expectations. *See Penn Central Transp. Co. v. City of N.Y.*, 438 U.S. 104 (1978). In practice, regulatory takings claims are hard for plaintiffs to win; even substantial adjustments in property values are generally not sufficient to establish successful claims. But plaintiffs do win sometimes. And even when they do not, the idea that environmental regulators should not adjust established property rights holds powerful political force and can dissuade regulators from imposing constraints, even when those constraints might be constitutionally allowable.

V. STANDING

In addition to helping define the powers of Congress and the relationships between the federal government and the states, the United States Constitution also defines the role of the federal judiciary. It limits federal court jurisdiction to justiciable cases. The *American Electric Power Co.* litigation has already introduced you to the political question doctrine, which is one example of a limitation on the justiciability of cases. But the most important limitation, for purposes of environmental law, is the doctrine of standing.

A. INTRODUCTION

The doctrine of justiciability constrains the exercise of judicial authority to situations that are appropriate or suitable for adjudication by a court. In federal law, justiciability doctrine finds its source in Article III, § 2, of the U.S. Constitution, which provides that the judicial power is limited to "cases" and "controversies." Justiciability encompasses a series of more specific requirements: a case is not justiciable if there is not an actual controversy between the parties; if it seeks an advisory opinion; if it is unripe or moot; if it seeks judgment upon a political question; or if the plaintiff lacks standing.

This section focuses on standing, one requirement a case or controversy must meet to be justiciable. Standing presents the question of who can bring an otherwise justiciable suit. It requires a plaintiff to show a sufficient personal stake in a controversy.

The legal authority for standing requirements is constitutional— Article III's case or controversy requirement—but the Constitution does not explicitly impose standing requirements. Rather, courts have created standing requirements based on their interpretation of Article III's case or controversy requirement. These judicially created requirements have three elements:

- *Injury*: A plaintiff must show invasion of a legally protected interest which is (a) concrete and particularized, and (b) actual or imminent, not conjectural or hypothetical.

- *Causation*: A plaintiff's injury must be fairly traceable to the challenged action of the defendant, and not the result of the independent action of some third party not before the court.

- *Redressability*: It must be likely, as opposed to merely speculative, that the plaintiff's injury will be redressed by a favorable decision from the court.

See Lujan v. Defenders of Wildlife, 504 U.S. 555 (1992).

Standing becomes somewhat more complicated when the plaintiff is an organization. Courts have developed a prudential rule that plaintiffs ordinarily cannot bring lawsuits to vindicate the rights of others. An exception to that rule is that an organization can bring a lawsuit as the representative of one or more of its members if it meets three additional requirements:

- At least one member of the organization must have constitutional standing to sue in his or her own right.

- The interests the organization seeks to protect through the litigation must be germane to the organization's purpose.

- Participation of individual members in the lawsuit must be unnecessary to resolve either the claim asserted or relief requested.

Courts and scholars have identified three main benefits of enforcing standing requirements. First, in theory, standing promotes the proper *separation of powers* by limiting courts to vindicating personal interests, leaving debate over general public interests to the legislative and executive branches. Second, standing conserves scarce judicial resources and protects defendants from unnecessary suits. Third, standing maintains the appropriate role of courts by implementing the adversary system and sharpening the presentation of issues.

Other scholars and judges have contested whether standing really produces these benefits—or, in some circumstances, whether they really are benefits—and critics have charged that standing requirements also have significant disadvantages. Most important, standing requirements mean that some legal violations may be left unenforced. When a plaintiff lacks standing, its complaint is dismissed even if the defendant has violated the law. Second, according to its critics, standing selectively favors certain interests. For regulated entities, demonstrating standing will usually be easy; courts routinely recognize the economic injuries caused by regulatory controls as an appropriate basis for standing. But the beneficiaries of environmental regulation are often trying to vindicate interests that cannot easily be reduced to economic terms, and sometimes their claims of injury rest on complex or uncertain causal chains.[5] Courts have often allowed standing when plaintiffs are claiming uncertain, future, and non-economic injuries, but critics allege that getting into court still is harder for people advocating environmental regulation than for people opposing it. Relatedly, some critics allege that standing doctrine is excessively malleable, and that it gives courts too much ability to manage their dockets, effectively allowing them to duck cases brought by disfavored plaintiffs.

B. PROBLEM: PARTICULATE MATTER EMISSIONS FROM SHIPS

Many large ships engaged in international transport run on heavy, high-sulfur fuels that cause the ships to emit particulate matter into the air. These ships are just one of many sources of particulate matter emissions. Other sources of particulate matter emissions include agricultural operations, industrial processes, fuel combustion, construction activities, windblown dust, and wildfires. Among other harms, particulate matter can worsen symptoms of asthma, particularly in children, and can also trigger asthma in children who never have had asthma.

Suppose that EPA issues a regulation pursuant to the Clean Air Act limiting the amount of particulate matter that ships can emit when operating within 230 miles of the U.S. coast. Most shipping companies are expected to comply with the new regulation by switching to cleaner-burning fuels, which cost more than high-sulfur fuels.

Three different parties have filed separate petitions for review challenging EPA's new rule:

- Emma Jane Glennon, a twenty-three year old resident of an area with high levels of particulate matter pollution who worries about getting asthma and believes EPA should have promulgated more stringent emissions limits;

- Stop Asthma Now, a citizen group whose members are concerned about childhood asthma and believe EPA should have promulgated more stringent emissions limits; and

---

[5] The challenges are somewhat similar to those faced by plaintiffs bringing environmental tort claims. *See* pages 66–70, supra.

- Muo Shipping Supply Company, which resupplies ships with food and water when they are in U.S. ports and thinks EPA's new emissions limits are too stringent.

As an attorney working for EPA, you have been asked to evaluate whether each of these petitioners has standing to sue EPA to challenge the new regulation. Each petitioner has filed a declaration in support of his or her standing. Evaluate whether each declaration will suffice to establish the petitioner's standing. If you conclude that a petitioner's declaration does not suffice to establish the petitioner's standing, what additional facts would the petitioner have to allege, and then prove, to establish standing?

DECLARATION OF JUAN GUSTAVO HIDALGO, M.D., IN SUPPORT OF STANDING OF EMMA JANE GLENNON

I, Juan Gustavo Hidalgo, do hereby declare, under the penalty of perjury and the laws of the United States of America:

1. My name is Juan Gustavo Hildalgo. I am a physician licensed by the Medical Board of California to practice medicine in California. I am also certified by the American Board of Internal Medicine. I have a Doctor of Medicine degree from Columbia University and have been practicing internal medicine in California since 1993.

2. The petitioner in this litigation, Emma Jane Glennon, is a patient of mine and has been for three years.

3. Emma Jane is an eight-year-old female in good mental and physical health who resides in Riverside, California. She exercises regularly, including playing soccer in a youth recreational league in Riverside.

4. Emma Jane is exposed on a daily basis to particulate matter in the ambient air of Riverside. The City of Riverside, where Emma Jane lives, is located in Riverside County. Riverside County suffers from high levels of particulate matter pollution. In 2016, the American Lung Association issued a State of the Air report that gave Riverside County an "F" grade for particulate matter air quality.

5. Medical studies have found that exposure to particulate matter is significantly associated with the incidence of asthma among children, with the risk of asthma increasing with the amount of exposure.

6. My professional opinion is that Emma Jane is at risk of contracting asthma and other pulmonary diseases from her exposure to inhaled particulate matter. Were there to be less particulate matter in the ambient air in Riverside, Emma Jane's risk of contracting asthma would be reduced.

Pursuant to 28 U.S.C. § 1746, I declare under the penalty of perjury that the foregoing is true and correct.

Executed on this 12th day of August, 2016.

Respectfully Submitted,

/s/ Juan Gustavo Hidalgo

DECLARATION OF NIGEL AARON COSTELLO
IN SUPPORT OF STANDING

I declare under penalty of perjury:

1. My name is Nigel Aaron Costello. I am the elected President of Stop Asthma Now.

2. Stop Asthma Now is an organization of citizen activists concerned about childhood asthma.

3. I reside in Long Beach, California, approximately five miles from the Port of Long Beach.

4. Many of my friends and neighbors in Long Beach suffer from asthma. I believe exposure to particulate matter in the air is a cause of this asthma.

5. Ships docked in the Port of Long Beach emit large quantities of particulate matter.

6. A recent study by the American Thoracic Society and New York University's Marron Institute of Urban Management estimated that about 1,341 people die each year in the Los Angeles-Long Beach-Glendale area because of poor air quality.

7. As a member of Stop Asthma Now, I believe EPA should do more to reduce the amount of particulate matter in the air. If there were less particulate matter in the air, fewer residents would suffer from asthma and other pulmonary diseases.

I declare under penalty of perjury that the foregoing is true and correct.

Executed on this 23rd day of September, 2016.

Respectfully Submitted,

/s/ Nigel Aaron Costello

DECLARATION OF ALBERT MUO

1. My name is Albert Muo. I am the Chairman and Chief Executive Officer of Muo Shipping Supply Company (MSSC).

2. MSSC's primary business is to resupply ships with food and water when they are in U.S. ports. In 2015, MSSC had revenues of $50 million.

3. Recently the U.S. Environmental Protection Agency (EPA) issued a regulation limiting the amount of particulate matter that ships can emit when operating within 230 miles of the U.S. coast.

4. Most shipping companies will comply with the new EPA regulation by switching to cleaner-burning fuels, which cost more than high-sulfur fuels.

5. I expect that, as a result of the higher costs they will incur under the EPA regulation, fewer ships will use U.S. ports. There may be less international shipping into U.S. ports. Some international shipping companies may use ports in Canada and then move goods by rail or truck from Canada into the United States.

6. As a result of fewer ships using U.S. ports, I expect that demand for MSSC's services will decrease, causing concomitant reductions in MSSC's revenue.

7. If the new EPA regulation are held invalid, I expect that shipping will increase to prior levels, restoring MSSC's revenue to previous levels.

I certify under penalty of perjury that the foregoing is true and correct.

Executed on September 5, 2016.

/s/ Albert Muo

Because judges have defined the parameters of standing doctrine, your research focuses almost exclusively on case law. The following two cases each examine a standing issue. In reviewing and analyzing the cases' relevance to your problem, consider what facts pose a potential obstacle to the plaintiffs' standing in each case. Why are those facts relevant to the issue of standing? What rules does the court in each case apply to determine whether the plaintiffs have standing?

Massachusetts v. EPA
549 U.S. 497 (2007)

[Eds.: A group of private organizations petitioned EPA to begin regulating emissions of greenhouse gases under a provision of the Clean Air Act that directs to EPA to establish standards for the emission of air pollutants from new motor vehicles. EPA denied the petition, declining to issue the requested regulations. Petitioners, joined by intervening state and local governments, filed a petition for review in the D.C. Circuit challenging EPA's denial of the petition. A divided panel of the D.C. Circuit rejected the petition for review, with one judge issuing an opinion on the merits of the petitioners' claims, one concurring in the judgment on the ground that petitioners lacked standing to sue, and one judge dissenting.]

■ JUSTICE STEVENS delivered the opinion of the Court.

* * * Article III of the Constitution limits federal-court jurisdiction to "Cases" and "Controversies." Those two words confine "the business of federal courts to questions presented in an adversary context and in a form historically viewed as capable of resolution through the judicial process." It is therefore familiar learning that no justiciable "controversy" exists when parties seek adjudication of a political question, when they ask for an advisory opinion, or when the question sought to be adjudicated has been mooted by subsequent developments. This case suffers from none of these defects.

The parties' dispute turns on the proper construction of a congressional statute, a question eminently suitable to resolution in federal court. Congress has moreover authorized this type of challenge to EPA action. See 42 U.S.C. § 7607(b)(1). That authorization is of critical importance to the standing inquiry: "Congress has the power to define injuries and articulate chains of causation that will give rise to a case or controversy where none existed before." *Lujan v. Defenders of Wildlife*, 504 U.S. 555, 580 (1992) (Kennedy, J., concurring in part and concurring in judgment). "In exercising this power, however, Congress must at the very least identify the injury it seeks to vindicate and relate the injury to the class of persons entitled to bring suit." *Ibid.* We will not, therefore, "entertain citizen suits to vindicate the public's nonconcrete interest in the proper administration of the laws." *Id.*, at 581.

EPA maintains that because greenhouse gas emissions inflict widespread harm, the doctrine of standing presents an insuperable jurisdictional obstacle. We do not agree. At bottom, "the gist of the question of standing" is whether petitioners have "such a personal stake in the outcome of the controversy as to assure that concrete adverseness which sharpens the presentation of issues upon which the court so largely depends for illumination." As Justice Kennedy explained in his *Lujan* concurrence:

> "While it does not matter how many persons have been injured by the challenged action, the party bringing suit must show that the action injures him in a concrete and personal way. This requirement is not just an empty formality. It preserves the vitality of the adversarial process by assuring both that the parties before the court have an actual, as opposed to professed,

stake in the outcome, and that the legal questions presented . . . will be resolved, not in the rarified atmosphere of a debating society, but in a concrete factual context conducive to a realistic appreciation of the consequences of judicial action." 504 U.S., at 581 (internal quotation marks omitted).

To ensure the proper adversarial presentation, *Lujan* holds that a litigant must demonstrate that it has suffered a concrete and particularized injury that is either actual or imminent, that the injury is fairly traceable to the defendant, and that it is likely that a favorable decision will redress that injury. See *id.*, at 560–561. However, a litigant to whom Congress has "accorded a procedural right to protect his concrete interests," *id.* at 572 n.7—here, the right to challenge agency action unlawfully withheld, § 7607(b)(1)—"can assert that right without meeting all the normal standards for redressability and immediacy," ibid. When a litigant is vested with a procedural right, that litigant has standing if there is some possibility that the requested relief will prompt the injury-causing party to reconsider the decision that allegedly harmed the litigant. *Ibid.*

Only one of the petitioners needs to have standing to permit us to consider the petition for review. We stress here, as did Judge Tatel below, the special position and interest of Massachusetts. It is of considerable relevance that the party seeking review here is a sovereign State and not, as it was in *Lujan,* a private individual.

Well before the creation of the modern administrative state, we recognized that States are not normal litigants for the purposes of invoking federal jurisdiction. As Justice Holmes explained in *Georgia v. Tennessee Copper Co.,* 206 U.S. 230, 237 (1907), a case in which Georgia sought to protect its citizens from air pollution originating outside its borders:

"The case has been argued largely as if it were one between two private parties; but it is not. The very elements that would be relied upon in a suit between fellow-citizens as a ground for equitable relief are wanting here. The State owns very little of the territory alleged to be affected, and the damage to it capable of estimate in money, possibly, at least, is small. This is a suit by a State for an injury to it in its capacity of *quasi*-sovereign. In that capacity the State has an interest independent of and behind the titles of its citizens, in all the earth and air within its domain. It has the last word as to whether its mountains shall be stripped of their forests and its inhabitants shall breathe pure air."

Just as Georgia's "independent interest . . . in all the earth and air within its domain" supported federal jurisdiction a century ago, so too does Massachusetts' well-founded desire to preserve its sovereign territory today. That Massachusetts does in fact own a great deal of the "territory alleged to be affected" only reinforces the conclusion that its stake in the outcome of this case is sufficiently concrete to warrant the exercise of federal judicial power.

When a State enters the Union, it surrenders certain sovereign prerogatives. Massachusetts cannot invade Rhode Island to force reductions in greenhouse gas emissions, it cannot negotiate an emissions treaty with China or India, and in some circumstances the exercise of its police powers to reduce in-state motor-vehicle emissions might well be pre-empted. See *Alfred L. Snapp & Son, Inc. v. Puerto Rico ex rel. Barez,* 458 U.S. 592, 607 (1982) ("One helpful indication in determining whether an alleged injury to the health and welfare of its citizens suffices to give the State standing to sue *parens patriae* is whether the injury is one that the State, if it could, would likely attempt to address through its sovereign lawmaking powers").

These sovereign prerogatives are now lodged in the Federal Government, and Congress has ordered EPA to protect Massachusetts (among others) by prescribing standards applicable to the "emission of any air pollutant from any class or classes of new motor vehicle engines, which in [the Administrator's] judgment cause, or contribute to, air pollution which may reasonably be anticipated to endanger public health or welfare." 42 U.S.C. § 7521(a)(1). Congress has moreover recognized a concomitant procedural right to challenge the rejection of its rulemaking petition as arbitrary and capricious. § 7607(b)(1). Given that procedural right and Massachusetts' stake in protecting its quasi-sovereign interests, the Commonwealth is entitled to special solicitude in our standing analysis.

Drawing on *Massachusetts v. Mellon,* 262 U.S. 447 (1923), and *Alfred L. Snapp & Son, Inc. v. Puerto Rico ex rel. Barez,* 458 U.S. 592 (1982) (citing *Missouri v. Illinois,* 180 U.S. 208 (1901)), The Chief Justice claims that we "overloo[k] the fact that our cases cast significant doubt on a State's standing to assert a quasi-sovereign interest . . . against the Federal Government." Not so. *Mellon* itself disavowed any such broad reading when it noted that the Court had been "called upon to adjudicate, not rights of person or property, not rights of dominion over physical domain, [and] *not quasi sovereign rights actually invaded or threatened.*" 262 U.S., at 484–485 (emphasis added). In any event, we held in *Georgia v. Pennsylvania R. Co.,* 324 U.S. 439, 447 (1945), that there is a critical difference between allowing a State "to protect her citizens from the operation of federal statutes" (which is what *Mellon* prohibits) and allowing a State to assert its rights under federal law (which it has standing to do). Massachusetts does not here dispute that the Clean Air Act *applies* to its citizens; it rather seeks to assert its rights under the Act.

With that in mind, it is clear that petitioners' submissions as they pertain to Massachusetts have satisfied the most demanding standards of the adversarial process. EPA's steadfast refusal to regulate greenhouse gas emissions presents a risk of harm to Massachusetts that is both "actual" and "imminent." *Lujan,* 504 U.S., at 560 (internal quotation marks omitted). There is, moreover, a "substantial likelihood that the judicial relief requested" will prompt EPA to take steps to reduce that risk. EPA's steadfast refusal to regulate greenhouse gas emissions presents a risk of harm to Massachusetts that is both "actual" and "imminent." *Lujan,* 504 U.S., at 560 (internal quotation marks omitted). There is, moreover, a "substantial likelihood that the judicial relief requested" will prompt EPA to take steps to reduce that risk.

The Injury

The harms associated with climate change are serious and well recognized. Indeed, the NRC Report itself-which EPA regards as an "objective and independent assessment of the relevant science"-identifies a number of environmental changes that have already inflicted significant harms, including "the global retreat of mountain glaciers, reduction in snow-cover extent, the earlier spring melting of rivers and lakes, [and] the accelerated rate of rise of sea levels during the 20th century relative to the past few thousand years . . . ."

Petitioners allege that this only hints at the environmental damage yet to come. According to the climate scientist Michael MacCracken, "qualified scientific experts involved in climate change research" have reached a "strong consensus" that global warming threatens (among other things) a precipitate rise in sea levels by the end of the century, "severe and irreversible changes to natural ecosystems," a "significant reduction in water storage in winter snowpack in mountainous regions with direct and important economic consequences," and an increase in the spread of disease. He also observes that rising ocean temperatures may contribute to the ferocity of hurricanes.[18]

That these climate-change risks are "widely shared" does not minimize Massachusetts' interest in the outcome of this litigation. See *Federal Election Comm'n v. Akins,* 524 U.S. 11, 24 (1998) ("[W]here a harm is concrete, though widely shared, the Court has found 'injury in fact' "). According to petitioners' unchallenged affidavits, global sea levels rose somewhere between 10 and 20 centimeters over the 20th century as a result of global warming. These rising seas have already begun to swallow Massachusetts' coastal land. Because the Commonwealth "owns

---

[18] In this regard, MacCracken's 2004 affidavit-drafted more than a year in advance of Hurricane Katrina-was eerily prescient. Immediately after discussing the "particular concern" that climate change might cause an "increase in the wind speed and peak rate of precipitation of major tropical cyclones (i.e., hurricanes and typhoons)," MacCracken noted that "[s]oil compaction, sea level rise and recurrent storms are destroying approximately 20–30 square miles of Louisiana wetlands each year. These wetlands serve as a 'shock absorber' for storm surges that could inundate New Orleans, significantly enhancing the risk to a major urban population."

a substantial portion of the state's coastal property," it has alleged a particularized injury in its capacity as a landowner. The severity of that injury will only increase over the course of the next century: If sea levels continue to rise as predicted, one Massachusetts official believes that a significant fraction of coastal property will be "either permanently lost through inundation or temporarily lost through periodic storm surge and flooding events." Remediation costs alone, petitioners allege, could run well into the hundreds of millions of dollars.[21]

Causation

EPA does not dispute the existence of a causal connection between man-made greenhouse gas emissions and global warming. At a minimum, therefore, EPA's refusal to regulate such emissions "contributes" to Massachusetts' injuries.

EPA nevertheless maintains that its decision not to regulate greenhouse gas emissions from new motor vehicles contributes so insignificantly to petitioners' injuries that the agency cannot be haled into federal court to answer for them. For the same reason, EPA does not believe that any realistic possibility exists that the relief petitioners seek would mitigate global climate change and remedy their injuries. That is especially so because predicted increases in greenhouse gas emissions from developing nations, particularly China and India, are likely to offset any marginal domestic decrease.

But EPA overstates its case. Its argument rests on the erroneous assumption that a small incremental step, because it is incremental, can never be attacked in a federal judicial forum. Yet accepting that premise would doom most challenges to regulatory action. Agencies, like legislatures, do not generally resolve massive problems in one fell regulatory swoop. They instead whittle away at them over time, refining their preferred approach as circumstances change and as they develop a more-nuanced understanding of how best to proceed. That a first step might be tentative does not by itself support the notion that federal courts lack jurisdiction to determine whether that step conforms to law.

And reducing domestic automobile emissions is hardly a tentative step. Even leaving aside the other greenhouse gases, the United States transportation sector emits an enormous quantity of carbon dioxide into the atmosphere-according to the MacCracken affidavit, more than 1.7 billion metric tons in 1999 alone. That accounts for more than 6% of

---

[21] In dissent, The Chief Justice dismisses petitioners' submissions as "conclusory," presumably because they do not quantify Massachusetts' land loss with the exactitude he would prefer. He therefore asserts that the Commonwealth's injury is "conjectur[al]." Yet the likelihood that Massachusetts' coastline will recede has nothing to do with whether petitioners have determined the precise metes and bounds of their soon-to-be-flooded land. Petitioners maintain that the seas are rising and will continue to rise, and have alleged that such a rise will lead to the loss of Massachusetts' sovereign territory. No one, save perhaps the dissenters, disputes those allegations. Our cases require nothing more.

worldwide carbon dioxide emissions. To put this in perspective: Considering just emissions from the transportation sector, which represent less than one-third of this country's total carbon dioxide emissions, the United States would still rank as the third-largest emitter of carbon dioxide in the world, outpaced only by the European Union and China. Judged by any standard, U.S. motor-vehicle emissions make a meaningful contribution to greenhouse gas concentrations and hence, according to petitioners, to global warming.

The Remedy

While it may be true that regulating motor-vehicle emissions will not by itself reverse global warming, it by no means follows that we lack jurisdiction to decide whether EPA has a duty to take steps to slow or reduce it. See also *Larson v. Valente*, 456 U.S. 228, 244 n.15 (1982) ("[A] plaintiff satisfies the redressability requirement when he shows that a favorable decision will relieve a discrete injury to himself. He need not show that a favorable decision will relieve his every injury"). Because of the enormity of the potential consequences associated with man-made climate change, the fact that the effectiveness of a remedy might be delayed during the (relatively short) time it takes for a new motor-vehicle fleet to replace an older one is essentially irrelevant. Nor is it dispositive that developing countries such as China and India are poised to increase greenhouse gas emissions substantially over the next century: A reduction in domestic emissions would slow the pace of global emissions increases, no matter what happens elsewhere.

We moreover attach considerable significance to EPA's "agree[ment] with the President that 'we must address the issue of global climate change,'" and to EPA's ardent support for various voluntary emission-reduction programs. As Judge Tatel observed in dissent below, "EPA would presumably not bother with such efforts if it thought emissions reductions would have no discernable impact on future global warming."

In sum-at least according to petitioners' uncontested affidavits-the rise in sea levels associated with global warming has already harmed and will continue to harm Massachusetts. The risk of catastrophic harm, though remote, is nevertheless real. That risk would be reduced to some extent if petitioners received the relief they seek. We therefore hold that petitioners have standing to challenge the EPA's denial of their rulemaking petition.[24] * * *

---

[24] In his dissent, The Chief Justice expresses disagreement with the Court's holding in *United States v. Students Challenging Regulatory Agency Procedures (SCRAP)*, 412 U.S. 669, 687–688 (1973). He does not, however, disavow this portion of Justice Stewart's opinion for the Court:

"Unlike the specific and geographically limited federal action of which the petitioner complained in *Sierra Club* [*v. Morton*, 405 U.S. 727 (1972)], the challenged agency action in this case is applicable to substantially all of the Nation's railroads, and thus allegedly has an adverse environmental impact on all the natural resources

[Eds.: CHIEF JUSTICE ROBERTS, joined by JUSTICE SCALIA, JUSTICE THOMAS, and JUSTICE ALITO, dissented. They would have held, among other things, that Massachusetts lacked standing.]

Natural Resources Defense Council v. EPA ("Methyl Bromide")
464 F.3d 1 (D.C. Cir. 2006)

■ RANDOLPH, CIRCUIT JUDGE.

The United States and other countries entered into the Montreal Protocol on Substances that Deplete the Ozone Layer, Sept. 16, 1987 ("Montreal Protocol"), a treaty in which the signatory nations agreed to reduce the use of certain substances, including methyl bromide, that degrade the stratospheric ozone layer. The Environmental Protection Agency issued a rule implementing "critical use" exemptions from the treaty's general ban on production and consumption of methyl bromide. We dismissed the Natural Resources Defense Council's petition for judicial review for lack of standing. *Natural Res. Def. Council v. EPA*, 440 F.3d 476, 477–78 (D.C. Cir. 2006) ("*NRDC I*"). In their respective petition for and opposition to rehearing, NRDC and EPA offered new information that has led us to change our view of the standing issue. We therefore grant the petition for rehearing, withdraw our previous opinion, and decide the merits. Fed. R. App. P. 40(a)(4)(A).

I.

In the mid-1970s, scientists discovered that certain man-made chemicals can destroy the layer of ozone gas in the stratosphere approximately ten to twenty-five miles above the Earth's surface. Stratospheric ozone absorbs ultraviolet radiation; as the ozone layer thins, less radiation is absorbed. Increased human exposure to ultraviolet radiation is linked to a range of ailments, including skin cancer and cataracts.

Amidst growing international concern about ozone depletion, the United States and twenty-four other nations entered into the Montreal Protocol. The Protocol requires signatory nations—which now number 189—to reduce and eliminate their production and use of ozone-depleting

---

of the country. Rather than a limited group of persons who used a picturesque valley in California, all persons who utilize the scenic resources of the country, and indeed all who breathe its air, could claim harm similar to that alleged by the environmental groups here. But we have already made it clear that standing is not to be denied simply because many people suffer the same injury. Indeed some of the cases on which we relied in *Sierra Club* demonstrated the patent fact that persons across the Nation could be adversely affected by major governmental actions. *To deny standing to persons who are in fact injured simply because many others are also injured, would mean that the most injurious and widespread Government actions could be questioned by nobody.* We cannot accept that conclusion." *Ibid.* (citations omitted and emphasis added).

chemicals in accordance with agreed-upon timetables. Montreal Protocol arts. 2–2I. The Senate ratified the treaty in 1988, and Congress incorporated its terms into domestic law through the Clean Air Act Amendments of 1990. Since then, the United States has reduced its use of methyl bromide to less than 39% of its 1991 baseline.

In 1997, the Parties "adjusted" the Protocol to require developed-country Parties to cease "production" and "consumption" of methyl bromide by 2005. *See* Montreal Protocol art. 2H(5). In response, Congress amended the Clean Air Act to require EPA to "promulgate rules for reductions in, and terminate the production, importation, and consumption of, methyl bromide under a schedule that is in accordance with, but not more stringent than, the phaseout schedule of the Montreal Protocol Treaty as in effect on October 21, 1998." 42 U.S.C. § 7671c(h).

Methyl bromide is a naturally occurring gas produced by oceans, grass and forest fires, and volcanoes. It is also man-made and used as a broad-spectrum pesticide. Methyl bromide is typically injected into soil as a fumigant before several types of crops are planted. * * *

In light of methyl bromide's wide use and the lack of comparable substitute pesticides, the Protocol allows exemptions from the general ban "to the extent that the Parties decide to permit the level of production or consumption that is necessary to satisfy uses agreed by them to be critical uses." Montreal Protocol art. 2H(5); *see also* 42 U.S.C. § 7671c(d)(6) ("To the extent consistent with the Montreal Protocol, the [EPA] Administrator . . . may exempt the production, importation, and consumption of methyl bromide for critical uses."). The Parties to the Protocol meet annually to "decide to permit the level of production or consumption that is necessary to satisfy uses agreed by them to be critical uses." Montreal Protocol art. 2H(5). * * *

The Parties reached agreement at their First Extraordinary Meeting in March 2004. They granted the United States critical uses in sixteen categories, amounting to 8,942 metric tons of methyl bromide. To satisfy these critical uses, the Parties authorized 7,659 metric tons of new production and consumption, with the remainder (1,283 metric tons) to be made up from existing stocks of methyl bromide. Decision Ex.I/3 noted that "each Party which has an agreed critical use should ensure that the criteria in paragraph 1 of decision IX/6 are applied when . . . authorizing the use of methyl bromide and that such procedures take into account available stocks."

With Decision Ex.I/3 in hand, EPA proposed rules to implement the critical-use exemption. Many parties, including NRDC, submitted comments. The Final Rule, issued in December 2004, authorized new production and consumption up to the limit established in Decision

Ex.I/3. It also authorized the use of stocks as permitted by the decision, and permitted noncritical users to draw upon existing stocks.

NRDC believes the Final Rule violated Decision IX/6 and Decision Ex.I/3 because EPA failed to disclose the full amount of existing stocks, failed to offset new production and consumption by the full amount of these stocks, and failed to reserve the stocks for critical uses, and because the total amount of methyl bromide critical use the Final Rule authorized is not the technically and economically feasible minimum. These claims depend upon the legal status of Decisions IX/6 and Ex.I/3. * * *

II.

In order for this court to have Article III jurisdiction, NRDC had to establish that at least one of its members has standing to sue in his own right, the interests the association seeks to protect are germane to its purpose, and individual members need not participate in the lawsuit themselves. *Sierra Club v. EPA,* 292 F.3d 895, 898 (D.C. Cir. 2002) (citing *Hunt v. Wash. State Apple Adver. Comm'n,* 432 U.S. 333, 342–43 (1977)). We have no reason to doubt that NRDC meets the second and third requirements. As to the first, NRDC had to demonstrate that at least one member satisfied the "irreducible constitutional minimum" of standing: injury-in-fact, causation, and redressability. *Lujan v. Defenders of Wildlife,* 504 U.S. 555, 560 (1992).

NRDC claimed that its members faced increased health risks from EPA's rule. Although this claim does not fit comfortably within the Supreme Court's description of what constitutes an "injury in fact" sufficient to confer standing—such injuries must be "actual or imminent, not 'conjectural' or 'hypothetical,'" *Whitmore v. Arkansas,* 495 U.S. 149, 155 (1990) (quoting *City of Los Angeles v. Lyons,* 461 U.S. 95, 101–02 (1983))—we have recognized that increases in risk can at times be "injuries in fact" sufficient to confer standing. *See Mountain States Legal Found. v. Glickman,* 92 F.3d 1228, 1234–35 (D.C. Cir. 1996). Environmental and health injuries often are purely probabilistic. We have cautioned that this category of injury may be too expansive. "[W]ere all purely speculative 'increased risks' deemed injurious, the entire requirement of 'actual or imminent injury' would be rendered moot, because all hypothesized, nonimminent 'injuries' could be dressed up as 'increased risk of future injury.'" *Ctr. for Law & Educ. v. Dep't of Educ.,* 396 F.3d 1152, 1161 (D.C. Cir. 2005). We therefore generally require that petitioners demonstrate a "substantial probability" that they will be injured. *See Sierra Club,* 292 F.3d at 898, 899; *Am. Petroleum Inst. v. EPA,* 216 F.3d 50, 63–64, 67 (D.C. Cir. 2000); *La. Envtl. Action Network v. EPA,* 172 F.3d 65, 68 (D.C. Cir. 1999). *Mountain States Legal Foundation v. Glickman,* which found that an increased risk of forest fire created by a Forest Service logging rule was enough to support standing, held that the relevant variations in risk must be "non-trivial," 92 F.3d at

1235, and "sufficient . . . to take a suit out of the category of the hypothetical," *id.* at 1234–35 (quoting *Vill. of Elk Grove Vill. v. Evans,* 997 F.2d 328, 329 (7th Cir. 1993)).

NRDC's expert quantified the increased risk posed by EPA's rule in an affidavit stating that "it is reasonable to expect more than 10 deaths, more than 2,000 nonfatal skin cancer cases, and more than 700 cataract cases to result from the 16.8 million pounds of new production and consumption allowed by the 2005 exemption rule." Intervenor Methyl Bromide Industry Panel argued that the probability of injury to NRDC's members is too small. In *NRDC I,* we found the annualized risk posed to NRDC members to be trivial. 440 F.3d at 481–82 & n.8, 484. The parties vigorously dispute whether we were correct to hold as a quantitative matter that NRDC's alleged injury was trivial or whether, in NRDC's words, any "scientifically demonstrable increase in the threat of death or serious illness," is sufficient for standing. This question has given rise to a conflict among the circuits. *Compare Baur v. Veneman,* 352 F.3d 625, 634 (2d Cir. 2003); *Cent. Delta Water Agency v. United States,* 306 F.3d 938, 947–48 (9th Cir. 2002); *Friends of the Earth, Inc. v. Gaston Copper Recycling Corp.,* 204 F.3d 149, 160 (4th Cir. 2000) (en banc), *with Shain v. Veneman,* 376 F.3d 815, 818 (8th Cir. 2004); *Baur,* 352 F.3d at 651 & n. 3 (Pooler, J., dissenting). On reconsideration, we have determined that the question is one we do not have to answer in this case. EPA's expert, who built the quantitative model on which both sides rely, now informs us that "[e]xpressing the risk in annualized terms is not practical" and "it is more appropriate to express the risk as a population's cumulative or lifetime risk." The lifetime risk that an individual will develop nonfatal skin cancer as a result of EPA's rule is about 1 in 200,000 by the intervenor's lights, or 1 in 129,000 by EPA's. Even if a quantitative approach is appropriate—an issue on which we express no opinion—this risk is sufficient to support standing. One may infer from the statistical analysis that two to four of NRDC's nearly half a million members will develop cancer as a result of the rule.

As to causation, NRDC's asserted injuries are linked to EPA's action through a fairly straightforward chain: EPA has permitted too much new production and consumption of methyl bromide, which will result in more emissions, which will increase ozone depletion, which will adversely affect the health of NRDC's members. This injury can be redressed if EPA does not permit such excessive production and consumption of methyl bromide. * * *

[Eds.: The court proceeded to find that NRDC's claim failed on the merits, and on that basis denied the petition for review.]

———————————

Once you have read the *Massachusetts* and *Methyl Bromide* cases, consider the three petitioners you have been asked to analyze for this problem. What rules from *Massachusetts* and *Methyl Bromide* will apply to determine whether each petitioner has standing? What facts will be necessary to establish each of those petitioners' standing? Has the petitioner alleged those facts?

NOTES

1.   In addition to the standing issues raised by this problem, several others often come up in environmental cases. One issue is sometimes referred to as procedural standing. Sometimes an environmental plaintiff will object to an agency's alleged failure to follow required decision-making procedures, yet there is no guarantee that the agency would have done what the plaintiff wanted even if it had followed the requisite procedures. In other words, there is no certainty that fixing the procedural violation would fix the environmental problem about which the plaintiff is really complaining. In that circumstance, does the plaintiff have standing? The general answer is a qualified yes. If the agency's decision threatens a concrete and particularized interest of the plaintiff, and if following the correct procedure might avoid or reduce harm to that interest, then the general rule is that the plaintiff does have standing. *See Lujan v. Defenders of Wildlife*, 504 U.S. 555, 572 & n.7 (1992).

2.   The cases above address circumstances where (a) a court has good reason to believe that people will be harmed, but it cannot identify the particular persons who will suffer that harm; and (b) a massive environmental problem is going to harm people, but the defendant's contribution to that problem is only incremental. What about a third circumstance, in which the plaintiff is not certain that environmental harm will occur at all? The Supreme Court addressed that circumstance in *Friends of the Earth v. Laidlaw Environmental Services (TOC), Inc.*, 528 U.S. 167 (2000). *Laidlaw* involved a challenge against a company that had been discharging mercury-contaminated effluent into the North Tyger River. There was no dispute that the discharges violated the company's Clean Water Act permit, but the plaintiffs had not produced any firm evidence of environmental harm. They instead alleged that their fear of pollution had caused them to avoid the part of the river where Laidlaw was discharging its effluent, and that this lost use was their harm. The Supreme Court (over a vigorous dissent by Justice Scalia) agreed that this was a sufficient basis for standing. It wrote:

> The relevant showing for purposes of Article III standing, however, is not injury to the environment but injury to the plaintiff. * * * Unlike the dissent, we see nothing "improbable" about the proposition that a company's continuous and pervasive illegal discharges of pollutants into a river would cause nearby residents

to curtail their recreational use of that waterway and would subject them to other economic and aesthetic harms. The proposition is entirely reasonable * * *.

Id. at 181–85

VI. ENFORCEMENT

"The law in books is different from the law in action. Enforcement determines the distance between the two." Margaret H. Lemos, *State Enforcement of Federal Law*, 86 N.Y.U. L. REV. 698, 699 (2011). That, at least, is conventional legal thought, and most environmental lawyers would readily agree that one cannot understand environmental law without knowing how it is—and whether it is—enforced. But environmental law enforcement is complicated, and enforcement personnel face recurring questions about who should bring enforcement actions, how often they should do so, whether enforcement strategies should be primarily punitive or primarily collaborative, and, if punitive strategies are imposed, what sanctions should be used. Regulated entities also face many questions: what should they do to prepare for possible enforcement, for example, and if an enforcement action does occur, should they collaborate with government personnel or strike a more adversarial stance? These same questions animate many political debates about environmental law, and this unit will introduce you to some of these issues.

A. BASIC ENFORCEMENT STRUCTURES

Like most elements of environmental law, understanding enforcement begins with reading statutes. With the exception of NEPA, all of the major environmental statutes covered in this book contain enforcement provisions. Those provisions generally specify who can bring enforcement actions and what types of enforcement actions can be brought. The enforcement provision of the Resource Conservation and Recovery Act (RCRA)—which is a hazardous waste management statute, and is also the subject of Chapter VI in this book—appears below. It is typical in many respects.

RCRA § 3008, 42 U.S.C. § 6928. Federal enforcement

(a) Compliance orders

(1) Except as provided in paragraph (2), whenever on the basis of any information the Administrator determines that any person has violated or is in violation of any requirement of this subchapter, the Administrator may issue an order assessing a civil penalty for any past or current violation, requiring compliance immediately or

within a specified time period, or both, or the Administrator may commence a civil action in the United States district court in the district in which the violation occurred for appropriate relief, including a temporary or permanent injunction.

(2) In the case of a violation of any requirement of this subchapter where such violation occurs in a State which is authorized to carry out a hazardous waste program under section 6926 of this title, the Administrator shall give notice to the State in which such violation has occurred prior to issuing an order or commencing a civil action under this section.

(3) Any order issued pursuant to this subsection may include a suspension or revocation of any permit issued by the Administrator or a State under this subchapter and shall state with reasonable specificity the nature of the violation. Any penalty assessed in the order shall not exceed $25,000 per day of noncompliance for each violation of a requirement of this subchapter. In assessing such a penalty, the Administrator shall take into account the seriousness of the violation and any good faith efforts to comply with applicable requirements.

(b) Public hearing

Any order issued under this section shall become final unless, no later than thirty days after the order is served, the person or persons named therein request a public hearing. Upon such request the Administrator shall promptly conduct a public hearing. In connection with any proceeding under this section the Administrator may issue subpoenas for the attendance and testimony of witnesses and the production of relevant papers, books, and documents, and may promulgate rules for discovery procedures.

(c) Violation of compliance orders

If a violator fails to take corrective action within the time specified in a compliance order, the Administrator may assess a civil penalty of not more than $25,000 for each day of continued noncompliance with the order and the Administrator may suspend or revoke any permit issued to the violator (whether issued by the Administrator or the State).

(d) Criminal penalties

Any person who—

(1) knowingly transports or causes to be transported any hazardous waste identified or listed under this subchapter to a facility which does not have a permit under this subchapter, or pursuant to title I of the Marine Protection, Research, and Sanctuaries Act (86 Stat. 1052) [33 U.S.C.A. § 1411 et seq.],

(2) knowingly treats, stores, or disposes of any hazardous waste identified or listed under this subchapter—

(A) without a permit under this subchapter or pursuant to title I of the Marine Protection, Research, and Sanctuaries Act (86 Stat. 1052) [33 U.S.C.A. § 1411 et seq.]; or

(B) in knowing violation of any material condition or requirement of such permit; or

(C) in knowing violation of any material condition or requirement of any applicable interim status regulations or standards;

(3) knowingly omits material information or makes any false material statement or representation in any application, label, manifest, record, report, permit, or other document filed, maintained, or used for purposes of compliance with regulations promulgated by the Administrator (or by a State in the case of an authorized State program) under this subchapter;

(4) knowingly generates, stores, treats, transports, disposes of, exports, or otherwise handles any hazardous waste or any used oil not identified or listed as a hazardous waste under this subchapter (whether such activity took place before or takes place after November 8, 1984) and who knowingly destroys, alters, conceals, or fails to file any record, application, manifest, report, or other document required to be maintained or filed for purposes of compliance with regulations promulgated by the Administrator (or by a State in the case of an authorized State program) under this subchapter;

(5) knowingly transports without a manifest, or causes to be transported without a manifest, any hazardous waste or any used oil not identified or listed as a hazardous waste under this subchapter required by regulations promulgated under this subchapter (or by a State in the case of a State program authorized under this subchapter) to be accompanied by a manifest;

(6) knowingly exports a hazardous waste identified or listed under this subchapter (A) without the consent of the receiving country or, (B) where there exists an international agreement between the United States and the government of the receiving country establishing notice, export, and enforcement procedures for the transportation, treatment, storage, and disposal of hazardous wastes, in a manner which is not in conformance with such agreement; or

(7) knowingly stores, treats, transports, or causes to be transported, disposes of, or otherwise handles any used oil not identified or listed as a hazardous waste under this subchapter—

(A) in knowing violation of any material condition or requirement of a permit under this subchapter; or

(B) in knowing violation of any material condition or requirement of any applicable regulations or standards under this chapter;

shall, upon conviction, be subject to a fine of not more than $50,000 for each day of violation, or imprisonment not to exceed two years (five years in the case of a violation of paragraph (1) or (2)), or both. If the conviction is for a violation committed after a first conviction of such person under this paragraph, the maximum punishment under the respective paragraph shall be doubled with respect to both fine and imprisonment.

(e) Knowing endangerment

Any person who knowingly transports, treats, stores, disposes of, or exports any hazardous waste identified or listed under this subchapter or used oil not identified or listed as a hazardous waste under this subchapter in violation of paragraph (1), (2), (3), (4), (5), (6), or (7) of subsection (d) of this section who knows at that time that he thereby places another person in imminent danger of death or serious bodily injury, shall, upon conviction, be subject to a fine of not more than $250,000 or imprisonment for not more than fifteen years, or both. A defendant that is an organization shall, upon conviction of violating this subsection, be subject to a fine of not more than $1,000,000.

(f) Special rules

For the purposes of subsection (e) of this section—

(1) A person's state of mind is knowing with respect to—

(A) his conduct, if he is aware of the nature of his conduct;

(B) an existing circumstance, if he is aware or believes that the circumstance exists; or

(C) a result of his conduct, if he is aware or believes that his conduct is substantially certain to cause danger of death or serious bodily injury.

(2) In determining whether a defendant who is a natural person knew that his conduct placed another person in imminent danger of death or serious bodily injury—

(A) the person is responsible only for actual awareness or actual belief that he possessed; and

(B)   knowledge possessed by a person other than the defendant but not by the defendant himself may not be attributed to the defendant;

Provided, That in proving the defendant's possession of actual knowledge, circumstantial evidence may be used, including evidence that the defendant took affirmative steps to shield himself from relevant information.

(3)   It is an affirmative defense to a prosecution that the conduct charged was consented to by the person endangered and that the danger and conduct charged were reasonably foreseeable hazards of—

(A)   an occupation, a business, or a profession; or

(B)   medical treatment or medical or scientific experimentation conducted by professionally approved methods and such other person had been made aware of the risks involved prior to giving consent.

The defendant may establish an affirmative defense under this subsection by a preponderance of the evidence.

(4)   All general defenses,. affirmative defenses, and bars to prosecution that may apply with respect to other Federal criminal offenses may apply under subsection (e) of this section and shall be determined by the courts of the United States according to the principles of common law as they may be interpreted in the light of reason and experience. Concepts of justification and excuse applicable under this section may be developed in the light of reason and experience.

(5)   The term "organization" means a legal entity, other than a government, established or organized for any purpose, and such term includes a corporation, company, association, firm, partnership, joint stock company, foundation, institution, trust, society, union, or any other association of persons.

(6)   The term "serious bodily injury" means—

(A)   bodily injury which involves a substantial risk of death;

(B)   unconsciousness;

(C)   extreme physical pain;

(D)   protracted and obvious disfigurement; or

(E)   protracted loss or impairment of the function of a bodily member, organ, or mental faculty.

(g) Civil penalty

Any person who violates any requirement of this subchapter shall be liable to the United States for a civil penalty in an amount not to exceed $25,000 for each such violation. Each day of such violation shall, for purposes of this subsection, constitute a separate violation.

(h) Interim status corrective action orders

(1) Whenever on the basis of any information the Administrator determines that there is or has been a release of hazardous waste into the environment from a facility authorized to operate under section 6925(e) of this title, the Administrator may issue an order requiring corrective action or such other response measure as he deems necessary to protect human health or the environment or the Administrator may commence a civil action in the United States district court in the district in which the facility is located for appropriate relief, including a temporary or permanent injunction.

(2) Any order issued under this subsection may include a suspension or revocation of authorization to operate under section 6925(e) of this title, shall state with reasonable specificity the nature of the required corrective action or other response measure, and shall specify a time for compliance. If any person named in an order fails to comply with the order, the Administrator may assess, and such person shall be liable to the United States for, a civil penalty in an amount not to exceed $25,000 for each day of noncompliance with the order.

Federal environmental statutes also generally include citizen suit provisions, which allow private entities to bring actions directly against violators. Plaintiffs bringing successful citizen suit claims can often recover attorneys' fees if they prevail, either under the citizen suit provision itself or under the Equal Access to Justice Act. The prevalence of these provisions helps explain why so many of the cases you will read in this book were initiated by environmental groups. But those authorizations come with limitations, as you will see from the example below. In general, a citizen plaintiff must provide the defendant and potential government enforcers with notice prior to filing a lawsuit, and citizen enforcement cannot proceed if the state or federal government is "diligently prosecuting" the same alleged violations.

The Endangered Species Act's citizen suit provision appears below.

ESA § 11, 16 U.S.C. § 1540. Penalties and enforcement

(g) Citizen suits

(1) Except as provided in paragraph (2) of this subsection any person may commence a civil suit on his own behalf—

(A) to enjoin any person, including the United States and any other governmental instrumentality or agency (to the extent permitted by the eleventh amendment to the Constitution), who is alleged to be in violation of any provision of this chapter or regulation issued under the authority thereof; or

(B) to compel the Secretary to apply, pursuant to section 1535(g)(2)(B)(ii) of this title, the prohibitions set forth in or authorized pursuant to section 1533(d) or 1538(a)(1)(B) of this title with respect to the taking of any resident endangered species or threatened species within any State; or

(C) against the Secretary where there is alleged a failure of the Secretary to perform any act or duty under section 1533 of this title which is not discretionary with the Secretary.

The district courts shall have jurisdiction, without regard to the amount in controversy or the citizenship of the parties, to enforce any such provision or regulation, or to order the Secretary to perform such act or duty, as the case may be. In any civil suit commenced under subparagraph (B) the district court shall compel the Secretary to apply the prohibition sought if the court finds that the allegation that an emergency exists is supported by substantial evidence.

(2)(A) No action may be commenced under subparagraph (1)(A) of this section—

(i) prior to sixty days after written notice of the violation has been given to the Secretary, and to any alleged violator of any such provision or regulation;

(ii) if the Secretary has commenced action to impose a penalty pursuant to subsection (a) of this section; or

(iii) if the United States has commenced and is diligently prosecuting a criminal action in a court of the United States or a State to redress a violation of any such provision or regulation.

(B) No action may be commenced under subparagraph (1)(B) of this section—

(i) prior to sixty days after written notice has been given to the Secretary setting forth the reasons why an emergency is thought to exist with respect to an endangered species or a threatened species in the State concerned; or

(ii) if the Secretary has commenced and is diligently prosecuting action under section 1535(g)(2)(B)(ii) of this title to determine whether any such emergency exists.

(C) No action may be commenced under subparagraph (1) (C) of this section prior to sixty days after written notice has been given to the Secretary; except that such action may be brought immediately after such notification in the case of an action under this section respecting an emergency posing a significant risk to the well-being of any species of fish or wildlife or plants.

(3)(A) Any suit under this subsection may be brought in the judicial district in which the violation occurs.

(B) In any such suit under this subsection in which the United States is not a party, the Attorney General, at the request of the Secretary, may intervene on behalf of the United States as a matter of right.

(4) The court, in issuing any final order in any suit brought pursuant to paragraph (1) of this subsection, may award costs of litigation (including reasonable attorney and expert witness fees) to any party, whenever the court determines such award is appropriate.

(5) The injunctive relief provided by this subsection shall not restrict any right which any person (or class of persons) may have under any statute or common law to seek enforcement of any standard or limitation or to seek any other relief (including relief against the Secretary or a State agency).

While these provisions narrow the discretion of governmental and private plaintiffs, they still leave many questions to be resolved. The following questions arise with particular frequency.

Federal or State. Because many environmental statutes employ cooperative federalism systems, states with approved implementation programs have discretion to enforce the statute. But what happens if EPA still wants to initiate an enforcement proceeding, either because the state is not doing anything or because the state is not prosecuting the action as aggressively as EPA would prefer? Under RCRA, to provide one example, the general rule is that EPA may bring its case if a state is not acting. But there is a circuit split on whether EPA may "overfile"—that is, file its own case in a matter on which the state already has its own enforcement proceeding. *Compare United States v. Power Eng'g Co.*, 303 F.3d 1232 (10th Cir. 2002) (allowing overfiling), *with Harmon Indus. v.*

Browner, 191 F.3d 894 (8th Cir. 1999) (rejecting overfiling). Of course, even in circuits where the courts have said that EPA *can* overfile, EPA staff still must decide whether, as a matter of comity, EPA *should not* overfile, and should instead let state actions proceed without federal involvement.

Civil or Criminal. Environmental statutes generally allow for civil or criminal enforcement. In practice, the vast majority of environmental enforcement proceedings are civil, and agencies tend to reserve criminal enforcement authority for particularly egregious violations or for cases that combine environmental violations with dishonesty or malicious motives.

Administrative or Judicial Forum. Criminal enforcement actions can only be initiated in courts. But in civil enforcement matters, EPA generally can choose between bringing the action before an administrative law judge, who works within the agency, or in federal district court. An action brought within the agency is appealable to EPA's Environmental Appeals Board, and the EAB's decisions may then be challenged in federal court.

Sanctions. Like most environmental statutes, RCRA provides for a range of sanctions. Criminal enforcement proceedings can result in fines and imprisonment. 42 U.S.C. § 6928(d). Civil enforcement actions typically result in financial penalties. Those financial penalties go to the federal treasury, not to the budget of the agency bringing the enforcement proceeding. RCRA, like many statutes, also empowers EPA to issue compliance orders, which demand immediate compliance with statutory requirements. 42 U.S.C. § 6928(a).

Punishment or Collaboration. While government agencies can seek penalties and even sometimes send violators to prison, they can also use less punitive enforcement strategies. Just as highway patrol officers let some speeders off with warnings, or simply let them drive by, environmental regulators do not prosecute every violation. Sometimes that may mean settling cases for lesser penalties than the law might allow, and sometimes it means not bringing a formal enforcement proceeding at all. Those softer strategies can be coupled with outreach and education. In this latter mode, agency enforcement staff may serve primarily as educators and compliance cheerleaders rather than as punishers.

In debates over enforcement, industry groups and their political supporters typically favor the latter mode of enforcement, or prefer complete non-enforcement, while many agency staff members and environmental advocates strongly favor the former. But the positions of both regulated entities and regulators are sometimes more nuanced. Some studies, for example, have found that firms with good compliance records appreciate punitive enforcement against competitors whose compliance is lax. That enforcement reassures the compliant firm that its efforts were worthwhile, and that it is not suffering a competitive disadvantage from following the law. Conversely, some relatively neutral observers have concluded that collaborative enforcement efforts effectively generate higher levels of compliance.

Resource Challenges. Environmental enforcement personnel do not have access to unlimited funding, and their ability to inspect facilities and bring enforcement proceedings is therefore limited. For some environmental programs, staffing and resources are so limited that hardly any enforcement occurs. These funding shortfalls create recurring challenges for agency personnel. How can they best detect violations when inspectors can visit only a small percentage of regulated facilities? How can they direct their limited resources toward the most important enforcement proceedings? And what kinds of enforcement strategies will produce the greatest public benefit with the smallest amount of government money and time?

Forcing Government Enforcement. In many circumstances, citizen suits allow private plaintiffs to act as "private attorneys general" and step into the shoes of government enforcers. Private plaintiffs also can sue the government to stop unlawful action, or to compel actions, like administrative rulemakings, that are required by law. But can citizen plaintiffs also sue government agencies to compel those agencies to initiate enforcement proceedings? The general answer is no. In a series of cases, some environmental and some in other realms, the United States Supreme Court has stated that governmental exercises of prosecutorial discretion deserve an extremely high level of judicial deference. *See, e.g., Norton v. Southern Utah Wilderness Alliance,* 542 U.S. 55 (2004); *Heckler v. Chaney,* 470 U.S. 821 (1987) (noting "the general unsuitability for judicial review of agency decisions to refuse enforcement").

What is the best way to respond to these challenges—and to many others? The excerpt below describes how a model enforcement program ought to function.

David L. Markell & Robert L. Glicksman, *A Holistic Look at Agency Enforcement*

93 N.C. L. REV. 11, 13–26 (2014)

Although it is possible to describe the components of effective regulation in many ways, we think at least five features are relevant to the design of a successful regulatory enforcement and compliance program: norm clarity, norm achievability, compliance verifiability, an appropriate mix of sanctions and rewards, and indicia of legitimacy, as we illustrate in Table 1.

Table 1: Components of Effective Regulation

Norm Clarity

Norm Achievability

Verifiability

The Mix of Rewards and Sanctions

Indicia of Legitimacy

1.   Clarity

It is axiomatic that it is important to consider the clarity of regulatory norms in designing effective regulations. There are good reasons for regulators to strive to create clear expectations for acceptable (and unacceptable) conduct. It is difficult for a regulated entity to comply with its regulatory responsibilities, or for others to assess whether it has done so, without understanding what those responsibilities are. Participants across the spectrum of interested stakeholders recognize the value of establishing clear standards for regulated parties to meet. Complaints about indeterminacy are heard from regulated parties as well as members of the public. The government has internalized this message as well, with the head of EPA's enforcement office recently acknowledging that "we should focus on greater simplicity and clarity [in our regulations]. One of the principles we have learned over years of hard experience is that compliance is better when the rules are simple and clear." This message is most obviously salient for the development of regulations, but it is also important in the development of guidance and the exercise of enforcement discretion.

Achieving clarity requires attention during multiple stages of the regulatory process. An obvious starting point is the regulatory norms themselves. A second important aspect of clarity, however, involves education, especially education of the regulated community. Studies have shown that extra effort to educate regulated parties about their legal obligations can pay significant dividends in terms of improved compliance. A recent Colorado compliance initiative involving hazardous waste rules, for example, found that an innovative state effort to increase understanding of regulatory requirements led to significant improvements in compliance, thereby dramatically reducing the need for enforcement.

Clarity, however, may also come at a cost. Statutory and regulatory schemes often cover a large number of actors, and not all are similarly situated. Thus, environmental policymakers often need to make choices about whether to use one-size-fits-all approaches or, alternatively, to tailor treatment of different sub-groups within the regulated community. In some situations it is possible to use fairly bright lines for such tailoring. The Resource Conservation and Recovery Act's ("RCRA") use of thresholds to distinguish between standard generators and de minimis generators is an example. Sometimes, however, efforts to regulate "fairly" require much more ad hoc judgments about whether particular members of the regulated community qualify for special treatment. Especially in the latter situations, where there are no bright-line rules or tests, there is a clear tension between clarity and "fair" treatment.

Regardless of the precise weight policymakers and others attach to clarity as a component of effective regulation in a particular context, it seems relatively uncontested that clarity of norms and expectations is a factor that at a minimum deserves attention in regulatory design.

2. Achievability

A second key component of effective regulation is its capacity to achieve (including the agency's ability to effectively implement) regulatory requirements. Using EPA's terminology, achievability involves the extent to which strategies "will work in the real world—rules with compliance built in." A recent example of EPA's emphasis on achievability in developing a particular regulatory regime relates to the agency's proposal of emission control regulations for oil and gas producers under the Clean Air Act ("CAA"). EPA adopted the strategy of allowing producers simply to inform EPA that they are using air pollution control equipment that EPA has certified rather than testing the equipment themselves. EPA explained that its purpose in using this approach was to "make compliance easier and less costly, while improving results . . . ."

Achievability has not always trumped other values in policy design. Congress has insisted that regulatory standards be set with little if any attention given to achievability because of the weight it attached to other values, such as attaining a particular level of health or environmental protection. In the environmental laws, for example, Congress in some cases has directed EPA *not* to consider costs in developing regulatory standards. In other regulatory schemes, Congress did not prohibit consideration of cost, but nevertheless made it clear that it was permissible for EPA to attach relatively little weight to it, and apply a relatively loose definition of achievability. At least in some contexts, technology-forcing regulatory approaches have been used successfully to substantially improve normatively desired outcomes notwithstanding questions at the outset about the achievability of such approaches.

Independent of any particular regime, scholars have debated the value of including hortatory language in environmental statutes because of the gap between objectives and likely results. Some suggest that setting the bar high has had a positive influence on performance. Others have been more skeptical. Regardless of the weight that should be attached to achievability in the design of any particular regulatory regime, the larger, conceptual point is that, when developing regulatory approaches, it is important to consider the extent to which regulated parties are likely to achieve regulatory standards.

3.   Verifiability

A third key component of effective regulation and of strategies to induce compliance involves what we term "verifiability." We define verifiability as the capacity to monitor compliance with regulatory requirements. There is little question that the ability to monitor compliance with legal requirements is a critical component of effective regulation.

The major federal environmental regulatory statutes generally provide broad monitoring authority that includes, at a minimum, authority for the government to inspect an operation's compliance with regulatory requirements, as well as an obligation for the regulated party to monitor its own performance. Yet, monitoring schemes come in various shapes and sizes. For example, New York implemented a statewide strategy that sought to enhance verifiability by requiring facilities with especially significant compliance concerns to hire independent third-party monitors whose role was to complement both government inspection efforts and the facility's own compliance efforts.

As a practical matter, the nature and extent of monitoring that occurs is likely to depend on a variety of features of the particular regulatory regime involved, including the availability of government resources; the complexity associated with monitoring compliance and the training required to monitor credibly; the availability, cost, and reliability of monitoring equipment; the trustworthiness of regulated parties and their commitment to self-monitoring; and the capacity of non-governmental interests to participate in monitoring.

Some commentators have highlighted the importance of broader transparency to the public as an aspect of verifiability. Transparency can be enhanced in a variety of ways. For example, the CWA requires permittees to submit discharge monitoring reports ("DMRs") that demonstrate compliance or noncompliance with legal requirements and, in addition, requires that these DMRs be easily accessible to interested citizens. The transparency of the CWA in revealing noncompliance is a principal reason why most of the citizen suit activity against alleged violators of major environmental laws has occurred under that statute. Other reporting requirements, such as those for hazardous substance releases above a reportable quantity, or pursuant to EPA's toxics release inventory ("TRI") program, are useful for monitoring and verifying compliance with legal requirements while also serving other purposes.

Considerable evidence shows that in many circumstances inadequate verification contributes to lower-than-desired levels of compliance with environmental requirements. To offer an example from international environmental law, the Kyoto Protocol's Clean Development Mechanism ("CDM") has suffered from weak verifiability, which has undermined the Mechanism's effectiveness. The Canadian Auditor General similarly found that monitoring shortcomings weakened the enforcement and compliance performance of a Canadian environmental program. On the other hand, enhanced reporting has led to dramatically improved compliance in some cases. In a recent article, EPA's Assistant Administrator for Enforcement highlighted a 2008 study in Massachusetts that found that requiring drinking water systems to mail compliance information to customers reduced both environmental regulatory violations and severe health violations significantly. She noted that "EPA's efforts to make our data more available are only starting to scratch the surface of the ways transparency can improve results."

In short, while the optimal parameters for incorporating a verification component into a particular regulatory regime will depend on a wide variety of factors, the literature demonstrates that verification is a foundational element of an effective regulatory scheme.

4.   The Mix of Rewards and Sanctions

A fourth component of an effective regulatory scheme is its capacity to incentivize regulated parties to comply with regulatory obligations through the use of both carrots and sticks. Conceptually, an optimal level of compliance maximizes net social benefits. Strategies that embody a mix of rewards and sanctions have the potential to contribute to achieving desired compliance levels.

EPA, on its own and in tandem with environmental or community non-governmental organizations ("NGOs") and regulated parties, has a rich array of options for promoting compliance. These include litigation options such as criminal prosecutions under many of the environmental statutes, civil judicial actions, and administrative enforcement actions, some of which may, like their judicial counterparts, seek penalties and other relief. Beyond these types of formal enforcement litigation, EPA uses strategies that employ "carrots," or a mix of "carrots and sticks," to promote compliance. An active debate continues about the relative effectiveness of various enforcement strategies in different contexts.

At the ground level, EPA has developed a library full of enforcement response and penalty policies that seek to prioritize violations that warrant different levels of enforcement attention. The agency has generally attempted to focus on "significant violations" and "high priority" violations, while giving less or different types of attention to minor instances of noncompliance. It has also developed a substantial set of compliance promotion and incentive policies that reflect a mix of strategies. In short, effective compliance promotion is most likely to derive from the use of a combination of traditional enforcement activity, facilitated by robust monitoring and reporting regimes, and efforts to induce regulated entities to comply through financial and other positive and negative incentives. Determinations of how best to combine those elements will inevitably be context specific.

5. Legitimacy

Finally, we suggest that an important component of effective regulation is its capacity to promote legitimacy, which we define to include enhancing confidence of the public and others. We believe that, in designing and implementing regulatory enforcement and compliance mechanisms, it is appropriate for policymakers to ask whether a particular regulatory design will enhance or diminish public confidence in the government's ability and willingness to promote compliance with it. A regulatory scheme that leads to a public perception that government is corrupt, overbearing, or selective in its enforcement of the law may lead to a loss of confidence and trust that undermines effective regulation in many ways, including by exacerbating budget pressures if public support for necessary funding diminishes. As one of us has noted elsewhere, "[t]he legitimacy of a regulatory system also [may] turn[ ] on the degree to which it protects against deviation from legislative goals due to capture of regulators by special interests," and on whether decisionmakers are perceived as honest, unbiased, or competent. Polling results showing the American public's loss of confidence in the federal government highlights the salience of perception by different audiences and constituencies in designing the enforcement aspects of regulatory programs.

B. Regulated Entities' Perceptions of Enforcement

Markell and Glicksman's description focuses on the optimal design of an enforcement system, and does so primarily from the perspective of that system's governmental architects. But another interesting, and important, way to consider enforcement is from the perspective of regulated entities. The excerpt below, while it focuses on regulation more generally, provides some useful insights into institutional responses to enforcement actions.

Garry C. Gray & Susan S. Silbey, *Governing Inside the Organization: Interpreting Regulation and Compliance*

120 AM. J. SOC. 96 (2014)

* * * We observed workers in a steel plant, independent and firm truck drivers, and scientists (lab technicians, students, professors) in university laboratories. Across these three fields, the safety, health, and environmental regulations about which we report were always subordinate to the dominant institutional logics of profit that prevailed in manufacturing and trucking and knowledge production that prevailed as the grounds of professional status in science.

* * * Across three different research sites, we observed that employees within the same organization interpreted the nature of the regulator's capacity and role in very different ways. However, we also noticed similar variations in the ways in which regulators were constructed by organizational actors occupying similar statuses across the different organizations. * * *

On the basis of our inductive analysis of the data from the three sites, we developed a typology of the regulator to depict the observed variations in the ways in which regulators are interpreted by organizational actors. * * * [T]he typology identifies three common variations: (a) regulator as threat, (b) regulator as ally, and (c) regulator as obstacle. * * *

Regulator as Threat

Often, frontline individuals in an organization know very little about regulators. Most of their experience with legal regulation stems from what is gleaned during informal workplace conversations, that is, "water cooler talk" or "banana time." In most cases, the result is an implicit sense that an inspector poses a threat to one's employer and thus indirectly to one's own job status. Sometimes, however, the danger is experienced as direct: the individual fears that she or he will be held personally responsible for regulatory noncompliance. Across organizational settings, regulators are routinely perceived as potentially threatening to the daily practices of work, no less to the financial and legal status of the organization. Indeed, inspectors are often described as seeking evidence only of noncompliance, of being preoccupied with issuing citations or other forms of punishment. They are seen as having a limited tool kit with which to secure compliance to legal rules and thus to meet the public interest embodied in their legal mandate. The academic literature on regulatory compliance often describes organizational compliance practices as primarily efforts to avoid sanction.

This construction of the regulator as a punitive threat is also one of the most common characterizations invoked in public political debates by those opposed to government regulation of business or government standard setting as a means of promoting responsible organizational performance. When the regulator is interpreted as a threat, compliance is understood to be like a compliance check on a computer, a process that demands perfect correspondence with ostensibly objective criteria, as opposed to a thermostat that maintains variation within limits. Here, compliance demands conformity because variation implies deviance, unacceptable difference rather than variation around a norm.

The construction of the regulator as a threat leads to individual and organizational efforts to "look compliant," regardless of whether or not the appearance of compliance corresponds to the espoused goals of regulation (i.e., "appearing safe vs. being safe"). This pattern of looking compliant was illustrated across our collective research settings and is often evidenced by extraordinary efforts to perform in the presence of and for the regulators, perhaps more often when the organizational actor is less familiar with the regulators or has less autonomy or expertise.

* * * Laboratory workers were observed to aggressively clean and straighten the labs in anticipation of semiannual inspections. Some of this laboratory housecleaning was so frantic that it not infrequently led to accidents. For instance, in the process of hastily dealing with waste before the inspectors arrived (waste must be appropriately capped, labeled, and put into designated holding areas), highly reactive chemicals that must be stored separately were occasionally poured into a single container, with consequently uncontrolled reactions with noxious fumes that took hours to subside or sometimes led to small explosions. Regulators were viewed as threats by lab technicians, who, lacking autonomy, secure position, or advanced degrees, occupy the lowest ranks in the laboratory hierarchy and routinely perform scripted and repetitive procedures. * * *

Regulator as Ally

When organizational actors construct the regulator as an ally, there is, if not an explicit, an implicit, tacit understanding that regulators are willing to work with the organization through a set of continuing relationships in which legal agents and organizational actors collaborate to produce compliance.

When experienced, interpreted, and responded to as an ally, the regulator is acknowledged to possess relevant expertise: knowledge of the specific and technical work of the organization, a range of possibly alternative compliant processes, the formal legal requirements, and a range of legal options. A regulator might function as an ally during official inspections or audits but may also serve as a backstage ally, who can be consulted, perhaps confidentially and certainly unofficially, if a regulatory issue becomes problematic among members within the organization or within the regulatory agency. In these situations, regulators are treated as resources available for internal management of uncertainty and risk. For many regulators, this is how they wish to be seen by organizational actors. * * *

Compliance officers who develop collaborative relationships with the regulated are more often closely situated in time and space to provide assistance to the regulated. That is, they are physically proximate, have lower caseloads, or have greater autonomy within their own organizations. However, simply as a matter of interactional efficiency and limited time, collaborative relationships with regulators cannot be formed with all organizational actors, so that the ally construction is unlikely to be widely shared across the organization (except through circulating narratives rather than firsthand experiences). * * *

Regulator as an Obstacle

In some cases, organization members interpret a regulatory agent as neither an ally nor a threat. Actors regard the regulator as an obstacle to compliance when the regulator is believed to lack expert knowledge about the organization's work processes or has insufficient additional resources or status to engage organizational actors. The regulator may have designed compliance requirements that are inadequately connected to the underlying regulatory goals * * *. Or the regulator may be unable to provide meaningful guidance and engagement that works to orient an organization's work processes toward meeting regulatory goals. With regard to the pollution prevention program, the EPA attorneys shared information about other universities' programs, providing additional grounds for the university staff to regard the EPA lawyers as allies.

* * * Our research in university laboratories provided abundant examples of scientists describing regulators—both compliance managers within the university and inspectors from government agencies—not as merely obstacles but as incompetent. At the most general level, the scientists explain that the standard state and federal environmental health and safety regulations that have been written for industrial plants can never work in research laboratories. Industrial sites carry out the same activities over and over again. Because of the repetitive actions, the practices of industrial safety can, like the work, also be routinized. They can be easily scripted for both performance and monitoring by the organization and the government inspectors.[6] In contrast to industrial production, the scientists claim, research laboratories, especially

---

6   Eds.: In a footnote in the paper, the authors note that this perception of industrial operations is often inaccurate. But university staff did have this perception. One of your casebook authors engaged in environmental compliance work for universities during this period and heard these same complaints.

nonbiological laboratories, perform a vast array of different activities, some of them infrequently and many only one time. Research laboratories also typically perform these acts on a considerably smaller scale, using small quantities of chemicals of nonetheless potentially hazardous materials. Because of the variation in processes, low volumes, and infrequency, it is difficult to anticipate the kinds of dangers and the substances that might turn out to be risky. "There are lots of things," one of the chemists said, "for which hazards are not known. They're new substances we've created as part of our research. And so . . . the laws that are being applied to us really are not relevant." In other words, the dangers that attach to research laboratories are to a significant degree unspecifiable in advance. And the regulators cannot possibly understand or know what is happening, what is being created in the laboratories, unless they, too, are research scientists. Our informant continued, "Chemists understand chemistry, and also the health effects and other things much more. . . . We understand why something's carcinogenic, we understand why something is corrosive, we understand things like that. Well, in our minds, that elevates the respect for the hazards." After all, how could the regulators know what should be done if the scientists are creating new knowledge? * * *

Interestingly, from the researchers' perspective, the regulators' deficiencies were not only scientific, which we might expect, but also bureaucratic and legal. Often the lab members could not understand what the compliance managers and by implication the government regulators expected of them. While the technicians fretted about this, worrying about being punished, the professors and senior scientists delegated these concerns to subordinates but also complained about what they saw as the nonsense expressed in the rules. For example, the regulations of the 1976 Resource Conservation and Recovery Act (40 CFR, pts. 260–80) require that, until removed off site, that is, out of the laboratory and then within 90 days off campus, waste must be kept in a "satellite accumulation area," at the place of generation, in the laboratory, with one active container per waste stream of up to 55 gallons or one quart of acutely hazardous waste. All waste must be labeled with a tag provided by the contractor. The label must indicate what type of waste material is enclosed (e.g., "waste acetone") as well as the associated hazards (e.g., "ignitable") and the date. The description must be in English, not in diagrams of molecular structure or chemical symbols. The containers must be situated so that the labels are clearly visible. All containers must be in good condition and all jars capped.

Although this latter requirement seems simple and basic enough, it was impossible to understand, according to the scientists:

> What does it mean capped? How tightly capped? Acids cannot
> be tightly capped or they will explode. What does it mean all jars

must be capped? If 72 of the 75 unsealed chemicals in the lab are capped, will we be cited for noncompliance? How can my graduate students possibly know? They are going to say 72 out of 75 is good enough. And so I don't know. Then what happens? You get an enormous amount of information in some central database, where someone is sitting with their feet on the desk in their office, like monitoring their computer. . . . I mean they're people. I don't know. . . . What are they going to do, sit around looking at this highly edited, uncertain information, provided by graduate students, which is a very crude level and determine if we are compliant?

The inspection and auditing forms, tools designed to help the regulators work trying to encourage, if not ensure, compliance, were regarded as inadequate, if not silly. As a consequence, senior scientists and professors would avoid calling the compliance staff for help until accidents occurred. Short of an accident, they delegated to their students and staff the work of meeting regulatory requirements. Sometimes, however, they tried to manage on their own. * * *

Test your knowledge with a Chapter 2 online quiz in CasebookPlus™.

CHAPTER 3

AIR POLLUTION

The Salt Lake City area of Utah is known for providing outstanding opportunities for outdoor recreation, which include easy access to world-class skiing, hiking, and cycling in the majestic Wasatch Mountains that rise over the city. Unfortunately, on many winter days a heavy blanket of air pollution cloaks the city, obscuring views of the mountains and besmirching Salt Lake City's reputation as a health-conscious community. Salt Lake City's pollution includes fine particulate matter, tiny particles that can pass through the upper respiratory system and lodge in the lungs or even the cardiovascular system. Exposure to fine particulate matter can cause coughing, wheezing, and shortness of breath; exacerbate lung conditions such as asthma and bronchitis; and aggravate heart conditions such as congestive heart failure and coronary heart disease. Children, the elderly, and people who exercise outdoors are particularly vulnerable. Salt Lake City's air pollution arises from a complex mix of factors:

- *Emissions.* About one-third of Utah's fine particle pollution is the direct result of combustion at sources such as power plants, vehicles, and fireplaces and woodstoves. The remaining two-thirds forms when chemicals emitted by sources such as factories and vehicles react in the atmosphere. Large industrial sources such as power plants contribute only about eleven percent of fine particle pollution in the Salt Lake City area, with the remainder coming from small industrial, commercial, and residential sources and vehicles.

- *Weather.* Under normal weather conditions, air is somewhat warmer in the lower atmosphere and cooler above. As warm air naturally rises, these layers mix. When pollutants are emitted, they thus diffuse throughout the atmosphere. Weather conditions known as inversions change these patterns. Inversions often occur after snowstorms. Fallen snow cools air near the surface while clear skies and heat reflected off the snow warm the air above, and the upper layer of warm air traps the cold air below it. The lack of vertical mixing, in turn, traps air pollutants close to the ground. The longer the inversion persists, the greater the accumulation of ambient pollution levels.

- *Topography.* Cold air blowing down from the mountains can push under warmer air rising from the valley, strengthening an inversion. The mountains also exacerbate the effect of an inversion by acting as a bowl that helps to trap the cooler, polluted air near the surface.

In addition to causing adverse health effects, air pollution negatively impacts Salt Lake City's quality of life, tourism, and economy. Schools cancel recess. Residents curtail their exercise. Visitors are confronted with unsightly haze. The Salt Lake City Chamber of Commerce has identified air quality as a top policy priority.

The example of Salt Lake City's air pollution problem illustrates some of the difficult challenges that air pollution poses to environmental law. On the one hand, addressing air pollution is vitally important. A 2015 article in the journal *Nature* estimated that air pollution exposure causes 3.3 million premature deaths each year worldwide, 55,000 in the United States. Jos Lelieveld et al., *The Contribution of Outdoor Air Pollution Sources to Premature Mortality on a Global Scale*, 525 NATURE 367 (2015). Another study estimated that air pollution causes between $71 billion and $277 billion of economic harm in the United States per year. Nicholas Z. Muller & Robert Mendelsohn, *Measuring the Damages of Air Pollution in the United States*, 54 J. ENVTL. ECON. & MGT. 1 (2007). On the other hand, air pollution is a ubiquitous byproduct of modern life. Whether driving a car, drinking water, or turning on a light, almost everything we do directly or indirectly emits air pollutants. Air pollution is also caused by a complex network of factors including emissions, weather, and topography. In recent years, the problem of global climate change from human emissions of greenhouse gases—air pollution at an even greater scale and with devastating potential consequences—has only amplified these challenges.

This chapter addresses the federal Clean Air Act, the primary environmental statute aimed at air pollution. We begin with a brief overview of the causes and effects of air pollution and the history of air pollution law in the United States. We then turn to the Clean Air Act itself, focusing on the structure of the Act's primary regulatory programs.

I. THE CHALLENGE OF AIR QUALITY

To understand the purposes and structure of air pollution law, it is helpful to know something about air pollution. We therefore begin with a brief summary discussion of the extent, sources, and consequences of air pollution in the United States.

A. SCOPE OF THE PROBLEM

As with many environmental problems in the United States, the problem of air pollution exhibits two clear overall trends. On the one hand, as Figure 3.1 illustrates, air quality in the United States overall has improved dramatically. On the other hand, as Figure 3.2 shows, air quality affects many Americans.

Figure 3.1: Trends in National Air Quality Concentrations for Common Air Pollutants (1980–2015)

Pollutant	Change in Concentration
Carbon Monoxide	−84%
Lead	−99%
Nitrogen Dioxide (annual)	−60%
Nitrogen Dioxide (1-hour)	−59%
Ozone	−32%
Sulfur Dioxide	−84%

Source: U.S. EPA, Air Quality—National Summary,
https://www.epa.gov/air-trends/air-quality-national-summary.

Figure 3.2

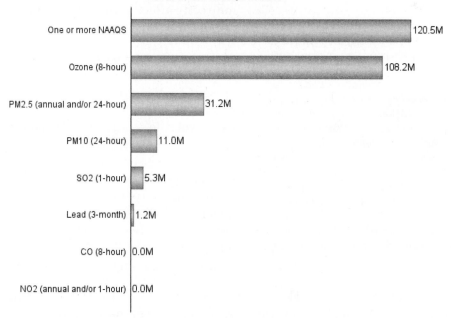

Number of People Living in Counties with Air Quality Concentrations Above the Level of the NAAQS in 2015

Source: U.S. EPA, Air Quality—National Summary,
https://www.epa.gov/air-trends/air-quality-national-summary.

B. POLLUTANTS, SOURCES, AND CONSEQUENCES

U.S. EPA, Our Nation's Air: Status and Trends Through 2010
Pp. 3–4 (2012)

Health and Environmental Impacts

Air pollution can affect our health in many ways. Numerous scientific studies have linked air pollution to a variety of health problems including: (1) aggravation of respiratory and cardiovascular disease; (2) decreased lung function; (3) increased frequency and severity of respiratory symptoms such as difficulty breathing and coughing; (4) increased susceptibility to respiratory infections; (5) effects on the nervous system, including the brain, such as IQ loss and impacts on learning, memory, and behavior; (6) cancer; and (7) premature death. Some sensitive individuals appear to be at greater risk for air pollution-related health effects, for example, those with pre-existing heart and lung diseases (e.g., heart failure/ischemic heart disease, asthma, emphysema, and chronic bronchitis), diabetics, older adults, and children.

Air pollution also damages our environment. For example, ozone can damage vegetation, adversely impacting the growth of plants and trees. These impacts can reduce the ability of plants to uptake carbon dioxide (CO2) from the atmosphere and indirectly affect entire ecosystems.

Precursors are substances that, when emitted into the air, react to form air pollutants. Air pollutants formed in the air from precursors are known as *secondary air pollutants*. For example, emissions of NO_x and VOCs, which are themselves air pollutants regulated under the Clean Air Act, react in sunlight to form ozone. NO_x and VOCs are, therefore, precursors to the secondary air pollutant ozone. One of the reasons the Clean Air Act regulates emissions of precursors is to reduce levels of secondary air pollutants in the air.

Sources of Air Pollution

Air pollution consists of gas and particle contaminants that are present in the atmosphere. Gaseous pollutants include SO_2, NO_x, ozone, CO, volatile organic compounds (VOCs), certain toxic air pollutants, and some gaseous forms of metals. Particle pollution ($PM_{2.5}$ and PM_{10}) includes a mixture of compounds. The majority of these compounds can be grouped into five categories: sulfate, nitrate, elemental (black) carbon, organic carbon, and crustal material.

Some pollutants are released directly into the atmosphere. Other pollutants are formed in the air. Ground-level ozone forms when emissions of NO_x and VOCs react in the presence of sunlight. Similarly, some particles are formed from other directly emitted pollutants. For example, sulfate particles are formed from complex reactions in the atmosphere of SO_2 emissions from power plants and industrial facilities. Weather plays an important role in the formation of secondarily formed air pollutants * * *

Generally, emissions come from large stationary fuel combustion sources (such as electric utilities and industrial boilers), industrial and other processes (such as metal smelters, petroleum refineries, cement kilns, manufacturing facilities, and solvent utilization), and mobile sources including highway vehicles and non-road sources (such as recreational and construction equipment, marine vessels, aircraft, and locomotives). Sources emit different combinations of pollutants. For example, electric utilities release SO_2, NO_x, and particles.

Sources and Health Effects of Air Pollution

Pollutant	Sources	Health Effects
Ozone (O_3)	Secondary pollutant typically formed by chemical reaction of volatile organic compounds (VOCs) and NO_x in the presence of sunlight.	Decreases lung function and causes respiratory symptoms, such as coughing and shortness of breath; aggravates asthma and other lung diseases leading to increased medication use, hospital admissions, emergency department (ED) visits, and premature mortality.
Particulate Matter (PM)	Emitted or formed through chemical reactions; fuel combustion (e.g., burning coal, wood, diesel); industrial processes; agriculture (plowing, field burning); and unpaved roads.	Short-term exposures can aggravate heart or lung diseases leading to respiratory symptoms, increased medication use, hospital admissions, ED visits, and premature mortality; long-term exposures can lead to the development of heart or lung disease and premature mortality.
Lead	Smelters (metal refineries) and other metal industries; combustion of leaded gasoline in piston engine	Damages the developing nervous system, resulting in IQ loss and impacts on learning, memory, and behavior in children.

	aircraft; waste incinerators; and battery manufacturing.	Cardiovascular and renal effects in adults and early effects related to anemia.
Oxides of Nitrogen (NOx)	Fuel combustion (e.g., electric utilities, industrial boilers, and vehicles) and wood burning.	Aggravate lung diseases leading to respiratory symptoms, hospital admissions, and ED visits; increased susceptibility to respiratory infection.
Carbon Monoxide (CO)	Fuel combustion (especially vehicles).	Reduces the amount of oxygen reaching the body's organs and tissues; aggravates heart disease, resulting in chest pain and other symptoms leading to hospital admissions and ED visits.
Sulfur Dioxide (SO2)	Fuel combustion (especially high-sulfur coal); electric utilities and industrial processes; and natural sources such as volcanoes.	Aggravates asthma and increased respiratory symptoms. Contributes to particle formation with associated health effects.

NOTE

As EPA's report notes, air pollution poses significant risks to public health. The health effects of air pollutant exposure are often not perceptible, however, even to those affected. This is because air pollution tends to increase the incidence of health impacts, such as asthma or pulmonary disease, that already are occurring in the population for other reasons. It is thus often difficult or impossible to link any particular individual's health problem to air pollution. In such situations, the impact can only be discerned in the aggregate, as a heightened incidence of the problem across the entire population.

II. HISTORY

Concerns over air pollution have lengthy historical roots. In the thirteenth and fourteenth centuries, for example, English monarchs attempted to prohibit the burning of coal in London due to poor air quality. Prior to modern environmental statutes, the law addressed air pollution concerns with common law nuisance suits against sources of excessive smoke or particularly noxious emissions. *See, e.g., Appeal of*

Pennsylvania Lead Co., 96 Pa. 116 (1881) (enjoining lead smelter as a nuisance). But, as discussed in Chapter 2, nuisance doctrine required courts to balance the harms from pollution against the economic benefits of the polluting activity, making it difficult to win a nuisance claim against a polluter.

The first anti-pollution statutes were air pollution ordinances enacted by local governments. But because of limited budgets and lack of scientific understanding of what air pollutants were emitted or what their effects might be, these ordinances often simply classified heavy emissions of black smoke or pungent odors as nuisances. *See, e.g., City of St. Louis v. Heitzeberg Packing & Provision Co.*, 141 Mo. 375, 42 S.W. 954, 954 (1897) (describing a "Smoke Ordinance" providing that "the emission into the open air of dense black or thick gray smoke within the corporate limits of the city of St. Louis is hereby declared to be a nuisance"); *see generally* Arnold W. Reitze, Jr., *A Century of Air Pollution Control Law: What's Worked; What's Failed; What Might Work*, 21 ENVTL. L. 1549, 1576–81 (1991).

Federal programs to address air pollution began in the early twentieth century and focused on research. Meanwhile, air pollution worsened. On smoggy days in Los Angeles, parents kept their children out of school and athletic events were canceled. In October 1948 in Donora, Pennsylvania, a lethal combination of heavy pollutant emissions from industry and a strong temperature inversion led to a pollutant-laden fog that caused 20 deaths and 400 hospitalizations among the town's 14,000 residents.

Smog in New York City, 1953

Source: Library of Congress

Highly visible incidents like this, and generally increasing public awareness about air pollution, created pressure for Congress to act. As the Supreme Court later explained,

> Congress initially responded to the problem of air pollution by offering encouragement and assistance to the States. In 1955 the Surgeon General was authorized to study the problem of air pollution, to support research, training, and demonstration projects, and to provide technical assistance to state and local governments attempting to abate pollution. In 1960 Congress directed the Surgeon General to focus his attention on the health hazards resulting from motor vehicle emissions. The Clean Air Act of 1963 authorized federal authorities to expand their research efforts, to make grants to state air pollution control agencies, and also to intervene directly to abate

interstate pollution in limited circumstances. Amendments in 1965 and in 1966 broadened federal authority to control motor vehicle emissions and to make grants to state pollution control agencies.

The focus shifted somewhat in the Air Quality Act of 1967. It reiterated the premise of the earlier Clean Air Act "that the prevention and control of air pollution at its source is the primary responsibility of States and local governments." Its provisions, however, increased the federal role in the prevention of air pollution, by according federal authorities certain powers of supervision and enforcement. But the States generally retained wide latitude to determine both the air quality standards which they would meet and the period of time in which they would do so.

The response of the State to these manifestations of increasing congressional concern with air pollution was disappointing. Even by 1970, state planning and implementation under the Air Quality Act of 1967 had made little progress. Congress reacted by taking a stick to the States in the form of the Clean Air Amendments of 1970, enacted on December 31 of that year. These Amendments sharply increased federal authority and responsibility in the continuing effort to combat air pollution. Nonetheless, the Amendments explicitly preserved the principle: "Each State shall have the primary responsibility for assuring air quality within the entire geographic area comprising such State . . . ." The difference under the Amendments was that the States were no longer given any choice as to whether they would meet this responsibility. For the first time they were required to attain air quality of specified standards, and to do so within a specified period of time.

Train v. Natural Resources Defense Council, 421 U.S. 60, 63–65 (1975).

III. CLEAN AIR ACT OVERVIEW

The Clean Air Act is the most complex regulatory program in U.S. environmental law. The statute is lengthy, spanning almost 300 pages in the U.S. Code. It creates a diversity of programs, many of which are highly technical and detailed in their requirements. This statutory complexity reflects the complicated nature of air pollution itself, a problem involving numerous different pollutants emitted from a variety of sources and drifting over long distances, including across state lines and national borders. These characteristics make air pollution an extremely challenging problem to address.

Despite these characteristics, the Clean Air Act has been a dramatic success on several levels. The pollution reduction achieved under the Act has prevented hundreds of thousands of premature deaths and hospitalizations. New vehicles now emit a fraction of the pollutants emitted by past models. Moreover, the Act has become the leading regulatory program for reducing the United States' greenhouse gas emissions that cause climate change. This section provides an overview and introduction to the statute—a big-picture view before we dive into particular programs that constitute the Act.

The Clean Air Act includes both regulatory provisions (i.e., those that control or restrict by law) and nonregulatory provisions. Examples of regulatory provisions include air quality standards, implementation plans, performance standards, permits, recordkeeping, monitoring and reporting, and inspections. This chapter will focus almost exclusively on these regulatory aspects. It is important, however, to be aware that the Clean Air Act, as with most environmental statutes, includes nonregulatory provisions as well. Examples of topics addressed by nonregulatory provisions include research, grants, training, and various committees, commissions, and agencies.

The Clean Air Act is best understood as a system of related regulatory programs, all aimed at working in combination to reduce air pollution to levels that will not harm human health and the environment.

- *National Ambient Air Quality Standards (NAAQS)*. Clean Air Act section 109 instructs EPA to establish uniform national standards for air quality for widespread air pollutants, known as criteria air pollutants. 42 U.S.C. § 7409. The NAAQS are environmental quality-based standards, to be set at a level that protects public health and welfare against the adverse effects of air pollution. The NAAQS do not themselves regulate emissions, but they create an important goal for many of the Act's regulatory programs.

- *State Implementation Plans (SIPs)*. Clean Air Act section 110 and other provisions direct states to develop state implementation plans aimed at bringing local air quality into compliance with the NAAQS. 42 U.S.C. § 7410. Although EPA establishes uniform NAAQS for the entire country, states have considerable discretion when developing and implementing their SIPs to decide how to regulate air pollutant emissions.

- *New Source Review (NSR)*. Clean Air Act section 165 requires anyone planning on building a major new stationary source of air pollution to obtain a permit before commencing construction of the source. 42 U.S.C. § 7475. The permitting process for these new sources is called New Source Review and is designed to ensure that a new source will not unduly degrade air quality and will use the most stringent emissions controls that are feasible for the source.

- *New Source Performance Standards (NSPS).* Clean Air Act section 111 directs EPA to establish standards of performance for categories of new stationary sources of emissions that contribute significantly to air pollution. 42 U.S.C. § 7411.

- *National Emission Standards for Hazardous Air Pollutants (NESHAPs).* The Clean Air Act regulates hazardous air pollutants separately from other air pollutants. Clean Air Act section 112 requires EPA to set technology-based limits on emissions of hazardous air pollutants for categories of new and existing stationary sources of hazardous air pollutant emissions. 42 U.S.C. § 7412.

- *Mobile Sources.* Clean Air Act section 202 instructs EPA to set emissions standards that limit pollution from mobile sources. 42 U.S.C. § 7521. Clean Air Act section 211 also directs EPA to regulate vehicle fuels and fuel additives that contribute to air pollution. 42 U.S.C. § 7545.

The Clean Air Act includes other regulatory programs too—such as the Regional Haze Program, which regulates emissions that impair visibility in wilderness areas and national parks; the Acid Rain Program, which regulates emissions of sulfur dioxide to reduce acid deposition; and the Stratospheric Ozone Protection Program, which limits the production and use of substances that deplete stratospheric ozone. For the purposes of this book, we have focused on the Clean Air Act's most significant regulatory programs, listed in the bullet points above.

The requirements of each of the Clean Air Act's regulatory programs can be quite complex, and multiple regulatory programs may apply to a single source. To assist in enforcement and compliance, Title V of the Clean Air Act requires sources regulated under the Act to obtain a permit to operate. The permit includes all air pollution requirements that apply to the source—including emissions limits, monitoring, recordkeeping, and reporting—under any of the Act's regulatory programs. 42 U.S.C. §§ 7661–7661f.

The relationship among the Clean Air Act's major regulatory programs is sometimes complicated. The SIP program, for example, builds directly on the NAAQS, establishing mechanisms for states to reach the air quality goals established by the NAAQS for criteria air pollutants. The NESHAPs, on the other hand, involve different pollutants, mostly separate from the criteria air pollutants. Yet many sources of air pollution emit both criteria air pollutants and hazardous air pollutants, and are therefore subject to both regulation under SIPs and NESHAPs. There also are pollutants—greenhouse gases are currently the most important examples—that are regulated under some stationary and mobile source controls but not under NESHAPs or SIPs. In thinking about the organization of the Clean Air Act's regulatory programs, it may be helpful to keep in mind the following questions:

1. *Is the source a stationary source or a mobile source?*

   - New Source Review (NSR), New Source Performance Standards (NSPS), National Emission Standards for Hazardous Air Pollutants (NESHAPs), and Title V Permits apply only to stationary sources of air pollution—that is, sources that do not move.

   - Mobile sources are regulated under their own regulatory program. Mobile sources include motor vehicles, locomotives, aircraft, and non-road engines such as generators.

   - State Implementation Plans (SIPs) primarily regulate stationary sources, but sometimes involve elements that regulate mobile sources.

2. *What kind of air pollutant is involved?*

   - State Implementation Plans regulate criteria air pollutants and their precursors.

   - New Source Performance Standards regulate sources of "air pollution which may reasonably be anticipated to endanger public health of welfare," 42 U.S.C. § 7411(b)(1)(A), a definition essentially identical to the principal requirement for listing a criteria air pollutant. Because of this congruence, the list of NSPS pollutants largely mirrors the list of criteria air pollutants, with a few additional pollutants. NSPS does not apply to hazardous air pollutants.

   - New Source Review regulates new sources of "air pollutants," which generally is interpreted to mean pollutants (other than hazardous air pollutants) regulated under the Clean Air Act—for the most part, but not always, criteria air pollutants.

   - NESHAPs regulate hazardous air pollutants.

   - The Mobile Source Program regulates pollutants that when emitted from mobile sources "endanger public health or welfare," 42 U.S.C. § 7521(a)(1), which encompasses some criteria air pollutants, a hazardous air pollutant, and greenhouse gases.

- Title V Permits apply to virtually every stationary source regulated under the Act, without differentiating between criteria and hazardous air pollutants.

In practice, this means that the Act's regulatory programs primarily regulate either criteria air pollutants (SIPs, NSPS, NSR), hazardous air pollutants (NESHAPs), or both criteria and hazardous air pollutants (Title V, Mobile Source). Some pollutants, like greenhouse gases, fall into neither category but nonetheless are regulated under some regulatory programs like NSPS, NSR, or the mobile source program.

3. *Is the source a new or existing source?* Like most environmental statutes, the Clean Air Act regulates new sources—that is, sources that postdate the promulgation of the environmental standard—more stringently than it regulates existing sources.

    - New Source Review and New Source Performance Standards primarily regulate only new sources, although those programs also count sources that are substantially modified as new sources.

    - The Mobile Source Program primarily regulates new sources, but includes some continuing requirements that extend over the "useful life" of the source.

    - NESHAPs regulate both new and existing sources, but regulate new sources more rigorously than existing sources.

    - SIPs regulate both new and existing sources, and because they incorporate New Source Review and NSPS requirements may regulate new sources more stringently than existing sources.

4. *Is the source located in a Prevention of Significant Deterioration (PSD) area or in a nonattainment area?* Some Clean Air Act programs differentiate between areas with air quality that meets the goal specified in the NAAQS, known as PSD areas, and areas with air quality that does not meet the NAAQS, known as nonattainment areas.

    - SIPs and New Source Review generally regulate sources in nonattainment areas more strictly than similar sources in a PSD area.

- NSPS and NESHAPs do not differentiate between nonattainment areas and PSD areas. The differentiation between nonattainment and PSD matters only for criteria air pollutants, because only criteria air pollutants have NAAQS. NESHAPs regulate air pollutants that are not criteria air pollutants, and NSPS regulates criteria air pollutants but some additional pollutants as well.

- The Mobile Source Program also does not differentiate between nonattainment areas and PSD areas, both because it regulates additional pollutants and because mobile sources can travel between nonattainment areas and PSD areas, making differentiation difficult to administer.

The diagram below illustrates how these distinctions collectively determine the mix of Clean Air Act regulatory programs that apply to any particular situation. Keep in mind that a particular source may have different characteristics for different programs. For example, a source may be considered a major source under the hazardous air pollutant program because of its emissions of hazardous air pollutants, but not a major source for purposes of New Source Review because of its emissions of criteria air pollutants. Similarly, a source may be considered a new source for purposes of the New Source Review program, because it was constructed after 1977, but an existing source for purposes of the New Source Performance Standards, because it was constructed before the promulgation of the relevant performance standards. You can see why the Clean Air Act has a reputation for being complex. But if you analyze each program's application carefully, you can navigate the Clean Air Act maze.

Figure 3.3. Simplified Conceptual Map of the Clean Water Act

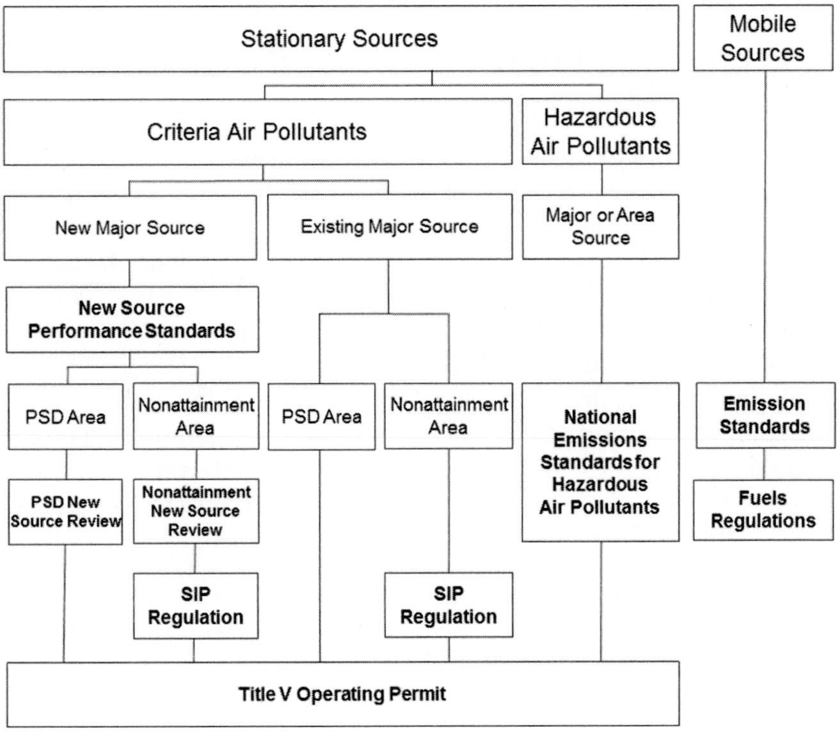

```
┌─────────────────────────────────────────────────┐   ┌──────────────┐
│              Stationary Sources                 │   │   Mobile     │
│                                                 │   │   Sources    │
└─────────────────────────────────────────────────┘   └──────────────┘

┌──────────────────────────────────┐  ┌──────────────┐
│      Criteria Air Pollutants     │  │  Hazardous   │
│                                  │  │ Air Pollutants│
└──────────────────────────────────┘  └──────────────┘

┌────────────────┐  ┌────────────────┐  ┌────────────┐
│ New Major Source│  │Existing Major  │  │ Major or Area│
│                │  │    Source      │  │   Source    │
└────────────────┘  └────────────────┘  └────────────┘

┌────────────────┐
│  New Source    │
│Performance     │
│  Standards     │
└────────────────┘

┌────────┐┌──────────┐  ┌────────┐┌──────────┐  ┌────────────┐  ┌────────────┐
│PSD Area││Nonattain-│  │PSD Area││Nonattain-│  │  National  │  │  Emission  │
│        ││ment Area │  │        ││ment Area │  │ Emissions  │  │  Standards │
└────────┘└──────────┘  └────────┘└──────────┘  │Standards for│  └────────────┘
                                                 │ Hazardous  │
┌────────┐┌──────────┐                           │Air Pollutants│ ┌────────────┐
│PSD New ││Nonattain-│                           │            │  │   Fuels    │
│Source  ││ment New  │                           │            │  │Regulations │
│Review  ││Source    │                           └────────────┘  └────────────┘
└────────┘│Review    │
          └──────────┘
       ┌──────────┐       ┌──────────┐
       │   SIP    │       │   SIP    │
       │Regulation│       │Regulation│
       └──────────┘       └──────────┘

┌─────────────────────────────────────────────────┐
│           Title V Operating Permit              │
└─────────────────────────────────────────────────┘
```

In addition to the aforementioned questions, which help to determine *which* Clean Air Act regulatory program(s) applies, the question of *who* issues standards and permits under a regulatory program also is important. The Clean Air Act, like most federal pollution statutes, follows a *cooperative federalism* model. *See supra* Chapter 2. Pursuant to the cooperative federalism model, for most Clean Air Act programs, state environmental agencies or local air quality regulators have the option to assume responsibility for implementing the program. While attorneys often refer generically to state delegation, EPA distinguishes between states with *approved programs* and states with *delegated permitting authority*. For approved programs, EPA authorizes the state to implement its own permitting program, providing that the state program is at least as stringent as the federal standards in the Clean Air Act and EPA regulations. For delegated programs, EPA delegates its permitting authority under the federal standards to the state—that is, the state implements the federal standards, not its own state-specific standards. Tribal governments, too, may have approved programs or delegated permitting authority. Finally, sometimes, such as for a state or tribe that does not have its own approved program or delegated permitting authority, EPA itself administers the program. The Clean Air Act's major exception to the cooperative federalism model is the Mobile Source Program, which with limited exceptions preempts state regulation.

IV. CRITERIA AIR POLLUTANTS AND NATIONAL AMBIENT AIR QUALITY STANDARDS

Although the Clean Air Act regulates an array of pollutants across its different programs, the heart of the Act's efforts to improve air quality focuses on a few common air pollutants known as the *criteria air pollutants*. The Act instructs EPA to establish *National Ambient Air Quality Standards* (NAAQS) for the criteria air pollutants and then requires states to develop state implementation plans (SIPs) aimed at bringing local air quality into attainment with the NAAQS. The first step in understanding this network of programs is to understand the requirements for listing a substance as a criteria air pollutant. The Clean Air Act does not directly designate the criteria air pollutants, but instead instructs EPA to create a list of pollutants based on three criteria set forth in section 108(a):

CAA § 108, 42 U.S.C. § 7408. Air quality criteria and control techniques

(a) Air pollutant list; publication and revision by Administrator; issuance of air quality criteria for air pollutants

(1) For the purpose of establishing national primary and secondary ambient air quality standards, the Administrator shall within 30 days after December 31, 1970, publish, and shall from time to time thereafter revise, a list which includes each air pollutant—

(A) emissions of which, in his judgment, cause or contribute to air pollution which may reasonably be anticipated to endanger public health or welfare;

(B) the presence of which in the ambient air results from numerous or diverse mobile or stationary sources; and

(C) for which air quality criteria had not been issued before December 31, 1970, but for which he plans to issue air quality criteria under this section.

The air quality criteria mentioned in section 108(a)(1)(C) is a science-based document EPA uses to regulate air pollutants. This is why EPA refers to substances listed under section 108(a) as criteria air pollutants, even though that phrase is not used in the Act.

Soon after Congress enacted the Clean Air Act, EPA stated that it planned to designate more than twenty criteria pollutants under Clean Air Act section 108(a) within only a few years. Instead, the list of criteria air pollutants has been small and very stable over time, with only limited changes since EPA first listed pollutants in 1970. In 1975, the Natural Resources Defense Council sued EPA to force the agency to add lead to the list, resulting in a court order and listing by EPA in 1976. EPA also has modified the way it defines some criteria air pollutants. For example, total suspended particles became particulate matter, with a differentiation between coarse particulate matter and fine particulate matter. Photochemical oxidants became ozone.

Once EPA has listed a substance as a criteria air pollutant under section 108(a), section 109(a) instructs EPA to issue a primary NAAQS and a secondary NAAQS for the pollutant. 42 U.S.C. § 7409(a). Primary NAAQS aim to protect public health; secondary NAAQS aim to prevent environmental and property damage. Clean Air Act section 109(b) instructs EPA how to choose NAAQS levels:

CAA § 109, 42 U.S.C. § 7409. National primary and secondary ambient air quality standards

* * *

(b) Protection of public health and welfare

(1) National primary ambient air quality standards, prescribed under subsection (a) of this section shall be ambient air quality standards the attainment and maintenance of which in the judgment of the Administrator, based on such criteria and allowing an adequate margin of safety, are requisite to protect the public health. Such primary standards may be revised in the same manner as promulgated.

(2) Any national secondary ambient air quality standard prescribed under subsection (a) of this section shall specify a level of air quality the attainment and maintenance of which in the judgment of the Administrator, based on such criteria, is requisite to protect the public welfare from any known or anticipated adverse effects associated with the presence of such air pollutant in the ambient air. Such secondary standards may be revised in the same manner as promulgated.

Understanding the statutory mandates for the NAAQS is one thing; understanding how to read an actual NAAQS regulation is another. Both are important. Consider, as an example of NAAQS, the following regulations for sulfur dioxide:

40 C.F.R. § 50.4. National primary ambient air quality standards for sulfur oxides (sulfur dioxide)

(a) The level of the annual standard is 0.030 parts per million (ppm), not to be exceeded in a calendar year. The annual arithmetic mean shall be rounded to three decimal places (fractional parts equal to or greater than 0.0005 ppm shall be rounded up).

(b) The level of the 24-hour standard is 0.14 parts per million (ppm), not to be exceeded more than once per calendar year. The 24-hour averages shall be determined from successive nonoverlapping 24-hour blocks starting at midnight each calendar day and shall be rounded to two decimal places (fractional parts equal to or greater than 0.005 ppm shall be rounded up).

(c) Sulfur oxides shall be measured in the ambient air as sulfur dioxide by the reference method described in appendix A to this part or by an equivalent method designated in accordance with part 53 of this chapter.

(d) To demonstrate attainment, the annual arithmetic mean and the second-highest 24-hour averages must be based upon hourly data that are at least 75 percent complete in each calendar quarter. A 24-hour block average shall be considered valid if at least 75 percent of the hourly averages for the 24-hour period are available. In the event that only 18, 19, 20, 21, 22, or 23 hourly averages are available, the 24-hour block average shall be computed as the sum of the available hourly averages using 18, 19, etc. as the divisor. If fewer than 18 hourly averages are available, but the 24-hour average would exceed the level of the standard when zeros are substituted for the missing values, subject to the rounding rule of paragraph (b) of this section, then this shall be considered a valid 24-hour average. In this case, the 24-hour block average shall be computed as the sum of the available hourly averages divided by 24.

(e) The standards set forth in this section will remain applicable to all areas notwithstanding the promulgation of SO_2 national ambient air quality standards (NAAQS) in § 50.17. The SO_2 NAAQS set forth in this section will no longer apply to an area one year after the effective date of the designation of that area, pursuant to section 107 of the Clean Air Act, for the SO_2 NAAQS set forth in § 50.17; except that for areas designated nonattainment for the SO_2 NAAQS set forth in this section as of the effective date of § 50.17, and areas not meeting the requirements of a SIP call with respect to requirements for the SO_2 NAAQS set forth in this section, the SO_2 NAAQS set forth in this section will apply until that area submits, pursuant to section 191 of the Clean Air Act, and EPA approves, an implementation plan providing for attainment of the SO₂ NAAQS set forth in § 50.17.

[61 FR 25579, May 22, 1996; 75 FR 35592, June 22, 2010]

40 C.F.R. § 50.17. National primary ambient air quality standards for sulfur oxides (sulfur dioxide)

(a) The level of the national primary 1-hour annual ambient air quality standard for oxides of sulfur is 75 parts per billion (ppb, which is 1 part in 1,000,000,000), measured in the ambient air as sulfur dioxide (SO_2).

(b) The 1-hour primary standard is met at an ambient air quality monitoring site when the three-year average of the annual (99th percentile) of the daily maximum 1-hour average concentrations is less than or equal to 75 ppb, as determined in accordance with appendix T of this part.

(c) The level of the standard shall be measured by a reference method based on appendix A or A–1 of this part, or by a Federal Equivalent Method (FEM) designated in accordance with part 53 of this chapter.

[75 FR 35592, June 22, 2010]

Note from this example a few important characteristics of the NAAQS:

- NAAQS set a goal for the concentration of air pollutants in the ambient air (air quality). They do not directly address the amount of pollutants emitted by sources (emissions). Of course, the amount of pollutants emitted into the air affects the amount of pollutants in the air. But the relationship between emissions and air quality can be quite complicated, dependent on a complex mix of factors including time, weather, and topography. Moreover, although NAAQS do not themselves regulate emissions, they create the goal for many of the Act's regulatory programs that do regulate emissions. Once EPA establishes a NAAQS, the Clean Air Act directs a state to develop a state implementation plan (SIP) specifying how the state will regulate emissions to achieve attainment of the NAAQS within that state.

- NAAQS specify both a concentration of air pollutants and a time frame for averaging such concentrations. Averaging times account for the fact that the concentration of an air pollutant at any moment can shift dramatically with wind direction and atmospheric conditions. The health effects of exposure also increase with time; momentary exposure to a high concentration of a pollutant may have much less effect than longer-term exposure to a low concentration of that same pollutant. Some NAAQS—such as the sulfur dioxide NAAQS in § 50.4—establish two standards for a single pollutant, one based on shorter-term exposure (in this case, 24-hour) and a second based on longer-term exposure (in this case, annual).

• Because the NAAQS set a uniform standard but air quality at any particular time varies significantly within an area, the method for determining whether an area's air quality meets the NAAQS standard is quite complex. This is why both of the sulfur dioxide regulations incorporate technical appendices that spell out in detail how to measure an area's compliance with a NAAQS.

• NAAQS are uniform national standards for the entire country. States thus have discretion through their state implementation plans to decide how to attain the NAAQS, but they lack any control over the NAAQS themselves. That said, the Clean Air Act generally does not preempt states from pursuing air quality goals that are more stringent than the NAAQS.

• EPA revises NAAQS from time to time. 42 U.S.C. § 9609(d)(1). In the meantime, states are developing and then enforcing their state implementation plans to reach attainment with the existing NAAQS. As a result, when EPA issues a new NAAQS, as it did for sulfur dioxide in 2010, *see* 40 C.F.R. § 50.17, the new NAAQS is phased in over time. This phase-in process for the new sulfur dioxide standard is explained in 40 C.F.R. § 50.4(e).

• NAAQS are an environmental quality-based standard set to protect the public health and welfare.

> The NAAQS are based on how an air pollutant affects public health and welfare. They set an environmental goal, and then direct EPA to select the regulatory standard that will accomplish the goal. This is known as an *environmental quality-based standard*, sometimes also called a *health-based standard*.
>
> Other environmental requirements, including many Clean Air Act standards, direct EPA to select a standard that is economically and technically feasible for the regulated industry. This type of standard is known as *technology-based*.

Nothing in section 109(b) indicates that EPA should consider, in choosing a NAAQS, the economic impacts or technical feasibility of achieving the standard. That said, as the following problem shows, it would naïve to think that such considerations never factor into the decision to issue or revise a NAAQS.

PROBLEM: REVISING THE OZONE STANDARD

You are an attorney in 2011 working for an environmental advocacy organization. President Barack Obama has just directed the EPA not to issue a new regulation that would have strengthened the ozone NAAQS to make it more protective of human health and the environment. Was the President's decision good policy or bad policy? Did the President's decision violate the Clean Air Act?

Let's start with some background. Clean Air Act section 109(d)(1) directs EPA to review the NAAQS for criteria air pollutants every five years and, if warranted, to revise the standards as may be appropriate. 42 U.S.C. § 7409(d)(1). Although EPA has not kept up with the five-year interval, the agency has periodically reviewed and revised NAAQS levels, including the standard for ozone. Since initially establishing an ozone NAAQS in 1971, *see* 36 Fed. Reg. 8186 (Apr. 30, 1971), EPA has reviewed the ozone standard five times, revising it three times. In 1997, for example, EPA set the primary and secondary ozone NAAQS at a level of 0.080 ppm measured as an eight-hour average. *See* 62 Fed. Reg. 38,856 (July 18, 1997). When EPA subsequently reviewed the ozone NAAQS again in the mid-2000s, the agency considered revising the standard downward to make it more stringent in response to additional scientific studies showing adverse health effects from ozone at lower levels of exposure. The Clean Air Scientific Advisory Committee (CASAC), which is an independent group of scientific experts which, under Clean Air Act section 109(d)(2), has responsibility to review NAAQS, 42 U.S.C. § 7409(d)(2), repeatedly recommended an eight-hour average ozone NAAQS within the 0.060 to 0.070 range to protect public health. Ultimately, however, EPA chose to revise the standard only to the 0.075 ppm level, more stringent than the 1997 level but less stringent than recommended by the CASAC. *See* 73 Fed. Reg. 16,436 (Mar. 27, 2008). The CASAC sent a letter to EPA Administrator Stephen Johnson strongly objecting to the agency's decision and complaining that it lacked scientific basis.

In 2009, following the election of President Obama, EPA Administrator Lisa Jackson decided to revisit the 2008 standard. As part of this review, the CASAC reiterated its prior recommendation to lower the ozone NAAQS to within the range of 0.060 ppm to 0.070 ppm. In 2010, EPA proposed to revise the ozone NAAQS to a level within this range:

National Ambient Air Quality Standards for Ozone

75 Fed. Reg. 2938 (proposed Jan. 19, 2010)

* * * This section presents the rationale for the Administrator's proposed decision that the O_3 primary standard, which was set at a level of 0.075 ppm in the 2008 final rule, should instead be set at a lower level within the range from 0.060 to 0.070 ppm. As discussed more fully below, the rationale for the proposed range of standard levels is based on a thorough review of the latest scientific information on human health effects associated with the presence of O_3 in the ambient air presented in the 2006 Criteria Document. * * *

In this proposed rule, EPA has drawn upon an integrative synthesis of the entire body of evidence, published through early 2006, on human health effects associated with the presence of O_3 in the ambient air. * * * [T]his body of evidence addresses a broad range of health endpoints associated with exposure to ambient levels of O_3, and includes over one hundred epidemiologic studies conducted in the U.S., Canada, and many countries around the world. In reconsidering this evidence, EPA focuses on those health endpoints that have been demonstrated to be caused by exposure to O_3, or for which the 2006 Criteria Document judges associations with O_3 to be causal, likely causal, or for which the evidence is highly suggestive that O_3 contributes to the reported effects. * * *

[A] substantial amount of new research conducted since the 1997 review of the O_3 NAAQS was available to inform the 2008 final rulemaking, with important new information coming from epidemiologic studies as well as from controlled human exposure, toxicological, and dosimetric studies. The research studies newly available in the 2008 final rulemaking that were evaluated in the 2006 Criteria Document and the exposure and risk assessments presented in the 2007 Staff Paper have undergone intensive scrutiny through multiple layers of peer review and many opportunities for public review and comment. While important uncertainties remain in the qualitative and quantitative characterizations of health effects attributable to exposure to ambient O_3, and while different interpretations of these uncertainties can result in different public health policy judgments, the review of this information has been extensive and deliberate. In the judgment of the Administrator, this intensive evaluation of the scientific evidence provides an adequate basis for this reconsideration of the 2008 final rulemaking. * * *

———

Business groups mounted a vigorous lobbying campaign in opposition to the proposed rule. They met with Administrator Jackson and top White House officials, including Chief of Staff William Daley, and argued that a standard within the range EPA had proposed would be too costly for industry to absorb. At the time, President Obama was facing a very difficult reelection campaign. A majority of Americans disapproved of his job performance. The country was still in the depths of what would become known as the Great Recession. The unemployment rate was over nine percent, and Republicans were blaming the President and EPA for "job-killing" regulations that purportedly prolonged the economic downturn:

> President Barack Obama seems more concerned with appeasing environmental extremists in his administration than he is with the lost jobs of poor Americans. He's letting the environmentalists run wild with long pent-up schemes to force a change in the American way of life that includes small cars, small apartments and, for many, a return to an idealized 19th century lifestyle. It's not China that's responsible for American job losses; it's Washington's fault for shutting down whole industries and preventing new jobs from being created.

Jon Basil Utley, *Job-Killing Environmentalists*, REASON.COM (Nov. 10, 2010), http://reason.com/archives/2010/11/10/job-killing-environmentalists; *see also* Eric Cantor, *Removing the Obstacles to Economic Growth*, WASH. POST, Aug. 21, 2011.

In the midst of this political battle, on July 11, 2011, EPA submitted a draft final rule to the White House for approval. Rumors circulated that the draft final rule would revise the eight-hour ozone standard to a level of 0.070 ppm. On September 2, 2011, however, the President instructed EPA to withdraw and reconsider its draft final rule:

Letter from Cass R. Sunstein, Administrator, Office of Information and Regulatory Affairs (OIRA), Office of Management and Budget, to Lisa Jackson, Administrator, U.S. EPA

Sept. 2, 2011

On July 11, 2011, the Environmental Protection Agency (EPA) submitted a draft final rule, "Reconsideration of the 2008 Ozone Primary and Secondary National Ambient Air Quality Standards," for review by the Office of Information and Regulatory Affairs (OIRA) under Executive Orders 13563 and 12866. The President has instructed me to return this rule to you for reconsideration. He has made it clear that he does not support finalizing the rule at this time.

OIRA shares EPA's strong and continued commitment to using its regulatory authorities, including the Clean Air Act (the Act), to protect public health and welfare. Over the last two and a half years, EPA has issued a significant number of rules to provide such protection. We also recognize that the relevant provisions of the Clean Air Act forbid EPA to consider costs in deciding on the stringency of national ambient air quality standards, both primary and secondary.

Nonetheless, we believe that the draft final rule warrants your reconsideration. We emphasize three related points:

1. Under the Act, finalizing a new standard now is not mandatory and could produce needless uncertainty. The Act explicitly sets out a five-year cycle for review of National ambient air quality standards. The current cycle began in 2008, and EPA will be compelled to revisit the most recent standards again in 2013. The new scientific work related to those forthcoming standards has already started (see point 2 below). A key sentence of Executive Order 13563 states that our regulatory system "must promote predictability and reduce uncertainty." In this light, issuing a final rule in late 2011 would be problematic in view of the fact that a new assessment, and potentially new standards, will be developed in the relatively near future.

2. The draft reconsideration necessarily depends on the most recent recommendations of the Clean Air Scientific Advisory Committee (CASAC), which in turn rely on a review of the scientific literature as of 2006. Executive Order 13563 explicitly states that our regulatory system "must be based on the best available science." As you are aware, work has already begun on a new and forthcoming scientific review, "based on the best available science." We urge you to reconsider whether to issue a final rule in late 2011, based on evidence that is no longer the most current, when a new scientific assessment is already underway.

3. Under your leadership, EPA has taken a series of strong and unprecedented steps to protect public health by reducing harmful air pollution in general and ozone in particular. For example, EPA and the Department of Transportation recently finalized the first joint rule reducing air pollution (including ozone) from heavy-duty trucks, with overall net benefits of $33 billion. EPA also recently finalized its Cross-State Air Pollution Rule, which will reduce air pollution (including ozone) and which is projected to prevent 13,000 to 34,000 deaths annually, producing annual estimated net benefits in excess of $100 billion. In addition, EPA has proposed national standards for mercury and other toxic pollutants; EPA's preliminary estimates, now out for public comment, suggest that these standards will prevent 6,800 to 18,000 premature deaths annually. These standards, whose annual net benefits are currently estimated to exceed $40 billion, are projected to reduce ozone as well. Cumulatively, these and other recently proposed and finalized rules count as truly historic achievements in protecting public health by

decreasing air pollution levels, including ozone levels, across the nation.

As noted, Executive Order 13563 emphasizes that our regulatory system "must promote predictability and reduce uncertainty." Executive Order 12866, incorporated in Executive Order 13563, states that each "agency shall avoid regulations that are inconsistent, incompatible, or duplicative with its other regulations . . . ." Executive Order 12866 also states that the "Administrator of OIRA shall provide meaningful guidance and oversight so that each agency's regulatory actions are consistent with . . . the President's priorities . . . ." In light of these requirements, and for the foregoing reasons, I am requesting, at the President's direction, that you reconsider the draft final rule.

More generally, the President has directed me to continue to work closely with all executive agencies and departments to implement Executive Order 13563 and to minimize regulatory costs and burdens, particularly in this economically challenging time. The President has instructed me to give careful scrutiny to all regulations that impose significant costs on the private sector or on state, local, or tribal governments.

We look forward to continuing to work with you to create, in the words of Executive Order 13563, a regulatory system that will "protect public health, welfare, safety, and our environment while promoting economic growth, innovation, competitiveness, and job creation."

Recall that Clean Air Act sections 108 and 109 set forth the process and substantive legal standard by which EPA is to issue air quality criteria and set NAAQS for ozone and other criteria air pollutants. In reviewing the language of sections 108 and 109, consider how the standards they create compare to the factors cited in OIRA's letter to EPA:

CAA § 108, 42 U.S.C. § 7408. Air quality criteria and control techniques

(a) Air pollutant list; publication and revision by Administrator; issuance of air quality criteria for air pollutants

(1) For the purpose of establishing national primary and secondary ambient air quality standards, the Administrator shall within 30 days after December 31, 1970, publish, and shall from time to time thereafter revise, a list which includes each air pollutant—

(A)   emissions of which, in his judgment, cause or contribute to air pollution which may reasonably be anticipated to endanger public health or welfare;

(B)   the presence of which in the ambient air results from numerous or diverse mobile or stationary sources; and

(C)   for which air quality criteria had not been issued before December 31, 1970 but for which he plans to issue air quality criteria under this section.

(2)   The Administrator shall issue air quality criteria for an air pollutant within 12 months after he has included such pollutant in a list under paragraph (1). Air quality criteria for an air pollutant shall accurately reflect the latest scientific knowledge useful in indicating the kind and extent of all identifiable effects on public health or welfare which may be expected from the presence of such pollutant in the ambient air, in varying quantities. The criteria for an air pollutant, to the extent practicable, shall include information on—

(A)   those variable factors (including atmospheric conditions) which of themselves or in combination with other factors may alter the effects on public health or welfare of such air pollutant;

(B)   the types of air pollutants which, when present in the atmosphere, may interact with such pollutant to produce an adverse effect on public health or welfare; and

(C)   any known or anticipated adverse effects on welfare. * * *

CAA § 109, 42 U.S.C. § 7409. National primary and secondary ambient air quality standards

(a) Promulgation

(1)   The Administrator—

(A)   within 30 days after December 31, 1970, shall publish proposed regulations prescribing a national primary ambient air quality standard and a national secondary ambient air quality standard for each air pollutant for which air quality criteria have been issued prior to such date; and

(B)   after a reasonable time for interested persons to submit written comments thereon (but no later than 90 days after the initial publication of such proposed standards) shall by regulation promulgate such proposed national primary and secondary ambient air quality standards with such modifications as he deems appropriate.

(2) With respect to any air pollutant for which air quality criteria are issued after December 31, 1970, the Administrator shall publish, simultaneously with the issuance of such criteria and information, proposed national primary and secondary ambient air quality standards for any such pollutant. The procedure provided for in paragraph (1)(B) of this subsection shall apply to the promulgation of such standards.

(b) Protection of public health and welfare

(1) National primary ambient air quality standards, prescribed under subsection (a) of this section shall be ambient air quality standards the attainment and maintenance of which in the judgment of the Administrator, based on such criteria and allowing an adequate margin of safety, are requisite to protect the public health. Such primary standards may be revised in the same manner as promulgated.

(2) Any national secondary ambient air quality standard prescribed under subsection (a) of this section shall specify a level of air quality the attainment and maintenance of which in the judgment of the Administrator, based on such criteria, is requisite to protect the public welfare from any known or anticipated adverse effects associated with the presence of such air pollutant in the ambient air. Such secondary standards may be revised in the same manner as promulgated. * * *

(d) Review and revision of criteria and standards; independent scientific review committee; appointment; advisory functions

(1) Not later than December 31, 1980, and at five-year intervals thereafter, the Administrator shall complete a thorough review of the criteria published under section 7408 of this title and the national ambient air quality standards promulgated under this section and shall make such revisions in such criteria and standards and promulgate such new standards as may be appropriate in accordance with section 7408 of this title and subsection (b) of this section. The Administrator may review and revise criteria or promulgate new standards earlier or more frequently than required under this paragraph.

(2)(A) The Administrator shall appoint an independent scientific review committee composed of seven members including at least one member of the National Academy of Sciences, one physician, and one person representing State air pollution control agencies.

(B) Not later than January 1, 1980, and at five-year intervals thereafter, the committee referred to in subparagraph (A) shall complete a review of the criteria published under section 7408 of

> this title and the national primary and secondary ambient air quality standards promulgated under this section and shall recommend to the Administrator any new national ambient air quality standards and revisions of existing criteria and standards as may be appropriate under section 7408 of this title and subsection (b) of this section.
>
> (C) Such committee shall also (i) advise the Administrator of areas in which additional knowledge is required to appraise the adequacy and basis of existing, new, or revised national ambient air quality standards, (ii) describe the research efforts necessary to provide the required information, (iii) advise the Administrator on the relative contribution to air pollution concentrations of natural as well as anthropogenic activity, and (iv) advise the Administrator of any adverse public health, welfare, social, economic, or energy effects which may result from various strategies for attainment and maintenance of such national ambient air quality standards.

The Supreme Court interpreted Clean Air Act section 109 in the 2001 case of *Whitman v. American Trucking Associations*. Christine Todd Whitman was the EPA Administrator at the time. As you read the *Whitman* decision, consider how the factors cited in OIRA's letter to EPA compare to the Court's description of the basis on which EPA is supposed to promulgate a NAAQS under section 109.

Whitman v. American Trucking Associations, Inc.
531 U.S. 457 (2001)

■ JUSTICE SCALIA delivered the opinion of the Court.

* * * Section 109(a) of the CAA, as added, 84 Stat. 1679, and amended, 42 U.S.C. § 7409(a), requires the Administrator of the EPA to promulgate NAAQS for each air pollutant for which "air quality criteria" have been issued under § 108, 42 U.S.C. § 7408. Once a NAAQS has been promulgated, the Administrator must review the standard (and the criteria on which it is based) "at five-year intervals" and make "such revisions . . . as may be appropriate." CAA § 109(d)(1), 42 U.S.C. § 7409(d)(1). These cases arose when, on July 18, 1997, the Administrator revised the NAAQS for particulate matter and ozone. * * *

In *Lead Industries Assn., Inc. v. EPA,* the District of Columbia Circuit held that "economic considerations [may] play no part in the promulgation of ambient air quality standards under Section 109" of the CAA. In the present cases, the court adhered to that holding, as it had done on many other occasions. * * *

Section 109(b)(1) instructs the EPA to set primary ambient air quality standards "the attainment and maintenance of which . . . are requisite to protect the public health" with "an adequate margin of safety." 42 U.S.C. § 7409(b)(1). Were it not for the hundreds of pages of briefing respondents have submitted on the issue, one would have thought it fairly clear that this text does not permit the EPA to consider costs in setting the standards. The language, as one scholar has noted, "is absolute." The EPA, "based on" the information about health effects contained in the technical "criteria" documents compiled under § 108(a)(2), 42 U.S.C. § 7408(a)(2), is to identify the maximum airborne concentration of a pollutant that the public health can tolerate, decrease the concentration to provide an "adequate" margin of safety, and set the standard at that level. Nowhere are the costs of achieving such a standard made part of that initial calculation. * * *

Accordingly, to prevail in their present challenge, respondents must show a textual commitment of authority to the EPA to consider costs in setting NAAQS under § 109(b)(1). And because § 109(b)(1) and the NAAQS for which it provides are the engine that drives nearly all of Title I of the CAA, 42 U.S.C. §§ 7401–7515, that textual commitment must be a clear one. Congress, we have held, does not alter the fundamental details of a regulatory scheme in vague terms or ancillary provisions—it does not, one might say, hide elephants in mouseholes. Respondents' textual arguments ultimately founder upon this principle.

Their first claim is that § 109(b)(1)'s terms "adequate margin" and "requisite" leave room to pad health effects with cost concerns. * * * [W]e find it implausible that Congress would give to the EPA through these modest words the power to determine whether implementation costs should moderate national air quality standards.

The same defect inheres in respondents' next two arguments: that while the Administrator's judgment about what is requisite to protect the public health must be "based on [the] criteria" documents developed under § 108(a)(2), see § 109(b)(1), it need not be based *solely* on those criteria; and that those criteria themselves, while they must include "effects on public health or welfare which may be expected from the presence of such pollutant in the ambient air," are not necessarily *limited* to those effects. Even if we were to concede those premises, we still would not conclude that one of the unenumerated factors that the agency can consider in developing and applying the criteria is cost of implementation. That factor is *both* so indirectly related to public health *and* so full of potential for canceling the conclusions drawn from direct health effects that it would surely have been expressly mentioned in §§ 108 and 109 had Congress meant it to be considered. Yet while those provisions describe in detail how the health effects of pollutants in the ambient air are to be calculated and given effect, see § 108(a)(2), they say not a word about costs. * * *

The text of § 109(b), interpreted in its statutory and historical context and with appreciation for its importance to the CAA as a whole, unambiguously bars cost considerations from the NAAQS-setting process, and thus ends the matter for us as well as the EPA. We therefore affirm the judgment of the Court of Appeals on this point.

■ [JUSTICE THOMAS filed a concurring opinion. JUSTICE STEVENS filed an opinion concurring in part and concurring in the judgment, in which JUSTICE SOUTER joined. JUSTICE BREYER filed an opinion concurring in part and concurring in the judgment.]

If you were an attorney in 2011 working for an environmental advocacy organization such as the Environmental Defense Fund, which supported EPA's draft rule, how would you have responded to the decision not to finalize the ozone NAAQS? Was the decision good policy or bad policy? Did the decision violate the Clean Air Act?

V. STATE IMPLEMENTATION PLANS

A. KEY ELEMENTS

The Clean Air Act requires states to adopt and submit *state implementation plans (SIPs)*. 42 U.S.C. §§ 7407(a), 7410(a). State implementation plans have several key elements:

- *Attainment of NAAQS.* The primary objective of a state implementation plan is to enable each air quality control region within a state to reach attainment—or maintain attainment, if the region already is in attainment—with the NAAQS. *See* 42 U.S.C. § 7407(a).

- *Reasonable further progress.* Congress faced a dilemma in imposing attainment deadlines on states. On the one hand, states need time to implement the emissions limitations necessary to achieve attainment. On the other hand, because limiting emissions to reach attainment can be economically and politically painful, states face a strong incentive to delay action as long as possible. To balance these two competing considerations, Congress imposed the requirement of *reasonable further progress*. 42 U.S.C. § 7502(c)(2). Reasonable further progress requires a state to demonstrate annual incremental reductions in emissions such that the state will achieve attainment by the applicable statutory deadline. *Id.* § 7501(1).

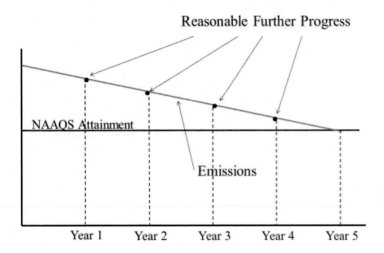

• *Emissions limitations.* As an additional means of nudging states toward limiting emissions, especially in nonattainment areas, the Clean Air Act also requires states to impose certain levels of emissions controls on sources. The level of emissions control depends on the type of source (new versus existing) and the type of area (attainment or nonattainment):

	Nonattainment Area	Attainment Area
New or Modified Source	Lowest Achievable Emission Rate (LAER)	Best Available Control Technology (BACT)
Existing Source	Reasonably Available Control Technology (RACT)	

The Clean Air Act defines each of these levels of emissions control based on factors EPA or the state is to consider in establishing an emissions limitation for a source. The lowest achievable emission rate is defined as the most stringent emission limitation that applies to a comparable source. 42 U.S.C. § 7501(3). A control technology may entail add-on equipment, such as a filter, or modification of a production process or method. Clean Air Act section 110 requires state implementation plans to incorporate the requirements of the Clean Air Act, which include applicable control technologies. *Id.* § 7410(a)(2)(A).

- *Permits for new sources.* A state implementation plan must require any "new or modified major stationary sources" in a nonattainment area to obtain a permit prior to construction. 42 U.S.C. § 7502(c)(5).

- *Emissions offsets.* New sources in nonattainment areas must obtain offsetting emissions reductions from existing sources in the area. 42 U.S.C. § 7503(a)(1). Offsets require new sources to secure emissions reductions from existing sources that offset the emissions increase from the new source, such that air quality improves despite the addition of a new source of emissions.

Contrary to the image that these descriptions may conjure, state implementation plans are not a single document labeled as such. Rather, a state implementation plan encompasses all of a state's statutes, regulations, policies, and programs that regulate air pollutant emissions.

B. TIMING AND PROCESS

The process that results in a state implementation plan involves multiple steps of state submissions and EPA approvals:

- Once EPA has established or revised a NAAQS for a criteria air pollutant, states—subject to EPA approval—designate all areas within the states as nonattainment, attainment, or unclassifiable. 42 U.S.C. § 7407(d). As these terms suggest, an area is nonattainment if it does not meet the NAAQS standard, is attainment if it does, and is unclassifiable if it cannot be classified on the basis of available information. States must submit their initial designations within one year after promulgation of a new NAAQS, and EPA must finalize the designations within two years of the new NAAQS.

- Once an area has been designated, a state must submit a proposed state implementation plan to EPA. 42 U.S.C. § 7410(a). It must submit the proposed plan within three years of the promulgation of a new NAAQS. For all the reasons (discussed in the Introduction to this chapter) that air pollution is a complex problem, developing a state implementation plan is a difficult and complicated task. In particular, to be effective in accomplishing its goals, a state implementation plan must reduce emissions from thousands—sometimes millions—of sources to a level that will result in air quality that meets the NAAQS. Many of these emissions reductions impose significant economic costs of compliance on sources. Developing a state implementation plan thus entails a long, difficult, and often contentious process. The steps necessary to prepare a plan include the following:

– Identify, locate, and quantify all emissions sources within the area.

– Identify potential emissions controls that could reduce emissions within the area.

– Develop a model to predict how various emissions reductions will affect air quality in the area.

– Select a set of emissions controls that the model shows will reduce emissions to a level that will result in air quality that meets the NAAQS.

Outside of including the key elements required in Clean Air Act section 110(a), states have considerable discretion in developing a state implementation plan to choose how to regulate air pollutant emissions to reach attainment. Thus, during the development of a state implementation plan, particular categories of sources are able to argue that they should be regulated less stringently. In addition, if a state adopts a state implementation plan that regulates a source more stringently than it thinks is warranted, the source may request a variance.

• Once a state has submitted a complete implementation plan, EPA has one year in which to approve, partially approve, or disapprove the plan. 42 U.S.C. § 7410(k). EPA must approve a proposed plan if it meets the statutory criteria. *Train v. Natural Resources Defense Council*, 421 U.S. 60 (1975).

• Once EPA has approved a SIP, the state must implement its terms so as to move the area toward attainment with the NAAQS. Clean Air Act section 172 establishes a general deadline requiring nonattainment areas to reach attainment with the applicable NAAQS within five years of the date the area was designated nonattainment. 42 U.S.C. § 7502(a)(2)(A). EPA can grant two one-year extensions of these deadlines. *Id.* § 7502(a)(2)(C).

Because of the persistent difficulty that many states faced in reaching the goal of attainment, the Clean Air Act Amendments of 1990 established pollutant-specific programs for nonattainment areas. These programs extend the statutory deadlines for these nonattainment areas to achieve attainment, but in return also impose more stringent requirements on state implementation plans for such areas. *See, e.g.,* 42 U.S.C. § 7511 (extending attainment deadlines for ozone nonattainment areas to up to twenty years); 42 U.S.C. § 7511a (imposing more stringent requirements, including motor vehicle inspections, for ozone nonattainment areas).

C. ENFORCEMENT AND SANCTIONS

To be effective, the Clean Air Act's provisions requiring state implementation plans must be implemented and enforced. This implementation and enforcement occurs on three different levels:

- EPA must meet its obligation to require adequate states to submit adequate implementation plans. If EPA fails to meet its obligations, it may be subject to a citizen suit that compels the agency to take action.

- States must submit adequate implementation plans. If a state fails to submit an implementation plan or submits an implementation plan that does not include the required elements, the Clean Air act authorizes EPA to impose sanctions that include mandating a federal implementation plan in lieu of a state plan, increasing the amount of offsets required for new or modified sources in the state, or barring any federal transportation aid. 42 U.S.C. §§ 7410(c), 7509. EPA has never actually withheld federal transportation funding, but its ability to do so—in connection with the other, more likely but less powerful potential sanctions—creates a strong incentive for states to cooperate so as not to risk that possibility.

- States must actually carry out and enforce their implementation plans. To have its implementation plan approved by EPA, a state must show that it has adequate legal authority and resources to implement the plan and a program to enforce emissions limitations. 42 U.S.C. § 7410(a)(2)(C), (E).

PROBLEM: A NEW FACTORY IN CHICAGO

This problem addresses the question whether the Illinois Environmental Protection Agency, the state agency charged with implementing the Clean Air Act in Illinois, should issue a permit for a new source of nitrogen oxides (NO_x) emissions in the Chicago area. The regulation of new sources is an important aspect of a state implementation plan.

As you read earlier in this chapter in the Ozone NAAQS Problem, EPA promulgated an 8-hour ozone standard in 1997 at the level of 0.08 parts per million. 62 Fed. Reg. 38,856 (July 18, 1997). In 2008, EPA revised the 8-hour ozone standard downward from 0.08 ppm to 0.075 ppm. 73 Fed. Reg. 16,436 (Mar. 27, 2008). EPA subsequently published rules designating and classifying areas under the 2008 8-hour ozone standard. 77 Fed. Reg. 30,088 (May 21, 2012). These 2012 rules designated the Chicago area, among others, as marginal nonattainment for the 2008 8-hour ozone standard.

Beginning in the 1960s, the Chicago Petro Company owned and operated a petroleum refinery in the Chicago area. The refinery processed crude oil into petroleum products such as gasoline, liquefied petroleum gas, propylene, and asphalt. Many of the refinery processes emitted, among other pollutants, significant quantities of NO_x. In 2005, when the refinery was at its peak level of production, it emitted 1,400 tons of NO_x.

When the Great Recession hit the U.S. economy in 2008, demand for the refinery's products fell dramatically. In 2009, Chicago Petro, already heavily in debt, stopped production at the refinery and laid off most of the workers. Some efforts were made with limited resources to maintain the facility in case economic conditions improved, in the hopes that it could reopen, but the equipment and site fell into increasing disrepair.

It is now 2013. The refinery has been closed since 2009. Chicago Petro, wary of continuing to invest in maintenance, is looking for a buyer for the refinery. Several potential purchasers have examined the refinery but declined to make an offer because of the amount of investment that would be needed to bring the refinery back into operable condition. Chicago Petro has continued to file annual emissions reports for the facility—showing no emissions because of the lack of production—in accordance with Illinois law.

Meanwhile, Big City Manufacturing is planning to open a large new manufacturing facility in the Chicago area. The new facility would utilize industrial boilers that emit 1,200 tons of NO_x per year. NO_x is both an ozone precursor and a criteria air pollutant in its own right. Because of Chicago's ozone nonattainment, any increase in NO_x, as an ozone precursor, is of concern.

Recall that Clean Air Act section 173 requires new sources in nonattainment areas to obtain emissions offsets from existing sources in the area. 42 U.S.C. § 7503(a)(1). Because EPA designated the Chicago area as nonattainment for ozone in 2012, Clean Air Act section 173 requires Illinois to ensure that any emissions of NO_x from new sources in the Chicago area are more than offset by emissions reductions from existing sources.

Big City and Chicago Petro have reached an agreement whereby Big City will pay Chicago Petro $24 million to acquire the NO_x emissions reduction credits for Chicago Petro's refinery site. If Illinois EPA approves, the agreement will allow Big City to use Chicago Petro's refinery as a source of emissions offsets for Big City's new manufacturing facility, based on the amount of NO_x the refinery is permitted to emit but is not emitting because it is not operating. On the basis of this agreement, Big City has applied for a new source permit from Illinois EPA.

As an attorney for Illinois EPA, you have been assigned to make a recommendation regarding whether to allow Big City Manufacturing to use emissions reduction credits from Chicago Petro's refinery.

Clean Air Act section 172 states the requirements for state implementation plans for nonattainment areas such as Chicago. What, if anything, does section 172 say about emissions offsets? Which, if any, of the provisions in section 172 are relevant to the question of whether Big City Manufacturing can use emissions reduction credits from Chicago Petro's refinery?

CAA § 172, 42 U.S.C. § 7502. Nonattainment plan provisions in general

* * *

(c) Nonattainment plan provisions

The plan provisions (including plan items) required to be submitted under this part shall comply with each of the following:

(1) In general

Such plan provisions shall provide for the implementation of all reasonably available control measures as expeditiously as practicable (including such reductions in emissions from existing sources in the area as may be obtained through the adoption, at a minimum, of reasonably available control technology) and shall provide for attainment of the national primary ambient air quality standards.

(2) RFP

Such plan provisions shall require reasonable further progress.

(3) Inventory

Such plan provisions shall include a comprehensive, accurate, current inventory of actual emissions from all sources of the relevant pollutant or pollutants in such area, including such periodic revisions as the Administrator may determine necessary to assure that the requirements of this part are met.

(4) Identification and quantification

Such plan provisions shall expressly identify and quantify the emissions, if any, of any such pollutant or pollutants which will be allowed, in accordance with section 7503(a)(1)(B) of this title, from the construction and operation of major new or modified stationary sources in each such area. The plan shall demonstrate to the satisfaction of the Administrator that the emissions quantified for this purpose will be consistent with the achievement of reasonable further progress and will not interfere with attainment of the applicable national ambient air quality standard by the applicable attainment date.

(5)   Permits for new and modified major stationary sources

Such plan provisions shall require permits for the construction and operation of new or modified major stationary sources anywhere in the nonattainment area, in accordance with section 7503 of this title. * * *

Clean Air Act section 172 refers to a permit program for new and modified sources under "section 7503 of this title." Based on this reference, you examine the text of 42 U.S.C. § 7503, also known as Clean Air Act section 173:

CAA § 173, 42 U.S.C. § 7503. Permit requirements

(a) In general

The permit program required by section 7502(b)(6)–[1] of this title shall provide that permits to construct and operate may be issued if—

(1)   in accordance with regulations issued by the Administrator for the determination of baseline emissions in a manner consistent with the assumptions underlying the applicable implementation plan approved under section 7410 of this title and this part, the permitting agency determines that—

(A)   by the time the source is to commence operation, sufficient offsetting emissions reductions have been obtained, such that total allowable emissions from existing sources in the region, from new or modified sources which are not major emitting facilities, and from the proposed source will be sufficiently less than total emissions from existing sources (as determined in accordance with the regulations under this paragraph) prior to the application for such permit to construct or modify so as to represent (when considered together with the plan provisions required under section 7502 of this title) reasonable further progress (as defined in section 7501 of this title); or

(B)   in the case of a new or modified major stationary source which is located in a zone (within the nonattainment area) identified by the Administrator, in consultation with the Secretary of Housing and Urban Development, as a zone to which economic development should be targeted, that emissions of such pollutant resulting from the proposed new or modified major stationary source will not cause or contribute to emissions levels which exceed the allowance permitted for such pollutant for such area from new or modified major stationary sources under section 7502(c) of this title;

(2) the proposed source is required to comply with the lowest achievable emission rate;

(3) the owner or operator of the proposed new or modified source has demonstrated that all major stationary sources owned or operated by such person (or by any entity controlling, controlled by, or under common control with such person) in such State are subject to emission limitations and are in compliance, or on a schedule for compliance, with all applicable emission limitations and standards under this chapter; and [2]

(4) the Administrator has not determined that the applicable implementation plan is not being adequately implemented for the nonattainment area in which the proposed source is to be constructed or modified in accordance with the requirements of this part; and

(5) an analysis of alternative sites, sizes, production processes, and environmental control techniques for such proposed source demonstrates that benefits of the proposed source significantly outweigh the environmental and social costs imposed as a result of its location, construction, or modification.

Any emission reductions required as a precondition of the issuance of a permit under paragraph (1) shall be federally enforceable before such permit may be issued. * * *

As with many issues, the statutory language addresses the concept of emissions offsets only generally. Accordingly, you research EPA regulations in the Code of Federal Regulations and find the following "Interpretative Ruling," first issued in 1978 and included as an appendix in the Code.

Emission Offset Interpretative Ruling
40 C.F.R. Pt. 51, app. S

This appendix sets forth EPA's Interpretative Ruling on the preconstruction review requirements for stationary sources of air pollution (not including indirect sources) under 40 CFR subpart I and section 129 of the Clean Air Act Amendments of 1977, Public Law 95–95, (note under 42 U.S.C. 7502). A major new source or major modification which would locate in any area designated under section 107(d) of the Act as attainment or unclassifiable for ozone that is located in an ozone transport region or which would locate in an area designated in 40 CFR part 81, subpart C, as nonattainment for a pollutant for which the source or modification would be major may be allowed to construct only if the stringent conditions set forth below are met. These conditions are designed to insure that the new source's emissions will be controlled to the greatest degree possible; that more than equivalent offsetting emission reductions (emission offsets) will be obtained from existing sources; and that there will be progress toward achievement of the NAAQS. * * *

IV. Sources That Would Locate in a Designated Nonattainment Area

A. Conditions for approval. If the reviewing authority finds that the major stationary source or major modification would be constructed in an area designated in 40 CFR 81.300 *et seq.* as nonattainment for a pollutant for which the stationary source or modification is major, approval may be granted only if the following conditions are met:

Condition 1. The new source is required to meet an emission Limitation 4 which specifies the lowest achievable emission rate for such source.

Condition 2. The applicant must certify that all existing major sources owned or operated by the applicant (or any entity controlling, controlled by, or under common control with the applicant) in the same State as the proposed source are in compliance with all applicable emission limitations and standards under the Act (or are in compliance with an expeditious schedule which is Federally enforceable or contained in a court decree).

Condition 3. Emission reductions (offsets) from existing sources in the area of the proposed source (whether or not under the same ownership) are required such that there will be reasonable progress toward attainment of the applicable NAAQS. Except as provided in paragraph IV.G.5 of this Ruling (addressing PM2.5 and its precursors), only intrapollutant emission offsets will be acceptable (e.g., hydrocarbon increases may not be offset against SO_2 reductions).

Condition 4. The emission offsets will provide a positive net air quality benefit in the affected area (see Section IV.D. below). Atmospheric simulation modeling is not necessary for volatile organic compounds and NO_x. Fulfillment of Condition 3 and Section IV.D. will be considered adequate to meet this condition.

Condition 5. The permit applicant shall conduct an analysis of alternative sites, sizes, production processes and environmental control techniques for such proposed source that demonstrates that the benefits of the proposed source significantly outweigh the environmental and social costs imposed as a result of its location, construction or modification. * * *

C.   Baseline for determining credit for emission and air quality offsets. The baseline for determining credit for emission and air quality offsets will be the SIP emission limitations in effect at the time the application to construct or modify a source is filed. Thus, credit for emission offset purposes may be allowable for existing control that goes beyond that required by the SIP. Emission offsets generally should be made on a pounds per hour basis when all facilities involved in the emission offset calculations are operating at their maximum expected or allowed production rate. The reviewing agency should specify other averaging periods (e.g., tons per year) in addition to the pounds per hour basis if necessary to carry out the intent of this Ruling. When offsets are calculated on a tons per year basis, the baseline emissions for existing sources providing the offsets should be calculated using the actual annual operating hours for the previous one or two year period (or other appropriate period if warranted by cyclical business conditions). Where the SIP requires certain hardware controls in lieu of an emission limitation (e.g., floating roof tanks for petroleum storage), baseline allowable emissions should be based on actual operating conditions for the previous one or two year period (i.e., actual throughput and vapor pressures) in conjunction with the required hardware controls.

1.   No meaningful or applicable SIP requirement. Where the applicable SIP does not contain an emission limitation for a source or source category, the emission offset baseline involving such sources shall be the actual emissions determined in accordance with the discussion above regarding operating conditions.

Where the SIP emission limit allows greater emissions than the uncontrolled emission rate of the source (as when a State has a single particulate emission limit for all fuels), emission offset credit will be allowed only for control below the uncontrolled emission rate. * * *

3.   Emission Reduction Credits from Shutdowns and Curtailments.

(i)   Emissions reductions achieved by shutting down an existing source or curtailing production or operating hours may be generally credited for offsets if they meet the requirements in paragraphs IV.C.3.i.1. through 2 of this section.

(1)   Such reductions are surplus, permanent, quantifiable, and federally enforceable.

(2)   The shutdown or curtailment occurred after the last day of the base year for the SIP planning process. For purposes of this paragraph, a reviewing authority may choose to consider a prior shutdown or curtailment to have occurred after the last day of the base year if the projected emissions inventory used to develop the attainment demonstration explicitly includes the emissions from such previously

shutdown or curtailed emission units. However, in no event may credit be given for shutdowns that occurred before August 7, 1977.

(ii) Emissions reductions achieved by shutting down an existing source or curtailing production or operating hours and that do not meet the requirements in paragraphs IV.C.3.i.1. through 2 of this section may be generally credited only if:

(1) The shutdown or curtailment occurred on or after the date the new source permit application is filed; or

(2) The applicant can establish that the proposed new source is a replacement for the shutdown or curtailed source, and the emissions reductions achieved by the shutdown or curtailment met the requirements of paragraphs IV.C.3.i.1. through 2 of this section. * * *

G.   Offset Ratios.

1.   In meeting the emissions offset requirements of paragraph IV.A, Condition 3 of this Ruling, the ratio of total actual emissions reductions to the emissions increase shall be at least 1:1 * * *

Which of the requirements set forth in the Interpretative Ruling are most relevant to the issue you are addressing? Additional research finds two court decisions, an EPA administrative order, and an EPA letter that apply the Interpretative Ruling. How well do these analyses match the language of EPA's Interpretative Ruling? Do the analyses modify or clarify any aspects of the Interpretative Ruling? How well do the facts of these cases match the facts of your case? Are those factual differences important? Which, if any, of these documents are binding on Illinois EPA? If not binding, what precedential weight should Illinois EPA give each of them?

Citizens Against the Refinery's Effects v. U.S. EPA

643 F.2d 183 (4th Cir. 1981)

■ K.K. HALL, CIRCUIT JUDGE.

Citizens Against the Refinery's Effects (CARE) appeals from a final ruling by the Administrator of the Environmental Protection Agency (EPA) approving the Virginia State Implementation Plan (SIP) for reducing hydrocarbon pollutants. The plan requires the Virginia Highway Department to decrease usage of a certain type of asphalt, thereby reducing hydrocarbon pollution by more than enough to offset expected pollution from the Hampton Roads Energy Company's (HREC) proposed refinery. We affirm the action of the administrator in approving the state plan.

The Act

The Clean Air Act establishes National Ambient Air Quality Standards (NAAQS) for five major air pollutants. 42 U.S.C. § 7409. The EPA has divided each state into Air Quality Control Regions (AQCR) and monitors each region to assure that the national standard for each pollutant is met. 42 U.S.C. § 7407. Where the standard has not been attained for a certain pollutant, the state must develop a State Implementation Plan designed to bring the area into attainment within a certain period. 42 U.S.C. § 7410. * * *

EPA recognized the need to develop a program that encouraged attainment of clean air standards without discouraging economic growth. Thus the agency proposed an Interpretive Ruling in 1976 which allowed the states to develop an "offset program" within the State Implementation Plans. 41 Fed. Reg. 55,524 (1976). The offset program, later codified by Congress in the 1977 Amendments to the Clean Air Act, permits the states to develop plans which allow construction of new pollution sources where accompanied by a corresponding reduction in an existing pollution source. 42 U.S.C. §§ 7502(b)(6), 7503. In effect, a new emitting facility can be built if an existing pollution source decreases its emissions or ceases operations as long as a positive net air quality benefit occurs. * * *

The Refinery

HREC proposes to build a petroleum refinery and offloading facility in Portsmouth, Virginia. Portsmouth has been unable to reduce air pollution enough to attain the national standard for one pollutant, photochemical oxidants, which is created when hydrocarbons are released into the atmosphere and react with other substances. Since a refinery is a major source of hydrocarbons, the Clean Air Act prevents construction of the HREC plant until the area attains the national standard.

In 1975, HREC applied to the Virginia State Air Pollution Control Board (VSAPCB) for a refinery construction permit. The permit was issued by the VSAPCB on October 8, 1975, extended and reissued on October 5, 1977 after a full public hearing, modified on August 8, 1978, and extended again on September 27, 1979. The VSAPCB, in an effort to help HREC meet the clean air requirements, proposed to use the offset ruling to comply with the Clean Air Act.

On November 28, 1977, the VSAPCB submitted a State Implementation Plan to EPA which included the HREC permit. The Virginia Board proposed to offset the new HREC hydrocarbon pollution by reducing the amount of cutback asphalt used for road paving operations in three highway districts by the Virginia Department of Highways. By switching from "cutback" to "emulsified" asphalt, the state can reduce hydrocarbon pollutants by the amount necessary to offset the pollutants from the proposed refinery.

EPA requested some changes in the state plan, including certain monitoring changes and verification from the Virginia Attorney General that the offset program was legally enforceable. The plan was transmitted by the EPA Region III director to EPA headquarters on September 9, 1978. Notices of the proposed plan were published on October 10, 1978 and again on May 1, 1979. 43 Fed. Reg. 46554 (1978). 44 Fed. Reg. 25471 (1979). Numerous comments were received, including several from CARE. The EPA administrator carefully considered the comments and approved the Virginia offset plan on January 31, 1980. * * *

For several years, Virginia has pursued a policy of shifting from cutback asphalt to the less expensive emulsified asphalt in road-paving operations. The policy was initiated in an effort to save money, and was totally unrelated to a State Implementation Plan. Because of this policy, CARE argues that hydrocarbon emissions were decreasing independent of this SIP and therefore are not a proper offset against the refinery. They argue that there is not, in effect, an actual reduction in pollution.

The Virginia voluntary plan is not enforceable and therefore is not in compliance with the 1976 Interpretive Ruling which requires that the offset program be enforceable. 41 Fed. Reg. 55526 (1976). The EPA, in approving the state plan, obtained a letter from the Deputy Attorney General of Virginia in which he stated that the requisites had been satisfied for establishing and enforcing the plan with the Department of Highways. Without such authority, no decrease in asphalt-produced pollution is guaranteed. In contrast to the voluntary plan, the offset plan guarantees a reduction in pollution resulting from road-paving operations. * * *

Conclusion

In approving the state plan, EPA thoroughly examined the data, requested changes in the plan, and approved the plan only after the changes were made. There is no indication that the agency acted in an arbitrary or capricious manner or that it stepped beyond the bounds of the Clean Air Act. We affirm the decision of the administrator in approving the state plan.

Sierra Club v. Georgia Power Co.

365 F. Supp. 2d 1287 (2004)

■ SMITH, DISTRICT JUDGE.

* * * Plaintiffs bring this suit as a citizen's suit authorized by the Clean Air Act ("CAA"). *See* 42 U.S.C. § 7604. Plaintiffs challenge Defendant Georgia Power Company's ("Georgia Power") emissions of hazardous air pollutants from its Wansley Steam-Electric Generating Plant in Heard County, Georgia, on numerous grounds. In Count IV, Plaintiffs specifically challenge Plant Wansley's Title V Permit issued under Georgia's State Implementation Plan pursuant to the CAA. Georgia Power wishes to construct new power generation units at Plant Wansley, which will increase Nitrous Oxide ("NOx") emissions; therefore, the Title V Permit requires Georgia Power to obtain "offsets," or reductions in similar emissions elsewhere. This Order addresses whether the required offsets comply with the CAA.

> Unlike most cases you will read in this book, Sierra Club's suit here is not seeking judicial review of an EPA action. Instead, Sierra Club brought its suit pursuant to Clean Air Act section 304, a "citizen suit" provision, which allows private citizens to bring civil suits against those committing certain violations of the Clean Air Act. 42 U.S.C. § 7604(a)(1). The citizen suit provision also allows private citizens to sue EPA if the agency has failed to perform a mandatory duty under the Act. 42 U.S.C. § 7604(a)(2). Many federal environmental statutes contain similar citizen suit provisions. *See, e.g.*, 33 U.S.C. § 1365 (Clean Water Act provision).

I. Background

A. The CAA and Georgia's State Implementation Plan

The CAA, 42 U.S.C. §§ 7401–7671q, requires all states to adopt "State Implementation Plans" ("SIPs") for attaining and maintaining National Ambient Air Quality Standards ("NAAQS"). NAAQS are based on maximum allowable levels of certain air pollutants, including ground-level ozone, which is formed by a chemical reaction between nitrogen oxides ("NOx") and volatile organic compounds. Once a State's SIP is approved by the U.S. Environmental Protection Agency (the "EPA"), it is enforceable by the State, the EPA, or by citizens through the CAA's citizen suit provision. 42 U.S.C. § 7604.

Plaintiffs bring a citizen suit alleging that Georgia Power's Wansley Plant, one of the largest power plants in the country, emits excessive amounts of toxic pollutants into the air. Plaintiffs allege that these emissions contribute to the high levels of ground-level ozone present in the Atlanta metropolitan area. Plaintiffs contend that Plant Wansley's excessive emissions damage human health, wildlife, vegetation, visibility, and property throughout the state. It is undisputed that Plant Wansley's emissions, because of the Plant's location, contribute to the Atlanta metropolitan area's designation as a "non-attainment area" as a result of ground-level ozone pollution.

Georgia's EPA-approved SIP includes specific measures to reduce the amount of ground-level ozone in the non-attainment area. The Atlanta metropolitan area has exceeded NAAQS for ground-level ozone for 22 years. Georgia's SIP requires that the owner or operator of any new or modified major stationary source of NO_x emissions obtain emission "offsets" prior to operation of the new or modified source. Ga. Comp. R. & Regs. R. 391–3–1–.03(8)(c)1. "Offsets" are reductions in NO_x emissions from other existing major stationary sources of NO_x emissions in the non-attainment area. These NO_x emission offsets must be real, permanent, quantifiable, enforceable, and surplus. *Id*. R. 391–3–1–.03(8)(c)12(iii), 391–3–1–.03(13)(b)(1). * * *

B.   Undisputed Facts

Most historic facts necessary to decide the present motions are not disputed. EPD amended the Title V permit[1] for Georgia Power's Wansley Plant in July 2000 to allow construction and operation of a "combined cycle facility," which consists of four natural-gas combustion turbines. Because the new turbines emit NO_x, Georgia Power's amended Wansley Permit requires Georgia Power to obtain NO_x emission offsets, at a ratio of 1.1 to 1, from its other emission sources. Specifically, condition 3.4.7 of the Wansley Permit provides:

> The Permittee shall obtain 572.4 tons of NO_x offsetting emissions reductions by the date that Phase I [i.e., two of the four new combustion turbines] commences operation. The NO_x offsetting emissions reductions must be real, permanent, quantifiable, enforceable, surplus, and have occurred after December 31, 1996 and by the date that Phase I commences operation. For purposes of this condition, "commences operation" shall mean the date when the emissions unit on which construction occurred becomes operational and begins to emit NO_x emissions.

On June 25, 2002, EPD amended condition 3.4.7 of the Wansley Permit to require only 457.9 tons of NO_x emission offsets. Two of the four new combustion turbines at the Wansley Plant (Phase I) began operating on or before July 9, 2002.

---

[1]   Eds.: We will examine the Title V permit program later in this chapter. For now, recall from the introduction to the chapter that Title V permits include all the Clean Air Act requirements applicable to a source. For purposes important to this case, those requirements incorporated into a Title V permit include SIP requirements.

To obtain the offsets required by condition 3.4.7, Georgia Power obtained amendments to its Bowen Plant Permit (the "Bowen Permit") and to seven of its electric generating plants in the non-attainment area (the "7-Plant Permits"). The Bowen Permit amendment limited NO_x emissions from Unit One and Unit Two of the Bowen Plant's four steam generating units ("units") for the 2002 ozone season. The 7-Plant Permit amendments limited NO_x emissions from seven Georgia Power plants for the 2003 ozone season and beyond. Plant Bowen is one of the seven plants. The ozone season runs from May 1 through September 30 each year.

During the 2002 ozone season, Georgia Power reduced NO_x emissions from units one and two at its Bowen Plant by 5,896.2 tons. Georgia Power primarily achieved these NO_x emissions by utilizing selective catalytic reduction ("SCR") air pollution controls on units one and two at the Bowen Plant. Georgia Power is currently complying with the new emission limitations imposed in the 7-Plant Permits for the 2003 ozone season and beyond.

Plaintiffs allege in Count IV of their Complaint that Georgia Power violated condition 3.4.7 of its Wansley Permit by not obtaining 459.7 tons of NO_x offsets that are real, permanent, quantifiable, enforceable, and surplus. Georgia Power moves for summary judgment on Count IV, contending that . . . the Bowen Permit created proper offsets for the 2002 ozone season. * * *

III. Analysis

* * *

B.   There is no Genuine Issue of Material Fact Regarding Whether Georgia Power Obtained Offsets that are Real, Permanent, Quantifiable, Enforceable, and Surplus

Georgia's SIP provides that "[i]n order to be used as an offset under this subsection, emission reductions must satisfy the criteria in section (13), subsections (a) and (b)." Ga. Comp. R. & Regs. R. 391–3–1–.03(8)(c) 12(iii). Subsection (13)(b) of the Rule provides that "a reduction in emissions must be real, permanent, quantifiable, enforceable, and surplus." *Id*. R. 391–3–1–.03(13)(b).3 Subsection (13)(i) defines the terms "real," "enforceable," "permanent," "quantifiable," and "surplus." *Id*. R. 391–3–1–.03(13)(i).

Although Plaintiffs allege in Count IV of their Complaint that Georgia Power's purported offsets for the Wansley Plant's combined cycle facility are not quantifiable, they did not address this requirement in their opposition to Georgia Power's summary judgment motion. Thus, Plaintiffs have abandoned any claim that the offsets are not quantifiable. *See Resolution Trust Corp. v. Dunmar Corp.*, 43 F.3d 587, 598–99 (11th Cir. 1995) ("[T]he onus is upon the parties to formulate arguments;

grounds alleged in the complaint but not relied upon in summary judgment are deemed abandoned.") (citing *Road Sprinkler Fitters Local Union No. 669 v. Indep. Sprinkler Corp.*, 10 F.3d 1563, 1568 (11th Cir. 1994)).

i.   The Offsets are Real and Enforceable

An offset is "real" if there is "a reduction in actual emissions emitted into the air." Ga. Comp. R. & Regs. R. 391–3–1–.03(13)(i)6. EPD amended the Bowen Permit to reduce the allowable NO_x emissions for units one and two for the 2002 ozone season, and the amended permit also reduced the two units' actual NO_x emissions below prior years' emissions. It is undisputed that Georgia Power reduced 2002 NO_x emissions from units one and two at the Bowen Plant below the new limit. Condition 3.4.7 of the Wansley Plant Permit required an offset of only 457.9 tons of NO_x emissions for the 2002 ozone season.

Plaintiffs argue that the offsets were not real because of the potential for "emissions leakage" from units one and two to units three and four at the Bowen Plant. "Emissions leakage" occurs when emissions from one or more units at a plant are reduced, but emissions from other units at the same plant are increased, thereby resulting in no net reduction in overall plant emissions. Plaintiffs contend that Georgia Power could simply shift production—and, thus, NO_x emissions—from units one and two to units three and four to obtain the emissions reductions required by the amended Bowen Permit.

Plaintiffs' speculation and emphasis of the "potential" for emissions leakage at the Bowen Plant does not create a genuine issue of fact as to whether the Bowen Plant actually reduced NO_x emissions during the 2002 ozone season. Indeed, the undisputed evidence shows that Georgia Power significantly reduced the Bowen Plant's 2002 ozone season NO_x emissions below prior years' emissions. EPD's Program Manager for its Stationary Source Permitting Program provided an undated internal evaluation to Plaintiffs' counsel that stated "[i]n the 2002 ozone season, Georgia Power emitted 13,385 tons at all 4 Units combined at Plant Bowen, a decrease from the baseline of 6,915 tons." Plaintiffs have presented no evidence to create an issue of fact regarding this finding. Their speculation, unsupported by any evidence in the record, as to what could have happened at the Bowen Plant cannot overcome the undisputed evidence showing "a reduction in actual emissions emitted into the air" during the 2002 ozone season. *See* Ga. Comp. R. & Regs. R. 391–3–1–.03(13)(i)6.

Alternatively, EPD observed that "[i]t is not possible to decrease utilization at one unit and increase utilization at another unit because all the units are already operating near full capacity and therefore it is not possible for any of them to operate significantly more than they already do." Thus, not only did Georgia Power reduce actual NO_x emissions from units one and two at the Bowen Plant during the 2002 ozone season, the uncontroverted evidence suggests that it could not have emitted more NO_x from units three and four, via emissions leakage or otherwise, because the entire plant was operating near full capacity. Plaintiffs have presented no evidence contradicting this and may not merely rest on their pleadings to create a genuine issue of fact in this regard.

An offset is "enforceable" if it is "enforceable by the [EPD]." *Id*. R. 391–3–1–.03(13)(i)2. Methods for ensuring that offsets are enforceable "include . . . conditions in air quality construction or operating permits issued by the [EPD]." *Id*. It is undisputed that EPD amended the Bowen and 7-Plant Permits, specifically the conditions requiring NO_x emission reductions from certain operating units at each plant. These NO_x emission limitations, which serve as the offsets for the Wansley Plant's new emissions, are fully enforceable by EPD. *See* O.C.G.A. §§ 12–9–6(b), 12–9–7(e); Ga. Comp. R. & Regs. R. 391–3–1–.09. Indeed, Plaintiffs have presented no evidence suggesting the offsets are not enforceable by EPD. Thus, there is no genuine issue of material fact as to whether Georgia Power's offsets are real and enforceable.

ii.   The Offsets are Permanent

An offset is "permanent" if it is "assured for the life of the corresponding Emission Reduction Credit through an enforceable mechanism such as a permit condition." Ga. Comp. R. & Regs. R. 391–3–1–.03(13)(i)4. As discussed in Part III.B, supra, the Rules provide that the criteria and definitions for emission reduction credits apply to emission offsets. *See id*. R. 391–3–1–.03(8)(c)12(iii). Thus, the definitions in Section (13) of the Rules apply to emission offsets. EPD's Manager of the NO_x Permitting Unit described in a May 17, 2001 letter to Georgia Power the interplay of the Rules as follows:

> Condition[ ] 3.4.7 . . . of [Plant Wansley's] Title V Permit . . . state[s] that the offsets must be real, permanent, quantifiable, enforceable, surplus. . . . The Emission Reduction Credit (ERC) Rule, found in 391–3–1–.03(13), contains definitions for these terms. It is EPD's policy that any offsets required under Georgia Rule 391–3–1–.03(8)(c) must meet the same criteria as an ERC banked under 391–3–1–.03(13). EPD is currently going through the rulemaking process to include this policy directly in Rule 391–3–1–.03(8)(c).

Indeed, even Plaintiffs cite the ERC Rule for the proposition that "[t]hese offsets must be real, permanent, quantifiable, enforceable and surplus."

Plaintiffs further contend that, even if the ERC Rule's definition of "permanent" applies, Georgia Power's offsets are not "assured for the life" of condition 3.4.7 of the Wansley Permit, which is infinite in duration. Because Georgia Power had obtained offsets for only the 2002 ozone season when Phase I of the Wansley Plant's combined cycle facility commenced operations, Plaintiffs argue that Georgia Power had not obtained permanent offsets as required by condition 3.4.7.

Georgia's SIP does not use the common dictionary definition of "permanent" for purposes of regulating ERCs and emission offsets. Thus, contrary to Plaintiffs' interpretation, the SIP did not require Georgia Power to obtain by July 9, 2002 emission offsets for 2002 and every year thereafter. Rather, the SIP required Georgia Power to obtain offsets that "are assured for the life of the corresponding . . . [c]redit," which in this case is the Bowen Plant's emission reductions for the 2002 ozone season.

It is undisputed that EPD amended the Bowen Permit to limit NO_x emissions from that plant during the 2002 ozone season by an additional 572.4 tons, the amount initially required as an offset under condition 3.4.7 of the amended Wansley Permit. The additional emission limitations contained in the amended Bowen Permit were the only "corresponding . . . [c]redit" EPD gave Georgia Power before July 9, 2002 for the Wansley Plant's new NO_x emissions. The "life" of this corresponding credit was the 2002 ozone season, and the amended Bowen Permit "assured" these emission reductions for this time period. Therefore, there is no genuine issue of fact as to whether the offsets obtained via the Bowen Plant's emission reductions for the 2002 ozone season are permanent under Rule 391–3–1–.03(13)(i)4.

iii.   *The Offsets are Surplus*

An offset is "surplus" if it is "not required by any local, state, or federal law, regulation, order, or requirement" and is "in excess of reductions used by the [EPD] in issuing any other permit or to demonstrate attainment of [NAAQS] or reasonable further progress towards achieving attainment of [NAAQS]." Ga. Comp. R. & Regs. R. 391–3–1–.03(13)(i)7. Essentially, the Rule prohibits owners or operators of major stationary sources of air emissions from "double-counting" emission reductions to satisfy multiple legal requirements. * * *

[I]t is undisputed that on July 9, 2002, the date by which Phase I of the Wansley Plant's combined cycle facility had begun emitting NO_x, neither EPA's pending lawsuit nor EPA's NO_x SIP Call were "law[s], regulation[s], order [s], or requirement[s]" applicable to Georgia Power, and it is undisputed that the Bowen Plant's 2002 NO_x emission reductions used as offsets for the Wansley Plant exceeded the reductions required by Title IV of the CAA. Furthermore, there is no evidence in the record suggesting that EPD used the emission reductions imposed in the Bowen and 7-Plant Permits in issuing any permit other than the amended Wansley Permit or for the purpose of attaining NAAQS.

Therefore, there is no genuine issue of fact as to whether Georgia Power's offsets are surplus under the plain meaning of Georgia's SIP and in accordance with condition 3.4.7 of the Wansley Plant Permit. *See* Ga. Comp. R. & Regs. R. 391–3–1–.03(13)(i)7.

IV. Conclusion

For the foregoing reasons, Georgia Power's motion for partial summary judgment is GRANTED as to Count IV of Plaintiffs' Complaint. * * *

In re Monroe Electric Generating Plant Entergy Louisiana, Inc. Proposed Operating Permit
EPA Administrator (1999)

On February 9, 1999, Ms. Merrijane Yerger, Managing Director of the Citizens for Clean Air & Water ("CCAW" or "Petitioner"), petitioned the Environmental Protection Agency ("EPA"), pursuant to section 505 (b) of the Clean Air Act ("CAA" or "the Act"), to object to issuance of a proposed State operating permit to Entergy Louisiana, Inc.'s Monroe Electric Generating Plant in Monroe, Louisiana ("Monroe plant"). The proposed operating permit for the Monroe plant was proposed for issuance by the Louisiana Department of Environmental Quality ("LDEQ") pursuant to title V of the Act, CAA §§ 501–507, the federal implementing regulations, 40 CFR Part 70, and the State of Louisiana regulations, Louisiana Administrative Code ("L.A.C."), Title 33, Part III, Chapter 5, sections 507 *et seq.*

Petitioner has requested that EPA review, investigate, and make an administrative determination on the entire matter of the proposed operating permit and planned restart of the Monroe plant, pursuant to section 505(b) of the Act and 40 CFR § 70.B(c). Petitioner alleges that the proposed operating permit is not in compliance with appli9able requirements of the Act including Prevention of Significant Deterioration ("PSD") permitting requirements and New Source Performance Standards ("NSPS"). Petitioner also alleges that Entergy's operating permit application fails to adequately demonstrate compliance with hazardous waste disposal requirements under the Resource Conservation and Recovery Act ("RCRA").

For the reasons set forth below, I find that the proposed title V permit does not assure compliance with applicable PSD requirements as set forth in the Louisiana State Implementation Plan ("SIP"). I therefore grant the Petitioner's request in part and object to issuance of the proposed title V permit unless the permit is revised in accordance with this Order. I deny the Petitioner's remaining claims. * * *

II. Background

The Monroe plant, located in Monroe, Louisiana, currently consists of three units (Units 10, 11 and 12), each with a boiler and ancillary equipment, which were installed in 1961, 1963, and 1968, respectively. Each boiler is fired primarily with natural gas, but is also capable of being fired with diesel fuel oil.

The rated capacities of the units are 23 megawatts ("MW"), 41 MW, and 74 MW, respectively. The total heat input for the units is 1,961 million British thermal units ("MMBtu"). Installation of these boilers was not subject to PSD review because it predated the PSD program.

On July 1, 1988, Louisiana Power & Light ("LP&L"), predecessor to Entergy Louisiana, Inc. ("Entergy"), placed the plant's three units in extended reserve shutdown ("ERS"). According to Entergy, these units were placed in extended reserve shutdown because of the addition of new electric generating capacity in the area. At the time of shutdown, LP&L projected that Units 10, 11 and 12 would not be needed for three to five years. That period grew to eleven years as a result of "many factors," according to Entergy, including increased competition and demand-side management.

Some time around September, 1966, LP&L initiated a number of activities at the Monroe plant to prepare the plant for extended shutdown, including draining, disconnecting and covering equipment, and installing and operating dehumidification equipment to prevent corrosion of the units. During shutdown, LP&L/Entergy conducted some inspection and maintenance activities, primarily in response to problems with the dehumidification system. During this period, LP&L/Entergy also maintained relevant environmental permits for the Monroe plant, including payment of air quality maintenance fees to LDEQ (between $1,100 and $1,300 per year), maintenance of water permits, and applications for an acid rain permit (received October 23, 1996) and a title V operating permit.

Entergy now proposes to restart Units 10, 11 and 12 at the Monroe plant beginning this summer. On September 16, 1996, Entergy submitted a title V permit application to LDEQ. The total estimated annual emissions of air pollutants associated with the plant, in tons per year ("tpy"), are as follows: nitrogen oxides ("NO_x"), 4,972.65 tpy; sulfur dioxide ("SO_2"), 679.84 tpy; carbon monoxide ("CO"), 361.65 tpy; particulate matter ("PM_{10}"), 32.46 tpy; and volatile organic compounds ("VOCs"), 12.74 tpy. These projected annual emission rates are incorporated as annual emission limits in the proposed title V permit. The requested operating permit includes no limitations on the hours of operation or the capacities at which the units would operate. Most relevant for purposes of this Order, neither the permit application nor the proposed permit provides for obtaining a PSD permit for the units prior to restart, under the Louisiana PSD program.

LDEQ submitted a proposed title V permit to EPA Region VI for review on November 16, 1998. The permit went out for public comment on November 25, 1998. Public commenters requested a public hearing. Notice of a public hearing was published on January 16, 1999. A public hearing was held by LDEQ on February 18, 1999. The public comment period ended April 20, 1999. EPA's 45-day review period expired on December 31, 1998. On February 9, 1999, Citizens for Clean Air & Water filed a timely petition with EPA pursuant to section 505 (b) (2) of the Clean Air Act requesting that EPA object to issuance of the proposed permit for the Entergy Monroe plant. As of this date, no final permit has been issued. * * *

IV. PSD Applicability Analysis * * *

EPA has a well-established policy that reactivation of a permanently shutdown facility will be treated as operation of a new source for purposes of PSD review. The key determination to be made under this policy is whether the facility to be reactivated was "permanently shutdown." In general, EPA has explained that whether or not a shutdown should be treated as permanent depends on the intention of the owner or operator at the time of shutdown based on all facts and circumstances. Shutdowns of more than two years, or that have resulted in the removal of the source from the State's emissions inventory, are presumed to be permanent. In such cases it is up to the facility owner or operator to rebut the presumption.

To determine the intent of the owner or operator, EPA has examined factors such as the amount of time the facility has been out of operation, the reason for the shutdown, statements by the owner or operator regarding intent, cost and time required to reactivate the facility, status of permits, and ongoing maintenance and inspections that have been conducted during shutdown. No single factor is likely to be conclusive in the Agency's assessment of these factors, and the final determination will often involve a judgment as to whether the owner's or operator's actions at the facility during shutdown support or refute any express statements regarding the owner's or operator's intentions.

While the policy suggests that the key determination is whether, rat the time of shutdown, the owner or operator intended shutdown to be permanent, in practice, after two years, statements of original intent are not considered determinative. Instead, EPA assesses whether the owner or operator has demonstrated a continuous intent to reopen. To make this assessment, EPA looks at activities during time of shutdown that evidence the continuing validity of the original intent not to permanently shut down.

Thus, to preserve their ability to reopen without a new source permit, EPA believes owners and operators of shutdown facilities must continuously demonstrate concrete plans to restart the facility sometime in the reasonably foreseeable future. If they cannot make such a demonstration, it suggests that for at least some period of the shutdown, the shutdown was intended to be permanent. Once it is found that an owner or operator has no real plan to restart a particular facility, such owner or operator cannot overcome this suggestion that the shutdown was intended to be permanent by later pointing to the most recent efforts to reopen the facility. * * *

Letter from U.S. EPA Region 10 to Colville Tribal Enterprise Corp.

Sept. 7, 2001

UNITED STATES ENVIRONMENTAL PROTECTION AGENCY
REGION 10

1200 Sixth Avenue
Seattle, Washington 98101
September 7, 2001

Re: Startup of Quality Veneer & Lumber Facility—Air Pollution Control Regulatory Applicability

This letter responds to your letters of June 15 and July 23, 2001, in which you requested EPA's views on a number of regulatory matters under the Clean Air Act (CAA) related to the Colville Tribal Enterprise Corporation's (CTEC) proposed purchase and operation of the Quality Veneer & Lumber plywood facility (QVL facility) located in Omak, Washington. As you have indicated, CTEC is in the process of purchasing the QVL facility, which has been shutdown since July 2000. It is our understanding that the QVL facility was, at the time of shutdown, a major source of air pollutants for purposes of both the Prevention of Significant Deterioration (PSD) construction permits program under Title I of the CAA and the Part 71 operating permits program (Part 71) under Title V of the CAA. We base the following responses to your questions on the information provided by CTEC and its consultant to EPA in your letters of June 15 and July 23, 2001, and in your telephone call with Dan Meyer of my staff on August 6, 2001.

1. Would CTEC's Startup of the QVL facility be Considered Construction of a New Source or the Continued Operation of an Existing Source?

Based on the information provided by CTEC and its consultant, EPA would not consider the startup of the QVL facility by CTEC to be a new source for purposes of the PSD program, but instead would consider it the restart of an existing PSD facility. According to EPA guidance,

> A source which had been shut down would be a new source for PSD purposes if the shutdown was permanent. Conversely, it would not be a new source if the shutdown was not permanent. Whether a shutdown was permanent depends upon the intention of the owner or operator at the time of the shutdown as determined from all the facts and circumstances, including the cause of the shutdown and the handling of the shutdown by the State. A shutdown lasting for two years or more, or resulting in removal of the source form the emissions inventory of the State, should be presumed permanent.

The information provided by CTEC does not indicate that the shutdown of the QVL facility was intended to be permanent. Even before the QVL facility ceased operation, CTEC entered into negotiations to acquire the QVL facility with the clear intent of operating the facility. Negotiations continued after the shutdown of the facility in July 2000 until a tentative agreement was reached in September 2000 for CTEC's purchase of the facility. QVL filed for bankruptcy under Chapter 11 in October 2000 in an effort to reorganize its business, and negotiations for CTEC's purchase of the facility continued during this time. It is our understanding that CTEC and the Bankruptcy Trustee are currently finalizing agreements for CTEC's purchase of the QVL facility. Based on these facts and the fact that facility has been shutdown less than two years, we agree with CTEC's contention that the QVL facility was never intended to be shutdown permanently. Therefore, EPA concludes that the QVL facility should not be considered a new source for purposes of PSD upon startup. Assuming CTEC resumes operation of the QVL facility by July 2002, the QVL facility will have been shut down for less than two years. Therefore, based on EPA guidance, EPA does not presume the shutdown was permanent. * * *

Sincerely,

Douglas E. Hardesty, Manager
Federal and Delegated Air Programs

For Illinois EPA to allow a transfer of emissions reduction credits from Chicago Petro to Big City, the emissions offsets must be consistent with Illinois state law as well as the Clean Air Act and EPA policy. The Illinois Administrative Code includes provisions regarding emissions offsets for new major stationary sources in nonattainment areas. Do the Illinois regulations include any additional requirements beyond what EPA requires under federal law?

35 Ill. Admin. Code Part 203. Major Stationary Sources Construction and Modification

§ 203.302. Maintenance of Reasonable Further Progress and Emission Offsets

a) The owner or operator of a new major source or major modification shall provide emission offsets equal to or greater than the allowable emissions from the source or the net increase in emissions from the modification sufficient to allow the Agency to determine that the source or modification will not interfere with reasonable further progress as set forth in Section 173 of the Clean Air Act.

 1) For new major sources or major modifications in ozone nonattainment areas the ratio of total emission reductions provided by emission offsets for volatile organic material or nitrogen oxides to total increased emissions of such contaminants shall be at least as follows:

   A) 1.1 to 1 in areas classified as marginal;

   B) 1.15 to 1 in areas classified as moderate;

   C) 1.2 to 1 in areas classified as serious;

   D) 1.3 to 1 in areas classified as severe; and

   E) 1.5 to 1 in areas classified as extreme.

 2) The offset requirement provided in subsection (1) above shall not be applicable in extreme areas to a modification of an existing source:

   A) if such modification consists of installation of equipment required to comply with the implementation plan or the Clean Air Act; or

   B) if the owner or operator of the source elects to offset the increase by a greater reduction in emissions of such pollutant from other discrete operations, units, or activities within the source at an internal offset ratio of at least 1.3 to 1.

b) The Agency shall allow the use of all or some portion of the available growth margin to satisfy subsection (a) above if the owner or operator can present evidence that the possible sources of emission offsets were investigated, none were available at that time and the new or modified major stationary source is located in a zone (within the nonattainment area) identified by United States Environmental Protection Agency, in consultation with the Secretary of Housing and Urban Development, as a zone to which economic development should be targeted.

(Source: Amended at 17 Ill. Reg. 6973, effective April 30, 1993)

§ 203.303. Baseline and Emission Offsets Determination

a) An emission offset must be obtained from a source in operation prior to the permit application for the new or modified source. Emission offsets must be effective prior to start-up of the new or modified source.

b) The emission offsets provided:

1) Must be of the same pollutant and further be of a type with approximately the same qualitative significance for public health and welfare as that attributed to the increase from a particular change;

2) Must, in the case of a fuel combustion source, be based on the type of fuel being burned at the time the permit application is filed, and, if offset is to be produced by a future switch to a cleaner fuel, be accompanied by evidence that long-term supplies of the clean fuel are available and a commitment to a specified alternative control measure which would achieve the same degree of emission reduction of the dirtier fuel is proposed;

3) Must, in the case of a past shutdown of a source or permanent curtailment of production or operating hours, have occurred since April 24, 1979, or the date of area is designated a nonattainment area for the pollutant, whichever is more recent, and, until the United States Environmental Protection Agency (USEPA) has approved the attainment demonstration and state trading or marketing rules for the relevant pollutant, the proposed new or modified source must be a replacement for the shutdown or curtailment;

4) Must be federally enforceable by permit; and

5) Must not have been previously relied on, as demonstrated by the Agency, in issuing any permit pursuant to 35 Ill. Adm. Code 201.142 or 201.143 or this Part, or for demonstrating attainment or reasonable further progress.

c) The baseline for determining the extent to which emission reductions are creditable as offsets shall be the actual emissions of the source from which the offset is to be obtained, to the extent they are within any applicable emissions limitations of this Chapter or the Act or any applicable standards adopted by USEPA pursuant to Section 111 and 112 of the Clean Air Act, and made applicable in Illinois pursuant to Section 9.1 of the Environmental Protection Act (Ill. Rev. Stat. 1991, ch. 111 1/2, par. 1009.1) [415 ILCS 5/9.1].

d)   The location of sources providing the emission reductions to fulfill the offset requirements of this Section:

1)   Must be achieved in the same nonattainment area as the increase being offset, except as provided as follows:

A)   An owner or operator may obtain the necessary emission reductions from another nonattainment area where such other area has an equal or higher nonattainment classification than the area in which the source is located, and

B)   The emission reductions from such other area contribute to a violation of the national ambient air quality standard in the nonattainment area in which the new or modified source is located.

2)   Must, for particulate matter, sulfur dioxide and carbon monoxide, be such that, relative to the site of the proposed new or modified source, the location of the offset, together with its effective stack height, ensures a positive net air quality benefit. This shall be demonstrated by atmospheric simulation modeling, unless the sources providing the offset are on the same premises or in the immediate vicinity of the new or modified source and the pollutants disperse from substantially the same effective stack height. In determining effective stack height, credit shall not be given for dispersion enhancement techniques. The owner or operator of a proposed new or modified source shall perform the analysis to demonstrate the acceptability of the location of an offset, if the Agency declines to make such analysis. Effective stack height means actual stack height plus plume rise. Where actual stack height exceeds good engineering practices, as determined pursuant to 40 CFR 51.100 (1987) (no future amendments or editions are included), the creditable stack height shall be used.

e)   Replacement of one volatile organic material with another of lesser reactivity does not constitute an emission reduction.

f)   Emission reductions otherwise required by the Clean Air Act (42 U.S.C. 7401 et seq.) shall not be creditable for purposes of any such offset requirement. Incidental emission reductions which are not otherwise required by the Clean Air Act shall be creditable as emission reductions for such purposes if such emissions reductions meet the requirements of this subpart.

(Source: Amended at 17 Ill. Reg. 6973, effective April 30, 1993)

NOTE

Interstate air pollution. The primary goal of state implementation plans is to limit air pollutant emissions within an air quality control area so that air quality within the area complies with the NAAQS standards. But what about air pollution that crosses state lines? Pollutants emitted in one upwind state can travel hundreds of miles, affecting air quality in downwind states. On a given day in southeastern Pennsylvania, for example, more than half of the air pollution may come from sources outside of Pennsylvania. To address interstate air pollution, Congress included a Good Neighbor Provision in Clean Air Act section 110. Clean Air Act section 110(a)(2)(D)(i) requires state implementation plans "to prohibit * * * any source or other type of emissions activity within the State from emitting any air pollutant in amounts which will * * * contribute significantly to nonattainment in, or interfere with maintenance by, any other State with respect to any national primary or secondary ambient air quality standard." 42 U.S.C. § 7410(a)(2)(D)(i).

One of the key issues in implementing the Good Neighbor Provision has been determining what constitutes a significant contribution to nonattainment that violates the Provision. Any particular downwind state's pollution may be caused by sources within the state and sources in multiple upwind states, and the Good Neighbor Provision does not specify how EPA is to allocate the necessary reductions in emissions. Between 1998 and 2011, EPA three times issued regulations implementing the Good Neighbor Provision. Controversially, all three regulations to some extent used the cost of achieving emissions reductions as a factor in identifying when an upwind state's contribution to pollution in a downwind state was significant within the meaning of the Good Neighbor Provision. The Supreme Court upheld EPA's 2011 rule, known as the Cross-State Air Pollution Rule, holding that the Rule reasonably used costs as a basis for setting emissions limitations. *EPA v. EME Homer City Generation, LP*, 134 S. Ct. 1584 (2014).

VI. NEW SOURCE REVIEW

Two regulatory programs within the Clean Air Act address new stationary sources specifically. First, New Source Review (NSR) requires *new major sources* of emissions to obtain permits before they start construction. Second, New Source Performance Standards, codified in EPA regulations, set forth regulatory requirements that pertain to categories of new sources. This section will address New Source Review; the next section will address New Source Performance Standards.

The New Source Review program regulates differently depending on whether a new source is located in a nonattainment area or in an area that is in attainment and therefore subject to the Prevention of Significant Deterioration program (PSD). As you would expect, new sources in nonattainment areas, where air quality is worse, are regulated more stringently than new sources in other areas with better air quality. Before addressing the differences between Nonattainment New Source Review and PSD New Source Review, we will examine some aspects that are common to both:

> The Clean Air Act imposes more stringent regulatory requirements on new sources of air pollution than it does on existing sources. This differential treatment, common to many regulatory programs and sometimes referred to as *new source bias*, reflects the fact that new sources can more readily take advantage of technological innovations and equipment that reduces emissions. Because of these advantages, it is both less costly and seems fairer to regulate new sources more strictly than we regulate existing sources. But regulating new sources more stringently than existing sources creates disincentives for companies to replace aging and inefficient facilities, hampering efforts to reduce emissions.

- *New Sources.* New Source Review applies only to new or modified sources. A source must obtain its permit prior to commencing construction. Not every change to a source constitutes a modification that triggers New Source Review. EPA regulations govern what changes to equipment are significant enough to trigger New Source Review. The challenge for regulators is to allow relatively routine maintenance and upgrades without burdening sources with permitting requirements, while also not allowing owners to modify their sources in ways that will substantially increase emissions without obtaining a new permit.

- *Pollutants.* New Source Review applies only to sources that emit "air pollutants." 42 U.S.C. §§ 7479(1), 7602(j). EPA regulations interpret the term *air pollutant* in this context to mean an air pollutant regulated under a Clean Air Act program other than the hazardous air pollutant program. 40 C.F.R. § 52.21(b)(50).

- *Major Source.* New Source Review applies only to major sources. Whether a source is categorized as major depends on its potential pollutant emissions—that is, its emissions if it were operated 24 hours per day, 365 days per year. As explained below, the threshold amounts for what qualifies a source as *major* differ between nonattainment areas and

PSD areas. In addition, a source often emits several different pollutants in varying amounts. Thus, a source may emit some pollutants in quantities that exceed the threshold for a major source and other pollutants in quantities below the threshold. When a source exceeds the threshold for any pollutant, it is considered major—and therefore subject to New Source Review—for all the regulated pollutants it emits. This principle is known as "Major for One, Major for All."

A. PREVENTION OF SIGNIFICANT DETERIORATION NEW SOURCE REVIEW

1. DEFINITION OF MAJOR EMITTING FACILITY

PSD New Source Review requires any new or modified "major emitting facility" in an area that is in attainment or unclassifiable with the NAAQS to obtain a permit prior to commencing construction. 42 U.S.C. § 7475(a). A major emitting facility is one that emits, or has the potential to emit, either 100 tons per year or 250 tons per year, depending on the type of source, of a pollutant for which the area is in nonattainment. *Id.* § 7479(1). The 100 tons-per-year threshold applies to 28 specific categories of large industrial sources; the 250 tons-per-year threshold applies to all other sources. *Id.* § 7479(1).

2. REQUIREMENTS

The Clean Air Act imposes several requirements on sources subject to PSD New Source Review. 42 U.S.C. § 7475. The most significant of these requirements are installation of Best Available Control Technology and air quality analysis.

- Sources subject to PSD New Source Review are subject to emissions limitations that reflect the *Best Available Control Technology (BACT)*. 42 U.S.C. § 7475(a)(4). To determine the appropriate BACT for a source, the permitting authority (usually a state environmental agency) determines the most stringent emission control option that is technically feasible (defined as commercially available and applicable to the source) and that is not ruled out on the basis of adverse energy, environmental, and economic impacts. EPA maintains a database of emissions limitations for permitted sources, known as the RACT/BACT/LAER Clearinghouse, which allows states to access information about what has been required in prior air permits for similar sources.

- Sources also must undergo an *air quality analysis*. The
  purpose of the air quality analysis is to determine whether
  the new pollutant emissions from the source will cause or
  contribute to a violation of a NAAQS or a *PSD increment*. A
  NAAQS, as you recall, is the maximum allowable
  concentration of a pollutant in the ambient air. PSD
  increments establish maximum annual increases in air
  pollutant concentrations, with the goal of keeping air
  quality even cleaner than the minimum of what is required
  by the NAAQS.

B. NONATTAINMENT NEW SOURCE REVIEW

1. DEFINITION OF MAJOR STATIONARY SOURCE

Nonattainment New Source Review requires any "new or modified
major stationary sources" in a nonattainment area to obtain a permit
prior to construction. 42 U.S.C. § 7502(c)(5). A major stationary source is
one that "emits, or has the potential to emit, one hundred tons per year
of any air pollutant." *Id.* § 7602(j).

2. REQUIREMENTS

The Clean Air Act requires several elements for nonattainment New
Source Review. 42 U.S.C. § 7503. Two of these elements stand out as
particularly significant:

- New sources in nonattainment areas must comply with
  emissions limitations based on a control technology known
  as the *lowest achievable emission rate* (LAER). 42 U.S.C.
  § 7503(a)(2). The lowest achievable emission rate is defined
  as the most stringent emission limitation that applies to a
  comparable source. *Id.* § 7501(3). In determining LAER for
  a particular source, the cost of a control technology is
  considered only to the extent that the cost is so great that a
  major new source could not be constructed or operated,
  rendering the control technology not achievable in practice.

- As examined earlier in this chapter in the Chicago factory
  problem, new sources in nonattainment areas also must
  obtain *emission offsets* from existing sources in the area. 42
  U.S.C. § 7503(a)(1). In addition, Clean Air Act section 182
  establishes higher offset ratios for moderate, serious, and
  severe ozone nonattainment areas. *Id.* § 7511a(a)(4), (b)(5),
  (c)(10), (d)(2), (e)(1).

PROBLEM: FIRE MOUNTAIN POWER PLANT, PART I

Coal-fired power plants burn coal to create steam to generate electricity. Most coal-fired power plants use a pulverized coal process in which coal is ground into fine particles to increase the coal's surface area and allow it to combust more efficiently. Power plants combust the pulverized coal in a furnace, the heat from the combustion creates steam, the steam drives the blades of a turbine, and the rapidly rotating turbine blades generate electricity. Coal combustion emits several different air pollutants, including nitrogen oxides (NO_x), sulfur dioxide (SO_2), and particulate matter (PM), all of which are criteria air pollutants regulated under the Clean Air Act.

Mountain Energy is planning to build a new 1000-megawatt coal-fired power plant near the rural community of Fire Mountain, Idaho. The Fire Mountain area is in attainment of the NAAQS for all six criteria air pollutants. Mountain Energy plans to install two 500-megawatt turbine generators at the Fire Mountain plant. Each turbine would burn 250 tons of coal per-hour using a pulverized coal process. The plant would emit significant amounts of several criteria air pollutants, including 10,000 tons per year of SO_2 and 6,000 tons per year of NO_x.

To construct and operate the Fire Mountain plant, Mountain Energy must obtain a preconstruction permit from the Idaho Department of Environmental Quality (DEQ). As part of its permitting process, Idaho DEQ will have to determine the BACT for the Fire Mountain plant and then set emissions limitations for the plant based on that control technology.

A nonprofit organization, Clean Air Idaho (CAI), opposes the construction of the Fire Mountain plant, based on the proposed plant's air pollutant emissions. CAI has indicated it will argue that, if Idaho DEQ allows Mountain Energy to construct and operate the Fire Mountain plan, Mountain Energy should at least be required to use an integrated gasification combined cycle (IGCC) process instead of the planned pulverized coal process.

IGCC, an alternative to a pulverized coal design for a coal-fired power plant, involves heating and partially oxidizing coal to create synthesis gas, which is cooled, cleaned, and combusted in a gas turbine. Exhaust from the gas turbine is used to produce steam that powers a steam turbine. Both the gas turbine and the steam turbine produce power used to generate electricity. Because an IGCC system removes most pollutants from the syngas prior to combustion, it emits lower levels of pollutants than pulverized coal technologies. But IGCC systems also cost more and have not been not broadly utilized.

Mountain Energy is wary of investing in IGCC technology, which it regards as expensive and unproven. If Idaho DEQ requires Mountain Energy to incorporate IGCC into the design of the Fire Mountain plant, Mountain Energy may decide to abandon its plans for the plant altogether. As outside environmental counsel for Mountain Energy, you have been asked to explain and evaluate CAI's argument regarding IGCC technology at the proposed Fire Mountain plant.

The statutory requirements for preconstruction permits in PSD areas are set forth in Clean Air Act section 165, with some additional definitions in Clean Air Act section 169. To what types of sources do these provisions apply? Would the provisions apply to the Fire Mountain plant? If so, which statutory requirements are most relevant to the applicability of IGCC technology to the Fire Mountain plant?

CAA § 165, 42 U.S.C. § 7475.
Preconstruction requirements

(a) Major emitting facilities on which construction is commenced

No major emitting facility on which construction is commenced after August 7, 1977, may be constructed in any area to which this part applies unless—

(1) a permit has been issued for such proposed facility in accordance with this part setting forth emission limitations for such facility which conform to the requirements of this part;

(2) the proposed permit has been subject to a review in accordance with this section, the required analysis has been conducted in accordance with regulations promulgated by the Administrator, and a public hearing has been held with opportunity for interested persons including representatives of the Administrator to appear and submit written or oral presentations on the air quality impact of such source, alternatives thereto, control technology requirements, and other appropriate considerations;

(3) the owner or operator of such facility demonstrates, as required pursuant to section 7410(j) of this title, that emissions from construction or operation of such facility will not cause, or contribute to, air pollution in excess of any (A) maximum allowable increase or maximum allowable concentration for any pollutant in any area to which this part applies more than one time per year, (B) national ambient air quality standard in any air quality control region, or (C) any other applicable emission standard or standard of performance under this chapter;

(4) the proposed facility is subject to the best available control technology for each pollutant subject to regulation under this chapter emitted from, or which results from, such facility;

(5) the provisions of subsection (d) of this section with respect to protection of class I areas have been complied with for such facility;

(6)   there has been an analysis of any air quality impacts projected for the area as a result of growth associated with such facility;

(7)   the person who owns or operates, or proposes to own or operate, a major emitting facility for which a permit is required under this part agrees to conduct such monitoring as may be necessary to determine the effect which emissions from any such facility may have, or is having, on air quality in any area which may be affected by emissions from such source; and

(8)   in the case of a source which proposes to construct in a class III area, emissions from which would cause or contribute to exceeding the maximum allowable increments applicable in a class II area and where no standard under section 7411 of this title has been promulgated subsequent to August 7, 1977, for such source category, the Administrator has approved the determination of best available technology as set forth in the permit. * * *

CAA § 169, 42 U.S.C. § 7479. Definitions

For purposes of this part—

(1)   The term "major emitting facility" means any of the following stationary sources of air pollutants which emit, or have the potential to emit, one hundred tons per year or more of any air pollutant from the following types of stationary sources: fossil-fuel fired steam electric plants of more than two hundred and fifty million British thermal units per hour heat input, coal cleaning plants (thermal dryers), kraft pulp mills, Portland Cement plants, primary zinc smelters, iron and steel mill plants, primary aluminum ore reduction plants, primary copper smelters, municipal incinerators capable of charging more than fifty tons of refuse per day, hydrofluoric, sulfuric, and nitric acid plants, petroleum refineries, lime plants, phosphate rock processing plants, coke oven batteries, sulfur recovery plants, carbon black plants (furnace process), primary lead smelters, fuel conversion plants, sintering plants, secondary metal production facilities, chemical process plants, fossil-fuel boilers of more than two hundred and fifty million British thermal units per hour heat input, petroleum storage and transfer facilities with a capacity exceeding three hundred thousand barrels, taconite ore processing facilities, glass fiber processing plants, charcoal production facilities. Such term also includes any other source with the potential to emit two hundred and fifty tons per year or more of any air pollutant. This term shall not include new or modified facilities which are nonprofit health or education institutions which have been exempted by the State. * * *

(3) The term "best available control technology" means an emission limitation based on the maximum degree of reduction of each pollutant subject to regulation under this chapter emitted from or which results from any major emitting facility, which the permitting authority, on a case-by-case basis, taking into account energy, environmental, and economic impacts and other costs, determines is achievable for such facility through application of production processes and available methods, systems, and techniques, including fuel cleaning, clean fuels, or treatment or innovative fuel combustion techniques for control of each such pollutant. In no event shall application of "best available control technology" result in emissions of any pollutants which will exceed the emissions allowed by any applicable standard established pursuant to section 7411 or 7412 of this title. Emissions from any source utilizing clean fuels, or any other means, to comply with this paragraph shall not be allowed to increase above levels that would have been required under this paragraph as it existed prior to November 15, 1990. * * *

Given the importance of the determination of what constitutes BACT for a source, you might expect that EPA's method for determining BACT is codified in the agency's regulations. It is not. Instead, the agency's foundational description of its BACT methodology is contained in a draft document from 1990. Despite this somewhat questionable provenance, the 1990 Draft Workshop Manual is widely used throughout the agency and routinely cited as authoritative by judicial and administrative courts. Which provisions of the guidance document are most relevant to the question whether IGCC is BACT for the Fire Mountain plant?

New Source Review Workshop Manual (Draft)
EPA (Oct. 1990)

CHAPTER B: BEST AVAILABLE CONTROL TECHNOLOGY

I.   INTRODUCTION

During each BACT analysis, which is done on a case-by-case basis, the reviewing authority evaluates the energy, environmental, economic and other costs associated with each alternative technology, and the benefit of reduced emissions that the technology would bring. The reviewing authority then specifies an emissions limitation for the source that reflects the maximum degree of reduction achievable for each pollutant regulated under the Act. In no event can a technology be recommended which would not meet any applicable standard of performance under 40

CFR Parts 60 (New Source Performance Standards) and 61 (National Emission Standards for Hazardous Air Pollutants).

In addition, if the reviewing authority determines that there is no economically reasonable or technologically feasible way to accurately measure the emissions, and hence to impose an enforceable emissions standard, it may require the source to use design, alternative equipment, work practices or operational standards to reduce emissions of the pollutant to the maximum extent.

On December 1, 1987, the EPA Assistant Administrator for Air and Radiation issued a memorandum that implemented certain program initiatives designed to improve the effectiveness of the NSR programs within the confines of existing regulations and state implementation plans. Among these was the "top-down" method for determining best available control technology (BACT).

In brief, the top-down process provides that all available control technologies be ranked in descending order of control effectiveness. The PSD applicant first examines the most stringent—or "top"—alternative. That alternative is established as BACT unless the applicant demonstrates, and the permitting authority in its informed judgment agrees, that technical considerations, or energy, environmental, or economic impacts justify a conclusion that the most stringent technology is not "achievable" in that case. If the most stringent technology is eliminated in this fashion, then the next most stringent alternative is considered, and so on.

The purpose of this chapter is to provide a detailed description of the top-down method in order to assist permitting authorities and PSD applicants in conducting BACT analyses. * * *

II.   BACT APPLICABILITY

The BACT requirement applies to each individual new or modified affected emissions unit and pollutant emitting activity at which a net emissions increase would occur. Individual BACT determinations are performed for each pollutant subject to a PSD review emitted from the same emission unit. Consequently, the BACT determination must separately address, for each regulated pollutant with a significant emissions increase at the source, air pollution controls for each emissions unit or pollutant emitting activity subject to review.

III. A STEP BY STEP SUMMARY OF THE TOP-DOWN PROCESS

* * *

III.A.   STEP 1—IDENTIFY ALL CONTROL TECHNOLOGIES

The first step in a "top-down" analysis is to identify, for the emissions unit in question (the term "emissions unit" should be read to mean emissions unit, process or activity), all "available" control options. Available control options are those air pollution control technologies or techniques with a practical potential for application to the emissions unit and the regulated pollutant under evaluation. Air pollution control technologies and techniques include the application of production process or available methods, systems, and techniques, including fuel cleaning or treatment or innovative fuel combustion techniques for control of the affected pollutant. This includes technologies employed outside of the United States. As discussed later, in some circumstances inherently lower-polluting processes are appropriate for consideration as available control alternatives. The control alternatives should include not only existing controls for the source category in question, but also (through technology transfer) controls applied to similar source categories and gas streams, and innovative control technologies. * * *

III.B.   STEP   2—ELIMINATE   TECHNICALLY   INFEASIBLE OPTIONS

In the second step, the technical feasibility of the control options identified in step one is evaluated with respect to the source-specific (or emissions unit-specific) factors. A demonstration of technical infeasibility should be clearly documented and should show, based on physical, chemical, and engineering principles, that technical difficulties would preclude the successful use of the control option on the emissions unit under review. Technically infeasible control options are then eliminated from further consideration in the BACT analysis. * * *

III.C.   STEP 3—RANK REMAINING CONTROL TECHNOLOGIES BY CONTROL EFFECTIVENESS

In step 3, all remaining control alternatives not eliminated in step 2 are ranked and then listed in order of overall control effectiveness for the pollutant under review, with the most effective control alternative at the top. A list should be prepared for each pollutant and for each emissions unit (or grouping of similar units) subject to a BACT analysis. The list should present the array of control technology alternatives and should include the following types of information:

!   control efficiencies (percent pollutant removed);

!   expected emission rate (tons per year, pounds per hour);

!   expected emissions reduction (tons per year);

!   economic impacts (cost effectiveness);

!   environmental impacts (includes any significant or unusual other media impacts (e.g., water or solid waste), and, at a minimum, the impact of each control alternative on emissions of toxic or hazardous air contaminants);

!   energy impacts.

However, an applicant proposing the top control alternative need not provide cost and other detailed information in regard to other control options. In such cases the applicant should document that the control option chosen is, indeed, the top, and review for collateral environmental impacts.

III.D.   STEP 4—EVALUATE MOST EFFECTIVE CONTROLS AND DOCUMENT RESULTS

After the identification of available and technically feasible control technology options, the energy, environmental, and economic impacts are considered to arrive at the final level of control. At this point the analysis presents the associated impacts of the control option in the listing. For each option the applicant is responsible for presenting an objective evaluation of each impact. Both beneficial and adverse impacts should be discussed and, where possible, quantified. In general, the BACT analysis should focus on the direct impact of the control alternative.

If the applicant accepts the top alternative in the listing as BACT, the applicant proceeds to consider whether impacts of unregulated air pollutants or impacts in other media would justify selection of an alternative control option. If there are no outstanding issues regarding collateral environmental impacts, the analysis is ended and the results proposed as BACT. In the event that the top candidate is shown to be inappropriate, due to energy, environmental, or economic impacts, the rationale for this finding should be documented for the public record. Then the next most stringent alternative in the listing becomes the new control candidate and is similarly evaluated. This process continues until the technology under consideration cannot be eliminated by any source-specific environmental, energy, or economic impacts which demonstrate that alternative to be inappropriate as BACT.

III.E.   STEP 5—SELECT BACT

The most effective control option not eliminated in step 4 is proposed as BACT for the pollutant and emission unit under review. * * *

IV. TOP-DOWN ANALYSIS DETAILED PROCEDURE

IV.A.   IDENTIFY   ALTERNATIVE   EMISSION   CONTROL TECHNIQUES (STEP 1)

The objective in step 1 is to identify all control options with potential application to the source and pollutant under evaluation. Later, one or more of these options may be eliminated from consideration because they are determined to be technically infeasible or to have unacceptable energy, environmental or economic impacts.

Each new or modified emission unit (or logical grouping of new or modified emission units) subject to PSD is required to undergo BACT review. BACT decisions should be made on the information presented in the BACT analysis, including the degree to which effective control alternatives were identified and evaluated. Potentially applicable control alternatives can be categorized in three ways.

!   Inherently Lower-Emitting Processes/Practices, including the use of materials and production processes and work practices that prevent emissions and resulting lower "production-specific" emissions; and

!   Add-on Controls, such as scrubbers, fabric filters, thermal oxidizers and other devices that control and reduce emissions after they are produced.

!   Combinations of Inherently Lower Emitting Processes and Add-on Controls. For example, the application of combustion and post-combustion controls to reduce NO_x emissions at a gas-fired turbine. * * *

Historically, EPA has not considered the BACT requirement as a means to redefine the design of the source when considering available control alternatives. For example, applicants proposing to construct a coal-fired electric generator, have not been required by EPA as part of a BACT analysis to consider building a natural gas-fired electric turbine although the turbine may be inherently less polluting per unit product (in this case electricity). However, this is an aspect of the PSD permitting process in which states have the discretion to engage in a broader analysis if they so desire. Thus, a gas turbine normally would not be included in the list of control alternatives for a coal-fired boiler. However, there may be instances where, in the permit authority's judgment, the consideration of alternative production processes is warranted and appropriate for consideration in the BACT analysis. A production process is defined in terms of its physical and chemical unit operations used to produce the desired product from a specified set of raw materials. In such cases, the permit agency may require the applicant to include the inherently lower-polluting process in the list of BACT candidates. * * *

The 1990 Draft New Source Review Manual contrasts available control alternatives, which must be considered in determining BACT for a source, with alternative designs or processes that would redefine the source and need not be considered. But how exactly should an agency or court differentiate between available control alternatives and alternatives that would redefine the source? If a permit applicant such as Mountain Energy can limit the BACT determination based on how it defines the parameters of the source in its application—for example, specifying that the power plant will use a pulverized coal process—then this could exclude alternatives that may be readily available and cleaner. But if the source is defined too broadly—for example, providing 1000 MW of generation capacity—then the permitting agency can completely redefine the applicant's plan, perhaps determining that BACT would be to install solar or wind generation. Hence EPA's concern about allowing the alternatives analysis to redefine the source. The following case grapples with the question of how far an agency must go in pursuing alternatives through its BACT analysis.

Sierra Club v. EPA

499 F.3d 653 (7th Cir. 2007)

■ POSNER, CIRCUIT JUDGE.

The federal Environmental Protection Agency (actually, Illinois's counterpart to the EPA, exercising authority that the federal EPA had delegated to it, but we can ignore that detail) issued a permit to Prairie State Generating Company to build a 1,500-megawatt coal-fired electrical generating plant in southern Illinois, near St. Louis. Environmentalists asked the EPA's Environmental Appeals Board to reverse the issuance of the permit, and, the Board having refused, *In re Prairie State Generating Co.*, No. 05–05 (EAB Aug. 24, 2006), they renew the quarrel in this court. They claim that the EPA violated two provisions of the Clean Air Act. One requires as a condition of receiving a permit that a plant or other source of air pollution be designed to have the "best available control technology" for minimizing pollution emitted by the plant. 42 U.S.C. § 7475(a)(4). The other attaches the further condition that the plant's emissions not exceed the limits imposed by the Act's national ambient air quality standards. § 7475(a)(3). The petitioners' first claim relates to the sulfur dioxide that will be produced as a byproduct of the production of electricity by Prairie State's plant, the second to the ozone that it will produce.

The plant is to be what is called a "mine-mouth" plant because it has been sited at the location of a coal seam. The seam is believed to contain 240 million tons of recoverable coal—enough to supply the plant's fuel needs for 30 years. The siting of the plant will enable the coal to be brought by a conveyor belt, more than half a mile long, from the mine to the plant. Unfortunately, this coal has a high sulfur content. To burn low-sulfur coal Prairie State would have to arrange for it to be transported from mines more than a thousand miles away and would have to make changes in the design of the plant—specifically, the design of the plant's facilities for receiving coal. The petitioners argue that the EPA must decide whether hauling low-sulfur coal from afar would be the best available means of controlling air pollution from the plant.

The Clean Air Act defines "best available control technology" as the "emission limitation" achievable by "application of production processes and available methods, systems, and techniques, including fuel cleaning, clean fuels, or treatment of innovative fuel combustion techniques." 42 U.S.C. § 7479(3). A "proposed facility" that would if built be a "major emitting facility," as the proposed Prairie State plant would be, must have "the best available control technology for each pollutant subject to regulation," § 7475(4), including sulfur dioxide. The EPA's position is that "best available control technology" does not include redesigning the plant proposed by the permit applicant ("traditionally, EPA does not require a . . . [permit] applicant to change the fundamental scope of its project," *In re Old Dominion Electric Cooperative,* 3 E.A.D. 779, 793 n.38 (EPA Adm'r 1992); Environmental Protection Agency, "New Source Review Workshop Manual: Prevention of Significant Deterioration and Nonattainment Permitting" B.13 (Draft, Oct. 1990)), unless the applicant intentionally designs the plant in a way calculated to make measures for limiting the emission of pollutants ineffectual. *In re Prairie State Generating Co., supra,* slip op. at 30, 33–34. But that is not contended in this case. Another provision of the Act, distinct from the one requiring adoption of the best available control technology, directs the EPA to consider "alternatives" suggested by interested persons (such as the Sierra Club) to a proposed facility. 42 U.S.C. § 7475(a)(2); see, e.g., *In re NE Hub Partners, L.P.,* 7 E.A.D. 561, 583 (EAB 1998). But that provision has not been invoked by the petitioners. Only compliance with the "BACT" (best available control technology) requirement is in issue.

The Act is explicit that "clean fuels" is one of the control methods that the EPA has to consider. Well, nuclear fuel is clean, and so the implication, one might think, is that the agency could order Prairie State to redesign its plant as a nuclear plant rather than a coal-fired one, or could order it to explore the possibility of damming the Mississippi to generate hydroelectric power, or to replace coal-fired boilers with wind turbines. That approach would invite a litigation strategy that would make seeking a permit for a new power plant a Sisyphean labor, for there would always be one more option to consider. The petitioners to their credit shy away from embracing the extreme implications of such a strategy, which would stretch the term "control technology" beyond the breaking point and collide with the "alternatives" provision of the statute. But they do not suggest another stopping point.

Now it is true that a difference between this case and our nuclear hypothetical is that a plant designed to burn coal cannot run on nuclear fuel without being redesigned from the ground up, whereas Prairie State's proposed plant could burn coal transported to the plant from afar.

But to convert the design from that of a mine-mouth plant to one that burned coal obtained from a distance would require that the plant undergo significant modifications—concretely, the half-mile-long conveyor belt, and its interface with the mine and the plant, would be superfluous and instead there would have to be a rail spur and facilities for unloading coal from rail cars and feeding it into the plant.

So it is no surprise that the EPA, consistent with our nuclear hypothetical and the petitioners' concession regarding it, distinguishes between "control technology" as a means of reducing emissions from a power plant or other source of pollution and redesigning the "proposed facility" (the plant or other source)—changing its "fundamental scope." The agency consigns the latter possibility to the "alternatives" section of the Clean Air Act, which as we said is not involved in this case. Refining the statutory definition of "control technology"—"production processes and available methods, systems, and techniques, including fuel cleaning, clean fuels, or treatment of innovative fuel combustion techniques"—to exclude redesign is the kind of judgment by an administrative agency to which a reviewing court should defer. *Environmental Defense v. Duke Energy Corp.,* ___ U.S. ___, 127 S. Ct. 1423, 1434 (2007); *New York v. EPA,* 413 F.3d 3, 19–20 (D.C. Cir. 2005); *Alabama Power Co. v. Costle,* 636 F.2d 323, 397–98 (D.C. Cir. 1979).

But this opens the further and crucial question where control technology ends and a redesign of the "proposed facility" begins. As it is not obvious where to draw that line either, it makes sense to let the EPA, the author of the underlying distinction, draw it, within reason.

Suppose this were not to be a mine-mouth plant but Prairie State had a contract to buy high-sulfur coal from a remote mine yet could burn low-sulfur coal as the fuel source instead. Some adjustment in the design of the plant would be necessary in order to change the fuel source from high-sulfur to low-sulfur coal, but if it were no more than would be necessary whenever a plant switched from a dirtier to a cleaner fuel the change would be the adoption of a "control technology." Otherwise "clean fuels" would be read out of the definition of such technology. At the other end of the spectrum is our nuclear hypothetical. The plant proposed in this case falls between that hypothetical example and the example of a plant that has alternative off-site sources of high- and low-sulfur coal respectively.

We hesitate in a borderline case, such as this, to pronounce the EPA's decision arbitrary, the applicable standard for judicial review of its granting the permit. *Alaska Department of Environmental Conservation v. EPA,* 540 U.S. 461, 496–97 (2004). The decision required an expert judgment. The petitioners' brief, though long, contains nothing about mine-mouth power stations. The petitioners pitch their case on the naked proposition that if a plant is capable—with redesign—of burning a clean fuel, it must undergo a "best available control technology" analysis. But they flinch by carving an exception for the nuclear case without explaining the principle that distinguishes it from this case. Of course there is a distinction, but it is one of degree and the treatment of differences of degree in a technically complex field with limited statutory guidance is entrusted to the judgment of the agency that administers the regulatory scheme rather than to courts of generalist judges. *Chevron U.S.A. Inc. v. Natural Resources Defense Council, Inc.*, 467 U.S. 837, 842–43 (1984); *Sierra Club v. EPA*, 375 F.3d 537 (7th Cir. 2004).

What must give us pause, however, is the scantiness of the Environmental Appeals Board's discussion of the difference between, on the one hand, adopting a control technology, and, on the other hand, redesigning the proposed plant, in the specific setting of this case. Here are the critical passages: " 'With respect to alternate sources of coal, e.g., low-sulfur western coal from Wyoming or Montana, the proposed plant is being designed and developed to burn high-sulfur Illinois coal, the locally available coal. It would be inconsistent with the scope of the project to use coal from other regions of the country. Rather, the BACT [best available control technology] determination addresses the appropriate control technology for SO₂ [sulfur dioxide] emissions associated with use of this coal at the proposed plant. . . . The project that must be addressed when evaluating BACT is the project for which an application has been submitted, i.e., a proposed mine-mouth power plant. The source of coal for which the plant would be developed is a specific reserve of 240 million tons of recoverable coal, which would meet the needs of the proposed plant for more than 30 years. Accordingly, the use of a particular coal supply is an inherent aspect of the proposed project. To require an evaluation of an alternative coal supply . . . would constitute a fundamental change to the project.' " *In re Prairie State Generating Co., supra,* slip op. at 20–21. Alternative coal supplies would be " 'beyond the scope of the project, a power plant fueled from coal delivered by a conveyor belt from an adjacent dedicated mine.' " *Id.* at 23. " 'The development of a mine-mouth power plant is an intrinsic aspect of the proposed plant, which would be developed to use a specific reserve of fuel, which is adequate for the expected life of the plant.' . . . [C]onsideration of low-sulfur coal, *because it necessarily involves a fuel source other than the co-located mine,* would require Prairie State to redefine the fundamental purpose or basic design of its proposed Facility." *Id.* at 31, 36 (emphasis added).

These passages might be read as merging two separate issues: the difference between low-sulfur (clean) and high-sulfur (dirty) coal as a fuel source for a power plant, and the difference between a plant co-located with a coal mine and a plant that obtains its coal from afar. The former is a difference in control technology, the latter a difference in design (or so the EPA can conclude). We think it is sufficiently clear from the passages that we have quoted from the Environmental Appeals Board's opinion, and especially from the clause that we italicized, that the Board did not confuse the two issues; that it granted the permit not because it thinks that *burning* low-sulfur coal would require the redesign of Prairie State's plant (it would not), but because *receiving* coal from a distant mine would require Prairie State to reconfigure the plant as one that is not co-located with a mine, and this reconfiguration would constitute a redesign.

So the Board's ruling on the BACT issue must be upheld * * *

Based on the reasoning of the *Prairie State* case, should IGCC for the Fire Mountain plant be considered an available alternative, or can it be excluded on the ground that it would redefine the source? If IGCC is a potentially available alternative for the Fire Mountain plant, does Mountain Energy have to concede that it constitutes BACT for the plant? What other arguments might Mountain Energy have for excluding IGCC from consideration as BACT?

VII. NEW SOURCE PERFORMANCE STANDARDS

In addition to the New Source Review (NSR) permitting process, new stationary sources of air pollutant emissions must comply with New Source Performance Standards (NSPS). Clean Air Act section 111 establishes the NSPS program. 42 U.S.C. § 7411. For purposes of NSPS, a "new source" is any source built or modified after EPA proposes the standard applicable to that type of source. *Id.* § 7411(a)(2). Unlike the source-specific permitting process under New Source Review, which results in a set of permit conditions tailored to the specific source, NSPS are sets of regulations issued by EPA that apply uniformly to an entire category of sources. As a program, NSPS does not restrict its application to major sources, but specific NSPS regulations often limit their application to certain size sources. NSPS emissions limits must reflect the "best system of emission reduction * * * adequately demonstrated." *Id.* § 7411(a)(1). Also unlike New Source Review, NSPS do not differ based on whether a source is located in a PSD area or in a nonattainment area.

PROBLEM: FIRE MOUNTAIN POWER PLANT, PART II

This problem incorporates the facts from the preceding Fire Mountain Power Plant problem in this chapter. For this problem, assume that Mountain Energy is pursuing plans to construct its new 1000-megawatt coal-fired Fire Mountain Power Plant, utilizing a pulverized coal process. Mountain Energy plans to install two 500-megawatt turbine generators at the Fire Mountain plant. Each turbine would burn 250 tons of coal per-hour. The Fire Mountain Plant will emit several different air pollutants, including nitrogen oxides (NO_x), sulfur dioxide (SO_2), and particulate matter (PM).

As outside environmental counsel for Mountain Energy, you have been asked to determine what emissions standards under the NSPS program will apply to the Fire Mountain plant.

The statutory requirements for New Source Performance Standards are set forth in Clean Air Act section 111.

CAA § 111, 42 U.S.C. § 7411. Standards of performance for new stationary sources

(a) Definitions

For purposes of this section:

(1) The term "standard of performance" means a standard for emissions of air pollutants which reflects the degree of emission limitation achievable through the application of the best system of emission reduction which (taking into account the cost of achieving such reduction and any nonair quality health and environmental impact and energy requirements) the Administrator determines has been adequately demonstrated.

(2) The term "new source" means any stationary source, the construction or modification of which is commenced after the publication of regulations (or, if earlier, proposed regulations) prescribing a standard of performance under this section which will be applicable to such source.

(3) The term "stationary source" means any building, structure, facility, or installation which emits or may emit any air pollutant. Nothing in subchapter II of this chapter relating to nonroad engines shall be construed to apply to stationary internal combustion engines.

(4) The term "modification" means any physical change in, or change in the method of operation of, a stationary source which increases the amount of any air pollutant emitted by such source or which results in the emission of any air pollutant not previously emitted. * * *

(b) List of categories of stationary sources; standards of performance; information on pollution control techniques; sources owned or operated by United States; particular systems; revised standards

(1)(A) The Administrator shall, within 90 days after December 31, 1970, publish (and from time to time thereafter shall revise) a list of categories of stationary sources. He shall include a category of sources in such list if in his judgment it causes, or contributes significantly to, air pollution which may reasonably be anticipated to endanger public health or welfare.

(B) Within one year after the inclusion of a category of stationary sources in a list under subparagraph (A), the Administrator shall publish proposed regulations, establishing Federal standards of performance for new sources within such category. * * *

(2) The Administrator may distinguish among classes, types, and sizes within categories of new sources for the purpose of establishing such standards. * * *

Your research finds two sets of NSPS regulations that apply to steam generators at power plants. Which one applies to the Fire Mountain plant?

40 C.F.R. Subpart D. Standards of Performance for Fossil-Fuel-Fired Steam Generators

§ 60.40.   Applicability and designation of affected facility.

(a) The affected facilities to which the provisions of this subpart apply are:

(1)   Each fossil-fuel-fired steam generating unit of more than 73 megawatts (MW) heat input rate (250 million British thermal units per hour (MMBtu/hr)).

(2)   Each fossil-fuel and wood-residue-fired steam generating unit capable of firing fossil fuel at a heat input rate of more than 73 MW (250 MMBtu/hr). * * *

(e) Any facility subject to either subpart Da or KKKK of this part is not subject to this subpart.

40 C.F.R. Subpart DA. Standards of Performance for Electric Utility Steam Generating

§ 60.40Da.   Applicability and designation of affected facility.

(a) Except as specified in paragraph (e) of this section, the affected facility to which this subpart applies is each electric utility steam generating unit:

(1)   That is capable of combusting more than 73 megawatts (MW) (250 million British thermal units per hour (MMBtu/hr)) heat input of fossil fuel (either alone or in combination with any other fuel); and

(2) For which construction, modification, or reconstruction is commenced after September 18, 1978.

(b) An IGCC electric utility steam generating unit (both the stationary combustion turbine and any associated duct burners) is subject to this part and is not subject to subpart GG or KKKK of this part if both of the conditions specified in paragraphs (b)(1) and (2) of this section are met.

(1) The IGCC electric utility steam generating unit is capable of combusting more than 73 MW (250 MMBtu/h) heat input of fossil fuel (either alone or in combination with any other fuel) in the combustion turbine engine and associated heat recovery steam generator; and

(2) The IGCC electric utility steam generating unit commenced construction, modification, or reconstruction after February 28, 2005. * * *

Based on your reading of the applicability regulations, you examine the NSPS requirements for PM, SO_2, and NO_x that will apply to the Fire Mountain Plant. Like many environmental requirements, the regulations are complex. Looking at the following provisions, what specific facts about the Fire Mountain Plant will determine which emissions limits apply? Do you see why it can be to a source's great advantage to fall under one set of requirements rather than another? Regulatory requirements often differ considerably across categories of sources, with significant consequences both for the amount of pollutants emitted and the cost of limiting emissions. For this reason, environmental lawyers spend a lot of time arguing about how to categorize sources.

§ 60.42Da.   Standards for particulate matter (PM).

(a) Except as provided in paragraph (f) of this section, on and after the date on which the initial performance test is completed or required to be completed under § 60.8 [which requires a performance test within 180 days of startup], whichever date comes first, an owner or operator of an affected facility shall not cause to be discharged into the atmosphere from any affected facility for which construction, reconstruction, or modification commenced before March 1, 2005, any gases that contain PM in excess of 13 ng/J (0.03 lb/MMBtu) heat input. * * *

(c) Except as provided in paragraphs (d) and (f) of this section, on and after the date on which the initial performance test is completed or required to be completed under § 60.8, whichever date comes first, no owner or operator of an affected facility that commenced construction, reconstruction, or modification after February 28, 2005, but before

May 4, 2011, shall cause to be discharged into the atmosphere from that affected facility any gases that contain PM in excess of either:

(1)   18 ng/J (0.14 lb/MWh) gross energy output; or

(2)   6.4 ng/J (0.015 lb/MMBtu) heat input derived from the combustion of solid, liquid, or gaseous fuel. * * *

(e) Except as provided in paragraph (f) of this section [which is not relevant to this problem], the owner or operator of an affected facility that commenced construction, reconstruction, or modification commenced after May 3, 2011, shall meet the requirements specified in paragraphs (e)(1) and (2) of this section.

(1)   On and after the date on which the initial performance test is completed or required to be completed under § 60.8, whichever date comes first, the owner or operator shall not cause to be discharged into the atmosphere from that affected facility any gases that contain PM in excess of the applicable emissions limit specified in paragraphs (e)(1)(i) or (ii) of this section.

(i)   For an affected facility which commenced construction or reconstruction:

(A)   11 ng/J (0.090 lb/MWh) gross energy output; or

(B)   12 ng/J (0.097 lb/MWh) net energy output.

(ii)   For an affected facility which commenced modification, the emission limits specified in paragraphs (c) or (d) of this section.

(2)   During startup periods and shutdown periods, owners or operators of facilities subject to subpart UUUUU of part 63 of this chapter shall meet the work practice standards specified in Table 3 to subpart UUUUU of part 63 and use the relevant definitions in § 63.10042, and owners or operators of facilities subject to subpart DDDDD of part 63 shall meet the work practice standards specified in Table 3 to subpart DDDDD of part 63 and use the relevant definition used in § 63.7575. * * *

§ 60.43Da.   Standards for sulfur dioxide (SO_2).

(a) On and after the date on which the initial performance test is completed or required to be completed under § 60.8, whichever date comes first, no owner or operator subject to the provisions of this subpart shall cause to be discharged into the atmosphere from any affected facility which combusts solid fuel or solid-derived fuel and for which construction, reconstruction, or modification commenced before or on February 28, 2005, except as provided under paragraphs (c), (d), (f) or (h) of this section, any gases that contain SO_2 in excess of:

(1) 520 ng/J (1.20 lb/MMBtu) heat input and 10 percent of the potential combustion concentration (90 percent reduction);

(2) 30 percent of the potential combustion concentration (70 percent reduction), when emissions are less than 260 ng/J (0.60 lb/MMBtu) heat input;

(3) 180 ng/J (1.4 lb/MWh) gross energy output; or

(4) 65 ng/J (0.15 lb/MMBtu) heat input. * * *

(b) On and after the date on which the initial performance test is completed or required to be completed under § 60.8, whichever date comes first, no owner or operator subject to the provisions of this subpart shall cause to be discharged into the atmosphere from any affected facility which combusts liquid or gaseous fuels (except for liquid or gaseous fuels derived from solid fuels and as provided under paragraphs (e) or (h) of this section) and for which construction, reconstruction, or modification commenced before or on February 28, 2005, any gases that contain SO_2 in excess of:

(1) 340 ng/J (0.80 lb/MMBtu) heat input and 10 percent of the potential combustion concentration (90 percent reduction); or

(2) 100 percent of the potential combustion concentration (zero percent reduction) when emissions are less than 86 ng/J (0.20 lb/MMBtu) heat input.

(c) [Reserved by 77 FR 9450].

(d) Sulfur dioxide emissions are limited to 520 ng/J (1.20 lb/MMBtu) heat input from any affected facility which:

(1) Combusts 100 percent anthracite;

(2) Is classified as a resource recovery unit; or

(3) Is located in a noncontinental area and combusts solid fuel or solid-derived fuel.

(e) Sulfur dioxide emissions are limited to 340 ng/J (0.80 lb/MMBtu) heat input from any affected facility which is located in a noncontinental area and combusts liquid or gaseous fuels (excluding solid-derived fuels).

(f) The SO_2 standards under this section do not apply to an owner or operator of an affected facility that is operated under an SO_2 commercial demonstration permit issued by the Administrator in accordance with the provisions of § 60.47Da.

(g) Compliance with the emission limitation and percent reduction requirements under this section are both determined on a 30-day rolling average basis except as provided under paragraph (c) of this section. * * *

(i) Except as provided in paragraphs (j) and (k) of this section, on and after the date on which the initial performance test is completed or required to be completed under § 60.8, whichever date comes first, no owner or operator of an affected facility for which construction, reconstruction, or modification commenced after February 28, 2005, but before May 4, 2011, shall cause to be discharged into the atmosphere from that affected facility, any gases that contain SO_2 in excess of the applicable emissions limit specified in paragraphs (i)(1) through (3) of this section.

(1) For an affected facility which commenced construction, any gases that contain SO_2 in excess of either:

(i)   180 ng/J (1.4 lb/MWh) gross energy output; or

(ii)   5 percent of the potential combustion concentration (95 percent reduction).

(2) For an affected facility which commenced reconstruction, any gases that contain SO_2 in excess of either:

(i)   180 ng/J (1.4 lb/MWh) gross energy output;

(ii)   65 ng/J (0.15 lb/MMBtu) heat input; or

(iii)   5 percent of the potential combustion concentration (95 percent reduction).

(3) For an affected facility which commenced modification, any gases that contain SO_2 in excess of either:

(i)   180 ng/J (1.4 lb/MWh) gross energy output;

(ii)   65 ng/J (0.15 lb/MMBtu) heat input; or

(iii)   10 percent of the potential combustion concentration (90 percent reduction).

(j) On and after the date on which the initial performance test is completed or required to be completed under § 60.8, whichever date comes first, no owner or operator of an affected facility that commenced construction, reconstruction, or modification commenced after February 28, 2005, and that burns 75 percent or more (by heat input) coal refuse on a 12-month rolling average basis, shall caused to be discharged into the atmosphere from that affected facility any gases that contain SO_2 in excess of the applicable emission limitation specified in paragraphs (j)(1) through (3) of this section.

(1) For an affected facility for which construction commenced after February 28, 2005, any gases that contain SO_2 in excess of either:

(i)　180 ng/J (1.4 lb/MWh) gross energy output on a 30-day rolling average basis; or

(ii)　6 percent of the potential combustion concentration (94 percent reduction) on a 30-day rolling average basis.

(2)　For an affected facility for which reconstruction commenced after February 28, 2005, any gases that contain SO_2 in excess of either:

(i)　180 ng/J (1.4 lb/MWh) gross energy output on a 30-day rolling average basis;

(ii)　65 ng/J (0.15 lb/MMBtu) heat input on a 30-day rolling average basis; or

(iii)　6 percent of the potential combustion concentration (94 percent reduction) on a 30-day rolling average basis.

(3)　For an affected facility for which modification commenced after February 28, 2005, any gases that contain SO_2 in excess of either:

(i)　180 ng/J (1.4 lb/MWh) gross energy output on a 30-day rolling average basis;

(ii)　65 ng/J (0.15 lb/MMBtu) heat input on a 30-day rolling average basis; or

(iii)　10 percent of the potential combustion concentration (90 percent reduction) on a 30-day rolling average basis.

(k) On and after the date on which the initial performance test is completed or required to be completed under § 60.8, whichever date comes first, no owner or operator of an affected facility located in a noncontinental area for which construction, reconstruction, or modification commenced after February 28, 2005, but before May 4, 2011, shall cause to be discharged into the atmosphere from that affected facility any gases that contain SO_2 in excess of the applicable emissions limit specified in paragraphs (k)(1) and (2) of this section.

(1)　For an affected facility that burns solid or solid-derived fuel, the owner or operator shall not cause to be discharged into the atmosphere any gases that contain SO_2 in excess of 520 ng/J (1.2 lb/MMBtu) heat input.

(2)　For an affected facility that burns other than solid or solid-derived fuel, the owner or operator shall not cause to be discharged into the atmosphere any gases that contain SO_2 in excess of 230 ng/J (0.54 lb/MMBtu) heat input.

(l)　Except as provided in paragraphs (j) and (m) of this section, on and after the date on which the initial performance test is completed or required to be completed under § 60.8, whichever date comes first, no owner or operator of an affected facility for which construction, reconstruction, or modification commenced after May 3, 2011, shall cause to be discharged into the atmosphere from that affected facility, any gases that contain SO_2 in excess of the applicable emissions limit specified in paragraphs (l)(1) and (2) of this section.

(1) For an affected facility which commenced construction or reconstruction, any gases that contain SO_2 in excess of either:

(i)   130 ng/J (1.0 lb/MWh) gross energy output; or

(ii)   140 ng/J (1.2 lb/MWh) net energy output; or

(iii) 3 percent of the potential combustion concentration (97 percent reduction).

(2) For an affected facility which commenced modification, any gases that contain SO_2 in excess of either:

(i)   180 ng/J (1.4 lb/MWh) gross energy output; or

(ii)   10 percent of the potential combustion concentration (90 percent reduction).

(m) On and after the date on which the initial performance test is completed or required to be completed under § 60.8, whichever date comes first, no owner or operator of an affected facility located in a noncontinental area for which construction, reconstruction, or modification commenced after May 3, 2011, shall cause to be discharged into the atmosphere from that affected facility any gases that contain SO_2 in excess of the applicable emissions limit specified in paragraphs (m)(1) and (2) of this section.

(1) For an affected facility that burns solid or solid-derived fuel, the owner or operator shall not cause to be discharged into the atmosphere any gases that contain SO_2 in excess of 520 ng/J (1.2 lb/MMBtu) heat input.

(2) For an affected facility that burns other than solid or solid-derived fuel, the owner or operator shall not cause to be discharged into the atmosphere any gases that contain SO_2 in excess of 230 ng/J (0.54 lb/MMBtu) heat input.

§ 60.44Da.   **Standards for nitrogen oxides (NO$_x$).**

* * *

(d) Except as provided in paragraph (h) of this section, on and after the date on which the initial performance test is completed or required to be completed under § 60.8, whichever date comes first, no owner or operator of an affected facility that commenced construction, reconstruction, or modification after July 9, 1997, but before March 1, 2005, shall cause to be discharged into the atmosphere from that affected facility any gases that contain NO$_x$ (expressed as NO$_2$) in excess of the applicable emissions limit specified in paragraphs (d)(1) and (2) of this section as determined on a 30-boiler operating day rolling average basis.

(1) For an affected facility which commenced construction, any gases that contain NO$_x$ in excess of 200 ng/J (1.6 lb/MWh) gross energy output.

(2) For an affected facility which commenced reconstruction, any gases that contain NO$_x$ in excess of 65 ng/J (0.15 lb/MMBtu) heat input.

(e) Except as provided in paragraphs (f) and (h) of this section, on and after the date on which the initial performance test is completed or required to be completed under § 60.8, whichever date comes first, no owner or operator of an affected facility that commenced construction, reconstruction, or modification after February 28, 2005 but before May 4, 2011, shall cause to be discharged into the atmosphere from that affected facility any gases that contain NO$_x$ (expressed as NO$_2$) in excess of the applicable emissions limit specified in paragraphs (e)(1) through (3) of this section as determined on a 30-boiler operating day rolling average basis.

(1) For an affected facility which commenced construction, any gases that contain NO$_x$ in excess of 130 ng/J (1.0 lb/MWh) gross energy output.

(2) For an affected facility which commenced reconstruction, any gases that contain NO$_x$ in excess of either:

(i)   130 ng/J (1.0 lb/MWh) gross energy output; or

(ii)   47 ng/J (0.11 lb/MMBtu) heat input.

(3) For an affected facility which commenced modification, any gases that contain NO$_x$ in excess of either:

(i)   180 ng/J (1.4 lb/MWh) gross energy output; or

(ii)   65 ng/J (0.15 lb/MMBtu) heat input.

(f) On and after the date on which the initial performance test is completed or required to be completed under § 60.8, whichever date comes first, the owner or operator of an IGCC electric utility steam generating unit subject to the provisions of this subpart and for which construction, reconstruction, or modification commenced after February 28, 2005 but before May 4, 2011, shall meet the requirements specified in paragraphs (f)(1) through (3) of this section.

(1) Except as provided for in paragraphs (f)(2) and (3) of this section, the owner or operator shall not cause to be discharged into

the atmosphere any gases that contain NO_x (expressed as NO_2) in excess of 130 ng/J (1.0 lb/MWh) gross energy output.

(2)　When burning liquid fuel exclusively or in combination with solid-derived fuel such that the liquid fuel contributes 50 percent or more of the total heat input to the combined cycle combustion turbine, the owner or operator shall not cause to be discharged into the atmosphere any gases that contain NO_x (expressed as NO_2) in excess of 190 ng/J (1.5 lb/MWh) gross energy output.

(3)　In cases when during a 30-boiler operating day rolling average compliance period liquid fuel is burned in such a manner to meet the conditions in paragraph (f)(2) of this section for only a portion of the clock hours in the 30-day compliance period, the owner or operator shall not cause to be discharged into the atmosphere any gases that contain NO_x (expressed as NO_2) in excess of the computed weighted-average emissions limit based on the proportion of gross energy output (in MWh) generated during the compliance period for each of emissions limits in paragraphs (f)(1) and (2) of this section.

(g)　Except as provided in paragraphs (h) of this section and § 60.45Da, on and after the date on which the initial performance test is completed or required to be completed under § 60.8, whichever date comes first, no owner or operator of an affected facility that commenced construction, reconstruction, or modification after May 3, 2011, shall cause to be discharged into the atmosphere from that affected facility any gases that contain NO_x (expressed as NO_2) in excess of the applicable emissions limit specified in paragraphs (g)(1) through (3) of this section.

(1)　For an affected facility which commenced construction or reconstruction, any gases that contain NO_x in excess of either:

(i)　88 ng/J (0.70 lb/MWh) gross energy output; or

(ii)　95 ng/J (0.76 lb/MWh) net energy output.

(2)　For an affected facility which commenced construction or reconstruction and that burns 75 percent or more coal refuse (by heat input) on a 12-month rolling average basis, any gases that contain NO_x in excess of either:

(i)　110 ng/J (0.85 lb/MWh) gross energy output; or

(ii)　120 ng/J (0.92 lb/MWh) net energy output.

(3)　For an affected facility which commenced modification, any gases that contain NO_x in excess of 140 ng/J (1.1 lb/MWh) gross energy output. * * *

VIII. HAZARDOUS AIR POLLUTANTS

As we have seen, the Clean Air Act generally instructs EPA to regulate air pollutants that cause or contribute to air pollution that endangers public health or welfare—the standard, for example, for listing a criteria air pollutant under Clean Air Act section 108. Some air pollutants, however, are particularly dangerous; these pollutants are known or suspected to pose risks of serious health effects or adverse environmental effects. Clean Air Act section 112 creates a regulatory program for EPA to limit emissions of these hazardous air pollutants, also known as air toxics. Examples of hazardous air pollutants include formaldehyde and methylene chloride, both of which are widely used to make industrial products but also are suspected of causing cancer and other adverse health effects. Clean Air Act section 112 directs EPA to establish standards for controlling emissions of hazardous air pollutants from sources, based on emissions levels that are being achieved by the best-performing—that is, least-emitting—sources in an industry.

A. REGULATED SUBSTANCES

Clean Air Act section 112(b) addresses the listing of hazardous air pollutants. In the 1990 Clean Air Act Amendments, Congress jumpstarted the listing process by listing 189 hazardous air pollutants. 42 U.S.C. § 7412(b)(1). EPA can add to the list on its own initiative, *id.* § 7412(b)(2), and any person can petition EPA to add (or delete) a pollutant from the list. *Id.* § 7412(b)(3). Air pollutants may be listed as hazardous if they "present, or may present, through inhalation or other routes of exposure, a threat of adverse human health effects (including, but not limited to, substances which are known to be, or may reasonably be anticipated to be, carcinogenic, mutagenic, teratogenic, neurotoxic, which cause reproductive dysfunction, or which are acutely or chronically toxic) or adverse environmental effects." *Id.* § 7412(b)(2). Criteria air pollutants listed under CAA section 108 cannot be added to the list of hazardous air pollutants, although precursors to criteria air pollutants may be. *Id.* § 7412(b)(2)

B. REGULATED SOURCES

Clean Air Act section 112 directs EPA to develop emissions standards for major and "area" sources of hazardous air pollutants. 42 U.S.C. § 7412(c). A major source is one that has the potential to emit 10 tons per year or more of any hazardous air pollutant, or 25 tons per year of any combination of hazardous air pollutants. *Id.* § 7412(a)(1). All other stationary sources are area sources. *Id.* § 7412(a)(2). Clean Air Act section 112 requires EPA to regulate emissions from area sources that EPA determines "present[ ] a threat of adverse effects to human health or the environment (by such sources individually or in the aggregate) warranting regulation." *Id.* § 7412(c)(3).

C. EMISSIONS STANDARDS

Clean Air Act section 112 requires EPA to establish emissions standards for industrial categories of both new and existing major and area sources of hazardous air pollutants. 42 U.S.C. § 7412(d). These National Emissions Standards for Hazardous Air Pollutants (NESHAPs) require sources to employ the Maximum Achievable Control Technology (MACT) to limit their emissions of hazardous air pollutants.

- For new major sources—that is, sources constructed after EPA proposes the NESHAP that would apply to the source—MACT requires emissions limitations at least as stringent as the "best controlled similar source." 42 U.S.C. § 7412(d)(3).

- For existing major sources, MACT requires emissions limitations reflecting the average of the best performing 12 percent of existing sources or, for categories of fewer than 30 sources, the average of the best performing 5 sources. 42 U.S.C. § 7412(d)(3).

- For area sources, EPA may require, as an alternative to MACT, emissions limitations reflecting less stringent generally available control technologies. 42 U.S.C. § 7412(d)(5).

The hazardous air pollutant program regulates emissions only and does not establish goals for ambient air quality—i.e., the concepts of attainment and nonattainment for NAAQS have no application to hazardous air pollutants.

IX. TITLE V PERMITTING

One of the important innovations of the 1990 Clean Air Act Amendments was to add the Title V operating permit program. Title V requires sources regulated under the Clean Air Act to obtain an operating permit. This includes sources required to obtain a New Source Review permit, sources subject to New Source Performance Standards, sources subject to NESHAP standards, and sources that otherwise qualify as a "major source." 42 U.S.C. § 7661a. The general threshold for a major source is emissions of 100 tons per year of any regulated pollutant, *id.* § 7602(j), with lower thresholds that apply by EPA regulation in non-attainment areas.

The goal of Title V is to consolidate all the air pollution control requirements that apply to a source, including emissions limits and monitoring, recordkeeping, and reporting requirements, into a single, comprehensive operating permit. The consolidated operating permit simplifies compliance for sources and makes it easier for agencies and citizens to monitor and enforce requirements.

PROBLEM: TITLE V PERMITTING AND SOURCE DETERMINATION

Acme Energy Corporation owns and operates a natural gas processing plant and five compressor stations that connect to the plant via pipelines. The stations compress natural gas gathered from wells and send the gas to the plant for processing. The plant and compressor stations are in an area of West Virginia that is in attainment for nitrogen oxides (NO_x).

The compressor stations are located at various distances from the plant ranging from 0.5 miles to 12 miles. Acme owns the land on which the compressor stations and plant are located but does not own the land between them. Since the plant was first built in 1995, Acme has sent all the gas that is compressed at its stations to the company's plant. It would be possible, however, with the existing pipeline infrastructure, to send the gas to a gathering pipeline and processing plant owned by Acme's competitor or to send the gas directly from the compressor stations into interstate gas transmission lines without any processing. Until recently, the plant and compressor stations, even if counted as a single source, emitted 80 tons per year of NO_x. Recently, Acme has indicated that it plans to add a sixth compressor station, located 1 mile from the plant, and to expand the plant. The new compressor station, the original five compressor stations, and the expanded plant will emit 120 tons per years of NO_x.

You are an attorney for Clean the Air, an environmental group that advocates against air pollution. Clean the Air opposes Acme's expansion plans and is seeking to convince the West Virginia Department of Environmental Protection, which is the state air permitting agency, that the expansion would require Acme to obtain, among other things, a Title V operating permit. What legal arguments can you make to the state agency? What is the likelihood that those arguments will persuade the agency? If the agency does not require Acme to obtain a Title V permit, should Clean the Air sue to challenge the agency's decision?

Clean Air Act section 502 sets forth the key elements of the Title V permit program, including what sources are required to obtain a Title V permit. Clean Air Act section 501 defines some of the key terms in section 502.

CAA § 501, 42 U.S.C. § 7661. Definitions

As used in this subchapter—

(1) Affected source

The term "affected source" shall have the meaning given such term in subchapter IV-A of this chapter.

(2) Major source

The term "major source" means any stationary source (or any group of stationary sources located within a contiguous area and under common control) that is either of the following:

(A) A major source as defined in section 7412 of this title.

(B) A major stationary source as defined in section 7602 of this title or part D of subchapter I of this chapter. * * *

CAA § 502, 42 U.S.C. § 7661a. Permit programs

(a) Violations

After the effective date of any permit program approved or promulgated under this subchapter, it shall be unlawful for any person to violate any requirement of a permit issued under this subchapter, or to operate an affected source (as provided in subchapter IV-A of this chapter), a major source, any other source (including an area source) subject to standards or regulations under section 7411 or 7412 of this title, any other source required to have a permit under parts1 C or D of subchapter I of this chapter, or any other stationary source in a category designated (in whole or in part) by regulations promulgated by the Administrator (after notice and public comment) which shall include a finding setting forth the basis for such designation, except in compliance with a permit issued by a permitting authority under this subchapter. (Nothing in this subsection shall be construed to alter the applicable requirements of this chapter that a permit be obtained before construction or modification.) The Administrator may, in the Administrator's discretion and consistent with the applicable provisions of this chapter, promulgate regulations to exempt one or more source categories (in whole or in part) from the requirements of this subsection if the Administrator finds that compliance with such requirements is impracticable, infeasible, or unnecessarily burdensome on such categories, except that the Administrator may not exempt any major source from such requirements.

(b) Regulations

The Administrator shall promulgate within 12 months after November 15, 1990, regulations establishing the minimum elements of a permit program to be administered by any air pollution control agency. These elements shall include each of the following:

(1) Requirements for permit applications, including a standard application form and criteria for determining in a timely fashion the completeness of applications.

(2) Monitoring and reporting requirements.

(3)(A) A requirement under State or local law or interstate compact that the owner or operator of all sources subject to the requirement to obtain a permit under this subchapter pay an annual fee, or the equivalent over some other period, sufficient to cover all reasonable (direct and indirect) costs required to develop and administer the permit program requirements of this subchapter * * *.

(4) Requirements for adequate personnel and funding to administer the program.

(5) A requirement that the permitting authority have adequate authority to:

(A) issue permits and assure compliance by all sources required to have a permit under this subchapter with each applicable standard, regulation or requirement under this chapter;

(B) issue permits for a fixed term, not to exceed 5 years;

(C) assure that upon issuance or renewal permits incorporate emission limitations and other requirements in an applicable implementation plan;

(D) terminate, modify, or revoke and reissue permits for cause;

(E) enforce permits, permit fee requirements, and the requirement to obtain a permit, including authority to recover civil penalties in a maximum amount of not less than $10,000 per day for each violation, and provide appropriate criminal penalties; and

(F) assure that no permit will be issued if the Administrator objects to its issuance in a timely manner under this subchapter. * * *

Issuing a Title V permit is generally the responsibility of a state environmental agency or local air pollution control agency. In West Virginia, where Acme Energy Corporation's natural gas processing plant and compressor stations are located, the West Virginia Department of Environmental Protection has authority to issue Title V permits. West

Virginia regulations set forth the requirements for obtaining a Title V permit from the Department of Environmental Protection:

West Virginia Code of State Rules § 45–30.
Requirements for Operating Permits

§ 45–30–1.   General.

1.1.Scope.—This rule provides for the establishment of a comprehensive air quality permitting system consistent with the requirements of Title V of the Clean Air Act. * * *

§ 45–30–2.   Definitions.

* * *

2.26.   "Major source" means any stationary source (or any group of stationary sources that are located on one or more contiguous or adjacent properties, and are under common control of the same person (or persons under common control)) belonging to a single major industrial grouping and that is described in subdivisions 2.26.a, 2.26.b, or 2.26.c. For the purpose of defining "major source," a stationary source or group of stationary sources shall be considered part of a single industrial grouping if all of the pollutant emitting activities at such source or group of sources on contiguous or adjacent properties belong to same Major Group (i.e., all have the same two-digit code) as described in the Standard Industrial Classification Manual, 1987, except that a research and development facility may be treated as a separate source from other stationary sources that are part of the same industrial grouping, are located on contiguous or adjacent property, and are under common control.

2.26.a.   A major source under § 112 of the Clean Air Act, which is defined as:

2.26.a.1. For pollutants other than radionuclides, any stationary source or group of stationary sources located within a contiguous area and under common control that emits or has the potential to emit, in the aggregate, ten (10) tons per year (tpy) or more of any hazardous air pollutant which has been listed pursuant to § 112(b) of the Clean Air Act, or twenty-five (25) tpy or more of any combination of such hazardous air pollutants. Refer to Table 45–30A for a listing of hazardous air pollutants regulated pursuant to this rule. Notwithstanding the preceding sentence, emissions from any oil or gas exploration or production well (with its associated equipment) and emissions from any pipeline compressor or pump station shall not be aggregated with emissions from other similar units, whether or not such units are in a contiguous area or under common control, to determine whether such units or stations are major sources * * *

2.26.b. A major stationary source of air pollutants, as defined in § 302 of the Clean Air Act, that directly emits or has the potential to emit, one hundred (100) tpy or more of any air pollutant subject to regulation (including any major source of fugitive emissions of any such pollutant, as determined by rule of the Secretary). * * *

2.26.c. A major stationary source as defined in Part D of Title I of the Clean Air Act [applying to nonattainment areas] * * *

§ 45–30–3.   Applicability.

3.1. Permit requirement.

3.1.a. On and after the effective date of the operating permit program, no person shall violate any requirement of a permit issued under this rule nor shall any person operate any of the following sources, except in compliance with a permit issued under section 6:

3.1.a.1. Any major source;

3.1.a.2. Any source, including an area source, subject to a standard or other requirements promulgated under § 111 of the Clean Air Act;

3.1.a.3. Any source, including an area source, subject to a standard or other requirements under § 112 of the Clean Air Act, except that a source is not required to obtain a permit solely because it is subject to regulations or requirements under § 112(r) of the Clean Air Act;

3.1.a.4. Any affected source; and

3.1.b. If, on the effective date of the operating permit program, a source is not subject to enforceable emissions limitations or such other enforceable measures that require the continued operation and maintenance of air pollution control equipment and/or other operational limitations that make the source non-major, the source shall be treated as a major source subject to the requirements of this rule. * * *

What test do the federal statute and the state regulations establish for what constitutes a source that requires a Title V operating permit? What language in that test is most relevant to determining whether Acme Energy Corporation's processing plant and compressor stations constitute a source that requires an operating permit? In the following case, the Sixth Circuit Court of Appeals evaluated whether a natural gas production plant and associated production wells required a Title V permit:

Summit Petroleum v. EPA

690 F.3d 733 (6th Cir. 2012)

■ SUHRHEINRICH, CIRCUIT JUDGE.

This case arises from a final action of the Environmental Protection Agency (EPA) determining that a natural gas sweetening plant and various sour gas production wells commonly owned by Petitioner Summit Petroleum Corporation (Summit) and separately located within an area of approximately forty-three square miles constitute a single stationary source under the EPA's Clean Air Act Title V permitting program. Specifically at issue is the EPA's conclusion that Summit's facilities satisfy the regulatory requirement of being "located on . . . adjacent properties" because, although physically independent, they are "truly interrelated." Summit, together with Amici American Petroleum Institute and American Exploration and Production Counsel, argues that the EPA's determination that the physical requirement of adjacency can be established through mere functional relatedness is unreasonable and contrary to the plain meaning of the term "adjacent." We agree. For these and other reasons fully set forth herein, we VACATE the EPA's final determination and REMAND this case to the EPA to determine whether Summit's sweetening plant and sour gas wells are sufficiently physically proximate to be considered "adjacent" within the ordinary, i.e., physical and geographical, meaning of that requirement.

I. Background

A. Summit's Natural Gas Production Facilities

Summit is a producer of natural gas that owns and operates a natural gas sweetening plant in Rosebush, Michigan. Summit's plant "sweetens" the "sour" gas from approximately one hundred sour gas production wells by removing hydrogen sulfide so that the gas can be used. Summit owns all of the production wells and the subsurface pipelines that connect each of the wells to the sweetening plant. The wells themselves are located over an area of approximately forty-three square miles at varying distances from the plant—from five hundred feet to eight miles away—and Summit does not own the property between the individual well sites or the property between the wells and the plant. None of the well sites share a common boundary with each other, nor do any of the well sites share a common boundary with Summit's production plant. Flares work as part of the plant operations by burning off natural gas waste to relieve pressure on the gas collection equipment. The closest flare is located approximately one half-mile from the plant, while the remaining flares are each over one mile away.

The sweetening plant and the majority of Summit's gas production wells and flares are located within the territory of Michigan's Saginaw Chippewa Indian Tribe's Isabella Reservation. The sweetening plant, gas production wells, and flares emit sulfur dioxides and nitrous oxides, air pollutants subject to regulation under the Clean Air Act (CAA). The plant alone emits, or has the potential to emit, just under one hundred tons of these pollutants per year. Each flare and each well site emits, or has the potential to emit, much lower amounts of pollutants. However, if the emissions of sulfur dioxide from the plant and any one production well were to be combined, they would exceed one hundred tons of pollutants per year.

B.   The EPA's Title V Permitting Program

* * * Title V requires every "major source" of air pollution to obtain a Title V operating permit. 42 U.S.C. § 7661a(a). The EPA's Title V plan defines a major source to include "any stationary facility or source of air pollutants which directly emits, or has the potential to emit, one hundred tons per year of any pollutant," including nitrous oxides and sulfur dioxides (the pollutants emitted by Summit's operations). *See* 42 U.S.C. § 7602(j); *see also* 40 C.F.R. § 71.2. The EPA defines a "stationary source" as "any building, structure, facility, or installation which emits or may emit a regulated [air] pollutant." 40 C.F.R. § 52.21(b)(5). Multiple pollutant-emitting activities, such as Summit's sweetening plant and sour gas production wells, can be aggregated together and considered a "building, structure, facility, or installation," i.e., a single stationary source, under Title V only if they: (1) are under common control; (2) "are located on one or more contiguous or adjacent properties"; and (3) belong to the same major industrial grouping. 40 C.F.R. § 71.2. If the pollutant-emitting activities fail to satisfy any one of these three criteria, they are considered separate stationary sources and their emissions cannot be aggregated to meet the major source threshold for which a Title V permit is required.

C.   Major Source Determination Correspondence
Between Summit and the EPA

In January 2005, Summit, together with the Michigan Department of Environmental Quality (MDEQ), submitted a request to the EPA to determine whether Summit's facilities met the definition of a Title V major source of air pollution. * * *

The EPA responded to Summit's source determination request on April 26, 2007, * * * stating that it was "unable to conclude if the wells and plant constituted a single source for Title V purposes." The EPA * * * maintain[ed] that pollutant-emitting facilities *could be* aggregated to constitute a single stationary source under Title V if they operated under common control, were located on contiguous or adjacent properties, and belonged to the same industrial grouping. It then identified the proper procedure for determining a single stationary source in the oil and gas industry, outlined in an EPA guidance memorandum issued by Acting Assistant Administrator William Wehrum:

1)   Identify the surface sites,

2)   Evaluate whether each individual surface site qualifies as a separate stationary source, or if the emissions activities should be grouped together to form a stationary source (i.e., if their emission activities are under common control, belong to the same major industrial grouping, and are contiguous or adjacent), and

3)   Aggregate two or more stationary sources if they are under common control and are located in proximity of each other.

Memorandum from William L. Wehrum, Acting Assistant Adm'r, to Reg'l Adm'rs I–X (Jan. 12, 2007) (Wehrum Memorandum).

The EPA found that based on the information provided by Summit's request, its wells and production plant were undisputedly commonly owned, part of the same industrial grouping, and not located on contiguous surface sites. Accordingly, the agency concluded that it "must evaluate the adjacency, (i.e., the nearness or closeness) of the sour gas wells to the sweetening plant" to determine whether Summit's facilities constituted a single stationary source subject to regulation. Although it noted that "because the production wells supply the gas to the gas sweetening plant, we believe that the sites meet the common sense notion of a plant," the EPA found that the Wehrum Memorandum "makes clear that proximity is the most informative factor in making a source determination involving oil and gas activities." Finally, the EPA requested additional information—a map of Summit's facilities and a schematic of its processes that showed the connection between Summit's "exploration and production activities"—to assist it in reaching a decision.

Summit provided the requested information in a letter dated April 24, 2008. * * *

In July 2009, the EPA responded that even with Summit's supplemental materials, it was again unable to conclusively determine whether Summit's facilities constituted a single stationary source. The EPA * * * stressed that physical proximity was not the only factor in adjacency determinations, stating that "generally, the EPA determines whether two facilities are 'adjacent' based on a 'common sense' notion of a source and the functional interrelationship of the facilities, rather than simply on the physical distance between the facilities." * * *

On September 8, 2009, EPA issued its determination that Summit's sweetening plant and sour gas wells constituted a single stationary source, and were therefore a major source, under Title V. The EPA did not explain the basis for its decision, save for citing to its prior April 26, 2007 and April 16, 2009 letters to Summit. Shortly after the EPA issued its decision, it forwarded Summit a September 22, 2009 guidance memorandum prepared by the EPA's Office of Air and Radiation Assistant Administrator Gina McCarthy entitled "Withdrawal for Source Determinations for Oil and Gas Industries" (McCarthy Memorandum). In pertinent part, the McCarthy Memorandum reasoned that the simplified approach of the Wehrum Memorandum, with its emphasis on physical proximity in the determination of what constituted a stationary source, was no longer appropriate. The McCarthy Memorandum called permitting authorities to instead "rely foremost on the three regulatory criteria for aggregating emissions from multiple sources, . . . (1) whether the activities are under the control of the same person (or person under common control); (2) whether the activities are located on one or more contiguous or adjacent properties; and (3) whether the activities belong to the same industrial grouping." *Id.* (citing 40 C.F.R. § 52.21(b)(6)). The guidance memorandum nevertheless conceded that stationary source determinations should be made on a case-by-case basis and that "in some cases, 'proximity' may serve as the overwhelming factor in a permitting authority's source determination decision." *Id.* * * *

On October 18, 2010, the EPA sent Summit a final letter confirming that even with Summit's supplemental information, the EPA considered Summit's facilities a single stationary source, and thus a major source, under Title V. * * * The agency discussed its view that Summit's plant, wells, and flares worked together as a single unit that "together produced a single product" and found that Summit had failed to provide any evidence to demonstrate that the emissions sources were not "truly interdependent." The EPA thus concluded that given this functional interrelationship, Summit's facilities "should not be considered separate emission sources."

Summit filed a * * * Petition for Review in this Court on October 18, 2010. * * *

II. Analysis

* * *

The issue in the instant case is relatively straightforward. Summit, the EPA, and Amici agree * * * that Summit's production plant and sour gas wells are commonly owned and share a major industrial grouping, satisfying two parts of the three-part test for a stationary source under the EPA's Title V permitting program. All parties further agree that *if* Summit's plant and wells are aggregated into a single stationary source, the total emissions from this source would exceed the threshold required for a stationary source to be considered a major source, and Summit would be required to obtain a Title V permit to regulate its emissions of criteria pollutants. Finally, the parties agree that Summit's production plant and sour gas wells are not located on "contiguous," i.e., bordering, properties. Undisputedly, the sole disputed issue before us is whether Summit's facilities are "adjacent" to one another, thus converting them into a stationary source, and a major source, under Title V. * * *

Summit argues that the term "adjacent," both generally and as it appears in the EPA's regulatory requirement that aggregated activities be "located on contiguous or adjacent properties," is unambiguous. The EPA disagrees, submitting, *inter alia,* that the term "adjacent" is unquestionably ambiguous because the EPA has never defined a specific physical distance by which it is defined or with which it is simultaneous. * * *

This Court, and others as well, have often consulted dictionaries to ascertain the meaning of words. *See, e.g., Terrell v. United States,* 564 F.3d 442, 451 (6th Cir. 2009) (citing *MCI Telecomms. Corp. v. AT & T Co.,* 512 U.S. 218, 225 (1994)). Our research satisfies us that dictionaries agree that two entities are adjacent when they are "[c]lose to; lying near . . . [n]ext to, adjoining." American Heritage Dictionary of the English Language. The EPA does not cite, nor could we locate, any authority suggesting that the term "adjacent" invokes an assessment of the functional relationship between two activities. *See, e.g.,* Merriam-Webster Dictionary ("not distant: nearby <the city and *adjacent* suburbs>; having a common endpoint or border <*adjacent* lots> . . . ; immediately preceding or following); Oxford Dictionaries ("next to or adjoining something else; *adjacent rooms; the area adjacent to the fire station*"). * * *

The EPA argues that though they are not incorrect, dictionaries provide an incomplete definition of "adjacent," and that the functional interrelationship of two facilities *must* be considered because physical distance is meaningless without context. The notion that adjacency expands and contracts with context, true as it is, must not be overextended. In the first instance, it is certainly correct that two states could be adjacent to one another in the context of a country, just as two houses could be adjacent in the context of a neighborhood. It is noted, however, that the contextual element of the overall space within which one asks whether two things are adjacent does not fundamentally change the physical and geographical nature of the question. The EPA makes an impermissible and illogical stretch when it states that one must ask the *purpose* for which two activities exist in order to consider whether they are adjacent to one another. Whether the distance between two facilities enables a given relationship to exist between them is immaterial to the concept of adjacency—it merely answers the question of whether a certain activity can or cannot occur between two locations that were, and will continue to be regardless of whether they host the activity, physically distant or physically adjacent. * * *

Our decision finds support in many of the arguments raised in the brief of Amicus API. First, as a member of the oil and gas industry itself, API urges us to consider the fact that the EPA's interpretation of adjacency to include a measure of functional relationship is subjective and unpredictable, undermining the *Alabama Power* Court's mandate that the EPA's test give "explicit notice as to whether (and on what statutory authority) the EPA construes the term [stationary] source. . . ." *See Alabama Power [v. Costle]*, 636 F.2d [323,] 397 [D.C. Cir. 1979]. Relatedly, API criticizes the EPA for supporting its source determination with the concept of a "common sense notion of a plant," reasoning that this general principle is clearly meant to constrain, rather than enlarge, the EPA's definition of a single stationary source.

API also argues that the EPA's interpretation has led in this case, and will continue to lead, to absurd source determinations within the industry. In a context where oil and gas producers often have little say over where emission points are located and nearly every facility is connected to one another by pipeline (and thus, in a sense, functionally related), API argues, the aggregation of activities without regard to their physical proximity is inherently unreasonable. Indeed, with the concept of a "common sense notion of a plant" construed as facilitating the aggregation of operationally related but physically distant activities, there is little foreseeable limit to the aggregation of emission points spread out literally across the country. Moreover, API cautions that source determinations dependent on activities' functional relatedness will be quickly outdated as oil and gas producers add and remove emission points from their production systems, potentially requiring nearly constant renewed source determination requests and decisions.

We are particularly struck by API's final observation—that the EPA's source determination in this case is an ironic showcase of the very fears that caused the agency not to adopt a functional relatedness test for source determinations in the first instance. From Summit and MDEQ's joint source determination request in January 2005 to the final iteration of the EPA's decision, nearly five years passed. The parties engaged in at least twenty-five conference calls and exchanged "a small mountain of paper" within this period. Certainly, the cost for Summit to produce the data and schematics requested by the EPA, and the cost for the EPA to distill and understand the same, were high in terms of both monetary and capital resources. As API points out, this process produced exactly the "fine-grained" and administratively burdensome result the EPA sought to avoid in its drafting of its Title V stationary source test, and is strong evidence that the EPA's interpretation of its own regulation was unreasonable.

III. Conclusion

For the reasons stated, we VACATE the final agency determination of the EPA aggregating Summit's sour gas wells and sweetening plant into a single and major source under its Title V permitting plan. We REMAND this case to the EPA for a reassessment of Summit's Title V source determination request in light of the proper, plain-meaning application of the requirement that Summit's activities be aggregated only if they are located on physically contiguous or adjacent properties.

■ KAREN NELSON MOORE, CIRCUIT JUDGE, dissenting.

Congress passed the Clean Air Act ("CAA") "to protect and enhance the quality of the Nation's air resources so as to promote the public health and welfare and the productive capacity of its population." 42 U.S.C. § 7401(b)(1). Because the majority hamstrings the Environmental Protection Agency's ("EPA") ability to pursue this mission by refusing to defer to the agency's reasonable interpretation of its own regulation, I respectfully dissent. * * *

The EPA will aggregate the emissions of multiple stationary sources to determine if the sources together constitute a major source if those sources (1) "are under common control of the same person," (2) "are located on one or more contiguous or adjacent properties," and (3) "belong[ ] to a single major industrial grouping." 40 C.F.R. § 71.2. In this case, the EPA determined that Summit's sour-gas wells, flares, and gas-sweetening plant, which are connected by a dedicated underground pipeline and are used exclusively as part of a single, interconnected operation, together constituted a major source. As part of its determination that Summit's various stationary sources were located on adjacent properties, the EPA considered the fact that those sources were functionally interrelated. * * *

The majority peruses several dictionaries and concludes that "adjacent" refers to the physical or geographical relationship between two or more objects. The objects must be "not distant," "next to," "close to," or "immediately preceding or following." The EPA's interpretation of its Title V regulations to allow for consideration of functional interrelatedness in adjacency determinations does not contradict this plain meaning of the word "adjacent." The ultimate question remains whether two properties are physically close enough to be considered adjacent for the purposes of aggregation under Title V. The EPA's position is simply that other factors in addition to absolute physical distance can be relevant in determining whether two objects that are a given distance apart are close enough to be considered adjacent in this context. The EPA does not contend that multiple stationary sources are adjacent simply because they are functionally interrelated, and the majority either misunderstands or mischaracterizes the agency's position in so describing it.

In this more limited sense, "adjacent" is ambiguous. The fact that "adjacent" refers to the distance between two objects does not explain what factors go into a determination of whether two objects that are a given distance apart are "next to" each other, "close," or "immediately preceding or following." The cited definitions do not unambiguously foreclose the consideration of factors other than absolute physical distance. One object in a sequence "immediately preced[es] or follow[s]" the next item in the sequence, for example. Two objects that are physically connected fall "next to" each other along that connection. Two or more stationary sources that are functionally interrelated can similarly be described as "next to" each other; one follows the other in a common process.

Moreover, functional interrelatedness can inform the determination of whether two objects that are a given distance apart are adjacent. If two properties are close enough to each other to house stationary sources that contribute to the same interrelated operation, and only to that operation, those properties are more likely to be close enough reasonably to be considered adjacent. Likewise, the EPA could reasonably conclude that two or more sources that exist only as part of the same larger process or sequence will likely be close enough to each other to be considered adjacent. As the EPA recognizes, circumstances may exist in which the distance between two stationary sources is too great for those sources to be considered adjacent, even if they are functionally interrelated. This fact does not mean that interrelatedness can never be a factor, but that it will not support a finding of adjacency in that instance. * * *

The EPA's position thus comports with the plain meaning of the word "adjacent" as a description of the geographical relationship between two objects. The EPA uses interrelatedness only to determine whether two properties are close enough to each other to be considered adjacent. Functional interrelatedness thus operates only in that realm of adjacency that is ambiguous; it does not replace proximity, but serves as a means of determining proximity. Accordingly, deference is warranted. * * *

Because "adjacent" is ambiguous as to how to determine whether two objects that are a given distance apart should be considered adjacent, we should defer to the EPA's decision to consider functional interrelatedness as a means of making that determination. * * *

[T]oday's ruling frees the oil and gas industry to gerrymander its way out of Title V regulation. So long as sufficient distance exists between each well (so that they are not "adjacent" as the majority defines that term), or someone other than the drilling company owns parcels of land in between each well (so that they are not "contiguous"), the drilling operation cannot be classified as a major source through aggregation. Unlike the CAA provisions governing hazardous air pollutant emissions, *see* 42 U.S.C. § 7412(n)(4), Title V does not grant the oil and gas industry immunity from aggregation; this court should not effectively create such a provision when Congress has not done so. * * *

Because I believe that the EPA's consideration of functional interrelatedness as a factor along with physical distance in its adjacency determination was both reasonable (and thus worthy of deference) and correct, I would affirm its decision to aggregate the various stationary sources in Summit's drilling operation as a major source. * * *

West Virginia does not fall within the Sixth Circuit, so assume that *Summit Petroleum* is not binding authority for the question of whether Acme Energy Corporation's plant and compressor stations are a single source that requires a Title V operating permit. It nevertheless may, however, influence how the West Virginia Department of Environmental Protection interprets the applicable standard. How will the Department likely decide to treat Acme Energy Corporation's plant and compressor stations if the Department follows the *Summit Petroleum* majority's interpretation? What if the Department follows the dissent? Do Acme's plant and compressor stations present a closer question, or an easier question, than the facts of *Summit Petroleum*?

To gain an understanding of how the Department may view source aggregation, you research the Department's guidance documents. Guidance documents are an agency's nonbinding statements of policy or statutory or regulatory interpretation. Your research finds instructions for an operating permit application that address the issue of source aggregation:

West Virginia Department of Environmental Protection Division of Air Quality, Application Instructions and Forms for General Permit G70-A
P. 46 (2014)

Aggregation Discussion Guidance:

The information provided below is taken from outreach previously provided by WVDAQ regarding air permit issues related to the natural gas industry in regards to single source determinations. This discussion guidance is provided to communicate information that should be considered and included in the aggregation determination discussion that is provided with the G70-A registration applications. Aggregation Determinations are complex and made on a case-by-case basis. If additional information is required, it will be requested.

What does Aggregation mean?

- "Stationary source" is defined as any "building, structure, facility or installation which emits, or may emit any air pollutant".

- "Building, structure, facility, or installation" is defined as all the pollutant emitting activities which belong to the same major industrial grouping, are located on one or more contiguous or adjacent properties, and are under the control of the same person

- If a facility meets all of these criteria, emissions from all applicable sources must be aggregated in order to determine the facility's total emissions in regards to major source or PSD status

Three-prong test:

Same Industrial Grouping

- The sources belong to a single industrial grouping if they belong to the same "major group" (have the same two (2)-digit SIC code).

Common control of the same person

- The sources are under common of the same person (or persons under common control)

- Common control can be established through ownership. Control of the same person refers to corporate control, not site management. If two divisions of a corporation operate at the same site, even if each operation is managed separately, they will count as one source provided the other criteria are met because they are under control of the same company.

- Common control can be established if an entity has decision-making authority over the operations of a second entity

- Is there a contract for service relationship between two entities?

- Is there a support/dependency relationship between two entities?

Contiguous or Adjacent Properties

- The sources are located on one or more "contiguous or adjacent" properties

- "Contiguous or Adjacent" determinations are made on a "case by case" basis

- These determinations are based on the relationship between the activities in question (same industrial grouping, common control) Regulations do not define these terms.

- Dictionary Definitions:

  Contiguous—being in actual contact; touching along a boundary or at a point.

  Adjacent—not distant; nearby; having common endpoint or border.

- "Contiguous" or "adjacent" are proximity based

- Focus on proximity and the common sense notion of a plant

- Avoid aggregating pollutant emitting activities that as a group would not fit within the ordinary meaning of "building", "structure", "facility" or "installation"

- There is no defined distance

What can you do?

- Provide as much information as possible to support your aggregation determination

  This includes: (a) SIC code of facility; (b) ownership issues; (c) contiguous or adjacent issues; (d) proximity; (e) operational dependence or lack thereof; (f) what equipment is in question; and (g) why you made the aggregation decision

———

In light of this guidance, how will the West Virginia Department of Environmental Protection likely treat Acme Energy Corporation's natural gas processing plant and compressor stations? Does this guidance document give any indication whether the Department is more likely to follow the *Summit Petroleum* majority, dissent, or a different approach altogether? Is it to Clean the Air's advantage to seek a definitive resolution, from the Department and perhaps a court, of the issue under federal and West Virginia law?

X. MOBILE SOURCES

Thus far, our examination of the Clean Air Act has focused on stationary sources of air pollution. Title II of the Clean Air Act regulates mobile sources of air pollution—principally motor vehicles but also non-road engines. The category of non-road engines includes locomotives, aircraft, watercraft, diesel equipment, forklifts, generators, compressors, lawn and garden equipment, snowmobiles, dirt bikes, and all-terrain vehicles.

Motor vehicles are responsible for substantial air pollutant emissions: nearly half of smog-forming volatile organic compounds (VOCs); more than half of nitrogen oxide (NO_x) emissions; about half of the toxic air pollutant emissions; and three-quarters of carbon monoxide (CO) emissions nationwide. In the United States, there are more than 200 million cars and light-duty trucks currently on the road. Moreover, the total vehicle miles traveled in the United States have roughly tripled since the Clean Air Act was enacted in 1970, further complicating efforts to reduce total emissions from mobile sources.

A. REGULATED POLLUTANTS

Clean Air Act section 202 requires EPA to set emissions standards for "any air pollutant from any class or classes of new motor vehicles or new motor vehicle engines, which in his judgment cause, or contribute to, air pollution which may reasonably be anticipated to endanger public health or welfare." 42 U.S.C. § 7521(a)(1). Pursuant to this mandate, EPA regulates emissions of NO_x, CO, non-methane organic gases (NMOG), particulate matter (PM), formaldehyde, and greenhouse gases.

B. REGULATORY PROGRAMS

The Clean Air Act's Mobile Source Program under Title II establishes three types of primary requirements for mobile sources: emission standards, testing requirements, and fuels regulations.

- *Emission Standards.* Clean Air Act section 202 directs EPA to set emissions standards for new motor vehicles. 42 U.S.C. § 7521. Congress generally gave EPA discretion in setting these emissions standards, but instructed the agency that standards are not to go into effect until "after such period as the Administrator finds necessary to permit the development and application of the requisite technology." *Id.* § 7521(a)(2). Thus, emissions standards can be technology-forcing—that is, requiring the development of future technology not yet available—but must be feasible. Clean Air Act section 213 establishes a similar emissions standards program for nonroad engines and nonroad vehicles. *Id.* § 7547. As will be discussed more thoroughly later in the capstone policy problem at the end of this chapter, EPA relatively recently has issued regulations that impose fuel efficiency requirements on new motor vehicles under Clean Air Act section 202 as a means of indirectly reducing greenhouse gas emissions.

- *Testing Requirements.* Title II establishes a three-stage testing process to ensure that a class of vehicles complies with the relevant emissions standards. 42 U.S.C. §§ 7521, 7541.

  - First, EPA examines a prototype of a new vehicle prior to its manufacture to ensure that the design of the prototype complies with the applicable emissions standards. 42 U.S.C. § 7525(a).

  - Second, EPA examines sample new vehicles as they come off the assembly line to ensure that the vehicles as actually manufactured comply with the standards. 42 U.S.C. § 7525(b).

  - Third and finally, EPA tests sample vehicles during their useful life to determine whether they continue to satisfy emission standards. 42 U.S.C. § 7541(b). Clean Air Act section 207(a) requires manufacturers to warranty that their vehicles will comply with emissions standards throughout their useful life. *Id.* § 7541(a). Manufacturers must remedy, at their own expense, any problem. *Id.* § 7541(c). This makes it a responsibility of the manufacturers, not vehicle owners, if a vehicle turns out not to comply with emissions standards.

- *Fuels Regulations.* Clean Air Act section 211 requires EPA to regulate fuels and fuel additives that contribute to air pollution. 42 U.S.C. § 7545. EPA relied on its authority under section 211 to phase out lead from gasoline, dramatically reducing the amount of lead in ambient air. Clean Air Act section 211 also mandates the use of reformulated gasoline to reduce emissions in ozone nonattainment areas and oxygenated gasoline to reduce emissions in carbon monoxide nonattainment areas. *Id.* § 7545(k), (m).

C. FEDERALISM

As explained in Chapter 2, most federal environmental statutes, including the Clean Air Act, employ a model of cooperative federalism that allows states to regulate more stringently than required by federal law. If, for example, a state wants to limit a factory's air pollutant emissions to lower levels than the Clean Air Act allows, the state is free to do so.

Title II's Mobile Source Program is different. Clean Air Act section 209 preempts states from adopting their own emissions controls for new vehicles, 42 U.S.C. § 7543(a), but creates an exception for California, *id.* § 7543(b). Clean Air Act section 177 authorizes other states to adopt California's standards instead of the federal standards. *Id.* § 7507. Thus, in effect, states have two options: either adopt the federal standards or adopt California's standards. Recently, as part of a larger negotiation over emissions standards nationally, California has voluntarily adopted federal standards, creating uniform emissions standards nationwide. See Jody Freeman, *The Obama Administration's National Auto Policy: Lessons from the "Car Deal,"* 35 HARV. ENVTL. L. REV. 344 (2011).

Congress adopted this unusual preemption scheme because it did not want to allow states to create their own standards. Allowing a multiplicity of state standards could create chaos for vehicle manufacturers, who would either have to manufacture different vehicles for different states or simply comply with the most stringent state regulation. But Congress exempted California from preemption because California had emissions standards that preexisted the federal standards and California had special air pollution problems.

D. NON-TITLE II MOBILE SOURCE CONTROLS

Although Title II is devoted to mobile sources, some regulation of mobile sources also occurs through NAAQS-based regulation under state implementation plans. State implementation plans, although they apply primarily to stationary sources, can include *transportation control measures* that reduce mobile source emissions by reducing vehicle use or improving traffic flow. 42 U.S.C. § 7408(f). Examples of transportation control measures include improved public transit, improved traffic flow and added high-occupancy vehicle lanes on roads, facilities that make walking and biking easier, and flexible work schedules. *Id.* Requirements to equip vehicles with pollution-control devices or design features relating to emissions control do not count as transportation control measures, but rather are "standard[s] relating to the control of emissions from new motor vehicles or new motor vehicle engines" and therefore preempted by Clean Air Act section 209. *Engine Mfrs. Ass'n v. South Coast Air Quality Mgmt. Dist.*, 541 U.S. 246, 252–53 (2004).

State implementation plans also can regulate *indirect sources.* Indirect sources lie at the intersection of stationary sources and mobile sources, although they are not regulated as either. An indirect source is any "facility, building, structure, installation, real property, road, or highway which attracts, or may attract, mobile sources of pollution." 42 U.S.C. § 7410(a)(5)(C). Parking lots and structures are indirect sources. *Id.* The Clean Air Act allows, but does not require, states to regulate indirect sources in their state implementation plans. *Id.* § 7410(a)(5)(B).

XI. EMISSIONS TRADING

The emissions reduction credits in the Chicago Factory problem from earlier in this chapter are an example of emissions trading—also known as tradable permit rights—which we first introduced in Chapter 1. Emissions trading is an aspect of several different Clean Air Act regulatory programs, sometimes written into the statute itself and sometimes added by EPA to increase regulatory flexibility and reduce compliance burdens.

Emissions trading increases the economic efficiency of a permit program by allowing sources to trade surplus emissions reductions—that is, reductions in emissions that go beyond what the law requires—within the same source or across sources. Emissions trading increases efficiency because it allows a source with relatively low pollution control costs to reduce its emissions by more than what is required and then to sell its surplus emissions rights to another source with higher pollution control costs. Both sources benefit from the transaction, as does society by obtaining emissions reductions at less cost. Emissions trading poses several important questions for regulators, including the following:

- *What should be the scope of trading under the program?* The scope of emissions trading programs varies widely, ranging from programs that allow trading across a multi-state region to programs that only allow emissions averaging within a single facility. To maximize the efficiency benefits of a program, regulators may want it to encompass as many sources as possible. But broader programs encompassing more numerous and diverse sources are more difficult to administer. In addition, there are some natural limits on the scope of an emissions trading program. Transactions should trade emissions of the same pollutant or closely related pollutants—for example, nitrogen oxides (NO_x) emissions for NO_x emissions, not NO_x emissions for carbon monoxide emissions. Sources should be located within the same airshed, so that trades do not worsen air quality in one area for the benefit of another area. An area of reduced air quality because trading has concentrated emissions in the area is known as a *hotspot*.

- *How should emissions rights be allocated?* Economists generally favor assigning emissions rights by auction, which are thought to create more robust markets. Most trading systems, however, assign emissions rights based on recent historical emissions levels, effectively grandfathering in existing sources. If initial emissions rights are assigned based on past emissions, regulators must choose which year or years should be treated as the baseline. Emissions may fluctuate from year to year for a variety of reasons, and so choosing the baseline period will affect how much sources will be able to emit moving forward and may favor some sources over others. Also, if some sources already have invested in pollution control technology, reducing their emissions, using existing emissions levels as the baseline may effectively penalize early adopters who instead should be rewarded.

- *What ratio of avoided emissions to permitted emissions should be required?* Some programs allow one-for-one swaps of emissions reductions credits for new emissions. This maximizes the incentive for trading and therefore the number of trades. It also reduces the costs of the program to the regulated industry. Other programs require more emissions reductions for each new unit of emissions. This maximizes the environmental benefit of each trade, but may reduce the number of trades. Maximizing the overall economic benefit of the program depends on how cost-sensitive the regulated industry is—that is, how many fewer trades occur as the environmental benefits of each trade increase.

- *Can sources bank their emissions?* Allowing sources to bank their emissions—that is, save them for future use or trading—adds increased flexibility and facilitates trading. But allowing emissions banking may concentrate emissions in some periods, leading to air quality below the desired goal.

- *How should new sources be included?* Regulators generally want to allow new sources of emissions because they provide economic benefits in the form of growth and innovation. But allowing new sources with additional emissions undermines the environmental goals of the program. One way to achieve both economic and environmental goals is to require new sources to purchase credits from existing sources, so that new sources do not increase overall emissions. This is the approach can also occur outside of a broad trading program. For example, the Clean Air Act's requirements for new sources in nonattainment areas require offsets, as the New Factory in

Chicago problem illustrates. Another way is to set aside, in the initial allocation of emissions rights, some allocations for new sources. EPA has used new source set-asides in its interstate air pollution regulations.

The 1990 Clean Air Act Amendments created an emissions trading program to address the problem of acid rain. 42 U.S.C. §§ 7651–7651o. Using past, rather than current, years as the baseline prevented sources from strategically increasing their fuel consumption to increase their allowances. Using fuel consumption, rather than sulfur dioxide emissions, avoided biasing against early adopters of pollution control equipment. The program then gradually reduced the total number of allowances—and thus overall emissions—over time. The acid rain program is regarded as a highly innovative and successful emissions trading program, resulting in dramatic emissions reductions with lower compliance costs than expected. EPA has drawn on its experience with the acid rain program in designing other cap-and-trade systems for interstate air pollution, including the Cross-State Air Pollution Rule.

The following report from EPA's National Center for Environmental Economics summarizes how the agency has added emissions trading to many of the Clean Air Act's regulatory programs.

National Center for Environmental Economics, U.S. EPA, The United States Experience with Economic Incentives for Protecting the Environment
Pp. 69–74 (2001)[2]

The first trading of permitted rights to release any type of pollutant in the United States began in the 1970s as a mechanism to allow economic development in areas that failed to meet ambient air quality standards. EPA gradually broadened the offset policy to include emission bubbles, banking, and netting. These programs are described in the following paragraphs. * * *

6.2.1   Offset Program

In the mid-1970s, the EPA proposed the "offset" policy that permitted growth in non-attainment areas, provided that new sources install air pollution control equipment which met Lowest Achievable Emission Rate (LAER) standards. These sources also had to offset any excess emissions by acquiring greater emission reductions from other sources in the area.

---

² Eds.: We have reordered the material in the EPA report to move the summary of the pre-1990 programs to the front of the excerpt, followed by the trading programs added by the 1990 Amendments.

Through this process, growth could be accommodated while maintaining progress toward attaining national ambient air quality standards.

Of more than 10,000 offset trades (a few of which are described later in this section), over 90% have been in California. Nationwide, about 10% of offset trades are between firms; the remainder are between sources owned by the same firm. Most offset credits are created as a result of all or part of a facility being closed.

The offset policy, which was included in the 1977 amendments to the Clean Air Act, spawned three related programs: bubbles, banking, and netting. The common element in these programs is the Emission Reduction Credit (ERC), which is generated when sources reduce actual emissions below their permitted emissions and apply to the state for certification of the reduction. To be certified as an ERC, the state must determine that the reduction meets the following criteria: (1) that the reduction is surplus in the sense of not being required by current regulations in the State Implementation Plan (SIP); (2) that it is enforceable; (3) that it is permanent; and (4) that it is quantifiable. ERCs are normally denominated in terms of the quantity of pollutant in tons released over 1 year. By far the most common method of generating ERCs is closing the source or reducing its production. However, ERCs also can be earned by modifying production processes and installing pollution control equipment. Trades of ERCs most often involve stationary sources, although trades involving mobile sources are permitted. States have approved a variety of activities that sources may use to generate offset credits. The South Coast Air Quality Management District (SCAQMD) in California, for example, accepts the scrapping of older vehicles and lawn mowers as a means of generating credits. It then applies a formula to determine the magnitude of air pollution credits for each old car that is scrapped. * * *

6.2.2   Bubble Policy

The bubble policy, established in 1979, allows sources to meet emission limits by treating multiple emission points within a facility as if they face a single aggregate emission limit. The term bubble was used to connote an imaginary bubble over a source such as a refinery or a steel mill that had several emission points, each with its own emission limit. Within the "bubble," a source could propose to meet all of its emission control requirements for a criteria pollutant with a mix of controls that is different from those mandated by regulations—as long as total emissions within the bubble met the limit for all sources within the bubble. A bubble can include more than one facility owned by one firm, or it can include facilities owned by different firms. However, all of the emission points must be within the same attainment or non-attainment area.

Bubbles must be approved as a revision to an applicable State Implementation Plan (SIP), a factor that has discouraged their use. Prior to the 1986 final policy, EPA approved or proposed to approve approximately 50 source-specific bubbles. EPA approved 34 additional bubbles under EPA-authorized generic bubble rules. The EPA-approved, pre-1986 bubbles were estimated to save $300 million over conventional control approaches. State-approved, pre-1986 bubbles saved an estimated $135 million. No estimates are reported for the number of, or savings from, post-1986 bubbles. By design, bubbles are neutral in terms of environmental impact.

6.2.3   Banking

EPA's initial offset policy did not allow the banking of emission reduction credits for future use or sale. EPA contended that banking would be inconsistent with the basic policy of the Clean Air Act. But without a provision for storing or banking ERCs, the policy encouraged sources to continue operating dirty facilities until they needed credits for internal use. New and expanding firms without internal sources of ERCs had to engage in lengthy searches for other firms that were willing to create and supply credits.

The offset policy in the 1977 amendments to the Clean Air Act included provisions for the banking of emission reduction credits for future use or sale. Although the EPA approved several banks, there was limited use of the provision, most likely because of the uncertain nature of the banked ERC. * * *

6.2.4   Netting

Netting, the final component of EPA's 1986 emission trading policy statement, dates from 1980. Netting allows sources undergoing modification to avoid new source review if they can demonstrate that plant-wide emissions do not increase significantly. Netting is the most widely used of these early emission trading programs. * * *

Cost savings can arise in three ways. First, netting may allow a firm to avoid being classified as a major source, under which it would be subject to more stringent emission limits. Reductions in control costs in such a case would depend upon the control costs and emission limits that the firm must satisfy after netting. One source estimated that netting typically results in savings between $100,000 and $1 million per application (indicating aggregate savings of $500 million to as much as $12 billion). Second, the aggregate cost savings from avoiding the cost of going through the major source permitting process could range from $25 million to $300 million. Third, additional savings could arise from avoiding construction delays that are caused by the permitting process. * * *

Since 1990, EPA has significantly expanded the use of trading in Clean Air Act programs. Today, emissions trading is a standard tool of EPA's air quality program. Although not a panacea for every situation, trading is being used by EPA and states to help solve a variety of air pollution problems. A broad overview of these programs follows. * * *

Acid Rain: Perhaps the best-known example of trading is the Acid Rain Program's system of marketable pollution allowances for sulfur dioxide emissions for electric utilities. [The Acid Rain Program mandated reductions in sulfur dioxide emissions, primarily from coal-fired power plants owned by electric utilities, and allowed affected sources to market their unused emission allowances. The program was designed as a "cap and trade" system, whereby EPA first allocated allowances—each allowance permitted a source to emit one ton of sulfur dioxide per year— to affected sources based on their baseline fuel consumption in 1985, 1986, and 1987. Sources that reduced their emissions more than required could sell their surplus allowances to other sources, reducing compliance costs through "trade" while staying below the "cap" of total emissions allowed under the program.] * * *

Smog and Other Common Pollutants: EPA is working with states to promote trading and other market-based approaches to help achieve national air quality standards for smog, particulates, and other common pollutants that are regulated through national air quality standards. In addition, EPA has provided trading opportunities in virtually all federal rules that are aimed at cutting emissions from motor vehicles and fuels. These federal measures are essential to helping states meet federal air quality goals.

Under the Clean Air Act, states have primary responsibility for devising pollution control strategies for local areas, so states can meet national air quality standards. EPA has issued guidance to assist states in designing trading and other economic incentive programs, including economic incentives rules and guidance in 1994 (which, at present, are being revised); general guidance on State Implementation Plans (SIPs) in 1992; and the 1986 emissions trading policy statement. EPA also has assisted states in setting up trading programs, such as California's RECLAIM cap-and-trade program for sulfur dioxide and nitrogen oxides and the Ozone Transport Commission's (OTC) program for controlling nitrogen oxide emissions among states in the Northeast. Through a unique partnership, EPA and the OTC states are jointly implementing this NO_x budget system for the Northeast, which draws on the experience of the acid rain program.

In 1998, EPA issued a rule that established NO_x budgets for many states (the "NO_x SIP call") to combat the problem of transported ozone pollution in the eastern United States on a broader scale. To encourage an efficient market-based approach to reducing NO_x on a regional basis, EPA simultaneously provided states with a model cap-and-trade rule for utilities and large industrial sources. The experiences of the acid rain program and the OTC effort show that this approach holds the potential to achieve regional NO_x reductions in an efficient and highly cost-effective manner.

In the 1990 Clean Air Act Amendments, Congress called for EPA to help states meet their air quality goals by issuing federal standards to cut emissions from cars, trucks, buses, many types of non-road engines, and fuels. These rules cut toxic air pollution as well as reduced the amount of air pollutants, which were regulated through air quality standards.

EPA has provided trading opportunities in virtually all of these new standards, building on the early success of trading in the phased reduction of lead in leaded gasoline during the 1980s. These standards include rules for cleaner burning reformulated gasoline, which now accounts for approximately 30% of the nation's gasoline, and the national low-emission vehicle standards for cars and light-duty trucks that will be met nationwide by 2001. Opportunities for averaging, trading, and banking also are provided by new national emissions standards for heavy-duty trucks and buses, locomotives, heavy-duty off-road engines such as bulldozers, and small gasoline engines (e.g., those used in lawn and garden equipment).

Another recent example is the landmark Tier II/gasoline sulfur rule that President Clinton announced in December 1999. This rule would provide compliance flexibility to both vehicle manufacturers and fuel refiners by allowing them to use averaging, banking, and trading. In the case of automakers, EPA created different "bins" of emissions levels, rather than require a single NO_x emissions standard for each vehicle model. EPA required automakers to achieve a fleet average emissions rate of 0.07 grams of NO_x per mile (gpm). Automakers whose fleet average is below 0.07 gpm could generate credits that they could either use in a later model year or sell to another auto manufacturer. This rule does allow the production of certain higher polluting vehicles that consumers desire. However, it also provides a strong incentive for the industry to develop technology well beyond the 0.07 gpm standard, since any higher polluting vehicle will have to be offset by a lower polluting one.

Industrial Air Toxics: The 1990 Clean Air Act Amendments called on EPA to establish national emissions standards to control major industrial sources of toxic air pollution. EPA has used emissions averaging as one of several ways to provide compliance flexibility in these industry-by-industry standards. For example, emissions averaging is permitted by national air toxics emissions standards for petroleum refining, synthetic organic chemical manufacturing, polymers and resins manufacturing, aluminum production, wood furniture manufacturing, printing and publishing, and a number of other sectors. To avoid shifting

SECTION XII

CAPSTONE PROBLEM: SHOULD GREENHOUSE
GASES BE LISTED AS A NAAQS POLLUTANT?

271

risks from one area to another, toxics averaging is allowed only within individual facilities. With appropriate safeguards, EPA also has used other methods, including multiple compliance options, to help provide flexibility in complying with air toxics rules.

Ozone Layer Depletion: In gradually phasing out the production of chemicals that harm the stratospheric ozone layer, EPA is giving producers and importers the flexibility to trade allowances. Under the Montreal Protocol, the United States and other developed countries agreed to stop producing and importing CFCs (chlorofluorocarbons) and other chemicals that are destructive to the ozone layer. By 1996, production of the most harmful ozone-depleting chemicals, including CFCs, virtually ceased in the United States and other developed countries. Additional chemicals are to be phased out in the future. Provided the United States and the world community maintain their commitment to planned protection efforts, the stratospheric ozone layer is projected to recover by the middle of the 21st century.

The phase-out of these chemicals is being achieved by using trading rules developed by EPA, rules that have served as a model for programs in other countries. In part because of the flexible market-based approach, the phase-out of CFCs was much less expensive than predicted. In 1988, EPA estimated that a 50% reduction of CFCs by 1998 would cost $3.55 per kilogram. In 1993, the cost for a 100% phase-out by 1996 was reduced to $2.45 per kilogram.

––––––––––

Since EPA issued this report in 2001, the agency has continued to add emissions trading to its regulatory programs. Building on the NO_x SIP Call mentioned in the report, EPA's Cross-State Air Pollution Rule (mentioned above) issued in 2011 includes a substantial trading component. The Rule establishes a pollution limit for each of the twenty-three states it covers and then allows trading, with limits, of emissions allowances between power plants in the same state or across states. EPA's Clean Power Plan, summarized in the final capstone problem of this chapter, regulates greenhouse gas emissions from existing power plants and includes an option for states to join an interstate cap-and-trade program to reduce the costs of implementing emissions reductions.

––––––––––

XII. CAPSTONE PROBLEM: SHOULD GREENHOUSE GASES BE LISTED AS A NAAQS POLLUTANT?

By now, most Americans have some familiarity with the related concepts of global warming, climate change, and climate disruption. Global average temperatures near Earth's surface are increasing. They rose 1.5°F since 1900 and are projected to rise another 0.5 to 8.6°F in this century. Indeed, 14 of the 15 warmest years on record have occurred since 2000.

This global warming is causing, and will continue to cause, changes in climate. But the climate impacts vary and are more complicated than simply warming by a few degrees. Some areas will have more intense rainfall, leading to flooding and erosion. Some areas will have more drought. Some areas will experience more heat waves. Some areas may even experience cooling. Higher temperatures are melting glaciers and the polar ice caps. Oceans are warming and becoming more acidic, and sea levels are rising. The World Health Organization predicts that health impacts of climate change—increased malnutrition, malaria, diarrhea and heat stress—will cause approximately 250,000 additional deaths per year.

Scientists have little doubt that human activities are the primary cause of this warming and climate disruption. A variety of human activities, most importantly fossil fuel combustion, emit carbon dioxide and other greenhouse gases into the atmosphere. Greenhouse gases trap energy and cause atmospheric warming. In limited amounts, this is beneficial—indeed, necessary to sustain life. But when too much greenhouse gases are emitted and build up in the atmosphere, too much warming occurs, causing dangerous climate disruption.

The Organization for Environmental Litigation (OEL), a large and well-respected national environmental advocacy group, is considering petitioning EPA to list greenhouse gases as a criteria pollutant under the Clean Air Act. You are an attorney for OEL and have been asked to brief OEL's board, addressing the following questions:

   a.   How strong are the legal arguments in favor of listing greenhouse gases as a criteria air pollutant? What information or data would be necessary to support a petition to list greenhouse gases as a criteria air pollutant?

   b.   If EPA is inclined to deny the petition, what arguments is it likely to make?

   c.   What are the likely consequences of listing greenhouse gases as a criteria air pollutant? Would these consequences advance OEL's objective of more stringent regulation of greenhouse gas emissions?

   d.   If EPA denies the petition, should OEL file a lawsuit? What is the likelihood that OEL would prevail in such a lawsuit?

   e.   Should OEL wait to file a petition at least until after litigation over EPA's Clean Power Plan (described below) has concluded? How might listing greenhouse gases as a

criteria air pollutant affect the Clean Power Plan litigation,
and vice versa?

———————

Recall from earlier in this chapter that Clean Air Act section 108, 42
U.S.C. § 7408, establishes the standard for listing criteria air pollutants:

CAA § 108, 42 U.S.C. § 7408. Air quality criteria and control techniques

(a) Air pollutant list; publication and revision by Administrator;
issuance of air quality criteria for air pollutants

(1) For the purpose of establishing national primary and
secondary ambient air quality standards, the Administrator shall
within 30 days after December 31, 1970, publish, and shall from
time to time thereafter revise, a list which includes each air
pollutant—

(A) emissions of which, in his judgment, cause or contribute to
air pollution which may reasonably be anticipated to endanger
public health or welfare;

(B) the presence of which in the ambient air results from
numerous or diverse mobile or stationary sources; and

(C) for which air quality criteria had not been issued before
December 31, 1970, but for which he plans to issue air quality
criteria under this section.

Natural Resources Defense Council, Inc. v. Train
545 F.2d 320 (2d Cir. 1976)

■ J. JOSEPH SMITH, CIRCUIT JUDGE:

The Environmental Protection Agency, ("EPA"), and its Administrator,
Russell Train, appeal from an order of the United States District Court
for the Southern District of New York, Charles E. Stewart, Jr., Judge, in
an action under § 304 of the Clean Air Act, as amended, 42 U.S.C.
§ 1857h–2(a), requiring the Administrator of the EPA, within thirty days,
to place lead on a list of air pollutants under § 108(a)(1) of the Clean Air
Act, as amended, 42 U.S.C. § 1857c–3(a)(1), ("the Act"). We affirm the
order of the district court.

The 1970 Clean Air Act Amendments provide two different approaches
for controlling pollutants in the air. One approach, incorporated in
§§ 108–110, 42 U.S.C. §§ 1857c–3 to c–5, provides for the publication of a
list of pollutants adverse to public health or welfare, derived from

"numerous or diverse" sources, the promulgation of national ambient air quality standards for listed pollutants, and subsequent implementation of these standards by the states. The second approach of the Act provides for control of certain pollutants at the source, pursuant to §§ 111, 112, 202, 211 and 231 (42 U.S.C. §§ 1857c–6, c–7, f–1, f–6c, f–9).

The relevant part of § 108 reads as follows:

> (a)(1)   For the purpose of establishing national primary and secondary ambient air quality standards, the Administrator shall within 30 days after December 31, 1970, publish, and shall from time to time thereafter revise, a list which includes each air pollutant
>
>> (A) which in his judgment has an adverse effect on public health or welfare;
>>
>> (B) the presence of which in the ambient air results from numerous or diverse mobile or stationary sources; and
>>
>> (C) for which air quality criteria had not been issued before December 31, 1970, but for which he plans to issue air quality criteria under this section.

Once a pollutant has been listed under § 108(a)(1), §§ 109 and 110 of the Act are automatically invoked. These sections require that for any pollutant for which air quality criteria are issued under § 108(a)(1)(C) after the date of enactment of the Clean Air Amendments of 1970, the Administrator must simultaneously issue air quality standards. Within nine months of the promulgation of such standards, states are required to submit implementation plans to the Administrator.[3] § 110(a)(1). The Administrator must approve or disapprove a state plan within four months.[4] § 110(a)(2). If a state fails to submit an acceptable plan, the Administrator is required to prepare and publish such a plan himself. § 110(c). State implementation plans must provide for the attainment of primary ambient air quality standards no later than three years from the date of approval of a plan.[5] § 110(a)(2)(A)(i). Extension of the three-year period for attaining the primary standard may be granted by the Administrator only in very limited circumstances, and in no case for more than two years. § 110(e).

---

[3]   Eds.: The Act now gives states three years to submit their implementation plans. 42 U.S.C. § 7410(a)(1).

[4]   Eds.: The Act now gives EPA twelve months after a state has submitted a complete implementation plan to approve or disapprove the plan. 42 U.S.C. § 7410(k)(2).

[5]   Eds.: Clean Air Act § 172 now establishes a general deadline requiring nonattainment areas to reach attainment with the applicable NAAQS within five years of the date the area was designated nonattainment. 42 U.S.C. § 7502(a)(2)(A). Pollutant-specific programs for some nonattainment areas extend the statutory deadlines to as long as twenty years. See, e.g., CAA § 181, 42 U.S.C. § 7511. EPA can grant two one-year extensions of attainment deadlines. 42 U.S.C. § 7502(a)(2)(C).

SECTION XII

CAPSTONE PROBLEM: SHOULD GREENHOUSE
GASES BE LISTED AS A NAAQS POLLUTANT?

275

The EPA concedes that lead meets the conditions of §§ 108(a)(1)(A) and (B) that it has an adverse effect on public health and welfare, and that the presence of lead in the ambient air results from numerous or diverse mobile or stationary sources. The EPA maintains, however, that under § 108(a)(1)(C) of the Act, the Administrator retains discretion whether to list a pollutant, even though the pollutant meets the criteria of §§ 108(a)(1)(A) and (B). The EPA regards the listing of lead under § 108(a)(1) and the issuance of ambient air quality standards as one of numerous alternative control strategies for lead available to it. Listing of substances is mandatory, the EPA argues, only for those pollutants for which the Administrator "plans to issue air quality criteria." He may, it is contended, choose not to issue, i.e., not "plan to issue" such criteria, and decide to control lead solely by regulating emission at the source, regardless of the total concentration of lead in the ambient air. The Administrator argues that if he chooses to control lead (or other pollutants) under § 211, he is not required to list the pollutant under § 108(a)(1) or to set air quality standards. * * *

We agree with the district court and with appellees, National Resources Defense Council, Inc., et al., that the interpretation of the Clean Air Act advanced by the EPA is contrary to the structure of the Act as a whole, and that if accepted, it would vitiate the public policy underlying the enactment of the 1970 Amendments as set forth in the Act and in its legislative history. Recent court decisions are in accord, and have construed § 108(a)(1) to be mandatory if the criteria of subsections A and B are met. * * *

EPA has not to date listed greenhouse gases as a criteria air pollutant. The agency has, however, undertaken other regulatory initiatives under the Clean Air Act to limit greenhouse gas emissions. The genesis of these regulatory initiatives was a request by environmental advocacy groups in 1999 asking EPA to regulate greenhouse gas emissions from new motor vehicles under Clean Air Act § 202, 42 U.S.C. § 7521. When EPA denied the request at the inception of President George W. Bush's Administration, environmentalists and states sued EPA. The case ultimately made its way to the Supreme Court, resulting in the landmark decision, *Massachusetts v. EPA*.

Massachusetts v. EPA

549 U.S. 497 (2007)

■ JUSTICE STEVENS delivered the opinion of the Court.

* * *

I

Section 202(a)(1) of the Clean Air Act, as added by Pub. L. 89–272, § 101(8), 79 Stat. 992, and as amended by, inter alia, 84 Stat. 1690 and 91 Stat. 791, 42 U.S.C. § 7521(a)(1), provides:

> "The [EPA] Administrator shall by regulation prescribe (and from time to time revise) in accordance with the provisions of this section, standards applicable to the emission of any air pollutant from any class or classes of new motor vehicles or new motor vehicle engines, which in his judgment cause, or contribute to, air pollution which may reasonably be anticipated to endanger public health or welfare . . . ."

The Act defines "air pollutant" to include "any air pollution agent or combination of such agents, including any physical, chemical, biological, radioactive . . . substance or matter which is emitted into or otherwise enters the ambient air." § 7602(g). "Welfare" is also defined broadly: among other things, it includes "effects on . . . weather . . . and climate." § 7602(h). * * *

II

On October 20, 1999, a group of 19 private organizations filed a rulemaking petition asking EPA to regulate "greenhouse gas emissions from new motor vehicles under § 202 of the Clean Air Act." * * *

On September 8, 2003, EPA entered an order denying the rulemaking petition. The agency gave two reasons for its decision: (1) that contrary to the opinions of its former general counsels, the Clean Air Act does not authorize EPA to issue mandatory regulations to address global climate change; and (2) that even if the agency had the authority to set greenhouse gas emission standards, it would be unwise to do so at this time.

In concluding that it lacked statutory authority over greenhouse gases, EPA observed that Congress "was well aware of the global climate change issue when it last comprehensively amended the [Clean Air Act] in 1990," yet it declined to adopt a proposed amendment establishing binding emissions limitations. Congress instead chose to authorize further investigation into climate change. EPA further reasoned that Congress' "specially tailored solutions to global atmospheric issues,"—in particular, its 1990 enactment of a comprehensive scheme to regulate pollutants that depleted the ozone layer,—counseled against reading the general

SECTION XII

CAPSTONE PROBLEM: SHOULD GREENHOUSE
GASES BE LISTED AS A NAAQS POLLUTANT?

277

authorization of § 202(a)(1) to confer regulatory authority over greenhouse gases. * * *

III

Petitioners, now joined by intervenor States and local governments, sought review of EPA's order in the United States Court of Appeals for the District of Columbia Circuit. Although each of the three judges on the panel wrote a separate opinion, two judges agreed "that the EPA Administrator properly exercised his discretion under § 202(a)(1) in denying the petition for rule making." The court therefore denied the petition for review. * * *

VI

On the merits, the first question is whether § 202(a)(1) of the Clean Air Act authorizes EPA to regulate greenhouse gas emissions from new motor vehicles in the event that it forms a "judgment" that such emissions contribute to climate change. We have little trouble concluding that it does. In relevant part, § 202(a)(1) provides that EPA "shall by regulation prescribe . . . standards applicable to the emission of any air pollutant from any class or classes of new motor vehicles or new motor vehicle engines, which in [the Administrator's] judgment cause, or contribute to, air pollution which may reasonably be anticipated to endanger public health or welfare." 42 U.S.C. § 7521(a)(1). Because EPA believes that Congress did not intend it to regulate substances that contribute to climate change, the agency maintains that carbon dioxide is not an "air pollutant" within the meaning of the provision.

The statutory text forecloses EPA's reading. The Clean Air Act's sweeping definition of "air pollutant" includes "any air pollution agent or combination of such agents, including any physical, chemical . . . substance or matter which is emitted into or otherwise enters the ambient air . . . ." § 7602(g) (emphasis added). On its face, the definition embraces all airborne compounds of whatever stripe, and underscores that intent through the repeated use of the word "any." Carbon dioxide, methane, nitrous oxide, and hydrofluorocarbons are without a doubt "physical [and] chemical . . . substance[s] which [are] emitted into . . . the ambient air." The statute is unambiguous. * * *

While the Congresses that drafted § 202(a)(1) might not have appreciated the possibility that burning fossil fuels could lead to global warming, they did understand that without regulatory flexibility, changing circumstances and scientific developments would soon render the Clean Air Act obsolete. The broad language of § 202(a)(1) reflects an intentional effort to confer the flexibility necessary to forestall such obsolescence. Because greenhouse gases fit well within the Clean Air Act's capacious definition of "air pollutant," we hold that EPA has the statutory authority to regulate the emission of such gases from new motor vehicles.

VII

The alternative basis for EPA's decision—that even if it does have statutory authority to regulate greenhouse gases, it would be unwise to do so at this time—rests on reasoning divorced from the statutory text. While the statute does condition the exercise of EPA's authority on its formation of a "judgment," 42 U.S.C. § 7521(a)(1), that judgment must relate to whether an air pollutant "cause[s], or contribute[s] to, air pollution which may reasonably be anticipated to endanger public health or welfare," *ibid.* Put another way, the use of the word "judgment" is not a roving license to ignore the statutory text. It is but a direction to exercise discretion within defined statutory limits.

If EPA makes a finding of endangerment, the Clean Air Act requires the agency to regulate emissions of the deleterious pollutant from new motor vehicles. *Ibid.* (stating that "[EPA] shall by regulation prescribe . . . standards applicable to the emission of any air pollutant from any class of new motor vehicles"). EPA no doubt has significant latitude as to the manner, timing, content, and coordination of its regulations with those of other agencies. But once EPA has responded to a petition for rulemaking, its reasons for action or inaction must conform to the authorizing statute. Under the clear terms of the Clean Air Act, EPA can avoid taking further action only if it determines that greenhouse gases do not contribute to climate change or if it provides some reasonable explanation as to why it cannot or will not exercise its discretion to determine whether they do. Ibid. To the extent that this constrains agency discretion to pursue other priorities of the Administrator or the President, this is the congressional design. * * *

In short, EPA has offered no reasoned explanation for its refusal to decide whether greenhouse gases cause or contribute to climate change. Its action was therefore "arbitrary, capricious, . . . or otherwise not in accordance with law." 42 U.S.C. § 7607(d)(9)(A). We need not and do not reach the question whether on remand EPA must make an endangerment finding, or whether policy concerns can inform EPA's actions in the event that it makes such a finding. *Cf. Chevron U.S.A. Inc. v. Natural Resources Defense Council, Inc.*, 467 U.S. 837, 843–844 (1984). We hold only that EPA must ground its reasons for action or inaction in the statute.

VIII

The judgment of the Court of Appeals is reversed, and the case is remanded for further proceedings consistent with this opinion.

It is so ordered.

■ [JUSTICE SCALIA, joined by CHIEF JUSTICE ROBERTS, JUSTICE THOMAS, and JUSTICE ALITO, filed a dissenting opinion.]

SECTION XII

CAPSTONE PROBLEM: SHOULD GREENHOUSE
GASES BE LISTED AS A NAAQS POLLUTANT?

279

Massachusetts v. EPA is relevant to your analysis in two important respects. First, the case set in motion a chain of events that comprise EPA's regulatory program for addressing greenhouse gas emissions. As such, it is important to understand *Massachusetts v. EPA* as a step toward understanding EPA's climate change programs. The Supreme Court decided *Massachusetts v. EPA* in 2007, toward the end of President George W. Bush's term. President Barack Obama, who was inaugurated in early 2009, had campaigned on a platform that promised action to address climate change. In a 2012 decision, the D.C. Circuit explained what actions EPA took under President Obama to follow *Massachusetts v. EPA*'s directive:

> *Massachusetts v. EPA* spurred a cascading series of greenhouse gas-related rules and regulations. First, in direct response to the Supreme Court's directive, EPA issued an Endangerment Finding for greenhouse gases. *Endangerment and Cause or Contribute Findings for Greenhouse Gases Under Section 202(a) of the Clean Air Act* ("Endangerment Finding"), 74 Fed. Reg. 66,496 (Dec. 15, 2009). The Endangerment Finding defined as a single "air pollutant" an "aggregate group of six long-lived and directly-emitted greenhouse gases" that are "well mixed" together in the atmosphere and cause global climate change: carbon dioxide, methane, nitrous oxide, hydrofluorocarbons, perfluorocarbons, and sulfur hexafluoride. Following "common practice," EPA measured the impact of these gases on a "carbon dioxide equivalent basis," (CO_2e) which is based on the gases' "warming effect relative to carbon dioxide . . . over a specified timeframe." (Using the carbon dioxide equivalent equation, for example, a mixture of X amount of nitrous oxide and Y amount of sulfur hexafluoride is expressed as Z amount of CO_2e). After compiling and considering a considerable body of scientific evidence, EPA concluded that motor-vehicle emissions of these six well-mixed gases "contribute to the total greenhouse gas air pollution, and thus to the climate change problem, which is reasonably anticipated to endanger public health and welfare."
>
> Next, and pursuant to the CAA's requirement that EPA establish motor-vehicle emission standards for "any air pollutant . . . which may reasonably be anticipated to endanger public health or welfare," 42 U.S.C. § 7521(a)(1), the agency promulgated its Tailpipe Rule for greenhouse gases. *Light-Duty Vehicle Greenhouse Gas Emission Standards and Corporate Average Fuel Economy Standards; Final Rule* ("Tailpipe Rule"), 75 Fed. Reg. 25,324 (May 7, 2010). Effective January 2, 2011, the Tailpipe Rule set greenhouse gas emission standards for

cars and light trucks as part of a joint rulemaking with fuel economy standards issued by the National Highway Traffic Safety Administration (NHTSA).

Under EPA's longstanding interpretation of the CAA, the Tailpipe Rule automatically triggered regulation of stationary greenhouse gas emitters under two separate sections of the Act. The first, the Prevention of Significant Deterioration of Air Quality (PSD) program, requires state-issued construction permits for certain types of stationary sources—for example, iron and steel mill plants—if they have the potential to emit over 100 tons per year (tpy) of "any air pollutant." *See* 42 U.S.C. §§ 7475; 7479(1). All other stationary sources are subject to PSD permitting if they have the potential to emit over 250 tpy of "any air pollutant." *Id.* § 7479(1). The second provision, Title V, requires state-issued operating permits for stationary sources that have the potential to emit at least 100 tpy of "any air pollutant." *Id.* § 7602(j). EPA has long interpreted the phrase "any air pollutant" in both these provisions to mean any air pollutant that is regulated under the CAA. *See Requirements for Preparation, Adoption, and Submittal of Implementation Plans; Approval and Promulgation of Implementation Plans* ("1980 Implementation Plan Requirements"), 45 Fed. Reg. 52,676, 52,711 (Aug. 7, 1980) (PSD program); *Prevention of Significant Deterioration and Title V Greenhouse Gas Tailoring Rule* ("Tailoring Rule"), 75 Fed. Reg. 31,514, 31,553–54 (June 3, 2010) (discussing history of Title V regulation and applicability). And once the Tailpipe Rule set motor-vehicle emission standards for greenhouse gases, they became a regulated pollutant under the Act, requiring PSD and Title V greenhouse permitting.

Acting pursuant to this longstanding interpretation of the PSD and Title V programs, EPA issued two rules phasing in stationary source greenhouse gas regulation. First, in the Timing Rule, EPA concluded that an air pollutant becomes "subject to regulation" under the Clean Air Act—and thus subject to PSD and Title V permitting—only once a regulation requiring control of that pollutant takes effect. *Reconsideration of Interpretation of Regulations That Determine Pollutants Covered by Clean Air Act Permitting Programs* ("Timing Rule"), 75 Fed. Reg. 17,004 (Apr. 2, 2010). Therefore, EPA concluded, major stationary emitters of greenhouse gases would be subject to PSD and Title V permitting regulations on January 2, 2011— the date on which the Tailpipe Rule became effective, and thus, the date when greenhouse gases first became regulated under the CAA.

Next, EPA promulgated the Tailoring Rule. In the Tailoring Rule, EPA noted that greenhouse gases are emitted in far greater volumes than other pollutants. Indeed, millions of industrial, residential, and commercial sources exceed the 100/250 tpy statutory emissions threshold for CO_2e. Tailoring Rule, 75 Fed. Reg. at 31,534–36. Immediately adding these sources to the PSD and Title V programs would, EPA predicted, result in tremendous costs to industry and state permitting authorities. *See id.* As a result, EPA announced that it was "relieving overwhelming permitting burdens that would, in the absence of this rule, fall on permitting authorities and sources." Departing from the CAA's 100/250 tpy emissions threshold, the Tailoring Rule provided that only the largest sources—those exceeding 75,000 or 100,000 tpy CO_2e, depending on the program and project—would initially be subject to greenhouse gas permitting. *Id.* at 31,523. (The Tailoring Rule further provided that regulated sources must also emit greenhouse gases at levels that exceed the 100/250 tpy emissions threshold on a *mass* basis. That is, they must emit over 100/250 tpy of actual pollutants, in addition to exceeding the 75,000/100,000 tpy carbon dioxide equivalent.)

Coalition for Responsible Regulation, Inc. v. EPA, 684 F.3d 102, 114–16 (D.C. Cir. 2012) *aff'd in part, rev'd in part sub nom. Util. Air Regulatory Group v. EPA*, 134 S. Ct. 2427 (2015). Several of these EPA rules were at issue in the following case.

In addition to understanding *Massachusetts v. EPA* for its direct consequences, the case also set important precedent for future litigation over EPA's authority to regulate greenhouse gas emissions under the Clean Air Act. As to that issue, how does the statutory standard at issue in *Massachusetts v. EPA* compare to the statutory standard for listing criteria air pollutants? Given the Supreme Court's holding in *Massachusetts v. EPA*, is there any viable legal argument that greenhouse gases should not be listed as a criteria air pollutant?

The Supreme Court next addressed EPA's climate change program in its 2014 decision in *Utility Air Regulatory Group v. EPA*. Like *Massachusetts v. EPA*, *UARG* (as it is known) is important both for its direct consequences for EPA's regulatory programs and for its more indirect precedential impacts. Justice Scalia, who dissented in *Massachusetts v. EPA*, wrote the majority opinion in *UARG*.

———————

Utility Air Regulatory Group v. EPA
134 S. Ct. 2427 (2014)

■ JUSTICE SCALIA announced the judgment of the Court and delivered the opinion of the Court with respect to Parts I and II.

Acting pursuant to the Clean Air Act, 42 U.S.C. §§ 7401–7671q, the Environmental Protection Agency recently set standards for emissions of "greenhouse gases" (substances it believes contribute to "global climate change") from new motor vehicles. We must decide whether it was permissible for EPA to determine that its motor-vehicle greenhouse-gas regulations automatically triggered permitting requirements under the Act for stationary sources that emit greenhouse gases.

I.   Background

* * * Numerous parties, including several States, filed petitions for review in the D.C. Circuit under 42 U.S.C. § 7607(b), challenging EPA's greenhouse-gas-related actions. The Court of Appeals dismissed some of the petitions for lack of jurisdiction and denied the remainder. *Coalition for Responsible Regulation, Inc. v. EPA,* 684 F.3d 102 (2012) (*per curiam*). First, it upheld the Endangerment Finding and Tailpipe Rule. Next, it held that EPA's interpretation of the PSD permitting requirement as applying to "any regulated air pollutant," including greenhouse gases, was "compelled by the statute." The court also found it "crystal clear that PSD permittees must install BACT for greenhouse gases." Because it deemed petitioners' arguments about the PSD program insufficiently applicable to Title V, it held they had "forfeited any challenges to EPA's greenhouse gas-inclusive interpretation of Title V." Finally, it held that petitioners were without Article III standing to challenge EPA's efforts to limit the reach of the PSD program and Title V through the Triggering and Tailoring Rules. The court denied rehearing en banc, with Judges Brown and Kavanaugh each dissenting.

We granted six petitions for certiorari but agreed to decide only one question: " 'Whether EPA permissibly determined that its regulation of greenhouse gas emissions from new motor vehicles triggered permitting requirements under the Clean Air Act for stationary sources that emit greenhouse gases.' "

II.   Analysis

This litigation presents two distinct challenges to EPA's stance on greenhouse-gas permitting for stationary sources. First, we must decide whether EPA permissibly determined that a source may be subject to the PSD and Title V permitting requirements on the sole basis of the source's potential to emit greenhouse gases. Second, we must decide whether EPA permissibly determined that a source already subject to the PSD program because of its emission of conventional pollutants (an "anyway" source)

SECTION XII

CAPSTONE PROBLEM: SHOULD GREENHOUSE
GASES BE LISTED AS A NAAQS POLLUTANT?

283

may be required to limit its greenhouse-gas emissions by employing the "best available control technology" for greenhouse gases. The Solicitor General joins issue on both points but evidently regards the second as more important; he informs us that "anyway" sources account for roughly 83% of American stationary-source greenhouse-gas emissions, compared to just 3% for the additional, non-"anyway" sources EPA sought to regulate at Steps 2 and 3 of the Tailoring Rule.

We review EPA's interpretations of the Clean Air Act using the standard set forth in *Chevron U.S.A. Inc. v. Natural Resources Defense Council, Inc.,* 467 U.S. 837, 842–843 (1984). Under *Chevron,* we presume that when an agency-administered statute is ambiguous with respect to what it prescribes, Congress has empowered the agency to resolve the ambiguity. The question for a reviewing court is whether in doing so the agency has acted reasonably and thus has "stayed within the bounds of its statutory authority." *Arlington v. FCC,* 569 U.S. ___, ___, 133 S. Ct. 1863, 1868 (2013) (emphasis deleted).

A.   The PSD and Title V Triggers

We first decide whether EPA permissibly interpreted the statute to provide that a source may be required to obtain a PSD or Title V permit on the sole basis of its potential greenhouse-gas emissions.

1

EPA thought its conclusion that a source's greenhouse-gas emissions may necessitate a PSD or Title V permit followed from the Act's unambiguous language. The Court of Appeals agreed and held that the statute "compelled" EPA's interpretation. We disagree. The statute compelled EPA's greenhouse-gas-inclusive interpretation with respect to neither the PSD program nor Title V.

The Court of Appeals reasoned by way of a flawed syllogism: Under *Massachusetts,* the general, Act-wide definition of "air pollutant" includes greenhouse gases; the Act requires permits for major emitters of "any air pollutant"; therefore, the Act requires permits for major emitters of greenhouse gases. The conclusion follows from the premises only if the air pollutants referred to in the permit-requiring provisions (the minor premise) are the same air pollutants encompassed by the Act-wide definition as interpreted in *Massachusetts* (the major premise). Yet no one—least of all EPA—endorses that proposition, and it is obviously untenable.

The Act-wide definition says that an air pollutant is "any air pollution agent or combination of such agents, including any physical, chemical, biological, [or] radioactive . . . substance or matter which is emitted into or otherwise enters the ambient air." § 7602(g). In *Massachusetts,* the Court held that the Act-wide definition includes greenhouse gases because it is all-encompassing; it "embraces all airborne compounds of whatever stripe." 549 U.S., at 529. But where the term "air pollutant" appears in the Act's operative provisions, EPA has routinely given it a narrower, context-appropriate meaning.

That is certainly true of the provisions that require PSD and Title V permitting for major emitters of "any air pollutant." Since 1978, EPA's regulations have interpreted "air pollutant" in the PSD permitting trigger as limited to *regulated* air pollutants, 43 Fed. Reg. 26403, codified, as amended, 40 C.F.R. § 52.21(b)(1)–(2), (50)—a class much narrower than *Massachusetts*' "all airborne compounds of whatever stripe," 549 U.S., at 529. And since 1993 EPA has informally taken the same position with regard to the Title V permitting trigger, a position the Agency ultimately incorporated into some of the regulations at issue here. Those interpretations were appropriate: It is plain as day that the Act does not envision an elaborate, burdensome permitting process for major emitters of steam, oxygen, or other harmless airborne substances. It takes some cheek for EPA to insist that it cannot possibly give "air pollutant" a reasonable, context-appropriate meaning in the PSD and Title V contexts when it has been doing precisely that for decades.

Nor are those the only places in the Act where EPA has inferred from statutory context that a generic reference to air pollutants does not encompass every substance falling within the Act-wide definition. Other examples abound:

- The Act authorizes EPA to enforce new source performance standards (NSPS) against a pre-existing source if, after promulgation of the standards, the source undergoes a physical or operational change that increases its emission of "any air pollutant." § 7411(a)(2), (4), (b)(1)(B). EPA interprets that provision as limited to air pollutants *for which EPA has promulgated new source performance standards*. 36 Fed. Reg. 24877 (1971), codified, as amended, 40 C.F.R. § 60.2; 40 Fed. Reg. 58419 (1975), codified, as amended, 40 C.F.R. § 60.14(a).

- The Act requires a permit for the construction or operation in a nonattainment area of a source with the potential to emit 100 tons per year of "any air pollutant." §§ 7502(c)(5), 7602(j). EPA interprets that provision as limited to pollutants *for which the area is designated nonattainment*. 45 Fed. Reg. 52745 (1980), promulgating 40 C.F.R. § 51.18(j)(2), as amended, § 51.165(a)(2).

- The Act directs EPA to require "enhanced monitoring and submission of compliance certifications" for any source with the potential to emit 100 tons per year of "any air pollutant." §§ 7414(a)(3), 7602(j). EPA interprets that

SECTION XII

CAPSTONE PROBLEM: SHOULD GREENHOUSE
GASES BE LISTED AS A NAAQS POLLUTANT?

285

provision as limited to *regulated* pollutants. 62 Fed. Reg.
54941 (1997), codified at 40 C.F.R. §§ 64.1, 64.2.

- The Act requires certain sources of air pollutants that
  interfere with visibility to undergo retrofitting if they have
  the potential to emit 250 tons per year of "any pollutant."
  § 7491(b)(2)(A), (g)(7). EPA interprets that provision as
  limited to *visibility-impairing* air pollutants. 70 Fed. Reg.
  39160 (2005), codified at 40 C.F.R. pt. 51, App. Y, § II.A.3.

Although these limitations are nowhere to be found in the Act-wide
definition, in each instance EPA has concluded—as it has in the PSD and
Title V context—that the statute is not using "air pollutant" in
Massachusetts' broad sense to mean any airborne substance whatsoever.

Massachusetts did not invalidate all these longstanding constructions.
That case did not hold that EPA must always regulate greenhouse gases
as an "air pollutant" everywhere that term appears in the statute, but
only that EPA must "ground its reasons for action *or inaction* in the
statute" (emphasis added), rather than on "reasoning divorced from the
statutory text." EPA's inaction with regard to Title II was not sufficiently
grounded in the statute, the Court said, in part because nothing in the
Act suggested that regulating greenhouse gases under that Title would
conflict with the statutory design. Title II would not compel EPA to
regulate in any way that would be "extreme," "counterintuitive," or
contrary to " 'common sense.' " At most, it would require EPA to take the
modest step of adding greenhouse-gas standards to the roster of new-
motor-vehicle emission regulations. * * *

We need not, and do not, pass on the validity of all the limiting
constructions EPA has given the term "air pollutant" throughout the Act.
We merely observe that taken together, they belie EPA's rigid insistence
that when interpreting the PSD and Title V permitting requirements it
is bound by the Act-wide definition's inclusion of greenhouse gases, no
matter how incompatible that inclusion is with those programs'
regulatory structure.

In sum, there is no insuperable textual barrier to EPA's interpreting "any
air pollutant" in the permitting triggers of PSD and Title V to encompass
only pollutants emitted in quantities that enable them to be sensibly
regulated at the statutory thresholds, and to exclude those atypical
pollutants that, like greenhouse gases, are emitted in such vast
quantities that their inclusion would radically transform those programs
and render them unworkable as written.

2

Having determined that EPA was mistaken in thinking the Act
compelled a greenhouse-gas-inclusive interpretation of the PSD and Title
V triggers, we next consider the Agency's alternative position that its

interpretation was justified as an exercise of its "discretion" to adopt "a reasonable construction of the statute." Tailoring Rule 31517. We conclude that EPA's interpretation is not permissible. * * *

EPA itself has repeatedly acknowledged that applying the PSD and Title V permitting requirements to greenhouse gases would be inconsistent with—in fact, would overthrow—the Act's structure and design. In the Tailoring Rule, EPA described the calamitous consequences of interpreting the Act in that way. Under the PSD program, annual permit applications would jump from about 800 to nearly 82,000; annual administrative costs would swell from $12 million to over $1.5 billion; and decade-long delays in issuing permits would become common, causing construction projects to grind to a halt nationwide. The picture under Title V was equally bleak: The number of sources required to have permits would jump from fewer than 15,000 to about 6.1 million; annual administrative costs would balloon from $62 million to $21 billion; and collectively the newly covered sources would face permitting costs of $147 billion. Moreover, "the great majority of additional sources brought into the PSD and title V programs would be small sources that Congress did not expect would need to undergo permitting." EPA stated that these results would be so "contrary to congressional intent," and would so "severely undermine what Congress sought to accomplish," that they necessitated as much as a 1,000-fold increase in the permitting thresholds set forth in the statute. * * *

EPA's interpretation is also unreasonable because it would bring about an enormous and transformative expansion in EPA's regulatory authority without clear congressional authorization. When an agency claims to discover in a long-extant statute an unheralded power to regulate "a significant portion of the American economy," *FDA v. Brown & Williamson Tobacco Corp.*, 529 U.S. 120, 159 (2000), we typically greet its announcement with a measure of skepticism. We expect Congress to speak clearly if it wishes to assign to an agency decisions of vast "economic and political significance." *Id.*, at 160; see also *MCI Telecommunications Corp. v. American Telephone & Telegraph Co.*, 512 U.S. 218, 231 (1994); *Industrial Union Dept., AFL-CIO v. American Petroleum Institute*, 448 U.S. 607, 645–646 (1980) (plurality opinion). The power to require permits for the construction and modification of tens of thousands, and the operation of millions, of small sources nationwide falls comfortably within the class of authorizations that we have been reluctant to read into ambiguous statutory text. Moreover, in EPA's assertion of that authority, we confront a singular situation: an agency laying claim to extravagant statutory power over the national economy while at the same time strenuously asserting that the authority claimed would render the statute "unrecognizable to the Congress that designed" it. Since, as we hold above, the statute does not compel EPA's interpretation, it would be patently unreasonable—not to say outrageous—for EPA to insist on seizing expansive power that it admits the statute is not designed to grant.

3

EPA thought that despite the foregoing problems, it could make its interpretation reasonable by adjusting the levels at which a source's greenhouse-gas emissions would oblige it to undergo PSD and Title V permitting. Although the Act, in no uncertain terms, requires permits for sources with the potential to emit more than 100 or 250 tons per year of a relevant pollutant, EPA in its Tailoring Rule wrote a new threshold of *100,000* tons per year for greenhouse gases. * * *

We conclude that EPA's rewriting of the statutory thresholds was impermissible and therefore could not validate the Agency's interpretation of the triggering provisions. An agency has no power to "tailor" legislation to bureaucratic policy goals by rewriting unambiguous statutory terms. * * *

B.   BACT for "Anyway" Sources

For the reasons we have given, EPA overstepped its statutory authority when it decided that a source could become subject to PSD or Title V permitting by reason of its greenhouse-gas emissions. But what about "anyway" sources, those that would need permits based on their emissions of more conventional pollutants (such as particulate matter)? We now consider whether EPA reasonably interpreted the Act to require those sources to comply with "best available control technology" emission standards for greenhouse gases.

1

To obtain a PSD permit, a source must be "subject to the best available control technology" for "each pollutant subject to regulation under [the Act]" that it emits. § 7475(a)(4). The Act defines BACT as "an emission limitation based on the maximum degree of reduction of each pollutant subject to regulation" that is "achievable . . . through application of production processes and available methods, systems, and techniques, including fuel cleaning, clean fuels, or treatment or innovative fuel combustion techniques." § 7479(3). BACT is determined "on a case-by-case basis, taking into account energy, environmental, and economic impacts and other costs." *Ibid.*

Some petitioners urge us to hold that EPA may never require BACT for greenhouse gases—even when a source must undergo PSD review based on its emissions of conventional pollutants—because BACT is fundamentally unsuited to greenhouse-gas regulation. BACT, they say, has traditionally been about end-of-stack controls "such as catalytic converters or particle collectors"; but applying it to greenhouse gases will make it more about regulating energy use, which will enable regulators to control "every aspect of a facility's operation and design," right down to the "light bulbs in the factory cafeteria." * * *

2

The question before us is whether EPA's decision to require BACT for greenhouse gases emitted by sources otherwise subject to PSD review is, as a general matter, a permissible interpretation of the statute under *Chevron.* We conclude that it is.

The text of the BACT provision is far less open-ended than the text of the PSD and Title V permitting triggers. It states that BACT is required "for each pollutant subject to regulation under this chapter" (*i.e.,* the entire Act), § 7475(a)(4), a phrase that—as the D.C. Circuit wrote 35 years ago—"would not seem readily susceptible [of] misinterpretation." *Alabama Power Co. v. Costle,* 636 F.2d 323, 404 (1979). Whereas the dubious breadth of "any air pollutant" in the permitting triggers suggests a role for agency judgment in identifying the subset of pollutants covered by the particular regulatory program at issue, the more specific phrasing of the BACT provision suggests that the necessary judgment has already been made by Congress. The wider statutory context likewise does not suggest that the BACT provision can bear a narrowing construction: There is no indication that the Act elsewhere uses, or that EPA has interpreted, "each pollutant subject to regulation under this chapter" to mean anything other than what it says.

Even if the text were not clear, applying BACT to greenhouse gases is not so disastrously unworkable, and need not result in such a dramatic expansion of agency authority, as to convince us that EPA's interpretation is unreasonable. We are not talking about extending EPA jurisdiction over millions of previously unregulated entities, but about moderately increasing the demands EPA (or a state permitting authority) can make of entities already subject to its regulation. And it is not yet clear that EPA's demands will be of a significantly different character from those traditionally associated with PSD review. In short, the record before us does not establish that the BACT provision as written is incapable of being sensibly applied to greenhouse gases. * * *

To sum up: We hold that EPA exceeded its statutory authority when it interpreted the Clean Air Act to require PSD and Title V permitting for stationary sources based on their greenhouse-gas emissions. Specifically, the Agency may not treat greenhouse gases as a pollutant for purposes of defining a "major emitting facility" (or a "modification" thereof) in the PSD context or a "major source" in the Title V context. To the extent its regulations purport to do so, they are invalid. EPA may, however, continue to treat greenhouse gases as a "pollutant subject to regulation under this chapter" for purposes of requiring BACT for "anyway" sources.

SECTION XII

CAPSTONE PROBLEM: SHOULD GREENHOUSE
GASES BE LISTED AS A NAAQS POLLUTANT?

289

The judgment of the Court of Appeals is affirmed in part and reversed in part.

It is so ordered.

■ JUSTICE BREYER, with whom JUSTICE GINSBURG, JUSTICE SOTOMAYOR, and JUSTICE KAGAN join, concurring in part and dissenting in part.

* * * The Tailoring Rule solves the practical problems that would have been caused by the 250 tpy threshold. But what are we to do about the statute's language? The statute specifies a definite number—250, not 100,000—and it says that facilities that are covered by that number must meet the program's requirements. The statute says nothing about agency discretion to change that number. What is to be done? How, given the statute's language, can the EPA exempt from regulation sources that emit more than 250 but less than 100,000 tpy of greenhouse gases (and that also do not emit other regulated pollutants at threshold levels)?

The Court answers by (1) pointing out that regulation at the 250 tpy threshold would produce absurd results, (2) refusing to read the statute as compelling such results, and (3) consequently interpreting the phrase "*any* air pollutant" as containing an implicit exception for greenhouse gases. (Emphasis added.) Put differently, the Court reads the statute as defining "major emitting facility" to mean "stationary sources that have the potential to emit two hundred fifty tons per year or more of any air pollutant *except for those air pollutants, such as carbon dioxide, with respect to which regulation at that threshold would be impractical or absurd or would sweep in smaller sources that Congress did not mean to cover.*"

I agree with the Court that the word "any," when used in a statute, does not normally mean "any in the universe." Cf. *FCC v. NextWave Personal Communications Inc.,* 537 U.S. 293, 311 (2003) (BREYER, J., dissenting) (" 'Tell all customers that . . .' does not refer to every customer of every business in the world"). Rather, "[g]eneral terms as used on particular occasions often carry with them implied restrictions as to scope," *ibid.,* and so courts must interpret the word "any," like all other words, in context. As Judge Learned Hand pointed out when interpreting another statute many years ago, "[w]e can best reach the meaning here, as always, by recourse to the underlying purpose, and, with that as a guide, by trying to project upon the specific occasion how we think persons, actuated by such a purpose, would have dealt with it, if it had been presented to them at the time." *Borella v. Borden Co.,* 145 F.2d 63, 64 (C.A.2 1944). The pursuit of that underlying purpose may sometimes require us to "abandon" a "literal interpretation" of a word like "any." *Id.,* at 64–65.

The law has long recognized that terms such as "any" admit of unwritten limitations and exceptions. Legal philosophers like to point out that a statute providing that " '[w]hoever shall willfully take the life of another shall be punished by death' " need not encompass a man who kills in self-defense; nor must an ordinance imposing fines upon those who occupy a public parking spot for more than two hours penalize a driver who is unable to move because of a parade. See Fuller, The Case of the Speluncean Explorers, 62 Harv. L. Rev. 616, 619, 624 (1949); see also *United States v. Kirby,* 7 Wall. 482, 485–487 (1869) (holding that a statute forbidding knowing and willful obstruction of the mail contains an implicit exception permitting a local sheriff to arrest a mail carrier). The maxim *cessante ratione legis cessat ipse lex*—where a law's rationale ceases to apply, so does the law itself—is not of recent origin. See, *e.g., Zadvydas v. Davis,* 533 U.S. 678, 699 (2001) (citing 1 E. Coke, Institutes *70b); *Green v. Liter,* 8 Cranch 229, 249 (1814) (Story, J.) ("*cessante ratione, cessat ipsa lex*").

I also agree with the Court's point that "a generic reference to air pollutants" in the Clean Air Act need not "encompass every substance falling within the Act-wide definition" that we construed in *Massachusetts,* § 7602(g). As the Court notes, the EPA has interpreted the phrase "any air pollutant," which is used several times in the Act, as limited to "air pollutants *for which EPA has promulgated [new source performance standards]*" in the portion of the Act dealing with those standards, as limited to "*visibility-impairing* air pollutants" in the part of the Act concerned with deleterious effects on visibility, and as limited to "pollutants *for which the area is designated nonattainment*" in the part of the Act aimed at regions that fail to attain air quality standards.

But I do not agree with the Court that the only way to avoid an absurd or otherwise impermissible result in these cases is to create an atextual greenhouse gas exception to the phrase "any air pollutant." After all, the word "any" makes an earlier appearance in the definitional provision, which defines "major emitting facility" to mean "*any* . . . source with the potential to emit two hundred and fifty tons per year or more of any air pollutant." § 7479(1) (emphasis added). As a linguistic matter, one can just as easily read an implicit exception for small-scale greenhouse gas emissions into the phrase "any source" as into the phrase "any air pollutant." And given the purposes of the PSD program and the Act as a whole, as well as the specific roles of the different parts of the statutory definition, finding flexibility in "any source" is far more sensible than the Court's route of finding it in "any air pollutant."

The implicit exception I propose reads almost word for word the same as the Court's, except that the location of the exception has shifted. To repeat, the Court reads the definition of "major emitting facility" as if it referred to "any source with the potential to emit two hundred fifty tons per year or more of any air pollutant *except for those air pollutants, such as carbon dioxide, with respect to which regulation at that threshold*

SECTION XII

CAPSTONE PROBLEM: SHOULD GREENHOUSE
GASES BE LISTED AS A NAAQS POLLUTANT?

291

would be impractical or absurd or would sweep in smaller sources that Congress did not mean to cover." I would simply move the implicit exception, which I've italicized, so that it applies to "source" rather than "air pollutant": "any *source* with the potential to emit two hundred fifty tons per year or more of any air pollutant *except for those sources, such as those emitting unmanageably small amounts of greenhouse gases, with respect to which regulation at that threshold would be impractical or absurd or would sweep in smaller sources that Congress did not mean to cover.*"

From a legal, administrative, and functional perspective—that is, from a perspective that assumes that Congress was not merely trying to arrange words on paper but was seeking to achieve a real-world *purpose*—my way of reading the statute is the more sensible one. For one thing, my reading is consistent with the specific purpose underlying the 250 tpy threshold specified by the statute. The purpose of that number was not to prevent the regulation of dangerous air pollutants that cannot be sensibly regulated at that particular threshold, though that is the effect that the Court's reading gives the threshold. Rather, the purpose was to limit the PSD program's obligations to larger sources while exempting the many small sources whose emissions are low enough that imposing burdensome regulatory requirements on them would be senseless. * * *

An implicit source-related exception would serve this statutory purpose while going no further. The implicit exception that the Court reads into the phrase "any air pollutant," by contrast, goes well beyond the limited congressional objective. Nothing in the statutory text, the legislative history, or common sense suggests that Congress, when it imposed the 250 tpy threshold, was trying to undermine its own deliberate decision to use the broad language "any air pollutant" by removing some substances (rather than some facilities) from the PSD program's coverage. * * *

The Court's decision to read greenhouse gases out of the PSD program drains the Act of its flexibility and chips away at our decision in *Massachusetts.* What sense does it make to read the Act as generally granting the EPA the authority to regulate greenhouse gas emissions and then to read it as denying that power with respect to the programs for large stationary sources at issue here? It is anomalous to read the Act to require the EPA to regulate air pollutants that pose previously unforeseen threats to human health and welfare where "250 tons per year" is a sensible regulatory line but not where, by chemical or regulatory happenstance, a higher line must be drawn. And it is anomalous to read an unwritten exception into the more important phrase of the statutory definition ("any air pollutant") when a similar unwritten exception to less important language (the particular number used by the statute) will do just as well. The implicit exception preferred by the Court produces all of these anomalies, while the source-related exception I propose creates none of them. * * *

I agree with the Court's holding that stationary sources that are subject to the PSD program because they emit other (non-greenhouse-gas) pollutants in quantities above the statutory threshold—those facilities that the Court refers to as "anyway" sources—must meet the "best available control technology" requirement of § 7475(a)(4) with respect to greenhouse gas emissions. I therefore join Part II–B–2 of the Court's opinion. But as for the Court's holding that the EPA cannot interpret the language at issue here to cover facilities that emit more than 100,000 tpy of greenhouse gases by virtue of those emissions, I respectfully dissent.

■ JUSTICE ALITO, with whom JUSTICE THOMAS joins, concurring in part and dissenting in part.

In *Massachusetts v. EPA,* 549 U.S. 497 (2007), this Court considered whether greenhouse gases fall within the Clean Air Act's general definition of an air "pollutant." *Id.,* at 528–529. The Environmental Protection Agency cautioned us that "key provisions of the [Act] cannot cogently be applied to [greenhouse gas] emissions," but the Court brushed the warning aside and had "little trouble" concluding that the Act's "sweeping definition" of a pollutant encompasses greenhouse gases. 549 U.S., at 528–529. I believed *Massachusetts v. EPA* was wrongly decided at the time, and these cases further expose the flaws with that decision.

I

As the present cases now show, trying to fit greenhouse gases into "key provisions" of the Clean Air Act involves more than a "little trouble." These cases concern the provisions of the Act relating to the "Prevention of Significant Deterioration" (PSD), 42 U.S.C. §§ 7470–7492, as well as Title V of the Act, § 7661. And in order to make those provisions apply to greenhouse gases in a way that does not produce absurd results, the EPA effectively amended the Act. The Act contains specific emissions thresholds that trigger PSD and Title V coverage, but the EPA crossed out the figures enacted by Congress and substituted figures of its own.

I agree with the Court that the EPA is neither required nor permitted to take this extraordinary step, and I therefore join Parts I and II–A of the Court's opinion.

II

I do not agree, however, with the Court's conclusion that what it terms "anyway sources," *i.e.,* sources that are subject to PSD and Title V permitting as the result of the emission of conventional pollutants, must install "best available control technology" (BACT) for greenhouse gases. As is the case with the PSD and Title V thresholds, trying to fit greenhouse gases into the BACT analysis badly distorts the scheme that Congress adopted. * * *

[I]t is curious that the Court, having departed from a literal interpretation of the term "pollutant" in Part II–A, turns on its heels and adopts a literal interpretation in Part II–B. The coverage thresholds at issue in Part II–A apply to any "pollutant." The Act's general definition of this term is broad, and in *Massachusetts v. EPA, supra,* the Court held that this definition covers greenhouse gases. The Court does not disturb that holding, but it nevertheless concludes that, as used in the provision triggering PSD coverage, the term "pollutant" actually means "pollutant, other than a greenhouse gas."

In Part II–B, the relevant statutory provision says that BACT must be installed for any "pollutant subject to regulation under [the Act]." § 7475(a)(4). If the term "pollutant" means "pollutant, other than a greenhouse gas," as the Court effectively concludes in Part II–A, the term "pollutant subject to regulation under [the Act]" in § 7475(a)(4) should mean "pollutant, other than a greenhouse gas, subject to regulation under [the Act], and that is subject to regulation under [the Act]." The Court's literalism is selective, and it results in a strange and disjointed regulatory scheme.

Under the Court's interpretation, a source can emit an unlimited quantity of greenhouse gases without triggering the need for a PSD permit. Why might Congress have wanted to allow this? The most likely explanation is that the PSD permitting process is simply not suited for use in regulating this particular pollutant. And if that is so, it makes little sense to require the installation of BACT for greenhouse gases in those instances in which a source happens to be required to obtain a permit due to the emission of a qualifying quantity of some other pollutant that is regulated under the Act. * * *

BACT analysis, like the rest of the Clean Air Act, was developed for use in regulating the emission of conventional pollutants and is simply not suited for use with respect to greenhouse gases. I therefore respectfully dissent from Part II–B–2 of the opinion of the Court.

––––––––––

The Court's decision in *UARG* is relevant to our question—whether greenhouse gases should be listed as criteria air pollutants—in several ways. To make full use of *UARG*, it is important to disentangle these different threads of reasoning.

First, in assessing the consequences of listing greenhouse gases as a criteria air pollutant, it is important to understand which greenhouse gas emissions are regulated already. To that end, consider the following: What sources of greenhouse gas emissions were covered by the EPA regulations described in *UARG*? Which of these sources were excluded from regulation as a result of the *UARG* decision? What sources remain unregulated—at least with respect to their greenhouse gas emissions? What other Clean Air Act regulatory programs described in this chapter can EPA use to regulate greenhouse gas emissions if it lists greenhouse gases as a criteria air pollutant?

Second, *UARG* interprets the term "any air pollutant" in the Prevention of Significant Deterioration (PSD) and Title V programs. The similar term "air pollutant" is used in section 108(a)'s definition of a criteria air pollutant. How does the *UARG* majority interpret "any air pollutant" in the PSD and Title V programs? How does this interpretation of "any air pollutant" in the PSD and Title V programs compare to the *Massachusetts v. EPA* majority's interpretation of "air pollutant" in the mobile source program? What relevance does either interpretation have to the interpretation of "air pollutant" in the definition of a criteria air pollutant under section 108(a)?

Third, on what grounds does the *UARG* majority hold that EPA can interpret the term "any air pollutant" in the PSD and Title V programs to exclude greenhouse gases? Would similar grounds justify, or even require, EPA to interpret "air pollutant" in section 108(a)'s definition of a criteria air pollutant to exclude greenhouse gases.

Power Plant Performance Standards

Since the Supreme Court issued its decision in *UARG* in 2014, EPA has issued more climate change regulations. Understanding these rules may help you decide whether additional regulation of greenhouse gas emissions as a criteria air pollutant would be good policy.

In August 2015, EPA issued two rules aimed at limiting greenhouse gas emissions from power plants. First, the Carbon Pollution Standard for New Power Plants sets greenhouse gas emission standards of performance for new and modified power plants under the New Source Performance Standards program in Clean Air Act section 111(b). 80 Fed. Reg. 64,510 (Oct. 23, 2015). A more important rule, known as the Clean Power Plan, establishes greenhouse gas emissions standards of performance for existing power plants under Clean Air Act section 111(d). 80 Fed. Reg. 64,662 (Oct. 23, 2015).

Earlier in this chapter, we examined Clean Air Act section 111(b), which directs EPA to establish New Source Performance Standards. Clean Air Act section 111(d) directs EPA to establish standards of performance for existing sources. Once a relatively obscure provision, section 111(d) has become a cornerstone of EPA's efforts to regulate greenhouse gas emissions. In reading section 111(d), do you see why it

SECTION XII

CAPSTONE PROBLEM: SHOULD GREENHOUSE
GASES BE LISTED AS A NAAQS POLLUTANT?

295

has not been a major part of the Clean Air Act? Under what circumstances can EPA issue performance standards under § 111(d)?

CAA § 111, 42 U.S.C. § 7411. Standards of performance for new stationary sources

(a) Definitions

For purposes of this section:

(1) The term "standard of performance" means a standard for emissions of air pollutants which reflects the degree of emission limitation achievable through the application of the best system of emission reduction which (taking into account the cost of achieving such reduction and any nonair quality health and environmental impact and energy requirements) the Administrator determines has been adequately demonstrated.

(2) The term "new source" means any stationary source, the construction or modification of which is commenced after the publication of regulations (or, if earlier, proposed regulations) prescribing a standard of performance under this section which will be applicable to such source. * * *

(6) The term "existing source" means any stationary source other than a new source. * * *

(d) Standards of performance for existing sources; remaining useful life of source

(1) The Administrator shall prescribe regulations which shall establish a procedure similar to that provided by section 7410 of this title under which each State shall submit to the Administrator a plan which (A) establishes standards of performance for any existing source for any air pollutant (i) for which air quality criteria have not been issued or which is not included on a list published under section 7408(a) of this title or emitted from a source category which is regulated under section 7412 of this title but (ii) to which a standard of performance under this section would apply if such existing source were a new source, and (B) provides for the implementation and enforcement of such standards of performance. Regulations of the Administrator under this paragraph shall permit the State in applying a standard of performance to any particular source under a plan submitted under this paragraph to take into consideration, among other factors, the remaining useful life of the existing source to which such standard applies.

Carbon Pollution Standard for New Power Plants

The Carbon Pollution Standard for New Power Plants establishes greenhouse gas emission standards for two types of new, modified, and reconstructed power plants—fossil fuel-fired electric utility steam generating units (generally, coal- and oil-fired power plants) and natural gas-fired stationary combustion turbines. The emission standards are intended to embody the "best system of emissions reduction * * * adequately demonstrated" (BSER), as Clean Air Act section 111(a) provides. EPA determined that natural gas combined cycle technology is the best system of emission reduction for stationary combustion turbines, and the agency established a performance rate based on emissions from a combined cycle turbine. For steam generating units, EPA determined that partial carbon capture and sequestration is the best system of emission reduction, and established a performance rate based on about 20 percent capture. The performance rates are expressed in terms of pounds of CO_2 emitted per Megawatt-hour of electricity generated.

Although coal-fired power plants would have difficulty meeting the new standards, because carbon capture and sequestration is a still-developing technology, there is less concern in the electric power industry over the Carbon Pollution Standard for New Power Plants than for the Clean Power Plan for existing power plants. This is because economic factors—primarily, the low cost of natural gas—and other environmental regulations have independently created strong disincentives for the industry to construct new coal-fired power plants. In other words, since the industry is not inclined to construct new coal-fired power plants anyway, the new standard for coal-fired power plants is not currently affecting the industry.

Clean Power Plan

In promulgating the Clean Power Plan, EPA noted that such power plants "are by far the largest domestic stationary source of emissions of CO_2, the most prevalent of the GHGs that the EPA has determined endangers public health and welfare through its contribution to climate change." 80 Fed. Reg. at 64,664. The Clean Power Plan designates statewide goals for greenhouse gas emissions from existing power plants. These statewide goals reflect the performance rates for the two types of power plants (electric steam generating and stationary combustion) and each state's mix of power plants. States are to develop and implement plans for achieving their goals established under the Plan. The Plan includes interim goals for the period of 2022 to 2029 and final goals to be achieved by 2030. When fully implemented in 2030, the Plan will reduce CO_2 emissions from the utility power sector by 32% as compared with emission levels in 2005.

SECTION XII

CAPSTONE PROBLEM: SHOULD GREENHOUSE
GASES BE LISTED AS A NAAQS POLLUTANT?

297

The Clean Power Plan includes three "building blocks," which together comprise the best system of emissions reduction for existing power plants. Essentially, the three building blocks are options that EPA suggests states can use to meet their emissions goals under the Clean Power Plan. The three building blocks are (1) improving the efficiency of coal-fired power plants; (2) substituting increased generation from lower-emitting existing natural gas power plants for generation from coal-fired power plants; and (3) substituting increased generation from renewable energy for generation from fossil fuel-fired power plants.

The first building block resembles conventional environmental standards, in that it is based on changes that can be made within a particular source to reduce its emissions. The second and third building block, by contrast, attempt to look at the problem more broadly, by inquiring whether existing power plants as a system can be operated in a manner that reduces emissions. This has been called a "beyond the fenceline" approach, because it looks beyond the characteristics of individual sources.

Opponents of the Clean Power Plan argue that the "beyond the fenceline" approach exceeds EPA's authority under Clean Air Act section 111(d). EPA and other supporters of the Clean Power Plan contend that Clean Air Act section 111's reference to a "system of emissions reduction" empowers the agency to employ its "beyond the fenceline" approach and that the approach appropriately reflects the interdependency of power plants within the electric grid.

The Clean Power Plan is facing substantial legal and political obstacles. In October 2015, states, coal-related companies and associations, trade associations, and energy companies filed petitions for review in the D.C. Circuit Court of Appeals challenging the Clean Power Plan, raising the "beyond the fenceline" objection and other arguments. The petitioners asked the D.C. Circuit to stay—essentially, to enjoin—the Clean Power Plan pending the completion of the litigation. The D.C. Circuit denied the stay requests on January 21, 2016. On January 27, the petitioners requested a stay from the Supreme Court, which granted the requests on February 9, 2016. The vote was 5–4 in favor of the stay, with Justice Scalia among those favoring the stay. Justice Scalia died less than a week later, on February 13, 2016. The case is currently pending on the merits in the D.C. Circuit, and will probably eventually make its way to the Supreme Court. In addition, Donald Trump, when he was campaigning for President, pledged to eliminate the Clean Power Plan.

———————

EPA's climate change initiatives, like the Clean Air Act generally, involve a complex web of interrelated parts. What is the relationship, within this web, between Clean Air Act section 111(d), which EPA asserts authorizes the Clean Power Plan, and Clean Air Act section 108(a), which authorizes EPA to list criteria air pollutants? How will a decision by the courts either approving or disapproving the Clean Power Plan affect the question whether EPA should list greenhouse gases as a criteria air pollutant—as a matter of policy or as a legal matter? Is there also an effect in the other direction—if EPA were to list greenhouse gases as criteria air pollutants, might that affect the Clean Power Plan? How do these questions factor into your overall analysis of whether the Organization for Environmental Litigation should petition EPA to list greenhouse gases as a criteria air pollutant?

Test your knowledge with a Chapter 3 online quiz in CasebookPlus™.

CHAPTER 4

WATER POLLUTION

On August 2, 2014, state and local officials warned residents of Toledo, Ohio, and surrounding areas not to drink their tap water. Toledo draws its drinking water from Lake Erie, and algae blooms had formed on the lake surface near the city's intake pipes. Algae blooms, and the cyanobacteria they harbor, can be deadly. In EPA's words, they "produce extremely dangerous toxins that can sicken or kill people or animals," as well as creating dead zones in oceans and lakes and generating millions of dollars in treatment costs. EPA, Harmful Algal Blooms, http://www2. epa.gov/nutrientpollution/harmful-algal-blooms#effect. Lake Erie's blooms were fed by nutrients like phosphorous and nitrogen, which wash off thousands of farms and city streets and continue to pour out of wastewater treatment plants around the lake.

For Lake Erie, this might seem like a surprising turn of events. The lake once was legendary for its pollution, and by the time Congress enacted the Clean Water Act in 1972, some observers had pronounced Lake Erie "dead." The Clean Water Act led to dramatic improvements in water quality, however, and by the late 1980s, Lake Erie had become a popular poster-child for the Clean Water Act's successes. But those successes, as we will see in this chapter, were only partial—both at Lake Erie and across the rest of the United States. Toledo's algae blooms aptly illustrate the extent to which water quality remains an important practical, and legal, challenge.

This chapter addresses the environmental laws that govern water quality. Our primary focus will be the federal Clean Water Act, which remains the most important law in this realm. But we will also discuss the roles of common law and state law.

The chapter begins with a brief discussion of the causes and effects of water quality impairment. We then discuss the history of water quality law and then turn to the Clean Water Act. The materials focus on the scope of federal jurisdiction under the Clean Water Act; the structure and functions of the Act's primary regulatory programs, and the legal frontiers of water quality protection.

Readers should be aware of two important omissions from this chapter. First, this is not a chapter about the legal protection of *groundwater* quality. Most of the United States' liquid freshwater is located beneath the ground, and that groundwater is an important source of municipal, industrial, and domestic water supplies, as well as a key source of recharge flows to surface water bodies. For example, a 2010 study found that groundwater irrigates more than half of the acres of farmland in North America. S. Siebert et al., *Groundwater Use for Irrigation—A Global Inventory*, 14 HYDROL. EARTH SYST. SCI. 1863 (2010). Like surface water, pollution contaminates groundwater, and that contamination creates economic costs and poses public health threats. But different legal regimes protect groundwater and surface water. Under federal law, groundwater protection primarily arises from the Safe Drinking Water Act, which regulates injection of pollution underground, and from hazardous waste laws like the Resource Conservation and Recovery Act (RCRA) and the Comprehensive Environmental Response, Compensation, and Liability Act (CERCLA), which we discuss in detail in chapters 5 and 6. State and local laws also often distinguish between surface and groundwater.

Second, this chapter only briefly addresses legal rights to water *use*. Those rights are closely connected to water quality; high-quality water is more useful, and extracting water often affects the quality of water that remains in rivers, lakes, and streams. But the large and complicated set of laws that govern the allocation of water resources is typically the subject of a separate course in water law, and is not a focus of this chapter.

I.   THE CHALLENGE OF WATER QUALITY

To understand the purposes and structure of water pollution law, it is helpful to know something about water pollution. We therefore begin with a brief summary discussion of the extent, sources, and consequences of water pollution in the United States.

A.   SCOPE OF THE PROBLEM

As you will learn later in the chapter, the Clean Water Act requires states to set water quality standards. The Clean Water Act also requires states to monitor whether water bodies are attaining those standards, and section 305(b) of the Act requires states to report their monitoring results. The data tables below come from EPA's summaries of the states' data.

Assessed Waters of United States

Incomplete state reported information may lead to discrepancies and/or missing information in these reports.

Description of this table

	Size of Water							
	Rivers and Streams (Miles)	Lakes, Reservoirs, and Ponds (Acres)	Bays and Estuaries (Square Miles)	Coastal Shoreline (Miles)	Ocean and Near Coastal (Square Miles)	Wetlands (Acres)	Great Lakes Shoreline (Miles)	Great Lakes Open Water (Square Miles)
Good Waters	486,267	5,757,409	9,379	1,324	618	573,947	78	62
Threatened Waters	7,305	130,709						
Impaired Waters	519,783	12,060,042	23,612	7,215	1,059	538,492	4,353	53,270
Total Assessed Waters	1,013,355	17,948,160	32,990	8,539	1,677	1,112,438	4,431	53,332
Total Waters	3,533,205	41,666,049	87,791	58,618	54,120	107,700,000	5,202	60,546
Percent of Waters Assessed	28.7	43.1	37.6	14.6	3.1	1.0	85.2	88.1

In many waterways, water quality has improved dramatically since 1972, when the modern Clean Water Act emerged from Congress. Nevertheless, as these numbers make clear, water quality remains a widespread problem. Of the surveyed rivers and streams, 51.3% were impaired; 67.2% of lakes, ponds, and reservoirs were impaired, and a whopping 71.6% of surveyed estuaries and bays were impaired.

B. POLLUTANTS AND SOURCES

What pollutants cause that impairment? Here are EPA's statistics for rivers and streams:

National Summary
Causes of Impairment in Assessed Rivers and Streams
Description of this table

Cause of Impairment Group	Miles Threatened or Impaired
Pathogens	162,436
Sediment	128,626
Nutrients	104,063
Organic Enrichment/Oxygen Depletion	87,058
Polychlorinated Biphenyls (PCBs)	79,570
Metals (other than Mercury)	75,870
Temperature	68,728
Mercury	65,096
Habitat Alterations	63,766
Flow Alteration(s)	41,962
Cause Unknown	40,496
Cause Unknown - Impaired Biota	38,018
Salinity/Total Dissolved Solids/Chlorides/Sulfates	34,313
Turbidity	28,841
pH/Acidity/Caustic Conditions	28,769
Pesticides	18,096
Ammonia	12,336
Other Cause	12,099
Fish Consumption Advisory	10,267
Total Toxics	9,892
Toxic Inorganics	7,923
Algal Growth	6,080
Toxic Organics	4,943
Dioxins	4,600
Oil and Grease	3,084
Biotoxins	2,150
Nuisance Exotic Species	1,448
Trash	1,233
Taste, Color and Odor	854
Chlorine	732
Cause Unknown - Fish Kills	688
Radiation	677
Noxious Aquatic Plants	362
Nuisance Native Species	127

The leading causes of impairment for lakes, estuaries, and other waterways—which are not covered in this chart—are somewhat different. For example, mercury is the leading cause of impairment in most other categories. But this chart provides you with a general sense of the types of pollutants that commonly cause water quality problems.

Where do those pollutants come from? Here, again, EPA's statistics provide useful summaries. The statistics for rivers and streams again are reproduced below:

National Summary
Probable Sources of Impairments in Assessed Rivers and Streams
Description of this table

Probable Source Group	Miles Threatened or Impaired
Agriculture	129,016
Unknown	102,341
Atmospheric Deposition	100,207
Hydromodification	60,575
Urban-Related Runoff/Stormwater	58,941
Municipal Discharges/Sewage	56,382
Natural/Wildlife	52,521
Unspecified Nonpoint Source	48,040
Habitat Alterations (Not Directly Related To Hydromodification)	35,039
Resource Extraction	28,809
Silviculture (Forestry)	19,592
Industrial	17,201
Construction	12,995
Other	9,974
Land Application/Waste Sites/Tanks	9,047
Legacy/Historical Pollutants	5,640
Spills/Dumping	2,991
Recreation And Tourism (Non-Boating)	1,564
Aquaculture	304
Groundwater Loadings/Withdrawals	270
Recreational Boating And Marinas	142
Commercial Harbor And Port Activities	52
Military Bases	42

Several features of this chart (and the charts for other categories of water bodies) are worth noting. The first is the sheer variety of sources. As you will see, the Clean Water Act initially focused primarily on direct discharges of water pollution from industrial outfalls and municipal sewers. Those sources remain significant, but substantial quantities of pollution enter waterways from a variety of other sources and through a wide variety of pathways. Agriculture, not industry, constitutes the single largest source of water pollution, degrading 60 percent of impaired miles of river and half of impaired lakes. The phrase "atmospheric deposition" includes pollutants (mercury is a particularly common and problematic example) emitted from smokestacks and then carried by rain and snow down into surface water bodies. Urban stormwater runoff comes from a huge variety of sources, including thousands of roofs, parking lots, roads, and lawns, and it reaches surface waterways by a variety of pathways. These dispersed sources and pathways create a challenge for efforts to regulate water pollution, for there is no single, discrete category of sources upon which regulators may place their primary focus. Indeed, many water pollution sources fall outside the traditional parameters of water quality law, and originate from activities that are the traditional focus of the Clean Air Act or of state and local land use law.

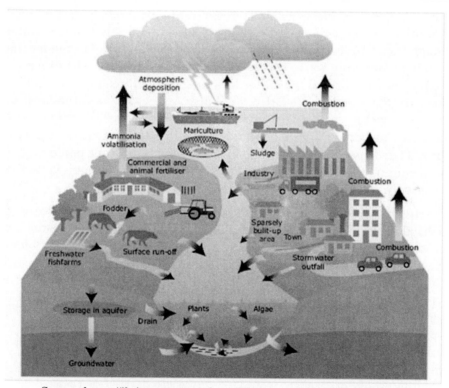

Source: https://ih-igcse-geography.wikispaces.com/1.8+Clean+Water

Second, many of these pollution sources work in combination. A single stream might be affected by agricultural runoff, depletion from water withdrawals, dams, loss of riparian habitat, invasive species, and urban stormwater runoff. Devising a regulatory regime that responds to all of those problems is a significant challenge. And if the regime focuses only on a subset of pollution sources, regulated entities are likely to complain that they have been unfairly singled out.

Third, many pollution sources are numerous and geographically dispersed. The most extreme example of this is the so-called Gulf of Mexico "dead zone"—an area where water is too anoxic to support most marine life—that forms annually at the mouth of the Mississippi River. The primary cause of that dead zone is nutrients from thousands of different farms throughout the Mississippi River basin. Similarly, even in a small urban watershed, stormwater pollution is likely to originate on hundreds, if not thousands, of different properties. Again, the dispersion of sources creates substantial challenges for regulatory system design.

C. CONSEQUENCES

Across the world, water quality impairment is a major threat to public health. Millions of people die each year from diseases and parasites attributable to lack of access to safe drinking water and basic sanitation. In the United States, the situation generally is much better, though the 2016 scandal in Flint, Michigan provided a sad reminder that even here, drinking water can be dangerously unhealthy. The difference is partly due to our ability to afford water treatment technology, and it is also partly due to the Safe Drinking Water Act, which sets standards for drinking water quality. Nevertheless, water quality impairment continues to impact public health and the environment in a variety of ways. That is particularly so for the small but significant percentage of the population whose drinking water comes from individual wells that are largely unregulated and rarely tested for contaminants.

Health impacts from poor water quality include exposure to pathogens, which can occur through drinking contaminated water and through direct exposure (typically swimming). Contact-related problems remain widespread. In many oceanfront areas, swimming during or soon after a rainstorm can result in exposure to pathogens washed into the sea with the pulse of urban stormwater runoff. As this example illustrates, water quality problems also can lead people who are fearful of health risks to avoid activities they otherwise would choose to pursue. Water quality problems can also lead to significant economic costs for water suppliers who must forego using, or apply expensive treatment to, polluted water supplies.

Another persistent health problem is exposure to contaminants in fish. Some contaminants, including mercury, *bioaccumulate*, which means that concentrations intensify up the food chain. A person who frequently eats fish from mercury-contaminated waters therefore can accumulate much of the mercury that those fish ate, and even seemingly low levels of environmental contamination can lead to high levels of exposure.

The environmental impacts of water contamination also can be significant. At the extreme, pollution can make water bodies uninhabitable for most life forms other than bacteria and algae. The Gulf of Mexico dead zone is an example of this phenomenon. Even more moderate levels of pollution can significantly change the number and type of species present in a waterway, as well as its clarity and aesthetic appearance. Recent studies, for example, have found that even a modest influx of urban stormwater runoff—at levels one might expect from sparse suburban development—typically correlates with a reduction in the number and diversity of native species in a stream.

II. HISTORY

The primary focus of this chapter is the Clean Water Act, which emerged in something close to its modern form in 1972 and was significantly amended in 1977 and again in 1987. But water pollution control laws first appeared in the United States much earlier, and a brief introduction to that history provides context for modern water pollution control law. For a more detailed discussion of that history (and for the main sources of the discussion below), see William L. Andreen, *The Evolution of Water Pollution Control in the United States—State, Local, and Federal Efforts, 1789–1972, Part I*, 22 STAN. ENVTL. L.J. 145 (2003), and William L. Andreen, *The Evolution of Water Pollution Control in the United States—State, Local, and Federal Efforts, 1789–1972, Part II*, 22 STAN. ENVTL. L.J. 215 (2003).

As Andreen explains, modern water pollution control began to emerge in the late nineteenth century, when a series of waterborne disease outbreaks revealed the threats posed by contaminated waterways. By that time, many urban waterways had become open sewers, and cities had not yet begun to invest in wastewater treatment plants. The United States' increasing industrialization also took a severe toll on waterways. Cities responded by investing in drinking water treatment plants, by empowering local health boards to regulate water pollution, and, occasionally, by bringing nuisance suits against upstream polluters. But drinking water treatment plants did nothing to remove pollutants from the waterways themselves, the health boards often lacked meaningful regulatory clout, and nuisance lawsuits often failed.

Over the first half of the twentieth century, the situation worsened. The United States' urban population centers continued to grow, leading to increased loading of human waste. Industrialization also accelerated, particularly during and immediately after World War II. Local health boards struggled to address the increasing pollution, and some states responded by empowering state agencies to regulate water quality. Those agencies often began by designating water quality standards, but they had difficulty establishing mechanisms for actually ensuring the attainment of those standards, and effective enforcement actions against polluters were rare. Congress did enact a series of water pollution control statutes, such as the Oil Pollution Act of 1824, the Rivers and Harbors Act of 1899, a weak water-quality statute in 1948, and a series of modest amendments in the two decades that followed, but until 1972, those statutes focused primarily on providing support for state regulatory action. Andreen summarizes the results:

> In the face of a growing population and rapidly expanding manufacturing activity, state regulatory efforts were proving too little, too late. In 1960, 3,500 cities and towns in the United States were still discharging the raw waste of 25 million Americans. Of the approximately 7,500 communities that had sewage treatment facilities, only two-thirds were served by secondary treatment plants; the rest made do with antiquated, primary treatment systems. Viewed in a more abstract way, the total effluent from both treated and untreated municipal sources in the United States in 1960 would have equaled the amount of raw sewage produced by 75 million people. Despite all this sewage, municipal sources were running "a distant second to industry in the water pollution derby." By 1968, eighty percent of the pollutant loading to American waters was industrial in origin, up from forty percent in 1900. Of the 22 billion gallons of wastewater which American industry discharged on a daily basis in 1970, only twenty-nine percent received any treatment whatsoever—regardless of whether the level of treatment was adequate.

The implications for water quality were appalling. In the 1960s, Lake Erie was experiencing accelerated eutrophication—a process that also adversely affected a number of other American waters including Lake Tahoe, the Great South Bay on Long Island, Lake Oneida in New York, and a number of bays along the southern shore of Lake Ontario. In 1968, the Buffalo River was described as "a repulsive holding basin for industrial and municipal wastes under the prevalent sluggish flow conditions. It [was] devoid of oxygen and almost sterile. Oil, phenols, color, oxygen-demanding materials, iron, acid, sewage, and exotic organic compounds [we]re present in large amounts." The Cuyahoga was described in equally graphic terms in 1968: "The lower Cuyahoga River and navigation channel throughout the Cleveland area is a waste treatment lagoon. At times, the river is choked with debris, oils, scums, and floating globs of organic sludge. Foul smelling gases can be seen rising from decomposing materials on the river's bottom." While these two rivers were among the most polluted in the United States in the late 1960s, appalling conditions afflicted countless streams and lakes across the country. For more and more Americans, water pollution was becoming intolerable.

22 STAN. ENVTL. L.J. at 197–98.[1]

By the late 1960s, many members of Congress perceived the states as ineffective regulators, and that perception eventually led to the emergence of the Federal Water Pollution Control Act Amendments of 1972, often called the Clean Water Act.

III. CLEAN WATER ACT OVERVIEW

The 1972 Clean Water Act amendments marked a dramatic departure from the previous decades of water quality regulation. Andreen summarizes the significance of the change:

> The Clean Water Act of 1972 was revolutionary in many ways. It made the federal government the dominant authority in an area where the states had long held sway. It instituted a new system of technology-based effluent limitations that would demand the same basic level of treatment for a particular industry, regardless of whether it was located in Georgia or New York, Louisiana or Wisconsin. No longer could an industry so effectively block state pollution control efforts by threatening to relocate to a more lenient jurisdiction. And no longer could discharge limitations be based solely upon the assimilative capacity of the receiving waterway and its ability to meet a designated use—which might well be only industrial or agricultural usage.
>
> To implement and monitor compliance with the new technology-based limitations, and any more stringent limits needed to meet state water quality standards, every discharger, municipal as well as industrial, was required to obtain a permit and comply with its terms. These permits transformed most of the Act's requirements into specific numerical limits that greatly simplified the enforcement process. No longer would one have to demonstrate actual endangerment or prove that a specific polluter had violated stream standards; instead one need only compare permit limits with a permittee's performance at the point of discharge. The Clean Water Act also expressed

---

[1] While this dismal assessment of pre-1972 state water quality regulation is widely shared, it has received some criticism. *See, e.g.,* Jonathan H. Adler, *Fables of the Cuyahoga: Reconstructing a History of Environmental Protection*, 14 FORDHAM ENVTL. L.J. 89 (2003). For a response defending the traditional view, see William L. Andreen, *Delegated Federalism Versus Devolution: Some Insights from the History of Water Pollution*, in PREEMPTION CHOICE: THE THEORY, LAW, AND REALITY OF FEDERALISM'S CORE QUESTION 257, 261–62 (William W. Buzbee ed., 2009).

Congress' skepticism about EPA's ability or even the willingness of EPA or any expert administrative agency to continuously and vigorously perform its regulatory mission. The Act thus limited administrative discretion by imposing a long series of mandatory duties, regulatory schedules, and deadlines, and by creating a judicial mechanism through which citizens could seek to compel administrative action and supplement, perhaps even stimulate, agency enforcement.

22 STAN. ENVTL. L.J. at 286.

This section provides an overview of these provisions, and the sections that follow explore them in more depth.

Figure 4.1. A Simplified Conceptual Map of the Clean Water Act

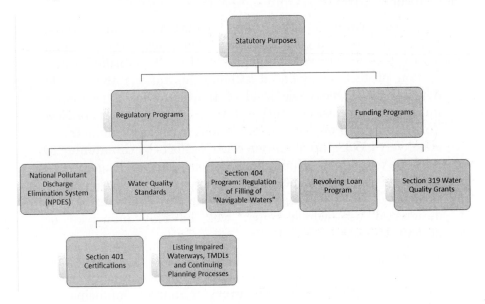

A. GOALS

One of the most distinctive features of the Clean Water Act is the ambition of its stated goals. Congress called for drastic reductions in, and even complete elimination of, water pollution, though it also sought to preserve a significant role for state governance.

CWA § 101, 33 U.S.C. § 1251. Congressional Declaration of Goals and Policy

(a) Restoration and maintenance of chemical, physical and biological integrity of Nation's waters; national goals for achievement of objective

The objective of this chapter is to restore and maintain the chemical, physical, and biological integrity of the Nation's waters. In order to achieve this objective it is hereby declared that, consistent with the provisions of this chapter—

(1) it is the national goal that the discharge of pollutants into the navigable waters be eliminated by 1985;

(2) it is the national goal that wherever attainable, an interim goal of water quality which provides for the protection and propagation of fish, shellfish, and wildlife and provides for recreation in and on the water be achieved by July 1, 1983;

(3) it is the national policy that the discharge of toxic pollutants in toxic amounts be prohibited;

(4) it is the national policy that Federal financial assistance be provided to construct publicly owned waste treatment works;

(5) it is the national policy that areawide waste treatment management planning processes be developed and implemented to assure adequate control of sources of pollutants in each State;

(6) it is the national policy that a major research and demonstration effort be made to develop technology necessary to eliminate the discharge of pollutants into the navigable waters, waters of the contiguous zone, and the oceans; and

(7) it is the national policy that programs for the control of nonpoint sources of pollution be developed and implemented in an expeditious manner so as to enable the goals of this chapter to be met through the control of both point and nonpoint sources of pollution.

(b) Congressional recognition, preservation, and protection of primary responsibilities and rights of States

It is the policy of the Congress to recognize, preserve, and protect the primary responsibilities and rights of States to prevent, reduce, and eliminate pollution, to plan the development and use (including restoration, preservation, and enhancement) of land and water resources, and to consult with the Administrator in the exercise of his authority under this chapter. It is the policy of Congress that the States manage the construction grant program under this chapter and implement the permit programs under sections 1342 and 1344 of this title. It is further the policy of the Congress to support and aid research relating to the prevention, reduction, and elimination of pollution, and to provide Federal technical services and financial aid to State and interstate agencies and municipalities in connection with the prevention, reduction, and elimination of pollution.

Needless to say, the ambitious goals stated in subsections (a)(1) and (a)(2) were not achieved by the stated deadlines, and we are still not close to attaining them today.

B. REGULATORY PROGRAMS

As you have probably learned by this point in your legal education, statutes often state ambitious goals (though not always this ambitious!) but contain more modest and nuanced substantive prohibitions. In that sense, the Clean Water Act is typical, though its substantive provisions still are demanding.

The CWA contains three primary regulatory programs. Two of those programs relate to Section 301 of the Act, which bans "discharges" of water pollutants unless they are authorized by certain types of permits. A "discharge" under the CWA, is a release of pollutants through some sort of discrete conveyance—typically, but not always, a pipe or ditch—into "navigable waters." In the readings below, we'll consider the meaning of each of those terms.

NPDES and Technology-Based Standards. The first, and traditionally most important, regulatory program is the National Pollutant Discharge Elimination System, or NPDES. The NPDES program is one of the two programs that allows "discharges" that otherwise would be prohibited by section 301. NPDES permit holders must comply with "technology-based" standards, which are in many ways analogous to the technology-based standards developed under the Clean Air Act. These standard generally specify how much pollution discharges may contain, and they also typically specify monitoring and reporting requirements.

During the early years of CWA implementation, the agencies implementing the NPDES permitting program focused primarily on major industrial sources and wastewater treatment plants. Those sources remain important, but in recent years, controlling stormwater discharges has emerged as the most important frontier in NPDES permitting.

Filling Wetlands and Waterways. The Clean Water Act's second key regulatory program addresses the filling of wetlands and waterways. Section 404 creates a permitting regime to allow these activities to occur without running afoul of section 301's prohibition on discharge. The permits are issued by the U.S. Army Corps of Engineers (Michigan and New Jersey have received delegated authority to implement part of the section 404 program, but otherwise the federal government retains control), and the Army Corps and EPA jointly oversee the program.

Prior to issuing a permit, the Army Corps generally requires applicants to ensure that they have avoided filling wetlands or waterways to the maximum extent practicable; that they have minimized the extent of any unavoidable impacts; and that they have compensated for any remaining impacts, generally through creating, restoring, enhancing, or protecting wetlands or waterways either elsewhere within the construction site or at some other location.

Water Quality Standards. One of the central innovations of the 1972 Clean Water Act was to add a technology-based regulatory program. But Congress did not abandon its prior commitment to water quality standards, and the statute still requires each state to adopt water quality standards for all of that state's waterways. The standards establish the *designated uses* to which that waterway will be put. The standards also contain *water quality criteria* which, if satisfied, will be sufficiently protective to preserve those uses. The water quality standards also include a *non-degradation policy* designed to ensure that the state moves toward, not away from, the national goals of eliminating discharges and ensuring fishable and swimmable waterways. States must periodically update their standards, and the initial standards and updates are subject to EPA review and approval. EPA can step in and establish standards itself if a state fails to do so.

In theory, water quality standards translate into regulatory controls on pollution in three ways. First, Clean Water Act section 401 requires federally-approved projects that discharge into navigable waterways to obtain *state certifications* that the project will comply with state water quality standards.

Second, section 303 of the Clean Water Act requires states to identify and publish lists of water bodies that do not meet state water quality standards. It also requires states to draft *total maximum daily loads* (TMDLs), which are essentially pollution budgets, for those water bodies, and to have a "continuing planning processes" for bringing water bodies into compliance. The entire program bears some similarity to the Clean Air Act's planning provisions, which use state implementation plans as a mechanism to rectify noncompliance with national ambient air quality standards. But, as you will see, there are dramatic differences in enforceability and effectiveness between water quality plans and state implementation plans.

Third, the Clean Water Act directs states (and EPA, in the few states where EPA administers the NPDES program) to factor water quality standards into NPDES permits. Where traditional technology-based controls alone will not be sufficient to bring a water body into compliance with water quality standards, states may then ratchet up the intensity of NPDES permit controls. However, the ratchet works only one way. States cannot rely on water quality standards as a basis for weakening NPDES permit requirements.

C. FUNDING PROGRAMS

For understandable reasons, lawyers tend to focus on the regulatory and enforcement provisions of statutes. To non-lawyers who work in the water quality field, however, and for lawyers advising prospective recipients of federal dollars, funding provisions are also important. The federal government provides several sources of funding for water quality projects.

Prior to 1987, the most important of these funding mechanisms was a construction grants program designed to help states build wastewater treatment plants. The Clean Water Act imposed ambitious and stringent obligations upon wastewater managers, many of which were municipal governments with limited budgets, and Congress viewed financial support as an essential complement to its regulatory mandates (some members of Congress also viewed a major construction program as a way to bring jobs to their districts). In 1987, Congress replaced the construction grants program with a broader revolving loan program. Under that program, EPA issues low-interest loans to states, and the states may use their loans to support a variety of different ways of building or maintaining water quality infrastructure.

In terms of dollars spent, the most important present-day source of water quality grant funding lies outside the Clean Water Act. Farm bills authorize major expenditures to control water pollution from agriculture. The United States Department of Agriculture, rather than EPA, administers those grants.

D. ENFORCEMENT PROVISIONS

As Andreen's historical account explains, one key concern about the Clean Water Act's predecessor regimes was their perceived lack of enforcement. Congress responded to those concerns by granting EPA and the states civil and criminal enforcement authority under the Clean Water Act, and it did not stop there. Like many environmental statutes, the Act also contains a citizen suit provision authorizing citizens to sue for violations of the Act.

E. PREEMPTION

The Clean Water Act preempts some of state and local regulatory authority and preserves other parts. The Act preempts states' ability to displace the Act with *weaker* state laws, but it preserves states' authority to enact more stringent water quality regulations. Some states have done so; some have not; and some have passed laws that expressly forbid their regulatory agencies from imposing any requirements that go beyond the floor set by federal law.

The Act's relationship to tort law is somewhat more complex. In the years prior to enactment of the Clean Water Act, plaintiffs sometimes turned to nuisance law in an attempt to abate water quality. They appealed to state common law and also, in interstate water disputes, federal common law. In *Milwaukee v. Illinois*, 451 U.S. 304 (1981) and *Middlesex County Sewerage Authority v. National Sea Clammers Ass'n*, 451 U.S. 1 (1981), the United States Supreme Court held that the Clean Water Act had displaced federal common law in the water quality field. Similarly, in *International Paper Company v. Ouellette*, 479 U.S. 481 (1987), the Court held that the Clean Water Act preempted a nuisance action brought by Vermont plaintiffs under Vermont common law against a point source in New York State, while allowing those plaintiffs to pursue their claim under New York Law. In other words, the Court held that the Clean Water Act preempted the common law of states experiencing the effects of pollution, but preserved the common law of states from which water pollution is emitted.

IV. SCOPE OF THE CLEAN WATER ACT

A. WATERS OF THE UNITED STATES

The Clean Water Act, as its name suggests, addresses water quality, and does not purport to be a land use statute. But activities on land affect water quality. Indeed, two leading watershed scientists recently asserted that "[t[he primary reason why so many rivers and streams are still being degraded today is poor land stewardship." Margaret A. Palmer & J. David Allan, *Restoring Rivers*, 22 ISSUES IN SCI. & TECH. 40, 42 (2006). And the boundaries between land and water are not always clear. Wetlands, for example, do not always have crisp edges, and many areas are wet during some parts of the year and dry during others. Streams and rivers change in size as precipitation waxes and wanes, and some streams flow only for a short period after a large precipitation event. The shifting boundaries and complex relationships between land and water raise a legal question: how much of the landscape does the Clean Water Act govern?

For practicing lawyers and property owners, this question is very important. If a wetland is subject to Clean Water Act jurisdiction, a developer cannot fill it without a permit, and obtaining that permit will require time and money. If an intermittent stream is subject to Clean Water Act jurisdiction, industrial facilities cannot discharge effluent into it without a permit. That permit also could be difficult to obtain, and compliance might require treating or even eliminating the discharge. On the other hand, if these activities are not subject to Clean Water Act jurisdiction, and if no state law fills the void, water quality in the wetland or intermittent stream, and in downstream waterways, could suffer, harming the environment and the economic interests of downstream water users. Businesses, regulators, consultants, and lawyers therefore invest a lot of effort into determining the geographic extent of Clean Water Act jurisdiction.

> Water quality lawyers spend much of their time negotiating, writing, and interpreting the terms of permits. That may sound rote, and sometimes it is. But permits can be structured in innovative and creative ways, and they can also be quite complicated. That complexity and those opportunities for innovation can make a permit-focused legal practice much more interesting than one might initially suspect.

The problems and materials below explore the somewhat ambiguous and evolving law applicable to the boundary between land and water. As you read the materials, you'll notice that there are many different sources of law that might govern, including statutes, regulations, Supreme Court decisions (the most recent of which lacks a majority opinion), and the United States Constitution. That creates a challenge for you (and for practicing lawyers): you'll need to figure out not just what each source of law says, but also where different legal sources might conflict and, if they do, which source controls.

PROBLEM: VERNAL POOLS AND INTERMITTENT STREAMS

A developer wishes to construct a new shopping mall on undeveloped land in State X. The land is bounded on one side by Shiner Brook, a small stream. Where it flows through the proposed construction site, Shiner Brook is ephemeral, which means it contains water only during and a few days after rainstorms. Three miles downstream, Shiner Brook discharges into the Trout River. The Trout River is currently popular among recreational canoers, and at the time State X became a state, the Trout River was navigated by commercial traders transporting furs.

The proposed site also contains a complex of vernal pools. Vernal pools are seasonal wetlands that lack permanent connections to surface water bodies. Because they are seasonal, and because they are usually isolated from surface water bodies, vernal pools cannot support fish populations, but they provide excellent breeding grounds for amphibians and many invertebrates. Their biological productivity can be remarkable; in some regions of the country, as much as half of the animal biomass in a forest is born in vernal pools. This biological productivity also attracts predators, including species of migratory and resident birds.

Vernal pools in Oregon

Vernal pools in Maine

As part of his development proposal, the developer would like to fill the vernal pools and a portion of Shiner Brook. He has asked the U.S. Army Corps of Engineers for a "jurisdictional determination"—that is, a determination that the pools and the streambed either are or are not subject to federal jurisdiction under the Clean Water Act. An Army Corps biologist has inspected the site and has come to the following conclusions:

- At the site, Shiner Brook typically contains water only during and for a few days after rainstorms. Only when a series of rainstorms occurs in succession does flow continue for weeks at a time.

- Despite its ephemeral flows, Shiner Brook does have a discernible streambed.

- The vernal pools are ¼ mile from Shiner Brook.

- The portion of Shiner Brook that might be filled is not within the Trout River's floodplain, and the vernal pools are not within the floodplains of Shiner Brook or the Trout River.

- About once every five years, surface water flows from the pools to Shiner Brook.

- Water from the pools flows into a groundwater aquifer and water from the aquifer flows into Shiner Brook downstream of the site, and then, eventually, to the Trout River.

- If the pools were filled and the site were developed, more stormwater runoff would reach Shiner Brook, and less groundwater would reach the brook. The quality of that stormwater runoff would be lower than the quality of the groundwater that currently reaches the brook.

- Animals often move between the vernal pools, Shiner Brook, and the Trout River. Some of the amphibians that breed in the pools live other parts of their life cycle in the brook and the river. Birds also often move between the habitats. The biologist concludes that filling the pools would diminish the biological richness of the brook and the river, but the change would be slight.

If you were an attorney for the Army Corps, would you advise it to assert jurisdiction over the vernal pools and/or Shiner Brook? If you were an attorney for the developer, and the Army Corps elected to assert jurisdiction, would you advise your client to challenge that jurisdictional determination? Assume that changing the project to avoid the vernal pools and the stream, either by reducing its scale or finding an alternate location, would cost hundreds of thousands of dollars. If you would advise a challenge, what arguments would you raise?

In researching this problem, you would quickly learn that "jurisdictional determinations"—that is, determinations about whether a particular waterway falls within federal jurisdiction—require consideration of three sources of law:

- Congress cannot exceed its authority under the Constitution. Questions about the scope of that authority have featured prominently in litigation over the scope of the Clean Water Act.

- Regulatory agencies like EPA and the Army Corps of Engineers cannot exceed the authority Congress vested in them, and also cannot stretch their authority beyond constitutional boundaries. For that reason, the meaning of the Clean Water Act's language has also been centrally important to litigation.

- EPA and the Army Corps of Engineers have issued regulations implementing the Clean Water Act. "Jurisdictional determinations" for individual sites must be consistent with those regulations.

The most important constitutional provision for jurisdictional determinations is the Commerce Clause, which appears below:

United States Constitution, art. I, § 8, cl.3

The Congress shall have Power * * * [t]o regulate Commerce with foreign Nations, and among the several States, and with the Indian Tribes.

In combination, several provisions of the Clean Water Act prohibit the discharge of pollutants into "navigable waters" unless that discharge occurs in compliance with a permit. The Clean Water Act also prohibits the discharge of fill materials into "navigable waters" except in compliance with a permit. The Clean Water Act's definition of "navigable waters" appears below.

CWA § 502, 33 U.S.C. § 1362. Definitions

(7) The term "navigable waters" means the waters of the United States, including the territorial seas.

The Clean Water Act empowers EPA and the Army Corps of Engineers—the two agencies with jurisdiction to implement the act—to promulgate regulations fleshing out the statute's requirements. EPA and the Army Corps have used that authority to define "waters of the United States." An excerpt from those regulations appears below. Importantly, these regulations were issued *after* the *Rapanos* decision, which you will read next. Many plaintiffs are currently challenging these regulations, arguing that they are inconsistent with the Clean Water Act, as interpreted by the Supreme Court in *Rapanos* and its predecessor decisions, and, also, that the regulations are unconstitutional. As this casebook goes to press, the regulations have been stayed by the Sixth Circuit, and the Trump Administration has criticized them. Their fate, in short, is highly uncertain. Nevertheless, for purposes of answering the problem, please assume that they do apply—if, of course, they are consistent with the Clean Water Act and the United States Constitution.

33 C.F.R. § 328.3. Definitions

(a) For purposes of the Clean Water Act, 33 U.S.C. 1251 et seq. and its implementing regulations, subject to the exclusions in paragraph (b) of this section, the term "waters of the United States" means:

(1) All waters which are currently used, were used in the past, or may be susceptible to use in interstate or foreign commerce, including all waters which are subject to the ebb and flow of the tide;

(2) All interstate waters, including interstate wetlands;

(3) The territorial seas;

(4) All impoundments of waters otherwise identified as waters of the United States under this section;

(5) All tributaries, as defined in paragraph (c)(3) of this section, of waters identified in paragraphs (a)(1) through (3) of this section;

(6) All waters adjacent to a water identified in paragraphs (a)(1) through (5) of this section, including wetlands, ponds, lakes, oxbows, impoundments, and similar waters;

(7) All waters in paragraphs (a)(7)(i) through (v) of this section where they are determined, on a case-specific basis, to have a significant nexus to a water identified in paragraphs (a)(1) through (3) of this section.

[Eds.: Paragraphs (a)(7)(i) through (v) then provide a series of categories of waters, none of which is at issue in this problem.]

. . . (8) All waters located within the 100-year floodplain of a water identified in paragraphs (a)(1) through (3) of this section and all waters located within 4,000 feet of the high tide line or ordinary high water mark of a water identified in paragraphs (a)(1) through (5) of this section where they are determined on a case-specific basis to have a significant nexus to a water identified in paragraphs (a)(1) through (3) of this section. For waters determined to have a significant nexus, the entire water is a water of the United States if a portion is located within the 100-year floodplain of a water identified in paragraphs (a)(1) through (3) of this section or within 4,000 feet of the high tide line or ordinary high water mark. Waters identified in this paragraph shall not be combined with waters identified in paragraph (a)(6) of this section when performing a significant nexus analysis. If waters identified in this paragraph are also an adjacent water under paragraph (a)(6), they are an adjacent water and no case-specific significant nexus analysis is required.

(b) The following are not "waters of the United States" even where they otherwise meet the terms of paragraphs (a)(4) through (8) of this section.

(1) Waste treatment systems, including treatment ponds or lagoons designed to meet the requirements of the Clean Water Act.

(2) Prior converted cropland. Notwithstanding the determination of an area's status as prior converted cropland by any other Federal agency, for the purposes of the Clean Water Act, the final authority regarding Clean Water Act jurisdiction remains with EPA.

(3) The following ditches:

(i) Ditches with ephemeral flow that are not a relocated tributary or excavated in a tributary.

(ii) Ditches with intermittent flow that are not a relocated tributary, excavated in a tributary, or drain wetlands.

(iii) Ditches that do not flow, either directly or through another water, into a water identified in paragraphs (a)(1) through (3) of this section.

(4) The following features:

(i) Artificially irrigated areas that would revert to dry land should application of water to that area cease;

(ii) Artificial, constructed lakes and ponds created in dry land such as farm and stock watering ponds, irrigation ponds, settling basins, fields flooded for rice growing, log cleaning ponds, or cooling ponds;

(iii) Artificial reflecting pools or swimming pools created in dry land;

(iv) Small ornamental waters created in dry land;

(v) Water-filled depressions created in dry land incidental to mining or construction activity, including pits excavated for obtaining fill, sand, or gravel that fill with water;

(vi) Erosional features, including gullies, rills, and other ephemeral features that do not meet the definition of tributary, non-wetland swales, and lawfully constructed grassed waterways; and

(vii) Puddles.

(5) Groundwater, including groundwater drained through subsurface drainage systems.

(6) Stormwater control features constructed to convey, treat, or store stormwater that are created in dry land.

(7) Wastewater recycling structures constructed in dry land; detention and retention basins built for wastewater recycling; groundwater recharge basins; percolation ponds built for wastewater recycling; and water distributary structures built for wastewater recycling.

(c) Definitions.

In this section, the following definitions apply:

(1) Adjacent.

The term adjacent means bordering, contiguous, or neighboring a water identified in paragraphs (a)(1) through (5) of this section, including waters separated by constructed dikes or barriers, natural river berms, beach dunes, and the like. For purposes of adjacency, an open water such as a pond or lake includes any wetlands within or abutting its ordinary high water mark. Adjacency is not limited to waters located laterally to a water identified in paragraphs (a)(1) through (5) of this section. Adjacent waters also include all waters that connect segments of a water identified in paragraphs (a)(1) through (5) or are located at the head of a water identified in paragraphs (a)(1) through (5) of this section and are bordering, contiguous, or neighboring such water. Waters being used for established normal farming, ranching, and silviculture activities (33 U.S.C. 1344(f)) are not adjacent.

(2) Neighboring.

The term neighboring means:

(i) All waters located within 100 feet of the ordinary high water mark of a water identified in paragraphs (a)(1) through (5) of this section. The entire water is neighboring if a portion is located within 100 feet of the ordinary high water mark;

(ii) All waters located within the 100-year floodplain of a water identified in paragraphs (a)(1) through (5) of this section and not more than 1,500 feet from the ordinary high water mark of such water. The entire water is neighboring if a portion is located within 1,500 feet of the ordinary high water mark and within the 100-year floodplain;

(iii) All waters located within 1,500 feet of the high tide line of a water identified in paragraphs (a)(1) or (a)(3) of this section, and all waters within 1,500 feet of the ordinary high water mark of the Great Lakes. The entire water is neighboring if a portion is located within 1,500 feet of the high tide line or within 1,500 feet of the ordinary high water mark of the Great Lakes.

(3) Tributary and tributaries.

The terms tributary and tributaries each mean a water that contributes flow, either directly or through another water (including an impoundment identified in paragraph (a)(4) of this section), to a water identified in paragraphs (a)(1) through (3) of this section that is characterized by the presence of the physical indicators of a bed and banks and an ordinary high water mark. These physical indicators demonstrate there is volume, frequency, and duration of flow sufficient to create a bed and banks and an ordinary high water mark, and thus to qualify as a tributary. A tributary can be a natural, man-altered, or man-made water and includes waters such as rivers, streams, canals, and ditches not excluded under paragraph (b) of this section. A water that otherwise qualifies as a tributary under this definition does not lose its status as a tributary if, for any length, there are one or more constructed breaks (such as bridges, culverts, pipes, or dams), or one or more natural breaks (such as wetlands along the run of a stream, debris piles, boulder fields, or a stream that flows underground) so long as a bed and banks and an ordinary high water mark can be identified upstream of the break. A water that otherwise qualifies as a tributary under this definition does not lose its status as a tributary if it contributes flow through a water of the United States that does not meet the definition of tributary or through a non-jurisdictional water to a water identified in paragraphs (a)(1) through (3) of this section.

(4) Wetlands.

The term wetlands means those areas that are inundated or saturated by surface or groundwater at a frequency and duration sufficient to support, and that under normal circumstances do support, a prevalence of vegetation typically adapted for life in saturated soil conditions. Wetlands generally include swamps, marshes, bogs, and similar areas.

(5) Significant nexus.

The term significant nexus means that a water, including wetlands, either alone or in combination with other similarly situated waters in the region, significantly affects the chemical, physical, or biological integrity of a water identified in paragraphs (a)(1) through (3) of this section. The term "in the region" means the watershed that drains to the nearest water identified in paragraphs (a)(1) through (3) of this section. For an effect to be significant, it must be more than speculative or insubstantial. Waters are similarly situated when they function alike and are sufficiently close to function together in affecting downstream waters. For purposes of determining whether or not a water has a significant nexus, the water's effect on downstream paragraph (a)(1) through (3) waters shall be assessed by evaluating the aquatic functions identified in paragraphs (c)(5)(i) through (ix) of this section. A water has a significant nexus when any single function or combination of functions performed by the water, alone or together with similarly situated waters in the region, contributes significantly to the chemical, physical, or biological integrity of the nearest water identified in paragraphs (a)(1) through (3) of this section. Functions relevant to the significant nexus evaluation are the following:

(i)   Sediment trapping,

(ii)   Nutrient recycling,

(iii) Pollutant   trapping,   transformation,   filtering,   and transport,

(iv)   Retention and attenuation of flood waters,

(v)   Runoff storage,

(vi)   Contribution of flow,

(vii) Export of organic matter,

(viii) Export of food resources, and

(ix)   Provision of life cycle dependent aquatic habitat (such as foraging, feeding, nesting, breeding, spawning, or use as a nursery area) for species located in a water identified in paragraphs (a)(1) through (3) of this section.

(6)   Ordinary high water mark.

The term ordinary high water mark means that line on the shore established by the fluctuations of water and indicated by physical characteristics such as a clear, natural line impressed on the bank, shelving, changes in the character of soil, destruction of terrestrial vegetation, the presence of litter and debris, or other appropriate means that consider the characteristics of the surrounding areas.

(7)   High tide line.

The term high tide line means the line of intersection of the land with the water's surface at the maximum height reached by a rising tide. The high tide line may be determined, in the absence of actual data, by a line of oil or scum along shore objects, a more or less continuous deposit of fine shell or debris on the foreshore or berm, other physical markings or characteristics, vegetation lines, tidal gages, or other suitable means that delineate the general height reached by a rising tide. The line encompasses spring high tides and other high tides that occur with periodic frequency but does not

> include storm surges in which there is a departure from the normal
> or predicted reach of the tide due to the piling up of water against
> a coast by strong winds such as those accompanying a hurricane or
> other intense storm.

Litigants have often challenged EPA's and the Army Corps' assertions
of regulatory jurisdiction, and the issue has repeatedly reached the United
States Supreme Court. The Court's most recent decision appears below, and
you will find summaries of two important earlier cases in the justices'
opinions. As you read, consider what legal standards emerge from this
decision, which produced three opinions and a four-one-four split among the
justices. Again, you should also consider whether the regulations you read
above are consistent with the case below—and, if you think that consistency
is not present, what that means for your client.

Rapanos v. United States
547 U.S. 715 (2006)

■ JUSTICE SCALIA announced the judgment of the Court and delivered
and opinion, in which THE CHIEF JUSTICE, JUSTICE THOMAS, and JUSTICE
ALITO join.

In April 1989, petitioner John A. Rapanos backfilled wetlands on a parcel
of land in Michigan that he owned and sought to develop. This parcel
included 54 acres of land with sometimes-saturated soil conditions. The
nearest body of navigable water was 11 to 20 miles away. Regulators had
informed Mr. Rapanos that his saturated fields were "waters of the
United States," 33 U.S.C. § 1362(7), that could not be filled without a
permit. Twelve years of criminal and civil litigation ensued.

The burden of federal regulation on those who would deposit fill material
in locations denominated "waters of the United States" is not trivial. In
deciding whether to grant or deny a permit, the U.S. Army Corps of
Engineers (Corps) exercises the discretion of an enlightened despot,
relying on such factors as "economics," "aesthetics," "recreation," and "in
general, the needs and welfare of the people," 33 C.F.R. § 320.4(a) (2004).
The average applicant for an individual permit spends 788 days and
$271,596 in completing the process, and the average applicant for a
nationwide permit spends 313 days and $28,915—not counting costs of
mitigation or design changes.[2] "[O]ver $1.7 billion is spent each year by
the private and public sectors obtaining wetlands permits." * * *

---

[2]   Eds: Later in this chapter, we'll explain the difference between an individual and a
general nationwide permit. The vast majority of 404 permits fall into the latter category.

The enforcement proceedings against Mr. Rapanos are a small part of the immense expansion of federal regulation of land use that has occurred under the Clean Water Act—without any change in the governing statute—during the past five Presidential administrations. In the last three decades, the Corps and the Environmental Protection Agency (EPA) have interpreted their jurisdiction over "the waters of the United States" to cover 270-to-300 million acres of swampy lands in the United States—including half of Alaska and an area the size of California in the lower 48 States. And that was just the beginning. The Corps has also asserted jurisdiction over virtually any parcel of land containing a channel or conduit—whether man-made or natural, broad or narrow, permanent or ephemeral—through which rainwater or drainage may occasionally or intermittently flow. On this view, the federally regulated "waters of the United States" include storm drains, roadside ditches, ripples of sand in the desert that may contain water once a year, and lands that are covered by floodwaters once every 100 years. Because they include the land containing storm sewers and desert washes, the statutory "waters of the United States" engulf entire cities and immense arid wastelands. In fact, the entire land area of the United States lies in some drainage basin, and an endless network of visible channels furrows the entire surface, containing water ephemerally wherever the rain falls. Any plot of land containing such a channel may potentially be regulated as a "water of the United States."

I

Congress passed the Clean Water Act (CWA or Act) in 1972. The Act's stated objective is "to restore and maintain the chemical, physical, and biological integrity of the Nation's waters." 86 Stat. 816, 33 U.S.C. § 1251(a). The Act also states that "[i]t is the policy of Congress to recognize, preserve, and protect the primary responsibilities and rights of States to prevent, reduce, and eliminate pollution, to plan the development and use (including restoration, preservation, and enhancement) of land and water resources, and to consult with the Administrator in the exercise of his authority under this chapter." § 1251(b).

One of the statute's principal provisions is 33 U.S.C. § 1311(a), which provides that "the discharge of any pollutant by any person shall be unlawful." "The discharge of a pollutant" is defined broadly to include "any addition of any pollutant to navigable waters from any point source," § 1362(12), and "pollutant" is defined broadly to include not only traditional contaminants but also solids such as "dredged spoil, . . . rock, sand, [and] cellar dirt," § 1362(6). And, most relevant here, the CWA defines "navigable waters" as "the waters of the United States, including the territorial seas." § 1362(7).

The Act also provides certain exceptions to its prohibition of "the discharge of any pollutant by any person." § 1311(a). Section 1342(a) authorizes the Administrator of EPA to "issue a permit for the discharge of any pollutant, . . . notwithstanding section 1311(a) of this title." Section 1344 authorizes the Secretary of the Army, acting through the Corps, to "issue permits . . . for the discharge of dredged or fill material into the navigable waters at specified disposal sites." § 1344(a), (d). It is the discharge of "dredged or fill material"—which, unlike traditional water pollutants, are solids that do not readily wash downstream—that we consider today. * * *

We first addressed the proper interpretation of 33 U.S.C. § 1362(7)'s phrase "the waters of the United States" in *United States v. Riverside Bayview Homes, Inc.,* 474 U.S. 121 (1985). That case concerned a wetland that "was adjacent to a body of navigable water," because "the area characterized by saturated soil conditions and wetland vegetation extended beyond the boundary of respondent's property to . . . a navigable waterway." *Id.,* at 131; see also 33 C.F.R. § 328.3(b). Noting that "the transition from water to solid ground is not necessarily or even typically an abrupt one," and that "the Corps must necessarily choose some point at which water ends and land begins," 474 U.S., at 132, we upheld the Corps' interpretation of "the waters of the United States" to include wetlands that "actually abut[ted] on" traditional navigable waters. *Id.,* at 135.

Following our decision in *Riverside Bayview,* the Corps adopted increasingly broad interpretations of its own regulations under the Act. For example, in 1986, to "clarify" the reach of its jurisdiction, the Corps announced the so-called "Migratory Bird Rule," which purported to extend its jurisdiction to any intrastate waters "[w]hich are or would be used as habitat" by migratory birds. 51 Fed. Reg. 41217. * * *

In *SWANCC,* we considered the application of the Corps' "Migratory Bird Rule" to "an abandoned sand and gravel pit in northern Illinois." 531 U.S., at 162. Observing that "[i]t was the *significant nexus* between the wetlands and 'navigable waters' that informed our reading of the CWA in *Riverside Bayview,*" *id.,* at 167 (emphasis added), we held that *Riverside Bayview* did not establish "that the jurisdiction of the Corps extends to ponds that are not adjacent to open water," 531 U.S., at 168 (emphasis deleted). On the contrary, we held that "nonnavigable, isolated, intrastate waters," *id.,* at 171—which, unlike the wetlands at issue in *Riverside Bayview,* did not "actually abu[t] on a navigable waterway," 531 U.S., at 167—were not included as "waters of the United States." * * *

II

In these consolidated cases, we consider whether four Michigan wetlands, which lie near ditches or man-made drains that eventually empty into traditional navigable waters, constitute "waters of the United States" within the meaning of the Act. Petitioners in No. 04–1034, the Rapanos and their affiliated businesses, deposited fill material without a permit into wetlands on three sites near Midland, Michigan: the "Salzburg site," the "Hines Road site," and the "Pine River site." The wetlands at the Salzburg site are connected to a man-made drain, which drains into Hoppler Creek, which flows into the Kawkawlin River, which empties into Saginaw Bay and Lake Huron. The wetlands at the Hines Road site are connected to something called the "Rose Drain," which has a surface connection to the Tittabawassee River. And the wetlands at the Pine River site have a surface connection to the Pine River, which flows into Lake Huron. It is not clear whether the connections between these wetlands and the nearby drains and ditches are continuous or intermittent, or whether the nearby drains and ditches contain continuous or merely occasional flows of water.

[Eds.: This decision actually addressed two consolidated cases. We have included some of the facts of the *Rapanos* case but not the facts of the *Carabell* case.]

* * *

We granted certiorari and consolidated the cases to decide whether these wetlands constitute "waters of the United States" under the Act, and if so, whether the Act is constitutional.

III

Rapanos petitioners contend that the terms "navigable waters" and "waters of the United States" in the Act must be limited to the traditional definition of *The Daniel Ball,* which required that the "waters" be navigable in fact, or susceptible of being rendered so. See 10 Wall., at 563. But this definition cannot be applied wholesale to the CWA. The Act uses the phrase "navigable waters" as a *defined* term, and the definition is simply "the waters of the United States." 33 U.S.C. § 1362(7). Moreover, the Act provides, in certain circumstances, for the substitution of state for federal jurisdiction over "navigable waters . . . *other than* those waters which are presently used, or are susceptible to use in their natural condition or by reasonable improvement as a means to transport interstate or foreign commerce . . . including wetlands adjacent thereto." § 1344(g)(1) (emphasis added). This provision shows that the Act's term "navigable waters" includes something more than traditional navigable waters. We have twice stated that the meaning of "navigable waters" in the Act is broader than the traditional understanding of that term, *SWANCC,* 531 U.S., at 167; *Riverside Bayview,* 474 U.S., at 133. We have also emphasized, however, that the qualifier "navigable" is not devoid of significance, *SWANCC, supra,* at 172.

We need not decide the precise extent to which the qualifiers "navigable" and "of the United States" restrict the coverage of the Act. Whatever the scope of these qualifiers, the CWA authorizes federal jurisdiction only over "waters." 33 U.S.C. § 1362(7). The only natural definition of the term "waters," our prior and subsequent judicial constructions of it, clear evidence from other provisions of the statute, and this Court's canons of construction all confirm that "the waters of the United States" in § 1362(7) cannot bear the expansive meaning that the Corps would give it.

The Corps' expansive approach might be arguable if the CWA defined "navigable waters" as "water of the United States." But "the waters of the United States" is something else. The use of the definite article ("the") and the plural number ("waters") shows plainly that § 1362(7) does not refer to water in general. In this form, "the waters" refers more narrowly to water "[a]s found in streams and bodies forming geographical features such as oceans, rivers, [and] lakes," or "the flowing or moving masses, as of waves or floods, making up such streams or bodies." Webster's New International Dictionary 2882 (2d ed. 1954) (hereinafter Webster's Second). On this definition, "the waters of the United States" include only relatively permanent, standing or flowing bodies of water.[5] The definition refers to water as found in "streams," "oceans," "rivers," "lakes," and "bodies" of water "forming geographical features." *Ibid.* All of these terms connote continuously present, fixed bodies of water, as opposed to ordinarily dry channels through which water occasionally or intermittently flows. Even the least substantial of the definition's terms, namely, "streams," connotes a continuous flow of water in a permanent channel—especially when used in company with other terms such as "rivers," "lakes," and "oceans." None of these terms encompasses transitory puddles or ephemeral flows of water.

The restriction of "the waters of the United States" to exclude channels containing merely intermittent or ephemeral flow also accords with the commonsense understanding of the term. In applying the definition to "ephemeral streams," "wet meadows," storm sewers and culverts, "directional sheet flow during storm events," drain tiles, man-made drainage ditches, and dry arroyos in the middle of the desert, the Corps has stretched the term "waters of the United States" beyond parody. The

---

[5] By describing "waters" as "relatively permanent," we do not necessarily exclude streams, rivers, or lakes that might dry up in extraordinary circumstances, such as drought. We also do not necessarily exclude *seasonal* rivers, which contain continuous flow during some months of the year but no flow during dry months—such as the 290-day, continuously flowing stream postulated by Justice STEVENS' dissent (hereinafter the dissent), *post,* at 2259–2260. Common sense and common usage distinguish between a wash and seasonal river.

plain language of the statute simply does not authorize this "Land Is Waters" approach to federal jurisdiction.

* * * As we noted in *SWANCC*, the traditional term "navigable waters"— even though defined as "the waters of the United States"—carries *some* of its original substance: "[I]t is one thing to give a word limited effect and quite another to give it no effect whatever." 531 U.S., at 172. That limited effect includes, at bare minimum, the ordinary presence of water. * * *

Even if the phrase "the waters of the United States" were ambiguous as applied to intermittent flows, our own canons of construction would establish that the Corps' interpretation of the statute is impermissible. As we noted in *SWANCC*, the Government's expansive interpretation would "result in a significant impingement of the States' traditional and primary power over land and water use." 531 U.S., at 174. Regulation of land use, as through the issuance of the development permits sought by petitioners in both of these cases, is a quintessential state and local power. See *FERC v. Mississippi,* 456 U.S. 742, 767–768, n. 30 (1982); *Hess v. Port Authority Trans-Hudson Corporation,* 513 U.S. 30, 44 (1994). The extensive federal jurisdiction urged by the Government would authorize the Corps to function as a *de facto* regulator of immense stretches of intrastate land—an authority the agency has shown its willingness to exercise with the scope of discretion that would befit a local zoning board. See 33 C.F.R. § 320.4(a)(1) (2004). We ordinarily expect a "clear and manifest" statement from Congress to authorize an unprecedented intrusion into traditional state authority. See *BFP v. Resolution Trust Corporation,* 511 U.S. 531, 544 (1994). The phrase "the waters of the United States" hardly qualifies.

Likewise, just as we noted in *SWANCC*, the Corps' interpretation stretches the outer limits of Congress's commerce power and raises difficult questions about the ultimate scope of that power. See 531 U.S., at 173. (In developing the current regulations, the Corps consciously sought to extend its authority to the farthest reaches of the commerce power. See 42 Fed. Reg. 37127 (1977).) Even if the term "the waters of the United States" were ambiguous as applied to channels that sometimes host ephemeral flows of water (which it is not), we would expect a clearer statement from Congress to authorize an agency theory of jurisdiction that presses the envelope of constitutional validity. See *Edward J. DeBartolo Corp. v. Florida Gulf Coast Building & Constr. Trades Council,* 485 U.S. 568, 575 (1988).

In sum, on its only plausible interpretation, the phrase "the waters of the United States" includes only those relatively permanent, standing or continuously flowing bodies of water "forming geographic features" that are described in ordinary parlance as "streams[,] . . . oceans, rivers, [and] lakes." See Webster's Second 2882. The phrase does not include channels through which water flows intermittently or ephemerally, or channels that periodically provide drainage for rainfall. The Corps' expansive interpretation of the "the waters of the United States" is thus not "based on a permissible construction of the statute." *Chevron U.S.A. Inc. v. Natural Resources Defense Council, Inc.,* 467 U.S. 837, 843 (1984).

IV

[Eds.: The Court then discussed when an "adjacent" wetland meets the Clean Water Act's definition of "navigable waters."]

* * * Therefore, *only* those wetlands with a continuous surface connection to bodies that are "waters of the United States" in their own right, so that there is no clear demarcation between "waters" and wetlands, are "adjacent to" such waters and covered by the Act. Wetlands with only an intermittent, physically remote hydrologic connection to "waters of the United States" do not implicate the boundary-drawing problem of *Riverside Bayview,* and thus lack the necessary connection to covered waters that we described as a "significant nexus" in *SWANCC.* 531 U.S., at 167. Thus, establishing that wetlands such as those at the Rapanos and Carabell sites are covered by the Act requires two findings: first, that the adjacent channel contains a "wate[r] of the United States," (*i.e.,* a relatively permanent body of water connected to traditional interstate navigable waters); and second, that the wetland has a continuous surface connection with that water, making it difficult to determine where the "water" ends and the "wetland" begins.

[Eds.: The Court remanded the case so the Sixth Circuit could apply this standard.]

[Eds.: Chief Justice Roberts' concurrence is omitted]

■ JUSTICE KENNEDY, concurring in the judgment.

These consolidated cases require the Court to decide whether the term "navigable waters" in the Clean Water Act extends to wetlands that do not contain and are not adjacent to waters that are navigable in fact. In *Solid Waste Agency of Northern Cook Cty. v. Army Corps of Engineers,* 531 U.S. 159 (2001) *(SWANCC),* the Court held, under the circumstances presented there, that to constitute " 'navigable waters' " under the Act, a water or wetland must possess a "significant nexus" to waters that are or were navigable in fact or that could reasonably be so made. *Id.,* at 167, 172. In the instant cases neither the plurality opinion nor the dissent by Justice STEVENS chooses to apply this test; and though the Court of Appeals recognized the test's applicability, it did not consider all the factors necessary to determine whether the lands in question had, or did not have, the requisite nexus. In my view the cases ought to be remanded to the Court of Appeals for proper consideration of the nexus requirement. * * *

The statutory term to be interpreted and applied in the two instant cases is the term "navigable waters." The outcome turns on whether that phrase reasonably describes certain Michigan wetlands the Corps seeks to regulate. Under the Act "[t]he term 'navigable waters' means the waters of the United States, including the territorial seas." § 1362(7). In a regulation the Corps has construed the term "waters of the United States" to include not only waters susceptible to use in interstate commerce—the traditional understanding of the term "navigable waters of the United States," *see, e.g., United States v. Appalachian Elec. Power Co.*, 311 U.S. 377, 406–408 (1940); *The Daniel Ball*, 10 Wall. 557, 563–564 (1871)—but also tributaries of those waters and, of particular relevance here, wetlands adjacent to those waters or their tributaries. 33 C.F.R. §§ 328.3(a)(1), (5), (7). * * *

Contrary to the plurality's description, wetlands are not simply moist patches of earth. They are defined as "those areas that are inundated or saturated by surface or ground water at a frequency and duration sufficient to support, and that under normal circumstances do support, a prevalence of vegetation typically adapted for life in saturated soil conditions. Wetlands generally include swamps, marshes, bogs, and similar areas." § 328.3(b). The Corps' Wetlands Delineation Manual, including over 100 pages of technical guidance for Corps officers, interprets this definition of wetlands to require: (1) prevalence of plant species typically adapted to saturated soil conditions, determined in accordance with the United States Fish and Wildlife Service's National List of Plant Species that Occur in Wetlands; (2) hydric soil, meaning soil that is saturated, flooded, or ponded for sufficient time during the growing season to become anaerobic, or lacking in oxygen, in the upper part; and (3) wetland hydrology, a term generally requiring continuous inundation or saturation to the surface during at least five percent of the growing season in most years. See Wetlands Research Program Technical Report Y–87–1 (on-line edition), pp. 12–34 (Jan. 1987), http://www.saj. usace.army.mil/permit/documents/87manual.pdf. Under the Corps' regulations, wetlands are adjacent to tributaries, and thus covered by the Act, even if they are "separated from other waters of the United States by man-made dikes or barriers, natural river berms, beach dunes and the like." § 328.3(c). * * *

II

Twice before the Court has construed the term "navigable waters" in the Clean Water Act. In *United States v. Riverside Bayview Homes, Inc.*, 474 U.S. 121 (1985), the Court upheld the Corps' jurisdiction over wetlands adjacent to navigable-in-fact waterways. *Id.*, at 139. * * * Recognizing that "[a]n agency's construction of a statute it is charged with enforcing is entitled to deference if it is reasonable and not in conflict with the expressed intent of Congress," *id.*, at 131 (citing *Chemical Mfrs. Assn. v.*

Natural Resources Defense Council, Inc., 470 U.S. 116, 125 (1985), and *Chevron U.S.A. Inc. v. Natural Resources Defense Council, Inc.*, 467 U.S. 837, 842–845 (1984)), the Court held that "the Corps' ecological judgment about the relationship between waters and their adjacent wetlands provides an adequate basis for a legal judgment that adjacent wetlands may be defined as waters under the Act," 474 U.S., at 134. The Court reserved, however, the question of the Corps' authority to regulate wetlands other than those adjacent to open waters. See *id.*, at 131–132, n. 8.

In *SWANCC*, the Court considered the validity of the Corps' jurisdiction over ponds and mudflats that were isolated in the sense of being unconnected to other waters covered by the Act. 531 U.S., at 171. The property at issue was an abandoned sand and gravel pit mining operation where "remnant excavation trenches" had "evolv[ed] into a scattering of permanent and seasonal ponds." *Id.*, at 163. Asserting jurisdiction pursuant to a regulation called the "Migratory Bird Rule," the Corps argued that these isolated ponds were "waters of the United States" (and thus "navigable waters" under the Act) because they were used as habitat by migratory birds. *Id.*, at 164–165. The Court rejected this theory. "It was the significant nexus between wetlands and 'navigable waters,' " the Court held, "that informed our reading of the [Act] in *Riverside Bayview Homes*." *Id.*, at 167. Because such a nexus was lacking with respect to isolated ponds, the Court held that the plain text of the statute did not permit the Corps' action. *Id.*, at 172.

* * * Taken together these cases establish that in some instances, as exemplified by *Riverside Bayview*, the connection between a nonnavigable water or wetland and a navigable water may be so close, or potentially so close, that the Corps may deem the water or wetland a "navigable water" under the Act. In other instances, as exemplified by SWANCC, there may be little or no connection. Absent a significant nexus, jurisdiction under the Act is lacking. Because neither the plurality nor the dissent addresses the nexus requirement, this separate opinion, in my respectful view, is necessary. * * *

The concerns addressed in *SWANCC* do not support the plurality's interpretation of the Act. In *SWANCC*, by interpreting the Act to require a significant nexus with navigable waters, the Court avoided applications—those involving waters without a significant nexus—that appeared likely, as a category, to raise constitutional difficulties and federalism concerns. Here, in contrast, the plurality's interpretation does not fit the avoidance concerns it raises. On the one hand, when a surface-water connection is lacking, the plurality forecloses jurisdiction over wetlands that abut navigable-in-fact waters—even though such navigable waters were traditionally subject to federal authority. On the other hand, by saying the Act covers wetlands (however remote) possessing a surface-water connection with a continuously flowing stream (however small), the plurality's reading would permit applications of the statute as far from traditional federal authority as are the waters it deems beyond the statute's reach. Even assuming, then, that federal regulation of remote wetlands and nonnavigable waterways would raise a difficult Commerce Clause issue notwithstanding those waters' aggregate effects on national water quality, *but cf. Wickard v. Filburn,* 317 U.S. 111 (1942); the plurality's reading is not responsive to this concern. As for States' "responsibilities and rights," § 1251(b), it is noteworthy that 33 States plus the District of Columbia have filed an *amici* brief in this litigation asserting that the Clean Water Act is important to their own water policies. These *amici* note, among other things, that the Act protects downstream States from out-of-state pollution that they cannot themselves regulate. * * *

[T]he plurality's overall tone and approach—from the characterization of acres of wetlands destruction as "backfilling . . . wet fields," to the rejection of Corps authority over "man-made drainage ditches" and "dry arroyos" without regard to how much water they periodically carry, to the suggestion, seemingly contrary to Congress' judgment, that discharge of fill material is inconsequential for adjacent waterways,—seems unduly dismissive of the interests asserted by the United States in these cases. Important public interests are served by the Clean Water Act in general and by the protection of wetlands in particular. To give just one example, *amici* here have noted that nutrient-rich runoff from the Mississippi River has created a hypoxic, or oxygen-depleted, "dead zone" in the Gulf of Mexico that at times approaches the size of Massachusetts and New Jersey. Scientific evidence indicates that wetlands play a critical role in controlling and filtering runoff. It is true, as the plurality indicates, that environmental concerns provide no reason to disregard limits in the statutory text, but in my view the plurality's opinion is not a correct reading of the text. The limits the plurality would impose, moreover, give insufficient deference to Congress' purposes in enacting the Clean Water Act and to the authority of the Executive to implement that statutory mandate. * * *

Consistent with *SWANCC* and *Riverside Bayview* and with the need to give the term "navigable" some meaning, the Corps' jurisdiction over wetlands depends upon the existence of a significant nexus between the wetlands in question and navigable waters in the traditional sense. The required nexus must be assessed in terms of the statute's goals and purposes. Congress enacted the law to "restore and maintain the chemical, physical, and biological integrity of the Nation's waters," 33 U.S.C. § 1251(a), and it pursued that objective by restricting dumping and filling in "navigable waters," §§ 1311(a), 1362(12). With respect to wetlands, the rationale for Clean Water Act regulation is, as the Corps has recognized, that wetlands can perform critical functions related to the integrity of other waters—functions such as pollutant trapping, flood control, and runoff storage. 33 C.F.R. § 320.4(b)(2). Accordingly, wetlands possess the requisite nexus, and thus come within the statutory phrase "navigable waters," if the wetlands, either alone or in combination with similarly situated lands in the region, significantly affect the chemical, physical, and biological integrity of other covered waters more readily understood as "navigable." When, in contrast, wetlands' effects on water quality are speculative or insubstantial, they fall outside the zone fairly encompassed by the statutory term "navigable waters." * * *

When the Corps seeks to regulate wetlands adjacent to navigable-in-fact waters, it may rely on adjacency to establish its jurisdiction. Absent more specific regulations, however, the Corps must establish a significant nexus on a case-by-case basis when it seeks to regulate wetlands based on adjacency to nonnavigable tributaries. Given the potential overbreadth of the Corps' regulations, this showing is necessary to avoid unreasonable applications of the statute. Where an adequate nexus is established for a particular wetland, it may be permissible, as a matter of administrative convenience or necessity, to presume covered status for other comparable wetlands in the region. That issue, however, is neither raised by these facts nor addressed by any agency regulation that accommodates the nexus requirement outlined here.

This interpretation of the Act does not raise federalism or Commerce Clause concerns sufficient to support a presumption against its adoption. To be sure, the significant-nexus requirement may not align perfectly with the traditional extent of federal authority. Yet in most cases regulation of wetlands that are adjacent to tributaries and possess a significant nexus with navigable waters will raise no serious constitutional or federalism difficulty. Cf. *Pierce County v. Guillen,* 537 U.S. 129, 147 (2003) (upholding federal legislation "aimed at improving safety in the channels of commerce"); *Oklahoma ex rel. Phillips v. Guy F. Atkinson Co.,* 313 U.S. 508, 525–526 (1941) ("[J]ust as control over the non-navigable parts of a river may be essential or desirable in the interests of the navigable portions, so may the key to flood control on a navigable stream be found in whole or in part in flood control on its tributaries .... [T]he exercise of the granted power of Congress to regulate interstate commerce may be aided by appropriate and needful control of activities and agencies which, though intrastate, affect that commerce"). As explained earlier, moreover, and as exemplified by *SWANCC,* the significant-nexus test itself prevents problematic applications of the statute. See 531 U.S., at 174. The possibility of legitimate Commerce Clause and federalism concerns in some circumstances does not require the adoption of an interpretation that departs in all cases from the Act's text and structure. See *Gonzales v.*

Raich, 545 U.S. 1, 17 (2005) ("[W]hen a general regulatory statute bears a substantial relation to commerce, the *de minimis* character of individual instances arising under that statute is of no consequence" (internal quotation marks omitted).

III

In both the consolidated cases before the Court the record contains evidence suggesting the possible existence of a significant nexus according to the principles outlined above. Thus the end result in these cases and many others to be considered by the Corps may be the same as that suggested by the dissent, namely, that the Corps' assertion of jurisdiction is valid. Given, however, that neither the agency nor the reviewing courts properly considered the issue, a remand is appropriate, in my view, for application of the controlling legal standard. * * *

In these consolidated cases I would vacate the judgments of the Court of Appeals and remand for consideration whether the specific wetlands at issue possess a significant nexus with navigable waters.

■ JUSTICE STEVENS, with whom JUSTICE SOUTER, JUSTICE GINSBURG, and JUSTICE BREYER join, dissenting.

* * *

The narrow question presented in No. 04–1034 is whether wetlands adjacent to tributaries of traditionally navigable waters are "waters of the United States" subject to the jurisdiction of the Army Corps; the question in No. 04–1384 is whether a manmade berm separating a wetland from the adjacent tributary makes a difference. The broader question is whether regulations that have protected the quality of our waters for decades, that were implicitly approved by Congress, and that have been repeatedly enforced in case after case, must now be revised in light of the creative criticisms voiced by the plurality and Justice KENNEDY today. Rejecting more than 30 years of practice by the Army Corps, the plurality disregards the nature of the congressional delegation to the agency and the technical and complex character of the issues at stake. Justice KENNEDY similarly fails to defer sufficiently to the Corps, though his approach is far more faithful to our precedents and to principles of statutory interpretation than is the plurality's.

In my view, the proper analysis is straightforward. The Army Corps has determined that wetlands adjacent to tributaries of traditionally navigable waters preserve the quality of our Nation's waters by, among other things, providing habitat for aquatic animals, keeping excessive sediment and toxic pollutants out of adjacent waters, and reducing downstream flooding by absorbing water at times of high flow. The Corps' resulting decision to treat these wetlands as encompassed within the term "waters of the United States" is a quintessential example of the Executive's reasonable interpretation of a statutory provision. See

Chevron U.S.A. Inc. v. Natural Resources Defense Council, Inc., 467 U.S. 837, 842–845 (1984). * * *

I would affirm the judgments in both cases, and respectfully dissent from the decision of five Members of this Court to vacate and remand. I close, however, by noting an unusual feature of the Court's judgments in these cases. It has been our practice in a case coming to us from a lower federal court to enter a judgment commanding that court to conduct any further proceedings pursuant to a specific mandate. That prior practice has, on occasion, made it necessary for Justices to join a judgment that did not conform to their own views. In these cases, however, while both the plurality and Justice KENNEDY agree that there must be a remand for further proceedings, their respective opinions define different tests to be applied on remand. Given that all four Justices who have joined this opinion would uphold the Corps' jurisdiction in both of these cases—and in all other cases in which either the plurality's or Justice KENNEDY's test is satisfied—on remand each of the judgments should be reinstated if *either* of those tests is met.

[Eds.: Justice Breyer's separate dissenting opinion is omitted.]

NOTES

1.   As the closing paragraph of Justice Stevens' dissent acknowledges, the *Rapanos* decision places lower courts in a difficult position. They must decide not only what standards the Justices' opinions create, but also, in some cases, which standard to apply. Some intercircuit confusion has resulted, with some courts applying only Justice Kennedy's "significant nexus" test, some applying Justice Scalia's test, and some following Justice Stevens' suggestion that courts find federal jurisdiction where the wetland in question meets either Justice Kennedy's test or Justice Scalia's test. *See* Robin Kundis Craig, *Agencies Interpreting Courts Interpreting Statutes: The Deference Conundrum of a Divided Supreme Court*, 61 EMORY L.J. 1, 59–60 (2011).

2.   Are there constitutional provisions other than the Commerce Clause that Congress could invoke as sources of authority to regulate water quality? Congress can enact laws to implement treaties with other countries, and that power represents a potential alternative or additional source of authority. In the *SWANCC* case discussed in *Rapanos*, the Court suggested that the Commerce Clause might not grant Congress power to regulate hydrologically isolated waters used as habitat by migratory birds. During that litigation, the United States did not argue that Congress has authority to protect migratory bird habitat to implement the 1916 Convention for the Protection of Migratory Birds between the United States and Great Britain (acting on behalf of Canada). That treaty might serve as an alternative source of authority to allow Congress to regulate certain waters that might fall outside

the Commerce Clause. *See* Chapter 2 (discussing the Treaty Power as a potential source of congressional power to enact environmental legislation).

3.   State water quality statutes may have somewhat different scope than the federal Clean Water Act. Among other things, state statutes are not limited to the scope of federal regulatory authority under the Commerce Clause. Pennsylvania's Clean Streams Law, 35 P.S. §§ 691.1–691.1001, for example, prohibits unauthorized discharges of "sewage," "industrial waste," or "pollution" into "waters of the Commonwealth," which it defines as "any and all rivers, streams, creeks, rivulets, impoundments, ditches, water courses, storm sewers, lakes, dammed water, ponds, springs and all other bodies or channels of conveyance of surface and underground water, or parts thereof, whether natural or artificial, within or on the boundaries of this Commonwealth." 35 P.S. § 691.1. Would the vernal pools or Shiner Brook, if located in Pennsylvania, constitute "waters of the Commonwealth"? To what extent would the reasoning of the *Rapanos* plurality, concurring, and dissenting opinions apply to interpreting the Clean Streams Law?

B. POINT SOURCE

Establishing that an aquatic resource is a "water of the United States" is a necessary precondition for protection under the Clean Water Act. But the kinds of protections that apply to a waterway also depend upon the pollution sources impacting that waterway. One distinction is particularly important: the Clean Water Act separates pollution sources into point source and non-point source categories. Because point sources are often stringently regulated, and nonpoint sources are generally subject to less stringent regulation or no regulation at all, this distinction is of great interest to environmental lawyers. The problem below introduces you to a particularly controversial application of that distinction.

PROBLEM: FIREWORKS

Every year around the Fourth of July, Wisconsin's lakes get a little bit louder. In Wisconsin, fireworks permits are readily available, and many people spend hundreds of dollars, or more, on spectacular displays, some of them above the state's many lakes. Many of the other homeowners enjoy their neighbors' displays, or at least view them as an inevitable and unavoidable consequence of lakefront homeownership. But a few residents have begun voicing concerns about consequences for water quality. Fireworks displays leave behind chemicals and debris, and while fireworks manufacturers and fireworks display sponsors argue that the quantities are de minimis, some water quality advocates disagree.

Recently, a homeowners' association on one lake decided to turn those concerns into legal action. It sent a letter to ten landowners, each of whom had held fireworks displays every year for the previous ten years, notifying them of the association's intent to bring suit under the citizens' suit provision of the Clean Water Act, 33 U.S.C. § 1365. The letter warned the fireworks aficionados that their displays had violated the Clean Water Act and could not proceed without permits.

Please consider this controversy from the following perspectives:

- You are an attorney with the Wisconsin John Muir Chapter of the Sierra Club. The homeowner's association has asked the chapter to join in filing a lawsuit. What will you advise? Legally, how strong are your potential arguments? Do you think bringing the lawsuit would be an effective advocacy strategy?

- You are an attorney with the Wisconsin Department of Natural Resources, which administers the NPDES program in Wisconsin. How will you respond to the notice letter? Will you bring your own enforcement action? Doing so would supplant the homeowners' association's suit and would put your department in charge of the litigation. Will you try to participate as an intervenor or amicus curiae? On which side, and with what arguments?

- You are an attorney for several of the homeowners who received the notice letter. What advice will you give them? If they elect to litigate (rather than settle), are they likely to prevail?

In researching the issue, you have identified some key passages from the Clean Water Act and one potentially important case, all of which appear below. You also have identified two other places where the application of the Clean Water Act to fireworks has become a controversial issue. One is San Diego, where the San Diego Regional Water Quality Control Board now requires permits for fireworks displays over "waters of the United States." The other is Lake Tahoe, where residents have initiated litigation against the sponsors of fireworks shows. Materials from both of those controversies also appear below.

If you were a real-world attorney considering this problem, you would consider not just whether fireworks displays are point sources, but also how those displays would be regulated if they are classified as point sources. For purposes of this problem, you should focus only on the former question. In the next unit, we'll consider how point sources are regulated.

CWA § 301, 33 U.S.C. § 1311. Effluent limitations

(a) Illegality of pollutant discharges except in compliance with law

Except as in compliance with this section and sections 1312, 1316, 1317, 1328, 1342, and 1344 of this title, the discharge of any pollutant by any person shall be unlawful. * * *

[Sections 1312, 1316, 1317, 1328, 1342, and 1344 set forth the requirements of the various permitting programs, including the NPDES program, under which pollutants may lawfully be discharged.]

CWA § 502, 33 U.S.C. § 1362. Definitions

(6) The term "pollutant" means dredged spoil, solid waste, incinerator residue, sewage, garbage, sewage sludge, munitions, chemical wastes, biological materials, radioactive materials, heat, wrecked or discarded equipment, rock, sand, cellar dirt and industrial, municipal, and agricultural waste discharged into water. This term does not mean (A) "sewage from vessels or a discharge incidental to the normal operation of a vessel of the Armed Forces" within the meaning of section 1322 of this title; or (B) water, gas, or other material which is injected into a well to facilitate production of oil or gas, or water derived in association with oil or gas production and disposed of in a well, if the well used either to facilitate production or for disposal purposes is approved by authority of the State in which the well is located, and if such State determines that such injection or disposal will not result in the degradation of ground or surface water resources. * * *

(12)   The term "discharge of a pollutant" and the term "discharge of pollutants" each means (A) any addition of any pollutant to navigable waters from any point source, (B) any addition of any pollutant to the waters of the contiguous zone or the ocean from any point source other than a vessel or other floating craft. * * *

(14)   The term "point source" means any discernible, confined and discrete conveyance, including but not limited to any pipe, ditch, channel, tunnel, conduit, well, discrete fissure, container, rolling stock, concentrated animal feeding operation, or vessel or other floating craft, from which pollutants are or may be discharged. This term does not include agricultural stormwater discharges and return flows from irrigated agriculture.

United States v. Plaza Health Laboratories

3 F.3d 643 (2d. Cir. 1992)

■ GEORGE C. PRATT, CIRCUIT JUDGE:

Defendant Geronimo Villegas appeals from a judgment entered in the United States District Court for the Eastern District of New York, Edward R. Korman, *Judge,* convicting him of two counts of knowingly discharging pollutants into the Hudson River in violation of the Clean Water Act ("CWA"). *See* 33 U.S.C. §§ 1311 and 1319(c)(2). * * *

Facts and Background

Villegas was co-owner and vice president of Plaza Health Laboratories, Inc., a blood-testing laboratory in Brooklyn, New York. On at least two occasions between April and September 1988, Villegas loaded containers of numerous vials of human blood generated from his business into his personal car, and drove to his residence at the Admirals Walk Condominium in Edgewater, New Jersey. Once at his condominium complex, Villegas removed the containers from his car and carried them to the edge of the Hudson River. On one occasion he carried two containers of the vials to the bulkhead that separates his condominium complex from the river, and placed them at low tide within a crevice in the bulkhead that was below the high-water line.

On May 26, 1988, a group of eighth graders on a field trip at the Alice Austin House in Staten Island, New York, discovered numerous glass vials containing human blood along the shore. Some of the vials had washed up on the shore; many were still in the water. Some were cracked, although most remained sealed with stoppers in solid-plastic containers or ziplock bags. Fortunately, no one was injured. That afternoon, New York City workers recovered approximately 70 vials from the area.

On September 25, 1988, a maintenance worker employed by the Admirals Walk Condominium discovered a plastic container holding blood vials wedged between rocks in the bulkhead. New Jersey authorities retrieved numerous blood vials from the bulkhead later that day.

Ten of the retrieved vials contained blood infected with the hepatitis-B virus. All of the vials recovered were eventually traced to Plaza Health Laboratories.

Based upon the May 1988 discovery of vials, Plaza Health Laboratories and Villegas were indicted on May 16, 1989, on two counts each of violating §§ 1319(c)(2) and (3) of the Clean Water Act. 33 U.S.C. §§ 1251 *et seq.* A superseding indictment charged both defendants with two additional CWA counts based upon the vials found in September 1988. * * *

Counts II and IV of the superseding indictment charged Villegas with knowingly discharging pollutants from a "point source" without a permit. *See* 33 U.S.C. §§ 1311(a), 1319(c)(2). Counts I and III alleged that Villegas had discharged pollutants, knowing that he placed others in "imminent danger of death or serious bodily injury". *See* 33 U.S.C. § 1319(c)(3). On January 31, 1991, following a trial before Judge Korman, the jury found Villegas guilty on all four counts. * * *

Villegas contends that one element of the CWA crime, knowingly discharging pollutants from a "point source", was not established in his case. He argues that the definition of "point source", 33 U.S.C. § 1362(14), does not include discharges that result from the individual acts of human beings. Raising primarily questions of legislative intent and statutory construction, Villegas argues that at best, the term "point source" is ambiguous as applied to him, and that the rule of lenity should result in reversal of his convictions. * * *

Discussion

* * *

A.   *Navigating the Clean Water Act.*

The basic prohibition on discharge of pollutants is in 33 U.S.C. § 1311(a), which states:

> Except as in compliance with this section and sections 1312, 1316, 1317, 1328, *1342,* and 1344 of this title, the *discharge* of any *pollutant* by any person shall be unlawful.

Id. (emphasis added).

The largest exception to this seemingly absolute rule is found in 33 U.S.C. § 1342, which establishes the CWA's national pollutant discharge elimination system, or NPDES:

> (a)   Permits for discharge of pollutants
>
> (1)   Except as provided in sections 1328 [aquaculture] and 1344 of this title [dredge and fill permits], the Administrator may, after opportunity for public hearing, issue a permit for the discharge of any pollutant . . . *notwithstanding section 1311(a) of this title,* upon condition that such discharge will meet . . . all applicable requirements under sections 1311, 1312, 1316, 1317, 1318, and 1343 of this title. . . .

33 U.S.C. § 1342(a) (emphasis added).

Reading § 1311(a), the basic prohibition, and § 1342(a)(1), the permit section, together, we can identify the basic rule, our rhumb line to clean waters, that, absent a permit, "the discharge of any pollutant by any person" is unlawful. 33 U.S.C. § 1311(a).

We must then adjust our rhumb line by reference to two key definitions— "pollutant" and "discharge". "Pollutant" is defined, in part, as "biological materials . . . *discharged* into water." 33 U.S.C. § 1362(6) (emphasis added). "Discharge", in turn, is "any addition of any pollutant to navigable waters *from any point source.* . . ." (emphasis added). 33 U.S.C. § 1362(12).

As applied to the facts of this case, then, the defendant "added" a "pollutant" (human blood in glass vials) to "navigable waters" (the Hudson River), and he did so without a permit. The issue, therefore, is whether his conduct constituted a "discharge", and that in turn depends on whether the addition of the blood to the Hudson River waters was "from any point source".

For this final course adjustment in our navigation, we look again to the statute.

> (14) The term "point source" means any discernible, confined and discrete conveyance, including but not limited to any pipe, ditch, channel, tunnel, conduit, well, discrete fissure, container, rolling stock, concentrated animal feeding operation, or vessel or other floating craft, from which pollutants are or may be discharged. This term does not include agricultural stormwater discharges and return flows from irrigated agriculture.

33 U.S.C. § 1362(14). * * *

As the parties have presented the issue to us in their briefs and at oral argument, the question is "whether a human being can be a point source". * * *

1.   Language and Structure of Act.

Human beings are not among the enumerated items that may be a "point source". Although by its terms the definition of "point source" is nonexclusive, the words used to define the term and the examples given ("pipe, ditch, channel, tunnel, conduit, well, discrete fissure", etc.) evoke images of physical structures and instrumentalities that systematically act as a means of conveying pollutants from an industrial source to navigable waterways.

In addition, if every discharge involving humans were to be considered a "discharge from a point source", the statute's lengthy definition of "point source" would have been unnecessary. It is elemental that congress does not add unnecessary words to statutes. Had congress intended to punish any human being who polluted navigational waters, it could readily have said: "any person who places pollutants in navigable waters without a permit is guilty of a crime."

The Clean Water Act generally targets industrial and municipal sources of pollutants, as is evident from a perusal of its many sections. Consistent with this focus, the term "point source" is used throughout the statute, but invariably in sentences referencing industrial or municipal discharges. *See, e.g.,* 33 U.S.C. § 1311 (referring to "owner or operator" of point source); § 1311(e) (requiring that effluent limitations established under the Act "be applied to all point sources of discharge"); § 1311(g)(2) (allows an "owner or operator of a point source" to apply to EPA for modification of its limitations requirements); § 1342(f) (referring to classes, categories, types, and sizes of point sources); § 1314(b)(4)(B) (denoting "best conventional pollutant control technology measures and practices" applicable to any point source within particular category or class); § 1316 ("any point source * * * which is constructed as to meet all applicable standards of performance"); § 1318(a) (administrator shall require owner or operator of any point source to install, use and maintain monitoring equipment or methods); and § 1318(c) (states may develop procedures for inspection, monitoring, and entry with respect to point sources located in state).

This emphasis was sensible, as "[i]ndustrial and municipal point sources were the worst and most obvious offenders of surface water quality. They were also the easiest to address because their loadings emerge from a discrete point such as the end of a pipe." David Letson, *Point/Nonpoint Source Pollution Reduction Trading: An Interpretive Survey*, 32 NAT. RESOURCES J. 219, 221 (1992).

Finally on this point, we assume that congress did not intend the awkward meaning that would result if we were to read "human being" into the definition of "point source". Section 1362(12)(A) defines "discharge of a pollutant" as "any addition of any pollutant to navigable waters from any point source". Enhanced by this definition, § 1311(a) reads in effect "the addition of any pollutant to navigable waters *from any point source by any person* shall be unlawful" (emphasis added). But were a human being to be included within the definition of "point source", the prohibition would then read: "the addition of any pollutant to navigable waters *from any person by any person* shall be unlawful", and this simply makes no sense. As the statute stands today, the term "point source" is comprehensible only if it is held to the context of industrial and municipal discharges.

2.   *Legislative History and Context.*

* * *

The legislative history of the CWA, while providing little insight into the meaning of "point source", confirms the act's focus on industrial polluters. Congress required NPDES permits of those who discharge from a "point source". The term "point source", introduced to the act in 1972, was intended to function as a means of identifying industrial polluters— generally a difficult task because pollutants quickly disperse throughout the subject waters. The senate report for the 1972 amendments explains:

> In order to further clarify the scope of the regulatory procedures in the Act the Committee had added a definition of point source to distinguish between control requirements where there are *specific confined conveyances, such as pipes,* and control requirements which are imposed to control runoff. The control of pollutants from runoff is applied pursuant to section 209 and the authority resides in the State or other local agency.

S. Rep. No. 92–414, *reprinted in* 1972 U.S.C.C.A.N. 3668, 3744. * * *

We accordingly conclude that the term "point source" as applied to a human being is at best ambiguous.

[Eds.: The court also concluded that the rule of lenity weighed against the government's reading of "point source."]

Convictions reversed; cross-appeal affirmed.

■ OAKES, CIRCUIT JUDGE, dissenting:

I agree that this is not the typical Clean Water Act prosecution—though, as criminal prosecutions under the Act are infrequent, or at least result in few published judicial opinions, what is "typical" is as yet ill-defined. I also agree that the prosecutors in this case may not have defined the theory of their case before proceeding to trial as well as they might have, thereby complicating the task of determining whether the jury was asked to resolve the proper factual questions. However, because I do not agree that a person can never be a point source, and because I believe that Mr. Villegas' actions, as the jury found them, fell well within the bounds of activity proscribed by the Clean Water Act's bar on discharge of pollutants into navigable waters, I am required to dissent.

Point source.

I begin with the proposition that the Clean Water Act bars "the discharge of any pollutant by any person," except as authorized elsewhere in the Act. 33 U.S.C. § 1311(a) (1988). The only limiting factors are definitional: the Act bars "discharges" from "point sources" of "pollutants" to "navigable waters."[1] It does not bar nonpoint source pollution, pollution of dry land or nonnavigable waters, or the movement of existing pollution within the navigable waters.

The key in this case is the definition of a point source. * * *

The language of this definition indicates that it encompasses a wide range of means of placing pollutants into navigable waters. The question before us is what, in addition to the listed examples, is a "discernible, confined and discrete conveyance."

I begin with the obvious, in hopes that it will illuminate the less obvious: the classic point source is something like a pipe. This is, at least in part, because pipes and similar conduits are needed to carry large quantities of waste water, which represents a large proportion of the point source pollution problem. Thus, devices designed to convey large quantities of waste water from a factory or municipal sewage treatment facility are readily classified as point sources. Because not all pollutants are liquids, however, the statute and the cases make clear that means of conveying solid wastes to be dumped in navigable waters are also point sources. *See, e.g.,* 33 U.S.C. § 1362(14) ("rolling stock," or railroad cars, listed as an example of a point source); *Avoyelles Sportsmen's League, Inc. v. Marsh,*

715 F.2d 897, 922 (5th Cir. 1983) (backhoes and bulldozers used to gather fill and deposit it on wetlands are point sources).

What I take from this look at classic point sources is that, at the least, an organized means of channeling and conveying industrial waste in quantity to navigable waters is a "discernible, confined and discrete conveyance." The case law is in accord: courts have deemed a broad range of means of depositing pollutants in the country's navigable waters to be point sources. * * * In short, the term "point source" has been broadly construed to apply to a wide range of polluting techniques, so long as the pollutants involved are not just humanmade, but reach the navigable waters by human effort or by leaking from a clear point at which waste water was collected by human effort. From these cases, the writers of one respected treatise have concluded that such a "man-induced gathering mechanism plainly is the essential characteristic of a point source" and that a point source, "[p]ut simply, . . . is an identifiable conveyance of pollutants." 5 Robert E. Beck, *Waters & Water Rights* § 53.01(b)(3) at 216–17 (1991), *citing Sierra Club v. Abston Constr. Co.,* 620 F.2d at 45 (miners channeled waters into sump pits which leaked after heavy rains). * * *

This broad reading of the term "point source" is essential to fulfill the mandate of the Clean Water Act, in that

> [t]he touchstone of the regulatory scheme is that those needing to use the waters for waste distribution must seek and obtain a permit to discharge that waste, with the quantity and quality of the discharge regulated. The concept of a point source was designed to further this scheme by embracing the broadest possible definition of any identifiable conveyance from which pollutants might enter the waters of the United States. * * *

> We believe it contravenes the intent of FWPCA and the structure of the statute to exempt from regulation any activity that emits pollution from an identifiable point.

Earth Sciences, 599 F.2d 368, 373.

Nonetheless, the term "point source" sets significant definitional limits on the reach of the Clean Water Act. Fifty percent or more of all water pollution is thought to come from nonpoint sources. S. Rep. 99–50, 99th Cong., 1st Sess. 8 (1985); William F. Pedersen, Jr., *Turning the Tide on Water Quality,* 15 ECOL. L.Q. 69, n.10 (1988). So, to further refine the definition of "point source," I consider what it is that the Act does not cover: nonpoint source discharges.

Nonpoint source pollution is, generally, runoff: salt from roads, agricultural chemicals from farmlands, oil from parking lots, and other substances washed by rain, in diffuse patterns, over the land and into navigable waters. The sources are many, difficult to identify and difficult to control. Indeed, an effort to greatly reduce nonpoint source pollution could require radical changes in land use patterns which Congress evidently was unwilling to mandate without further study. The structure of the statute—which regulates point source pollution closely, while leaving nonpoint source regulation to the states under the Section 208 program—indicates that the term "point source" was included in the definition of discharge so as to ensure that nonpoint source pollution would *not* be covered. Instead, Congress chose to regulate first that which could easily be regulated: direct discharges by identifiable parties, or point sources. * * *

While Villegas' activities were not prototypical point source discharges—in part because he was disposing of waste that could have been disposed of on land, and so did not need a permit or a pipe—they much more closely resembled a point source discharge than a nonpoint source discharge. * * *

Accordingly, I would affirm the rulings of the district court.

In the course of researching the controversy, you have come across some materials from similar controversies in California. Excerpts from some of those materials appear below. The first item is from an advocacy letter submitted to the San Diego Regional Water Control Board, a California government agency, on behalf of the La Jolla Community Fireworks Foundation. The second item is a legal memorandum produced by the California State Water Resources Control Board. The third item is a notice letter indicating the intent of homeowners along Lake Tahoe to bring a Clean Water Act Lawsuit. The fourth item is a letter from ten United States senators to EPA. As you read these materials, bear in mind that none of them contains binding legal authority. Instead, they will help you anticipate arguments that might be raised in your controversy.

Letter from Robert Howard, Latham & Watkins LLP, to San Diego Regional Water Quality Control Board

Dec. 9, 2010

Dear Mr. Gibson and Honorable Board Members:

Thank you for the opportunity to submit comments in advance of the December 16, 2010 workshop on Tentative Order No. R9–2010–0124 regarding General Waste Discharge Requirements for the Public Display of Fireworks in the San Diego Region ("Tentative Order"), released by the San Diego Regional Water Quality Control Board ("Regional Board") on

September 23, 20 I 0. We submit these comments on behalf of the La Jolla Community Fireworks Foundation ("LJCFF"), a non-profit corporation organized for the purpose of promoting patriotism and community spirit by preserving La Jolla's Fourth of July tradition with a public fireworks display.

We are very concerned that the Regional Board staff has proposed a new, unnecessary and nation-wide precedent-setting regulatory regime for future public fireworks displays, without any significant public input and, more importantly, without any scientific basis. Quite simply, the Tentative Order is a regulation seeking a problem. There have been no showing of problems or water quality issues presented to the Regional Board that justify the issuance of this Tentative Order and the onerous regulatory requirements set forth therein. The burdensome regulations, testing and reporting requirements will almost certainly prevent most coastal communities in the San Diego region from participating in a patriotic fireworks tradition that dates back over 200 years. Importantly, no regulatory body in the nation bas found it necessary or appropriate to regulate any one of the countless fireworks displays that have occurred during the almost forty years that the Clean Water Act has been in existence. And any attempt to justify the terms of the Tentative Order based on the current fireworks displays put on by Sea World is preposterous when one considers that the Sea World events occur for over 100 consecutive days from a barge in an enclosed, shallow bay, whereas, by way of example, Fourth of July fireworks are a once-a-year event that last a matter of mere minutes.

We would therefore request that the Regional Board withdraw this Tentative Order, and, as has been done for inland fireworks displays, issue a General National Pollution Discharge Elimination System ("NPDES") permit exemption for public fireworks displays that occur from the same coastal location between four to ten times a year. In the alternative, the Regional Board should revise the Tentative Order to implement a de minimis exception for those public fireworks displays which occur from the same coastal location less than ten times a year and/or detonate no more than a reasonable annual threshold of pyrotechnical material, a threshold that can be reached through consultation with water quality consultants.

I.   The Tentative Order Would Regulate Fourth of July Fireworks Out Of Existence

A.   Implementation of the Tentative Order Would Result in Cancellation of Most Coastal Community Fireworks Displays

First and foremost, the Regional Board must understand that the Tentative Order as it now stands would result in the cancellation of most, if not all, San Diego area community fireworks displays as a result of the high cost of compliance with the Tentative Order's demanding regulations, testing and reporting requirements. Financed by small individual community contributions, these long-standing patriotic celebrations would be permanently shut down if communities are forced to produce enough capital to comply with the unnecessary and duplicative provisions of the Tentative Order.

As an example, the La Jolla Cove fireworks display has been an annual community celebration for over 25 years. This year's 2010 display lasted 23 minutes, at a total cost of approximately $30,000. Yet the Tentative Order proposes water quality and sediment monitoring that local water quality consultants have estimated will cost between $30,000 and $100,000, thereby doubling or quadrupling the cost of the event and making any single event cost prohibitive.

* * *

II.   The Regional Board Has No Jurisdiction to Regulate Public Displays of Fireworks as They Are Not a "Point Source" Under Federal Clean Water Act

A.   Fireworks Are Not a "Point Source" Under the Clean Water Act

Even if San Diego communities could conceivably raise enough capital annually to finance the permit fee, water monitoring and sediment testing requirements of the Tentative Order, the Regional Board has no legal jurisdiction to require these community organizers to comply with the terms of the Tentative Order. As explained below, occasional public fireworks displays detonated above or near water cannot be considered a "point source" under the federal Clean Water Act (33 U.S.C. § 1251 et seq.) ("CWA"), and thus the Regional Board has no legal basis for regulating these displays.

The CWA empowers states to administer the NPDES permit program, under which entities such as the Regional Board are authorized to issue and administer NPDES permits. 33 U.S.C. § 1342(b). However, the CWA requires such permits only when pollutants are discharged from a "point source." 33 U.S.C. § 1362(12). As explained below, the legislative history of the CWA, EPA regulations, and federal case law all confirm that individual fireworks displays are not "point sources" under the CWA and thus cannot be regulated by the Regional Board under the NPDES program.

The CWA defines a point source as "any discernible, confined and discrete conveyance, including but not limited to any pipe, ditch, channel, tunnel, conduit, well, discrete fissure, container, rolling stock, concentrated animal feeding operation; or vessel or other floating craft, from which pollutants are or may be discharged." 33 U.S.C. § 1362(14). The legislative history of the Act suggests that Congress meant to cover discharges that were at least "frequent," or that resulted in some "measurable" waste entering the water. *Northwest Envtl. Def. Ctr. v. Brown*, 617 F.3d 1176, 1183 (9th Cir. 2010). Here, the evidence shows that occasional celebratory and civic public fireworks displays are neither "frequent" nor result any "measurable" amount of waste entering the water; thus, it makes sense that no regulatory body in the nation, including the U.S. Environmental Protection Agency ("EPA") which has primary jurisdiction for nationwide enforcement of the CWA, has ever attempted to regulate such displays as a "point source" under the CWA. * * *

The federal regulations interpreting the definition of "point source" focus on various industrial categories such as dairy products processing; grain mills; the textile industry; cement manufacturing; feed lots; fertilizer manufacturing; nonferrous metals manufacturing; steam electric power generating; leather tanning; asbestos manufacturing; and coal mining. 40 C.F.R. § 405 et seq. While the regulations include explosives manufacturing as a specified category of regulated point sources, fireworks displays are not referred to anywhere in the regulations. Given the breadth of regulations existing with regards to other potential "point sources," a logical conclusion from this conspicuous regulatory absence is that Congress does not consider occasional public fireworks displays detonated above water to constitute a "point source" discharge under the CWA.

Federal courts have held that activities and "sources" such as people, grazing cows, and even a building from which trash and runoff ran into a river are not "point sources." *United States v. Plaza Health Labs., Inc.*, 3 F.3d 643 (2d Cir. 1993); *Oregon Natural Desert Ass'n v. Dombeck*, 172 F.3d 1092 (9th Cir. 1998); *Hudson Riverkeeper Fund v. Harbor at Hastings Assocs.*, 911 F. Supp. 251 (S.D.N.Y. 1996). The Second Circuit has stated that the definition of "point source" and the examples given by Congress "evoke images of physical structures and instrumentalities that systematically act as a means of conveying pollutants from an industrial source to navigable waterways." *Plaza Health Labs., Inc.*, 3 F.3d at 646 (emphasis added). The individual fireworks displays at issue here do not systematically convey pollutants because they take place only once or twice per year, nor are they an industrial source of pollutants. Similarly, occasional fireworks displays are not comparable to the year-after-year deliberate bombing of water-based targets and disposal of millions of pounds of military munitions into the ocean surrounding Vieques Island. *Weinberger v. Romero-Barcelo*, 456 U.S. 305, 307 (1982).

By enacting the CWA, Congress intended to target "industrial and municipal production of pollutants," not infrequent activities such as fireworks displays. *Plaza Health Labs., Inc.*, 3 F.3d at 650. The Tentative Order would constitute the first and only interpretation in the country that public fireworks displays are a "point source" discharge under the

CWA. It simply cannot be reasonably argued that occasional coastal fireworks displays fall within the definition of "point source" discharge under federal law.

B.   Regulation of Fireworks as a "Point Source" Would Lead To Absurd Conclusions

Any attempt by the Regional Board to label occasional public fireworks display as a "point source" under the CWA would inevitably lead to a slippery slope of endless regulation with illogical results. For example, if once- or twice-yearly fireworks displays constitute a "point source," then the Regional Board by necessity must also require a NPDES permit for any plane flying over the ocean whose engines discharge particulates, or any person entering the ocean with non-waterproof sunscreen, or even a person caught littering in a body of water. All of these sources produce far more cumulative "pollutants" and occur infinitely more frequently than a 23-minute Fourth of July fireworks display; yet the Regional Board has correctly not seen fit to regulate any of these discharges as a point source under the CWA. No doubt the Regional Board recognizes that it does not have the legal authority to do so under the CWA, and such regulation would result in an endless permitting fiasco. The Regional Board should now apply those same principles here and provide a general NPDES permitting exemption for occasional public fireworks displays.

The characterization of Fourth of July fireworks displays as a "point source" is a fantastic and inappropriate expansion of the term as it is used in the CWA. * * * Occasional public fireworks events occurring between four and ten times per year (or which comprise no more than a certain threshold of pyrotechnics) should be treated as exempt from any NPDES permitting requirements. * * *

Very Truly Yours,

Robert M. Howard

Jessica M. Newman & Catherine George Hagan (Staff Counsel, California State Water Resources Control Board), Memorandum Analyzing Whether Fireworks Are Point Source Discharges under Clean Water Act

Apr. 20, 2011

Background

The Regional Water Quality Control Board, San Diego Region (San Diego Water Board) is considering adoption of a national pollutant discharge elimination system (NPDES) permit for residual firework pollutant waste discharges to waters of the United States. The permit would cover public displays of fireworks in the San Diego region and uses a tiered approach to regulating the firework displays. Several comment letters received by the San Diego Water Board expressed the view that fireworks are not a point source discharge that could be regulated through an NPDES permit.

Question Presented

Are fireworks that enter waters of the United States a point source discharge?

Brief Answer

Yes, fireworks are a point source. The definition of a point source must be read broadly to protect water quality. While courts have not considered the issue of whether fireworks are a point source, courts have found that ordnance from military aircraft, spent shot from a gun fired over water, and pesticides sprayed via airplane or helicopter over water are all point sources. For fireworks, the point source is the instrument that shoots the firework into the air and causes the discharge.

Discussion

* * *

In light of the goals of the CWA, courts have very broadly interpreted the definition of a point source. The Second Circuit Court of Appeals stated that the definition "embrac[es] the broadest possible definition of any identifiable conveyance from which pollutants might enter waters of the United States." (*Peconic Baykeeper, Inc. v. Suffolk County* (2d Cir. 2010) 600 F.3d 180, 188 (quoting *Cordiano v. Metacon Gun Club, Inc.* (2d. Cir. 2009) 575 F.3d 199, 219; *Dague v. City of Burlington* (2d Cir. 1991) 935 F.2d 1343, 1354–55); see also *Northwest Environmental Defense Center v. Brown* (9th Cir. 2010) 617 F.3d 1176, 1183; *United States v. Earth Sciences, Inc.* (10th Cir. 1979) 599 F.2d 368, 373.) One comment letter noted that the federal regulations interpreting the definition of a point source have focused on industrial sources. (Letter from Latham & Watkins on behalf of the La Jolla Community Fireworks Foundation (December 9, 2010) at p. 5.) While industrial sources may be common discharges, the definition of a point source is much broader than just that category of discharges. The Ninth Circuit Court of Appeals noted that Senate Committee Report "instructed that the [EPA] Administrator should not ignore discharges resulting from point sources other than pipelines or similar conduits . . . There are many other forms of periodic, though frequent, discharges of pollutants into the water through point sources such as barges, vessels, feedlots, trucks, and other conveyances." (*Northwest Environmental Defense Center v. Brown, supra,* 617 F.3d at p. 1183 (quoting S. Rep. No. 92–414, at p. 51 (1971).) Thus, a broad interpretation of "point source" must be used when determining whether fireworks are a point source.

While a court has not yet reviewed the specific issue of whether fireworks are point sources, courts have looked at similar discharges that are not explicitly identified in the definition of a point source. Ordnance fired from a military aircraft into the water has been held to be the addition of a pollutant from a point source that requires an NPDES permit. (*Romero-Barcelo v. Brown* (1st Cir. 1981) 643 F.2d 835, 861, rev'd sub nom. *Weinberger v. Romero-Barcelo* (1982) 456 U.S. 305).) The ordnance fired from the military aircraft included accidental bombings of the navigable waters and the occasional intentional bombing of water targets. (*Weinberger v. Romero-Barcelo* (1982) 456 U.S. 305, 307.) Even though the ordnances did not frequently enter the water, the military still needed an NPDES permit to comply with the CWA. The district court, when looking at the facts, held that an NPDES permit was required notwithstanding the fact that the Environmental Protection Agency did not have any regulations governing the issuance of an NPDES permit to cover ordnances entering the water, and that there was no evidence that the ordnances had measurable deleterious effects on the water. (*Romero-Barcelo v. Brown* (D.P.R. 1979) 478 F. Supp. 646, 664, aff'd in part, vacated in part, (1st Cir. 1981), 643 F.2d 835, rev'd sub nom. *Weinberger v. Romero-Barcelo* (1982) 456 U.S. 305.) When comparing fireworks to ordnances, both contain pollutants that are discharged from an untraditional source that had not been previously regulated.

Spent shot and target fragments from trap shooting over the water are also discharges of a pollutant over navigable waters. (*Stone v. Naperville Park Dist.* (N.D. Ill. 1999) 38 F. Supp. 2d 651, 655; see also *Connecticut Coastal Firemen's Association v. Remington Arms Co.* (2d Cir. 1993) 989 F.2d 1305, 1313 (finding that lead and steel shot are both "pollutants" under the CWA).) In *Stone*, the court held that the trap shooting range and each firing station were a "point source" under the CWA. (*Stone v. Naperville Park Dist., supra*, 38 F. Supp. 2d at p. 655.) The court found that the whole purpose of the facility was to "discharge pollutants" in the form of lead shot and fragmented targets and the facility was "discernible, confined and discrete." (*Ibid.*) Similarly, the point of the instruments that set off fireworks is to discharge pollutants, i.e. shoot the firework into the air to allow the firework to explode and produce the colorful effect we all see. The firework itself is the pollutant, much like the bullet is the pollutant at a firing range.

The interpretation of the instrument setting off the firework being the point source is confirmed by an analysis of the word "from" in the phrase ". . . addition of any pollutant to navigable waters from any point source." (33 U.S.C. § 1362(12).) When looking at pesticides sprayed into the air over navigable waters from a truck and helicopter, the Second Circuit

Court of Appeals found that the point source was not the air but rather the spray apparatus that was on the truck or helicopter. (*Peconic Baykeeper, Inc. v. Suffolk County* (2d. Cir. 2010) 600 F.3d 180, 188.) Even though the pesticides were being sprayed into the air, the spray apparatus was the starting point and so was the point source. (*Ibid.*) The same analysis applies to fireworks that explode in the air. The discharge comes from the instruments that shoot the fireworks into the air and not from the air after the fireworks explode. Therefore, the instruments the set off the fireworks are the point source from which the pollutants in the fireworks are discharged.

* * *

Letter from Michael R. Lozeau, Lozeau Drury LLP, to Carol Chaplin, Executive Director, Lake Tahoe Visitors Association, et al.

Sept. 5, 2013

Dear Ms. Chaplin, Mr. Souza, Mr. Dicks, and Mr. Gilfillan,

We write to notify you that Joan and Joseph Truxler, long-time residents of Zephyr Cove, Nevada, hereby notify the Lake Tahoe Visitors' Association ("LTVA"), Pyro Spectaculars North, Inc., Pyro Spectaculars, Inc., Pyro Spectaculars Productions, Inc., Carol Chaplin, James R. Souza, John E. Dicks, and Mathew Gilfillan that they are each in violation of the Federal Water Pollution Control Act, 33 U.S.C. §§ 1251–1376 (hereinafter "Clean Water Act" or "CWA") by discharging pollutants into Lake Tahoe without having obtained a National Pollutant Discharge Elimination System ("NPDES") permit during the biannual fireworks shows held in South Lake Tahoe on July 4th and Labor Day eve each year. By this letter, pursuant to 33 U.S.C. § 1365(a) and (b) of the CWA, the Truxlers are providing each of you with notice of their intent to file suit to address the violations of the Clean Water Act referenced in this letter.

I.   Discharging Firework Debris and Chemicals Into Lake Tahoe Without a NPDES Permit Are Violations of the Federal Clean Water Act.

Under the CWA, it is unlawful to discharge pollutants from a "point source" to navigable waters without obtaining and complying with a permit governing the quantity and quality of discharges. *Trustees for Alaska v. EPA*, 749 F.2d 549, 553 (9th Cir. 1984). Section 30l(a) of the Clean Water Act prohibits "the discharge of any pollutants by any person," except as in compliance with, among other sections of the Act, Section 402, the NPDES permitting requirements. 33 U.S.C. § 1311(a). The term "discharge of pollutants" means "any addition of any pollutant to navigable waters from any point source." 33 U.S.C. § 1362(12). Pollutants are deemed to include, among other examples, solid waste, garbage, munitions, chemical wastes, industrial waste, and municipal waste discharged into water. 33 U.S.C. § 1362(6). Debris and chemicals from detonated fireworks are pollutants. *See Weinberger v. Romero-Barcelo*, 456 U.S. 305, 309–310 (1982) (acknowledging lower courts' rulings that "the release of ordnance from aircraft or from ships into navigable waters is a discharge of pollutants"); *Barcelo v. Brown*, 478 F. Supp. 646, 664 (D.P.R. 1979) ("Defendant Navy is required to have an NPDES permit to cover the accidental or intentional release or firing of ordnance" into waters off of Puerto Rico); *Long Island Soundkeeper Fund v. New York Athletic Club*, 1996 U.S. Dist. LEXIS 3383 (S.D.N.Y. Mar. 20, 1996) ("shot and target debris generated by operation of defendant's trap shooting range constitute pollutants within the meaning of the CWA"). A point source is defined as "any discernable, confined and discrete conveyance, including but not limited to any pipe, ditch, channel, tunnel, [or] conduit . . . from which pollutants are or may be discharged." 33 U.S.C. § 1362(14). Each of the mortar tubes that discharges pollutants to Lake Tahoe is a distinct and separate point source. "Navigable waters" means "the waters of the United States." 33 U.S.C. § 1362(7). Lake Tahoe is a water of the United States.

This notice covers all violations occurring from September 5, 2008 to the present, as well as any violations described in this notice that occur after the date of this notice letter. Based on the information currently available to the Truxlers, LTV A, Carol Chaplin, Pyro Spectaculars North, Inc., Pyro Spectaculars, Inc., Pyro Spectaculars Productions, Inc., James R. Souza, John E. Dicks, and/or Mathew Gilfillan (collectively "LTVA and Pyro Spectaculars") have managed and operated a fireworks show offshore of South Lake Tahoe every Fourth of July and Labor Day eve for at least the last five years. The fireworks show consists of launching several thousand rockets, mortars, and other fireworks from an array of several hundred mortar tubes set up on one or more barges/boats floating in Lake Tahoe. The fireworks are fired over the Lake and, upon detonation, spread debris and chemicals upon the surface of Lake Tahoe. Over the past five years, discharges of pollutants to the Lake from mortar tubes mounted on fireworks barges or boats have occurred on or about July 4, 2009, September 6, 2009, July 4, 2010, September 5, 2010, July 4, 2011, September 4, 2011, July 4, 2012, September 3, 2012, July 4, 2013, and September 1, 2013. * * *

Pursuant to Section309(d) of the Act (33 U.S.C. § 1319(d)) and the Adjustment of Civil Monetary Penalties for Inflation (40 C.F.R. § 19.4) each separate violation of the Act subjects LTVA and Pyro Spectaculars to a penalty of up to $32,500 per day per violation for all violations occurring during the period commencing five years prior to the date of this Notice of Violations and Intent to File Suit through January 12, 2009, and a maximum of $37,500 per day per violation for all violations occurring after January 12, 2009. Each discharge from each point source, i.e., each mortar tube operated on the barges or boats, is a separate and distinct violation. In addition to civil penalties, the Truxlers will seek injunctive relief preventing further violations of the Act pursuant to Sections 505(a) and (d) (33 U.S.C. § 1365(a) and (d)) and such other relief as permitted by law. Lastly, Section 505(d) of the Act (33 U.S.C. § 1365(d)), permits the Truxlers as prevailing parties to recover costs and fees, including attorneys' fees from each of you.

The Truxlers believe this Notice of Violations and Intent to File Suit sufficiently states grounds for filing suit. The Truxlers intend to file a citizen suit under Section 50S(a) of the Act against LTVA and Pyro Spectaculars, and their agents for the above-referenced violations upon the expiration of the 60-day notice period. However, during the 60-day notice period, the Truxlers would be willing to discuss effective remedies for the violations noted in this letter. If you wish to pursue such discussions in the absence of litigation, we suggest that you initiate those discussions within the next 20 days so that they may be completed before the end of the 60-day notice period. The Truxlers do not intend to delay the filing of a complaint in federal court if discussions are continuing when that period ends.

Sincerely,

Michael R. Lozeau

Letter from Senator David Vitter, et al., to Gina McCarthy, Administrator, Environmental Protection Agency
July 1, 2014

Dear Administrator McCarthy:

As Independence Day approaches, we write to express concern for a cherished Fourth of July tradition: celebratory fireworks to commemorate our nation's founding. In the past few years, misguided citizen lawsuits have threatened community fireworks shows. We are concerned, on the eve of the celebration of this great nation's founding, that the Environmental Protection Agency (EPA) is set to foster expanded efforts to undermine this form of celebration. If finalized, EPA and the Army Corps of Engineers' (Corps) proposal to expand the Clean Water Act's definition of the "waters of the United States" may enable litigious environmental groups to jeopardize fireworks displays throughout the country.

In California, there is clearly a concerted effort to prevent local communities from conducting traditional Fourth of July fireworks shows. The Lake Murray July Fourth Music Fest and Fireworks Show has been cancelled three years in a row due to litigation uncertainty. Last month, the San Diego City Council agreed to pay an environmental lawyer $250,000 in order to end litigation over Fourth of July fireworks displays? At Lake Tahoe, officials nearly cancelled this year's Fourth of July fireworks show in response to an environmental lawsuit, but a settlement reached in April will apparently allow the show to go on as scheduled.

The Lake Tahoe lawsuit is particularly noteworthy, since it alleged that the locality's Fourth of July fireworks show violated the Clean Water Act. According to the plaintiffs' complaint, the fireworks show was unlawful because it resulted in the unpermitted discharge of pollutants into Lake Tahoe. The Lake Tahoe lawsuit also demanded that fireworks operators and municipal authorities pay $37,500 per day in civil penalties for each violation of the Clean Water Act. Similarly misguided approaches to the Clean Water Act have led some legal observers to question the future viability of community fireworks shows.

Unfortunately, EPA and the Corps' proposed "waters of the United States" rule could exacerbate this disturbing trend. By expanding federal Clean Water Act jurisdiction to include ditches, small streams, ponds, and other purely local waterbodies, EPA and the Corps may be exposing landowners and municipalities across the country to costly citizen suit litigation if they should attempt to conduct a neighborhood fireworks show. Recent history in California may set an ominous precedent for such challenges to fireworks displays in other states. If the proposed "waters of the United States" rule becomes final and serves as the eventual basis for future citizen suits against those who organize fireworks shows, we fear few homeowners, communities, or local organizations will be able to conduct fireworks displays as they have for decades or longer.

Commemorative fireworks displays have been a part of our nation's history since its founding. However, there are individuals and groups who would like to significantly limit this tradition through heavy-handed citizen suit litigation under the Clean Water Act and other laws. Finalization of the proposed "waters of the United States" rule could unduly encourage proponents of this tactic, lending further and additional reason for the withdrawal of the proposed rule. As we celebrate the Fourth of July later this week, we appreciate your attention to this important matter.

[Eds.: The letter was signed by Senators David Vitter, John Barrasso, Mike Enzi, Orrin Hatch, Jim Inhofe, Mike Johanns, Deb Fischer, Mike Lee, Saxby Chambliss, and John Hoeven]

NOTES

1.   The materials relating to the San Diego fireworks controversy note that the permitting decision will be made by the San Diego Regional Water Control Board, a California government agency. This reflects the important role that state government agencies play in implementing the Clean Water Act in states with approved programs.

2.   In many older cities, "combined sewer overflows" are particularly problematic kinds of point sources. A combined sewer system collects both stormwater and sanitary wastewater within a single set of pipes. During dry weather or mild precipitation events, the system conveys all of that water to a wastewater treatment plant. But during wet events, many systems now receive more stormwater runoff than they can handle. To avoid damaging wastewater treatment plants, those systems divert some of the sewage/stormwater mix into an overflow pipe, which then discharges the untreated mix directly into surface waterways. These CSOs are major sources of pollution, but removing a CSO generally requires expensive engineering, which can put sever strains on municipal budgets. That conflict has led to legal work, and many cities now are subject to consent decrees establishing schedules for removing their CSOs.

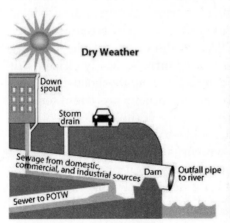 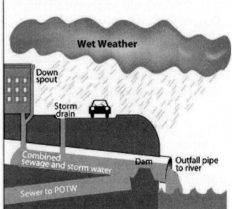

ADDITIONAL QUESTIONS

Decide whether each of the following factual scenarios involves a discharge of a pollutant from a point source.

1.   A paper mill is located on the banks of the Fox River in Wisconsin. The mill treats its effluent at an on-site wastewater treatment plant, then discharges that effluent through a pipe into the river. While the treatment plant removes most contaminants from the effluent, low quantities of tannins, cellulosic fibers, chlorinated compounds, and acids remain in the effluent.

2.   In eastern Colorado, a ditch conveys irrigation water to fields near a tributary to the Platte River. Not all of the water is consumed by crops, and a second ditch conveys excess water back into the stream. The returning water contains elevated concentrations of salt, sediment, and nutrients and trace quantities of herbicides and pesticides.

3.   In central Iowa, thousands of acres of farmland occupy lands that once were quite wet. Groundwater tables beneath those lands still can rise to the surface, flooding plants' root zones and destroying valuable crops. Farmers have responded to these flooding problems by constructing systems of tile drains. Tile drains are underground pipes that collect groundwater and convey it into surface ditches, which then drain into natural rivers and streams. While these systems are effective at protecting crops, they also convey fertilizers, pesticides, and herbicides that percolate downward through the soil and accumulate in groundwater. Indeed, lands irrigated by tile drain systems contribute much of the nutrient loading to the Mississippi River system, and thus are major contributors to the Gulf of Mexico dead zone beyond the Mississippi Delta. As of this writing, these tile drains never have been regulated as point sources. Should they be?

4.   A large system of municipal storm sewers collects stormwater runoff from Los Angeles and the surrounding cities and delivers that stormwater runoff into the Los Angeles River. The runoff generally begins its pathway to the river by pooling on parking lots, roofs, roadways, and other developed areas. It then flows over the ground surface to storm drains, and then flows through subsurface pipes to the river. As it flows, the stormwater picks up a variety of impurities, including metals scraped from brake pads, oil and grease from cars, and fertilizers and herbicides.

5.   A group of families intending to start a boating club recently purchased property along a river. The property is vacant, except for a pile of fertilizer left by the previous owner. Since the boating club bought the property, neighbors have told them that the fertilizer pile seems to be eroding into the river, loading the water with sediment and nutrients. Rumor has it that a local environmental group may be considering bringing suit under the Clean Water Act. The boating club has found someone willing to haul away the fertilizer sometime this summer, but in the meantime the club is concerned that it might be violating the Clean Water Act. It is considering attempting to build a berm between the fertilizer pile and the river, with the hopes of preventing runoff from reaching the river.

6.   In a town in eastern North Carolina, 10,000 pigs are raised in a complex of warehouse-like buildings. The pigs generate huge volumes of fecal waste, which are stored in adjacent open-air lagoons. During occasional heavy rainstorms, one of the lagoons overflows, and the waste travels through a small ditch and into the New River.

7.   A power company operates a hydroelectric plant between two rivers. Although the two rivers are only a few miles apart, one river flows at a higher elevation than the other, and the company generates power by shifting water

from the higher river to the lower one. The higher river has lower water quality, and shifting the water from the higher river to the lower river introduces sediment into the lower river system.

8.   An old coal-fired power plant discharges a variety of pollutants, including sulfur dioxide, nitrogen oxides, and mercury, through its stacks. Hundreds of miles away, many of these pollutants are carried back to earth by the rain. Some fall directly into waterways, and some flow overland into those waterways. They raise nutrient concentrations, lower the pH, and contribute to mercury loading within the waterway.

V. NPDES PROGRAM

Section 301 of the Clean Water Act prohibits the discharge of pollutants into navigable waters, unless that discharge occurs in compliance with one of the Clean Water Act's two major permitting programs. One of those permitting programs is the National Pollutant Discharge Elimination System, or NPDES. The other, which we discuss after the NDPES materials that follow, is the Section 404 program for permitting the dredging and filling of waters of the United States.

This section discusses the NPDES program in detail. Within that discussion, we initially focus on the regulation of effluent from large, discrete sources like industrial facilities and wastewater treatment plants. We will then discuss the NPDES program's approach to stormwater management.

PROBLEM: PHARMACEUTICAL MANUFACTURING

Although the Clean Water Act is considerably less complex than the Clean Air Act, it still is easy to get lost in the maze of statutory programs, terms, and cross-references. To gain an understanding of how the Clean Water Act actually works to regulate pollutant discharges from point sources, we will use the example of a hypothetical pharmaceutical manufacturing facility that wants to know how the Clean Water Act applies to its facility. What regulatory programs apply to the facility? What specific regulatory requirements apply to the facility? What characteristics of the facility affect what the Act requires? These are the types of issues that practicing environmental lawyers encounter in advising a client about obtaining a Clean Water Act permit, or enforcing the Clean Water Act, or in negotiating over possible violations of the Clean Water Act.

A. EFFLUENT LIMITATIONS

Recall that Clean Water Act section 301, 33 U.S.C. § 1311, prohibits "the discharge of any pollutant by any person" except as authorized by the Act. The NPDES program is the primary regulatory mechanism for authorizing a discharge of a pollutant that would otherwise be illegal under Clean Water Act section 301. The program involves technology-based standards that are set for specified categories of sources.

Let's consider how the program regulates pharmaceutical manufacturing. Manufacturing pharmaceutical products and medicines is an important industry in the United States. Approximately 2,000 facilities around the country employ over 200,000 people and generate over $188 billion in product. *See* U.S. Census Bureau, Snapshots: Pharmaceutical and Medicine Manufacturing. Pharmaceutical manufacturing facilities use different types of processes, each of which produces somewhat different wastewaters. *See* 60 Fed. Reg. 21,592, 21,603–04 (proposed May 2, 1995); U.S. EPA, Development Document for Final Effluent Limitations Guidelines and Standards for the Pharmaceutical Manufacturing Point Source Category (July 30, 1998). The four primary types of pharmaceutical manufacturing processes are as follows:

Fermentation uses an organism such as a yeast, mold, or fungus to induce chemical changes that produce a pharmaceutical active ingredient. Most antibiotics and steroids are produced through fermentation. Fermentation generally involves large-scale batch processing of a dilute fermentation broth—similar to brewing beer, in which yeast is used to ferment sugar into carbon dioxide and alcohol—followed by processing to extract the pharmaceutical active ingredient from the broth. Fermentation primarily generates wastewater from spent (used) fermentation broth and solvents and other substances used to extract the active ingredient from the broth.

Biological and natural extraction derives active ingredients from natural sources such as plants, animals, and fungi. The extraction process generates relatively small amounts of active ingredient from large quantities of natural sources, and is thus generally used only when no alternative types of processes will work. Extraction generates wastewater from spent raw materials such as plant or animal tissue residue, from washing floors and equipment, and from spent solvents used in the extraction process.

Chemical synthesis uses a series of chemical reactions to convert raw materials into active ingredients. Most pharmaceutical active ingredients are manufactured through chemical synthesis. Chemical synthesis generally uses a batch process to chemically synthesize active ingredients. Wastewaters produced from chemical synthesis include process wastewaters such as spent solvents and filtrates, and floor and equipment washes.

Mixing, compounding, and formulating puts active ingredients into dosage forms such as tablets, liquids, capsules, and ointments. These processes generate some wastewater from floor and equipment washes, wet scrubbers, and spills.

Some pharmaceutical manufacturing facilities discharge their wastewater into a sewer system that carries the wastewater to a publicly owned treatment works (POTW), which treats the waste before discharging it. Other facilities discharge their wastewater directly into a waterway such as a river. This brings us to a first general distinction in Clean Water Act regulation of point source discharges under the NPDES program:

- Facilities that discharge into sewer systems are known as *indirect dischargers*. 40 C.F.R. § 122.2. Because they are not discharging into waters of the United States, they do not require a NPDES permit. They are, however, subject to *pretreatment standards* that limit what they can discharge into the sewer system. *See* 33 U.S.C. § 1317(b)–(e).

- Facilities that discharge into waters of the United States are known as *direct dischargers*. *See* 40 C.F.R. § 122.2. They require a NPDES permit. *See* 33 U.S.C. §§ 1311 (a), 1342(a).

The wastewater streams generated by pharmaceutical manufacturing include different pollutants that pose varying threats to human and environmental health. All pollutants can cause harm at some level of exposure, but some are more hazardous or more difficult to remove from wastewater. For example, the materials in spent fermentation broth are relatively easy to remove through biological treatment processes, such as those used in POTWs. Other substances, such as cyanide, are highly dangerous and persistent in the environment and require different treatment. This brings us to a second general distinction in Clean Water Act regulation of point source discharges:

- *Conventional pollutants* are generally naturally occurring, biodegradable substances that traditionally have been the focus of wastewater treatment. 43 Fed. Reg. 32,857 (July 28, 1978). Congress designated four conventional pollutants (the first two of which are really groups of pollutants) in the Clean Water Act—biological oxygen demanding, suspended solids, fecal coliform, and pH. 33 U.S.C. § 1314(a)(3)(A). EPA has since added a fifth, oil and grease. 40 C.F.R. § 401.16.

- *Toxic pollutants* are toxic and persistent substances that cause serious biological abnormalities or malfunctions in organisms. 33 U.S.C. §§ 1317(a), 1362(13). Congress designated 65 pollutants as toxic in the Clean Water Act. 33 U.S.C. § 1317(a). Based on the list of toxic pollutants, which includes some groups of pollutants, EPA has developed a list of 126 specific *priority pollutants* for which it has developed analytical test methods and specific regulatory limits. 40 C.F.R. pt. 423 App. A.

- *Non-conventional pollutants* are those pollutants not classified as conventional or toxic pollutants. 33 U.S.C. §§ 1311(a), 1342(a). Aluminum, for example, is a non-conventional pollutant.

Some pharmaceutical manufacturing facilities have been operating for years and have invested in processes and equipment. Their commitment to that existing infrastructure limits their ability to change to conform to new regulatory requirements without incurring significant, perhaps even unaffordable, costs. Other facilities will not be built until after regulations are in place, and so have much greater ability to adopt particular processes or employ certain equipment at lower cost. For this reason, the Clean Water Act, like most environmental statutes, also distinguishes between facilities based on their age, which presents a third general distinction in Clean Water Act regulation of point source discharges:

- *New sources* are sources for which construction began after the publication of regulations addressing discharges from new sources in that industry. *See* 33 U.S.C. § 1316(a)(2); 40 C.F.R. § 122.2.

- *Existing sources* are sources other than new sources—that is, sources for which construction began before the publication of regulations addressing discharges from new sources in that industry. *See* 40 C.F.R. § 122.29(a)(3).

Together, these various distinctions—direct versus indirect dischargers, conventional versus toxic versus non-conventional pollutants, new source versus existing source—affect the stringency of the regulatory limits that apply to a particular discharge covered by the Clean Water Act. (Whether a waterway is meeting its water quality goals also may affect the applicable regulatory limits, a topic we address later in this chapter.) To some extent, these distinctions operate independently. For example, new sources are generally regulated more stringently than existing sources, for all types of pollutants and for both direct and indirect discharges. But the distinctions are also interrelated to some extent. In particular, because POTWs can effectively treat conventional pollutants, permits for indirect discharges—that is, discharges to sewer systems that flow into POTWs—often do not include limits for conventional pollutants. Toxic and non-conventional pollutants, by contrast, can interfere with the bacteria that treat sewage or pass through treatment works untreated, and so pretreatment standards for those pollutants are vitally important.

Recall that Clean Water Act § 402, 33 U.S.C. § 1342, establishes the NPDES program that allows point sources to discharge pollutants into waters of the United States without violating the Act. Section 402 requires permitted discharges to comply with other provisions of the Clean Water Act. Among the most important of these other provisions are Clean Water Act sections 301, 304, and 307, *id.* §§ 1311, 1314, 1317, which in combination direct EPA to establish, and periodically review, *effluent limitations* specifying the amount of pollutants that can be present in discharges covered by the Act. These effluent limitations are a type of *technology-based standard*, because they are based on EPA's determination of what levels of pollution prevention and control are technically and economically feasible for a particular industry. Despite their name, however, technology-based effluent limits do not require sources to use a specific pollutant control technology; instead, effluent limits identify specific maximum pollutant levels that are permitted in the sources' wastewater discharges. The technology-based standards imposed by the CWA are a variety of *performance standard*, discussed in chapter 1.

EPA approaches effluent limitations on an industry-by-industry basis, issuing sets of regulations (*effluent guidelines*) that specify effluent limitations for different types of facilities within a particular industry. Just as with the Clean Air Act, different types of sources within an industry are subject to different effluent limitations based on different control technologies. The types of dischargers are classified according to the various distinctions we have identified in this section:

- *Best Practicable Control Technology (BPT)* applies to direct discharges of all categories of pollutants (conventional, non-conventional, and toxic) from existing sources in the industry. EPA bases BPT effluent limitations on the average of the best performing existing sources within the industry. 33 U.S.C. § 1311(b)(1)(A) (directing effluent limitations requiring BPT); *id.* § 1314(b)(1) (defining BPT).

- *Best Conventional Pollutant Control Technology (BCT)* applies to direct discharges of conventional pollutants from existing sources in the industry. Thus, BCT overlaps in application with BPT, which applies to direct discharges of all pollutants from existing sources. BCT is what is known as a *second level of control*, because it potentially regulates sources more stringently than the first level of control under the BPT standard. The BCT standard allows EPA to establish effluent limitations at levels more stringent than the BPT standard, but only if the incremental additional stringency is cost-effective. If the additional stringency is at least as cost-effective as the BPT standard (known as the industry cost-effectiveness test), and not less cost-effective than a comparable increase in stringency in POTW treatment (known as the POTW test), then EPA establishes effluent limitations based on the BCT standard. 51 Fed. Reg. 24,974 (July 9, 1986); *Am. Paper Inst. v. EPA*, 660 F.2d 954 (4th Cir. 1981). If no method of pollutant control passes these cost-effectiveness tests, then EPA sets BCT effluent limitations at the same level as BPT effluent limitations. 33 U.S.C. § 1311(b)(2)(E) (directing effluent limitations requiring BCT for pollutants identified in § 1314(a)(4)); *id.* § 1314(a)(4) (defining conventional pollutants); *id.* 33 U.S.C. § 1314(b)(4) (defining BCT).

- *Best Available Technology Economically Achievable (BAT)* applies to direct discharges of non-conventional and toxic pollutants from existing sources in the industry. *See* 33 U.S.C. § 1311(b)(2) (directing effluent limitations requiring BAT for non-conventional and toxic pollutants); *id.* § 1314(b)(2) (defining BAT); *id.* § 1317(a) (defining toxic pollutant). Thus, just as BCT and BPT overlap in application with respect to discharges of conventional pollutants from existing direct dischargers, BAT overlaps in application with BPT with respect to direct discharges of non-conventional and toxic pollutants from existing sources. Like BCT, BAT is a second level of control that potentially results in more stringent effluent limitations than under BPT. EPA bases BAT effluent limitations guidelines on the best existing pollution control technology that is economically and technologically achievable for sources in the industry. Although cost is a factor under the BAT standard, BAT effluent limitations are not subject to the strict cost-effectiveness tests of the BCT standard.

- *New Source Performance Standards (NSPS)* apply to direct discharges of all types of pollutants from new sources in the industry. EPA bases new source performance standards on the best available demonstrated control technology. Because new sources can use the most efficient production processes and the most effective pollution control technologies, NSPS should generally be the most stringent effluent limitations for an industry. 33 U.S.C. § 1316.

- *Pretreatment Standards for Existing Sources (PSES)* apply to indirect discharges of pollutants (typically non-conventional and toxic pollutants)[3] from existing sources in the industry. Pretreatment standards are intended to prevent indirect discharges that pass through, interfere with, or are otherwise incompatible with the operation of a POTW. 33 U.S.C. § 1317(b). EPA bases pretreatment standards for existing sources on the same factors it employs to set effluent limitations for existing direct dischargers under the BAT standard.

- *Pretreatment Standards for New Sources (PSNS)* apply to indirect discharges of pollutants (typically non-conventional and toxic pollutants) from new sources in the industry. 33 U.S.C. § 1317(b). Pretreatment standards for existing sources on the same factors it employs to set effluent limitations for new direct dischargers in the NSPS.

As lawyers, it is important to understand these terms conceptually, but also to understand how the text of the Clean Water Act creates these control technologies and defines the types of discharges to which they apply. Unfortunately, the way the statute does this for direct dischargers is complicated and reminiscent of the Clean Air Act's many internal cross-references. Clean Water Act section 301(b) creates a timetable for EPA to establish effluent limitations for different categories of discharges and specifies the control technology that applies to each category of discharge. For example, section 301(b)(2)(E) directs EPA, by March 31, 1989, to issue effluent limitations that "require application of the best conventional pollutant control technology as determined in accordance with regulations by the Administrator pursuant to section 1314(b)(4)," for "pollutants identified pursuant to section 1314(a)(4)." Section 304, in turn, identifies the pollutants, *see, e.g.*, 33 U.S.C. § 1314(a)(4) (defining "conventional pollutants"), and the factors that are to be considered in determining each control technology, *see, e.g.*, *id.* § 1314(a)(4) (defining the best conventional pollutant control technology). The Clean Water Act's directive for pretreatment standards is mercifully simpler and for the most part contained in a single provision, *id.* § 1317(b).

---

[3]   EPA sometimes sets pretreatment standards for conventional pollutants, either as surrogates for toxic or nonconventional pollutants or when necessary to prevent interference with the operation of POTWs.

Type of Source		Conventional Pollutants	Non-Conventional Pollutants	Toxic Pollutants
Direct	New	NSPS	NSPS	NSPS
	Existing	BPT + BCT	BPT + BAT	BPT + BAT
Indirect	New		PSNS	PSNS
	Existing		PSES	PSES

Now let's apply this framework to pharmaceutical manufacturers. EPA issued its first effluent guidelines for pharmaceutical manufacturers in 1976. 41 Fed. Reg. 50,676 (Nov. 17, 1976). EPA revised and expanded the pharmaceutical effluent guidelines in 1983, 1986, and 1998. See 63 Fed. Reg. 50,388 (Sept. 21, 1998); 51 Fed. Reg. 45,094 (Dec. 16, 1986); 48 Fed. Reg. 49,808 (Oct. 27, 1983); see also 68 Fed. Reg. 12,266 (Mar. 13, 2003) (minor clarification); 64 Fed. Reg. 10,391 (Mar. 4, 1999) (technical correction). When EPA begins the process of establishing or revising effluent guidelines, it compiles information about the industry's processes, water use, wastewater characteristics, and treatment technologies. The extensive process leading to the 1998 amendments began with EPA developing a database of technical and cost information about how each of the facilities subject to the effluent guidelines for pharmaceutical manufacturers dealt with its wastewater. 60 Fed. Reg. 21,592, 21,602–03 (proposed May 2, 1995). Based on the information in the database, EPA identified various pollutant control processes and technologies, calculated the potential effluent characteristics of wastewater associated with each process and technology, and estimated the costs of these processes and technologies. *Id.* EPA published initial proposed regulations for public comment in 1995, 60 Fed. Reg. 21,592, and then published additional information for public comment in a 1997 notice, 62 Fed. Reg. 42,720 (Aug. 8, 1997). With the information gathered through this process, including from public comments, EPA issued final regulations in 1998 reflecting the agency's judgments about what effluent limitations were appropriate for each type of discharge, based on the relevant statutory factors:

For discharges of wastewater containing chemical oxygen demand— a non-conventional pollutant—from existing sources that use a fermentation or chemical synthesis process, EPA determined that advanced biological treatment was widely used in the industry and therefore consistent with the statutory factors that define the BPT. 63 Fed. Reg. at 50,396–99. EPA determined that implementation of advanced biological treatment could reduce discharges of chemical oxygen demand to a maximum daily concentration of 1675 parts per million (ppm) and a maximum monthly average concentration of 856 ppm. 40 C.F.R. §§ 439.13(c), 439.32(c).

With respect to the second level of control under the BCT standard for the direct discharge of conventional pollutants from existing sources, which as explained above requires any incremental limitation beyond what is required under BPT to be cost-effective, EPA determined that no technologies were available that would achieve greater removal of conventional pollutants than the BPT effluent limits and also satisfy the BCT cost test. 63 Fed. Reg. at 50,402. Accordingly, EPA promulgated BCT effluent limitations that are equal to BPT limitations for each category. 40 C.F.R. §§ 439.13, 439.23, 439.33, 439.43.

With respect to the second level of control under the BAT standard for the direct discharge of 31 non-conventional and toxic pollutants from existing sources that use a fermentation or chemical synthesis process, EPA determined that advanced biological treatment and biological nitrification was economically achievable and consistent with the statutory factors for BAT. 63 Fed. Reg. at 50,399–400. EPA promulgated maximum daily and maximum monthly average effluent limitations, applicable to fermentation and chemical synthesis processes, which it determined could be achieved through use of this technology. 40 C.F.R. §§ 439.14(a), 439.34(a).

For direct discharges of pollutants from new sources under the NSPS, EPA determined that it lacked data about the performance of control technologies that might reduce effluent levels below those prescribed for existing sources. 63 Fed. Reg. at 50,402. Accordingly, EPA promulgated effluent limitations for new sources equal to those for existing sources. 40 C.F.R. §§ 439.15, 439.25, 439.35, 439.45.

For indirect discharges of pollutants from existing sources using a fermentation or chemical synthesis process, EPA determined that steam stripping and nitrification would reduce levels of 23 volatile organic compounds and ammonia that otherwise would pass through POTWs. 63 Fed. Reg. at 50,400–02. EPA promulgated effluent limitations for existing indirect dischargers under the PSES for these pollutants. 40 C.F.R. §§ 439.16, 439.36. Because EPA could not identify a technology that would achieve lower effluent levels than steam stripping and nitrification, it promulgated effluent limitations for new indirect discharges under the PSNS standard equal to the limitations for existing sources under the PSES standard. 40 C.F.R. §§ 439.17, 439.37.

QUESTIONS

For each of the following hypotheticals, identify the type of source, applicable control technology standard, and apply the effluent guidelines for pharmaceutical manufacturing, 40 C.F.R. Part 439, to determine the maximum monthly discharge limit for the specified pollutants.

1.   Lee Pharmaceuticals has operated its plant since 1995. The plant produces pharmaceutical products by a fermentation process and discharges wastewater containing benzene into a sewer system, which then discharges to a wastewater treatment plant.

2.   Assume the same facts as in (1), but the plant discharges its wastewater into the Delaware River.

3.   Lee Pharmaceuticals is considering constructing a new plant along the Delaware River. The new plant will utilize an extraction process and will discharge wastewater into the river. Lee is concerned about limits on the amounts of total suspended solids in its wastewater.

4.   In 1995, Lee Pharmaceuticals constructed a plant that manufactures pharmaceutical products through chemical synthesis and produces wastewater containing cyanide. The plant currently discharges its wastewater directly into the Delaware River, but Lee is considering whether to alter its process so that it discharges to a sewer system. Lee wants to know whether and how such a change will affect the limits on the amount of cyanide in its wastewater.

5.   Assume that Lee Pharmaceuticals is operating the plant referenced in (3), and EPA issues a proposed rule that would amend section 439.23 to limit maximum monthly average discharges of total suspended solids to 20 ppm. Would this new limit apply to Lee's plant? Why or why not?

6.   Why do none of the pretreatment standards contain limits on discharges of total suspended solids?

B.   PERMITTING

Commonwealth Pharma Services operates a pharmaceutical manufacturing facility in Conshohocken, Pennsylvania.[4] The facility discharges approximately 56,000 gallons of wastewater per day into the Schuykill River. The Clean Water Act thus requires Commonwealth Pharma to operate under a NPDES permit that authorizes its discharges.

Role of States. The Clean Water Act, like the Clean Air Act, is a "cooperative federalism" statute. It grants states the option to take over implementation of the NPDES program, so long as the state's implementation program meets certain criteria. 33 U.S.C. § 1342(b). A state with delegated NPDES authority then becomes the primary source of NPDES permits and enforcement actions within that state's boundaries. Almost all of the states have taken advantage of this opportunity, and EPA directly administers the NPDES program in only a handful of states. Thus, the Pennsylvania Department of

---

[4]   The description in this section is based on an actual plant, but we have changed some of the information.

Environmental Protection—rather than EPA—issued Commonwealth's NPDES permit for the Conshohocken plant. A copy of the permit can be found on the course website.

Even where EPA has approved a state NPDES program, EPA still retains a central role in NPDES permitting. State permits are written in accordance with EPA's national effluent limitations. 33 U.S.C. § 1342(b)(1)(A). EPA retains oversight over state implementation of NPDES permitting, and, in theory, may revoke that authority. *Id.* § 1342(c)(3). EPA retains veto power over individual permits. *Id.* § 1342(d). EPA and the U.S. Justice Department—in addition to states— may take enforcement action against violations of state-issued permits, just as they can with EPA-issued permits. *Id.* § 1342(i).

That being said, although states with delegated authority must comply with the terms of the Clean Water Act in order to gain (and keep) EPA's approval, state agencies often have considerable leeway in implementing the Act, especially when there is ambiguity or controversy about the statute's meaning. Recall, for example, that the decision whether to require a permit for the San Diego fireworks displays was to be made at least in the first instance by the San Diego Regional Water Control Board, a California government agency—not by EPA. Unless EPA can credibly threaten to revoke its approval, a state agency such as the San Diego Board may be able to implement the Clean Water Act in ways that differ from what EPA would do. *See* Jessica Bulman-Pozen & Heather K. Gerken, *Uncooperative Federalism*, 118 YALE L.J. 1256, 1276 (2009) (noting that cooperative federalism under federal environmental statutes "lends the states considerable leverage, which they have sometimes used to challenge and reshape federal policy").

Permit Limits. A NPDES permit specifies the effluent limitations that apply to the permitted facility's discharges. A single permitted source may discharge from multiple *outfalls.* Thus, Commonwealth Pharma's Conshohocken plant has one outfall that discharges wastewater from its wastewater treatment plant, and another outfall that discharges stormwater runoff

> Technology-based standards set floors but not ceilings. A NPDES permit may contain more stringent limits if the waterway into which a source discharges has quality worse than regulatory standards. We will discuss water quality standards and their implications later in this Chapter in Section 3.D.

from parking lots, roof drains, and the manufacturing area. Each outfall has its own effluent limitations. The effluent limitations for the wastewater derive directly from EPA's effluent guidelines for pharmaceutical manufacturing. For example, Commonwealth Pharma's permit specifies that it may not discharge wastewater with an average monthly chemical oxygen demand of greater than 856 ppm or a maximum daily chemical oxygen demand of greater than 1,675 ppm, the same limits set forth in EPA's effluent guidelines regulations. 40 C.F.R. §§ 439.32(a), 439.34(a). For industries for which EPA has not yet issued effluent guidelines, Clean Water Act section 402(a)(1)(B), 33 U.S.C. § 1342(a)(1)(B), directs permitting authorities to apply "conditions as [the permitting authority] determines are necessary to carry out the provisions of [the CWA]"—which EPA regulations refer to as "Best Professional Judgment," 40 C.F.R. § 125.3. Consequently, even if EPA had not established effluent limitations for pharmaceutical manufacturers, Commonwealth Pharma's Conshohocken plant would need to secure a NPDES permit and that permit would limit the pollutants in the plant's effluent.

Monitoring and Reporting. Although effluent limitations are an essential element of NPDES permits, permits do more than simply require permittees to comply with effluent limits. Permits also require periodic effluent sampling; Johnson Matthey's permit requires it to sample for some pollutants daily, some weekly, and others monthly. Permittees must provide monthly *discharge monitoring reports* that transmit their monitoring results to regulators. Those reports then may be obtained by the public, which means that environmental groups have ready access to data on NPDES permit violations. The course website also contains Commonwealth Pharma's discharge reports for April and May 2014. Note how easy it is to determine whether Commonwealth Pharma was in compliance with its permit limits—the monitoring results and permit limits are both reported.

Given the penalties for violating a NPDES permit, you might wonder why a permittee would not falsify its discharge monitoring reports to conceal a discharge that exceeds the effluent limitations in its permit. While such behavior undoubtedly occurs, the Clean Water Act makes it a felony to knowingly falsify monitoring data. 33 U.S.C. § 1319(c)(4); *see, e.g., United States v. Hopkins*, 53 F.3d 533 (2d Cir. 1995); *United States v. Kuhn*, 165 F. Supp. 2d 639 (E.D. Mich. 2001). Moreover, states and EPA are generally relatively lenient in penalizing permittees who accurately report and diligently correct their permit violations.

Standard Clauses. In addition to effluent limitations and monitoring and reporting requirements, permits also include standard clauses regarding the administration and enforcement of the permit. For example, Commonwealth Pharma's permit requires the company to properly operate and maintain its facility, including all treatment and control equipment; authorizes the Pennsylvania Department of Environmental Protection and EPA to revoke the permit for cause; and authorize the agencies to enter the facility and perform inspections.

QUESTIONS

1.   Why do you think NPDES permits—see Commonwealth Pharma's permit at III.B.4 on page 15—restrict who may sign the discharge monitoring report?

2.   Commonwealth Pharma's permit (III.B.5 on page 15), in accordance with EPA regulations, 40 C.F.R. § 122.41(l)(4)(ii), dictates that if the permittee monitors more frequently than its permit requires, the permittee must report all of its monitoring data on its discharge monitoring report. Why do you think EPA regulations require this?

3.   If Commonwealth Pharma wanted to sell its Conshohocken plant to Lee Pharmaceuticals, would Lee Pharmaceuticals have to apply to the Pennsylvania Department of Environmental Protection for a new NPDES permit?

C. STORMWATER

The problems above focus on the application of the NPDES program to effluent discharges from industrial facilities. Because they have achieved enormous reductions in pollution loading, environmental lawyers often describe these requirements as among the most successful in all of environmental law. Similar requirements apply to discharges from municipal wastewater treatment plants, and those requirements have been similarly effective.

But there is another universe of sources that the NPDES program regulates less effectively. Stormwater regulation, and its associated challenges, have become one of the most important frontiers for water quality law. To understand why, one must first know something about why stormwater runoff is an important environmental concern. The excerpt below summarizes some of the key ways urbanization impacts water quality. Most of them derive from the ways stormwater moves through an urban landscape.

———————

Dave Owen, *Urbanization, Water Quality, and the Regulated Landscape*
82 U. COLO. L. REV. 431, 439–44 (2011)

Urbanized watersheds typically have very different hydrology from undeveloped watersheds. In the latter, some precipitation does not reach the ground and instead remains on leaves, branches, or grass. The rest typically lands on porous surfaces—either partly decayed leaves and duff or in meadows with matted layers of live and dead grass—which allow infiltration into the ground but impede surface flow. Once in the ground, some water is absorbed into root systems and transpired by plants, some remains as soil moisture, and the rest percolates downward to the water table. It then flows laterally, usually at a very slow rate, until it discharges to surface waters. Only in larger storm events, when the rate of precipitation exceeds the ground's capacity for infiltration or on landscapes with abundant bedrock or hard-packed soils, does precipitation produce significant quantities of surface runoff.

In several ways, that natural flow regime supports surface water quality. While surface flows tend to warm or cool to ambient surface temperatures, which vary widely over seasons and even days, subsurface conditions vary little, and streams recharged primarily by groundwater flow therefore have relatively stable temperatures. Shade vegetation creates a similar moderating effect, and trees also promote habitat diversity when they fall into waterways. An undeveloped landscape usually contains few pollutant sources, and some of the pollution carried with precipitation or deposited on the land surface filters out as water moves through the ground. And in undeveloped landscapes, waterways are directly connected to surrounding riparian and upland habitat, allowing species to move between habitat zones as they forage, shelter, and breed. For all of these reasons, the quality of waterways flowing through undeveloped landscapes tends to be quite high.

Urbanization introduces a series of detrimental changes to that hydrology. Human development almost invariably increases the extent of impervious surfaces—pavement and roofs, most importantly, but also compacted soils—which stop water from infiltrating the ground and force it to flow overland, usually to a system of storm drains and sometimes directly to receiving waters. Because these overland flows move much faster than groundwater, more water reaches streams during and shortly after rainstorms, which increases, often dramatically, the frequency and intensity of high flows. Meanwhile, groundwater flows diminish, and less water flows into streams between storm events. Water extractions can exacerbate this effect; lawns and landscaped vegetation usually require irrigation, which can increase pumping from aquifers already depleted by reductions in recharge. Consequently, urbanized watersheds frequently experience "flashy" flow, with higher flows, and often even floods, during storm events and lower or non-existent flows in dry periods.

For a variety of reasons, the composition of urban runoff also differs from runoff in undeveloped areas. Urbanization adds many pollutants: lawn fertilizers and pesticides; oil and grease from cars and machinery; heavy metals scraped from brake pads and tires; salts from snow and ice treatment; sediment from construction sites; and aromatic hydrocarbons from fuel combustion, among others. Loading of most of these pollutants increases in proportion to the area of impervious surfaces. Other pollutants, like animal feces or atmospherically deposited nitrogen or mercury, occur in both urban and undeveloped areas but are more easily washed into surface waters where impervious surfaces are present. Temperatures also change; urban landscapes often warm and sometimes cool runoff, leading to both greater temperature variability than in undeveloped landscapes and greater stress for many aquatic species. Often these pollutants arrive in pulses, particularly when rain falls after extended dry periods or, in colder regions, when snow melts. In watersheds with combined sewers, the pulses are particularly pronounced; runoff from small storm events may be treated, but larger storms can overflow treatment systems and discharge mixtures of untreated stormwater and raw sewage.

Urbanization also changes the physical structure of streams. With development, streams are often channelized, routed through culverts and dams, or even buried. Development often displaces riparian habitat, severing connections between streams and the surrounding habitat and removing shade vegetation. The loss of riparian vegetation limits the influx of large woody debris, which provides important habitat in healthy streams. Flow changes also affect the physical shape of streambeds. High flows tend to be erosive, and flashy flows will often widen and deepen a stream's bed. Habitat diversity typically diminishes, with riffles, pools, and bends replaced by a straighter stream with a more homogenous substrate.

The aggregate consequence of these physical and chemical changes usually is a stream with little resemblance to a stream in an undeveloped area. Native biodiversity decreases, with sensitive (and sometimes legally protected) species declining or disappearing. Streams can lose aesthetic appeal, with low, sluggish flows moving through wide, devegetated streambeds, except during occasional periods of high flow or flood. These changes are pervasive. Some survey studies conclude that water quality tends to decline when impervious surfaces cover more than 10 percent of a watershed, and that small watersheds with more than 25 percent impervious cover almost always exhibit highly degraded water quality. Even sparse exurban development, if spread across a watershed, will exceed the former threshold, and stream degradation therefore is a standard feature of the landscapes in which most Americans live, work, and shop. Other recent research suggests that impacts begin at even lower development levels; several studies have found a consistent onset of degradation at impervious cover levels below 5 percent. The correlation between impervious cover and degradation in larger watersheds is less clear; while larger watersheds are still impacted, studies have not yet tied degrees of degradation to specific levels of urbanization. But even with those remaining uncertainties, scientists know that thousands of urban streams, small rivers, and even larger watersheds are significantly degraded by stormwater pollution from roofs and pavement.

While urbanization almost invariably lowers water quality, a variety of mechanisms can mitigate the effects. Builders can reduce the footprints of buildings and the area of roads or can substitute pervious pavement and green roofs for traditional road surfaces and building designs. Impervious surfaces can drain into infiltration swales or rain gardens rather than into storm drainage systems. Prohibitions on toxic products, educational programs, and maintenance programs like street sweeping can reduce pollutant loading. Uncertainties about treatment remain; few watershed-scale studies document the effectiveness of mitigation programs, and most researchers expect that no amount of planning and engineering can turn an urbanized landscape into the hydrologic equivalent of a forest. These solutions also cost money—particularly when they require retrofitting already-developed areas—and financial constraints therefore could prevent full mitigation even if it were theoretically possible. But such measures, if transformed into standard practice, could slow the degradation of water quality in developing areas and improve it where development already has taken place.

Because of these impacts, stormwater has emerged as one the central issues confronting water pollution lawyers. But that focus is relatively new. In its 1972 incarnation, the Clean Water Act said nothing specific about stormwater. EPA initially focused its regulatory efforts on other discharges—primarily effluents from industrial processes and wastewater treatment plants—and it initially interpreted the Clean Water Act's definition of "point source" to exclude most forms of stormwater runoff. Administrative feasibility concerns were the primary reason for that exclusion; administrators believed that their newly-formed agency simply lacked the capacity to regulate tens of thousands of stormwater sources, and that their limited resources would be better spent elsewhere. *See NRDC v. Costle*, 568 F.2d 1369, 1372–73 (D.C. Cir. 1977).

Costle rejected EPA's attempts to exclude stormwater from point source controls. According to the court, "The wording of the statute, legislative history, and precedents are clear: the EPA Administrator does not have authority to exempt categories of point sources from the permit requirements of [section] 402. Courts may not manufacture for an agency a revisory power inconsistent with the clear intent of the relevant statute." The D.C. Circuit also noted that permitting huge numbers of point sources might not be as difficult as EPA claimed. It observed that EPA could use general permits, which establish standardized requirements for large groups of permittees, to reduce the transaction costs of permitting and to ease administrative burdens. The D.C. Circuit also observed that regulators could use controls other than effluent limitations, which EPA had argued would be a poor fit for stormwater

A "best management practice" ("BMP") is, as its name suggests, a practice thought to effectively control pollution. A BMP requirement therefore is different from an effluent limitation because the former requires an activity and the latter mandates an outcome—or, in other words, is a performance standard. Regulatory economists generally prefer performance standards because they allow regulated entities to find the cheapest way to produce the desired outcome, and environmental advocates also often prefer performance standards because they care more about the outcome than the method of achieving it. But where outcomes are difficult to measure—a common problem with stormwater runoff—a standard that prescribes a particular practice may be the best available regulatory option.

runoff. It noted that permits could require activities—which Clean Water Act lawyers refer to as "best management practices" or BMPs—designed to reduce stormwater pollution.

The D.C. Circuit's suggestions foreshadowed EPA's stormwater regulatory program, but that program still took years to emerge. A series of legislative amendments, court decisions, and rulemaking processes has redefined the legal scope of the NPDES stormwater program. That evolution continues to this day.

In its modern form, the program applies differently depending upon the type of stormwater source.

Agricultural stormwater runoff. In 1977, immediately following the *Costle* decision, Congress amended the Clean Water Act to (among other things) expressly exclude agricultural stormwater runoff from the Act's definition of "point source." Consequently, agricultural stormwater runoff is not part of the NPDES program, even when it reaches surface waterways through discrete conveyances that otherwise would meet the definition of a point source. States may regulate agricultural stormwater runoff if they choose, and the TMDLs and continuing planning processes required by Clean Water Act section 303—which you will read about in more detail in the pages to come—may help inform state regulatory efforts. In a few places, states also have attempted to create trading programs that allow traditional NPDES dischargers to purchase pollution reductions from agricultural sources and use the resulting "offsets" to avoid reductions in their own discharge limits. But other than these limited exceptions, agricultural stormwater runoff is simply not regulated by the CWA.

Silvicultural stormwater runoff. Runoff from timber harvesting, known as silvicultural runoff, also is largely exempted from NPDES permitting requirements, though for different reasons. For decades, EPA declined to require NPDES permits for all but a very limited set of activities associated with logging. In the mid-2000s, an environmental group challenged that exclusion. Its specific focus was runoff from logging roads, and it argued that neither the CWA nor EPA's regulations excluded logging road runoff from NPDES permitting. In 2013, however, the Supreme Court rejected the environmental group's challenge. *See Decker v. Northwest Envtl. Def. Ctr.*, 133 S. Ct. 1326 (2013). While the case was pending, EPA also promulgated new regulations designed to make the silvicultural stormwater exclusion more explicit. 77 Fed. Reg. 72,974 (2012). The net result is that silvicultural stormwater runoff, though quite possibly a form of "point source" pollution (the Supreme Court did not resolve that question), remains almost entirely outside the NPDES program.

Industrial stormwater discharges. By contrast, industrial stormwater discharges are subject to NPDES permitting. EPA creates general permits for different industrial sectors, and industrial dischargers also can pursue individual permits tailored to conditions at their facilities. The permits generally specify BMPs designed to limit stormwater pollution, and they also often require periodic monitoring of stormwater discharges. The effectiveness of industrial stormwater monitoring is subject to dispute. See Wendy E. Wagner, *Stormy Regulation: The Problems that Result when Stormwater (and other) Regulatory Programs Neglect to Account for Limitations in Scientific and Technical Information*, 9 CHAP. L. REV. 191 (2006). Wagner's core critique is that the program affords industrial dischargers too much flexibility to specify the terms of their own programs, allowing them to select BMPs that are cheap rather than effective and monitoring plans that maintain appearances rather than catching problems.

Municipal stormwater runoff. EPA also regulates municipal stormwater runoff. Most municipalities operate storm sewer systems—formally referred to as municipal separate storm sewer systems (MS4s)—which collect runoff from city streets and from public and private properties (many private properties have private stormwater collection systems, which may or may not flow into municipal systems). This public/private hybrid system sometimes puts cities in a difficult position. Because they own and manage the ultimate discharge points, they are the NPDES permit holders, and they are ultimately responsible for complying with NPDES permit terms. But because they do not directly manage much—often most—of the properties where pollution originates, they must assert regulatory authority over private and other public landowners in order to assure compliance.

EPA's stormwater regulations specify mandatory elements of MS4 permits, and these mandatory elements reflect the need for municipalities to assume a regulatory role. Each MS4 permit must contain:

A public education and outreach program. Much stormwater pollution is ultimately traceable to individual behaviors, like excessive fertilizer use or failure to clean up dog feces, that

are not easily addressed through regulatory controls. Education and outreach (a common and familiar example is the "No Dumping" stamps that appear next to many storm drains) may be better tactics to limit these kinds of pollution.

An illicit discharge detection and control program. The term "illicit discharge" refers to the addition of non-stormwater pollutants—for example, used motor oil or industrial waste—into storm sewer systems.

Controls for construction sites. Construction sites can be major sources of sediment and other pollutants. A municipal permit therefore must require BMPs (the hay bales one often sees at the edge of building sites are a common example) for construction sites.

Controls on post-construction runoff. Even after construction is completed, developed sites continue to be pollution sources, particularly if stormwater flows off impervious surfaces rather than infiltrating into the ground. Many post-construction controls therefore attempt to encourage on-site infiltration of stormwater.

A pollution prevention program. The goal of this program is to reduce the amount of pollution generated rather than to manage the flows that transport that pollution.

A monitoring program.

Stormwater also can be regulated, either within or outside the MS4 program, by state and local law. States with delegated NPDES authority issue and oversee MS4 permits, and they enjoy some discretion to specify permit requirements. States also can create independent regulatory programs for stormwater runoff, as can local governments. In developing those requirements, state and local governments can draw upon their TMDLs and upon the "continuing planning processes" required by CWA section 303(e).

For urban areas, at least, this might seem like a thorough regulatory program. But critics have several concerns:

- The industrial stormwater component of the NPDES program leaves out many forms of non-residential development. Commercial properties (like shopping malls and office parks) and institutional properties (like university campuses) are not included, even though some of these areas can be major sources of polluted stormwater runoff.

- For industrial properties that are covered, stormwater permits traditionally focus on keeping stormwater away from industrial process materials. That's important, but runoff from industrial roofs and parking lots may also be polluted even if the industrial plant does an excellent job protecting its process materials from the elements.

- Not all municipalities need MS4 permits. Phase I of the MS4 program covered only cities and some counties with populations over 100,000. Phase II applied to smaller urbanized areas (determined by residential population density). But most rural and many suburban areas are not required to have MS4 permits. Even some highly developed areas, like commercial shopping malls, are not covered by the MS4 program because of their low population density. In other words, some important point sources of stormwater are not subject to any NPDES permitting at all.

- Many municipalities are reluctant participants in the program. An effective stormwater control program generally requires money for monitoring, enforcement, maintenance, and, often, retrofitting of municipal streets and facilities. But many municipalities are cash-strapped. They also need that money for things like paying police and maintaining schools. An effective program also requires regulation of private landowners. But prospective land use controls are unpopular in many areas, and expensive retrofitting requirements are even more financially and politically difficult to impose. Similarly, finding and responding to stormwater violations may be an uncomfortable thing for local officials to do.

- Controls on non-point-source stormwater runoff are minimal. In environmental law and policy circles, it's quite common to hear people describe urban stormwater runoff as non-point source pollution. They aren't completely wrong. Most urban stormwater reaches surface waterways through ditches, pipes, or other discrete conveyances that meet the CWA's definition of "point sources." But some urban stormwater runoff travels as "sheet flow" which means it has not been channelized into any discrete conveyance. That runoff (if polluted, which it often is) really is non-point source pollution. While TMDLs may describe and establish budgets for that non-point runoff, it is subject to regulation only under state and local laws.

- State and local regulatory efforts are uneven. In some places, state or local governments have enacted extensive and stringent water quality protection programs. In others, however, they have done little or nothing. One reason for that inaction is a fear that heightened water quality protection requirements will deter economic development.

- The program doesn't seem to be working. EPA began regulating stormwater decades ago, but discrepancies between water quality standards and actual water quality remain pervasive in urban areas. Meanwhile, urban stormwater management has become the leading legal challenge in the water quality realm.

As this casebook goes to press, EPA has been working on a new draft rule addressing urban stormwater. That rule has been in the works for many years, however, and when it will emerge and what it will say both remain uncertain.

———

VI. THE 404 PROGRAM

The NPDES program isn't the only way to legally discharge pollutants into waters of the United States. Section 404 of the Clean Water Act also sets up a permitting program, which applies where applicants would like to dredge or fill waters of the United States. In practice, this is a very common situation. Particularly in relatively wet parts of the country, building a major development project, like a shopping mall, or a linear project, like a road or utility pipeline, without filling wetlands and waterways is very difficult. Indeed, some forms of construction—recreational docks, for example—are by definition water-dependent. Consequently, thousands of permits issue each year, and dealing with the requirements of Clean Water Act section 404 generates thousands of hours of work for attorneys.

The program is administered through a complicated arrangement. Except in the states of Michigan and New Jersey, which have authority to administer part of the 404 program, the Army Corps of Engineers processes and issues all of the permits. EPA holds veto authority over those permits (including permits issued by Michigan and New Jersey), and on very rare occasions EPA exercises that authority. The Army Corps and EPA jointly develop regulations and guidance governing the permitting program. Because permitting decisions trigger section 401 of the Clean Water Act (discussed in more detail later in this chapter) and, sometimes, the Endangered Species Act, state environmental agencies, the United States Fish and Wildlife Service, and the National Marine Fisheries Service also hold authority over permitting decisions.

Section 404 permits may take two forms:

- *Individual permits* are issued for individual activities and are tailored to that specific activity.

- *General permits* establish standard requirements and conditions for a class of similar activities. Such permits can be established on a local, statewide, regional, or national basis. General permits, while less flexible than individual permits, require much less effort (and therefore less money) to obtain, and the Army Corps typically uses general permits to address smaller and repeatedly-occurring dredging or filling projects.

While both individual and general permits allow the destruction of wetlands and waterways, they also place limits upon dredging and filling. A "no net loss" policy, which was first articulated by President George H.W. Bush and later written into joint EPA/Army Corps regulations, governs national wetland regulation. In accordance with that policy, the Army Corps generally requires permit applicants to analyze alternatives to dredging or filling waters of the United States, to avoid filling waters where it is possible; to minimize the extent of any dredging or filling that must occur; and to provide compensatory mitigation for any waters that must be impacted. That compensatory mitigation may be provided by creating new wetlands, restoring or enhancing damaged wetlands, or by preserving wetlands that are under threat. It also may be directly provided by the permit applicant or by third parties that the applicant pays to restore those wetlands. In concept, this compensatory mitigation system bears some similarity to the emissions trading systems we discussed when we studied the Clean Air Act. The basic premise is that permit applicants should be able to engage in an environmentally destructive and otherwise prohibited activity so long as they compensate by providing extra environmental protection somewhere or sometime else. *See* James Salzman & J.B. Ruhl, *Currencies and the Commodification of Environmental Law*, 53 STAN. L. REV. 607 (2000).

The section 404 program has been controversial. As the opening paragraphs of Justice Scalia's *Rapanos* opinion indicate, regulated entities have chafed at its cost. Environmental advocates have often charged that the Army Corps does a poor job fulfilling its no-net-loss mandate. They have been particularly critical of compensatory mitigation, which they argue has often produced ecologically dysfunctional substitute wetlands. In the 1990s and 2000s, a series of studies from the National Research Council and the Government Accountability Office substantiated many of those critiques. But the program continues to evolve, with increasing reliance on third-party mitigation techniques that are designed—in theory—to allocate money to coordinated protection or restoration of high-value wetlands. *See* ROYAL GARDNER, LAWYERS, SWAMPS, AND MONEY: U.S. WETLAND LAW, POLICY, AND POLITICS (2011).

VII. WATER QUALITY STANDARDS

While the NPDES and 404 programs have been primary foci of Clean Water Act lawyers, the statute also contains other regulatory programs. These include a series of measures that begin with state water quality standards and, in theory, translate those standards into controls on individual sources. This section discusses those programs, first explaining what water quality standards are and how they are created, and then exploring their potential consequences.

A. ELEMENTS

The obligation to set water quality standards derives from Clean Water Act section 303, which also requires states to submit their standards to EPA for approval. The Clean Water Act itself says little about the content of those standards, which instead is specified by EPA regulations. Those regulations require water quality standards to include the following core elements:

- designated and existing uses for individual waterways;

- criteria for measuring whether the water body is sufficiently clean to support its designated and existing uses; and

- a non-degradation policy designed to ensure that water quality progresses toward the overall goals of the Clean Water Act.

The process of setting and updating these standards therefore involves several steps. First, states make waterway-by-waterway determinations of designated and existing uses. The chosen uses might include, for example, providing drinking water, supporting a cold- or warm-water fishery, supporting contact or non-contact recreation, or providing agricultural or industrial water supplies. The CWA contemplates that those uses will vary from waterway to waterway, and they do. Sometimes states also designate different uses for different segments of the same waterway. EPA's regulations do provide some parameters, however, effectively creating a rebuttable presumption that states should designate water to at least support fishing and swimming.

Second, the states must select criteria for measuring whether water quality is sufficiently high to support designated uses. Those criteria can be expressed in a wide variety of ways: as numeric standards, like temperature thresholds or pollutant concentrations that the waterway should not exceed, or in narrative form. States also may choose many different proxies to measure water quality. Many criteria focus on concentrations of particular contaminants, and a few states use the number and diversity of native species as a key indicator of water quality attainment. EPA influences this process at both the front and back ends; it helps states by developing model criteria, and it holds approval authority over the ultimate standards. If states fail to set water quality standards, or set standards that fail to obtain EPA approval, the CWA obligates EPA to step in and develop the standards on its own.

B. IMPLICATIONS

There are, in theory, three primary ways in which state water quality standards can translate into controls on specific sources. The materials that follow discuss each. We begin with the certification process required by section 401 of the Clean Water Act, which gives state environmental regulators some ability to regulate federally-approved projects. We then discuss TMDLs. We then return to the NPDES program and explain how water quality standards and TMDLs can increase the stringency of NPDES permits.

1. WATER QUALITY CERTIFICATIONS

One key mechanism for translating water quality standards into pollution controls is supplied by Clean Water Act section 401. Section 401 applies to (a) any applicant for a federal license or permit to conduct any activity that (b) may result in a discharge. It obliges those applicants to obtain a certification from the state that the discharge will comply with applicable water quality standards. Those requirements may seem straightforward, but controversies arise regarding what activities require a water quality certification, when states can or must deny a certification, and what conditions states can attach to a certification.

PROBLEM: WATER QUALITY CERTIFICATION AND SECTION 404 PERMITS

Timber Creek flows through a forested region of your state. The primary economic activities in the Timber Creek watershed are timber harvesting and viticulture (growing wine grapes). The state's monitoring data show that the creek does not meet state water quality standards for sediment, temperature, dissolved oxygen, and several pesticides.

Your client, Timber Creek Vineyard, owns and operates a vineyard, inn, and restaurant along the banks of Timber Creek. Business is good, and Timber Creek Vineyard would like to expand the physical footprint of its buildings and its vineyards. The catch is that expanding will require building over, and partially filling, a small intermittent stream that flows into Timber Creek. The U.S. Army Corps of Engineers has informed you that it considers the intermittent stream to be a "water of the United States," a conclusion you think a court would uphold. Timber Creek Vineyard therefore will need a Clean Water Act section 404 permit if the project is to proceed. The Army Corps has signaled its willingness to issue the permit, but it has asked your client to obtain a section 401 certification from the state water quality agency. That certification would come with strings attached.

Specifically, the state agency has demanded that your client mitigate impacts to the stream channel by planting native riparian vegetation along another stretch of Timber Creek, and that your client reconstruct a small wetland area from which the small tributary stream drains (both areas are on Timber Creek Vineyard's property). According to the state, the replanting will provide shade for the stream, reducing temperature impacts associated with the land clearing your client proposes to do, and the reconstructed wetland will trap sediment, compensating for increased sedimentation associated with your client's land-clearing activities. To Timber Creek Vineyards, that sounds like a lot of demands. "Can they really force us to do this?" your client representative asks you. "I mean, we're asking for a federal permit to tinker with part of a little stream. And I'm fine with making sure we're careful about how we tinker with that stream. But it seems like now the state is trying to take over management of other parts of our property. Can they do that?"

How will you respond to this question?

CWA § 401, 33 U.S.C. § 1341. Certification

(a) Compliance with applicable requirements; application; procedures; license suspension

(1) Any applicant for a Federal license or permit to conduct any activity including, but not limited to, the construction or operation of facilities, which may result in any discharge into the navigable waters, shall provide the licensing or permitting agency a certification from the State in which the discharge originates or will originate, or, if appropriate, from the interstate water pollution control agency having jurisdiction over the navigable waters at the point where the discharge originates or will originate, that any such discharge will comply with the applicable provisions of sections 1311, 1312, 1313, 1316, and 1317 of this title. In the case of any such activity for which there is not an applicable effluent limitation or other limitation under sections 1311(b) and 1312 of this title, and there is not an applicable standard under sections 1316 and 1317 of this title, the State shall so certify, except that any such certification shall not be deemed to satisfy section 1371(c) of this title. Such State or interstate agency shall establish procedures for public notice in the case of all applications for certification by it and, to the extent it deems appropriate, procedures for public hearings in connection with specific applications. In any case where a State or interstate agency has no authority to give such a certification, such certification shall be from the Administrator. If the State, interstate agency, or Administrator, as the case may be, fails or refuses to act on a request for certification, within a reasonable period of time (which shall not exceed one year) after receipt of such request, the certification requirements of this subsection shall be waived with respect to such Federal application. No license or permit shall be granted until the certification required by this section has been obtained or has been waived as provided in the preceding sentence. No license or permit shall be granted if certification has been denied by the State, interstate agency, or the Administrator, as the case may be. * * *

(d) Limitations and monitoring requirements of certification

Any certification provided under this section shall set forth any effluent limitations and other limitations, and monitoring requirements necessary to assure that any applicant for a Federal license or permit will comply with any applicable effluent limitations and other limitations, under section 1311 or 1312 of this title, standard of performance under section 1316 of this title, or prohibition, effluent standard, or pretreatment standard under section 1317 of this title, and with any other appropriate requirement of State law set forth in

> such certification, and shall become a condition on any Federal license or permit subject to the provisions of this section.

The primary United States Supreme Court case considering section 401—and, therefore, a particularly important case for your client, appears below. Understanding the case is somewhat easier with visual aids, and the map below shows the proposed project considered in the case.[5] The petitioners proposed to build a hydroelectric project on Washington's Dosewallips River just east of Olympic National Park. The project would have operated by withdrawing water from the river just east of the park boundary, sending it through a tunnel (the black dashed line) that would run roughly parallel to the river, and discharging the water back into the river after it passed through the powerhouse, which is the small rectangular box near the eastern edge of the map. The dispute centered around the flows—or lack thereof—in the portion of the river between the intake and the powerhouse.

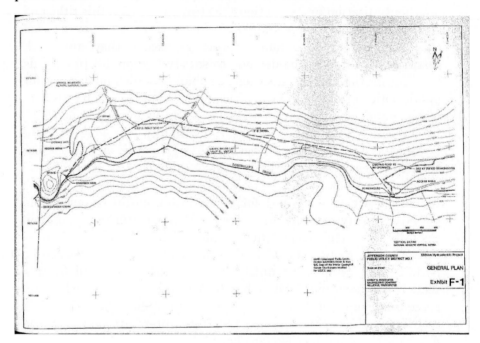

---

[5]   The authors thank Chris Maynard of the Washington Department of Ecology for finding this map.

PUD No. 1 of Jefferson County v. Washington Dept. of Ecology

511 U.S. 700 (1994)

■ JUSTICE O'CONNOR delivered the opinion of the Court.

Petitioners, a city and a local utility district, want to build a hydroelectric project on the Dosewallips River in Washington State. We must decide whether respondent state environmental agency (hereinafter respondent) properly conditioned a permit for the project on the maintenance of specific minimum stream flows to protect salmon and steelhead runs.

I.

This case involves the complex statutory and regulatory scheme that governs our Nation's waters, a scheme that implicates both federal and state administrative responsibilities. The Federal Water Pollution Control Act, commonly known as the Clean Water Act, 86 Stat. 816, as amended, 33 U.S.C. § 1251 *et seq.,* is a comprehensive water quality statute designed to "restore and maintain the chemical, physical, and biological integrity of the Nation's waters." § 1251(a). The Act also seeks to attain "water quality which provides for the protection and propagation of fish, shellfish, and wildlife." § 1251(a)(2).

To achieve these ambitious goals, the Clean Water Act establishes distinct roles for the Federal and State Governments. Under the Act, the Administrator of the Environmental Protection Agency (EPA) is required, among other things, to establish and enforce technology-based limitations on individual discharges into the country's navigable waters from point sources. See §§ 1311, 1314. Section 303 of the Act also requires each State, subject to federal approval, to institute comprehensive water quality standards establishing water quality goals for all intrastate waters. §§ 1311(b)(1)(C), 1313. These state water quality standards provide "a supplementary basis . . . so that numerous point sources, despite individual compliance with effluent limitations, may be further regulated to prevent water quality from falling below acceptable levels." *EPA v. California ex rel. State Water Resources Control Bd.,* 426 U.S. 200, 205, n. 12 (1976).

The State of Washington has adopted comprehensive water quality standards intended to regulate all of the State's navigable waters. See Washington Administrative Code (WAC) 173–201–010 to 173–201–120 (1986). The State created an inventory of all the State's waters, and divided the waters into five classes. 173–201–045. Each individual fresh surface water of the State is placed into one of these classes. 173–201–080. The Dosewallips River is classified AA, extraordinary. 173–201–080(32). The water quality standard for Class AA waters is set forth at

173–201–045(1). The standard identifies the designated uses of Class AA waters as well as the criteria applicable to such waters.

In addition to these specific standards applicable to Class AA waters, the State has adopted a statewide antidegradation policy. That policy provides:

> "(a) Existing beneficial uses shall be maintained and protected and no further degradation which would interfere with or become injurious to existing beneficial uses will be allowed.

> "(b) No degradation will be allowed of waters lying in national parks, national recreation areas, national wildlife refuges, national scenic rivers, and other areas of national ecological importance.

> . . .

> "(f) In no case, will any degradation of water quality be allowed if this degradation interferes with or becomes injurious to existing water uses and causes long-term and irreparable harm to the environment." 173–201–035(8).

As required by the Act, EPA reviewed and approved the State's water quality standards. See 33 U.S.C. § 1313(c)(3); 42 Fed. Reg. 56792 (1977). Upon approval by EPA, the state standard became "the water quality standard for the applicable waters of that State." 33 U.S.C. § 1313(c)(3).

States are responsible for enforcing water quality standards on intrastate waters. § 1319(a). In addition to these primary enforcement responsibilities, § 401 of the Act requires States to provide a water quality certification before a federal license or permit can be issued for activities that may result in any discharge into intrastate navigable waters. 33 U.S.C. § 1341. Specifically, § 401 requires an applicant for a federal license or permit to conduct any activity "which may result in any discharge into the navigable waters" to obtain from the State a certification "that any such discharge will comply with the applicable provisions of sections [1311, 1312, 1313, 1316, and 1317 of this title]." 33 U.S.C. § 1341(a). Section 401(d) further provides that "[a]ny certification . . . shall set forth any effluent limitations and other limitations, and monitoring requirements necessary to assure that any applicant . . . will comply with any applicable effluent limitations and other limitations, under section [1311 or 1312 of this title] . . . and with any other appropriate requirement of State law set forth in such certification." 33 U.S.C. § 1341(d). The limitations included in the certification become a condition on any federal license. *Ibid.*

II

Petitioners propose to build the Elkhorn Hydroelectric Project on the Dosewallips River. If constructed as presently planned, the facility would be located just outside the Olympic National Park on federally owned land within the Olympic National Forest. The project would divert water from a 1.2-mile reach of the river (the bypass reach), run the water through turbines to generate electricity and then return the water to the river below the bypass reach. Under the Federal Power Act (FPA), 41 Stat. 1063, as amended, 16 U.S.C. § 791a *et seq.*, the Federal Energy Regulatory Commission (FERC) has authority to license new hydroelectric facilities. As a result, petitioners must get a FERC license to build or operate the Elkhorn Project. Because a federal license is required, and because the project may result in discharges into the Dosewallips River, petitioners are also required to obtain state certification of the project pursuant to § 401 of the Clean Water Act, 33 U.S.C. § 1341.

The water flow in the bypass reach, which is currently undiminished by appropriation, ranges seasonally between 149 and 738 cubic feet per second (cfs). The Dosewallips supports two species of salmon, coho and chinook, as well as steelhead trout. As originally proposed, the project was to include a diversion dam which would completely block the river and channel approximately 75% of the river's water into a tunnel alongside the streambed. About 25% of the water would remain in the bypass reach, but would be returned to the original riverbed through sluice gates or a fish ladder. Depending on the season, this would leave a residual minimum flow of between 65 and 155 cfs in the river. Respondent undertook a study to determine the minimum stream flows necessary to protect the salmon and steelhead fishery in the bypass reach. On June 11, 1986, respondent issued a § 401 water quality certification imposing a variety of conditions on the project, including a minimum stream flow requirement of between 100 and 200 cfs depending on the season.

[Eds.: The Court then explained the prior procedural history of the matter, which culminated in the Washington Supreme Court holding in favor of the Washington Department of Ecology.]

III

The principal dispute in this case concerns whether the minimum stream flow requirement that the State imposed on the Elkhorn Project is a permissible condition of a § 401 certification under the Clean Water Act. To resolve this dispute we must first determine the scope of the State's authority under § 401. We must then determine whether the limitation at issue here, the requirement that petitioners maintain minimum stream flows, falls within the scope of that authority.

A.

There is no dispute that petitioners were required to obtain a certification from the State pursuant to § 401. Petitioners concede that, at a minimum, the project will result in two possible discharges—the release of dredged and fill material during the construction of the project, and the discharge of water at the end of the tailrace after the water has been used to generate electricity. Petitioners contend, however, that the minimum stream flow requirement imposed by the State was unrelated to these specific discharges, and that as a consequence, the State lacked the authority under § 401 to condition its certification on maintenance of stream flows sufficient to protect the Dosewallips fishery.

If § 401 consisted solely of subsection (a), which refers to a state certification that a "discharge" will comply with certain provisions of the Act, petitioners' assessment of the scope of the State's certification authority would have considerable force. Section 401, however, also contains subsection (d), which expands the State's authority to impose conditions on the certification of a project. Section 401(d) provides that any certification shall set forth "any effluent limitations and other limitations . . . necessary to assure that *any applicant*" will comply with various provisions of the Act and appropriate state law requirements. 33 U.S.C. § 1341(d) (emphasis added). The language of this subsection contradicts petitioners' claim that the State may only impose water quality limitations specifically tied to a "discharge." The text refers to the compliance of the applicant, not the discharge. Section 401(d) thus allows the State to impose "other limitations" on the project in general to assure compliance with various provisions of the Clean Water Act and with "any other appropriate requirement of State law." Although the dissent asserts that this interpretation of § 401(d) renders § 401(a)(1) superfluous, we see no such anomaly. Section 401(a)(1) identifies the category of activities subject to certification—namely, those with discharges. And § 401(d) is most reasonably read as authorizing additional conditions and limitations on the activity as a whole once the threshold condition, the existence of a discharge, is satisfied.

Our view of the statute is consistent with EPA's regulations implementing § 401. The regulations expressly interpret § 401 as requiring the State to find that "there is a reasonable assurance that the *activity* will be conducted in a manner which will not violate applicable water quality standards." 40 C.F.R. § 121.2(a)(3) (1993) (emphasis added). EPA's conclusion that *activities*—not merely discharges—must comply with state water quality standards is a reasonable interpretation of § 401, and is entitled to deference. See, *e.g., Arkansas v. Oklahoma,* 503 U.S. 91, 110 (1992); *Chevron U.S.A. Inc. v. Natural Resources Defense Council, Inc.,* 467 U.S. 837 (1984).

Although § 401(d) authorizes the State to place restrictions on the activity as a whole, that authority is not unbounded. The State can only ensure that the project complies with "any applicable effluent limitations and other limitations, under [33 U.S.C. §§ 1311, 1312]" or certain other provisions of the Act, "and with any other appropriate requirement of State law." 33 U.S.C. § 1341(d). The State asserts that the minimum stream flow requirement was imposed to ensure compliance with the state water quality standards adopted pursuant to § 303 of the Clean Water Act, 33 U.S.C. § 1313.

We agree with the State that ensuring compliance with § 303 is a proper function of the § 401 certification. Although § 303 is not one of the statutory provisions listed in § 401(d), the statute allows States to impose limitations to ensure compliance with § 301 of the Act, 33 U.S.C. § 1311. Section 301 in turn incorporates § 303 by reference. See 33 U.S.C. § 1311(b)(1)(C); see also H.R. Conf. Rep. No. 95–830, p. 96 (1977), U.S. Code Cong. & Admin. News 1977, pp. 4326, 4471 ("Section 303 is always included by reference where section 301 is listed"). As a consequence, state water quality standards adopted pursuant to § 303 are among the "other limitations" with which a State may ensure compliance through the § 401 certification process. This interpretation is consistent with EPA's view of the statute. See 40 C.F.R. § 121.2(a)(3) (1992). Moreover, limitations to assure compliance with state water quality standards are also permitted by § 401(d)'s reference to "any other appropriate requirement of State law." We do not speculate on what additional state laws, if any, might be incorporated by this language. But at a minimum, limitations imposed pursuant to state water quality standards adopted pursuant to § 303 are "appropriate" requirements of state law. * * *

■ JUSTICE THOMAS, with whom JUSTICE SCALIA joins, dissenting.

The Court today holds that a State, pursuant to § 401 of the Clean Water Act, may condition the certification necessary to obtain a federal license for a proposed hydroelectric project upon the maintenance of a minimum flow rate in the river to be utilized by the project. In my view, the Court makes three fundamental errors. First, it adopts an interpretation that fails adequately to harmonize the subsections of § 401. Second, it places no meaningful limitation on a State's authority under § 401 to impose conditions on certification. Third, it gives little or no consideration to the fact that its interpretation of § 401 will significantly disrupt the carefully crafted federal-state balance embodied in the Federal Power Act. Accordingly, I dissent.

NOTES

1.   In addition to clarifying a state's authority under section 401, the *PUD No. 1* decision was significant for two other reasons, neither of which is directly implicated by the problem. First, the case upheld states' ability to base the conditions they imposed on federal licenses on designated uses, even if those uses were expressed in narrative form, not just on quantitative water

quality criteria. Second, the Supreme Court emphatically rejected an argument that section 401 conditions could not address issues of water *quantity*. Many water lawyers, particularly in the west, had viewed water allocation and water quality protection as distinct legal spheres, with the latter sphere occupied by state water allocation law and the Federal Power Act—and with no room left for the Clean Water Act. But the Court rejected that view.

> Petitioners also assert more generally that the Clean Water Act is only concerned with water "quality," and does not allow the regulation of water "quantity." This is an artificial distinction. In many cases, water quantity is closely related to water quality; a sufficient lowering of the water quantity in a body of water could destroy all of its designated uses, be it for drinking water, recreation, navigation or, as here, as a fishery. In any event, there is recognition in the Clean Water Act itself that reduced stream flow, *i.e.*, diminishment of water quantity, can constitute water pollution. First, the Act's definition of pollution as "the man-made or man induced alteration of the chemical, physical, biological, and radiological integrity of water" encompasses the effects of reduced water quantity. 33 U.S.C. § 1362(19). This broad conception of pollution—one which expressly evinces Congress' concern with the physical and biological integrity of water—refutes petitioners' assertion that the Act draws a sharp distinction between the regulation of water "quantity" and water "quality."

511 U.S. at 719.

2.   TMDLs

The second mechanism for translating a water quality standard into actual water quality improvements involves the creation of TMDLs. TMDLs, as you have previously read, are essentially pollutant budgets for impaired waterways. The following problem asks you to think about the circumstances that trigger an obligation to create a TMDL, and the implications of creating a TMDL.

PROBLEM: IMPAIRED WATERBODIES AND TMDLS

This problem returns you to Timber Creek. Please assume, as before, that Timber Creek is listed as impaired for sediment, dissolved oxygen, nutrients, and several pesticides. The primary source of these pollution problems is stormwater runoff from timber harvesting activities and from vineyards. Please assume, also, that the state in which Timber Creek is located has not prepared a TMDL for the creek.

- If you represent the Timber Creek Alliance, an environmental group, and the state declines to prepare a TMDL, would you advise the alliance to sue to compel TMDL preparation? Assume that the alliance does not want to litigate if all it can obtain is a hollow legal victory. Your key questions, then, are not just whether a lawsuit demanding a TMDL is likely to prevail, but also whether preparation of a TMDL is likely to lead to actual water quality improvements.

- If you represent Timber Creek County, and your client asked you to explain the likely consequences of a TMDL, what would you say? Assume that your client is particularly concerned about the impacts on regulated industries in the county.

- How does the political climate of your state factor into your answer? Some states are committed to water quality protection, while others have passed laws precluding administrative agencies from imposing any constraint that is not clearly required by federal law. Does it matter which type of state you are in?

CWA § 303, 33 U.S.C. § 1313. Water quality standards and implementation plans

(d) Identification of areas with insufficient controls; maximum daily load; certain effluent limitations revision

(1)(A) Each State shall identify those waters within its boundaries for which the effluent limitations required by section 1311(b)(1)(A) and section 1311(b)(1)(B) of this title are not stringent enough to implement any water quality standard applicable to such waters. The State shall establish a priority ranking for such waters, taking into account the severity of the pollution and the uses to be made of such waters.

(B) Each State shall identify those waters or parts thereof within its boundaries for which controls on thermal discharges under section 1311 of this title are not stringent enough to assure protection and propagation of a balanced indigenous population of shellfish, fish, and wildlife.

(C) Each State shall establish for the waters identified in paragraph (1)(A) of this subsection, and in accordance with the priority ranking, the total maximum daily load, for those pollutants which the Administrator identifies under section 1314(a)(2) of this title as suitable for such calculation. Such load shall be established at a level necessary to implement the applicable water quality standards with seasonal variations and a margin of safety which takes into account any lack of knowledge concerning the relationship between effluent limitations and water quality.

(D) Each State shall estimate for the waters identified in paragraph (1)(B) of this subsection the total maximum daily thermal load required to assure protection and propagation of a balanced, indigenous population of shellfish, fish, and wildlife. Such estimates shall take into account the normal water temperatures, flow rates, seasonal variations, existing sources of heat input, and the dissipative capacity of the identified waters or parts thereof. Such estimates shall include a calculation of the maximum heat input that can be made into each such part and shall include a margin of safety which takes into account any lack of knowledge concerning the development of thermal water quality criteria for such protection and propagation in the identified waters or parts thereof.

(2) Each State shall submit to the Administrator from time to time, with the first such submission not later than one hundred and eighty days after the date of publication of the first identification of pollutants under section 1314(a)(2)(D) of this title, for his approval the waters identified and the loads established under paragraphs (1)(A), (1)(B), (1)(C), and (1)(D) of this subsection. The Administrator shall either approve or disapprove such identification and load not later than thirty days after the date of submission. If the Administrator approves such identification and load, such State shall incorporate them into its current plan under subsection (e) of this section. If the Administrator disapproves such identification and load, he shall not later than thirty days after the date of such disapproval identify such waters in such State and establish such loads for such waters as he determines necessary to implement the water quality standards applicable to such waters and upon such identification and establishment the State shall incorporate them into its current plan under subsection (e) of this section.

(3) For the specific purpose of developing information, each State shall identify all waters within its boundaries which it has not identified under paragraph (1)(A) and (1)(B) of this subsection and estimate for such waters the total maximum daily load with seasonal variations and margins of safety, for those pollutants which the Administrator identifies under section 1314(a)(2) of this title as suitable for such calculation and for thermal discharges, at a level that would assure protection and propagation of a balanced indigenous population of fish, shellfish, and wildlife.

(4) Limitations on revision of certain effluent limitations

   (A) Standard not attained

   For waters identified under paragraph (1)(A) where the applicable water quality standard has not yet been attained, any effluent limitation based on a total maximum daily load or other waste load allocation established under this section may be revised only if (i) the cumulative effect of all such revised effluent limitations based on such total maximum daily load or waste load allocation will assure the attainment of such water quality standard, or (ii) the designated use which is not being attained is removed in accordance with regulations established under this section.

(B)   Standard attained

For waters identified under paragraph (1)(A) where the quality of such waters equals or exceeds levels necessary to protect the designated use for such waters or otherwise required by applicable water quality standards, any effluent limitation based on a total maximum daily load or other waste load allocation established under this section, or any water quality standard established under this section, or any other permitting standard may be revised only if such revision is subject to and consistent with the antidegradation policy established under this section.

(e) Continuing planning process

(1)   Each State shall have a continuing planning process approved under paragraph (2) of this subsection which is consistent with this chapter.

(2)   Each State shall submit not later than 120 days after October 18, 1972, to the Administrator for his approval a proposed continuing planning process which is consistent with this chapter. Not later than thirty days after the date of submission of such a process the Administrator shall either approve or disapprove such process. The Administrator shall from time to time review each State's approved planning process for the purpose of insuring that such planning process is at all times consistent with this chapter. The Administrator shall not approve any State permit program under subchapter IV of this chapter for any State which does not have an approved continuing planning process under this section.

(3) The Administrator shall approve any continuing planning process submitted to him under this section which will result in plans for all navigable waters within such State, which include, but are not limited to, the following:

(A)   effluent limitations and schedules of compliance at least as stringent as those required by section 1311(b)(1), section 1311(b)(2), section 1316, and section 1317 of this title, and at least as stringent as any requirements contained in any applicable water quality standard in effect under authority of this section;

(B)   the incorporation of all elements of any applicable area-wide waste management plans under section 1288 of this title, and applicable basin plans under section 1289 of this title;

(C)   total maximum daily load for pollutants in accordance with subsection (d) of this section;

(D)   procedures for revision;

(E)   adequate authority for intergovernmental cooperation;

(F)   adequate implementation, including schedules of compliance, for revised or new water quality standards, under subsection (c) of this section;

(G)   controls over the disposition of all residual waste from any water treatment processing;

(H)   an inventory and ranking, in order of priority, of needs for construction of waste treatment works required to meet the applicable requirements of sections 1311 and 1312 of this title.

Subsections 303(d) and (e) have an interesting implementation history. On their face, they appear to create mandatory obligations. But for many years, states did not submit section 303(d) lists or TMDLs to EPA for approval. EPA also did not publish its own substitute lists or TMDLs. The entire program instead languished, and EPA and the states focused on implementing the NPDES program.

In the late 1980s and early 1990s, that all changed. Environmental groups began suing the EPA, arguing the states' failures to submit 303(d) lists and TMDLs amounted to the "constructive submission" of defective lists and TMDLs. EPA, the environmental groups argued, was therefore obligated to step in and prepare its own section 303(d) lists and TMDLs. The environmental groups prevailed in many of these lawsuits and settled many others, and EPA and the states soon found themselves subject to court orders and consent decrees setting schedules for submitting 303(d) lists and preparing TMDLs. *See* OLIVER A. HOUCK, THE CLEAN WATER ACT TMDL PROGRAM: LAW, POLICY, AND IMPLEMENTATION (2d ed. 2002). Tens of thousands of TMDLs have been prepared, and the key questions confronting lawyers now are whether individual TMDLs are legally sufficient and what legal obligations a completed TMDL creates.

The case below explores the answer to that second question. The core question raised was whether water bodies must be listed, and TMDLs prepared, where impairment results solely from non-point source pollution. The Pronsolinos—and, more generally, the agriculture and timber industries—argued that the TMDL requirements only applied where permitted point sources were present and traditional technology-based controls would not be sufficient to attain water quality standards. Under that interpretation, a river impaired only by non-point source runoff from timber harvesting or agriculture would not require TMDLs, even if its water quality failed to attain state standards. EPA interpreted section 303 to require TMDLs for any water body that failed to attain water quality standards regardless of the presence or absence of point sources. The Ninth Circuit, as you will see below, held in favor of EPA.

The Ninth Circuit's resolution of that question is of great historical importance, for a contrary holding would have excluded thousands of streams from TMDL requirements. That historic importance is one reason we have included the case, although, to conserve space, we have left out much of the detailed statutory analysis that led to that conclusion. The other reason, which is of greater practical importance looking forward, is what the Ninth Circuit has to say about the legal consequences of TMDLs.

Pronsolino v. Nastri

291 F.3d 1123 (9th Cir. 2002)

■ BERZON, CIRCUIT JUDGE.

The United States Environmental Protection Agency ("EPA") required California to identify the Garcia River as a water body with insufficient pollution controls and, as required for waters so identified, to set so-called "total maximum daily loads" ("TMDLs")—the significance of which we explain later—for pollution entering the river. Appellants challenge the EPA's authority under the Clean Water Act ("CWA" or the "Act") § 303(d), 33 U.S.C. § 1313(d), to apply the pertinent identification and TMDL requirements to the Garcia River. The district court rejected this challenge, and we do as well.

CWA § 303(d) requires the states to identify and compile a list of waters for which certain "effluent limitations" "are not stringent enough" to implement the applicable water quality standards for such waters. § 303(d)(1)(A). Effluent limitations pertain only to point sources of pollution; point sources of pollution are those from a discrete conveyance, such as a pipe or tunnel. Nonpoint sources of pollution are non-discrete sources; sediment run-off from timber harvesting, for example, derives from a nonpoint source. The Garcia River is polluted only by nonpoint sources. Therefore, neither the effluent limitations referenced in § 303(d) nor any other effluent limitations apply to the pollutants entering the Garcia River.

The precise statutory question before us is whether the phrase "are not stringent enough" triggers the identification requirement both for waters as to which effluent limitations apply but do not suffice to attain water quality standards and for waters as to which effluent limitations do not apply at all to the pollution sources impairing the water. We answer this question in the affirmative, a conclusion which triggers the application of the statutory TMDL requirement to waters such as the Garcia River.

I.   Statutory Background

* * *

Congress enacted the CWA in 1972, amending earlier federal water pollution laws that had proven ineffective. *EPA v. California,* 426 U.S. 200, 202 (1976). * * * In enacting sweeping revisions to the nation's water pollution laws in 1972, Congress began from the premise that the focus "on the tolerable effects rather than the preventable causes of pollution" constituted a major shortcoming in the pre 1972 laws. *Oregon Natural Desert Assoc. v. Dombeck,* 172 F.3d 1092, 1096 (9th Cir. 1998) (quoting *EPA v. State Water Resources Control Board,* 426 U.S. 200, 202–03 (1976)). The 1972 Act therefore sought to target primarily "the preventable causes of pollution," by emphasizing the use of technological controls. *Id.; Oregon Natural Res. Council v. United States Forest Serv.,* 834 F.2d 842, 849 (9th Cir. 1987).

At the same time, Congress decidedly did *not* in 1972 give up on the broader goal of attaining acceptable water quality. CWA § 101(a), 33 U.S.C. § 1251(a). Rather, the new statute recognized that even with the application of the mandated technological controls on point source discharges, water bodies still might not meet state-set water quality standards, *Natural Res. Def. Council,* 915 F.2d at 1316–17. The 1972 statute therefore put in place mechanisms other than direct federal regulation of point sources, designed to "restore and maintain the chemical, physical, and biological integrity of the Nation's waters." § 101(a).

In so doing, the CWA uses distinctly different methods to control pollution released from point sources and that traceable to nonpoint sources. *Oregon Natural Res. Council,* 834 F.2d at 849. The Act directly mandates technological controls to limit the pollution point sources may discharge into a body of water. *Dombeck,* 172 F.3d at 1096. On the other hand, the Act "provides no direct mechanism to control nonpoint source pollution but rather uses the 'threat and promise' of federal grants to the states to accomplish this task," *id.* at 1097 (citations omitted), thereby "recogniz[ing], preserv[ing], and protect[ing] the primary responsibilities and rights of States to prevent, reduce, and eliminate pollution, [and] to plan the development and use . . . of land and water resources . . . ." § 101(b).

B. *The Structure of CWA § 303, 33 U.S.C. § 1313*

* * *

2. *Section 303(d): "Identification of Areas with Insufficient Controls; Maximum Daily Load"*

* * *

For waters identified [as impaired] pursuant to § 303(d)(1)(A)(the "§ 303(d)(1) list"), the states must establish the "total maximum daily load" ("TMDL") for pollutants identified by the EPA as suitable for TMDL calculation.[2] § 303(d)(1)(C). "A TMDL defines the specified maximum amount of a pollutant which can be discharged or 'loaded' into the waters at issue from all combined sources." *Dioxin/Organochlorine Center v. Clarke,* 57 F.3d 1517, 1520 (9th Cir. 1995). The TMDL "shall be established at a level necessary to implement the applicable water quality standards . . . ." § 303(d)(1)(C).

Section 303(d)(2), in turn, requires each state to submit its § 303(d)(1) list and TMDLs to the EPA for its approval or disapproval. If the EPA approves the list and TMDLs, the state must incorporate the list and TMDLs into its "continuing planning process," the requirements for which are set forth in § 303(e). § 303(d)(2). If the EPA disapproves either the § 303(d)(1) list or any TMDLs, the EPA must itself put together the missing document or documents. *Id.* The state then incorporates any EPA-set list or TMDL into the state's continuing planning process. *Id.*

* * *

3. *Continuing Planning Process*

The final pertinent section of § 303, § 303(e), requiring each state to have a "continuing planning process," gives some operational force to the prior information-gathering provisions. The EPA may approve a state's continuing planning process only if it "will result in plans for all navigable waters within such State" that include, inter alia, effluent limitations, TMDLs, areawide waste management plans for nonpoint sources of pollution, and plans for "adequate implementation, including schedules of compliance, for revised or new water quality standards." § 303(e)(3).

The upshot of this intricate scheme is that the CWA leaves to the states the responsibility of developing plans to achieve water quality standards if the statutorily-mandated point source controls will not alone suffice, while providing federal funding to aid in the implementation of the state plans. *See Dombeck,* 172 F.3d at 1097; § 303(e); *see also* § 319(h), 33 U.S.C. § 1329(h) (providing for grants to states to combat nonpoint source pollution). TMDLs are primarily informational tools that allow the states to proceed from the identification of waters requiring additional planning to the required plans. *See Alaska Center for the Environment v. Browner,*

20 F.3d 981, 984–85 (9th Cir. 1994). As such, TMDLs serve as a link in an implementation chain that includes federally-regulated point source controls, state or local plans for point and nonpoint source pollution reduction, and assessment of the impact of such measures on water quality, all to the end of attaining water quality goals for the nation's waters.

II.   Factual And Procedural Background

A.   The Garcia River TMDL

In 1992, California submitted to the EPA a list of waters pursuant to § 303(d)(1)(A). Pursuant to § 303(d)(2), the EPA disapproved California's 1992 list because it omitted seventeen water segments that did not meet the water quality standards set by California for those segments. Sixteen of the seventeen water segments, including the Garcia River, were impaired only by nonpoint sources of pollution. After California rejected an opportunity to amend its § 303(d)(1) list to include the seventeen sub-standard segments, the EPA, again acting pursuant to § 303(d)(2), established a new § 303(d)(1) list for California, including those segments on it. California retained the seventeen segments on its 1994, 1996, and 1998 § 303(d)(1) lists.

California did not, however, establish TMDLs for the segments added by the EPA. Environmental and fishermen's groups sued the EPA in 1995 to require the EPA to establish TMDLs for the seventeen segments, and in a March 1997 consent decree the EPA agreed to do so. According to the terms of the consent decree, the EPA set March 18, 1998, as the deadline for the establishment of a TMDL for the Garcia River. When California missed the deadline despite having initiated public comment on a draft TMDL and having prepared a draft implementation plan, the EPA established a TMDL for the Garcia River. The EPA's TMDL differed only slightly from the state's draft TMDL.

The Garcia River TMDL for sediment is 552 tons per square mile per year, a sixty percent reduction from historical loadings. The TMDL allocates portions of the total yearly load among the following categories of nonpoint source pollution: a) "mass wasting" associated with roads; b) "mass wasting" associated with timber-harvesting; c) erosion related to road surfaces; and d) erosion related to road and skid trail crossings.

B.   The Appellants

In 1960, appellants Betty and Guido Pronsolino purchased approximately 800 acres of heavily logged timber land in the Garcia River watershed. In 1998, after re-growth of the forest, the Pronsolinos applied for a harvesting permit from the California Department of Forestry ("Forestry").

In order to comply with the Garcia River TMDL, Forestry and/or the state's Regional Water Quality Control Board required, among other things, that the Pronsolinos' harvesting permit provide for mitigation of 90% of controllable road-related sediment run-off and contain prohibitions on removing certain trees and on harvesting from mid-October until May 1. The Pronsolinos' forester estimates that the large tree restriction will cost the Pronsolinos $750,000.

Larry Mailliard, a member of the Mendocino County Farm Bureau, submitted a draft harvesting permit on February 4, 1998, for a portion of his property in the Garcia River watershed. Forestry granted a final version of the permit after incorporation of a 60.3% reduction of sediment loading, a requirement included to comply with the Garcia River TMDL. Mr. Mailliard's forester estimates that the additional restrictions imposed to comply with the Garcia River TMDL will cost Mr. Mailliard $10,602,000.

Bill Barr, another member of the Mendocino County Farm Bureau, also applied for a harvesting permit in 1998 for his property located within the Garcia River watershed. Forestry granted the permit after incorporation of restrictions similar to those included in the Pronsolinos' permit. A forester states that these additional restrictions, included to comply with the TMDL, will cost Mr. Barr at least $962,000. * * *

III. Analysis

A. Deference to the EPA

As this is a summary judgment case, our review of the district court's decision is, of course, de novo. *See Oregon Natural Res. Council,* 834 F.2d at 844. Harder to answer is the question of the degree of deference we owe the EPA's regulations and decisions interpreting and applying CWA § 303.

The EPA argues that we owe deference to the interpretation of § 303 embodied in its regulations, pursuant to *Chevron U.S.A., Inc. v. Natural Res. Def. Council,* 467 U.S. 837 (1984). An agency's statutory interpretation is entitled to *Chevron* deference if "Congress delegated authority to the agency generally to make rules carrying the force of law, and . . . the agency interpretation claiming deference was promulgated in the exercise of that authority." *United States v. Mead,* 533 U.S. 218, 226–27 (2001). If *Chevron* deference applies, we must defer to the agency's interpretation as long as it is reasonably consistent with the statute. *Id.* at 229.

[Eds.: The court held that EPA's interpretation should receive *Chevron* deference. It then concluded that the statutory language and structure strongly supported EPA's interpretation, and that the interpretation was reasonable. The court concluded its statutory analysis by considering the federalism implications of the competing interpretations. That portion of the analysis, which reveals much about the legal implications of a TMDL, appears below.]

C.   Federalism Concerns

The Pronsolinos finally contend that, by establishing TMDLs for waters impaired only by nonpoint source pollution, the EPA has upset the balance of federal-state control established in the CWA by intruding into the states' traditional control over land use. *See Solid Waste Agency of Northern Cook County v. United States Army Corps of Eng'rs,* 531 U.S. 159, 172–73 (2001). That is not the case.

The Garcia River TMDL identifies the maximum load of pollutants that can enter the Garcia River from certain broad categories of nonpoint sources if the river is to attain water quality standards. It does not specify the load of pollutants that may be received from particular parcels of land or describe what measures the state should take to implement the TMDL. Instead, the TMDL expressly recognizes that "implementation and monitoring" "are state responsibilities" and notes that, for this reason, the EPA did not include implementation or monitoring plans within the TMDL. EPA, *Garcia River Sediment Total Maximum Daily Load* 43 (Mar. 16, 1998).

Moreover, § 303(e) requires—separately from the § 303(d)(1) listing and TMDL requirements—that each state include in its continuing planning process "adequate implementation, including schedules of compliance, for revised or new water quality standards" "for all navigable waters within such State." § 303(e)(3). The Garcia River TMDL thus serves as an informational tool for the creation of the state's implementation plan, independently—and explicitly—required by Congress.

California chose both *if* and *how* it would implement the Garcia River TMDL. States must implement TMDLs only to the extent that they seek to avoid losing federal grant money; there is no pertinent statutory provision otherwise requiring implementation of § 303 plans or providing for their enforcement. *See* CWA § 309, 33 U.S.C. § 1319; CWA § 505, 33 U.S.C. § 1365. * * *

The decision of the district court is AFFIRMED.

———————

To environmental groups, the success of their lawsuits seeking to compel EPA and states to develop TMDLs seemed like cause for celebration. But what consequences have TMDLs actually produced, and what obligations might a TMDL create for polluters? That question is difficult to answer, partly because of the dearth of comprehensive data on TMDL implementation. But a recent General Accounting Office study provides some clues. Here is a summary:

To date, at least, the nation's most ambitious TMDL addresses the water pollution problems of Chesapeake Bay. Additional discussion of that TMDL appears in the capstone problem at the end of this chapter. For a recent judicial decision upholding the TMDL against a broad challenge, see *American Farm Bureau Federation v. U.S. EPA*, 792 F.3d 281 (3rd Cir. 2015).

General Accounting Office, Changes Needed if Key Program Is to Help Fulfill the Nation's Water Quality Goals

2013

Of about 50,000 TMDLs developed and approved, nearly 35,000 were approved more than 5 years ago, long enough for GAO to consider them long established. State officials GAO surveyed in its representative sample of 191 TMDLs reported that pollutants had been reduced in many waters, but few impaired water bodies have fully attained water quality standards.

The sample of 25 TMDLs reviewed by water resource experts GAO contacted seldom contained all features key to attaining water quality standards. According to the National Research Council and EPA, these features—some that are beyond the scope of EPA's existing regulations—include identifying pollution-causing stressors and showing how addressing them would help attain such standards; specifying how and by whom TMDLs will be implemented; and ensuring periodic revisions as needed. The experts found, however, that 17 of 25 long-established TMDLs they reviewed did not show that addressing identified stressors would help attain water quality standards; 12 contained vague or no information on actions that need to be taken, or by whom, for implementation; and 15 did not contain features to help ensure that TMDLs are revised if need be. GAO's review showed that EPA's existing regulations do not explicitly require TMDLs to include these key features, and without such features in TMDLs—or in addition to TMDLs—impaired water bodies are unlikely to attain standards.

In response to GAO's survey, state officials reported that long-established TMDLs generally do not exhibit factors most helpful for attaining water quality standards, particularly for nonpoint source pollution (e.g., farms and storm water runoff). The officials reported that landowner participation and adequate funding—factors they viewed as among the most helpful in implementing TMDLs—were not present in the implementation activities of at least two-thirds of long-established TMDLs, particularly those of nonpoint source TMDLs. Because the Clean Water Act addresses nonpoint source pollution largely through voluntary means, EPA does not have direct authority to compel landowners to take prescribed actions to reduce such pollution. In GAO's survey, state officials knowledgeable about TMDLs reported that 83 percent of TMDLs have achieved their targets for point source pollution (e.g., factories) through permits but that 20 percent achieved their targets for nonpoint source pollution. In 1987, when the act was amended to cover such pollution, some Members of Congress indicated that this provision was a starting point, to be changed if reliance on voluntary approaches did not significantly improve water quality. More than 40 years after Congress passed the Clean Water Act, however, EPA reported that many of the nation's waters are still impaired, and the goals of the act are not being met. Without changes to the act's approach to nonpoint source pollution, the act's goals are likely to remain unfulfilled.

NOTE

Some particularly interesting TMDL litigation has addressed so-called proxy TMDLs. These TMDLs use measures other than mass loading of pollutants, and therefore seek instead to set a budget for things like the amount of stormwater flow entering a waterway or the amount of impervious cover in a watershed. EPA and some states have argued that these TMDLs provide more useful diagnoses of the causes of water pollution, and that they prescribe more implementable responses, but challengers have argued that they violate the requirements of section 303(d). *See, e.g., Virginia Dep't of Transp. v. U.S. EPA*, No. 12–775, 2013 WL 53741 (E.D. Va. Jan. 3, 2013) (rejecting EPA's argument that regulating stormwater flow was a permissible proxy for regulating sediment).

3.   WATER QUALITY STANDARDS AND NPDES PERMITS

Water quality standards also can affect the terms of NPDES permits. States (or EPA, where it retains authority to implement the NPDES program) can increase the stringency of NPDES permits where technology-based standards alone would not be sufficient to ensure compliance with water quality standards (water quality standards cannot be used to *weaken* NPDES permits below the floor set by technology-based standards). In many states, a water quality analysis is an important part of the process of issuing NPDES permits. However, as you will see from the materials below, the circumstances under which water quality standards *compel* a state or EPA to issue more stringent NPDES permits—or to decline to issue a NPDES permit—are subject to some ambiguity and dispute.

PROBLEM: WATER QUALITY CERTIFICATION AND SECTION 402 PERMITS

This problem incorporates the facts from the two preceding Timber Creek problems. For this problem, assume that the state has listed Timber Creek as an impaired water and issued a TMDL with wasteload and load allocations, but the state has not yet developed a program to turn the load and wasteload allocations into enforceable controls on specific facilities. Please also assume that your client, Timber Creek Vineyard, owns and operates a small wastewater treatment plant, which discharges to Timber Creek. That wastewater treatment plant discharges some nutrients into the stream.

Business for Timber Creek Vineyard has been particularly good recently, and, building on its previous expansions, your client would like to construct a new inn, restaurant, and winery further upstream along Timber Creek. That will require building another wastewater treatment plant. Timber Creek Vineyard plans to build a state-of-the-art facility, which will use a combination of engineered wetlands and traditional wastewater treatment plant technology to reduce pollutant discharges to very low levels, but the new treatment facility would still discharge some pollutants into the stream. You have already advised Timber Creek Vineyards that the new wastewater treatment facility will need a NPDES permit.

In addition, Timber Creek Vineyard needs to make some upgrades to its existing wastewater treatment facility. To your client, working on two facilities at once sounds like a hassle. But the environmental engineers working on the project see an opportunity. By making some technological upgrades to the existing facility, they think that nutrient discharges can be reduced. In fact, they believe that the total nutrient discharges from the new facility and the upgraded but preexisting facility would be *less* than the current nutrient discharges from the existing facility. "If we promise to make those pollution reductions at the existing facility," they argue, "that should streamline the process of getting the new permit, shouldn't it?"

Your client wants to know the answer to that question. Can Timber Creek get a NPDES permit for the new facility? And would it streamline the permitting process to offset the pollutant discharges from the new facility with pollutant discharge reductions at the existing facility?

CWA § 302, 33 U.S.C. § 1312. Water quality related effluent limitations

(a) Establishment

Whenever, in the judgment of the Administrator or as identified under section 1314(l) of this title, discharges of pollutants from a point source or group of point sources, with the application of effluent limitations required under section 1311(b)(2) of this title, would interfere with the attainment or maintenance of that water quality in a specific portion of the navigable waters which shall assure protection of public health, public water supplies, agricultural and industrial uses, and the protection and propagation of a balanced population of shellfish, fish and wildlife, and allow recreational activities in and on the water, effluent limitations (including alternative effluent control strategies) for such point source or sources shall be established which can reasonably be expected to contribute to the attainment or maintenance of such water quality.

(b) Modifications of effluent limitations

[Eds.: Subsection (b) sets forth procedures for adopting the effluent limitations required under subsection (a), and also sets forth several circumstances under which EPA may make exceptions to the requirements of subsection (a).] * * *

---

40 C.F.R. § 122.4. Prohibitions

No permit may be issued:

* * *

(d) When the imposition of conditions cannot ensure compliance with the applicable water quality requirements of all affected States; * * *

(i) To a new source or a new discharger, if the discharge from its construction or operation will cause or contribute to the violation of water quality standards. The owner or operator of a new source or new discharger proposing to discharge into a water segment which does not meet applicable water quality standards or is not expected to meet those standards even after the application of the effluent limitations required by sections 301(b)(1)(A) and 301(b)(1)(B) of CWA, and for which the State or interstate agency has performed a pollutants load allocation for the pollutant to be discharged, must demonstrate, before the close of the public comment period, that:

(1) There are sufficient remaining pollutant load allocations to allow for the discharge; and

(2) The existing dischargers into that segment are subject to compliance schedules designed to bring the segment into compliance with applicable water quality standards. The Director may waive the submission of information by the new source or new discharger required by paragraph (i) of this section if the Director determines that the Director already has adequate information to evaluate the request. An explanation of the development of limitations to meet the criteria of this paragraph (i)(2) is to be included in the fact sheet to the permit under § 124.56(b)(1) of this chapter.

Friends of Pinto Creek v. U.S. EPA

504 F.3d 1007 (9th Cir. 2007)

■ HUG, CIRCUIT JUDGE:

In this case, we determine whether the Environmental Protection Agency ("EPA") properly issued a National Pollution Discharge Elimination System ("NPDES") permit under the Clean Water Act to Carlota Copper Company ("Carlota"). The permit allows mining-related discharges of copper into Arizona's Pinto Creek, a waterbody already in excess of water quality standards for copper. Based upon provisions of the Clean Water Act, the implementing regulations, and their applicability to the factual scenario of this case, we vacate the permit and remand.

I.   Factual Background

Pinto Creek is a desert river located near Miami, Arizona, approximately 60 miles east of Phoenix. It has been listed by the American Rivers Organization as one of the country's most endangered rivers due to threats from proposed mining operations. Pinto Creek and its riparian environs are home to a variety of fish, birds, and other wildlife, some of which are specially protected. Due to excessive copper contamination from historical mining activities in the region, Pinto Creek is included on Arizona's list of impaired waters under § 303(d) of the Clean Water Act, 33 U.S.C. § 1313(d), as a water quality limited stream due to non-attainment of water quality standards for dissolved copper.

Carlota proposed to construct and operate an open-pit copper mine and processing facility approximately six miles west of Miami, Arizona, covering over 3000 acres while extracting about 100 million tons of ore. Part of the operation plan includes constructing diversion channels for Pinto Creek to route the stream around the mine, as well as groundwater cut-off walls to block the flow of groundwater into the mine. * * *

Because the proposed action would involve the discharge of pollutants into Pinto Creek, Carlota applied to the EPA for an NPDES permit under § 402 of the Clean Water Act, 33 U.S.C. § 1342, in 1996. The EPA ultimately issued the permit, and the Environmental Appeals Board ("Appeals Board"), the internal appellate board of the EPA, denied review.

II.   Issues

A.   Whether the issuance of the permit to discharge a pollutant, dissolved copper, into Pinto Creek, which already exceeded the amount of dissolved copper allowed under the Section 303(d) Water Quality Standard, is in violation of the Clean Water Act and the applicable regulations.

B.   *Whether the EPA's failure to include and regulate all discharges from the Carlota Copper Mine in the NPDES permit violates the Clean Water Act and the applicable regulations.* * * *

IV.   Analysis

* * *

The Petitioners contend that as a "new discharger" Carlota's discharge of dissolved copper into a waterway that is already impaired by an excess of the copper pollutant violates the intent and purpose of the Clean Water Act. Under the NPDES permitting program, 40 C.F.R. § 122.4(i) addresses the situation where a new source seeks to permit a discharge of pollutants into a stream already exceeding its water quality standards for that pollutant. Section 122.4 states in relevant part:

No permit may be issued:

* * *

(i)   To a new source or a new discharger if the discharge from its construction or operation will cause or contribute to the violation of water quality standards. The owner or operator of a new source or new discharger proposing to discharge into a water segment which does not meet applicable water quality standards or is not expected to meet those standards . . . and for which the State or interstate agency has performed a pollutants load allocation for the pollutant to be discharged, must demonstrate, before the close of the public comment period, that:

(1)   There are sufficient remaining pollutant load allocations to allow for the discharge; and

(2)   The existing dischargers into that segment are subject to compliance schedules designed to bring the segment into compliance with applicable water quality standards.

40 C.F.R. § 122.4 (2000).

The plain language of the first sentence of the regulation is very clear that no permit may be issued to a new discharger if the discharge will contribute to the violation of water quality standards. This corresponds to the stated objectives of the Clean Water Act "to restore and maintain the chemical, physical, and biological integrity of the nation's waters." 33 U.S.C. § 1251(a) (1987). And that "it is the national policy that the discharge of toxic pollutants in toxic amounts be prohibited." 33 U.S.C. § 1251(a)(3) (1987).

The EPA contends that the partial remediation of the discharge from the Gibson Mine will offset the pollution. However, there is nothing in the Clean Water Act or the regulation that provides an exception for an offset when the waters remain impaired and the new source is discharging pollution into that impaired water.

The regulation does provide for an exception where a TMDL has been performed and the owner or operator demonstrates that *before the close of the comment period* two conditions are met, which will assure that the impaired waters will be brought into compliance with the applicable water quality standards. The plain language of this exception to the prohibited discharge by a new source provides that the exception does not apply unless the new source can demonstrate that, under the TMDL, the plan is designed to bring the waters into compliance with applicable water quality standards.

The EPA argues that under the requirements of clause (1), there are sufficient remaining load allocations to allow for the discharge because the TMDL provides a method by which the allocations could be established to allow for the discharge. There is no contention, however, that these load allocations represent the amount of pollution that is currently discharged from the point sources and nonpoint sources, and there is no indication of any plan that will effectuate these load allocations so as to bring Pinto Creek within the water quality standards. The TMDL merely provides for the manner in which Pinto Creek *could* meet the water quality standards if all of the load allocations in the TMDL were met, not that there are sufficient remaining pollutant load allocations under existing circumstances.

With regard to the requirements of clause (2), the EPA argues that the requirement of "compliance schedules" pertains only to point sources for which there is a permit. This does not correspond to the plain language of clause (2), which provides "the existing discharges into that segment [of Pinto Creek] are subject to compliance schedules designed to bring the segment into compliance with applicable water quality standards." 40 C.F.R. § 122.4(i)(2) (2000).

We examine that language utilizing the definitions provided in the regulation. The term "discharge" is defined to mean "the discharge of a pollutant." 40 C.F.R. § 122.2 (2000). The term "discharge of a pollutant," is defined as any addition of any "pollutant" or combination of pollutants to "waters of the United States" from *any point source*." *Id.* at § 122.2(a) (emphasis added). Thus, under the plain language of the regulation, compliance schedules are not confined only to "permitted" point source discharges, but are applicable to "any" point source.

The EPA contends that this would amount to a complete ban of the discharge of pollution to impaired waters. This is based on its misreading of the plain language of the regulation to state that the remediation has to be *completed* before Carlota's discharge. The plain language of clause (2) of the regulation, instead, provides that existing discharges into that segment (of the waters) are "subject to *compliance schedules* designed to bring the segment into compliance with applicable water quality standards." 40 C.F.R. § 122.4(i)(2) (2000) (emphasis added). This is not a complete ban but a requirement of schedules to meet the objective of the Clean Water Act. * * *

In Carlota's case, there are no plans or compliance schedules to bring the Pinto Creek segment "into compliance with applicable water quality standards," as required by § 122.4(i)(2), which Carlota and the EPA both acknowledge is the applicable section with which Carlota must comply. The error of both the EPA and Carlota is that the objective of that section is not simply to show a lessening of pollution, but to show how the water quality standard will be met if Carlota is allowed to discharge pollutants into the impaired waters.

The EPA has the responsibility to regulate discharges from point sources and the states have the responsibility to limit pollution coming into the waters from non-point sources. If point sources, other than the permitted point source, are necessary to be scheduled in order to achieve the water quality standard, then the EPA must locate any such point sources and establish compliance schedules to meet the water quality standard before issuing a permit. If there are not adequate point sources to do so, then a permit cannot be issued unless the state or Carlota agrees to establish a schedule to limit pollution from a nonpoint source or sources sufficient to achieve water quality standards. * * *

In this case, the Petitioners do not argue for an absolute ban on discharges into a waterway that is in violation of the water quality standards. Rather, the Petitioners point to the § 122.4(i) exception by which a new discharger can comply with the Clean Water Act requirements. Those requirements simply were not met. * * *

V.   Conclusion

Because the issuance of the NPDES Permit to Carlota Copper Mine was based on errors of law under the Clean Water Act, 40 C.F.R. § 122.4(i), and the NEPA, we vacate and remand the permit to the EPA for further proceedings consistent with this opinion.

NOTES

1.   The *Pinto Creek* decision addressed constraints on the issuance of *new* NPDES permits in areas with deficient water quality. It does not say what obligations the Clean Water Act establishes for the revision of *existing* permits in areas with deficient water quality. Nor are those obligations set forth elsewhere in the statute. In regulations implementing section 303(d), EPA has required that each TMDL include a "load allocation" for non-point source pollution and a "wasteload allocation" for point source pollution, and those budgets can provide starting points for reducing pollutant loading from existing point sources. But states retain discretion to allocate their budget between the load and wasteload allocations, and as the *Pronsolino* decision notes, they also retain discretion to decide whether or not to turn TMDLs into controls on non-point source pollution. That means a state has discretion to shield existing NPDES permit-holders by establishing a generous wasteload allocation and a small load allocation, and then can shield non-point source pollution sources by leaving the load allocation unimplemented.

2.   The *Pinto Creek* decision refers to something called an "offset." As with air quality, an offset is a reduction in pollution in one location or time to compensate for the introduction of pollution at some other time or place. Here, for example, the mining company argued, and EPA agreed, that several actions taken in the creation of the mine would lead to pollution reductions, which would offset the introduction of pollution from the new discharges.

While the Ninth Circuit was skeptical of the legal and factual basis of that argument (in an omitted footnote, it questioned whether the offset was real), other courts have distinguished *Pinto Creek* and have allowed new discharges, even in the absence of compliance schedules, where those discharges were to be offset by other pollution reductions. *See, e.g., Assateague Coastkeeper v. Md. Dept. of Envt.*, 28 A.3d 178, 205–09 (Md. 2011).

3.   On some waterways, EPA and states have tried to expand the offset concept and create environmental trading systems for water quality. The basic premise of these trading systems is that regulated entities can compensate for their pollution by paying some other entity for pollution reductions. In practice, this could happen by trading among NPDES permit holders—for example, one wastewater treatment plant could pay another plant for pollutant reductions, rather than reducing pollution itself.

Alternatively, NPDES permit holders could pay other polluters, including non-point sources, for pollution reductions. Thus, for example, wastewater treatment plants might sponsor measures to reduce nutrient loading from farms. Because reducing nutrient loading from farms is often much cheaper than squeezing additional pollutant reductions out of wastewater treatment plants, this approach seems potentially appealing.

Despite that seeming promise, and EPA's support, water quality trading is much less common than air quality trading. For an exploration of reasons why water quality trading lags behind some other forms of environmental trading, see Karen Fisher-Vanden & Sheila Olmstead, *Moving Pollution Trading from Air to Water: Potential, Problems, and Prognosis*, 27 J. ECON. PERSPECTIVES 147, 147 (2013).

4.   Does the Clean Water Act require municipal stormwater permits to ensure compliance with water quality standards? According to one court, the answer is no, though EPA or a state *may* demand such compliance if it chooses to do so. *See Defenders of Wildlife v. Browner*, 191 F.3d 1159 (9th Cir. 1999). In other circuits, the question remains open, and environmental groups have advocated for such requirements. The resolution of this question is potentially quite important, for many urban waterways do not currently comply with water quality standards, and stormwater discharges are important contributing causes.

VIII. CAPSTONE PROBLEM: CHESAPEAKE BAY TMDL[6]

Of all the United States' water quality controversies, none is more prominent—and more complicated—than the Chesapeake Bay. The Bay's watershed includes parts of Virginia, West Virginia, Maryland, Delaware, New York, Pennsylvania, and Washington, D.C., and its water quality problems therefore present a major interstate challenge. The Bay's pollution problems—which are long-lasting and serious—also derive from a wide variety of sources, including agricultural, wastewater treatment plant discharges, industrial discharges, and urban stormwater. For decades, the federal government and the Chesapeake Bay states have been discussing and attempting to implement fixes for those problems, so far with little success.

---

[6]   Created by, and adapted and reused with permission from, Bryan Franey, Manko, Gold, Thacher & Fox LLP.

In recent years, EPA and the states have turned to the TMDL process as a potential driver of reform. In 2010, EPA published a massive TMDL for sediment and nutrients entering Chesapeake Bay.

CHESAPEAKE BAY TMDL EXECUTIVE SUMMARY
EPA (Dec. 2010)

Introduction

The U.S. Environmental Protection Agency (EPA) has established the Chesapeake Bay Total Maximum Daily Load (TMDL), a historic and comprehensive "pollution diet" with rigorous accountability measures to initiate sweeping actions to restore clean water in the Chesapeake Bay and the region's streams, creeks and rivers.

Despite extensive restoration efforts during the past 25 years, the TMDL was prompted by insufficient progress and continued poor water quality in the Chesapeake Bay and its tidal tributaries. The TMDL is required under the federal Clean Water Act and responds to consent decrees in Virginia and the District of Columbia from the late 1990s. It is also a keystone commitment of a federal strategy to meet President Barack Obama's Executive Order to restore and protect the Bay.

The TMDL—the largest ever developed by EPA—identifies the necessary pollution reductions of nitrogen, phosphorus and sediment across Delaware, Maryland, New York, Pennsylvania, Virginia, West Virginia and the District of Columbia and sets pollution limits necessary to meet applicable water quality standards in the Bay and its tidal rivers and embayments. Specifically, the TMDL sets Bay watershed limits of 185.9 million pounds of nitrogen, 12.5 million pounds of phosphorus and 6.45 billion pounds of sediment per year—a 25 percent reduction in nitrogen, 24 percent reduction in phosphorus and 20 percent reduction in sediment. These pollution limits are further divided by jurisdiction and major river basin based on state-of-the-art modeling tools, extensive monitoring data, peer-reviewed science and close interaction with jurisdiction partners.

The TMDL is designed to ensure that all pollution control measures needed to fully restore the Bay and its tidal rivers are in place by 2025, with at least 60 percent of the actions completed by 2017. The TMDL is supported by rigorous accountability measures to ensure cleanup commitments are met, including short-and long-term benchmarks, a tracking and accountability system for jurisdiction activities, and federal contingency actions that can be employed if necessary to spur progress.

* * *

TMDL Background

The Clean Water Act (CWA) sets an overarching environmental goal that all waters of the United States be "fishable" and "swimmable." More specifically it requires states and the District of Columbia to establish appropriate uses for their waters and adopt water quality standards that are protective of those uses. The CWA also requires that every two years jurisdictions develop—with EPA approval—a list of waterways that are impaired by pollutants and do not meet water quality standards. For those waterways identified on the impaired list, a TMDL must be developed. A TMDL is essentially a "pollution diet" that identifies the maximum amount of a pollutant the waterway can receive and still meet water quality standards.

Most of the Chesapeake Bay and its tidal waters are listed as impaired because of excess nitrogen, phosphorus and sediment. These pollutants cause algae blooms that consume oxygen and create "dead zones" where fish and shellfish cannot survive, block sunlight that is needed for underwater Bay grasses, and smother aquatic life on the bottom. The high levels of nitrogen, phosphorus and sediment enter the water from agricultural operations, urban and suburban stormwater runoff, wastewater facilities, air pollution and other sources, including onsite septic systems. Despite some reductions in pollution during the past 25 years of restoration due to efforts by federal, state and local governments;

non-governmental organizations; and stakeholders in the agriculture, urban/suburban stormwater, and wastewater sectors, there has been insufficient progress toward meeting the water quality goals for the Chesapeake Bay and its tidal waters.

More than 40,000 TMDLs have been completed across the United States, but the Chesapeake Bay TMDL will be the largest and most complex thus far—it is designed to achieve significant reductions in nitrogen, phosphorus and sediment pollution throughout a 64,000-square-mile watershed that includes the District of Columbia and large sections of six states. The TMDL is actually a combination of 92 smaller TMDLs for individual Chesapeake Bay tidal segments and includes pollution limits that are sufficient to meet state water quality standards for dissolved oxygen, water clarity, underwater Bay grasses and chlorophyll-a, an indicator of algae levels. It is important to note that the pollution controls employed to meet the TMDL will also have significant benefits for water quality in tens of thousands of streams, creeks, lakes and rivers throughout the region.

* * *

Developing the Chesapeake Bay TMDL

Development of the Chesapeake Bay TMDL required extensive knowledge of the stream flow characteristics of the watershed, sources of pollution, distribution and acreage of the various land uses, appropriate best management practices, the transport and fate of pollutants, precipitation data and many other factors. The TMDL is informed by a series of models, calibrated to decades of water quality and other data, and refined based on input from dozens of Chesapeake Bay scientists. Modeling is an approach that uses observed and simulated data to replicate what is occurring in the environment to make future predictions, and was a critical and valuable tool to develop the Chesapeake Bay TMDL.

The development of the TMDL consisted of several steps:

1. EPA provided the jurisdictions with loading allocations for nitrogen, phosphorus and sediment for the major river basins by jurisdiction.

2. Jurisdictions developed draft Phase I WIPs to achieve those basin-jurisdiction allocations. In those draft WIPs, jurisdictions made decisions on how to further sub-allocate the basin-jurisdiction loadings to various individual point sources and a number of point and nonpoint source pollution sectors.

3. EPA evaluated the draft WIPs and, where deficiencies existed, EPA provided backstop allocations in the draft

TMDL that consisted of a hybrid of the jurisdiction WIP allocations modified by EPA allocations for some source sectors to fill gaps in the WIPs.

4. The draft TMDL was published for a 45-day public comment period and EPA held 18 public meetings in all six states and the District of Columbia. Public comments were received, reviewed and considered for the final TMDL.

5. Jurisdictions, working closely with EPA, revised and strengthened Phase I WIPs and submitted final versions to EPA.

6. EPA evaluated the final WIPs and used them along with public comments to develop the final TMDL. * * *

Ultimately, the TMDL is designed to ensure that by 2025 all practices necessary to fully restore the Bay and its tidal waters are in place, with at least 60 percent of the actions taken by 2017. The TMDL loadings * * * were determined using the best peer-reviewed science and through extensive collaboration with the jurisdictions and are informed by the jurisdictions' Phase I WIPs.

Accountability and Goals

The Chesapeake Bay TMDL is unique because of the extensive measures EPA and the jurisdictions have adopted to ensure accountability for reducing pollution and meeting deadlines for progress. The TMDL will be implemented using an accountability framework that includes WIPs, two-year milestones, EPA's tracking and assessment of restoration progress and, as necessary, specific federal contingency actions if the jurisdictions do not meet their commitments. This accountability framework is being established in part to provide demonstration of the reasonable assurance provisions of the Chesapeake Bay TMDL pursuant to both the Clean Water Act (CWA) and the Chesapeake Bay Executive Order, but is not part of the TMDL itself.

When EPA establishes or approves a TMDL that allocates pollutant loads to both point and nonpoint sources, it determines whether there is a "reasonable assurance" that the point and nonpoint source loadings will be achieved and applicable water quality standards will be attained. Reasonable assurance for the Chesapeake Bay TMDL is provided by the numerous federal, state and local regulatory and non-regulatory programs identified in the accountability framework that EPA believes will result in the necessary point and nonpoint source controls and pollutant reduction programs. The most prominent program is the CWA's National Pollutant Discharge Elimination System (NPDES) permit program that regulates point sources throughout the nation. Many nonpoint sources are not covered by a similar federal permit program; as a result, financial incentives, other voluntary programs and state-specific regulatory programs are used to achieve nonpoint source reductions. * * *

Beginning in 2012, jurisdictions (including the federal government) are expected to follow two-year milestones to track progress toward reaching the TMDL's goals. * * * If a jurisdiction's plans are inadequate or its progress is insufficient, EPA is committed to take the appropriate contingency actions to ensure pollution reductions. These include expanding coverage of NPDES permits to sources that are currently unregulated, increasing oversight of state-issued NPDES permits, requiring additional pollution reductions from point sources such as wastewater treatment plants, increasing federal enforcement and compliance in the watershed, prohibiting new or expanded pollution discharges, redirecting EPA grants, and revising water quality standards to better protect local and downstream waters.

Watershed Implementation Plans

The cornerstone of the accountability framework is the jurisdictions' development of WIPs, which serve as roadmaps for how and when a jurisdiction plans to meet its pollutant allocations under the TMDL. In their Phase I WIPs, the jurisdictions were expected to subdivide the Bay TMDL allocations among pollutant sources; evaluate their current legal, regulatory, programmatic and financial tools available to implement the allocations; identify and rectify potential shortfalls in attaining the allocations; describe mechanisms to track and report implementation activities; provide alternative approaches; and outline a schedule for implementation.

EPA provided the jurisdictions with detailed expectations for WIPs in November 2009 and evaluation criteria in April 2010. To assist with WIP preparation, EPA provided considerable technical and financial assistance. EPA worked with the jurisdictions to evaluate various "what if" scenarios—combinations of practices and programs that could achieve their pollution allocations.

The two most important criteria for a WIP is that it achieves the basin-jurisdiction pollution allocations and meets EPA's expectations for providing reasonable assurance that reductions will be achieved and maintained, particularly for non-permitted sources like runoff from agricultural lands and currently unregulated stormwater from urban and suburban lands.

After the draft Phase I WIP submittals in September 2010, a team of EPA sector experts conducted an intense evaluation process, comparing the submissions with EPA expectations. The EPA evaluation concluded that the pollution controls identified in two of the seven jurisdictions' draft WIPs could meet nitrogen and phosphorus allocations and five of the seven jurisdictions' draft WIPs could meet sediment allocations. The

EPA evaluation also concluded that none of the seven draft Phase I WIPs provided sufficient reasonable assurance that pollution controls identified could actually be implemented to achieve the nitrogen, phosphorus and sediment reduction targets by 2017 or 2025.

In response to its findings, EPA developed a draft TMDL that established allocations based on using the adequate portions of the jurisdictions' draft WIP allocations along with varying degrees of federal backstop allocations in all seven jurisdictions. Backstop allocations focused on areas where EPA has the federal authority to control pollution allocations through NPDES permits, including wastewater treatment plants, stormwater permits, and animal feeding operations. * * *

Final Watershed Implementation Plans and TMDL

Since submittal of the draft WIPs and release of the draft TMDL in September 2010, EPA worked closely with each jurisdiction to revise and strengthen its plan. Because of this cooperative work and state leadership, the final WIPs were significantly improved. * * *

These improvements enabled EPA to reduce and remove most federal backstops, leaving a few targeted backstops and a plan for enhanced oversight and contingency actions to ensure progress.

Backstop Allocations, Adjustments, and Actions

Despite the significant improvement in the final WIPs, one of the jurisdictions did not meet all of its target allocations and two of the jurisdictions did not fully meet EPA's expectations for reasonable assurance for specific pollution sectors. To address these few remaining issues, EPA included in the final TMDL several targeted backstop allocations, adjustments and actions. As a result of the jurisdictions' significant improvements combined with EPA's backstops, EPA believes the jurisdictions are in a position to implement their WIPs and achieve the needed pollution reductions. This approach endorses jurisdictions' pollution reduction commitments, gives them the flexibility to do it their way first, and signals EPA's commitment to fully use its authorities as necessary to reduce pollution. * * *

Enhanced Oversight and Contingencies

While final WIPs were significantly improved and the jurisdictions deserve credit for the efforts, EPA also has minor concerns with the assurance that pollution reductions can be achieved in certain pollution sectors in Pennsylvania, Virginia and West Virginia. EPA has informed these jurisdictions that it will consider future backstops if specific near-term progress is not demonstrated in the Phase II WIP. * * *

Ongoing Oversight of Chesapeake Bay Jurisdictions

EPA will carefully review programs and permits in all jurisdictions. EPA's goal is for jurisdictions to successfully implement their WIPs, but EPA is prepared to take necessary actions in all jurisdictions for insufficient WIP implementation or pollution reductions. Federal actions can be taken at any time, although EPA will engage particularly during two-year milestones and refining the TMDL in 2012 and 2017. Actions include:

- Expanding coverage of NPDES permits to sources that are currently unregulated

- Increasing oversight of state-issued NPDES permits

- Requiring additional pollution reductions from federally regulated sources

- Increasing federal enforcement and compliance

- Prohibiting new or expanded pollution discharges

- Conditioning or redirecting EPA grants

- Revising water quality standards to better protect local and downstream waters

- Discounting nutrient and sediment reduction progress if jurisdiction cannot verify proper installation and management of controls

Final TMDL

As a result of the significantly improved WIPs and the removal and reduction of federal backstops, the final TMDL is shaped in large part by the jurisdictions' plans to reduce pollution. Jurisdiction-based solutions for reducing pollution was a long-standing priority for EPA and why the agency always provided the jurisdictions with flexibility to determine how to reduce pollution in the most efficient, cost-effective and acceptable manner.

Now, the focus shifts to jurisdictions' implementation of the WIP policies and programs designed to reduce pollution on-the-ground and in-the-water. EPA will conduct oversight of WIP implementation and jurisdictions' progress toward meeting two-year milestones. If progress is insufficient, EPA will utilize contingencies to place additional controls on federally permitted sources of pollution, such as wastewater treatment plants, large animal agriculture operations and municipal stormwater systems, as well as target compliance and enforcement activities. * * *

The TMDL raises some interesting questions about the extent to which TMDLs can compel regulatory action and, relatedly, about the role of states and the federal government in addressing interstate water quality problems. *See Am. Farm Bureau Fed'n v. U.S. EPA*, 792 F.3d 281 (3rd Cir. 2015). For purposes of this problem, however, your focus is within one state—Pennsylvania—and, specifically the policy question of how Pennsylvania should go about complying with the obligations set forth in the TMDL.

The facts provided in this problem are based on the Chesapeake Bay TMDL but do not always match the actual facts. You should rely exclusively on the facts in the problem to develop your "factual" arguments. Do not make up facts. For any legal arguments, most of what you need is embedded in the fact pattern. You can develop additional legal arguments by looking at outside resources, but make sure that they fit within the fact pattern.

The Pennsylvania Department of Environmental Protection (DEP) has been tasked with developing a Watershed Implementation Plan (WIP) to describe how the Commonwealth will meet its obligations under the Chesapeake Bay TMDL to reduce nitrogen, phosphorus, and sediment loadings to the Bay. This problem, however, focuses only on nitrogen. As the chart below shows, the Commonwealth currently discharges 100 million pounds of nitrogen to the Chesapeake Bay. Under the Chesapeake Bay TMDL, the Commonwealth must reduce its loadings of nitrogen to the Bay to 75 million pounds of nitrogen.

	Million Pounds of Nitrogen Per Year		
Sector	Current Loadings	Adjustment	Future TMDL Allocation
Agriculture	56		
Natural Sources (e.g., forests)	20	−2	18
Point Source (POTWs)	10		
Point Source (Industrials)	3		
Stormwater (MS4s)	7		
Septic	3	−1	2
Air Deposition	1	−0.5	0.5
Totals	100		75

The purpose of the public hearing will be to debate and then determine how much each business sector will be required to reduce its loadings to the Bay. The class will be divided into six teams:

- Pennsylvania Farm Bureau, representing the agricultural sector;

- Association of Pennsylvania Publicly Owned Treatment Works (POTWs), representing the point source (POTW) category;

- Pennsylvania Municipal Authorities Association, representing municipalities that own separate storm sewer systems (MS4s);

- Pennsylvania Chamber of Commerce, representing industrial interests;

- PennFuture, representing general environmental interests; and

- DEP, responsible for allocating nitrogen loadings to each business sector.

You are the legal team representing your assigned interest group. Your client has asked you to attend the public hearing and give a brief presentation in support of your group's interests (i.e., how should DEP allocate the loading of nitrogen amongst the various sources). You will be provided with confidential information from your client to help you develop the presentation.

Your presentation should *briefly* state what group you represent, how that group discharges nitrogen to the Bay (i.e., how it will be impacted by the TMDL), and then provide several arguments in support of your client's position. The arguments can be based on the law, the facts provided, or policy. You can argue why your client should not have to reduce its loadings (or by only a certain amount), or you can argue why other groups should be forced to reduce their loads. You can also offer up certain reductions where you think your client should be willing to do so, particularly if you believe that this will avoid even more drastic reductions.

You will not have time to provide much background or context for your arguments, so keep your arguments short and simple. For example, if a team represented the "air deposition" source category, it could argue that its client should not be forced to reduce loadings to the Bay because its client's impact is already de minimis (1% of the problem), and any forced reductions would be an inefficient use of limited resources. In addition, the team could argue that EPA has already promulgated several rules that will have the co-benefit of reducing nitrogen deposition to the Chesapeake Bay, and further reductions would be duplicative and/or unduly burdensome.

After each group has had the opportunity to present, the members of the DEP team will meet and will decide what sectors will be required to reduce their loading of nitrogen and by how much. The reductions of the Septic, Forest, and Air Deposition categories have already been selected, so DEP will have to reduce nitrogen loadings by an additional 21.5 million pounds per year (refer to the chart above).

Publicly Available Information

The following information is available to all groups:

- Stormwater runoff from agriculture results in 39 million pounds of nitrogen loading per year.

- It is technically feasible for POTWs to install pollution prevention technology that will reduce that sector's loadings to 6 million pounds per year.

- It is technically feasible to reduce stormwater runoff into MS4s from 7 to 3 million pounds of nitrogen per year by implementing "best management practices" (BMPs).

- It is technically feasible for industrials that directly discharge to the Chesapeake Bay watershed to install pollution prevention technology that would reduce nitrogen discharges by 1 million pounds per year.

- Municipalities could reduce nitrogen loadings (2 million pounds per year) to the Chesapeake Bay by prohibiting the application of lawn fertilizer.

- Concentrated Animal Feeding Operations (CAFOs) contribute approximately 10 million pounds of nitrogen to the Bay each year.

Your instructor will provide your group with additional confidential information. Rumor has it that internal whistleblowers for some of the groups have leaked confidential information to PennFuture.

Here are examples of some additional resources that you can use to develop your arguments or find background information:

- Final Phase I and Phase II State Watershed Implementation Plans http://www.epa.gov/reg3wapd/tmdl/ ChesapeakeBay/EnsuringResults.html?tab2=1.

- Interest and Advocacy Group Webpages—*see, e.g.*, Food & Water Watch, Pennsylvania Farm Bureau.

- *American Farm Bureau Federation v. U.S. EPA*, 792 F.3d 281 (3rd Cir. 2015).

Test your knowledge with a Chapter 4 online quiz in CasebookPlus™.

CHAPTER 5

MANAGEMENT OF HAZARDOUS WASTE

A primary purpose of environmental law is to keep pollution from being released into the environment. Two of the statutes discussed in this book, the Clean Air Act and Clean Water Act, are designed specifically to reduce the pollution of the media they protect. Those protections are important for many reasons, but protection of the air and water omits a significant additional pathway for pollution: pollution placed on or within land.

Landfills have always been a popular way to dispose of trash. Archeologists around the world often sift through ancient refuse to learn about human history. No doubt future civilizations will study the trash we create today. And there is a lot of it! The United States creates hundreds of millions of tons of solid waste each year. Some of that waste is extremely dangerous. For example, it contains toxics chemicals, or it could explode.

Before the advent of laws governing hazardous waste management, businesses often disposed of their hazardous waste on-site or by sending it to municipal landfills. Many industrial sites and landfills are now highly contaminated as a result. We'll discuss the laws governing cleanup of such sites in the next chapter.

Environmental protection laws also create new hazardous solid waste. The control technologies required by the Clean Air Act and Clean Water Act can transform chemicals contained in liquids or gases into solid form—for example, sludge filtered out of wastewater during treatment at a publicly owned treatment works. While hazardous solid waste produced by environmental compliance may not be significant in quantity when compared to other sources, in the absence of regulation of hazardous waste disposal on land, air, and water, control technologies could simply shift pollution from one part of the environment to another.

In 1976, Congress enacted the Resource Conservation and Recovery Act (RCRA) to address the problem of hazardous solid waste and "eliminate[ ] the last remaining loophole in environmental law, that of unregulated land disposal of discarded materials and hazardous waste." H.R. Rep. No. 94–1491, at 4 (1976). RCRA creates a comprehensive "cradle to grave" regulatory regime for hazardous waste. Congress targeted hazardous waste for federal regulation both because of its potential to cause harm and because Congress viewed it as an unlikely candidate for cost-effective recycling and reuse. As Congress explained, "[w]ithout a regulatory framework, such hazardous waste will continue to be disposed of in ponds or lagoons or on the ground in a manner that results in substantial and sometimes irreversible pollution of the environment." *Id.*

Notwithstanding Congress's lofty goal of closing the final "loophole" in environmental law, RCRA only addresses hazardous materials once they become waste. A gallon of a highly toxic solvent that is being thrown away is subject to a multitude of requirements that dictate what type of container must be used to hold the solvent, where that container can be stored, and to whom it can be sent. The very same gallon of solvent is not subject to any requirements under RCRA if it is being stored for future use or sale. RCRA simply does not limit or regulate chemicals or compounds included in commercial products and provides no protection against the accidental release of hazardous materials into the environment from those products until they are discarded.

Other Federal Chemical Laws: RCRA only regulates hazardous waste, not hazardous products. Two other federal laws do address hazardous products, at least to an extent. The Federal Insecticide, Fungicide, and Rodenticide Act, 7 U.S.C. §§ 136–136y, requires pesticides to be registered with EPA before they are marketed, and an applicant must demonstrate that approved uses of pesticide "will not generally cause unreasonable adverse effects on the environment." 7 U.S.C. § 136a(c)(5)(D). The Toxic Substance Control Act (TSCA), 15 U.S.C. §§ 2601–2697, provides EPA with authority to regulate chemicals more generally, but for many years, EPA's burden for proving that a chemical was harmful was so high that the agency rarely exercised that authority. *See Corrosion Proof Fittings v. EPA*, 947 F.2d 1201 (5th Cir. 1991). On June 22, 2016, President Barack Obama signed legislation into law aimed to reform TSCA. Whether this reform will effectively create a federal regulatory regime for hazardous materials before they become waste remains to be seen.

Deciding what counts as hazardous waste is a very important question for lawyers practicing RCRA law. It is also a complex and often difficult question. We shall see several examples of this complexity over the course of the chapter. Once a hazardous waste has been identified, RCRA imposes obligations on three categories of entities: first, generators of hazardous waste; second, transporters of hazardous waste; and third, facilities that treat, store, or dispose of hazardous waste (TSDFs).

As you proceed through this chapter, keep in mind the Congressional findings that are reproduced below. Some of these findings were part of RCRA at its inception. Others, specifically the ones addressing disposal of hazardous waste in or on land, were added in 1984 when Congress enacted the Federal Hazardous and Solid Waste Amendments (HSWA), which further tightened hazardous waste regulation and limited land disposal of those wastes. While these findings have no direct regulatory consequences, they can inform both administrative and judicial interpretations of RCRA's substantive provisions.

RCRA § 1002, 42 U.S.C. § 6901. Congressional findings

(b) Environment and health

The Congress finds with respect to the environment and health, that—

(1) although land is too valuable a national resource to be needlessly polluted by discarded materials, most solid waste is disposed of on land in open dumps and sanitary landfills;

(2) disposal of solid waste and hazardous waste in or on the land without careful planning and management can present a danger to human health and the environment;

(3) as a result of the Clean Air Act [42 U.S.C.A. § 7401 et seq.], the Water Pollution Control Act [33 U.S.C.A. § 1251 et seq.], and other Federal and State laws respecting public health and the environment, greater amounts of solid waste (in the form of sludge and other pollution treatment residues) have been created. Similarly, inadequate and environmentally unsound practices for the disposal or use of solid waste have created greater amounts of air and water pollution and other problems for the environment and for health;

(4) open dumping is particularly harmful to health, contaminates drinking water from underground and surface supplies, and pollutes the air and the land;

(5) the placement of inadequate controls on hazardous waste management will result in substantial risks to human health and the environment;

(6) if hazardous waste management is improperly performed in the first instance, corrective action is likely to be expensive, complex, and time consuming; * * *

I. HAZARDOUS WASTE AND ITS SOURCES

Hazardous waste comes in all shapes and sizes. It also originates from many sources: chemical manufacturers, scientific laboratories, stores selling consumer goods, and power plants, to name a few. Household waste often also contains hazardous waste—think about the last time you threw away dead batteries, which contain toxic heavy metals—although households are typically exempted from RCRA.

We will talk more about the dangers that hazardous waste can pose to people and the environment in Chapter 6, when we discuss the cleanup of hazardous sites. For now, it is important to understand that hazardous waste can pose a wide range of health and environmental problems. Mere exposure to some toxins can make people sick or die. Some hazardous wastes can ignite, causing chemical fires, or even explode. And others are highly corrosive and can eat through metal at a rapid rate.

From an environmental perspective, we might think that ideally hazardous waste would either be recycled, so that the chemicals it contains can be reused, or treated, to neutralize any threat they might pose. Data suggest that those strategies are not common. Figure 5.1 includes data from EPA about the volume of hazardous waste generated over the course of the decade ending in 2011 and the management strategy that was used for that waste. As you can see, the vast majority of waste was disposed. Note also that non-disposal categories of waste management didn't increase over the course of the decade.

Figure 5.1

RCRA hazardous waste generation and management in the U.S., 2001– 2011

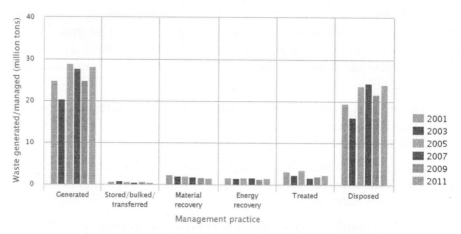

Source: https://cfpub.epa.gov/roe/indicator.cfm?i=54#

That most hazardous waste is disposed doesn't tell us exactly what is happening to it. As the congressional findings you just read suggest, RCRA contains a strong preference against land disposal of hazardous waste, although, as Section IV will discuss, land disposal can occur as long as it complies with disposal and treatment standards set by EPA. Where else can hazardous waste go? EPA has subdivided disposal into three categories, two of which involve disposal of hazardous waste on the surface of land. A third and vastly more popular option is to inject hazardous waste deep underground, in hopes that it will remain isolated from the environment. Figure 5.2 includes data about the amount of disposal that occurs in each category. As you can see, underground injection dwarfs the other options. If you're looking at the chart and wondering why it's missing the third category of disposal identified in the legend, that's because the volume of waste subject to "land treatment/land application" is so small that it doesn't even show up on a chart that includes the other two categories. In 2001, just over 0.02 million tons fell into that category, and the number dropped to only just over 0.001 million tons in 2011.

Figure 5.2

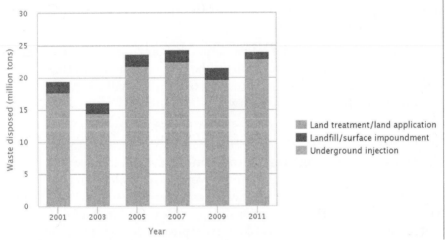

RCRA hazardous waste disposal to land in the U.S. by practice, 2001–2011

Source: https://cfpub.epa.gov/roe/indicator.cfm?i=54#2

Given the stringency of restrictions on land disposal, that most hazardous waste is disposed underground may come as no surprise. In many circumstances, underground injection may be safer than disposing of hazardous waste on the surface. Underground injection wells are regulated under the Safe Drinking Water Act, 42 U.S.C. §§ 300f to 300j–26, and wells are only approved for the disposal of hazardous waste where it is believed that waste will remain in place for at least 10,000 years. Typically, that means disposing of the waste thousands of feet below the surface. There are about 130 wells licensed for the disposal of hazardous waste, and most of them are in either Texas or Louisiana. *See* EPA, Class I Industrial and Municipal Waste Disposal Wells, https://www.epa.gov/uic/class-i-industrial-and-municipal-waste-disposal-wells. There have, however, been numerous instances in which hazardous waste and other materials from approved injection wells migrated into drinking water, and some have suggested that the use of these wells is a looming environmental disaster. *See* Abraham Lustgarten, *Injection Wells: The Poison Beneath Us: The Hidden Risks of Pumping Waste*

Underground, PROPUBLICA (June 21, 2012, 8:20 A.M.), https://www. propublica.org/article/injection-wells-the-poison-beneath-us.

II. OVERVIEW OF FEDERAL SOLID WASTE LAW

Congress enacted RCRA as an amendment to the Solid Waste Disposal Act (SWDA) and it comprises just one of the SWDA's subtitles, although perhaps the most important one for environmental lawyers. As initially enacted, the SWDA provided federal funds for solid or hazardous waste management but left regulation to state or local governments. Congress abandoned that more laisse faire approach when it enacted RCRA, creating extensive federal regulation of hazardous waste. Regulation of non-hazardous solid waste remains primarily the province of state law.

Here we provide a brief introduction to the two other most prominent subtitles of the SWDA, which will not be covered further in this Chapter, and also an overview of the aspects of RCRA that will be the focus of our discussion of hazardous waste law.

Subtitle D. Subtitle D of the SWDA includes programs aimed at non-hazardous solid waste. Subtitle D is generally not regulatory in nature. Congress primarily left regulating non-hazardous solid waste to state and local governments. The federal government's role with such waste is to "provid[e] technical and financial assistance." 42 U.S.C. § 6902(a)(1). Through Subtitle D, EPA generally provides guidance and support to state and local governments. For example, EPA has developed design criteria for solid waste landfills. While many states have adopted these criteria, they are not required to do so.

Subtitle I. The Hazardous and Solid Waste Amendments (HSWA) created Subtitle I, which regulates underground storage tanks that contain chemicals or petroleum. Unlike the other subtitles of RCRA, the requirements of Subtitle I apply even if an underground storage tank contains useful products, rather than waste. At the time of Subtitle I's enactment, there were more than 2 million underground storage tanks nationwide, many of which were leaking or at risk of leaking. Regulations implementing Subtitle I impose engineering requirements on tanks, require monitoring of nearby groundwater, and also create a notification and tracking system. Today, the number of underground storage tanks has shrunk by almost seventy-five percent; EPA now estimates that approximately 550,000 tanks remain. The number of leaking tanks has shrunk even more dramatically. Nevertheless, both leaks that occur in new tanks and the legacy effects of old tanks continue to generate major cleanup costs—and significant work for environmental lawyers—across the country.

Subtitle C. Subtitle C, which regulates hazardous waste, is the Subtitle referred to as RCRA and the primary focus of this Chapter. For RCRA to regulate a material, that material must generally satisfy two threshold criteria, and parties generating waste must determine if these criteria are met. They are:

- *Is the material solid waste?* Only materials that fall within this category are generally regulated under RCRA, although the phrase can be misleading. RCRA defines the term solid waste as including many liquids and even some gases. Another difficult feature of determining whether a material is a solid waste arises from reuse and recycling. Materials are treated as solid waste when they are reused or recycled in certain manners, but not in others.

- *Is the solid waste hazardous?* Solid waste that is also hazardous is regulated by RCRA. The category of hazardous waste is further subdivided in two subcategories.

  - A waste can be a *characteristic hazardous waste* because it exhibits any of four characteristics: corrosivity, ignitability, reactivity, or toxicity. Characteristic hazardous wastes are determined on a case-by-case basis by analyzing the nature of a particular waste and deciding if it meets any of the regulatory thresholds that define those characteristics.

  - A waste can also be a *listed hazardous waste* because EPA, by regulation, has designated it as such. This pathway is categorical. Any waste that falls within a listed category is a hazardous waste, although a major pathway by which EPA creates those categories is an assessment of whether a category of wastes is likely to exhibit the characteristics that would make it eligible to be a characteristic waste.

Once a hazardous waste exists, RCRA imposes regulatory obligations on three categories of parties:

- *Generators* are the sources of hazardous waste. For example, a laboratory that generates waste chloroform or an automobile repair shop that generates solvent-contaminated waste oil is a generator. RCRA divides these generators into three subcategories—large quantity generators, small quantity generators, and conditionally exempt small quantity generators, which you could think of as very small quantity generators. Regulatory requirements are increasingly stringent for generators that produce more hazardous waste.

- *Transporters* move hazardous waste from site to site. For example, a company that picks up waste trichloroethylene from a machine shop and transports that waste to a treatment facility would be a transporter.

- *Treatment, storage, and disposal facilities* (TSDFs), as their name suggests, treat, store, and/or dispose of hazardous waste. These include facilities that reclaim—in other words, process so that it can be reused—certain hazardous waste.

The requirements imposed on all of these entities can be voluminous, governing everything from the design of storage containers to training for employees. You will encounter some of those requirements in Section IV.

The HSWA also created something known as corrective action authority, under which EPA can compel regulated entities to clean up contaminated sites. In practice, the process by which corrective action cleanups occur closely resembles cleanups pursuant to CERCLA, the statute discussed in the next chapter.

RCRA and the States. As with many other environmental laws, RCRA creates a scheme of cooperative federalism. States may seek delegated authority for their own hazardous waste programs, and if they receive such delegation, the "State is authorized to carry out such program in lieu of the Federal program." 42 U.S.C. § 6926(b). A state program must be "equivalent to" the federal hazardous waste program; it must also be "consistent with" the hazardous waste programs of other states; and it must have adequate enforcement mechanisms. *Id.*

Forty-eight states (all but Alaska and Iowa) have at least some delegated authority under RCRA. Some of these states have chosen to designate certain wastes—petroleum is the most important example—as hazardous even if those wastes are not treated as hazardous waste under the federal program. As a result, facilities dealing with waste must understand whether that waste is considered hazardous under both federal law and state law. To make things more complicated, most states have only been delegated authority to implement specific aspects of RCRA, and, as a result, many entities engaging in activities subject to RCRA—particularly TSDFs, the entities subject to the most stringent regulations—must coordinate their activities with both state and federal regulators.

III. REGULATED MATERIALS

Most of the rest of this chapter focuses on three basic questions: *What* is regulated under RCRA? *Who* is regulated? And *how* are they regulated? We begin with the first question. In general terms, the answer to that question is simple: RCRA regulates hazardous waste. Determining whether something qualifies as hazardous waste, in turn, involves two inquiries:

1. Is the material a "solid waste?"

2. If so, then is the material a "hazardous" waste?

These are important questions for lawyers who assist private clients with environmental compliance. RCRA requires generators of waste to determine whether the waste they generate is a hazardous waste. A company that fails to properly do so can be subject to substantial penalties for noncompliance.

A. DEFINITION OF SOLID WASTE

RCRA applies to materials that are solid waste, although the statutory definition of that term, reproduced in the problem materials below, is broadly worded and includes materials that wouldn't seem at first blush to count as "solid" waste.

Sometimes identifying solid waste is easy. For example, materials that have been "abandoned" are waste. 40 C.F.R. § 261.2(b). In the preamble to EPA's first regulations addressing the definition of solid waste, the agency explained "[b]y saying 'abandoned,' we do not intend any complicated concept, but simply mean thrown away." Final Rule, Hazardous Waste Management System; Definition of Solid Waste, 50 Fed. Reg. 614, 627 (Jan. 4, 1985).

When is a solid waste not a solid? RCRA provides a powerful reminder of the importance of reading statutory definitions. A solid, as any schoolchild learns, is something different from a liquid or a gas; in normal parlance, the terms are mutually exclusive. But according to RCRA section 6903(27), the term "solid waste" includes wastes that are "solid, liquid, semisolid, or contained gaseous material." Can air pollution also count as solid waste? In 2006, a district court ruled that materials emitted from a smokestack could be solid waste if the gaseous emissions later deposited materials on the land. The court reasoned that RCRA is a broad remedial statute and that nothing in the definition of solid waste prevented it from applying to gases that deposited materials after being emitted. *See Citizens Against Pollution v. Ohio Power Co.,* 2006 W.L. 6870564 (S.D. Ohio 2006). The Ninth Circuit, however, has adopted an alternative analysis, holding that materials released as air emissions cannot be regulated as solid waste. *See Center for Community Action & Environmental Justice v. BNSF Railroad Co.,* 764 F.3d 1019 (9th Cir. 2014).

The determination becomes more complicated with materials that might be reused. Those generating hazardous waste have a substantial economic incentive to avoid RCRA regulation if at all possible. They also may generate materials that, while byproducts of one industrial process, are useful in another. Rather than throwing those materials away, a facility may instead decide to find someone willing to reuse them. Sometimes reuse and recycling complements RCRA's goal of reducing hazardous waste generation. Sometimes, however, recycling a material may create the very danger to the environment that RCRA is designed to avoid.

EPA has promulgated complicated regulations that identify circumstances where recycling counts as disposal, and therefore where recycled materials count as solid waste. These regulations require determination of whether a particular material is a "secondary material"—which we will discuss in the next paragraphs. If something is a secondary material, and it is being recycled in a prohibited fashion, then the regulations define it as a solid waste.

The courts have not, however, given EPA free rein to regulate recycled materials as solid waste. The D.C. Circuit in particular has interpreted the statutory language of RCRA to impose limits on EPA's regulatory authority. The upshot is that a material constitutes a solid waste if (1) it falls within one of EPA's regulations, and (2) it is not involved in a recycling process that D.C. Circuit precedent indicates does not fall within the meaning of the word "disposal" used in the statute.

Secondary Materials. EPA uses the phrase "secondary materials" to refer to a "material that potentially can be a solid and hazardous waste when recycled.'" 50 Fed. Reg. 614,616 n.4 (Jan. 4, 1985). While the phrase secondary material does not appear in the statute or regulations, it is used as short hand for several defined categories of materials, including "spent materials, sludges, by-products, scrap metal, and commercial products recycled in ways that differ from their normal use." *Id.*

Determining whether a material being recycled constitutes a secondary material can serve as a threshold to applying RCRA. A recycled material may only be a solid waste if it falls within one of the defined categories of secondary materials. Because EPA's definitions contain ambiguity, a regulated party may argue that a material is not a qualifying secondary material at all, and thus even if that material is recycled in a way that would be prohibited under the regulations, the material is not a solid waste.

The four primary types of secondary materials regulated by EPA are discussed below. Before we turn to those definitions, it's worth understanding that three of them—spent materials, by-products, and scrap metal—can be viewed as working together to define as a secondary material everything related to a manufacturing process other than the product the process is intended to produce.

Spent Material. EPA's regulations define a "spent material" as "any material that has been used and as a result of contamination can no longer serve the purpose for which it was produced without processing." 40 C.F.R. § 261.1(c)(1). EPA interprets that definition as including materials that are used, contaminated through use, and then put to a new, substantially different use.

Sludge. RCRA's statutory text defines the term "sludge" as "any solid, semisolid or liquid waste" generated from water treatment or air pollution control facilities. 42 U.S.C. § 6903(26A). In other words, the definition of sludge integrates RCRA into the frameworks created by other environmental statutes. When facilities regulated by the Clean Air Act or Clean Water Act implement controls to remove pollution from wastewater or air emissions, that pollution must then be disposed of pursuant to RCRA (assuming it is hazardous).

By-Products. EPA's regulations define "byproduct" as "a material that is not one of the primary products of a production process and is not solely or separately produced by the production process." 40 C.F.R. § 261.1(c)(3). In other words, by-products are outputs of a manufacturing process other than the product that the process is designed to produce.

Scrap Metal. EPA's regulations explain that " '[s]crap metal' is bits of metal parts (e.g.,[ ] bars, turnings, rods, sheets, wire) or metal pieces that may be combined together with bolts or soldering (e.g., radiators, scrap automobiles, railroad box cars), which when worn or superfluous can be recycled." 40 C.F.R. § 261.1(c)(6). Scrap metal, therefore, includes in the definition of solid waste metal that may come into contact with hazardous materials during a manufacturing process or during transportation or storage of hazardous materials.

Exclusions. Certain wastes are specifically excluded from the definition of "solid waste," and therefore are not subject to RCRA. RCRA § 1004(27) identifies four categories of exempt waste: domestic sewage, irrigation water, industrial discharges subject to a NPDES permit under the Clean Water Act, and certain nuclear materials. 42 U.S.C. § 6903(27). Notably, in a comment offered as part of its regulations, EPA has explained that the exception for NPDES permitted discharges "applies only to the actual point source discharge. It does not exclude industrial wastewaters while they are being collected, stored or treated before discharge, nor does it exclude sludges that are generated by industrial wastewater treatment." 40 C.F.R. § 261.4(2) (comment). That means that a facility may need to treat wastewater as hazardous waste under RCRA before discharging that wastewater pursuant to a valid NPDES permit.

By regulation, EPA has exempted certain other materials, many of which are industry or chemical specific. For example, "[p]ulping liquors * * * that are reclaimed in a pulping liquor recovery furnace and then reused in the pulping process" and "[s]pent sulfuric acid used to produce virgin sulfuric acid" are excluded from the definition of solid waste. 40 C.F.R. § 261.4(6)–(7).

As part of the 1980 amendments to RCRA, Congress enacted the Bevill and Bentsen Amendments, which identified categories of "special wastes" that were to be excluded from RCRA until EPA submitted an assessment of the risks posed by those wastes to Congress. 42 U.S.C. § 6921(b)(3)(A). Those categories encompassed wastes related to mining, cement manufacturing, and energy generation. The amendments directed EPA to determine whether to revoke the exclusion of these wastes from RCRA after submitting its assessment. EPA has since decided to continue to exempt from RCRA wastes including cement kiln dust, waste related to oil and gas exploration, and mining waste.

PROBLEM: UTILITY POLES, PART I

Utilities in the United States use millions of wooden utility poles to provide electricity, telecommunications, and other services. Many wooden utility poles are treated with pentachlorophenol (PCP), a chemical that kills bacteria, fungus, insects, and other organisms that degrade wood. PCP treatment extends the lifespan of wooden utility poles, saving utilities money and reducing wood usage and disposal. Over their life, wooden utility poles release PCP into the environment. Some releases occur during precipitation events when water coming into contact with the poles can absorb PCP. Small particles of PCP-impregnated wood also flake off of the poles.

You are an attorney in EPA's Office of Resource Conservation and Recovery and the following letter has been routed to your desk:

Director
Office of Resource Conservation and Recovery
U.S. Environmental Protection Agency

Dear Director:

I am writing on behalf of the American Utility Alliance (AUA) to seek advice about EPA's interpretation of the phrase "solid waste" for purposes of RCRA in contexts that may be important to utilities.

What are EPA's views about whether the following circumstances would involve a disposal of solid waste for purposes of RCRA: First, if precipitation comes into contact with a structure owned by a company—for example, a utility pole—and the precipitation absorbs a chemical from that structure, is that precipitation a solid waste when it carries the chemical into the ground? Second, if a structure owned by a company slowly and unavoidably sloughs off small amounts of material—for example, wood flaking off of a utility pole—and that material is impregnated with a chemical, are those small amounts of material a solid waste?

I am also seeking EPA's concurrence with AUA's view that the following two circumstance do not involve solid waste: First, a company removes old utility poles containing wood impregnated with PCP and sells those poles to a third-party who uses the poles to produce wood chips for landscaping. AUA does not believe the poles are a solid waste because they are being reused. Second, a company maintains an outdoor facility for treating utility poles and purchases PCP in ten gallon drums for its operations. Full and partially empty drums of PCP remain on the platform with lids affixed and are used as the company has need for new utility poles. The drums may be left in place for extended periods of time of up to two years. AUA does not believe the full or partially empty drums of PCP are a solid waste because they will be used by the company.

I would appreciate a response at your earliest convenience.

Sincerely,

Partner at law firm

EPA routinely receives requests for such guidance and publishes responses on a public website. *See* https://yosemite.epa.gov/osw/rcra.nsf/topics. Considering the materials below, how would you advise EPA to respond to this letter? Should these materials be treated as solid wastes?

RCRA § 1004, 42 U.S.C. § 6903. Definitions

(3) The term "disposal" means the discharge, deposit, injection, dumping, spilling, leaking, or placing of any solid waste or hazardous waste into or on any land or water so that such solid waste or hazardous waste or any constituent thereof may enter the environment or be emitted into the air or discharged into any waters, including ground waters. * * *

(27) The term "solid waste" means any garbage, refuse, sludge from a waste treatment plant, water supply treatment plant, or air pollution control facility and other discarded material, including solid, liquid, semisolid, or contained gaseous material resulting from industrial, commercial, mining, and agricultural operations, and from community activities, but does not include solid or dissolved material in domestic sewage, or solid or dissolved materials in irrigation return flows or industrial discharges which are point sources subject to permits under section 1342 of Title 33, or source, special nuclear, or byproduct material as defined by the Atomic Energy Act of 1954, as amended. * * *

40 C.F.R. § 261.2. Definition of solid waste

(a)(2)(i)   A discarded material is any material which is: (A) Abandoned, * * *; (B) Recycled. * * *; or (C) Considered inherently waste-like * * *.

(b) Materials are solid waste if they are abandoned by being:

(1)   Disposed of; or

(2)   Burned or incinerated; or

(3)   Accumulated, stored, or treated (but not recycled) before or in lieu of being abandoned by being disposed of, burned or incinerated; or * * *

(c) Materials are solid wastes if they are recycled—or accumulated, stored, or treated before recycling—as specified in paragraphs (c)(1) through (4) of this section.

(1)   Used in a manner constituting disposal.

(i)   [Certain] [m]aterials * * * are solid wastes when they are:

(A)   Applied to or placed on the land in a manner that constitutes disposal; or

(B)   Used to produce products that are applied to or placed on the land or are otherwise contained in products that are applied to or placed on the land (in which cases the product itself remains a solid waste). * * *

(2)   Burning for energy recovery.

(i)   [Certain] [m]aterials * * * are solid wastes when they are:

(A)   Burned to recover energy;

(B)   Used to produce a fuel or are otherwise contained in fuels (in which cases the fuel itself remains a solid waste). * * *

(4)   [Certain] [m]aterials * * * are solid wastes when accumulated speculatively.

(d) * * * The following materials are solid wastes when they are recycled in any manner [Eds.: A list of specific materials follows].

As you consider whether materials related to AUA's request constitute solid waste, you have discovered an EPA memorandum that may be helpful.

Memorandum from Suzanne Rudzinski, Director of the Office of Resource Conservation and Recovery to EPA Regional Offices

EPA (Apr. 23, 2013)

Subject: Checklist to Assist in Evaluating Whether Commercial Chemical Products are Solid and Hazardous Waste under the Resource Conservation and Recovery Act

This memorandum provides EPA regions and states a checklist designed to assist in evaluating the regulatory status under the Resource Conservation and Recovery Act (RCRA) hazardous waste management regulations of materials that would, under usual circumstances, be considered products. Under the RCRA regulations these materials are termed Commercial Chemical Products (CCP)* * *.

We developed this checklist in response to requests for assistance in evaluating the regulatory status of CCPs from regional and state regulators and from the regulated community. One common situation in which this question arises is during a facility inspection. As an example, an inspector who observes a material being stored on-site may question facility representatives about the regulatory status of the material. If the facility claims that the material is a product and not a solid or hazardous waste, yet the observed management of the material or other information suggests otherwise, the inspector should gather additional information to support a regulatory status evaluation. The attached checklist will assist in gathering the appropriate supporting information and in making a regulatory status evaluation for CCPs.

Abandoned CCPs can and have caused environmental damages through leaks, spills, volatilization, fires, and explosions. Such damages and the associated clean up costs can be significant. To avoid such situations, facility owners or operators should be aware that abandoned CCPs may be solid and hazardous waste, and if so should be managed under the hazardous waste regulations. These regulations are designed to ensure that hazardous waste is managed in ways that are protective of human health and the environment. Figures 1–4, found at the end of this memorandum, provide photographs of examples encountered during inspections that suggest abandonment of CCPs.

Applicable Regulations

EPA's authority under Subtitle C of RCRA covers management of solid and hazardous wastes, but does not extend to management of materials that are products. Note, however, that there may be regulations applicable to products under other environmental regulations, such as the regulation of toxic substances in products under the Toxic Substances Control Act (TSCA), or under programs managed by other federal agencies, such as the Occupational Safety and Health Administration (OSHA) and the Food and Drug Administration (FDA).

In the RCRA hazardous waste management regulations the term commercial chemical product generally refers to materials that would, under usual circumstances, be considered products and not wastes, but if they are solid wastes would be hazardous because they are listed as hazardous waste or exhibit a characteristic of hazardous waste.

The RCRA regulatory definition of solid waste, found in 40 CFR 261.2, prescribes what materials are solid wastes because they are discarded, and thus are potentially hazardous waste* * *.

[The regulations] establish that:

- CCPs are *not* solid waste if they are:

  o Appropriately stored or managed for use,

  o Legitimately reclaimed, or

  o Appropriately stored or managed for legitimate reclamation

- CCPs *are* solid waste if they are:

  o Abandoned by being accumulated, or by being stored, or treated before, or as a means of, being disposed.

The attached checklist is designed to assist in applying this regulatory structure to specific situations and evaluating whether a particular CCP, managed in a particular way, is a solid waste.

If a CCP is a solid waste, it then must be determined if the CCP is listed as a hazardous waste in 40 CFR part 261 subpart D, or exhibits a characteristic of hazardous waste as described in 40 CFR part 261 subpart C. If the CCP is a solid and hazardous waste, it must be managed in compliance with the RCRA Subtitle C hazardous waste management regulations.

In order to conduct this analysis, EPA and state inspectors have the authority to gather information when they encounter CCPs that appear abandoned or are being managed in a questionable manner. In fact, both EPA and the states have successfully enforced against facilities that falsely claimed that their abandoned materials were CCPs.

* * *

Attachment A

CHECKLIST: To Assist in Evaluating Whether Commercial Chemical Products are Solid and Hazardous Waste under the Resource Conservation and Recovery Act (RCRA)

* * *

Section 1:   Does the facility appear to be managing the material being evaluated in a manner that suggests it is a product (as opposed to being abandoned or stored in lieu of abandonment)?

1.   Are the containers used to store the material in good condition (vs. crushed, bulging, corroded, dusty, leaking, incompatible with the contents, open, or overpacked)?

2.   Are the containers of concern stored in a manner that suggests the material has value? (For example, is the material protected from precipitation, locked-up when the facility is not operating, or stored in a fenced/secure area?)

3.   Does the management of the containers appear to preserve the material's integrity and serve to prevent the material from becoming unstable, unusable or contaminated?

4.   Do the containers have labels that identify the contents as product?

5.   Do the container labels have information, such as lot number, manufacture date, or expiration date, to help determine the age/viability of the material, particularly if a recommended expiration date has been exceeded?

6.   If a container is not labeled, can the facility support a claim that the contents is a product (e.g., provide analytical testing results to verify that the material meets specifications for use, or explain that it recently had to transfer contents to a new container due to damage to the original container and can provide record of purchase)?

7.   Does the condition of the material suggest it is a valuable product? (For example, no crystals have formed inside or outside the container, the material is not discolored, there is no phase separation evident)?

8.   Does the facility manage the material as a valuable commodity by limiting access to the material and having security procedures in place to prevent unauthorized removal of the material?

Section 2:   Does the facility appear to be using the material being evaluated in the production of its products or in support of production operations (as opposed to being abandoned or stored in lieu of abandonment)?

1.   Can the facility describe how the material is used or show where the material is used in the facility?

2.   Do the containers storing the material in question appear to be stored in an appropriate location?

  –   Is the material stored according to manufacturer recommendations (e.g., recommended temperatures, light)?

  –   Are the containers accessible?

–   Are the materials being stored in the same location as other similar product materials?

3.   Do product specifications exist for the material or process in which it is to be used (e.g., minimum concentration of an active ingredient, maximum concentrations of contaminants, or dates beyond which the material should not be used)?

4.   Is there a process in place for the facility to compare the properties of the material in question to specifications that must be met in order for the material to be used for the claimed purpose, or is documentation available to support a facility claim that the material meets such specifications?

5.   Does it appear that the facility has purchased new material that will be used for the same purpose as the material in question? * * *.

6.   Are records available to demonstrate that the facility has NOT written off the material as a loss (indicating that the facility still believes that the material has a use)?

Section 3:   Does the facility appear to be selling into commerce the material being evaluated (as opposed to being abandoned or stored in lieu of abandonment)?

1.   Does the facility have "active" customers or a market for the material?

2.   If yes, can the facility provide a list of such customers and document recent shipments of the material for subsequent distribution in commerce, or provide copies of contracts from past or future sales? Note: The inspector may want to obtain contact information for the receiving facility or facilities (e.g., distributors, customers).

3.   Can the facility identify any competitors for the sale of the material to support a claim that there is an existing or potential market for the material?

4.   Can the facility provide a list of inactive or past customers that purchased the material?

5.   Can the facility provide any information about a future market for the material?

6.   Is a Material Safety Data Sheet (MSDS) or SDS under OSHA's new Globally Harmonized System available for the material (supporting a claim that the material has been in, or will enter, commerce)?

7.   Does the facility have a system for accepting/managing returned or off-specification products it produced and utilizing that material to produce a new product? If so, is this system documented?

8.   Has the material been recalled or returned from a customer? If so, can the facility explain how it intends to use the material? Is there a market for the returned material?

Bottom Line:

Overall, does the facility appear to be managing the material in question as a valuable commodity; i.e., in a manner that preserves the material's integrity and does not cause it to become unusable? * * *

Materials are reused all the time, and the legal issues you are facing are not new. You have uncovered several cases to help you determine whether the recycled utility poles AUA is asking about may be regulated as solid waste. The first relates to EPA's statutory authority to regulate recycled materials. This issue has come up numerous time in the D.C. Circuit, and you will find a short summary of other relevant cases after this first case.

American Mining Congress v. EPA

824 F.2d 1177 (D.C. Cir. 2000)

■ STARR, CIRCUIT JUDGE:

These consolidated cases arise out of EPA's regulation of hazardous wastes under the Resource Conservation and Recovery Act of 1976 ("RCRA"), as amended, 42 U.S.C. §§ 6901–6933 (1982 & Supp. III 1985). Petitioners, trade associations representing mining and oil refining interests, challenge regulations promulgated by EPA that amend the definition of "solid waste" to establish and define the agency's authority to regulate secondary materials reused within an industry's ongoing production process. In plain English, petitioners maintain that EPA has exceeded its regulatory authority in seeking to bring materials that are not discarded or otherwise disposed of within the compass of "waste."

I

RCRA is a comprehensive environmental statute under which EPA is granted authority to regulate solid and hazardous wastes. * * *

Congress' "overriding concern" in enacting RCRA was to establish the framework for a national system to insure the safe management of hazardous waste. H.R. Rep. No. 1491, 94th Cong., 2d Sess. 3 (1976). In passing RCRA, Congress expressed concern over the "rising tide" in scrap, discarded, and waste materials. 42 U.S.C. § 6901 (a)(2). As the statute itself puts it, Congress was concerned with the need "to reduce the amount of waste and unsalvageable materials and to provide for proper and economical solid waste disposal practices." *Id.* § 6901 (a)(4). Congress thus crafted RCRA "to promote the protection of health and the environment and to conserve valuable material and energy resources." *Id.* § 6902.

RCRA includes two major parts: one deals with non-hazardous solid waste management and the other with hazardous waste management. Under the latter, EPA is directed to promulgate regulations establishing a comprehensive management system. *Id.* § 6921. EPA's authority, however, extends only to the regulation of "hazardous waste." Because "hazardous waste" is defined as a subset of "solid waste," *id* § 6903(5), the scope of EPA's jurisdiction is limited to those materials that constitute "solid waste." That pivotal term is defined by RCRA as

> any garbage, refuse, sludge from a waste treatment plant, water supply treatment plant, or air pollution control facility *and other discarded material*, including solid, liquid, semisolid or contained gaseous material, resulting from industrial, commercial, mining, and agricultural operations, and from community activities * * *.

42 U.S.C. § 6903(27) (emphasis added). As will become evident, this case turns on the meaning of the phrase, "and other discarded material," contained in the statute's definitional provisions. * * *

[Eds.: We have omitted the court's description of regulatory history]

EPA issued its final rule on January 4, 1985. 50 Fed. Reg. 614 (1985). Under the final rule, materials are considered "solid waste" if they are abandoned by being disposed of, burned, or incinerated; or stored, treated, or accumulated before or in lieu of those activities. In addition, certain recycling activities fall within EPA's definition. EPA determines whether a material is a RCRA solid waste when it is recycled by examining both the material or substance itself and the recycling activity involved. The final rule identifies five categories of "secondary materials" (spent materials, sludges, by-products, commercial chemical products, and scrap metal). These "secondary materials" constitute "solid waste" when they are disposed of; burned for energy recovery or used to produce a fuel; reclaimed; or accumulated speculatively. *Id.* at 618–19, 664. Under the final rule, if a material constitutes "solid waste," it is subject to RCRA regulation *unless* it is directly reused as an ingredient or as an effective substitute for a commercial product, or is returned as a raw material substitute to its original manufacturing process. *Id.* In the jargon of the trade, the latter category is known as the "closed-loop" exception. In either case, the material must not first be "reclaimed" (processed to recover a usable product or regenerated). *Id.* EPA exempts these activities "because they are like ordinary usage of commercial products." *Id.* at 619.

II

Petitioners, American Mining Congress ("AMC") and American Petroleum Institute ("API"), challenge the scope of EPA's final rule. Relying upon the statutory definition of "solid waste," petitioners contend that EPA's authority under RCRA is limited to controlling materials that are *discarded* or *intended for discard*. They argue that EPA's reuse and recycle rules, as applied to in-process secondary materials, regulate materials that have not been discarded, and therefore exceed EPA's jurisdiction. To understand petitioners' claims, a passing familiarity with the nature of their industrial processes is required.

Petroleum. Petroleum refineries vary greatly both in respect of their products and their processes. Most of their products, however, are complex mixtures of hydrocarbons produced through a number of interdependent and sometimes repetitious processing steps. In general, the refining process starts by "distilling" crude oil into various hydrocarbon streams or "fractions." The "fractions" are then subjected to a number of processing steps. Various hydrocarbon materials derived from virtually all stages of processing are combined or blended in order to produce products such as gasoline, fuel oil, and lubricating oils. Any hydrocarbons that are not usable in a particular form or state are returned to an appropriate stage in the refining process so they can eventually be used. Likewise, the hydrocarbons and materials which escape from a refinery's production vessels are gathered and, by a complex retrieval system, returned to appropriate parts of the refining process. Under EPA's final rule, this reuse and recycling of materials is subject to regulation under RCRA.

Mining. In the mining industry, primary metals production involves the extraction of fractions of a percent of a metal from a complex mineralogical matrix (i.e., the natural material in which minerals are embedded). Extractive metallurgy proceeds incrementally. Rome was not built in a day, and all metal cannot be extracted in one fell swoop. In consequence, materials are reprocessed in order to remove as much of the pure metal as possible from the natural ore. Under EPA's final rule, this reprocessed ore and the metal derived from it constitute "solid waste." What is more, valuable metal-bearing and mineral-bearing dusts are often released in processing a particular metal. The mining facility typically recaptures, recycles, and reuses these dusts, frequently in production processes different from the one from which the dusts were originally emitted. The challenged regulations encompass this reprocessing, to the mining industry's dismay.

Against this factual backdrop, we now examine the legal issues presented by petitioners' challenge.

III

* * *

[Eds.: The court explains that it will apply *Chevron* deference.]

B

Guided by these principles, we turn to the statutory provision at issue here. Congress, it will be recalled, granted EPA power to regulate "solid waste." Congress specifically defined "solid waste" as "discarded material." EPA then defined "discarded material" to include materials destined for reuse in an industry's *ongoing* production processes. The challenge to EPA's jurisdictional reach is founded, again, on the proposition that in-process secondary materials are outside the bounds of EPA's lawful authority. Nothing has been *discarded*, the argument goes, and thus RCRA jurisdiction remains untriggered.

1

The first step in statutory interpretation is, of course, an analysis of the language itself. As the Supreme Court has often observed, "the starting point in every case involving statutory construction is 'the language employed by Congress.' " *CBS v. FCC*, 453 U.S. 367, 377 (1981), (quoting *Reiter v. Sonotone Corp.*, 442 U.S. 330, 337 (1979)). In pursuit of Congress' intent, we "start with the assumption that the legislative purpose is expressed by the ordinary meaning of the words used." *Securities Industry Ass'n v. Board of Governors*, 468 U.S. 137, 149 (1984) (quoting *Richards v. United States*, 369 U.S. 1, 9 (1962)). These sound principles governing the reading of statutes seem especially forceful in the context of the present case. Here, Congress defined "solid waste" as "discarded material." The ordinary, plain-English meaning of the word "discarded" is "disposed of," "thrown away" or "abandoned." Encompassing materials retained for immediate reuse within the scope of "discarded material" strains, to say the least, the everyday usage of that term. * * *

[But] a complete analysis of the statutory term "discarded" calls for more than resort to the ordinary, everyday meaning of the specific language at hand. For, "the sense in which [a term] is used in a statute must be determined by reference to the purpose of the particular legislation." *Burnet v. Chicago Portrait Co.*, 285 U.S. 1, 6 (1932). The statutory provision cannot properly be torn from the law of which it is a part; context and structure are, as in examining any legal instrument, of substantial import in the interpretive exercise. *See, e.g., Stafford v. Briggs*, 444 U.S. 527, 535 (1980); *Offshore Logistics, Inc. v. Tallentire*, 477 U.S. 207 (1986); *Pennhurst State School v. Halderman*, 451 U.S. 1, 18–19 (1981).

As we previously recounted, the broad objectives of RCRA are "to promote the protection of health and the environment and to conserve valuable material and energy resources. . . ." 42 U.S.C. § 6902. But that goal is of majestic breadth, and it is difficult, as *Dimension Financial* taught us, to pour meaning into a highly specific term by resort to grand purposes. Somewhat more specifically, we have seen that RCRA was enacted in response to Congressional findings that the "rising tide of scrap, discarded, and waste materials" generated by consumers and increased industrial production has presented heavily populated urban communities with "serious financial, management, intergovernmental, and technical problems in the disposal of solid wastes." *Id.* § 6901(a). In light of this problem, Congress determined that "federal action through financial and technical assistance and leadership in the development, demonstration, and application of new and improved methods and processes to reduce the amount of waste and unsalvageable materials and to provide for proper and economical solid waste disposal practices was necessary." *Id.* Also animating Congress were its findings that "disposal of solid and hazardous waste" without careful planning and management presents a danger to human health and the environment; that methods to "separate usable materials from solid waste" should be employed; and that usable energy can be produced from solid waste. *Id.* § 6901(b), (c), (d).

The question we face, then, is whether, in light of the National Legislature's expressly stated objectives and the underlying problems that motivated it to enact RCRA in the first instance, Congress was using the term "discarded" in its ordinary sense—"disposed of" or "abandoned"—or whether Congress was using it in a much more open-ended way, so as to encompass materials no longer useful in their original capacity though destined for immediate reuse in another phase of the industry's ongoing production process.

For the following reasons, we believe the former to be the case. RCRA was enacted, as the Congressional objectives and findings make clear, in an effort to help States deal with the ever-increasing problem of solid waste *disposal* by encouraging the search for and use of alternatives to existing methods of disposal (including recycling) and protecting health and the environment by regulating hazardous wastes. To fulfill these purposes, it seems clear that EPA need not regulate "spent" materials that are recycled and reused in an *ongoing* manufacturing or industrial process. These materials have not yet become part of the waste disposal problem; rather, *they are destined for beneficial reuse or recycling in a continuous process by the generating industry itself.*

* * *

[Eds.: The dissent of Judge Mikva is omitted]

_____

In your research, you have located several D.C. Circuit cases that follow the *American Mining Congress* case excerpted above, which is often referred to as *AMC I*. They include:

American Mining Congress v. EPA, 907 F.2d 1179 (1990). This case, brought by the same lead petitioner, is often referred to as *AMC II*. It involved sludge that mining companies stored in surface impoundments. The companies argued that they were storing the sludge for possible reclamation in the future, and that therefore it had not been discarded. This time the court sided with EPA, deferring to the agency's judgment that materials managed in a land disposal unit after an industrial process had ended could be regulated as solid waste regardless of whether a company might seek to reuse them in the future.

American Petroleum Institute v. EPA, 906 F.2d 729 (1990). This case, referred to as *API I*, dealt with waste materials that companies sent to reclamation facilities. The court held that the materials could be regulated as solid waste. It distinguished *AMC I* by explaining that these materials were "delivered to a [reclamation] facility not as part of an '*ongoing* manufacturing or industrial process' within 'the generating industry,' but as part of a mandatory waste treatment plan prescribed by EPA." *Id*. At 741 (quoting *AMC I*).

American Petroleum Institute v. EPA, 216 F.3d 50 (D.C. Cir. 2000). This case, referred to as *API II*, dealt with treatment of oil-laden waste water during the refining process. EPA believed that the waste water was a solid waste when it was sent for primary treatment,[1] but the industry argued that primary treatment was a step in the refining process that recovered valuable hydrocarbons. The Court explained:

> At bottom, the parties disagree over the proper characterization of primary treatment. Is it simply a step in the act of discarding? Or is it the last step in a production process before discard? * * * It may be permissible for EPA to determine that the predominant purpose of primary treatment is discard. Legal abandonment of property is premised on determining the intent to abandon, which requires an inquiry into facts and circumstances. * * * Where an industrial by-product may be characterized as discarded or "in process" material, EPA's choice of characterization is entitled to deference.

Id. at 57. The Court then considered EPA's explanation for characterizing primary treatment as part of discarding the wastewater. "EPA has noted two purposes of primary treatment and concludes, 'clearly, wastewater

_____

[1]   As you may remember from the Clean Water Act chapter, primary treatment means on-site treatment of liquid effluent that then will be treated again at an off-site wastewater treatment plant.

treatment is the main purpose.' * * * As English teachers have long taught, a conclusion is not 'clear' or 'obvious' merely because one says so." *Id*. The court then remanded to allow EPA to elaborate on its explanation.

Even if EPA has the statutory authority to regulate recycled utility poles, its assertion of that authority must also be consistent with agency regulations. The case below addresses the regulatory definition of "spent material," which you believe is the closest fit for the situation you are analyzing.

Howmet Corporation v. EPA
614 F.3d 544 (D.C. Cir. 2010)

■ BROWN, CIRCUIT JUDGE:

The Environmental Protection Agency (EPA or the Agency) says Howmet Corporation (Howmet) violated the Resource Conservation and Recovery Act and the Hazardous and Solid Waste Amendments of 1984, 42 U.S.C. §§ 6901 *et seq.* (collectively RCRA), and its implementing regulations. Howmet says its actions were permitted by the regulations. Whether viewed as a syntactical ambiguity or a semantic squabble, the dispute focuses on one question: when is a material no longer serving "the purpose for which it was produced?" The EPA insists the initial use of the material is determinative; Howmet contends the initial use is irrelevant. The question matters because "spent material" is subject to RCRA's hazardous waste regulations, but material that has not been spent is not. Howmet insisted that used KOH (liquid potassium hydroxide) sent to a fertilizer manufacturer for use as a fertilizer ingredient was not "spent material" and thus not subject to RCRA regulations. After Howmet lost this argument before an administrative law judge (ALJ) and the Environmental Appeals Board (EAB), the district court rejected Howmet's Administrative Procedure Act claim and granted the EPA's cross-motion for summary judgment, holding the EPA's interpretation of its "spent material" regulation was not arbitrary and capricious * * *. We affirm.

* * *

III

We review the district court's grant of summary judgment de novo, *see Steele v. Schafer*, 535 F.3d 689, 692 (D.C. Cir. 2008), and must set aside the EPA's final determination if "arbitrary, capricious, an abuse of discretion, or otherwise not in accordance with law," 5 U.S.C. § 706(2)(A).

We accord an agency's interpretation of its own regulations a "high level of deference," accepting it "unless it is plainly wrong." *Gen. Elec. Co. v. EPA*, 53 F.3d 1324, 1327 (D.C. Cir. 1995)[.] * * *

A.   *The definition of "spent material" is ambiguous*

Both parties seem to agree our analysis should begin with determining whether the regulatory text of the EPA's spent material definition, as applied to Howmet's KOH shipments to Royster, is clear on its face. Howmet argues the EPA's definition is unambiguous. It claims both the dictionary definition of "purpose" ("the object . . . for which something exists"), as well as the context of the regulation, are relevant and support its position. Howmet insists the plain language of the definition—"the purpose for which it was *produced*"—looks retrospectively to a material's intended purpose at the time it was produced, not prospectively to the first use made of the material following its production and therefore does not permit the interpretation adopted by the EPA. The EPA, on the other hand, argues the word "purpose" is ambiguous, both taken alone and in context, and that the phrase "the purpose for which it was produced" could relate to a material's use, especially where, as here, the producer of the material does not itself put the material to use, but rather creates the product for sale. We agree with the EPA.

Neither the word "purpose" nor the phrase "the purpose for which it was produced" are defined in the EPA's regulations, and the dictionary definition relied on by Howmet provides little help in determining the meaning of either the word or phrase, as they are used in 40 C.F.R. § 261.1. The everyday meanings of the term and phrase also do not provide any clarity as to whether the initial use of a material is relevant to determining the purpose for which the material was produced. In sum, the text of the EPA's definition is simply ambiguous with respect to whether we should adopt Howmet's "multiple, original purposes" approach to determining when a material is "spent," or whether we should, instead, adopt the "original use"-based purpose test advanced by the EPA.

B.   *The EPA's interpretation of the "spent material" regulation is reasonable*

Having concluded the plain language of the EPA's "spent material" definition does not answer the question whether the used KOH sent to Royster was a spent material, we examine whether the EPA's interpretation of the definition is reasonable. *See, e.g., Gorman v. NTSB*, 558 F.3d 580, 589 (D.C. Cir. 2009) * * *. In so doing, we look to the EPA's overall regulatory framework under RCRA, as well as the regulatory history of the Agency's "spent material" definition. Both establish the EPA's interpretation is reasonable and consistent with the Agency's prior interpretations.

1. *Regulatory History of the EPA's "Spent Material" Definition*

* * *

In 1983, the EPA proposed the rule containing the current hazardous waste regulations. *See* Hazardous Waste Mgmt. Sys., 48 Fed. Reg. 14,472 (proposed Apr. 4, 1983) (to be codified at 40 C.F.R. pts. 260, 261, 264, 265, 266). * * * The revised definition of "solid waste" stated that five types of recycling activities, including "[u]se constituting disposal . . . which involves the direct placement of wastes onto the land," would be within the EPA's jurisdiction. *Id.* at 14,476. The five categories were further divided according to the type of waste involved. One such type of waste was "spent material," which the EPA described in the preamble as "materials that have been used and are *no longer fit for use* without being regenerated, reclaimed, or otherwise re-processed." *Id.* (emphasis added). The EPA explained that "processes using spent materials may be more logical candidates for regulation because spent materials (having already fulfilled their *original use*) are more inherently waste-like." *Id.* at 14,488 (emphasis added). The proposed regulation itself defined "spent material" as "any material that has been used and has served its *original purpose.*" *Id.* at 14,508 (proposed 40 C.F.R. § 261.2(b)(1)) (emphasis added). [ ] [T]he EPA's synonymous use of the singular term "original use" and the term "original purpose" reveals the Agency viewed the two concepts as closely connected and interrelated.

The EPA finalized the proposed regulations in 1985. *See* Hazardous Waste Mgmt. Sys.; Definition of Solid Waste, 50 Fed. Reg. 614 (Jan. 4, 1985). Although the EPA stated it "was continuing to define spent materials as those which have been used and are no longer fit for use without being regenerated, reclaimed, or otherwise reprocessed," *id.* at 624, the EPA acknowledged its "reference to original purpose [in the 1983 proposed regulations] was ambiguous when applied to situations where a material can be used further without being reclaimed, but the further use is not identical to the initial use." *Id.* The Agency therefore stated it was "clarifying what [it] mean[t] by spent materials," *id.*, and, accordingly, revised the wording of the definition to read as it does today: "A 'spent material' is any material that has been used and as a result of contamination can no longer serve the purpose for which it was produced without processing," 40 C.F.R. § 261.1(c)(1) (1985). In the preamble, the EPA provided an example of a product used for a subsequent purpose not identical to its original use that would *not* be considered a spent material:

> [W]here solvents used to clean circuit boards are no[ ] longer pure enough for that continued use, but are still pure enough for use as metal degreasers. These solvents are not spent materials when used for metal degreasing. The practice is simply continued use of a solvent (This is analogous to using/reusing a secondary material as an effective substitute for commercial

> products.). The reworded regulation clarifies this by stating that spent materials are those that have been used, and as a result of that use become contaminated by physical or chemical impurities, and can no longer serve the purpose for which they were produced.

50 Fed. Reg. at 624.

* * * [W]e recognize an agency's preamble guidance generally does not have the binding force of the agency's regulations. Nonetheless, it is at least informative. The example the EPA provided is illustrative of the type of subsequent use of a material it sought to regulate under RCRA. The example suggested certain "continued use[s]" of a material sufficiently similar to or consistent with the material's *initial* use would be considered "a purpose for which [the material] was produced" and thus permitted under the Agency's "spent material" definition. Thus, the example makes clear the EPA was, in both 1983 and 1985, associating the concept of "purpose" with "initial use." * * * The EPA's accompanying explanation further indicates the Agency intended to place limits on the types of reuse allowable under its regulations. The Agency's acknowledgement that its spent material definition was ambiguous when applied to situations where a material's "further use *is not identical* to [its] initial use" implies the Agency intended to create a distinction between certain types of reuse. In fact, had the EPA intended, as Howmet insists, to allow *any* reuse that is a "normal use" of a material, its clarification of situations where "the further use is not identical to the initial use" would have been superfluous.

2.   *RCRA's overall purpose*

In addition to being inconsistent with the regulatory history of the EPA's "spent material" definition, we find Howmet's position to be incompatible with the overall thrust of RCRA and its implementing regulations. Congress described the national policy objective of RCRA as, wherever feasible, reducing or eliminating "the generation of hazardous waste." 42 U.S.C. § 6902(b). "Waste that is nevertheless generated should be treated, stored, or disposed of so as to minimize the present and future threat to human health and the environment." *Id.* Congress recognized that "disposal of solid waste and hazardous waste in or on the land without careful planning and management can present a danger to human health and the environment." *Id.* § 6901(b)(2). Moreover, Congress acknowledged that materials being reused and recycled "can indeed be solid and hazardous wastes and that these various recycling activities may constitute hazardous waste treatment, storage, or disposal." H.R.REP. NO. 98–198(I), at 46 (1983), *reprinted in* 1984 U.S.C.C.A.N. 5576, 5605. Congress thus conceded that certain recycled materials must be regulated in order to further its overall goal of "protect[ing] human health and the environment." *Id.*

Consistent with Congress's guidance, the EPA's regulations recognize that recyclable materials, if not managed properly, may present significant risks to public health and the environment. Congress and the EPA have also indicated their concerns are heightened when materials and applications applied to the land are involved. *See* 48 Fed. Reg. at 14,474 * * *.

Under the EPA's regulations, certain recycled materials are not treated as solid wastes when "[u]sed or reused as ingredients in an industrial process to make a product, provided the materials are not being reclaimed" or "[u]sed or reused as effective substitutes for commercial products." 40 C.F.R. § 261.2(e)(1)(i), (ii). However, "[m]aterials used in a manner constituting disposal, or used to produce products that are applied to the land," *id*. § 261.2(e)(2)(i), are treated as solid wastes, regardless, "even if the recycling involves use, reuse, or return to the original process," *id*. § 261.2(e)(2). Accordingly, when a material has become contaminated, and a party seeks to use the contaminated material for a purpose substantially different from its original use by applying it to the land, the party seeking to reuse the material has an obligation to examine the material, disclose its hazardous characteristics, and treat it as a hazardous waste. Fertilizer is indisputably a product "applied to the land." Thus, the shipment of a corrosive material such as used KOH to be used to produce fertilizer appears to be the type of activity the EPA sought to regulate under RCRA.

Having determined the Agency's interpretation is reasonable, we need not evaluate the reasonableness of Howmet's proposed interpretation. Once it is established that an agency has adopted a reasonable interpretation of an ambiguous regulation, the agency's interpretation stands even if a regulated entity has proposed an interpretation that might comport with the statutory scheme equally well or even better.

[Eds.: Judge Kavanaugh's dissent is omitted.]

NOTES

1.   The decision in *Sierra Club v. EPA*, 755 F.3d 968 (D.C. Cir. 2014), suggests further refinement of the D.C. Circuit's approach to the definition of solid waste. The court struck down an EPA rule that exempted from RCRA "certain hazardous residuals left over from the petroleum refining process," *id*. at 970, when those residuals were reused at the same facility to produce fuel. EPA justified its rule as an application of the principle that material immediately reused in the same manufacturing process is not solid waste. In vacating the rule, the court explained that the *AMC I* decision related to the "general definitional section pertaining to 'solid waste,'" and not other provisions identifying hazardous waste for regulation. *Id*. at 979. The court

viewed RCRA's mandate that EPA regulate all facilities producing fuels from characteristic or listed hazardous waste, 42 U.S.C. § 6924(q), as making the general solid waste definition inapplicable. Because, in the court's view, the residuals were indisputably characteristic or listed hazardous waste, EPA could not exempt them from RCRA. How does this view of RCRA comport with the general approach taken by EPA and the courts that require a material to be both a solid waste and a hazardous waste before it is subject to regulation?

2.   As you read the checklist excerpted above, you may have wondered who uses this document, and how. Its primary users are state and federal agency staff members who inspect hazardous waste generators, transporters, and treat, storage, and disposal facilities (TSDFs) to ensure compliance with RCRA. RCRA requires "any person who generates, stores, treats, transports, disposes of, or otherwise handles or has handled hazardous waste" to allow EPA or state officials "to enter at reasonable times any establishment or other place where hazardous waste are or have been generated, stored, treated, disposed of, or transported from," 42 U.S.C. § 6927(a), and requires an inspection of every TSDF at least every two years. *Id.* § 6927(e)(1). Regional offices of EPA and states with delegated authority to implement RCRA develop and implement plans governing inspections of generators and transporters. The checklist reproduced above is designed to assist state or federal inspectors in carrying out their duties during inspections.

3.   You may also have wondered, how much legal force does the checklist hold? The checklist is non-binding and the document is not regulatory in nature. Nevertheless, such documents promote standardization among inspectors and also provide information about the facts the agency views as important. Checklists like this one are also of considerable value to those subject to inspections. Private business can use documents like the checklist to detect problems at their own facilities. Businesses often audit their own RCRA compliance, and savvy general counsel will use all of the materials that EPA provides to the public to inform those audits, and to identify and rectify potential violations before EPA inspectors show up.

B. DEFINITION OF HAZARDOUS WASTE

Even if a material is a *solid* waste, it must also be a *hazardous* waste to be subject to RCRA. Determining whether waste is hazardous can sometimes be a technical process, which requires the skills of engineers and scientists as much as it demands legal analysis. But legal questions do arise.

Section 3001 of RCRA required EPA to "develop and promulgate criteria for identifying the characteristics of hazardous waste, and for listing hazardous waste." 42 U.S.C. § 6921(a). By regulation, EPA has developed two approaches to defining hazardous waste—one categorical in nature, and one that requires case-by-case analysis. First, EPA specially lists certain wastes as hazardous waste. Wastes that fall within these listed categories are always considered listed hazardous waste. Second, EPA has identified criteria to evaluate four characteristics of waste: ignitability, corrosivity, reactivity, and toxicity. If a waste satisfies the criteria specified by the regulation, then the waste is characteristic hazardous waste. Making that determination will often require testing.

With a few exceptions, RCRA requires any entity that "generates a solid waste" to "determine if that waste is a hazardous waste." 40 C.F.R. § 262.11. (One of those exceptions is for household waste, so you are not legally obliged to test the trash from your home.)

Data provided in EPA's 2011 RCRA Hazardous Waste Report indicate that 58% of hazardous waste was classified as hazardous solely based on its characteristics. Of that waste, nearly sixty percent exhibited more than one characteristic that would require the waste to be treated as hazardous. Listed wastes are somewhat rarer. Only 12% of hazardous waste was classified solely because it constituted a listed waste, and an additional 30% of waste was qualified as both characteristic and listed waste.

1.   LISTED HAZARDOUS WASTE

EPA has listed wastes in several ways.

- F-List wastes contain specific *substances*. 40 C.F.R. § 261.31(a). For example, F001 waste includes certain "spent halogenated solvents used in degreasing," such as trichloroethylene. Waste containing trichloroethylene is, therefore, a listed hazardous waste when that chemical is used for degreasing by entities in any industry.

- K-List wastes are produced by certain *processes*. 40 C.F.R. § 261.32(a). For example, K001 waste includes "[b]ottom sediment sludge from the treatment of wastewaters from wood preserving processes that use creosote and/or pentachlorophenol." The sludge resulting from identified wood preservation processes is thus a K-List hazardous waste, but sludge of identical chemical composition would not be so listed if produced through an alternative process (although it might fall within another listed category or constitute characteristic waste).

- P-List and U-List wastes identify discarded commercial chemical products that are listed wastes. For example, P003 waste consists of any discarded quantity of the chemical acrolein.

2.   CHARACTERISTIC HAZARDOUS WASTE

Wastes that do not fall within one of the categories EPA has designated as listed hazardous waste may still be hazardous waste if they exhibit one of four characteristics that EPA identified in its regulations. 40 C.F.R. §§ 261.20–24. These characteristics are as follows:

> A standard method for determining whether something qualifies as a characteristic hazardous waste for toxicity is the *toxicity characteristic leaching potential (TCLP) test*. To run the TCLP test, an acid solution is dripped through a sample of the substance (much like hot water being dripped through coffee grounds), and the composition of the liquid is then measured. The test is designed to simulate, in accelerated form, the effects of precipitation filtering through a landfill. *See* U.S. E.P.A., *Method 1311: Toxicity Characteristic Leaching Procedure* (1992).

- *Ignitability.* Ignitable wastes pose a risk of fire under certain conditions. These wastes are defined by the technical specifications listed in the regulation. Among other things, a waste will generally be characteristic for ignitability if it has a flash point of less than 140° F or is spontaneously combustible. 40 C.F.R. § 261.21.

- *Corrosivity.* Corrosive wastes have a pH less than or equal to 2 or greater than or equal to 12.5. These levels are designed to identify acidic and basic wastes that would threaten to corrode metal containers that might be used to store them. 40 C.F.R. § 261.22.

- *Reactivity.* Reactive wastes are those that are "unstable" under ordinary conditions or when mixed with water. This includes wastes that may explode or release toxic gases. 40 C.F.R. § 261.23.

- *Toxicity.* Toxic wastes are those that contain more than a certain amount of any of forty chemicals known to be harmful to human health. Each chemical has a specified regulatory level, and any waste containing more than the regulatory level is characteristic for toxicity. For example, wastes containing more than 5 mg/L of arsenic or 1 mg/L of selenium are toxic characteristic wastes. 40 C.F.R § 261.24.

3.   DESIGNATING A LISTED HAZARDOUS WASTE

RCRA does not itself designate wastes as listed hazardous wastes. Instead, this is done by EPA through notice-and-comment rulemaking. There are three pathways that EPA can use to designate a waste as a listed hazardous waste. First, EPA may designate a waste as a listed hazardous waste if it exhibits a characteristic that would qualify it as a characteristic hazardous waste. 40 C.F.R. § 261.11(a)(1). For example, if EPA determines that a particular waste stream is too corrosive, it can designate that waste stream as a listed hazardous waste. Second, EPA may designate a waste as a listed hazardous waste if "[i]t has been found to be fatal to humans in low doses" or fatal to animals at certain other doses. 40 C.F.R. § 261.11(a)(2). These wastes are referred to as "acute hazardous wastes," and various provisions of RCRA impose particularly stringent requirements with respect to them. Third, EPA may designate a waste as a listed waste because it contains "toxic constituents" if the agency concludes, after considering eleven factors, that because of those toxic constituents waste "is capable of posing a substantial present or potential hazard to human health or the environment when improperly treated, stored, transported or disposed of, or otherwise managed." 40 C.F.R. § 261.11(a)(3).

4. DELISTING

The generator of a waste that otherwise qualifies as a listed hazardous waste may petition EPA to have its waste "delisted"—i.e. designated as a nonhazardous waste despite falling within a listed category. 40 C.F.R. § 260.22(a). The petitioner must demonstrate that its waste does not meet any of the criteria upon which EPA based its initial decision to list the waste and that there is no other basis for treating the waste as hazardous. *Id.* § 260.22(a)(1). So, for example, if EPA designated the waste stream from battery manufacturers as a listed hazardous waste because it generally contains toxic levels of heavy metals, a particular battery manufacturer could file a delisting petition. That petition would need to contain information demonstrating that the waste from that manufacturer contains only safe levels of heavy metals and is not otherwise toxic.

PROBLEM: UTILITY POLES, PART II

Assume that, after reviewing the materials associated with the first part of this problem, you have decided that the utility poles sent to the wood-chipping company are solid waste. EPA has sent a response to AUA expressing those views.

A second letter has now been routed to your desk:

Director
Office of Resource Conservation and Recovery
U.S. Environmental Protection Agency

Dear Director:

Thank you for responding to my earlier letter. I write again on behalf of the American Utility Alliance (AUA) to seek further guidance from EPA.

I am seeking EPA's concurrence with AUA's view that, even if used utility poles sent to wood-chipping facilities are solid waste, they are not hazardous waste. I do not believe used utility poles fall within either of the two listed waste types involving pentachlorophenol (PCP), which are F021 or F027, because the poles are neither waste from the production or manufacturing of PCP, nor are they discarded formulations of that chemical. Therefore, they could only be hazardous by virtue of being characteristic hazardous waste. TCLP results for new utility poles are generally around 150 mg/L of PCP, but over time PCP leaches out of the poles. Utility poles that have been in use for more than ten years generally produce TCLP results less than 100 mg/L PCP, and therefore are not characteristic hazardous wastes. Utility poles that are retired after less than ten years produce TCLP results over 100 mg/L of PCP when tested on their own. But they are not hazardous waste when reused to make wood chips because, through the wood chipping process, the material from the used poles mixes with other wood material and the resulting wood chips test at less than 100 mg/L of PCP.

I also seek EPA's concurrence with AUA's view that unused PCP that a company has decided not to use is not a hazardous waste so long as the company dilutes it with sufficient water so that the resulting mixture produces TCLP results of less than 100 mg/L of PCP.

I would appreciate a response at your earliest convenience.

Sincerely,

Partner at law firm

You have been asked to prepare a response for EPA. Your response should identify the potential wastes that exist in the processes described by the AUA letter and analyze whether they are properly characterized as hazardous waste. For purposes of this exercise, you can assume that wood chips constitute "products that are applied to or placed on the land" under the definition of solid waste.

RCRA § 1004, 42 U.S.C. § 6903. Definitions

(5) The term "hazardous waste" means a solid waste, or combination of solid wastes, which because of its quantity, concentration, or physical, chemical, or infectious characteristics may—

    (A)   cause, or significantly contribute to an increase in mortality or an increase in serious irreversible, or incapacitating reversible, illness; or

    (B)   pose a substantial present or potential hazard to human health or the environment when improperly treated, stored, transported, or disposed of, or otherwise managed. * * *

Most of the regulations you have read involve lots of words that describe legal obligations or processes. Some, like the regulatory provisions below, provide information in other formats. Here, that information is contained in tables. As you review these regulations, examine the definition of listed wastes F012 and F027 to determine if either unused PCP diluted with water, or the contaminated utility poles used to produce wood chips, qualify as listed wastes. If they do not, are they characteristic wastes for toxicity?

---

40 C.F.R. § 261.24. Toxicity characteristic

(b) A solid waste that exhibits the characteristic of toxicity has the EPA Hazardous Waste Number specified in Table 1 which corresponds to the toxic contaminant causing it to be hazardous.

TABLE 1—MAXIMUM CONCENTRATION OF CONTAMINANTS FOR THE TOXICITY CHARACTERISTIC

EPA HW No.[1]	Contaminant	CAS No.[2]	Regulatory Level (mg/L)
D004	Arsenic	7440-38-2	5.0
D005	Barium	7440-39-3	100.0
D018	Benzene	71-43-2	0.5
D006	Cadmium	7440-43-9	1.0
D019	Carbon tetrachloride	56-23-5	0.5
D020	Chlordane	57-74-9	0.03
D021	Chlorobenzene	108-90-7	100.0
D022	Chloroform	67-66-3	6.0
D007	Chromium	7440-47-3	5.0
D023	o-Cresol	95-48-7	[4]200.0
D024	m-Cresol	108-39-4	[4]200.0
D025	p-Cresol	106-44-5	[4]200.0
D026	Cresol		[4]200.0
D016	2,4-D	94-75-7	10.0
D027	1,4-Dichlorobenzene	106-46-7	7.5
D028	1,2-Dichloroethane	107-06-2	0.5
D029	1,1-Dichloroethylene	75-35-4	0.7
D030	2,4-Dinitrotoluene	121-14-2	[3]0.13
D012	Endrin	72-20-8	0.02
D031	Heptachlor (and its epoxide)	76-44-8	0.008
D032	Hexachlorobenzene	118-74-1	[3]0.13
D033	Hexachlorobutadiene	87-68-3	0.5
D034	Hexachloroethane	67-72-1	3.0
D008	Lead	7439-92-1	5.0
D013	Lindane	58-89-9	0.4
D009	Mercury	7439-97-6	0.2
D014	Methoxychlor	72-43-5	10.0
D035	Methyl ethyl ketone	78-93-3	200.0
D036	Nitrobenzene	98-95-3	2.0
D037	Pentachlorophenol	87-86-5	100.0
D038	Pyridine	110-86-1	[3]5.0
D010	Selenium	7782-49-2	1.0
D011	Silver	7440-22-4	5.0
D039	Tetrachloroethylene	127-18-4	0.7
D015	Toxaphene	8001-35-2	0.5
D040	Trichloroethylene	79-01-6	0.5
D041	2,4,5-Trichlorophenol	95-95-4	400.0
D042	2,4,6-Trichlorophenol	88-06-2	2.0
D017	2,4,5-TP (Silvex)	93-72-1	1.0
D043	Vinyl chloride	75-01-4	0.2

[1]Hazardous waste number.

[2]Chemical abstracts service number.

[3]Quantitation limit is greater than the calculated regulatory level. The quantitation limit therefore becomes the regulatory level.

[4]If o-, m-, and p-Cresol concentrations cannot be differentiated, the total cresol (D026) concentration is used. The regulatory level of total cresol is 200 mg/l.

40 C.F.R. § 261.31. Hazardous waste from non-specific sources

(a) The following solid wastes are listed hazardous wastes from non-specific sources unless they are excluded under §§ 260.20 and 260.22 and listed in appendix IX.

Industry and EPA hazardous waste No.	Hazardous waste	Hazard code
Generic:		
* * *		
F021	Wastes (except wastewater and spent carbon from hydrogen chloride purification) from the production or manufacturing use (as a reactant, chemical intermediate, or component in a formulating process) of pentachlorophenol, or of intermediates used to produce its derivatives	(H)
* * *		
F027	Discarded unused formulations containing tri-, tetra-, or pentachlorophenol or discarded unused formulations containing compounds derived from these chlorophenols. (This listing does not include formulations containing Hexachlorophene sythesized from prepurified 2,4,5-trichlorophenol as the sole component.)	(H)

In addition to rules governing specific kinds of listed wastes, EPA's rules also address wastes that are mixed with other materials. These rules are known as the Mixture and Derived-From Rules, and your research has revealed that they may be relevant to determining whether the company's waste streams qualify as hazardous waste. The regulatory section involved is lengthy and includes a series of cross-references that make it difficult to digest. It is codified at 40 C.F.R. § 261.3. Trying to make sense of the regulation, you have located the Federal Register notice that EPA published when it proposed the current incarnation of these rules. That notice provides an overview of the rules.

For purposes of your research, you need to understand whether the Mixture and Derived-From Rules apply to the various waste streams at issue. That analysis begins with the determination of whether the used utility poles or the left-over PCP are either characteristic hazardous wastes or listed hazardous wastes. How does that determination affect application of the Mixture and Derived-From Rules? Does that determination for the used utility poles and left-over PCP dictate whether the wood chips and PCP-water mixture are hazardous waste? Based on EPA's justification for the rules, does distinguishing between characteristic hazardous waste and listed hazardous waste make sense?

———————

Hazardous Waste Identification Rule (HWIR): Identification and Listing of Hazardous Wastes

64 Fed. Reg. 63,382, 63,385-90 (proposed Nov. 19, 1999)

Background

* * *

III. Why Is EPA Proposing To Retain the Mixture and Derived-From Rules?

A.   What Are the Mixture and Derived-From Rules?

The mixture and derived-from rules are a part of the RCRA regulations that define which wastes are considered to be hazardous and therefore subject to RCRA Subtitle C regulations. The mixture rule discussed in today's notice refers specifically to 40 CFR 261.3(a)(2)(iii) and (iv). Under the mixture rule, a solid waste becomes regulated as a hazardous waste if it is mixed with one or more listed hazardous wastes The derived-from rule discussed in today's notice refers specifically to 40 CFR 261.3(c)(2)(i). Under the derived-from rule, any solid waste generated from the treatment, storage, or disposal of a hazardous waste remains regulated as a hazardous waste. These derived-from wastes include wastes such as sludges, spill residues, ash, emission control dust, and leachate.

B.   What Is the Legal History of the Mixture and Derived-From Rules?

EPA promulgated the mixture and derived-from rules in 1980 as part of the comprehensive "cradle to grave" requirements for managing hazardous waste. 45 FR 33066 (May 19, 1980). Numerous industries that generate hazardous wastes challenged the 1980 mixture and derived-from rules in *Shell Oil Co. v. EPA*, 950 F. 2d 741 (D.C. Cir. 1991). In December 1991 the D.C. Circuit Court of Appeals vacated the rules because they had been promulgated without adequate notice and opportunity to comment. [Eds. We omit a the discussion of the history of the rule after the 1991 decision]

C.   Why Is EPA Proposing To Retain the Mixture and Derived-From Rules?

The mixture and derived-from rules are necessary to regulate hazardous wastes in a way that protects human health and the environment. Mixtures and residuals of hazardous waste represent a large and varied universe. Many hazardous wastes continue to be toxic after they have been mixed with other waste or have been treated. As explained below, without the mixture and derived-from rules, such wastes could easily escape coverage of RCRA Subtitle C regulations, while nevertheless posing risks to human health and the environment.

We believe that without the mixture and derived-from rules, some generators would alter their waste to the point it no longer meets the listing description without detoxifying, immobilizing, or otherwise actually treating the waste. For example, without a "mixture" rule, generators of hazardous wastes could escape regulatory requirements by mixing listed hazardous wastes with other hazardous wastes or nonhazardous solid wastes to create a "new" waste that arguably no longer meets the listing description, but continues to pose a serious hazard. Similarly, without a "derived-from" rule, hazardous waste generators could potentially evade regulation by minimally processing or managing a hazardous waste and claiming that the resulting residue is no longer the listed waste, despite the continued hazards of the residue. (See 57 Fed. Reg. 7628). It is therefore necessary for protection of human health and the environmental to capture mixtures and derivatives of listed hazardous waste in the universe of regulated hazardous wastes. A hazardous waste regulatory system that allowed hazardous waste to leave the system as soon as it was modified to any degree by being mixed or marginally treated would be ineffective and unworkable. Such a system could act as a disincentive to adequately treat, store and dispose of listed hazardous waste.

We know that mixtures and residuals of hazardous waste can be hazardous based on our experience in identifying and regulating hazardous waste. For example, during the listing process, we review data on specific waste streams generated from a number of industrial processes to determine whether these wastes would pose hazards to human health or the environment if mismanaged. Through the listing process, we have determined risks arising from the disposal of waste mixtures and derived-from wastes. Leachate generated from hazardous wastes is a particularly good example of residuals of hazardous wastes that contain toxic chemicals that can endanger environmental or human receptors. Our risk analyses have shown that multi-source leachate derived from hazardous waste landfills can contain very high concentrations of toxic organic compounds and metals. (Preliminary Data Summary for the Hazardous Waste Treatment Industry, EPA/OW, 1989). Other derived-from wastes that, because of their treatment process, can result in higher concentrations of chemicals (especially metals) than their parent wastes include wastewater treatment sludge and combustor ash. As a result of either wastewater treatment or combustion, the wastes would have their volumes greatly reduced, but could still contain the same amount of inorganic chemicals, thus resulting in a higher concentration of chemicals.

Our experience with delisting petitions also supports the need to regulate as hazardous mixtures and residuals of listed hazardous waste in order to protect human health and the environment. Generators can petition us under 40 CFR 260.22 to exclude a waste produced at a particular facility from the definition of hazardous waste. Such petitions must demonstrate that the waste does not meet any of the criteria for which it was listed nor has other attributes that might result in the waste being hazardous. As of March 27, 1995, we have denied or dismissed 139 of 809 (17%) of delisting petitions received. This estimate does not include 543 petitions (67% of the total) that were withdrawn (311), mooted (198) or referred to the State authority (34). The chief reason for denying or dismissing most of the 139 delisting petitions was failure by the petitioner to supply adequate information. However, in at least 13 cases, we denied delisting petitions for mixtures or residuals of listed waste because risk analyses indicated that the toxicity and leaching potential of hazardous chemicals in those wastes posed unacceptable risk to human health (see *Disposition of Delisting Petitions for Derived-From/Mixture Wastes,* U.S. EPA memorandum, 1992 and *Analysis of the Delisting Petition Data Management System,* U.S. EPA, September 1998). We have also identified damage cases associated with mixture and derived-from wastes. For example, there are Superfund sites that contain mixture and derived-from wastes (See 50 FR 658). In many cases, determining when the environmental damage occurs on a site is difficult, but we have identified at least nine sites that involve the mismanagement of mixture and derived-from wastes. (see "Releases of Hazardous Constituents Associated with Mixture and Derived-from Wastes," EPA 1999). These waste types are also associated with RCRA corrective actions where high concentrations of hazardous chemicals were found in the vicinity of units that contained a listed waste. (*Data on Mixture and Derived-from Wastes from Closures and Corrective Action at Hazardous Waste Management Facilities,* EPA, 1992).

In addition, through the development of the LDR program, we have considered the appropriateness and effectiveness of various hazardous waste treatment technologies. Treatments specified within the LDR regulations, promulgated under 40 CFR 268, are required for hazardous waste to be land disposed. However, technology-based treatment standards do not always equate with low risk. In addition, treatment that is not performed properly or is not fully optimized may result in residues that present some risk. Further discussion and examples of LDR treatment are presented in a background document entitled *Memorandum to the Docket from Larry Rosengrant Regarding Section 3004(m) of the Hazardous and Solid Waste Amendments,* U.S. EPA January 21, 1992. Since treatment standards are based on the limits of technology, residuals can still pose sufficient risk to warrant continued regulation under RCRA Subtitle C.

D.   Does EPA Have the Legal Authority To Retain the Mixture and Derived-From Rules?

We have had, and we continue to have the statutory and regulatory authority to promulgate the mixture and derived-from rules. The mixture and derived-from rules, particularly with the revisions proposed today, ensure that hazardous wastes that are mixed with other wastes or treated in some fashion do not escape regulation as long as they are reasonably likely to threaten human health and the environment. These rules retain jurisdiction over listed hazardous wastes and clarify that such wastes do not automatically exit the Subtitle C system when they are mixed or treated, however minimally.

The mixture and derived-from rules are valid exercises of our authority to list hazardous waste under section 3001 of RCRA. We have consistently interpreted section 3001(a) as providing EPA with flexibility in deciding whether to list or identify a waste as hazardous, that is to consider the need for regulation. Specifically, section 3001 requires that EPA, in determining whether to list a waste as hazardous waste, or to otherwise identify a waste as hazardous waste, decided whether a waste "should be subject to the requirements of Subtitle C." Hence, section 3001 authorizes us to determine when Subtitle C regulation is appropriate. The statute directs EPA to regulate hazardous waste generators (section 3002(a)), hazardous waste transporters (section 3003(a)), and hazardous waste treatment, storage, and disposal facilities (section 3004(a)) "as necessary to protect human health and the environment." By extension, the decision of when waste should be subject to the regulatory requirements of Subtitle C is essentially a question of whether regulatory controls promulgated under sections 3002–3004 are necessary to protect human health and the environment. We have therefore consistently interpreted section 3001 to give us broad flexibility in fashioning criteria for hazardous wastes to enter or exit the Subtitle C regulatory system. *See, Military Toxics Project v. EPA*, 146 F.3d 948, 958 (D.C. Cir. 1998).

EPA's 1980 criteria authorize the listing of classes of hazardous wastes when we have reason to believe that wastes in the class are typically or frequently hazardous. See 40 CFR 261.11(b). As discussed Section III.C. above, EPA has ample reasons for classifying mixtures and residuals of listed hazardous waste as hazardous wastes.

In addition to providing the context in which the determination of whether a waste "should be subject to the requirements of Subtitle C," sections 3002–3004 allow us to impose requirements on waste handlers until wastes have "cease[d] to pose a hazard to the public." *Shell Oil Co. v. EPA*, 959 F.2d 741, 754 (D.C. Cir. 1991). *See also Chemical Manufacturers Assoc. v. EPA*, 959 F.2d 158, 162–65 (D.C. Cir. 1990) (EPA may regulate the disposal of nonhazardous wastes in a hazardous waste impoundment under section 3004) and *Chemical Waste Management, Inc. v. EPA*, 976 F.2d 2, 8, 13–14 (D.C. Cir. 1992) (EPA may require further treatment of wastes under section 3004 even though they cease to exhibit a hazardous characteristic). * * *

NOTES

1.   When EPA first issued its Mixture and Derived-From Rules, it interpreted the rules as applying to environmental media—like groundwater or soil. This is sometimes referred to as the "contained in" policy—soil and groundwater containing hazardous waste are themselves hazardous waste. The D.C. Circuit upheld that interpretation in *Chemical Waste Management, Inc. v. EPA*, 869 F.2d 1526 (D.C. Cir. 1989). That interpretation is important because hazardous waste sites often contain large volumes of contaminated soil and groundwater. Managing that soil and groundwater as hazardous waste is costly, and owners of contaminated sites would generally prefer to avoid that expense. But managing contaminated soil and groundwater as hazardous waste can also prevent injuries to workers and environmental harms.

2.   Designation of a waste as a hazardous waste substantially increases the costs faced by those that handle that waste. In some circumstances, this may have perverse consequences. For example, batteries disposed by consumers are not hazardous waste under the household waste exclusion, but such batteries could be hazardous waste if collected by a store to facilitate more environmentally-friendly disposal. EPA has addressed this problem by identifying four "universal wastes" that are widely generated, and by creating special rules for those that wish to collect these wastes to facilitate better disposal. *See* 40 C.F.R. Part 273. These universal wastes include batteries, pesticides, mercury-containing equipment, and light bulbs. An entity collecting those wastes is subject to less stringent regulatory requirements than those that would otherwise apply under RCRA.

3.   Pharmaceuticals have posed a challenge under RCRA. Those materials may contain a variety of unique or rare compounds, including antibiotics, hormones, and other bioactive substances, that can significantly affect human health and the environment. And as the introductory chapter discussed, those substances are getting into the environment. A study by the U.S. Geological Survey in 1999 and 2000 found that 80% of 139 streams sampled contained pharmaceuticals. Dana W. Kolpin et al., USGS, *Pharmaceuticals, Hormones, and Other Organic Wastewater Contaminants in U.S. Streams, 1999–2000: A National Reconnaissance*, 36 ENVIRONMENTAL SCIENCE & TECHNOLOGY 1202 (2002). Despite the nearly ubiquitous presence of pharmaceuticals in the environment, and the potential for them to cause significant harm, EPA has done little to regulate these compounds under RCRA. In 1980, EPA identified 31 chemicals used in pharmaceuticals as qualifying as hazardous waste, but that list has never been updated, despite the fact that other federal agencies have identified more than 100 drugs as hazardous. In 2008, EPA proposed adding hazardous pharmaceuticals to the list of universal wastes, *see* 73 Fed. Reg. 73,520 (Dec. 2, 2008), but has since announced that it plans to pursue an alternative, as-of-yet unspecified, approach.

This lack of action has not gone unnoticed. In 2012, EPA's Office of Inspector General, an office within the agency charged with providing an independent assessment of the agency's activities, released a report criticizing EPA for failing to implement a process to identify and review pharmaceuticals that may qualify as hazardous waste. *See* EPA OFFICE OF INSPECTOR GENERAL, EPA INACTION IN IDENTIFYING HAZARDOUS WASTE PHARMACEUTICALS MAY RESULT IN UNSAFE DISPOSAL (2012). The report concludes:

> For more than 30 years, EPA has not used its RCRA authority to determine whether pharmaceuticals may qualify as hazardous waste. This may mean some drugs are disposed and managed in ways that are not safe for humans and the environment. EPA's belief that there is widespread noncompliance in the health care industry with RCRA hazardous waste regulations further compounds the potential risks to human health and the environment from unregulated HWPs [Hazardous Waste Pharmaceuticals]. In addition, the idle status of EPA's rule to improve management of HWPs, coupled with its primary reliance on "best management practices" to ensure human health and environmental protection, represent small steps in an environment where hundreds of pharmaceutical products are widely used throughout the nation. EPA has recently published its intent to develop another proposal to address the management of pharmaceutical wastes at health care facilities. Over 100 drugs have been identified by other federal agencies as hazardous pharmaceuticals, whereas EPA has identified 31 hazardous pharmaceutical compounds. If EPA's hazardous waste rules do not keep up with new drug development or ensure that regulated entities understand and comply with their obligations, uncertainties about human health and environmental risks from hazardous pharmaceuticals are likely to grow.

Id. at 9.

One challenging aspect of this problem is that many pharmaceuticals may enter the environment because of the actions of individual consumers. Since 1980, EPA has exempted household waste from RCRA by regulation. *See* 40 C.F.R. § 261.4(b)(1) (exempting "any material * * * derived from households (including single and multiple residences, hotels and motels [and others]"). It is hard to imagine how regulators could address the actions of individuals who dispose of their medications in the trash or down the drain— but perhaps you can come up with an idea.

IV. REGULATED ENTITIES

So far, we have considered *what* material RCRA regulates: hazardous waste. In this section, we will learn *who* is subject to regulation. We will also learn about some, although far from all, of the obligations that RCRA imposes on regulated entities.

As the introductory materials explained, RCRA imposes obligations on three types of entities: generators; transporters; and treatment, storage, and disposal facilities (TSDFs). Some of the obligations imposed by RCRA apply across categories. For example, RCRA requires the generator of a hazardous waste to create a hazardous waste manifest that must accompany the waste during transport and eventual treatment or disposal. Other requirements limit what can be done with hazardous waste by particular categories of entities. Perhaps most importantly, the RCRA amendments of 1984 prohibited any land disposal of a hazardous waste unless EPA has affirmatively authorized a particular form of such disposal.

A. GENERATORS

The RCRA regulatory framework begins when an entity generates a hazardous waste. While generators do not need to secure permits, they must comply with significant requirements related to the storage of such waste, to the process of transferring that waste to transporters, and to ensuring that waste ultimately reaches a licensed TSDF.

RCRA regulations identify three classes of generators based on the amount of hazardous waste generated—large-quantity generators, small-quantity generators, and conditionally exempt small-quantity generators—and impose decreasingly stringent requirements on those categories. Conditionally exempt small-quantity generators produce up to 100 kg of hazardous waste a month and may have up to 1000 kg of hazardous waste stored on-site at any one time. Small-quantity generators produce between 100 kg and 1000 kg of hazardous waste a month and may have up to 6000 kg of hazardous waste stored on-site at any one time. Large-quantity generators produce more than 1000 kg of hazardous waste a month. These quantity thresholds are calculated anew each calendar month, so that a generator could be a conditionally exempt small-quantity generator one month and a large generator the next month, entirely depending on the volume of hazardous waste generated during the relevant timeframe. Conditionally exempt small-quantity generators are, as their designation suggests, exempt from many—but not all—of the requirements that apply to generators. Small-quantity generators are subject to most of the same general types of requirements that apply to large-quantity generators, although sometimes the requirements for them are less stringent.

Generators are subject to an array of requirements. Some of the most important are:

- *Storage, Labeling, and Training.* To avoid accidental releases of waste, and to minimize the risks associated with any releases that do occur, generators must label their wastes. They also face a variety of requirements related to storage, including requirements that waste storage areas have secondary containment—that is, an additional level of containment in case the primary container leaks—and that incompatible wastes be kept separate. Personnel who work with hazardous wastes also must receive specialized training.

- *Hazardous Waste Determination.* EPA's regulations require that any "person who generates a solid waste * * * must determine if that waste is a hazardous waste." 40 C.F.R. § 262.11. The regulations identify three primary steps in carrying out such a hazardous waste determination. First, a generator of solid waste must determine if it has produced a waste exempt from regulation. Second, the generator must determine if it has produced a listed waste. And third, if the waste is not listed or is listed and destined for land disposal, the generator must determine whether the waste is a characteristic waste.

- *Use of Properly Licensed TSDF.* To avoid improper disposal of hazardous waste that could endanger the public or the environment, RCRA requires large-quantity generators and small-quantity generators to dispose of their hazardous waste at a permitted TSDF, although in some circumstances (not discussed here) generators may treat hazardous waste themselves. *See* 40 C.F.R. § 262.20(a)–(c). Sending waste to a TSDF can be quite expensive, and EPA's regulations allow conditionally-exempt small-quantity generators to dispose of their waste at either TSDFs or some municipal solid waste facilities. *See id.* § 261.5(f)(3), (g)(3).

- *Accumulation Before Disposal or Treatment.* A generator may have significant economic incentive to accumulate waste before sending it to a TSDF, both because such accumulation will delay having to pay for disposal or treatment and because the generator may reduce its cost by shipping and arranging for treatment or disposal of fewer batches of larger volumes of waste. At the extreme, were there no limits, a generator could potentially evade regulation by simply keeping hazardous waste on site permanently. Prolonged storage can also increase the risk of releases or accidents, particularly for wastes that deteriorate over time or are corrosive. For these reasons, RCRA limits storage times. *See* 40 C.F.R. §§ 262.34(a)–(d). Waste can also only be accumulated for so long. Large-quantity generators may only accumulate hazardous waste for 90 days, *id.* § 262.34(b), while small-quantity generators may do so for 180 days, although the regulations provide a longer time period for small-quantity generators that have to ship waste long distances, *id.* §§ 262.34(d)(2)–(3).

- *Identification Number.* EPA and authorized state agencies must keep track of the many entities that are involved in the generation, transportation, and disposal of hazardous waste. EPA's regulations therefore require small-quantity and large-quantity generators (along with transporters and TSDFs) to obtain an EPA-issued identification number. *See* 40 C.F.R § 262.12.

- *Manifest Requirement.* EPA and authorized state agencies also track hazardous waste to ensure that if problems arise, waste can be tracked back to its source. To accomplish that task, small-quantity and large-quantity generators must create a manifest to track their waste. *See* 40 C.F.R. §§ 262.20–.27. The manifest is a single paper form with multiple copies that identifies and characterizes the waste, provides handling instructions, and includes a signature line for all parties involved in the disposal process. It also includes the identification number for the various entities that encounter the hazardous waste. The generator, any transporter, and the TSDF each retain a copy of the manifest, and the TSDF returns a final copy to the generator once it has received the waste.[2]

- *Waste Minimization.* RCRA also aims to reduce the amount of hazardous waste that is created. To achieve that goal, small-quantity and large-quantity generators must try to minimize the amount of hazardous waste they generate. This requirement is imposed under the manifest system; generators must certify that they have undertaken the required steps when signing a manifest. Small-quantity generators must only engage in good faith effort to engage

---

[2]   In 2012, Congress enacted the Hazardous Waste Electronic Manifest Establishment Act to require EPA to develop digital manifests that regulated entities could voluntarily use as a replacement to the paper forms. Pub. L. No. 112–195, 126 Stat. 1452 (Oct. 5, 2012) (codified at 42 U.S.C. § 6939g). EPA promulgated a final rule authorizing voluntary use of an electronic manifest in 2014, but that rule only authorizes use of a system that EPA will eventually create. 79 Fed. Reg. 7518 (Feb. 7, 2014). Due in part to a lack of congressionally appropriated funds, the e-manifest system is not yet available. EPA maintains a website tracking the development of the system at https://www.epa.gov/hwgenerators/hazardous-waste-electronic-manifest-system-e-manifest.

in waste minimization, while large-quantity generators must have implemented a program to "reduce the volume and toxicity of waste generated to the degree" the generator has determined is economically practicable. 40 C.F.R. § 262.27.

- *Record Keeping and Reporting.* Small-quantity and large-quantity generators must keep records of hazardous waste determinations, including any test results used to make such determinations, and must maintain copies of manifests. *See* 40 C.F.R. § 262.40. Large-quantity generators must also submit a biannual report to either EPA or an authorized state agency providing information about the volume and nature of hazardous waste they have generated. *Id.* § 262.41.

- *Closure Requirements.* Large-quantity generators must develop plans to govern closure of their facilities and must properly dispose or decontaminate all equipment, structures, and soils associated with their facilities. *See* 40 C.F.R. §§ 265.111(a), 265.114.

PROBLEM: RESTORATION PAINTS

You are general counsel for Restoration Paints, a boutique paint company that produces interior house paint for high-end residential construction. The company purchases dyes of various colors, mixes those dyes, and adds an adhesive. The resulting paint is sold to a few general contractors in 100 gallon drums. Inevitably, some of the dyes are improperly mixed and the resulting paint is sent to a landfill.

You receive the following email:

To: General Counsel
Subject: Cadmium in Red Paint
From: CEO

Hi,

I think we may have a small problem and I'm trying to figure out how we should proceed. We just received a shipment of red dye from the usual manufacturer. For the first time ever, a notice was affixed to the container that says that the dye "contains 10 mg/L cadmium." I called the company and they told me the dye has always contained cadmium, they've just recently started reporting that on the label. I'm shocked! I've been in the paint industry twenty years and I thought the industry standard was non-toxic paint these days.

Unfortunately, we make some of our best-selling paint using this dye and I would like to keep using it if we can. But I need to know what this means for us. I looked in the records for those hazardous waste determinations forms you make me fill out, and over the last year, we've sent 150 kg of paint to the landfill each month that contained at least some of the red dye. I wrote on the form that I was determining that the waste wasn't hazardous based on my knowledge of the paint industry.

Did we violate the law by sending that paint to the landfill? More importantly, now that we know there is cadmium in the red dye, how should we determine whether waste paint is hazardous moving forward?

If you could get back to me on this quickly, I'd appreciate it.

    CEO

Use the materials below to answer the questions posed by the CEO.

---

40 C.F.R. § 262.11. Hazardous waste determination

A person who generates a solid waste, as defined in 40 CFR 261.2, must determine if that waste is a hazardous waste using the following method:

(a) He should first determine if the waste is excluded from regulation under 40 CFR 261.4.

(b) He must then determine if the waste is listed as a hazardous waste in subpart D of 40 CFR part 261.

NOTE: Even if the waste is listed, the generator still has an opportunity under 40 CFR 260.22 to demonstrate to the Administrator that the waste from his particular facility or operation is not a hazardous waste.

(c) * * * the generator must then determine whether the waste is identified in subpart C of 40 CFR part 261 [which identifies characteristic wastes] by either:

    (1) Testing the waste according to the methods set forth in subpart C of 40 CFR part 261, or according to an equivalent method approved by the Administrator under 40 CFR 260.21; or

    (2) Applying knowledge of the hazard characteristic of the waste in light of the materials or the processes used. * * *

You've also come upon a decision by the Environmental Appeals Board (EAB), which is an appellate panel of administrative law judges within EPA. Proceedings before the EAB closely resemble judicial proceedings, and EAB's decisions are the final decision of the agency, unless the EPA Administrator personally reverses the decision. When courts review EAB decisions, they apply traditional administrative law deference principles, so environmental lawyers take the views of the EAB very seriously.

In re: Chem-Solv, Inc., Formerly Trading as Chemicals and Solvents, Inc. and Austin Holdings-Va, LLC

Environmental Appeals Board (2015)

Leslye M. Fraser and Randolph L. Hill

FINAL DECISION AND ORDER

* * * III. *SUMMARY OF RELEVANT FACTS*

Chem-Solv operates a chemical blending and distribution facility located in Roanoke. Jamison Glenn Austin was Chem-Solv's vice president and general manager at all times relevant to this case. Chem-Solv primarily purchases unblended substances from producers or wholesalers and then resells these substances to customers, either directly or after repackaging. Chem-Solv also blends substances to make products meeting customer requests. The facility is approximately four acres in size and is spread over several parcels of land. The violations alleged in this case are focused primarily on a relatively small area of the facility referred to as the "acid pad" and a 1,900-gallon subgrade tank collecting liquids from the acid pad, referred to as the "pit" or the "pit tank." The remaining violations concern a 55-gallon drum of sodium hydrosulfide and aerosol cans observed elsewhere at the facility.

Chem-Solv used the acid pad area to repackage and blend materials from bulk storage tanks. After filling drums with various chemicals, the lines from the bulk tanks were flushed to a drain on the floor of the acid pad and were collected in the pit tank. In addition, Chem-Solv placed the filled drums on the acid pad and washed the outside of the drums to remove chemical residue (including "incidental product drippage"), dirt, and debris before shipping them to customers. The waste liquids from this washing activity also flowed into the pit tank. Prior to 2000, Chem-Solv also rinsed the interior of drums on the acid pad. When liquid in the pit tank (referred to as "pit water") reached a certain level, Chem-Solv pumped the liquid into a nearby aboveground storage tank for temporary storage.

EPA and state inspectors from the Virginia Department of Environmental Quality ("VDEQ") inspected the facility on several occasions between 1999 and 2007.

On several occasions, EPA sought information from Chem-Solv concerning the source, composition, and disposition of the pit water and other materials. In responding to these information requests, Chem-Solv provided information concerning the shipment of pit water off-site.

In January 2008, Chem-Solv removed the contents of the pit tank and placed the material into 32 drums. In February 2008, Chem-Solv removed the pit tank itself and sent the drums containing waste from the pit tank, along with the 55-gallon drum of sodium hydrosulfide, to be disposed as hazardous waste at an off-site facility.

On March 31, 2011, the Region filed its complaint in this matter alleging that Chem-Solv owned and operated an unpermitted hazardous waste storage facility and had accumulated and stored hazardous materials, i.e., the pit water, pit sludge, and the 55-gallon drum of sodium hydrosulfide, in an unlawful manner. The complaint alleged further that Chem-Solv had failed to make hazardous waste determinations as required by 40 C.F.R. § 262.11. Chem-Solv alleged various defenses to these assertions. In particular, Chem-Solv asserted that the pit water was not a solid waste within the meaning of 40 C.F.R. § 261.2 because it was reused to rinse the exterior of drums and as a raw ingredient in the manufacture of FreezeCon, a "freeze conditioning agent" Chem-Solv sold to customers to apply to coal. Chem-Solv argued further that because the pit water was reused, it was exempt from regulation under 40 C.F.R. § 261.4(c) (manufacturing process unit exemption). With regard to the 55-gallon drum of sodium hydrosulfide, Chem-Solv asserted that the material was not a hazardous waste because it was a marketable product in Chem-Solv's inventory.

On June 5, 2014, the ALJ issued her initial decision finding Chem-Solv and Austin Holdings liable for the violations alleged in Counts I and III-VII of the complaint and Chem-Solv solely liable for the violation alleged in Count II of the complaint. In so doing, the ALJ rejected Chem-Solv's assertion that the pit water was not a solid waste because it was reused or recycled and concluded that the preponderance of the evidence showed that the material in the pit was simply accumulated until it was shipped offsite for disposal. Similarly, the ALJ rejected the assertion that the 55-gallon drum of sodium hydrosulfide observed at the facility was a useful product in inventory and therefore not a solid waste. Rather, the ALJ concluded that the preponderance of the evidence demonstrated that the 55-gallon drum was an abandoned material being accumulated and stored before or in lieu of disposal. Finally, the ALJ held that the Region had met its burden of establishing that Chem-Solv failed to perform the hazardous waste determinations (required by 40 C.F.R. § 262.11) for the pit materials, the 55-gallon drum of sodium hydrosulfide, and aerosol cans observed at the facility. As stated above, the ALJ assessed a civil penalty of $597,026.28 against Chem-Solv, Inc. and Austin Holdings-VA, LLC, jointly and severally, and an additional penalty of $15,312.50 against Chem-Solv, Inc., individually. This appeal followed.

After careful review of the record on appeal, the Board finds that the ALJ's determination is supported by a preponderance of evidence. Accordingly, the Board affirms the ALJ's Initial Decision in its entirety.

IV. *STANDARD OF REVIEW*

The Board reviews an administrative law judge's factual and legal conclusions on a *de novo* basis. *See* 40 C.F.R. § 22.30(f). However, as this Board has made clear, where, as here, an ALJ has had the opportunity to observe and evaluate witness testimony, the Board typically will grant considerable deference to the ALJ's determinations regarding witness credibility as well as any factual findings based thereon. *See In re Smith Farm Enters., LLC*, CWA Appeal No. 08–02, slip op. at 7 (EAB Mar. 16, 2011). The Board generally defers to an ALJ's factual findings when those findings rely on witness testimony and when the credibility of the witnesses is a factor in the ALJ's decisionmaking. *See In re Ocean State Asbestos Removal, Inc.*, 7 E.A.D. 522, 530 (EAB 1998).

V. *ANALYSIS* * * *

C. *The ALJ Did Not Err in Determining That Chem-Solv Failed to Make Required Waste Determinations*

Count II of the complaint alleged that from at least May 23, 2007, until February 1, 2008, Chem-Solv failed to perform a hazardous waste determination on the pit water, pit sludge, or discarded aerosol cans treated, stored, and/or disposed at the facility in violation of 40 C.F.R. § 262.11. This section requires that persons generating solid wastes determine whether or not the wastes are hazardous wastes. In making this determination, generators may engage in testing of the wastes or, in the alternative, apply their own "knowledge of the hazardous characteristics of the waste in light of the materials or the processes used." 40 C.F.R. § 262.11(c)(2). As the preamble to the regulation states, "[this] determination is the crucial, first step in the regulatory system, and the generator must undertake this responsibility seriously [and the determination] must be based on factors which are subject to objective review." Standards Applicable to Generators of Hazardous Waste, 45 Fed. Reg. 12,724, 12,727 (Feb. 26, 1980). *Generators must keep records of this determination, whether completed through testing or reliance on generator knowledge, and maintain these records for at least three years from the date the waste was shipped off-site for disposal. See* 40 C.F.R. § 262.40(c).

Chem-Solv argued before the ALJ that it performed the required waste determinations for the pit water and pit sludge. First, with regard to the pit water, Chem-Solv asserted that it had performed a waste determination using generator knowledge and concluded that the pit water was not a hazardous waste. Upon consideration of the evidence presented at the hearing, however, the ALJ found that Chem-Solv failed to produce any documentation, as required by 40 C.F.R. § 262.40(c), or testimony demonstrating that it performed the required waste determination. Chem-Solv does not dispute this finding on appeal.

Rather, Chem-Solv merely repeats its assertion that "it had no reason to believe that [the pit water] was hazardous." Because the record is devoid of any documentation establishing that Chem-Solv performed the required waste determination, as required by EPA regulations, either through testing or generator knowledge, the Board affirms the ALJ's determination. Moreover, as discussed above, the analytical results from samples of pit water collected during the May 23, 2007 inspection demonstrated that the pit water contained levels of chloroform above the regulatory threshold and was therefore a hazardous waste. Thus, if indeed Chem-Solv performed a hazardous waste determination of the pit water, that characterization was inaccurate or not representative of conditions in the pit at all times.[30] Under these circumstances, and given the lack of documentation relating to this alleged waste determination, the record does not support Chem-Solv's assertion that it conducted a waste determination in compliance with the requirements of 40 C.F.R. § 262.11.

Second, with regard to the pit sludge, Chem-Solv asserts that it believed the pit sludge was not hazardous based on testing performed in May of 2006 and on generator knowledge. In support of this assertion, Chem-Solv cites to a May 24, 2006 analytical report prepared on Chem-Solv's behalf by ProChem Analytical, Inc. That report indicated that the sampled material did not contain hazardous concentrations of trichloroethylene or tertrachloroethylene. The record, however, suggests that the material sampled by Pro-Chem in May of 2006 consisted not only of pit sludge, but of a combination of pit sludge and materials from a storm water drainage swale. Thus, the 2006 analysis is of little value and does not constitute an adequate waste determination. Further, as with the pit water, Chem-Solv has not provided any documentation that it conducted a waste determination based on generator knowledge. Under these circumstances, the Board agrees with the ALJ that Chem-Solv did not conduct a waste determination as required by 40 C.F.R. § 262.11.

---

[30] The Board notes that Chem-Solv states that it blends and packages chemicals in response to customer orders, and rinses off the outside of the filled drums to remove excess chemicals, dirt, and debris before shipping the drums to the customers. The rinse water from this washing operation flows into the pit. Given that it is unlikely that Chem-Solv prepared the same materials every day or every week, or the same amount of chemical, dirt, or debris would exist on every drum washed, or the same amount of water was used to wash every drum, it is implausible that Chem-Solv could believe that the concentration in the pit tank would remain constant. And given the different chemicals involved, it is also not improbable that chemical reactions from the materials in the rinse water could be occurring in the pit. These observations are supported by statements by Mr. Lester that periodically Chem-Solv would have to treat the pit water to adjust the pH, which could range from below 2.0 to above 12.5, before it could ship it for disposal. See Tr. I at 97–98 (Lohman); Appeal at 14 (stating that Chem-Solv employees adjusted the pH of the pit water prior to disposal). Thus, the Board does not find Chem-Solv's argument that it relied on generator knowledge to even be a reasonable attempt at complying with this regulatory obligation. The fact that the pit water changed in concentration and content has no bearing on the liability finding in this case, as a preponderance of the evidence in the record demonstrates that the pit water, pit sludge, and sodium hydrosulfide drums were hazardous wastes when analyzed.

Finally, in response to an information request letter from the Region seeking information about any waste determinations conducted on the aerosol cans, Chem-Solv's only response was "N/A." This response indicates that Chem-Solv did not perform a waste determination. Further, as with the pit water and pit sludge, the record does not contain any evidence that Chem-Solv conducted a hazardous waste determination in compliance with 40 C.F.R. § 262.11.

NOTE

Most generators have a good idea that they are producing hazardous waste. That has not always been true, however, for the retail sector—meaning businesses that sell goods to the public. EPA has recognized that the retail sector faces particular problems when it comes to managing hazardous waste: "The retail sector handles a large number of diverse product * * *, many of which may potentially become regulated as hazardous waste under RCRA when discarded. * * * [R]etailers are required to make numerous hazardous waste determinations at thousands of sites, generally by store employees with limited experience with the RCRA hazardous waste regulations." 79 Fed. Reg. 8,928 (Feb. 14, 2014). Since 2008, EPA has been considering whether to develop specialized rules that govern the applicability of RCRA to this sector and in 2014 issued a Notice of Data Availability to collect information to inform a potential rulemaking process. EPA maintains a website addressing this issue at http://www2.epa.gov/hwgenerators/hazardous-waste-management-and-retail-sector.

B. TRANSPORTERS

RCRA also sets standards for transporters of hazardous waste. These transporters also must comply with extensive regulation by the Department of Transportation (DOT) pursuant to the Hazardous Materials Transportation Act, 49 U.S.C. §§ 5101 *et seq.*, which regulates transportation of hazardous materials including hazardous waste. DOT's regulations for hazardous waste transport lie beyond the scope of this chapter, but they are extensive and, for transporters, important. Fortunately for transporters, EPA's regulations provide that a transporter who complies with all DOT regulations "will be deemed in compliance with" the RCRA transporter regulations, although EPA retains independent authority to enforce such regulations. 40 C.F.R. § 263.10 (note).

Like generators and TSDFs, transporters must properly use a hazardous waste manifest to track transportation of waste. *See* 40 C.F.R. § 263.20. They must also comply with various standards, largely established by DOT, governing transport itself. For example, transporters must use designated containers and must comply with all applicable routing restrictions. If any hazardous waste is discharged, a transporter must take immediate action to address the problem. *See id.* § 263.30. Like generators, transporters do not need a permit under RCRA, although depending on the nature of the hazardous waste, they may need a DOT-issued hazardous materials safety permit. Transporters must, however, obtain an EPA identification number. *Id.* § 263.11. During transportation, hazardous waste may be stored at a waste transfer facility for up to ten days—so long as it is stored in an appropriate container—without subjecting the transporter to regulation as a TSDF. *See id.* § 263.12.

PROBLEM: CHEMCO

You are an EPA inspector carrying out a routine inspection at Chemco, a chemical manufacturing company, which is a large quantity generator of hazardous waste. The company operates five chemical manufacturing plants on different properties within a 20-mile radius. The largest of the plants includes a waste storage building. Each day, the company brings waste from the other four plants to the waste storage building. The company stores all of its waste in the waste storage building until it is picked up by a licensed transporter and then brought to a licensed TSDF, which usually occurs about once a month. Assuming that the company is complying with the standards applicable to a large quantity generator, is it also subject to regulation as a transporter? If so, how long could Chemco store waste in the waste storage building without also becoming a TSDF? Is there a strategy you can recommend to Chemco that might reduce its regulatory burden while still complying with the applicable regulations?

---

40 C.F.R. § 260.10. Definitions

On-site means the same or geographically contiguous property which may be divided by public or private right-of-way, provided the entrance and exit between the properties is at a cross-roads intersection, and access is by crossing as opposed to going along, the right-of-way. Non-contiguous properties owned by the same person but connected by a right-of-way which he controls and to which the public does not have access, is also considered on-site property.

40 C.F.R. § 263.10. Scope

(a) These regulations establish standards which apply to persons transporting hazardous waste within the United States if the transportation requires a manifest under 40 CFR part 262.

(b) These regulations do not apply to on-site transportation of hazardous waste by generators or by owners or operators of permitted hazardous waste management facilities.

---

40 C.F.R. § 263.12. Transfer facility requirements

A transporter who stores manifested shipments of hazardous waste in [approved] containers * * * at a transfer facility for a period of ten days or less is not subject to regulation [as a TSDF] * * * with respect to the storage of those wastes.

40 C.F.R. § 263.30. Immediate action

(a) In the event of a discharge of hazardous waste during transportation, the transporter must take appropriate immediate action to protect human health and the environment (e.g., notify local authorities, dike the discharge area).

C. TREATMENT, STORAGE, AND DISPOSAL FACILITIES

RCRA reserves its most stringent level of regulation for treatment, storage, and disposal facilities (TSDFs). This makes sense because hazardous waste may reside at these facilities indefinitely. That waste could be released into the environment even decades after disposal, with dramatic consequences for the environment and public health.

Unlike other entities regulated by RCRA, TSDFs generally must have a permit issued by EPA, or by a state to which EPA has delegated RCRA authority. Regulations govern a range of TSDF characteristics, including facility design, treatment methods, the monitoring of soil and groundwater conditions at the site, the amount of funds set aside for eventual closure and remediation of a facility, and cleanup of contamination discovered while a facility remains operational.

Here we will look at some of the more significant requirements for TSDFs. We will pay particular attention to three questions often raised by RCRA's coverage of TSDFs.

- First, who qualifies as a TSDF? The distinction between generators and TSDFs is very important, because the regulatory requirements applicable to the former are different from and less stringent than the latter, but sometimes a generator can inadvertently turn itself into a TSDF by making a mistake in its handling of waste.

- Second, what methods can a TSDF use to treat waste? In a perfect world, TSDFs might turn every waste into useful raw materials or environmentally benign substances, but in the real world, that level of treatment is often impossible, or at least prohibitively expensive. EPA and TSDFs therefore have had to wrestle with what degrees and methods of cleanup are permissible. As the problem below illustrates, that question can be particularly difficult when the wastes in question would be generated by attempts to clean up a site that otherwise would remain contaminated.

- Third, what are the implications of the "land disposal restrictions," or LDR, that Congress enacted in the 1984 amendments to RCRA?

The excerpt below is from an EPA document written to provide a general overview of the requirements for TSDFs. This background information will provide you context for the problem that will follow.

Training Module, Introduction to Treatment, Storage and Disposal Facilities
EPA (Sept. 2005)

1. INTRODUCTION

The final link in RCRA's cradle-to-grave concept is the treatment, storage, and disposal facility (TSDF) that follows the generator and transporter in the chain of waste management activities. The regulations pertaining to TSDFs are more stringent than those that apply to generators or transporters. They include general facility standards as well as unit-specific design and operating criteria. The general facility standards consist of good housekeeping provisions for any facility that handles hazardous waste. The unit-specific technical requirements are designed to prevent the release of hazardous waste into the environment. The regulations also address the different types of hazardous waste units available to treatment, storage, and disposal facilities.

This training module presents an overview of the general TSDF standards found in 40 CFR Part 264/265, Subparts A through E. The unit-specific standards will be addressed in other training sessions. * * *

2. REGULATORY SUMMARY

RCRA § 3004 requires that EPA develop standards for both existing TSDFs that were immediately subject to regulation at the time the statute was enacted and for facilities that would be built after regulations were established. Congress also mandated that the standards for both types of facilities should only be different where absolutely necessary. To make allowances for existing facilities that would not be able to comply with the full regulatory program immediately, EPA promulgated interim status standards in Part 265. New facilities, on the other hand, would be constructed after the regulations were promulgated, thus enabling these facilities to be designed and built to meet the standards EPA deemed necessary to protect human health and the environment. The standards for new facilities are found in Part 264. While the standards in Part 264 are more stringent than those in Part 265, the standards are nearly identical except in the limited circumstances where the standards for new facilities would be impracticable for existing facilities to implement immediately. * * *

Congress directed EPA to establish a system for issuing TSDFs permits (RCRA § 3005). * * * A permit is an authorization, license, or equivalent control document issued by EPA or an authorized state to implement the TSDF requirements. TSDF permits are facility-specific and are issued after a documentation and review process. Generators and transporters are not required to obtain permits for several reasons: they generally handle smaller amounts of waste for shorter periods of time and their operations are more changeable, which is not conducive to the long and detailed process of permitting. A TSDF, on the other hand, is a permanent facility in operation for the purpose of making a profit from waste management. * * *

2.1 APPLICABILITY: SUBPART A

With some exceptions, the Part 264/265 regulations apply to facilities that treat, store, and dispose of hazardous wastes. The terms "facility," "treat," "store," and "dispose" all have specific definitions found in § 260.10. A facility includes all contiguous land, structures, and appurtenances on or in the land used for treating, storing, or disposing of hazardous waste. A single facility may consist of several types or combinations of operational units. Treatment is defined as any method, technique, or process designed to change the physical, chemical, or biological character or composition of any hazardous waste so as to neutralize such waste, or so as to recover energy or material resources from the waste, or so as to render such waste non-hazardous, or less hazardous; safer to transport, store or dispose of; or amenable for recovery, amenable for storage, or reduced in volume. Storage is defined as holding hazardous waste for a temporary period, at the end of which the hazardous waste is treated, disposed of, or stored elsewhere. Disposal is the discharge, deposit, injection, dumping, spilling, leaking, or placing of any solid or hazardous waste on or in the land or water. A disposal facility is any site where hazardous waste is intentionally placed and at which the waste will remain after closure. If an area meeting the definition of a facility is engaged in treatment, storage, and/or disposal, it must be in compliance with the standards under Part 264/265.

TSDF is a term of convenience, grouping all such facilities together for the purpose of discussing the regulations. In practice, there are storage facilities, treatment and disposal facilities, and every other combination possible. A facility becomes subject to Part 264/265 if it chooses to perform any of these three regulated activities. * * *

2.2 GENERAL FACILITY STANDARDS: SUBPART B

If a TSDF is not exempt, the owner and operator must comply with the requirements in Part 264/265. The general facility standards cover a variety of good housekeeping requirements that are required for any non-exempt TSDF. These provisions include recordkeeping requirements, personnel training requirements, and other safety requirements. Most of the standards are the same for permitted and interim status facilities, but notations are made where they are different.

IDENTIFICATION NUMBER

All TSDF owners and operators must obtain site-specific EPA identification numbers (§ 264/265.11).

WASTE ANALYSIS

TSDFs need to verify the composition (i.e., hazardous constituents and characteristics) of incoming waste in order to treat, store, or dispose of the waste properly. A waste analysis plan (WAP) outlines the verification procedures, including specific sampling methods, necessary to ensure proper treatment, storage, or disposal (§ 264/265.13). The WAP must be written and kept on site. * * *

INSPECTION REQUIREMENTS

The owner or operator must visually inspect the facility for malfunction, deterioration, operator errors, and discharges (§ 264/265.15). The inspection provisions are carried out according to a written inspection schedule that is developed and followed by the owner or operator and kept at the facility. The schedule must identify the types of problems to be looked for, and set the frequency of inspection, which may vary. Areas subject to spills, such as loading and unloading areas, must be inspected daily when in use. Unit-specific inspections or requirements also must be included in the schedule (e.g., § 265.226 for surface impoundments). The owner or operator must record inspections in a log or summary, and must remedy any problems identified during inspections. The records must include the date and time of inspection, the name of the inspector, notation of observations, and the date and nature of any necessary repairs or other remedial actions, and must be kept at the facility for three years. * * *

LOCATION STANDARDS

As mentioned earlier, the location standards differ between new and existing facilities. The location standards for new facilities provided in § 264.18 place restrictions on siting new facilities, including restrictions on locating TSDFs in floodplains or earthquake-sensitive areas. Existing facilities are not subject to the floodplains and seismic considerations because the facilities are already in operation.

Both interim status and permitted TSDFs may not place noncontainerized or bulk liquid hazardous waste in a salt dome, salt bed formation, or underground mine or cave. Congress has granted one exception to this rule: the Department of Energy's Waste Isolation Pilot Project (WIPP) in New Mexico (§§ 264.18(c)/265.18).

CONSTRUCTION QUALITY ASSURANCE

Interim status and permitted landfills, waste piles, and surface impoundments are required to implement a construction quality assurance (CQA) program pursuant to § 264/265.19. The CQA program ensures that all design criteria are met during the construction of a unit. A written CQA plan is required, and the CQA officer (i.e., a registered professional engineer) must certify that the unit meets all design criteria and permit specifications before waste can be received in the unit.

2.3 PREPAREDNESS AND PREVENTION: SUBPART C

The preparedness and prevention standards are intended to minimize and prevent emergency situations at TSDFs. Facilities must be operated and maintained in a manner that minimizes the possibility of a fire, explosion, or any unplanned sudden or nonsudden release of hazardous waste or hazardous waste constituents to air, soil, or surface water. The regulations require maintenance of equipment, alarms, minimum aisle space, and provisions for contacting local authorities. Specifically, § 264/265.32 mandates that a facility must have an internal communication or alarm system, a phone or radio capable of summoning emergency assistance, fire-fighting equipment, and adequate water supply. Sections 264/265.33 and 264/265.34 require that this equipment be maintained and tested regularly, and that all personnel have access to an alarm system or emergency communication device. In addition, the facility must have aisle space that is sufficient to ensure easy movement of personnel and equipment unless the owner/operator demonstrates that it is unnecessary (§ 264/265.35).

Facilities must also have provisions for contacting local authorities that might be involved in emergency responses at the facility. The local authorities must be familiar with the facility and properties of the hazardous waste(s) handled at the facility (§ 264/265.37). Local authorities include police, fire department, hospitals, and emergency response teams. Where more than one local authority is involved, a lead authority must be designated. Where state or local authorities decline to enter into such arrangements, the owner and operator must document the refusal in the operating record (§ 264/265.37(b)).

2.4 CONTINGENCY PLAN AND EMERGENCY PROCEDURES: SUBPART D

Because even strict adherence to the Part 264/265 preparedness and prevention standards will not eliminate the possibility of an emergency situation, the Part 264/265, Subpart D regulations are designed to limit the extent of damage resulting from an emergency. These provisions help facilities respond to a fire, explosion, or any unplanned release of hazardous waste or hazardous constituents into the environment. Owners and operators must maintain contingency plans on site at all times and carry out these plans in the event of an actual emergency. * * *

2.5 MANIFEST SYSTEM, RECORDKEEPING, AND REPORTING: SUBPART E

The paperwork required by Part 264/265, Subpart E, is designed to track hazardous waste from cradle to grave. The manifest system tracks each shipment of hazardous waste while the operating record and Biennial Report summarize facility activity over time.

MANIFEST

TSDFs that accept waste from off site are the final signatories to the manifest. When a manifested waste shipment is received, all copies of the manifest are signed and dated by the facility owner or operator. The transporter and the TSDF keep signed copies of the manifest, and a copy is sent to the generator within 30 days to verify acceptance of the waste (§ 264/265.71). If the owner or operator of a TSDF sends the waste on to another TSDF for further treatment or disposal, a new manifest with a new designated facility must be initiated.

MANIFEST DISCREPANCIES

Manifest discrepancies include significant differences between the quantity or type of hazardous waste designated on the manifest and the quantity or type of hazardous waste that a facility actually receives; rejected wastes; and container residues. More specifically, significant differences are any discrepancies in weight (for bulk shipments, over 10 percent), piece count (for batch or containerized waste shipments, one container per truckload), or waste type. Upon discovering a significant difference in quantity or type, the owner or operator must try to reconcile the discrepancy with the generator or transporter. Any discrepancies not resolved within 15 days of waste receipt must be reported to the Regional Administrator with an explanatory letter and a copy of the manifest (§ 264/265.72). * * *

OPERATING RECORD

Until closure, the owner and operator are required to keep a written operating record on site describing all waste received, methods and dates of treatment, storage, and disposal, and the wastes' location within the facility as detailed in Appendix I of Part 264/265 (§ 264/265.73). All information should be cross-referenced with the manifest number. The operating record also must include waste analysis results, details of emergencies requiring contingency plan implementation, inspection results (for three years), groundwater monitoring data, land treatment and incineration monitoring data, and closure and post-closure cost estimates.

BIENNIAL REPORT

Biennial Reports must be filed with the Regional Administrator by March 1 of each even-numbered year, covering the facility's activities for the previous year (§ 264/265.75). For example, the Biennial Report covering 2003 activities would be due March 1, 2004. The facility owner or operator must send the report (Form 8700–13A/B) to its implementing agency (i.e., state or EPA region) and maintain a copy on site for three years. * * *

The EPA manual excerpt above omits two important issues. The first is closure. Hazardous waste may remain at disposal site in perpetuity, but that doesn't mean a TSDF will forever remain in business. As a condition of receiving a permit to operate, a TSDF must maintain a plan to govern the closure of the facility once it has reached the end of its operational life. 40 C.F.R. § 264.112. Closure is heavily regulated, and the plan must identify the means by which the facility will be closed so as to "minimiz[e] or eliminate[ ], to the extent necessary to protect human health and the environment, post-closure escape of hazardous waste." *Id.* § 264.111. In addition to preparing a closure plan, a TSDF must provide financial assurances, demonstrating that it has adequate financial resources to carry out the closure plan. *See id.* §§ 264.142–.146

Best Demonstrated Available Technology (BDAT): Many hazardous waste treatment standards are based on BDAT, which imposes a numerical standard for treatment based on the technology that best minimizes the mobility or toxicity of toxic constituents within a waste (or both). EPA has not promulgated a regulation expressly defining BDAT, but rather has incorporated the definition into treatment standards for specific hazardous wastes. EPA maintains documents identifying treatment standards based on BDAT at http://www3.epa.gov/epawaste/inforesources/pubs/bdat.htm.

Finally, TSDFs (and everyone else) are subject to special restrictions on land disposal of hazardous waste. These arise out of the 1984 amendments to RCRA, through which Congress created section 3004 to significantly limit land disposal. This section, sometimes referred to as LDR, differs from most other environmental laws. Rather than authorizing EPA to regulate if the agency believed it necessary, the LDR outright banned land disposal unless EPA affirmatively found that such a ban was *not* necessary to protect human health or the environment. EPA was also authorized to identify standards for treatment of hazardous waste to "substantially diminish" toxicity or "substantially reduce the likelihood of migration." 42 U.S.C. § 6924(m). Land disposal could occur only under the treatment standards issued under section 3004(m). In other words, the LDR created a presumption against land disposal that EPA could overcome by regulation. Regulated entities therefore wanted EPA to promulgate exception rules as quickly as possible, and EPA did indeed promulgate treatment standards for all classes of hazardous waste before the blanket land disposal prohibition came into force. EPA has interpreted its authority under section 3004(m) to authorize it to establish treatment standards based either on available technologies or on considerations related to risks that particular wastes pose to the environment, an approach that the D.C. Circuit upheld in *Hazardous Waste Treatment Council v. EPA*, 886 F.2d 355 (D.C. Cir. 1989). EPA has, however, issued technology-based standards, called the best demonstrated available technology (BDAT), for most toxic constituents found in hazardous waste.

When issuing those standards, EPA often faces a difficult challenge. Setting the standards at very strict levels can sometimes ensure high levels of treatment. But sometimes, high standards will encourage TSDFs to use alternative treatment technologies, like incineration, that might be more environmentally harmful than land disposal. And where hazardous waste already is in the land—for example, at abandoned hazardous waste sites—a stringent cleanup standard might actually discourage environmental remediation. That dilemma is at the heart of the problem below.

PROBLEM: ENVIRONMENTAL REHAB WORKS

You work in EPA's Office of Solid Waste and have been assigned to consider a petition for rulemaking filed by Environmental Rehab Works (ERW), a private, for-profit company. The petition asks EPA to issue a rule, under RCRA section 3004(m), adopting a new technology-based treatment standard for water in surface impoundments at contaminated sites.

ERW has filed this petition to advance its business model, which is to acquire, clean up, and sell abandoned industrial sites. That business model works so long as ERW can buy sites at a steep discount and then sell them for less than the cost of acquisition, financing, and cleanup. That will be easier to do, of course, if the cleanup costs are lower.

The sites ERW hopes to acquire and clean have remained in a contaminated state for years because their original owners are bankrupt and therefore can't be compelled to engage in cleanup under CERCLA—the statute we will cover in Chapter 6. Some of the industrial sites that ERW would like remediate have impoundments—in other words, small, artificial surface ponds—that are contaminated with heavy metals.

ERW's petition explains that complying with the current BDAT, which is the treatment standard EPA has adopted for water contaminated by each of the heavy metals at issue, would be costly because each constituent heavy metal could require a different treatment technology. Consequently, the petition asks the agency to authorize use of a technology known as the Universal Water Filtration System, or UWFS, to treat all contaminated surface waters containing heavy metals as an alternative to complying with BDAT. The petition contains the following information and arguments:

- UWFS removes approximately 95 percent of most heavy metals from contaminated water, although it only removes 80 percent of a few heavy metals.

- In most cases, water treated by UWFS would contain heavy metal concentrations less than ten times the Universal Treatment Standard (UTS). That level of cleanup—ten times the UTS—is the standard that most hazardous waste cleanup efforts must achieve.

- Authorizing UWFS as an alternative treatment standard would reduce the cost of treating contaminated water by two thirds.

> *Universal Treatment Standards* ("UTS"): For many hazardous constituents, EPA has established UTS, which are numeric standards that treatment should achieve before hazardous waste can be disposed. These UTS take the form of a concentration level; typically there is one for wastewater set in terms of milligrams per liter and a second for non-wastewater set in terms of milligrams per kilogram. *See* 40 C.F.R. § 268.48. Under UTS, a treatment for a hazardous waste containing acetone, for example, should result in material containing no more than 160 mg/kg of that substance.

- Water treated by UWFS would primarily be discharged into settling ponds and allowed to evaporate.

- Some water containing residual heavy metals could migrate from the settling ponds into groundwater. But the contaminated surface waters that ERW would like to remediate pose similar risks. Indeed, the degree of risk will depend largely on the locations of both existing and remedial ponds, and the care with which the remediation process is monitored.

- After evaporation occurs, remaining heavy metals would remain in the soil under the ponds. That soil would be collected and sent to a landfill under EPA's existing rule for contaminated soils. Sites would need to be monitored to ensure that the soil is removed before contamination levels exceed ten times the UTS.

- The majority of the sites that would make good candidates for remediation by ERW are located in neighborhoods that are disproportionately poor and disproportionately communities of color.

EPA has never approved an alternative treatment standard for contaminated water associated with environmental remediation, but as the materials below indicate, EPA has issued a rule for similar contaminated soils. A contaminated water rule would be a first for the agency, and you have been asked to make a recommendation to EPA on the petition. Assume that granting the petition will lead to more contaminated sites in socioeconomically disadvantaged communities and communities of color being cleaned up more quickly, but that after cleanup efforts are completed, such sites will remain more contaminated and will pose a greater threat to groundwater than they would be if EPA denies the petition—and if cleanup actually occurs. This recommendation will require you to both consider whether EPA has authority to approve an alternative treatment standard— in other words, does RCRA leave EPA discretion to grant the petition—but probably more importantly, whether doing so would be good policy. You also must consider whether to simply adopt or deny ERW's requested rule or, alternatively, to promulgate a rule that partially fulfills ERW's request. And answering all those questions will require you to consider whether granting the petition would advance or retard environmental justice—and how much your answer to that question matters.

Your discretion to grant or deny a rulemaking petition is always bounded by statutory terms, and the starting point of your analysis must be the statute itself. Keep in mind, as you read, the standard of review that would apply to any challenge to your statutory interpretation.

RCRA § 3004, 42 U.S.C. § 6924. Standards applicable to owners and operators of hazardous waste treatment, storage, and disposal facilities

(a) In general

[EPA shall establish] performance standards[ ] applicable to owners and operators of facilities for the treatment, storage, or disposal of hazardous waste * * * as may be necessary to protect human health and the environment. * * * Such standards shall include, but need not be limited to, requirements respecting—

(1) maintaining records * * * ;

(2) satisfactory reporting, monitoring, and inspection and compliance with the manifest system referred to in section 6922(5) of this title;

(3) treatment, storage, or disposal of all such waste received by the facility pursuant to such operating methods, techniques, and practices as may be satisfactory to the Administrator;

(4) the location, design, and construction of such hazardous waste treatment, disposal, or storage facilities;

(5) contingency plans for effective action to minimize unanticipated damage from any treatment, storage, or disposal of any such hazardous waste; * * *

(d) Prohibitions on land disposal of specified wastes

(1) Effective 32 months after November 8, 1984 * * *, the land disposal of the hazardous wastes referred to in paragraph (2) is prohibited unless the Administrator determines the prohibition on one or more methods of land disposal of such waste is not required in order to protect human health and the environment for as long as the waste remains hazardous, taking into account—

(A) the long-term uncertainties associated with land disposal,

(B) the goal of managing hazardous waste in an appropriate manner in the first instance, and

(C) the persistence, toxicity, mobility, and propensity to bioaccumulate of such hazardous wastes and their hazardous constituents.

For the purposes of this paragraph, a method of land disposal may not be determined to be protective of human health and the environment for a hazardous waste referred to in paragraph (2) (other than a hazardous waste which has complied with the pretreatment regulations promulgated under subsection (m) of this section), unless, upon application by an interested person, it has been demonstrated to the Administrator, to a reasonable degree of certainty, that there will be no migration of hazardous constituents from the disposal unit or injection zone for as long as the wastes remain hazardous. * * *

(k) "Land disposal" defined

For the purposes of this section, the term "land disposal", when used with respect to a specified hazardous waste, shall be deemed to include, but not be limited to, any placement of such hazardous waste in a landfill, surface impoundment, waste pile, injection well, land treatment facility, salt dome formation, salt bed formation, or underground mine or cave.

(m) Treatment standards for wastes subject to land disposal prohibition

(1) Simultaneously with the promulgation of regulations under subsection (d), (e), (f), or (g) of this section prohibiting one or more methods of land disposal of a particular hazardous waste, and as appropriate thereafter, the Administrator shall, after notice and an opportunity for hearings and after consultation with appropriate Federal and State agencies, promulgate regulations specifying those levels or methods of treatment, if any, which substantially diminish the toxicity of the waste or substantially reduce the likelihood of migration of hazardous constituents from the waste so that short-term and long-term threats to human health and the environment are minimized.

(2) If such hazardous waste has been treated to the level or by a method specified in regulations promulgated under this subsection, such waste or residue thereof shall not be subject to any prohibition promulgated under subsection (d), (e), (f), or (g) of this section and may be disposed of in a land disposal facility which meets the requirements of this subchapter. Any regulation promulgated under this subsection for a particular hazardous waste shall become effective on the same date as any applicable prohibition promulgated under subsection (d), (e), (f), or (g) of this section.

Your research quickly leads you to EPA's regulations for land disposal of treated contaminated soil. As you read the excerpt, bear in mind that these regulations are not binding legal authority for your present dilemma, for they govern soil contamination, not groundwater contamination. The regulations are relevant only to the extent that they provide a potential model—and non-binding precedent—for your regulatory approach to groundwater contamination.

40 C.F.R. § 268.49. Alternative LDR treatment standards for contaminated soil

(c) Treatment standards for contaminated soils. Prior to land disposal, contaminated soil * * * must be treated according to all the standards specified in this paragraph or according to the Universal Treatment Standards specified in 40 CFR 268.48 [Eds.: These are the generally applicable treatment standards].

(1) All soils. Prior to land disposal, all constituents subject to treatment must be treated as follows:

(A) For non-metals except carbon disulfide, cyclohexanone, and methanol, treatment must achieve 90 percent reduction in total

> constituent concentrations, except as provided by paragraph (c)(1)(C) of this section.
>
> (B) For metals and carbon disulfide, cyclohexanone, and methanol, treatment must achieve 90 percent reduction in constituent concentrations as measured in leachate from the treated media (tested according to the TCLP) or 90 percent reduction in total constituent concentrations (when a metal removal treatment technology is used), except as provided by paragraph (c)(1)(C) of this section.
>
> (C) When treatment of any constituent subject to treatment to a 90 percent reduction standard would result in a concentration less than 10 times the Universal Treatment Standard for that constituent, treatment to achieve constituent concentrations less than 10 times the universal treatment standard is not required.
> * * *
>
> (2) Soils that exhibit the characteristic of ignitability, corrosivity or reactivity. In addition to the treatment required by paragraph (c)(1) of this section, prior to land disposal, soils that exhibit the characteristic of ignitability, corrosivity, or reactivity must be treated to eliminate these characteristics.

Many regulations are easier to understand after you have read the preamble produced when they are promulgated, and that preamble also can explain policy considerations that might be relevant to future rulemaking decisions. An excerpt from the preamble for the soil treatment regulations therefore appears below.

Land Disposal Restrictions Phase IV

63 Fed. Reg. 28,556, 28,602-06 (May 26, 1998)

VII. LDR Treatment Standards for Soil

* * *

A. Application of Land Disposal Restriction Treatment Standards to Contaminated Soil and Justification for Soil Specific LDRs

Prior to today's rule, soil that contained listed hazardous waste or exhibited a characteristic of hazardous waste were prohibited from land disposal unless they had been treated to meet the treatment standards promulgated for pure industrial hazardous waste. This means the same treatment standards which apply to a pure, industrial hazardous waste were also applied to contaminated soil. 61 FR at 18804 (April 29, 1996) and other sources cited therein. In most cases then, contaminated soils were subject to the treatment standards listed in 40 CFR 268.40, and the associated treatment standards in 40 CFR 268.48(a) table Universal Treatment Standards (UTS).

As EPA has discussed many times, the treatment standards developed for pure, industrial hazardous waste may be unachievable in contaminated soil or may be inappropriate for contaminated soil due to particularities associated with the soil matrix and the remediation context under which most contaminated soil is managed, as discussed below. For that reason, EPA is promulgating today's LDR treatment standards specifically tailored to contaminated soil and to the remedial context.

With respect to the soil matrix, the treatment standards developed for pure hazardous waste (i.e., the universal treatment standards) are generally either technically unachievable or technically or environmentally inappropriate. * * *

Although EPA has data showing that some soils can be treated to the existing universal treatment standards for metals using stabilization and high temperature metals recovery, the Agency continues to believe that tailored soil treatment standards are appropriate for metal contaminated soil to ensure that the wide variety of soils can be effectively treated to meet the treatment standards. In addition, the soil treatment standards will have the added environmental benefit of encouraging greater use of innovative soil treatment technologies such as soil or enhanced soil (acid) washing. * * *

With respect to the remedial context, EPA, the states, and the regulated and environmental communities have long recognized that application of the LDR treatment standards developed for pure, industrial hazardous waste to contaminated soil can be counterproductive. * * * Application of LDRs developed for pure, industrial hazardous waste to contaminated soil often presents remediation project managers with only two choices: pursue a legal option of capping or treating hazardous contaminated soil in place thereby avoiding a duty to comply with LDRs, or excavate the soil and treat it to the full extent of best demonstrated available technology, usually, for organic constituents, incineration. EPA has found that this situation often creates an incentive to select remedies that minimize application of LDRs (e.g., remedies that involve capping or leaving untreated soil in place) a result obviously not contemplated by Congress in enacting the LDR program. * * *

Because of the differences between the remedial context (responding to wastes which have already been released to the environment) and regulation of wastes generated by on-going industrial process (preventing wastes from being released into the environment in the first instance), EPA has rejected the conclusion that treatment standards for soil must be based upon the performance of the "best" demonstrated available treatment technology in the way the Agency has historically interpreted these terms. Instead, the Agency has chosen to develop soil treatment standards that can be achieved using a variety of treatment technologies which achieve substantial reductions in concentration or mobility of hazardous constituents and, because they are generally used to treat contaminated soils in remedial settings, do not present site managers with the type of dilemma described above. As EPA has long maintained, the strong policy considerations that argue for using the traditional BDAT analysis as the basis for LDR treatment standards for hazardous wastes generated by on-going industrial operations do not apply when evaluating BDAT in the remedial context. In the remedial context, for example, waste minimization is not an issue and the additional increment of treatment necessary to achieve traditional BDAT may yield little if any environmental benefit over other treatment options that adequately protect human health and the environment. 54 FR 41568 (October 19, 1989). Indeed there is a legitimate question as to whether a technology whose use results in foregoing other substantial environmental benefits (such as more aggressive, permanent remedies) can be considered a "best" technology. *Portland Cement Association v. Ruckelshaus*, 486 F. 2d 375, 385–86 at n.42 (D.C. Cir. 1973); *Essex Chemical Corp. v. Ruckelshaus*, 486 F. 2d 427, 439 (D.C. Cir. 1973). This issue was discussed fully in the April 29, 1996 proposal and in a number of other EPA documents, see, for example, 54 FR 41568 (October 19, 1989) and 61 FR at 18808 (April 29, 1996) and other sources cited therein.

The soil treatment standards promulgated today will significantly improve management of contaminated soil and remediations that involve contaminated soil. However, the Agency emphasizes that today's rule does not resolve the larger, more fundamental issues associated with application of RCRA Subtitle C to remediation generally. The Agency maintains that additional reform is needed to address, more fundamentally, the application of certain RCRA subtitle C requirements to all remediation wastes, including contaminated soil. The Agency will continue to participate in discussions of potential legislation to promote this additional needed reform. If legislation is not forthcoming, the Agency may reexamine its approach to remediation waste management, including the soil treatment standards.

B.   Detailed Analysis of Soil Treatment Standards

All land disposal restriction treatment standards must satisfy the requirements of RCRA section 3004(m) by specifying levels or methods of treatment that "substantially diminish the toxicity of the waste or substantially reduce the likelihood of migration of hazardous constituents from that waste so that short-term and long-term threats to human health and the environment are minimized." As EPA has discussed many times, the RCRA Section 3004(m) requirements may be satisfied by technology-based standards or risk-based standards. * * * Today's treatment standards for contaminated soils are primarily technology-based; however, a variance from the technology-based standards is allowed when EPA or an authorized state makes a site-specific determination that threats posed by land disposal of any given volume of contaminated soil are minimized at higher concentrations.

1.   Technology Basis for Soil Treatment Standards

The land disposal restriction treatment standards for soil require that concentrations of hazardous constituents subject to treatment be reduced by ninety percent (90%) with treatment for any given constituent capped at ten times the universal treatment standard (10 × UTS). In other words, if treatment of a given constituent to meet the 90% reduction standard would reduce constituent concentrations to less than 10 × UTS, treatment to concentrations less than 10 × UTS is not required. This is commonly referred to as "90% capped by 10xUTS." * * *

For contaminated soil, the Agency has chosen to establish technology-based soil treatment standards at levels that are achievable using a variety of common remedial technologies which destroy, remove or immobilize substantial amounts of hazardous constituents. 58 FR 48129 (September 14, 1993). The levels chosen—90% reduction capped at 10 × UTS—are within the zone of reasonable levels the Agency could have selected as treatment standards for contaminated soil. * * *

Furthermore, the Agency has concluded that it is appropriate to express the soil treatment standards as a treatment performance goal capped by specific treatment levels. More specific standards, for example, a single numerical standard for all soil, could be counterproductive—less often achievable—given the varying combinations of hazardous constituents and soil properties that might be encountered in the field. 58 FR 48130 (September 14, 1993). An express objective of this rule is to increase the range of appropriate treatment alternatives available to achieve the LDR treatment standards in soil to increase the likelihood that more remediations will include treatment as a component of the remedy. This objective could be impeded by adopting single numeric values as treatment standards, since that approach would reduce needed flexibility. The resulting soil treatment standards, while still technology-based, thus depart from EPA's past methodology developed for process wastes in that they are not based exclusively on the application of the most aggressive technology to the most difficult to treat waste and are not expressed as a single numeric value.

Like any land disposal restriction treatment standard, the soil treatment standards may be achieved using any treatment method except treatment methods which involve impermissible dilution (e.g., addition of volume without destroying, removing or immobilizing hazardous constituents or transfer of hazardous constituents from soil to another medium such as air). * * *

2.   The Soil Treatment Standards Satisfy RCRA Section 3004(m) Requirements

The technology-based "90% capped by 10 × UTS" treatment standard for contaminated soil is sufficiently stringent to satisfy the core requirement of RCRA Section 3004(m) that short-term and long-term threats to human health and the environment posed by land disposal are minimized. Technology-based standards provide an objective measure of assurance that hazardous wastes are substantially treated before they are land disposed, thus eliminating the "long-term uncertainties associated with land disposal." Eliminating these uncertainties was a chief Congressional objective in prohibiting land disposal of untreated hazardous wastes. *Hazardous Waste Treatment Council v. EPA*, 886 F.2d at 361–64. In addition, the extent of treatment required, 90% reduction capped at treatment to concentrations within an order of magnitude of the UTS, "substantially" reduces mobility or total concentrations of hazardous constituents within the meaning of RCRA Section 3004(m)(1). * * *

In an important but subtle way, EPA's regulations for contaminated soils differ from the regulations requested by ERW. The case below may help you recognize that difference, and it also might point toward an intermediate option between promulgating the rule as requested by ERW and denying the petition.

Association of Battery Recyclers, Inc. v. EPA
208 F.3d 1047 (D.C. Cir. 2000)

■ RANDOLPH, CIRCUIT JUDGE:

These are consolidated petitions for judicial review of Environmental Protection Agency regulations promulgated on May 26, 1998, under the Resource Conservation and Recovery Act of 1976 ("RCRA"), Pub. L. No. 94–580, 90 Stat. 2795. The regulations—known collectively as the "Land Disposal Restrictions Phase IV" Rule—deal with residual or secondary materials generated in mining and mineral processing operations and EPA's classification of these materials as "solid waste"; with the treatment standards for a specific category of hazardous waste; and with EPA's test for determining whether certain wastes are hazardous. Our opinion is in three parts. The first part decides whether EPA properly defined "solid waste." We are unanimous that it did not. The second part decides, again unanimously, that EPA's treatment standards for a particular category of hazardous waste are lawful. The third part, written by Judge Ginsburg and joined by Judge Silberman, decides that EPA's test for determining toxicity is valid for certain wastes but not for others. I disagree with their conclusion for the reasons stated in my dissenting opinion. * * *

II. ALTERNATIVE TREATMENT STANDARDS

A.

Once it is determined that materials are hazardous waste and thus subject to RCRA, EPA is required to take several steps, one of which is to promulgate regulations prohibiting land disposal of certain hazardous wastes. *See* 42 U.S.C. § 6924(d), (e) & (g). If a waste falls under this disposal restriction, it cannot be disposed of "unless the waste is treated so as to minimize the short-term and long-term threats to human health and the environment posed by toxic and hazardous constituents . . . or unless the EPA finds that no migration of hazardous constituents from the facility will occur after disposal." *Chemical Waste Management, Inc. v. EPA*, 976 F.2d 2, 8 (D.C. Cir. 1992) (citing 42 U.S.C. § 6924 (g)(5), (m)). We are concerned in this portion of the opinion with the first option—the land disposal restriction ("LDR") treatment standards.

EPA originally promulgated technology-based LDR treatment standards, *see Hazardous Waste Treatment Council v. EPA*, 886 F.2d 355, 361–66 (D.C. Cir. 1989), usually examining the available treatment data and requiring use of the "best demonstrated available technology" ("BDAT"), *see* 61 Fed. Reg. 18,780, 18,807 (1996). Beginning in 1991, *see* 56 Fed. Reg. 55,160, 55,172–77 (1991), EPA began to rethink whether BDAT standards should apply to all soils containing hazardous wastes. While continuing to believe that BDAT standards are best for newly-generated wastes, the agency doubted that this was also true for wastes generated during remediation of contaminated soils. *See* 61 Fed. Reg. 18,780, 18,808 (1996). BDAT standards "create an incentive to generate less of the affected waste in the first instance." *Id.* This incentive is what EPA desires in the context of newly-generated wastes, but in the remediation context it serves as a barrier to desirable cleanup efforts. *See id.*

EPA thus proposed, and promulgated in the rule before us, alternative treatment standards for soils. Rather than requiring BDAT, the alternative standards allow any treatment that results in a ninety percent reduction in the concentration of hazardous constituents, unless the ninety percent reduction would result in a concentration less than ten times the Universal Treatment Standard (based on BDAT) for that constituent. *See* 40 C.F.R. § 268.49(c)(1). In that case, the concentrations can be reduced only to ten times the Universal Treatment Standard. *See id.* § 268.49(c)(1)(C).

The final rule applies solely to soils that are placed "into a land disposal unit." *See id.* § 268.49(a). Four industry groups representing electric and gas utilities challenge the regulation because it departed from the proposed rules, which petitioners contend applied to any "land disposal" of soils. The practical effect of this difference is that the alternative standards do not apply to soils that are recycled into products placed on land. *See* 63 Fed. Reg. at 28,609. These petitioners prefer the proposed rule because in their efforts to clean up manufactured gas plant sites, they often recycle contaminated soils into asphalt, brick, or cement— products that are placed on land. Petitioners * * * argue that the final rule should be set aside as "arbitrary and capricious." *See* 5 U.S.C. § 706(2)(A). * * *

D.

This brings us to the arbitrary and capricious challenge. EPA concluded that soils recycled into products placed on land should continue to be treated with the "best treatment available" because these products "can be placed virtually anywhere, compounding potential release mechanisms, exposure pathways, and human and environmental receptors." 63 Fed. Reg. at 28,610. The agency stressed the "uncertainties posed by this method of land disposal" in refusing to apply the alternative LDR standards. *See id.* at 28,609–10.

Petitioners claim this "uncertainty" is not a rational basis for agency decisionmaking and that EPA did not adequately support its environmental concerns with recycled soils placed on land. There is nothing to this. EPA decided not to apply alternative standards unless it was certain the new standards would result in safe disposal. "[N]othing [in RCRA] requires the Administrator to determine that a method of land disposal is not safe before prohibiting it. Rather, the statute commands the Administrator to promulgate prohibitory regulations unless he has made an affirmative determination of safety." *Natural Resources Defense Council, Inc. v. EPA*, 907 F.2d 1146, 1153 (D.C. Cir. 1990). EPA applies a similar presumption in granting variances from treatment standards. *See* 40 C.F.R. § 268.44. EPA also sufficiently supported its view that environmental risks exist when soils are recycled into products placed on land. *See* 63 Fed. Reg. at 28,610 (citing 53 Fed. Reg. at 31,197–98); J.A. 2131–32. It engaged in reasoned decisionmaking in finding that contaminated soils placed on the ground as asphalt or cement pose greater environmental risks than similar soils placed in land disposal units.

The materials below pertain to hazardous waste TSDFs, not to abandoned and contaminated properties. But they still underscore a larger, and relevant, point: there is compelling evidence that, on average, people of color disproportionately bear the burdens of many important environmental problems. How will that circumstance affect your rulemaking decision?

Robert D. Bullard et al., *Toxic Wastes and Race at Twenty: Why Race Still Matters After All of these Years*
38 ENVTL. L. 371, 392-407 (2008)

VI. Assessment of Current Disparities

In 2001, industry in the United States generated approximately 41 million tons of hazardous wastes. Under the Resource Conservation and Recovery Act of 1976 (RCRA), hazardous wastes must be managed by specially designed facilities referred to as treatment, storage, and disposal facilities (TSDFs). Companies operating such facilities are required to obtain permits from state and sometimes federal environmental agencies and conform to local land use regulations. However, as the November 2006 explosion of stored hazardous wastes in Danvers, Massachusetts illustrates, TSDFs can adversely impact nearby residents even when operated according to accepted specifications. The city of East Palo Alto was home to Romic Environmental Technologies, a commercial facility that had endangered workers and the surrounding community by operating with only a provisional permit and releasing large amounts of hazardous air pollutants into the environment. Indeed, hazardous waste facilities are well known as serious risks to health, property, and quality of life. As a result of these threats, public opposition to siting of TSDFs is nearly universal, especially for high-profile facilities such as incinerators and landfills, and new facility sitings have tended to follow the path of least political resistance. Although in recent decades communities of color have begun to mount their own resistance, their limited scientific, technical, and legal resources have historically made such communities vulnerable to facility sitings. * * *

A.   National Findings

Over nine million people are estimated to live within three kilometers (1.8 miles) of the nation's 413 commercial hazardous waste facilities. This represents 3.3% of the U.S. population. More than 5.1 million people of color, including 2.5 million Hispanics or Latinos, 1.8 million African Americans, 616,000 Asians/Pacific Islanders, and 62,000 Native Americans, live in neighborhoods with one or more TSDF (see Table 1). Indeed, these host neighborhoods are densely populated, with over 870 persons per square kilometer (2300 per mi²), compared to 30 persons per square kilometer (77 per mi²) in non-host areas. Not surprisingly, 343 facilities (83%) are located in metropolitan areas.

For 2000, neighborhoods within three kilometers of a TSDF are 56% people of color whereas non-host areas are 30% people of color (see Table 1). Thus, percentages of people of color as a whole are 1.9 times greater in host neighborhoods than in non-host areas. Percentages of African Americans, Hispanics/Latinos, and Asians/Pacific Islanders in host neighborhoods are 1.7, 2.3, and 1.8 times greater (20% vs. 12%, 27% vs. 12%, and 6.7% vs. 3.6%), respectively.

Table 1 also reveals significant socioeconomic disparities. Poverty rates in the host neighborhoods are 1.5 times greater than those in non-host areas (18% vs. 12%) and mean annual household incomes in host neighborhoods are 15% lower ($48,234 vs. $56,912).

Table 1: Racial and Socioeconomic Disparities for the Nation's 413 TSDFs
(2000 Census)

	Host Neighborhoods	Non-Host Areas	Difference	Ratio
Population				
Total Population (1000s)	9,222	272,200	-262,979	0.03
Population Density (persons/sq. km.)	870	29.7	840	29.0
Race/Ethnicity				
% People of Color	55.9%	30.0%	25.9%	1.86
% African American	20.0%	11.9%	8.0%	1.67
% Hispanic or Latino	27.0%	12.0%	15.0%	2.25
% Asian/Pacific Islander	6.7%	3.6%	3.0%	1.83
% Native American	0.7%	0.9%	-0.2%	0.77
Socioeconomics				
Poverty Rate	18.3%	12.2%	6.1%	1.50
Mean Household Income	$48,234	$56,912	-$8,678	0.85
Mean Owner-Occpd. Housing Value	$135,510	$159,536	-$24,025	0.85
% with 4-Year College Degree	18.5%	24.6%	-6.1%	0.75
% Professional "White Collar" Occp.	28.0%	33.8%	-5.8%	0.83
% Employed in "Blue Collar" Occp.	27.7%	24.0%	3.7%	1.15

NOTES: Data computed using areal apportionment method (see Figure 1D). Differences and ratios are between host neighborhood and non-host area. Differences may not precisely correspond to other values due to rounding off.

Mean owner-occupied housing values are also disproportionately low in TSDF host neighborhoods. These data reveal depressed economic conditions in host neighborhoods of the nation's hazardous waste facilities. Education and employment disparities also can be noted in Table 1. The percentage of persons twenty-five years and over with a four-year college degree are much lower in host neighborhoods than in non-host areas (18% vs. 25%, respectively). Similar disparities exist for the percentage of persons employed in professional "white collar" occupations, while percentages employed in "blue collar" occupations are disproportionately high in host neighborhoods. These racial and socioeconomic disparities are statistically significant (p<0.001).

* * * [N]eighborhoods with clustered facilities, i.e., multiple facilities, have higher percentages of people of color than those with non-clustered facilities, i.e., a single facility (69% vs. 51%). In addition, percentages of African Americans and Hispanics in the neighborhoods with clustered facilities are significantly higher than neighborhoods with non-clustered facilities (29% vs. 16% and 33% vs. 25%, respectively). Although Asians/Pacific Islanders are disproportionately located in all host neighborhoods * * *, they are found in lower percentages in the neighborhoods with clustered facilities than in non-clustered facility neighborhoods (4.3% vs. 7.8%). Native American percentages are very small and nearly equal (0.7%) in clustered and non-clustered facility host neighborhoods.

Poverty rates in the neighborhoods with clustered facilities are high compared to non-clustered facility neighborhoods (22% vs. 17%), mean household incomes are 10% lower in neighborhoods with clustered facilities ($44,600 vs. $49,600), and mean housing values are 14% lower ($121, 200 vs. $141,000). All of these racial and socioeconomic disparities between neighborhoods with clustered facilities and non-clustered facility host neighborhoods are statistically significant (p<0.01). These findings are similar to those of the 1987 Toxic Wastes and Race report and the 1994 Toxic Wastes and Race Revisited update, both of which found that zip codes with higher levels of hazardous waste activity were home to higher percentages of people of color and had higher poverty rates. In 2000, people of color and the poor thus continue to be particularly vulnerable to the various negative impacts of hazardous waste facilities. Moreover, the present findings show that this is the case for African Americans, Hispanics, and Asians/Pacific Islanders. * * *

D.   The Matter of Race

Toxic Wastes and Race in the United States found race to be more important than socioeconomic status in predicting the location of the nation's commercial hazardous waste facilities. Thus, it is appropriate to ask whether the racial disparities reported above in the current distribution of hazardous wastes are a function of neighborhood socioeconomic characteristics. Because race is often highly correlated with socioeconomic status, it is difficult to tell if race plays an independent role in accounting for facility locations without conducting statistical tests (i.e., multivariate analyses) to isolate the effect of race alone.

To determine the independent effect of race, socioeconomic factors believed to be associated with race must be statistically controlled. * * * [A multivariate analysis of the data finds that] [a]ll race variables (percentages of Hispanics, African Americans, and Asians/Pacific Islanders) are highly significant independent predictors of the facility locations ($p<0.001$). * * * [T]he higher the people of color percentages, the more likely a census tract is to be within three kilometers of a commercial hazardous waste facility. Among the indicators of socioeconomic status, mean income and percent employed in blue collar occupations are significant predictors ($p<0.001$). These variables are therefore independently associated with hazardous waste facility locations. Mean housing value is statistically significant ($p<0.002$), but in an unexpected direction (i.e., it has a positive coefficient).

Some socioeconomic variables are not statistically significant. For example, the percentage employed in management and professional (i.e., white collar) occupations is not a significant predictor. Likewise, the percentage of persons with a college degree does not quite achieve the threshold ($p<0.05$) necessary to be considered statistically significant, though it is trending that way. It also has a positive coefficient, which is in the unexpected direction. The results show that race continues to be a significant and robust predictor of commercial hazardous waste facility locations when socioeconomic and other non-racial factors are taken into account. * * *

VII. Conclusions and Policy Recommendations

Twenty years after the release of Toxic Wastes and Race, significant racial and socioeconomic disparities persist in the distribution of the nation's commercial hazardous waste facilities. Although the current assessment uses newer methods that better match where people and hazardous waste facilities are located, the conclusions are very much the same as they were in 1987. In fact, people of color are found to be more concentrated around hazardous waste facilities than previously shown. People of color are particularly concentrated in neighborhoods and communities with the greatest number of hazardous waste facilities. Furthermore, racial disparities are widespread throughout the country, whether one examines states or metropolitan areas. Race clearly still matters. * * *

D. CORRECTIVE ACTION

Chapter 7 will introduce you to CERCLA, the flagship federal statute governing hazardous waste site cleanups. RCRA has similar provisions that receive much less attention. This may seem odd, because corrective actions have been initiated at sites encompassing 18 million acres, an area larger than the state of West Virginia and significantly larger than the number of acres subject to remediation under CERCLA. But RCRA corrective action issues are considerably less likely to find their way into court, because in most circumstances they involve a single, financially solvent TSDF that is willing to cooperate with federal or state regulators because it does not want to jeopardize its permit to operate.

Because there is significant overlap between corrective action and the issues we will discuss in the next chapter, we provide only a brief overview in the form of an excerpt from a report EPA recently released celebrating the success of the program.

RCRA Corrective Action: Case Studies Report

EPA (2013)

I. INTRODUCTION TO RCRA CORRECTIVE ACTION

A. Purpose of the Program

During more than a century of American industrial development, waste disposal—left unchecked—progressively polluted our air, water, and land. Recognizing the need for careful waste management to protect human health and the environment, Congress passed the Resource Conservation and Recovery Act of 1976 (RCRA) to require, among other things, a system to identify and properly manage hazardous waste. Congress amended RCRA in November 1984 to expand cleanup provisions. Under the amended law, owners or operators of facilities where hazardous waste was or is treated, stored, or disposed (i.e., TSDs) must clean up contamination from any past and present releases, including contamination that may have spread beyond site boundaries. Coordinated by EPA and its state partners, the RCRA Corrective Action Program ensures that these cleanups occur.

RCRA Corrective Action facilities include current and former chemical manufacturing plants, oil refineries, lead smelters, wood preservers, steel mills, commercial landfills, and a variety of other types of entities. Sites range in size from hazardous waste treatment facilities of less than one acre to former military bombing ranges covering 2 million acres. Sites of all sizes, however, can threaten human health and the environment. Due to poor practices prior to environmental regulations, Corrective

Action facilities have left large stretches of river sediments laden with PCBs; deposited lead in residential yards and parks beyond site boundaries; polluted drinking water wells in rural areas with chlorinated solvents; tainted municipal water supplies used by millions with components of rocket fuel; and introduced mercury into waterways, necessitating fish advisories.

EPA and state regulators work with facilities and communities to design cleanup remedies based on the contamination, geology, and anticipated use unique to each site. Program goals, however, are the same for all sites: (1) to protect human health and the environment, and (2) to keep or return land to productive use, thereby supporting jobs, a healthy tax base, and other values from the land, as determined by local communities.

B.   Human Health Benefits

EPA estimates that more than 35 million people, roughly 12 percent of the U.S. population, live within one mile of a RCRA Corrective Action site. The presence of hazardous constituents in contaminated soil, sediments, groundwater, surface water, and air at, or emanating from, RCRA Corrective Action sites can increase the risk of adverse health effects to exposed populations. This can be especially critical for minority and poor communities—as well as sensitive sub-populations such as children, pregnant women, and the elderly—who can be disproportionately affected. Dangers include acute health effects, such as poisoning and injuries from fire or explosions, and long-term effects, such as cancers, birth defects, and other chronic non-carcinogenic effects (e.g., damage to kidney, liver, nervous and endocrine systems). By reducing exposures to contaminants * * *, RCRA Corrective Action cleanups protect the health of local residents, site workers, and others. Corrective Action sites can, and often do, contain more than one contaminant.

C.   Environmental Benefits

Contamination of soil, groundwater, surface water, and other media degrade the functioning of ecosystems by affecting the health of various plant and animal species. The effects vary widely from site to site depending on the species, contaminant, and ecosystem involved, but the overall impact is a change to an ecosystem's species composition and functioning.

In addition to harming plant and animal communities, these changes can lead to a reduction in the benefits—both direct and indirect—that ecosystems provide humans. RCRA Corrective Action cleanups help to protect and restore these benefits, often referred to as ecosystem services. * * *

D.   Community Benefits

While the RCRA Corrective Action Program's primary objective is the protection of human health and the environment, cleaning up and redeveloping contaminated sites also results in positive economic and social benefits for many communities. RCRA Corrective Action cleanups not only eliminate or reduce real and perceived health and environmental risks associated with hazardous waste sites, but they also reduce liabilities associated with reusing these contaminated sites. As a result, the program helps convert vacant and underutilized land into productive resources; reduces blight, uncertainty, and other negative perceptions; improves aesthetics and general well-being; and are likely to boost property values in communities surrounding facilities.

Redevelopment of RCRA Corrective Action sites can also function as a catalyst for additional development in areas near these sites. Both on-site and off-site development generates jobs, income, and tax revenue for local governments. Since many Corrective Action sites are in built up areas—66% are associated with census-defined urban areas—that might have otherwise gone to greenfield sites, redevelopment generally results in reduced energy use, fewer emissions of greenhouse gases and other pollutants, and decreased stormwater runoff.

E.   Relationship of RCRA Corrective Action to Other EPA Cleanup Programs

Since 1980, Congress has mandated that several programs be established to clean up contaminated land. Four main programs are listed below, together with: year of establishment, features that distinguish one program from another, and the current number of acres addressed by each program.

• *Superfund (1980):* sites that are abandoned, bankrupt, or have multiple responsible parties and uncontrolled releases of hazardous substances (3.9 million acres)

• *RCRA Corrective Action (1984):* sites with viable owners or operators that have treated, stored, or disposed of hazardous waste since 1980 and released hazardous constituents to the environment (18 million acres)
* * *

The same hazardous constituents contaminate RCRA Corrective Action and Superfund sites, and cleanups result in similar benefits. Each program has a significant number of large, complex cleanups that will require many years to complete, and sites occasionally move between the two programs. While similarities exist, important distinctions also exist and are discussed below.

Figure 1: Acres Addressed per Cleanup Program

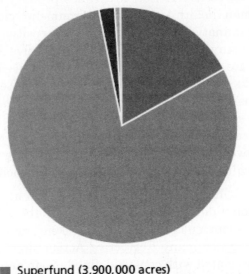

■ Superfund (3,900,000 acres)
■ RCRA Corrective Action (18,000,000 acres)
■ Underground Storage Tanks (507,000 acres)
■ Brownfields (164,000 acres)

The *RCRA Corrective Action Program* addresses facilities with *viable owners or operators*, many of whom are still engaged in manufacturing or other business operations at the site (e.g., 105 operating petroleum refineries that, together, process 90 percent of all oil refined in the U.S.). In all cases, even if the specific facility has closed, site *owners or operators are required to fund the cleanup* work and provide financial assurance to cover cleanup costs in case of bankruptcy. Regulators provide oversight and take enforcement actions where appropriate.

Operating facilities provide advantages in that they generally employ members of the local community, produce tax revenue for local governments, and have a vested interest in maintaining a safe and healthy work environment. They also have revenues which may be used to pay for cleanup work. Operating facilities provide challenges as well; committing money to cleanup may be difficult for financially-struggling facilities, and operations themselves can make areas of contamination difficult to access. Regulators play a vital role in ensuring the timely achievement of cleanup goals, but the financial capacity of site owners can also control the pace of cleanup work.

EPA *authorizes states* to implement the RCRA Corrective Action Program. To date, 42 authorized states and one territory lead implementation at their Corrective Action facilities, with assistance from EPA grants. EPA regional offices have work-sharing agreements with both authorized and unauthorized states, with whom they meet regularly to discuss sites and topic areas where states need regional help. * * *

The *Superfund Program* typically addresses *abandoned* hazardous waste sites (including sites of spills or illegal dumping) and sites where uncontrolled releases demand an immediate response. Superfund provides funding to clean up dangerous sites when no viable responsible party can be found, or when action is necessary before disputes over liability can be resolved. In such cases, the Superfund program seeks to recover costs after the fact from one or more responsible parties, if they can be identified. Generally, recovered funds do not cover the full cost, and cleanup actions are *partially taxpayer-funded*. Although states play a critical role, federal Superfund programs are *not delegated* to the states, and EPA regional offices oversee individual Superfund cleanups.

In creating the RCRA Corrective Action program, Congress provided a powerful tool to prevent current hazardous waste management facilities (i.e., RCRA facilities) from becoming future Superfund sites. RCRA compels facility owners and operators to take responsibility for hazardous waste contamination arising from their operations before costs can be externalized onto the public.

V. CAPSTONE PROBLEM: ENFORCING RCRA AT MIT

As with other environmental statutes, enforcement plays a major part in determining the effectiveness of RCRA's regulatory regime. But enforcement also raises a variety of challenging questions for parties on all sides. On the governmental side, attorneys and policymakers must consider how they will detect violations; which industries and facilities deserve the closest attention; whether to rely on punitive or collaborative enforcement strategies, or some combination of both; and what sort of remedies to demand—among many other questions. On the defense side, attorneys must advise their clients about how to avoid enforcement problems, and they must decide how to respond once an enforcement proceeding begins. Should they advise their clients to take an adversarial or a collaborative approach? And are there ways, other than just paying penalties, to bring an enforcement proceeding to a mutually beneficial resolution?

The problem below will not introduce you to all of these issues. And it will provide you a window into some of the key questions that recur in many enforcement proceedings.[3]

---

[3] The authors are grateful to MIT, EPA, and the United States Department of Justice for agreeing to share the documents excerpted in this problem, as well as other documents that informed the development of the problem. At the request of MIT, we have altered the specific

For this exercise, you will be negotiating a settlement—or, at least, attempting to do so; if your negotiations break down, litigation also is an option. Some of you will represent EPA Region 1, which initiated the enforcement proceeding at issue in the settlement negotiations. Some of you will represent the Massachusetts Institute of Technology (MIT), which is the object of EPA's enforcement. Your central goal, for either client, is to negotiate a settlement that best serves your client's interests.

Background

Our story is set in 2001.[4] But the backstory begins a few years earlier and on another university campus. In 1995, EPA inspectors conducted an environmental compliance inspection of Yale University. For EPA, this inspection marked a change of focus; since the passage of RCRA, enforcement had focused primarily on manufacturers and other industrial actors. But the EPA team inspecting Yale found no shortage of problems, particularly in research laboratories. After extensive negotiations, Yale agreed to pay over half a million dollars, partly in contributions to environmental programs and partly as a fine. *Many New England Colleges Break Environmental Rules*, BOSTON GLOBE, May 27, 1996.

The Yale inspection sparked EPA Region 1's interest, and it began investigating other universities, finding similar problems and levying similar fines. Universities, it seemed, were chronic violators of hazardous waste laws. Several reasons for this chronic non-compliance quickly emerged. One—which the Gray and Silbey article, which you read excerpts from in Chapter II, alluded to—is that universities use many hazardous chemicals and produce a wide variety of wastes. A typical research university has dozens of science laboratories, and a single chemistry or biochemistry laboratory can contain dozens of bottles, vials, and other containers of hazardous chemicals. Wastes can turn up in other surprising places on campus—art rooms, for example—and the university's facilities management team and groundskeepers are also likely to store and use hazardous chemicals. Keeping track of so many chemicals in so many places is no easy task.

The governance structures of universities also cause waste management challenges. Within universities, power tends to be

---

penalty amounts (including MIT's request for a modification for extraordinary cooperation) in both EPA's and MIT's proposals. Those numbers are entirely fictional.

Some readers may note similarities to the Hawaii Volcanoes case study from the Stanford Law School case studies series. In part, those similarities arise because RCRA enforcement matters—which are the common subject matter of both studies—tend to result in certain common questions. But the similarities also arise because this case study was partly inspired by that earlier work.

[4] Despite this time setting for the story, we have used current regulations and guidance documents. In some circumstances, those documents are identical to the ones that existed in 2001, but some other documents have changed.

decentralized, and individual laboratories act somewhat like fiefdoms over which lead researchers reign. Personnel within those labs tend to turn over frequently; many different students and post-docs can share a lab, and most of them will be present only for a few years at most. Universities also have career environmental health and safety staff, but in the 1990s, those staffs were generally quite small, and the clout of an environmental health and safety staff member rarely approached that of a star professor. Consequently, effective hazardous waste management at universities generally requires overseeing, training, and retraining a huge group of constantly changing people, and also requires gaining cooperation from dozens of people over whom the health and safety department holds little leverage. In any workplace setting, environmental compliance can be challenging; it requires picky attention to detail and can distract people from what they perceive as their primary jobs. But the operational complexities and institutional cultures of universities can make compliance particularly difficult.

In EPA's view, another issue exacerbated these problems. Because universities had not been enforcement targets, they may have felt little motivation—until the Yale audit—to develop robust environmental compliance programs. Tools to improve compliance did exist; Harvard University, to provide on outlying example, had hired and empowered a relatively large environmental health and safety staff. And few universities wanted the bad publicity that could come from news stories about environmental or safety problems. But at many universities, these incentives were not enough—or at least that is what EPA staff began to think. Perhaps the threat of enforcement could be a better way to improve compliance.

EPA's Inspection of MIT

On May 19–22 and on June 10, 1998, inspectors visited MIT. They walked through dozens of buildings, looked at thousands of hazardous waste containers, interviewed dozens of personnel, reviewed university records of hazardous waste management and storage, and found many RCRA violations. One of the documents in the supporting materials summarizes the site team's findings.

After the inspection was complete, EPA decided to begin a civil judicial enforcement proceeding. But it also offered to engage MIT in settlement discussions, and MIT accepted that offer. Your problem is set partway through those settlement discussions. MIT and EPA have exchanged proposals and counterproposals but continue to disagree on several key points. If you can resolve those disagreements, you will be able to settle the case. If you cannot, the matter will proceed to litigation.

The Negotiations

You are heading into a meeting through which EPA and MIT hope to develop a final settlement. As you will see below, EPA and MIT have already exchanged documents laying out their respective positions, and this meeting is an opportunity to try to resolve differences.

Your task is to discuss and resolve the amount of civil penalty that MIT will pay and how, if at all, that amount should reflect a Supplemental Environmental Project (SEP) that MIT has proposed.

The first set of issues relates to how large a penalty MIT should pay in the absence of any SEP. The basic sticking points are as follows:

- EPA's latest penalty offer was $674,000. MIT has offered to settle for $419,000. So the parties are still far apart.

- EPA's offer incorporates an overall $25,000 reduction in the penalty because of MIT's "extraordinary cooperation." MIT argues that this amount should be higher. It currently values that cooperation at $125,000.

- A key factor in EPA's penalty calculations is the sheer number of violations. But MIT argues that EPA also found many more containers that *were* properly labeled; found many more records that *were* properly maintained; and interviewed many more people who *were* properly trained. Viewed out of context, MIT argues, the aggregate number of violations may look large, but that large number really represents a small part of MIT's vast operations.

- The severity of the violations is also at issue. EPA argues that the practices of failing to properly train employees, maintain thorough records, label wastes, separate incompatible wastes, and move wastes off-site in a timely fashion all made MIT a ticking time bomb. But MIT points out that EPA has not alleged any actual release of hazardous materials to the environment. EPA's arguments that violations were severe instead all share the common contention that something bad *could have* happened.

- Underlying MIT's arguments is a larger theme. The university makes no claim that its compliance was acceptable, and it is actively working to improve its hazardous waste management practices. But it does argue that its problems were at least understandable. Complying with hazardous waste laws at a university with so many labs, containers, and personnel is very difficult, and MIT argues that that difficulty weighs against imposing a massive penalty.

In addition to issues that have become sticking points, a second issue has emerged and not yet been thoroughly discussed. That issue is how much the amount of MIT's penalty should be reduced, if at all, because of MIT's proposed SEP. A SEP is an environmentally beneficial project that a defendant completes in return for a reduction of its financial penalty. EPA policy encourages SEPs, but those SEPs have to meet certain criteria, which are spelled out in more detail in the supporting materials below. These criteria are designed to ensure that SEPs provide genuine environmental benefits and that they respond to the same kinds of environmental problems that led to the enforcement action. So long as a SEP meets those criteria, it can take a wide variety of forms, and defendants can be quite creative in designing SEP proposals.

Here, MIT developed a particularly innovative proposal. That proposal had two key elements. First, MIT proposed to provide environmental education programming for the City of Cambridge's public schools (MIT is located in Cambridge, Massachusetts). Second, MIT proposed to create an on-line teaching program designed to assist other universities with their hazardous waste compliance efforts. The supporting materials describe that proposal in more detail.[5] At the stage in which you will pick up the negotiations, EPA has not yet decided whether to accept this proposal as is, to demand changes, or to reject it. If EPA does accept the proposal, it also will need to determine how much, if at all, MIT's financial penalty should be reduced.

To sum up, there are a few key questions for each side to address independently, and then through negotiations:

- What penalty is appropriate? Here, rather than discussing how each violation fits within EPA's penalty matrix (which would be an important part of the work of a practicing attorney), you should focus on more general questions, like the extent to which MIT's cooperation, management reforms, or status as a university might justify penalty adjustments.

- Is the proposed SEP consistent with EPA's guidelines (and if it is not, does that matter)?

- How might the SEP proposal be improved?

- How much of a penalty reduction does the SEP justify?

The worksheet below summarizes those questions, and may be useful as you proceed through the problem. You will want to fill in your team's column prior to beginning the negotiation. You do have some license to

---

[5] In the actual enforcement proceeding upon which this problem is based, MIT also proposed to construct a new stormwater management facility. We have left that element of the SEP out of this problem.

be creative, however, and neither your initial position nor your final agreement needs to fit exactly with the categories on this sheet.

	EPA's proposal	MIT's proposal	Agreement
Initial penalty for violations			
Adjustment factors (e.g. for cooperation)			

Budget for accepted SEPs (if any)
  SEP 1: Cambridge Schools
  SEP 2: Virtual Hazwaste Program
  Alternative SEP proposal			

Total SEP expenditures			
Penalty Adjustment to account for SEPs			
Total Penalty = (Initial penalty × adjustment factor) − (total SEP expenditures × penalty adjustment for SEPs)			

As in most areas of environmental law, statutes provide and circumscribe EPA's enforcement authority. The excerpt below includes key parts of RCRA's enforcement provisions.

RCRA § 3008, 49 U.S.C. § 6928. Federal Enforcement

(a) Compliance orders

(1) Except as provided in paragraph (2), whenever on the basis of any information the Administrator determines that any person has violated or is in violation of any requirement of this subchapter, the Administrator may issue an order assessing a civil penalty for any past or current violation, requiring compliance immediately or within a specified time period, or both, or the Administrator may commence a civil action in the United States district court in the district in which the violation occurred for appropriate relief, including a temporary or permanent injunction.

* * * (3) * * * Any penalty assessed in the order shall not exceed $25,000 per day of noncompliance for each violation of a

> requirement of this subchapter. In assessing such a penalty, the Administrator shall take into account the seriousness of the violation and any good faith efforts to comply with applicable requirements. * * *
>
> (g) Civil penalty
>
> Any person who violates any requirement of this subchapter shall be liable to the United States for a civil penalty in an amount not to exceed $25,000 for each such violation. Each day of such violation shall, for purposes of this subsection, constitute a separate violation. * * *

In conducting its negotiations, EPA is guided by the following policy document. This document is not formally binding, but serves as a guidepost that EPA attorneys and defense counsel use to negotiate settlements.

As you will see, the guidance document provides detailed numeric guidelines (some of which we have not included) for assigning dollar values to particular violations. A practicing attorney handling an enforcement proceeding like this would probably spend hours comparing each individual violation to these guidelines and developing arguments for violation-by-violation discussions of penalty calculations. In this exercise, however, we have not provided a detailed accounting of every violation; there were too many. You therefore should read these guidelines primarily to get a sense of the overall policy considerations that drive penalty calculations. In negotiating, you may assume that the disparity between EPA's and MIT's prior positions derives partly from their disagreement about the severity of the underlying violations.

RCRA Civil Penalty Policy

EPA (June 2003)

I.   SUMMARY OF THE POLICY

The penalty calculation system established through U.S. Environmental Protection Agency's RCRA Civil Penalty Policy ("Penalty Policy" or "Policy") is based upon Section 3008 of RCRA, 42 U.S.C. § 6928. Under this section, the seriousness of the violation and any good faith efforts to comply with applicable requirements are to be considered in assessing a penalty. Consistent with this statutory direction, this Penalty Policy consists of: (1) determining a gravity-based penalty for a particular violation, from a penalty assessment matrix, (2) adding a "multi-day" component, as appropriate, to account for a violation's duration, (3) adjusting the sum of the gravity-based and multi-day components, up or down, for case specific circumstances, and (4) adding to this amount the appropriate economic benefit gained through non-compliance. More specifically, the revised RCRA Civil Penalty Policy establishes the following penalty calculation methodology:

> Penalty Amount = gravity-based component + multi-day component +/− adjustments + economic benefit

In administrative civil penalty cases, EPA will perform two separate calculations under this Policy: (1) to determine an appropriate amount to seek in the administrative complaint and subsequent litigation, and (2) to explain and document the process by which the Agency arrived at the penalty figure it has agreed to accept in settlement. The methodology for these calculations will differ only in that no downward adjustments (other than those reflecting a violator's good faith efforts to comply with applicable requirements) will usually be included in the calculation of the proposed penalty for the administrative complaint. In those instances where the respondent or reliable information demonstrates prior to the issuance of the complaint that applying further downward adjustment factors (over and above those reflecting a violator's good faith efforts to comply) is appropriate, enforcement personnel may in their discretion (but are not required to) make such further downward adjustments in the amount of the penalty proposed in the complaint.

In determining the amount of the penalty to be included in the complaint, enforcement personnel should consider all possible ramifications posed by the violation and resolve any doubts (e.g., as to the application of adjustment factors or the assumptions underlying the amount of the economic benefit enjoyed by the violator) against the violator in a manner consistent with the facts and findings so as to preserve EPA's ability to litigate for the strongest penalty possible. It should be noted that assumptions underlying any upward adjustments or refusal to apply downward adjustments in the penalty amount are subject to revision later as new information becomes available.

In civil judicial cases, EPA will use the narrative penalty assessment criteria set forth in the Policy to explain the penalty amount agreed to in settlement. In litigation, the penalty that is sought should be based on the statutory factors set forth in Section 3008, 42 U.S.C. § 6928 as well as relevant case law. * * *

MATRIX[1]

Extent of Deviation from Requirement

		MAJOR	MODERATE	MINOR
Potential for Harm	MAJOR	$27,500 to 22,000	$21,999 to 16,500	$16,499 to 12,100
	MODERATE	$12,099 to 8800	$8,799 to 5,500	$5,499 to 3,300
	MINOR	$3,299 to 1,650	$1,649 to 550	$549 to 110

* * * III. RELATIONSHIP TO AGENCY PENALTY POLICY

The RCRA Civil Penalty Policy sets forth a method for calculating penalties consistent with the established goals of the Agency's Policy on Civil Penalties which was issued on February 16, 1984. These goals are:

- deterrence;

- fair and equitable treatment of the regulated community; and

- swift resolution of environmental problems.

* * * V. RELATIONSHIP BETWEEN PENALTY AMOUNT SOUGHT IN AN ADMINISTRATIVE ACTION AND ACCEPTED IN SETTLEMENT

* * * The Agency expects that the dollar amount of the proposed penalty that will be sought in the administrative hearing will often exceed the amount of the penalty the Agency would accept in settlement.

This may be so for several reasons. First, at the time the complaint is filed, the Agency will often not be aware of mitigating factors (then known only to the respondent) on the basis of which the penalty may be adjusted downward. Second, it is appropriate that the Agency have the enforcement discretion to accept in settlement a lower penalty than it has sought in its complaint, because in settling a case the Agency is able to avoid the costs and risks of litigation. Moreover respondents must perceive that they face some significant risk of higher penalties through litigation to have appropriate incentives to agree to penalty amounts acceptable to the Agency in settlement. Therefore, Agency enforcement personnel should, as necessary, prepare two separate penalty calculations for each administrative proceeding—one to support the initial proposed penalty and the other to be placed in the administrative file as support for the final penalty amount the Agency accepts in settlement. In calculating the amount of the proposed penalty to be sought in an administrative proceeding, Agency personnel should total: (1) the gravity-based penalty amount (including any multi-day component), and (2) an amount reflecting upward adjustments of the penalty, and subtract from this sum an amount reflecting any downward adjustments in the penalty based solely on respondent's "good faith efforts to comply with applicable requirements." This total should then be added to the amount of any economic benefit accruing to the violator. The result will be the proposed penalty the Agency will seek in the administrative proceeding.

The methodology for determining and documenting the penalty figure the Agency accepts in settlement should be basically identical to that employed in calculating the proposed penalty, but should also include consideration of: (1) any new and relevant information obtained from the violator or elsewhere, and (2) all other downward adjustment factors (in addition to the "good faith efforts" factor weighed in calculating the proposed penalty).

* * * VI. DETERMINATION OF GRAVITY-BASED PENALTY AMOUNT RCRA

Section 3008(a)(3) states that the seriousness of a violation must be taken into account in assessing a penalty for the violation. The gravity-based component is a measure of the seriousness of violation. The gravity-based penalty amount should be determined by examining two factors:

- potential for harm; and
- extent of deviation from a statutory or regulatory requirement.

A. POTENTIAL FOR HARM

The RCRA requirements were promulgated in order to prevent harm to human health and the environment. Thus, noncompliance with any RCRA requirement can result in a situation where there is a potential for harm to human health or the environment. In addition to those violations that involve actual or potential contamination from the release of hazardous wastes, violations such as failure to comply with recordkeeping requirements create a risk of harm to the environment or human health as well as undermine the integrity of the RCRA regulatory program. Accordingly, the assessment of the potential for harm resulting from a violation should be based on two factors:

- the risk of human or environmental exposure to hazardous waste and/or hazardous constituents that may be posed by noncompliance, and

- the adverse effect noncompliance may have on statutory or regulatory purposes or procedures for implementing the RCRA program.

* * * Enforcement personnel should evaluate whether the potential for harm is major, moderate, or minor in a particular situation. The degree of potential harm represented by each category is defined as:

MAJOR:

(1) The violation poses or may pose a substantial risk of exposure of humans or other environmental receptors to hazardous waste or constituents; and/or

(2) the actions have or may have a substantial adverse effect on statutory or regulatory purposes or procedures for implementing the RCRA program.

MODERATE:

(1) The violation poses or may pose a significant risk of exposure of humans or other environmental receptors to hazardous waste or constituents; and/or

(2) the actions have or may have a significant adverse effect on statutory or regulatory purposes or procedures for implementing the RCRA program.

MINOR:

(1) The violation poses or may pose a relatively low risk of exposure of humans or other environmental receptors to hazardous waste or constituents; and/or

(2) the actions have or may have a small adverse effect on statutory or regulatory purposes or procedures for implementing the RCRA program.

* * * B. EXTENT OF DEVIATION FROM REQUIREMENT

1. Evaluating the Extent of Deviation

The "extent of deviation" from RCRA and its regulatory requirements relates to the degree to which the violation renders inoperative the requirement violated. In any violative situation, a range of potential noncompliance with the subject requirement exists. In other words, a violator may be substantially in compliance with the provisions of the requirement or it may have totally disregarded the requirement (or a point in between).

In determining the extent of the deviation, the following categories should be used:

MAJOR: The violator deviates from requirements of the regulation or statute to such an extent that most (or important aspects) of the requirements are not met resulting in substantial noncompliance.

MODERATE: The violator significantly deviates from the requirements of the regulation or statute but some of the requirements are implemented as intended.

MINOR: The violator deviates somewhat from the regulatory or statutory requirements but most (or all important aspects) of the requirements are met.

* * * VII. MULTIPLE AND MULTI-DAY PENALTIES

A. PENALTIES FOR MULTIPLE VIOLATIONS

1.   Multiple Violations Criteria

In certain situations, EPA may find that a facility has violated several different RCRA requirements. A separate penalty should be proposed in an administrative proceeding and obtained in settlement or litigation for each separate violation that results from an independent act (or failure to act) by the violator and is substantially distinguishable from any other claim in the complaint for which a penalty is to be assessed. * * * For litigation or settlement purposes, each of the violations should be assessed separately and the amounts added to determine a total penalty to pursue.

* * * B. PENALTIES FOR MULTI-DAY VIOLATIONS

RCRA provides EPA with the authority to assess in administrative actions or seek in court civil penalties of up to $27,500 per day of non-compliance for each violation of a requirement of Subtitle C (or the regulations which implement that subtitle). This language explicitly authorizes the Agency to consider the duration of each violation as a factor in determining an appropriate total penalty amount. Accordingly, any penalty assessed should consist of a gravity-based component, economic benefit component, and to the extent that violations can be shown or presumed to have continued for more than one day, an appropriate multi-day component. The multi-day component should reflect the duration of the violation at issue * * *.

After it has been determined that any of the violations alleged has continued for more than one day, the next step is to determine the length of time each violation continued and whether a multi-day penalty is mandatory, presumed, or discretionary. In most instances, the Agency should only seek to obtain multi-day penalties, if a multi-day penalty is appropriate, for the number of days it can document that the violation in question persisted. However, in some circumstances, reasonable assumptions as to the duration of a violation can be made. * * *

C.   CALCULATION OF THE MULTI-DAY PENALTY

After the duration of the violation has been determined, the multi-day component of the total penalty is calculated, pursuant to the Multi-Day Matrix, as outlined below.

Step 1:   Determine the gravity-based designations for the violation, e.g., major-major, moderate-minor, or minor-minor;

Step 2:   Determine, for the specific violation, whether multi-day penalties are mandatory, presumed, or discretionary, as follows:

Mandatory multi-day penalties—Multi-day penalties are considered mandatory for days 2–180 of all violations with the following gravity-based designations: major-major, major-moderate. The only exception is when they have been waived or reduced, in "highly unusual cases," as described below. Multi-day penalties for days 181+ are discretionary.

Presumption in favor of multi-day penalties—Multi-day penalties are presumed appropriate for days 2–180 of violations with the following gravity-based designations: major-minor, moderate-major, moderate-moderate. Therefore, multi-day penalties should be sought, unless case-specific facts overcoming the presumption for a particular violation are documented carefully in the case files. The presumption may be overcome for one or more days. Multi-day penalties for days 181+ are discretionary.

Discretionary multi-day penalties—Multi-day penalties are discretionary, generally, for all days of all violations with the following gravity-based designations: minor-major, moderate-minor, minor-moderate, minor-minor. In these cases, multi-day penalties should be sought where case-specific facts support such an assessment. Discretionary multi-day penalties may be imposed for some or all days. The bases for decisions to impose or not impose any discretionary multi-day penalties must be documented in the case files.

MULTI-DAY MATRIX OF MINIMUM DAILY PENALTIES (in dollars)

Extent of Deviation from Requirement

		MAJOR	MODERATE	MINOR
Potential for Harm	MAJOR	$5,500 to 1,100	$4,400 to 825	$3,300 to 605
	MODERATE	$2,420 to 440	$1,760 to 275	$1,100 to 165
	MINOR	$660 to 110	$330 to 110	$110

The policy then discusses penalty adjustments to account for economic benefits gained from non-compliance—a factor you need not consider for this problem—and then lists a series of other adjustment factors. Those factors are:

- Good faith effort to comply (downward adjustment)

- Lack of good faith effort to comply (upward adjustment)

- Degree of willfulness/negligence (upward or downward adjustment)

- History of noncompliance (upward adjustment only)

- Ability to pay (downward adjustment only)

- Other unique factors.

The discussion of adjustment factors also includes the paragraph below.]

e.　*Environmental Projects (downward adjustment only)*

Under certain circumstances the Agency may consider adjusting the penalty amount downward in return for an agreement by the violator to undertake an appropriate environmentally beneficial project. All proposals for such projects should be evaluated in accordance with EPA's May 1, 1998, Supplemental Environmental Projects Policy and any subsequent amendments to the SEP Policy.

Supplemental Environmental Projects (SEP) Policy 2015 Update

EPA (Mar. 2015)

* * * I.　INTRODUCTION

A.　*Background*

A Supplemental Environmental Project (SEP) is an environmentally beneficial project or activity that is not required by law, but that a defendant agrees to undertake as part of the settlement of an enforcement action. SEPs are projects or activities that go beyond what could legally be required in order for the defendant to return to compliance, and secure environmental and/or public health benefits in addition to those achieved by compliance with applicable laws. In settlements of environmental enforcement cases, the United States Environmental Protection Agency (the EPA or the Agency) requires alleged violators to achieve and maintain compliance with federal environmental laws and regulations, take action to remedy the harm or risk caused by past violations, and/or to pay a civil penalty. In certain instances, SEPs may be included in the settlement. The primary purpose of the SEP Policy is to encourage and obtain environmental and public health protection and benefits that may not otherwise have occurred in the settlement of an enforcement action.

The Agency encourages the use of SEPs that are consistent with this Policy. Case teams should consider SEPs early in the settlement process and, in appropriate cases, provide SEP ideas to defendants. SEPs are an important component of the EPA's enforcement program, but may not be appropriate in the settlement of all cases. Even in the absence of a SEP, enforcement settlements provide substantial benefits to communities and the environment. Penalties promote environmental compliance by deterring future violations by the defendant and other members of the regulated community. Penalties also help ensure a national level playing field for the regulated community. Injunctive relief measures ensure that compliance is achieved and maintained, and redress the harm caused by a violation, thereby providing long-term significant environmental and public health benefits to the impacted community. Where a proposed project could reasonably comprise part of the injunctive relief portion of a settlement, it should not be a SEP.

B.   Using this Policy

This Policy establishes a framework for the EPA to use in exercising its enforcement discretion in determining appropriate settlements. To include a proposed project in a settlement as a SEP, Agency enforcement and compliance personnel should:

1.   Ensure that the project conforms to the basic definition of a SEP (Section III);

2.   Ensure that all legal guidelines are satisfied (Section IV);

3.   Ensure that the project fits within one (or more) of the designated categories of SEPs (Sections V and VI);

4.   Determine the appropriate amount of penalty mitigation to reflect the project's environmental and/or public health benefits using the evaluation criteria (Sections VIII and IX); and

5.   Ensure that the project satisfies all of the EPA procedures, settlement requirements and other criteria (Sections X-XII).

* * * III. DEFINITION AND KEY CHARACTERISTICS OF A SEP

Supplemental environmental projects are defined as *environmentally beneficial projects* which a defendant agrees to undertake *in settlement of an enforcement action*, but which the defendant, or any other third party, *is not otherwise legally required to perform*. The three bolded key parts of this definition are described in more detail below.

A.   *"Environmentally beneficial"* means a SEP must improve, protect, or reduce risks to public health or the environment.

While in some cases a SEP may provide the alleged violator with certain benefits, there must be no doubt that the project primarily benefits public health and/or the environment.

B. *"In settlement of an enforcement action"* means:

1. The defendant's commitment to perform the SEP is included in a legally enforceable settlement document;

* * * C. *"Not otherwise legally required to perform"* means the project or activity is not required by any federal, state, or local law or regulation or achievable under applicable environmental and other federal laws

IV. LEGAL GUIDELINES

The EPA has broad discretion to settle cases, including the discretion to include SEPs as an appropriate part of a settlement. The evaluation of whether a proposed SEP is within the EPA's authority and consistent with all statutory and Constitutional requirements may be a complex task. Accordingly, this Policy uses the following legal guidelines to ensure that SEPs are within the Agency's and a federal court's authority, and do not run afoul of any Constitutional or statutory requirements. Legal guidelines may not be waived, and are described below.

A. Nexus

1. All projects must have sufficient nexus. Nexus is the relationship between the violation and the proposed project. Nexus ensures the proper exercise of the EPA's prosecutorial discretion and enables appropriate penalty mitigation for including the SEP in the settlement.

2. A project may not be inconsistent with any provision of the underlying statutes that are the basis of the enforcement action. All projects must advance at least one of the objectives of the environmental statutes that are the basis of the enforcement action.

3. Projects must relate to the underlying violation(s) at issue in the enforcement action. The project must demonstrate that it is designed to reduce:

a. The likelihood that similar violations will occur in the future;

b. The adverse impact to public health and/or the environment to which the violation at issue contributes; or

c. The overall risk to public health and/or the environment potentially affected by the violation at issue.

4.   SEPs may not be agreements to spend a certain amount on a project that will be defined later. For a case team to properly evaluate a SEP's characteristics (the "what, where, when" of the SEP), and establish the connection to the underlying violation being resolved, the type and scope of each project must be specifically described and defined. Without a well-defined project with clear environmental or public health benefit, the EPA cannot demonstrate nexus.

* * * V.   CATEGORIES OF SEPs

The EPA has identified seven specific categories of projects which may qualify as SEPs. Many SEPs may fall into more than one category. In addition, there is an eighth category for "Other" projects that meet all conditions of the SEP Policy but do not readily fit in one of the seven specific categories.

A.   Public Health

Public health projects include those that provide diagnostic, preventative and/or health care treatment related to the actual or potential harm to human health caused by the violation. This includes, but is not limited to, epidemiological data collection and analysis, medical examinations of potentially affected persons, collection and analysis of blood/fluid/tissue samples, medical treatment and rehabilitation therapy. Examples of public health SEPs include blood lead level testing, asthma screening and treatment and mobile health clinics. Public health SEPs may also include projects such as mosquito eradication programs or donation of antimicrobial products to assist in natural disaster situations. Public health SEPs are acceptable only where the primary beneficiary of the project is the population that was harmed or put at risk by the violations.

B.   Pollution Prevention

A pollution prevention project prevents pollution at its source, before it is generated. It includes any practice that reduces the quantity and/or toxicity of pollutants entering a waste stream prior to recycling, treatment, or disposal. After the pollutant or waste stream has been generated pollution prevention is no longer possible, and the waste must be handled by appropriate recycling, treatment, containment, or disposal methods (i.e., pollution reduction). * * *

C.   Pollution Reduction

If the pollutant or waste stream already has been generated or released, a pollution reduction approach which employs recycling, treatment, containment or disposal techniques may be appropriate. A pollution reduction project is one which results in a decrease in the amount and/or toxicity of any hazardous substance, pollutant, or contaminant entering any waste stream or otherwise being released into the environment by an operating business or facility by a means which does not qualify as "pollution prevention." * * *

D. Environmental Restoration and Protection

An environmental restoration and protection project is one which enhances the condition of the ecosystem or immediate geographic area adversely affected by the violation. These projects may be used to restore or protect natural environments and address environmental contamination and similar issues in man-made environments, and may include any project that protects the ecosystem from actual or potential damage resulting from the violation or that improves the overall condition of the ecosystem. * * *

E. Assessments and Audits

There are three types of projects in the assessments and audits category: (1) pollution prevention assessments; (2) environmental quality assessments; and (3) compliance audits. These assessments and audits are only acceptable as SEPs when the defendant agrees to provide the EPA with a copy of the report and the results are made available to the public, except to the extent they constitute confidential business information (CBI) pursuant to 40 C.F.R. Section 2, Subpart B. * * *

F. Environmental Compliance Promotion

An environmental compliance promotion project provides training or technical support to other members of the regulated community in order to: (1) identify, achieve, and maintain compliance with applicable statutory and regulatory requirements or (2) go beyond compliance by reducing the generation, release, or disposal of pollutants beyond legal requirements. For these types of projects, the defendant may lack the experience, knowledge, or ability to implement the project itself and, if so, the defendant should be required to contract with an appropriate expert to develop and implement the compliance promotion project. Acceptable projects may include, for example, producing a seminar directly related to correcting widespread or prevalent violations within the defendant's economic sector. Environmental compliance promotion SEPs are acceptable only where the primary impact of the project is focused on the same regulatory program requirements that were violated and where the EPA has reason to believe that compliance in the sector would be significantly advanced by the proposed project. For example, if the alleged violations involved Clean Water Act (CWA) pretreatment violations, the compliance promotion SEP must be directed at ensuring compliance with pretreatment requirements. Environmental compliance promotion SEPs require the special approvals described in Section XII.A.4.

G. Emergency Planning and Preparedness

An emergency planning and preparedness project provides assistance, such as computers and software, communication systems, chemical emission detection and inactivation equipment, HAZMAT equipment, or training, to a responsible state or local emergency response or planning entity. * * *

H. Other Types of Projects

Projects that do not fit within one of the seven categories above, but have environmental and/or public health benefits and are otherwise fully consistent with all other provisions of this Policy, are allowable as SEPs subject to the approval requirements in Section XII.A.4.

VI. PROJECTS NOT ACCEPTABLE AS SEPs

The following are examples of the types of projects that are not allowable as SEPs. This list is not exhaustive.

A. General public educational or public environmental awareness projects (e.g., sponsoring public seminars, conducting tours of environmental controls at a facility, or promoting recycling in a community);

B. Contributions to environmental research at a college or university;

C. Cash donations to community groups, environmental organizations, state/local/federal entities, or any other third party;

D. Projects for which the defendant does not retain full responsibility to ensure satisfactory completion;

E. Projects which, though beneficial to a community, are unrelated to environmental protection (e.g., making a contribution to a non-profit, public interest, environmental or other charitable organization, donating playground equipment, etc.);

F. Studies or assessments without a requirement to address the problems identified in the study (except as provided for in Section V.E above);

G. Projects which the defendant, SEP recipient, or SEP implementer will undertake, in whole or in part, with federal loans, federal contracts, federal grants, or other forms of federal financial assistance or non-financial assistance;

H. Projects that are expected to become profitable to the defendant within the first five years of implementation (within the first three years for SEPs implemented by defendants that are small businesses or small communities). * * *

I.   Projects that provide raw materials only, with no commitment from the defendant for a completed project utilizing the raw materials (e.g., donating rail ties and gravel for a fish ladder but not actually ensuring that the ladder is built);

J.   Projects that are not complete, discrete actions with environmental or public health benefits;

K.   Projects for which completion depends on the actions or contributions of individuals or entities that are neither party to the settlement nor hired by the defendant as an implementer;

L.   Except in very limited circumstances, as described in Section XI.B, SEPs may not include actions that a third party is legally required to perform by any federal, state, or local law or regulation (also referred to as "third-party compliance" projects). * * *

IX. CALCULATION OF THE FINAL SETTLEMENT PENALTY

A primary incentive for a defendant to propose a SEP is the potential mitigation of its civil penalty. In settling enforcement actions, the EPA requires alleged violators to promptly cease the violations and, to the extent feasible, remediate any harm caused by the violations. The EPA also seeks substantial penalties in order to deter noncompliance. Penalties promote environmental compliance and help protect public health by deterring future violations by the same violator and other members of the regulated community. Penalties help maintain a national level playing field by ensuring that violators do not obtain an unfair economic advantage over their competitors who made the necessary expenditures to comply on time. Thus, any mitigation of penalties must be carefully considered.

A.   Components of the Settlement Penalty

* * * Settlements that include a SEP must always include a settlement penalty that recoups the economic benefit a violator gained from noncompliance with the law, as well as an appropriate gravity-based penalty reflecting the environmental and regulatory harm caused by the violation(s).

SEPs are not penalties, nor are they accepted in lieu of a penalty. However, a violator's commitment to perform a SEP is a relevant factor for the EPA to consider in establishing an appropriate settlement penalty. All else being equal, the final settlement penalty will be lower for a violator who agrees to perform an acceptable SEP, compared to the violator who does not.

B.   Minimum and Maximum Penalty Requirements When SEPs Are Included in Settlement

1.   Minimum Penalty Requirements

Settlements that include a SEP must always also include a penalty. In settlements in which defendants commit to conduct a SEP, the final settlement penalty must equal or exceed either:

> a.   The economic benefit of noncompliance plus ten percent (10%) of the gravity component; or
>
> b.   Twenty-five percent (25%) of the gravity component only; whichever is greater.

* * *

C.   Mitigation of the Penalty When SEPs Are Included in Settlement

1.   General Approach to Penalty Mitigation

Penalty mitigation for performance of a SEP is considered only after all other appropriate mitigation factors in the applicable penalty policies have been applied and a bottom-line settlement penalty determined.

The amount of penalty mitigation given for a SEP should be equivalent to a percentage of the estimated cost to implement the SEP and should not exceed eighty percent (80%) of that estimated cost. * * *

2.   Exceptions to General Penalty Mitigation Approach

> a.   For defendants that are small businesses, government agencies or entities, or non-profit organizations, the penalty mitigation amount may be set as high as one hundred percent (100%) of the estimated SEP cost, if the defendant can demonstrate the project is of outstanding quality. * * *

The preceding materials provide the legal backdrop for the negotiation upon which you are embarking. The following materials specifically relate to EPA's enforcement case against MIT. The enforcement files for this proceeding contain several hundred pages of documents. From those pages, we have selected a few excerpts. The first document below, an internal memorandum from EPA's files, summarizes MIT's RCRA violations. As you read, consider how severe these violations seem, both individually and collectively. Are heavy penalties appropriate?

DRAFT RCRA VIOLATIONS—CONFIDENTIAL

Name and address: Massachusetts Institute of Technology
                           77 Massachusetts Avenue
                           Cambridge, MA 02139

Facility EPA ID Number: MAD001425594

Date of Inspection: May 19, 20, 21,22 and June 10, 1998

Inspectors: [REDACTED] RCRA Technical Office
                           [REDACTED] RCRA Technical Office

Summary of RCRA Violations

1.   Failure to label or mark clearly each container holding hazardous waste with required information, as required by 310 CMR 30.340(1)(b(1),(2) and (3). Containers were not marked with the words "Hazardous Waste" or without the hazardous waste described in words or without the hazard associated with the waste. Specifically, EPA inspectors identified one hundred-eighty-eight (188) containers of hazardous waste without proper labels. * * *

2.   Failure to label or mark containers holding hazardous waste with accumulation dates, as required by 310 CMR 30.340(l)(b)(4). Specifically, EPA inspectors identified one hundred-forty-eight (148) containers holding hazardous waste without markings or labels indicating the accumulation date. * * *

3.   Failure to keep containers holding hazardous waste closed when waste is not being added or removed, as required by 310 CMR 30.685, as referenced by 310 CMR 30.340(I)(a)(c). Specifically, a one-gallon container of acetone and water waste located in Lab 426 of Building 18 was open at the time of the inspection.

4.   Failure to separate incompatible wastes or any other waste or material that is incompatible by means of a dike, berm, wall or other device, as required by 310 CMR 30.688(4). Incompatible wastes were stored in the same secondary containment unit in seven locations. First, in Building 12A—Shelf A1, a container of lanthanium nitrate (oxidizer) was incompatible with both a container of palladium cyanide and zinc sulfide (reducer). Second, in Building 12A—Shelf B1, a container of aluminum nitrate was incompatible with several containers of halogenated organic, amine, and ignitable wastes. These containers held Freon, tetramethylethylenediamine, dinonylphthalates(sp) and thiorhene(sp). Third, in Building 12A—Shelf E3 contained seven containers of acids, a container of sodium cyanide and a container of calcium hypochlorite (oxidizer); all of which are incompatible with each other. Fourth, in Building 12A-Shelf F3, a container of sodium hydroxide/ethanol was stored with multiple containers of acids. Fifth, in

Building 12A—Shelf G2, a container with tetra-n-butyl ammonium hydroxide was incompatible with a container of 1,1,1, trichloroethane. Sixth, in Building 68—Lab 611, a container of chromic and sulfuric acids were stored with a container of chloroform and phenol and a container of ethanol. Seventh, in Building 56—Lab 561, a container of pyropargol alcohol was stored with containers with the organic acids, propionic acid and chloroperoxybenzoic acid.

5.   Failure to have an adequate containment system for storage of containers holding hazardous wastes that contain free liquids, as required by 310 CMR 30.687(2)(c). Along the outside wall of Building 12A there was an approximately 4 inch high berm providing secondary containment for the building. This containment structure existed for both rooms. However, inside the West entrance to each room of the building there was a grate under which ran a steam pipe which was used for heating purposes for both rooms. The trench in which the steam pipe ran was open to the ground along its entire length. This negated any secondary containment in both rooms.

6.   Failure to determine whether a waste is hazardous, as required by 310 CMR 30.302 and 40 C.F.R. § 268.7. Forty-four (44) individual containers and one waste stream did not have determinations made at the time of the inspection.

* * *

7.   Failure to operate the facility in a manner which prevents and minimizes the possibility of any threat to public health, safety, or welfare, or the environment from a fire, explosion, or any other unplanned sudden or non-sudden release of hazardous waste to the air, soil, surface water, or ground water, as required by 310 CMR 30.524(1) as referenced by 310 CMR 30.340(d)(2). There were three instances of this violation. First, in Building 18, Lab 330 a four liter container was clamped to a support over the sink. This container held acetone/hexane/ethyl acetate/palladium. There was no secondary containment. Second, outside room 119 in Building NW21 the storage area was seriously overcrowded. Hazardous waste containers were stacked on the floor and there were multiple layers of secondary containment buckets on single shelves. Third, in Building 56, Lab 522 there was a four liter bottle of water/ethanol/acetic acid waste strapped to the wall next to and above the sink. There was no secondary containment.

8.   Failure to have a device capable of summoning emergency assistance immediately available at the accumulation area, as required by 310 CMR 30.524(2)(b). The storage area outside room 119 in Building NW21 did not have a phone available in the area, the only phone was location in a locked lab. This lab is always locked. The storage area in Lab 171 in

Building E–18 did not have a phone available in the area. The closest emergency telephone was located in the lobby of E–18.

9.   Failure to obtain a Permit prior to the treatment and storage of hazardous waste, as required by 310 CMR 30.801. Specifically, MIT stored hazardous wastes for greater than ninety days in four locations;

- Building 66, Lab 557—one container of butyl alcohol dated 9/13/97 and one container of formamide/pump oil dated 3/14/96.

- Building 66, Lab 463—one container of contaminated glassware dated 9/4/97.

- Building N10, Room207—two containers of MIBK, and one container of waste silicone all dated 8/1/91.

- Building 56, Lab 561—seven containers of various wastes, all dated 1/7/98. In addition, at Building NW21 in Room 167, wastes were treated prior to disposal. In a fume hood, rags soaked with 111-TCA used in cleaning and degreasing are allowed to evaporate prior to [disposal] in the trash.

10. Failure to conduct weekly inspections of hazardous waste accumulation areas for leaking and deterioration of containers or containment system, as required by 310 CMR 30.686 as referenced by 310 CMR 30.340(1)(a)l.d and 310 CMR 30.696(1). Specifically, there were thirty-six (36) areas operating as less-than ninety day storage areas identified during the inspection, even though they had been identified as satellite storage locations. These areas were not included in the weekly scheduled inspection program conducted by the Safety Office. * * * In addition, a partial review of inspection records identified one hundred and fifty (150) missed inspections. For those areas reviewed, it was found that there were missing logs from the record. The following list identify the number of missing logs for each area.

Building 2, lab 115—4 missed

Building 2, lab 308—20 missed

Building 6, lab 431—7 missed

Building 13, lab 5128—34 missed

Building 18, lab 125—5 missed

Building 18, lab 271—11 missed

Building 18, lab 304—9 missed

Building 18, lab 33 1—12 missed

Building 18, lab 332—3 missed

Building 18, lab 349—8 missed

Building 18, lab 363—1 missed

Building 18, lab 546—36 missed

11. Failure to have an adequate Contingency Plan (CP), as required by 310 CMR 30.521(10) & (11). The CP does not list the location of all emergency response equipment throughout the campus. It does state that certain pieces of equipment are located in various locations, but does not give those locations. The CP does not list the home phone numbers for the Emergency Coordinators, and also the CP does not list all the hazardous waste storage locations. The areas identified above in violation #10, do not appear in the CP.

There are contradictions in emergency response procedures within the CP. On page 3 of the CP, the plan states that when a call is received dispatchers will call either 1) the MIT Emergency Response Group, 2) the Safety Office, 3) EMS or 4) the Cambridge Fire Department. On page 11 of the same plan, it is stated that the dispatcher will call an Emergency Coordinator from the Safety Office and perhaps the Cambridge Fire Dept. This section goes on to state that the Emergency Coordinator (EC), will determine if emergency responders are needed including Cambridge Fire.

There are contradictions in spill response procedures within the CP and combined with departmental Chemical Hygiene Plan (CHPs). In the CP, the Emergency Coordinator has the responsibility to determine the identity, character, source and amount of a HW spill. In addition, the EC will determine when to call emergency responders or clean-up contractors. Under the "Specific Emergency Procedures" section of the CP. the EC is more specifically required to determine the potential threat to the environment, and [the] most effective way to contain and collect spills of hazardous materials. To do this the EC must determine what has spilled, how much and how it might spread. Small spills may be cleaned up by trained members of the MIT staff under the direction and [advice] of the EMS. More serious spills require a broader response. In CHPs a different response to spills are outlined. First, the CHPs state that department/lab personnel are responsible for cleaning up spills in their areas. The campus emergency number is listed if the individual needs [advice] from the Safety Office or EMS.

12. Failure to provide and/or failure to provide adequate hazardous waste training, as required by 310 CMR 30.516(1) as referenced by 310 CMR 30.340(1)(d)1. Many personnel and students at MIT did not receive adequate training for the level of their respective RCRA duties. Satellite accumulation area (SAA) operators in nearly all areas inspected were managing hazardous wastes. The SAAs were responsible for making hazardous waste determinations, labeling and dating containers, transporting the waste to less-than-90 day (LT90) storage areas and in

some locations potentially responsible for transporting wastes to Building 12A Group Safety Coordinators (GSC), LT90 operators (if not GSCs) and Lab Supervisors (faculty, principal investigators) were responsible for compliance and management of the LT90 storage areas. All of these individuals received training in their department's Chemical Hygiene Plan (CHP). The level of RCRA information presented in the CHP is not sufficient for those operating LT90 storage areas. In addition, GSCs, Chemical Hygiene Officers and Lab Supervisors are responsible for training new staff and students in hazardous waste management practices. None of these individuals have had sufficient specific RCRA training to be instructors.

A review of Safety Office personnel training records show that REDACTED did not receive annual training in 1995, 1996, 1997 and 1998, REDACTED did not receive annual training in 1995 and 1996, REDACTED did not receive annual training in 1995 and 1996, and REDACTED did not receive annual training in 1997. Additionally, there was no training for the following persons who signed manifests for MIT in 1997 and 1998: [six names redacted]. Finally, there were no records of training received for REDACTED, anyone from Environmental Medical Services, the MIT Emergency Response Group or the MIT Police Department—all of whom are listed as first responders to HW incidents.

13. Failure to have an adequate training plan and failure to maintain documentation of hazardous waste training, as required by 310 CMR 30. 516(1) as referenced by 310 CMR 30.340(l)(d)1.

The MIT Training Plan does not identify job titles for those persons involved with emergency response. Other job titles are mentioned in passing in the Plan.

The Plan does not include descriptions for some titles presented. For example, lab personnel managing satellite and less-than-90 (LT90) day accumulation areas as well as emergency responders are mentioned but there are no descriptions of their duties.

There are no descriptions of skills or qualifications needed for any position in the Plan.

The Plan does not list any individuals that need training. Some positions that are listed that do not have a description of any training. For example, technicians in the Safety Office have a detailed description of [their] duties but there is no description of the type and amount of training necessary for the position. Some training lists positions for which there are no descriptions, such as, Responder Level training. The sole position description requiring response to emergencies is the one person filling the Chemical Waste Program Manager position, although the training description states that there are many others.

Nowhere in the Plan is there a discussion of the required amount of introductory or continuing training.

No CHP calls for the training courses identified in the Plan. The Plan apparently had not made it to the department level CHPs address what the training requirements are for the department and those requirements are only to be trained on the CHP.

At the department/lab level, there are indications from the CHPs that documentation is supposed to be maintained for initial training on the CHP. However, when inspectors asked to see such data it was not available for review. In the Chemistry Department (the largest generators), annual training records were not maintained at all. According to REDACTED, Chemistry CHO and Deputy Dept. Chair, professors are only verbally asked if training has occurred the previous year in their group.

14. Shipping hazardous waste without a manifest, as required by 310 CMR 30.311(1).

On May 27, 1997 a shipment of waste mercury was sent to Radiac Research Corp. 261 Kent Ave. Brooklyn, NY 11211 on a Bill of Lading. The shipment included two thirty gallon drums of the mercury waste that Radiac has stated was destined to be recycled. Hazardous wastes shipped to be recycled must be shipped on a Hazardous Waste Manifest.

15. Failure to properly file exception reports, as required by 310 CMR 30.333.

During the review of 1997 and 1998, it was discovered that there were many missing return copies of manifests from the receiving facilities. MIT personnel were asked about these manifests and as a follow-up to the inspection, MIT attempted to locate missing manifests. At the time of the inspection, the key personnel in the Safety Office responsible for waste shipments did not know of the missing copies or of any exception reporting. However, MIT later submitted to the EPA inspector, a letter to [the Massachusetts Department of Environmental Protection] dated April 22, 1998 documenting that for thirty-nine manifests from 3/3/95 to 2/26/98 no return copies were received and that after repeated attempts to get copies they were unsuccessful.

16. Proper use of manifest violations—to come

EPA's next step was to provide MIT with a detailed accounting of these violations and the associated penalty amounts and rationales. MIT then responded with a detailed response arguing for reduced penalties and providing its rationales for those reductions. Additional correspondence followed. These documents are long—the initial proposal and counterproposal both contain about ninety pages—and the excerpt below, from an MIT counterproposal, is designed to give you a sense of the discussion. As you negotiate, we suggest that you avoid getting bogged down in detailed discussions about where each of these violations fits within EPA's penalty matrix. While getting bogged down in those discussions would likely be an important part of a real-world settlement negotiation, your task here instead is to stay focused on the general questions. How severe are these violations (bearing in mind that this is just a partial sampling from a much longer discussion)? How might you tailor a settlement to discourage their recurrence? And how much credit should MIT receive for the efforts described in its cover letter?

Letter from Chief, Civil Division, U.S. Attorney's Office and U.S. EPA to MIT

Feb. 7, 2000

CONFIDENTIAL AND FOR PURPOSES OF SETTLEMENT ONLY

RE: MIT's Counterproposal to EPA/Justice Department December 21, 1999 Penalty Demand

Dear REDACTED:

This letter and its enclosures constitute the Massachusetts Institute of Technology's ("MIT") counter-proposal in response to your letter of December 21, 1999. Your letter and its attachments allege various violations of the Resource Conservation and Recovery Act, Clean Water Act and Clean Air Act identified by the Environmental Protection Agency ("EPA") in a May, 1998 inspection at MIT's Cambridge, Massachusetts campus, and demand associated penalties.

As a threshold matter, thank you for including detailed penalty calculations and rationales with your December 21st letter. This courtesy not only made MIT's review of your demand more efficient, but also allowed us to focus on your principal concerns. MIT has taken the same approach in our counterproposal, and has enclosed detailed calculations and rationales for your review. Hopefully, this approach will allow us to most productively engage in settlement negotiations and foster a prompt resolution.

As I indicated in my recent telephone conversation with the enclosed calculations and rationales support a considerably lower penalty than the demanded penalty. In deriving MIT's counterproposal, however, we have been careful to employ only what we believe are reasonable interpretations and applications of EPA's penalty policies. MIT also has identified and enclosed additional information and documentation that we believe further mitigate the penalty demanded. In an effort to expedite settlement, we have not proposed as extensive a reduction in penalties for litigation risk as we might have.

MIT appreciates your determination that we have been "exceptionally cooperative" in our response to EPA's enforcement. Having made this determination, you provided a 10% reduction in the penalties demanded. During and after EPA's inspection, MIT provided access to our facilities and records, answered questions and provided requested documentation promptly and cooperatively. MIT has always tried to be responsible in our approach to the environment; and although we recognize some shortcomings in our past organizational approach and follow through, there are no allegations of actual damage to the environment. EPA's inspection did reveal a need for MIT to develop a more organized approach to environmental management, and we have made every attempt to respond to this need even before resolving this enforcement.

Since the time of EPA's inspection, MIT has taken definitive action and made a significant economic investment to improve our organizational structure around environmental matters. The President and Executive Vice President of MIT have created a senior management position, the Managing Director for Environmental Programs and Risk Management, and Senior Counsel, that reports to the Executive Vice President and is responsible for environmental compliance as well as for coordinating the implementation of positive environmental initiatives at MIT. In July, 1999, I was hired to fill this position. All of the service departments at MIT that oversee and administer environmental compliance and positive initiatives report to the Managing Director. Two of these departments are the Safety Office and the Environmental Medical Service. The third department is a new department, the Environmental Management Office, that has been broken out of, and elevated to equal status as, the Safety Office, and is responsible for administering environmental compliance and positive initiatives. This new position and organizational structure has elevated the visibility and importance of environmental matters on campus. This new organizational structure also is enabling MIT to establish clearer roles, responsibilities and accountability for each of the environmental regulatory programs and to pursue a comprehensive program of positive initiatives as well.

In addition to creating an enhanced organizational capacity, as Managing Director I have developed, with input by staff and faculty, a preliminary plan for an innovative environmental, health and safety management system ("EMS"). This plan for an EMS goes beyond what is required for compliance, and integrates environmental compliance and good safety and health practices with positive initiatives and education (both as required by regulations and in support of positive attitudes and practices among students, staff and faculty). This integrated approach recognizes that compliance, positive practices and initiatives and education are all components of responsible environmental stewardship. This plan for an EMS is a model for higher education and is made possible in part by MIT's investing responsibility for both compliance and positive initiatives in the same position. A single responsible position avoids the typical isolation of compliance from the kinds of positive initiatives that can reap real benefits for the environment while reducing the burdens of compliance. The EMS will embody a comprehensive environmental management approach, rather than a limited compliance approach. In furtherance of this plan, I have assembled a team comprising staff of the environmental service departments, the Information Systems Department, and representatives of the regulated community at MIT, to further define, develop and implement the plan. (Implementation of the plan may have to be phased, or possibly not be fully realized, due to the potential of very high implementation costs. However, components of the plan will be prioritized, and there will be substantial value in designing an EMS that is a model and could be implemented over time.) MIT's Provost has directed the Deans to identify faculty representatives to participate in this effort as well.

President REDACTED on January 12, 2000 announced a campus-wide environmental initiative to make MIT's campus more sustainable in an economically and administratively feasible manner. An Environmental Programs Task Force convened in the summer of 1999, led by the Managing Director and comprising students and staff across MIT, already has vastly expanded MIT's recycling program, has commenced a food com posting pilot program, has initiated a green building task force to develop guidelines for the design of greener buildings on campus, and has implemented the first phase (focussing on paper procurement) of a green goods procurement program. MIT is not only responding to EPA's compliance requirements, but also seeks to assume a leadership role in its overall approach to the environment on campus.

In addition to these substantial commitments, MIT has supported EPA's Clean Charles 2005 Initiative. MIT's support has included donating a boat and graduate student for one year to assist in clean-up activities, being a founding member of the Clean Charles Coalition, offering to contribute a graduate student and some funding toward a storm water competition, and assisting in public promotions of EPA's Initiative.

In view of these actions and this level of cooperation, MIT respectfully requests that you consider at least a 30% reduction in the penalty assessed against MIT. EPA's enforcement guidelines allow up to a 30% reduction in penalties for "unique" factors; and we hope that you will consider MIT's cooperation and commitment worthy of at least a 20% reduction.

As we have discussed, MIT would like to perform Supplemental Environmental Projects ("SEP") in lieu of monetary penalties to the fullest extent permissible. I have had some preliminary discussions with and others at EPA about the comprehensive model EMS integrating compliance, positive initiatives and education as a potential SEP. We look forward to further discussing the details of this proposal, and potentially others, with you and then to submitting a written SEP proposal. MIT's settlement counterproposal is subject to EPA allowing MIT to invest in SEP(s) in lieu of 75% (the highest allowable percentage) of the final penalties assessed pursuant to EPA's SEP policy. Our counterproposal also is subject to EPA giving MIT full credit against the final penalties, dollar for dollar, for our investment in any approved SEP(s), because MIT is a nonprofit entity.

We have agreed with you on a schedule for settlement discussions this month and next, and I look forward to beginning this process in a few weeks. In the meantime, please feel free to contact me if you have any questions concerning the enclosed counterproposal. While each of us must responsibly and zealously represent our clients, I look forward to continuing the cooperative and constructive dialogue we have had, as we progress to the next stage of this matter.

Very truly yours,

REDACTED

Managing Director for Environmental Programs
And Risk Management, and
Senior Counsel

MIT'S PENALTY CALCULATIONS FOR THE RCRA VIOLATIONS

I.   Alleged failure to label or mark clearly each container holding hazardous waste with information regarding its contents, as required by 310 C.M.R. 30.340(1)(b)(1), (2), and (3) and 40 C.F.R. 262.34(c) and 262.34(a)(3).

A.   Application of the Penalty Policy:

1.   Category of Violation: Moderate/Minor

(a)   Potential for Harm—Moderate—For purposes of settlement MIT has not proposed changing EPA's determination of the "Potential for Harm."

(b)   Extent of Deviation—Minor—MIT proposes to adjust the extent of deviation from the regulatory requirement to minor for the following reasons. MIT estimates that EPA inspected over 2000 containers, and alleged only 188, mostly small containers had some labeling issues. This represents less than 10% of the total containers inspected. EPA also recognized that most of the 188 containers had some identifying information. Also, out of the nearly 2000 laboratories and other facilities on campus, EPA observed only 30 locations with alleged violations; many of these thirty rooms only had one container alleged to be missing one of the three pieces of identifying information required by the Massachusetts regulations.

2.   Penalty Assessment:

(a)   Matrix Cell Range (Range for Moderate/Minor violations is $3,000–$4,999):

Gravity-Based Component: Penalty Amount Proposed: $3,200. MIT proposes the low end of the matrix range because the potential for harm from this violation could easily have been deemed minor. First, at the time of EPA's inspection, MIT had (and still has) a procedure in place for resolving waste container labeling problems. The waste technicians check for labeling discrepancies at the time of pick-up (in the lab) and again during the shelving of the waste in the main storage area, Building 12A. The main storage area is inspected weekly (as a less than 90-day storage area) when the HW labels are again reviewed. Outside vendors' chemists again check the labels during the bi-weekly waste pick-ups at the main storage area. Also, most containers that EPA identified were in flammable storage cabinets and were small. The number of locations where EPA identified violations is a small percentage of all sites on campus where waste is stored and a small percentage of the overall number of containers inspected.

(b)   Multiple/multi-day: Although EPA has discretion with a Moderate/Minor violation to forego multiple penalties, in order to facilitate settlement MIT has included a multi-day component in its penalty counteroffer. The matrix cell for *Moderate/Minor* violations has a range of $150–$1,000. For the reasons discussed above, MIT has proposed that the low end of the matrix range be used. We have also accepted EPA's proposal for the number of instances.

Instance 2–30 are assessed at $160 per instance

Penalty = ($160 × 29) = $4,640

* * *

(d)   Adjustment to Penalty Amount for Unique Factors: MIT appreciates EPA's determination that MIT has made exceptional efforts to cooperate with EPA and support EPA's initiatives. * * * These efforts include, among others, creating the senior management position of Managing Director for Environmental Programs (filled by REDACTED) to lead all of the offices at MIT with responsibility for environmental management, to overhaul MIT's environmental management systems, and to coordinate the implementation of positive environmental programs. REDACTED has initiated (without awaiting the resolution of this matter) significant efforts to improve environmental management at MIT. MIT has also assisted EPA in undertaking and promoting the Clean Charles 2005 initiative and has quickly and comprehensively responded to all of EPA's information requests in this matter. MIT has also responded promptly to correct conditions identified by EPA. Given this level of cooperation and commitment, EPA's RCRA Penalty Policy allows as much as a 40% reduction. MIT requests under these circumstances that EPA consider a greater than 10% downward adjustment, such as a 30% adjustment. 30% deflation factor = $2,292.

(e) Adjustment to Penalty Amount for Willfulness/negligence: None.

(f) Adjustment to Penalty Amount for History of Noncompliance: MIT proposes that there be no upward adjustment for "History of Non-compliance." Although EPA did not specify the "History" upon which it relies, MIT has not received any notice of non-compliance from either EPA or the Massachusetts Department of Environmental Protection ("MADEP") under RCRA for almost ten years. MIT believes it promptly responded satisfactorily to the issues identified by the MADEP ten years ago. Particularly since the length of time that has elapsed is an important factor in EPA's RCRA Civil Penalty Policy for determining if a history of non-compliance adjustment is appropriate, MIT requests that no upward adjustment be made.

(g) Economic benefit: None.

Total Penalty Amount= $6,876

II. Alleged failure to label or mark containers holding hazardous waste with the date that accumulation began, as required by 310 C.M.R. 30.340(1)(b)(4) and 40 C.F.R. 262.34(a)(2).

A. Application of the Penalty Policy:

1. Category of Violation:

(a) Potential for Harm—Moderate. MIT proposes to adjust the potential for harm from major to moderate for a number of reasons. First, virtually all of the waste EPA observed was in small containers. Also, of the 137 containers identified, at least 123 were in satellite accumulation areas where Massachusetts' regulations do not require that the date be placed on containers. Moreover, the potential for harm should not be major because the basis of EPA's allegation that many of these satellite accumulation areas were being operated as less than ninety day areas was that more than one container was collecting similar waste streams. This practice is not even a requirement for maintaining satellite accumulation status in EPA's regulations at 40 C.F.R. § 262.34 or in other Region 1 states. Also, as discussed above, there was no major potential for harm since MIT had (and still has) a procedure in place for catching labeling discrepancies. In the unlikely event that a container is mislabeled or unlabeled, MIT technicians will correct any deficiencies during the weekly inspections of the main storage area or the biweekly waste pick-ups at the laboratories (e.g. dating full containers, checking hazard class, etc.). The fact that all but one of the hundreds of containers in Building 12A, the central waste storage building for the campus were labeled with accumulation dates reinforces that MIT's procedures provide a good back-up and reduce the potential for harm from these allegations from major to moderate. In addition, although MIT is allowed to store waste for 90 days, it is MIT's policy and usual practice to pick up waste from Building 12A at a minimum of every two weeks. This further reduces the likelihood that waste will remain on campus for greater than 90 days and thus the potential for harm is minimized. For these reasons it might be possible to justify a "minor" designation, but in the interest of settlement, MIT has not proposed to do so.

(b)   Extent of Deviation—Minor. MIT agrees that the extent of deviation is minor.

2.   Penalty Assessment:

(a)   Matrix Cell Range (Range for Moderate/Minor violations is $3,000–$4,999): Gravity-Based Component: Penalty Amount Proposed: $3,800.

(b)   Multiple/multi-day: As discussed above, for moderate/minor penalties EPA can forego multi-day penalties. However, for settlement purposes, MIT has included a multi-day component in its proposal. The matrix cell for Moderate/Minor violations is $150–$1,000. Instances 2–22 are assessed at $400 per instance

Penalty= ($400 × 21) = $8,400

* * *

(d)   Adjustment to Penalty Amount for Unique Factors: As discussed above in greater detail, MIT requests EPA's consideration of a 30% downward adjustment for what EPA has determined to be MIT's exceptional cooperation. Although MIT believes that there is some litigation risk associated with the portion of this allegation that is based on the alleged failure to date containers in satellite storage areas, we have not proposed any additional downward adjustment in an effort to reach a quick settlement. Deflation factor = $3,660

(e)   Adjustment to Penalty Amount for Willfulness/negligence: None.

(f)   Adjustment to Penalty Amount for History of Noncompliance: None. See discussion above.

(g)   Economic benefit: None.

Total Penalty Amount = $8,540

* * *

———————

In the document above, MIT's cover letter mentions the possibility of developing a SEP. MIT and EPA continued to pursue that option, and the discussion below explains MIT's proposal. To simplify the problem we have omitted the portion of the original SEP proposal that described a new stormwater containment facility.

Letter from MIT to Chief, Civil Division, U.S. Attorney's Office and U.S. EPA

June 22, 2000

CONFIDENTIAL AND FOR PURPOSES OF SETTLEMENT ONLY

RE: MIT SEP Proposal

Dear: Redacted

Thank you for providing MIT with the opportunity to explore a public school Supplemental Environmental Project (SEP) with the Cambridge School system on the schedule required by the City of Cambridge. Our initial discussions with school officials have been fruitful and, although we have more work to do with the City to formalize our understanding, we are now able to enclose that preliminary SEP proposal, as well as MIT's other SEP proposals, for your review. As you will see, we have tentatively proposed subject to the conditions outlined below, to undertake * * * the following SEPs: (1) an outreach and education program in the Cambridge Public School system that will integrate programs of environmental awareness, education, hazardous materials use and waste reduction, technical issues, and improvements to existing curricula (cost estimate $150,000); and (3) the development of a "Virtual Campus" that will provide an interactive guide and educational resource for hazardous material and waste management in the university setting (cost estimate $275,000). These SEPs are intended to respond to EPA's and the US Attorney's office's previously expressed interest in MIT's pursuit of * * * a public benefit project, and a virtual campus program.

The attached SEP proposals provide a more detailed description of the [two] SEPs, and our initial estimate of budgets and schedules. The total cost of the two SEPs is estimated to be $425,000, which * * * exceeds the SEP credit necessary under * * * MIT's [$419,000 total for cash penalty and SEPs settlement proposal. That cost would offset part of the government's $674,000 settlement proposal.]

As we discussed with REDACTED this morning, MIT is nonetheless excited about the significant environmental

> To be clear, what MIT is asking here is that the amount of any penalty it pays to the U.S. Treasury be reduced by a percentage of the cost of the SEPs. This is a standard practice with SEPs, but the key question—if EPA accepts the SEPs—is how much of a reduction is appropriate. EPA's SEP guidance (excerpted above) discusses that question.

benefits offered by these [two] SEPs and is willing to implement them, if EPA agrees to accept MIT's settlement proposal of $419,000 on the further terms outlined below.

Under any reasonable analysis, the overall mitigation credit from these two SEPs is greater than required under either party's settlement proposal, and more than bridges the approximately $254,000 gap between MIT's and the Government's positions. If MIT's settlement offer were not accepted, and we were able to negotiate an agreeable total settlement figure, MIT would propose to implement SEPs that may exceed, but are more in line with, the amount of the necessary SEP credit.

Our offer to undertake up to [two] of the SEPs described in this letter is contingent on negotiating consent decree language that (1) would legally require MIT to expend 75% of the total settlement amount [i.e. 314,250] or such greater amount as may be necessary to complete the SEPs, rather than citing the greater amount that MIT is likely to expend, and (2) would allow MIT to reallocate SEP funds among the projects if they individually cost more or less than we have estimated. We discussed the second point with REDACTED. I also understand there is precedent in other consent decrees for such an approach. This settlement proposal is further contingent on the Government allowing MIT to mitigate the maximum allowable percentage of overall penalties under EPA's SEP Policy (in this case 75% of the total penalties, as MIT has not realized any significant economic benefit from the alleged violations), and our receiving dollar-for-dollar credit for the SEPs. Thus, we are proposing to pay a cash penalty of $104,750, with the $314,250 remainder of the $419,000 penalty being mitigated by * * * the SEPs described in this submission.

MIT is enthusiastic about the prospect of undertaking these SEP proposals and we are available to discuss the details of this settlement proposal with you. Please contact me or REDACTED at REDACTED to arrange a time to discuss MIT's proposal or to address any questions you may have as you review our proposal. Thank you for your consideration; we look forward to hearing from you soon.

Very truly yours,

REDACTED

Confidential—For Settlement Purposes Only

Scope of Work
Supplemental Environmental Project #2
Cambridge Public School System Outreach and Education Program
Consent Decree and Order
Docket No. ___
Massachusetts Institute of Technology (MIT)
77 Massachusetts Avenue
Cambridge, MA 02139

Proposed SEP Description

Following the success of earlier programs, in 1997 MIT formed the Center for Environmental Initiatives ("CEI"). The Program for Environmental Education and Research ("PEER") was established within CEI and given the explicit mission to act as its education and outreach arm. MIT proposes to develop through PEER, the MIT Center for Environmental Initiatives, and the MIT Chemistry Department a curriculum module for use in the Cambridge High School system. The module would be used in the Cambridge High Schools to integrate programs of environmental awareness, education, technical issues, and improvements to existing curricula, including hazardous waste reduction and pollution prevention. In order to undertake this SEP, the Cambridge School System will have to agree to collaborate with MIT and incorporate the new curricula into existing science curricula.

In preliminary conversations with Cambridge School Department leaders, officials have responded positively and have proposed that MIT officials work collaboratively with a team of science teachers and the Science Coordinator for the City of Cambridge Schools to develop such environmental curricula. This program may be both classroom and laboratory oriented. School officials are hopeful that such a project could build upon the smaller curricula initiatives presently implemented in the system. The Cambridge School System has signaled a willingness to collaborate with MIT in the development and implementation of a program plan and to negotiate a memorandum of understanding with MIT to outline the program's purpose and goals.

MIT is already collaborating successfully with the School System to develop and implement many other unrelated projects of varying subjects, which demonstrates MIT's ability to work well with the Cambridge School System. A summary of these activities is available upon request.

Public Health and Environmental Benefit

Implementation of this SEP will be environmentally beneficial. Incorporating pollution prevention and "green chemistry" concepts into the Cambridge Public School System will educate current and future users of hazardous materials in the safe and efficient management of hazardous materials, reduction in hazardous waste, and pollution prevention, as well as promoting important lifetime environmental values. This will reduce risks to public health and the environment at large. The Education and Outreach program will also have the immediate effect of focusing the Cambridge School System's attention on its current hazardous materials use and waste generation, and provide a mechanism to evaluate areas where chemical use and waste generation can be reduced.

Cambridge School officials indicate that such a project could raise awareness of environmental issues and increase positive environmental performance of both the Cambridge Schools and homes of the families of students in the City of Cambridge.

The Cambridge Public School System Outreach and Education Program Satisfies the SEP Policy.

The Cambridge Public School System Outreach and Education Program meets the definition and key characteristics of a SEP contained in the SEP Policy. The project fits within the basic definition of a SEP since, as is discussed above, it is an environmentally beneficial project. This project also would provide significant public environmental benefits to Cambridge. MIT conceived of this project in response to EPA's notification of alleged violations of the Resource Conservation and Recovery Act (RCRA), well after EPA conducted its inspection at the Institute. MIT is not otherwise required to assist the Cambridge Public School System. This SEP falls, among others, under the Pollution Prevention Assessment and the Environmental Compliance Promotion categories in the SEP Policy.

This SEP also satisfies EPA's legal guidelines for a SEP. First, it has adequate nexus to the RCRA violations identified by EPA. It will reduce the likelihood of similar violations in the future by educating the faculty and students of the Cambridge Public School System—current and future users of hazardous materials and generators of hazardous waste—regarding the importance of safe and responsible use of hazardous materials and minimization of hazardous waste. The SEP will be implemented in Cambridge, which is in the "immediate geographic area" of EPA's alleged violations. Second, the Program will clearly advance the objectives of the Resource Conservation and Recovery Act. Third, although MIT welcomes EPA's input on the details of the Program, MIT is not proposing that EPA play any role in managing SEP funds or controlling the performance of it. Finally, no EPA appropriations are to be used in performing this SEP.

Cost of Project

The estimated costs that MIT expects to incur in its work on this project are listed below. These preliminary estimates, which are subject to change and refinement as we develop more detailed curricula with the City of Cambridge, are based on developing and pilot testing the program and implementing it for one school year, after which the Cambridge School System would be in a position to effectively use the curriculum on its own.

Administration of the Program	3,990
Research Assistant Stipend	26,500
Graduate Student Stipend	18,750
Peer Services Charge—MIT Faculty Advisor	18,000
Hardware and Software	8,000
Reproduction Costs	46,760
City of Cambridge Implementation	28,000
Grand Total	125,000

Schedule for Implementation

MIT anticipates that the initial development of environmental curriculum materials could be completed within a period of approximately 24 months. The materials could then be pilot tested in one or more high school science classes as soon thereafter as the Cambridge School System determines is feasible, based on the timing of the academic year. MIT would propose an implementation schedule in the development phase of this project. If completion of the development phase does not coincide with the beginning of a school year, implementation may need to wait for the next school year. Adjustments will be made during the pilot implementation, and the program can then be more widely implemented. The City of Cambridge will be asked to commit to using the materials for at least one school year but would be equipped to continue their use. We would like to discuss with EPA the best way to address the schedule for this SEP in the consent decree.

Confidential—For Settlement Purposes Only

Scope of Work
Supplemental Environmental Project #3
Design & Development of a "Virtual Campus"
Consent Decree and Order
Docket No. ___
Massachusetts Institute of Technology (MIT)
77 Massachusetts Avenue
Cambridge, MA 02139

Proposed SEP Description

Among the biggest challenges facing the regulated community is the sheer number of environmental regulations that govern its activities. Universities, hospitals, and similar research directed, highly decentralized institutions are particularly challenged by these regulatory requirements. Adequately addressing proper waste generation, handling and disposal, and training a diverse population of researchers, administrators, and students, requires innovative management strategies. The transient nature of such settings, with significant turnover at least three times annually, exacerbates the situation.

MIT proposes to develop an innovative, computer-based "virtual campus" designed to help to address these challenges. The project, which will involve content and software development and the procurement of computer hardware, will allow users to "navigate" the virtual campus and identify the regulatory requirements applicable to various locations. These will include laboratories, central waste storage areas, power plant facilities, and potentially, certain other areas (e.g., storm drains, garages) where regulated activities are conducted. MIT is also willing to discuss the virtual campus concept and content with EPA, within the general scope of our proposal.

The SEP will require the following tasks:

- development of the storyboard and shoot list (content and photography planning and development)
- shooting video and taking still photographs
- digitizing and editing video and photos
- production of the technical content underlying the user interface
- software coding to produce package
- a dedicated server purchase

Public Health and Environmental Benefit

This SEP will be environmentally beneficial. The innovative "virtual campus" will create a highly effective training tool for campus environmental management including compliance. This tool will be as useful to researchers as it is to students and every level of administrative staff, by clearly and graphically demonstrating the regulatory requirements and good management practices applicable to a variety of areas on campus where hazardous materials or wastes are generated, stored or otherwise managed. The virtual campus will clearly identify the areas subject to compliance requirements, and make that information widely and easily available. MIT would like to discuss with EPA appropriate access to the use of this virtual campus software for a limited number of other colleges or universities that lack the means to develop their own program.

The Virtual Campus Satisfies the SEP Policy

The Virtual Campus Project meets the definition and key characteristics of an SEP contained in the SEP Policy. The project fits within the basic definition of an SEP since, as is discussed above, it is an environmentally beneficial project. MIT is not otherwise required to develop the virtual campus. This SEP falls, among others, under the Pollution Prevention Assessment and the Environmental Compliance Promotion categories of the SEP Policy.

This SEP also satisfies EPA's legal guidelines for a SEP. First, it has adequate nexus to the Resource Conservation and Recovery Act and Clean Water Act violations alleged by EPA. EPA expressed concern about MIT's training programs, and this SEP will provide an excellent training tool for a wide variety of constituents in the regulated community. It will improve MIT's ability, beyond that required in the regulations, to respond to the violations alleged by EPA, by helping us to maximize knowledge of good management and regulatory provisions relating to labeling, compatibility of storage, accumulation dates, LDR information, and record keeping. The SEP also will be implemented at MIT's campus where EPA alleged violations, and is therefore in the "immediate geographic area" of the alleged violations. Second, by enhancing MIT's ability to achieve and maintain compliance, good management practices and excellence in training, the project will clearly advance the objectives of the Resource Conservation and Recovery Act, the Clean Air Act and the Clean Water Act, the three federal statutes underlying EPA's action. Third, although MIT welcomes EPA's input on the technical details, MIT is not proposing that EPA play any role in managing SEP funds or controlling the performance of it. Finally, no EPA appropriations are to be used in performing this SEP.

Cost of Project

We do not anticipate the significant use of outside consultants to perform the work, with the possible exceptions of the photography and video development and some content development. However, the implementation of this project is not currently included in staff time budgets and we will be required to pay a service charged to MIT's Information Systems Group for the development of this program. For cost estimating purposes, we have used a loaded cost of $100 per hour for IS staff and senior departmental staff for the technical content. There are also expected to be other related costs (not included here) such as subscriptions to regulatory databases and MSDS libraries, but these should be small compared to the overall project costs. The following cost proposal reflects a preliminary order of magnitude cost estimate. Actual costs could range from $100,000 to over $235,000. We continue to develop more cost information and will provide updated information within the next month.

Phase	*Estimated Costs*
1) Software Development and Project Management	$80,000
2) Develop Technical Content-Staff Time	70,000
3) Technical Content-Photography and Movies	17,500
4) Pilot/Beta Testing System	17,500
5) Server Procurement and Installation	8,000
6) Consulting services support for content and/or system development and software tools	82,000
Total:	$275,000

Implementation Schedule

[Eds.: The proposal describes implementation and reporting over a two-year period.]

NOTE

In another excerpt of their article about compliance, Gray and Silbey describe efforts at "Eastern University" to implement a settlement with EPA. One passage describes the roles played by the lawyers:

> With a team of graduate students, Susan Silbey conducted an ethnographic study as Eastern University developed a management system (MS) for containing EHS hazards in its research laboratories. The MS was part of a negotiated agreement with the EPA following an inspection of the laboratories. Although

the EPA had not recorded one spill, emission, or instance of environmental damage, the agency faulted the university for not having a documented system for managing laboratory hazards and for not being able to account for the variation in compliance or violations that the EPA observed among the many laboratories inspected. The university's attorney and chief risk manager, along with several compliance managers (e.g., the head of environmental programs and the director of the EHS Office), were obligated to meet semiannually with EPA staff attorneys to develop the MS in accordance with terms of the negotiated consent decree.

Going beyond the required semiannual meetings, the university compliance managers regularly met and consulted with the EPA lawyers. The university's attorney, however, was not present at these meetings, during which the EHS compliance managers often sought advice about alternative models for policies, programs, and procedures they were developing.

For example, as part of the EHS-MS, the university was required to create a pollution prevention program. As the committee designing the system began to work on the pollution prevention component, the requirements became indeterminate, as was often the case with each of the consent decree's mandates. So the committee members met with the EPA attorney to discuss possible alternative ways that the design committee had come up with to reduce consumption of potentially polluting substances. They inquired about the decree's language to see what room for maneuver and degrees of freedom they had. For instance, would the inventory system they were developing, combined with research on alternative, less toxic solvents, and a program to encourage adoption of these alternative solvents, meet the goal of a pollution prevention program? In the course of these back-and-forth discussions, the university compliance managers established an easygoing, almost collegial relationship that involved ongoing dialogue about the university's local culture, resources, and pragmatic considerations; at the same time they would often exchange stories about other universities' and public entities' struggles with environmental compliance. Although the EPA attorneys would not prescribe what should be done and how the EHS-MS should look in its details, they were a source of information about what other institutions were doing, how one procedure worked better than another, and under what conditions.

The EPA did not have a script for compliance. The entire purpose of creating a management system to achieve sustainable environmental health and safety was premised on the notion that the university had to institute means of self-observation and the capacity to respond by and for itself. The central trope here is of a regulatory mechanism that will bring routine practices and behavior within acceptable boundaries, similar to a thermostat. Although all parties were ostensibly bound by the governing federal (and state and local) statutes, as well as the court-sanctioned consent decree, the EPA attorney's stance was more pedagogical and informational than prescriptive or proscriptive. Moreover, the EPA did not expect perfectly uniform performance. It acknowledged the inevitable variation but wanted to limit the scope and frequency of those violations. Not infrequently, these conversations were punctuated by humorous quips about the administration in Washington as well as the difficulties of managing arrogant professors. Each side of the table offered confessions concerning their most intransigent colleagues. The EPA and university managers had become allies in the effort to herd the scientific cats of academia, working together to develop a system that would produce safer and more environmentally sustainable research laboratories.

In contrast, throughout the duration of the consent decree, Eastern's attorney interacted with and anticipated interactions with the EPA quite differently. He rarely spoke with EPA attorneys outside the semiannual reports; his transactions were scripted and curt. When he prepared documents, he assumed that they would be interpreted to the detriment of the university. Although an attorney should anticipate that opposing parties may exploit textual lacunae and indeterminacies to serve their interests, experienced attorneys usually adjust their expectations to the particular situation, learning through the various transactions what the work style of the opposing lawyer is, and what kinds of responses to expect, and they adjust tactics accordingly. When negotiations are successful, this can be a process of mutual exploration and adjustment. The university's attorney had successfully negotiated with this EPA attorney what the university leadership assessed to be a very reasonable settlement. Yet, even as the development of the EHS-MS proceeded, and even into the final weeks of the consent decree's time frame, the university's attorney adopted an adversarial stance with the EPA. At times, he became so distrusting and hostile that the university's compliance managers found themselves repeatedly engaged in repair work with the EPA attorneys. Expressing disappointment in this variation in treatment from the university's agents (the attorney as compared to the managers with whom he allied), the EPA attorney said one day, "Doesn't he see the person behind the role? Who does he think he is dealing with? Haven't we been working on this for years now? Am I the enemy?" To the university's attorney, the EPA was the enemy, a threat rather than an ally. Here, an internal compliance officer with almost complete autonomy—the university attorney—lacking technical expertise in the hazards and infrequently interacting with the EPA personnel did not form alliances or regard the external regulators as allies, as did some of the other internal compliance staff. Thus, internal compliance staff may themselves be either compliance promoting or compliance limiting, depending, we argue, not on their formal position alone but on their expertise, autonomy, and interactional frequency with the regulators.

Gray & Silbey, *supra*, at 121–23.

Test your knowledge with a Chapter 5 online quiz in CasebookPlus™.

CHAPTER 6

CONTAMINATED SITE CLEANUP

Between 1957 and 1971, paper companies released more than 250,000 pounds of polychlorinated biphenyls (PCBs) into the Lower Fox River of Wisconsin. PCBs, we now know, are highly toxic chemicals, but these releases likely broke no federal statutory law. Congress did not enact the modern Clean Water Act until 1972, and EPA did not ban the use of PCBs in manufacturing until 1979. Yet, as a result of the actions of these paper companies, and to a lesser extent of other polluters, PCBs contaminated more than 10 million tons of sediment along a 40-mile stretch of the Lower Fox River and a 1,000 square mile portion of Lake Michigan's Green Bay, into which the river flows. Controversy over the resulting cleanup has lasted decades. When all of the final bills come due, that cleanup will cost well over $1 billion.

The Comprehensive Environmental Response, Compensation, and Liability Act (CERCLA), sometimes referred to as the Superfund statute, is the federal law governing the remediation of contaminated sites like the Lower Fox River. CERCLA does this partly by authorizing EPA to set standards governing the process of cleaning up sites contaminated by hazardous substances. But its primary importance—and the reason that it once was the single most important statute for practicing environmental lawyers—is that it assigns liability for environmental problems that have already occurred. In other words, CERCLA determines who pays the often-massive bills for sites like the Lower Fox River. And, as you will see, CERCLA is among the most aggressive liability laws ever created, imposing liability that is generally strict, joint and several, and retroactive. That means any company that releases hazardous substances into a site like the Lower Fox River could be on the hook for the entire cost of cleanup. There are exceptions to that principle; as you will also learn, CERCLA does provide polluters with ways to avoid or reduce liability. But the single most important thing to know about CERCLA is that the dollar figures associated with liability for contaminated sites can be huge.

The federal government is not alone in requiring polluters to clean up areas that they have contaminated. Many states have their own laws governing environmental remediation, and many cleanup efforts are initiated and supervised by state, rather than federal, agencies. This means that representing entities with liability at contaminated sites often requires attorneys to navigate both federal and state law and negotiate with both federal and state agencies. While lawyers specializing in the cleanup of contaminated sites will need to master their state's cleanup laws, we focus here on the obligations and liability provisions of federal law. Since many of those state laws are modeled upon federal law, understanding CERCLA should also give you a good start toward understanding state laws addressing contaminated sites.

We will begin this chapter with a brief introduction to the science and history of hazardous contamination and then provide a statutory overview. The problems and materials that follow will take you through a series of questions: (1) Who can be liable under CERCLA? (2) How can a potentially liable party avoid liability? (3) What sorts of cleanup processes does CERCLA require? (4) How can a liable party shift some of its liability to other polluters? And (5) how does CERCLA deal with the harms—commonly referred to as natural resource damages—that cannot be undone even by cleaning up a site?

Throughout the chapter, another persistent question will emerge: what kinds of incentives does this statute create? CERCLA has many critics. They argue that the costs the statute imposes are not worth the benefits it creates; that it serves primarily to enrich lawyers;[1] and, perhaps most concerning, that it encourages the abandonment of old industrial sites and pushes development to urban fringes. As you read, consider whether you agree with these critiques, and consider also whether you think the steps Congress and EPA have taken to respond to these critiques make sense.

———————

I. THE PROBLEM OF ENVIRONMENTAL CONTAMINATION

Contaminated sites often have their own distinctive histories and problems, but there are some common characteristics. Understanding a little bit about where contamination often comes from, what gets contaminated, which contaminants are common, and how sites are generally cleaned up can be helpful for a lawyer. In practice, you will typically work with engineers, geologists, and other specialists with much greater technical knowledge about contamination, but a contaminated site lawyer needs to have some basic information about the technical side of site identification and cleanup. The materials that follow therefore provide a quick primer.

A. WHERE DOES HAZARDOUS SUBSTANCE CONTAMINATION COME FROM?

Many human activities have created sites contaminated by hazardous substances. Large industrial sources like factories may be the

———————

[1] Lest this raise your hopes too high, we should warn you that CERCLA does not enrich lawyers as effectively now as it did in the 1980s and 1990s. The United States is not making contaminated sites like it used to, which means less CERCLA work.

first to come to mind, and industrial activities are indeed a significant source of contamination. But other activities also significantly contribute. Modern regulatory standards for waste landfills are strict, but that was not always true, and chemicals placed into solid waste dumps often mixed with precipitation and leached into the underlying soil and water. Many smaller businesses, like machine shops or dry cleaners, have spilled toxic solvents. And government properties— military bases are particularly frequent culprits—often have costly contamination issues. Sometimes contamination issues arise where one would least expect. The bucolic campus of Wellesley College, for example, includes a contaminated site cleanup of residual pollution from a nineteenth century paint factory.

B. WHAT GETS CONTAMINATED?

Hazardous contaminants wind up in a variety of places on and off the sites where they were leaked or discarded.

- Contaminated soil is present at most contaminated sites.

- Contaminated groundwater is also a pervasive problem. Often contaminants in soil will flow downward, particularly if they are in soils that are exposed to precipitation. When those contaminants reach the groundwater table, they can dissolve and then flow laterally, sometimes forming contaminated plumes that extend under neighboring properties. Insoluble contaminants will pool on top of the groundwater table (if, like oil, they are lighter than water) or sink through it (if, like some common industrial solvents, they are heavier).

  One of the United States's most infamous contaminated sites is Wells G and H, in Woburn, Massachusetts. Long after the municipal groundwater wells were contaminated by industrial solvents from several nearby industrial sites, the City of Woburn continued distributing the well water to its residents, who were exposed primarily when they showered and the solvents evaporated out of solution and filled the surrounding air. The result was a cluster of leukemia cases, many of them fatal. For a gripping retelling of the story, as well as the groundbreaking legal case that followed, the authors highly recommend Jonathan Harr's book *A Civil Action*.

- Sometimes contaminated sites contain contaminated buildings.

- Sometimes contaminants are present in waste drums or other containers that have not yet leaked.

- In sites along surface waterways, contaminants are often present in the sediments beneath the water. This is a particularly common problem with relatively immobile contaminants like PCBs and heavy metals.

- Sometimes contaminants are present in gaseous form. This often happens when volatile contaminants (that is, contaminants that evaporate easily) are present in soil or groundwater. Those contaminants then can evaporate into the air in pore spaces in the soil, and can eventually migrate up and into overlying buildings in a process known as vapor intrusion.

- Sometimes contaminants are present in plants and animals that have been exposed to contaminated soils or waters.

C. WHAT ARE SOME COMMON CONTAMINANTS?

EPA compiles a "priority list of hazardous substances" to identify those hazardous substances that are of the greatest concern at the most heavily contaminated sites within the United States. The list is based on the frequency, toxicity, and potential for human exposure of each of the 275 hazardous substances EPA considers. Table 6.1 identifies the top ten substances included on EPA's 2013 list. The table reveals the diverse array of chemicals that pose threats to human health and the environment—from household names like lead and mercury, which can be found in a variety of consumer products and manufacturing processes, to more obscure compounds like benzo(b)fluouranthene, which is associated with coal and petroleum products. PCBs are currently ranked number five on EPA's priority list of hazardous substances. Conspicuously absent from this list are fuel oil and gasoline, which, in their pure form, are exempted from CERCLA's list of hazardous substances. But many sites contaminated with hazardous substances are also contaminated with petroleum products.

Table 6.1: 2015 Substance Priority List

Rank	Substance
1	Arsenic
2	Lead
3	Mercury
4	Vinyl Chloride
5	Polychlorinated Biphenyls
6	Benzene
7	Cadmium
8	Benzo(A)Pyrene
9	Polycyclic Aromatic Hydrocarbons
10	Benzo(B)Fluoranthene

Here, we have reproduced only the top ten contaminants from the list, and there are many more possibilities. Many contaminated sites also contain mixtures of a variety of different kinds of hazardous substances.

D. HOW ARE PEOPLE EXPOSED TO HAZARDOUS SUBSTANCES AT CONTAMINATED SITES?

Over the course of your life, you have probably been in close proximity to hazardous substance cleanup sites dozens, if not hundreds, of times. You probably never knew about the sites, and you probably also were subject to very little risk of exposure. That is because at most sites, hazardous substance contamination is relatively contained. But people are sometimes exposed to hazardous substances from contaminated sites, and the list below explains a few common pathways.

Figure 6.1. Illustration of Sources of Hazardous Contamination

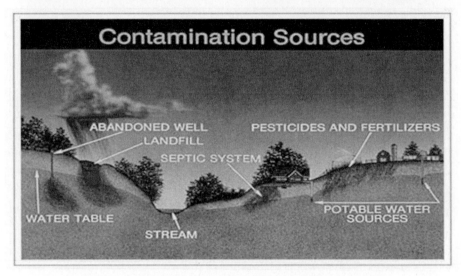

Source: http://www.epa.gov/region1/eco/drinkwater/pc_
sourcewater_assessment.html

- *Through drinking water.* If a contaminated site contaminates groundwater, and that water enters nearby private wells or public drinking water systems, people will be exposed to hazardous substances when they drink or bathe. Or, alternatively, people may have to find new water sources, sometimes at significant expense.

- *Through on-site disturbance of contaminated materials.* Construction workers may encounter hazardous substance contamination as they excavate a site, particularly if they did not know hazardous substances might be present. Similarly, if hazardous substance contamination is in a residential area, homeowners (particularly children) may be exposed if they dig into the dirt. This can occur through direct contact with the soil, or by inhaling dust kicked up by disturbing soils. And while the people who investigate and remediate hazardous contamination sites take measures to limit their exposure risk, some possibility of harm always remains.

- *Through bioaccumulation.* Chemicals that accumulate in aquatic sediments can be absorbed by plants and animals and then can be passed up the food chain, often in increasing quantities, until they are absorbed by something eaten by people. This is a particularly common problem for mercury and PCBs.

- *Through exposure to vapors.* Some common hazardous substance contaminants are volatile, which means that they evaporate easily. People at or near a contaminated site with volatile contaminants in soil or groundwater can inhale gaseous vapors.

E. WHAT ARE THE CONSEQUENCES OF EXPOSURE TO HAZARDOUS SUBSTANCES?

Exposure to hazardous substances can result in many adverse consequences. Hazardous substance exposure can change the behavior of people and wildlife. It can cause physical abnormalities, birth defects, cancer, other diseases, and, sometimes, death.

Such effects can be distinguished based on how fast they manifest. Acute toxicity occurs when exposure to a hazardous substance results in an immediate or rapid health consequence. You might more commonly think of this as poisoning. Chronic toxicity occurs when health problems manifest gradually over time. *See* EPA, Health and Ecological Hazards Caused by Hazardous Substances, http://www2.epa.gov/emergency-response/health-and-ecological-hazards-caused-hazardous-substances. Because the effects of chronic toxicity may not become apparent for years or decades, scientists may have difficulty fully understanding the risks created by hazardous substances.

People can often avoid these health risks by avoiding exposure pathways. But avoidance behaviors carry their own costs. If people cannot drink water from their wells, or a city has to abandon wells that tap a contaminated aquifer, finding replacement sources can be expensive. Similarly, if people avoid redeveloping contaminated land, then the abandoned area can become blighted. Cleaning a site up is another way of avoiding exposure, but that is not cheap.

F. HOW ARE CONTAMINATED SITES CLEANED UP?

Because contaminated sites are distinctive, cleanups also are distinctive. But there are a few standard cleanup approaches.

- *Site characterization.* Before any contaminated site cleanup can start, investigators must figure out what contaminants are present and where within the site they can be found. On large industrial sites with long histories, this can be a very time-consuming process; it may require extensive historical research and drilling hundreds of soil borings and monitoring wells. Investigators will generally continue to monitor site conditions during and after the cleanup.

- *Removing contaminated materials.* One of the most common ways to clean up a contaminated site is to excavate contaminated soils (or dredge contaminated sediments) and transport them to a hazardous waste landfill.

- *Pumping and treating contaminated groundwater.* To treat contaminated groundwater, engineers often build systems to pump groundwater out of the ground, remove contaminants (often by evaporating them from the groundwater), and then pump the treated groundwater back into the ground. The process can go on for decades.

- *Containment in place.* Sometimes, instead of cleaning up or removing a site, engineers will instead design a containment system (often an impervious clay layer) that keeps people from contacting the contaminated materials and that keeps precipitation from leaching through contaminated soil. Often containment in place is much cheaper than excavating and disposing soil and treating groundwater.

- *Partial cleanups and activity-and-use limitations.* A similar option (with similar cost-savings) is to partially clean up a site and then place legal restrictions on its future use. Those legal restrictions are generally designed to keep particularly vulnerable people—often children—away from the site, and to limit particularly dangerous uses, like growing vegetables for human consumption.

G. PCBs AND THE FOX RIVER: A CASE STUDY OF THE HAZARDS OF CONTAMINATION

We began this chapter with the Lower Fox River and its PCBs, and learning a little more about the lifecycle of those PCBs may help you understand the risks posed by contaminated sites.

PCBs are a class of chemical compounds that include a biphenyl molecule surrounded by between one and ten chlorine atoms. Because those chlorine atoms can occupy multiple locations in the compound, there are 209 PCB molecules, each of which is referred to as a congener. The chemical company Monsanto manufactured virtually all PCBs in the United States, including those used by paper companies along the Lower Fox River, and it sold them using the trade name Aroclor. Different Aroclors contained different concentrations of multiple congeners to create mixtures with properties useful for different applications.

The chemical properties of PCBs—they are relatively inert, heat resistant, and good at storing electricity—meant that they were deployed in numerous industries. Paper companies used them to produce carbonless copy paper, which was big business before the advent of photocopiers. They were also used to manufacture paints and plastics.

And while their production has been banned in the United States for decades, they are still present in some older electrical transformers and capacitors.

The toxicity of PCBs varies by congener. In general, the more chlorine atoms, the greater the toxicity, although the arrangement of the atoms also matters. Twelve congeners are regarded as particularly toxic, although all congeners have some toxic properties. By extension, the greater the proportion of high-chlorine congeners contained in an Aroclor, the greater the risk that the particular commercially sold chemical poses.

The diversity of the potential uses of PCBs can make it difficult to identify the source of contamination at any particular location, something that is made even more difficult by the fact that each Aroclor includes numerous congeners and, therefore, can be mistaken for one another. Along the Lower Fox River, paper manufacturers hotly contested what proportion of contamination originated with the paper industry, rather than other industries, and part of that dispute involved determining the relative concentration of the Aroclor used in paper manufacturing as compared to other Aroclors.

PCBs, like many hazardous substances, "bio-accumulate," meaning that low concentrations in the tissue of organisms low on the food chain turn into higher concentration in higher-level organisms. The diagram below shows how PCBs move from contaminated soils into invertebrates, fish, mammals and birds.

Figure 6.2. Contamination pathways

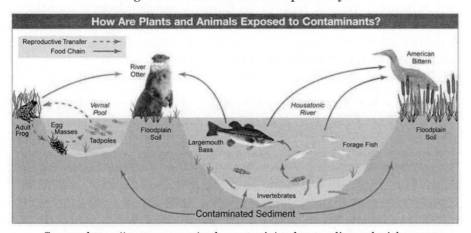

Source: https://www.epa.gov/ge-housatonic/understanding-pcb-risks-ge-pittsfieldhousatonic-river-site

If you add someone fishing to the diagram, you will see one of the pathways by which people can be exposed to PCBs. This is typical of many hazardous substances. Human exposure often results from consuming fish or other contaminated foods. Bio-accumulation magnifies that exposure because people tend to prefer to catch and eat larger fish that tend to be higher on the food chain. To guard against these hazards, states often issue advisories about fish consumption. For example, the Wisconsin Department of Natural Resources has issued the fish advisory provided below to guide consumption of fish along the Lower Fox River. Some consumption warnings apply everywhere. You've probably heard that pregnant women (and really everyone) should limit the amount of tuna they eat. That's because tuna are high on the oceanic food chain and their tissue may contain high concentrations of mercury, which also bio-accumulates.

Because PCBs are relatively heavy molecules and are not soluble in water, bioaccumulation is the primary pathway through which people are exposed. But there are other risks. People who stir up contaminated sediments could also be directly exposed, as could anyone who comes in physical contact with old transformers or other PCB-containing materials.

Hazardous substances pose a range of health risks, and PCBs are no exception. While some uncertainty remains, available evidence, much of which involves animal testing, indicates that PCBs threaten to, among other things, disrupt the endocrine system, increase cancer risks, damage the nervous system, suppress the immune system, and cause negative reproductive and developmental effects. These effects may take many years to reveal themselves, particularly because once PCBs enter the human body, they can remain for a long time. Depending on the congener and dose to which a person is exposed, studies have estimated that PCBs may have a half-life in humans ranging from 6 months to 133.33 years. *See* AGENCY FOR TOXIC SUBSTANCES AND DISEASE REGISTRY, ASTDR CASE STUDIES IN ENVIRONMENTAL MEDICINE: POLYCHLORINATED BIPHENYLS (PCBS) TOXICITY (2014), *available at* http://www.atsdr.cdc.gov/csem/pcb/docs/pcb.pdf.

Figure 6.3. Fish advisory for portion of the Lower Fox River

Species	Unrestricted	Eat no more than 1 meal/week	Eat no more than 1 meal/month	Eat no more than 1 meal every 2 months	Do Not Eat
Fox River from the De Pere Dam downstream to the mouth					
Black crappie, Bluegill, Lake whitefish, Rock bass, Smallmouth bass, White sucker, Yellow perch			All Sizes		
White perch				All sizes	
Northern pike			Under 33"	Over 33"	
Sheepshead			Under 19"	19" - 23"	Over 23"
Walleye			Under 21"	21" - 25"	Over 25"
Carp, Channel catfish, Big-mouth buffalo, White bass					All Sizes

Source: http://dnr.wi.gov/topic/fishing/documents/GreenBayFoxRiver2012.pdf

PCBs also harm wildlife. For example, the Forster's tern is believed to have experienced reduced hatching success, embryonic deformities, and behavioral effects, and the brown trout is believed to have experienced cancer, disease, physiological malfunction, and deformation, as a result of exposure to PCBs in the Lower Fox River. *See* STATUS CONSULTING INC., RESTORATION AND COMPENSATION DETERMINATION PLAN (RCDP): LOWER FOX RIVER/GREEN BAY NATURAL RESOURCE DAMAGE ASSESSMENT (Oct. 25, 2000).

II. HISTORY

RICHARD LAZARUS, THE MAKING OF ENVIRONMENTAL LAW
Pp. 107–110 (2004)

The single statute * * * that most transformed environmental law and the environmental profession in the 1980s was the Comprehensive Environmental Response, Compensation, and Liability Act (CERCLA), which * * * became law in December 1980. Unlike all the other major environmental laws of the preceding decade, CERCLA, popularly known as "Superfund," was a *liability* rather than *regulatory* statute. By imposing monetary liability on those entities that contributed to releases and threatened releases of hazardous substances, CERCLA sought the numerous abandoned and inactive hazardous waste sites littering the nation's landscape.

The existence of such sites was partly the result of decades of underregulation of disposal activities by state and local governments. Absent regulatory oversight, companies would dispose of hazardous wastes either on- or off-site in unsecured containers, often burying waste in landfills lacking any liners, leachate collection systems, or monitors. Unless one is in the waste control business, waste is inherently a nonproductive aspect of most activities. Neither a business seeking to maximize profits nor a governmental agency seeking to minimize costs is likely to spend any more on waste control than the minimum required by law.

But the hazardous waste sites targeted by CERCLA were also partly the result of the tough regulatory statutes that Congress and the states had enacted in the 1970s. Because of the expense of complying with those statutes, many hazardous waste disposal businesses shut down. The unintended consequence of tough prospective laws was, consequently, even more abandoned dump sites across the nation with hundreds and sometimes thousands of barrels and tanks eroding and leaking into the land and nearby surface waters and groundwaters. By their nature, waste disposal laws are difficult to monitor and to enforce. There are many clandestine ways to dispose of hazardous wastes, making violations easy to commit, difficult to discover, and, if the cost of compliance is high, a seemingly easy way for a business to save a lot of money.

Driven by public concern over publicized hazardous waste sites such as Love Canal in Buffalo, which reportedly leeched suspected carcinogens "into the backyards and basements of 100 homes and a public school," Congress intended CERCLA to be a drastic, short-lived remedy for a national emergency. It imposed monetary liability for the costs of cleanup on those responsible for creating the hazardous waste sites. It also imposed a tax on the chemical industry (later amended to apply to corporations in general) to create a fund to pay for the cleanup costs. This "Superfund" was used to pay for cleanup costs in advance of the recovery of those costs from those legally responsible and to pay for cleanup at those orphan sites where no solvent responsible parties could be identified.

The standard of liability was strict, meaning that it did not depend on any showing that those responsible for creating the site had, at the time of their actions, acted negligently, recklessly, or in an otherwise legally culpable manner. As further interpreted by the courts, CERCLA also imposed liability on a "joint and several" basis in those circumstances in which the injury to be redressed was deemed legally "indivisible." Joint and several liability allows a plaintiff to compel any one of several legally responsible parties to pay the *entirety* of damages—here, the cleanup cost of the site. Moreover, because of the combined effect of deliberate mixing and leaking, poor recordkeeping at the sites, and the ways in which the forces of natures (namely, wind and water) further commingle contaminants, most Superfund sites were legally indivisible.

What made strict, joint and several liability so transformative of the law, however, was its potential scope of application. CERCLA identified as potentially responsible parties not only the current owners and operators of the sites were hazardous substances were located and those who transported the substances to the site. It also extended liability to (1) all past owners and operators at the time of disposal and (2) any entity that arranged for the transportation of disposal or discarded hazardous substances.

The category of past owners and operators extended the scope of liability back in time to prior landowners who might have had no active involvement in the waste disposal activity beyond passive ownership of the property. The impact of such temporal expansion of liability on a strict, joint and several basis was tremendous. Not only did it retrospectively sweep in persons and entities who had long assumed that their responsibilities had ended with formal relinquishment of land ownership, but it also sent a strong signal throughout the real estate and banking industry regarding the implications of the ownership of land.

The result has been that few purchasers of real estate now consider the transaction without detailed inquiries into the past uses of the property, including the possible presence of hazardous substances. Possible environmental liability became a normal part of the negotiations of real estate transactions, especially of industrial properties. At the very least, the price of such property reflected possible cleanup costs, and some sales of contract made cleanup an express condition of sale. Several states made investigation into possible contamination and remediation of any environmental hazards discovered a formal condition of a lawful sale.

The practical impact of CERCLA's extending its liability scheme to so-called arrangers was, however, even greater. The federal statute did not make liable only current and past owners and operators of the site and those who transported the hazardous substances to them. It also singled out for liability those persons who "arranged" for the transportation, treatment, storage, and disposal of hazardous substances now located at the sites and requiring cleanup. The single most significant category of such arrangers comprises the original generators of the hazardous substances. This category of responsible parties is extraordinarily broad, including representatives of nearly every manufacturing and industrial activity in the United States, ranging from the most powerful Fortune 500 company to the family-owned neighborhood dry cleaner. It also reaches many federal agencies, all municipal governments and hospitals, and public and private universities and colleges. Under CERCLA, each was potentially subject to strict, joint and several liability for the cleanup of all hazardous substances located at the same site where their own hazardous substances had been disposed.

After CERCLA became law, liability for environmental contamination was no longer just someone else's problem. It became everyone's problem, and the impact of this change was immediate and far-reaching. It generated a huge demand for environmental lawyers to represent those concerned about their potential exposure. It also made public and private entities more aware of the implications of not taking every possible measure to guard against liability based on future activities. Indeed, although CERCLA was formally only a liability law concerned with existing conditions based largely on past conduct, CERCLA's greatest impact was likely on future behavior. The threat of such sweeping liability in the future indirectly prompted industry proactively to seek out ways to change their manufacturing processes to minimize the production of hazardous wastes.

Congress passed CERCLA in a hurry, and "[i]t has been criticized frequently for inartful drafting and numerous ambiguities attributable to its precipitous passage." *Artesian Water Co. v. Gov't of New Castle*

County, 851 F.2d 643, 648 (3d Cir. 1988); *see also Exxon Corp v. Hunt*, 475 U.S. 355 (1986) (explaining that a particular provision of CERCLA "is not a model of legislative draftsmanship"). This occurred because CERCLA was a hard-fought compromise enacted in November 1980 during the lame duck session of the 96th Congress at a moment in which leadership in the Senate was about to switch parties. Despite that impending change, there was tremendous political pressure for Congress to act swiftly due to swelling concern about abandoned hazardous waste sites—most famously, a site in Niagara Falls, New York, called Love Canal.

Since 1980, Congress has amended CERCLA on several occasions, usually to address problems that the original drafters of the law did not foresee. Two amendments are particularly important. In 1986, Congress enacted the Superfund Amendments and Reauthorization Act (SARA), which added provisions to induce liable parties to settle their CERCLA liability. SARA also enhanced the ability of liable parties to initiate lawsuits amongst themselves in order to spread the costs of cleanup. Congress passed SARA, at least in part, because of the massive cost of litigating CERCLA claims. By some estimates, the majority of funds during the early years of CERCLA went to pay lawyers, rather than to fund cleanups. *See United States v. Charter Int'l Oil Co.*, 83 F.3d 510, 520 n.14 (1st Cir. 1996) (collecting sources).

In 2002, Congress enacted the Small Business Liability Relief and Brownfields Reauthorization Act, which again made important, if less substantial, revisions to CERCLA. Those amendments added and modified statutory defenses to CERCLA liability in order to allow parties to purchase and make use of contaminated sites without automatically assuming full liability for cleanup.

III. CERCLA OVERVIEW

CERCLA has two primary aims: "The Act was designed to promote the timely cleanup of hazardous waste sites and to ensure that the costs of such cleanup efforts were borne by those responsible for the contamination." *Burlington N. & Santa Fe Ry. Co. v. United States*, 556 U.S. 599, 603 (2009) (quotation marks omitted). CERCLA accomplishes these goals by authorizing EPA to remediate contaminated sites or compel the parties responsible for polluting those sites to engage in cleanups. CERCLA also allows government entities and private parties to sue those that contributed to environmental contamination to recover the cost of cleanup.

A. SCOPE

CERCLA applies when there has been a "release" of a "hazardous substance" into the "environment." 42 U.S.C. § 9604(a)(1). Each of these three threshold terms—"release," "hazardous substance," and "environment"—is broadly defined.

The term "release," with a few specific exceptions, covers virtually any means by which a hazardous substance enters or moves through the environment. It includes both mechanisms that involve affirmative human action—such as "emitting" and "dumping"—and those that do not—such as "leaking" and "leaching." 42 U.S.C. § 9601(22). As a result of that broad definition, CERCLA applies not only to landfills and other hazardous waste disposal sites, but also other sites that have been contaminated by hazardous substances. The term release does not, however, include engine exhaust, the ordinary use of fertilizer, or certain types of disposal of nuclear materials. *Id.*

The term "hazardous substance" includes substances that EPA designates under CERCLA and also substances subject to regulation under a number of other environmental laws. 42 U.S.C. § 9601(14). For example, any substance treated as a hazardous air pollutant under the Clean Air Act or a toxic pollutant under the Clean Water Act is deemed a hazardous substance for purposes of CERCLA. *Id.*

Certain substances are, however, expressly exempted. The most significant such exemption is for "petroleum, * * * natural gas, natural gas liquids, liquefied natural gas, or synthetic gas usable for fuel (or mixtures of natural gas and such synthetic gas)." *Id.* These oil and gas substances are subject to a different cleanup regime under the Oil Prevention Act. *See* 33 U.S.C. §§ 2701–2762.

Determining the scope of the oil and gas exclusion can be tricky. EPA and the courts have generally taken the view that the exclusion only applies to unadulterated oil and gas materials. *See, e.g., United States v. Alcan Aluminum Corp.*, 964 F.2d 252, 266–67 (3d. Cir. 1992). As a result, releasing oil and gas into the environment can trigger CERCLA liability if the released material has itself become contaminated by hazardous substances.

B. SITE DISCOVERY

EPA can only address hazardous substances in the environment if the agency knows that a site has been contaminated. CERCLA itself creates one mechanism by which such information may come to light. Section 103 requires anyone in charge of "a vessel or an onshore or offshore facility" to immediately report any release of hazardous substances in excess of certain amounts, referred to as a *reportable quantity*, to the National Response Center, which is an agency within the United States Coast Guard. 42 U.S.C. § 9603(a). Hazardous substances have reportable quantities that range from one pound to 5,000 pounds.

Section 111 also requires those responsible for releases of hazardous substances to "provide reasonable notice to potentially injured parties by publication in local newspapers serving the affected areas." 42 U.S.C. § 9611(g). Even though reporting the release of a hazardous substance may result in significant cleanup liability, reports occur frequently, no doubt in part because people violating section 103 face criminal and civil penalties. *Id.* § 9603(b). In 2015, for example, the National Response Center received more than 25,000 reports of hazardous substance releases. The Center provides details about those reports on its website at www.nrc.uscg.mil.

Section 103 can only bring new releases of hazardous substances to EPA's attention. There are, of course, many sites across the country that have been contaminated for decades. EPA may receive notification about these sites from virtually anyone—concerned citizens, other governmental agencies, businesses, or environmental

> Many *federal facilities* are contaminated with hazardous substances. Military installations may be the first to come to mind, but many agencies have contaminated sites. For example, on December 22, 2008, a dike at the Kingston Fossil Plant operated by the Tennessee Valley Authority (TVA) dramatically failed, resulting in the release of 1.7 million cubic yards of coal waste, which covered hundreds of acres of land and polluted the Emory River.
>
> Federal agencies like TVA must report new releases of hazardous substances into the environment under CERCLA section 103, and also face numerous other legal obligations to report on environmental conditions.
>
> Federal agencies, just like private PRPs, often enter settlements with EPA to resolve CERCLA liability. In the Emory River example, EPA and TVA entered into an administrative settlement on May 11, 2009, to govern cleanup. That the United States is often both a plaintiff and a defendant in CERCLA cases creates interesting dynamics within the federal government. Agencies with contaminated sites have an interest in interpreting CERCLA narrowly, while EPA generally supports expansive interpretation of the statute. When such intra-governmental conflicts arise in the context of litigation, the Department of Justice may ultimately serve as a mediator.

organizations, to name a few. If EPA has reason to believe that a site is contaminated by hazardous substances, section 104 authorizes the agency to "undertake such investigations, monitoring, surveys, testing, and other information gathering" necessary to determine what, if any, threat the contamination poses to the public health or welfare. 42 U.S.C. § 9604(b).

Once EPA learns about a potentially contaminated site, it initiates a pre-screening process to determine whether that site should be added to EPA's database of contaminated sites and undergo a formal site assessment. Sites are excluded from further action in the pre-screening process for a variety of reasons, including if final cleanup of a site has been initiated through a state or tribal remediation program. The vast majority of sites remain subject to state authority; CERCLA tends to catch just the few (but often particularly large or heavily contaminated) sites that states are not addressing on their own.[2] The sites managed by the states, rather than EPA, are generally owned by companies that are currently solvent, continuing to operate at the site, and inclined toward exercising a greater degree of control over the cleanup than CERCLA typically allows. If a site is not excluded through pre-screening, EPA investigates contamination at the site and begins to identify PRPs.

C. POTENTIALLY RESPONSIBLE PARTIES

Section 107 identifies four types of PRPs that are liable under the statute. Those include (1) current owners or operators of facilities; (2) some past owners or operators of facilities, (3) those that arrange for the disposal of hazardous substances, and (4) some parties that transport hazardous substances for disposal or treatment. 42 U.S.C. § 9607(a). These categories are expansive. Often there will be a large number of PRPs at a contaminated site.

Section 107, in combination with other provisions of CERCLA, also exempts from liability certain classes of parties that would otherwise be PRPs. Some of these exemptions relate to the manner in which hazardous substances enter the environment. For example, releases caused by acts of war do not create CERCLA liability. 42 U.S.C. § 9607(b)(2). Other exemptions relate to the nature of the PRP. For example, owners of contaminated property are often exempted from liability if hazardous substances seeped onto their property from adjoining land. *Id.* § 9607(q).

D. EPA-INITIATED CLEANUP

CERCLA authorizes EPA to initiate remediation of a contaminated site in two fashions. Section 104 allows EPA itself to lead cleanups. Specifically, EPA can engage in long-term cleanups, called "remedial actions," or short-term cleanups, called "removal actions." 42 U.S.C. § 9604(a). Section 106 allows EPA to compel PRPs to engage in cleanup either through an administrative order or through a civil action seeking an injunction. *Id.* § 9606(a).

As mentioned in the introductory materials for this chapter, remediation of contaminated sites often is directed by state agencies rather than EPA. CERCLA doesn't specifically authorize any particular type of activity by state agencies. Rather, state agencies that engage in cleanup activities, or compel private parties to do so, invoke authority

---

[2]   In addition to the many sites addressed under state authority, many contaminated sites are regulated through RCRA's corrective action provisions, discussed in Chapter 5.

invested in them by state law. Often, although far from always, when a state agency takes the lead, it will do so in coordination with EPA.

E. CLEANUP STANDARDS AND NATIONAL CONTINGENCY PLAN

Section 121 requires cleanup efforts under CERCLA to achieve a degree of cleanliness that "at a minimum * * * assures protection of human health and the environment." 42 U.S.C. § 9621(d)(1). This standard is very protective and, as a result, cleanups under CERCLA are usually thorough and expensive. Under section 105, EPA has promulgated extensive regulations to implement that standard. *Id.* § 9605(a). These regulations are part of the National Contingency Plan (NCP), which governs cleanup of hazardous substances under CERCLA and petroleum products under other statutory authority.

Section 105 also requires creation of a national priorities list, or NPL, to identify sites of the highest priority for cleanup based on the risks they pose to human health and the environment. *Id.* § 9605(c). EPA adds sites to the NPL by regulation. While there are more than 1,300 NPL sites across the country, some of the most significant cleanups, including the cleanup of the Lower Fox River, have occurred without EPA ever adding a site to the NPL.[3]

F. COST RECOVERY AND LIABILITY

Section 107 identifies three categories of costs for which PRPs are liable. First, and most importantly, PRPs must reimburse cleanup costs incurred by the federal, state, and tribal governments to remediate a site in accordance with the NCP and also similar costs incurred by certain private parties, although, as we discuss later, precisely which private parties can seek cost recovery under section 107 is not always clear. 42 U.S.C. §§ 9607(a)(4)(A)–(B). Second, PRPs must pay for damage to natural resources. *Id.* § 9607(a)(4)(C). And third, PRPs must pay for certain health-related studies. *Id.* § 9607(a)(4)(D). CERCLA does not, however, require PRPs to pay damages (except for natural resource damage payments to certain government trustees—a subject we will revisit later in the chapter). That means that people who suffer damage to their health, property, or business cannot rely on CERCLA, but must instead file a lawsuit under state tort law.

G. SETTLEMENTS

EPA can enter judicial or administrative settlements under which a settling party resolves its CERCLA liability in exchange for its

---

[3]   In 1998, EPA did propose listing the Fox River, partly as an attempt to spur progress on cleanup efforts. The proposal was never finalized.

agreement to carry out or fund cleanup activities. EPA generally can make use of administrative settlements for removal actions, but must seek judicial approval of a consent decree for a remedial action. 42 U.S.C. § 9622(d). CERCLA generally requires EPA to seek public comment on consent decrees, although EPA may use expedited procedures to settle the liability of *de minimis* PRPs, whom the agency finds bear relatively little responsibility for contamination at a site. *Id.* § 9622(g).

H. CONTRIBUTION

Because liability under section 107 is typically joint and several, one or more PRPs may find themselves burdened with a disproportionate share of cleanup costs. The law provides multiple options for addressing that perceived unfairness.

Mirroring common law rules for joint and several liability, CERCLA section 113 allows PRPs who fall in certain procedural circumstances to seek "contribution." At common law, contribution is "[o]ne tortfeasor's right to collect from joint tortfeasors when, and to the extent that, the tortfeasor has paid more than his or her proportionate share to the injured party, the shares being determined as percentages of causal fault." BLACK'S LAW DICTIONARY (2016). In other words, while joint and several liability allows a plaintiff to sue a single defendant, or a subset of defendants, to recover everything, contribution allows such a defendant or defendants to sue other liable parties to recover an equitable share.

In three circumstances, PRPs may seek contribution under CERCLA section 113. First, a PRP can bring contribution actions if that PRP has been compelled, though a lawsuit brought under CERCLA section 106, to engage in remediation. 42 U.S.C. § 9613(f)(1). Second, a PRP can bring a contribution action if it has been compelled, through a lawsuit brought under CERCLA section 107, to reimburse cleanup costs incurred by other parties. *Id.* Third, a PRP can seek contribution if it enters into a judicial or administrative settlement to either fund or carry out a cleanup or to reimburse a government agency for the cleanup costs that the agency has incurred. *Id.* § 9613(f)(3)(B). Section 113 also creates a significant incentive for PRPs to enter settlement negotiations with EPA or a state. Under its provisions, any PRP that has entered into a settlement with EPA or a state agency receives a statutory shield to protect it from a contribution suit brought by another PRP. *Id.* § 9613(f)(2).

PRPs who do not fall into one of those categories—generally meaning PRPs who engage in cleanup on their own initiative or who complied with "unilateral administrative orders" (discussed later in this chapter)—may seek cost recovery from other PRPs under section 107. 42 U.S.C. § 9607(a)(4)(B).

IV. LIABILITY

As the name of the statute suggests, assigning liability is at the core of CERCLA. The work of many lawyers, particularly those representing private clients, often begins with determining whether a client is a PRP. This question can arise when a client wants to assess existing exposure or when a client wants to determine whether taking some action—like purchasing property or another company—will create liability.

This section begins with an overview of fundamental principles of CERCLA liability. It then turns to the statutory provisions that identify PRPs and provide defenses to liability. Because CERCLA liability is particularly important to corporate attorneys, the section concludes by considering how corporate law can sometimes shield companies from the liabilities of their subsidiaries or predecessors.

A. RULES FOR LIABILITY

CERCLA is among the most aggressive liability statutes in federal law. Environmental remediation is expensive, and Congress enacted CERCLA partly to protect taxpayers from shouldering the financial burden caused by the conduct of private polluters. As a result, liability under CERCLA is:

Strict. Under CERCLA, parties releasing hazardous substances into the environment are strictly liable for costs of environmental remediation. Section 107(a) does not speak directly to the imposition of strict liability. Indeed, no provision of CERCLA uses the term "strict liability." The text of CERCLA does, however, link liability under the statute to the standard of liability under a section of the Clean Water Act, which the courts at the time had interpreted to involve strict liability. *See* 42 U.S.C. § 9601(32). Based on this cross-reference, and the legislative history, courts have uniformly found that strict liability applies. *See, e.g., New York v. Shore Realty Corp.*, 759 F.2d 1032 (2d Cir. 1985) (citing legislative history).

Strict liability means that a party is liable under CERCLA even if the party released hazardous substances into the environment accidently and while exercising due care. Such a party—acting neither negligently, recklessly, or intentionally—is just as liable under section 107(a) for the cost of remediating a contaminated site as a party who engages in intentional conduct. Such differences in culpability may, however, be considered by a district court in allocating costs in a contribution action between two or more PRPs.

Joint and Several. Liability under CERCLA is generally, but not always, joint and several. That means that any PRP at a site can be liable for all of the response costs incurred by the government at that site. As with strict liability, CERCLA's text makes no mention of joint and several liability. Courts drew the joint and several liability scheme from background principles of common law. *See, e.g., United States v. Chem-Dyne Corp.*, 572 F. Supp. 802 (S.D. Ohio 1983).

While joint and several liability is CERCLA's default standard, it does not always apply. A PRP may prove, by a preponderance of the evidence, the existence of a reasonable basis for apportioning the harm, and if successful in that effort, the PRP will only be subject to several liability. This doctrine, often called *divisibility*, is discussed further in the *Burlington Northern* case, reproduced below.

Divisibility, which is also referred to as apportionment, also derives from the common law. The doctrine provides an affirmative defense to a party otherwise subject to joint and several liability if that party can prove "there is a reasonable basis for determining the contribution of each cause to a single harm." Restatement (Second) of Torts § 433A(1)(b), p. 434 (1963–1964).

While it might seem superficially easy for a PRP to prove such a basis, hazardous substances released into the environment tend to mix together, and remediation efforts designed to remove one contaminant simultaneously remove other contaminants. To prove divisibility, a PRP must prove that its releases of hazardous substances would not have justified incurring the response costs at issue. Because evidence about the precise quantities and locations of hazardous substances is often difficult to obtain, placing the burden of proof on PRP defendants means courts rarely allow several (as opposed to joint and several) liability.

Retroactive. CERCLA creates retroactive liability, meaning that a PRP is liable for response costs even if it released hazardous substances into the environment prior to the enactment of CERCLA. Like strict liability and joint and several liability, retroactivity is not expressly set out in the statutory text. Courts have nonetheless relied on legislative history, textual clues, and the general nature of the statute to find that a party is liable regardless of when it engaged in the actions that made it a PRP. *See, e.g., United States v. Ne. Pharm. & Chem. Co.*, 810 F.2d 726 (8th Cir. 1986) ("Although CERCLA does not expressly provide for retroactivity, it is manifestly clear that Congress intended CERCLA to have retroactive effect.").

No minimum quantity requirement (in some circuits). Liability under CERCLA can seem particularly severe because most courts have interpreted it to render a party liable based on any release of a hazardous substance, no matter how small. This understanding of the statute arises from the omission of any mention of quantity in the statute's definitions of the terms hazardous substance and release. *See* 42 U.S.C. §§ 9601(14), (22).

The lack of a minimum quantity requirement can matter a great deal where multiple parties have contributed environmental contaminants to a site. In *United States v. Alcan Aluminum Corp.*, 964 F.2d 252 (3d Cir. 1992), Alcan Aluminum Corporation's production process created a liquid wastewater with trace quantities of heavy metals. Alcan contracted with another company to dispose of its wastewater, but rather than properly doing so, that company simply dumped it down a mine shaft also contaminated with an array of other hazardous substances. In 1985, 100,000 gallons of liquid from the mine discharged in to the Susquehanna River and EPA undertook a costly cleanup of the mine. The Third Circuit held that, despite the minute quantity of hazardous substances in Alcan's waste water, Alcan was a PRP at the site because "the statute does not, on its face, impose any quantitative or concentration level on the definition of 'hazardous substances.' " *Id.* at 260.

The Fifth Circuit took a different approach in *Amoco Oil Co. v. Borden, Inc.*, 889 F.2d 664 (5th Cir. 1989). It held that a party is only a PRP if it releases a sufficient quantity of hazardous substances to have " 'caus[ed] the incurrence of response costs.' " *Id.* at 670 (quoting § 9607(a)(4) and alteration in original).

PROBLEM: LIABILITY ALONG THE LOWER FOX RIVER

1.   You are an attorney in Monsanto's general counsel's office. Monsanto was the United States' primary manufacturer of PCBs. It never owned or operated any of the paper factories on the Fox River, but those factories did buy most of their PCBs from Monsanto. Some of the companies and municipalities involved in the Fox River cleanup have made public statements about holding Monsanto liable for part of the cleanup cost, and your boss has asked you whether CERCLA liability is a real threat. Is Monsanto a responsible party?

As you answer the question, please assume you have found evidence that Monsanto knew that many of its customers were spilling PCBs into the environment.

2.   You are an attorney in the general counsel's office of Wisconsin Recycling Company (WRC). WRC recycled used carbon paper, among other things. But it did so only from 1960 to 1965. WRC's recycling process produced liquid effluent that contained PCBs.

Figure 6.4. Lower Fox River Schematic

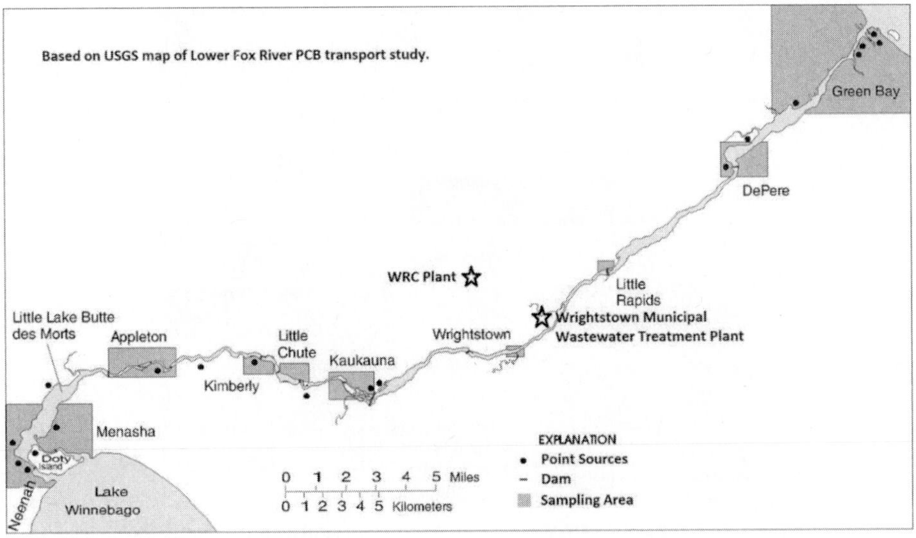

Based on: http://wi.water.usgs.gov/pubs/FS-116-96/pcbfig1a.GIF

Because the WRC Plant was located two miles inland, it did not directly discharge its wastewater into the river. Instead, the WRC Plant piped wastewater to the Wrightstown Municipal Treatment Plant. That municipal facility treated the WRC Plant wastewater, along with other industrial and residential wastewater within its service area. But the wastewater treatment plant did not remove PCBs, and virtually all of the PCBs in the WRC Plant's wastewater were ultimately discharged into the Lower Fox River. Based on the amount of paper WRC recycled between 1960 and 1965, WRC's engineers estimate that the wastewater from the WRC Plant contained approximately 1,000 pounds of PCBs. Records indicate that between 1960 and 1965, the directors and officers of WRC did not know that PCBs threatened human health or the environment.

In total from all sources, about 600,000 pounds of PCBs entered the Lower Fox River between 1957 and 1971. Almost all of those PCBs have settled into sediments at the bottom of the river. But river sediments move downstream (the river flows from southwest to northeast), particularly when the river experiences high flows, and the PCBs have moved with the sediments. Consequently, PCBs are now present throughout the Lower Fox River and in Green Bay.

EPA has designated the Lower Fox River as a single site. But for purposes of designing and implementing a remediation plan, the agency has divided the site into the five operable units (OUs), pictured on the map above. Those OUs are separated by dams, although some OUs span multiple dams. Wastewater from the Wrightstown Municipal Wastewater Treatment Plant was discharged below the Wrightstown dam in the middle of OU–2.

Figure 6.5. Map of Operating Units on Lower Fox River

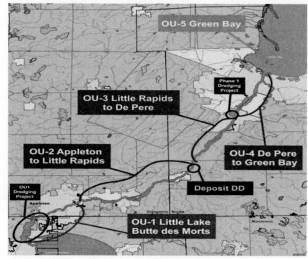

Source: https://www3.epa.gov/region5/cleanup/foxriver/
pdf/foxriver_rod_200706.pdf

You have been asked to consider two issues. First, is WRC a PRP because it sent its wastewater to the Wrightstown Municipal Wastewater Treatment Plant, which then discharged PCBs originating at WRC into the Lower Fox River? Second, if WRC is a PRP, can it avoid being joint and severally liable for the entire cost of remediating the Lower Fox River?

The starting point for any determination of CERCLA liability is section 107 of the statute, which is reproduced (along with a key excerpt from the statutory definitions) below.

CERCLA § 101, 42 U.S.C. § 9601. Definitions

(9) The term "facility" means (A) any building, structure, installation, equipment, pipe or pipeline (including any pipe into a sewer or publicly owned treatment works), well, pit, pond, lagoon, impoundment, ditch, landfill, storage container, motor vehicle, rolling stock, or aircraft, or (B) any site or area where a hazardous substance has been deposited, stored, disposed of, or placed, or otherwise come to be located; but does not include any consumer product in consumer use or any vessel.

CERCLA § 107, 42 U.S.C. § 9607. Liability

(a) Notwithstanding any other provision or rule of law, and subject only to the defenses set forth in subsection (b) of this section—

  (1) the owner and operator of a vessel or a facility,

(2)   any person who at the time of disposal of any hazardous substance owned or operated any facility at which such hazardous substances were disposed of,

(3)   any person who by contract, agreement, or otherwise arranged for disposal or treatment, or arranged with a transporter for transport for disposal or treatment, of hazardous substances owned or possessed by such person, by any other party or entity, at any facility or incineration vessel owned or operated by another party or entity and containing such hazardous substances, and

(4)   any person who accepts or accepted any hazardous substances for transport to disposal or treatment facilities, incineration vessels or sites selected by such person, from which there is a release, or a threatened release which causes the incurrence of response costs, of a hazardous substance, shall be liable for—

(A)   all costs of removal or remedial action incurred by the United States Government or a State or an Indian tribe not inconsistent with the national contingency plan;

(B)   any other necessary costs of response incurred by any other person consistent with the national contingency plan;

(C)   damages for injury to, destruction of, or loss of natural resources, including the reasonable costs of assessing such injury, destruction, or loss resulting from such a release; and

(D)   the costs of any health assessment or health effects study carried out under section 9604(i) of this title.

Unlike most areas of environmental law, EPA regulations play only a small role in many aspects of CERCLA practice. Instead, CERCLA liability law has primarily evolved through judicial decisions that interpret the statute and, often, integrate traditional principles of common law liability. The United States Supreme Court's most recent CERCLA decision appears below, along with a subsequent court of appeals decision involving a similar issue.

Burlington Northern & Santa Fe
Railway Co. v. United States
556 U.S. 599 (2009)

■ JUSTICE STEVENS delivered the opinion of the Court.

* * *

I

In 1960, Brown & Bryant, Inc. (B & B), began operating an agricultural chemical distribution business, purchasing pesticides and other chemical products from suppliers such as Shell Oil Company (Shell). Using its own equipment, B & B applied its products to customers' farms. B & B opened its business on a 3.8 acre parcel of former farmland in Arvin, California, and in 1975, expanded operations onto an adjacent .9 acre parcel of land owned jointly by the Atchison, Topeka & Santa Fe Railway Company, and the Southern Pacific Transportation Company (now known respectively as the Burlington Northern and Santa Fe Railway Company and Union Pacific Railroad Company) (Railroads). * * *

During its years of operation, B & B stored and distributed various hazardous chemicals on its property. Among these were the herbicide dinoseb, sold by Dow Chemicals, and the pesticides D-D and Nemagon, both sold by Shell. * * *

When B & B purchased D-D, Shell would arrange for delivery by common carrier, f.o.b. destination. When the product arrived, it was transferred from tanker trucks to a bulk storage tank located on B & B's primary parcel. From there, the chemical was transferred to bobtail trucks, nurse tanks, and pull rigs. During each of these transfers leaks and spills could—and often did—occur. Although the common carrier and B & B used buckets to catch spills from hoses and gaskets connecting the tanker trucks to its bulk storage tank, the buckets sometimes overflowed or were knocked over, causing D-D to spill onto the ground during the transfer process.

Aware that spills of D-D were commonplace among its distributors, in the late 1970's Shell took several steps to encourage the safe handling of its products. Shell provided distributors with detailed safety manuals and instituted a voluntary discount program for distributors that made improvements in their bulk handling and safety facilities. Later, Shell revised its program to require distributors to obtain an inspection by a qualified engineer and provide self-certification of compliance with applicable laws and regulations. B & B's Arvin facility was inspected twice, and in 1981, B & B certified to Shell that it had made a number of recommended improvements to its facilities.

Despite these improvements, B & B remained a " '[s]loppy' [o]perator." * * * Over the course of B & B's 28 years of operation, delivery spills, equipment failures, and the rinsing of tanks and trucks allowed Nemagon, D-D and dinoseb to seep into the soil and upper levels of ground water of the Arvin facility. In 1983, the California Department of Toxic Substances Control (DTSC) began investigating B & B's violation of hazardous waste laws, and the United States Environmental Protection Agency (EPA) soon followed suit, discovering significant contamination of soil and ground water. Of particular concern was a plume of contaminated ground water located under the facility that threatened to leach into an adjacent supply of potential drinking water.

Although B & B undertook some efforts at remediation, by 1989 it had become insolvent and ceased all operations. * * *

In 1991, EPA issued an administrative order to the Railroads directing them, as owners of a portion of the property on which the Arvin facility was located, to perform certain remedial tasks in connection with the site. The Railroads did so, incurring expenses of more than $3 million in the process. Seeking to recover at least a portion of their response costs, in 1992 the Railroads brought suit against B & B in the United States District Court for the Eastern District of California. In 1996, that lawsuit was consolidated with two recovery actions brought by DTSC and EPA against Shell and the Railroads.

The District Court conducted a 6-week bench trial in 1999 and four years later entered a judgment in favor of the Governments. In a lengthy order supported by 507 separate findings of fact and conclusions of law, the court held that both the Railroads and Shell were potentially responsible parties (PRPs) under CERCLA—the Railroads because they were owners of a portion of the facility, see 42 U.S.C. §§ 9607(a)(1)–(2), and Shell because it had "arranged for" the disposal of hazardous substances through its sale and delivery of D-D, see § 9607(a)(3).

Although the court found the parties liable, it did not impose joint and several liability on Shell and the Railroads for the entire response cost incurred by the Governments. The court found that the site contamination created a single harm but concluded that the harm was divisible and therefore capable of apportionment. Based on three figures—the percentage of the total area of the facility that was owned by the Railroads, the duration of B & B's business divided by the term of the Railroads' lease, and the Court's determination that only two of three polluting chemicals spilled on the leased parcel required remediation and that those two chemicals were responsible for roughly two-thirds of the overall site contamination requiring remediation—the court apportioned the Railroads' liability as 9% of the Governments' total response cost. Based on estimations of chemical spills of Shell products, the court held Shell liable for 6% of the total site response cost. * * *

II

CERCLA imposes strict liability for environmental contamination upon four broad classes of PRPs [including] * * *

> "(3) any person who by contract, agreement, or otherwise arranged for disposal or treatment, or arranged with a transporter for transport for disposal or treatment, of hazardous substances owned or possessed by such person, by any other party or entity, at any facility or incineration vessel owned or operated by another party or entity and containing such hazardous substances. * * * " 42 U.S.C. § 9607(a).

Once an entity is identified as a PRP, it may be compelled to clean up a contaminated area or reimburse the Government for its past and future response costs. See *Cooper Industries, Inc. v. Aviall Services, Inc.*, 543 U.S. 157 (2004).In these cases, it is undisputed that the Railroads qualify as PRPs under both §§ 9607(a)(1) and 9607(a)(2) because they owned the land leased by B & B at the time of the contamination and continue to own it now. The more difficult question is whether Shell also qualifies as a PRP under § 9607(a)(3) by virtue of the circumstances surrounding its sales to B & B.

To determine whether Shell may be held liable as an arranger, we begin with the language of the statute. As relevant here, § 9607(a)(3) applies to an entity that "arrange[s] for disposal . . . of hazardous substances." It is plain from the language of the statute that CERCLA liability would attach under § 9607(a)(3) if an entity were to enter into a transaction for the sole purpose of discarding a used and no longer useful hazardous substance. It is similarly clear that an entity could not be held liable as an arranger merely for selling a new and useful product if the purchaser of that product later, and unbeknownst to the seller, disposed of the product in a way that led to contamination. See *Freeman v. Glaxo Wellcome, Inc.*, 189 F.3d 160, 164 (CA2 1999); *Florida Power & Light Co. v. Allis Chalmers Corp.*, 893 F.2d 1313, 1318 (CA11 1990). Less clear is the liability attaching to the many permutations of "arrangements" that fall between these two extremes—cases in which the seller has some knowledge of the buyers' planned disposal or whose motives for the "sale" of a hazardous substance are less than clear. In such cases, courts have concluded that the determination whether an entity is an arranger requires a fact-intensive inquiry that looks beyond the parties' characterization of the transaction as a "disposal" or a "sale" and seeks to discern whether the arrangement was one Congress intended to fall within the scope of CERCLA's strict-liability provisions. See *Freeman*, 189 F.3d, at 164; *Pneumo Abex Corp. v. High Point, Thomasville & Denton R. Co.*, 142 F.3d 769, 775 (CA 4 1998) (" '[T]here is no bright line between a sale and a disposal under CERCLA. A party's responsibility . . . must by necessity turn on a fact-specific inquiry into the nature of the transaction'" (quoting *United States v. Petersen Sand & Gravel,* 806 F. Supp. 1346, 1354 (N.D. Ill. 1992))); *Florida Power & Light Co.,* 893 F.2d, at 1318.

Although we agree that the question whether § 9607(a)(3) liability attaches is fact intensive and case specific, such liability may not extend beyond the limits of the statute itself. Because CERCLA does not specifically define what it means to "arrang[e] for" disposal of a hazardous substance, see, *e.g., United States v. Cello-Foil Prods., Inc.,* 100 F.3d 1227, 1231 (CA 6 1996); *Amcast Indus. Corp. v. Detrex Corp.,* 2 F.3d 746, 751 (CA 7 1993); *Florida Power & Light Co.,* 893 F.2d, at 1317, we give the phrase its ordinary meaning. *Crawford v. Metropolitan Government of Nashville and Davidson Cty.,* 555 U.S. 271 (2009); *Perrin v. United States,* 444 U.S. 37 (1979). In common parlance, the word "arrange" implies action directed to a specific purpose. See Merriam-Webster's Collegiate Dictionary 64 (10th ed. 1993) (defining "arrange" as "to make preparations for: plan[;] . . . to bring about an agreement or understanding concerning"); see also *Amcast Indus. Corp.,* 2 F.3d, at 751 (words "'arranged for' . . . imply intentional action"). Consequently, under the plain language of the statute, an entity may qualify as an arranger under § 9607(a)(3) when it takes intentional steps to dispose of a hazardous substance. See *Cello-Foil Prods., Inc.,* 100 F.3d, at 1231 ("[I]t would be error for us not to recognize the indispensable role that state of mind must play in determining whether a party has 'otherwise arranged for disposal . . . of hazardous substances'").

The Governments do not deny that the statute requires an entity to "arrang[e] for" disposal; however, they interpret that phrase by reference to the statutory term "disposal," which the Act broadly defines as "the discharge, deposit, injection, dumping, spilling, leaking, or placing of any solid waste or hazardous waste into or on any land or water." 42 U.S.C. § 6903(3); see also § 9601(29) (adopting the definition of "disposal" contained in the Solid Waste Disposal Act). The Governments assert that by including unintentional acts such as "spilling" and "leaking" in the definition of disposal, Congress intended to impose liability on entities not only when they directly dispose of waste products but also when they engage in legitimate sales of hazardous substances knowing that some disposal may occur as a collateral consequence of the sale itself. Applying that reading of the statute, the Governments contend that Shell arranged for the disposal of D-D within the meaning of § 9607(a)(3) by shipping D-D to B & B under conditions it knew would result in the spilling of a portion of the hazardous substance by the purchaser or common carrier. See Brief for United States 24 ("Although the delivery of a useful product was the ultimate *purpose* of the arrangement, Shell's continued participation in the delivery, with knowledge that spills and leaks would result, was sufficient to establish Shell's intent to dispose of hazardous substances"). Because these spills resulted in wasted D-D, a result Shell anticipated, the Governments insist that Shell was properly found to have arranged for the disposal of D-D.

While it is true that in some instances an entity's knowledge that its product will be leaked, spilled, dumped, or otherwise discarded may provide evidence of the entity's intent to dispose of its hazardous wastes, knowledge alone is insufficient to prove that an entity "planned for" the disposal, particularly when the disposal occurs as a peripheral result of the legitimate sale of an unused, useful product. In order to qualify as an arranger, Shell must have entered into the sale of D-D with the intention that at least a portion of the product be disposed of during the transfer process by one or more of the methods described in § 6903(3). Here, the facts found by the District Court do not support such a conclusion.

Although the evidence adduced at trial showed that Shell was aware that minor, accidental spills occurred during the transfer of D-D from the common carrier to B & B's bulk storage tanks after the product had arrived at the Arvin facility and had come under B & B's stewardship, the evidence does not support an inference that Shell intended such spills to occur. To the contrary, the evidence revealed that Shell took numerous steps to encourage its distributors to *reduce* the likelihood of such spills, providing them with detailed safety manuals, requiring them to maintain adequate storage facilities, and providing discounts for those that took safety precautions. Although Shell's efforts were less than wholly successful, given these facts, Shell's mere knowledge that spills and leaks continued to occur is insufficient grounds for concluding that Shell "arranged for" the disposal of D-D within the meaning of § 9607(a)(3). Accordingly, we conclude that Shell was not liable as an arranger for the contamination that occurred at B & B's Arvin facility.

III

Having concluded that Shell is not liable as an arranger, we need not decide whether the Court of Appeals erred in reversing the District Court's apportionment of Shell's liability for the cost of remediation. We must, however, determine whether the Railroads were properly held jointly and severally liable for the full cost of the Governments' response efforts.

The seminal opinion on the subject of apportionment in CERCLA actions was written in 1983 by Chief Judge Carl Rubin of the United States District Court for the Southern District of Ohio. *United States v. Chem-Dyne Corp.,* 572 F. Supp. 802. After reviewing CERCLA's history, Chief Judge Rubin concluded that although the Act imposed a "strict liability standard," *id.,* at 805, it did not mandate "joint and several" liability in every case. See *id.,* at 807. Rather, Congress intended the scope of liability to "be determined from traditional and evolving principles of common law[.]" *Id.,* at 808. The *Chem-Dyne* approach has been fully embraced by the Courts of Appeals. * * *

[A]pportionment is proper when "there is a reasonable basis for determining the contribution of each cause to a single harm." Restatement (Second) of Torts § 433A(1)(b), p. 434 (1963–1964) (hereinafter Restatement).

Not all harms are capable of apportionment, however, and CERCLA defendants seeking to avoid joint and several liability bear the burden of proving that a reasonable basis for apportionment exists. See *Chem-Dyne Corp.,* 572 F. Supp., at 810 (citing Restatement § 433B (1976)) (placing burden of proof on party seeking apportionment). When two or more causes produce a single, indivisible harm, "courts have refused to make an arbitrary apportionment for its own sake, and each of the causes is charged with responsibility for the entire harm." *Id.* § 433A, Comment *i,* p. 440 (1963–1964).

Neither the parties nor the lower courts dispute the principles that govern apportionment in CERCLA cases, and both the District Court and Court of Appeals agreed that the harm created by the contamination of the Arvin site, although singular, was theoretically capable of apportionment. The question then is whether the record provided a reasonable basis for the District Court's conclusion that the Railroads were liable for only 9% of the harm caused by contamination at the Arvin facility.

The District Court criticized the Railroads for taking a " 'scorched earth,' all-or-nothing approach to liability," failing to acknowledge any responsibility for the release of hazardous substances that occurred on their parcel throughout the 13-year period of B & B's lease. According to the District Court, the Railroads' position on liability, combined with the Governments' refusal to acknowledge the potential divisibility of the harm, complicated the apportioning of liability. See App. to Pet. for Cert. in No. 07–1601, at 236a–237a ("All parties . . . effectively abdicated providing any helpful arguments to the court and have left the court to independently perform the equitable apportionment analysis demanded by the circumstances of the case"). Yet despite the parties' failure to assist the court in linking the evidence supporting apportionment to the proper allocation of liability, the District Court ultimately concluded that this was "a classic 'divisible in terms of degree' case, both as to the time period in which defendants' conduct occurred, and ownership existed, and as to the estimated maximum contribution of each party's activities that released hazardous substances that caused Site contamination." *Id.,* at 239a. Consequently, the District Court apportioned liability, assigning the Railroads 9% of the total remediation costs.

The District Court calculated the Railroads' liability based on three figures. First, the court noted that the Railroad parcel constituted only 19% of the surface area of the Arvin site. Second, the court observed that the Railroads had leased their parcel to B & B for 13 years, which was only 45% of the time B & B operated the Arvin facility. Finally, the court found that the volume of hazardous-substance-releasing activities on the B & B property was at least 10 times greater than the releases that occurred on the Railroad parcel, and it concluded that only spills of two chemicals, Nemagon and dinoseb (not D-D), substantially contributed to the contamination that had originated on the Railroad parcel and that those two chemicals had contributed to two-thirds of the overall site contamination requiring remediation. The court then multiplied .19 by .45 by .66 (two-thirds) and rounded up to determine that the Railroads were responsible for approximately 6% of the remediation costs. "Allowing for calculation errors up to 50%," the court concluded that the Railroads could be held responsible for 9% of the total CERCLA response cost for the Arvin site. *Id.,* at 252a. * * *

[W]e conclude that the facts contained in the record reasonably supported the apportionment of liability. The District Court's detailed findings make it abundantly clear that the primary pollution at the Arvin facility was contained in an unlined sump and an unlined pond in the southeastern portion of the facility most distant from the Railroads' parcel and that the spills of hazardous chemicals that occurred on the Railroad parcel contributed to no more than 10% of the total site contamination, see *id.,* at 247a–248a, some of which did not require remediation. With those background facts in mind, we are persuaded that it was reasonable for the court to use the size of the leased parcel and the duration of the lease as the starting point for its analysis. Although the Court of Appeals faulted the District Court for relying on the "simplest of considerations: percentages of land area, time of ownership, and types of hazardous products," 520 F.3d, at 943, these were the same factors the court had earlier acknowledged were *relevant* to the apportionment analysis. See *id.,* at 936, n. 18 ("We of course agree with our sister circuits that, if adequate information is available, divisibility may be established by 'volumetric, chronological, or other types of evidence,' including appropriate geographic considerations" (citations omitted)).

The Court of Appeals also criticized the District Court's assumption that spills of Nemagon and dinoseb were responsible for only two-thirds of the chemical spills requiring remediation, observing that each PRP's share of the total harm was not necessarily equal to the quantity of pollutants that were deposited on its portion of the total facility. Although the evidence adduced by the parties did not allow the court to calculate precisely the amount of hazardous chemicals contributed by the Railroad parcel to the total site contamination or the exact percentage of harm caused by each chemical, the evidence did show that fewer spills occurred on the Railroad parcel and that of those spills that occurred, not all were carried across the Railroad parcel to the B & B sump and pond from which most of the contamination originated. The fact that no D-D spills on the Railroad parcel required remediation lends strength to the District Court's conclusion that the Railroad parcel contributed only Nemagon and dinoseb in quantities requiring remediation.

The District Court's conclusion that those two chemicals accounted for only two-thirds of the contamination requiring remediation finds less support in the record; however, any miscalculation on that point is harmless in light of the District Court's ultimate allocation of liability, which included a 50% margin of error equal to the 3% reduction in liability the District Court provided based on its assessment of the effect of the Nemagon and dinoseb spills. Had the District Court limited its apportionment calculations to the amount of time the Railroad parcel was in use and the percentage of the facility located on that parcel, it would have assigned the Railroads 9% of the response cost. By including a two-thirds reduction in liability for the Nemagon and dinoseb with a 50% "margin of error," the District Court reached the same result. Because the District Court's ultimate allocation of liability is supported by the evidence and comports with the apportionment principles outlined above, we reverse the Court of Appeals' conclusion that the Railroads are subject to joint and several liability for all response costs arising out of the contamination of the Arvin facility.

IV

For the foregoing reasons, we conclude that the Court of Appeals erred by holding Shell liable as an arranger under CERCLA for the costs of remediating environmental contamination at the Arvin, California facility. Furthermore, we conclude that the District Court reasonably apportioned the Railroads' share of the site remediation costs at 9%. The judgment is reversed, and the cases are remanded for further proceedings consistent with this opinion.

It is so ordered.

[Eds.: Justice Ginsburg's dissenting opinion is omitted]

United States v. P.H. Glatfelter Co.

768 F.3d 662 (7th Cir. 2014)

■ TINDER, CIRCUIT JUDGE.

* * *

I. BACKGROUND

The Superfund Site at issue encompasses both the Lower Fox River and Green Bay. * * * [S]uffice it to say that several paper mills discharged wastewater containing polychlorinated biphenyls (PCBs) into the River from the mid-1950s through the 1970s, and since 1998, the Site has been the subject of massive remedial efforts conducted pursuant to CERCLA. * * *

NCR and Glatfelter are PRPs under CERCLA § 107(a), 42 U.S.C. § 9607(a), because they or their corporate predecessors formerly owned and operated paper mills that discharged wastewater containing PCBs into the River. NCR is responsible for two mills that produced carbonless copy paper using an emulsion containing PCBs and then discharged PCB-contaminated wastewater into OU2. Glatfelter is responsible for a mill that re cycled scraps of carbonless copy paper unusable by the original manufacturer and then discharged PCB-contaminated wastewater into OU1. * * *

II. SUMMARY JUDGMENT RULINGS

The district court's summary judgment rulings came after the parties filed cross-motions for summary judgment on the propriety of the remedy, and the United States moved for summary judgment on the OU1 Defendants' liability. * * *

B. GLATFELTER'S LIABILITY

Next, Glatfelter challenges the district court's entry of summary judgment on the issue of its liability for response costs in OU4, where remediation work is ongoing. Section 107(a) of CERCLA imposes strict liability for response costs upon four classes of responsible parties. 42 U.S.C. § 9607(a). With respect to Glatfelter, the relevant class is any former owner or operator of a facility at which hazardous substances were disposed of and "from which there is a release, or a threatened release which causes the incurrence of response costs, of a hazardous substance." *Id.* This is because Glatfelter is the corporate successor to Bergstrom Paper Company, which formerly operated a paper recycling mill in Neenah, Wisconsin, and discharged PCB-contaminated wastewater into Little Lake Butte des Morts.

The question we must decide is whether the government established Glatfelter's liability for response costs in OU4, even though the Bergstrom Mill was located at the upstream end of OU1. In this regard,

Glatfelter argues that the government should have been required to prove that PCB discharges from the Bergstrom Mill made their way into OU4 in sufficient quantities to "cause [ ] the incurrence of response costs" there. The district court disagreed, holding that

> there need be no "nexus" between a given defendant's release and a specific response cost incurred—it is enough that (a) the defendant released a pollutant and (b) response costs were incurred to clean up "a" release. If the defendant truly released a minimal amount, that speaks not to its own liability (for which there is no *de minimis* defense) but to whether that liability is divisible.

On appeal, Glatfelter argues that the district court improperly relieved the government of its burden of proof on causation by instead requiring Glatfelter to disprove causation in relation to its divisibility defense. * * *

Where Glatfelter's argument goes astray is in its assumption that the government must prove all of the elements of liability in relation to each operable unit of the Site. Such a requirement is nowhere to be found in the statute. Instead, once it is established that a party is responsible for a facility "from which there is a release, or a threatened release which causes the incurrence of response costs, of a hazardous substance," that party "shall be liable for . . . all costs of removal or remedial action incurred by the United States Government or a State or an Indian tribe not inconsistent with the national contingency plan." 42 U.S.C. § 9607(a).

In short, even assuming that a release for which the defendant is responsible must have caused the incurrence of response costs, nothing in the statute limits the defendant's liability to the response costs its release caused. Instead, the defendant is liable for all response costs "not inconsistent with the national contingency plan." *Id.* The national contingency plan authorizes removal or remedial action at the "site," 40 C.F.R. §§ 300.415, 300.435, and it defines "on-site" to mean "the areal extent of contamination and all suitable areas in very close proximity to the contamination necessary for implementation of the response action," *id.* § 300.5. Where, as here, releases from multiple facilities contaminate an interconnected environmental system like a river, the entire system falls within this definition. Thus, in this case, the Site was properly defined to include the entire Lower Fox River and Green Bay, and so long as PCBs released from the Bergstrom Mill caused the incurrence of *some* response costs within the Site, Glatfelter may be held liable for *all* response costs within the Site.

Glatfelter does not dispute that PCB discharges from the Bergstrom Mill caused the incurrence of response costs in Little Lake Butte des Morts, which is within the Site. Yet it insists that its liability should not extend to OU4, where discharges from the Bergstrom Mill may not have caused the incurrence of response costs. In essence, Glatfelter wants us to treat OU4 as a separate site for which the government must establish liability. But this is inconsistent with the national contingency plan, which defines an operable unit as "a discrete action that comprises an incremental step toward comprehensively addressing site problems." *Id.* To put it simply, operable units are not separate sites; thus, they do not determine the extent of a party's liability.

Of course, an operable unit "may address geographical portions of a site," *id.,* and in some cases, a divisibility defense may prevail based upon those same geographic portions. However, the burden to prove divisibility rests on the defendant. The government need not prove each party's liability in relation to each geographic unit of a site the first instance. It need only prove each party's liability as to the site as a whole. In this case, the undisputed facts establish Glatfelter's liability as to the Lower Fox River and Green Bay Site.

Glatfelter protests that holding it liable for response costs in OU4 is like holding it liable for "the Sheboygan River or the Hudson River, two other, unrelated, sediment PCB sites." But of course, OU4 is not unrelated to OU1, nor is it a separate site; rather, OU1 and OU4 are part of the same site. Glatfelter cannot be held liable for cleanup in the Sheboygan River or the Hudson River because EPA could not define the Site to include those rivers, which are not part of "the areal extent of contamination and all suitable areas in very close proximity to the contamination necessary for implementation of the response action." *Id.* However, as Glatfelter concedes, EPA properly defined the Site to include the entire Lower Fox River. Therefore, Glatfelter may be held liable for cleanup costs there, and the district court properly granted summary judgment to the government on the issue of Glatfelter's liability. * * *

NOTES

1.   In *Burlington Northern*, the Supreme Court was, in theory, reviewing a trial court's factual findings under an abuse of discretion standard. Might that standard of review have determined the outcome of the case? Would the Supreme Court have similarly held joint and several liability unavailable had the district court found to the contrary? In the years since *Burlington Northern*, courts have tended to reject divisibility claims and continue to impose joint and several liability on PRPs.

2.   Courts often divide the divisibility analysis in two. In *United States v. NCR Corp.*, 688 F.3d 833 (7th Cir. 2012), an earlier decision from the same Fox River litigation that produced *P.H. Glatfelter Co.*, the Seventh Circuit addressed this methodology for assessing a divisibility argument.

This analysis proceeds in two steps. First, we must determine whether the harm at issue is theoretically "capable of apportionment." [*Burlington Northern*, 556 U.S. at 614]. The Restatement instructs that this is "a question of law, and is for the decision of the court in all cases." Restatement (Second) of Torts § 434, cmt. d. By that, we understand that the ultimate question is one that is allocated to the court for decision, but that as is often the case, there will be underlying findings of fact on which the court's decision will rest. For example, the district court will need to decide what type of pollution is at issue, who contributed to that pollution, how the pollutant presents itself in the environment after discharge, and similar questions. In reviewing the district court's findings of the facts that underlie the ultimate decision, our review, as noted previously, proceeds under the clear error standard. Second, if the harm is capable of apportionment, the fact-finder must determine how actually to apportion the damages, which is "a question of fact." *Id*. At all times, the burden remains on the party seeking apportionment—here NCR—to "prove[ ] that a reasonable basis for apportionment exists. *Burlington Northern*, 556 U.S. at 614.

NCR Corp., 688 F.3d at 838.

3.   One category of PRPs is entities that owned or operated a facility *during* the period when the disposal of a hazardous substance occurred. But what if a party (a) owned a piece of property that was contaminated *prior to* that party's ownership; (b) did not dump or spill more hazardous substances during its period of ownership or operation; and (c) later sold or ceased operating at the property? The question is important because some older sites may have passed through a series of owners and operators between the time when contamination occurred and the time when remedial efforts begin and CERCLA liability must be assigned.

The answer to that question turns on the definition of the word "disposal." More specifically, the key question is whether, during the party's period of ownership or operation of the site, hazardous substances migrated or moved in ways that qualify as disposal.

CERCLA does not independently define the term "disposal," but rather refers to the definition included in RCRA section 1004, which provides that

'disposal' means the discharge, deposit, injection, dumping, spilling, leaking, or placing of any solid waste or hazardous waste into or on any land or water so that such solid waste or hazardous waste or any constituent thereof may enter the environment or be emitted into the air or discharged into any waters, including ground waters.

42 U.S.C. § 6903(3). In interpreting that language, courts have often required some active spreading of hazardous substances, rather than just passive migration, but they have also drawn some subtle distinctions. One

example of this trend is *Carson Harbor Village, Ltd. v. Unocal Corp.*, 270 F.3d 863 (9th Cir. 2001). The current owner of a mobile home park had sued the previous owner to recover costs related to cleaning up contamination that had occurred prior to both of their periods of ownership. The plaintiff argued that a "disposal" had occurred because contaminants had spread through the ground while the defendant owned the land. The Ninth Circuit disagreed, explaining that the word "disposal" did not encompass "the gradual passive migration of contamination through the soil." The court acknowledged, however, that had the contaminants been buried in underground barrels, which had leaked during the defendants' ownership, that would have constituted a "disposal." *See also Sycamore Indus. Park Assocs. v. Ericsson*, 546 F.3d 847 (7th Cir. 2008).

4.   CERCLA also provides that parties are liable if they "accept[ ] * * * any hazardous substances for transport to disposal or treatment facilities, incineration vessels or sites selected by such person." 42 U.S.C. § 9607(a)(4). In other words, the transporter itself must play a role in choosing the location for treatment or disposal. But what, precisely, does it mean to select a site? Must a transporter be solely responsible for determining where it brings hazardous substances? The prevailing rule requires something less. In *Tippins Inc. v. USX Corp.*, 37 F.3d 87, 94–95 (3d Cir. 1994), the Third Circuit explained that

> [A] person is liable as a transporter not only if it ultimately selects the disposal facility, but also when it actively participates in the disposal decision to the extent of having had substantial input into which facility was ultimately chosen. The substantiality of the input will be a function, in part, of whether the decisionmaker relied upon the transporter's special expertise in reaching its final decision. In other words, the selection process is a continuum and, in the circumstances we have described, the selection is done jointly.

5.   A PRP who releases hazardous substances into the environment is also responsible for the cost of environmental testing, even if that testing reveals that environmental conditions already meet the cleanup standard required by the National Contingency Plan (NCP). As the Eighth Circuit has explained,

> CERCLA allocates to the generator of hazardous substances the cost of ascertaining the danger posed by an actual or threatened released of hazardous substances, even if such testing determines the levels do not warrant cleanup action." Imposing a requirement that a party release a certain amount of hazardous substances before becoming liable would run counter to the "policy decision Congress has already made: that the threat posed by hazardous substances does not depend upon a minimum concentration or quantity.

Johnson v. James Langley Operating Co., Inc., 226 F.3d 957, 963 (8th Cir. 2000).

B. DEFENSES TO LIABILITY

CERCLA liability can be financially catastrophic. This has several advantages. First, it discourages releasing hazardous substances in the first place. Second, it strongly encourages prospective purchasers of land or of companies to investigate the potential CERCLA liabilities associated with their purchases. In combination with the statute's reporting requirements, that incentive to investigate has provided regulators and the public with abundant information about contaminated sites. Less intuitively, perhaps, the robustness of CERCLA liability also creates incentives for PRPs to cooperate with EPA and state regulators in hopes of entering a settlement that commits them only to specific, defined cleanup obligations.

The robustness of CERCLA liability also has disadvantages. Two are particularly important. First, notions of fairness suggest that some parties that otherwise fall within the provisions of section 107(a) should not be financially responsible for all cleanup costs. For example, owner liability would apply to a homeowner whose property has been contaminated by hazardous substances seeping through the ground from a nearby industrial facility.

Second, CERCLA liability creates harmful incentives. Potential liability can discourage sales of property that is known to have been contaminated, or where, based on the property's history, there is a reasonable suspicion of contamination. Such properties are often located in urbanized, developed areas close to potential workers and to transportation routes—exactly the places where a land use planner would usually want new development to go. But in the absence of a defense, few companies would purchase contaminated sites—often referred to as "brownfields"—and find productive and safe uses for those sites.

To address these problems, section 107(b) provides several defenses. Below, we briefly summarize four rarely-used defenses that allow someone that would appear to fall within the categories of PRP set forth in section 107(a) to avoid liability. Then, the problem that follows addresses three other defenses that insulate certain parties from liability—and that are, in practice, very important.

Act of God Defense. Like many environmental statutes, CERCLA provides a defense to liability if an "act of God" resulted in a release of hazardous substances. 42 U.S.C. § 9607(b)(1). A PRP may be able to escape liability by proving that a natural disaster, such as a tornado, earthquake, hurricane, flood, or wildfire, caused the release. But section

101(1) limits the availability of this defense. A natural disaster only constitutes an "act of God" if its effects "could not have been prevented or avoided by the exercise of due care or foresight." *Id.* § 9601(1). In other words, a PRP invoking the defense must prove not only that a natural disaster caused the release, but that the PRP could not have taken reasonable precautions to prevent the release from occurring.

As a result, courts have construed the "act of God" defense narrowly. This issue was addressed by the district court in the *United States v. Alcan Aluminum Corp.* case, discussed earlier in this chapter. Recall that the case involved a company whose waste was dumped into a mineshaft. Subsequently waste from the mineshaft entered the Susquehanna River during torrential rainfall caused by Hurricane Gloria. The district court explained:

> Alcan's reliance on the act of God defense must be rejected for at least three reasons. First, no reasonable factfinder could conclude that Hurricane Gloria was the sole cause of the release and resulting response costs. Two million gallons of hazardous wastes were not dumped into the borehole by an act of God, and were it not for the unlawful disposal of this hazardous waste Hurricane Gloria would not have flushed 100,000 gallons of this chemical soup into the Susquehanna River.

> Second, the effects of Hurricane Gloria could "have been prevented or avoided by the exercise of due care or foresight." 42 U.S.C. § 9601(1). Clearly, exercise of due care or foresight would have militated against dumping hazardous wastes into mine workings that inevitably lead to such a significant natural resource as the Susquehanna River.

> Finally, as the Court in [*United States v. Stringfellow*, 661 F. Supp. 1053 (C.D. Cal. 1987)] recognized, heavy rainfall is "not the kind of 'exceptional' natural phenomenon to which the act of God exception applies." 661 F. Supp. at 1061. Accordingly, it is appropriate to enter judgment in favor of the Government on Alcan's act of God defense.

United States v. Alcan Aluminum Corp., 892 F. Supp. 648, 658 (M.D. Pa. 1995).

Act of War Defense. Many statutory regimes also exempt individuals from liability for events caused by an "act of war," and CERCLA is no different. 42 U.S.C. § 9607(b)(2). The statute does not define an act of war, and what little case law exists suggests a narrow interpretation. For example, in *United States v. Shell Oil Co.*, 294 F.3d 1045, 1062 (9th Cir. 2002), the Ninth Circuit rejected the view that "any governmental act taken by authority of the War Powers Clause is an 'act of war.'" In so doing, the court held that a company dumping hazardous substances as part of "wartime production" could not invoke the defense. *Id.*

The act of war defense has interesting implications in the context of domestic terrorism. Is a company liable for releases of hazardous substances caused by a terrorist attack? Would that analysis depend in part on whether the group carrying out the terrorist attack was a domestic or foreign group? The Second Circuit addressed this issue in its decision in *In re September 11 Litigation*, 751 F.3d 86 (2d Cir. 2014). The case involved a real estate developer seeking to recover response costs from the owners and lessees of the World Trade Center for the cost of removing pulverized dust that had contaminated the developer's property. The court held that the act of war defense applied.

Lender Defense. The definition of "owner or operator" in section 101(20) exempts "a person who, without participating in the management of a vessel or facility, holds indicia of ownership primarily to protect his security interest in the vessel or facility." 42 U.S.C. § 9601(20)(E)(i). This means that a bank or other financial institution does not become a PRP just because it holds a mortgage over property that would qualify as a facility. This protection extends even where a lender forecloses on the property so long as the lender simply has the property sold and collects the proceeds. *Id.* § 9601(20)(E)(ii).

That exemption provides major protection to lenders, who once faced major risks from foreclosing on contaminated land. But if you represent such an institution, beware! Any activity that could be construed as management of the facility can open a lender up to liability. And even if your client does not become liable for cleanup costs at a property it forecloses upon, it still has taken possession of an asset with compromised value.

Municipal Solid Waste Exemption. Section 107(p) provides that the owners of residential property, small businesses, and non-profit organizations are exempt from arranger liability—but not other categories of PRPs—if their status as an arranger would arise solely because they sent their waste to a municipal solid waste facility. 42 U.S.C. § 9607(p)(1). This defense is not absolute, however, and does not apply if EPA determines that an entities waste "contributed significantly or could contribute significantly, either individually or in aggregate, to the cost of the response action or natural resource restoration with respect to the facility." *Id.* § 9607(p)(2)(A). That seemingly open-ended standard could seriously erode the utility of the exemption. Based on the legislative history, EPA has explained, however, that the phrase "in aggregate" does not mean the aggregate of all waste from similarly exempt individuals at a site, but rather, the total amount of waste a single entity has sent to all sites. EPA further explains that the exception "will apply relatively infrequently." Joint Memorandum from EPA and

DOJ, Interim Guidance on the Municipal Solid Waste Exemption under CERCLA Section 107(p) (Aug. 20, 2003). Moreover, PRPs at a site cannot drag covered entities into litigation by arguing that they contributed significantly to response costs. EPA's decision about whether the exception to the defense applies is not subject to judicial review. 42 U.S.C. § 9607(p)(3).

All of these defenses are of limited importance to most lawyers who work with CERCLA. Three other defenses—the bona fide prospective purchaser defense, the innocent landowner defense, and the contiguous property owner defense—are different. These defenses are very important to purchasers of real estate, particularly if that real estate has historically been used for industrial purposes. Through these defenses, a purchaser may acquire and make use of valuable property while avoiding thousands, if not millions, of dollars of liability. If your future practice will involve working with real estate transactions, these are essential defenses to know. The problem below requires you to consider each of them.

PROBLEM: PURCHASING CONTAMINATED PROPERTY

You represent a residential development company called Elite Residential Living (ERL).[4] The CEO of ERL has a friend from college who owns a ten-acre undeveloped lot located along Green Bay not far from the mouth of the Lower Fox River. The CEO believes that purchasing the lot for residential development is a great business opportunity.

The shoreline along the ten-acre lot is contaminated with PCBs. While most of the contamination lies below the ordinary high-water line (which, under Wisconsin law, marks the boundary between private and state land), some contamination is located above that line, and thus on the property that ERL would like to purchase. The remedial action plan approved by EPA for OU–5 of the Lower Fox River site requires that contaminated soils from above the waterline and to a depth of ten feet be moved offsite. This will be accomplished using water-born dredges and land-based heavy equipment, which will operate in the area within thirty feet of the water. The lot ERL would like to buy is scheduled to be remediated within the next five years, although completion of the remedial action plan in its entirety is likely to take more than a decade.

The remedial action plan for OU–5 also identifies the need for a local zoning ordinance prohibiting any development or surface-disturbing activity within 50 feet of the shore prior to completion of the OU–5 remedial action. The City of Green Bay has not yet enacted such a zoning ordinance.

---

[4]   While Green Bay does in fact contain PCB-contaminated sediments, the specific facts in this problem related to PCB contamination of the shore of Green Bay and EPA's remedial action plan are fictional.

If ERL purchases the property, it would like to immediately begin constructing three residential towers, all of which would be more than fifty feet from the shore. ERL would also like to landscape the shoreline and build recreational facilities—such as a swimming area and small dock—for residents. ERL believes that it can make a decent profit on the condominiums even before the remediation plan is completed, but that once it is finished, the value of its property will significantly increase.

ERL does not want to proceed with this project if purchasing the lot will make it a PRP for the Lower Fox River site. Your client has asked you to assess whether ERL could invoke the innocent third party defense, the contiguous landowner defense, or the bona fide purchaser defense if it buys the lot. Also, your client wants to know if there are steps that ERL should take to ensure that it falls within those defenses. Finally, does invoking those defenses impose any obligations on ERL?

You have discovered that the statutory provisions that address the three defenses relevant to your client are lengthy and include a range of cross-references and detailed obligations. Here are some of the core provisions.

CERCLA § 101, 42 U.S.C. § 9601. Definitions

(35)(A) The term "contractual relationship", for the purpose of section 9607(b)(3) of this title, includes, but is not limited to, land contracts, deeds, easements, leases, or other instruments transferring title or possession, unless the real property on which the facility concerned is located was acquired by the defendant after the disposal or placement of the hazardous substance on, in, or at the facility, and * * *

> (i)   At the time the defendant acquired the facility the defendant did not know and had no reason to know that any hazardous substance which is the subject of the release or threatened release was disposed of on, in, or at the facility. * * *

(40) Bona fide prospective purchaser

The term "bona fide prospective purchaser" means a person (or a tenant of a person) that acquires ownership of a facility * * * and establishes * * * :

> (H) No affiliation
>
> The person is not—
>
> > (i)   potentially liable, or affiliated with any other person that is potentially liable, for response costs at a facility through—
> >
> > > (I)   any direct or indirect familial relationship; or
> > >
> > > (II)   any contractual, corporate, or financial relationship (other than a contractual, corporate, or financial relationship that is created by the instruments by which title to the facility

---

is conveyed or financed or by a contract for the sale of goods or services); or

(ii)   the result of a reorganization of a business entity that was potentially liable.

CERCLA § 107, 42 U.S.C. § 9607. Liability

(b) Defenses. There shall be no liability under section (a) of this section for a person * * * who can establish * * * that the release or threat of release of a hazardous substance * * * was caused solely by—

(3)   an act or omission of a third party other than an employee or agent of the defendant, or than one whose act or omission occurs in connection with a contractual relationship, existing directly or indirectly, with the defendant * * *, if the defendant establishes * * * that (a) he exercised due care with respect to the hazardous substance concerned, taking into consideration the characteristics of such hazardous substance, in light of all relevant facts and circumstances, and (b) he took precautions against foreseeable acts or omissions of any such third party and the consequences that could foreseeably result from such acts or omissions; * * *

(q) Contiguous properties

(1)   Not considered to be an owner or operator

(A)   In general

A person that owns real property that is contiguous to or otherwise similarly situated with respect to, and that is or may be contaminated by a release or threatened release of a hazardous substance from, real property that is not owned by that person shall not be considered to be an owner or operator of a vessel or facility under paragraph (1) or (2) of subsection (a) of this section solely by reason of the contamination if—

(i)   the person did not cause, contribute, or consent to the release or threatened release;

(ii)   [Eds.: This provision is materially identical to the "no affiliation" provision in § 101(40(H)] * * *

(C)   Bona fide prospective purchaser

Any person that does not qualify as a person described in this paragraph because the person had, or had reason to have, knowledge specified in subparagraph (A)(viii) at the time of acquisition of the real property may qualify as a bona fide prospective purchaser under section 9601(40) of this title * * *.

(r) Prospective purchaser and windfall lien

(1) Limitation on liability

Notwithstanding subsection (a)(1) of this section, a bona fide prospective purchaser whose potential liability for a release or threatened release is based solely on the purchaser's being considered to be an owner or operator of a facility shall not be liable as long as the bona fide prospective purchaser does not impede the performance of a response action or natural resource restoration.

(2) Lien

If there are unrecovered response costs incurred by the United States at a facility for which an owner of the facility is not liable by reason of paragraph (1), * * * the United States shall have a lien on the facility * * * for the unrecovered response costs.

(3) Conditions * * *

(B) Fair market value

The response action increases the fair market value of the facility above the fair market value of the facility that existed before the response action was initiated. * * *

You have also discovered EPA guidance that describes the operation of the relevant defenses. An excerpt from that guidance document follows.

Memorandum from Susan E. Bromm, Director of Office of Site Remediation and Enforcement, to EPA Regional Offices

EPA (Mar. 6, 2003)

Subject: Interim Guidance Regarding Criteria Landowners Must Meet in Order to Qualify for Bona Fide Prospective Purchaser, Contiguous Property Owner, or Innocent Landowner Limitations on CERCLA Liability ("Common Elements")

I. Introduction

The Small Business Liability Relief and Brownfields Revitalization Act, ("Brownfields Amendments"), Pub. L. No. 107–118, enacted in January 2002, amended the Comprehensive Environmental Response, Compensation and Liability Act ("CERCLA"), to provide important liability limitations for landowners that qualify as: (1) bona fide prospective purchasers, (2) contiguous property owners, or (3) innocent landowners (hereinafter, "landowner liability protections" or "landowner provisions").

To meet the statutory criteria for a landowner liability protection, a landowner must meet certain threshold criteria and satisfy certain continuing obligations. Many of the conditions are the same or similar under the three landowner provisions ("common elements"). * * *

III. Discussion

A party claiming to be a bona fide prospective purchaser, contiguous property owner, or section 101(35)(A)(i) innocent landowner bears the burden of proving that it meets the conditions of the applicable landowner liability protection. Ultimately, courts will determine whether landowners in specific cases have met the conditions of the landowner liability protections and may provide interpretations of the statutory conditions. EPA offers some general guidance below regarding the common elements. This guidance is intended to be used by Agency personnel in exercising enforcement discretion. Evaluating whether a party meets these conditions will require careful, fact-specific analysis.

A.   *Threshold Criteria*

To qualify as a bona fide prospective purchaser, contiguous property owner, or innocent landowner, a person must perform "all appropriate inquiry" before acquiring the property. Bona fide prospective purchasers and contiguous property owners must, in addition, demonstrate that they are not potentially liable or "affiliated" with any other person that is potentially liable for response costs at the property.

1.   All Appropriate Inquiry

* * * The Brownfields Amendments require EPA, not later than January 2004, to promulgate a regulation containing standards and practices for all appropriate inquiry and set out criteria that must be addressed in EPA's regulation. CERCLA § 101(35)(B)(ii), (iii). * * *

2.   Affiliation

To meet the statutory criteria of a bona fide prospective purchaser or contiguous property owner, a party must not be potentially liable or affiliated with any other person who is potentially liable for response costs. Neither the bona fide prospective purchaser/contiguous property owner provisions nor the legislative history define the phrase "affiliated with," but on its face the phrase has a broad definition, covering direct and indirect familial relationships, as well as many contractual, corporate, and financial relationships. It appears that Congress intended the affiliation language to prevent a potentially responsible party from contracting away its CERCLA liability through a transaction to a family member or related corporate entity. EPA recognizes that the potential breadth of the term "affiliation" could be taken to an extreme, and in exercising its enforcement discretion, EPA intends to be guided by Congress' intent of preventing transactions structured to avoid liability.

The innocent landowner provision does not contain this "affiliation" language. In order to meet the statutory criteria of the innocent landowner liability protection, however, a person must establish by a preponderance of the evidence that the act or omission that caused the release or threat of release of hazardous substances and the resulting damages were caused by a third party with whom the person does not have an employment, agency, or contractual relationship. Contractual relationship is defined in section 101(35)(A).

B. *Continuing Obligations*

Several of the conditions a landowner must meet in order to achieve and maintain a landowner liability protection are continuing obligations. This section discusses those continuing obligations * * *

1. Land Use Restrictions and Institutional Controls

The bona fide prospective purchaser, contiguous property owner, and innocent landowner provisions all require compliance with the following ongoing obligations as a condition for maintaining a landowner liability protection: [1] the person is in compliance with any land use restrictions established or relied on in connection with the response action and [2] the person does not impede the effectiveness or integrity of any institutional control employed in connection with a response action. CERCLA §§ 101(40)(F), 107(q)(1)(A)(V), 101(35)(A). Initially, there are two important points worth noting about these provisions. First, because institutional controls are often used to implement land use restrictions, failing to comply with a land use restriction may also impede the effectiveness or integrity of an institutional control, and vice versa. As explained below, however, these two provisions do set forth distinct requirements. Second, these are ongoing obligations and, therefore, EPA believes the statute requires bona fide prospective purchasers, contiguous property owners, and innocent landowners to comply with land use restrictions and to implement institutional controls, even if the restrictions or institutional controls were not in place at the time the person purchased the property.

Institutional controls are administrative and legal controls that minimize the potential for human exposure to contamination and protect the integrity of remedies by limiting land or resource use, providing information to modify behavior, or both. For example, an institutional control might prohibit the drilling of a drinking water well in a contaminated aquifer or disturbing contaminated soils. EPA typically uses institutional controls whenever contamination precludes unlimited use and unrestricted exposure at the property. Institutional controls are often needed both before and after completion of the remedial action. Also, institutional controls may need to remain in place for an indefinite duration and, therefore, generally need to survive changes in property ownership (i.e., run with the land) to be legally and practically effective.

Generally, EPA places institutional controls into four categories: (1) governmental controls (e.g., zoning); (2) proprietary controls (e.g., covenants, easements); (3) enforcement documents (e.g., orders, consent decrees); and (4) informational devices (e.g., land record/deed notices).

Institutional controls often require a property owner to take steps to implement the controls, such as conveying a property interest (e.g., an easement or restrictive covenant) to another party such as a governmental entity, thus providing that party with the right to enforce a land use restriction; applying for a zoning change; or recording a notice in the land records.

Because institutional controls are tools used to limit exposure to contamination or protect a remedy by limiting land use, they are often used to implement or establish land use restrictions relied on in connection with the response action. However, the Brownfields Amendments require compliance with land use restrictions relied on in connection with the response action, even if those restrictions have not been properly implemented through the use of an enforceable institutional control. Generally, a land use restriction may be considered "relied on" when the restriction is identified as a component of the remedy. * * *

An institutional control may not serve the purpose of implementing a land use restriction for a variety of reasons, including: (1) the institutional control is never, or has yet to be, implemented; (2) the property owner or other persons using the property impede the effectiveness of the institutional controls in some way and the party responsible for enforcement of the institutional controls neglects to take sufficient measures to bring those persons into compliance; or (3) a court finds the controls to be unenforceable. For example, a chosen remedy might rely on an ordinance that prevents groundwater from being used as drinking water. If the local government failed to enact the ordinance, later changed the ordinance to allow for drinking water use, or failed to enforce the ordinance, a landowner is still required to comply with the groundwater use restriction identified as part of the remedy to maintain its landowner liability protection. Unless authorized by the regulatory agency responsible for overseeing the remedy, if the landowner fails to comply with a land use restriction relied on in connection with a response action, the owner will forfeit the liability protection and EPA may use its CERCLA authorities to order the owner to remedy the violation, or EPA may remedy the violation itself and seek cost recovery from the noncompliant landowner. * * *

3.   Cooperation, Assistance, and Access

The Brownfields Amendments require that bona fide prospective purchasers, contiguous property owners, and innocent landowners provide full cooperation, assistance, and access to persons who are authorized to conduct response actions or natural resource restoration at the vessel or facility from which there has been a release or threatened release, including the cooperation and access necessary for the installation, integrity, operation, and maintenance of any complete or partial response action or natural resource restoration at the vessel or facility. CERCLA §§ 101(40)(E), 107(q)(1)(A)(iv), 101(35)(A).

The innocent land owner and bona fide prospective purchaser defenses require investigation of property before purchase. EPA has provided a factsheet describing what the scope of those investigations should be.

Factsheet, All Appropriate Inquiries Final Rule
EPA (Feb. 2014)

What is "All Appropriate Inquiries"?

"All appropriate inquiries" is the process of evaluating a property's environmental conditions and assessing potential liability for any contamination.

Why Did EPA Establish Standards For Conducting All Appropriate Inquiries?

The 2002 Brownfields Amendments to CERCLA require EPA to promulgate regulations establishing standards and practices for conducting all appropriate inquiries.

Stakeholder Collaboration

A Negotiated Rulemaking Committee consisting of 25 diverse stakeholders developed the proposed rule. Following publication of the proposed rule, EPA provided for a three month public comment period. EPA received over 400 comments from interested parties. Based upon a review and analysis of issues raised by commenters, EPA developed the final rule.

When Did the Rule Go Into Effect?

The final rule was effective on November 1, 2006—one year after being published in the Federal Register.

Who is Affected?

The final All Appropriate Inquiries requirements are applicable to any party who may potentially claim protection from CERCLA liability as an innocent landowner, a bona fide prospective purchaser, or a contiguous property owner. Parties who receive grants under the EPAs Brownfields Grant program to assess and characterize properties must comply with the All Appropriate Inquiries Rule.

When Must All Appropriate Inquiries Be Conducted?

All appropriate inquiries must be conducted or updated within one year prior to the date of acquisition of a property. If all appropriate inquiries are conducted more than 180 days prior to the acquisition date, certain aspects of the inquiries must be updated.

What Specific Activities Does the Rule Require?

Many of the rule's required activities must be conducted by, or under the supervision or responsible charge of, an individual who qualifies as an "environmental professional" as defined in the final rule.

The inquiry of the environmental professional must include:

- interviews with past and present owners, operators and occupants;
- reviews of historical sources of information;
- reviews of federal, state, tribal and local government records;
- visual inspections of the facility and adjoining property;
- commonly known or reasonably ascertainable information; and
- degree of obviousness of the presence or likely presence of contamination at the property and the ability to detect the contamination.

"Additional inquiries" that must be conducted by or for the prospective landowner or grantee include: searches for environmental cleanup liens; assessments of any specialized knowledge or experience of the prospective landowner (or grantee); an assessment of the relationship of the purchase price to the fair market value of the property, if the property was not contaminated; and commonly known or reasonably ascertainable information.

Who Qualifies as an Environmental Professional?

To ensure the quality of all appropriate inquiries, the final rule includes specific educational and experience requirements for an environmental professional.

The final rule defines an environmental professional as someone who has:

> (1) a state or tribal issued certification or license and three years of relevant full-time work experience; or

> (2) a Baccalaureate degree or higher in science or engineering and five years of relevant full-time work experience; or

> (3) ten years of relevant full-time work experience.

* * *

NOTES

1. As originally drafted, CERCLA inadvertently discouraged the reuse of brownfields because anyone purchasing a site contaminated with hazardous substances would thereafter be liable as a PRP. This resulted in sites being left unused even after environmental remediation had occurred. EPA estimates that there are more than 450,000 brownfield sites in the United States, so a large amount of land was affected by this dynamic. When President Bush signed the 2002 Brownfields Amendments into law, he addressed this issue in his signing statement:

> The law I sign today addresses the problem of land which has already been developed and then abandoned. American cities have many such eyesores; anywhere from 500,000 to a million brownfields are across our Nation. These areas once supported manufacturing and commerce, and now lie empty, adding nothing of value to the community and sometimes only causing problems.

> Many communities and entrepreneurs have sought to redevelop brownfields. Often they could not, either because of excessive regulation or because of the fear of endless litigation. As a consequence, small businesses and other employers have located elsewhere, pushing development farther and farther outward, taking jobs with them and leaving cities empty * * * *

> [B]enefit[s from the law] will come as businesses recycle older properties and spare surrounding lands from development. There has been a lot of talk about urban sprawl. Well, one of the best ways to arrest urban sprawl is to develop brownfields and make them productive pieces of land where people can find work and employment. By one estimate, for every acre of redeveloped brownfields, we save 4½ acres of open space * * *

Statement by President George W. Bush Upon Signing H.R. 2869, 2002 U.S.C.C.A.N. 1780 (Jan. 11, 2002).

2. After 2002, a redeveloper of a brownfield can now avoid becoming a PRP. What about a third party that would like to purchase a site in order to clean

it up? Why would such parties, typically referred to as Good Samaritans, face potential liability under CERCLA? EPA has tried to address this problem and encourage third parties to undertake cleanup efforts through a variety of administrative tools, including entering settlements with Good Samaritans to resolve any potential CERCLA liability in exchange for the Good Samaritan undertaking specific cleanup obligations. This strategy has not been entirely successful, however, because many Good Samaritans seek to address sites that cause water quality problems, and as a result they also face potential liability under the Clean Water Act. *See* EPA Memorandum, Clean Water Act § 402 National Pollution Discharge Elimination System (NPDES) Permit Requirements for "Good Samaritans" at Orphan Mine Sites (Dec. 12, 2012).

3.   Good Samaritans are increasingly important for cleanups of abandoned mines. Such sites are plentiful. Colorado alone is home to an estimated 18,000 abandoned mine features, such as mine openings and waste rock piles, just within National Forests. And many sites contain worrying levels of contaminants. A survey conducted by the Colorado Geological Survey identified about 900 sites that have environmental problems that require investigation. *See* Colorado Geological Survey, Abandoned Mine Land Inventory Project, http://coloradogeologicalsurvey.org/water/abandoned-mine-land/united-states-forest-hazard-abandoned-mine-land-inventory-project/. In 2008, the organization Trout Unlimited became the first to party to enter into a Good Samaritan agreement with EPA, spending more than one million dollars to treat 60 acres of mine tailings along seventeen miles of Kerber Creek in Colorado. *See* Trout Unlimited, Press Release, *EPA Agrees to give Trout Unlimited Liability Protection for Colorado Abandoned Mine Cleanup* (Aug. 24, 2010).

C.   CERCLA LIABILITY AND CORPORATE LAW

In the *Burlington Northern* case, the district court found that an agricultural chemical distributor called Brown & Bryant Inc. was responsible for eighty-five percent of the cleanup at issue. 556 U.S. 599, 606 (2009). But soon after cleanup began, that company went bankrupt, leaving two railroads, which bore relatively little responsibility for contamination, as the only solvent PRPs. This is not a rare circumstance, and the financial consequences are significant for the PRPs that remain solvent and for the public. An analysis conducted by the Center for Public Integrity found that just four companies by themselves avoided more than $700 million in cleanup costs by declaring bankruptcy. *See* Kevin Bogardus, *Bankrupt Companies Avoid More than $700 Million in Cleanup Costs*, https://www.publicintegrity.org/2007/05/03/5620/bankrupt-companies-avoid-more-700-million-cleanup-costs.

There are several reasons for CERCLA's uncomfortably close relationship with bankruptcy law. First, cleanup costs can drive a company into bankruptcy. Second, CERCLA often assigns liability for releases that occurred many decades ago, and even without cleanup liability, companies tend to come and go over those long time spans. Third, in some circumstances, a bankruptcy proceeding may be part of a broader scheme to shield assets from environmental liabilities. This could occur, for example, if a PRP attempts to transfer its assets but not its liabilities to a second company with the same owners, and then has the original company declare bankruptcy. Or, alternatively, a company might spin off a poorly-capitalized subsidiary to pursue a venture—opening a new mine, perhaps—that carries a high risk of CERCLA liability. The parent company might then reap the profits of the venture while letting the subsidiary shoulder the risk.

As we have seen, Congress was aware of the potential for gamesmanship when it created the innocent third party defense, contiguous property owner defense, and bona fide purchaser defense. In each case, a party cannot invoke the defense if it had certain types of relationships, like a business relationship, with the prior or contiguous owner. But these limitations to CERCLA defenses do not end the matter. One of the basic purposes of corporate law is to shield investors from liability for the actions of companies in which they invest. Absent such protection, the theory goes, investment would be diminished, innovation would occur less, and the economy would be much weaker. But that basic policy goal often stands in direct tension with CERCLA's goal of avoiding public liability for cleanups, because companies can attempt to use the corporate form to evade CERCLA liability. The materials that follow address this issue.

PROBLEM: LIABLE PARENT COMPANIES

You are an attorney in the Office of Enforcement and Compliance Assurance (OECA) within EPA's Region 5 Office, which has jurisdiction over six states in the Midwest, including Wisconsin. EPA has already identified and either settled with or sued most of the primary PRPs at the Lower Fox River site. One of your tasks is to identify any additional PRPs.

You recently became aware of a small paper products factory called the De Pere Plant that has, until now, escaped notice. The De Pere Plant is owned by Little Apple Paper Co. (Little Apple). Little Apple is a subsidiary of Big Apple Paper Co. (Big Apple), which also owns a dozen other paper products factories in the Midwest. The De Pere Plant currently manufactures wrapping paper using soy ink, but in the 1960s, it produced specialty carbonless paper products using NCR Paper. As a result, it probably released Aroclor 1242 into the Lower Fox River. Big Apple is a Delaware corporation, and the corporate filing you obtained indicates it is a closely held company, and that it has been closely held since the 1960s. During that period, it had four owners: Willie and Carey Flores and Clyde and Maureen Lisle, each of whom serve on the board of directors, with Willie Flores serving as the President.

You sent Little Apple a notice of liability informing it that it was a probable PRP. The response informed you that Little Apple was entering a bankruptcy proceeding. A little investigation verifies this claim, and also convinces you that Little Apple is unlikely to emerge from the proceeding with any assets that it can contribute to the cleanup. That means redirecting your attention to Big Apple.

The 1960s were a long time ago, but your records requests produce some information about management of the plant, and you are also able to find a former employee who remembers how the plant operated during that time. From those investigations, you learn a few key facts about Little Apple in the 1960s (and assume you have sufficient evidence to prove each of these facts in court):

- Little Apple had a board of directors with five members. Willie Flores, Carey Flores, and Clyde Lisle both sat on Little Apple's Board. The other two board members were not formally affiliated with Big Apple.

- Little Apple was a wholly owned subsidiary of Big Apple. In other words, no other entity had an ownership share of Little Apple.

- Little Apple's day-to-day operations were handled primarily by Francis Jordan, the company's president. He generally made operational decisions about how equipment was managed. On a weekly basis, however, he would meet with Willie Flores to discuss market needs, key customers, and Little Apple's cash flow. Willie Flores often made suggestions about financial decisions. Francis Jordan (who is retired but still alive) told you, "Willie was always pushing me to cut costs, cut costs. He didn't want us to buy any new equipment unless we had too. But he was a money guy, not an engineer. He didn't tell me how to run the machines."

Is Big Apple liable for PCB pollution in the Lower Fox River?

The Supreme Court decision below remains the most important precedent about the role that state corporate law plays in establishing CERCLA liability.

United States v. Bestfoods

524 U.S. 51 (1998)

■ JUSTICE SOUTER delivered the opinion of the Court.

* * *

II

In 1957, Ott Chemical Co. (Ott I) began manufacturing chemicals at a plant near Muskegon, Michigan, and its intentional and unintentional dumping of hazardous substances significantly polluted the soil and ground water at the site. In 1965, respondent CPC International Inc. incorporated a wholly owned subsidiary to buy Ott I's assets in exchange for CPC stock. The new company, also dubbed Ott Chemical Co. (Ott II), continued chemical manufacturing at the site, and continued to pollute its surroundings. CPC kept the managers of Ott I, including its founder, president, and principal shareholder, Arnold Ott, on board as officers of Ott II. Arnold Ott and several other Ott II officers and directors were also given positions at CPC, and they performed duties for both corporations.

In 1972, CPC sold Ott II to Story Chemical Company, which operated the Muskegon plant until its bankruptcy in 1977. Shortly thereafter, when respondent Michigan Department of Natural Resources (MDNR) examined the site for environmental damage, it found the land littered with thousands of leaking and even exploding drums of waste, and the soil and water saturated with noxious chemicals. MDNR sought a buyer for the property who would be willing to contribute toward its cleanup, and after extensive negotiations, respondent Aerojet-General Corp. arranged for transfer of the site from the Story bankruptcy trustee in 1977. Aerojet created a wholly owned California subsidiary, Cordova Chemical Company (Cordova/California), to purchase the property, and Cordova/California in turn created a wholly owned Michigan subsidiary, Cordova Chemical Company of Michigan (Cordova/Michigan), which manufactured chemicals at the site until 1986.

By 1981, the federal Environmental Protection Agency had undertaken to see the site cleaned up, and its long-term remedial plan called for expenditures well into the tens of millions of dollars. To recover some of that money, the United States filed this action under § 107 in 1989, naming five defendants as responsible parties: CPC, Aerojet, Cordova/California, Cordova/Michigan, and Arnold Ott. (By that time, Ott I and Ott II were defunct.) After the parties (and MDNR) had launched a flurry of contribution claims, counterclaims, and cross-claims, the District Court consolidated the cases for trial in three phases: liability, remedy, and insurance coverage. So far, only the first phase has been completed; in 1991, the District Court held a 15-day bench trial on the issue of liability. Because the parties stipulated that the Muskegon plant was a "facility" within the meaning of 42 U.S.C. § 9601(9), that hazardous substances had been released at the facility, and that the United States had incurred reimbursable response costs to clean up the site, the trial focused on the issues of whether CPC and Aerojet, as the parent corporations of Ott II and the Cordova companies, had "owned or operated" the facility within the meaning of § 107(a)(2). * * * [The district court ruled that CPC and Aerojet were operators within the meaning of section 107(a)(1). The Sixth Circuit sitting en banc reversed holding that a "parent will be liable only when the requirements necessary to pierce the corporate veil [under state law] are met."]

We granted certiorari, 522 U.S. 1024 (1997), to resolve a conflict among the Circuits over the extent to which parent corporations may be held liable under CERCLA for operating facilities ostensibly under the control of their subsidiaries. We now vacate and remand.

III

It is a general principle of corporate law deeply "ingrained in our economic and legal systems" that a parent corporation (so-called because of control through ownership of another corporation's stock) is not liable for the acts of its subsidiaries. Douglas & Shanks, Insulation from Liability Through Subsidiary Corporations, 39 Yale L.J. 193 (1929) (hereinafter Douglas)[.] * * * Although this respect for corporate distinctions when the subsidiary is a polluter has been severely criticized in the literature, see, *e.g.,* Note, Liability of Parent Corporations for Hazardous Waste Cleanup and Damages, 99 Harv. L. Rev. 986 (1986), nothing in CERCLA purports to reject this bedrock principle, and against this venerable common-law backdrop, the congressional silence is audible. Cf. *Edmonds v. Compagnie Generale Transatlantique,* 443 U.S. 256, 266–267 (1979) ("[S]ilence is most eloquent, for such reticence while contemplating an important and controversial change in existing law is unlikely"). The Government has indeed made no claim that a corporate parent is liable as an owner or an operator under § 107 simply because its subsidiary is subject to liability for owning or operating a polluting facility.

But there is an equally fundamental principle of corporate law, applicable to the parent-subsidiary relationship as well as generally, that the corporate veil may be pierced and the shareholder held liable for the corporation's conduct when, *inter alia,* the corporate form would otherwise be misused to accomplish certain wrongful purposes, most notably fraud, on the shareholder's behalf[.] * * * Nothing in CERCLA purports to rewrite this well-settled rule, either. CERCLA is thus like many another congressional enactment in giving no indication that "the entire corpus of state corporation law is to be replaced simply because a plaintiff's cause of action is based upon a federal statute," *Burks v. Lasker,* 441 U.S. 471, 478 (1979), and the failure of the statute to speak to a matter as fundamental as the liability implications of corporate ownership demands application of the rule that "[i]n order to abrogate a common-law principle, the statute must speak directly to the question addressed by the common law," *United States v. Texas,* 507 U.S. 529, 534 (1993) (internal quotation marks omitted). The Court of Appeals was accordingly correct in holding that when (but only when) the corporate veil may be pierced, may a parent corporation be charged with derivative CERCLA liability for its subsidiary's actions.

IV

A

If the Act rested liability entirely on ownership of a polluting facility, this opinion might end here; but CERCLA liability may turn on operation as well as ownership, and nothing in the statute's terms bars a parent corporation from direct liability for its own actions in operating a facility owned by its subsidiary. As Justice (then-Professor) Douglas noted almost 70 years ago, derivative liability cases are to be distinguished from those in which "the alleged wrong can seemingly be traced to the parent through the conduit of its own personnel and management" and "the parent is directly a participant in the wrong complained of." Douglas 207, 208. In such instances, the parent is directly liable for its own actions. See H. Henn & J. Alexander, Laws of Corporations 347 (3d ed. 1983) (hereinafter Henn & Alexander) ("Apart from corporation law principles, a shareholder, whether a natural person or a corporation, may be liable on the ground that such shareholder's activity resulted in the liability"). The fact that a corporate subsidiary happens to own a polluting facility operated by its parent does nothing, then, to displace the rule that the parent "corporation is [itself] responsible for the wrongs committed by its agents in the course of its business," *Mine Workers v. Coronado Coal Co.,* 259 U.S. 344, 395 (1922), and whereas the rules of veil piercing limit derivative liability for the actions of another corporation, CERCLA's "operator" provision is concerned primarily with direct liability for one's own actions. See, *e.g., Sidney S. Arst Co. v. Pipefitters Welfare Ed. Fund,* 25 F.3d 417, 420 (CA7 1994) ("[T]he direct, personal liability provided by CERCLA is distinct from the derivative liability that results from piercing the corporate veil" (internal quotation marks omitted)). It is this direct liability that is properly seen as being at issue here.

Under the plain language of the statute, any person who operates a polluting facility is directly liable for the costs of cleaning up the pollution. See 42 U.S.C. § 9607(a)(2). This is so regardless of whether that person is the facility's owner, the owner's parent corporation or business partner, or even a saboteur who sneaks into the facility at night to discharge its poisons out of malice. If any such act of operating a corporate subsidiary's facility is done on behalf of a parent corporation, the existence of the parent-subsidiary relationship under state corporate law is simply irrelevant to the issue of direct liability. * * *

So, under CERCLA, an operator is simply someone who directs the workings of, manages, or conducts the affairs of a facility. To sharpen the definition for purposes of CERCLA's concern with environmental contamination, an operator must manage, direct, or conduct operations specifically related to pollution, that is, operations having to do with the leakage or disposal of hazardous waste, or decisions about compliance with environmental regulations.

B

With this understanding, we are satisfied that the Court of Appeals correctly rejected the District Court's analysis of direct liability. But we also think that the appeals court erred in limiting direct liability under the statute to a parent's sole or joint venture operation, so as to eliminate any possible finding that CPC is liable as an operator on the facts of this case.

1

By emphasizing that "CPC is directly liable under section 107(a)(2) as an operator because CPC actively participated in and exerted significant control over Ott II's business and decision-making," 777 F. Supp., at 574, the District Court applied the "actual control" test of whether the parent "actually operated the business of its subsidiary," *id.*, at 573, as several Circuits have employed it, see, *e.g., United States v. Kayser-Roth Corp.,* [910 F.2d 24, 27 (CA1 1990)] (operator liability "requires active involvement in the affairs of the subsidiary"); *Jacksonville Elec. Auth. v. Bernuth Corp.,* 996 F.2d 1107, 1110 (CA11 1993) (parent is liable if it "actually exercised control over, or was otherwise intimately involved in the operations of, the [subsidiary] corporation immediately responsible for the operation of the facility" (internal quotation marks omitted)).

The well-taken objection to the actual control test, however, is its fusion of direct and indirect liability; the test is administered by asking a question about the relationship between the two corporations (an issue going to indirect liability) instead of a question about the parent's interaction with the subsidiary's facility (the source of any direct liability). If, however, direct liability for the parent's operation of the facility is to be kept distinct from derivative liability for the subsidiary's own operation, the focus of the enquiry must necessarily be different under the two tests. "The question is not whether the parent operates the subsidiary, but rather whether it operates the facility, and that operation is evidenced by participation in the activities of the facility, not the subsidiary. Control of the subsidiary, if extensive enough, gives rise to indirect liability under piercing doctrine, not direct liability under the statutory language." Oswald 269; see also *Schiavone v. Pearce,* 79 F.3d

248, 254 (CA2 1996) ("Any liabilities [the parent] may have as an *operator,* then, stem directly from its control over the plant"). The District Court was therefore mistaken to rest its analysis on CPC's relationship with Ott II, premising liability on little more than "CPC's 100-percent ownership of Ott II" and "CPC's active participation in, and at times majority control over, Ott II's board of directors." 777 F. Supp., at 575. The analysis should instead have rested on the relationship between CPC and the Muskegon facility itself.

In addition to (and perhaps as a reflection of) the erroneous focus on the relationship between CPC and Ott II, even those findings of the District Court that might be taken to speak to the extent of CPC's activity at the facility itself are flawed, for the District Court wrongly assumed that the actions of the joint officers and directors are necessarily attributable to CPC. The District Court emphasized the facts that CPC placed its own high-level officials on Ott II's board of directors and in key management positions at Ott II, and that those individuals made major policy decisions and conducted day-to-day operations at the facility[.] * * *

In imposing direct liability on these grounds, the District Court failed to recognize that "it is entirely appropriate for directors of a parent corporation to serve as directors of its subsidiary, and that fact alone may not serve to expose the parent corporation to liability for its subsidiary's acts." *American Protein Corp. v. AB Volvo,* 844 F.2d 56, 57 (CA2), *cert. denied,* 488 U.S. 852 (1988); *see also Kingston Dry Dock Co. v. Lake Champlain Transp. Co.,* 31 F.2d 265, 267 (CA2 1929) (L. Hand, J.) ("Control through the ownership of shares does not fuse the corporations, even when the directors are common to each"); Henn & Alexander 355 (noting that it is "normal" for a parent and subsidiary to "have identical directors and officers").

This recognition that the corporate personalities remain distinct has its corollary in the "well established principle [of corporate law] that directors and officers holding positions with a parent and its subsidiary can and do 'change hats' to represent the two corporations separately, despite their common ownership." *Lusk v. Foxmeyer Health Corp.,* 129 F.3d 773, 779 (CA5 1997); see also *Fisser v. International Bank,* 282 F.2d 231, 238 (CA2 1960). Since courts generally presume "that the directors are wearing their 'subsidiary hats' and not their 'parent hats' when acting for the subsidiary," P. Blumberg, Law of Corporate Groups: Procedural Problems in the Law of Parent and Subsidiary Corporations § 1.02.1, p. 12 (1983); see, *e.g., United States v. Jon-T Chemicals, Inc.,* 768 F.2d 686, 691 (CA5 1985), *cert. denied,* 475 U.S. 1014 (1986), it cannot be enough to establish liability here that dual officers and directors made policy decisions and supervised activities at the facility. The Government would have to show that, despite the general presumption to the contrary, the officers and directors were acting in their capacities as CPC officers and directors, and not as Ott II officers and directors, when they committed those acts. The District Court made no such enquiry here, however, disregarding entirely this time-honored common-law rule.

In sum, the District Court's focus on the relationship between parent and subsidiary (rather than parent and facility), combined with its automatic attribution of the actions of dual officers and directors to the corporate parent, erroneously, even if unintentionally, treated CERCLA as though it displaced or fundamentally altered common-law standards of limited liability. Indeed, if the evidence of common corporate personnel acting at management and directorial levels were enough to support a finding of a parent corporation's direct operator liability under CERCLA, then the possibility of resort to veil piercing to establish indirect, derivative liability for the subsidiary's violations would be academic. There would in essence be a relaxed, CERCLA-specific rule of derivative liability that would banish traditional standards and expectations from the law of CERCLA liability. But, as we have said, such a rule does not arise from congressional silence, and CERCLA's silence is dispositive.

2

We accordingly agree with the Court of Appeals that a participation-and-control test looking to the parent's supervision over the subsidiary, especially one that assumes that dual officers always act on behalf of the parent, cannot be used to identify operation of a facility resulting in direct parental liability. Nonetheless, a return to the ordinary meaning of the word "operate" in the organizational sense will indicate why we think that the Sixth Circuit stopped short when it confined its examples of direct parental operation to exclusive or joint ventures, and declined to find at least the possibility of direct operation by CPC in this case.

In our enquiry into the meaning Congress presumably had in mind when it used the verb "to operate," we recognized that the statute obviously meant something more than mere mechanical activation of pumps and valves, and must be read to contemplate "operation" as including the exercise of direction over the facility's activities. * * * The Court of Appeals recognized this by indicating that a parent can be held directly liable when the parent operates the facility in the stead of its subsidiary or alongside the subsidiary in some sort of a joint venture. See 113 F.3d, at 579. We anticipated a further possibility above, however, when we observed that a dual officer or director might depart so far from the norms of parental influence exercised through dual officeholding as to serve the parent, even when ostensibly acting on behalf of the subsidiary in operating the facility. * * * Yet another possibility, suggested by the facts of this case, is that an agent of the parent with no hat to wear but the parent's hat might manage or direct activities at the facility.

Identifying such an occurrence calls for line-drawing yet again, since the acts of direct operation that give rise to parental liability must necessarily be distinguished from the interference that stems from the normal relationship between parent and subsidiary. Again norms of corporate behavior (undisturbed by any CERCLA provision) are crucial reference points. Just as we may look to such norms in identifying the limits of the presumption that a dual officeholder acts in his ostensible capacity, so here we may refer to them in distinguishing a parental officer's oversight of a subsidiary from such an officer's control over the operation of the subsidiary's facility. "[A]ctivities that involve the facility but which are consistent with the parent's investor status, such as monitoring of the subsidiary's performance, supervision of the subsidiary's finance and capital budget decisions, and articulation of general policies and procedures, should not give rise to direct liability." Oswald 282. The critical question is whether, in degree and detail, actions directed to the facility by an agent of the parent alone are eccentric under accepted norms of parental oversight of a subsidiary's facility.

There is, in fact, some evidence that CPC engaged in just this type and degree of activity at the Muskegon plant. The District Court's opinion speaks of an agent of CPC alone who played a conspicuous part in dealing with the toxic risks emanating from the operation of the plant. G.R.D. Williams worked only for CPC; he was not an employee, officer, or director of Ott II, see Tr. of Oral Arg. 7, and thus, his actions were of necessity taken only on behalf of CPC. The District Court found that "CPC became directly involved in environmental and regulatory matters through the work of . . . Williams, CPC's governmental and environmental affairs director. Williams . . . became heavily involved in environmental issues at Ott II." 777 F. Supp., at 561. He "actively participated in and exerted control over a variety of Ott II environmental matters," *ibid.,* and he "issued directives regarding Ott II's responses to regulatory inquiries," *id.,* at 575.

We think that these findings are enough to raise an issue of CPC's operation of the facility through Williams's actions, though we would draw no ultimate conclusion from these findings at this point. Not only would we be deciding in the first instance an issue on which the trial and appellate courts did not focus, but the very fact that the District Court did not see the case as we do suggests that there may be still more to be known about Williams's activities. Indeed, even as the factual findings stand, the trial court offered little in the way of concrete detail for its conclusions about Williams's role in Ott II's environmental affairs, and the parties vigorously dispute the extent of Williams's involvement. Prudence thus counsels us to remand, on the theory of direct operation set out here, for reevaluation of Williams's role, and of the role of any other CPC agent who might be said to have had a part in operating the Muskegon facility. * * *

NOTES

1.   In *Bestfoods*, the Court talks about the common law governing corporations. Should that common law be state corporate law or a uniform federal common law rule? In a footnote, the Supreme Court acknowledged that the lower courts have divided on that question, but declined to resolve the issue. 524 U.S. 51, 63 n.9 (1998). As an example of this conflict, in *United States v. Davis*, the First Circuit expressed the view that "the majority rule is to apply state law 'so long as it is not hostile to the federal interests animating CERCLA.'" 261 F.3d 1, 54 (1st Cir. 2001). In *United States v. General Battery Corp.*, the Third Circuit disagreed, applying a federal common law rule based on "the general doctrine of successor liability in operation in most states." 423 F.3d 294, 298 (3d Cir. 2005). For a more detailed analysis of this issue, see Michael Carter, Comment, *Successor Liability under CERCLA: It's Time to Fully Embrace State Law*, 156 U. PENN. L. REV. 767 (2008) (arguing that federal courts should apply state corporate law). *But see* Lawrence P. Schnapf, *CERCLA and the Substantial Continuity Test: A Unifying Proposal for Imposing CERCLA Liability Asset on Purchasers*, 4 ENVTL. L. 435 (1998) (arguing for a unified approach to successor liability under CERCLA).

2.   The *Bestfoods* case and the problem above focus on the relationship between a parent company and its subsidiary. But issues of corporate form also arise through corporate sales. For example, a corporation might dissolve and distribute its assets to shareholders or owners. Do they then inherit CERCLA liabilities as well? Or, alternatively, a company's purchaser might purport to purchase only the company's assets, rather than purchasing the company in its entirety. Do CERCLA liabilities transfer with the sale?

For discussion of the first issue, see *March v. Rosenbloom*, 499 F.3d 165 (2d Cir. 2007). In *March,* the Second Circuit decided that the shareholders of a defunct corporation could not be sued after the state's statutory wind-up period for a corporate dissolution. The court explained that the state's limitation on shareholder liability post dissolution did not thwart CERCLA's goals because the state's law "require[s] corporations to provide security that will be reasonably likely to be sufficient to cover claims that have not been made known to the corporation or that, based on the facts known to the corporation, are likely to arise within a period after dissolution." *Id.* at 180.

On the latter question, corporate law traditionally differentiates between a merger or consolidation, through which a purchasing company acquires all of the liabilities and obligations of the selling company, *see, e.g.,* 8 Del. C. § 259(a), and an asset sale, through which the purchaser acquires only those liabilities it specifically agrees to assume, *see, e.g., Polius v. Clark Equip. Co.*, 802 F.2d 75, 77–78 (3d Cir. 1986). Ordinarily, the difference between a merger and asset sale will be governed by the formal structure of the deal reached between the companies. In some instances, however, a court will find that a transaction structured as an asset sale is a de facto merger. The court in *Philadelphia Electric Co. v. Hercules, Inc.*, 762 F.2d 303, 311 (3d Cir. 1985), examined this issue and explained:

> In determining whether a particular transaction amounts to a de facto merger as distinguished from an ordinary purchase and sale of assets most courts look to the following factors:
>
> (1) There is a continuation of the enterprise of the seller corporation, so that there is continuity of management, personnel, physical location, assets, and general business operations.
>
> (2) There is a continuity of shareholders which results from the purchasing corporation paying for the acquired assets with shares of its own stock, this stock ultimately coming to be held by the shareholders of the seller corporation so that they become a constituent part of the purchasing corporation.
>
> (3) The seller corporation ceases its ordinary business operations, liquidates, and dissolves as soon as legally and practically possible.
>
> (4) The purchasing corporation assumes those obligations of the seller ordinarily necessary for the uninterrupted continuation of normal business operations of the seller corporation.

3.   If you represent a company that is purchasing another company with potential CERCLA liabilities, and you want to protect your client from those liabilities—without playing games with corporate forms—what can you do? There are a few options. The simplest is to accept the liability but negotiate a lower purchase price. If your client is comfortable taking on a cleanup and shouldering some liability risk, it may actually be able to get a good deal. Another alternative is to negotiate an indemnity agreement that allocates liability by contract. That won't stop EPA from coming after your client to fund a cleanup—it cannot use a contract to erase its status as a PRP—but you can provide your client with a clear legal basis to obtain reimbursement from the seller.

4.   CERCLA's drafters recognized that environmental liability could bankrupt companies, leaving taxpayer on the hook for the cost of cleanup. To address this issue, CERCLA section 108(b) requires EPA to identify classes of industrial actors that must provide "financial assurances" before handling hazardous materials. 42 U.S.C. § 9608(b). Those financial assurances would guarantee that cleanup funds would be available if a hazardous substance release occurs.

EPA was supposed to implement section 108(b) no later than December 11, 1983, but the agency took no action for decades. In 2008, the Sierra Club sued, alleging that the agency had failed to undertake a nondiscretionary duty, and in 2009 a district court agreed. *See Sierra Club v. Johnson*, 2009 WL 482248 (N.D. Cal. Feb. 25, 2009). Later that year, EPA issued a notice that it planned to identify "classes of facilities within the hard-rock mining industry as its priority for the development of financial responsibility requirements." 74 Fed. Reg. 37,213 (July 28, 2009). Again, however, EPA did not act. In 2014, six environmental organizations sued to compel EPA to finalize financial assurance requirements for hard rock mining companies and other categories of potential polluters. On January 29, 2016, the D.C. Circuit entered a consent decree resolving the litigation. *In re Idaho Conservation League*, 811 F.3d 502 (D.C. Cir. 2016). Under the terms of the decree, EPA promised to initiate a rulemaking for the hardrock mining industry by December 1, 2016, and finalize a rule one year later. The consent decree also requires EPA to consider whether to issue regulations for other industries. As of the date of this writing, however, EPA has not issued a final rule.

For a discussion of the way that EPA's § 108(b) rules intersect with the parent-subsidiary relationship, see Stacey L. Sklaver, *Parents Know Best: A Legal and Economics Analysis of Financial Assurances under CERCLA Section 108(b) and the Parent-Subsidiary Relationship*, 18 J. L. BUS. & ETH. 169 (2012).

V. CLEANUP PROCESS

We've seen who is responsible for the costs of cleanup, but how does cleanup actually occur? More specifically, what is the process for proceeding through a cleanup, and what legal authority does EPA have to actually clean up a site, or to compel PRPs to do so? And what procedural or substantive constraints cabin that authority? The summary discussion below explains the process and describes the key legal levers.

A. CLEANUP PROCESS

The CERCLA process begins when EPA receives notification that a release of hazardous substances has occurred. State environmental agencies also receive notification, and EPA may defer to state oversight.

CERCLA does not itself authorize states to engage in such cleanup, nor does it directly impose standards on such cleanups. If the state does take the lead, then the investigation and remediation of the site will proceed under state law, with the state either carrying out the cleanup or, more often, providing regulatory oversight as the responsible parties move through the process. Federal law, however, is not irrelevant in such circumstances. In practice, when states themselves carry out cleanups, they typically follow the guidelines and standards contained in the National Contingency Plan (NCP) because only then can they recover their costs under section 107. Also, some state laws directly reference the NCP. California law, for example, generally only authorizes use of state money to fund cleanups that are "consistent with the priorities, guidelines, criteria, and regulations contained in the national contingency plan." Cal. Health & Safety Code § 26350. And EPA (and sometimes state regulators) can use the threat of federal authority to motivate recalcitrant PRPs.

Because state-law cleanups occur under a variety of regulatory regimes, we have not described them in detail here. The paragraphs below instead describe what happens if EPA assumes control.

Preliminary Assessment and Site Investigation. After EPA receives notification of a release of hazardous substances, the next step is to complete a prescreening process. If EPA decides further investigation is warranted, the agency then commences a preliminary assessment and site investigation, also referred to as a PA/SI. The first step of that process is to investigate the site to determine what, if any, hazardous substances exist and what, if any, response is required.

The distinction between a removal action and a remedial action is sometimes a source of controversy. In *United States v. W.R. Grace & Co.*, 429 F.3d 1224 (9th Cir. 2005), for example, EPA had taken extensive measures to abate large-scale asbestos pollution, in Libby, Montana. EPA labeled the action a removal action, and W.R. Grace argued that the action really was a remedial action—and that, because EPA had not followed the NCP's requirements for remedial actions, the federal government's expenses were not reimbursable under section 107. The Ninth Circuit rejected W.R. Grace's argument. After noting that "[w]e cannot escape the fact that people are sick and dying as a result of this continue exposure," it deferred to EPA's characterization of the actions as removal actions.

EPA has three choices for its response. First, if it can initiate a *removal action*, a short-term action to "abate, prevent, minimize, stabilize, mitigate, or eliminate the release or threat of release" of a hazardous substance that poses a "threat to public health or welfare * * * or the environment." 40 CF.R. § 300.415(b)(1); *see* 42 U.S.C. § 9601(23) (defining "removal").

Second, EPA can plan for a longer-term response, which is known as a *remedial action. See* 42 U.S.C. § 9601(24) (defining "remedial action"). The authority for such responses comes from CERCLA section 104(a), which authorizes EPA to take any response action consistent with the NCP. 42 U.S.C. § 9704(a).[5]

Third, if the concentrations of hazardous substances are sufficiently low such that the site meets

---

[5]   Many sections of CERCLA, including sections 104 and 106, vest authority directly in the president, but executive orders have delegated that authority primarily to EPA, although the Departments of Defense, Energy, and Interior have also been assigned responsibilities. *See* Executive Order No. 12580, 52 Fed. Reg. 2923 (Jan. 23, 1987); *see also* Executive Order 13016, 61 Fed. Reg. 45871 (Aug. 28, 1996) (amending executive order 12580).

applicable cleanup standards, EPA can decide that *no response* is necessary.

National Priorities List. Based on information produced during the PA/SI, EPA develops a Hazardous Ranking System (HRS) score for a site. The HRS score includes a numerical evaluation of factors, taking account of the amount and nature of any hazardous substances released into the environment, the extent to which those hazardous substances have contaminated ground water, surface water, soil and air, and the likely effect on human health or sensitive environments. Based on all of those considerations, EPA assigns a single HRS score, between 0 and 100. A site that receives a HRS score above a 28.5 is eligible for listing on the National Priorities List (NPL). If EPA decides to proceed with such a listing, it must consult with state agencies and undergo a public administrative process.

According to EPA, NPL listings primarily serve an informational purpose. The agency can initiate removal or remedial actions, and can demand private responses, with or without an NPL listing. But NPL listings still are sometimes controversial, largely because state and local governments believe a stigma accompanies such listings.

The Lower Fox River provides an example of those controversies. Efforts to address its contamination began in the mid-1980s. Initially, the Wisconsin Department of Natural Resources (WDNR) was the primary government player involved, although the U.S. Fish and Wildlife Service, U.S. Army Corps of Engineers, and the Oneida and Menominee Tribes were also involved. WDNR engaged in a lengthy process to develop a cleanup plan with PRPs along the river. By the mid-1990s, no plan had been finalized. Frustrated by the lack of progress, EPA sent a letter to WDNR in 1997 indicating that it planned to propose listing the Lower Fox River on the NPL and asking for the state to support the proposal. Shortly thereafter, a Milwaukee newspaper ran an article that included the following passages:

> Some familiar with the decades-long Fox River cleanup project are skeptical that peace is at hand in the political standoff between the federal Environmental Protection Agency and the state Department of Natural Resources.
>
> The inter-agency dispute was supposedly averted by the July 11 announcement of an agreement between the EPA and the DNR to work together on the project. * * *
>
> The agreement is aimed at resolving whether the EPA would be the lead agency on the Fox River cleanup as a federal Superfund site, or whether the state DNR should take the lead. * * *
>
> Under the agreement, the EPA will work with the DNR and local entities already seeking a solution. But the EPA reserves

the right to designate the Fox River a Superfund site and do the cleanup the EPA's way, said Jim Hahnenberg, remedial project manager at the EPA regional office in Chicago.

The state accepted the EPA's involvement in the planning reluctantly, said Bruce Baker, the DNR's deputy administrator for water.

The DNR has been working cooperatively with companies along the river for several years on a solution to the contamination problem along the Fox River. Within the next 12 months, it is set to do test cleanup projects at certain points along the waterway, Baker said.

But if the EPA stepped in and established the river as a federal Superfund site, he said, that would only slow down the existing cleanup process.

"The way I like to analogize it is that we were already traveling 50 miles an hour down the road and the EPA is trying to jump in and we hope they don't slow us down," Baker said.

But a leading environmentalist said the state is hardly racing toward a solution on its own.

"You can't slow down something that isn't moving," said Brett Hulsey, Great Lakes program director for the Sierra Club in Madison. * * *

The DNR has been working on PCB contamination of the river for 10 years, he said, but "the state has not cleaned up one pound of the Fox River." * * *

Robert Mullins, *Agency Truce May Streamline Fox River Cleanup*, MILWAUKEE BUS. J., Aug. 3, 1997.

Despite the agreement discussed in the article, EPA formally proposed listing the Lower Fox River on the NPL on July 28, 1998. 63 Fed. Reg. 40247 (July 28, 1998). EPA never finalized the listing, but it did assume much more control of the cleanup process.

For an excellent teaching case study based on the Fox River NPL listing controversy, see Mary Decker & Barton H. Thompson, Jr., *The Lower Fox River* (Stanford Law School Case Studies Series, 1998).

Remedial Investigation and Feasibility Study. This stage, often referred to as the RI/FS, occurs if EPA determines that a remedial action is required at a site. The RI/FS involves two separate exercises, which are usually performed at the same time. The Remedial Investigation involves a detailed characterization of the site and the risks that it poses. In accomplishing that task, EPA also develops "acceptable exposure levels for use in developing remedial alternatives." 40 C.F.R.

§ 300.430(d)(4). In other words, the RI requires EPA to fully assess the hazardous substances at the site, the threats the substances pose, and the degree of cleanup necessary. The Feasibility Study then develops alternative approaches to remedying the contamination.

Proposed Plan. Based on the RI/FS, EPA releases a proposed plan describing an intended remedy that will achieve the required degree of cleanup. Section 117 requires the agency to release a "brief analysis of the proposed plan" and provide a "reasonable opportunity" for public comment. 42 U.S.C. § 9617(a).

Record of Decision. After receiving public comment on the proposed plan, EPA issues the record of decision (ROD) to select a remedy. The ROD remains somewhat general in nature. It explains the contours of the selected remedy and how the remedy will achieve the required degree of cleanup.

Remedial Design and Remedial Action. After EPA selects a remedy through the ROD, the RD/RA fills in the technical details of how that remedy will be accomplished. Once the RD/RA is completed, implementation of the remedy can begin.

Figure 6.6. Flow Chart of an EPA-led Cleanup

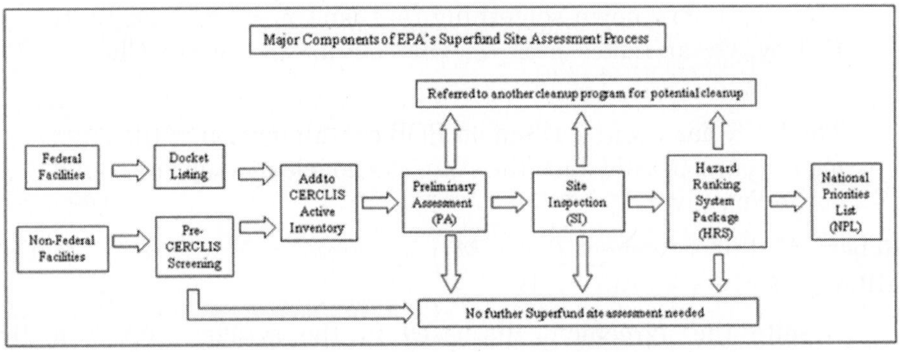

Source: https://www.epa.gov/sites/production/files/styles/large/
public/2015-07/assessproc.gif

Degree of Cleanup Required. Section 121 of CERCLA requires all remediation efforts in which the EPA is involved to "attain a degree of cleanup * * * at a minimum which assures protection of human health and the environment" and to meet "all applicable or relevant and appropriate requirements" (ARARs). 42 U.S.C. § 9612(d). ARARs are standards for environmental quality established by other state or federal laws. The potential suite of sources for such standards is large, and as a result, lawyers focusing on CERCLA cleanups need broad expertise in many other areas of environmental law.

A good place to start in considering what ARARs may be involved at any particular site is EPA's *CERCLA Compliance with Other Laws*

Manual. The manual, which only exists in an interim final form, is published in two parts and extends over hundreds of pages. EPA explains that the specific standards derived from these other sources of law come in at least three categories: "health- or risk-based numerical values or methodologies," "technology- or activity-based requirements or limitations," or "[l]ocation-specific requirements * * * placed on the concentrations of hazardous substances or the conduct of activities solely because they occur in special locations." EPA, CERCLA COMPLIANCE WITH OTHER LAW MANUAL PART I: INTERIM FINAL at xiv (1988).

The Role of the Superfund. When CERCLA was enacted, Congress created the Hazardous Substance Superfund Trust Fund, commonly referred to as the Superfund, which was supposed to provide EPA with the money necessary to carry out environmental cleanups. Prior to 1995, the Superfund was fueled by an excise tax on petroleum and chemical feedstocks. That tax provided nearly 70 percent of the money in the Superfund, although EPA also obtained money from direct congressional appropriations and as the result of cost recovery lawsuits and settlements. The excise tax expired in 1995 and has never been reauthorized. After reaching a peak of $4.7 billion in 1997, the balance in the Superfund has dwindled to nearly nothing; at the beginning of 2007, the Superfund contained just $173 million.

EPA does still have money to spend on environmental remediation. Congress continues to appropriate money to the agency on an annual basis, although those appropriations have declined from about $2 billion in 1999 to $1 billion in 2013. *See* GOVERNMENT ACCOUNTABILITY OFFICE, TRENDS IN FEDERAL FUNDING AND CLEANUP OF EPA'S NONFEDERAL NATIONAL PRIORITIES LIST SITES (2015); GOVERNMENT ACCOUNTABILITY OFFICE, EPA'S ESTIMATED COSTS TO REMEDIATE EXISTING SITES EXCEED CURRENT FUNDING LEVELS, AND MORE SITES ARE EXPECTED TO BE ADDED TO THE NATIONAL PRIORITIES LIST (2010). As a result, EPA funds fewer cleanups than it once did and instead relies on its power to compel PRPs to act.

B. COMPELLING CLEANUPS

Because of its limited funding, and because of the legal wrangling associated with cost recovery actions, government-led cleanups are rarely EPA's preferred option. Instead, the agency generally prefers for PRPs to fund and carry out cleanups, and it has a variety of legal tools to make sure that happens. Two of the most important of these tools are unilateral administrative orders (UAOs) and administrative orders on consent (AOCs).

A UAO is, as its name suggests, a unilateral order from EPA to a PRP ordering that PRP to undertake cleanup actions at a site. Authority for UAOs comes directly from the statute itself; section 106(a) states that "[t]he President may also, after notice to the affected state, take other action under this section including, but not limited to, issuing such orders as may be necessary to protect public health and welfare and the environment." 42 U.S.C. § 9606(a). A UAO is not subject to judicial review until after a PRP has complied with the order's terms. *Id.* § 9606(b)(2), 9613(h). This means that even a party who believes it has a valid defense to liability cannot raise that defense in court in response to a UAO. Such a party can refuse to comply and await EPA filing a civil action to enforce the UAO. But such a strategy is very risky and rarely pursued. Failure to comply with a valid UAO can result in stiff fines and even punitive damages. *Id.* §§ 9606(b), 9607(c)(3). PRPs have tried to challenge this statutory scheme as violating constitutional due process requirements, so far without success. *See Gen. Elec. Co. v. Jackson*, 610 F.3d 110 (D.C. Cir. 2010).

Understanding UAOs is crucial for any environmental lawyer who represents private companies with CERCLA liabilities. The district court decision in *General Electric* explained that "[b]etween August 16, 1982 and May 25, 2006—a period of 285 months—EPA issued 1,705 UAOs to more than 5,400 PRPs. * * * On average, then, EPA has issued approximately six UAOs to nineteen PRPs every *month*." *Gen. Elec. Co. v. Jackson*, 595 F. Supp. 2d 8, 33 (D.D.C. 2009). The prevalence of UAOs is consistent with EPA's policy statements. In a memorandum sent to EPA's regional administrators, the EPA office charged with implementing and enforcing CERCLA explained the role of UAOs as follows:

> Unilateral orders should be considered as one of the primary enforcement tools to obtain RD/RA response by PRPs. Unilateral orders can provide an incentive for PRPs to settle, can help to control settlement negotiation deadlines, and can be used to force commencement of work at the site when settlement cannot be reached. Unilateral orders can also help to encourage the organization and coalescence of disorganized PRPs. Because many PRPs promptly comply with unilateral orders, they also help to conserve the limited funds available for government-financed cleanup.

OSWER Directive Number 9833.0–1a, Guidance on CERCLA Section 106(a) Unilateral Administrative Orders for Remedial Designs and Remedial Actions at 3 (Mar. 7, 1990).

CERCLA section 122 also authorizes EPA to issue orders that enter administrative settlements with PRPs. Such AOCs have proven attractive to PRPs. By entering into an AOC, a liable party can avoid costly litigation and has the opportunity to negotiate over the extent of financial responsibility it will bear for the cleanup and influence the cleanup process itself. In exchange, section 122(f) authorizes EPA to provide a settling party with a covenant guaranteeing that the federal government will not bring any further judicial action against that party. 42 U.S.C. § 9622(f). A party entering into a settlement with EPA receives protection from lawsuits for contribution brought by other liable parties, *id.* § 9613(f)(2)—an issue discussed in more detail in the next problem.

Despite their appeal to EPA and some PRPs, other PRPs and some academic commentators have criticized EPA's practice of settling CERCLA claims through AOCs and consent decrees, arguing that the agency may use that technique to benefit preferred PRPs. For that reason, non-settling parties often seek to block consent decrees. The Lower Fox River provides an example. EPA negotiated consent decrees with a number of parties the agency determined bear insignificant responsibility for PCB contamination. NCR and Appleton Paper, the companies that EPA determined bear the majority of responsibility, intervened in the lawsuit to oppose entry of the consent decrees, arguing that they required too little financial contribution from the parties involved. The Seventh Circuit ultimately disagreed, holding that the district court had appropriately considered the public interest in entering the consent decrees. *See United States v. George A. Whiting Paper*, 644 F.3d 368 (7th Cir. 2011).

As the preceding materials reveal, there are many legal pathways through a site cleanup. The chart below summarizes the key mechanisms. As you review it, keep in mind that actions that fall into multiple boxes may occur at a single site. For example, an EPA-led removal action may be followed by an EPA-ordered but PRP-led cleanup, or a site may initially be managed by a state but then may shift to federal control.

Cleanup Actions Carried out by EPA:	Removal actions to provide short-term response Remedial actions to provide permanent remedy
Cleanup Actions Ordered by EPA under CERCLA Authority:	Unilateral Administrative Orders Administrative Orders on Consent
Non-CERCLA Cleanup Actions:	State-led cleanup actions State-regulated cleanup actions EPA-Initiated RCRA corrective action

VI. DISTRIBUTION OF COSTS AMONG PRPs

CERCLA imposes liability on a broad range of PRPs. In general, under the principle of joint and several liability, each PRP is potentially liable for the entire cost of cleanup. But CERCLA provides mechanisms for liable parties to avoid that consequence. One possibility, which you have already learned about from the *Burlington Northern* case, is for PRPs to argue that contamination is divisible and, therefore, liability for the contamination can be apportioned among the PRPs. That defense limits the ability of EPA or a state to hold a PRP jointly and severally liable for the full cost of cleanup, and compels EPA or the state to either recover money from other PRPs or stick the public with the bill. But CERCLA sections 107 and 113 also provide other mechanisms for PRPs to seek financial contributions from their fellow polluters.

The resulting negotiations and litigation are frequent and have high stakes. Because environmental remediation can cost so much money, PRPs often invest heavily in lawsuits against other PRPs. To provide just one example, a lawsuit between mining companies in the Pinal Creek basin in Arizona began in 1991. After nearly two decades and more than 2,000 docket entries in the district court, the case finally settled in 2010, just days before it was scheduled for oral argument in its second trip to the Ninth Circuit.

Attorneys involved in inter-PRP negotiations and litigation often confront two sets of issues. The first set of questions turns on the availability of claims against other PRPs. CERCLA does not provide PRPs with blanket authorization to sue other PRPs whenever justice allows. Instead, the ability of PRPs to bring claims against, and to be sued by, their fellow PRPs, turns partly on factors like whether they have been sued by, or have settled with, EPA. These limitations create traps for the unwary, and PRPs' attorneys must think carefully about those traps not just as they deal with each other but also as they negotiate or litigate with the government.

The second set of questions involves the merits of the claim one PRP brings against another. Section 113(f)(1) provides that a court may allocate cleanup costs between the parties in a contribution action based on "such equitable factors as the court determines are appropriate." 42 U.S.C. § 9613(f)(1). This leaves district court judges with broad discretion. To guide that discretion, courts often look to factors that were proposed as an amendment to the Superfund Amendments and Reauthorization Act (SARA) by then-Representative Al Gore. *See, e.g., Boeing Co. v. Cascade Corp.*, 207 F.3d 1177, 1187 (9th Cir, 2000). These factors, referred to as the "Gore Factors," include:

(i)　the ability of the parties to demonstrate that their contribution to a discharge, release or disposal of a hazardous waste can be distinguished;

(ii)　the amount of hazardous waste involved;

(iii)　the degree of toxicity of the hazardous waste involved;

(iv) the degree of involvement by the parties to the generation, transportation, treatment, storage, or disposal of the hazardous waste;

(v) the degree of care exercised by the parties with respect to the hazardous waste concerned, taking into account the characteristics of such waste; and

(vi) the degree of cooperation by the parties with Federal, State, or local officials to prevent any harm to the public health or the environment.

126 Cong. Rec. H9461 (1980). Because the Gore Factors are part of an unenacted amendment, they are not binding on a district court in equitably allocating costs in a contribution action. *See Boeing Co.*, 207 F.3d at 1187. They do, however, serve as a useful starting point for analyzing the fair share of the PRPs at a site.

A PRP's claim under section 107(a) for cost recovery, unlike a claim for contribution, is not governed directly by equitable considerations. Once a plaintiff PRP has brought such a cost recovery claim, however, the defendant PRP will generally file a contribution counterclaim under section 113(f)(1). In most circumstances, this effectively transforms cost recovery claims into contribution claims.

The problem below addresses the first set of questions: when is a cost recovery claim available at all? The capstone problem that follows integrates those issues alongside questions about the merits of CERCLA 107 and 113 claims.

PROBLEM: FILING LAWSUITS ON BEHALF OF PRPs

You represent one of the paper companies along the Lower Fox River. Your company has joined a coalition of PRPs, all of which have pledged to negotiate jointly with EPA and the Wisconsin Department of Natural Resources (WDNR), on the theory that EPA will otherwise divide and conquer the PRPs with a series of unfavorable (from your perspective) judicial verdicts or settlements. But you understand perfectly well that this united front has all the durability of an alliance on *Game of Thrones* or *Survivor*. Your client would turn on its allies/competitors the moment a favorable deal from EPA and WDNR is offered, and the other coalition members would likely do the same.

Because of the alliance's fragility, your client has asked you two questions. First, it wants to know whether cutting a deal with EPA will (a) limit its ability to bring claims against other PRPs; and (b) protect it from claims brought by other PRPs. Second, your client wants to know essentially the same question in reverse: if it holds out, and forces EPA to litigate section 107 claims against it, will that enhance or inhibit its ability to bring claims or defend claims against its fellow PRPs? A simple matrix summarizes the dilemma:

TO SETTLE OR NOT TO SETTLE		Is it in a better or worse position for. . .	
		. . . defending against a suit from a fellow PRP	. . . filing a suit against a fellow PRP
If your client. . .	. . . settles with EPA		
	. . . refuses to settle		

As you answer, please assume that neither EPA nor WDNR has sued your client under CERCLA section 107. Because everyone professes hope for a voluntary cleanup, no litigation has yet been filed.

To answer these questions, the key statutory excerpts come from CERCLA sections 107 and 113.

CERCLA § 107, 42 U.S.C. § 9607. Liability

(a)(4)   [PRPs are liable for]

(A) all costs of removal or remedial action incurred by the United States Government or a State or an Indian tribe not inconsistent with the national contingency plan;

(B) [PRPs shall be liable for] any other necessary costs of response incurred by any other person consistent with the national contingency plan.

CERCLA § 113, 42 U.S.C. § 9613. Civil Proceedings

(f)(1)   Contribution

Any person may seek contribution from any other person who is liable or potentially liable under section 9607(a) of this title, during or following any civil action under section 9606 of this title or under section 9607(a) of this title. Such claims shall be brought in accordance with this section and the Federal Rules of Civil Procedure, and shall be governed by Federal law. In resolving contribution claims, the court may allocate response costs among liable parties using such equitable factors as the court determines are appropriate. Nothing in this subsection shall diminish the right of any person to bring an action for contribution in the absence of a civil action under section 9606 of this title or section 9607 of this title.

---

(2) Settlement

A person who has resolved its liability to the United States or a State in an administrative or judicially approved settlement shall not be liable for claims for contribution regarding matters addressed in the settlement. Such settlement does not discharge any of the other potentially liable persons unless its terms so provide, but it reduces the potential liability of the others by the amount of the settlement.

(3) Persons not party to settlement

(A) If the United States or a State has obtained less than complete relief from a person who has resolved its liability to the United States or the State in an administrative or judicially approved settlement, the United States or the State may bring an action against any person who has not so resolved its liability.

(B) A person who has resolved its liability to the United States or a State for some or all of a response action or for some or all of the costs of such action in an administrative or judicially approved settlement may seek contribution from any person who is not party to a settlement referred to in paragraph (2).

(C) In any action under this paragraph, the rights of any person who has resolved its liability to the United States or a State shall be subordinate to the rights of the United States or the State. Any contribution action brought under this paragraph shall be governed by Federal law. * * *

In the past two decades, CERCLA section 113 has generated two important Supreme Court cases. Heavily excerpted versions of each appear below.

Cooper Industries, Inc. v. Aviall Services, Inc.

543 U.S. 157 (2004)

■ JUSTICE THOMAS delivered the opinion of the Court.

Section 113(f)(1) of the Comprehensive Environmental Response, Compensation, and Liability Act of 1980 (CERCLA) allows persons who have undertaken efforts to clean up properties contaminated by hazardous substances to seek contribution from other parties liable under CERCLA. Section 113(f)(1) specifies that a party may obtain contribution "during or following any civil action" under CERCLA § 106 or § 107(a). The issue we must decide is whether a private party who has not been sued under § 106 or § 107(a) may nevertheless obtain contribution under § 113(f)(1) from other liable parties. We hold that it may not.

I

* * * After CERCLA's enactment in 1980, litigation arose over whether § 107, in addition to allowing the Government and certain private parties to recover costs from PRPs, also allowed a PRP that had incurred response costs to recover costs from other PRPs. More specifically, the question was whether a private party that had incurred response costs, but that had done so voluntarily and was not itself subject to suit, had a cause of action for cost recovery against other PRPs. Various courts held that § 107(a)(4)(B) and its predecessors authorized such a cause of action. See, *e.g.*, *Wickland Oil Terminals v. Asarco, Inc.*, 792 F.2d 887, 890–892 (CA 9 1986); *Walls v. Waste Resource Corp.*, 761 F.2d 311, 317–318 (CA 6 1985); *Philadelphia v. Stepan Chemical Co.*, 544 F. Supp. 1135, 1140–1143 (E.D. Pa. 1982).

After CERCLA's passage, litigation also ensued over the separate question whether a private entity that had been sued in a cost recovery action (by the Government or by another PRP) could obtain contribution from other PRPs. [Eds.: The Court then discussed lower court decisions that concluded—dubiously—that such a cause of action was available.] * * *

Congress subsequently amended CERCLA in the Superfund Amendments and Reauthorization Act of 1986 (SARA), 100 Stat. 1613, to provide an express cause of action for contribution, codified as CERCLA § 113(f)(1):

> Any person may seek contribution from any other person who is liable or potentially liable under section 9607(a) of this title, during or following any civil action under section 9606 of this title or under section 9607(a) of this title. Such claims shall be brought in accordance with this section and the Federal Rules of Civil Procedure, and shall be governed by Federal law. In resolving contribution claims, the court may allocate response costs among liable parties using such equitable factors as the court determines are appropriate. Nothing in this subsection shall diminish the right of any person to bring an action for contribution in the absence of a civil action under section 9606 of this title or section 9607 of this title." *Id.*, at 1647, as codified in 42 U.S.C. § 9613(f)(1).

SARA also created a separate express right of contribution, § 113(f)(3)(B), for "[a] person who has resolved its liability to the United States or a State for some or all of a response action or for some or all of the costs of such action in an administrative or judicially approved settlement." In short, after SARA, CERCLA provided for a right to cost recovery in certain circumstances, § 107(a), and separate rights to contribution in other circumstances, §§ 113(f)(1), 113(f)(3)(B).

II

This case concerns four contaminated aircraft engine maintenance sites in Texas. Cooper Industries, Inc., owned and operated those sites until 1981, when it sold them to Aviall Services, Inc. Aviall operated the four sites for a number of years. Ultimately, Aviall discovered that both it and Cooper had contaminated the facilities when petroleum and other hazardous substances leaked into the ground and ground water through underground storage tanks and spills.

Aviall notified the Texas Natural Resource Conservation Commission (Commission) of the contamination. The Commission informed Aviall that it was violating state environmental laws, directed Aviall to clean up the site, and threatened to pursue an enforcement action if Aviall failed to undertake remediation. Neither the Commission nor the EPA, however, took judicial or administrative measures to compel cleanup.
* * *

III

A

Section 113(f)(1) does not authorize Aviall's suit. The first sentence, the enabling clause that establishes the right of contribution, provides: "Any person *may* seek contribution . . . *during or following* any civil action under section 9606 of this title or under section 9607(a) of this title," 42 U.S.C. § 9613(f)(1) (emphasis added). The natural meaning of this sentence is that contribution may only be sought subject to the specified conditions, namely, "during or following" a specified civil action.

Aviall answers that "may" should be read permissively, such that "during or following" a civil action is one, but not the exclusive, instance in which a person may seek contribution. We disagree. First, as just noted, the natural meaning of "may" in the context of the enabling clause is that it authorizes certain contribution actions—ones that satisfy the subsequent specified condition—and no others.

Second, and relatedly, if § 113(f)(1) were read to authorize contribution actions at any time, regardless of the existence of a § 106 or § 107(a) civil action, then Congress need not have included the explicit "during or following" condition. In other words, Aviall's reading would render part of the statute entirely superfluous, something we are loath to do. See, *e.g., Hibbs v. Winn*, 542 U.S. 88, 101 (2004). Likewise, if § 113(f)(1) authorizes contribution actions at any time, § 113(f)(3)(B), which permits contribution actions after settlement, is equally superfluous. There is no reason why Congress would bother to specify conditions under which a person may bring a contribution claim, and at the same time allow contribution actions absent those conditions.

The last sentence of § 113(f)(1), the saving clause, does not change our conclusion. That sentence provides: "Nothing in this subsection shall diminish the right of any person to bring an action for contribution in the absence of a civil action under section 9606 of this title or section 9607 of this title." 42 U.S.C. § 9613(f)(1). The sole function of the sentence is to clarify that § 113(f)(1) does nothing to "diminish" any cause(s) of action for contribution that may exist independently of § 113(f)(1). In other words, the sentence rebuts any presumption that the express right of contribution provided by the enabling clause is the exclusive cause of action for contribution available to a PRP. The sentence, however, does not itself establish a cause of action; nor does it expand § 113(f)(1) to authorize contribution actions not brought "during or following" a § 106 or § 107(a) civil action; nor does it specify what causes of action for contribution, if any, exist outside § 113(f)(1). Reading the saving clause to authorize § 113(f)(1) contribution actions not just "during or following" a civil action, but also before such an action, would again violate the settled rule that we must, if possible, construe a statute to give every word some operative effect. See *United States v. Nordic Village, Inc.*, 503 U.S. 30, 35–36 (1992).

Our conclusion follows not simply from § 113(f)(1) itself, but also from the whole of § 113. As noted above, § 113 provides two express avenues for contribution: § 113(f)(1) ("during or following" specified civil actions) and § 113(f)(3)(B) (after an administrative or judicially approved settlement that resolves liability to the United States or a State). Section 113(g)(3) then provides two corresponding 3-year limitations periods for contribution actions, one beginning at the date of judgment, § 113(g)(3)(A), and one beginning at the date of settlement, § 113(g)(3)(B). Notably absent from § 113(g)(3) is any provision for starting the limitations period if a judgment or settlement never occurs, as is the case with a purely voluntary cleanup. The lack of such a provision supports the conclusion that, to assert a contribution claim under § 113(f), a party must satisfy the conditions of either § 113(f)(1) or § 113(f)(3)(B).

Each side insists that the purpose of CERCLA bolsters its reading of § 113(f)(1). Given the clear meaning of the text, there is no need to resolve this dispute or to consult the purpose of CERCLA at all. As we have said: "[I]t is ultimately the provisions of our laws rather than the principal concerns of our legislators by which we are governed." *Oncale v. Sundowner Offshore Services, Inc.*, 523 U.S. 75, 79 (1998). Section 113(f)(1), 100 Stat. 1647, authorizes contribution claims only "during or following" a civil action under § 106 or § 107(a), and it is undisputed that

Aviall has never been subject to such an action.[9] Aviall therefore has no § 113(f)(1) claim.

B

[Eds.: The Court declined to address the question of whether Aviall could bring suit to recover its costs under CERCLA § 107(a)(4)(B)].

C

In addition to leaving open whether Aviall may seek cost recovery under § 107, Part III–B, *supra,* we decline to decide whether Aviall has an implied right to contribution under § 107. Portions of the Fifth Circuit's opinion below might be taken to endorse the latter cause of action, 312 F.3d, at 687; others appear to reserve the question whether such a cause of action exists, *id.,* at 685, n. 15. To the extent that Aviall chooses to frame its § 107 claim on remand as an implied right of contribution (as opposed to a right of cost recovery), we note that this Court has visited the subject of implied rights of contribution before. See *Texas Industries,* 451 U.S., at 638–647; *Northwest Airlines,* 451 U.S., at 90–99. We also note that, in enacting § 113(f)(1), Congress explicitly recognized a particular set (claims "during or following" the specified civil actions) of the contribution rights previously implied by courts from provisions of CERCLA and the common law. Cf. *Transamerica Mortgage Advisors, Inc. v. Lewis,* 444 U.S. 11, 19 (1979). Nonetheless, we need not and do not decide today whether any judicially implied right of contribution survived the passage of SARA.

* * *

We hold only that § 113(f)(1) does not support Aviall's suit. We therefore reverse the judgment of the Fifth Circuit and remand the case for further proceedings consistent with this opinion.

It is so ordered.

■ JUSTICE GINSBURG, with whom JUSTICE STEVENS joins, dissenting.

Aviall Services, Inc., purchased from Cooper Industries, Inc., property that was contaminated with hazardous substances. Shortly after the purchase, the Texas Natural Resource Conservation Commission notified Aviall that it would institute enforcement action if Aviall failed to remediate the property. Aviall promptly cleaned up the site and now seeks reimbursement from Cooper. In my view, the Court unnecessarily defers decision on Aviall's entitlement to recover cleanup costs from Cooper. * * *

I see no cause for protracting this litigation by requiring the Fifth Circuit to revisit a determination it has essentially made already: Federal courts, prior to the enactment of § 113(f)(1), had correctly held that PRPs could "recover [under § 107] a proportionate share of their costs in actions for contribution against other PRPs," 312 F.3d, at 687; nothing in § 113 retracts that right, *ibid.* (noting that § 113(f)'s saving clause preserves all preexisting state and federal rights of action for contribution, including the § 107 implied right this Court recognized in *Key Tronic,* 511 U.S., at 816 (1960). Accordingly, I would not defer a definitive ruling by this Court on the question whether Aviall may pursue a § 107 claim for relief against Cooper.

United States v. Atlantic Research Corp.

551 U.S. 128 (2007)

■ JUSTICE THOMAS delivered the opinion of the Court.

Two provisions of the Comprehensive Environmental Response, Compensation, and Liability Act of 1980 (CERCLA)—§§ 107(a) and 113(f)—allow private parties to recover expenses associated with cleaning up contaminated sites. 42 U.S.C. §§ 9607(a), 9613(f). In this case, we must decide a question left open in *Cooper Industries, Inc. v. Aviall Services, Inc.,* 543 U.S. 157 (2004): whether § 107(a) provides so-called potentially responsible parties (PRPs), 42 U.S.C. §§ 9607(a)(1)–(4), with a cause of action to recover costs from other PRPs. We hold that it does.

I

A

Courts have frequently grappled with whether and how PRPs may recoup CERCLA-related costs from other PRPs. The questions lie at the intersection of two statutory provisions—CERCLA §§ 107(a) and 113(f). Section 107(a) defines four categories of PRPs, 42 U.S.C. §§ 9607(a)(1)–(4), and makes them liable for, among other things:

> "(A) all costs of removal or remedial action incurred by the United States Government or a State or an Indian tribe not inconsistent with the national contingency plan; [and]

> (B) any other necessary costs of response incurred by any other person consistent with the national contingency plan." §§ 9607(a)(4)(A)–(B).

Enacted as part of the Superfund Amendments and Reauthorization Act of 1986 (SARA), 100 Stat. 1613, § 113(f) authorizes one PRP to sue another for contribution in certain circumstances. 42 U.S.C. § 9613(f).

Prior to the advent of § 113(f)'s express contribution right, some courts held that § 107(a)(4)(B) provided a cause of action for a private party to recover voluntarily incurred response costs and to seek contribution after having been sued. See *Cooper Industries, supra,* at 161–162, (collecting cases); *Key Tronic Corp. v. United States,* 511 U.S. 809, 816, n. 7 (1994) (same). After SARA's enactment, however, some Courts of Appeals believed it necessary to "direc[t] traffic between" § 107(a) and § 113(f). 459 F.3d 827, 832 (CA 8 2006) (case below). As a result, many Courts of Appeals held that § 113(f) was the exclusive remedy for PRPs. See *Cooper Industries, supra,* at 169 (collecting cases). But as courts prevented PRPs from suing under § 107(a), they expanded § 113(f) to allow PRPs to seek "contribution" even in the absence of a suit under § 106 or § 107(a). *Aviall Servs., Inc. v. Cooper Industries, Inc.,* 312 F.3d 677, 681 (CA5 2002) (en banc).

In *Cooper Industries,* we held that a private party could seek contribution from other liable parties only after having been sued under § 106 or § 107(a). 543 U.S., at 161. This narrower interpretation of § 113(f) caused several Courts of Appeals to reconsider whether PRPs have rights under § 107(a)(4)(B), an issue we declined to address in *Cooper Industries. Id.,* at 168. After revisiting the issue, some courts have permitted § 107(a) actions by PRPs. See *Consolidated Edison Co. of N.Y. v. UGI Utilities, Inc.,* 423 F.3d 90 (CA 2 2005); *Metropolitan Water Reclamation Dist. of Greater Chicago v. North American Galvanizing & Coatings, Inc.,* 473 F.3d 824 (CA7 2007). However, at least one court continues to hold that § 113(f) provides the exclusive cause of action available to PRPs. *E.I. DuPont de Nemours & Co. v. United States,* 460 F.3d 515 (CA3 2006). Today, we resolve this issue.

B

In this case, respondent Atlantic Research leased property at the Shumaker Naval Ammunition Depot, a facility operated by the Department of Defense. At the site, Atlantic Research retrofitted rocket motors for petitioner United States. Using a high-pressure water spray, Atlantic Research removed pieces of propellant from the motors. It then burned the propellant pieces. Some of the resultant wastewater and burned fuel contaminated soil and ground water at the site.

Atlantic Research cleaned the site at its own expense and then sought to recover some of its costs by suing the United States under both §§ 107(a) and 113(f). After our decision in *Cooper Industries* foreclosed relief under § 113(f), Atlantic Research amended its complaint to seek relief under § 107(a) and federal common law. The United States moved to dismiss, arguing that § 107(a) does not allow PRPs (such as Atlantic Research) to recover costs. * * *

II

A

The parties' dispute centers on what "other person[s]" may sue under § 107(a)(4)(B). The Government argues that "any other person" refers to any person not identified as a PRP in §§ 107(a)(1)–(4). In other words, subparagraph (B) permits suit only by non-PRPs and thus bars Atlantic Research's claim. Atlantic Research counters that subparagraph (B) takes its cue from subparagraph (A), not the earlier paragraphs (1)–(4). In accord with the Court of Appeals, Atlantic Research believes that subparagraph (B) provides a cause of action to anyone except the United States, a State, or an Indian tribe—the persons listed in subparagraph (A). We agree with Atlantic Research.

Statutes must "be read as a whole." *King v. St. Vincent's Hospital,* 502 U.S. 215, 221 (1991). Applying that maxim, the language of subparagraph (B) can be understood only with reference to subparagraph (A). The provisions are adjacent and have remarkably similar structures. Each concerns certain costs that have been incurred by certain entities and that bear a specified relationship to the national contingency plan. Bolstering the structural link, the text also denotes a relationship between the two provisions. By using the phrase "other necessary costs," subparagraph (B) refers to and differentiates the relevant costs from those listed in subparagraph (A).

In light of the relationship between the subparagraphs, it is natural to read the phrase "any other person" by referring to the immediately preceding subparagraph (A), which permits suit only by the United States, a State, or an Indian tribe. The phrase "any other person" therefore means any person other than those three. See 42 U.S.C. § 9601(21) (defining "person" to include the United States and the various States). Consequently, the plain language of subparagraph (B) authorizes cost-recovery actions by any private party, including PRPs. See *Key Tronic,* 511 U.S., at 818 (stating in dictum that § 107 "impliedly authorizes private parties to recover cleanup costs from *other* PRP[s]" (emphasis added)).

* * *

B

The Government also argues that our interpretation will create friction between §§ 107(a) and 113(f), the very harm courts of appeals have previously tried to avoid. In particular, the Government maintains that our interpretation, by offering PRPs a choice between §§ 107(a) and 113(f), effectively allows PRPs to circumvent § 113(f)'s shorter statute of limitations. See 42 U.S.C. §§ 9613(g)(2)–(3). Furthermore, the Government argues, PRPs will eschew equitable apportionment under § 113(f) in favor of joint and several liability under § 107(a). Finally, the Government contends that our interpretation eviscerates the settlement bar set forth in § 113(f)(2).

We have previously recognized that §§ 107(a) and 113(f) provide two "clearly distinct" remedies. *Cooper Industries,* 543 U.S., at 163, n. 3. "CERCLA provide[s] for a *right to cost recovery* in certain circumstances,

§ 107(a), and *separate rights to contribution* in other circumstances, §§ 113(f)(1), 113(f)(3)(B)." *Id.*, at 163, (emphasis added). The Government, however, uses the word "contribution" as if it were synonymous with any apportionment of expenses among PRPs. Brief for United States 33, n. 14 ("Contribution is merely a form of cost recovery, not a wholly independent type of relief"); see also, *e.g., Pinal Creek Group v. Newmont Mining Corp.*, 118 F.3d 1298, 1301 (CA9 1997) ("Because all PRPs are liable under the statute, a claim by one PRP against another PRP necessarily is for contribution"). This imprecise usage confuses the complementary yet distinct nature of the rights established in §§ 107(a) and 113(f).

Section 113(f) explicitly grants PRPs a right to contribution. Contribution is defined as the "tortfeasor's right to collect from others responsible for the same tort after the tortfeasor has paid more than his or her proportionate share, the shares being determined as a percentage of fault." Black's Law Dictionary 353 (8th ed.2004). Nothing in § 113(f) suggests that Congress used the term "contribution" in anything other than this traditional sense. The statute authorizes a PRP to seek contribution "during or following" a suit under § 106 or § 107(a). 42 U.S.C. § 9613(f)(1). Thus, § 113(f)(1) permits suit before or after the establishment of common liability. In either case, a PRP's right to contribution under § 113(f)(1) is contingent upon an inequitable distribution of common liability among liable parties.

By contrast, § 107(a) permits recovery of cleanup costs but does not create a right to contribution. A private party may recover under § 107(a) without any establishment of liability to a third party. Moreover, § 107(a) permits a PRP to recover only the costs it has "incurred" in cleaning up a site. 42 U.S.C. § 9607(a)(4)(B). When a party pays to satisfy a settlement agreement or a court judgment, it does not incur its own costs of response. Rather, it reimburses other parties for costs that those parties incurred.

Accordingly, the remedies available in §§ 107(a) and 113(f) complement each other by providing causes of action "to persons in different procedural circumstances." *Consolidated Edison,* 423 F.3d, at 99; see also *E.I. DuPont de Nemours,* 460 F.3d, at 548 (Sloviter, J., dissenting). Section 113(f)(1) authorizes a contribution action to PRPs with common liability stemming from an action instituted under § 106 or § 107(a). And § 107(a) permits cost recovery (as distinct from contribution) by a private party that has itself incurred cleanup costs. Hence, a PRP that pays money to satisfy a settlement agreement or a court judgment may pursue § 113(f) contribution. But by reimbursing response costs paid by other parties, the PRP has not incurred its own costs of response and therefore cannot recover under § 107(a). As a result, though eligible to seek contribution under § 113(f)(1), the PRP cannot simultaneously seek to recover the same expenses under § 107(a). Thus, at least in the case of reimbursement, the PRP cannot choose the 6-year statute of limitations for cost-recovery actions over the shorter limitations period for § 113(f) contribution claims.[6]

For similar reasons, a PRP could not avoid § 113(f)'s equitable distribution of reimbursement costs among PRPs by instead choosing to impose joint and several liability on another PRP in an action under § 107(a).[7] The choice of remedies simply does not exist. In any event, a defendant PRP in such a § 107(a) suit could blunt any inequitable distribution of costs by filing a § 113(f) counterclaim. 459 F.3d, at 835; see also *Consolidated Edison, supra,* at 100, n.9 (collecting cases). Resolution of a § 113(f) counterclaim would necessitate the equitable apportionment of costs among the liable parties, including the PRP that filed the § 107(a) action. 42 U.S.C. § 9613(f)(1) ("In resolving contribution claims, the court may allocate response costs among liable parties using such equitable factors as the court determines are appropriate").

Finally, permitting PRPs to seek recovery under § 107(a) will not eviscerate the settlement bar set forth in § 113(f)(2). That provision prohibits § 113(f) contribution claims against "[a] person who has resolved its liability to the United States or a State in an administrative or judicially approved settlement . . . ." 42 U.S.C. § 9613(f)(2). The settlement bar does not by its terms protect against cost-recovery liability under § 107(a). For several reasons, we doubt this supposed loophole would discourage settlement. First, as stated above, a defendant PRP may trigger equitable apportionment by filing a § 113(f) counterclaim. A district court applying traditional rules of equity would undoubtedly consider any prior settlement as part of the liability calculus. Cf. 4 Restatement (Second) of Torts § 886A(2), p. 337 (1977) ("No tortfeasor can be required to make contribution beyond his own equitable share of the liability"). Second, the settlement bar continues to provide significant protection from contribution suits by PRPs that have inequitably reimbursed the costs incurred by another party. Third, settlement carries the inherent benefit of finally resolving liability as to the United States or a State.

---

[6]   We do not suggest that §§ 107(a)(4)(B) and 113(f) have no overlap at all. *Key Tronic Corp. v. United States,* 511 U.S. 809, 816 (1994) (stating the statutes provide "similar and somewhat overlapping remed[ies]"). For instance, we recognize that a PRP may sustain expenses pursuant to a consent decree following a suit under § 106 or § 107(a). See, *e.g., United Technologies Corp. v. Browning-Ferris Industries, Inc.,* 33 F.3d 96, 97 (CA1 1994). In such a case, the PRP does not incur costs voluntarily but does not reimburse the costs of another party. We do not decide whether these compelled costs of response are recoverable under § 113(f), § 107(a), or both. For our purposes, it suffices to demonstrate that costs incurred voluntarily are recoverable only by way of § 107(a)(4)(B), and costs of reimbursement to another person pursuant to a legal judgment or settlement are recoverable only under § 113(f). Thus, at a minimum, neither remedy swallows the other, contrary to the Government's argument.

[7]   We assume without deciding that § 107(a) provides for joint and several liability.

III

Because the plain terms of § 107(a)(4)(B) allow a PRP to recover costs from other PRPs, the statute provides Atlantic Research with a cause of action. We therefore affirm the judgment of the Court of Appeals.

It is so ordered.

NOTE

Section 113(g) provides statutes of limitation for cost recovery suits brought under section 107 and contribution suits brought under section 113. 42 U.S.C. § 9613(g). There are three different statutes of limitation for cost recovery actions. A suit to recover the cost of a removal action must be brought within three years of the completion of that action. A suit to recover the costs of a remedial action must be brought within six years of the time that physical construction of the remedial action began. Those two rules are easy to apply. Sometimes, however, a removal action is performed in preparation for a remedial action. In such circumstances, CERCLA provides a special rule to avoid duplicate litigation. If physical construction of a remedial action begins within three years of the completion of a removal action, then a single lawsuit seeking to recover the costs of both may be brought within six years of the beginning of physical construction of the remedial action. The statutes of limitations for contribution claims are more straightforward. A lawsuit under sections 113(f)(1) or 113(f)(3)(B) must be brought within three years of either a civil judgment or a settlement or consent decree.

VII. NATURAL RESOURCES DAMAGES

The provisions of CERCLA we have discussed so far all relate to cleanup of hazardous substances. Sometimes, however, environmental remediation cannot return the environment to its original condition. And cleanups also do not compensate the public for the environmental damage that occurred before the cleanup was complete. Consider the Lower Fox River: even with an aggressive cleanup, it will be years before PCB concentrations in fish tissue are low enough for fish to be safely consumed, and it could be centuries before background conditions return. CERCLA allows government trustees to seek monetary compensation for these environmental impacts. In keeping with its mission to make polluters pay for the harm they cause, CERCLA makes PRPs liable for "natural resource damages."

Unlike other provisions of CERCLA, natural resource damages assessment occurs under a regulatory regime established by the Department of Interior, rather than the EPA. Natural resource damage assessment, or NRDA as it is often called, is a complex process. The statutory authority for the program is, however, relatively concise. The key statutory provisions appear below.

CERCLA § 101, 42 U.S.C. § 9601. Definitions

(16)   The term "natural resources" means land, fish, wildlife, biota, air, water, ground water, drinking water supplies, and other such resources belonging to, managed by, held in trust by, appertaining to, or otherwise controlled by the United States (including the resources of the fishery conservation zone established by the Magnuson-Stevens Fishery Conservation and Management Act [16 U.S.C.A. § 1801 et seq.]), any State or local government, any foreign government, any Indian tribe, or, if such resources are subject to a trust restriction on alienation, any member of an Indian tribe. * * *

CERCLA § 107, 42 U.S.C. § 9607. Liability

(a) Covered persons; scope; recoverable costs and damages; interest rate; "comparable maturity" date

Notwithstanding any other provision or rule of law, and subject only to the defenses set forth in subsection (b) of this section * * * [a PRP] shall be liable for * * *

   (C) damages for injury to, destruction of, or loss of natural resources, including the reasonable costs of assessing such injury, destruction, or loss resulting from such a release * * *

(f)(1)   Natural resources liability; designation of public trustee of natural resources

In the case of an injury to, destruction of, or loss of natural resources under subparagraph (C) of subsection (a) of this section liability shall be to the United States Government and to any State for natural resources within the State or belonging to, managed by, controlled by, or appertaining to such State and to any Indian tribe for natural resources belonging to, managed by, controlled by, or appertaining to such tribe, or held in trust for the benefit of such tribe, or belonging to a member of such tribe if such resources are subject to a trust restriction on alienation[.] * * * Sums recovered by the United States Government as trustee under this subsection shall be retained by the trustee, without further appropriation, for use only to restore, replace, or acquire the equivalent of such natural resources. Sums recovered by a State as trustee under this subsection shall be available for use only to restore, replace, or acquire the equivalent of such natural resources by the State. The measure of damages in any action under subparagraph (C) of subsection (a) of this section shall not be limited

> by the sums which can be used to restore or replace such resources.
> * * *

Implementation of these provisions raises several recurring issues. Some of the key questions are:

Who are the natural resource trustees?

Natural resource damages can only be recovered by government entities that serve as trustees of the natural environment for the public. Identifying the proper trustee can be tricky where multiple governmental entities arguably have jurisdiction over particular natural resources. One case addressing this issue, *Coeur D'Alene Tribe v. Asarco Inc.*, 280 F. Supp. 2d 1094 (D. Idaho 2003), involved contamination in the Coeur D'Alene Basin caused by a century of mining activities. That activity released hazardous substances throughout the basin. Alleged damage to natural resources included: 1) rivers and streams containing heavy metals in excess of water quality standards, 2) groundwater containing heavy metals in excess of drinking water standards, and 3) harm to vegetation, fish, and aquatic invertebrate species. The State of Idaho settled its claim for natural resource damages with the mining company PRPs, but the Coeur D'Alene Tribe and the federal government filed their own suits seeking natural resource damages related to the same resources.

In its initial decision, the court ruled that neither the tribe nor the federal government was a proper trustee for many of the natural resources at issue. The court reasoned that the state exercised "management and control of the natural resources," and although the federal government and the tribes had legal authority to engage in such management, "[p]ower that is not exercised is not management or control even though in a legal sense the resource may belong in part or appertain to that party." *Id.* at 1116. Two years later, however, the court reversed course, ruling that the tribe and federal government were proper trustees because they possessed "trusteeship duties." *United States v. Asarco Inc.*, 471 F. Supp. 2d 1063 (D. Idaho 2005). The court further concluded that Idaho's settlement did not preclude a damage award to the tribe and federal government as "co-trustees," because CERCLA "dictates that a co-trustee acting individually or collectively with the other co-trustees may go after the responsible party or parties for the full amount of the damage, less any amount that has already been paid as a result of a settlement to another trustee by a responsible party." *Id.* at 1068. Does the court's decision threaten PRPs with the prospect of double recovery, meaning that they could face payment for the same damages to the state, federal, and tribal governments?

What can natural resource damages be used for?

Section 107(f)(1) provides that any natural resource damages recovered from a PRP can only be used to restore or replace the natural resources that experienced the damages. 42 U.S.C. § 9607(f)(1). In other words, natural resource damages, unlike civil penalties imposed under other environmental statutes, are a source of dedicated funding and do not become general treasury funds.

Often it is fairly obvious what actions count as restoring or replacing damaged resources. For example, if contamination destroys wildlife habitat, rehabilitating other degraded habitat could constitute replacement. But sometimes questions arise. For example, what if the Lower Fox River trustees wanted to compensate for damage to the Lower Fox River and Green Bay by improving recreational parks along those waterways? PCB pollution has limited public access to the river and bay, and improving parks benefits public access. But is the nexus between ecological damage and recreational improvements tight enough?

What is the amount of the damages?

With natural resource damages, no question is harder than determining the value of the damaged resources. Think back, for a moment, to the environmental uncertainty issues discussed at the very beginning of the book; almost every one of them is likely to arise in a natural resource damages case. It may be very difficult to determine just how much harm natural resources have suffered from exposure to toxins, largely because research on the reactions of species to pollution exposure is likely to be quite limited. Placing an economic value on those harms also can be hard, particularly if the impacted species are not themselves articles of commerce. And the challenges are compounded by the need to assess damages relatively early in the process of environmental recovery, and well before scientists can complete the kinds of long-term studies that might provide more certainty about actual damages. These challenges do not stop trustees from calculating damages and seeking awards, but they have caused some commentators to warn that assessments may be much too low—or, in some circumstances, too high. *See generally* Sanne Knudsen, *The Long-Term Tort: In Search of a New Causation Framework for Natural Resources Damages*, 108 NW. U. L. REV. 475 (2014).

VIII. CAPSTONE PROBLEM: OVERLAPPING PRIVATE CAUSES OF ACTION

In the wake of the Supreme Court's decisions in *Cooper Industries* and *Atlantic Research*, reproduced above, the boundary between the right to recover response costs under section 107 and the right to share liability through contribution under section 113 is not entirely clear. When a PRP reimburses response costs paid by another party because of liability incurred under a settlement or judgment, it will clearly have a right to contribution. And when it incurs response costs by funding cleanup directly without being sued or having settled, then it clearly has a claim for cost recovery under section 107. But what happens when a PRP engages in cleanup activities pursuant to an injunction or an AOC—that is, when it incurs response costs by virtue of a finding of liability or a settlement? Because EPA routinely enters into AOCs that obligate PRPs to assume responsibility for cleanup activities, this circumstance is common.

Reconciling sections 107 and 113 is primarily a question of statutory interpretation and requires consideration of relatively little text. It also requires analysis of the *Cooper Industries* and *Atlantic Research* cases. Robust arguments have been made for interpreting the statute either to allow settling PRPs to have the option of suing under section 107 or 113 or to allow them only to sue under section 113. The text and those cases are excerpted in Section VI of this Chapter. The materials below are modeled after a case that settled before it was argued in the Ninth Circuit. The problem asks you to marshal textual arguments to advance a client's position. In considering the problem, you may want to refer to Chapter 2's discussion of statutory interpretation.

You are a staff attorney in EPA's Office of General Counsel. You have received the assignment memo below from one of the Deputy General Counsels. It asks you to assist in developing EPA's legal position in a case between two private parties. Once EPA has developed its position, it will transmit a memorandum to the U.S. Department of Justice requesting that the United States participate in the case as *amicus curiae*. The Deputy General Counsel has scheduled a meeting at which you and your colleagues will provide a briefing on the arguments you believe EPA should make. You are now meeting with the other staff attorneys assigned to the briefing to discuss the issues, identify the arguments you believe EPA should present in the case, and assess the strengths and weakness of those arguments.

———————

ASSIGNMENT MEMO:

To: Staff Attorneys

From: Deputy General Counsel, Environmental Protection Agency

RE: Assignment for *Power-Tech, Inc. v. United Power Corporation*

As you know, EPA has a significant interest in lawsuits private parties bring against one another under CERCLA, because such lawsuits can affect the incentives that PRPs have to settle with EPA. EPA is, however, typically not a party to these lawsuits between private parties.

One such lawsuit is ongoing between Power-Tech, Inc. and United Power Corp., and I would like EPA to participate as *amicus curiae*. While Power-Tech has acted more productively over the course of the cleanup at issue in that suit—entering into a settlement with the state to carry out a remediation plan—Power-Tech is taking a legal position contrary to EPA's interests and asserting that it can sue United Power for cost recovery under section 107, despite having entered a settlement that qualifies it for bringing a claim for contribution under section 113(f)(3)(B). Power-Tech initially filed both 107 and 113 claims, and the district court entered an order dismissing Power-Tech's cost recovery claim. The court of appeals has granted an interlocutory appeal of that decision.

I am asking you to identify arguments that EPA can make in a brief we plan to file as *amicus*. The issue in the case is whether section 107 provides a cause of action to a PRP like Power-Tech that has been sued by a state, and entered into a consent decree to resolve that suit, thereby falling within the conditions addressed in sections 113(f)(1) and 113(f)(3)(B). I would like you to argue that Power-Tech is limited to seeking contribution under those provisions of section 113 and may not choose, instead, to assert a claim under section 107(a)(4)(B). You should also consider why EPA is interested in this case at all.

Background

The Linal Creek basin contains significant mineral resources and has been heavily mined for more than a century. As a result of mining activities, groundwater underlying the basin became contaminated with a variety of hazardous substances associated with mining. In 1995, the state department of environmental quality (DEQ) commenced a site investigation. In 1999, DEQ adopted a plan to remediate groundwater.

In coordination with DEQ, several mining interests, including Power-Tech, Inc., formed the Linal Creek Group in 2000 to engage in environmental cleanup. In 2001, the Linal Creek Group sued United Power Corp. and other companies owning mines in the basin that had not joined the Linal Creek Group under section 107(a)(4)(B) to recover the costs of cleanup efforts. In a 2002 decision that predated *Cooper Industries* and *Atlantic Research*, the court of appeals affirmed dismissal of that lawsuit, holding that a PRP may never bring suit under section 107 and may only seek contribution under section 113.

In 2004, DEQ filed a complaint against the Linal Creek Group, along with a proposed consent decree alleging claims under section 107(a) and state law. The district court entered the consent decree in 2005. Under its terms, the Linal Creek Group agreed to pay past and future costs incurred by DEQ and to carry out DEQ's groundwater remediation plan.

Prior to filing its 2004 suit, DEQ had approached other mining companies including United Power Corp. and asked them to cooperate in the cleanup effort. United Power Corp. had refused and was not included in the DEQ's complaint or the consent decree.

In 2008, Linal Creek Group filed a second lawsuit against United Power Corp. and other mining companies that had not participated in the cleanup effort. The complaint pled claims for contribution under section 113(f)(3)(B) and claims for cost recovery under section 107(a)(4)(B). Over the next three years, the Linal Creek Group reached settlements with all of the defendants other than United Power Corp. In 2011, the other members of the Linal Creek Group voluntarily dismissed their claims, leaving only Power-Tech, Inc. and United Power Corp. as parties to the case.

Due to a series of mistakes that occurred during discovery, the district court entered sanctions against Power-Tech that prevented it from introducing evidence of the respective quantities of mining waste released by United Power and Power-Tech. As a result, Power-Tech is unlikely to be able to prevail in its claim for contribution. United Power filed a motion to dismiss Power-Tech's claim for cost recovery under section 107, and the district court granted that motion. The court of appeals has agreed to interlocutory review that order.

Because EPA plans to file as *amicus* in support of United Power, only Power-Tech's brief is available. An excerpt of that brief appears below:

BRIEF OF POWER-TECH CORPORATION[6]

ISSUES PRESENTED

1.   Does section 107(a) of CERCLA, 42 U.S.C. § 9607(a), authorize a potentially responsible party ("PRP") that has incurred cleanup costs to hold other PRPs jointly and severally liable for those costs?

2.   Does section 107(a) authorize a PRP to recover costs incurred in performing a cleanup pursuant to a judicially approved consent decree?

ARGUMENT

I.   Section 107 Permits Any Person to Hold Any Potentially Responsible Party Jointly and Severally Liable for All Cleanup Costs

    A.   The Plain Language of Section 107 Imposes Liability on Any Potentially Responsible Party for All Cleanup Costs, Including Costs Incurred by a PRP such as Power-Tech

---

[6]   This brief on behalf of a fictitious company is a heavily modified and excerpted version of a brief filed on behalf of Canadian Oxy Offshore Production Co. in *Phelps Dodge Miami, Inc. v. CanadianOxy Offshore Production Co.*, Docket No. 08-17614 (9th Cir. 2008), which was settled before oral argument.

Section 107(a) makes four classes of PRPs liable for costs incurred in cleaning up hazardous substances. 42 U.S.C. § 9607(a). It provides that "any person" associated with the use, transport or disposal of hazardous substances, "shall be liable for . . . (B) any other necessary costs of response incurred by any other person consistent with the national contingency plan." *Id*. §§ 9607(a)(4)(A), (B).

The statute thus makes "*any*" PRP liable for "*any other necessary costs*" that are "incurred by *any other person*" in cleaning up hazardous substances. Subparagraph (B) addresses costs incurred by persons other than the governmental entities, which are addressed in subparagraph (A). For such non-governmental costs, the only conditions for liability are that the costs (i) be "necessary," (ii) be "costs of response," i.e., costs relating to the cleanup of hazardous substances, and (iii) be "consistent with the national contingency plan" that Congress directed the President to develop regarding cleanups of hazardous substances. Congress imposed these three conditions and only these three conditions. It imposed no condition that a person's costs must be incurred "voluntarily" or without any lawsuit having been filed or independently of any order or consent decree.

Nor did Congress impose any limitation in subparagraph (B) regarding the "person" that incurred the costs. It is now settled that the term "any other person" in subparagraph (B) includes PRPs. *Atlantic Research*, 127 S. Ct. at 2336. Just as the term "any other person" does not exclude PRPs, neither does it exclude any subcategory of PRPs. It does not exclude PRPs that have been sued or PRPs that have settled. Section 107(a) imposes liability for costs incurred without regard to any of these circumstances.

There is no limit on a PRP's potential liability for such costs. To the contrary, section 107(a) states that "any" PRP "shall be liable" for "all" qualifying costs under subparagraph (A) and "any other" qualifying costs under subparagraph (B). In other words, it makes *any* PRP strictly liable (subject to a very few affirmative defenses not relevant here) for *all* qualifying costs. It recognizes no limit on the liability of a PRP for costs incurred by another PRP, including another PRP that has been sued or has settled claims against it. Section 107(a) makes no mention of any of these circumstances.

The absence of such limitations in section 107(a) must be regarded as purposeful, not only because the plain language admits no other construction, but also because Congress knew how to distinguish PRPs from other possible claimants. In the immediately preceding provision, section 106, Congress authorized persons who are ordered by the President to take responsive action to recover their costs from the Superfund, but prohibited PRPs from recovering certain costs from the fund, *see* 42 U.S.C. § 9606(b)(2)(C) ("[T]o obtain reimbursement, the petitioner shall establish by a preponderance of the evidence that it is not liable for response costs under section 9607(a) . . . ."), while permitting them to recover others, *see id.* § 9606(b)(2)(D) (permitting Superfund recovery by PRPs where "the response action ordered was arbitrary and capricious or was otherwise not in accordance with law"). Congress could in section 107(a) have similarly provided for different treatment of PRPs or of costs incurred by PRPs—such as costs incurred after being sued or pursuant to a consent decree—but did not do so.

Accordingly, taking as true Power-Tech's allegations that United Power is a PRP and that Power-Tech has incurred costs in cleaning up Linal Creek that are covered by section 107(a)(4)(B) (ER 11–12 ¶¶ 53–54, 216 ¶ 60), United Power is liable for Power-Tech's cleanup costs. The plain language of the statute compels this conclusion.

B. Section 107 Confers a Right to Recover Jointly and Severally Against Any PRP

It is well settled that section 107(a), by imposing liability on PRPs for cleanup costs, also authorizes persons that incur such costs to recover them from PRPs. *Atlantic Research*, 127 S. Ct. at 2334 (section 107(a) provides a PRP "with a cause of action to recover costs from other PRPs"). In keeping with section 107(a)'s declaration that "any" PRP shall be liable for "all" cleanup costs, courts have recognized that a person that incurs cleanup costs can recover jointly and severally against any PRP. *See Mardan Corp. v. C.G.C. Music, Ltd.*, 804 F.2d 1454, 1457 n.3 (9th Cir. 1986) (noting that most courts have "interpreted section 107 of CERCLA to impose, as a matter of federal law, joint and several liability for indivisible injuries with a correlative right of contribution").

Power-Tech has alleged that the contamination of Linal Creek is a harm for which United Power is a PRP. Thus a person that incurs costs in cleaning up Linal Creek can hold United Power jointly and severally liable for those costs. This conclusion requires no novel analysis but rather is dictated by the statute's plain language and the cases cited above.

C. A Claim by a PRP to Recover Cleanup Costs Is Not a Claim for Contribution but a Claim Under Section 107 for Joint and Several Recovery

The text of section 107(a) supplies no basis for treating a claim by a PRP differently than the claim of any other person. For this reason, the Supreme Court held in *Atlantic Research* that a PRP, like any other person that incurs cleanup costs, can sue under section 107(a) to recover those costs. The Supreme Court explained that section 107(a) provides "*a right to cost recovery* in certain circumstances," 127 S. Ct. at 2337 (quoting *Cooper Indus.*, 543 U.S. at 163), by permitting a person to recover "the costs it has 'incurred' in cleaning up a site," *id.* at 2338. The Court contrasted this right to recover cleanup costs "incurred" with the "*separate rights to contribution* in other circumstances" that are conferred by section 113(f). *Id.* at 2337.

Atlantic Research rejected the notion that a claim by a PRP to recover cleanup costs that it has incurred directly should be treated as a claim for contribution.

The Court explained that if a PRP incurs cleanup costs directly, it has a claim under section 107(a) to recover those costs. If a PRP incurs a liability to another person, such as a judgment or settlement that compels reimbursement of costs incurred in the first instance by someone else, the PRP has a claim under section 113(f)(1) or (3) for contribution. In this case, Power-Tech has asserted claims of both kinds: It seeks to recover under section 107(a) cleanup costs that it has incurred directly, both before and after entering into the consent decree, and it seeks contribution under section 113(f) for its payments that reimbursed the State for costs that the State incurred.

In *Atlantic Research*, the Supreme Court considered the possibility that, despite the different circumstances addressed by sections 107(a) and 113(f), the two remedies might, under some conditions, overlap. *Id.* at 2338 n.6. The Court did not treat that possibility as problematic. To the contrary, it stated:

> [W]e recognize that a PRP may sustain expenses pursuant to a consent decree following a suit under § 106 or § 107(a). In such a case, the PRP does not incur costs voluntarily but does not reimburse the costs of another party. We do not decide whether these compelled costs of response are recoverable under § 113(f), § 107(a), or both. For our purposes, it suffices to demonstrate that costs incurred voluntarily are recoverable only by way of § 107(a)(4)(B), and costs of reimbursement to another person pursuant to a legal judgment or settlement are recoverable only under § 113(f)." *Id.* (citation omitted).

This case in part presents the question not reached in *Atlantic Research*. The answer is nevertheless clear in view of the plain language of section 107(a) and the analytical framework laid down by the Supreme Court. As discussed above, the statute imposes liability on PRPs for *all* cleanup costs incurred by "*any other person.*" This categorically inclusive language permits no carveouts for particular kinds of cleanup costs, such as costs incurred in compliance with a consent decree. Within the framework of section 107(a), there is no difference between the cleanup costs incurred by the PRP-plaintiff in *Atlantic Research* and the cleanup costs incurred by a PRP under a consent judgment. The plain language of section 107(a) sweeps all such costs within its scope, and there the matter ends. *See, e.g., Estate of Cowart v. Nicklos Drilling Co.*, 505 U.S. 469, 475 (1992) ("[W]hen a statute speaks with clarity to an issue judicial inquiry into the statute's meaning, in all but the most extraordinary circumstance, is finished.").

Nor is it problematic that a PRP that incurs cleanup costs could hold another PRP liable for amounts exceeding the defendant-PRP's own equitable share—i.e., for amounts that would equitably be allocated to other, absent PRPs. The possibility of disproportionate liability is, after all, a standard feature of the joint and several liability regime imposed by section 107(a), and would apply if the plaintiff were not a PRP. If the State, for example, had incurred costs, it could sue any PRP for the entirety of its costs, without regard to that PRP's equitable share. The possible harshness of that result is mitigated by section 113(f)(1), which permits a PRP charged with liability for cleanup costs in excess of its own equitable share to "seek contribution from any other person who is liable or potentially liable." 42 U.S.C. § 9613(f)(1). A PRP held liable under section 107(a) accordingly can seek contribution from any other PRPs that can be found, in proportion to their respective equitable shares of responsibility.

D.   Construing Section 107 to Permit Power-Tech to Recover Jointly and Severally Is Consistent with the Public Policy Favoring Consent Decrees

Construing section 107(a) to permit a PRP to recover jointly and severally for cleanup costs incurred pursuant to a consent decree is not only required by the plain language of the statute, it is also consistent with the public policy of promoting private party cleanups under negotiated consent decrees. A contrary interpretation, by contrast, would undermine that policy objective by discouraging PRPs that are conducting cleanups from entering into consent decrees.

Courts have recognized that CERCLA's core objective of cleaning up hazardous substances is advanced by encouraging cleanups under negotiated consent decrees. Such "[c]onsent decrees are an alternative means for government agencies to ensure that cleanup takes place." *Intel Corp. v. Hartford Accident & Indem. Co.*, 952 F.2d 1551, 1564 (9th Cir. 1991). Indeed, "they are a favored method," because they permit "more rapid, and less costly, cleanup than does full scale litigation." *Id.*; *see also* H.R. Rep. No. 99–253, pt. 5, at 58 (1st Sess. 1985), *reprinted in* 1986 U.S.C.C.A.N. 3124, 3181 (noting that section 122 amendments were "intended to encourage" the "negotiated private party cleanup of hazardous substances").

PRPs that conduct cleanups under consent decrees should not lose the ability to recover jointly and severally as a result of cooperating with the government, because that result would only discourage private party cleanups under consent decrees. Nor is there any reason why the threat of joint and several liability faced by a non-settling PRP should *decrease* because another PRP has agreed to conduct the cleanup. Here, for example, if the State instead of Power-Tech had incurred the cleanup costs, there is no question that the State would be able to hold United Power jointly and severally liable for all of its cleanup costs. United Power has done nothing that should limit its exposure. The threat of such exposure is intended to induce PRPs to settle claims and to fund cleanups. To prevent a PRP that has conducted a cleanup from recovering jointly and severally would reduce that threat—and would thereby reduce the incentives to agree to a cleanup in the first place.

II.   The District Court Erred in Holding that Power-Tech Could Not Recover Under Section 107 Because It Had Been Sued by the State

The District Court denied Power-Tech's motion to reinstate its claim for joint and several liability on the grounds that Power-Tech had been sued by the state before entering into its consent decree, unlike the plaintiff in *Atlantic Research*, which according to the District Court had "voluntarily cleaned a contaminated site at its own expense without being subject to suit." The District Court erred in treating the State's suit as relevant to Power-Tech's claim.

A.   Section 107 Does Not Require that Cleanup Costs Must Be Incurred "Voluntarily"

As already discussed, section 107(a) authorizes recovery by any person that has incurred cleanup costs. It contains no exception that denies recovery to persons that have been sued. Nor does it limit recovery to costs incurred before a lawsuit was filed or to costs incurred "voluntarily." Section 107(a) makes PRPs liable for all cleanup costs incurred by any person, under any circumstances. The concepts of compulsion and volition are altogether foreign to its plain language.

Accordingly, to disallow recovery by a PRP that incurred costs "involuntarily" or after being sued would create an exception that Congress did not see fit to make. In providing that section 107(a) governs "any" cleanup costs incurred by "any" person, Congress chose clear, unambiguous language that precludes any inference that persons that have been sued themselves are ineligible to recover cleanup costs they incur. *See, e.g., Salinas v. United States*, 522 U.S. 52, 57 (1997) ("The word 'any' ... undercuts the attempt to impose [a] narrowing construction.").

Atlantic Research did not hold or even imply that a PRP can recover only costs incurred "voluntarily." The Supreme Court distinguished between "incurring" costs directly and "reimbursing" others' expenses, not between voluntary and involuntary action. The Court explained that when a party "reimburses other parties for costs that those parties incurred," it can seek contribution. 127 S. Ct. at 2338. By contrast, a party "that has itself incurred cleanup costs" can seek "cost recovery (as distinct from contribution).” *Id.* Nothing in this explanation suggests that a party must incur costs “voluntarily” to have such a remedy.

B.   Section 113 Does Not Preclude Cost Recovery Under Section 107 by a PRP that Has Been Sued

The District Court also erred insofar as it denied Power-Tech's motion on the grounds that Power-Tech can instead seek contribution under section 113(f)(1). Section 113(f) of CERCLA, which was enacted as part of the Superfund Amendments and Reauthorization Act of 1986 (“SARA”), 100 Stat. 1613(f), authorizes private parties to seek contribution in two circumstances. Section 113(f)(1) provides that any person may seek contribution “from any other person who is liable or potentially liable” under section 107(a), provided that a civil action under section 106 or section 107(a) has been filed. 42 U.S.C. § 9613(f)(1); *see also Cooper Indus.*, 543 U.S. at 168. Section 113(f)(3)(B) authorizes an action for contribution by any person “who has resolved its liability to the United States or a State for some or all of a response action or for some or all of the costs of such action.” 42 U.S.C. § 9613(f)(3)(B). Neither of these provisions supplies any basis for limiting Power-Tech to contribution rather than cost recovery.

The contribution remedies are “clearly distinct” from cost recovery under section 107(a). *Atlantic Research*, 127 S. Ct. at 2337. As discussed above, section 113(f) provides a right to contribution for liabilities to third parties, such as reimbursement of others' cleanup costs. *See id.* at 2338 (“by reimbursing response costs paid by other parties” a PRP is “eligible to seek contribution under section 113(f)(1)”). It accordingly authorizes Power-Tech to seek contribution from other PRPs for amounts that Power-Tech reimbursed the State of Arkarodo for costs that the State incurred. Section 107(a), however, by its plain text authorizes Power-Tech to obtain cost recovery for costs that it has “incurred,” whether or not Power-Tech may also be able to seek contribution for those costs under section 113(f).

Neither section 113(f)(1) nor section 113(f)(3)(B) purports to provide an exclusive means of recovery. Section 113(f)(1) states that a person “may” seek contribution when permitted, not that contribution is the sole remedy in those circumstances. Section 113(f)(3)(B) likewise provides that a person that has settled “may seek contribution,” but does not preclude other claims. Any argument that either of these provisions precludes a claim under section 107(a) for a party that has been sued or has settled is an improper attempt to read into these provisions restrictions that they do not contain, and should be rejected.

Nor is it problematic that a party might in some limited set of circumstances be able either to recover costs under section 107(a) or to seek contribution under section 113(f)(1) or 113(f)(3)(B). At the point that it was sued by the State, PowerTech became eligible to seek contribution under section 113(f)(1). When PowerTech settled with the State, it became eligible to seek contribution under section 113(f)(3)(B). And when it incurred cleanup costs directly, it became eligible to recover those costs under section 107(a). None of these overlaps creates any difficulty under the statute. Indeed, as noted above, in *Atlantic Research* the Supreme Court took pains to avoid suggesting that the two provisions "have no overlap at all." 127 S. Ct. at 2338 n.6. And it entertained the possibility that a PRP that incurred costs under a consent decree (i.e., "compelled costs of response") might be entitled to seek recovery under either one "or both." *Id.*

The Supreme Court has repeatedly stated that partially overlapping remedies in statutory schemes are not uncommon, and that courts are not to choose between them when both apply. *See, e.g., J.E.M. Agric. Supply, Inc. v. Pioneer Hi-Bred Int'l, Inc.*, 534 U.S. 124, 144 (2001) (rejecting argument that "dual protection" for certain patents cannot exist, and noting that "this Court has not hesitated to give effect to two statutes that overlap, so long as each reaches some distinct cases").

The rights to contribution conferred by section 113(f) provide no basis for construing section 107(a) as not permitting recovery where a party has been sued under section 107 or has settled. Section 107(a) contains no such limitation, and neither do the provisions of section 113(f). It is not for the courts to invent one.

Test your knowledge with a Chapter 6 online quiz in CasebookPlus™.

CHAPTER 7

ENVIRONMENTAL IMPACT ANALYSIS

In the late 1960s, as the environmental movement in the United States was becoming a political force, the federal government was in the midst of a prolonged construction blitz. For decades, major public works projects had been broadly celebrated as a triumph of America's advanced civilization. Federal agencies constructed massive dams and waterworks across the nation and the interstate highway system, just a decade old, was rapidly expanding. A book published in 1941 expressed a common sentiment: "No other achievement of peaceful civilization during the last two decades on this war-torn earth has contributed more to the welfare of future generations than the building of dams in this country." PAUL ZUCKER, AMERICAN BRIDGES AND DAMS (1941). At the same time, some federal regulatory and land management agencies, like the Atomic Energy Commission or the Forest Service, were widely viewed as boosters for American industry, and industrial activities brought their own environmental consequences.

The resulting environmental impacts were large and, as the environmental movement came into its own, increasingly controversial. But many of the federal agencies that were altering the American landscape, or were authorizing private changes, had shown little inclination to consider the environmental consequences of their actions. Some even argued that they had no authority to take environmental impacts into account. Those arguments and practices convinced many lawmakers that federal agencies should give more thought to the environmental consequences of their actions, and that some federal agencies would pay attention to those environmental consequences only if compelled to do so.

The result was the United States' first major addition to the pantheon of modern environmental laws. On January 1, 1970, Richard Nixon ushered in a decade of environmental legislation by signing the National Environmental Policy Act (NEPA). The statute's requirements were brief and straightforward, particularly in comparison to the technically complex Clean Air Act that Congress would pass just a few months later. NEPA directed federal agencies to take into account the environmental consequences of their actions, to consider alternatives courses of action, and to disclose their analyses to the public. More specifically, it directed those agencies to prepare something that has come to be known as an environmental impact statement, or EIS, before taking any action that might have significant impacts upon the human environment.

That seemingly simple mandate has transformed the field of environmental law. NEPA cases are an important component of the federal courts' environmental caseload, and NEPA litigation remains an important part of environmental groups' legal arsenals. The time devoted to NEPA cases also is just the tip of the iceberg. Most NEPA processes do not result in litigation, but attorneys are routinely involved in preparing, reviewing, and commenting upon NEPA documents. Indeed, preparing NEPA documents has now become a major part of the day-to-day work of many administrative agencies.

NEPA also has generated many imitators (and had a few important predecessors; some states had passed laws like NEPA before the federal government acted). Sixteen states now have "baby NEPAs"—statutes that establish NEPA-like requirements for state agencies. *See* Council on Environmental Quality, State NEPA Contacts. Those statutes also can be influential. In California, for example, the California Environmental Quality Act dominates environmental law practice; no other law equals its importance. Across the world, dozens of countries also have statutes modeled on NEPA, and the International Court of Justice has held that where a project may have significant transboundary environmental impacts, an environmental impact assessment requirement is now part of customary international law. Pulp Mills on the River Uruguay (Argentina v. Uruguay), para. 204 (Int'l Ct. Justice Apr. 20, 2010). Even some quasi-governmental or private institutions, like the World Bank, now incorporate NEPA-like requirements into their operating procedures.

In this chapter, we will consider the requirements, and the consequences, of this so-called "Magna Carta of environmental laws." We'll first consider when an environmental impact statement must be prepared, and, then, what information that environmental impact statement must contain. We'll close by considering two issues at the current cutting edge of NEPA practice: when, if at all, are exemptions from NEPA processes appropriate, and how should agencies factor climate change into their NEPA compliance?

Throughout, you will also confront some basic questions about environmental impact assessment statutes. Most importantly, are these statutes effective? Do they in fact promote better decision-making and more transparent governance? Or are they fatally weak, excessively time-consuming, or overly focused on generating voluminous documents? Debates about these questions have been continuous since NEPA first emerged in 1970, and these debates continue in the chambers of Congress, the halls of state legislatures, and the offices of agencies even today.

I. NEPA OVERVIEW

A. STATUTE

Unlike the other statutes you will study in this course, NEPA is elegantly simple. Its first section declares the broad purposes of the statute, and its second section contains the most important operative mandates. Other sections follow, but none is particularly important to the day-to-day work of a NEPA lawyer. Indeed, the key language is sufficiently brief that we have quoted nearly all of it in the excerpts below.

NEPA § 101, 42 U.S.C. § 4331. Congressional Declaration of National Environmental Policy

(a) The Congress, recognizing the profound impact of man's activity on the interrelations of all components of the natural environment, particularly the profound influences of population growth, high-density urbanization, industrial expansion, resource exploitation, and new and expanding technological advances and recognizing further the critical importance of restoring and maintaining environmental quality to the overall welfare and development of man, declares that it is the continuing policy of the Federal Government, in cooperation with State and local governments, and other concerned public and private organizations, to use all practicable means and measures, including financial and technical assistance, in a manner calculated to foster and promote the general welfare, to create and maintain conditions under which man and nature can exist in productive harmony, and fulfill the social, economic, and other requirements of present and future generations of Americans.

(b) In order to carry out the policy set forth in this chapter, it is the continuing responsibility of the Federal Government to use all practicable means, consistent with other essential considerations of national policy, to improve and coordinate Federal plans, functions, programs, and resources to the end that the Nation may—

    (1) fulfill the responsibilities of each generation as trustee of the environment for succeeding generations;

    (2) assure for all Americans safe, healthful, productive, and esthetically and culturally pleasing surroundings;

    (3) attain the widest range of beneficial uses of the environment without degradation, risk to health or safety, or other undesirable and unintended consequences;

---

(4)   preserve important historic, cultural, and natural aspects of our national heritage, and maintain, wherever possible, an environment which supports diversity and variety of individual choice;

(5)   achieve a balance between population and resource use which will permit high standards of living and a wide sharing of life's amenities; and

(6)   enhance the quality of renewable resources and approach the maximum attainable recycling of depletable resources.

(c) The Congress recognizes that each person should enjoy a healthful environment and that each person has a responsibility to contribute to the preservation and enhancement of the environment

NEPA § 102, 42 U.S.C. § 4332. Cooperation of agencies; reports; availability of information; recommendations; international and national coordination of efforts

The Congress authorizes and directs that, to the fullest extent possible: (1) the policies, regulations, and public laws of the United States shall be interpreted and administered in accordance with the policies set forth in this chapter, and (2) all agencies of the Federal Government shall—

(A) utilize a systematic, interdisciplinary approach which will insure the integrated use of the natural and social sciences and the environmental design arts in planning and in decisionmaking which may have an impact on man's environment;

(B) identify and develop methods and procedures, in consultation with the Council on Environmental Quality established by subchapter II of this chapter, which will insure that presently unquantified environmental amenities and values may be given appropriate consideration in decisionmaking along with economic and technical considerations;

(C) include in every recommendation or report on proposals for legislation and other major Federal actions significantly affecting the quality of the human environment, a detailed statement by the responsible official on—

(i)   the environmental impact of the proposed action,

(ii)   any adverse environmental effects which cannot be avoided should the proposal be implemented,

(iii) alternatives to the proposed action,

(iv) the relationship between local short-term uses of man's environment and the maintenance and enhancement of long-term productivity, and

(v) any irreversible and irretrievable commitments of resources which would be involved in the proposed action should it be implemented.

Prior to making any detailed statement, the responsible Federal official shall consult with and obtain the comments of any Federal agency which has jurisdiction by law or special expertise with respect to any environmental impact involved. Copies of such statement and the comments and views of the appropriate Federal, State, and local agencies, which are authorized to develop and enforce environmental standards, shall be made available to the President, the Council on Environmental Quality and to the public as provided by [the Administrative Procedure Act] and shall accompany the proposal through the existing agency review processes;

[subsection (D), which allows federal agencies to use environmental impact statements prepared by the states, is omitted.]

(E) study, develop, and describe appropriate alternatives to recommended courses of action in any proposal which involves unresolved conflicts concerning alternative uses of available resources;

[subsections (F), (G), (H), and (I) are omitted.]

Lawyers generally view section 102(2)(C), which requires EIS preparation, as the most important part of these passages and as the true heart of the statute.

NEPA is also notable for what it does not contain. Most importantly, NEPA lacks any binding substantive constraint on agency decisions. Early NEPA plaintiffs argued that the broad language in section 101 obligated federal agencies to take affirmative steps to protect the environment. The federal courts have consistently and repeatedly rejected that claim. "It is well settled," the Supreme Court once put it, "that NEPA itself does not impose substantive duties mandating particular results, but simply prescribes the necessary process for preventing uninformed—rather than unwise—agency action." *Robertson v. Methow Valley Citizens Council*, 490 U.S. 332, 333 (1989). Accordingly, as long as an agency adequately considers alternatives and identifies environmental impacts, nothing in NEPA prevents the agency from choosing to undertake an action with adverse environmental consequences. That said, agencies generally do not like to be known for causing avoidable adverse environmental impacts. NEPA's procedural mandate to prepare an EIS thus has important substantive implications for agency decisionmaking.

B. REGULATIONS

Administrative agencies often flesh out the requirements of statutes by promulgating regulations, and NEPA involves no exception to this general practice. Indeed, the brevity of the statute means that implementing regulations (and court cases) have been particularly important for NEPA. Those implementing regulations typically come from two sources.

One is an agency known as the Council on Environmental Quality (CEQ). Within the federal government, the CEQ holds primary responsibility for developing NEPA regulations, and its regulations are much more detailed and extensive than the statutory language itself. Administrative lawyers have occasionally raised questions about the extent to which the CEQ regulations can bind other federal agencies. *See, e.g., NRDC v. Callaway*, 524 F.2d 79, 86 n.8 (2d Cir. 1975). In practice, however, courts and other federal agencies tend to defer to the CEQ regulations. *See id.* (granting them "significant weight"). *But see Nevada v. Department of Energy*, 457 F.3d 78, 87 n. 5 (D.C. Cir. 2006) ("Because the CEQ has no express regulatory authority under NEPA—it was empowered to issue regulations only by executive order—the binding effect of CEQ regulations is far from clear." (citations, quotations, and alterations omitted)). Practicing NEPA lawyers therefore often spend more time focusing on the language of the regulations than on the statute itself.

Many federal agencies also have adopted their own regulations for implementing NEPA. Sometimes those regulations incorporate the CEQ regulations by reference, which does away with any question about whether the CEQ regulations bind that particular agency. Additionally, agency regulations often go beyond the basic requirements set forth by the CEQ regulations and specify additional requirements or procedures for that particular agency, including how the NEPA process should fit into the agency's overall decision procedures.

Both the CEQ and individual federal agencies also can issue guidance documents. These documents provide non-binding, but often influential, guidance explaining how particular NEPA problems should be addressed. *See, e.g.,* CEQ, *Final Guidance for Federal Departments and Agencies on Consideration of Greenhouse Gas Emissions and the Effects of Climate Change in National Environmental Policy Act Reviews* (August 1, 2016); U.S. Army Corps of Engineers, *Environmental Evaluation and Planning within the SMART Planning Framework* (2015).

C. NEPA Processes

So how does a NEPA process actually work? One might think, from just reading the statutory language, that most of the legal work associated with NEPA processes goes into the preparation and review of EISs. Preparing, reviewing, and critiquing EISs is indeed an important part of NEPA practice. A study of 53 federal agencies between 1998 and 2006 found that 2,236 EISs were prepared during those years and on average took 3.4 years to complete. Piet deWitt & Carole A. de Witt, *How Long Does It Take to Prepare an Environmental Impact Statement?*, 10 Envtl. Prac. 164 (2008). An even more common issue, however, is whether an EIS even needs to be prepared. For the vast majority of federal agency actions— more than 99 percent—some more streamlined form of NEPA compliance takes place.

The CEQ regulations specify two alternative ways in which federal agencies can comply with NEPA without preparing an EIS. First, agencies may prepare something known as an "environmental assessment," which, in theory, is a shorter environmental study designed to assess the need for an EIS. If an environmental assessment reveals that an EIS is unnecessary—usually because whatever environmental impacts it identifies will not be significant—then the agency may issue something known as a "finding of no significant impact," a document often referred to as a "FONSI." The project may then proceed without the preparation of an EIS. Alternatively, if an EA reveals that a project might have a significant impact, the agency will often adopt project modifications or mitigation measures designed to reduce that impact to a less-than-significant level. The agency then will typically adopt a "mitigated FONSI," which approves the project in reliance on the adjustments or mitigation measures. Again, the project may then proceed without preparing an EIS. While EAs are substantially more common than EISs, they also account for only a small proportion—less than 5 percent—of federal agencies' NEPA compliance documents.

> It is very difficult to understand the realities of NEPA practice, or to begin to evaluate NEPA's effectiveness, without spending some time reading EISs, environmental assessments, and other NEPA documents. For that reason, we have included a small library of NEPA documents on the course website. We recommend that you spend some time skimming at least one or two of those documents. Consider, as you read, what kind of time investment went into preparing the documents and who would have been involved. Consider, also, whether those documents would help you understand the proposed action's environmental impacts, and take an informed position on that action, if you were a government decision-maker or a concerned member of the public.

Second, federal agencies may avoid an EIS requirement by approving projects pursuant to something known as a "categorical exclusion." Approximately 95% of federal agency actions fall into this category. According to the CEQ regulations, a

> '[c]ategorical exclusion' means a category of actions which do not individually or cumulatively have a significant effect on the human environment and which have been found to have no such effect in procedures adopted by a Federal agency in implementation of these regulations [ ] and for which, therefore, neither an environmental assessment nor an environmental impact statement is required.

40 C.F.R. 1508.4. For example, the United States Forest Service has determined that certain routine maintenance projects individually and cumulatively lack significant impacts. It therefore has promulgated a regulation creating a categorical exclusion for: "Repair and maintenance of administrative sites. Examples include but are not limited to: (i) [M]owing lawns at a district office; (ii) Replacing a roof or storage shed; (iii) Painting a building; or (iv) Applying registered pesticides for rodent or vegetation control." 36 C.F.R. § 220.6. Approval of such activities would presumptively be covered under that categorical exclusion. Barring exceptional circumstances, no EISs or environmental assessments would be prepared.

Figure 7.1. A United States Forest Service
NEPA Process Flowchart

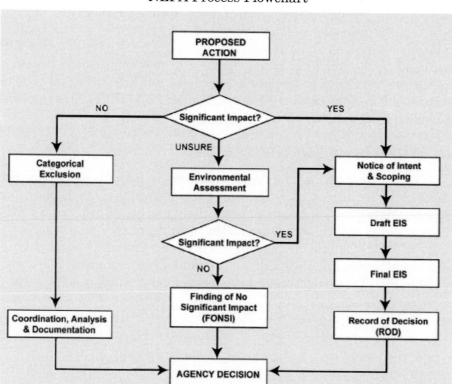

Why would agencies want to avail themselves of these alternative paths to NEPA compliance? The reasons, ultimately, are time and money. A 2003 report estimated that the typical EIS costs between $250,000 and $2 million to prepare. *See* NEPA TASK FORCE, REPORT TO THE COUNCIL ON ENVIRONMENTAL QUALITY, MODERNIZING NEPA IMPLEMENTATION (2003). That expense arises from processes that many agency staff perceive as cumbersome. If an agency does prepare an EIS, it will begin with a "scoping" process, in which the agency seeks comments from the public and from other agencies about issues and alternatives they would like the EIS to address. The agency then will prepare a draft EIS, which will then be made available for public comment. For a major infrastructure project, the draft EIS could be hundreds of pages long and rely on dozens of other studies about various potential impacts of the project. Once the comment period has elapsed, and if the agency still wishes to proceed with the action, it will prepare a final EIS, which will include both updates to the analysis and responses—often detailed—to the comments the agency received on its draft. Then, after the EIS is complete and some additional time for public deliberation has passed, the agency can issue a "record of decision,"

which, as its name suggests, records the agency's decision to proceed with the action. NEPA compliance efforts typically draw on the expertise of a variety of professional disciplines, and the resulting documents, at their best, can be impressive compilations of information. But the process typically takes several years, and sometimes longer. And if, after the EIS is complete, the proposed action changes, or new information emerges, the agency may need to prepare a "supplemental EIS," which can mean starting much of the process all over again. An EA/FONSI or a categorical exclusion is often a much faster way to proceed.

II. WHEN IS AN EIS NECESSARY?

NEPA generates many legal questions, a handful of which are particularly recurrent. First among them is whether an agency can appropriately proceed, or has appropriately proceeded, without an EIS. That question in turn depends upon the meaning of a few words in NEPA section 102(2)(C), which requires an EIS for "major Federal actions significantly affecting the quality of the human environment." 42 U.S.C. § 4332(2)(C). Those words tend to generate a few recurring sub-issues:

- *What counts as an _action_?*[1] Federal agencies are doing things all the time. But federal agencies cannot possibly go through NEPA compliance processes for every single thing they do. Instead, out of necessity, NEPA compliance must focus on certain discrete decision points. Figuring out what counts as such a decision point is often a central question in NEPA litigation. *See, e.g., Kleppe v. Sierra Club*, 427 U.S. 390 (1976) (considering whether the United States Bureau of Land Management's increased emphasis on mineral extraction in the northern Great Plains constituted an agency action).

- *What counts as _federal_ action?* Sometimes it is very clear that a federal agency is acting. But if a federal agency grants a permit to a private actor, or provides funds that support a state project, is that a federal action within the meaning of NEPA? The answer to both questions is generally yes, but sometimes complications arise. For example, what if a federal agency authorizes or funds just a segment of a larger highway system, or some other piece of a larger project? Is NEPA compliance necessary then, and if so, how much of the larger project must the analysis

---

[1]   Interestingly, a question that does *not* typically arise is whether a federal action qualifies as major. In its regulations, the CEQ has stated that whether an action is major, for purposes of NEPA, depends on the significance of its environmental consequences. 40 C.F.R. 1508.18 ("Major reinforces but does not have a meaning independent of significantly."). That effectively collapses the "major action" inquiry into the "significant impact" inquiry.

address? *See, e.g., Ohio Valley Environmental Coalition v. Aracoma Coal Co.,* 556 F.3d 177 (4th Cir. 2009) (upholding environmental assessments that considered only the portion of an action subject to federal authority, not the action as a whole). Or, what if a federal agency provides technical assistance to a state or local agency undertaking a project? Does that assistance transform the state's project into a federal action? *See, e.g., Ka Makani O'Kohala Ohana Inc. v. County of Hawai'i Department of Water Supply,* 295 F.3d 955 (9th Cir. 2002) (holding that a state water project was not a federal action just because a federal agency partially funded and participated in preliminary studies to assess groundwater).

- *What counts as an environmental impact?* Some impacts, like changes to air or water quality, clearly qualify as environmental. But what about a change that might increase street crime or congestion on public transit, or might affect the historic character of a neighborhood? What about the psychological consequences of perceived increases in risk? In an abundance of caution, agencies often address these kinds of impacts in their NEPA documents. But questions do sometimes arise about whether an impact, though real and perhaps significant, qualifies as environmental. *See, e.g., Metropolitan Edison Co. v. People Against Nuclear Energy,* 460 U.S. 766 (1983) (finding that perceptions of increased risk of nuclear accidents, and the fears associated with those perceived risks, were not environmental impacts).

- *What counts as a significant environmental impact?* Of all of these questions, the most common one is whether an environmental impact rises to a level of significance. The mere inclusion of the word "significant" implies that not just any environmental impact will necessitate preparation of an EIS. But "significant" is an imprecise term, and a term that NEPA does not define (the statute has no definitions section). The NEPA regulations do define "significant," but, as you will see, that definition is not very precise. That imprecision often generates legal uncertainty about just how large an impact must be before it triggers the need for an EIS. Closely related is another recurring question: if, after preparing an EA, an agency is still unsure about the scale or likelihood of a potential impact, is it obligated to prepare an EIS?

- *What if the lead agency lacks __discretion__?* Occasionally, federal agencies have no choice but to take actions with significant environmental consequences, because governing statutory law leaves them with no discretion to forego or alter the mandated action. In those circumstances, the Supreme Court has held, the agency has no obligation to prepare an EIS, for preparation would be pointless if the agency has no discretion to act upon the EIS's conclusions. *Department of Transportation v. Public Citizen,* 541 U.S. 752 (2004). That legal principle may sound straightforward, but applying it can be difficult. Sometimes determining the scope of a federal agency's discretion raises complex legal questions, and the necessity of an EIS is unclear.

The problem below does not raise all of these questions, and this list of questions does not exhaust the field. But the problem does illustrate the kinds of dilemmas that often confront federal agencies as they decide whether or not to prepare EISs.

PROBLEM: JAMES RIVER UTILITY LINE CROSSING, PART I

The James River arises in the Blue Ridge Mountains of western Virginia and flows east across the state, passing by Richmond and Williamsburg before it discharges into Chesapeake Bay. Its lower reaches are as rich in history as any place in the United States. Jamestown, the first successful British colony in North America, was founded along the river's north bank, a short distance from Williamsburg, which became Virginia's first colonial capitol. On the nearby York River, just a few miles above its confluence with the James, General George Washington and his French allies laid siege to British troops at Yorktown, ultimately winning the climactic battle of the American Revolutionary War.

Between these historic sites, the Dominion Virginia Power, a major energy supplier, would like to build a new utility line across the river (Dominion refers to the proposed line as the Skiffes Creek Project). Dominion once burned coal to generate much of its energy. But because of a combination of market pressures and increasingly stringent environmental regulations, coal is a decreasingly viable energy source, and Dominion plans to shutter several coal-fired power plants, including one in Yorktown. With the plant closure will come a need to deliver energy along different pathways, and that means building new utility lines. One of them, according to Dominion, must cross the James River.[2]

Building that line will require placing a series of 300-foot-tall towers in the river itself. Constructing those towers will require Clean Water Act permits from the U.S. Army Corps of Engineers, a federal agency (Chapter 5

---

[2]   Project opponents dispute the necessity of the new transmission line, and later in this chapter you will consider how the Corps's NEPA compliance efforts should address alternative proposals.

contains more detailed discussion of the Army Corps of Engineers' role in implementing the Clean Water Act). Federal action, in other words, must be taken for the project to proceed. But must the Army Corps prepare an EIS before issuing permits to Dominion?

As you read the materials below, consider that question from the perspective of the U.S. Army Corps of Engineers, Dominion, the National Parks Conservation Association (a non-profit organization dedicated to protecting the scenic, natural, and historic values of national parks, monuments, and historic sites), and the Lower James Riverkeeper, an environmental group dedicated to protecting the James River. What position(s) would your client take on the basic question of whether an EIS should be prepared? What arguments would you use to advocate for that position? What legal risks, if any, do you perceive?

Figure 7.2. Map of the Proposed James River Utility Line Crossing

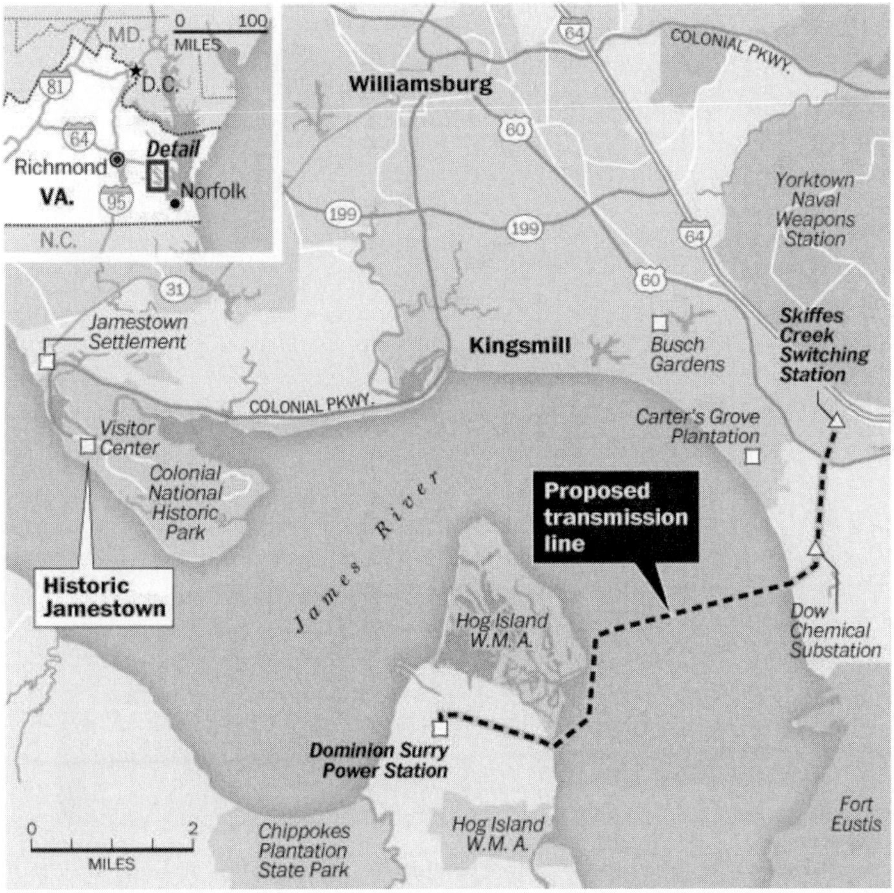

In the battle over NEPA compliance for the proposed crossing, three issues have become particularly salient. The first, and most important, is the impact of the crossing on the historic character of the area. As you will see from the materials below, preservation advocates, including the National

Parks Conservation Association, and the National Park Service have argued that history comes alive at Jamestown partly because the area has retained much of its historic character. That sense of history will be damaged, they argue, if the utility line crossing is installed. But does that change qualify as an environmental impact? And if it does, is it significant?

Second, many opponents are concerned about aesthetics. Those aesthetics are part of the historic preservation argument against the crossing, of course, but the aesthetic concerns are not just about history. The James River remains a recreational and scenic resource, and the Lower James Riverkeeper and others are concerned about how the project will look from many viewpoints, not just the shores of Jamestown Island. Dominion counters that aesthetic impacts like these are quite routine, particularly in an area that already hosts significant cities and major industrial sites.

Figure 7.3. A National Parks Conservation Association poster opposing the proposed transmission line

Third, the project may affect biological resources. Of many possible consequences, some of the most controversial involve Atlantic sturgeon, an endangered species of fish. Sturgeon migrate between fresh and salt water, and are present for part of the year in the James River basin. The utility crossing might affect them in several ways. Building the utility towers will require pile driving, and the resulting loud noises can disturb aquatic species, including sturgeon. Building the towers also will temporarily raise sediment levels in the river, as construction equipment stirs up the sediments on the river bottom. And the towers, once built, will occupy habitat. The National Marine Fisheries Service, a federal agency with responsibility for managing and protecting sturgeon, has informed the Army Corps of Engineers that these impacts are likely to be so small in scale that they can readily be discounted. But the Lower James Riverkeeper is not so sure.

As you try to determine whether these impacts should, or must, be counted as significant, it may help to have some sense of the U.S. Army Corps of Engineers' standard practices. In 2014, the agency issued more than 50,000 permits for filling wetlands and waterways, and the agency also builds, operates, and maintains many water projects of its own. *See* INSTITUTE FOR WATER RESOURCES, THE MITIGATION RULE RETROSPECTIVE: A REVIEW OF THE 2008 REGULATIONS GOVERNING COMPENSATORY MITIGATION FOR LOSS OF AQUATIC RESOURCES 26 (2015). Preparing an individual EIS for each one of those permits would be prohibitively time-consuming and expensive, and the Corps does not do so. Instead, the Corps often just prepares EAs, even for projects that are substantial in scale. To provide one example, in the mid-2000s, the Corps often issued mining companies permits that allowed them to fill miles of small streams with leftover rubble from surface mining operations, and it generally prepared EAs, not EISs, for those projects. In *Ohio Valley Environmental Coalition v. Aracoma Coal Co.*, 556 F.3d 177 (4th Cir. 2009), the Fourth Circuit upheld this method of NEPA compliance.

Dominion has argued that an EIS would be both harmful and unnecessary. On its project website, Dominion offers a series of answers to frequently asked questions. Two are included below:

> If the US Army Corps of Engineers–Norfolk District calls for an Environmental Impact Study [sic], what impact would it have?

> An EIS is not a requirement for this project. The Corps has been working toward the completion of an Environmental Assessment (EA) of the Skiffes Creek project for months. An EIS would likely delay the project an additional **12–18 months**. That delay would consequently remove any chance at all for completing the Skiffes Creek project before the retirement of the two coal units at Yorktown by April 2017, putting the entire Peninsula region at risk for rotating blackouts.

> Why does Dominion believe an Environmental Impact Study [sic] is not needed for this project?

> Through extensive public comment opportunities, as well as face to face meetings, the US Army Corps of Engineers has done an excellent job collecting a large amount of useful input from stakeholders. The input will be analyzed by the Corps in the Environmental Assessment (EA) process which is very thorough.

Dominion, and third-party consultants, do not believe that an EIS is required because the chosen route will not have a significant adverse impact on the scenic assets, historic districts, and the environment of the area. The Supreme Court of Virginia's unanimous upholding of the State Corporation Commission's 2013 order approving the construction of a proposed 500-kilovolt (500kV) overhead transmission line across the James River confirms this.

NEPA cases—and cases under analogous state statutes—typically involve voluminous administrative records. NEPA and its state counterparts also have produced large bodies of case law, which can make NEPA lawyering rather research-intensive. Fortunately for you, we cannot reproduce that research-intensive experience in a casebook. But we have provided a small subset of the regulatory materials, cases, and other documents that might be relevant to resolving this controversy.

As you review these materials, and as you think about the relevant facts and statutory language you have already read, you should consider not just whether the Army Corps of Engineers *should* prepare an EIS, but also whether it is *obligated* to do so. In other words, if the Army Corps of Engineers chooses to rely on an EA/FONSI, and someone does not like that choice, will that someone be able to persuade a court to compel the Corps to withdraw its FONSI? Based on your answers to those questions, what strategies would you recommend for your client, if your client is the Army Corps, Dominion, the National Parks Conservation Association, or the Lower James Riverkeeper?

Also, as you read, consider one other question. Why wouldn't the Corps just prepare an EA, see what it reveals, and then, if necessary, prepare an EIS? That is exactly the approach the CEQ regulations seem to envision. But agencies rarely choose that pathway. Can you figure out why not?

The starting point for your analysis is NEPA's statutory language, which we have quoted above. You will also want to look carefully at the CEQ's regulations, excerpts of which appear below.

---

40 C.F.R. § 1508.9. Environmental assessment

"Environmental assessment":

(a) Means a concise public document for which a Federal agency is responsible that serves to:

    1.   Briefly provide sufficient evidence and analysis for determining whether to prepare an environmental impact statement or a finding of no significant impact.

    2.   Aid an agency's compliance with the Act when no environmental impact statement is necessary.

    3.   Facilitate preparation of a statement when one is necessary.

(b) Shall include brief discussions of the need for the proposal, of alternatives as required by section 102(2)(E), of the environmental impacts of the proposed action and alternatives, and a listing of agencies and persons consulted.

40 C.F.R. § 1508.13. Finding of no significant impact

"Finding of no significant impact" means a document by a Federal agency briefly presenting the reasons why an action, not otherwise excluded (Sec. 1508.4), will not have a significant effect on the human environment and for which an environmental impact statement therefore will not be prepared. * * *

40 C.F.R. § 1508.27. Significantly

Significantly as used in NEPA requires considerations of both context and intensity:

(a) Context. This means that the significance of an action must be analyzed in several contexts such as society as a whole (human, national), the affected region, the affected interests, and the locality. Significance varies with the setting of the proposed action. For instance, in the case of a site-specific action, significance would usually depend upon the effects in the locale rather than in the world as a whole. Both short- and long-term effects are relevant.

(b) Intensity. This refers to the severity of impact. Responsible officials must bear in mind that more than one agency may make decisions about partial aspects of a major action. The following should be considered in evaluating intensity:

(1) Impacts that may be both beneficial and adverse. A significant effect may exist even if the Federal agency believes that on balance the effect will be beneficial.

(2) The degree to which the proposed action affects public health or safety.

(3) Unique characteristics of the geographic area such as proximity to historic or cultural resources, park lands, prime farmlands, wetlands, wild and scenic rivers, or ecologically critical areas.

(4) The degree to which the effects on the quality of the human environment are likely to be highly controversial.

(5) The degree to which the possible effects on the human environment are highly uncertain or involve unique or unknown risks.

(6) The degree to which the action may establish a precedent for future actions with significant effects or represents a decision in principle about a future consideration.

(7) Whether the action is related to other actions with individually insignificant but cumulatively significant impacts. Significance exists if it is reasonable to anticipate a cumulatively significant impact on the environment. Significance cannot be avoided by terming an action temporary or by breaking it down into small component parts.

(8) The degree to which the action may adversely affect districts, sites, highways, structures, or objects listed in or eligible for listing in the National Register of Historic Places or may cause loss or destruction of significant scientific, cultural, or historical resources.

(9) The degree to which the action may adversely affect an endangered or threatened species or its habitat that has been determined to be critical under the Endangered Species Act of 1973.

(10) Whether the action threatens a violation of Federal, State, or local law or requirements imposed for the protection of the environment.

Questions about whether EISs are necessary have come up in many NEPA controversies, and a substantial body of caselaw addresses these issues. Below, we have included excerpts from two relevant cases.

Ocean Advocates v. U.S. Army Corps of Engineers
402 F.3d 846 (9th Cir. 2004)

■ D.W. NELSON, SENIOR CIRCUIT JUDGE.

Ocean Advocates (OA), an environmental group, appeals a summary judgment ruling in favor of the U.S. Army Corps of Engineers (the Corps) and BP West Coast Products (BP). OA challenges the issuance and extension of a permit allowing BP to build an addition to its existing oil refinery dock in Cherry Point, Washington. * * *

STANDARD OF REVIEW

* * * The Administrative Procedure Act (APA) governs our review of the Corps' action, conclusions, and findings of fact. Section 10(a), 5 U.S.C. § 702, sets out the standard for judicial review of decisions involving NEPA, *Lujan v. Nat'l Wildlife Fed'n,* 497 U.S. 871, 882–83 (1990) * * *. We must set aside the Corps' actions, findings, or conclusions if they are "arbitrary, capricious, an abuse of discretion, or otherwise not in accordance with law." 5 U.S.C. § 706(2)(A).

This review is "searching and careful," but the arbitrary and capricious standard is narrow, and we cannot substitute our own judgment for that of the Corps. *Citizens to Preserve Overton Park, Inc. v. Volpe,* 401 U.S. 402, 416 (1971), *overruled on other grounds by Califano v. Sanders,* 430 U.S. 99 (1977). We ask "whether the [Corps'] decision was based on a consideration of the relevant factors and whether there has been a clear error of judgment." *Citizens to Preserve Overton Park,* 401 U.S. at 416. We also "must determine whether the [Corps] articulated a rational connection between the facts found and the choice made." *Ariz. Cattle Growers' Ass'n v. United States Fish & Wildlife,* 273 F.3d 1229, 1236 (9th Cir.2001). Our review "must not 'rubber-stamp' . . . administrative decisions that [we] deem inconsistent with a statutory mandate or that frustrate the congressional policy underlying a statute." *Id.* (quoting *NLRB v. Brown,* 380 U.S. 278, 291–92 (1965)) (first alteration in original).

DISCUSSION

* * * III. NEPA

OA challenges the Corps' failure to prepare an EIS prior to granting BP's permit application and permit extension application.

The relevant provision of NEPA provides that "all agencies of the Federal Government shall . . . include in every recommendation or report on . . . major Federal actions significantly affecting the quality of the human environment, a detailed statement by the responsible official." 42 U.S.C. § 4332(2)(C). This report, or EIS, considers the environmental impact of the proposed project.

Not every project necessitates an EIS. Where an EIS is not categorically required, the agency must prepare an Environmental Assessment to determine whether the environmental impact is significant enough to warrant an EIS. 40 C.F.R. §§ 1501.3, 1508.9; *Metcalf v. Daley,* 214 F.3d 1135, 1142 (9th Cir.2000). If the action will significantly affect the environment, an EIS must be prepared, while if the project will have only an insignificant effect, the agency issues a FONSI. 40 C.F.R. §§ 1501.3, 1501.4.

NEPA aims to establish procedural mechanisms that compel agencies, such as the Corps, to take seriously the potential environmental consequences of a proposed action. We have termed this crucial evaluation a "hard look." *Kern v. United States Bureau of Land Mgmt.,* 284 F.3d 1062, 1066 (9th Cir. 2002). The Corps cannot avoid preparing an EIS by making conclusory assertions that an activity will have only an insignificant impact on the environment. *See Alaska Ctr. for Env't v. United States Forest Serv.,* 189 F.3d 851, 859 (9th Cir. 1999). If an agency, such as the Corps, opts not to prepare an EIS, it must put forth a "convincing statement of reasons" that explain why the project will impact the environment no more than insignificantly. *Blue Mountains Biodiversity Project v. Blackwood,* 161 F.3d 1208, 1212 (9th Cir. 1998). This account proves crucial to evaluating whether the Corps took the requisite "hard look" at the potential impact of the dock extension. *Id.*

"[A]n EIS *must* be prepared if 'substantial questions are raised as to whether a project . . . *may* cause significant degradation of some human environmental factor.'" *Idaho Sporting Cong. v. Thomas,* 137 F.3d 1146, 1149 (9th Cir. 1998) (quoting *Greenpeace Action v. Franklin,* 14 F.3d 1324, 1332 (9th Cir. 1992)). "To trigger this requirement a 'plaintiff need not show that significant effects *will in fact occur,*' [but] raising 'substantial questions whether a project may have a significant effect' is sufficient." *Id.* at 1150 (quoting *Greenpeace,* 14 F.3d at 1332).

The Council on Environmental Quality has adopted regulations governing the implementation of NEPA. In determining whether a federal action requires an EIS because it significantly affects the quality of the human environment, an agency must consider what "significantly" means. The regulations give it two components: context and intensity. 40 C.F.R. § 1508.27. Context refers to the setting in which the proposed action takes place, in this case Cherry Point. *See id.* § 1508.27(a). Intensity means "the severity of the impact." *Id.* § 1508.27(b).

In considering the severity of the potential environmental impact, a reviewing agency may consider up to ten factors that help inform the "significance" of a project, such as the unique characteristics of the geographic area, including proximity to an ecologically sensitive area; whether the action bears some relationship to other actions with individually insignificant but cumulatively significant impacts; the level of uncertainty of the risk and to what degree it involves unique or unknown risks; and whether the action threatens violation of an environmental law. *Id.* § 1508.27(b)(3), (5), (7), (10). We have held that one of these factors may be sufficient to require preparation of an EIS in appropriate circumstances. *See Nat'l Parks & Conservation Ass'n v. Babbitt,* 241 F.3d 722, 731 (9th Cir. 2001).

The Corps has failed to provide the requisite convincing statement of reasons explaining why the dock extension would have only a negligible impact on the environment and therefore has left us unpersuaded that it took a "hard look" at the environmental impact of the dock extension. Moreover, the permit necessitated an EIS because OA raised a substantial question as to whether the dock extension *may* cause *significant* degradation of the environment. *See Idaho Sporting Cong.,* 137 F.3d at 1149.

A.   Convincing Statement of Reasons

In granting the 1996 permit, the Corps made a finding of no significant impact:

Performance of this work, in accordance with the standard conditions of the permit, will not significantly affect the quality of the human environment. Further, [the Corps has] determined that the issuance of this particular permit is a Federal action not having a significant impact on the environment. [The Corps has] thus concluded that the preparation of a formal Environmental Impact Statement is not required.

This finding fails to provide *any* reason, let alone a convincing one, why the Corps refrained from preparing an EIS. The only portion of the 1996 permit that *might* be considered a statement of reasons—if construed quite liberally—is the Corps' discussion of the FWS' concern about the cumulative impact of the pier extension. We conclude, however, that this neither qualifies as a statement of reasons nor convinces us that a comprehensive environmental impact report was unnecessary.

The Corps recounted the concerns that the FWS raised, namely increased tanker traffic that would raise the risk of an oil spill, and BP's response to those concerns in the text of the 1996 permit. The Corps then concluded:

The new pier also should reduce the chance of oil spills during bunkering of tankers at dock, as the ships will be surrounded with containment booms while moored at the dock. The project will also reduce turnaround time for tankers at anchorage, thus reducing the chance for oil spills while at anchor. The Corps concludes that the proposed facility should result in a reduction in the chances for oil spills.

We find this determination unsatisfactory, even if it could be interpreted as a statement of reasons obviating the need for an EIS. First, the Corps never explicitly adopted the claim that the project could result in an increase in tanker traffic, leaving us to guess whether it took a hard look at, or even considered, this obvious potential impact. Second, the Corps notes in its summation of BP's arguments that the dock "will not lead to an increase in the [BP] refinery capacity, as the refinery is already working at maximum capacity." This statement cannot possibly qualify as a fully informed and well-reasoned basis for failing to give more careful attention to the potential for increased traffic. BP alleged that its refinery was operating "at capacity," but the Corps never explicitly adopted or relied on this contention, and OA later disproved this claim when it sought to reopen the permit. A patently inaccurate factual contention can never support an agency's determination that a project will have "no significant impact" on the environment. Third, the Corps relied wholly on BP's claims that the project would reduce oil spills because of containment booms and reduced anchoring time to conclude that the dock extension would decrease the potential for an oil spill. This claim alone, without a reasoned evaluation of the potential for increased traffic, which is at least in part due to the Corps' erroneous conclusion that the refinery was operating at full capacity, does not inspire any confidence that the Corps took the hard look that we require. * * *

B. Substantial Question as to a "Significant" Impact on the Environment

OA has raised a substantial question as to the dock extension's potential significant impact on the environment. As just discussed, the Corps did not consider the potential for increased tanker traffic when it granted the 1996 permit, other than to mention—erroneously—in its recitation of BP's contentions that the dock extension would not result in increased tanker traffic because the refinery was operating at maximum capacity. The 2000 permit extension decision did not revisit this omission, instead relying exclusively on BP's expedient assertion that the project would not increase tanker traffic.

Without even considering the factors outlined by the Council on Environmental Quality, OA has raised a substantial question about the intensity of the impact that increased tanker traffic would have on Puget Sound; in fact, the "severity of the impact" would be unquestionably severe. The Corps ignored record evidence that the dock could not handle much additional traffic. In its 1992 permit application, BP noted that the use of the pier increased incrementally since the mid1980s and that the pier was operating at seventy-four percent of its capacity, a figure it termed "a very high utilization rate that is considered close to, if not maximum practical utilization." In addition, a report that BP commissioned from an outside consultant expected "marine traffic, especially tanker traffic" to increase upon project completion. Because the new platform would double the berthing capacity of the dock, this factor also would contribute to an increase in the number of vessels able to and actually accessing the refinery. When added to the other traffic demands on the Cherry Point area, the accumulation of tanker traffic may well have a significant impact on the environment, and OA has raised a substantial question about this effect.

Since BP applied for the permit in 1992, its traffic has increased. Between 1995 and 1999, the refinery's throughput increased by 672,000 gallons per day on average. Tanker traffic accessing the BP refinery cannot continue to increase ad infinitum, especially if the dock was operating at or near capacity in 1992. This record evidence raises a substantial question as to whether the dock extension will result in increased tanker traffic.

We agree with the Corps and BP that market forces also would increase tanker traffic to the BP facility. The dock extension, however, also increases the facility's ability to handle increased tanker traffic. Were the dock extension never constructed, BP could handle some additional tanker traffic caused by increasing market demands. With the dock extension, though, the BP facility can handle even greater increases in traffic, should market forces dictate such increases. Because a "reasonably close causal relationship" exists between the Corps' issuance of the permit, the environmental effect of increased vessel traffic, and the attendant increased risk of oil spills, the Corps had a duty to explore this relationship further in an EIS. *Dep't of Transp. v. Public Citizen,* 541 U.S. 752 (2004) (quoting *Metro. Edison Co. v. People Against Nuclear Energy,* 460 U.S. 766, 774 (1983)).

Increased tanker traffic elevates the risk of oil spills—an undeniable and patently apparent risk of harm to Puget Sound. An oil spill could destroy and disrupt ecosystems and kill or injure critical numbers of threatened and endangered species that live, and thrive, in the Cherry Point Region. The Corps failed to appreciate that the permitted activity would lead to increased tanker traffic, an error about the fundamental nature and severity of the impact that the dock extension would have. The obvious severity of the impact that increased tanker traffic poses is enough to warrant reversal on OA's NEPA claim. Were we unconvinced, however, some of the Council on Environmental Quality factors also demonstrate the significance of increased tanker traffic on this ecologically sensitive area, particularly cumulative significant impacts and uncertain environmental impacts. * * *

ii.   Uncertainty

Where the environmental effects of a proposed action are highly uncertain or involve unique or unknown risks, an agency must prepare an EIS. 40 C.F.R. § 1508.27(b)(5); *Nat'l Parks,* 241 F.3d at 731–32. "Preparation of an EIS is mandated where uncertainty may be resolved by further collection of data or where the collection of such data may prevent 'speculation on potential . . . effects. The purpose of an EIS is to obviate the need for speculation. . . .'" *Nat'l Parks,* 241 F.3d at 732 (quoting *Sierra Club v. United States Forest Serv.,* 843 F.2d 1190, 1195 (9th Cir. 1988)) (citation omitted) (alteration in original).

The amount that tanker traffic might increase in relation to the dock extension was largely unknown. Presumably, data collection or projection analysis could have determined the likely increase in tanker traffic, considering market forces, the dock extension, and the cumulative impact of the existing and pending facilities in the area. No such analysis is evident in the EA, nor is there a " 'justification regarding why more definitive information could not be provided.'" *Blue Mountains,* 161 F.3d at 1213 (quoting *Neighbors of Cuddy Mountain,* 137 F.3d at 1380). The Corps' "lack of knowledge does not excuse the preparation of an EIS; rather it requires [the Corps] to do the necessary work to obtain it." *Nat'l Parks,* 241 F.3d at 733. Concluding that a general risk, but not one attendant to the pier, exists, does not qualify as a hard look that would allow the Corps to skirt preparing an EIS.

Advocates for Transportation Alternatives, Inc. v. U.S. Army Corps of Engineers

453 F. Supp. 2d 289 (D. Mass. 2006)

■ YOUNG, DISTRICT JUDGE.

I.   INTRODUCTION

The plaintiffs Advocates for Transportation Alternatives, Inc. and individual Massachusetts residents (collectively, the "Advocates") allege that the U.S. Army Corps of Engineers ("Corps") violated federal environmental statutes by issuing a permit pursuant to the Clean Water Act to the Massachusetts Bay Transportation Authority ("MBTA") to restore commuter rail service on the Greenbush Line between Braintree and Scituate, Massachusetts.

* * * A.   The Corps Section 404 Permit

As a necessary part of the Greenbush commuter rail restoration, the MBTA applied for a Clean Water Act Section 404 permit ("Permit") for the discharge of dredged or fill materials into 7.6 acres of jurisdictional waters and wetlands (4.2 acres of temporary impacts, 3.4 acres of permanent impacts). As a result, the Corps examined the environmental impacts of all the MBTA's proposed activities over a 250-foot-wide corridor along the entire 18-mile Greenbush commuter rail line. Through its own analysis and consultation with federal and state agencies and the general public, the Corps identified issues that would be addressed in its permit review process.

In order to determine if an EIS was needed for the Greenbush Project, the Corps prepared an environmental assessment ("Assessment") that examined in detail the MBTA's proposal and alternatives such as ferry service and transportation systems management. * * * After considering the "localized adverse impacts to wetlands, historic resources, property values, and other environmental or social impacts" and mitigation projects that would lessen those impacts, the Corps concluded that the Greenbush Project did not require an EIS because the Corp's decision to approve the Permit was "not a major federal action significantly affecting the quality of the human environment." * * *

III. DISCUSSION

A.   COUNTS I, II, III, and IV: NEPA Violations

The Advocates claim that the Corps's Assessment and resulting FONSI violated NEPA because they failed substantively to: (1) take a hard look at the environmental impacts of the proposed Greenbush Project; (2) address the required factors in determining whether to prepare an EIS;

and (3) provide a convincing statement of reasons for declining to prepare an EIS. The Advocates allege that the Corps' FONSI and its failure to prepare an EIS were arbitrary and capricious and an abuse of discretion.

* * * The Advocates allege that the adverse impacts upon historic resources associated with the Greenbush Project mandate the preparation of an EIS. Pls.'s Mem. at 5–7. The NEPA Council regulations look to "[t]he degree to which the action may adversely affect" such historic resources to determine whether there is an impact of sufficient significance to warrant an EIS. 40 C.F.R. § 1508.27(b)(8). * * * It is undisputed that the Greenbush Project will have adverse impacts on twenty-seven historic properties and thirty-four historic districts in the area affected by the Greenbush Project. AR I:11998, 12030–32. These adverse effects include the introduction of noise, vibration, traffic, and aesthetic impacts. AR I:11998.

* * * In conducting its NEPA analysis, the Corps appropriately can consider the relative significance of the different types of impacts [to historic resources]. Thus, while a number of historic properties will be impacted by the Greenbush Project, the Corps determined that these impacts do not rise to the level of NEPA significance. AR I:12030 ("No buildings that are listed or eligible for listing on the National Register of Historic Places will be taken, destroyed, or negatively altered because of this project.").

For example, the Record reveals that while a number of properties eligible for listing on the National Register will be affected by vibration from trains above detectable threshold levels, none will occur at levels that will cause even cosmetic damage to fragile historic structures. AR III:8851 (threshold of 95 VdB for potential cosmetic damage to fragile historic structures); AR III:8930–9004 (no vibration impacts reach 95 VdB). Likewise, the visual impacts and effects to the setting of historic properties do not rise to the level of significance under NEPA, as the MBTA will be taking extensive mitigation measures such as building a tunnel beneath a Hingham historic district and utilizing plantings, fencing, and dark colored project fixtures, as well as numerous other measures. AR I:11916–59, 12044.

f.   Conclusion of the Court's Substantive Review: the FONSI is neither Arbitrary nor Capricious.

* * * [T]he Record establishes that the Corps took a hard look at most of the identified environmental concerns. *See id.* The Corps reasonably addressed factors in determining whether to prepare an EIS by properly identifying, reviewing, and considering the environmental impacts associated with the Greenbush Project. The Corps' conclusion that the degree of these impacts did not rise to the level of significant impact as defined by the NEPA Council regulations was neither arbitrary nor

capricious and was reasonably based on technical and scientific review.
* * *

To assess visual impacts, a picture can be worth more than a thousand words, and a video can be worth even more than a picture. On the course website, you will find two videos, one produced by a contractor for Dominion, and one produced by the National Parks Conservation Association. Each contains computer-generated images purporting to show what the completed utility lines will look like.

The videos also appear at https://www.dom.com/corporate/what-we-do/electricity/transmission-lines-and-projects/surry-skiffes-creek-500kv-and-skiffes-creek-whealton-230kv-projects#collapse1514238891   (the Dominion video) and at https://www.youtube.com/watch?v=Bg-cJzqAz0c (the NPCA video). Please take a few minutes to view each.

Many interested parties also have expressed opinions about the visual and historical impacts of the project. A sample of those opinions appears below.

Office of the Director

United States Department of the Interior

NATIONAL PARK SERVICE
1849 C Street, N.W.
Washington, D.C. 20240

DEC 1 1 2015

Lieutenant General Thomas P. Bostick
US Army Chief of Engineers and Commanding General
US Army Corps of Engineers
441 G Street NW
Washington, DC 20314-1000

Dear General Bostick:

The National Park Service would like to convey our serious concerns about the impacts of the proposed Dominion Surry-Skiffes Creek-Whealton Transmission Line project. This project would seriously impact irreplaceable, nationally significant resources. Running power lines through the landscape where the earliest days of American history were written will forever change the ability of Americans to experience and understand our nation's earliest days.

The proposed overhead line would mar the historic setting that represents the very beginnings of and the military defense of our nation. It would be a massive and modern industrial intrusion into a landscape that retains the feeling and appearance of long ago. It would cross directly over the open water of the Captain John Smith Chesapeake National Historic Trail. It would be within sight of Jamestown Island and the Colonial Parkway. It would set a precedent for additional development and cumulative effects. It would forever degrade, damage, and destroy the historic setting of these iconic resources. This is not acceptable for resources designated by Congress to ensure their permanent protection.

* * * We know from decades of experience protecting and managing nationally significant historic resources such as the John Smith Chesapeake Trail, Jamestown Island, and the Colonial Parkway that people value and understand their history and heritage through experiencing it in place. The historic setting of these resources is integral to being able to understand each and their connection to each other. It is a setting that has survived intact for over 400 years and the reasons presented by the utility company should not compel you to permanently mar this national resource.

* * * The NPS has not participated in discussions regarding mitigation because the Section 106[3] Assessment of Effects has not been sufficiently completed, nor has the Army Corps' NEPA compliance considered other viable alternatives. We understand the USACE has determined the proposal would have an adverse effect to historic resources in the area, but repeat that the specific effects have not been fully clarified and the severity of those effects has not yet been identified or agreed on. The severity of the Dominion overhead line proposal in such an iconic landscape requires thorough and complete assessment. Once that assessment has been sufficiently completed we believe the sheer magnitude of irreversible impacts will be clear and point to one conclusion: an overhead power line proposal is unsuitable in this location. No amount of mitigation could possibly counteract the severity of the effects that would be caused by this proposal. We urge the USACE to deny the permit for the proposed overhead line and to encourage Dominion Virginia Power to further examine the many other solutions available through an Environmental Impact Statement.

On the eve of the centennial of the NPS, this proposal has become one of the most serious threats to our nationally significant historic resources. This nation has only one Jamestown.

Thank you for your continued serious attention on this matter.

---

³   Eds: Here, Mr. Jarvis is referring to section 106 of the National Historic Preservation Act.

Sincerely,

Jonathan B. Jarvis
Director

cc: Major General Donald E. Jackson, Jr., US Army Corps of Engineers
cc: Assistant Secretary JoEllen Darcy, Department of Defense
cc: Molly Ward, Secretary of Natural Resources, Commonwealth of
Virginia

In assessing the significance, or lack thereof, of impacts on Atlantic sturgeon, much of the relevant documentation comes from the National Marine Fisheries Service, which is one of the two federal agencies primarily responsible for implementing the Endangered Species Act. The first document below is a fact sheet summarizing NMFS's general assessment of the status of Atlantic sturgeon. The second document provides a more specific assessment of the likely effects of this project upon Atlantic sturgeon. As you read that second document, bear in mind that you are reading conclusions excerpted from a much longer letter.

National Marine Fisheries Service, Fact Sheet: Atlantic Sturgeon Chesapeake Bay Distinct Population Segment: Endangered

Based on the best available science, we determined that the Chesapeake Bay distinct population segment of Atlantic sturgeon is endangered because it is currently in danger of extinction throughout its range due to: (1) precipitous declines in population sizes and the protracted period in which sturgeon populations have been depressed; (2) the limited amount of current spawning; and (3) the impacts and threats that have and will continue to prevent population recovery.

Population

Numbers of Atlantic sturgeon in the Chesapeake Bay distinct population segment are extremely low compared to historical levels and have remained so for the past 100 years.

- Prior to 1890, when a sturgeon fishery began, it was estimated that approximately 20,000 adult females inhabited the Chesapeake Bay and its tributaries.

- Currently, the existing spawning population in the James River is estimated to have less than 300 spawning adults per year.

- The spawning population of this distinct population segment is thought to be one to two orders of magnitude below historical levels.

Spawning

In addition to having fewer fish spawning, some spawning populations have been completely eliminated.

- There is only one known spawning population in the James River. Spawning may also occur in the York River as well.

- Historical evidence suggests the Potomac, Susquehanna, and Rappahannock Rivers were also Atlantic sturgeon spawning rivers. Current evidence of Atlantic sturgeon spawning in these other rivers of the Chesapeake Bay distinct population segment is lacking.

Threats

Threats to already depressed populations of Atlantic sturgeon from habitat degradation, vessel strikes and being accidentally caught and potentially injured or killed by fishermen are working in combination to put the distinct population segment in danger of extinction.

- Dredging, which occurs throughout in the Chesapeake Bay distinct population segment (e.g., the James River), can displace sturgeon while it is occurring and affect the quality of the habitat afterwards by changing the depth, sediment characteristics, and prey availability.

- Water quality has been degraded in areas throughout the range of the Chesapeake Bay distinct population segment. This has occurred as a result of runoff from agriculture, industrialization (e.g., paper mills), and the alteration of some river systems by dams.

- Vessel strikes occur in the James River. Eleven Atlantic sturgeon were reported to have been struck by vessels from

2005 through 2007. Several of these were mature individuals. Studies have shown that Atlantic sturgeon can only sustain low levels of mortality. The loss of even a few adult female Atlantic sturgeon could impact recovery of Atlantic sturgeon in the James River.

- Fisheries known to incidentally catch Atlantic sturgeon occur throughout the marine range of the species and in some riverine waters as well. Because Atlantic sturgeon mix extensively in marine waters and may use multiple river systems for spawning, foraging, and other life functions, they are subject to being caught in multiple fisheries throughout their range.

UNITED STATES DEPARTMENT OF COMMERCE
National Oceanic and Atmospheric Administration
NATIONAL MARINE FISHERIES SERVICE
GREATER ATLANTIC REGIONAL FISHERIES OFFICE
55 Great Republic Drive
Gloucester, MA 01930-2276

JAN 2 8 2016

Randy L. Steffey
Project Manager, Southern Virginia Regulatory Section
Department of the Army
Corps of Engineers, Norfolk District
803 Front Street
Norfolk, VA 23510-1096

> US Army Corps of
> Engineers
> Norfolk District
> Regulatory Office
> Received by: RLS
> Date: Jan 28, 2016

Re: NAO-2012-00080 Dominion Surry-Skiffes Creek-Whealton Transmission Line Project

Dear Mr. Steffey,

On April 16, 2014, we completed informal consultation, pursuant to section 7 of the Endangered Species Act (ESA) of 1973, as amended, with the Army Corps of Engineers, Norfolk District (ACOE) regarding Dominion Virginia Power's proposed Surry-Skiffes Creek-Whealton 500 kV aerial transmission line project on the James River. In your June 10, 2015 letter, you requested re-initiation of that consultation to consider changes to the proposed action, as well as to consider new information about listed species in the action area, and you determined that effects of the modified project are not likely to adversely affect any ESA listed species under our jurisdiction. After receiving a follow-up letter on November 25, 2015, and additional information on December 17, 2015 and December 29, 2015, we have reviewed all materials related to the project.

Summary of Noise Effects

Because the [time of year restrictions; hereinafter TOYR] will be adhered to in deep water habitat for construction of the towers (towers 21, 22, and 24–26) and fender systems located therein, there will be no effects from increased noise related to 24-inch steel or 30-inch fiber pile driving. * * * No pile driving will be performed in deep water portions of the action area * * * between February 15th and November 15th, which encompasses the times of year that spring and fall spawning fish migrate through the deep water portion of the action area and fall spawning fish stage there, while feeding and resting. * * *

Pile driving of 24-inch steel piles in shallow water habitat in the action area within an approximate 60,653,000 square foot cross-sectional portion of shallow water habitat within the James River around river mile 30, where Atlantic sturgeon are known to occur, will proceed during the TOYR (from February 15th to November 15th). This includes construction of towers 12–20, 23, 27, and 28. As discussed, Atlantic sturgeon stage for fall spawning in the deep water portions of the action area, however, they may opportunistically forage in shallow water habitat where prey is available. As detailed above, fish are able to move away from ensonified areas when pile driving is occurring. These ensonified areas will only encompass a small percentage of the overall habitat available in the river (230 foot radius from pile being driven where the width of the river is 14,767 feet wide), and in a cross-sectional portion of the river where the entire length of the transmission line will occur of 132,903,000 square feet. As such, we concur that all effects from pile driving while fish are present within the action area, are insignificant and/or discountable, and thus we concur that all pile driving activities will not likely adversely affect Atlantic sturgeon.

Water Quality Effects

The tower and fender system construction may cause a temporary increase in the amount of turbidity in the action area; however, suspended sediment is expected to settle out of the water column within a few hours and any increase in turbidity will be short term and limited in scope.

* * * Studies of the effects of turbid water on fish suggest that concentrations of suspended solids can reach thousands of milligrams per liter before an acute toxic reaction is expected (Burton 1993). The TSS levels expected for pile driving (5 to 10 mg/L) are below those shown to have adverse effect on fish (580 mg/L for the most sensitive species, with 1,000 mg/L more typical; see summary of scientific literature in Burton 1993) and benthic communities (390 mg/L (EPA 1986)). As the TSS levels will not reach levels that are toxic to benthic communities, the proposed action is extremely unlikely to result in reductions in the quality or

quantity of sturgeon prey currently available. TSS is most likely to affect sturgeon if a plume causes a barrier to normal behaviors. However, the increase in TSS levels expected for pile driving (5 to 10 mg/L) is so minor that any effect of sediment plumes caused by the proposed action on sturgeon movements or behavior will be undetectable because we expect sturgeon to either swim through the plume or make small evasive movements to avoid it. Additionally, this increase in turbidity is below levels known to adversely affect benthic communities and as such, any effects to sturgeon prey will be undetectable. Based on the best available information, the effects of suspended sediment resulting from pile installation on sturgeon will be insignificant.

Habitat Effects

The tower and fender system piles will permanently alter portions of the substrate in the action area by direct removal of habitat (permanent river bottom impact from pile driving and fender installation), and shading (subtidal encroachment). Shading from the installation of the towers and fender systems can impact the benthic communities by reducing photosynthesis in these areas, which forms the basis of benthic food chains. This may reduce the overall forage base in the shaded area. Although some benthic habitat will be permanently shaded, the area covered by the towers and fender system within the action area is small compared to the cross-section of available habitat at river mile 30 of the James River that includes the linear length of the transmission line along the western shore and across the river.

The applicant has estimated that approximately 2,712 square feet of permanent impacts to the river bottom will occur as a result of the action. This equates to 0.002% of the 132,930,000 square foot cross section of the James River that includes the shore length extent and cross river extent of the transmission line, inclusive of the action area. When broken down further, approximately 0.003% of the 72,250,000 square feet of deep water habitat will be permanently altered in the same cross sectional area, and 0.0014% of shallow water habitat will be permanently altered. Approximately 0.04% of the total cross sectional area will be shaded because of the action, and similarly 0.04% of deep and shallow water habitat, separately, will be shaded. Overall, this equates to very small reductions in available benthic habitat due to permanent alteration and shading, as a result of the action. If Atlantic sturgeon are in the action area, the action will not measurably reduce their ability to opportunistically forage, rest, and migrate in nearby suitable habitat near river mile 30, which has been identified as an aggregation area for sturgeon. Any reductions in foraging, resting, or migration as a result of habitat loss related to the action will be so small they cannot be detected.
* * *

Vessel Interactions

While the exact number of Atlantic sturgeon killed as a result of being struck by boat hulls or propellers is unknown, it is a concern in some areas. During project construction, small incremental increases in vessel traffic in the James River will occur (i.e., barges, support vessels, etc.). Regardless of the number of barges and trips used for the proposed project (one crane barge and one material barge, 1–2 tugboats, and several crew vessels during operations), there is still the potential that Atlantic sturgeon could be struck by a vessel during its transit to and from action area or within the action area. We have considered the likelihood that an increase in vessel traffic associated with the project increases the risk of interactions between sturgeon and vessels in the project area, compared to baseline conditions. Given the large volume of traffic in the action area, the increase in traffic associated with the project (only at most 5–7 additional vessels) is extremely small. * * *

Conclusions

Based on the analysis that any effects to ESA-listed species will be insignificant or discountable, we are able to concur with your determination that re-initiation of this consultation was necessary and that the modified proposed action is not likely to adversely affect any listed species under our jurisdiction. Therefore, no further consultation pursuant to section 7 of the ESA is required. * * *

Sincerely,

Kimberly Damon-Randall
Assistant Regional Administrator
for Protected Resources

NOTES

1.   Suppose the Army Corps of Engineers elects to prepare an EA/FONSI, and the National Parks Conservation Association sues and wins. What will the remedy be? In that circumstance, courts will rarely just order the agency to prepare an EIS. Instead, they will generally hold that the EA/FONSI was arbitrary and capricious and remand the matter to the agency. In theory, the agency might then issue another EA/FONSI, this time with a more reasoned justification. But as a practical matter, the reasoning of the reviewing court's decision may effectively compel an EIS.

A related remedial question is what to do about the project in the meantime. In general, the preferred remedy for a NEPA violation includes an injunction against proceeding with the action. The core purpose of NEPA, according to the CEQ regulations and most courts, is to promote informed decision-making *before* action occurs, and allowing an action to proceed before NEPA compliance is complete would defeat that basic purpose. *See Sierra Club v. Marsh*, 872 F.2d 497, 500–01 (1st Cir. 1989). But sometimes issues arise about the appropriate scope of the injunction, particularly for agency actions that are large in scale. *See, e.g., Monsanto Co. v. Geertson Seed Farms*, 561 U.S. 139 (2010) (setting aside a lower court's nationwide injunction against the planting of a genetically modified plant).

Finally, sometimes a project is completed before a court finds that a federal agency violated NEPA. Although agencies often cannot undo completed projects, courts have generally still required them to comply with NEPA, reasoning that the agency could engage in mitigation after adequately considering environmental impacts. *See, e.g., Oregon Natural Resources Council v. U.S. Bureau of Land Management*, 470 F.3d 818 (9th Cir. 2006) (concluding that although timber harvest had already occurred, NEPA claim was not moot because agency could still mitigate environmental impacts).

2.   One of the most common issues at the EA/EIS decision point—and an issue the problem above does *not* directly raise—is what to do about cumulative impacts. A cumulative impact is an impact that would arise partly from the action at issue and partly from other actions. In other words, it is an impact to which the proposed action would contribute, but for which it would not be solely responsible.

Cumulative impacts can be tricky in the NEPA context—and in many other environmental contexts—because of a basic problem. The contribution an individual action makes to a larger environmental problem may seem small. Indeed, that contribution may not even seem noticeable unless the impacts of the proposed action are considered in combination with the consequences of other related actions. For example, a timber harvest on public land might displace some animals that otherwise would nest or feed in the harvested area. On its own, that might not seem like a major impact, particularly if the timber sale covers a small area; one might think that the affected animals could just go somewhere else. But if that timber sale is just one of many in the affected area, a NEPA analysis that focuses solely on that one timber sale may miss the possibility that the animals will have nowhere else to go.

To respond to that problem, the CEQ regulations explicitly call for analysis of cumulative impacts. In one of its clearest directives, section 1508.27 of those regulations states that "[s]ignificance exists if it is reasonable to anticipate a cumulatively significant impact on the environment." That may seem sensible, but it also causes headaches for agencies. Analyzing the impacts of one project on its immediate environment can be challenging. Broadening that analysis to include many other projects and their effects can make the NEPA process seem even more burdensome, at least from the perspective of federal agencies and project proponents. For that reason, cumulative impact analysis is often a key battleground in NEPA litigation. For general discussion of cumulative impacts and NEPA, see Council on Environmental Quality, *Considering Cumulative Effects under the National Environmental Policy Act* (1997).

3.   To streamline their NEPA processes, and to address cumulative impacts, agencies sometimes engage in a practice known as tiering. This process is particularly appealing where an agency is developing a broad management plan of some kind, and then later will implement that plan through a series of site-specific decisions. The agency can then begin by preparing a broad EIS for the overall program of action, and then more focused EISs or EA/FONSIs for site-specific actions. The focused EISs and EA/FONSIs will generally incorporate the broader EIS by reference and will rely on it for cumulative impact analysis and, sometimes, for identification of measures to mitigate environmental impacts.

4.   Sometimes the initial environmental review of a project will reveal impacts that are arguably significant. As discussed above, a common agency response to that circumstance is to adopt mitigation measures designed to reduce the impacts to a less-than-significant level, and to approve the project in reliance on a "mitigated finding of no significant impact" instead of preparing an EIS. The CEQ and the courts have generally endorsed this practice.

        Courts do not, however, always approve mitigated FONSIs, particularly where an agency cannot be certain that a mitigation measure will be implemented. A mitigated FONSI, like other environmental review documents, does not by itself require any particular action. Once a federal agency issues a permit or otherwise authorizes private-party activities, that agency may have limited authority to compel the private party to perform mitigation measures. Moreover, even if a mitigation measure is implemented, it may not be implemented well, or it may simply not be effective. For those reasons, project opponents often argue that uncertain mitigation measures cannot be the basis for a finding of no significant impact. *See, e.g., Friends of Back Bay v. U.S. Army Corps of Engineers*, 681 F.3d 581, 587–89 (2012) (rejecting a mitigated FONSI where the Corps was merely "hopeful" that a mitigation measure would be implemented).

        Relatedly, once a mitigated FONSI has been issued and a project commenced, it may be unclear how, and whether, anyone will make sure the mitigation measures actually are implemented—and implemented effectively. Neither NEPA itself nor the CEQ implementing regulations prescribe any method or requirement for monitoring the effectiveness of mitigation measures. Often, it just is not done. *See* Bradley C. Karkkainen, *Toward a Smarter NEPA: Monitoring and Managing Government's Environmental Performance*, 102 COLUM. L. REV. 993 (2002) (criticizing this lack of monitoring, and proposing reforms).

5.   Another recurring NEPA issue is whether an EIS needs to be supplemented. Often federal agency actions evolve over time, and sometimes the project that gets implemented is not the same as the project the agency reviewed during its NEPA process. Additionally, new information can emerge after an EIS is complete and a decision made, but before the agency has finished implementing the project. What, then, is the agency obligated to do? Must it prepare a "supplemental EIS" every time circumstances change or new information emerges? Or is its NEPA process done once it issues a record of decision, no matter what happens next?

In *Marsh v. Oregon Natural Resources Council*, 490 U.S. 360 (1989), the Supreme Court provided an intermediate answer to this question. *Marsh* involved an Army Corps of Engineers' project to build the Elk Creek Dam on a tributary to the Rogue River in Oregon. After the Corps issued a final EIS, but before the dam itself was completed, two documents emerged (from agencies other than the Corps) suggesting that the impacts of the project would be more severe than had previously been thought. Dam opponents argued that the Corps was obligated to prepare a supplemental EIS addressing this new information before proceeding with the project. The Supreme Court disagreed. It acknowledged that project changes or new information could obligate a federal agency to prepare a supplemental EIS. But it held that the necessity of a supplemental EIS was subject to a "rule of reason," which would accommodate the reality that projects often evolve and new information often emerges. On the facts before it—and given the deferential arbitrary and capricious standard of review—the Court held that no supplemental EIS was required.[4]

III. CONTENTS OF AN EIS (OR AN EA)

What must an EIS or EA include? The statute itself provides only the tersest of language explaining what an EIS must contain and says nothing about EAs. But a combination of regulations, court cases, guidance documents, and the evolving conventions of agencies and environmental consultants have generated a fairly standardized format for EISs and EAs (for examples of those formats, please look at some of the NEPA documents available on the casebook website).

Despite that increasing standardization, the content (or alleged lack thereof) of EISs and EAs often raises two sets of legal questions. The first set of questions concerns whether particular impacts were adequately analyzed. Often plaintiffs will argue that a federal agency failed to analyze some important environmental consequence, or analyzed that

---

[4]   The Supreme Court's *Marsh* decision was just one episode in the remarkable legal history of the Elk Creek Dam. For a timeline of that history—and an example of just how complex environmental law battles can be—see http://www.oregonwild.org/waters/rivers-and-dams/elk-creek-dam/timeline.

A typical final EIS would use the following outline:

I.   Introduction

II.   Purpose and Need for the Action

III. Alternatives to the Action

IV.   Affected Environment and Environmental Consequences

V.   List of Preparers

VI.   Responses to Comments

Appendices

The structure of a draft EIS would be similar, except, of course, that the responses to comments chapter would not appear.

consequence in a misleading way, or predicated its analysis on false assumptions.

The second set of questions involves alternatives. Section 102(2)(C)(iii) requires an EIS to include an analysis of "alternatives to the proposed action." 42 U.S.C. § 4332(2)(C)(iii). CEQ's regulations require agencies to include a similar analyses of alternatives in EAs. 40 C.F.R. § 1508.9(b). Quite often, a project's opponents will argue that these alternatives analyses were insufficient, either because the federal agency simply did not look at enough alternatives or because it excluded a promising alternative from the analysis. Perhaps the Forest Service should have authorized a smaller timber sale; perhaps a highway project should have followed another route; or perhaps an energy conservation project would have been preferable to leasing public land for oil drilling. In a world of unlimited time and resources, federal agencies could respond to these concerns by studying every conceivable alternative, but time and resources are limited. Federal agencies therefore have strong incentives to limit the scope of their analyses. Additionally, a strategic agency (or project proponent) that is wedded to a particular course of action may not want alternatives analyzed precisely because closer examination might reveal them to be desirable. This can put agencies in a difficult spot. Any time a project is initiated by an applicant, the agency must define goals for someone else's project and, sometimes, analyze alternatives that the project proponent does not want. The question that then arises is whether an agency's analysis of alternatives was broad enough.

The problem below, which returns you to the James River and Dominion's proposed utility crossing, exemplifies some of the legal and policy questions raised by NEPA analyses and project alternatives.

PROBLEM: JAMES RIVER UTILITY LINE CROSSING, PART II

As you read above, Dominion, a major utility, is proposing to construct a new utility line across the James River near Williamsburg, Virginia. Dominion argues that the impending closure of two coal-fired power plants requires new power delivery infrastructure, and that crossing the James

River is the best—really, the only—way to adjust to the closures. Opponents disagree. They generally concede that some changes are necessary, but they argue that several alternative approaches, including energy conservation, a different crossing location, or a subsurface utility line, merit close analysis.

In addition to deciding whether to prepare an EA or an EIS, the Army Corps needs to decide which alternatives to analyze. For purposes of answering this question, please assume that the Corps is leaning toward an analysis that considers three alternatives: (1) Dominion's preferred crossing route (the Surry-Skiffes-Whealton route), with above-ground utility lines; (2) an alternative route, known as the Chickahominy-Skiffes-Whealton route; and (3) no action. The Corps and other interested parties have identified a wide variety of other alternatives, including different routes, underground utility lines with a range of different voltage levels, and demand-side management (which means managing gaps between energy supply and demand by reducing or managing demand rather than by maintaining or increasing supply). But, based on its preliminary analysis, the Corps does not intend to give additional consideration to those alternatives.

That will not sit well with project opponents, who have specifically emphasized two alternatives. First, the Save the James Alliance argues that Dominion should continue to run Yorktown 2 (one of the two plants slated for closure) using natural gas, which burns more cleanly than coal, for several years, and use the interim period to upgrade existing utility lines and make serious investments in demand-side management. These changes, they argue, could obviate the need for new lines. Second, The National Parks Conservation Association, along with a coalition of allies, has argued that even if the James River crossing must be built, it should be built under the river, thus avoiding the aesthetic impacts associated with above-ground towers and power lines.

Beyond these suggestions, the opponents offer two general objections to the way the Corps has considered alternatives. The Corps, they argue, has been overly reliant on information submitted by Dominion. That information, opponents claim, has been slanted to promote the alternatives Dominion wants to pursue. Second, they argue that the bind in which Dominion currently finds itself is largely of Dominion's own creation. Had Dominion invested earlier in a shift away from coal, it would not need such a rapid fix now and would have time for other alternatives—or so project opponents claim. A public agency's choices, they argue, should not be constrained by a private entity's poor business planning.

Consider this situation from a series of perspectives. If you represent the Corps, would you advise your client that the three alternatives the Corps plans to include in its EA will be adequate? Or would you recommend analyzing additional alternatives? If you represent one of the environmental or historic preservation groups opposed to the crossing, do you think you could successfully challenge the Corps's proposed alternatives analysis for being unduly narrow? Such a challenge, if you bring it, would not be ripe until the Corps issues a FONSI or a record of decision. That means you have time for additional advocacy before seeking judicial redress. What will you do during that time? And if you represent Dominion, how might you advocate for the Corps to adopt your preferred position?

As you consider the question, please also assume that the Corps has decided to prepare an EIS. Issues do sometimes arise about the appropriate scope and depth of an alternatives analysis in an EA, but for purposes of this problem, you do not need to confront those issues.

---

40 C.F.R. § 1502.14. Alternatives including the proposed action

This section is the heart of the environmental impact statement. Based on the information and analysis presented in the sections on the Affected Environment (§ 1502.15) and the Environmental Consequences (§ 1502.16), it should present the environmental impacts of the proposal and the alternatives in comparative form, thus sharply defining the issues and providing a clear basis for choice among options by the decisionmaker and the public. In this section agencies shall:

(a) Rigorously explore and objectively evaluate all reasonable alternatives, and for alternatives which were eliminated from detailed study, briefly discuss the reasons for their having been eliminated.

(b) Devote substantial treatment to each alternative considered in detail including the proposed action so that reviewers may evaluate their comparative merits.

(c) Include reasonable alternatives not within the jurisdiction of the lead agency.

(d) Include the alternative of no action.

(e) Identify the agency's preferred alternative or alternatives, if one or more exists, in the draft statement and identify such alternative in the final statement unless another law prohibits the expression of such a preference.

(f) Include appropriate mitigation measures not already included in the proposed action or alternatives.

Challenges to NEPA alternatives analyses (and to alternatives analyses prepared pursuant to state environmental assessment laws) have produced an abundance of court decisions. Two particularly well-known decisions appear below. The first decision reflects one general trend: as has often happened with these kinds of claims, the plaintiffs lost. But, as the second decision illustrates, challenges to alternatives analyses are not always unsuccessful.

Citizens Against Burlington v. Busey
938 F.2d 190 (D.C. Cir. 1991)

■ CLARENCE THOMAS, CIRCUIT JUDGE:

The city of Toledo decided to expand one of its airports, and the Federal Aviation Administration decided to approve the city's plan. In this petition for review of the FAA's order, an alliance of people who live near the airport contends that the FAA has violated several environmental statutes and regulations. We hold that the FAA has complied with all of the statutes and all but one of the regulations.

I.

The Toledo Express Airport, object of the controversy in this case, lies about twenty-five miles to the west of downtown Toledo. Half a mile to the southwest of the airport, surrounded by four highways and intersected by three more, lies the Oak Openings Preserve Metropark, used by joggers, skiers, and birders, and site of one of the world's twelve communities of oak savannas. * * * The Toledo-Lucas County Port Authority, one of the intervenors, wants to make the city of Toledo a cargo hub. Burlington Air Express, Inc., the other intervenor, wants to move its operations to Toledo. [Opponents of the project] have formed Citizens Against Burlington, Inc. to stop them.

* * * On May 11, 1990, the FAA published a final environmental impact statement. The first chapter of the statement explained that the Port Authority needed the FAA's approval for its plan to expand the Toledo Express Airport and described the role in that process that Congress meant for the agency to play. The second chapter of the EIS reviewed the particulars of the Port Authority's plan, listed the fourteen separate federal statutes and regulations that applied to the Port Authority's proposal, briefly described some alternatives to acting on the Port Authority's plan, and explained why the agency had decided not to discuss those possibilities more fully. The FAA then concluded that it had to consider in depth the environmental impacts of only two alternatives: the approval of the Port Authority's plan to expand the airport, and no action. * * *

* * * This case concerns the most important responsibility that NEPA demands—that an agency reviewing proposals for action prepare an environmental impact statement, and, more specifically, that the agency discuss in its statement alternatives to the action proposed. We consider here whether the FAA has complied with NEPA in publishing an

environmental impact statement that discussed in depth two alternatives: approving the expansion of the Toledo Express Airport, and not approving the expansion of the Toledo Express Airport.

(1)

Federal agencies must prepare environmental impact statements when they contemplate "major Federal actions significantly affecting the quality of the human environment." NEPA § 102(2)(C), 42 U.S.C. § 4332(2)(C). An EIS must discuss, among other things, "alternatives to the proposed action," NEPA § 102(2)(C)(iii), 42 U.S.C. § 4332(2)(C)(iii), and the discussion of alternatives forms "the heart of the environmental impact statement." 40 C.F.R. § 1502.14; *see Alaska v. Andrus,* 580 F.2d 465, 474 (D.C. Cir.), *vacated in part as moot sub nom. Western Oil & Gas Ass'n v. Alaska,* 439 U.S. 922 (1978).

The problem for agencies is that "the term 'alternatives' is not self-defining." *Vermont Yankee Nuclear Power Corp. v. Natural Resources Defense Council, Inc.,* 435 U.S. 519, 551 (1978). * * *

Recognizing the harm that an unbounded understanding of alternatives might cause, *see id.* at 549–55, CEQ regulations oblige agencies to discuss only alternatives that are feasible, or (much the same thing) reasonable. 40 C.F.R. §§ 1502.14(a)–(c), 1508.25(b)(2); *see* Forty Most Asked Questions Concerning CEQ's NEPA Regulations, 46 Fed. Reg. 18,026, 18,026 (1981) [hereinafter *Forty Questions*]. But the adjective "reasonable" is no more self-defining than the noun that it modifies. Consider two possible alternatives to our nuclear reactor in Vernon. Funding research in cold fusion might be an unreasonable alternative by virtue of the theory's scientific implausibility. But licensing a reactor in Lake Placid, New York might also be unreasonable, even though it passes some objective test of scientific worth. In either case, the proposed alternative is reasonable only if it will bring about the ends of the federal action—only if it will do what the licensing of the reactor in Vernon is meant to do. *See City of New York v. Department of Transp.,* 715 F.2d 732, 742–43 (2d Cir. 1983) (construing NEPA § 102(2)(E), 42 U.S.C. § 4332(2)(E) (discussion of alternatives in environmental assessments)), *cert. denied,* 465 U.S. 1055 (1984); *see also City of Angoon v. Hodel,* 803 F.2d 1016, 1021 (9th Cir. 1986) (per curiam) ("When the purpose is to accomplish one thing, it makes no sense to consider the alternative ways by which another thing might be achieved."), *cert. denied,* 484 U.S. 870 (1987). If licensing the Vernon reactor is meant to help supply energy to New England, licensing a reactor in northern New York might make equal sense. If licensing the Vernon reactor is meant as well to stimulate the Vernon job market, licensing a reactor in Lake Placid would be far less effective. The goals of an action delimit the universe of the action's reasonable alternatives.

We have held before that an agency bears the responsibility for deciding which alternatives to consider in an environmental impact statement. *See North Slope Borough v. Andrus*, 642 F.2d 589, 601 (D.C. Cir. 1980). We have also held that an agency need follow only a "rule of reason" in preparing an EIS, *see Natural Resources Defense Council, Inc. v. Morton*, 458 F.2d 827, 834, 837 (D.C. Cir. 1972), and that this rule of reason governs "both *which* alternatives the agency must discuss, and the *extent* to which it must discuss them," *Alaska v. Andrus,* 580 F.2d at 475; *see Allison v. Department of Transp.*, 908 F.2d 1024, 1031 (D.C. Cir. 1990). It follows that the agency thus bears the responsibility for defining at the outset the objectives of an action. *See* City of Angoon v. Hodel, 803 F.2d at 1021; *cf.* 40 C.F.R. § 1502.13. As the phrase "rule of reason" suggests, we review an agency's compliance with NEPA's requirements deferentially. We uphold an agency's definition of objectives so long as the objectives that the agency chooses are reasonable, and we uphold its discussion of alternatives so long as the alternatives are reasonable and the agency discusses them in reasonable detail.

We realize, as we stated before, that the word "reasonable" is not self-defining. Deference, however, does not mean dormancy, and the rule of reason does not give agencies license to fulfill their own prophecies, whatever the parochial impulses that drive them. Environmental impact statements take time and cost money. Yet an agency may not define the objectives of its action in terms so unreasonably narrow that only one alternative from among the environmentally benign ones in the agency's power would accomplish the goals of the agency's action, and the EIS would become a foreordained formality. *See City of New York v. Department of Transp.*, 715 F.2d at 743. Nor may an agency frame its goals in terms so unreasonably broad that an infinite number of alternatives would accomplish those goals and the project would collapse under the weight of the possibilities.

Instead, agencies must look hard at the factors relevant to the definition of purpose. When an agency is asked to sanction a specific plan, *see* 40 C.F.R. § 1508.18(b)(4), the agency should take into account the needs and goals of the parties involved in the application. *See, e.g., Louisiana Wildlife Fed'n v. York*, 761 F.2d 1044, 1048 (5th Cir. 1985) (per curiam); *Roosevelt Campobello Int'l Park Comm'n v. EPA,* 684 F.2d 1041, 1046–47 (1st Cir. 1982). Perhaps more importantly, an agency should always consider the views of Congress, expressed, to the extent that the agency can determine them, in the agency's statutory authorization to act, as well as in other congressional directives. *See City of New York v. Department of Transp.*, 715 F.2d at 743–45 (Congress instructed the Department of Transportation to create safety regulations for carrying nuclear fuel by interstate highway; the Department was not required to discuss the unreasonable alternative of carrying nuclear fuel around New

York City by barge); *cf. Izaak Walton League of Am. v. Marsh*, 655 F.2d 346, 372 (D.C. Cir.) ("When Congress has enacted legislation approving a specific project, the implementing agency's obligation to discuss alternatives in its [EIS] is relatively narrow."), *cert. denied*, 454 U.S. 1092 (1981).

Once an agency has considered the relevant factors, it must define goals for its action that fall somewhere within the range of reasonable choices. We review that choice, like all agency decisions to which we owe deference, on the grounds that the agency itself has advanced. *See SEC v. Chenery Corp.*, 332 U.S. 194, 196 (1947).

(2)

The EIS * * * describes five alternatives: approving the Port Authority's plan for expanding Toledo Express, approving other geometric configurations for expanding Toledo Express, approving other ways of channelling airplane traffic at Toledo Express, no action by the agency at all, and approving plans for other airports both in the Toledo metropolitan area and out of it, including Baer Field in Fort Wayne. Finally, the EIS briefly explains why the agency eliminated all the alternatives but the first and the fourth. See 40 C.F.R. § 1502.14(a).

* * * The FAA's reasoning fully supports its decision to evaluate only the preferred and do-nothing alternatives. The agency first examined Congress's views on how this country is to build its civilian airports. As the agency explained, Congress has told the FAA to nurture aspiring cargo hubs. *See* AAIA § 502(a)(7), (11), 49 U.S.C. app. § 2201(a)(7), (11). At the same time, however, Congress has also said that the free market, not an ersatz Gosplan for aviation, should determine the siting of the nation's airports. * * * Congress has expressed its intent by statute, and the FAA took both of Congress's messages seriously.

The FAA also took into account the Port Authority's reasons for wanting a cargo hub in Toledo. In recent years, more than fifty major companies have left the Toledo metropolitan area, and with them, over seven thousand jobs. The Port Authority expects the cargo hub at Toledo Express to create immediately more than two hundred permanent and six hundred part-time jobs with a total payroll value of more than $10 million. After three years, according to the Port Authority, the hub should create directly more than one thousand permanent jobs at the airport and one hundred and fifty other, airport-related jobs. The University of Toledo estimates that the new Toledo Express will contribute at least $42 million to the local economy after one full year of operation and nearly $68 million per year after three. In addition, the Port Authority expects the expanded airport, and Burlington's presence there, to attract other companies to Toledo. All of those factors, the Port

Authority hopes, will lead to a renaissance in the Toledo metropolitan region.

Having thought hard about these appropriate factors, the FAA defined the goal for its action as helping to launch a new cargo hub in Toledo and thereby helping to fuel the Toledo economy. The agency then eliminated from detailed discussion the alternatives that would not accomplish this goal. Each of the different geometric configurations would mean technological problems and extravagant costs. So would plans to route traffic differently at Toledo Express, or to build a hub at one of the other airports in the city of Toledo. None of the airports outside of the Toledo area would serve the purpose of the agency's action. The FAA thus evaluated the environmental impacts of the only proposal that might reasonably accomplish that goal-approving the construction and operation of a cargo hub at Toledo Express. It did so with the thoroughness required by law. *See* 40 C.F.R. § 1502.16.

We conclude that the FAA acted reasonably in defining the purpose of its action, in eliminating alternatives that would not achieve it, and in discussing (with the required do-nothing option) the proposal that would. The agency has therefore complied with NEPA.

(3)

Citizens agrees that the FAA need only discuss reasonable, not all, alternatives to Toledo Express. Relying on *Van Abbema v. Fornell,* 807 F.2d 633 (7th Cir. 1986), however, Citizens argues that "the evaluation of 'alternatives' mandated by NEPA is to be an evaluation of alternative means to accomplish the *general* goal of an action; it is not an evaluation of the alternative means by which a particular applicant can reach his goals." *Id.* at 638 (construing NEPA § 102(2)(E), 42 U.S.C. § 4332(2)(E)). According to Citizens, the "general goal" of the Port Authority's proposal is to build a permanent cargo hub for Burlington. Since, in Citizens' view, Fort Wayne (and perhaps Peoria) will accomplish this general goal just as well as Toledo, if not better, Baer Field is a reasonable alternative to Toledo Express, and the FAA should have discussed it in depth. Since it did not, this court should force the FAA to prepare a new (or supplemental) environmental impact statement.

We see two critical flaws in *Van Abbema,* and therefore in Citizens' argument. The first is that the *Van Abbema* court misconstrued the language of NEPA. *Van Abbema* involved a private businessman who had applied to the Army Corps of Engineers for permission to build a place to "transload" coal from trucks to barges. *See* 807 F.2d at 635. The panel decided that the Corps had to survey "feasible alternatives . . . to the applicant's proposal," or alternative ways of accomplishing "the general goal [of] deliver[ing] coal from mine to utility." *Id.* at 638; *see also Trout Unlimited v. Morton,* 509 F.2d 1276, 1286 (9th Cir. 1974). In commanding agencies to discuss "alternatives to the proposed action," however, NEPA plainly refers to alternatives to the "major *Federal* actions significantly affecting the quality of the human environment," and not to alternatives to the applicant's proposal. NEPA § 102(2)(C), 42 U.S.C. § 4332(2)(C) (emphasis added). An agency cannot redefine the goals of the proposal that arouses the call for action; it must evaluate alternative ways of achieving *its* goals, shaped by the application at issue and by the function that the agency plays in the decisional process. Congress did expect agencies to consider an applicant's wants when the agency formulates the goals of its own proposed action. Congress did not expect agencies to determine for the applicant what the goals of the applicant's proposal should be.

The second problem with *Van Abbema* lies in the court's assertion that an agency must evaluate "alternative means to accomplish the general goal of an action," 807 F.2d at 638 (emphasis deleted)-a statement that troubles us even if we assume that the panel was alluding to the general goals of the federal action instead of to the goals of the private proposal. Left unanswered in *Van Abbema* and Citizens' brief (and at oral argument) is why and how to distinguish general goals from specific ones and just who does the distinguishing. *Someone* has to define the purpose of the agency action. Implicit in *Van Abbema* is that the body responsible is the reviewing court. As we explained, however, NEPA and binding case law provide otherwise. * * *

■ BUCKLEY, CIRCUIT JUDGE, dissenting in part:

Burlington Air Express and the Federal Aviation Administration might be right: On substantial economic and environmental balance, Toledo Express Airport may well be the only suitable site for Burlington's air cargo hub. The public cannot know for certain, however, and neither can the FAA. By refusing to inquire into the feasibility of sites rejected by Burlington, the agency sidestepped its obligation to prepare "a detailed statement ... on ... alternatives to the proposed action." 42 U.S.C. § 4332(2)(C) (1988). The majority endorses this evasion. I cannot, and therefore I dissent from part II(A) of the majority opinion. While "the concept of 'alternatives' is an evolving one," *Vermont Yankee Nuclear Power Corp. v. NRDC,* 435 U.S. 519, 552 (1978), judicial evolution may not reduce it to a vermiform appendix.

I.

In a narrow sense, the only federal action that is involved when a non-federal applicant seeks federal approval or funding is the agency's decision to grant or deny the applicant's request. No one disputes, however, that the agency's environmental impact statement ("EIS") must inquire into reasonable alternatives to the applicant's proposal. The only controversy is over the nature of the alternatives that the EIS should consider. *See, e.g., Friends of the River v. FERC,* 720 F.2d 93, 104–05 (D.C. Cir. 1983) (permit to operate hydroelectric plant; alternative of purchasing power from other producers); *Mason County Med. Ass'n v. Knebel,* 563 F.2d 256, 262–63 (6th Cir. 1977) (permit to build coal-fired steam electric generator; alternatives of nuclear, geothermal, conservation, purchased power, and others); *North Carolina v. FPC,* 533 F.2d 702, 707 (D.C. Cir.) (permit to build hydroelectric plant; alternative of conservation), *vacated on other grounds,* 429 U.S. 891 (1976).

* * * I cannot fault the FAA for the attention given Burlington and its preferences. While both Toledo and Burlington are indispensable to the enterprise, Burlington is plainly the dominant partner; its requirements and desires shaped the project from the start. As the agency points out in its Record of Decision ("ROD"), "[t]he demand for this project is clearly based on a business decision by Burlington Air Express and the interest of a local airport sponsor, the Toledo-Lucas County Port Authority, in accommodating and facilitating this decision." ROD at 29.

I do fault the agency for failing to attend to its own business, which is to examine all alternatives "that are practical or feasible from the technical and economic standpoint . . . rather than simply desirable from the standpoint of the applicant." Forty Most Asked Questions Concerning CEQ's National Environmental Policy Act Regulations ("Forty Questions"), 46 Fed. Reg. 18,026, 18,027 (1981) (emphasis omitted). As far as I can tell, the FAA never questioned Burlington's assertions that of the ones considered, Toledo Express is the only airport suitable to its purposes. Instead, the agency simply accepted Burlington's "Toledo-or-bust" position. * * *

I do not suggest that Burlington is untrustworthy, only that the FAA had the duty under NEPA to exercise a degree of skepticism in dealing with self-serving statements from a prime beneficiary of the project. It may well be that none of the sixteen other alternatives examined by Burlington and its consultants could be converted into a viable air cargo hub at acceptable cost. That, however, was something that the FAA should have determined for itself instead of accepting as a given. Under NEPA, "the federal agency must itself determine what is reasonably available." *Trinity Episcopal School Corp. v. Romney,* 523 F.2d 88, 94 (2d Cir. 1975); *see Van Abbema v. Fornell,* 807 F.2d 633, 642 (7th Cir. 1986) (condemning agency's "blind reliance on material prepared by the applicant"). By allowing the FAA to abandon this requirement, the majority establishes a precedent that will permit an applicant and a third-party beneficiary of federal action to define the limits of the EIS inquiry and thus to frustrate one of the principal safeguards of the NEPA process, the mandatory consideration of reasonable alternatives. * * *

III.

The EIS requirement "seeks to ensure that each agency decision maker has before him and takes into proper account all possible approaches to a particular project . . . which would alter the environmental impact and the cost-benefit balance." *Calvert Cliffs' Coordinating Comm., Inc. v. AEC,* 449 F.2d 1109, 1114 (D.C. Cir. 1971). With its uncritical dismissal of alternatives and its myopic view of economic consequences, the EIS here fell short of this objective. As a result, we cannot be confident that in approving Toledo's applications, the FAA took the pertinent environmental as well as economic and technical considerations into the balance. And that, of course, is the purpose of the National Environmental Policy Act.

Simmons v. U.S. Army Corps of Engineers
120 F.3d 664 (7th Cir. 1997)

■ CUDAHY, CIRCUIT JUDGE.

Eight years have elapsed since the City of Marion, Illinois, first proposed building a new water reservoir in the southernmost tip of Illinois. In those eight years a tale has unfolded that is all too familiar. Lawsuits have stopped the project short; the case has visited the district court twice; and Marion still is no closer to a new water supply. As is routine in American administrative law, the litigation has little to do with what anybody really cares about. One side wants a dam built and a new lake created, and the other does not. Instead, the dispute, now in and out of federal court for five years, has centered on procedures-whether the U.S. Army Corps of Engineers fulfilled its procedural obligations under federal environmental law. All this is true. But the case provides a textbook vindication of the wisdom of Congress in insisting that agencies follow those procedures in the first place.

I.

* * *

NEPA mandates a searching inquiry into alternatives, but says nothing about which to choose. It binds federal officials to justify their plans in public, after a full airing of alternatives. It thus blends a faith in technocratic expertise with a trust in democracy. Officials must think through the consequences of-and alternatives to-their contemplated acts; and citizens get a chance to hear and consider the rationales the officials offer. *Robertson v. Methow Valley Citizens Council*, 490 U.S. 332, 349 (1989). But, if a federal agency has heard all the objections to a plan and considered all the sensible options before it, the agency has fulfilled its duty. *Robertson*, 490 U.S. at 350.

When a federal agency prepares an Environmental Impact Statement (EIS), it must consider "all reasonable alternatives" in depth. 40 C.F.R. § 1502.14. No decision is more important than delimiting what these "reasonable alternatives" are. That choice, and the ensuing analysis, forms "the heart of the environmental impact statement." 40 C.F.R. § 1502.14. To make that decision, the first thing an agency must define is the project's purpose. *See Citizens Against Burlington, Inc. v. Busey,* 938 F.2d 190, 195–96 (D.C. Cir. 1991). The broader the purpose, the wider the range of alternatives; and vice versa. The "purpose" of a project is a slippery concept, susceptible of no hard-and-fast definition. One obvious way for an agency to slip past the strictures of NEPA is to contrive a purpose so slender as to define competing "reasonable alternatives" out of consideration (and even out of existence). The federal courts cannot condone an agency's frustration of Congressional will. If the agency constricts the definition of the project's purpose and thereby excludes what truly are reasonable alternatives, the EIS cannot fulfill its role. Nor can the agency satisfy the Act. 42 U.S.C. § 4332(2)(E).

We are confronted here with an example of this defining-away of alternatives. In 1989, the City of Marion applied to the U.S. Army Corps of Engineers (the Corps) for permission to build a dam and reservoir, as required by § 404 of the Clean Water Act, 33 U.S.C. § 1344. The dam would block up Sugar Creek, a free-flowing stream in southern Illinois running seven miles southeast of Marion. Marion envisioned that the resulting Sugar Creek Lake would supply water not just to Marion, but to the Lake of Egypt Water District, which encompasses six counties and 15,000 rural customers. Sugar Creek Lake would drown a substantial area, with the usual environmental effects of drowning, including the transformation or obliteration of the riverine habitats of several species.

We discuss the details of the project's history below, but the case boils down to no more than those bare facts. From the beginning, Marion and the Corps have defined the project's purpose as supplying two users (Marion and the Water District) from a single source-namely, a new lake. Accordingly, when the Corps prepared an environmental impact statement, it confined the analysis to single-source alternatives. And therein lies the difficulty. At no time has the Corps studied whether this single-source idea is the best one-or even a good one. Marion and the Lake of Egypt Water District share a common problem, a thirst for water. From this fact the Corps adduces the imperative for a common solution. We disagree. A single source may well be the best solution to the putative water shortages of Marion and the Lake of Egypt Water District. The Corps' error is in accepting this parameter as a given. To conclude that a common problem *necessarily* demands a common solution defies common sense. We conclude that the U.S. Army Corps of Engineers defined an impermissibly narrow purpose for the contemplated project. The Corps therefore failed to examine the full range of reasonable alternatives and vitiated the EIS. We reverse. * * *

III.

Logic and law dictate that every time an agency prepares an environmental impact statement, it must answer three questions in order. First, what is the purpose of the proposed project (major federal action)? Second, given that purpose, what are the reasonable alternatives to the project? And third, to what extent should the agency explore each particular reasonable alternative? *See City of Carmel-by-the-Sea v. United States Dep't of Transportation*, 95 F.3d 892, 903 (9th Cir. 1996); *City of Grapevine, Texas v. Dep't of Transportation*, 17 F.3d 1502, 1506 (D.C. Cir. 1994). These are questions for an agency (the Corps) to resolve in the first instance. We owe and accord deference to the Corps on whether the Corps resolved those three questions in a permissible way. "[I]t is not our role to second-guess" the Corps. *Van Abbema*, 807 F.2d at 636. We ensure only that "the Corps followed required procedures, evaluated relevant factors and reached a reasoned decision." *Id.*

The Corps rigged the environmental impact statement on the question of purpose, contend the plaintiffs. The Corps defined the project's purpose as finding or creating a single source to supply both Marion and the Lake of Egypt Water District. (Actually, the Corps never did so explicitly; the district court had to "fill in the blanks" to ascribe this purpose to the Corps.) The Corps' imputed definition, the plaintiffs say, is unreasonable: the project's real purpose is supplying Marion and the Water District with more water, and there are reasonable alternatives to that beyond relying on a single reservoir. Marion, for instance, could hook its water-treatment plant up to an existing pipeline stemming from Rend Lake and lying only seven miles away. (Marion's water-treatment plant is twelve miles away from Sugar Creek Lake.)

As its first line of defense, the Corps essentially passes the buck to Marion. Marion wanted a single reservoir to supply it and the Lake of Egypt Water District. Since Marion is the proposer and will construct the project, the Corps must accept its definition. This is a losing position in the Seventh Circuit. Over a decade ago, we held that "the evaluation of 'alternatives' mandated by NEPA is to be an evaluation of alternative means to accomplish the general goal of an action." *Van Abbema*, 807 F.2d at 638 (emphasis added); 40 C.F.R. § 1502.13 ("The [EIS] shall briefly specify the *underlying* purpose and need") (CEQ regulations) (emphasis added). The general goal of Marion's application is to supply water to Marion and the Water District-*not* to build (or find) a single reservoir to supply that water. Indeed, in *Van Abbema*, we specifically rejected the Corps' present position. An agency cannot restrict its analysis to those "alternative means by which a particular applicant can reach *his* goals." *Van Abbema*, 807 F.2d at 638 (emphasis added); *contra*,

Busey, 938 F.2d at 198–99. This is precisely what the Corps did in this case. The Corps has "the duty under NEPA to exercise a degree of skepticism in dealing with self-serving statements from a prime beneficiary of the project." *Busey,* 938 F.2d at 209 (Buckley, J., dissenting). And that is exactly what the Corps has not shown in its wholesale acceptance of Marion's definition of purpose.

We turn then to probe the reasonableness of the Corps' looking only to single-source alternatives to damming Sugar Creek. Here the Corps argues that Marion and the Lake of Egypt Water District share the same problem-a shortage of water-and that they are contiguous. Hence, a single source is the obvious solution. Maybe, even probably, the Corps is right. Alternatives might fail abjectly on economic grounds. But the Corps and, more important, the public cannot know what the facts are until the Corps has tested its presumption. It is axiomatic that the Corps need not examine every conceivable alternative. Identifying, assessing and comparing alternatives costs time and money, Metropolitan Edison v. People *vs. Nuclear Energy*, 460 U.S. 766, 776 (1983), and an agency should focus its energies only on the potentially feasible, not the unworkable. 40 C.F.R. §§ 1502.14(a)–(c), 1508.25(b)(2). As a matter of logic, however, supplying Marion and the Water District from two or more sources is not absurd-which it must be to justify the Corps' failure to examine the idea at all. In fact, the plaintiffs have advanced at least one concrete alternative that seems reasonable: for Marion to build a shorter pipeline that would ultimately feed water from the extant *Rend Lake. Alaska Wilderness Recreation & Tourism v. Morrison*, 67 F.3d 723, 729 (9th Cir. 1995) (" 'The existence of a viable but unexamined alternative renders an environmental impact statement inadequate.' " (citation omitted)). What other alternatives exist we do not know, because the Corps has not looked. Perhaps the Corps is relying on a contract between Marion and the Water District for Marion to supply the Water District with water *if* it succeeds in damming Sugar Creek. But this condition depends on meeting environmental requirements, which, in turn, demand exploration of alternatives free of contractual arrangements. The public interest in the environment cannot be limited by private agreements. * * *

IV.

If NEPA mandates anything, it mandates this: a federal agency cannot ram through a project before first weighing the pros and cons of the alternatives. In this case, the officials of the Army Corps of Engineers executed an end-run around NEPA's core requirement. By focusing on the single-source idea, the Corps never looked at an entire category of reasonable alternatives and thereby ruined its environmental impact statement. We presume that the Corps' failure to satisfy NEPA was inadvertent, notwithstanding the Corps' failure to heed the admonitions of Judge Foreman on this point. We believe that Judge Foreman was right at the time of his decision, and remains right.

Before an agency prepares an environmental impact statement—and, sometimes, before it prepares an environmental assessment—it will often conduct a preliminary analysis of alternatives, just as the FAA did in the *Citizens Against Burlington* case. That preliminary analysis helps inform the development of NEPA documents, and it may also assist the action agency in making decisions under other laws, as well as informing other agencies. For the proposed James River utility crossing, that preliminary analysis came in multiple steps. Dominion submitted a thirty-one page alternatives analysis, backed with extensive appendices, to the Corps. The Corps then prepared a shorter summary of alternatives, which largely adopts the analysis and conclusions of the Dominion study, and which appears, in heavily excerpted form, below.

USACE Preliminary Alternatives Conclusions White Paper

RE: NAO–2012–0080/13–V0408

October 1, 2015

The Norfolk District Regulatory Branch (Corps) is currently reviewing an application from Dominion Virginia Power (Dominion) who proposes to construct a new high voltage aerial electrical transmission line, known as the Surry-Skiffes Creek-Whealton project. The proposed project consists of three components; (1) Surry-Skiffes Creek 500 kilovolt (kV) aerial transmission line, (2) Skiffes Creek 500 kV–230 kV–115 kV Switching Station, and (3) Skiffes Creek-Whealton 230 kV aerial transmission line. In total, the proposed project will permanently impact 2,712 square feet (0.06 acres) of subaqueous river bottom and 281 square feet (0.01 acres) of non-tidal wetlands, and convert 0.56 acres of palustrine forested wetlands to scrub shrub non-tidal wetlands.

* * * In response to several public notices the Corps has received numerous comments both supporting and in opposition to the project. Opposition to the project is largely focused on the potential impacts to historic and cultural resources. Many commenters have suggested Dominion explore alternatives to the proposed action including burial or relocation of the proposed line.

As part of its initial application materials Dominion provided information on alternatives to the proposed work. At the request of the Corps, and in response to comments, Dominion has provided further information on alternatives. The Corps has considered Dominion's alternatives analysis and supplemental information as well as information on alternatives supplied through public, agency, and consulting party comments. The Corps has also considered the basic purpose and need for the project. We have evaluated each alternative against the purpose and need and review criteria in light of all information supplied to date. Following is a general summary of our preliminary findings:

Project Need: Dominion currently supplies power to the North Hampton Roads Load Area (NHRLA) via generation from the Yorktown Power Station (approximately 1,141 Mw) and two transmission corridors that deliver power into the service area. * * * Due to environmental restrictions Dominion can only operate Yorktown 3 intermittently (8% of year) and the unit has an approximately 3 day start up time. Additionally, Dominion anticipates retiring Yorktown 3 by 2020.

With current configurations and without additional power input into the service area by 2019, Dominion would be unable to maintain compliance with the North American Electric Reliability Corporation (NERC) standards. The NHRLA is currently dependent on power generated from the Yorktown Power Station (approximately 1,141 Mw) and two transmission corridors that deliver power into the service area. Dominion's power flow studies project the demand for electricity in this area will grow by 8% between 2015 and 2020. This increase will cause a load growth that will exceed Dominion's ability to remain compliant with NERC standards given the current configuration. NERC has confirmed that these standards are absolute requirements that have no waiver provision. NERC has the authority to impose fines of up to $1 million per day, per violation.

In December 2011, the United States Environmental Protection Agency (EPA) passed the Mercury Air and Toxics Standards (MATS) Rule requiring power generation facilities to reduce toxic air pollutant emissions. Dominion's Yorktown Power Station, specifically Yorktown Units 1 and 2, is subject to these required reductions. The MATS rule requires that facilities be compliant by April 2015. However, facilities may request a one-year extension from the state regulatory agency with jurisdiction over the area where the facility is located—here, the Virginia Department of Environmental Quality. After April 2016, the Environmental Protection Agency can exercise its enforcement discretion to allow facilities to operate for up to one additional year under an Administrative Order. To achieve compliance with MATS, Dominion must retrofit, repower or decommission Yorktown Units 1 and 2. EPA has confirmed that this interpretation of timelines is accurate.

Project Purpose:

(1) Basic: To continue providing the North Hampton Roads Load Area (NHRLA) with reliable, cost effective, bulk electrical service consistent with mandatory North American Electric Reliability Corporation (NERC) Reliability Standards for transmission facilities and planning criteria.

(2) Overall: Provide sustainable electrical capacity into the NHRLA in a manner that addresses future load growth deficiencies, replaces aging infrastructure, complies with Federal regulations, including MATS, and maintains compliance with NERC Reliability Standards.

Alternatives Considerations:

Dominion has provided information on various alternatives to the proposed action explored as part of its initial project evaluation as well as in response to Corps inquiries and public comment. These include generation alternatives, upgrades to existing facilities, use of existing transmission lines, and the construction of new transmission at varying capacities.

* * *

Decommission: Loss of the generation capacity of Yorktown 1 and 2 creates violations of NERC Category B, C and D. Absent an improvement to the load area upon implementation of the EPA MATS Rule and the retirement of Yorktown Units 1 and 2, Dominion will be required to implement pre-contingency load shedding (i.e., rolling blackouts) in the NHRLA to prevent the possibility of cascading outages impacting the reliability of the interconnected transmission system. The load flow modeling evidence establishes a need for new electric infrastructure to address approaching reliability violations projected for Dominion's transmission system.

Retrofitting: Retrofitting of the Yorktown facility alone would not increase capacity and would be cost prohibitive. The Yorktown units are nearly 60 years old and would require substantial structural and environmental upgrades to become compliant with MATS. Dominion estimates that these upgrades would cost over $1 billion. Additionally, since retrofitting would not substantially increase output capacity, additional projects would be needed before 2019 to avoid NERC non-compliance.

Repowering: Dominion examined the potential to repower some or all of the Yorktown units to natural gas. There is currently no sufficient gas supply to support year-round operation of gas-fired generation at Yorktown and significant expansion of the regional gas supply would be required. Currently, the region does not have adequate infrastructure to support this expansion and there is no certainty when this infrastructure may be in place.

New Generation: Upon the determination that Yorktown Units 1 and 2 should be retired, Dominion considered new generation options throughout the area. Options such as combined-cycle, combustion turbine and coal generation were considered. Also considered were small scale generation sources such as biomass, wind and solar. A standalone generation solution was found to be $633 million to satisfy 2016 NERC reliability criteria. An additional $722 million would be required to provide sufficient generation by 2021, bringing the total cost of a standalone generation solution to an estimated $1.3 billion. Stand-alone generation would also face siting, permitting and construction timeline constraints.

[Eds.: we have deleted discussion of several alternative routes, each of which the Corps concluded would not be feasible.]

Chickahominy-Skiffes Creek 500 kV: The Chickahominy-Skiffes Creek alternative utilizes a ROW currently owned by Dominion that extends approximately 37.9 miles from the Chickahominy Substation in Charles City County to the proposed Skiffes Creek Switching Station in James City County. Approximately 13 miles of this route is existing, cleared ROW while the remaining 24.9 miles is unimproved ROW that would require clearing for construction of the proposed line. The Chickahominy-Skiffes Creek 500 kV resolves the NERC reliability violations due to the retirement of Yorktown Units 1 and 2 by 2016.

Surry-Skiffes Creek 500 kV Underground (Alternating Current): The placement of an underground Alternating Current (AC) 500 kV line of this capacity is on the cutting edge of technology. Underground lines in general present reliability and operational concerns, as locating and repairing damaged underground lines is significantly more difficult than locating and repairing overhead lines. Existing underground projects were examined for comparison while evaluating the feasibility of this alternative. This comparison supported information supplied by Dominion regarding the concerns with this alternative.

Surry-Skiffes Creek 500 kV Underground (High Voltage Direct Current): An HVDC alternative would require the conversion of AC power to DC, the installation of an underground HVDC crossing in the James River, and the conversion of DC power back to AC. This alternative is presented with routing and siting constraints, land acquisition requirements, reliability concerns, cost, increased environmental and cultural impacts and time constraints.

Surry-Skiffes Creek-Whealton 500 kV Overhead (Dominion's Preferred Alternative): This alternative consists of three components; (1) Surry-Skiffes Creek 500 kilovolt (kV) aerial transmission line, (2) Skiffes Creek

500 kV–230 kV–115 kV Switching Station, and (3) Skiffes Creek-Whealton 230 kV aerial transmission line. This alternative fully resolves the NERC criteria violations with the retirement of Yorktown Units 1 and 2.

* * *

Hybrid Alternatives: Several combinations of retrofitting, repowering and retirement combined with transmission construction were also evaluated. These included several configurations of 230 kV lines, both overhead and underground, combined with retention of generation at Yorktown. None of these combination alternatives can resolve all NERC Reliability Violations in 2016 without the construction of additional transmission or generation.

Save The James Alliance Alt Solution: This alternative includes the closing of Yorktown 1 and continued operation of Yorktown 2, while building an underground 230kV line across James River, and constructing future generation facilities. Continued operation of Yorktown 2 in its present condition is not compliant with MATS. This hybrid alternative would require Dominion to run Yorktown 2 in violation of MATS indefinitely or long enough to retrofit or repower one or both of the Yorktown Units or to develop new generation. For this reason, this alternative presents the same obstacles of retrofitting, repowering and new generation as discussed above.

Demand-Side Management (DSM): Rather than approaching power usage from the supply side, DSM resources include activities and programs undertaken to influence the amount and timing of electricity use, as well as market purchases from outside power generators to reduce overall demand. DSM resources are already included in the transmission planning process. Additional amounts cannot be assumed to be available to address NERC reliability violations due to transient and voluntary nature of these resources.

* * *

Preliminary Findings:

The Corps fully considered all information supplied to date from both Dominion and the public. Additionally, Corps Electrical Engineers have evaluated the information for technical accuracy. In screening the various alternatives, the Corps focused on the ability to sustain sufficient power supply to meet current demand and predicted future growth, existing technology, implementation cost and ability to maintain/achieve compliance with federal laws.

At this time, most alternatives, including Dominion's preferred alternative would potentially require Dominion to operate Yorktown in violation of MATS in order to ensure uninterrupted service to NHRLA.

However, there is substantial difference among the alternatives in the length of time of noncompliance. Increasing time of non-compliance increases Dominion's exposure to legal action and increasing fines thereby, increasing cost and affecting the practicability of alternatives.

Based on information supplied to date, many of these alternatives could be eliminated based on cost alone. The costs used in this analysis include alignment acquisition and construction. Dominion's preferred alternative is estimated to cost $180 million to fully implement. The next lowest cost alternative is the Chickahominy-Skiffes-Whealton 500kV alternative at approximately $265 million. Other alternatives have substantially greater costs but also present technical challenges and/or substantially increase the time Dominion would be non-compliant with regulations.

Therefore, based on information presented to date, our preliminary finding is that two alternatives appear to meet the project purpose while reasonably complying with the evaluation criteria. These are Surry-Skiffes-Whealton 500 kV OH (AC) (Dominion's Preferred) and Chickahominy-Skiffes-Whealton 500kV. We have determined that other alternatives are unavailable due to cost, engineering constraints and/or logistics. Please note this is not a decision on whether Dominion's preferred alternative is or is not permittable, nor does it exclude further consideration of alternatives should new information become available.

Project opponents also have spoken out on the alternatives issue. Excerpts from a lengthy letter submitted by the James River Alliance appear below. Consider, as you read, whether the information quoted or summarized here is likely to be effective at persuading the Army Corps of Engineers to pursue a different course. Consider, also, whether similar information would be likely to persuade a court to overturn the Corps's alternatives analysis.

Save the James Alliance, Response to Dominion Virginia's Surry-Skiffes Creek Alternatives Analysis Preliminary Review by the U.S Army Corps of Engineers
Nov. 13, 2015

Thank you for forwarding the Army Corps' Preliminary Alternatives Analysis of Dominion Virginia Power's (the Applicant) Surry-Skiffes Creek project. We have reviewed this document and we continue to find the methodology of these analyses fundamentally flawed because all conclusions are based upon data submitted by or on behalf of the

Applicant in such a way as to distort the factual record. We have been consistent in our requests for analytical conclusions that are based upon independently-derived analysis, facts, statistics and opinion. Until such an independent process is undertaken, the true impacts, costs and intentions of this project will not be known. While the Applicant's clever use of cherry-picked information is not surprising to us, the Corps may not have the necessary heightened awareness of the company's history of using such tactics. The Corps must raise their awareness to these distortions and recognize that the appropriate depth of review can only take place within the EIS framework. If nothing else, it should be abundantly obvious by now that the Applicant has an answer for everything.

The fact remains that the Applicant has been intractably intransigent regarding the route of Surry-Skiffes Creek from Day 1. They have provided absolutely no alternatives. None. And, the so-called Chickahominy route is, and always has been, a straw man, not a true alternative. They have budged not one iota. How many problems in life ever have just one solution? Very few. Yet, this Applicant has been mind-numbingly devoid of any other solutions, defying any reasonableness standard, in suggesting that theirs is the only answer. If the construction of this project were to impact "just another" viewshed, one might just roll one's eyes at the noise of only "one solution," suck it up and accept it, but, this is a singular moment where their so-called "only one solution" meets a truly "one-of-its-kind place," America's Founding River at Jamestown Island, VA. Therefore, their (lack of) solutions, statements, protestations and those of their paid consultants, whose paychecks rely on insuring agreement with their client, must withstand not just a reasonableness test, but also the most thorough of reviews as to corporate integrity and veracity. Our purpose, thus, is to present documented background and surrounding information that we believe is critical to the Corps' thinking, conclusions and objectives. This information clearly reveals that the Applicant has been disingenuous, at best, in their ham-handed, bully-like inflexibility. More than sufficient questions are raised by the supporting information to justify the Corps undertaking an independent analysis through an Environmental Impact Study (EIS). To support our statements we appreciate the opportunity to submit the following.

Let us be clear from the beginning—Dominion's decisions that led to the Surry/Skiffes Creek proposal were purely and simply business profitability decisions. These decisions were not made to "protect the grid," to "provide reliable power" or to "meet NERC reliability standards." (Those same, tired, reasons can be found in every filing Dominion makes.) Long before the Surry-Skiffes Creek (S-SC) project was proposed, the Applicant made other decisions, including those related to Yorktown Power Station that were designed to improve its own bottom line, without thought or caring about the external consequences of those actions. The company states pointedly in their filings and public statements that decisions are the results of their economic analysis of the projects, decisions that measure only costs to the Applicant. Given that the primary goal of any company is to satisfy their stakeholders, it comes as no surprise that their motive is profit. Nonetheless, Dominion has the luxury of business decisions made in the uniquely rarified air of a regulated monopoly, one that protects them from the financial assaults and course corrections inherent in doing business in a competitive marketplace.

The powerful combination of monopoly and regulation stirred together in the exclusive, Member's Only stratosphere of doing business in Virginia, particularly in Richmond, has created over time a corporate mindset, convinced of its own grandeur which must not to be questioned or scrutinized, its hubris growing unchecked. We believe that it is only because of those decisions, made by Dominion in such a vacuum, seemingly without any appreciation for the massive costs imposed by the externalities of those decisions, that the grid may now be in potential jeopardy, that electric reliability may be questioned and that NERC standards might be subject to violation. Dominion brings its predicament upon itself. And, so, it is Dominion who must be made to incur the financial costs of these thoughtless judgements.

* * * The Applicant must be told something by the Corps that their Virginia-based fraternity will not, that this time the devastating consequences of their insular, corporate decisions will not be allowed to be imposed on the landscape of this national treasure, America's Founding River, the James. The ticking clock the Applicant finds itself up against is in its own mind and of its own making. Their timeline must not be ours. * * *

The Save the James Alliance alternative, a so-called hybrid alternative, put forth to the Corps in the summer of 2015, envisioned a two-step solution. The first step, a shorter-term solution, is designed to meet relatively immediate needs. It calls for retrofitting YPS Unit #2 to burn natural gas, in combination with the build of a underground 230 kV line from Surry. The 230 submerged option was acknowledged by PJM Interconnect[5] in its 2012 Regional Baseline Reliability Assessment, as meeting the NERC Reliability standards, albeit, somewhat less robustly. Nonetheless, combined with the retrofit of YPS #2 to gas, the problem would be resolved for the short-term, which would allow the Applicant the time to move to the longer-term phase, building new generation capacity in Hampton Roads.

---

5 Eds.: PJM is a private company responsible for energy transmission in thirteen states, including Virginia.

[Eds.: The Alliance then included extensive quotes from a 2011 plan published by Dominion. That plan, according to the Alliance, identified the 230 kV line as a preferred alternative and showed that it could meet regional grid reliability needs.]

In Dominion's unbroken rebukes of options, the Applicant has cited repeatedly either insufficient pipeline capacity or inadequate supply of natural gas as reasons why a number of alternative are not viable. Like much that the company asserts, this statement is not supported by the facts. Allow us to share with you what is publically available regarding supply and infrastructure for natural gas in the region, generally, and on the Hampton Roads Peninsula, specifically.

[Eds.: The Alliance then included lengthy quotes from statements by Virginia Natural Gas, another public utility, describing new pipelines and increased capacity (but also describing a history of supply/demand mismatches) in the general vicinity of the proposed James River utility crossing.]

While distributive pipelines may to necessary to reach the Yorktown Power Station site from the main transmission pipelines that currently exist, that would be a relatively minor undertaking in the larger context of the project. The National Pipeline Mapping System indicates that a VNG transmission line is no further away than about five miles. Additionally, other pipelines already exist in a corridor stretching from the VNG transmission line vicinity to YPS. Since refueling Yorktown Unit #2 for natural gas was their PREFERRED plan, a plan they describe as well analyzed and based upon many factors, including adequate supply and infrastructure, one should assume that the required pipelines may, perhaps, already be in place near the YPS site. Thus, with this knowledge, it is quite impossible to believe the Applicant's recent statements, made when rejecting the STJA proposal, of insufficient pipeline infrastructure or insufficient supplies of gas with existing pipeline. As we have shown, independent sources directly contradict the self-serving accounts of the company. The Army Corps must seek independent answers. * * *

VNG's testimony states, unequivocally, that there is sufficient natural gas and infrastructure. So, why the disconnect? The dilemma from Dominion's standpoint is that they don't own it, Dominion's definition of "inadequate." The company appears to have adopted a business strategy of using only gas they own since relying on outside suppliers subjects them to the price volatility of open market purchases or the lock-in of long-term supply contracts that can go against them on price, or both. Make no mistake; although, the Applicant may not be the owner of this particular gas supply, gas is abundant, as is the necessary pipeline capacity. In fact, their desire to use only gas they own within their facilities is why they have undertaken yet another controversial project, the Atlantic Coast Pipeline (ACP), and, ACP may help explain why the Applicant has made no plans to replace the generation it wants to shutter within Hampton Roads.

[The Alliance next argued, again at length, that Dominion's energy forecasts overstated demand and understated the potential achievements of demand side management. The concluding paragraph that follows summarizes that argument.]

The double whammy—1.) overestimations by PJM's forecast load model in tandem with 2.) overestimations of both historic and future economic growth in Hampton Roads, does not support Dominion's rationale for needed expansion on the Peninsula, at least not in Phase I, the short term, of the suggested alternative. Hoped for economic growth would be a component of planning for replacement generation, which must be physically located in Hampton Roads, but that comes in Phase II, the long-term. So, there appear to be absolutely no burgeoning pressures on the system due to economic growth that must be addressed in the very short-run, and that gives the Applicant time to return to the drawing board to devise a plan that incorporates the latest technology, to build it in Hampton Roads, that contains innovative thinking about solving this problem and provides the solution that avoids destroying America's John Smith Trail at Williamsburg.

NOTES

1. The problem focuses primarily on alternatives to the proposed action, but EISs (and EAs, as you read earlier) also often identify mitigation measures designed to reduce the environmental impacts of a project. While NEPA establishes no legal *obligation* for agencies to adopt those mitigation measures, they sometimes choose to do so.

2. For the proposed James River utility crossing, NEPA is not the only environmental law that applies. The Clean Water Act also requires the Army Corps of Engineers to analyze the environmental impacts of, and proposed alternatives to, the crossing. And the Army Corps of Engineers also must consult with the Fish and Wildlife Service and the National Marine Fisheries Service about the potential impacts of the project on threatened and endangered species. This is not an atypical situation. Often major infrastructure projects trigger a suite of environmental laws, and attorneys devote substantial time to figuring out how to coordinate the NEPA process with other compliance processes. They also must consider the implications of statements in an EA or EIS for efforts to comply (or demonstrate non-compliance) with other environmental laws.

3. As you read through the materials, you may have wondered if it is common practice for one agency to write a letter opposing another federal

agency's project. Other federal and state agencies do often comment on EISs, though the vehemence of this particular letter is not typical of correspondence among federal agencies. Section 309 of the Clean Air Act also obligates EPA to review and evaluate EISs, and EPA gives each EIS a kind of grade. These agency comments are often influential. *See* Michael C. Blumm & Andrea Lang, *Shared Sovereignty: The Role of Expert Agencies in Environmental Law*, 42 ECOLOGY L.Q. 609 (2015). Can you guess why? Consider how a negative comment from EPA, or another federal agency with environmental expertise, might affect the deference a court would normally accord to a lead agency's analysis.

4.   As discussed earlier in this Chapter, producing an EIS is an expensive undertaking. Funding an EIS may could consume substantial federal financial resources. Is that an appropriate use of taxpayer money, particularly where a federal agency is considering approving something of value to a private party? For instance, should the Army Corps of Engineers fund an EIS to consider the effects of granting Clean Water Act permits to Dominion? In general, federal agencies require those that apply for federal permits or licenses to pay for many aspects of the environmental review process. Alternatively, federal agencies may simply rely on information produced by the applicant. Because private parties often shoulder much of the cost of NEPA compliance, the environmental review process can substantially increase the cost of projects that require federal approval. Such cost shifting may also raise questions about whether an agency is receiving unbiased information, particularly where federal agencies rely on information provided by the project applicant.

IV. NEPA's Frontiers

NEPA is now almost half a century old, and, unlike the other statutes you will study, it has never been amended in any significant way. Because of that legislative stasis, and because the law itself is quite short, you might think that the law and politics of NEPA, and of equivalent state laws, are fairly well settled. But that is not the case. The statute remains controversial, and new NEPA issues continue to emerge.

In the pages that follow, you will encounter two of the most salient of those issues. The first issue is how, if at all, NEPA's requirements should apply to climate change. The second is whether and when legislative exemptions from NEPA are appropriate. Each issue implicates deeper questions, for it is difficult to develop a position on either issue without also forming an idea about the value of the procedures that NEPA mandates. The problems therefore will require you to focus on those broader policy issues, rather than just zeroing in on the application of environmental law to a particular situation.

A. NEPA AND CLIMATE CHANGE

If a federal action will cause greenhouse gas emissions, do those emissions qualify as impacts that require analysis in NEPA documents? Do they qualify as *significant* impacts? And if NEPA documents should supply analysis, what depth of analysis should they provide? Prior to the early 2000s, hardly anyone had considered those questions. But they soon arose in both federal and state courts as well as non-judicial forums. The short problem below introduces you to some of the resulting issues.

PROBLEM: NEPA, CLIMATE CHANGE, AND MINERAL LEASING

The United States Department of the Interior ("DOI") manages huge swaths of land, particularly in the western United States. It also holds jurisdiction over submerged offshore lands in the Gulf of Mexico and off the shores of Alaska. Beneath some of that land are deposits of coal, oil, and natural gas. For years, DOI has allowed private companies to mine and drill those energy resources, generally by offering companies the opportunity to purchase mineral leases. The decision to offer minerals for sale generally is discretionary.

Imagine that you are an attorney at DOI. The agency is considering drafting a guidance document explaining how its offices should factor climate change impacts into NEPA reviews for mineral leases. You've been tasked with developing a draft version of that guidance. To do so, you will need to address a few specific questions:

- Should all DOI lease sale NEPA documents address climate change? Some of them? None of them?

- If some, but not all, of the lease sale documents should address climate change, how should project managers decide whether their proposed action triggers thresholds for NEPA analysis?

- Should the consequences of greenhouse gas emissions from *some* lease sales—or, perhaps, *all* lease sales—qualify as significant environmental impacts, thus necessitating review in an EIS?

- If some lease sales will trigger significance findings, but not all will, how will the lines be drawn?

As you consider your answers to those questions, make a few assumptions. First, assume that individual lease sales will increase global greenhouse gas emissions. That will happen partly through the fugitive emissions associated with mineral extraction, and partly because increased mineral extraction will increase energy supplies, decreasing prices and thus encouraging greater consumption. Second, assume that any individual lease sale will increase global greenhouse gas emissions only by a tiny fraction of a percentage. In other words, each lease sale will accelerate global climate change, but only to a very small extent. Third, assume that a large portion of the United States' fossil fuel extraction occurs on federal lands. One telling (and real) statistic indicates the importance of federal leasing: in 2016, Secretary of Interior Sally Jewell observed that "[o]ver the last few years, approximately 41 percent of the Nation's annual coal production has come from Federal land." Sally Jewell, Order No. 3338: Discretionary Programmatic Environmental Impact Statement to Modernize the Federal Coal Program (Jan. 15, 2016).

As you research this question, you would normally start with the language of the statute and any regulations directly on point. But the statute says nothing specific about climate change, and the regulation most directly on point is 40 C.F.R. § 1508.27, which defines "significantly"—but which also lacks any direct reference to climate change. Your most useful authority, instead, is likely to come from cases and agency guidance.

Beginning in the mid-2000s, a series of cases have addressed NEPA's applicability to climate change. One of those decisions appears below.

High Country Conservation Advocates v. United States Forest Service

52 F. Supp. 3d 1174 (D. Colo. 2014)

■ R. BROOKE JACKSON, UNITED STATES DISTRICT JUDGE

The North Fork Valley in western Colorado is blessed with valuable resources. The area hosts several coal mines as well as beautiful scenery, abundant wildlife, and outstanding recreational opportunities. And as is sometimes the case in rich places like this, people disagree about how to manage the development of those resources. In the case before the Court, the plaintiff environmental organizations seek judicial review of three agency decisions that together authorized on-the-ground mining exploration activities in a part of the North Fork Valley called the Sunset Roadless Area. * * * Plaintiffs allege that these three agency decisions failed to comply with the National Environmental Policy Act ("NEPA") and the Administrative Procedure Act ("APA") and must be set aside. * * *

I.   BACKGROUND

* * * B.   Coal Leasing on Federal Land

The [United States Bureau of Land Management] manages coal leases underlying Forest Service Land pursuant to the Mineral Leasing Act, 30 U.S.C. § 181 et seq. Because the Forest Service retains management authority over the surface lands overlying these leases, the BLM must first obtain the consent of the Forest Service before approving leases. 30 U.S.C. §§ 201(a)(3)(iii), 207(a); 43 C.F.R. § 3425.3(b).

Prior to granting consent, the Forest Service is authorized to impose conditions to protect forest resources. Id. * * *

[The court then described the agency decisions and EISs at issue. The procedural history is complex, but in essence, the agency decisions were part of a larger compromise agreement that would preserve some of Colorado's roadless areas but would also allow coal mining in some other areas that had not previously been accessible. The court noted that, according to the FEIS, those decisions would "lead to the production of 5.6 million tons of coal from adjacent private lands and 3.3 million tons from adjacent federal lands."]

* * * Plaintiffs allege three NEPA violations in the Lease Modification FEIS: (1) the agencies failed to disclose the impact to adjacent public and private lands in sufficient detail, (2) the agencies failed to disclose the social, environmental, and economic impacts of GHG emissions resulting from the lease modifications, and (3) the agencies failed to analyze direct volatile organic compound ("VOC") emissions associated with methane venting on the modified lease. Overall, as the record demonstrates, the agencies did an excellent job of disclosing the effects of the Lease Modifications and analyzing those effects. Nonetheless, their explanation of the social, economic, and environmental effects of methane emissions from the development of the Lease Modification was arbitrary and appears to have either "entirely failed to consider an important aspect of the problem, . . . offered an explanation for its decision that runs counter to the evidence before the agency, or is so implausible that it could not be ascribed to a difference in view or the product of agency expertise." *New Mexico ex. rel. Richardson*, 565 F.3d at 704.

* * * ii. The Lease Modification FEIS Inadequately Disclosed the Effects of GHG Emissions.

While the agencies provided an adequate disclosure of effects on adjacent lands, their treatment of the costs associated with GHG emissions from the mine was arbitrary and capricious. The agencies apparently do not dispute that they are required to analyze the indirect effects of GHG emissions in some fashion, but they contend that their general discussion of the effects of global climate change was sufficient under NEPA. The FEIS, however, justifies this approach with a statement that is incorrect and ignores evidence in the record. And the post-hoc rationales provided by counsel in this case, even if they could save the FEIS, suffer from problems of their own.

One of the foreseeable effects of the Lease Modification approval is the likely release of methane gas from the expanded mining operations. As explained above, an EIS must disclose and evaluate all of the effects of a proposed action—direct, indirect, and cumulative. NEPA further defines impacts or effects to include "ecological[,] . . . economic, [and] social" impacts of a proposed action. 40 C.F.R. § 1508.8(b). The agencies do not argue that they could ignore these effects. In fact, they acknowledged that there might be impacts from GHGs in the form of methane emitted from mine operations and from carbon dioxide resulting from combustion of the coal produced. Beyond quantifying the amount of emissions relative to state and national emissions and giving general discussion to the impacts of global climate change, they did not discuss the impacts caused by these emissions. Instead, they offered a categorical explanation that such an analysis is impossible.

> Standardized protocols designed to measure factors that may contribute to climate change, and to quantify climatic impacts, are presently unavailable. . . .

> Predicting the degree of impact any single emitter of [greenhouse gases] may have on global climate change, or on the changes to biotic and abiotic systems that accompany climate change, is not possible at this time. As such, . . . the accompanying changes to natural systems cannot be quantified or predicted at this time.

But a tool is and was available: the social cost of carbon protocol. Interagency Working Group on Social Cost of Carbon, Technical Support Document (Feb. 2010). The protocol—which is designed to quantify a project's contribution to costs associated with global climate change— was created with the input of several departments, public comments, and technical models. The protocol is provisional and was expressly designed to assist agencies in cost-benefit analyses associated with rulemakings, but the EPA has expressed support for its use in other contexts. * * *

In case there was any doubt about the protocol's potential for inclusion in the Lease Modification EIS, the agencies included it in the draft EIS. The draft weighed several specific economic benefits—coal recovered, payroll, associated purchases of supplies and services, and royalties— against two costs: the cost of disturbing forest and the cost of methane emissions from the mine (measured in terms of dollars per ton of carbon dioxide as estimated by the social cost of carbon protocol). The BLM included a similar analysis in its preliminary EA on the Lease Modifications.

As noted above, these attempts at quantification of the Lease Modification's contribution to the costs of global climate change were abandoned in the FEIS. The analysis was removed, in part it seems, in response to an email from one of the BLM's economists that pointed out that the social cost of carbon protocol is "controversial."

> Placing quantitative values on greenhouse gas emissions is still controversial. Social cost estimates for a ton of carbon dioxide emitted range from $5 to over $800 (Interagency Working Group

2010; F. Ackerman & E. Stanton, Climate Risks and Carbon Prices: Revising the Social Costs of Carbon, 2010). Considering the 1.23 million tons of carbon dioxide equivalent emissions [from methane] the West Elk mine emits annually, the cost could range from a moderate $6 million per year to an overwhelming $984 million per year.

Email of D. Epstein, Economist, BLM State Office to N. Mortenson, Forest Service (July 19, 2012 6:08 PM). The final, however, retained the quantification of the benefits associated with the Lease Modifications and even added some additional benefits.

Therefore the FEIS, on its face, offers a factually inaccurate justification for why it omitted the social cost of carbon protocol. A tool existed, and indeed it was in the draft EIS. This justification "runs counter to the evidence before the agency [and] is so implausible that it could not be ascribed to a difference in view or the product of agency expertise. . . ." *New Mexico ex rel. Richardson*, 565 F.3d at 704.

Furthermore, this error is more than a mere "flyspeck." The agencies expressly relied on the anticipated economic benefits of the Lease Modifications in justifying their approval.

Even though NEPA does not require a cost-benefit analysis, it was nonetheless arbitrary and capricious to quantify the benefits of the lease modifications and then explain that a similar analysis of the costs was impossible when such an analysis was in fact possible and was included in an earlier draft EIS. See also 40 C.F.R. § 1502.23; *Hughes River Watershed Conservancy*, 81 F.3d at 446–48 ("it is essential that the EIS not be based on misleading economic assumptions"); *Sierra Club v. Sigler*, 695 F.2d 957, 979 (5th Cir. 1983) (agency choosing to "trumpet" an action's benefits has a duty to disclose its costs). In effect the agency prepared half of a cost-benefit analysis, incorrectly claimed that it was impossible to quantify the costs, and then relied on the anticipated benefits to approve the project.

* * * [E]ven if the agencies had argued the protocol was controversial because it is imprecise, the only evidence in the record that appears to support that rationalization is the economist's email noting that there is no scientific consensus about the exact dollar amount to assign to carbon emissions. *See supra* Email of D. Epstein, Economist, BLM State Office to N. Mortenson, Forest Service (July 19, 2012 6:08 PM). As he noted, there is a wide range of estimates about the social cost of GHG emissions. But neither the BLM's economist nor anyone else in the record appears to suggest the cost is as low as $0 per unit. Yet by deciding not to quantify the costs at all, the agencies effectively zeroed out the cost in its quantitative analysis. *See Ctr. for Biological Diversity v. Nat'l Highway Traffic Safety Admin.*, 538 F.3d 1172, 1217 (9th Cir. 2008) (holding that

NEPA requires agencies to analyze the effects of its actions on global climate change); *id.* at 1200 (finding it arbitrary and capricious to assign a cost of $0/ton to emissions when none of the identified estimates was that low); *Border Power Plant Working Grp. v. U.S. Dep't of Energy*, 260 F. Supp. 2d 997, 1028–29 (S.D. Cal.2003) (same).

[Eds.: The court then turned to the second EIS. For similar reasons, it found that second EIS's analysis of greenhouse gas emissions to be arbitrary and capricious. Then, in the two paragraphs that follow, the court addressed another argument: that the approval or disapproval of a particular project would have no effect on the aggregate amount of coal burned, and thus on global greenhouse gas emissions.]

Third and finally, the agencies argue that the same amount of coal will be burned whether or not the CRR exempts the North Fork Valley. The agency concluded that there would be perfect substitution between coal provided by the North Fork Valley and coal mined elsewhere. In other words, coal is a global commodity, and if the coal does not come out of the ground in the North Fork consumers will simply pay to have the same amount of coal pulled out of the ground somewhere else—overall GHG emissions from combustion will be identical under either scenario. The agencies reached this conclusion in part by relying on a U.S. Department of Energy report forecasting a small annual increase in the demand for coal. CRR–0080586. Based on that assumption, the agency concluded that perfect substitution would occur.

I cannot make sense of this argument, and I am persuaded by an opinion from the Court of Appeals for the Eighth Circuit that rejected a nearly identical agency justification for not analyzing the future effects of coal combustion. In *Mid States Coalition for Progress v. Surface Transportation Board*, the court held that an agency violated NEPA when it failed to disclose and analyze the future coal combustion impacts associated with the agency's approval of a railroad line. 345 F.3d 520, 549 (8th Cir. 2003). In that case—like this one—the agency argued that emissions would occur regardless of whether the railroad line were approved because "the demand for coal will be unaffected by an increase in availability and a decrease in price." *Id.* The court rejected this argument as "illogical at best" and noted that "increased availability of inexpensive coal will at the very least make coal a more attractive option to future entrants into the utilities market when compared with other potential fuel sources, such as nuclear power, solar power, or natural gas." *Id.* The same dynamic is at play here. The production of coal in the North Fork exemption will increase the supply of cheap, low-sulfur coal. At some point this additional supply will impact the demand for coal relative to other fuel sources, and coal that otherwise would have been left in the ground will be burned. This reasonably foreseeable effect must

be analyzed, even if the precise extent of the effect is less certain. *Id.* at
549–50.

———

Your client, if it proceeds, would not be the first federal agency to
draft guidance explaining how climate change impacts should be
addressed in NEPA documents. In 2010, the CEQ issued draft guidance
addressing NEPA and climate change. CEQ never finalized that
guidance. Instead, in December, 2014, it released a separate draft
guidance document. Finally, in the summer of 2016, it finalized that
document. Excerpts appear below.

———

EXECUTIVE OFFICE OF THE PRESIDENT
COUNCIL ON ENVIRONMENTAL QUALITY
WASHINGTON, D.C. 20503

August 1, 2016

MEMORANDUM FOR HEADS OF FEDERAL DEPARTMENTS AND AGENCIES

FROM: CHRISTINA GOLDFUSS
               COUNCIL ON ENVIRONMENTAL QUALITY

SUBJECT: Final Guidance for Federal Departments and Agencies on
               Consideration of Greenhouse Gas Emissions and the Effects of
               Climate Change in National Environmental Policy Act Reviews

I.   INTRODUCTION

The Council on Environmental Quality (CEQ) issues this guidance to
assist Federal agencies in their consideration of the effects of greenhouse
gas (GHG) emissions and climate change when evaluating proposed
Federal actions in accordance with the National Environmental Policy
Act (NEPA) and the CEQ Regulations Implementing the Procedural
Provisions of NEPA (CEQ Regulations). This guidance will facilitate
compliance with existing NEPA requirements, thereby improving the
efficiency and consistency of reviews of proposed Federal actions for
agencies, decision makers, project proponents, and the public. The
guidance provides Federal agencies a common approach for assessing
their proposed actions, while recognizing each agency's unique

circumstances and authorities. Climate change is a fundamental environmental issue, and its effects fall squarely within NEPA's purview. Climate change is a particularly complex challenge given its global nature and the inherent interrelationships among its sources, causation, mechanisms of action, and impacts. Analyzing a proposed action's GHG emissions and the effects of climate change relevant to a proposed action—particularly how climate change may change an action's environmental effects—can provide useful information to decision makers and the public. CEQ is issuing the guidance to provide for greater clarity and more consistency in how agencies address climate change in the environmental impact assessment process. This guidance uses longstanding NEPA principles because such an analysis should be similar to the analysis of other environmental impacts under NEPA. The guidance is intended to assist agencies in disclosing and considering the reasonably foreseeable effects of proposed actions that are relevant to their decision-making processes. It confirms that agencies should provide the public and decision makers with explanations of the basis for agency determinations.

* * *

As discussed in this guidance, when addressing climate change agencies should consider: (1) The potential effects of a proposed action on climate change as indicated by assessing GHG emissions (e.g., to include, where applicable, carbon sequestration) and, (2) The effects of climate change on a proposed action and its environmental impacts.

* * *

III. CONSIDERING THE EFFECTS OF GHG EMISSIONS AND CLIMATE CHANGE

This guidance is applicable to all Federal actions subject to NEPA, including site-specific actions, certain funding of site-specific projects, rulemaking actions, permitting decisions, and land and resource management decisions. This guidance does not—and cannot—expand the range of Federal agency actions that are subject to NEPA. Consistent with NEPA, Federal agencies should consider the extent to which a proposed action and its reasonable alternatives would contribute to climate change, through GHG emissions, and take into account the ways in which a changing climate may impact the proposed action and any alternative actions, change the action's environmental effects over the lifetime of those effects, and alter the overall environmental implications of such actions.

This guidance is intended to assist agencies in disclosing and considering the effects of GHG emissions and climate change along with the other reasonably foreseeable environmental effects of their proposed actions. This guidance does not establish any particular quantity of GHG emissions as "significantly" affecting the quality of the human environment or give greater consideration to the effects of GHG emissions and climate change over other effects on the human environment.

A.   GHG Emissions as a Proxy for the Climate Change Impacts of a Proposed Action

In light of the global scope of the impacts of GHG emissions, and the incremental contribution of each single action to global concentrations, CEQ recommends agencies use the projected GHG emissions associated with proposed actions as a proxy for assessing proposed actions' potential effects on climate change in NEPA analysis. This approach, together with providing a qualitative summary discussion of the impacts of GHG emissions based on authoritative reports such as the USGCRP's National Climate Assessments and the Impacts of Climate Change on Human Health in the United States, a Scientific Assessment of the USGCRP, allows an agency to present the environmental and public health impacts of a proposed action in clear terms and with sufficient information to make a reasoned choice between no action and other alternatives and appropriate mitigation measures, and to ensure the professional and scientific integrity of the NEPA review.

Climate change results from the incremental addition of GHG emissions from millions of individual sources, which collectively have a large impact on a global scale. CEQ recognizes that the totality of climate change impacts is not attributable to any single action, but are exacerbated by a series of actions including actions taken pursuant to decisions of the Federal Government. Therefore, a statement that emissions from a proposed Federal action represent only a small fraction of global emissions is essentially a statement about the nature of the climate change challenge, and is not an appropriate basis for deciding whether or to what extent to consider climate change impacts under NEPA. Moreover, these comparisons are also not an appropriate method for characterizing the potential impacts associated with a proposed action and its alternatives and mitigations because this approach does not reveal anything beyond the nature of the climate change challenge itself: the fact that diverse individual sources of emissions each make a relatively small addition to global atmospheric GHG concentrations that collectively have a large impact. When considering GHG emissions and their significance, agencies should use appropriate tools and methodologies for quantifying GHG emissions and comparing GHG quantities across alternative scenarios. Agencies should not limit themselves to calculating a proposed action's emissions as a percentage of sector, nationwide, or global emissions in deciding whether or to what extent to consider climate change impacts under NEPA.

1.   GHG Emissions Quantification and Relevant Tools

This guidance recommends that agencies quantify a proposed agency action's projected direct and indirect GHG emissions. Agencies should be guided by the principle that the extent of the analysis should be commensurate with the quantity of projected GHG emissions and take into account available data and GHG quantification tools that are suitable for and commensurate with the proposed agency action. The rule of reason and the concept of proportionality caution against providing an in-depth analysis of emissions regardless of the insignificance of the quantity of GHG emissions that would be caused by the proposed agency action.

Quantification tools are widely available, and are already in broad use in the Federal and private sectors, by state and local governments, and globally. Such quantification tools and methodologies have been developed to assist institutions, organizations, agencies, and companies with different levels of technical sophistication, data availability, and GHG source profiles. When data inputs are reasonably available to support calculations, agencies should conduct GHG analysis and disclose quantitative estimates of GHG emissions in their NEPA reviews. These tools can provide estimates of GHG emissions, including emissions from fossil fuel combustion and estimates of GHG emissions and carbon sequestration for many of the sources and sinks potentially affected by proposed resource management actions. * * *

NEPA reviews for proposed resource extraction and development projects typically include the reasonably foreseeable effects of various phases in the process, such as clearing land for the project, building access roads, extraction, transport, refining, processing, using the resource, disassembly, disposal, and reclamation. Depending on the relationship between any of the phases, as well as the authority under which they may be carried out, agencies should use the analytical scope that best informs their decision making. * * *

* * * 3.   Alternatives

Considering alternatives, including alternatives that mitigate GHG emissions, is fundamental to the NEPA process and accords with NEPA Sections 102(2)(C) and 102(2)(E). * * *

4.   Direct and Indirect Effects

If the direct and indirect GHG emissions can be quantified based on available information, including reasonable projections and assumptions, agencies should consider and disclose the reasonably foreseeable direct and indirect emissions when analyzing the direct and indirect effects of the proposed action.[42] Agencies should disclose the information and any assumptions used in the analysis and explain any uncertainties. To compare a project's estimated direct and indirect emissions with GHG emissions from the no-action alternative, agencies should draw on existing, timely, objective, and authoritative analyses, such as those by the Energy Information Administration, the Federal Energy Management Program, or Office of Fossil Energy of the Department of Energy. In the absence of such analyses, agencies should use other available information. When such analyses or information for quantification is unavailable, or the complexity of comparing emissions from various sources would make quantification overly speculative, then the agency should quantify emissions to the extent that this information is available and explain the extent to which quantified emissions information is unavailable while providing a qualitative analysis of those emissions. As with any NEPA analysis, the level of effort should be proportionate to the scale of the emissions relevant to the NEPA review.

5.   Cumulative Effects

"Cumulative impact" is defined in the CEQ Regulations as the "impact on the environment that results from the incremental impact of the action when added to other past, present, and reasonably foreseeable future actions regardless of what agency (Federal or non-Federal) or person undertakes such other actions." All GHG emissions contribute to cumulative climate change impacts. However, for most Federal agency actions CEQ does not expect that an EIS would be required based solely on the global significance of cumulative impacts of GHG emissions, as it would not be consistent with the rule of reason to require the preparation of an EIS for every Federal action that may cause GHG emissions regardless of the magnitude of those emissions.

Based on the agency identification and analysis of the direct and indirect effects of its proposed action, NEPA requires an agency to consider the cumulative impacts of its proposed action and reasonable alternatives. As noted above, for the purposes of NEPA, the analysis of the effects of GHG emissions is essentially a cumulative effects analysis that is subsumed within the general analysis and discussion of climate change impacts. Therefore, direct and indirect effects analysis for GHG emissions will adequately address the cumulative impacts for climate change from the proposed action and its alternatives and a separate cumulative effects analysis for GHG emissions is not needed.

---

[42]   For example, where the proposed action involves fossil fuel extraction, direct emissions typically include GHGs emitted during the process of exploring for or extracting the fossil fuel. The indirect effects of such an action that are reasonably foreseeable at the time would vary with the circumstances of the proposed action. For actions such as a Federal lease sale of coal for energy production, the impacts associated with the end-use of the fossil fuel being extracted would be the reasonably foreseeable combustion of that coal.

[In its remaining pages, the guidance emphasizes the importance of analyzing mitigation measures that would reduce greenhouse gas emissions. It also urges agencies to consider how climate change will interact with other project impacts, and to use the NEPA process as an opportunity to plan for adaptation to a changing climate change.]

NOTES

1.   Among the court decisions addressing NEPA and climate change, one of the most prominent is *Center for Biological Diversity v. National Highway Traffic Safety Administration*, 538 F.3d 1172 (9th Cir. 2008). In *CBD v. NHTSA*, the Ninth Circuit considered an EA for new federal automobile fuel economy standards—which the decision refers to as "CAFE standards." Environmental groups and some states had challenged those standards, which they thought were less stringent than the Energy Policy and Conservation Act required them to be. They also alleged that the NHTSA's EA for the project (the agency had not prepared an EIS) provided an inadequate analysis of the greenhouse gas emissions that would be caused by the new rule. The Ninth Circuit agreed. In a key passage, it wrote:

> The impact of greenhouse gas emissions on climate change is precisely the kind of cumulative impacts analysis that NEPA requires agencies to conduct. Any given rule setting a CAFE standard might have an "individually minor" effect on the environment, but these rules are "collectively significant actions taking place over a period of time." 40 C.F.R. § 1508.7; *see also Native Ecosystems Council,* 304 F.3d at 897 (holding that the Forest Service's road density standard amendments must be subject to cumulative impacts analysis because otherwise, "the Forest Service will be free to amend road density standards throughout the forest piecemeal, without ever having to evaluate the amendments' cumulative environmental impacts."); *City of Los Angeles v. NHTSA,* 912 F.2d 478, 501 (D.C. Cir. 1990) (Wald, C.J., dissenting) ("[W]e cannot afford to ignore even modest contributions to global warming. If global warming is the result of the cumulative contributions of myriad sources, any one modest in itself, is there not a danger of losing the forest by closing our eyes to the felling of the individual trees?"), *overruled on other grounds by Fla. Audubon Soc. v. Bentsen,* 94 F.3d 658 (D.C. Cir. 1996). Thus, NHTSA must provide the necessary contextual information about the cumulative and incremental environmental impacts of the Final Rule in light of other CAFE rulemakings and other past, present, and reasonably foreseeable future actions, regardless of what agency or person undertakes such other actions.

How far does that principle extend? In theory, that argument might reach every federal agency action that emits even the tiniest puff of greenhouse gases, and every such project might require an EIS. *See* Madeline June Kass, *A NEPA Climate Paradox: Taking Greenhouse Gases into Account in Threshold Significance Determinations*, 42 IND. L. REV. 47 (2009). To date, no federal court has been willing to go that far. But if they do not go that far, how can courts, or agencies, draw a principled dividing line between impacts that are large enough to be significant and those are too small to count?

An alternative approach, which California now uses for agencies implementing the California Environmental Quality Act, is to set thresholds of significance for different types of projects. If a project's emissions exceed those thresholds, a significance finding is mandatory. And because the California Environmental Quality Act, unlike NEPA, requires avoidance or mitigation of significant impacts if that avoidance or mitigation is feasible, project proponents must mitigate emissions that exceed significance thresholds. *See, e.g.,* South Coast Air Quality Management District, Greenhouse Gases (GHG) Significance Thresholds, http://www.aqmd.gov/docs/default-source/ceqa/handbook/scaqmd-air-quality-significance-thresholds.pdf.

Would you recommend that the Department of the Interior adopt similar thresholds of significance for its NEPA analyses?

2.   The problem above asks you to consider how the Department of Interior should go about addressing the negative impacts its mineral leasing program could have upon the climate. Some federal agency actions are likely to have positive impacts, however; certain land management practices can promote carbon sequestration, and leasing federal land for renewable energy development arguably can help displace carbon-intensive energy sources. Looking beyond climate impacts, many federal agency actions are designed to improve environmental conditions. How should these positive impacts be addressed in NEPA analyses? For general discussion of this question, see Shaun A. Goho, *NEPA and the "Beneficial Impact" EIS*, 36 WM. & MARY ENVTL. L. & POL'Y REV. 367 (2012) (arguing that EISs are not required, and should not be required, for projects that have only environmentally beneficial effects).

B. REFORMING ENVIRONMENTAL ASSESSMENT LAWS?

NEPA has never been significantly amended, but that is not for lack of trying. Criticism of the law arose almost as soon as NEPA was enacted. To many environmentalists, the law isn't nearly strong enough. To many of the federal agencies responsible for compliance, and the state and private entities whose permits depend on federal compliance, the law is just a massive generator of paperwork, cost, and delay.

Sometimes those critiques have led to calls for outright repeal of the law, or of its state counterparts. But another reform model comes from several recent controversies in California. There, several state laws have granted exemptions from the California Environmental Quality Act ("CEQA")—NEPA's state-law counterpart—for projects that (a) fall within certain pre-defined classifications and (b) meet certain pre-specified environmental performance standards. So, for example, a California statute passed in 2012 allows the following basic tradeoffs for infill development projects:[6]

If project meets performance standards for:	It can obtain some procedural streamlining measures like:
<ul><li>Greenhouse gas emissions;</li><li>Energy efficiency;</li><li>Induced traffic;</li><li>Water use efficiency;</li><li>Transit-oriented development; and</li><li>Public health protections.</li></ul>	<ul><li>No need to consider impacts previously considered in prior environmental studies;</li><li>No need to consider impacts where the project meets performance standards for that kind of impact;</li><li>No need to prepare an environmental impact report at all if the project meets performance standards for all potentially significant impacts;</li><li>Narrower environmental review, including truncated alternatives analyses, for projects that do necessitate an environmental impact report.</li></ul>

In other words, an infill project that meets certain environmental/smart growth performance standards may receive a complete exemption from CEQA's requirements, or it may receive streamlined environmental review.

That preferential treatment reflects a widely-shared view that infill development is better for the environment than development at urban fringes, particularly if development meets demanding environmental performance standards. But infill development still creates environmental impacts that the performance standards do not address, and that neighbors or other members of the community might care about. To those neighbors, requiring better environmental performance for infill development may not seem like sufficient compensation for the loss of a broad environmental review process.

---

[6] Infill development is development within areas that already are urbanized.

Are these reforms positive or problematic? And should they be imitated? Imagine that you are a state legislator considering analogous reforms to your state environmental assessment statute, or a member of Congress considering analogous reforms to NEPA. Would you support them? Might you even argue for more ambitious uses of this type of reform? Stepping back to a broader question, what should the future of environmental assessment law be?

To provide a truly informed answer to that question, you might wish to have empirical evidence of the environmental benefits produced by NEPA and its state counterparts, and the associated costs. After all, detailed studies have helped commentators and legislators assess the value of the Clean Air Act, to provide perhaps the most prominent example. *See* United States EPA, Benefits and Costs of the Clean Air Act, https://www.epa.gov/clean-air-act-overview/benefits-and-costs-clean-air-act (linking to three studies). For NEPA, however, the evidence, though extensive, is almost entirely anecdotal, and designing a study that assesses the environmental benefit of additional procedures is a difficult thing to do. The article we have excerpted below is not an empirical study of NEPA's effects. But it does provide a particularly concise summary some of the most widespread views.

Bradley C. Karkkainen, *Whither NEPA?*
12 N.Y.U. ENVTL. L.J. 333, 338–51 (2004)

Observers hold divergent views on NEPA's effectiveness and its value as an environmental policy tool. As a baseline, we might describe one prevalent view as that of the "NEPA optimist." The optimist argues that NEPA is working reasonably well to achieve the objectives set out by Congress. By forcing agencies to confront information they otherwise might not have considered, the environmental impact assessment process as set out by NEPA leads straightforwardly to better informed, more rational, and environmentally enlightened decision-making. At the same time, the optimist argues, NEPA-mandated procedures have the democracy-enhancing virtue of opening the policy process to greater public scrutiny and public participation, thus enhancing transparency and democratic accountability. The twin goals of better-informed decision-making and enhanced public oversight seem to have been the original public policy justifications for NEPA, and the Act's most ardent defenders insist it has largely succeeded on both fronts.

The optimist's rosy assessment can be distinguished from the darker, more cynical view of the "NEPA monkey wrencher." The monkey wrencher is often critical of the quality of the information generated by environmental impact assessments and skeptical that agencies compelled to observe the rituals of NEPA procedure are actually influenced by the information thus generated. The monkey wrencher nonetheless places a high value on NEPA because it affords extraordinary opportunities to throw up procedural roadblocks that may delay or kill projects the monkey wrencher opposes. A full-scale environmental impact statement (EIS), in particular, is usually costly and time-consuming to produce.

NEPA litigation—either to decide whether an EIS is required or to determine its adequacy once it is produced—adds further costs and delays. Fear of judicial review pushes agencies toward ever-lengthier and more elaborate EISs, responding to all major comments received in the public notice and comment period. NEPA thus becomes a highly effective tool that environmental NGOs and others can use to raise the financial and political costs of projects they oppose and stretch out decisions over an extended time frame, giving time to rally political opposition. In some cases these delays and associated financial and political costs may be enough to derail the project entirely. In other cases, their ability to erect procedural obstacles may give project opponents leverage in the larger political bargaining that surrounds the decision, which they may use to force desired modifications in project design.

When used in this way, NEPA is largely a negative weapon—an obstructionist tool. Its use is predicated upon an understanding that the EIS process is by its very nature so inefficient and cumbersome that it may be used to thwart or constrain agency decision-making through selective, tactical application of extreme transaction costs. Environmental NGOs often deploy NEPA in this way, producing environmentally beneficial outcomes in particular cases; some NGOs justify NEPA's continued utility on these grounds. In the aggregate, however, a decision-making process that depends upon high transaction costs and tactical obstructionism looks like a sub-optimal way to run a government. As to particular applications, there is no way to sort the good cases from the bad; anyone with an obstructionist agenda, a skilled lawyer, and constitutional standing can wield the procedural monkey wrench to try to block or delay government projects, making NEPA (and state-level "little NEPAs") a favorite tool of NIMBY-ism as well as environmentalism.

A third position, roughly reflecting the longstanding view of some agency officials and many in the extractive industries operating on federal lands, is that of the "NEPA skeptic." This view is roughly the flip-side of the monkey wrencher's. For all the reasons environmental NGOs love NEPA, agency managers and affected industry parties tend to hate it. They see it as a tool of unprincipled obstructionism, a roadblock to progress, and a pointless and burdensome paperwork exercise that leads to delays and adds to project costs. Some NEPA skeptics also see its obstructionist potential as a fundamentally undemocratic device that gives "special interest lobbies" (the monkey wrenchers) undue influence over governmental decision-making. The skeptics' underlying analysis of NEPA's operative mechanisms is in important respects quite similar to that of the monkey wrenchers, yet, as the parties who bear the costs of delay, they are on the other side of the fence with respect to the desirability of tactical obstructionism.

A fourth view, prevalent in the legal academic literature, is that of the "legalist critic." The legalist's view of NEPA is also generally negative, but her complaint here is not that NEPA is too robust, but rather that it is too anemic. Legalists charge that although NEPA was intended to have substantive as well as procedural requirements, the statute has been eviscerated by the courts and especially by the Supreme Court—a forum in which environmental NGOs have never won a NEPA case. The Court held that NEPA's substantive requirements were merely precatory and not judicially enforceable; NEPA's requirements, the Court said, are "essentially procedural." Mandatory procedure without substantive legal standards is held in low regard by the legalist critics. In addition, the Court has eliminated even the more detailed procedures that lower courts had begun to require. The effect of these decisions, in the view of the legalist critic, is to expand the range of agency discretion and weaken NEPA's influence.

This brief inventory does not exhaust the range of views concerning NEPA's effectiveness. Nor are the four positions caricatured here mutually exclusive. Some environmental NGOs, for example, may simultaneously hold optimist and monkey wrencher views, valuing NEPA both because it produces better-informed and more environmentally enlightened agency decisions, and because it allows them to intervene to block especially undesirable projects. Other monkey wrenchers may share the legalist critic's view that judicially enforceable substantive standards would make for a stronger and more effective NEPA, but in the meantime they are willing to use the procedural tools at their disposal. Precisely because they think that procedure without substance is likely to be ineffective, some legalist critics may share the skeptic's view that observance of NEPA's procedural formalities is dilatory, costly, and a waste of scarce agency resources.

Nor are these various positions always held in such stark terms as I pose them here; actual views extend across a continuum of intensity. Still, the caricatures depicted here roughly capture the principal poles in the debate.

II   NEPA's Effectiveness: An Alternative View

In a recent article, I came down somewhere between NEPA's enthusiasts and its critics, but with a twist. I argued that NEPA has accomplished a good deal—certainly more than its most vociferous critics acknowledge. These results have not come about, however, through the mechanisms usually identified by NEPA's supporters. Instead, progress has been achieved mainly through a back-handed and unintentional incentive mechanism, one that is poorly understood and deserves a good deal more scholarly attention than it has received to date.

NEPA demands of the reporting agency a great deal of information all at once: a one-time-only, purely ex ante, panoptic assessment of all the environmental consequences of a proposed action; all reasonably foreseeable alternatives to that action; and any reasonably foreseeable mitigation measures necessary to reduce the adverse environmental impacts. That's quite a mouthful even to say, but stating it that way suggests the enormous burden that such an open-ended information production requirement places on the agency.

Another critical feature of NEPA is that its environmental impact assessment requirements are purely predictive in character. Simply put, NEPA asks reporting agencies to tell us everything that's going to happen. It does not ask for subsequent verification that the agency's predictions were accurate. The emphasis is not on actual impacts, but on predicted impacts. This may seem puzzling, but NEPA—written in the latter stages of an era when we had great confidence in "comprehensive bureaucratic rationality"—apparently assumes that expert bureaucrats armed with sharp pencils and green eyeshades will have the capacity to predict, accurately and comprehensively, how things will turn out, given a particular course of action and taking all relevant factors into account.

We have subsequently learned that the world is more complicated than that. Ecological systems are complex, dynamic, and non-linear, consisting of numerous mutually interdependent components and processes, interacting in complex and hard-to-calculate ways, and exhibiting numerous threshold effects and high levels of "inherent stochasticity." Our scientific understanding of basic ecosystem components and processes is riddled with gaps and uncertainties, and even the most thoroughly studied and best understood ecosystems tend to produce surprises—sometimes quite large surprises—over time.

This background of ecological complexity and interconnectedness contributes to the burdensomeness of the EIS requirement. Comprehensive assessments of environmental impacts are costly and time-consuming, as the monkey wrenchers well recognize; it is precisely for this reason that the EIS has become the favorite tool of those seeking to kill or delay projects. The background of ecological complexity also creates opportunities for monkey wrenchers to challenge the substantive adequacy of the EISs that are produced, since they can often find some impact, alternative, or mitigation measure that the agency has failed to consider. This, predictably, drives agencies to try to write even more comprehensive "kitchen sink" EISs so as to preempt the possibility of judicial reversal, further adding to the length of the process, the size of the EIS document, and the costs of EIS production.

* * * Due to the time it takes to produce, the EIS will also typically arrive too late in the process to inform and influence the agency's decision. Typically, agencies will commit resources to producing an EIS only if they have already determined that it is unavoidable; that is, if the project is so environmentally damaging than an EIS will be required, but the agency calculates that project benefits outweigh the costs and delay added by EIS production. Consequently, we tend to get EISs only for the most environmentally harmful projects, after the agency has already decided (though not as a formal legal matter) to proceed despite the adverse environmental consequences.

As an unintended corollary, agencies have a strong incentive to avoid EIS production in the first instance if at all possible. For the vast majority of projects, avoiding EIS production turns out to be reasonably easy. NEPA requires that an agency produce an EIS only if its proposed action "significantly affects the quality of the human environment." The term "significantly affects" is not defined in the statute or in the CEQ regulations, leaving that judgment to agency discretion—albeit policed by the possibility of NGO lawsuits and judicial intervention. Most NEPA compliance effort these days goes not into producing full-scale EISs, but into producing slimmed-down documents called environmental assessments (EAs), designed to produce just enough information to justify a "Finding of No Significant Impact" (FONSI) to get the agency off the hook.

The numbers tell the story: each year federal agencies produce about 50,000 EAs leading to FONSIs. In contrast, across the entire federal government only about 500 EISs are produced annually, and since every Final EIS must be preceded by a Draft EIS (and may be followed by a Supplemental EIS), this figure really represents approximately 250 federal actions per year that trigger the EIS production process—a vanishingly small number given the scale and scope of federal operations.

Many of the 50,000 FONSIs are so-called "mitigated FONSIs," in which the proposed project is redefined at an early stage to include some mitigation measures that, if implemented, will bring the expected environmental impacts below the EIS-triggering threshold of "significant." To enthusiasts of the EIS process, the mitigated FONSI looks like an unprincipled evasion of NEPA's core requirement. If the agency starts out expecting the project to have "significant" impacts, a full-scale EIS is ordinarily required to compel the agency to examine environmental impacts, reasonable alternatives, and the full range of mitigation measures, so that a "fully informed" agency can reassess its alternatives and mitigation options in light of the information thus revealed. With a mitigated FONSI, the agency takes a procedural shortcut, short-circuiting the prescribed decision-making path by choosing mitigation measures before the results of a full EIS analysis are in, and on that basis redefining the project so it is no longer expected to have "significant effects." To the mitigated FONSI's critics, this looks like cheating.

I say, "Bravo!" to the use of mitigated FONSIs—at least, up to a point. The widespread use of the mitigated FONSI is the best evidence we have that NEPA is actually altering agency decision-making and improving environmental performance. Agencies are redefining projects to include mitigation measures that reduce adverse environmental impacts below the "significant" threshold. Moreover, through use of the mitigated FONSI, they are presumably achieving these environmentally beneficial results at a lower cost and in less time than would be required if they went through the full-blown EIS process. That is a positive outcome, not a negative one. It is evidence that NEPA works. Of course, it may not be working in quite the way it was intended to work. Rather than serving as the vehicle for fully informed agency decision-making, the EIS operates as a penalty-default rule, creating an incentive for agencies to avoid its onerous requirements by upgrading environmental standards at an earlier stage of project design.

III   A Smarter NEPA?

I said "Bravo!" to the mitigated FONSI, but only up to a point. The missing elements here are verification, transparency, and accountability—shortcomings in the entire NEPA system, but especially in the netherworld of FONSIs and mitigated FONSIs, where most NEPA compliance efforts occur outside the glare of public scrutiny.

Environmental impact assessment should be reoriented toward monitoring and reporting on actual outcomes, rather than relying exclusively on ex ante predictions. We should begin by recognizing that agency experts do not have perfect information, and consequently we cannot trust that their predictions will turn out to be accurate. If we want to ensure that mitigation measures are achieving environmentally beneficial results, at some point we need to see what has actually happened and to know whether the predictions were correct.

Without question, there is value in a pre-project analytical exercise that generates science-based predictions concerning the expected environmental consequences of a proposed action. However, because ecological processes are complex and typically less than fully understood, such predictions are often highly uncertain, as are expectations concerning the effectiveness of mitigation measures that might be included in the project. Yet no follow-up monitoring or verification of the accuracy of pre-project predictions is required once the project is in place.

NEPA thus assumes an unattainable level of clairvoyance at the pre-project stage, and naively relies on the uncertain information thus generated. My first proposal is simply that we require follow-up monitoring to verify the accuracy of any predictions we can identify at the pre-project analytical stage as resting on uncertain foundations. Follow-up monitoring would produce multiple benefits. It would provide baseline data that should allow us to improve scientific understanding of ecological processes and human impacts, and thereby improve our predictive capacity over time. In addition, it would create the possibility of post-project adjustments in mitigation measures, enhancing their prospects for success. Finally, it would give the political branches and the public a better opportunity to hold agencies accountable for actual, as opposed to merely predicted, environmental performance.

NOTES

1.   In addition to the views expressed by Karkkainen, some observers have asserted that NEPA has helped protect the environment by transforming agency cultures. According to this argument, complying with NEPA (and with other environmental laws) has compelled federal agencies to hire more environmental scientists, and those environmental scientists have brought more environmental awareness to the agencies for which they work.

2.   For a good case study of NEPA in the trenches, see Robert Adler, *In Defense of NEPA: The Case of the Legacy Parkway*, 26 J. LAND RESOURCES & ENVTL. L. 297 (2007). Adler describes NEPA battles over the Legacy Parkway, a highway project near the shores of Great Salt Lake in Utah. The process was protracted and litigious, yet Adler describes it as ultimately positive:

> The Legacy Parkway NEPA process is notable more for its flaws than for its strengths. It took far longer than intended, was fraught with divisive controversy, and ultimately the FEIS was rejected by the U.S. Court of Appeals for the Tenth Circuit. Despite all of those problems, however, in the end the NEPA process (and the accompanying Clean Water Act analysis) served its intended purposes. It facilitated a broader public discussion of the values at stake in the controversy, and a wider consideration of alternatives. Litigation is never the preferred way to resolve disputes, and can be expensive, time-consuming, and even painful. The end result, however, was a project that will better serve the transportation needs of the corridor, but with less impact to the internationally significant wetlands and wildlife resources in the Great Salt Lake ecosystem.

Id. at 318.

3. While Congress has never amended NEPA, it does occasionally authorize exemptions from NEPA compliance. For example, the REAL ID Act of 2005 provided that Secretary of Homeland Security with the authority to waive any law, including NEPA, if necessary to "ensure expeditious construction" of structures along the United States' border with Mexico. On September 22, 2005, Homeland Security Secretary Michael Chertoff exercised that authority to exempt construction of a border fence in San Diego from seven environmental laws including NEPA. *See* CHAD C. HADDAL, ET AL., CONGRESSIONAL RESEARCH SERVICE, BORDER SECURITY: BARRIERS ALONG THE U.S. INTERNATIONAL BORDER (2009).

Test your knowledge with a Chapter 7 online quiz in CasebookPlus™.

CHAPTER 8

BIODIVERSITY PROTECTION

For many students, law school begins with a fox. In addition to being a property law classic, *Pierson v. Post* is a reminder that wild animals and plants have long been important to the law. Indeed, laws governing wild plants and animals have been part of the American political tradition for centuries, and were well developed years before the term "environmental law" came into common use. With the emergence of modern environmental law, the law of wild, non-human living things— which we will refer to as the law of biodiversity—has taken on new dimensions and prominence. Now, in many parts of the country, some of the most salient environmental issues involve regulatory protection of things like wolves, prairie chickens, and two-inch-long fish.

This chapter addresses one part of biodiversity law: the federal Endangered Species Act (ESA). That is a relatively narrow focus, for the ESA is just one component of a broader legal field, much of which cannot be covered in an introductory environmental law course. *See generally* JOHN COPELAND NAGLE ET AL., THE LAW OF BIODIVERSITY AND ECOSYSTEM MANAGEMENT (2013). At the federal level, laws like the Lacey Act, the Migratory Bird Treaty Act, the Magnuson-Stevens Fishery Act, and the Marine Mammal Protection Act all play important roles in protecting biodiversity, as do traditional pollution control statutes like the Clean Water Act. State biodiversity law is also extensive, and often extends to species not protected under federal laws. Internationally, numerous treaties, like the Convention on Biodiversity, the International Convention for the Regulation of Whaling, and the Convention on International Trade in Endangered Species of Wild Fauna and Flora, protect biodiversity. But among all of these bodies of law, the ESA stands out. We focus upon it here because it is a particularly influential and controversial law, and because the ESA captures themes that echo across the field of environmental regulation.

This chapter begins with background materials on biodiversity, explaining why it is diminishing, why we might want to reverse that trend, and why people might have reservations about biodiversity protection. We then provide a brief overview of the ESA before exploring ways in which key statutory provisions are applied.

I. WHY (AND WHY NOT) PROTECT BIODIVERSITY?

For most people, at least some of the common reasons for protecting air and water quality, or for keeping hazardous waste out of the ground, will seem obvious. People need clean air and clean water to survive.

There are similarly obvious arguments for protecting some forms of biodiversity; a world without pollinators, for example, would be a much worse place for people. But some of the arguments for biodiversity protection are less intuitive. This section therefore explains why biodiversity is threatened and why we might want law to respond to those threats—as well as some of the reasons why we might be cautious about such legal responses.

A. BIODIVERSITY AND EXTINCTION

According to paleontologists, the earth's history includes five major extinction events, when a very large percentage of the earth's plant and animal species disappeared. Some ecologists argue that we are now in the midst of the sixth major extinction, with humans serving as the primary cause.

Humans cause biodiversity loss in a variety of ways. *See* David S. Wilcove et al., *Quantifying Risks to Imperiled Species in the United States*, 48 BIOSCIENCE 607 (1998). The most important threat is habitat degradation and loss. Across the globe, humans have put massive areas of land, and many of our aquatic ecosystems, to agricultural, industrial, and urban use. Some species can adapt as their habitats are transformed, but many cannot, and they are forced to retreat to increasingly smaller remnants of their former range. Even where some relatively undisturbed habitat remains, its configuration can cause problems. If habitat is reduced to isolated patches, species are likely to lose their genetic diversity. They also may not be able to repopulate isolated habitat areas if populations are wiped out by natural disturbances or disease.

Invasive species are another major threat. Sometimes deliberately and sometimes accidentally, humans have moved many species around the world, often introducing them into habitats where they have few natural predators and where potential prey species have developed few defenses to their new neighbors. These invasive species can decimate native populations. They also can become valued species in their own right; to provide one example, many fish species have populated habitats outside their native ranges precisely because anglers put them there. For that reason, efforts to exterminate invasive species sometimes raise tricky questions about what environmental conditions we value, and why. Whatever value invasive species have, their aggregate effects on native biodiversity have clearly been negative and widespread.

In the United States, hunting and harvesting of rare species is generally not a major issue; gone are the days when the American commercial hunting industry could drive bison to the brink of extinction—and drive passenger pigeons over that brink. But globally, trade in wildlife remains a huge, and sometimes illicit, industry. According to one recent estimate, illegal trade in endangered species is worth between eight and ten billion dollars annually, with the extent of trade rising rapidly in recent years. KATHERINE LAWSON & ALEX VINES, GLOBAL IMPACTS OF THE ILLEGAL WILDLIFE TRADE viii (2014). In the United States, targeted hunting remains controversial for several rare species, including the recovering wolf populations of the northern Rocky Mountains. Incidental catches of rare species also are an ongoing issue for the fishing industry.

Finally, pollution threatens many species. To provide one example, widespread use of DDT, a potent pesticide, contributed to drastic reductions in the United States' population of bald eagles. This particular story has a happy ending; DDT was banned, and bald eagle populations have recovered enough that they are no longer listed as threatened or endangered. But for many species, pollution remains a continuing threat.

More recent studies also identify climate change as a major risk factor for large numbers of species. *See, e.g.,* Michelle Staudinger et al., IMPACTS OF CLIMATE CHANGE ON BIODIVERSITY, ECOSYSTEMS, AND ECOSYSTEM SERVICES: TECHNICAL INPUT TO THE 2013 NATIONAL CLIMATE ASSESSMENT (2012). By moving climate zones toward the poles and to higher elevations, shifting precipitation patterns, and raising sea levels, among other consequences, climate change is likely to have profound effects upon many ecosystems and upon the species that inhabit them.

These threats often work in combination. Climate change, for example, is likely to be a greater threat where habitat loss and fragmentation have limited a species' ability to migrate to more suitable climate zones. Habitat loss also can expose a species to higher levels of predation, particularly if that habitat loss pushes it into zones where it must compete with, or be preyed upon by, invasive species. And pollution can weaken living things, leaving them more vulnerable to other threats like climate change or disease.

B. REASONS FOR PROTECTING BIODIVERSITY

That humans are causing a dramatic loss of biodiversity is beyond dispute. But why should we care? And, more specifically, why should laws protect biodiversity? After all, for much of our nation's history, many laws did the opposite; government-sponsored bounty systems encouraged the extermination of species, like wolves and bears, that the ESA would later protect. And while most of those bounty systems are gone, there are many places—our homes, yards, and agricultural fields, for example— where biodiversity is something we actively suppress, usually without any second thoughts. But long before the enactment of the ESA, other laws reflected a growing belief that species should not be lost. The excerpt below introduces you to some of the traditional arguments supporting that belief.

Holly Doremus, Comment, *Patching the Ark: Improving Legal Protection of Biological Diversity*
18 ECOLOGY L.Q. 265, 269–75 (1991)

[T]he arguments for preservation of biological diversity can be divided into three categories: utilitarian, esthetic, and moral. * * *

1.   The Utilitarian Basis for Preservation of Diversity

The utilitarian justification for the preservation of diversity rests on the direct and indirect usefulness of biological resources to humanity. Individual species provide us with a number of direct benefits. For example, we have domesticated our food crops, both plant and animal, from wild species. Other species might provide new crops. Wild relatives of current crop species can also provide a source of useful genetic traits. * * *

Biological diversity is also a useful source of new medicinal drugs. Chemicals derived from higher plants form the major ingredient in about a quarter of all prescriptions written in the United States; chemicals derived from lower plants and microbes account for another eighth. Many of these drugs can be produced more cheaply by extraction than by chemical synthesis. Numerous species have yet to be examined for their medicinal properties. Thus, many undiscovered medicinally useful chemicals may exist in the natural world.

A number of animal species serve another important function in medicine as model systems for the study of human diseases. For obvious reasons, researchers cannot deliberately infect human subjects to facilitate laboratory study of the progress and properties of a disease. However, they can and do use animals as laboratory subjects. Examples include the use of desert pupfish to study kidney disease and of armadillos to study leprosy. Recently AIDS has been induced in rhesus monkeys, allowing researchers to develop a clinical model for the disease.

* * * Nature may also serve more subtle needs. Human beings may have "a deep-rooted need" for contact with other living things. Such contact may promote both mental and physical health.

Besides the direct benefits described above, ecosystems provide a number of indirect benefits to humanity. These "ecosystem services" include climate control, oxygen production, removal of carbon dioxide from the atmosphere, soil generation, nutrient cycling, and purification of freshwater supplies. Some of these functions could probably be performed by managed systems, at least on a small scale, but management of such systems on a global scale is presently beyond our technological capability.

Moreover, some of these processes, such as nutrient cycling, are highly complex and not yet fully understood.

Proponents of the utilitarian value of biological diversity often raise the argument that the potential uses of many biotic resources are not yet known, both because many species have not been fully investigated and because we cannot know in advance the needs of future generations. Thus, they argue, all (or as much as possible) of the biota must be preserved, in order to preserve those organisms which may ultimately prove useful. These advocates frequently cite Aldo Leopold's statement that "[t]o keep every cog and wheel is the first precaution of intelligent tinkering."

2.   The Esthetic Basis for Preservation of Diversity

Many people find beauty in the natural world, viewing natural objects, both living and nonliving, with a sense of admiration, wonder, or awe. Esthetic interest in nature is demonstrated in a variety of ways. For example, millions of Americans visit national parks and wildlife refuges every year. Some sixty million Americans participate in bird watching, and millions more engage in other forms of wildlife-related recreation. Nature photography and gardening are enormously popular hobbies. A perennial audience exists for television nature documentaries.

Individual species and specific natural areas may also come, over time, to be imbued with powerful symbolic value. They may embody the cultural or political identity of a people. The bald eagle is one such symbolic species; Mt. Fuji is an example of a symbolic natural feature. This symbolism provides further evidence of the esthetic attractions of nature.

* * * The esthetic value of diversity extends to ecosystem, species, and genetic diversity. Each species is an irreplaceable work of nature. A value similar to that given to works of art can be assigned to species. Ecosystems have esthetic value beyond that of the species they contain because the interactions that occur among species, and the way the system as a whole responds to perturbations, are themselves interesting. And genetic diversity is esthetically valuable both because the differences among individuals may fascinate us (as in the case of our own species), and because it provides the building blocks from which new manifestations of nature's wonder can be constructed. To perhaps overstrain the art analogy, ecosystems can be seen as the whole canvas, species as the elements which make up the composition, and genetic variability as the pigments with which the work is produced.

3.   The Ethical Basis for Preservation of Diversity

In 1949, Aldo Leopold advocated the extension of ethical obligations to the relations between man and nature, calling for the development of an "ecological conscience" reflecting "a conviction of individual responsibility for the health of the land." Since then, several commentators have argued that nonhuman organisms, and even nonliving natural objects, have or should have rights based on their intrinsic value. Under such a view, human beings have an ethical obligation not to destroy these creatures and objects, at least in the absence of a strong countervailing value.

* * * Ethical obligations to nature need not rest on such a nonanthropocentric foundation. Several philosophers and theologians, while not granting "rights" similar to those held by human beings to other species or to natural systems, have appealed to a tradition of human responsibility for stewardship of the Earth. The theological argument for stewardship proceeds from the premise that God created nature in part for his own enjoyment. The nature of the creation gives rise to a three-fold role for man with respect to nature: man is both overlord, wondering onlooker, and caretaker. The combination of these roles requires that man, insofar as possible, allow nature to flourish and to continue in its place.

These arguments in favor of protection may sound powerful, but protection often comes with costs, many of which will become clearer as you work through the materials that follow. Trees that are protected for northern spotted owls cannot be harvested. Land preserved for tiger salamanders cannot be developed. Water that must remain instream to sustain salmon cannot be used to irrigate agricultural fields. The list of conflicts could go on and on, and the common theme is straightforward: protecting endangered species often means limiting other human activities. The tradeoffs are not always negative; sometimes protecting species provides incidental benefits like preserving recreational opportunities or enhancing water quality. But the conflicts between species protection and other activities are nevertheless responsible for the ESA's reputation as perhaps the most controversial of all of the United States' environmental laws.

II. HISTORY

During the United States' first century, the federal government did very little to protect wildlife. Wildlife management authority instead rested primarily with the states. *See* Shannon Peterson, *Congress and Charismatic Megafauna: A Legislative History of the Endangered Species Act*, 29 ENVTL. L. 463 (1999).[1] In the late nineteenth and early twentieth centuries, the federal government began enacting legislation designed to protect specific kinds of wildlife, like the Migratory Bird Treaty Act, or to restrain trade in wildlife, like the Lacey Act. Broader federal protections for rare species did not emerge until the 1960s. Much like

---

[1] The history recounted in these paragraphs draws heavily on Peterson's article.

contemporaneous air and water quality statutes, the federal government's first efforts to protect endangered species lacked strong regulatory teeth and instead largely relied on voluntary action. By the early 1970s, both the Nixon Administration and many members of Congress perceived a need for stronger regulatory authority, and bills that would become the Endangered Species Act of 1973 emerged.

Though members of Congress wanted to strengthen protections, very few members seem to have realized just how strong a law they were enacting. As Peterson explains,

> Congress debated little over the various provisions of these bills. Moreover, the few congressional concerns centered not on sections 4, 7, or the application of the section 9 prohibition to habitat modification, but on issues relatively inconsequential to later developments. The most significant topic debated was the potential preemption of traditional state authority to manage wildlife. . . . These concerns, however, were minor, and congressional support for the bills soon became widespread and enthusiastic. In the Senate especially, debate over the ESA was almost nonexistent.
>
> The mutually beneficial nature of the proposed law seemed especially true because no significant special interest group came forward to oppose the ESA. During the Senate hearings in June of 1973, numerous administrative agency experts and every major environmental organization testified in support of the ESA. Even the National Rifle Association urged the passage of a stronger act. The only opposition came from a few groups representing state fish and game agencies, which worried about the preemption of state authority, and from the fur industry. Lack of significant special interest opposition was also evident during the House hearings. With "little open opposition to the bills," there appeared to be no reason, "except congressional inertia, for inaction."
>
> Few at the time opposed the ESA because no one anticipated how the Act might significantly interfere with economic development or personal property interests. One leading advocate of the ESA observed, "since someone does not necessarily have to combat vested economic interests, some politicians use the issue to parade themselves as environmentalists knowing they will not seriously offend corporate interests." The timber industry, other natural resource industries, and private property groups declined to fight the ESA in 1973 because they failed to see how the law might affect their interests. In addition, unlike today, no

organized anti-environmental coalition existed to probe and protest proposed environmental legislation.

Id. at 474. Consequently, Congress passed, by nearly unanimous votes, what the Supreme Court would later describe as "the most comprehensive legislation for the preservation of endangered species ever enacted by any nation." *Tenn. Valley Auth. v. Hill*, 437 U.S. 153, 180 (1978).

The statute's history did not end in 1973. Five years later, the Supreme Court decided *Tennessee Valley Authority v. Hill*,[2] a case famously viewed as pitting a two-inch fish against the mighty TVA, and the power of the new law became starkly clear. Congress immediately contemplated amendments to the statute, with the goal of adding additional flexibility. But it did not gut the ESA. The amendments, as you will see, allow exceptions to some of the act's primary mandates and allow some harms to species, but those exceptions are available only in very limited circumstances. Congress amended the statute again in 1982, and this time the changes involved trading regulatory flexibility in some areas for heightened conservation in others. The statutory amendments then ceased. Proposals for major amendments to the ESA emerged again in the 1990s and the 2000s, but to date, none has ever made it through Congress. Instead, in the past three decades, the primary—and significant—changes to ESA implementation have occurred at the administrative level.

III. ESA OVERVIEW

The Endangered Species Act begins with a bold statement of purpose:

---

16 U.S.C. § 1531. Congressional findings and declaration of purposes and policy

The Congress finds and declares that—

(1) various species of fish, wildlife, and plants in the United States have been rendered extinct as a consequence of economic growth and development untempered by adequate concern and conservation;

(2) other species of fish, wildlife, and plants have been so depleted in numbers that they are in danger of or threatened with extinction;

---

[2] An excerpted version of *TVA v. Hill* appears on pages 775–780.

(3) these species of fish, wildlife, and plants are of esthetic, ecological, educational, historical, recreational, and scientific value to the Nation and its people; * * *

(b) Purposes

The purposes of this chapter are to provide a means whereby the ecosystems upon which endangered species and threatened species depend may be conserved, to provide a program for the conservation of such endangered species and threatened species, and to take such steps as may be appropriate to achieve the purposes of [a series of treaties that commit the United States to protecting biodiversity].

To give effect to the ESA's purposes, Congress included several key substantive provisions in the Act.

The Act delegates primary implementing authority to the United States Fish and Wildlife Service (FWS), a sub-agency within the Department of the Interior, and the National Marine Fisheries Service (NMFS), a sub-agency within the United States Department of Commerce. FWS has jurisdiction over terrestrial species, and NMFS has jurisdiction over most marine and diadromous species.[3] In addition to the authority conferred on NMFS and FWS, all federal agencies have responsibilities to conserve species, as described in more detail below.

To receive protection under the act, species must be listed as threatened or endangered, and *section 4* (along with ESA's definitions section) specifies substantive criteria for judging whether species qualify for listing and procedures for completing the listing process. Importantly, section 4 also provides public petition rights and creates deadlines for agency action, and that combination allows non-governmental entities to initiate the listing process and to accelerate its completion. Listing petitions and subsequent litigation have become an increasingly common aspect of practice under the ESA, leading to frequent complaints that the listing process has been wrested from governmental control. See Eric Biber & Berry Brosi, *Officious Intermeddlers or Citizen Experts? Petitions and Public Production of Information in Environmental Law*, 58 UCLA L. REV. 321, 336 (2010).

Section 4 also requires the designation of critical habitat for listed species, and it authorizes FWS to draft recovery plans and protective regulations.

Section 7 requires federal agencies to take affirmative steps to "conserve" listed species, although courts have generally viewed this as

---

[3]   Diadromous species spend part of their life cycle in freshwater and part in saltwater. For ESA purposes, the most important diadromous species are anadromous, which means they are born in fresh water and then migrate to saltwater. Most salmon, for example, are anadromous.

an unenforceable obligation. It also limits those agencies' ability to harm species. More specifically, it precludes federal agencies from authorizing, funding, or carrying out actions likely to "jeopardize" the continued existence of listed species or to adversely modify their critical habitat. Section 7 also specifies a process, commonly known as "consultation," that requires federal agencies to work with FWS or NMFS to ensure that their actions will not result in jeopardy or in adverse modification of critical habitat. ESA litigation frequently involves questions about whether a federal agency has adequately consulted with FWS and NMFS and whether it will successfully avoid jeopardy and adverse modification.

Section 9 prohibits trade in endangered fish and wildlife species. It also forbids "takes" of such species, and that prohibition extends to anyone, not just federal agencies. Section 9 provides somewhat lesser protection to endangered plant species. As you will see from the materials below, prohibited "takes" can occur through habitat modifications, and questions about whether habitat modifications constitute "takes" recur often in ESA implementation and litigation.

While the text of section 9 explicitly applies only to endangered species, the ESA authorizes FWS and NMFS to extend section 9's protections to threatened species. The two agencies have taken different approaches to exercising that authority. In 1978, FWS issued a "blanket" rule extending the take prohibition to all threatened species unless the agency specially limited such protections for a specific species. See 50 C.F.R. § 17.31. NMFS, on the other hand, decides on a case-by-case basis whether to affirmatively extend the take prohibition to threatened species, usually at the time that species is listed.

Sections 7 and 10 provide exceptions to section 9's general prohibition on takes. Section 7 allows federal agencies that complete a consultation process and implement "reasonable and prudent measures," which are measures designed to minimize takes, to obtain "incidental take authorization." Section 10 allows regulated entities to obtain "incidental take permits," but only so long as they prepare and implement, and FWS or NMFS approves, something known as a "habitat conservation plan."

Several other provisions of the ESA authorize FWS and NMFS to use land purchases to protect species and to cooperate with states and with other countries on protective initiatives.

Finally, *section 11* of the ESA contains enforcement provisions. It authorizes civil or criminal enforcement by government entities, and it also contains a sweeping citizen suit provision and an attorney fee provision. As you learned when reading *Lujan v. Defenders of Wildlife*, 504 U.S. 555 (1992), the Supreme Court has placed limits on that citizen suit provision. Plaintiffs must have standing, notwithstanding statutory language that seems to authorize any person to prosecute any violation. But the combination of extensive petition rights, a citizen suit provision, and an attorney fee provision has made litigation an important part of ESA implementation.

The map below illustrates these key relationships. It is not a complete depiction of the ESA; several provisions (including the citizen suit provision) are missing. But it should help you understand the interrelationships of the provisions covered in depth in the pages that follow.

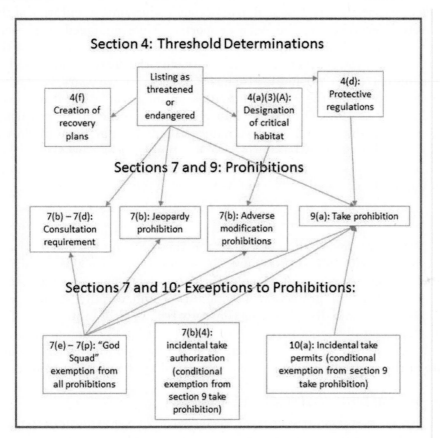

What has all of this accomplished? The excerpt below provides a brief summary of the extensive literature on ESA implementation.

Dave Owen, *The Endangered Species Act*

in GLOBAL CLIMATE CHANGE AND U.S. LAW 187–88 (Michael B. Gerrard & Jody Freeman, eds.; 2d ed. 2014)

So does the ESA work? Even after nearly forty years of implementation, answers to that question are decidedly mixed. Multiple studies do show that the ESA reduces the risk of extinctions. Conversely, few listed species have recovered. These contrasting results suggest that the Act has been effective primarily at stabilizing species, or at least slowing their decline, but not at nursing them back to health.

The even greater question about the Act is whether its successes are worth its costs. To many of the ESA's critics, the answer is obviously not; they argue that the Act has imposed major financial burdens while generating few positive results. In recent decades, Congress also has seemed rather unsympathetic to the ESA, sometimes passing budgetary measures specifically designed to undercut agency implementation of the statute. Nevertheless, the Act's supporters have managed to prevent statutory amendments, and many of the ESA's supporters argue that the value of its protections does greatly outweigh the costs it imposes. The calculus of costs and benefits also has changed over the years, for agency implementation of the ESA is quite different now from what it was even as recently as 1990. On the one hand, increases in the number of listed species and the amount of designated critical habitat have made the statute a far more pervasive presence. But the Services have also worked hard to find more flexible ways of implementing the statute, perhaps softening the economic impact of its increased reach.

IV. LISTING SPECIES

The gateway to protection under the ESA is section 4, which establishes criteria and procedures for listing species as "threatened" or "endangered." Much is at stake with listing decisions. A listed species will receive the full protection of section seven and, usually, sections nine and ten, while non-listed species generally receive ESA protection only if they incidentally benefit from protections accorded to other species. For that reason, listing decisions often receive ample political attention and are at the center of litigation—as exemplified by the problem below.

PROBLEM: LISTING ATLANTIC SALMON?

Many Endangered Species Act controversies have involved salmon. Particularly in the Pacific Northwest, where enormous salmon runs have largely been extirpated by dams, water withdrawals, fishing, logging, and a variety of other human activities, ESA litigation involving salmon has been constant. Those controversies also have touched the East Coast. Atlantic salmon, once abundant in most rivers from the Hudson north, have nearly disappeared. Dams, pollution, and overfishing eliminated salmon from southern New England's rivers, and only in Maine do a few rivers retain indigenous runs. Even in those rivers, populations are severely depleted.

Image from NOAA.gov

You are an attorney with the United States Fish and Wildlife Service (for Atlantic salmon, your agency and the National Marine Fisheries Service share jurisdiction). For several years, both agencies have been considering whether to list Atlantic salmon. Two years ago, FWS and NMFS declined to list the species. They concluded that Atlantic salmon populations in Maine were not sufficiently distinct from Canadian populations (some of which remain abundant) to justify a listing, and also that conservation efforts by the state of Maine obviated the need for a listing. Elected officials in Maine were pleased with that decision. Environmental groups, some of which had petitioned for the listing, were not.

More recently, FWS and NMFS shifted course. They issued a proposed rule that would list Atlantic salmon populations in seven Maine rivers as endangered. Your task, now, is to evaluate the legal implications of finalizing that proposal. As you will see from the materials below, the state of Maine has warned that it will sue if Maine's Atlantic salmon are listed. Environmental groups will probably sue if Maine's Atlantic salmon are *not* listed. And your bosses would like to know whether either course of action, or both, will stand up in court.

As you review the materials, please consider the legal implications of several points of controversy—each of which exemplifies issues that often arise from listing decisions:

The economic consequences of listing. Participants in three important industries in northeastern coastal Maine[4]—blueberry growing, aquaculture, and forestry—adamantly oppose the listing. The blueberry growers worry that if the salmon runs are listed, growers will be compelled to withdraw less groundwater from aquifers that ultimately discharge into salmon streams, and may also be compelled to reduce their pesticide use. Both changes would put them at a severe competitive disadvantage, they claim, against Canadian blueberry growers, who will be subject to no such restrictions. Salmon aquaculture farmers are likewise concerned about increased regulation. Many environmental advocates have warned that salmon farms can incubate disease and that interbreeding with escaped farmed salmon can weaken the fitness and genetic diversity of natural stocks. The salmon farmers are therefore concerned that listing will lead to restrictions on the scale and location of their operations. The timber industry worries about restrictions

---

4   Mainers refer to this region as "Downeast Maine."

on where and when it can harvest. All three groups warn of potentially devastating economic consequences in an already-poor region.

Do these economic concerns provide a legal basis for declining to list the salmon?

Federalism concerns. The state of Maine has flatly stated that it opposes any "federalization" of salmon management. In 2007, it developed and began implementing a management plan designed to preclude the need for a listing. The state claims that its plan's sensitivity to local needs makes it a preferable alternative to the blunt and inflexible ESA. Senior officials in FWS, NMFS, and the White House have some sympathy for this view. They would like the threat of ESA listings to lead to effective *state* protection of species, without listings actually occurring.

Do these federalism concerns provide a legal basis for declining to list the salmon?

Geography and genetics. While Atlantic salmon are almost gone from the United States, healthy populations remain in a few Canadian rivers, and those populations do not seem likely to go extinct. Your biologists tell you that Maine's population is *not* sufficiently distinct that it would be classified (using a biological definition) as a separate species. But they have also concluded that the Atlantic salmon in Maine's rivers are genetically distinct from those in Canadian rivers and from those raised in Maine's many aquaculture pens. These differences, they tell you, have helped Maine's Atlantic salmon adapt to life at the southern edge of its range, and therefore may be important to the species' future survival in Maine and, potentially, southern Canada.

If your scientists are correct, can Maine's population of Atlantic salmon be listed? Must it?

Climate change. Salmon are a cold-water species, but climate change is gradually warming Maine rivers, and is expected to continue to do so in the future. Even if global emissions are curbed, some continued warming is inevitable, and Maine's climate could eventually become warmer than areas outside of Atlantic salmon's historic range. What this means for salmon isn't certain, but it is possible that Maine's runs are now doomed no matter what changes occur in management of the rivers themselves.

How should climate change affect your listing decision?

The starting point for your research is the text of section 4, which appears below. As you read, you will want to pay close attention to the criteria for listing decisions. Which of the factors described above are specifically recognized as important, and which, if any, are excluded from the analysis?

16 U.S.C. § 1532. Definitions

(5)(A) The term "critical habitat" for a threatened or endangered species means—

(i)   the specific areas within the geographical area occupied by the species, at the time it is listed in accordance with the provisions of section 1533 of this title, on which are found those physical or biological features (I) essential to the conservation of the species and (II) which may require special management considerations or protection; and

(ii) specific areas outside the geographical area occupied by the species at the time it is listed in accordance with the provisions of section 1533 of this title, upon a determination by the Secretary that such areas are essential for the conservation of the species.
* * *

(6) The term "endangered species" means any species which is in danger of extinction throughout all or a significant portion of its range other than a species of the Class Insecta determined by the Secretary to constitute a pest whose protection under the provisions of this chapter would present an overwhelming and overriding risk to man.
* * *

(16) The term "species" includes any subspecies of fish or wildlife or plants, and any distinct population segment of any species of vertebrate fish or wildlife which interbreeds when mature.

* * *

(20) The term "threatened species" means any species which is likely to become an endangered species within the foreseeable future throughout all or a significant portion of its range.

16 U.S.C. § 1533. Determination of endangered species and threatened species

(a) Generally

(1)   The Secretary shall by regulation promulgated in accordance with subsection (b) of this section determine whether any species is an endangered species or a threatened species because of any of the following factors:

(A)   the present or threatened destruction, modification, or curtailment of its habitat or range;

(B)   overutilization for commercial, recreational, scientific, or educational purposes;

(C) disease or predation;

(D) the inadequacy of existing regulatory mechanisms; or

(E) other natural or manmade factors affecting its continued existence. * * *

(3)(A) The Secretary, by regulation promulgated in accordance with subsection (b) of this section and to the maximum extent prudent and determinable—

(i) shall, concurrently with making a determination under paragraph (1) that a species is an endangered species or a threatened species, designate any habitat of such species which is then considered to be critical habitat; and

(ii) may, from time-to-time thereafter as appropriate, revise such designation. * * *

(b) Basis for determinations

(1)(A) The Secretary shall make determinations required by subsection (a)(1) of this section solely on the basis of the best scientific and commercial data available to him after conducting a review of the status of the species and after taking into account those efforts, if any, being made by any State or foreign nation, or any political subdivision of a State or foreign nation, to protect such species, whether by predator control, protection of habitat and food supply, or other conservation practices, within any area under its jurisdiction, or on the high seas. * * *

(2) The Secretary shall designate critical habitat, and make revisions thereto, under subsection (a) (3) of this section on the basis of the best scientific data available and after taking into consideration the economic impact, the impact on national security, and any other relevant impact, of specifying any particular area as critical habitat. The Secretary may exclude any area from critical habitat if he determines that the benefits of such exclusion outweigh the benefits of specifying such area as part of the critical habitat, unless he determines, based on the best scientific and commercial data available, that the failure to designate such area as critical habitat will result in the extinction of the species concerned.

The article below is one of the many news stories written about the fight over the salmon listing. Note, as you read, that this story was written after an initial decision *not* to list the salmon. The proposal you're considering would reverse that initial decision.

———————

Orna Izakson, *Feds OK Salmon Plan, Agencies Forgo Endangered Listing*

BANGOR DAILY NEWS, Dec. 16, 1997

U.S. Secretary of Interior Bruce Babbitt cracks a smile during the applause after his statement about Maine salmon not being listed as an endangered species. Babbitt was with Gov. Angus King on Monday at the State House in Augusta.

At issue were remnant runs of wild Atlantic salmon in the Sheepscot, Ducktrap, Pleasant, Machias, East Machias, Dennys and Narraguagus rivers that were being considered for protection as a threatened species.

Instead, the U.S. Fish and Wildlife Service and the National Marine Fisheries Service decided that a state conservation plan removed the threats to those fish. The day's speakers all hailed the decision as a national model for protecting species locally with minimal federal intervention.

"The announcement today is short and sweet," Babbitt told the assembled lawmakers, state officials, industry leaders and environmentalists. "We are here gratefully and happily to say to the people of the great state of Maine that the petition to list the Atlantic salmon is hereby withdrawn."

The statement was followed by a protracted round of applause.

"We thought that would be a crowd pleaser," Babbitt said.

But not all the people who filled the State House's Hall of Flags were happy with the announcement.

"We're very concerned that this could turn out to be a national model plan for species extinction," said Jym St. Pierre, the Maine director for the group that first petitioned the federal agencies to protect the fish, RESTORE: The North Woods. "It really sounded like this decision . . . is being based primarily on politics, not on biology or what the law actually says."

St. Pierre said that the presence of the entire Maine congressional delegation and top players from the federal fish-protection agencies was unprecedented. "When you have a situation like this it's because you're trying to hide the lack of substance with a great deal of form."

King, the department heads and Maine's congressional delegation all said the state effort would go further to protect Atlantic salmon than federal intervention would. Babbitt said the move represents a change in the way the federal law is implemented to one that will be less dominated by litigation while still helping species at risk.

"Will the government be sued over this plan? It usually happens," Babbitt said. "I have absolute confidence that this plan will prevail."

Maine is the second state to successfully sell a plan based largely on beefed-up enforcement of existing regulation to the federal government in lieu of listing salmon.

NMFS approved a $30 million Oregon plan in April, also arguing that local efforts and goodwill backed by state government were the best way to protect the 35,000 coho salmon returning to the state's coastal streams.

In Maine, King has pledged $1.2 million for the plan to protect the roughly 200 fish that return to the seven Maine rivers each year, although the Legislature has made few specific allocations. The federal agencies have pledged an additional $11.4 million to the effort, and industry will spend $3.7 million.

* * * Bill Vail, director of the Maine Forest Products Council, who also served as commissioner of Fish and Wildlife in Maine from 1987 to 1993, said he was pleased with Monday's announcement.

"This really strengthens . . . the Endangered Species Act," he said. "It shows that the act can be flexible and focus on the goal rather than on the bureaucratic steps that tend to be so unforgiving or difficult. So we're going to get to the same end, but in a way that respects and accommodates people."

Sen. Susan Collins quoted Vail as saying that if the fish received federal protection, the Atlantic salmon would become the "spotted owl of the East," bringing to her mind visions of closed businesses and a wrecked Down East economy. "I'm delighted that we've avoided that outcome," she said.

Sen. Olympia Snowe tied the decision to the season.

"We thank you for the Christmas gift you have given the state," she said, adding that the result was based on a great deal of hard work. "Christmas has come early."

––––––––––––

FWS and NMFS use notice-and-comment rulemakings under section 553 of the Administrative Procedure Act to make listing decisions. 5 U.S.C. § 553. The preamble to a proposed or final rule typically contains a detailed summary of the status of and threats to the species, all based on the evidence before the agency. That preamble therefore becomes a key part of the administrative record in any litigation challenging the rule.

Below, we have included portions of the preamble to the proposed Atlantic salmon listing. The passages below are heavily excerpted—the actual document would be much longer—but they should give you good overview of the agency's evidence and its current reasoning. Because these statements also would be part of the administrative record for any judicial proceeding, and you should also consider whether they would support or undermine a listing or non-listing decision.

National Marine Fisheries Service and U.S. Fish and Wildlife Service, Endangered and Threatened Species; Proposed Endangered Status for a Distinct Population Segment of Anadromous Atlantic Salmon (Salmo salar) in the Gulf of Maine

64 Fed. Reg. 62,627, 62,631–38 (proposed Nov. 17, 1999)

Population Abundance of the Gulf of Maine DPS

Species abundance is a critical concern in assessing the population status of a species under the ESA. An examination of current abundance compared to historical levels and analysis of recent trends were used to determine the status of Atlantic salmon * * *. Total documented natural (wild & stocked fry) Gulf of Maine DPS spawner returns to the [eight rivers at issue] were: 1995 (83); 1996 (74); 1997 (35); 1998 (23); 1999 (29) (preliminary data). * * *

Given the data reviewed in this section, the Services conclude that naturally reproducing Atlantic salmon populations of the Gulf of Maine DPS are at extremely low levels of abundance. This conclusion is based principally on the facts that spawner abundance is below 10 percent of the number required to maximize juvenile production, juvenile abundance indices are lower than historical counts, and freshwater smolt production is less than a third of estimated capacity. * * *

Summary of Factors Affecting the Species

Section 4 of the ESA (16 U.S.C. 1533) and regulations promulgated to implement the listing provisions of the ESA (50 CFR part 424) set forth the procedures for adding species to the Federal list. Section 4 also requires that listing determinations be based solely on the best scientific and commercial data available, without consideration of possible economic or other impacts of such determinations. A species may be determined to be endangered or threatened due to one or more of the five factors described in section 4(a)(1) of the ESA. These factors and their application to the * * * Atlantic salmon are described below.

(a) The Present or Threatened Destruction, Modification, or Curtailment of Habitat or Range

Demonstrated and potential impacts to Atlantic salmon habitat within the (eight) watersheds result from the following causes: (1) Water extraction; (2) sedimentation; (3) obstructions to passage including those caused by beaver and debris dams and poorly designed road crossings;

(4) input of nutrients; (5) chronic exposure to insecticides, herbicides, fungicides, and pesticides (in particular, those used to control spruce budworm); (6) elevated water temperatures from processing water discharges; and (7) removal of vegetation along streambanks. The most obvious and immediate threat is posed by water extraction on some rivers within the DPS range, as it has the potential to expose or reduce salmon habitat.

* * * Although there does not appear to be one particular habitat issue which poses a significant threat by itself, the cumulative impacts from habitat degradation discussed above may reduce habitat quality and limit habitat quantity available to Gulf of Maine DPS salmon at various stages in their life history within freshwater. Given current low levels of abundance, it is critical that efforts be undertaken to better understand, avoid, minimize and mitigate these factors.

(b) Overutilization for Commercial, Recreational, Scientific, or Educational Purposes

Atlantic salmon smolts leave their natal rivers in New England in the spring and begin their extensive ocean migration. The migration brings them into Newfoundland waters in the spring, along the Labrador and Greenland coasts in summer, and on what is believed to be a return migration back into Newfoundland waters by early fall. * * * Over the past decade, only 90,000 wild Atlantic salmon (annual average) have returned to spawn in U.S. (3 percent) and Canadian (97 percent) rivers. Fishery managers believe that the annual number of returning spawners needed to sustain these stocks is 184,000 (ICES-NASWG, 1999).

[The report then describes increasingly restrictive regulation of salmon fisheries, both within and outside the United States.]

* * * Both commercial and recreational harvest of Atlantic salmon historically played a role in the decline of the Gulf of Maine DPS of Atlantic salmon. * * * The best available scientific data support the advice of technical experts in Maine that no directed recreational catch and release fishery should be carried out given existing stock conditions. Continuation of the existing directed catch and release fishery poses a threat of mortality or injury to the Gulf of Maine DPS of Atlantic salmon. Recreational fishing targeting other species also has the potential to result in incidental catch of various life stages of Atlantic salmon that could result in their injury or death. These fisheries also pose a potential threat to Atlantic salmon. The one documented poaching event in 1998 indicates that poaching continues to pose a potential threat to Atlantic salmon. Continued enforcement efforts and adequate penalties are essential to minimize this threat.

(c) Disease or Predation

Fish diseases have always represented a source of mortality to Atlantic salmon in the wild, though the threats of major loss due to disease are generally associated with salmon aquaculture. The level of threat from disease has remained relatively static until the last 3 years. Three recent events that have increased our concern for disease as a threat to the DPS are: (1) The appearance of ISA virus in 1996 on the North American continent within the range of possible exposure of migrant DPS salmon; (2) the discovery in 1998 of the retrovirus SSSV within the DPS population; and (3) the new information available in 1999 on the potential impact of coldwater disease (CWD) on salmon. * * *

(d) Inadequacy of Existing Regulatory Mechanisms

A variety of State and Federal statutes and regulations seek to address potential threats to Atlantic salmon and their habitat. These laws are complemented by international actions * * * and many interagency agreements and State-Federal cooperative efforts. Implementation and enforcement of these laws and regulations could be strengthened to further protect Atlantic salmon. The appropriate State and Federal agencies have established coordination mechanisms and have joined with private industries and landowners in partnerships for the protection of Atlantic salmon. These partnerships will be critical to the recovery of the species. Existing regulatory mechanisms either lack the capacity or have not been implemented adequately to decrease or remove the threats to wild Atlantic salmon. The discussion that follows will focus on those laws which are not sufficient to deal with threats, or, if adequate, are not being applied or enforced. Major threats continue to be poor marine survival, water withdrawals, recreational fishing mortality, disease, and aquaculture impacts, especially interaction with European strain and hybrid (European/North American) salmon.

(1) Water Withdrawals

Maine has made substantial progress in regulating water withdrawal for agricultural use. * * * The State Department of Environmental Protection is developing a rule to address withdrawals on a state-wide basis. At this point, water withdrawals in unorganized towns[5] are not regulated.

(2) Recreational Fishing Mortality

Maine currently allows catch and release salmon fishing in the DPS rivers. * * * In 1998, the Maine Atlantic Salmon Technical Advisory Committee advised that there should be no directed catch and release fishery for Atlantic salmon. Despite that advice, the fishery remains

---

5   Eds: An unorganized town is an area outside of an incorporated municipality.

open. However, regulations to close the directed fishery have been proposed recently.

(3) Disease

The European ISA virus has become established in North American aquaculture fish in proximity to Atlantic salmon in the DPS. Also, the occurrence of a heretofore unknown retrovirus, SSSV, is not yet specifically addressed by any regulations. These recent disease episodes have impacted the Services' river-specific stocking program in that Pleasant River broodstock had to be destroyed.

(4) Aquaculture

The risks inherent in wild stocks interacting with aquaculture escapees have increased significantly from 2 years ago when the Services believed that certain restrictions on the importation and use of foreign salmon stocks were in place and enforced. The Maine State law (PL 1991 c381 sub section 2) restricts importing of fish and eggs but fails to restrict importing of European milt, thus enabling expansion of the use of hybrids between European and North American salmon in aquaculture. Also, permit holders have continued to use European strain or hybrids in violation of their U.S. Army Corps of Engineers permits, which were issued in reliance on applications which stated that no European strain or hybrids would be placed in cages.

(e) Other Natural or Manmade Factors Affecting Its Continued Existence

* * * Atlantic salmon that escape from farms and hatcheries pose a threat to native Atlantic salmon populations in coastal Maine rivers. Escapement and resultant interactions with native stocks are expected to increase given the continued operation of farms and growth of the industry under current practices. * * * Comprehensive protective solutions to minimize the threat of interactions between wild and aquaculture salmon have not been implemented. In 1997 and 1998, the Services worked with industry and State representatives in an attempt to eliminate further importation of European stocks, remove pure European strain from marine cages, and phase out the holding of North American/European hybrids. These discussions were unsuccessful. In July of 1999 the Services initiated discussions directly with the Maine Department of Marine Resources (the State agency responsible for aquaculture industry regulation). These discussions were only partially successful.

Marine survival rates continue to be low for U.S. stocks of Atlantic salmon, and the subsequent low abundance of salmon impedes recovery of the DPS. Scientists have attributed natural mortality in the marine environment to sources that include stress, predation, starvation, disease and parasites, and abiotic factors. In addition, scientific studies indicate that year-to-year variation in return rates of U.S. salmon stocks is generally synchronous with other North Atlantic stocks. This information suggests that the trend in return rates is the result of factors that occur when the stocks are in the North Atlantic, particularly the Labrador Sea. Scientists have concluded that a significant proportion of the variation in recruitment or return rate is attributed to post-smolt survival. However, the factors responsible for reduced post-smolt survival are not well understood. * * *

Proposed Determination

* * * The Services propose to list this DPS of anadromous Atlantic salmon as endangered under the ESA. At present, the DPS is known to include populations of Atlantic salmon in the Sheepscot, Ducktrap, Narraguagus, Pleasant, Machias, East Machias and Dennys Rivers and Cove Brook. Both the naturally reproducing populations of the Gulf of Maine DPS of Atlantic salmon and those river-specific hatchery populations cultured from them are included. In the future, DPS populations may be identified in additional rivers based on ongoing stream surveys and continuing genetic analyses.

The revised proposal provoked a vigorous reaction from political leaders in Maine. Below is a synopsis of their concerns and arguments, few of which are unique to this particular controversy.

Governor Angus King, *Restoration not Regulation*
Dec. 2, 1999

A little less than two weeks ago, the Federal Government proposed to list the Atlantic salmon in eight Maine Rivers under the federal Endangered Species Act. * * *

Included is a vast swath of Maine, containing about one-third of our population, all of the agricultural economy of the Downeast region, a major portion of our forests and related industries, and virtually all of our newly developed aquaculture industry. This entire region—its people, lands and industries—will feel the impact, mostly negative I'm afraid, if the proposal to list Atlantic salmon under the Endangered Species Act is approved.

It's this proposal that I want to address tonight, not in a spirit of anger or confrontation, but rather in sadness and disappointment. * * *

For make no mistake, the return of the majestic Atlantic salmon would be a tremendous achievement for Maine, both in terms of what it would say about the quality of our environment and what it would mean for the recreational and economic life of the state. But a listing under the Endangered Species Act, under the circumstances which apply in Maine, will not bring back the fish. It will trivialize the purposes of the Act itself. It will divide those who should be working together, and will be a devastating economic blow to a region of the state least able to endure it.

The public should understand clearly that a listing in and of itself will not and cannot bring back the salmon—largely because many if not most of the problems affecting Maine salmon lie outside our borders. Most of the life cycle of the salmon takes place—and is subject to risks—far from our shores. From the West Greenland fishery (where they're still catching salmon by the ton with the assent of our federal government), to huge increases in federally protected predators like seals and cormorants— cormorants are called shags Downeast and in one study, a single cormorant's stomach contained 55 salmon tags!—to ocean temperature changes and the resurgent striped bass, salmon have to run a gauntlet of dangers that have nothing to do with Maine.

* * * What we in Maine do have some control over is the habitat in and around the streams where the salmon return to spawn, and where the young grow before returning to the sea. Protecting this habitat cannot bring back salmon lost at sea or consumed by predators before ever getting out, but it will assure the needed environment for the spawning and growth of young fish if and when the federal government is able to help us rectify those things under its control.

And the best hope for restoring and protecting this habitat is the Maine Salmon Conservation Plan. Drawn up over more than three years, involving everyone from federal officials to relevant state departments, local conservation groups, affected businesses, farmers, and riverside residents, the Plan—which was supposed to last five years—is a comprehensive, cooperative approach that identifies every threat to the salmon within our control and sets about mitigating or eliminating them.

* * * Since 1997, the State has committed over a million dollars to this effort, not including thousands of hours by myself, members of my staff, and personnel of the various departments involved. This has included everything from coordinating meetings right here in my office, to permitting and constructing weirs on the Pleasant and Dennys Rivers to catch any salmon that escape from aquaculture pens.

We've formed watershed councils to oversee implementation of the plan on each of the seven rivers, completed habitat mapping of critical spawning and nursery areas, implemented a loss control code for the aquaculture industry, adopted strict new rules governing fish health, and did the first ever water withdrawal study Downeast, and we're now putting in place tough new standards concerning the use of water from these seven rivers for irrigation by the blueberry industry. We've added warden patrols to cut down on poaching, beefed up environmental enforcement, and undertook a tremendous effort to compile the annual status report on the Conservation Plan that was filed this past spring.

Could we have done more? Undoubtedly. I haven't seen a problem around here yet that couldn't use more time or money. But remember, we were just getting started and there is no question that we have made a good-faith effort to implement the Plan—and there is no reason associated with our performance that justifies its abandonment after such a promising start.

But what about the Endangered Species Act itself? "If the returns to the Downeast rivers are low, governor, shouldn't we list, whether or not the Plan is working?" The short answer is the law simply does not apply in this situation—the fish in question are neither endangered nor a species.

The central purpose of the Endangered Species Act is just what its name implies—to save a species—a family of animals or plants—that is in danger of extinction, of being wiped out forever. * * *

But by no stretch should this definition apply to the Atlantic salmon. At any given moment, there are at least a million of these fish in the rivers of Maine, New England, and eastern Canada, in the waters off our collective shores and along the West Coast of Greenland. A million fish. There are an additional fifteen million in aquaculture pens off the coasts of Maine, New Brunswick, and Nova Scotia. There are thousands more held for breeding in hatcheries here and in Canada.

It's hard for me to understand how an animal that numbers in the millions can possibly be in danger of extinction.

Because of this troublesome fact, those who would justify listing are forced to argue that the salmon returning to Maine—just those salmon in Maine—are a subspecies unto themselves—something called a "Distinct Population Segment," animals different enough from their Canadian and aquaculture cousins to merit the protection of the Act.

Now if you think about it, the first problem with this argument is that if you carry it too far, everything is an endangered species: I guarantee that a mouse in Waterville, Maine is different in some ways from a mouse in Watertown, New York—in what it eats, how it lives, probably in some small way in its genetic makeup. But does that make either of them different species or subspecies? Or how about the white-tailed deer that once roamed the hills and swamps where Boston now stands? There are thousands of white-tailed deer in Maine but they are surely scarce around Fenway Park. Does that make them endangered?

* * * Remember, there's a funny thing about rules [like those of the ESA]. Rules can keep people from doing wrong things, but they can't make people do good things. And I believe it's these good things, these positive

attitudes and acts, that no one, not even the federal government, can compel. It's the positive acts that will make the difference for the salmon.

* * * It's been my experience that regulations always elicit the minimum required response, in other words, you meet the rule, whereas cooperation often takes you beyond compliance to a partnership that produces real results. * * *

Secondly, after a listing, the tables turn dramatically in favor of the federal government. In its scope and likely effects, it's not an exaggeration to say that what we are facing here really amounts to a partial takeover by the federal government of Washington, Penobscot, and the other counties involved. They will have enormous influence over all development, including municipal discharge, agricultural practices, forest practices, aquaculture, sport fishing, and other aspects of our lives we can't even now imagine.

So where do we go from here? * * * I respect the authority of Washington, but I believe just as strongly that Maine has authority here as well, and I deeply resent the arrogant assumption that the Federal Government knows better than we do how to protect this state's environment.

* * * And so I invite the federal government to reconsider listing once again and to join with us in a renewed commitment to a comprehensive, cooperative approach that truly hold the best hope for restoring salmon to Maine.

* * * The state of Maine will fight for the salmon.

The only real question is whether the federal government will force us to fight them as well.

The first news story you read mentioned a state salmon protection plan in Oregon and a federal decision, made in reliance on that state plan, to avoid listing a species. Environmentalists challenged that decision, leading to the court decision below. Although a federal district court case from Oregon would not bind a Maine court, the decision is potentially persuasive authority—particularly because other courts have reached similar conclusions in analogous cases.

Oregon Natural Resources Council v. Daley

6 F. Supp. 2d 1139 (D. Or. 1998)

■ STEWART, UNITED STATES MAGISTRATE JUDGE.

Plaintiffs, a group of environmental organizations, challenge the determination by defendants William M. Daley, the Secretary of

Commerce, and Rolland A. Schmitten, the Director of the National Marine Fisheries Service ("NMFS"), that the Oregon Coast evolutionarily significant unit of coho (silver) salmon (*Oncorhynchus kisutch*) ("Oregon Coast ESU") did not warrant listing as a threatened or endangered species under the Endangered Species Act ("ESA"), 16 USC §§ 1531–1544. 62 Fed Reg 24,588, 24,607–08 (May 6, 1997). This determination was based, among other reasons, on the expectation that the recently adopted Oregon Coastal Salmon Restoration Initiative ("OCSRI") would reverse the decline of the Oregon Coast ESU.

[Eds.: The court then described the OCSRI, which involved several different measures designed to protect salmon. After discussing several other legal issues, it returned to the OCSRI.]

* * * Plaintiffs also argue that the OCSRI's provisions are generally unimplemented, future, voluntary actions which are insufficient to support a "no list" decision. Defendants counter that (1) the NMFS may properly consider future and voluntary state conservation efforts and (2) many of the OCSRI provisions are currently implemented.

As previously noted, one section of the ESA requires the Secretary to consider five factors in a listing decision; the fourth factor is "the adequacy of existing regulatory mechanisms." 16 USC § 1533(a)(1)(D). The next section of the ESA requires the Secretary to consider these five factors based upon the best available data "after taking into account those efforts, if any, being made by any State . . . to protect such species, whether by predator control, protection of habitat and food supply, or other conservation practices." 16 USC § 1533(b)(1)(B). Plaintiffs argue that the two sections read together permit the Secretary to consider only state protective efforts that are regulatory and currently operational, and not state protective efforts that are voluntary in nature and rely on future action. Defendants respond that § 1533(b)(1)(B) does not state that state conservation efforts have to be existing, and only refers to protective measures, not regulatory measures. Thus, defendants conclude that the Secretary may consider state protective efforts even if they are to be taken in the future and rely on voluntary action.

The statutory reference to "existing regulatory mechanisms" in § 1533(a)(1)(D) is precise and unambiguous and, if standing alone, would preclude consideration of any future or voluntary conservation efforts which, by definition, are not "existing" or "regulatory." However, the language of § 1533(b)(1)(B) concerning "efforts" and "other conservation practices" is much broader and, if standing alone, would permit the Secretary to consider non-regulatory efforts. The question is whether § 1533(b)(1)(B) should be read merely to clarify what types of "existing regulatory mechanisms" may be considered as the fourth factor in § 1533(a)(1)(D) or whether it should be interpreted to expand upon the five factors by, in effect, adding yet another factor.

First, with respect to future actions, the answer is straightforward. Even the broad language of § 1533(b)(1)(B) cannot reasonably be interpreted to include future efforts, whether regulatory or non-regulatory. It speaks only in the present tense in terms of "efforts, if any, being made," and not future efforts which have yet to be made. The few courts that have addressed this issue have concluded that reliance on future actions is not permitted by the ESA.

* * * This court finds persuasive the reasoning in these cases and similarly concludes that according to the plain language of the ESA, the Secretary may not rely on plans for future actions to reduce threats and protect a species as a basis for deciding that listing is not currently warranted. The NMFS may only consider conservation efforts that are currently operational, not those promised to be implemented in the future.

The more difficult issue is whether the ESA permits consideration of voluntary actions, as opposed to regulatory actions. Since the reference to "regulatory mechanisms" in § 1533(a)(1)(D) could easily include conservation efforts embodied in state regulations, it is difficult to understand why § 1533(b)(1)(B) specifically refers to "efforts" by states to "protect such species, whether by predator control, protection of habitat and food supply, or other conservation practices." Such efforts could be regulatory and, hence, properly considered as "regulatory mechanisms" under § 1533(a)(1)(D). The parties have failed to shed any light on Congressional intent through the use of this language.

* * * [F]or the same reason that the Secretary may not rely on future actions, he should not be able to rely on unenforceable efforts. Absent some method of enforcing compliance, protection of a species can never be assured. Voluntary actions, like those planned in the future, are necessarily speculative, * * * Therefore, voluntary or future conservation efforts by a state should be given no weight in the listing decision. Instead, the NMFS must base its decision on current, enforceable measures.

NOTES

1.   In addition to requiring the listing of qualifying species, section four also requires FWS and NMFS to designate "critical habitat" for listed species. Critical habitat, according to the statute, is habitat that is essential to the species' survival or that requires special management considerations. *See* 16 U.S.C. § 1532(5)(A). A critical habitat designation generally cannot include all of a species' habitat and—in marked contrast to listing decisions—FWS and NMFS may consider economic consequences when issuing a critical habitat designation.

Critical habitat has been, in one law professor's words, "an agony of the ESA." Oliver Houck, *The Endangered Species Act and its Implementation by the U.S. Departments of Interior and Commerce*, 64 U. COLO. L. REV. 277, 297 (1993). FWS has argued that critical habitat designations take up agency time and effort without providing any significant conservation benefit to species. *See, e.g.* David J. Hayes et al., *A Modest Role for a Bold Term: Critical Habitat under the Endangered Species Act*, 43 ENVTL. L. REP. 10671, 10672 (2013). At least partly because of this view, the agency for many years declined to designate critical habitat. Beginning in the late 1990s, environmental groups often filed lawsuits demanding designations, and they often won. *See* Amy Sinden, *The Economics of Endangered Species: Why Less Is More in the Economic Analysis of Critical Habitat Designations*, 28 HARV. ENVTL. L. REV. 129, 157–59 (2004). FWS and NMFS now routinely designate critical habitat, though not always on the statutory timetable, and not without continued grumbling about wasted time and effort. Notwithstanding these government assurances that critical habitat designations are of little consequence, critical habitat designations often provoke outcry and litigation from regulated industries.

2.   Section four also provides for the creation of "recovery plans," which specify criteria for evaluating when a listed species has recovered and measures that can be taken to aid recovery. External commentary on recovery plans has often been critical, with skeptics charging that they are written in vague and open-ended terms and therefore have little ability to compel action. *See, e.g.,* Federico Cheever, *The Road to Recovery: A New Way of Thinking about the Endangered Species Act*, 23 ECOLOGY L.Q. 1 (1996). But some studies have found that species with recovery plans are more likely to recover, or at least have stable populations, than species without. *See* Martin F.J. Taylor et al., *The Effectiveness of the Endangered Species Act: A Quantitative Analysis*, 55 BIOSCIENCE 360, 363–64 (2005).

3.   In addition to governing the listing of species, section four also governs the removal of species from the list. Delistings have been infrequent events, but they do sometimes occur, and they too can provoke significant public attention. Perhaps the best example of this is a series of recent controversies over the delisting of several populations of wolves. *See, e.g., Humane Soc'y of the U.S. v. Jewell*, 76 F. Supp. 3d 69 (D.D.C. 2014); *Defenders of Wildlife v. Jewell*, 68 F. Supp. 3d 193 (D.D.C. 2014). Environmental groups have opposed wolf delistings because they fear that populations will be decimated under state management. Congress has also been interested in delisting wolves. After environmentalists convinced a district court judge to vacate FWS's initial delisting decision, Congress enacted an "appropriations rider" in 2011 directing FWS to reinstate its decision. In 2012, the Ninth Circuit rejected a challenge to that rider. *See Alliance for Wild Rockies v. Salazar*, 672 F.3d 1170 (9th Cir. 2012).

4.   One key issue in the Atlantic salmon listing controversy was the legal significance of the state's protective plans for the species. This issue comes up often. States, local governments, or private entities often will take steps

to protect species, or at least describe steps they could take, in an effort to keep those species off the list.

From the perspective of FWS and NMFS, this is desirable—if the steps are meaningful. As Secretary Babbitt's comments in the first news story demonstrate, the federal agencies generally state a preference for state- or private-led conservation rather than federal intervention. To formalize these arrangements, FWS and NMFS now sometimes use "candidate conservation agreements," which are agreements that specify steps non-federal actors will take to protect a species that is a candidate for listing. *See* U.S. Fish & Wildlife Service, Candidate Conservation Agreements, at http://www.fws.gov/endangered/what-we-do/cca.html. In reliance on those agreements, FWS or NMFS then will decline to list the species.

Federal agencies may also develop conservation measure for federal public lands to obviate the need for a listing. In 2015, for example, the U.S. Bureau of Land Management and the U.S. Forest Service put in place conservation plans for 165 million acres of habitat for the greater sage grouse. Because of those plans, FWS determined that it was unnecessary to list the species. *See* 80 Fed. Reg. 59,858 (Oct. 2, 2015).

5.   The problem posed a question about whether climate change might be a reason to *decline* to list the Atlantic salmon. In recent years, a more frequent question has been whether climate change *compels* listing. For a series of species, including polar bears, ribbon seals, and several varieties of coral, climate change has been an important factor in listing decisions, and it also played a central role in leading courts to reject a decision to remove grizzly bears from ESA protection. *See Greater Yellowstone Coalition v. Servheen*, 672 F. Supp. 2d 1105, 1118–20 (9th Cir. 2011); Owen, *The Endangered Species Act, supra*, at 189–91.

In then-Governor Angus King's statement opposing the Atlantic salmon listing, he painted a dark picture of the consequences of a listing decision. That decision, he claimed, would amount to a "partial takeover by the federal government" of a significant portion of Maine, with devastating economic consequences. Similar fears animate much of the opposition to species listings. But how much do listings really change the legal landscape? To understand the answer to that question, you must know something about the legal protections listed species receive, and we turn to those protections in the sections that follow.

V. JEOPARDY, ADVERSE MODIFICATION, AND THE CONSULTATION PROCESS

Once species are listed, they can receive protection in a variety of ways. Section five of the ESA authorizes FWS and NMFS to acquire lands in order to protect species. Section six authorizes FWS and NMFS to cooperate with the states on protective initiatives, and section eight authorizes cooperation with foreign governments. But the guts of the statute, at least from a lawyer's perspective, are the regulatory provisions contained in sections seven, nine, and ten.

In the pages that follow, you will read about each of those sections, beginning with section seven. Section seven contains several primary elements, each with its own internal complexities:

Section 7(a)(1) directs federal agencies other than NMFS and NOAA "utilize their authorities in furtherance of the purposes of this chapter by carrying out programs for the conservation of endangered species and threatened species." 16 U.S.C. § 1536(a)(1). That may sound powerful, but because the mandate is open-ended, courts have generally rejected assertions that it requires any particular action. *See generally* J.B. Ruhl, *Section 7(a)(1) of the 'New' Endangered Species Act: Rediscovering and Redefining the Untapped Power of Federal Agencies' Duty to Conserve Species*, 25 ENVTL. L. 1107 (1995).

Section 7(a)(2) is the substantive heart of section 7, and, perhaps, the most important part of the statute. It prohibits federal agencies from authorizing, funding, or carrying out actions likely to "jeopardize" listed species or to "result in the destruction or adverse modification of critical habitat." 16 U.S.C. § 1536(a)(2).

Sections 7(a), (b), (c), and (d) specify procedures for fulfilling the substantive mandate of section 7(a)(2). The overall process is known as "consultation." The "action agency"—that is, the federal agency taking, authorizing, or funding the activity in question—works with FWS or NMFS to determine whether its action is likely to cause jeopardy or adverse modification. The process often also involves adjusting the project to minimize its adverse consequences for protected species.

The consultation process also provides a shield against liability under ESA section 9. Section 9 prohibits "take" of listed species—a mandate whose meaning we will examine at the end of this chapter—but a federal agency may obtain "incidental take authorization" if it completes the section seven process and abides by "reasonable and prudent measures" designed to limit takes. *See* 16 U.S.C. §§ 1536(b)(4)(iv), (o).

Even by the somewhat warped standards of environmental law, ESA section 7 is a prodigious generator of specialized terms. This mini-glossary may help you remember some of the most important ones.

The *action agency* is the federal agency proposing to take, authorize, or fund an action that might affect listed species.

Formal consultation is the process of fulfilling the consultation steps specifically referred to in the ESA itself.

Informal consultation is a process (often occurring before or concurrently with formal consultation) through which the action agency and NMFS or FWS discuss a proposed action and its impacts on species. Sometimes that process just leads to agreement that there will not be adverse impacts on species. Sometimes the agencies will negotiate over project changes designed to minimize a project's negative impacts on species and to avoid a jeopardy or adverse modification finding.

A *biological assessment* is a document, prepared by the action agency, that describes the proposed action and its consequences for listed species. If the action agency's BA concludes that the action will not adversely affect listed species, and FWS or NMFS concurs in that conclusion, then the consultation process comes to an end.

A *biological opinion* is a document, prepared by FWS or NMFS, that describes the action, assesses its impacts upon listed species, and reaches conclusions about whether the project will cause jeopardy or adverse modification. The biological opinion also will often contain *conservation measures*, which are steps to minimize the action's adverse impact on species. The action agency must take those steps for the biological opinion's conclusions to remain valid. The biological opinion also will often contain *conservation recommendations*, which are non-binding protective measures that the action agency could carry out.

If a biological opinion reaches a jeopardy or adverse modification conclusion, it will include a *reasonable and prudent alternative* (unless no such alternative is available). A reasonable and prudent alternative is an alternative course of action that would fulfill the action agency's goals, or at least most of them, without causing jeopardy or adverse modification.

For many action agencies, a key goal of the consultation process is to obtain *incidental take authorization*. But for its authorization to be valid, the action agency must implement *reasonable and prudent measures* (not to be confused with reasonable and prudent alternatives), which are measures designed to minimize takes.

The final subsections of section 7 all govern a process through which federal agencies may obtain exemptions from the jeopardy and adverse modification prohibitions. The federal agency must seek permission from a committee of high-level administrative officials (the committee is widely referred to as "the God Squad" because of its supposed power to decide whether a species lives or dies). Applications to the God Squad have been exceedingly rare.

So what results does section 7 produce? Several empirical studies have considered the outcomes of consultation processes, and all share one central conclusion: jeopardy and adverse modification opinions are rare, and rarer still are decisions that actually block projects. The most recent and most comprehensive of these studies found only two jeopardy findings, one adverse modification finding, and no stopped projects in a pool of 88,290 FWS consultations. Jacob W. Malcolm & Ya-Wei Li, *Data Contradict Common Perceptions about a Controversial Provision of the US Endangered Species Act*, 112 PROC. NAT'L ACAD. SCI. 15,844 (2015). Earlier studies found higher rates of jeopardy and adverse modification findings, but those rates were still quite low. *See, e.g.,* Dave Owen, *Critical Habitat and the Challenge of Regulating Small Harms*, 64 FLA. L. REV. 141, 165 (2011); Oliver A. Houck, *The Endangered Species Act and Its Implementation by the U.S. Departments of Interior and Commerce*, 64 U. COLO. L. REV. 277, 321 (1993). A focus primarily on jeopardy and adverse modification opinions may miss a large part of the story, however. Nearly every project that goes through formal consultation gets modified, usually in ways designed to protect species. *See* Owen, *supra*, at 168. And while this effect is harder to measure, the mere prospect of a consultation process may sometimes deter federal agencies from even starting to pursue, authorize, or fund actions with potential adverse effects on listed species.

Much of the section 7 process involves research, writing, and communication by agency scientists and environmental consultants. But lawyers also play important roles. They often help clients determine when consultation is necessary, participate in negotiations over project changes, and, sometimes, challenge or defend the adequacy of agencies' efforts to comply with section 7. Broadly speaking, the resulting cases tend to raise two categories of questions.

The first category involves the necessity of consultation. Only discretionary federal actions that might adversely impact species require formal consultation, and questions therefore often arise about whether a federal action is present, whether that action is discretionary, and whether the action might adversely impact listed species. *See, e.g., Cal. Sportfishing Prot. Alliance v. Fed. Energy Regulatory Comm'n*, 472 F.3d 593, 594–95 (9th Cir. 2006) (considering whether any federal action had been taken); *Nat'l Ass'n of Home Builders v. Defenders of Wildlife*, 551 U.S. 644 (2007) (holding that EPA was not obliged to consult before engaging in actions the Court viewed as non-discretionary). The second category of questions involves the adequacy of a jeopardy or adverse modification determination or, sometimes, the legality of a reasonable and prudent alternative. The problem below falls within this latter category.

PROBLEM: STILLWATER BUSINESS PARK

On the outskirts of Redding, a city at the northern edge of California's Central Valley, is a site that planners and developers think would be an ideal location for a proposed Stillwater Business Park. The site is close to transportation hubs; an airport and a major highway are nearby. But the site also lies on the banks of a creek and contains a complex of vernal pools, which are seasonal wetlands that generally lack a surface connection to permanent surface waterways. Because of their unique hydrology, vernal pools often contain species that cannot survive elsewhere. Three of those species—two varieties of shrimp and a plant called slender Orcutt grass—are present in the vernal pools on the site.

California's Central Valley once contained thousands of these pools. But with the conversion of natural habitats to agricultural, commercial, and residential use, most of those pools have disappeared. FWS scientists estimate that seventy-five percent of the Central Valley's pools are gone. Many of the remaining pools have been impacted by surrounding land uses, and the remaining pool habitat is highly fragmented. Agency scientists expect habitat loss and fragmentation to continue, albeit at a slower pace. As the pools have disappeared, so too have the shrimp species and the slender Orcutt grass. In 1993, the FWS listed the shrimp as threatened species, and in 1997, slender Orcutt grass was also listed as threatened. Several years later, FWS designated critical habitat for all three species.

The designated critical habitat includes portions of the Stillwater site. Those designations include the pools themselves as well as adjacent upland habitat. All three species (and many other species that live in vernal pools) depend on

A fairy shrimp. Image from fws.gov.

upland habitat to filter stormwater and provide nutrients to the pools, and many other vernal pool-dependent species live significant portions of their life cycles in adjacent upland habitat. But developing the site will require filling some of those pools and clearing some of the upland habitat. Because "waters of the United States" cannot be filled without a federal permit (see Chapter 4), the developer has sought permits from the US Army Corps of Engineers. It also has sought grant funding from the federal Department of Housing and Urban Development (HUD).

Before granting those permits and providing funding, the Army Corps and HUD must comply with ESA section 7. Acting as their delegate, the City of Redding prepared a biological assessment describing the project and summarizing its impacts, and FWS has used that biological assessment to prepare a biological opinion for the project. Excerpts from the biological opinion appear below.

Imagine that you represent Defenders of Wildlife, an environmental group concerned with the protection of rare species. Should you bring a court action challenging the permit? And if you represent the government agencies or the developer, could you successfully defend against such a challenge?

ESA § 7, 16 U.S.C. § 1536. Interagency cooperation

(a)(2)   Each Federal agency shall, in consultation with and with the assistance of the Secretary, insure that any action authorized, funded, or carried out by such agency (hereinafter in this section referred to as an "agency action") is not likely to jeopardize the continued existence of any endangered species or threatened species or result in the destruction or adverse modification of habitat of such species which is determined by the Secretary, after consultation as appropriate with affected States, to be critical, unless such agency has been granted an exemption for such action by the Committee pursuant to subsection (h) of this section. In fulfilling the requirements of this paragraph each agency shall use the best scientific and commercial data available.

(3) Subject to such guidelines as the Secretary may establish, a Federal agency shall consult with the Secretary on any prospective agency action at the request of, and in cooperation with, the prospective permit or license applicant if the applicant has reason to believe that an endangered species or a threatened species may be present in the area affected by his project and that implementation of such action will likely affect such species.

* * *

(b) Opinion of Secretary

> * * * (3)(A) Promptly after conclusion of consultation under paragraph (2) or (3) of subsection (a) of this section, the Secretary shall provide to the Federal agency and the applicant, if any, a written statement setting forth the Secretary's opinion, and a summary of the information on which the opinion is based, detailing how the agency action affects the species or its critical habitat. If jeopardy or adverse modification is found, the Secretary shall suggest those reasonable and prudent alternatives which he believes would not violate subsection (a)(2) of this section and can be taken by the Federal agency or applicant in implementing the agency action.
>
> * * * (4) If after consultation under subsection (a)(2) of this section, the Secretary concludes that—

(A)   the agency action will not violate such subsection, or offers reasonable and prudent alternatives which the Secretary believes would not violate such subsection;

(B)   the taking of an endangered species or a threatened species incidental to the agency action will not violate such subsection; and

(C)   if an endangered species or threatened species of a marine mammal is involved, the taking is authorized pursuant to [the Marine Mammal Protection Act];

the Secretary shall provide the Federal agency and the applicant concerned, if any, with a written statement that—

(i)   specifies the impact of such incidental taking on the species,

(ii)   specifies those reasonable and prudent measures that the Secretary considers necessary or appropriate to minimize such impact,

(iii)   in the case of marine mammals, specifies those measures that are necessary to comply with [the Marine Mammal Protection Act] with regard to such taking, and

(iv)   sets forth the terms and conditions (including, but not limited to, reporting requirements) that must be complied with by the Federal agency or applicant (if any), or both, to implement the measures specified under clauses (ii) and (iii).

(c) Biological assessment

(1) To facilitate compliance with the requirements of subsection (a) (2) of this section, each Federal agency shall, with respect to any agency action of such agency for which no contract for construction has been entered into and for which no construction has begun on November 10, 1978, request of the Secretary information whether any species which is listed or proposed to be listed may be present in the area of such proposed action. If the Secretary advises, based on the best scientific and commercial data available, that such species may be present, such agency shall conduct a biological assessment for the purpose of identifying any endangered species or threatened species which is likely to be affected by such action. * * *

If any lawsuit is filed, FWS's biological opinion will be a crucial document. Challengers would try to attack its reasoning and to argue that its conclusions cannot be reconciled with the evidence before the agency. Biological opinions can be long documents—for complicated projects, they can be several hundred pages in length—and we have reproduced only a small portion of the biological opinion for this project. Nevertheless, the materials below should help you understand FWS's reasoning and the evidence upon which it rested its decision. Importantly, the materials below also should help you evaluate whether the FWS's conclusions and rationales seem reasonable enough to withstand judicial review.

Biological Opinion for the Proposed Stillwater Business Park Project

Environmental Compliance Manager
City of Redding
777 Cypress Avenue
Redding, California 96001
Subject: Formal Endangered Species Consultation on the Proposed Stillwater Business Park Project, Shasta County, California

Dear [Redacted][6]:

This is in response to your October 17, 2006, letter and supporting documentation requesting section 7 consultation for the proposed Stillwater Business Park project (proposed project) in Shasta County, California. * * * This response is in accordance with section 7 of the Endangered Species Act of 1973, as amended (16 U.S.C. 1531 *et seq.*) (Act).

At issue are potential adverse effects to the federally-threatened vernal pool fairy shrimp *(Branchinecta lynchi),* the endangered vernal pool tadpole shrimp *(Lepidurus packardi),* * * * and the threatened slender Orcutt grass *(Orcuttia tenuis);* and critical habitat for the vernal pool fairy shrimp, vernal pool tadpole shrimp, and slender Orcutt grass. The Service has determined that the proposed project will adversely affect the vernal pool fairy shrimp, vernal pool tadpole shrimp, * * * and slender Orcutt grass.

* * * Consultation History

April 29, 2005: The Service provided comments in a letter to the City of Redding regarding the *Stillwater Business Park Draft Environmental Impact Statement/Environmental Impact Report* (1–1–05–TA–1116). The Service raised concerns regarding the proposed project's adverse effects to federally-listed species and designated critical habitat and recommended that the City find an alternative site for the proposed business park.

---

6   Eds.: We have removed the names of all of the people mentioned in this biological opinion.

May 19, 2005: Representatives of the City of Redding, U.S. Army Corps of Engineers (Corps), EPA, California Department of Fish and Game (CDFG), the Service, and U.S. Congressman Wally Herger's office met to discuss the proposed project. The resource agencies recommended that the City of Redding utilize a different site for the business park to avoid adverse effects to this critical habitat area.

June 2, 2005: Representatives of the City of Redding, the Corps, the EPA, CDFG, the Service, and U.S. Congressman Wally Herger's office met to discuss the proposed project.

June 9, 2005: Representatives of the City of Redding, CDFG, and the Service attended a field visit at the proposed Stillwater Business Park project.

July 8, 2005: Representatives of the City of Redding, the Corps, the EPA, CDFG, the Service, and U.S. Congressman Wally Herger's office met to discuss the proposed project.

January 20, 2006: The City of Redding requested that the Service review the January 2006, *Draft City of Redding Stillwater Business Park Project, Biological Assessment for Wildlife and Plants.*

February 9, 2006: The Service provided comments to the City of Redding for the January 2006, *Draft City of Redding Stillwater Business Park Project, Biological Assessment for Wildlife and Plants.*

March 8, 2006: [A FWS biologist and a city representative] discussed the January 2006, *Draft City of Redding Stillwater Business Park Project, Draft Biological Assessment for Wildlife and Plants* by telephone.

March 29, 2006: Representatives of the City of Redding, the Corps, the EPA, CDFG, the Service, and U.S. Congressman Wally Herger's office met to discuss the proposed project.

June 1, 2006: The City of Redding provided the May 26, 2006, *City of Redding Stillwater Business Park Project Draft Biological Assessment for Wildlife and Plants* to the Service.

June 30, 2006: The City of Redding provided revisions to the May 26, 2006, *City of Redding Stillwater Business Park Project Draft Biological Assessment for Wildlife and Plants* to the Service.

October 17, 2006: The City of Redding initiated formal section 7 consultation with the Service and provided the October 10, 2006, *City of Redding Stillwater Business Park Project Biological Assessment for Wildlife and Plants.*

Description of the Proposed Action

The City of Redding has proposed the development of a business park, related infrastructure and roads, public services, and utilities components. The proposed project is located on 678 acres, of which approximately 390 acres would be developed. The proposed project site is located near the Redding Municipal Airport in Redding, Shasta County, along Stillwater Creek and Airport Road. The proposed project site is adjacent to the Stillwater Plains Conservation Bank. * * *

Core Facilities. Initially two phases or development thresholds based on square footage are proposed. Phase 1 entails development of up to 3,245,300 square feet of primarily light industrial, general industrial, and high tech cluster uses. Phase 2 encompasses the development of up to 1,165,100 square feet of the same uses on those remaining parcels that have not been developed under Phase 1.

[Eds.: The biological opinion then describes road construction, storm drainage systems, and utility construction for the industrial park.]

* * * *Environmental Baseline for the vernal pool fairy shrimp, vernal pool tadpole shrimp, and slender Orcutt grass*

The vernal pool fairy shrimp, vernal pool tadpole shrimp, and slender Orcutt grass are imperiled by a variety of human-caused activities, primarily urban development, water supply/flood control projects, and land conversion for agricultural use. Habitat loss occurs from direct destruction and modification of vernal pools due to filling, grading, disking, leveling, and other activities, as well as modification of surrounding uplands which alters vernal pool watersheds. Other activities which adversely affect these species include off-road vehicle use, certain mosquito abatement measures, and pesticide/herbicide use.

In addition to direct habitat loss, the vernal pool habitat for these three listed species has been, and continues to be, highly fragmented throughout their ranges due to conversion of natural habitat for urban and agricultural uses. This fragmentation results in small isolated vernal pool tadpole shrimp, vernal pool fairy shrimp, and slender Orcutt grass populations. Such populations may be highly susceptible to extirpation due to chance events, inbreeding depression, or additional environmental disturbance (Gilpin and Soule 1986; Goodman 1987a, 1987b). If an extirpation event occurs in a population that has been fragmented, the opportunities for recolonization would be greatly reduced due to geographical isolation from other source populations.

Holland (1978) estimated that between 67 and 88 percent of the area within the Central Valley of California which once supported vernal pools had been destroyed by 1973. In the ensuing years, threats to this habitat type have continued and resulted in a substantial amount of vernal pool habitat being converted for human uses in spite of federal regulations implemented to protect wetlands. Rapid urbanization and agricultural conversion throughout the range of these species continues to pose the most severe threat to the continued existence of the vernal pool tadpole shrimp, vernal pool fairy shrimp, and slender Orcutt grass.

Development projects within the Redding area have reduced the number of vernal pool complexes. Urban development is continuing in the vicinity of Redding and could eliminate much of the remaining habitat and occurrences of listed species in this area. * * * [Other planned d]evelopment projects within the Redding Core Recovery Area * * *, once built, will reduce the number of vernal pool complexes within the area and will result in both direct and indirect effects to vernal pools, resulting in a decline in vernal pool fairy shrimp, vernal pool tadpole shrimp, and slender Orcutt grass occurrences. Although the decline of federally-listed vernal pool crustacean and plant populations has not been quantified, the acreage of lost habitat continues to grow. Despite these adverse effects, city and county governments continue to implement development projects within the area.

Environmental Baseline for Critical Habitat for Vernal Pool Crustaceans

There are 35 critical habitat units designated for the vernal pool fairy shrimp, totaling 597,821 acres. There are 18 critical habitat units designated for the vernal pool tadpole shrimp, totaling 228,785 acres (Service 2006). The reduction and fragmentation of habitat due to urban development, flood control projects, highway development, and agricultural land conversion threaten many of these critical habitat units for the two vernal pool crustaceans. Critical habitat units near areas that are rapidly developing are under the greatest degree of risk. * * *

Environmental Baseline for Critical Habitat for Slender Orcutt Grass

There are six critical habitat units designated for slender Orcutt grass, totaling 94,213 acres (Service 2006). The reduction and fragmentation of habitat due to urban development, flood control projects, highway development, and agricultural land conversion threaten the six critical habitat units for slender Orcutt grass. * * *

EFFECTS OF THE PROPOSED ACTION

While the proposed business park has minimal direct effects to habitat for federally-listed species, the project would have significant indirect effects and contribute to a local and rangewide trend of habitat loss and degradation, the principal reasons that the * * * vernal pool fairy shrimp, vernal pool tadpole shrimp, and slender Orcutt grass were federally-listed. The proposed project will contribute to the fragmentation and reduction of the acreage of the remaining federally-listed vernal pool habitat located in the Redding Core Recovery Area, as well as critical habitat for the vernal pool fairy shrimp (unit 5), vernal pool tadpole shrimp (unit 1), and slender Orcutt grass (unit 2), and throughout the range of these listed vernal pool species.

* * * Direct Effects

* * * *Vernal Pool Crustaceans*

The development component of the proposed project would result in the direct loss of 0.56 acre of vernal pool crustacean habitat and the death of an unknown number of vernal pool fairy shrimp and vernal pool tadpole shrimp that are present in vernal pool habitat. In addition, the proposed project would result in the loss of 390 acres of upland habitat within the proposed action area. The loss of these 390 acres would be significant, as upland habitat supports the aquatic habitat that the two vernal pool species require for survival (see *Direct and Indirect Effects to Critical Habitat* section, below).

The City of Redding has proposed to preserve 1.12 acres of aquatic vernal pool crustacean habitat to offset direct effects to 0.56 acre of habitat. Preservation will occur through a combination of both on-site and off-site locations. The off-site locations have not been determined at this time, but are subject to Service-approval. In addition, the City has proposed to create/restore vernal pool crustacean habitat at a 1:1 ratio for a total of 0.56 acre. The City proposes to accomplish this creation/restoration by either: (1) purchasing credits sufficient to preserve 0.56 acre of created vernal pool crustacean habitat at a vernal pool conservation bank, such as the Stillwater Plains Conservation Bank; or (2) creating/restoring 0.56 acre of vernal pool crustacean habitat at a site deemed acceptable by the Service.

The City of Redding has proposed to preserve 0.6 acre of upland habitat for every one acre of upland critical habitat destroyed. The City of Redding has not proposed to preserve habitat to offset losses of upland habitat occurring in areas outside of critical habitat.

Slender Orcutt Grass

The proposed project would result in the direct loss of 0.07 acre of suitable Slender Orcutt grass habitat. In addition, the proposed project would result in the loss of 390 acres of upland habitat within the proposed action area. The loss of these 390 acres would be significant, as upland habitat supports the aquatic habitat that the two vernal pool species require for survival (see *Direct and Indirect Effects to Critical Habitat* section, below).

The City of Redding has proposed to preserve 0.14 acre of slender Orcutt grass habitat to offset direct effects resulting from the proposed project. Preservation will occur through a combination of both on-site and off-site locations. The off-site locations have not been determined at this time, but are subject to Service-approval. The City of Redding has also proposed to preserve 0.14 acres of restored/created habitat for slender Orcutt grass at a Service-approved conservation bank, such as Stillwater Plains Conservation Bank.

The City of Redding has proposed to preserve 0.6 acre of upland habitat for every one acre of upland critical habitat destroyed. The City of Redding has not proposed to preserve habitat to offset losses of upland habitat occurring in areas outside of critical habitat.

Indirect Effects

The Service considers indirect effects to include all habitat supported by future destroyed upland areas and swales, and all habitat otherwise damaged by loss of watershed, human intrusion, introduced species, and pollution that will be caused by the proposed project.

*** *Vernal Pool Crustaceans*

The proposed project would indirectly affect 6.42 acres of aquatic vernal pool crustacean habitat. The City of Redding has proposed to: (1) preserve habitat at 2:1 for aquatic habitat outside of critical habitat; and (2) preserve habitat at 4:1 for habitat within critical habitat. In addition, the proposed project would result in indirect affects to upland habitat within the proposed action area. This acreage amount of upland habitat has not been quantified at this time. However, the Service believes that it is reasonable to conclude that the majority of aquatic habitat, and the upland habitat that supports the aquatic habitat, within the proposed 678-acre project area would be indirectly affected to some degree.

A description of potential indirect effects to vernal pool habitat follows.

[The biological opinion then describes how development will contribute to erosion, hydrologic changes, introduction of non-native species, chemical contamination, and a variety of forms of human intrusion.]

In addition to the adverse effects detailed above, the proposed project will contribute to a local and range-wide trend of habitat loss and degradation, the principal reasons that vernal pool fairy shrimp and vernal pool tadpole shrimp were federally-listed. The proposed project would contribute to the fragmentation and reduction of the acreage of the remaining listed vernal pool crustacean habitat located in critical habitat for the vernal pool fairy shrimp (unit 5) and the vernal pool tadpole shrimp (unit 1), the Redding Core Recovery Area, and throughout the range of these two listed vernal pool species.

Slender Orcutt grass

The proposed project would result in indirect effects to 4.33 acres of slender Orcutt grass habitat. Indirect effects would likely result from erosion, changes in hydrology, introduction of non-native plant species, chemical contamination, human intrusion, and habitat fragmentation, as discussed above in the *Indirect Effects* section for vernal pool crustaceans. The City of Redding has proposed habitat compensation to offset these indirect effects. In addition, the proposed project would result in indirect effects to upland habitat, which supports the aquatic habitat that slender

Orcutt requires for survival. This acreage amount of indirectly affected upland habitat has not been quantified at this time. However, the Service believes that it is reasonable to conclude that the majority of aquatic habitat, and the upland habitat that supports the aquatic habitat, within the proposed 678-acre project area would be indirectly affected to some degree.

Direct and Indirect Effects to Critical Habitat

Critical Habitat for Vernal Pool Crustaceans

The proposed project is within critical habitat unit 5 for the vernal pool fairy shrimp and unit 1 for the vernal pool tadpole shrimp. These two units share the same boundary, and total 4,338 acres. The 678-acre proposed project site contains 356.6 acres of critical habitat units 1 and 5. The proposed project would result in the destruction of 234.5 acres of critical habitat within the proposed project study area, which is 5.4 percent of critical habitat in units 1 and 5 for the two vernal pool crustaceans. Of the 0.56 total acreage amount of directly affected aquatic vernal pool crustacean habitat, 0.37 acre is within critical habitat for the two vernal pool crustaceans. The proposed project would indirectly affect 2.44 acres of aquatic critical habitat.

Based on the primary constituent elements previously described in the *Status of the Species* section for the two vernal pool crustaceans, any form of construction associated with the proposed project that occurs in or near vernal pool habitat has the potential to disrupt vernal pool crustacean critical habitat through direct and indirect effects. These effects include altered hydrologic regimes that affect the surrounding upland areas, vernal pools, and swale complexes such that they fail to function properly from altered influxes of water; changes in inundation periods and depths; altered water quality or temperature; changes in soil moisture content; and increases in anthropocentric activities within vernal pool habitat (e.g., urbanization, recreational uses, *etc.*).

The proposed project would result in direct affects to uplands within critical habitat for these two species, which is a primary constituent element of critical habitat. The acreage amount of critical habitat uplands that would be destroyed as a result of the proposed project has not been quantified. However, the proposed project would destroy 356.6 acres of vernal pool crustacean critical habitat, so the total amount of critical habitat uplands destroyed would be 356.6 acres minus aquatic features and existing roads and structures. This amount is likely still close to 356.6 acres. In addition, because the City of Redding has not determined where preservation of vernal pool habitat would occur at this time, the Service is unable to quantify the amount of upland habitat that would be preserved within critical habitat or outside of critical habitat. The City of Redding has proposed to preserve 0.6 acre of upland habitat for every one acre of upland critical habitat that is destroyed, which would result in an overall loss of upland habitat. The City of Redding has not proposed to preserve habitat to offset losses of non-critical habitat uplands.

Critical Habitat for Slender Orcutt Grass

A total of 500 acres of critical habitat units 2a, 2b, and 2c for slender Orcutt grass occurs within the proposed project study area boundaries. The proposed project would result in the loss of 242.2 acres of critical habitat units 2a, 2b, and 2c, which is 3.7 percent of critical habitat unit 2 (which includes sub-units a, b, c, and d). The proposed project would directly affect 0.07 acre of suitable aquatic habitat within critical habitat for slender Orcutt grass. The proposed project would result in indirect effects to 3.5 acres of critical habitat unit 2c for this species.

Based on the primary constituent elements previously described in the *Status of the Species* section for slender Orcutt grass, any form of construction associated with the proposed project that occurs in or near vernal pool habitat has the potential to disrupt slender Orcutt grass critical habitat through direct and indirect effects. These effects include altered hydrologic regimes that affect the surrounding upland areas, vernal pools, and swale complexes such that they fail to function properly from altered influxes of water; changes in inundation periods and depths; altered water quality or temperature; changes in soil moisture content; and increases in anthropocentric activities within vernal pool habitat (*e.g.,* urbanization, recreational uses, *etc.*).

The proposed project would result in direct effects to uplands within the critical habitat of these two species, which is a primary constituent element of critical habitat. The acreage amount of critical habitat uplands within units 2a, 2b, and 2c that would be destroyed as a result of the proposed project has not been quantified. However, the proposed project would destroy 242.2 acres of slender Orcutt grass critical habitat, so the total amount of critical habitat uplands destroyed would be 242.2 acres minus aquatic features and existing roads and structures. This amount is likely still close to 242.2 acres. In addition, because the City of Redding has not determined where preservation of vernal pool habitat would occur at this time, the Service is unable to quantify the amount of upland habitat that would be preserved within critical habitat or outside of critical habitat. The City of Redding has proposed to preserve 0.6 acre of upland habitat for every one acre of upland critical habitat that is destroyed, which would result in an overall loss of upland habitat. The City of Redding has not proposed to preserve habitat to offset losses of noncritical habitat uplands.

Cumulative Effects

Cumulative effects include the effects of future State, Tribal, local or private actions that are reasonably certain to occur in the action area considered in this biological opinion. Future Federal actions that are unrelated to the proposed action are not considered in this section because they require separate consultation pursuant to section 7 of the Act.

* * * *Vernal Pool Species*

Because the vernal pool tadpole shrimp, vernal pool fairy shrimp, and slender Orcutt grass are endemic to vernal pools in the Central Valley, coast ranges, and a limited number of sites in the transverse range and Santa Rosa Plateau of California, the Service anticipates that a wide range of activities will affect these species. Such activities include, but are not limited to urban, water, flood control, highway, and utility projects, chemical contaminants, as well as conversion of vernal pools to agricultural use. Many of these activities will be reviewed under section 7 of the Act as a result of the Federal nexus provided by section 404 of the Clean Water Act.

Critical Habitat for Vernal Pool Species

Primary constituent elements for critical habitat for the vernal pool crustaceans and slender Orcutt grass will likely be affected by these future projects. Future projects will have the potential to alter hydrologic regimes that affect the surrounding upland areas, vernal pools, and swale complexes such that they fail to function properly from altered influxes of water; change the inundation periods and depths; alter water quality or temperature; change in soil moisture content; and increase in anthropocentric activities within vernal pool habitat *(e.g.,* housing developments, recreational uses, *etc.).* These cumulative effects will likely lead to the continued loss of the primary constituent elements for the designated critical habitat units 5, 1, and 2a, 2b, and 2c, respectively, for vernal pool fairy shrimp, vernal pool tadpole shrimp, and slender Orcutt grass, which in turn will negatively influence the function and conservation role of the critical habitat units for these three species.

Conclusion

The Service has reviewed the current status of the * * * vernal pool fairy shrimp, vernal pool tadpole shrimp, and slender Orcutt grass, the environmental baseline for the area covered by this biological opinion, the effects of the proposed project, and the cumulative effects. It is the Service's biological opinion that the Stillwater Business Park project, as proposed, is not likely to jeopardize the continued existence of the * * * vernal pool fairy shrimp, vernal pool tadpole shrimp, and slender Orcutt grass.

The Service has determined that the proposed project would not result in the adverse modification or destruction of critical habitat for vernal pool fairy shrimp, vernal pool tadpole shrimp, or slender Orcutt grass. * * *

However, the proposed project would contribute to a local and range-wide trend of habitat loss and degradation, the principal reasons that the * * * vernal pool fairy shrimp, vernal pool tadpole shrimp, and slender Orcutt grass were federally-listed. The proposed project will contribute to the fragmentation and reduction of the acreage of the remaining listed vernal pool species habitat located in critical habitat, the Redding Core Recovery Area, and throughout the range of these federally-listed species.

The business park would be constructed adjacent to the Stillwater Plains Conservation Bank. The ecological value and integrity of the conservation bank is of particular concern because it has been utilized as compensation for many development projects. The proposed project would also directly and indirectly affect hundreds of acres of upland habitat that supports the aquatic habitat that is required for the survival of the three vernal pool species addressed in this biological opinion.

In addition to the adverse effects detailed above, the proposed project would avoid on-site vernal pool habitat, but would degrade it substantially by development, thereby decreasing its conservation value. The proposed project would preserve created vernal pool habitat, but these wetlands would not have the same conservation value as the vernal pool crustacean habitat that would be directly and indirectly affected by the proposed project. Long-term success of created vernal pools has yet to be determined, and in some cases, created vernal pools do not support federally-listed vernal pool crustacean species.

The City of Redding has not indicated in the Biological Assessment or in additional information how the proposed conservation measures address the Service's 2005 Recovery Plan for the Redding Core Recovery Area. While, Service Recovery Plans are guidance documents and are not to be interpreted as a requirement when permitting projects, they do represent the "best scientific and commercial data available" (Section 7(a)(2) of the Act). We believe the conservation strategies developed in Recovery Plans are important to consider and, in lieu of alternate strategies, would assist in the recovery of vernal pool species if consistently implemented in permit issuance.

INCIDENTAL TAKE STATEMENT

[Eds.: The biological opinion then includes an incidental take statement for each of the protected species. It also includes several pages of "reasonable and prudent measures." While the legal purpose of the reasonable and prudent measures is to limit take, many of the measures would also likely reduce impacts to critical habitat. The biological opinion also includes conservation recommendations, which are non-mandatory actions that the action agency could choose to implement.]

REINITIATION-CLOSING STATEMENT

This concludes formal consultation on the proposed Stillwater Business Park Project. As provided in 50 CFR § 402.16, reinitiation of formal consultation is required where discretionary Federal agency involvement or control over the action has been maintained (or is authorized by law) and if: (1) the amount or extent of incidental take is exceeded; (2) new information reveals effects of the agency action that may affect listed species or critical habitat in a manner or to an extent not considered in this opinion; (3) the agency action is subsequently modified in a manner that causes an effect to the listed species or critical habitat that was not considered in this opinion; or, (4) a new species is listed or critical habitat designated that may be affected by the action. In instances where the amount or extent of incidental take is exceeded, any operations causing such take must cease pending reinitiation.

Please contact [staff biologists] if you have any questions regarding this biological opinion on the proposed Stillwater Business Park project.

Sincerely,

Acting Field Supervisor
cc:
U.S. Army Corps of Engineers, Redding, California
U.S. Environmental Protection Agency, San Francisco, California
California Department of Fish and Game, Redding, California

So how would a court go about reviewing a challenge brought under section 7? *Tennessee Valley Authority v. Hill*, reproduced below, was the first section 7 case to reach the Supreme Court, and remains one of most famous environmental protection (and statutory interpretation) cases in United States history. The second decision, a more recent case out of the Florida Everglades, zeroes in on a question often confronted by contemporary courts: what degree of habitat change qualifies as jeopardy or adverse modification?

Tennessee Valley Authority v. Hill
437 U.S. 153 (1978)

■ MR. CHIEF JUSTICE BURGER delivered the opinion of the Court.

The Little Tennessee River originates in the mountains of northern Georgia and flows through the national forest lands of North Carolina into Tennessee, where it converges with the Big Tennessee River near Knoxville. The lower 33 miles of the Little Tennessee takes the river's clear, free-flowing waters through an area of great natural beauty. * * *

In this area of the Little Tennessee River the Tennessee Valley Authority, a wholly owned public corporation of the United States, began constructing the Tellico Dam and Reservoir Project in 1967, shortly after Congress appropriated initial funds for its development. Tellico is a multipurpose regional development project designed principally to stimulate shoreline development, generate sufficient electric current to heat 20,000 homes, and provide flatwater recreation and flood control, as well as improve economic conditions in "an area characterized by underutilization of human resources and outmigration of young people." Hearings on Public Works for Power and Energy Research Appropriation Bill, 1977, before a Subcommittee of the House Committee on Appropriations, 94th Cong., 2d Sess., pt. 5, p. 261 (1976). Of particular relevance to this case is one aspect of the project, a dam which TVA determined to place on the Little Tennessee, a short distance from where the river's waters meet with the Big Tennessee. When fully operational, the dam would impound water covering some 16,500 acres—much of which represents valuable and productive farmland—thereby converting the river's shallow, fast-flowing waters into a deep reservoir over 30 miles in length.

The Tellico Dam has never opened, however, despite the fact that construction has been virtually completed and the dam is essentially ready for operation. Although Congress has appropriated monies for Tellico every year since 1967, progress was delayed, and ultimately stopped, by a tangle of lawsuits and administrative proceedings [including litigation under NEPA]. * * *

A few months prior to the District Court's decision dissolving the NEPA injunction, a discovery was made in the waters of the Little Tennessee which would profoundly affect the Tellico Project. Exploring the area around Coytee Springs, which is about seven miles from the mouth of the river, a University of Tennessee ichthyologist, Dr. David A. Etnier, found a previously unknown species of perch, the snail darter, or *Percina (Imostoma) tanasi*. This three-inch, tannish-colored fish, whose numbers are estimated to be in the range of 10,000 to 15,000, would soon engage the attention of environmentalists, the TVA, the Department of the Interior, the Congress of the United States, and ultimately the federal courts, as a new and additional basis to halt construction of the dam.

Until recently the finding of a new species of animal life would hardly generate a cause célèbre. This is particularly so in the case of darters, of which there are approximately 130 known species, 8 to 10 of these having been identified only in the last five years. The moving force behind the snail darter's sudden fame came some four months after its discovery, when the Congress passed the Endangered Species Act of 1973 (Act), 87 Stat. 884, 16 U.S.C. § 1531 *et seq.* (1976 ed.). This legislation, among other things, authorizes the Secretary of the Interior to declare species of animal life "endangered" and to identify the "critical habitat" of these creatures. When a species or its habitat is so listed, the following portion of the Act—relevant here—becomes effective:

"The Secretary [of the Interior] shall review other programs administered by him and utilize such programs in furtherance of the purposes of this chapter. All other Federal departments and agencies shall, in consultation with and with the assistance of the Secretary, utilize their authorities in furtherance of the purposes of this chapter by carrying out programs for the conservation of endangered species and threatened species listed pursuant to section 1533 of this title and *by taking such action necessary to insure that actions authorized, funded, or carried out by them do not jeopardize the continued existence of such endangered species and threatened species or result in the destruction or modification of habitat of such species* which is determined by the Secretary, after consultation as appropriate with the affected States, to be critical." 16 U.S.C. § 1536 (1976 ed.) (emphasis added).

In January 1975, the respondents in this case and others petitioned the Secretary of the Interior to list the snail darter as an endangered species. After receiving comments from various interested parties, including TVA and the State of Tennessee, the Secretary formally listed the snail darter as an endangered species on October 8, 1975. 40 Fed. Reg. 47505–47506; see 50 C.F.R. § 17.11(i) (1976). * * * [T]he Secretary determined that the snail darter apparently lives only in that portion of the Little Tennessee River which would be completely inundated by the reservoir created as a consequence of the Tellico Dam's completion. *Id.*, at 47506. The Secretary went on to explain the significance of the dam to the habitat of the snail darter:

> [T]he snail darter occurs only in the swifter portions of shoals over clean gravel substrate in cool, low-turbidity water. Food of the snail darter is almost exclusively snails which require a clean gravel substrate for their survival. *The proposed impoundment of water behind the proposed Tellico Dam would result in total destruction of the snail darter's habitat." Ibid.* (emphasis added).

Subsequent to this determination, the Secretary declared the area of the Little Tennessee which would be affected by the Tellico Dam to be the "critical habitat" of the snail darter. 41 Fed. Reg. 13926–13928 (1976) (to be certified as 50 CFR § 17.81). Using these determinations as a predicate, and notwithstanding the near completion of the dam, the Secretary declared that pursuant to § 7 of the Act, "all Federal agencies must take such action as is necessary to insure that actions authorized, funded, or carried out by them do not result in the destruction or modification of this critical habitat area." 41 Fed. Reg. 13928 (1976) (to be codified as 50 CFR § 17.81(b)). This notice, of course, was pointedly directed at TVA and clearly aimed at halting completion or operation of the dam.

[Eds.: The Court then described Congress's involvement in the controversy, which included continuing to appropriate money for the Tellico Dam even after Congress learned of the snail darter's presence.]

II

We begin with the premise that operation of the Tellico Dam will either eradicate the known population of snail darters or destroy their critical habitat. * * *

Starting from the above premise, two questions are presented: (a) Would TVA be in violation of the Act if it completed and operated the Tellico Dam as planned? (b) If TVA's actions would offend the Act, is an injunction the appropriate remedy for the violation? For the reasons stated hereinafter, we hold that both questions must be answered in the affirmative.

(A)

It may seem curious to some that the survival of a relatively small number of three-inch fish among all the countless millions of species extant would require the permanent halting of a virtually completed dam for which Congress has expended more than $100 million. The paradox is not minimized by the fact that Congress continued to appropriate large sums of public money for the project, even after congressional Appropriations Committees were apprised of its apparent impact upon the survival of the snail darter. We conclude, however, that the explicit provisions of the Endangered Species Act require precisely that result.

One would be hard pressed to find a statutory provision whose terms were any plainer than those in § 7 of the Endangered Species Act. Its very words affirmatively command all federal agencies "to *insure* that actions *authorized, funded,* or *carried out* by them do not *jeopardize* the continued existence" of an endangered species or "*result* in the destruction or modification of habitat of such species . . . ." 16 U.S.C. § 1536 (1976 ed.). (Emphasis added.) This language admits of no exception. Nonetheless, petitioner urges, as do the dissenters, that the Act cannot reasonably be interpreted as applying to a federal project which was well under way when Congress passed the Endangered Species Act of 1973. To sustain that position, however, we would be forced to ignore the ordinary meaning of plain language. It has not been shown, for example, how TVA can close the gates of the Tellico Dam without "carrying out" an action that has been "authorized" and "funded" by a federal agency. Nor can we understand how such action will "*insure*" that the snail darter's habitat is not disrupted. Accepting the Secretary's determinations, as we must, it is clear that TVA's proposed operation of the dam will have precisely the opposite effect, namely the *eradication* of an endangered species.

Concededly, this view of the Act will produce results requiring the sacrifice of the anticipated benefits of the project and of many millions of dollars in public funds. But examination of the language, history, and structure of the legislation under review here indicates beyond doubt that Congress intended endangered species to be afforded the highest of priorities.

[Eds.: The Court then described prior efforts, largely unsuccessful, to protect endangered species through less stringent legislation, and then provided extensive discussion of the legislative history of the 1973 ESA. It summed up that history by noting: "The legislative proceedings in 1973 are, in fact, replete with expressions of concern over the risk that might lie in the loss of *any* endangered species."]

* * * As it was finally passed, the Endangered Species Act of 1973 represented the most comprehensive legislation for the preservation of endangered species ever enacted by any nation. Its stated purposes were "to provide a means whereby the ecosystems upon which endangered species and threatened species depend may be conserved," and "to provide a program for the conservation of such . . . species . . . ." 16 U.S.C. § 1531(b) (1976 ed.). In furtherance of these goals, Congress expressly stated in § 2(c) that "all Federal departments and agencies *shall* seek *to conserve endangered species* and threatened species . . . ." 16 U.S.C. § 1531(c) (1976 ed.). (Emphasis added.) Lest there be any ambiguity as to the meaning of this statutory directive, the Act specifically defined "conserve" as meaning "to use and the use of *all methods and procedures which are necessary* to bring *any endangered species or threatened species* to the point at which the measures provided pursuant to this chapter are no longer necessary." § 1532(2). * * *

It is against this legislative background that we must measure TVA's claim that the Act was not intended to stop operation of a project which, like Tellico Dam, was near completion when an endangered species was discovered in its path. While there is no discussion in the legislative history of precisely this problem, the totality of congressional action makes it abundantly clear that the result we reach today is wholly in accord with both the words of the statute and the intent of Congress. The plain intent of Congress in enacting this statute was to halt and reverse the trend toward species extinction, whatever the cost. This is reflected not only in the stated policies of the Act, but in literally every section of the statute. All persons, including federal agencies, are specifically instructed not to "take" endangered species, meaning that no one is "to harass, harm, pursue, hunt, shoot, wound, kill, trap, capture, or collect" such life forms. 16 U.S.C. §§ 1532(14), 1538(a)(1)(B) (1976 ed.). Agencies in particular are directed by §§ 2(c) and 3(2) of the Act to "use . . . *all methods* and procedures which are necessary" to preserve endangered species. 16 U.S.C. §§ 1531(c), 1532(2) (emphasis added) (1976 ed.). In addition, the legislative history undergirding § 7 reveals an explicit congressional decision to require agencies to afford first priority to the declared national policy of saving endangered species. The pointed omission of the type of qualifying language previously included in endangered species legislation reveals a conscious decision by Congress to give endangered species priority over the "primary missions" of federal agencies.

It is not for us to speculate, much less act, on whether Congress would have altered its stance had the specific events of this case been anticipated. In any event, we discern no hint in the deliberations of Congress relating to the 1973 Act that would compel a different result than we reach here. Indeed, the repeated expressions of congressional concern over what it saw as the potentially enormous danger presented by the eradication of *any* endangered species suggest how the balance would have been struck had the issue been presented to Congress in 1973. * * *

(B)

Having determined that there is an irreconcilable conflict between operation of the Tellico Dam and the explicit provisions of § 7 of the Endangered Species Act, we must now consider what remedy, if any, is appropriate. It is correct, of course, that a federal judge sitting as a chancellor is not mechanically obligated to grant an injunction for every violation of law. * * *

Here we are urged to view the Endangered Species Act "reasonably," and hence shape a remedy "that accords with some modicum of common sense and the public weal." *Post,* at 2302. But is that our function? We have no expert knowledge on the subject of endangered species, much less do we have a mandate from the people to strike a balance of equities on the side of the Tellico Dam. Congress has spoken in the plainest of words, making it abundantly clear that the balance has been struck in favor of affording endangered species the highest of priorities, thereby adopting a policy which it described as "institutionalized caution."

Our individual appraisal of the wisdom or unwisdom of a particular course consciously selected by the Congress is to be put aside in the process of interpreting a statute. Once the meaning of an enactment is discerned and its constitutionality determined, the judicial process comes to an end. * * *

■ [JUSTICE POWELL'S dissent, which JUSTICE BLACKMUN joined, is omitted, as is JUSTICE REHNQUIST'S separate dissent.]

Miccosukee Tribe of Indians of Florida v. United States

566 F.3d 1257 (11th Cir. 2011)

■ CARNES, CIRCUIT JUDGE:

For centuries, a broad, shallow sheet of fresh water that covered most of South Florida flowed south from Lake Okeechobee to the Florida Bay. This phenomenon was the "river of grass" or Everglades, which supported unique and fragile flora and fauna. As so often happens with natural treasures, people sought to control and manipulate the Everglades for their own ends. After the State of Florida's efforts to tame the Everglades failed, in 1948 the Army Corps of Engineers got involved.

The Corps undertook the Central & Southern Florida Flood Project, which it hoped would control flooding, divert water away from developing areas, provide a source for irrigating crops, facilitate recreation, and "enhance" wildlife. *See Miccosukee Tribe of Indians v. United States*, 980 F. Supp. 448, 454 (S.D. Fla. 1997). In order to bend the water to its will, the Corps created thousands of miles of canals and levees supported by scores of pumps, gates, and dams. This massive plumbing project drained the northern portion of the original Everglades for agricultural use and diverted water into distinct, deeper Water Conservation Areas for controlled release into the southern part of the original area, which became Everglades National Park. There followed what the government artfully calls "unplanned environmental consequences." This case involves one of those consequences, which pits a sparrow against a hawk.

I.

The Cape Sable seaside sparrow, which we will refer to as simply "the sparrow," lives primarily in and around Everglades National Park. It was listed as endangered in 1967 and received critical habitat designation in 1977. The fragility of the sparrow as a species stems from two of its attributes. It has a short lifespan, and its nesting success depends on specific kinds of vegetation and water levels. If it is to survive, this species must have favorable breeding conditions without long periods of interruption. The sparrow exists in six subpopulations, all of which live in or around the Everglades. One of them is located apart from the others, which might provide the species with a measure of protection against extinction if some calamity were to wipe out the other five subpopulations. This important outlying group, called "Subpopulation A," lives directly south of the S–12 gates—outside of the bird's designated critical habitat—and it decreased from more than 2,600 birds in 1992 to 112 birds in 2006. The Corps' method of releasing water into the

Everglades, specifically at its S–12 gates, has been blamed for that decline.

The Everglade Snail Kite, a type of hawk, lives in the marshes of Florida and Cuba. Like the sparrow, the kite was also listed as endangered in 1967 and received critical habitat designation in 1977. And like the sparrow, the kite's survival depends on specific water levels. Kites feed primarily on apple snails, which require periods of inundation to reproduce, but the birds nest in woody vegetation that dies off if that inundation lasts too long or if the water level goes too high. It is, in that respect, a Goldilocks kind of bird when it comes to water levels—not too low, not too high. During a period of regional drought, Florida's total kite population declined from 3,400 birds in 1999 to 1,700 in 2002, but it appears to have stabilized since then. The kite's designated critical habitat includes more than 841,000 acres, of which just over a third are directly north of the S–12 gates in Water Conservation Area 3A (WCA–3A).

* * * In the early 1980s Congress authorized a restructuring of the Corps' water management system in order to restore wildlife in the Everglades. Someone decided that the best way to figure out how to correct the unplanned environmental consequences was to undertake a series of trial-and-error tests, each lasting several years. During each test, water would be released from various gates in varying amounts. Under one of these, "Test 7," the Corps began releasing large amounts of water through the S–12 gates. Those gates are located just to the north of the Everglades between the habitats of the endangered kites and the endangered sparrows. Test 7, which began in 1995, was scheduled to continue until 1999.

In 1998 the Service and the Corps, whose eyes were on the sparrow, began to modify their water releases in response to a dramatic decline in the sparrow's population below the S–12 gates. To avoid flooding the little bird into extinction, the Corps created an "Interim Structural and Operational Plan" that altered Test 7 by closing the gates during sparrow breeding season. In 1999 the Service issued a biological opinion concluding that continued flooding through S–12 would lead to the extinction of the sparrow but also warning that "stacking" high water above S–12 might adversely impact the kite.

Between 1999 and 2002, the Corps and the Service consulted and developed the "Interim Operational Plan for the Protection of the Cape Sable Seaside Sparrow" (Interim Plan). During the same period, a regional drought cut the number of kites statewide in half, from 3,400 to 1,700 birds. The Service issued a second biological opinion in 2002, this time analyzing the Interim Plan and concluding it would not jeopardize the kite or adversely modify its habitat. The Corps then implemented the Interim Plan, which changed the S–12 water release schedule to create at least sixty continuous days each year, during sparrow breeding season, in which water below the gates would remain under 6.0 feet above sea level. Water began to back up north of the gates—in the kites' critical habitat and on Miccosukee tribal land. Birds cannot sue, but a tribe can and this one did. * * *

Biological opinions are final agency actions subject to judicial review under the Administrative Procedure Act, 5 U.S.C. § 706(2)(A). *Bennett v. Spear,* 520 U.S. 154, 178 (1997). Specifically, the standard is whether the biological opinion is "arbitrary, capricious, an abuse of discretion, or otherwise not in accordance with law." 5 U.S.C. § 706(2)(A); *Fund for Animals, Inc. v. Rice,* 85 F.3d 535, 541 (11th Cir. 1996) ("On appeal, this court, in reviewing the administrative record, applies the . . . arbitrary and capricious standard of review.").

The arbitrary and capricious standard is "exceedingly deferential." *Sierra Club v. Van Antwerp,* 526 F.3d 1353, 1360 (11th Cir. 2008) (quotation marks omitted). We are not authorized to substitute our judgment for the agency's as long as its conclusions are rational. *Id.* We may, however, find an agency action arbitrary and capricious where the agency has relied on factors which Congress has not intended it to consider, entirely failed to consider an important aspect of the problem, offered an explanation for its decision that runs counter to the evidence before the agency, or is so implausible that it could not be ascribed to a difference in view or the product of agency expertise. *Alabama-Tombigbee Rivers Coal. v. Kempthorne,* 477 F.3d 1250, 1254 (11th Cir. 2007) (citing *Motor Vehicle Mfrs. Ass'n v. State Farm Mut. Auto. Ins. Co.,* 463 U.S. 29, 43 (1983)). The Supreme Court has instructed us that when an agency "is making predictions, within its area of special expertise, at the frontiers of science . . . as opposed to simple findings of fact, a reviewing court must generally be at its most deferential." *Balt. Gas & Elec. Co. v. Natural Res. Def. Council,* 462 U.S. 87, 103 (1983).

* * * The 2006 biological opinion concedes that the Interim Plan will continue to harm the kite habitat by flooding it. * * * The opinion concludes:

> Continued [Interim Plan] operations are expected to result in continued habitat degradation within WCA–3A, which has been one of the most significant areas of kite habitat within the past 30 years. In addition, [Interim Plan] operations are expected to result in reduced nest success of kites within WCA–3A, reduced foraging habitat suitability, and reduced abundance of the kite's primary prey. These impacts are expected to limit population growth in WCA–3A and possibly cause further reductions in the overall kite population. However, because snail kites are long-lived, have high rates of adult survival, and continue to successfully nest in other portions of their range in southern

Florida, these impacts are not anticipated to appreciably reduce the likelihood of survival and recovery of the species in the wild.

Degradation of designated critical habitat within WCA–3A is expected to continue under [the Interim Plan], but this is reversible with improved hydrologic conditions. No permanent loss of critical habitat is expected.

In other words, despite all of the harm that it will cause the kite and kite habitat, the Service believes that Interim Plan's S–12 closings during sparrow breeding season will not jeopardize the continued existence of the kite or adversely modify its critical habitat within the meaning of the Act. *See generally* 16 U.S.C. § 1536(a)(2) (federal agency action must not be likely to "jeopardize the continued existence of any endangered species or result in the destruction or adverse modification of [the critical] habitat of such species"). Evidently the Service is under the impression that flooding twenty percent of the kites' critical habitat to a depth that kills the woody vegetation the bird likes to perch on, that drives off the apple snails it likes to eat, and that reduces its nesting success is not "adverse modification" of critical habitat within the meaning of the Act. The Service asserts that "no *permanent* loss of critical habitat is expected." (emphasis added) But the Service does not cite, and we are unable to find, any decision holding that negative impacts on a species' critical habitat must be permanent to amount to "adverse modification." * * *

Whether short-term impacts on critical habitat amount to "adverse modification" depends to a large extent on the life cycle of the species. Some species may be eradicated if their habitats are negatively affected even for a relatively short time. Restoration of a habitat cannot resurrect the dead. In *Pacific Coast Federation of Fishermen's Ass'ns v. United States Bureau of Reclamation,* 426 F.3d 1082, 1094 (9th Cir. 2005), the National Marine Fisheries Service suggested a multi-phase project to restore adequate water flow to the endangered coho salmon. The problem was that the coho had only a three-year life cycle, and under the agency's plan eight years would pass before water flows were restored to meet the coho's need. *Id.* Understandably, the Court noted that "all the water in the world in 2010 and 2011 will not protect the coho, for there will be none [left] to protect. It is not sufficient for the agency to impose these flows without explaining how the flows will protect critical habitat and ensure that sufficient water is in the main stem for coho to survive during these first five generations." *Id.; see also Pac. Coast Fed'n of Fishermen's Ass'ns v. Nat'l Marine Fisheries Serv.,* 265 F.3d 1028, 1038 (9th Cir. 2001) ("Given the importance of the near-term period on the listed species' survival it is difficult to justify [the agency's] choice not to assess degradation over a time frame that takes into account the actual behavior of the species in danger.").

The point of the two *Pacific Coast* decisions is that adverse modification must be measured by taking into account the life cycle and behavioral pattern of the endangered species in question. Any biological opinion that plans to allow short-term habitat degradation—presumably, as part of a longer-term plan that anticipates the species' future recovery—must carefully consider the life cycles and behavioral patterns of the species to avoid crippling that recovery. It is not enough that the habitat will recover in the future if there is a serious risk that when that future arrives the species will be history.

That principle, however, is not fatal to the 2006 biological opinion's conclusion. The opinion does not focus solely on whether the loss of critical habitat will be permanent; it also determines effect on the species by taking into account the kite's life cycle and behavior. The opinion states, and the Tribe does not dispute, that the kite is a long-lived bird with a high adult survival rate and an enormous range covering 841,000 acres—more than 1,300 square miles—of designated critical habitat. Nor does the Tribe contend that the kite will be extinct after several more years of high water covering twenty percent of this critical habitat. Indeed, S–12 closings have occurred since 1998, and the kite population, though also afflicted by a drought between 1999 and 2002, appears to have stabilized since 2002. So far the kite has survived the adverse impact of the gate closings, making this case distinguishable from the *Pacific Coast* cases. *See Pacific Coast*, 426 F.3d at 1094 (observing that no coho salmon could possibly survive to enjoy their restored habitat after five generations without enough water).

Moreover, as we pointed out earlier, we do owe a high level of deference to the Service's scientific determinations. The deference owed the 2006 biological opinion is especially strong because the agency had to predict future hydrologic conditions and estimate the likelihood, extent, and duration of injury to a species. Balt. Gas & Elec., 462 U.S. at 103, 103 S. Ct. at 2255 (noting that when an agency "is making predictions, within its area of special expertise, at the frontiers of science . . . as opposed to simple findings of fact, a reviewing court must generally be at its most deferential").

We limit our conclusion, of course, to the facts of this case. Those facts involve a long-term program for restoring the Everglades' natural flow in a way that would cause temporary flooding of twenty percent of the critical habitat of a long-lived species of kite with a high adult survival rate and a wide range. The flooding is being done in an effort to avoid the extinction of an endangered sparrow in the area. The aim is to eventually restore the natural flow of the Everglades, a restoration which hopefully will benefit both endangered birds. In light of these facts, the Service's determination in its 2006 biological opinion that the action will not jeopardize the kite or adversely modify its habitat within the meaning of the Endangered Species Act is not arbitrary and capricious.

ADDITIONAL PROBLEMS

1.   You are an attorney with the Federal Energy Regulatory Commission (FERC), which is responsible for permitting liquefied natural gas (LNG) terminals. FERC is reviewing a private application for a permit for an LNG terminal on the coast of Maine. Your staff biologists tell you that shipping traffic to and from the terminal might impact a listed whale species. Must FERC engage in consultation before issuing the permit?

2.   You are still an attorney with the FERC, which also issues licenses to state and private hydroelectric projects. Twenty years ago, FERC issued a forty-year license to the Northern City Department of Water and Power to operate a dam on the Sturgeon River. Like most FERC licenses, this particular license included a "re-opener clause," which gives FERC discretion to re-open the licensing proceeding and amend the license if FERC determines that new environmental information might justify a license amendment.

In 2009, the species of sturgeon that inhabits the Sturgeon River was listed as endangered (it was not listed when FERC granted the original forty-year license) and an environmental group promptly asked FERC to use the re-opener clause to change Dam Co.'s license. FERC ignored the request. The environmental group now has sent FERC a notice letter threatening a lawsuit. In the letter, the group claims that before declining the group's request to re-open the license, FERC needed to engage in section 7 consultation with the Fish and Wildlife Service. Is the environmental group correct?

3.   In recent years, a series of studies has identified climate change as a threat to many species. Some, like piping plovers, monk seals, and sea turtles, are imperiled by rising seas, which will inundate their breeding and nesting sites. Others, like polar bears and salmon, are imperiled directly by warming temperatures, which will move their habitat zones further north or uphill, shrinking those zones along the way. And some, like grizzly bears in and around Yellowstone National Park, are imperiled by the potential loss of species upon which they depend for food. All of these species are listed.

As you learned in Chapter 1, the overwhelming scientific consensus holds that climate change results from human emissions of greenhouse gases, and that most of those human greenhouse gas emissions are emitted though the combustion of fossil fuels. Fossil fuel combustion, in other words, is a key cause of climate change.

That causal chain has led to questions about a pipeline that would transport oil from northern Alberta to refineries in the southern United States, where it would be processed and shipped into the global petroleum market. Ultimately, almost all of that petroleum would be burned. Authorization of interstate pipelines requires approval by the State Department, a federal agency, and the State Department now must consider what obligations, if any, it has under section seven of the Endangered Species Act. Specifically, it must answer one or, depending on its first answer, three questions;

Must it consult with FWS or NMFS on the pipeline approval?

If the State Department must consult, is FWS or NMFS likely to find jeopardy?

If the State Department must consult, is FWS or NMFS likely to find adverse modification?

In answering the question, please assume that the State Department's own studies have found that the existence of the pipeline will increase greenhouse gas emissions by approximately 24 million metric tons per year.[7] That number represents approximately 0.06% of global greenhouse gas emissions. It is also roughly equivalent to the emissions caused by driving an average car about sixty billion miles.

NOTES

1.　Many ESA lawyers refer to section 7 as "the jeopardy prohibition," without mentioning the prohibition on adverse modification. In practice, the agencies have largely collapsed the two inquiries into one. But environmental groups have argued that the standards should be distinct, and some court decisions have treated the inquiries separately. *See generally* Dave Owen, *Critical Habitat and the Challenge of Regulating Small Harms*, 64 FLA. L. REV. 141 (2012) (providing an empirical study of agency and judicial practices).

2.　The last problem asked you to consider whether FWS or NMFS should find jeopardy or adverse modification, or even consult at all, when a federal agency action would contribute to climate change. In guidance documents, the services' answer to that question has been an emphatic "no." According to an internal agency memorandum, "where the effect at issue is climate change in the form of increased temperatures, a proposed action that involves emission of [greenhouse gases] cannot pass the 'may affect' test and is not subject to consultation under the ESA and its implementing regulations." Memorandum from Office of the Solicitor, U.S. Department of Interior, to Director, U.S. Department of Interior (Oct. 3, 2008). In its decision listing the polar bear as threatened, FWS followed a similar course, explaining:

> the best the best scientific data available today are not sufficient to
> draw a causal connection between GHG emissions from a facility in
> the conterminous 48 States to effects posed to polar bears or their

---

[7]　This is a made-up fact. In the real world, the extent of any pipeline's impact on emissions is likely to be uncertain and hotly contested.

habitat in the Arctic, nor are there sufficient data to establish that such impacts are 'reasonably certain to occur' to polar bears. Without sufficient data to establish the required causal connection—to the level of 'reasonable certainty'—between a new facility's GHG emissions and impacts to polar bears, section 7 consultation would not be required to address impacts to polar bears.

73 Fed. Reg. 28,300 (May 15, 2008). Do you agree?

3.   In the Riverside Industrial Park problem, consultation was necessary partly because the developers applied for a permit from the U.S. Army Corps of Engineers. But under today's legal standards—including the Supreme Court's decisions in *SWANCC* and *Rapanos* and the EPA and Army Corps' 2015 waters of the United States rule, discussed in Chapter 4—would the Army Corps still have jurisdiction over those vernal pools? A vernal pool is a seasonal wetland that generally lacks a surface connection to perennial waters. But vernal pools are often hydrologically connected to other surface waters through groundwater flow, and many animal species move between vernal pools and surrounding landscapes, including streams and other surface waters.

4.   Following the Supreme Court's decision in *TVA v. Hill*, Congress amended the ESA to add the "God Squad" provisions discussed above. TVA then invoked those provisions seeking an exemption to allow completion of the Tellico Dam. On January 23, 1979, the members of the God Squad unanimously voted to deny the exemption. In July 1979, Congress interceded again, this time passing an appropriations rider directing TVA to complete construction of the dam, which it did later that year. The Tellico Dam did not, however, result in the extinction of the snail darter, as other populations of the species were discovered. For an in depth history of the Tellico Dam, written by counsel for the plaintiffs in *TVA v. Hill*, see ZYGMUNT J.B. PLATER, THE SNAIL DARTER AND THE DAM: HOW PORK-BARREL POLITICS ENDANGERED A LITTLE FISH AND KILLED A RIVER (2013).

VI. TAKE PROHIBITION AND ITS EXCEPTIONS

While ESA section seven contains a powerful mandate, that mandate only extends to actions authorized, funded, or carried out by the federal government. Unless the federal government is involved, section seven does not cover actions taken by private entities or by state or local governments. For those entities, the most important ESA constraints instead come from section nine.

A. TAKE PROHIBITION

Much of section nine governs trade in listed species, and in products derived from such species. But the primary focus of lawyers within the United States—and, therefore, our primary focus—will be on the "take" prohibition. Section nine makes it "unlawful for any person subject to the jurisdiction of the United States to * * * take any [endangered fish or wildlife] species within the United States or the territorial sea of the United States" or on the high seas. 16 U.S.C. § 1538(a). Section nine itself does not extend that prohibition to *threatened* species, but section 4 authorizes FWS and NMFS to do so by regulation, and most threatened fish and wildlife species also enjoy protection from takes. Listed plants, by contrast, receive a somewhat lesser level of protection under ESA section 9(a)(2).

ESA section nine has enjoyed a fearsome reputation. On its face, it appears to be a far-reaching statutory provision: anyone can be liable; liability can be civil or criminal; and enforcement can occur through government actions or citizen suits. Moreover, the wildlife services, by regulation, have extended take protection to most threatened fish and wildlife species. Consequently, many species—and, therefore, many actions—are addressed by the take prohibition, and much of the outcry against the ESA has focused on section nine.

What activities are prohibited under section nine? According to the statutory definition, "[t]he term 'take' means to harass, harm, pursue, hunt, shoot, wound, kill, trap, capture, or collect, or to attempt to engage in any such conduct." 16 U.S.C. § 1532(19). That definition clearly encompasses some traditional activities like hunting and fishing for protected species. But one key question has been whether it extends to modification of the habitat upon which listed species depend.

In regulations first promulgated in 1975, FWS and NMFS agreed that the take prohibition did preclude some habitat modification. Regulations adopted by those agencies provide that "[h]arm in the definition of 'take' in the Act means an act which actually kills or injures wildlife. Such acts may include significant habitat modification or degradation where it actually kills or injures wildlife by significantly impairing essential behavioral patterns, including breeding, feeding or sheltering." 50 C.F.R. § 17.3.

By the early 1990s, that definition had become a flashpoint. Some of the fiercest disputes involved the timber industry. In the Pacific Northwest, listing of the northern spotted owl, a species dependent upon old growth forests, threatened to compel major changes in timber harvesting practices. In the southeast, the listing of the red-cockaded woodpecker created a similar clash between timber harvesting and species protection. *See, e.g., Sierra Club v. Yeutter*, 926 F.2d 429 (5th Cir. 1990). Those controversies played out partly on public lands, where they implicated ESA section seven as well as NEPA and the National Forest Management Act. But as interpreted by FWS, ESA section nine governed timber harvest on private land, too. The timber industry responded with legal challenges, one of which ultimately made its way to the Supreme Court.

In *Babbitt v. Sweet Home Chapter of Communities for a Great Oregon*, 515 U.S. 687 (1995), the Court upheld the services' definition of harm. The majority employed a variety of statutory interpretation techniques, including semantic canons of construction, legislative history, a focus on the overall statutory structure, and *Chevron* deference, to conclude that the term harm could be interpreted to encompass habitat modifications that unintentionally but foreseeably harmed members of listed species. But both the majority and Justice O'Connor, who wrote a concurring opinion, emphasized that a take could occur only if the action at issue was in fact the proximate cause of identifiable injuries to members of the species. This qualifying language was not enough for Justice Scalia, who penned one of his more memorable dissents. "The Court's holding," he warned, "that the hunting and killing prohibition incidentally preserves habitat on private lands imposes unfairness to the point of financial ruin—not just upon the rich, but upon the simplest farmer who finds his land conscripted to national zoological use." 515 U.S. at 714.

Some section nine cases might seem to validate Justice Scalia's sense that section nine contains a powerful and far-reaching prohibition. Actual or threatened section nine liability has played a role in preventing or limiting a wide variety of activities that could impact species. *See, e.g., Animal Welfare Institute v. Beech Ridge Energy*, LLC, 675 F. Supp. 2d 540 (D. Md. 2009) (wind energy development); *GDF Realty Investments, Ltd. v. Norton*, 326 F.3d 622 (5th Cir. 2003), *certiorari denied*, 545 U.S. 1114 (2005) (shopping mall, housing, and office development); *National Ass'n of Home Builders v. Babbitt*, 130 F.3d 1041 (D.C. Cir. 1997), *certiorari denied*, 524 U.S. 937 (hospital construction); *Strahan v. Coxe*, 127 F.3d 155 (9th Cir. 1997), *certiorari denied*, 525 U.S. 830 (1998) (issuing permits to lobstermen); *Gibbs v. Babbitt*, 214 F.3d 483 (4th Cir. 2000), *certiorari denied*, 531 U.S. 1145 (shooting a red wolf that a farmer thought was threatening his livestock). Nevertheless, there are also several reasons to suspect that section nine is less consequential than its fearsome reputation might suggest.

First, following the Supreme Court's *Sweet Home* decision, courts have generally found that section nine liability depends upon a fairly direct causal connection between the challenged activity and harm to members of a species. Yet species harms often arise from complex causal mechanisms and from combinations of stressors, typically in circumstances where potential plaintiffs have limited data to draw upon. In such circumstances, finding a sufficient basis to assign section nine liability to any particular actor may be difficult. *See, e.g., The Aransas Project v. Shaw*, 775 F.3d 641 (5th Cir. 2014) (declining to find take liability where the defendant state agency authorized water withdrawals that allegedly caused a die-off of whooping cranes). Second, many actions that adversely affect species may not constitute takes. Habitat modifications that occur while species are not present, for example, are not likely to give rise to take liability. Third, enforcement resources are thin. FWS and NMFS do not have enough staff dedicated to section nine enforcement to go looking for violations, and citizen suits, though sometimes prominent, are relatively rare. Most ESA lawyers suspect that a large number of unreported violations occur—a phenomenon commonly referred to as "shoot, shovel, and shut up"—but no one knows just how prevalent that practice is.

Some section nine critics offer a different reason for questioning the prohibition's effectiveness. The purpose of section nine is to protect species, but it arguably creates perverse incentives and unfairness. A simple hypothetical illustrates the problem. Because of section nine liability, Neighbor A, who has endangered species on his property, is generally worse off (assuming that Neighbor A places no value on the

species, which might not be true) than Neighbor B, who has no such species. Yet the reason Neighbor A has such species and Neighbor B does not may be that Neighbor A has protected wildlife habitat while Neighbor B has developed his land. Neighbor A's reward for good environmental stewardship, in other words, is increased legal burdens. Though the action would be criminal, neighbor A might benefit economically if he could eradicate endangered species from his land without anyone noticing. And if those species are not present, but suitable habitat remains, his most economically advisable course of action might be to destroy that habitat to ensure that species do not repopulate his land. While the real-world impact of these incentives is very difficult to assess, there is empirical evidence that these

Is ESA section 9 constitutional? In a series of cases, plaintiffs have argued that it is not, at least as applied to rare species with small ranges on non-federal land. Their core argument is that the Commerce Clause of the United State Constitution does not empower the federal government to provide regulatory protection to entirely intrastate species for which there is no commercial market. *See, e.g., San Luis & Delta-Mendota Water Authority v. Salazar*, 638 F.3d 1163 (9th Cir. 2011) (water diversions and delta smelt); *Alabama-Tombigbee Rivers Coalition v. Kempthorne*, 477 F.3d 1250 (11th Cir. 2007) (Alabama sturgeon); *Rancho Viejo v. Norton*, 323 F.3d 1062 (D.C. Cir. 2003); *GDF Realty Investments, Ltd. v. Norton*, 326 F.3d 622 (5th Cir. 2003) (cave invertebrates). So far the federal government has won all of the circuit court decisions in these cases, and the Supreme Court has not yet granted a cert petition. But in 2014, plaintiffs prevailed in *People for the Ethical Treatment of Property Owners v. U.S. Fish & Wildlife Serv.*, 57 F. Supp. 3d 1337 (D. Utah 2014), a case involving prairie dogs. As of this writing, the case is on appeal.

dynamics do occur. *See, e.g.,* Dean Lueck & Jeffrey A. Michael, *Preemptive Habitat Destruction Under the Endangered Species Act*, 46 J.L. & ECON. 27 (2003).

In the 1990s, FWS and NMFS sought to address these perverse incentives through a series of administrative reforms. The first, called the "Safe Harbors Policy," is designed to provide a regulatory shield to landowners who (a) formally enroll their land in the Safe Harbors program; (b) allow suitable habitat to establish itself on their land; and (c) later want to return that land to its original condition. U.S. FISH AND WILDLIFE SERVICE & NATIONAL MARINE FISHERIES SERVICE, ENDANGERED SPECIES HABITAT CONSERVATION PLANNING HANDBOOK 3–41 (1996). The basic premise of the program is that creating suitable habitat, even on a temporary basis, is something the ESA should reward, not discourage. The second reform, known as the "No Surprises Policy," encourages landowners to enter into deals to protect species, and promises them that if they do enter such a deal, any additional commitments needed for species protection will come on the government's dime. *Id.* at 3–28 to 3–31.

The No Surprises Policy relates to a third major policy reform, something known as "habitat conservation planning," which requires a bit more explanation. That explanation comes after the problems below.

PROBLEMS

1.   A utility owns and operates a hydroelectric dam. A fish ladder helps salmon reach their spawning grounds upstream of the dam, and juvenile salmon later travel downstream to reach the ocean. As those juvenile salmon pass through the dam's turbines, some are killed or injured. Could the utility be liable for takes?

2.   In a Florida county, many beachfront homeowners like to use floodlights to illuminate the public beach in front of their houses. Florida law directs counties to implement ordinances to protect their environment, and the county has generally banned beachfront lighting, except in two exempted areas, where beachfront lights remain prevalent. Endangered sea turtles have traditionally used those areas to lay their eggs. But the sea turtles prefer to lay their eggs in the dark, and they avoid the lighted areas. That crowds the turtles into smaller portions of the beach, leading to egg mortality as turtles climb over and dig up each other's nests. Could the beachfront homeowners be liable for takes? What about the county?

3.   A farmer clears his field, and soon after, a heavy rainstorm sweeps through the area, eroding the exposed soil and carrying it into a nearby stream. The elevated silt levels in the stream lower dissolved oxygen levels, suffocating many of the fish that live there. The dead fish include several specimens of an endangered species of shiner. Has the farmer committed a take?

4.   A landowner in the Texas Hill Country clears a patch of juvenile shin oak trees from his property. Black-capped vireos, an endangered species, often nest in juvenile shin oak trees. The landowner's property is located within black-capped vireo critical habitat, but no black-capped vireos were present when the landowner cut the trees (they are a migratory species, and the landowner cut the trees while the vireos were wintering in Mexico). Did the landowner commit a take?

B.   Exceptions to the Take Prohibition

As it was originally drafted, the take prohibition lacked exceptions. But a prohibition without exceptions can create challenges. How, for example, could someone pursue an environmental restoration project that might kill a few listed species in the short term but would provide major conservation benefits in the long term? And what if a developer wants to build something in marginally valuable habitat used by an endangered species and is willing to compensate for the impacts by restoring higher-value habitat somewhere else? Under the original ESA, either action would have violated section 9. But in 1982, Congress added two key provisions that allow threatened and endangered species to be taken without violating the law.

The first of these exceptions, which you have already read about, comes from ESA section 7. A federal agency that completes a consultation and complies with "reasonable and prudent measures" may receive "incidental take authorization" that allows it to proceed with its action, even if some members of the species are harmed or even killed. Nearly every formal consultation process now produces an incidental take authorization, and that authorization is often a key motivator for federal agencies, and the state or private entities upon which those federal agencies confer funding or permits, to engage in consultation.

The second exception comes from ESA section 10. Section 10 authorizes any entity to obtain an "incidental take permit" that allows incidental takes of listed species, but only so long as that entity prepares and complies with a "habitat conservation plan." That habitat conservation plan must specify measures to minimize the extent of the take and to ensure that those takes that do occur leave the species no worse off than it otherwise would have been. Often, that means compensating for takes by preserving or restoring habitat elsewhere.

The key statutory language governing HCPs appears below:

ESA § 10, 16 U.S.C. § 1539. Exceptions

(a) Permits

(1)   The Secretary may permit, under such terms and conditions as he shall prescribe—

(A)   any act otherwise prohibited by section 1538 of this title for scientific purposes or to enhance the propagation or survival of the affected species, including, but not limited to, acts necessary for the establishment and maintenance of experimental populations pursuant to subsection (j) of this section; or

(B)   any taking otherwise prohibited by section 1538(a)(1)(B) of this title if such taking is incidental to, and not the purpose of, the carrying out of an otherwise lawful activity.

(2)(A)   No permit may be issued by the Secretary authorizing any taking referred to in paragraph (1)(B) unless the applicant therefor submits to the Secretary a conservation plan that specifies—

(i)   the impact which will likely result from such taking;

(ii)   what steps the applicant will take to minimize and mitigate such impacts, and the funding that will be available to implement such steps;

(iii)   what alternative actions to such taking the applicant considered and the reasons why such alternatives are not being utilized; and

(iv)   such other measures that the Secretary may require as being necessary or appropriate for purposes of the plan.

(B) If the Secretary finds, after opportunity for public comment, with respect to a permit application and the related conservation plan that—

(i)   the taking will be incidental;

(ii)   the applicant will, to the maximum extent practicable, minimize and mitigate the impacts of such taking;

(iii)   the applicant will ensure that adequate funding for the plan will be provided;

(iv)   the taking will not appreciably reduce the likelihood of the survival and recovery of the species in the wild; and

(v)   the measures, if any, required under subparagraph (A)(iv) will be met;

and he has received such other assurances as he may require that the plan will be implemented, the Secretary shall issue the permit. The permit shall contain such terms and conditions as the Secretary deems necessary or appropriate to carry out the purposes of this paragraph, including, but not limited to, such reporting requirements as the Secretary deems necessary for determining whether such terms and conditions are being complied with.

(C) The Secretary shall revoke a permit issued under this paragraph if he finds that the permittee is not complying with the terms and conditions of the permit. * * *

(d) Permit and exemption policy

The Secretary may grant exceptions under subsections (a)(1)(A) and (b) of this section only if he finds and publishes his finding in the Federal Register that (1) such exceptions were applied for in good faith, (2) if granted and exercised will not operate to the disadvantage of such endangered species, and (3) will be consistent with the purposes and policy set forth in section 1531 of this title.

To guide the process of HCP development, FWS and NMFS have developed a handbook. As guidance, the handbook is not binding law. But because it interprets laws that are binding, and because it prescribes procedures and standards that agency staff generally follow, lawyers generally take its contents fairly seriously.

U.S. Department of the Interior and U.S. Department of Commerce, Habitat Conservation Planning and Incidental Take Permit Processing Handbook
Pp. 7–2 to 7–6 (1996)

Section 10(a)(2)(B) of the ESA requires the following criteria to be met before the FWS or NMFS may issue an incidental take permit. If these criteria are met and the HCP and supporting information are statutorily complete, the permit must be issued.

1. The taking will be incidental.

Under the ESA, all taking of federally listed fish and wildlife species as detailed in the HCP must be incidental to otherwise lawful activities and not the purpose of such activities. For example, deliberate shooting or wounding a listed species ordinarily would not be considered incidental take and would not qualify for an incidental take permit. Conversely, the destruction of an endangered species or its habitat by heavy equipment during home construction or other land use activities generally would be construed as incidental and could be authorized by an incidental take permit.

* * * 2. The applicant will, to the maximum extent practicable, minimize and mitigate the impacts of such taking.

The applicant decides during the HCP development phase what measures to include in the HCP (though, obviously, the applicant does so in light of discussions with and recommendations from FWS or NMFS). However, the Services ultimately decide, at the conclusion of the permit application processing phase, whether the mitigation program proposed by the applicant has satisfied this statutory issuance criterion.

This finding typically requires consideration of two factors: adequacy of the minimization and mitigation program, and whether it is the maximum that can be practically implemented by the applicant. To the extent maximum that the minimization and mitigation program can be demonstrated to provide substantial benefits to the species, less emphasis can be placed on the second factor. However, particularly where the adequacy of the mitigation is a close call, the record must contain some basis to conclude that the proposed program is the maximum that can be reasonably required by that applicant. This may require weighing the costs of implementing additional mitigation, benefits and costs of implementing additional mitigation, the amount of mitigation provided by other applicants in similar situations, and the abilities of that particular applicant. Analysis of the alternatives that would require additional mitigation in the HCP and NEPA analysis, including the costs to the applicant is often essential in helping the Services make the required finding.

3.   The applicant will ensure that adequate funding for the HCP and procedures to deal with unforeseen circumstances will be provided.

* * * The Services must ensure that funding sources and levels proposed by the applicant are reliable and will meet the purposes of the HCP, and that measures to deal with unforeseen circumstances are adequately addressed. Without such findings, the section 10 permit cannot be issued.

* * * 4.   The taking will not appreciably reduce the likelihood of survival and recovery of the species in the wild.

This is a critically important criterion for incidental take permits because it establishes a fundamental "threshold" standard for any listed species affected by an HCP. Furthermore, the wording of this criterion is identical to the "jeopardy" definition under the section 7 regulations (50 CFR Part 402.02), which defines the term "jeopardize the continued existence of" as "to engage in an action that reasonably would be expected, directly or indirectly, to reduce appreciably the likelihood of both the survival and recovery of a listed species in the wild by reducing the reproduction, numbers, or distribution of that species."

* * * 5. The applicant will ensure that other measures that the Services may require as being necessary or appropriate will be provided.

This criterion is equivalent to the requirement that HCPs include other measures as necessary or appropriate for purposes of the plan. Because the HCP process deals with numerous kinds of proposals and species, this criterion authorizes the Services to impose additional measures to protect listed species where deemed necessary. * * *

6. The Services have received such other assurances as may be required that the HCP will be implemented.

The applicant must ensure that the HCP will be carried out as specified. Since compliance with the HCP is a condition of the permit, the authority of the permit is a primary instrument for ensuring that the HCP will be implemented. When developed, Implementing Agreements also provide assurances that the HCP will be properly implemented. Where a local government agency is the applicant, the Agreement should detail the manner in which local agencies will exercise their existing authorities to effect land or water use as set forth in the HCP. Under an HCP, government entities continue to exercise their duly constituted planning, zoning, and permitting powers. However, actions that modify the agreements upon which the permit is based (e.g., rezoning an area contrary to land uses specified in the HCP) could invalidate the permit. In addition, failure to abide by the terms of the HCP and Implementing Agreement (if required) is likely to result in suspension or revocation of the permit.

Some HCPs may involve interests other than the applicant or permittee. In these cases, the applicant must have specific authority over the other parties affected by the HCP and be willing to exercise that authority, or must secure commitments from them that the terms of the HCP will be upheld. In the latter case, agreements between the FWS or NMFS and the other groups, or legally binding contracts between the applicant and such individuals or interests, may be necessary to bind all parties to the terms of the HCP.

HCPs have an interesting history. For several years after Congress first added section 10 to the ESA, HCPs were rare, and most HCPs covered small areas. That changed in the mid-1990s, when attorneys at the Department of the Interior decided that they were going to need to come up with some creative implementation strategies if the ESA was going to survive a hostile Congress. One of their strategies was to begin preparing "area-wide" HCPs. Often, these HCPs would cover huge land areas, encompass multiple property owners, both public and private, address multiple species (including species that had not yet been listed), and set terms for permitting a variety of activities. The overall goal was to use extensive up-front planning to achieve both better-coordinated protection and greater streamlining and certainty for regulated entities. Small-scale HCPs still exist, as the excerpt below explains, but much of the effort and controversy now involves landscape-scale initiatives.

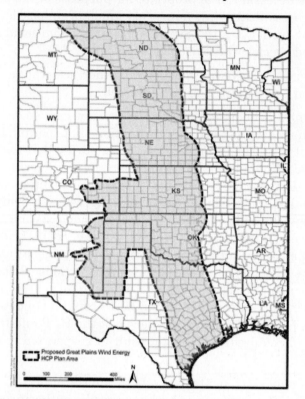

The proposed Great Plains Wind Energy Habitat Conservation Plan would cover the largest geographic area of any HCP to date.

MANAGEMENT SYSTEMS INTERNATIONAL, AN INDEPENDENT EVALUATION OF THE U.S. FISH AND WILDLIFE SERVICE'S HABITAT CONSERVATION PLAN PROGRAM

2009

The first HCP, the San Bruno Mountain HCP (California), was approved in 1983 and covers 3,500 acres. Since that time, more than 500 HCPs have been approved and currently cover over 46 million acres of non-federal land. The number of acres covered under HCPs increased dramatically from 1998 onward.

HCPs vary substantially from one plan to the next, with many being relatively small, e.g. five acres or less, and others covering a million acres or more, e.g. the Washington State Forest Practices HCP, which covers nine million acres. Among current HCPs:

99.3% of all acres covered by HCPs are covered by 57 HCPs (out of nearly 584 plans);

34% of all HCPs (196) cover less than an acre of land (the average coverage of the 196 HCPs is 0.43 acres); and

50% of all HCPs (292) provide coverage of approximately 0.001% of total acres covered under the program.

The number of species covered by individual HCPs also varies, with many of the smaller HCPs providing coverage for a single species, and some of the larger HCPs providing coverage for upwards of 140 species.

The basic types of HCPs include:

HCPs to individuals: The majority of these permits cover residential housing construction. Species most commonly covered under these types of HCPs include the Florida Scrub Jay, the six listed subspecies of Beach Mouse in Florida and Alabama, and the Houston Toad. A majority of the permits for these species cover five acres or less, and many cover less than an acre.

HCPs to companies or non-federal governments to cover development or business activities: HCPs typical of this category include real estate developments, timber harvest operations, and site-specific county development activities, such as school or road construction.

Area-wide HCPs: Area-wide HCPs are agreements with city, county, or state governments to cover a range of activities that fall under a government's permit or regulatory authority. HCPs that fall into this category include the issuance of state-wide timber harvesting permits (Washington State), the issuance of commercial and residential housing construction permits (Alabama, Florida and California), and agreements that guide countywide land use planning and development (California). These agreements may have multiple permittees and generally cover multiple species. Area-wide HCPs cover the most acreage of any type of HCP and are the most complicated, time consuming and expensive to develop.

[Eds.: Later, the report turned to an evaluation of the HCP program's successes and weaknesses. Excerpts from that discussion appear below.]

Program Effectiveness: This evaluation has concluded that the HCP program is a highly effective mechanism to protect endangered and listed species and their required habitats. In virtually every large HCP reviewed in detail, this evaluation found that HCPs are meeting the program's avoidance, minimization and mitigation mandate and most

HCPs are going beyond minimum requirements and making a positive contribution to species recovery.

The HCP program has significant and proven potential to contribute to endangered species protection and recovery due to the following:

- The HCP program provides a total conservation package, which includes: landscape-scale conservation and development planning; generation and use of science for HCP development; the ability to leverage significant funding; the collection of vast amounts of scientific data to monitor implementation progress; and the establishment of conservation management structures, which may take the form of non-profit entities, government programs or committees, or multiorganizational task forces.

- Substantial amounts of land are being brought under conservation protection through HCP management.

- Newer HCPs are focusing on landscape level regional planning. Landscape-scale conservation planning can result in the creation of large contiguous blocks of protected habitat which, in many cases, may be of a higher ecological value than the habitat lost as a result of development.

[Eds.: The study concludes that many HCPs are leaving species better off, helping leverage conservation funding, and advancing scientific research. But it also noted some downsides.]

The time and cost of developing HCPs is significant and serves as a disincentive to the development of additional agreements, especially for large area-wide plans. As an example, large scale area-wide HCPs being managed out of FWS' Sacramento Regional Office typically cost millions of dollars. The length of development time is due to a combination of factors, including the complexity of the agreements, the need to conduct scientific studies, protracted negotiations over appropriate mitigation strategies, FWS staffing constraints, and the applicant's sometimes wavering focus on HCP development due to resource constraints and competing demands.

* * * The HCP Program is understaffed and under-resourced. The under-resourced nature of the program manifests itself in the following ways: 1) FWS staff often does not have time to respond to applicant needs in a timely way, which increases the amount of time required to develop HCPs; and 2) Compliance monitoring does not receive an adequate level of attention (because most of staff time goes toward HCP development). These issues affect both the efficiency and effectiveness of the program.

VII. CAPSTONE PROBLEM: THE NORTHERN ROCKIES HCP

The northern Rocky Mountains contain some of the most spectacular scenery in the United States. They also are rich in natural resources and biodiversity. That combination sometimes creates conflicts, and this problem examines the potential role of HCPs in addressing those conflicts.

Image from Wikimedia Commons; Jaix Chaix, photographer.

For purposes of this exercise, you will play one of six roles (each of you will receive additional, confidential instructions describing your role in more detail):

The *Facilitators Team* has been hired by the participants to facilitate a negotiated, consensus resolution. If consensus cannot be achieved, the facilitators hope to bring as many parties as possible to agreement, and to develop an agreement that the non-agreeing parties cannot challenge—at least not successfully—in court.

The *Fish and Wildlife Service Team* represents the agency ultimately responsible for approving a HCP and issuing an incidental take permit. While that approval authority theoretically gives FWS staff the ability to veto any proposal, everyone involved is well aware that the FWS staff are under heavy pressure to achieve resolution with a minimum of conflict.

The *Northern Rockies Environmental Foundation Team* represents an umbrella organization representing environmental groups (there are many) that are interested in protecting the landscapes and biodiversity of the northern Rockies. They would like the most protective HCP possible, and in the past, they have often used litigation to attempt to compel higher levels of protection.

The *Local Government Team* represents a group of cities and counties in or near the potential HCP area. The economies of these cities and counties once relied heavily on extractive industries. Those industries are now less important, though still present, and construction and tourism have displaced resource extraction as the dominant economic drivers. The area's political culture is traditionally quite libertarian, and residents tend to distrust regulation in any form, particularly when it comes from the federal government, and to prefer low taxes. But there is a vocal minority within those cities and counties that favors strong environmental protections and is willing to spend for them.

The *Forest Products Industry Team* represents the interests of the forest products industry. Those interests generally include (a) maximizing the amount and profitability of timber harvesting from both private and public lands; and (b) avoiding a boom-bust cycle in timber harvesting.

The *State Governor's Team* wears multiple hats. The residents of the area are constituents, as are some of the people who come from outside the area to work or recreate. The state also is a major manager of land within the potential HCP area. Those state lands are "trust lands," which means that they are held in trust for the benefit of the state's people. The governor's job—and, by extension, her representative's job—is to fulfill that trustee responsibility and to balance the interests represented by the other teams, and of the public at large.

The Setting and its Uses

The potential HCP area (which we will call the Northern Rockies HCP Area, or NRHCPA) contains mountains and river valleys in a state in the northern Rockies. The mountainsides are heavily forested. In an undeveloped condition, the valleys would contain a mix of forest and rangeland.

While the federal government owns much of the northern Rockies, the NRHCPA area is primarily in state and private ownership. The state owns approximately 175,000 acres of land, all of it in state forest "trust lands." By state law, those lands are to be managed for multiple uses, including resource extraction, public recreation, and environmental protection. Revenues from management of those lands support a variety of public benefits, including public schools and state universities, hospitals, and land acquisitions that add to the state forest area. Most of the state lands are at middle and higher elevations, and the lands remain heavily forested.

Those forests are commercially valuable. Many decades of logging have changed the state forest, so that large, old growth trees are relatively rare and dense secondary growth is more common. But ample harvestable timber still remains. Under current management systems, eighty percent of the state forest is legally available for timber harvesting. The forest produces thousands of board feet of timber every year, and output has gradually increased over the past two decades. That harvesting produces several economic benefits. Timber sales (the state sells the right to harvest timber to private logging companies) are the primary source of revenue from the forests, and timber harvesting also brings jobs to the surrounding communities. Timber harvesting on federal and private lands has declined in the past two decades, and the timber industry views the timber on state lands as vital to its continued existence.

Outside the state lands, the primary economic activities are real estate development and tourism. The valleys' scenery and natural amenities attract many visitors, and some of those visitors decide to build or purchase seasonal or permanent homes. Particularly in the river valleys and rangeland, five to twenty-acre ranchettes have become increasingly prevalent.

All of this economic activity is occurring in a biologically rich region. The area is home to a wide variety of species, including large populations of deer, elk, moose, and black bear. Its forests and rangelands host small populations of grizzly bears and Canada lynx, both of which are listed as threatened species in the lower forty-eight states. Its rivers and streams contain bull trout, also a threatened species. They also contain westslope cutthroat trout and Columbia redband trout. Neither of these species is currently listed, but federal and state biologists are watching their populations with concern.

Timber harvesting impacts these species. Grizzly bears and Canada lynx generally avoid human activity and therefore shy away from areas with logging roads and vehicular traffic. When they do frequent those areas, they can be hit by vehicles. Streams often become warmer after timber harvests (because of the loss of shade) and contain elevated sediment levels because of runoff from clearcuts and roads. Both are problematic for all of the trout species, which depend upon clear, cold streams with rocky or gravelly bottoms.

Perhaps the greatest long-term threat to all species comes from real estate development. Like logging, development increases human activity, driving bears and lynx away from some areas and increasing the odds of vehicle strikes and other problematic interactions. Real estate development also tends to impact particularly high-value bear habitat. Before and after denning season, bears prefer to forage at lower elevations, where they can find more lush vegetation and more fish and meat. But those lower elevations are generally the same places people want to build their homes. And real estate development is different from logging in one other key way. Forests regrow, but once houses are built, they are unlikely to ever go away.

At a landscape scale, both logging and real estate development create another problem for wildlife: they tend to fragment habitat. Wildlife populations tend to be more resilient—that is, more able to rebound from stresses like fires, difficult winters, or disease outbreaks— if they are interconnected. Interconnections allow animals to move to habitat that remains suitable; to repopulate areas after they recover from disturbances like timber harvesting or fire; and to maintain genetic diversity within a population. But even if the overall habitat area remains substantial, timber harvesting and real estate development can divide an area into relatively isolated habitat chunks.

Because of this combination of threats, federal and state agency biologists believe that populations of grizzly bears, Canada lynx, and bull trout in the NRHCPA are in an unsteady but moderate decline. Indeed, if present trends continue, they anticipate that populations of all three listed species could dip below viable levels over the next century, although that prediction is fraught with uncertainty. They are also concerned about similar trends for the two non-listed trout species. The NRHCPA is not the only area where these species live, and nearby federal, state, and private lands could continue to host populations. But the threats affecting the NRCHPA also are recurring throughout much of the West.

History of the Proposed NRHCP

As in many parts of the West, the NRHCPA's conflicts between resource use, development, and environmental protection have played out partly in the courtroom. In an effort to protect species and wild landscapes, environmental groups have challenged timber sales, land use plans and subdivision approvals, and new road-building projects. To date, ESA section 9 has not been one of their preferred legal instruments, and FWS has not brought any section 9 enforcement actions. But those actions loom as an enticing possibility for some environmentalists, and as a threat for timber harvesters and developers.

In an attempt to turn that threat into a positive compromise, the state, local governments, and FWS have all worked together to craft an area-wide HCP. After three years of public outreach, meetings, research, and drafting, that plan now is in draft form. Getting to this point has not been easy. In its current form, the preferred alternative plan contains compromises that no one is entirely comfortable with. And many participants distrust the larger process and their fellow participants. Animosity between environmental groups, resource users, and developers can be intense, and all of those groups tend to think that the federal government is too cozy with, or at least cowed by, their opponents. The state holds better standing among resource users and developers, but only slightly. Consequently, the partially-completed HCP process remains in a fragile state.

> ### HCPs, ESA Section 7, and NEPA
>
> A key goal of the HCP process is to allow FWS or the NMFS to issue an incidental take permit. Issuing that permit is a federal agency action that, almost by definition, can impact listed species, as well as the environment more generally. FWS or NMFS therefore must comply with the National Environmental Policy Act and section 7 of the ESA. Large-scale HCPs like the NRHCP therefore are typically accompanied by EISs and biological opinions. In this circumstance, the relevant service will be both the consulting agency and the action agency. In other words to fulfill its obligations under section 7, the service will consult with itself.

To attempt to resolve this fragility, the state, local governments, and FWS have all agreed to participate, and to invite other interested parties to participate in, a meeting run by a professional facilitator. The goal of that meeting is to reach some consensus agreement on the content of the HCP, and to avoid having participants run to the courts, the state legislature, or Congress to make an end run around the HCP process.

The Draft HCP

The basic concept of the draft HCP is straightforward: trade preservation in some areas for development or exploitation in others, and trade landowners' and local governments' commitments to provide protection now for assurances that future protection, if it becomes necessary, will occur solely through voluntary donations or federal purchases, not through additional regulation.[8] But the devil is in the details, and here, those details include deciding how to strike that balance and figuring out how to fund the whole enterprise.

More specifically, several key issues have arisen:

The Forest Preserve. One component of the preferred alternative approach is a "Forest Preserve" within the state forest. In that area, timber harvesting activities would be categorically prohibited. Outside of that area, timber harvesting areas would receive expedited permitting. Environmental groups and the FWS would prefer for the Forest Preserve to exist, and to be as large as possible. In fact, FWS's biological opinion and EIS have concluded that a forest preserve of at least 60,000 acres

---

[8] That commitment would extend to species that are not presently listed.

(out of a total state forest area of 150,000 acres) is necessary if listed species populations are to be stabilized. But the size of the forest preserve is inversely proportional to timber company profits and to state trust revenues. The forest products industry has suggested instead using seasonal restrictions on harvesting, with the goal of keeping timber harvesting out of areas in which Canada lynx and grizzly bears are active. FWS's biological opinion and EIS express some skepticism about this approach but also conclude that it would be more effective than providing no regulatory protection at all.

The Private Lands Preserve. The HCP also calls for a preserve on what are presently private lands The preserve would be created by (a) placing development restrictions on private lands within the preserve area; (b) generating funds, either through development fees on unrestricted areas, through federal or state general funding, or through some other mechanism; and then (c) purchasing either conservation easements or fee simple title to compensate the landowners within the restricted area for the restrictions upon their land uses. FWS and conservation groups perceive this private preserve as a key element of the protective strategy, and the EIS and biological opinion conclude that the private lands preserve will need to contain at least 15,000 acres (out of approximately 30,000 acres of private land in the NRHCPA) if species populations are to be stabilized.

> A conservation easement is a legal instrument through which a landowner relinquishes the ability to engage in some environmentally harmful activity, or set of activities (often including development), on all or part of her land. Sometimes landowners donate conservation easements as gifts, and sometimes they are compensated.

They also argue that the private lands preserve will bring ancillary benefits to area residents. By shunting development toward already-developed areas, FWS and environmental groups argue, the preserve will protect open space and water quality, maintain recreational opportunities and scenery, and reduce government service costs. Many area residents are much more ambivalent about the concept. Some opposition is economic; real estate development is a major local industry, and many landowners are skeptical that they will receive adequate compensation for restrictions on their land. Some opposition is ideological. Many area residents perceive any land use restrictions as unjustified incursions upon their liberty.

Riparian Buffers. FWS and environmental groups have argued that the HCP should include riparian buffers, which are zones along the sides of rivers and streams in which timber harvesting and development are generally prohibited. Riparian buffers protect water quality by maintaining shade, filtering pollutants, reducing erosion, and keeping aquatic and riparian habitats interconnected. In developed areas, they also can protect public safety by keeping people out of the way of floods. But often the tallest, straightest trees grow in riparian soils, which makes riparian areas particularly desirable for timber harvesting. And many landowners prefer to build in close proximity to water. Riparian buffers therefore have costs, and timber harvesters and developers would prefer to keep these buffers as small as possible. The EIS and biological opinion state that riparian buffers are important to grizzly bears and crucially important to bull trout, and the larger the buffers are, the more protection they will provide.

Annual Monitoring Budget. Implementing an HCP generally requires monitoring. Someone has to make sure that regulatory commitments are being honored, follow trends in species populations, and determine whether habitat protection or restoration on acquired lands is proceeding appropriately. But that takes time and money. For HCPs at comparable scales, monitoring budgets have been as high as $1,000,000 per year. But every dollar spent on monitoring either takes dollars away from land acquisition or other HCP implementation measures or, if it increases the overall budget, increases costs for regulated entities or taxpayers.

Overall Funding. Administering the HCP could require millions of dollars every year, with much of that money going to land acquisitions. The money must come from somewhere. HCPs have traditionally drawn upon a variety of funding sources, including fees on developers or resource users, local, state, or federal taxpayer funds, and private donations. No private donor has offered to fund the NRHCP, so the participants must find some other source.

The NRHCP Draft EIS describes several alternatives, each involving a different suite of approaches to these basic issues. The table below summarizes the range of alternatives. Your task is to decide which of these alternatives—or some new alternative of your own creation—the participants will tentatively agree to. Of course, if you think you would be better off with no HCP at all, you may refuse to join any agreement.

Alternative	Forest preserve	Private lands preserve	Riparian buffers	Annual monitoring budget	Estimated annual overall budget (including monitoring)	Funding mechanism
No action[9]	None	None	50 feet in state forest No buffers elsewhere	None	None	None
Intermediate alternative	50,000 acres	10,000 acres	75 feet in state forest 50 feet elsewhere	$250,000	$3 million	Timber harvest fees (10%) Development fees (50%) State taxpayer funds (15%) Federal grant money (25%)
Environmental alternative	75,000 acres	20,000 acres	100 feet everywhere	$500,000	$4.5 million	Timber harvest fees (10%) Development fees (60%) State taxpayer funds (15%) Federal grant money (15%)

Test your knowledge with a Chapter 8 online quiz in CasebookPlus™.

---

[9]   Under the no-action alternative, no area-wide HCP would be developed. Individual developers or timber harvesters might develop smaller-scale HCPs, and timber harvesters and developers would have no legal shield against section 9 enforcement actions.

INDEX

References are to Pages